Handbook *of*
European
Union Politics

Handbook *of*
European
Union Politics

Edited by
Knud Erik Jørgensen,
Mark A. Pollack
and Ben Rosamond

SAGE Publications
London ● Thousand Oaks ● New Delhi

Introduction and Editorial Arrangement © Knud Erik Jørgensen,
Mark A. Pollack and Ben Rosamond 2007
Chapters 1–29 © SAGE Publications Ltd 2007

First published 2006

 SAGE Publications Ltd
1 Oliver's Yard
55 City Road
London EC1Y 1SP

SAGE Publications Inc.
2455 Teller Road
Thousand Oaks, California 91320

SAGE Publications India Pvt Ltd
B-42, Panchsheel Enclave
Post Box 4109
New Delhi 110 017

British Library Cataloguing in Publication data

A catalogue record for this book is available from
the British Library

ISBN-10 1-4129-0875-2   ISBN-13 978-1-4129-0875-7

Library of Congress Control Number: 2006904390

Typeset by C&M Digitals (P) Ltd., Chennai, India
Printed in Great Britain by The Cromwell Press Ltd, Trowbridge, Wiltshire
Printed on paper from sustainable resources

Contents

Contributors

Ian Bache is Senior Lecturer in Politics at the University of Sheffield. Between 2003–2005, Dr Bache convened the UACES Study Group and ESRC Seminar Series on *The Europeanization of British Politics and Policy-Making?* His publications include: *The Politics of European Union Regional Policy* (1998, UACES/Sheffield Academic Press); *Multi-level Governance* (with Matthew Flinders) (2004, Oxford University Press); *Politics in the European Union*, 2nd edn (with Stephen George) (2006, Oxford University Press); and *The Europeanization of British Politics* (with Andrew Jordan) (2006, Palgrave Macmillan). He is currently writing a book on *Europeanization and Multi-level Governance* for Rowman and Littlefield.

Tanja A. Börzel is Professor of Political Science and holds the Chair of European Integration at the Free University of Berlin. She completed her PhD at the European University Institute, Florence, Italy, in 1999. Between 1999–2004, she held positions at the Max-Planck Institute for Common Goods, Bonn, at the Humboldt University of Berlin, and at the University of Heidelberg. Her teaching and research interests include international institutions, compliance, European politics, comparative federalism, and the implementation of EU policies. She has published several articles on these subjects, as well as two books: *States and Regions in the European Union* (2002, Cambridge University Press), and *Environmental Leaders and Laggards in Europe* (2003, Ashgate). Her current research projects are on compliance with EU norms and rules in member states, accession countries, and neighbourhood countries.

Walter Carlsnaes is Professor of Political Science in the Department of Government, Uppsala University, and Adjunct Professor at the Norwegian Institute of International Affairs. He has published seven books, of which four are co-edited volumes, including the *Handbook of International Relations* (2002, Sage). He was also founding editor of the *European Journal of International Relations*. His main research interests are in foreign policy analysis, IR theory, and the philosophy of social science, EU external relations, as well as Swedish and South African foreign and security policy.

Dario Castiglione teaches Political Theory at the University of Exeter. His main research interests are in the history and theory of political thought and European constitutionalism. His publications include co-edited volumes on *The Constitution in Transformation* (1996, Blackwell), *The History of Political Thought in National Context* (2001, Cambridge University Press), *The Culture of Toleration in Diverse Societies* (2003, Manchester University Press), *Making European Citizens* (2006, Palgrave), and *The Language Question in Europe and Diverse Societies* (2006, Hart).

Jeffrey T. Checkel is Professor of Political Science and a Research Professor at the ARENA Centre for European Studies, both at the University of Oslo. His research and teaching interests are international relations theory (international institutions, constructivism, transnational politics), European integration (research methods, socialization dynamics, identity), qualitative methods, politics in East and West Europe (former USSR, Germany), and human rights. His publications have appeared in *American Political Science Review, Comparative Political Studies, European Journal of International Relations, European Union Politics, Europe–Asia Studies, International Organization, International Studies Quarterly, Journal of European Public Policy, Review of International Studies, Slavic Review* and *World Politics*. In addition, he is the author of *Ideas and International Political Change* (1997, Yale University Press) and recently edited a special issue of the journal *International Organization* (Fall 2005) on international socialization in Europe. Checkel serves on the Board of Editors of *International Organization*, and co-edits the Sage series *Foundations of International Relations*.

Manuele Citi graduated *cum laude* in Political Science at the University of Pisa. He is presently a doctoral student in the Department of Political and Social Sciences at the European University Institute, Florence, Italy, writing a thesis on the determinants of the evolution of EU science and technology policy.

Lisa Conant is Associate Professor of Political Science at the University of Denver and author of the book, *Justice Contained: Law and Politics in the European Union* (2002, Cornell University Press). She has engaged in research on the comparative study of law and society as a Jean Monnet fellow at the European University Institute and a fellow at the Berlin Program for Advanced German and European Studies. Her ongoing research concentrates on transformations in the rights and obligations of citizenship that derive from European Union law and the European Convention on Human Rights.

Patrick M. Crowley is an international economist and Associate Professor of Economics at Texas A&M University in Corpus Christi, Texas, USA. He specializes in studies of regional integration, with particular emphasis on the European Union. He has published widely in journals such as the *Journal of Common Market Studies*, the *Journal of Economic Integration*, and the *International Trade Journal*, and has been the editor for several edited volumes on Europe, including the volume entitled *Before and Beyond EMU* (2002, Routledge). Crowley is currently co-chair of the economics interest section of the European Union Studies Association of the US, and is also co-editor of the journal *Current Politics and Economics of Europe*. In 2004–2005 Crowley was a visiting research scholar at the Bank of Finland in Helsinki, Finland.

Adrian Favell is Associate Professor of Sociology at UCLA. He is the author of *Philosophies of Integration: Immigration and the Idea of Citizenship in France and Britain* (1998, Macmillan), and has published work on migration, mobility and multiculturalism in Europe, the integration of immigrants, EU immigration policy, and the sociology of European integration. He is currently finalising a new book, *Eurostars and Eurocities*, which examines the impact of free movement in the EU on three cities – Amsterdam, London and Brussels – through the experiences of foreign resident professionals.

Andreas Føllesdal is Professor of Politics and Director of Research in the Norwegian Centre for Human Rights at the University of Oslo. His research focuses on the political philosophy of the European Union, on topics of distributive justice, federalism, minority rights, deliberative democracy, subsidiarity, and European citizenship, published in such journals as *Journal of Political Philosophy*, *Law and Philosophy*, *Journal of European Public Policy*, *Journal of Peace Research*, and *International Journal on Minority and Group Rights*. He has edited books on democracy, the welfare state, consultancy, and on the European constitution. He is Founding Series Editor of *Themes in European Governance* (Cambridge University Press).

Andrew Geddes is Professor of Politics and Director of the Centre for International Policy Research at the University of Sheffield, UK. His particular area of research interest is European and EU migration and asylum policy and politics. Recent publications include *Immigration and European Integration: Towards Fortress Europe?* (2000, Manchester University Press), *The Politics of Migration and Immigration in Europe* (2003, Sage), and *The European Union and British Politics* (2004, Palgrave).

Mark Hallerberg is Associate Professor in the Department of Political Science at Emory University. His research focuses on fiscal institutions and fiscal policy, coalition governments, and the consequences of internationalization for European Union countries. He is the author of one book and has published over 20 peer-reviewed articles in academic journals in political science and economics. He has held visiting scholar positions at the University of Amsterdam, University of Bonn, University of Mannheim, and University of Munich.

Simon Hix is Professor of European and Comparative Politics at the London School of Economics and Political Science. He is author of *The Political System of the European Union* (2005, Palgrave), and co-author (with Abdul Noury and Gerard Roland) of *Democratic Politics in the European Parliament* (2006, Cambridge University Press). He has published articles in the *American Journal of Political Science*, *World Politics*, *British Journal of Political Science*, *Comparative Political Studies*, *European Journal of Political Research*, *Journal of Common Market Studies*, and *West European Politics*. He is also Director of the European Parliament Research Group and Associate Editor of the journal *European Union Politics*.

Markus Jachtenfuchs is Professor of European and International Governance at the Hertie School of Governance in Berlin. He holds a PhD from the European University Institute, in Florence, Italy, and served in various positions at the Mannheim University, Greifswald University and International University Bremen. His research interests are in the field of European governance, international institutions, and the transformation of the state.

Knud Erik Jørgensen is Jean Monnet Professor in the Department of Political Science at the University of Aarhus. He has been a visiting fellow at Chatham House, the European University Institute and the University of Toronto. He is the former editor of the journal *Cooperation and Conflict* and editor or co-editor of *Reflective Approaches to European Governance* (1997, Macmillan), *European Approaches to Crisis Management* (1997,

Kluwer), (with Thomas Christiansen and Antje Wiener) *The Social Construction of Europe* (2001, Sage), (with Karin Fierke) *Constructing International Relations* (2001, ME Sharpe) and (with Tonny B. Knudsen) *International Relations in Europe. Traditions, Perspectives and Destinations* (2006, Routledge). He has contributed chapters to numerous edited volumes and published articles in journals such as the *Journal of European Public Policy*, *European Journal of International Relations, Governance, Journal of Common Market Studies,* and *Cooperation and Conflict.* He is currently preparing a monograph on European foreign policy and a new textbook on IR Theory.

R. Daniel Kelemen is University Lecturer in Comparative European Politics in the Department of Politics and International Relations and Fellow and Tutor in Politics at Lincoln College, Oxford. Kelemen's research interests include European Union politics, comparative political economy, comparative federalism, judicial politics, and environmental policy. He is currently conducting an ESRC funded research project on the judicialization of public policy in Europe entitled: Suing for Europe: Adversarial Legalism and European Governance. A book based on this research, to be entitled, *Suing for Europe? The Rise of Adversarial Legalism in the European Union* will appear with Harvard University Press in 2007. Together with Keith Whittington and Greg Caldeira, he is co-editing *The Oxford Handbook on Law and Politics* (forthcoming 2007, Oxford University Press).

Andrea Lenschow is junior Professor of Political Science and European Integration at the faculty of social sciences at the University of Osnabrück (since 2003). Previously, she was assistant Professor (Hochschulassistentin) at Salzburg University and held fellowships at the European University Institute in Florence and at the Erasmus University of Rotterdam. She received her PhD in Political Science at New York University, and Masters Degrees in Political Science and public administration at Pennsylvania State University. She has published widely on comparative and EU environmental policy, theories of institutional and policy change, Europeanization, policy implementation, and policy convergence.

Ian Manners is a senior researcher at the Danish Institute for International Studies. His publications include *Substance and Symbolism: an Anatomy of Cooperation in the New Europe* (2000, Ashgate); with Richard Whitman (eds) *The Foreign Policies of European Union Member States* (2000, Manchester University Press); with Sonia Lucarelli (eds) *Values and Principles in European Union Foreign Policy* (2006, Routledge); and *Europe and the World: Between Regional Integration and Globalisation* (forthcoming, Palgrave). His article 'Normative Power Europe: a Contradiction in Terms?' won the prize for the best article in the *Journal of Common Market Studies* for 2002.

David G. Mayes is Advisor to the Board at the Bank of Finland, Professor of Economics at London South Bank University, and Honorary Professor of Banking and Financial Institutions at the University of Stirling. He is advisor to central banks in several of the new member states and in those that hope to become members. He has published widely on European integration particularly in the financial, monetary, trade, and single market fields. He was Director of the ESRC research programme on the Single Market and a member of the Maas Group on the single currency. His latest book is on *Adjusting to EMU* (2005, Palgrave-Macmillan).

Gail McElroy is Assistant Professor in the Department of Political Science at Trinity College, Dublin. Her research interests include legislative organization and the comparative study of political parties. She has recently published articles on committee structure and political competition in the European Parliament. Her current work focuses on the nature of multi-level party competition in the European Union, with particular reference to the creation and maintenance of transnational political groups.

Alan S. Milward is Professor Emeritus of European Integration Studies, European University Institute, in Florence, Italy, and is currently an Official Historian at the Cabinet Office in the UK. He is the author of several books, including *The Reconstruction of Western Europe, 1945–1951* (1984, University of California Press), and *The European Rescue of the Nation-State*, 2nd edn (2000, Routledge). He is currently working on the official history of Great Britain and the Common Market, the first volume of which was *The Rise and Fall of a National Strategy, 1945–1963* (2002, Frank Cass).

Kalypso Nicolaïdis is University Lecturer in International Relations at Oxford University, and a Fellow at St Antony's College. She teaches in European integration, international relations, international political economy and game theory. In the academic year 2004–2005, she was Vincent Wright Chair at Sciences-Po, Paris. She has published on the EU as well as other issues in international affairs in numerous journals including *Foreign Affairs, Foreign Policy, The Journal of Common Market Studies, Journal of European Public Policy*, and *International Organization*. Her latest publications include: *Whose Europe? National Models and the Constitution of the European Union* (2003, Oxford University Press), and *The Federal Vision: Legitimacy and Levels of Governance in the US and the EU* (2001, Oxford University Press).

Mark A. Pollack is Associate Professor of Political Science at Temple University. His research focuses on the role of international institutions in global and regional governance, with specific projects examining the delegation of powers to the supranational organizations of the EU, the creation of new mechanisms for the governance of the transatlantic relationship, and the 'mainstreaming' of gender issues in international organizations. He is the author of *The Engines of European Integration: Delegation, Agency and Agenda Setting in the EU* (2003, Oxford University Press), and co-editor of six books, including most recently *Policy-Making in the European Union*, with Helen Wallace and William Wallace (2005, Oxford University Press), as well as over two dozen articles and book chapters.

Elisabeth Prügl is Associate Professor in the Department of International Relations at Florida International University. Her current research foci include gender and agricultural policy reform in the European Union; gender mainstreaming in atypical arenas, including security policy; and the theoretical intersection of feminist and constructivist approaches in International Relations. Professor Prügl spent the 2001/2002 academic year as a Fulbright Senior Scholar at the University of Bremen. Her recent publications include 'Feminism and constructivism: Worlds apart or sharing the middle ground?' with Birgit Locher in *International Studies Quarterly* (March 2001) and *The Global Construction of Gender: Home-Based Work in the Political Economy of the 20th Century* (1999, Columbia University Press).

Tapio Raunio is Professor of Political Science at the University of Turku. His research interests include the role of national legislatures and parties in European integration, the European Parliament, and the Finnish political system, and he has published articles in journals such as the *European Journal of Political Research, Journal of Common Market Studies, Party Politics*, and *Scandinavian Political Studies*.

Leonard Ray is Associate Professor of Political Science at the Louisiana State University and Agricultural and Mechanical College in Baton Rouge, Louisiana. He earned a doctorate in Political Science from the University of North Carolina at Chapel Hill, and has published several scholarly articles on public support for the European Union in journals such as the *Journal of Politics, European Journal of Political Research, Political Behaviour*, and *European Union Politics*. His work has focused on the role of political parties and ideology is structuring opinions about the EU. His current research examines cultural solidarity and support for EU expansion, as well as the relationship between European identities and support for EU institutions.

Martin Rhodes is Professor of Political Economy, Graduate School of International Studies, University of Denver, in Denver, Colorado. Between 1999–2006 he was Professor of Public Policy in the Department of Political and Social Sciences at the European University Institute, Florence, Italy, and from 2004–2006, Scientific Director of the EU Framework 6 Integrated Project NEWGOV (New Modes of Governance). He is the author of over 100 book chapters and journal articles on globalization, EU policy-making and comparative European public policy and political economy, relating especially to labour markets, pension systems and welfare states.

Jeremy Richardson has held Chairs at the Universities of Strathclyde, Warwick, and Essex. His most recent post was as Professorial Fellow at Nuffield College, Oxford, where he is now an Emeritus Fellow. He is editor of *The Journal of European Public Policy* and has recently published the third edition of his textbook on the EU, *European Union: Power and Policy-making* (2006, Routledge).

Thomas Risse is Professor of International Politics at the Freie Universität Berlin. Major recent publications include, (ed. with R. K. Herrmann and M. Brewer) *Transnational Identities. Becoming European in the European Union* (2004, Rowman & Littlefield), (ed. with W. Carlsnaes and B. Simmons) *The Handbook of International Relations* (2002, Sage), (ed. with M.G. Cowles and J. Caporaso) *Transforming Europe. Europeanization and Domestic Change* (2001, Cornell University Press), (ed. with S. C. Ropp and K. Sikkink) *The Power of Human Rights: International Norms and Domestic Change* (1999, Cambridge University Press), and *Cooperation among Democracies. The European Influence on U.S. Foreign Policy* (1995, Princeton University Press). Professor Risse was also Associate Editor of *International Organization* (until 2006), and Coordinator of the Research Centre 'Governance in Areas of Limited Statehood' at the FU Berlin.

Ben Rosamond is Professor of Politics and International Studies at the University of Warwick where he is also an Associate Fellow of the Centre for the Study of Globalization and Regionalization. He has held visiting positions at Aarhus University, the Australian

National University, Columbia University, the Copenhagen Business School, the University of Oxford, and New York University. He is founding co-editor of the journal *Comparative European Politics* and author of *Theories of European Integration* (2000, Macmillan/ St Martin's Press), and *Globalization and the European Union* (forthcoming, Palgrave Macmillan). He is the author of around 50 refereed articles and book chapters on theories of regional and European integration, the role of ideas and discourses in national and supranational policy–making, and British political economy.

Justus Schönlau holds a PhD from the University of Reading and is currently an Honorary Fellow at the University of Exeter (School of Humanities and Social Sciences) and associate research fellow at the Centre for European Policy Studies, Brussels. He has been working on the EU's constitutional process both as an academic (in the EU-funded research projects EURCIT and CIDEL) and as a researcher to the chairman of the Constitutional Affairs Committee in the European Parliament. He is the author of *Drafting the EU Charter: Rights, Legitimacy and Process* (2005, Palgrave). He lives and works in Brussels.

Michael Smith is Professor of European Politics and Jean Monnet Chair in the Department of Politics, International Relations and European Studies at Loughborough University, UK. He has written very widely on the external policies of the EU. His most recent publications include *International Relations and the European Union* (2005, Oxford University Press, edited with Christopher Hill), and *The European Union's Roles in International Politics* (2006, Routledge, edited with Ole Elgström) as well as many other books and articles. Currently he is working on a jointly-authored volume dealing with EU–US relations (due for publication 2007), and on a longer-term project dealing with crises and crisis management in the Euro-American system.

Jonas Tallberg is Associate Professor at Stockholm University and Research Fellow at the Swedish Institute of International Affairs. His primary research interests are delegation to international institutions, compliance and legalization in international cooperation, and multilateral negotiations, with a regional specialization in European Union politics. He is the author of *Leadership and Negotiation in the European Union* (2006, Cambridge University Press), and *European Governance and Supranational Institutions: Making States Comply* (2003, Routledge). He has published articles in journals such as *International Organization, European Journal of International Relations, Journal of Common Market Studies, Journal of European Public Policy,* and *West European Politics.*

Helen Wallace is Director of the Robert Schuman Centre for Advanced Studies at the European University Institute, Florence. From 1998 she was Director of the British Economic and Social Research Council's *One Europe or Several?* Programme (1998–2001). She is currently a member of several editorial advisory boards of journals. She is a member of the Advisory Group to DG Research of the European Commission on Social Sciences and Humanities and of the Group of Political Analysis, which advises President Barroso of the European Commission. She is a Companion of the Order of St Michael and St George and a Fellow of the British Academy. Her recent publications include *The Council of Ministers of the European Union* with Fiona Hayes-Renshaw (1997,

Macmillan); (ed.) *Interlocking Dimensions of European Integration* (2001, Palgrave); contributed to Bruno de Witte (ed.) *Ten Reflections on the Constitutional Treaty for Europe* (2003, EUI); (co-author) *An Agenda for a Growing Europe* (2004, Oxford University Press); *Policy-Making in the European Union*, 5th edn, with William Wallace and Mark A. Pollack (2005, Oxford University Press). She has published articles in numerous journals, including the *Journal of Common Market Studies* and *Governance*.

William Wallace is emeritus Professor of International Relations at the London School of Economics. He was director of studies at the Royal Institute of International Affairs in London from 1978–1990, and a fellow of St Antony's College, Oxford, from 1990–1995. He was a member of the (British) House of Lords European Union Committee from 1996–2001, and chair of its sub-committee on Justice and Home Affairs from 1997–2000. He has written extensively on European international politics and transatlantic relations, in particular on cooperation in foreign policy and defence.

Alex Warleigh-Lack is Professor of Politics and International Relations at Brunel University. He is Chair of UACES (University Association for Contemporary European Studies, www.uaces.org) between September 2006 and September 2009. His most recent research monograph is *Democracy in the European Union: Theory, Practice and Reform* (2003, Sage) and his main research interests are reform of the EU and comparative regional integration/regionalization.

Ramses A. Wessel is Professor of the Law of the European Union and other International Organizations and Co-Director of the Centre for European Studies of the University of Twente, the Netherlands. He is Director of European Studies and Senior Research Fellow of the Institute for Governance Studies. Additional functions include: Editor-in-Chief and founder of the *International Organizations Law Review* and Editor-in-Chief of the Dutch journal and yearbook on peace and security, *Vrede en Veiligheid*. He is a Senior Member of the Netherlands Institute of Government (NOB) and Associate Member of the research school Ius Commune. He graduated in 1989 at the University of Groningen in International Law and International Relations. He wrote his PhD at Utrecht University on *The European Union's Foreign and Security Policy*. His research interests lie in the field of international and European institutional law, with a focus on international organizations, multi-level regulation, and EU external relations.

Alasdair R. Young is Senior Lecturer in international politics at the University of Glasgow. His teaching and research focus on the interaction between trade and regulatory policies and politics, with particular reference to the European Union and the World Trade Organization. His publications include: *Extending European Cooperation: The European Union and the 'New' International Trade Agenda* (2002, Manchester University Press), and (with Helen Wallace) *Regulatory Politics in the Enlarging European Union* (2000, Manchester University Press), as well as articles in *Global Environmental Politics*, *Journal of Common Market Studies*, and *World Politics*. He is co-editor of *Politics* and the *JCMS Annual Review of the European Union*.

Introduction

KNUD ERIK JØRGENSEN, MARK A. POLLACK
AND BEN ROSAMOND

A volume that is self-advertised as a 'handbook' requires some justification. 'Handbook' is suggestive of a claim to some sort of authority. It further connotes a manual or a one-stop guide to its subject. The organization and compilation of a handbook for an academic field is a risky enterprise, not least because the chances of conforming to the expectations and understandings of all of that field's practitioners are slim (to say the least).

Most readers will probably have a good sense of what the study of EU politics entails. Yet, of course, it is pretty much impossible to get past first base in a foundation level course in politics without entering the elementary, but insoluble, discussion about the boundaries of the political. Moreover, scholars of politics cannot escape the complex questions that attend debates about how to approach the study of politics. Much of this boils down to two fundamental questions. First, is one way of studying politics superior to others and, second, should the discipline of political science be the primary focus for those of us seeking to capture an area of study? Let us say a few words about how these two questions have been approached in relation to this book.

We are acutely aware of the struggles over and around 'political science'. How these intersect with the study of EU politics is dealt with more fully in Chapter 1 of this volume. For now, we should simply observe that the book as a whole does not seek to 'carry the can' for a particular view of how EU politics should be studied. Of course, this does not mean that the field lacks interventions that make claims on behalf of certain approaches over others. Indeed, having recruited a cross-section of some of the world's leading scholars to survey their particular areas of specialization, we would have been surprised if our contributors had not offered arguments on behalf of their preferred approaches. This will perhaps be most apparent in Part One, which examines the diversity of metatheoretical and disciplinary starting points for the study of the EU. However, the same is true of the twin chapters (6 and 7) that offer up quite distinct accounts of the EU polity. As such we are confident that the *Handbook* reflects the diversity of the spirit of pluralism that inheres within the field.

The second question really cuts to the heart of what the field is. Our approach here has been – for reasons of spatial necessity – perhaps more partial. The vast bulk of the material we survey emanates from what is broadly understood to be political science and its constituent subfields (conventionally: international relations, comparative politics, political theory and political economy). We are not saying that the only way to study EU politics is through the diverse lenses supplied by political science. Rather, what the book seeks to acknowledge is the richness and diversity of work on the EU politics that has been delivered by practitioners of political science. However, we could not leave out serious discussion of the contributions of scholars whose work sits beyond these formal boundaries. Hence, the inclusion of a lengthy composite Chapter 5, in which the separate contributions to the study of EU politics from History, Legal Studies, Economics and Sociology are presented by leading practitioners of those disciplines.

Our intention in preparing the *Handbook of European Union Politics* has been to deliver a volume that (a) provides a state of the art guide to the state of the field suitable for both established scholars and students of EU politics, (b) reflects upon and contributes to the debates about the nature of the field of EU studies and (c) explores in detail the development of the many approaches to the study of EU politics. Moreover, the book is not intended to pursue a particular or sectarian agenda. We commence from the premise that EU Studies is a diverse and open field. The EU is addressed from many theoretical and methodological points of departure and we are keen that the book taps into the considerable debate about the most appropriate and effective ways of developing a social science of the EU. Thus, we do not aspire to duplicate existing textbook treatments of the EU. The emphasis is less upon reporting what is going on in the EU, but rather to explore the various theoretical subdivisions and substantive empirical sub-areas within EU studies (past and present) – thereby providing a guidebook for scholars and advanced students alike.

We thought long and hard about how best to operationalize these aims. As a prerequisite to surveying the field we had, of course, to pre-define both its scope and its subdivisions. Lest it be felt that we have been fast and loose in 'playing god' with the field of EU politics, we should acknowledge that there is more than one way to organize a book such as this. Our strategy was to proceed in two stages. In the first, we sought to organize the *Handbook* into broad sections that made sense in terms of the different approaches and substantive areas in the literature, without presupposing the superiority of any single approach. In the second, we were faced with the task of devising a list of individual chapters that represent fairly the various topics in the study of EU politics.

As it happens, we alighted fairly quickly on the book's four-part structure, with each part to be introduced by an overview chapter. Part One, not surprisingly perhaps, deals with the theorization of European integration. Here we depart from the standard cleavage structure found in most textbooks to explore, not individual theories, but rather broader social theoretic (or 'second order') points of departure. This has the advantage of showing the social scientific context of EU studies, a point reinforced we believe by the inclusion of chapters on disciplinary history and the academic discourses on EU politics of other (non-political science) disciplines. Part Two, as suggested already, is organized around the controversy over the type of polity the EU might be. The chapters in this section move from the conventional categories of empirical political analysis (legislative politics, executive politics, judicial politics and so on) to hugely important questions of normative political theory and the ways in which these run through the case of the EU. Part Three deals with politics and policy-making in the EU. Again, this part of the book offers thorough discussions of the way in which the EU might perform the tasks of a conventional state (regulation, redistribution and so on) before considering the distinctiveness of EU governance and the complex interplay between the supranational and domestic levels in contemporary European politics. Part Four deals with the EU's constitution in the international system and the global political economy. The external relations of the EU make a complex and diverse field and we had to select aspects. We decided to include research on general foreign policy and issue areas such as development policy, trade policy and ending the volume with a chapter on comparative regionalism in the context of globalization. If the casual reader of the contents page fears that this section is too brief, then we would offer reassurance that questions of the EU's interaction with world politics is elemental to much of the rest of the book as well.

Unsurprisingly, given the scale of the book, we have many people to thank for their contributions to this collective effort. Sage editor

Lucy Robinson first approached us several years ago with the idea of producing a state-of-the-art handbook summarizing the state of the field, and her successor David Mainwaring has been equally efficient and patient with us as we moved from conception to finished product. Our early efforts to formulate an extensive and inclusive structure to the book was greatly aided by our editorial board of eminent EU scholars: James A. Caporaso, Peter Katzenstein, Alberta Sbragia, Helen Wallace and Wolfgang Wessels. Our thanks also go to our editorial assistant, Ulla Veronica Willner, who meticulously prepared and standardized each chapter for submission, and to Liz Steel and Mary Flannery at the Keyword Group, who shepherded a large manuscript and a huge cast of contributors through copy-editing and proofs to the production stage. Our greatest thanks, however, go to our contributors, who have produced a set of genuinely definitive statements on their respective fields of study. Our aim from the beginning of this project was to recruit the world's leading scholars on various aspects of EU politics, and to impress on them that we were looking for contributions that were comprehensive, up-to-date, and pointed in their analyses of the state of the field. It has been our good fortune that a superb cast of contributors responded to our demanding mandate. We have learned a great deal from our colleagues in the editing of this volume, and we are pleased to share that knowledge with the readers of this Handbook.

PART I

Process: Theorizing European Integration

The Political Sciences of European Integration: Disciplinary History and EU Studies

BEN ROSAMOND

INTRODUCTION

The task of writing disciplinary history is far from straightforward.[1] Like all history, the composition of a narrative about a field is undertaken at a particular time and in a particular place – from a particular 'subject position' that may reflect certain biases which in turn follow from a multiplicity of concerns that follow from those temporal and spatial coordinates. 'Formal' disciplinary histories in any field are relatively rare, while stock-taking, 'state of the art' exegeses are found rather more often. More common still, though largely unacknowledged as exercises in disciplinary history, are those acts of framing and story-telling about a field's past that routinely pepper scholarship in an area of enquiry. In other words scholarly activity is characterized by the constant flow of stories, which offer claims about routes to progress through the rectification of past errors and classify the field's development over time. Thus, interventions in a field's *present* routinely make arguments about that field's *past*. The net result could well be

that the history of a field 'is known more by reputation than readership' (Fuller 2003: 29).

The most prominent recent historian of the discipline of international relations (IR) argues that there 'is an intimate link between disciplinary identity and the manner in which we understand the history of the field' (Schmidt 2002: 16). If regular interventions in a field of enquiry habitually offer constructions of the field's past in order to justify intellectual moves made in the present, then critical engagement with disciplinary history also – by definition – shines an inquisitive torchlight on the disciplinary present. The task of such work is to interrogate 'the retrospective teleology of discipline-history' (Collini et al. 1983: 7). If this is not done then

> [t]he present theoretical consensus of the discipline, or possibly some polemical version of what that consensus should be, is in effect taken as definitive, and the past is then reconstituted as a teleology leading up to and fully manifested in it (Collini et al. 1983: 4).

This chapter does not pretend to offer a single definitive account of the field of EU politics, but it does investigate the various formal and informal accounts that exist in terms of the above observations. It begins with two short preparatory discussions. The first identifies six issues that intercept any attempt to write disciplinary history in this area, while the second supplies a rough 'anatomy' of the field of EU studies/EU politics in an effort to adjudicate some fundamental issues surrounding the substance of this area of study. In so doing, it perhaps justifies this chapter's focus on what appears to be an Anglophone academic mainstream. It then moves to describing and offering critical engagement with standard accounts of the field with a view to showing how, overwhelmingly, extant stories about the evolution of EU studies are bound up with particular claims about the organization of knowledge in the *present*. Indeed the argument here suggests that disciplinary history is used to adjudicate disputes about the proper scope and substance of the study of EU politics, which in turn connect to some quite fundamental struggles for the soul of political science.

Thus, the chapter is also attentive to sociology of knowledge questions. These remind us that our knowledge about the world is produced amidst broad scientific and more specific disciplinary structures, norms, practices and institutions – what Jørgensen (2000) neatly calls the 'cultural-institutional context' of academic work. It follows that the evolution of a field is (at the very least) partly a function of developments *within* the field. These in turn might reflect much broader path-dependent pathologies, which take us back to the intellectual and socio-political conditions of disciplinary foundation (Mancias 1987). This 'internalist' take on disciplinary history might not necessarily provide a full explanation of why scholars of EU politics address particular puzzles at particular moment, but it does offer a framework for understanding why particular theories and approaches dominate at particular times (Schmidt 1998; Wæver 2003). At the same time, many would prefer to argue for an 'externalist' understanding of disciplinary evolution, where the main academic innovations are largely construed as responses to the changing anatomy of the field's primary object

of study (the EU/the politics of European integration).

THE STUDY OF EU POLITICS: SIX PERENNIAL ISSUES

The field of EU studies, or for the purposes of this volume, the study of 'EU politics', brings with it some particular local complications. These issues render problematic any attempt to establish what Wessels (2006: 233) calls the *'acquis academique'*, let alone trace its evolution.

First, it does not necessarily follow that 'EU politics' and 'the political science of the EU' are synonymous. 'Political science' may connote a set of techniques for study of political phenomena and there are those who argue that the most 'progress' has been made in EU studies at those points where the intellectual technologies most associated with mainstream political science have been applied most rigorously. However, it might be that the fullest picture of EU politics is obtained through the collective and sometimes collaborative efforts of several disciplinary communities.

Second, we are then led into some complex arguments about disciplines, subdisciplines and disciplinary/subdisciplinary boundaries. Within political science (broadly defined), we find a co-existing array of modes of enquiry, which often organize themselves into coherent fields such as public administration, policy analysis and political economy – each of which may by prefixed by 'comparative' or 'international'. Scholars of politics tend to auto-define themselves in terms of these sub-tribes, whilst retaining an overall affiliation to the label 'political scientist', although a dividing line is often drawn between IR and political science – not least in a good deal of the EU studies literature.

A third related point grows out of the question of disciplines and disciplinarity. Is EU studies a branch of (a particular) social science or is it a form of 'area studies'? It might also presuppose a clear stance on the status of alternative forms of knowledge generation: 'deductive' vs 'inductive', 'nomothetic' vs 'idiographic' and so on (Lustick 1997; Wallace 2000: 96; Jupille 2006; see also Calhoun 2003).

Fourth, is territoriality a key variable? On the face of it, the intellectual community of EU studies is multi-national and polyglot as well as being multi-disciplinary. Are there distinct inter-national or inter-regional cleavages in how the EU has been and is studied? Obviously, we might expect scholars from different parts of the world to bring 'local' (empirical or social scientific) preoccupations to the study of the EU. For example, is there a distinctively British/continental/European approach to the study of the EU and does it contrast with an American/US variant? Do these produce distinctive readings of EU politics? How embedded are these national or regional approaches? Do national/regional social scientific traditions and institutional constellations prevail as determinants of how EU politics is studied in particular places? Or has EU studies gradually converged or globalized (perhaps Americanized?) around a set of core propositions, puzzles and forms of knowledge production?

Fifth, there is the deceptively simple question: when did EU studies begin? The rather obvious response is to insist that a defined field of study begins when its object of study (the EU and its antecedents) is founded (1951 in the case of the ECSC). However, of course, fields of study can never have a precise 'year zero' in that the study of any social scientific object will draw upon both long standing and ephemeral intellectual resources. Thus, as Follesdal notes in this volume (Chapter 16), the normative case for a European federation pre-dates post-World War II institutional forms by at least two centuries. If the Communities are read as solutions to the problem of war, then the emergent discipline of IR had been dealing with such questions for decades (though see Schmidt 1998; Smith 2003). Moreover, if we think more broadly and historically about European *integration*, then the EU can be read as but a recent institutional expression of some very long-standing and long studied historical processes (Wallace 2002).

Finally, there is one further quite distinctive issue, namely the extent to which the EU itself has been integral to the promotion of the discipline(s) that seek to analyse it. The Commission's Jean Monnet Project (*Action Jean Monnet*) is well known as a major benefactor of teaching and research in European integration studies within Europe. The project's database lists a cumulative total of 2477 Monnet chairs, permanent courses, modules and centres of excellence, of which 509 are designated as falling within the remit of 'European political science'.[2] As well as further support for the creation of transnational research groups, the Commission contributes funds towards five major institutions across the continent: The College of Europe (campuses in Bruges, founded 1949, and Natolin, Warsaw, 1992), The European University Institute (Florence, founded 1975), the European Institute of Public Administration (Maastricht, 1981), the Academy of European Law (*Europäische Rechtsackademie*, Trier, 1992) and the International Centre for European Training (*Centre international de formation européenne*, Nice, 1954). More recently, the Commission's sixth framework programme made a particular point of ring fencing monies for the creation of European academic networks to study citizenship and governance issues. The Commission has also been a major funder of EU-related scholarship in the US. Ten EU Centers (EUCs – made up of individual universities or consortia of geographically adjacent institutions) were created in 1998 with funding averaging $500 000 per centre for 3 years. A total of 15 EUCs have received funding (Keeler 2005).[3]

Any attempt to make an argument about the history of EU studies or the study of EU politics needs to grapple with these questions. It is also true that each of the six problems introduced above represent ongoing controversies *within* the field. The contention here is that a crucial part of the history of EU studies, particularly within the last decade, has been about alternative representations of the history of the field and that these alternative representations bring with them consequences.

THE ANATOMY OF A FIELD

As noted above, the study of EU politics might be organized in a number of ways. Two stylized

Table 1.1   *Largest ECSAs.*

	Country (Association)	Membership	% of membership 'political science'
1	US (EUSA)	1600	78
2	UK (UACES)	1000	50
3	Japan (EUSA Japan)	487	30
4	Germany (AEI)	438	30
5	France (CEDECE)	410	20
6	Italy (AUSE)	300	18
7	China (CSEUS)	256	32
8	Russia (AES Russia)	230	26
9	Taiwan (EUSA-Taiwan)	207	20
10	Rep of Korea (ECSA Korea)	200	3

Source: http://www.ecsanet.org (accessed 7 February 2006).

Table 1.2   *ECSAs with at least 50% of membership identified as 'political science'.*

Country (Association)	% of membership 'political science'	Membership
US (EUSA)	78	1600
Norway (NFEF)	75	56
Denmark (DSE)	60	100
UK (UACES)	50	1000
Canada (ECSA-C)	50	150
Hong Kong (HKMAES)	50	110

Source: http://www.ecsanet.org (accessed 7 February 2006).

alternatives spring to mind. In the first, the study of EU politics would be the domain of political scientists, while lawyers would produce scholarship on European law, economists would focus on the EU economy and so on. At the other pole sits the claim that the study of EU politics should be an inherently multi- (perhaps inter-) disciplinary affair.

Academic Associations

One way to provide a snapshot of the disciplinary composition of EU studies involves examining the membership data provided by those organizations which explicitly purport to organize scholarship in the field. EU studies is most obviously organized through a network of European Community Studies Associations (ECSAs). Tables 1.1 and 1.2 are derived from information supplied by the overarching ECSA organization.[4] Table 1.1 simply ranks the world's 10 largest ECSAs and reproduces information on the proportion of the membership that is designated as 'political science'. Table 1.2

(again straightforwardly) lists the half dozen ECSAs where the 'political science' membership is said to be greater than or equal to 50%. It is worth noting that there are no fewer than 52 formally constituted ECSAs, suggesting that barely 10% can claim a majority 'political science' membership.

Yet, the total global ECSA membership (excluding associations for which there is incomplete data) is 6896, of whom 2957 are identified as 'political science' (43%). Of these, 1748 are members of just two national associations (EUSA, US and UACES, UK), suggesting that some 59% of the EU studies political science community is based in (or at least affiliated to) the two main Anglophone academic communities (42% are EUSA members alone). Indeed if EUSA and UACES members are removed, then the proportion of political scientists among the total global ECSA population falls to 23%. Of course, EUSA's membership extends beyond the territorial reach of the US, indeed it might reflect a perception of EUSA as the nodal point for scholars of EU politics worldwide. Indeed, EUSA's own membership statistics would seem to confirm this perception. Of a total membership in 2006 of 871,[5] 480 scholars (55%) are based in North America (of whom the majority – 459 or 53%– come from the US). Some 377 (43%) come form Europe. Of the European membership of EUSA, the British contingent numbers 119 (or 14% of the total membership). The other national groupings claiming in excess of 50 members are Belgium and Germany with 59 each.[6] EUSA's apparently cosmopolitan character is evidenced by the participation patterns at EUSA's biennial conferences, where a majority of delegates in 2005 were based in European institutions (Keeler 2005: 574).

The pre-eminent role of EUSA as a hub for the study of EU politics suggests that English is the dominant medium of communication and that scholars in the field regard Anglophone academic work – rightly or wrongly – as the generator of the most important writing about European integration. More benignly, it might simply reflect the status of English as the *de facto* academic *lingua franca* (Wessels 2006: 235).

However, the facts that (a) so much work is produced in English and (b) scholars across the globe appear to cluster around the US-based professional association tell us little about whether academic work on the EU is converging around a particular set of knowledge production norms. An obvious question concerns the extent to which the dominant approaches found in US political science dominate in turn the study of EU politics? Do the standard intellectual technologies act as a global benchmark for what counts as 'quality' work or 'progressive' research. An alternative hypothesis might speculate that the large numbers of non-US scholars working on the EU has brought particular theoretical traditions and local epistemologies into Anglophone work on EU politics and European integration.

Academic Journals and the EU Studies 'Mainstream'

These questions are discussed in more detail below, but for now it is worth examining the extent to which explicitly non-mainstream work (i.e. that which eschews in one way or another the dominant epistemological and methodological preoccupations of US political science) engages with the mainstream. One way of measuring this is to look at the venues in which such work appears. In this volume, Ian Manners (Chapter 4) provides a systematic overview of 'critical' studies of European politics. Manners' extensive bibliography cites 53 papers published in academic journals, with a total of 32 journals mentioned. Of these, the two citations of pieces in *European Union Politics* (*EUP*) should be bracketed as 'non-critical' sources. Of the remainder, only two papers appear in journals (*International Organization* and *International Studies Quarterly*) normally associated with the practices of the US mainstream.[7] Many of the other papers are scattered across (British) IR, critical political economy, critical legal studies, sociology and women's studies journals. Perhaps, therefore, we might speculate that while 'dissenting' or 'critical' work on the EU abounds, it is usually presented to and discussed within non-EU studies/political science academic communities. That would be to ignore the 13 cited articles that have been published by the two most prominent EU studies journals: the *Journal of Common Market Studies* (*JCMS* – four citations) and the *Journal of European Public Policy* (*JEPP* – nine citations).

Table 1.3 presents the six journals that self-identify as outlets for the discussion of EU politics/European integration (as opposed to European politics more generally).[8] Of these, one (*European Integration Online Papers*) is a refereed working paper series and three (including *JCMS* and *JEPP*) possess ISI accreditation, meaning that articles appear in the Social Science Citation Index. The editorial balance is overwhelmingly UK/European, although the bi-lingual *Journal of European Integration/Revue d'Intégration Européenne* (*JEI*) was edited from Canada for many years.

With the outlier exception of *EUP*, each of these journals has identified itself (and by implication EU studies) as a place for conversations between disciplines. Kitzinger's (1962a: v)[9] editorial in the first number of *JCMS* announced the journal's aspiration to become

Table 1.3   *(English language) journals with a focus on 'EU politics'.*

Title	Founded	Current editorial base	ISI status
European Foreign Affairs Review	1996	UK	
European Integration Online Papers	1998	Austria	
European Union Politics	2000	Germany/UK/US	✓
Journal of Common Market Studies	1962	UK	✓
Journal of European Integration/Revue d'Intégration Européenne	1978	UK	
Journal of European Public Policy	1994	UK	✓

'a forum of high-level exchanges between scholars and policy-makers in different fields'. The *JEI* describes its focus as 'interdisciplinary or multidisciplinary … thus integrating politics, economics, law, history and sociology'.[10] The founding editorial of *JEPP* speaks of the journal's intention to draw upon the widest possible range of social scientific disciplines (Richardson and Lindley 1994). *JCMS* editorials penned at moments of editorial change have always reaffirmed this founding commitment. However, they also provide important insights into how senior figures in EU studies were thinking about the field at particular moments in its development. Take Tsoukalis's (1980: 215) argument when he assumed the helm at the *JCMS* in 1980: 'integration theory has been run into the ground, probably because we have been slow in realizing that this new and complex phenomenon could not be studied by our conventional tools of analysis'. This stands in remarkably sharp contrast to those arguing the precise contrary: that the problem in the study of the EU has been the *failure* to properly embrace and apply conventional political/social scientific tools of analysis (see *inter alia* Hix 1994, 1996, 1998, 2005; Moravcsik 1997, 1998, 1999a, b; Dowding 2000; Schneider et al. 2000; McLean 2003; Pahre 2005). New editors have also been keen to foresee their journals as responsive to conceptual and epistemological trends within the social sciences. *JEPP*, for example, is conceived as an expression of the maturity of policy analysis and its status as a 'rigorous scientific activity' (Richardson and Lindley 1994: 1). Back in 1980 at the *JCMS*, Tsoukalis (1980: 215) was noting the affinities between the journal's scope and the emergent sub-disciplinary project of

international political economy (IPE) (see also Katzenstein et al. 1998; Murphy and Nelson 2001; Verdun 2005). Bulmer and Scott's (1991) tenure would be attentive to the significance of legal scholarship and the points at which it might intersect with economics and political science (see also Shaw and More 1995). Their successors (Begg and Peterson 1999) identified 'globalization' and 'governance' as new key macro-themes that would influence the study of the EU and suggested that scholarship would need to grapple with the institutional consequences of a wealth of local EU developments such as monetary union and the growth of foreign and security policy competence. The most recent *JCMS* editorial statement – attentive perhaps to the controversies raised by the 'perestroika' movement in US political science – moved on from statements about multi- and post-disciplinarity to claim the journal as a non-sectarian refuge for methodological and epistemological pluralism (Paterson and Rollo 2004). Additionally there is a tendency to describe the focal point of these outlets as rather more than the EU (and its precursors). Indeed the *JCMS*, though obviously stimulated by the European experiments of the 1950s, was always keen to publish work on the growth of customs unions and common markets across the world as evidenced by the appointment of the Mexican-based Miguel Wionczek as joint editor in 1966.[11]

Stark contrast is provided by the one EU politics journal, already identified as an 'outlier', *EUP*. While the opening editorial (Schneider et al. 2000) anticipates contributions from across the social science spectrum and even intimates that the likes of postmodernism might find a place in the journal, there are some very clear pointers to the type of work that is likely to be (indeed has been) published.[12] One of the most interesting features of *EUP*'s first few years has been the publication of pieces by scholars who come from beyond the conventional orbit of EU studies, but are noted as leading protagonists in particular areas of political scientific enquiry. These papers review the 'progress' of the study of EU politics in light of clearly rationalist benchmarks (see Dowding (2000) on rational choice institutionalism and McLean (2003) on the analytic narratives approach). Take also what might be called the two 'founding complaints' of the journal. First there is an argument that work on EU politics was dominated by 'grand' IR theories (Schneider et al. 2000: 6). Second, the journal's existence is justified because the study of EU politics 'does not yet possess an outlet that concentrates on the most advanced and methodologically sophisticated research papers' (Schneider et al. 2000: 6). This, of course, implies that none of the extant journals on the EU perform this task adequately. Instead the best papers are held to be scattered throughout a range of general political science journals and *EUP* is designed to act as a rallying point for such work.

It is of course true that a full audit of research on EU politics cannot be confined to the output of sources that are auto-defined as 'EU journals'. Keeler's (2005) extensive mapping of the development of EU studies between 1960–2001 sought data on the publication patterns of 24 journals, thereby looking at not only EU studies periodicals, but also the primary political science journals of five countries and over a dozen more general politics and IR outlets. To examine the trends of EU studies within the US, Jupille (2006) opts to examine the EU-related output of two journals in each of two main sub-fields (comparative politics and IR) in American political science. It is difficult to miss the importance of *International Organization* (*IO*) as a long-standing arena for the discussion of European integration and the dynamics of EU politics (Katzenstein et al. 1998). Indeed, to ignore *IO*'s

output in the 1960s and early 1970s in favour of, say, the *JCMS* would almost certainly leave the reader with a very skewed impression of the significance of and the internal discussions within neofunctionalism.

CONVENTIONAL NARRATIVES OF THE STUDY OF EU POLITICS

Within EU studies, there are several very well established claims about the history of the field and scholars have provided multiple reconfigurations of the past. The story is usually told sequentially in terms of a number of staging-posts. Theoretical debate and evolution is the most obvious hook upon which the narrative is hung. However, precisely how this is done and with what purposes and consequences varies.

Within the mainstream Anglophone literature it is relatively easy to identify a series of theoretical points of reference around which much EU studies work has been organized (see Rosamond 2000 for a full account). Normative federalist thinking is often bracketed with David Mitrany's functionalist theory of institutional design and Karl Deutsch's transactionalist account of the formation of security communities to form a set of precursor theories, which fed – in various ways – into the thinking of the first generation of scholars to grapple properly with the institutions of postwar integration – the neofunctionalists. Neofunctionalism, in its classical incarnation, is thought to be bounded at one end by the publication in 1958 of Haas's (1958) *The Uniting of Europe* and at the other by a couple of essays from the mid 1970s, also by Haas (1975, 1976), in which regional integration theory was declared 'obsolescent'. In the interim neofunctionalism had been exposed to a powerful intergovernmentalist critique (Hoffmann 1966 is always cited; see also Hansen 1969), but for many its primary problem was its incapacity to build a general predictive theory of regional integration from its inductive engagement with the early

European experience. A cautionary theoretical atmosphere came over EU studies throughout much of the 1970s as social science more generally became less enamoured with the ambitions of grand theory, choosing instead to focus on the 'mid range'.

Events within the Communities during the 1980s yielded a series of attempts to revive and update neofunctionalism, but also induced the composition of a systematic liberal intergovernmentalist theory (Moravcsik 1998). Meanwhile, scholars from comparative politics and policy analytic traditions flocked to the EU as an object of study, bringing with them a host of concepts and theories. This led to the EU being theorized less as a case of 'integration' and more as a 'polity' or a 'political system', although there remained some quite profound disagreements about whether the object was a transcendent or familiar phenomenon. The EU came to be treated variously as a classic Lasswellian polity, a proto-federation, a system of (multi-level) governance or as a test case for one of the three emergent 'new institutionalist' paradigms.

By the late 1990s, there was significant momentum in three further areas. First, despite the powerful arguments of comparativists and policy analysts, the growth of EU foreign policy competence seemed to clear the way for theories of IR and foreign policy-making to (re-)enter EU studies (White 2001; Jørgensen 2004; Andreatta 2005). Second, the injection of constructivism into EU studies (largely from IR, but also from European social theory) provided a major theoretical challenge to the repertoire of 'rationalist' approaches to both integration and the EU polity and took debate in EU studies into the domain of metatheory. Third, concerns about the EU's legitimacy and democratic credentials fed a growing interest of the application of normative political theory to the EU. Beneath these broad umbrellas sit a diverse array of theories and approaches.

The creation of a narrative (such as that of the previous paragraphs) is a far from neutral exercise. For example, there is a clear implication, tackled more systematically in what follows, that one of the major stimuli for change

or reordering in the EU studies theoretical repertoire has been the changing nature of the EU itself. Moreover, simply by telling the story sequentially, such accounts are naturally prone to privilege present theoretical efforts over those of the past – or at the very least it begets the unexamined assumption that the theoretical work of 30–40 years ago was beset with problems and difficulties.

ORGANIZING STORIES ABOUT EU STUDIES

The standard story of EU studies may be straightforward enough, but it can be organized in different ways and with different purposes. As a prelude to the final sections of this chapter, which explore some of the standard modes of organizing this story, this section examines three 'meta' issues of concern. These are, respectively, whether there should be a (disciplinary) mainstream in EU studies and the derivative questions of what constitutes 'progress' in the field and to what conceptions of social science should EU scholars subscribe.

Mainstreaming vs Pluralism

Much of the foregoing points to an ongoing disagreement within the field of EU politics about both its proper scope as a branch of social scientific enquiry and the appropriate way(s) in which is should seek to accumulate knowledge. Table 1.4 presents a heavily and deliberately stylized ideal-typical version of this debate, representing the opposition between two broad ideal types – labelled here the 'mainstreaming' model and the 'pluralistic' model. Each model contains three functionally equivalent propositions designed to show the potential scope of disagreement within the field about (a) disciplinary co-ordinates, (b) epistemological and methodological commitments and (c) the ontological relationship between the object (the EU polity) and the intellectual tools needed to study it.

The debate is presented in this simplified version for heuristic purposes. It might be that

Table 1.4   *Two models of the study of EU politics.*

The mainstream model	The pluralistic model
The study of EU politics is best served by the standard tools of political science.	The study of EU politics is an inherently multidisciplinary affair.
Good political science conforms to a set of standardized epistemological positions and methodological rules of thumb.	The study of EU politics benefits from the input of work from diverse epistemological and methodological standpoints.
The EU is a polity 'like any other' that lends itself to the intellectual technologies developed over time by mainstream political science.	The EU is a new type of polity. The tools of standard political science may not be appropriate.

these two positions are better thought of as a continuum, with most scholars taking up a position somewhere along a line plotted between these two polar views. In particular it is important not to fall into the trap of assuming that all work on the EU emanating from formal theory and using quantitative methods sits at the extreme 'mainstreaming' end of the continuum (Pahre 2005). Moreover, from one angle at least, these two broad images of the field are not wholly incommensurable. From the position of the pure 'pluralist', enquiry building upon the propositions of the 'mainstreaming' model is perfectly acceptable – so long as it remains one approach amongst many (Wallace 2000). The 'ultra' version of the mainstreaming model, however, takes an extreme Kuhnian stance in that its understanding of science and scientific progress is predicated upon the idea of scholarly communities working around tightly policed sets of norms ('normal science') where there is little space for deviance or dissent (Kuhn 1996; on EU studies implications see Manners 2003). Of course, these arguments and oppositions are not confined to EU studies. Controversies of scientific exclusivity vs methodological/epistemological pluralism sit at the heart of the 'perestroika' movement's critique of the allegedly exclusionary practises of mainstream American political science (see *inter alia* Mearsheimer 2001; Dryzek 2002; Lubomudrov 2002; and, more popularly, Cohn 1999).

The pluralistic position is obviously tolerant of the so-called critical approaches discussed in this volume by Manners (Chapter 4), regardless of their epistemological credentials.

As we move towards the 'mainstreaming' pole, so the quality of 'critical' work comes to be scrutinized for the extent to which it fits a standard model of theory building (Pahre 2005). For example, one of the interesting debates within the constructivist tradition (see Checkel, Chapter 3) – a debate that has been played out explicitly within EU studies – concerns the extent to which constructivism should seek to share the same epistemological territory as rationalism (Pollack, chapter 2). Self-defined 'constructivist' work on the EU actually covers a vast metatheoretical territory (Christiansen et al. 2001) with scholars dispersed across a continuum between 'rationalist' and 'reflectivist' poles (Keohane 1988). There would seem to be two distinct 'constructivist' positions, one of which leans significantly towards the 'mainstreaming' pole. The debate between Checkel (2001a, b) and Moravcsik (2001a) is organized around the degree to which constructivist work on the EU *can* conform to standardized theory building norms (an aspiration clearly associated with the IR constructivist project of Wendt (1999); see also Wendt (2001) and Fearon and Wendt (2002)). Moravcsik's (1999b, 2001b) various critiques of the more reflectivist work on EU constructivism assess such contributions in relation to a series of benchmark definitions of 'good' social science practice (the formulation of explicit hypotheses that make possible disconfirmation and research design that allows replication – see also Moravcsik (1997, 1998: ch. 1)).[13]

A further question that follows from the presentation of the two models is quite simply to wonder whether they are reflective of different traditions in the study of politics: crudely, one 'American' (aspiring to scientific naturalism, theory driven, aspiring to 'normal scientific' synthesis),[14] the other 'non-American' (historicist, influenced more by broader social theoretic currents) (Wæver 1998: 724; Wallace 2000: 103). This contrast is drawn frequently enough. The assumption of a historic transatlantic divide in EU studies has achieved the status of a 'stylized fact', to coin a favourite rationalist phrase. Verdun (2005), for example, draws a contrast between theory-oriented 'American' research on the EU and 'European' case study-oriented work. The latter are – in effect – 'EU-ists' first and foremost, while the latter are 'political scientists' who use the EU as a case. The first British evaluations of the early American work on the communities seems to predict the 'two traditions', with reviews apparently bewildered by the use of theory. Take the founding editor's discussion of Haas's *The Uniting of Europe* in the *JCMS*: '[t]he conceptual discussions of the first chapter are tough going and British readers might be tempted to ask if the ponderous terminology assists as much as it impresses the ordinary student' (Kitzinger 1962b: 189).[15] There is an ongoing scepticism about (American) deductive, theory-driven work, which – allegedly – privileges theory over the accumulation of empirical knowledge. Much of the historical work on the EU (see Milward's essay in Chapter 5 of this volume) is built around a powerful defence of inductive research strategies in opposition to the supposed simplifications of history that characterized the first generation of deductive integration scholarship (Milward 1992; Milward and Sørensen 1993; Dinan 2006; Kaiser 2006).

Yet, we have to be very careful with such bold 'two camp' characterizations of EU studies. In particular, a literal understanding of this divide as purely geographic is likely to miss significant nuances. More productive is a sociological use of the terms 'European' and 'American' as signifiers of distinctive epistemological commitments, themselves embedded within distinctive cultural-institutional contexts (Wæver 1998). So, for example, we cannot understand the conduct of work on the EU that emanates from political scientists within US institutions, without understanding (a) the various scholarly norms that govern the admissibility and quality of academic research and (b) the incentive structures that prevail within the profession (Whitley 1984; Wagner et al. 1991). Therefore, the interesting question surrounds the extent to which culturally bound modes of knowledge production become influential beyond their locale (i.e. to what extent are they globalized?). Geography matters in so far as the social sciences (indeed disciplinarity more generally) are strongly rooted within the logic of nation-state (Mancias 1987), but it is the spread of scholarly styles and their capacity to penetrate 'alien' academic cultures that provokes interest.

The assumption of a straightforward geographic divide between 'American' and 'British' and/or 'European' approaches to EU politics can miss some key arguments. Jupille (2006) offers a very helpful cartography of approaches that exist at a level higher than precise theoretical choice (say neofunctionalism vs intergovernmentalism; sociological vs rational choice institutionalism), but which at the same time helps us to understand why scholars make those theoretical choices and make particular methodological commitments. It helps us to gather together some of the points made already. The first three cleavages identified by Jupille (*ontology, epistemology* and *social theory*) in effect account for the divisions between and the debates within the three broad schools of theory – rationalism, constructivism, critical approaches – that the three following chapters review. The fourth and fifth cleavages are, respectively, *disciplinarity* and *scholarly style*. As suggested already, *a priori* stances towards both of these are likely to be profoundly influential upon how scholars formulate puzzles, make theoretical choices and conduct the research process. A comparativist based in a top 10 US political science department with an interest in EU politics will make her own theoretical and methodological choices, but not altogether within conditions of her own choosing (see also Wiener and Diez 2004).

'Progress' in the Study of EU Politics

Different locations on an imaginary continuum between the 'mainstreaming' and the 'pluralist' position bring with them alternative understandings of *progress* in the field. The stylized 'mainstreaming' position is confident in political science's capacity to improve progressively its intellectual technologies over time. As such, the stock of secure social scientific knowledge is improved. The advantage of 'mainstreaming' as a strategy is precisely that it exposes scholars of the EU to the most advanced techniques available. Empirical advancement is inevitable, particularly since such techniques provide insurance that appropriate levels of analytical leverage are achieved (i.e. the EU is not reduced to the status of a single *n*). At the other end of the scale, 'pluralists' (some of whom – particular strands of postmodern science in particular – are actively hostile to the disciplining notion of 'progress') are cautious about bold claims of advancement, particularly if they amount to arguments that some traditions of work should be discounted as useless. A pluralist take on the study of EU politics would imagine the productive coexistence of multiple approaches, each with its own internal understanding of scholarly advancement. This, of course, threatens a kind of intellectual 'Balkanization', where a series of academic tribes co-exist, but rarely communicate (Jupille 2006). The solution – from a pluralist stance – is to facilitate communication without imposing one tribe's version of how research is justified and evaluated.

Social Science and the Study of EU Politics

The two models rather obviously have different understandings of the kind(s) of social science we need to know in order to study EU politics. By definition, the 'mainstreaming' pole of the continuum takes the view that the authorized mainstream of political science supplies the reference stock for the scholar of the EU. Scholars should be 'trained' according to the standard manuals of (US) graduate courses (for example, King et al. 1994), be acquainted with the latest ideas in how to provide rigour to case-based empirical work (for example Bates et al. 1998), understand the latest formal and statistical techniques and draw inspiration from the best research published in the world's leading political science journals (which in all likelihood will investigate cases other than the EU). As these norms spread and become embedded, so progressive research programmes on EU politics – umbilically linked to other research programmes – will emerge and empirical knowledge will advance.

The alternative position imagines that wide and eclectic reading should inform the study of EU politics. It distrusts the secure foundations attributed to standard political science by the 'mainstreamers', and perhaps draws attention to very broad meta-developments across intellectual life that closed Kuhnian communities miss (Manners 2003). Inevitably this becomes an argument for multi- or interdisciplinarity (Rumford and Murray 2003; Cini 2006) and places its advocates towards the 'complexity' side of what Hay (2002: 34–7) labels the 'parsimony-complexity trade off'. However, it also forces us to examine arguments that, instead of privileging discipline-based knowledge production, actively celebrate studies of 'the particular'. These arguments in turn are not comfortable with ideas such as Bates' (1996: 1) maxim that 'area studies has failed to generate scientific knowledge', seeing them as imperializing interventions on behalf of particular approaches (Johnson 1997). Pure disciplinarity brings with it a search for global/universal laws of political motion. This assumes, *a priori*, that localities/regions are, at a crucial level, not context bound and subject to particularistic dynamics (Appadurai 1996). This axis of debate has been particularly important to discussions about European studies in the US

(Calhoun 2003), where expectations brought by disciplinarity norms have been read as threats to the nurturing of area and regional expertise (Hancock 1999; Rosenthal 1999).

UNDERSTANDING THE COURSE OF THE STUDY OF EU POLITICS

It follows, of course, that quite different readings of the history of EU studies follow from the various oppositions that emerge from alternative models of the study of EU politics. For example, an assumption of the progressive advancement of political science over time carries the axiological consequence that EU studies is in a *better* place now than it was in the past, precisely because of the recent arrival into the field of *advanced* techniques. It is not just the structure of the narrative, but its substance which is at stake. As we move towards the 'mainstreaming' position, so the story of the study of EU politics comes to be more and more about application of political science to the EU, at the expense of other starting points. In other words, it is easy to slip into a way of telling history that (a) places the 'present' as the *telos* to which all hitherto existing theory leads and (b) treats earlier phases of work as necessarily 'prototypical of the present' (Gunnell 2005: 597). Conventional (textbook) narratives of IR have been criticized precisely because of this tendency towards 'presentism' (Schmidt 1998, 2002; Smith 2000b; Wæver 2003; Williams 2005). Thus, the oft heard claim that IR is about the problem of interstate war actively excludes work from the canon that is not premised on the discussion of this topic. Auto-definition produces a narrative (and polices the discipline's borders) in ways that confirm the authority of that auto-definition. The same is true of IR's theoretical canon, where recent scholarship suggests that the linear link (assumed by both neorealists and their critics) between realism and neorealism is dependent on serious misconstrual and simplification of the breadth and substance of classical realist writings (Murray 1997; Williams 2005). Claims about the past of the

field are – in effect – moves that frame notions of disciplinary and theoretical authenticity in the present. The story of the field is likely to be told differently by observers with diverse takes on the present state of the art. Three ways of organizing the state of knowledge in EU politics are presented here.

The first is to map theoretical change against empirical change. The presumption here is that there is and should be a close relationship between (a) the study of EU politics and (b) the 'real world' conduct of that politics and the institutional contexts within which it takes place. Thus, Anderson (1995) argues that the opposition between neofunctionalism and intergovernmentalism is rendered yet more sterile by the growing complexity of the EU from the 1980s on. The 'old' theories produce 'narrow puzzles that differ only at the margins and that lack empirical and theoretical reach' (Anderson 1995: 455). The solution is to turn to tools from comparative political economy (theories of negotiating and bargaining), rational choice theory, policy analysis (policy network analysis) and political science (the new institutionalisms). Diez and Wiener's (2004) classification of EU theory relies upon a three phase movement, where each phase is defined by a macro-puzzle, which in turn corresponds to a particular phases in the EU's history. The first phase sees scholarship seeking to 'explain integration' (1960s onwards) following the founding Treaties. The second phase (from the mid-1980s) is organized around the analysis of 'governance' and the EU polity (following the SEA). The third phase (from the 1990s), labelled 'constructing the EU' reflects the important appearance of constructivist analysis, but also addresses the important normative and constitutional implications of recent treaty reforms. In a slightly different light, Keeler (2005) divides EU studies into three phases in which the fortunes of academic work wax and wane in a co-variant way with the fortunes of the EU: the 'launch era', where the empirical driver was the Treaty of Rome (and presumably the Treaty of Paris before it) and debate was organized around the opposition between neofunctionalist and intergovernmentalist theories of integration; the 'doldrums' era after the 'empty chair crisis' in which theoretical work stagnated and grand theorizing became a no-go area in EU studies; and the renaissance/boom era that followed the *relance* of integration from the mid-1980s.[16]

A second common way of thinking about the evolution of EU studies involves the organization of classifications of the present field in ways that rely upon a kind of intellectual 'throat clearing' in which the history of EU studies past is reconstructed. This is very commonplace in the EU studies literature, so only a few prominent and interestingly contrasting examples are offered here. Hix (2005) presents the field in the here and now as clustered into three broad schools: liberal intergovernmentalism (LI – as elaborated by Moravcsik), an assortment of approaches that share the central concept of 'governance', and rational choice institutionalism. Of course, these are hardly functional equivalents. LI is – to all intents and purposes – the intellectual project of a single scholar (Schimmelfennig 2004),[17] whereas the governance school is a loose coalition of sub-schools with variable epistemological commitments. Meanwhile, rational choice institutionalism is characterized by a rather more coherent intellectual community that intervenes in the study of EU politics from the epicentre of US political science. These three approaches deserve their status as inductees into the present state of the art because they represent departures from at least one of two errors of previous work. In the first place, each contains the potential to generate *testable* propositions in the empirical context of the EU – a deep problem of EU studies past (see also Moravcsik 1997, 1998). Second, each of the three represents an escape from the disciplinary straitjacket of IR, which cast the study of EU politics as a series of puzzles about 'integration', when in fact the EU had come to function as a polity/political system (on which, see Hix 1994, 1996). The most obvious casualty of *both* the move away from IR *and* the appeal for rigorous academic standards is neofunctionalism. As Moravcsik (2005: 357) notes, '[f]rom 1958 to the late 1980s, neofunctionalism was the only game in town'. In many ways the neofunctionalist scholars were responsible for the totality of integration theory for much of the 1960s and

1970s.[18] Therefore, to deny neofunctionalism a place at the contemporary table is to cast very serious doubt on the credentials of the entire field's past.

Hooghe (2001) lists three contenders as rival 'macrotheoretic' models for the study of EU politics – united by (the political scientific) aspiration to produce comparative insights across cases. They are LI, a revised version of neofunctionalism (associated with Sandholtz and Stone Sweet 1998) and multi-level governance (MLG). This is a slightly revised version of the position developed earlier by the MLG school, where MLG is presented as an emerging and coherent rival to LI (Marks et al. 1996a). As such, MLG seems, initially at least, to have displaced neofunctionalism as the main pole of non-intergovernmentalist thinking on the EU. MLG scholars were very keen to show how their approach spoke directly to the changing nature of the EU (Marks et al. 1996a: 373), where new, multi-layered, multi-actor, fluid modes of governance made the simplistic, two-level game imagery of LI appear both empirically sterile and analytically limited (Marks et al. 1996a, b). Moreover, the MLG literature on European integration was but a small segment of a wider analytical and normative literature found in local government studies, public policy analysis, comparative federalism and IR on the changing forms and spatialities of governance (Hooghe and Marks 2003).

In contrast, Pollack (2005a, b) prefers to depict the state of the art as consisting of three coexistent communities, within which the degree of scholarly consensus varies from fundamental metatheoretical disagreements to the practice of something resembling a Kuhnian 'normal science'. The first of these is the (IR) debate between rationalist-constructivist *approaches*, which Pollack sees as displacing the rivalry between the two classical rationalist *theories* (neofunctionalism and intergovernmentalism).[19] Pollack's second community finds a 'spiritual home' in *EUP* (Pollack 2005b: 370) and clusters together those scholars who have brought the tools of (mainstream rationalist) comparative political science to bear upon the study of legislative, executive and judicial politics of the EU. This work proceeds via the maxims of 'normal science' and quite obviously builds upon insights from mainstream *American* political science about aspects of *American* politics. More diverse, potentially less rationalist and certainly less 'American' is the group of public policy, ideational and social theoretic approaches which utilize the concept of 'governance' (on the growth of the concept see van Kersbergen and van Waarden (2004)). The development of these three traditions in EU studies, once again, is seen as a vast improvement upon the analytical blind alley of neofunctionalism vs intergovernmentalism.

The third narrative of evolution of the study of EU politics follows the second's implicit progressivism – but others are much more explicit in their claims that the EU is in a far superior state of health now than in was in the past. More often than not, this move cites as the primary drivers of this new rigour the growth of formal and statistical modelling in EU studies and the appearance of work that openly subscribes to the theory building norms of US political science. Following the publication of Moravcsik's (1998) *The Choice for Europe,* Caporaso (1999: 161) maintained that '[s]tandards that apply in other sub-fields, for example, with regard to research design, data collection, and analysis, are more likely to extend to regional integration studies also'. In a jointly authored paper, one of the editors of EUP has written that '[n]eoinstitutionalist research has played a central role in the *professionalisation* of EU politics, and it does not seem inconceivable that the sub-field will become an exporter of new analytical tools rather than the passive importer it has been for decades' (Schneider and Aspinwall 2001: 177, my emphasis). McLean (2003: 499, my emphasis), welcoming the arrival of game theoretic work and theories of social choice into EU studies, reflects that '[f]or the first three decades of the existence of the EU and its predecessor organizations, almost all social science literature on it of which I am aware was *purely descriptive'.* Dowding (2000) writes approvingly of rational choice institutionalist work as *the* 'normal science' of EU studies.

It should be quite clear from the foregoing that these disciplinary histories narrate the evolution of the study of EU politics in often quite distinct ways, perhaps reflecting a particular theoretical or social scientific preference located in the *present.* Having said that, there does seem to be some common ground – around the likes of (a) the existence of a period of theoretical decline/stagnation that coincided with the Communities' own crises/Eurosclerosis of the 1960s and 1970s, (b) the displacement of IR in general and neofunctionalism in particular, (c) the rise to prominence quite recently of comparative politics and governance approaches, and (d) a general sense of improvement and progress in the field that some associate with the insertion of rigour and a logic of 'mainstreaming' into a hitherto 'backward' and 'ghettoized' field.

'INTERNALIST' AND 'EXTERNALIST' ACCOUNTS OF EU STUDIES

What also follows from these narratives of EU studies history is an understanding that changes in the object of study (the EU) have accounted for the changing anatomy of the field in terms of the theoretical traditions and scholarly communities that populate it. As Wæver (2003) notes, the intellectual evolution of a field is often thought of as being closely tied to developments within the object of study. Thus, it might be argued that the trajectory of EU studies in general, and its theoretical repertoire in particular, is a function of the changing nature of the EU over time. So to pick out some random examples, neofunctionalism might be read as an intellectual expression of the strategies employed by European elites that were embodied in the Schuman Declaration of 1950 and the subsequent institutional design of the early Communities. Similarly, the appearance of intergovernmental critiques and the collapse of the neofunctionalist project appear to be reactions to the growing visibility of national executives and intergovernmental institutional expressions in the Community system from the mid-1960s. The increasing tendency of current literature to conceptualize the EU as a political system can be traced to the obvious salience of the EU as a supplier of authoritative outputs and the attendant complexity of the multi-actor policy process that surrounds the EU's institutions. Finally, the rapid recent growth of studies of the external dimensions of European integration may seem an obvious consequence of (a) the growth of foreign, security and defence policy agendas and competencies, (b) the emerging status of the Euro as an alternative reserve currency and (c) the widening issue base of international trade that has forced issues of European integration (such as the Common Agricultural Policy) onto the agenda of the World Trade Organization.

Following Wæver (2003; see also Schmidt 1998), there are two variants of such an externalist position. The first celebrates this process as a sign of disciplinary progress in which EU studies has drawn valuable lessons from its object of study though a process of intellectual 'catch-up'. From this stance, it is imperative that EU remains an academic expression of the 'real world' of European integration and EU governance. Therefore, approaches to the EU that no longer 'fit' their object are candidates for disposal, although there may be cases where reinstatement is merited if the tide of integration shifts back in the direction of certain perspectives. The second position is rather more critical. Here scholarship is interrogated for its potential to act as the intellectual legitimation of particular ideologies associated with the object of study. A good example from EU studies is to be found in Milward and Sørensen's (1993) energetic critique of neofunctionalism, where the latter is portrayed as both (a) a Cold War theory offering an intellectual justification for US foreign policy priorities of the 1950s and (b) an attractive set of categories for the emerging supranational European elite to deploy in defence of their claims for the growth of Community-level governance capacity (see also White 2003).

Wæver (2003: 5) maintains that 'external explanations can sometimes … be better at accounting for the overall directions of change [in a field], but they can never explain the form that theory takes'. So, for example, institutionalist

approaches may appear to sit well with the broad treaty-induced and path-dependent pattern of EU politics, but this cannot explain why *rational choice* institutionalism (for example) has been applied so readily to the EU and why rationalist epistemologies are claimed to offer the basis for a coherent research programme that brings together the various insights of the three institutionalisms (Schneider and Aspinwall 2001; see also Jupille and Caporaso 1999). Pollack's (2005a, b) ascription of the term 'normal science' to a body of comparative work on the EU is highly appropriate because it proceeds from a set of shared axioms about the construction, evaluation and epistemological foundations of research, which together constitute measures of 'quality' that apply especially within the dominant circuits of US political science. If work aspires to the 'kite mark' of quality (with all that implies), then it is barely surprising that so much emerging American work on EU politics conforms to this tradition.

Wæver's distinction between 'externalist' and 'internalist' readings of disciplinary history resonates with Wessels' (2006) discussion of 'pull' factors (from the EU) and 'push' factors (from the discipline) that together act as drivers of the changing shape of EU studies. Any proper discussion of the study of EU politics needs to understand both of these dimensions. Indeed, the 'external'/'push' and 'internal'/'pull' framework gives us a useful way into critical analysis of the various extant formal and informal disciplinary histories of EU studies. It also shows how academic work operates within certain 'conditions of possibility', governed by both its object and the sociology of academic enquiry at different points in time. We should also recognize that 'external'/'push' and 'internal'/'pull' factors do not operate independently of one another.

Put simply, how we read the evolution of the EU is a function of the intellectual lenses we use. The description of the EU at particular moments in its history is an act that cannot occur independently of an *a priori* conceptual vocabulary that facilitates that description. Thus, the EU can be defined in ways that favour either standard political science treatments or less orthodox, cross disciplinary or 'critical' approaches (on the latter, see Geyer 2003). Moreover, descriptions of the EU are also often re-descriptions of a particular phase in the EU's history from a point where new disciplinary conditions of possibility apply. A good example, is the presumption of the period of 'Eurosclerosis' between *circa* 1966 and 1985 – a period whose 'bookends' are the empty chair crisis and the Luxembourg compromise in the 1960s and the publication of the Commission's White Paper on the internal market in the 1980s. Wincott (1995) shows how an intergovernmentalist reading of the Communities, with its expectation that key integration moments coincide with grand member-state bargains, is bound to construct this period as sterile because it brackets as insignificant everyday institutional interaction and key acts of jurisprudence by the European Court of Justice (see Weiler 1991; Christiansen and Jørgensen 1999).

Keeler's (2005) discovery of a 'doldrums' period in academic research on European integration that coincides with the 'Eurosclerosis' period is an important finding, but it might show a prevailing *perception* amongst established scholars and prospective doctoral students, armed as they were with particular intellectual technologies, that there were few (perhaps no) interesting academic puzzles resident within the Communities. That perception relies upon a description and the description in turn may represent the limitations of the political science of the time, rather than anything inherent within the Community system. At the time, one prominent scholar of the Community system was arguing that de Gaulle's interventions were not brakes on integration, but rather attempts to re-calibrate the nuances of the balance of policy-making forces within an already institutionalized Community model (Lindberg 1966; see also Inglehart 1967). Pushed to its post-positivist limits, this type of argument leads to complex arguments about the co-constitution of subject and object. Smith (2000a: 33, emphasis added) discussed the application of 'rationalist' theory to European integration as follows: 'far from being the explanatory theory that it claims to be, instead provides a political and normative account of

European integration whereby (positivist) notions of how to explain a given "reality" in fact *constitute* the reality of European integration' (see also Bailey 2006).

Figure 1.1 offers a broad framework for engaging with standard disciplinary histories of EU studies/the study of EU politics. It places emphasis on the importance of and the inter-action between 'internal' and 'external' drivers of the field's development. It adds a third driver, which is identified explicitly by Hooghe (2001). She suggests that the appearance from the 1980s of comparative politics research on the EU had much to do with the fact that systematic EU-level data sets were created and became available to the academic community. Thus, the archive of Eurobarometer data, the appearance (from 1979) of European Parliament electoral data and the vast amounts of material generated by the Commission through Eurostat created a resource that allowed scholars of a particular inclination to utilize the EU (or parts of it) as a case. This important observation reinforces the point, developed above, that our objects of study do not exist independently of our readings of them. It also pushes the idea that objects of study are responsible for defining *themselves* in ways that allow academic analysis. To this should be added the array of supports for EU studies research and pedagogy that were identified earlier in this chapter. Thus, the 'knowa-bility' of the EU to political science is something that develops and changes over time.

How then might such a framework be used to make an intervention in the discussion of the development of work on EU politics? The foregoing ought to suggest that it is very difficult to write singular histories of the field and that perhaps the task of intellectual historians to perform a kind of 'double reading' where existing accounts are exposed to critical scrutiny in light of the framework presented here. This might involve the identification and evaluation of the types of moves that are made in the writing of stories of the field, not simply to judge the empirical plausibility of those moves (for example, is the rejection of neo-functionalism justified when we re-read the

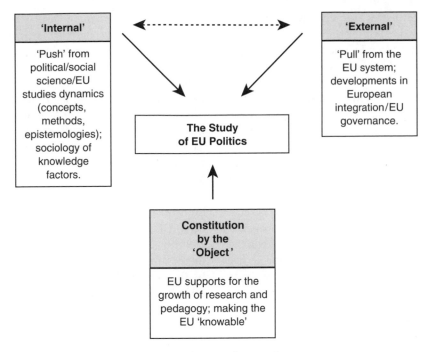

Figure 1.1   *A framework for critical disciplinary history of EU studies.*

original neofunctionalist texts?), but also to understand the reasons why such narrative moves are made in the first place (for example, does the rejection of neofunctionalism clear the way for certain claims about the appropriate theoretical scope of the field in the present?).

For illustrative purposes, the remainder of this chapter is devoted to the interrogation of two broad and recurrent claims, which tend to point an accusatory finger at neofunctionalism (see also Rosamond 2005): (a) the idea that the study of EU politics has moved beyond the sterility of IR and (b) the idea that EU studies past was characterized by unrigorous descriptive work that had no potential for the achievement of analytical leverage.

It is certainly true that Haas (2004: xiv) understood his own coordinates (and by extension those of neofunctionalism) as lying within a series of recurrent IR debates (Kreisler 2000). However – crucially – Haas's project involved assaulting the prevailing realist and liberal wisdoms from two flanks: one empirical and the other epistemological–methodological. The

second of these was directly connected to a commitment to the professionalized norms of standard contemporaneous political science (Ruggie et al. 2005). This casts doubt on any attempt to classify neofunctionalist work with the (in this case) pejorative label of 'IR'. Haas (2001) described such acts of labelling as 'silly'. Indeed, Haas and the neofunctionalists drew much breath from the growth of pluralist political science in the US. This meant not only that integration and the emergent EU system were conceived as analogous to the operation of domestic pluralist polities, but also that the standards of theory building (the specification of variables and the postulation of testable hypotheses) were mainstream and – by the standards of the time – highly sophisticated. If this was IR, then it was IR that operated at political science's cutting edge (see in particular the contributions to Lindberg and Scheingold 1971).

Much of the integration theory project of the 1960s and 1970s was actually conducted largely in terms of a nuanced conversation *among* neofunctionalists. The scattered intergovernmentalist critiques (particularly that of Hoffmann

1966; less so that of Hansen 1969) were taken very seriously. For example, the authorial Preface to the second edition of *The Uniting of Europe* (Haas 1968) worked through intergovernmentalist objections and provided a clear statement of neofunctionalist propositions. These in turn reflected the significant work done within the neofunctionalist circle on the importance of background conditions (including societal pluralism) as variables to explain both the initiation and the embedding of regional integration. One of the potential consequences of posing the theoretical past in terms of the titanic clash between two grand theories is the likelihood that both will be posed in simplistic, stylized and static terms. Neofunctionalism is often reduced to a set of propositions about the salience of non-state actors and the primacy of the spillover dynamic, which inevitably directs attention away from the neofunctionalists' extensive work on background conditions, societal pluralism prior to and within regional orders and the significance of knowledge and cognition in the integration process (see Schmitter 2004; Rosamond 2005, for summary and discussion).

This raises questions of what neofunctionalism was actually able to achieve in its heyday. It is commonplace to assume that the theory did little more than uncover (i.e. describe) a series of local dynamics in the European setting and thereby lost any potential for analytical leverage and comparative potential. Yet, it has been argued that neofunctionalism provided effective accounts of how and why integration might not take off or succeed in particular contexts (a theory of *disintegration* as well as integration – Schmitter 2004). Indeed, Haas and Schmitter (1964) arguably used neofunctionalist premises (although not necessarily those familiar in standard representations) to successfully predict the *failure* of Latin American integration. Also, the idea that scholars have only recently begun to think about the EU in political systemic terms must come under scrutiny when the Eastonian-influenced work of Lindberg (1965, 1966, 1967; Lindberg and Scheingold 1970) began to take shape some 40 years ago.

Intergovernmentalism too suffers from caricature. One of the first articles in *EUP* announced that '[D]espite some refinements, European integration theory still revolves around the debate between *neorealism* and neofunctionalism' (Schmidt 2000: 39, emphasis added). The bottling of Moravcsik (and for that matter Hoffmann before him) as 'neorealist' helps to discursively construct the classical terms of engagement in EU studies as hopelessly entrapped in an unproductive IR problematic. In so doing, it also misunderstands both (a) the nuances of Hoffmann's intergovernmentalism (about which Hoffmann (1989, 1995) has written in some detail) and (b) the important neo-liberal institutionalist turn in IR that spawned Moravcsik's liberal intergovernmentalist work on European integration. Neoliberal institutionalism has stood for at least decade and a half as the principal *rival* to neorealist IR in the US debate.[20] As indicted already, Moravcsik's work is as indebted to the standard (American) political science norms of the 1990s as Haas's was to those of the 1960s. And, while the full range of intellectual technologies (formal modelling, statistical and mathematical techniques, etc.) may have changed, the basic precepts of mainstream political science appear to be rather more static (Kaiser 1965; de Vree 1972).

Interestingly, in his last essay on European integration, Haas (2004) undertook a rare exercise by attempting to re-read neofunctionalism through contemporary lenses. This thought experiment classified neofunctionalist theory as epistemologically 'soft rationalist' and, via the elaboration of a 'pragmatic constructivist' ontology, sought to show how a revised form of neofunctionalism could enter into dialogue with some of the softer variants of constructivism and sociological institutionalism. For the most part, complex evolving theoretical movements like neofunctionalism (1958–1976) are not subject to the kind of scrutiny that would allow such contemporary parallels to be made. While statements of the present *acquis academique* often follow from honest attempts to develop analytical leverage and avoid various *sui generis* traps, they might contribute to a situation where the analytical potential of neofunctionalism (revised or otherwise) is never properly investigated. And, because the integration theory/neofunctionalism project is associated with a misconceived to develop predictive science of regional integration studies out of inductive work on the European case, a failure to reinvestigate the credentials of the theory might act as a potential block on the study of European integration re-entering the area of comparative studies of regional orders (see Warleigh, Chapter 29 of this volume). It is not simply the case that neofunctionalism *was* influenced by the interaction of 'external' and 'internal' drivers of the field during its period of pre-eminence. The way in which neofunctionalism – and integration theory more generally – is placed within disciplinary histories of EU studies *is* influenced by the same factors.

CONCLUSIONS

This chapter has sought to show that the way in which we construe the evolution of scholarly engagement with EU politics is a far from banal exercise. Indeed as a dynamic field characterized by vibrant debate over epistemology, theory and method, it is perhaps a sign of health that the past is so frequently constructed as a series of propositions that carry implications for the present. There are clearly many conceptions of what constitutes 'scientific progress' in EU studies. That said, there are some dangers of buying into such classifications without critical engagement. Claims about history are claims about the present and, as such, may well carry within them logics of 'necessity' and 'appropriateness'. These in turn (consciously or unconsciously) shape the parameters of possible enquiry in ways that might be consistent with the 'mainstreaming' ideal type outlined above. However, there is also an interesting yet under-researched relationship between the object of study (EU politics) and the way we as scholars seek to interpret, analyse and describe it. As such, it is important to recognize the dynamic qualities of fields like EU studies, not simply in terms of evolution and change, but also in terms of

how the ways we understand EU politics connect with and feed back into our broader social scientific preoccupations. There are also pedagogical issues here because the way in which we conceptualize the field's history is intimately connected to how we describe the field's present in terms of disciplinary location, key puzzles and relevant literature. Unless it is our intention to devise a completely 'mainstreamed' EU studies that obeys the dictums of Kuhnian 'normal science', then one interesting way of keeping the vibrant debate about the nature of the field open would be to throw the question back at our students.

NOTES

1. I am indebted to my fellow editors and Ian Manners for insightful comments on earlier drafts of this chapter.

2. http://europa.eu.int/comm/dg10/university/ajm/dbajmon. html, accessed 9 March 2006.

3. It is difficult to measure the impact of these funding efforts, particularly since we have no way of establishing 'value added' indices (i.e. would research output have differed significantly *without* Commission seed funding?). That said, Keeler's (2005: 566, fn 23) data point to the fact that EUCs were consistently responsible for the highest numbers of doctoral dissertations produced on EU topics between 1990–2001. It is important to recognize that the Commission has not been the sole source of funding for EU studies programmes in the US. The US Department of Education's 'Title VI' (National Resource Centers) programme and the German Academic Exchange Service (DAAD) have also been important funding sources. Keeler (2005: 565) shows that only one externally funded centre existed in the US in 1976, whereas 30 were being underwritten by the major grant awarding organizations in 2001.

4. The precision of some of these statistics is questionable. At best many seem to be estimates that do not necessarily correspond to membership data available from national ECSAs themselves. I present them here on the assumption that they more or less accurately reflect the broad compositional pattern of EU studies worldwide.

5. Note the discrepancy with the macro data supplied by ECSA.

6. All data quoted here is obtained from http://www.eustudies.org/organ.html, accessed 6 March 2006

7. Respectively, Ruggie (1993) and Smith (2004).

8. To these we might add major book series such as Palgrave Macmillan's 'European Union Series' and the 'New European Union Series' published by Oxford University Press. While these series are predominantly designed to produce textbooks, several other publishers such as Manchester University Press, Routledge and

Rowman and Littlefield have marketed monographs on EU politics within the series format.

9. The *JCMS* has always been edited by a mixture of scholars of politics and economics. The journal was edited exclusively by economists between 1980–1991 (Loukas Tsoukalis, 1980–1984 and Peter Robson, 1984–1991). Since 1991, the *JCMS* has followed a dual discipline editorial policy: Simon Bulmer (political scientist) and Andrew Scott (economist turned legal scholar), 1991–1999; Iain Begg (economist) and John Peterson (political scientist), 1999–2004; William E. Paterson (political scientist) and James Rollo (economist), 2004–present.

10. http://www.tandf.co.uk/journals/printviw/?issn=0703-6337, accessed 9 March 2006.

11. Wionczek remained as joint editor until 1979.

12. Jupille (2006: 225) finds *EUP* to be, in methodological terms, the *most* formal and statistical and the *least* qualitative of the five journals he surveys (the others are the *European Journal of International Relations*, *International Organization*, *JCMS* and *JEPP*).

13. For an aggressive critique of Moravcsik's work in its own methodological terms, see Lieshout et al. (2004).

14. See Milner (1998) on this particular point

15. Again, caution should be urged. Volume 4, number 1 of the *JCMS* contained an important, though now rarely cited, paper by Kaiser (1965) on the virtues of the American theory-driven approach, while volume 5, number 4 (1967) contained pieces by Haas and Lindberg.

16. Keeler's conclusions follow a quantitative analysis of dissertation production and journal article production between 1960–2001 rather than an analysis of changing theoretical trends.

17. As Schimmelfennig (2004: 75) rightly notes, LI emerges out of the rationalist (liberal) institutionalist tradition in IR (see also Rosamond 2000: 142).

18. The significance of this point will vary with the extent to which neofunctionalism is understood as a static theory (see below and Rosamond 2005).

19. Haas (2004: xvii, fn 5) remarked on the metatheoretical similarity between neofunctionalism and LI. Both constructivists and rationalists seem keen to claim neofunctionalism for their own side of the divide (see Börzel 2006).

20. It should be noted that Moravcsik's work is also crucially dependent upon liberal theory, which problematizes the formational of national preferences.

REFERENCES

Anderson, J.J. (1995) 'The state of the (European) Union: from the singular event to general theories', *World Politics*, 47(3): 441–65.

Andreatta, F. (2005) 'Theory and the European Union's international relations', in C. Hill and M. Smith (eds), *International Relations and the European Union*. Oxford: Oxford University Press, pp. 18–38.

Appadurai, A. (1996) *Modernity at Large: Cultural Dimensions of Globalization*. Minneapolis, University of Minnesota Press

Bailey, D.J. (2006) 'Governance or the crisis of governmentality? Applying critical state theory at the European level', *Journal of European Public Policy*, 13(1): 16–33.

Bates, R.E. (1996) 'Letter from the President: area studies and the discipline', *APSA-CP Newsletter of the APSA Organized Section in Comparative Politics*, 7(1): 1–2.

Bates, R., Greif, A., Levi, M., Rosenthal, J.-L. and Weingast, B. (1998) *Analytical Narratives*. Princeton, NJ: Princeton University Press.

Begg, I. and Peterson, J. (1999) 'Editorial', *Journal of Common Market Studies*, 37(1): 1–12.

Börzel, T. (ed.) (2006) *The Disparity of European Integration: Revisiting Neofunctionalism in Honour of Ernst B. Haas*. London: Routledge.

Bulmer, S. and Scott, A. (1991) 'Editorial', *Journal of Common Market Studies*, 29(6): 573–4.

Calhoun, C. (2003) 'European studies: always already there and still in formation', *Comparative European Politics*, 1(1): 5–20.

Caporaso, J.A. (1999) 'Toward a normal science of regional integration', *Journal of European Public Policy*, 6(1): 160–4.

Checkel, J.T. (2001a) 'From meta- to substantive theory? Social constructivism and the study of Europe', *European Union Politics*, 2(2): 219–28.

Checkel, J.T. (2001b) 'Constructivism and integration theory: crash landing or safe arrival?', *European Union Politics*, 2(2): 240–5.

Christiansen, T. and Jørgensen, K.E. (1999) 'The Amsterdam process: a structurationist perspective on EU treaty making', *European Integration Online Papers*, 3(10). Available online at: http://eiop.or.at/eiop/texte/1999-001a.htm, accessed 7 September 2006.

Christiansen, T., Jørgensen, K.E. and Wiener, A. (2001) 'Introduction', in T. Christiansen, K.E. Jørgensen and A. Wiener (eds), *The Social Construction of Europe*. London: Sage. pp. 1–19.

Cini, M. (2006) 'The "state of the art" in EU studies: from politics to interdisciplinarity (and back again?)', *Politics*, 26(1): 38–46.

Cohn, J. (1999) 'Irrational exuberance. When did political science forget about politics?', *The New Republic*, 25 October: 25–31.

Collini, S., Winch, D. and Burrow, J.W (1983) *That noble science of politics: a study in nineteenth century intellectual history*. Cambridge: Cambridge University Press.

De Vree, J.K. (1972) *Political Integration: The Formation of Theory and its Problems.* The Hague: Mouton.

Diez, T. and Wiener, A. (2004) 'Introducing the mosaic of integration theory', in A. Wiener and T. Diez (eds) *European Integration Theory.* Oxford: Oxford University Press. pp.1–21.

Dinan, D. (2006) 'The historiography of European integration', in D. Dinan (ed.), *Origins and Evolution of the European Union.* Oxford: Oxford University Press. pp. 297–324.

Dowding, K. (2000) 'Institutional research on the European Union: a critical review', *European Union Politics,* 1(1): 125–44.

Dryzek, J.S. (2002) 'A pox on perestroika, a hex on hegemony: toward a critical political science', Annual Conference of the American Political Science Association, Boston, MA, 29 August–1 September.

Fearon, J. and Wendt, A. (2002) 'Rationalism v constructivism: a skeptical view', in W. Carlsnaes, T. Risse and B.A. Simmons (eds), *Handbook of International Relations.* London: Sage. pp. 52–72.

Fuller, S. (2003) *Kuhn vs. Popper: the Struggle for the Soul of Science.* London: Icon Books.

Geyer, R. (2003) 'European integration, the problem of complexity and the revision of theory', *Journal of Common Market Studies,* 41(1): 15–35.

Gunnell, J.G. (2005) 'Political science on the cusp: recovering a discipline's past', *American Political Science Review,* 99(4): 597–609.

Hass, E.B. (1958) *The Uniting of Europe: Political, Social and Economic Forces, 1950–1957.* Stanford, CA: Stanford University Press.

Haas, E.B. (1968) *The Uniting of Europe: Political, Social and Economic Forces, 1950–1957,* 2nd edn. Stanford, CA: Stanford University Press.

Haas, E.B. (1975) 'The obsolescence of regional integration theory', Working paper, Berkeley: Institute of International Studies.

Haas, E.B. (1976) 'Turbulent fields and the study of regional integration', *International Organization,* 30(2): 173–212.

Haas, E.B. (2001) 'Does constructivism subsume neofunctionalism?', in T. Christiansen, K.E. Jørgensen and A. Wiener (eds), *The Social Construction of Europe.* London: Sage. pp. 22–31.

Haas, E.B. (2004) 'Introduction: institutionalism or constructivism?', in *The Uniting of Europe: Political, Social and Economic Forces, 1950–1957,* 3rd edn. Notre Dame, IN: University of Notre Dame Press. pp. xiii–lvi

Haas, E.B. and Schmitter, P.C. (1964) 'Economics and differential patterns of integration: projections about unity in Latin America', *International Organization,* 18(4): 705–37.

Hancock, M.D. (1999) 'The study of Europe in the United States: the Makins Report', *ECSA Review,* 12(1). Available online at: http://aei.pitt.edu/57/01/makinsforum.htm, accessed 7 September 2006.

Hansen, R.D. (1969) 'European integration: reflections on a decade of theoretical efforts', *World Politics,* 21(2): 242–71.

Hay, C. (2002) *Political Analysis: A Critical Introduction.* Basingstoke: Palgrave.

Hix, S. (1994) 'The study of the European Community: the challenge to comparative politics', *West European Politics,* 17(1): 1–30.

Hix, S. (1996) 'IR, CP and the EU: a rejoinder to Hurrell and Menon', *West European Politics,* 19(4): 802–4.

Hix, S. (1998) 'The study of the European Union II: the "new governance" agenda and its rival', *Journal of European Public Policy,* 5(1): 38–65.

Hix, S. (2005) *The Political System of the European Union,* 2nd edn. Basingstoke and New York: Palgrave Macmillan.

Hoffmann, S. (1966) 'Obstinate or obsolete? The fate of the nation-state and the case of Western Europe', *Daedalus,* 95(3): 862–915.

Hoffmann, S. (1989) 'A retrospective', in J. Kruzel and J.N. Rosenau (eds), *Journeys Through World Politics: Autobiographical Reflections of Thirty-four Academic Travelers.* Lexington, MA: Lexington Books.

Hoffmann, S. (1995) *The European Sisyphus: Essays on Europe, 1964–1994.* Boulder, CO: Westview.

Hooghe, L. (2001) *The European Commission and the Integration of Europe: Images of Governance.* Cambridge: Cambridge University Press.

Hooghe, L. and Marks, G. (2003) 'Unravelling the central state, but how? Types of multi-level governance', *American Political Science Review,* 97(2): 233–43.

Inglehart, R. (1967) 'An end to European integration', *American Political Science Review,* 61(1): 91–106.

Johnson, C. (1997) 'Preconception vs. observation, or the contributions of rational choice and area studies to contemporary political science', *PS: Political Science and Politics,* 30(June): 170–4.

Jupille, J. (2006) 'Knowing Europe: metatheory and methodology in European Union studies', in M. Cini and A.K. Bourne (eds), *Palgrave Advances in European Union Studies.* Basingstoke: Palgrave Macmillan. pp. 209–33.

Jupille, J. and Caporaso, J.A. (1999) 'Institutionalism and the European Union: beyond internationalism and comparative politics', *Annual Review of Political Science,* 2: 429–44.

Jørgensen, K.E. (2000) 'Continental IR theory: the best kept secret', *European Journal of International Relations*, 6(1): 9–42.

Jørgensen, K.E. (2004) 'European foreign policy: conceptualising the domain', in W. Carlsnaes, H. Sjursen and B. White (eds), *Contemporary European Foreign Policy*. London: Sage. pp. 32–56.

Kaiser, K. (1965) 'L'Europe des Savants: European integration and the social sciences', *Journal of Common Market Studies*, 4(1): 36–47.

Kaiser, K. (2006) 'From state to society? The historiography of European integration', in M. Cini and A.K. Bourne (eds), *Palgrave Advances in European Union Studies*. Basingstoke: Palgrave Macmillan. pp. 190–208.

Katzenstein, P., Keohane, R.O. and Krasner, S. (1998) 'International Organization and the study of world politics', *International Organization*, 52(4): 645–85.

Keeler, J.S. (2005) 'Mapping EU studies: the evolution from boutique to boom field 1960–2001', *Journal of Common Market Studies*, 43(3): 551–82.

Keohane, R.O. (1988) 'International institutions: two traditions', *International Studies Quarterly*, 32(4): 379–96.

King, G., Keohane, R.O. and Verba, S. (1994) *Designing Social Inquiry: Scientific Inference in Quantitative Research*. Princeton, NJ: Princeton University Press.

Kitzinger, U. (1962a) 'Editorial', *Journal of Common Market Studies*, 1(1): v–vi.

Kitzinger, U. (1962b) 'The state of the literature in 1960', *Journal of Common Market Studies*, 1(2): 187–93.

Kreisler, H. (2000) 'Science and progress in international relations: conversation with Ernst B. Haas', October 30. Available online at: http://globetrotter.berkeley.edu/people/Haas/haas-con0.html, accessed 19 October 2004.

Kuhn, T. (1996) [1962] *The Structure of Scientific Revolutions*. Chicago: University of Chicago Press.

Lieshout, R.H., Segers, M.L.L. and van der Vleuten, A.M. (2004) 'De Gaulle, Moravcsik and *The Choice for Europe*', *Journal of Cold War Studies*, 6(4): 89–139.

Lindberg, L.N. (1965) 'Decision-making and integration in the European Community', *International Organization*, 19(1): 56–80.

Lindberg, L.N. (1966) 'Integration as a source of stress on the European Community system', *International Organization*, 20(2): 233–66.

Lindberg, L.N. (1967) 'The European Community as a political system: notes toward the construction of a model', *Journal of Common Market Studies*, 5(4): 344–88.

Lindberg, L.N. and Scheingold, S.A. (1970) *Europe's Would-Be Polity: Patterns of Change in the European Community*. Englewood Cliffs, NJ: Prentice Hall.

Lindberg, L.N. and Scheingold, S.A. (eds) (1971) *Regional Integration: Theory and Research*. Cambridge, MA: Harvard University Press

Lubomudrov, A.Y. (2002) 'Perestroika, epistemology, and discipline: redefinitions of a political science', Portland State University, mimeo.

Lustick, I.S. (1997) 'The disciplines of political science: studying the culture of rational choice as a case in point', *PS: Political Science and Politics*, 30(June): 175–9.

Mancias. P. (1987) *A History and Philosophy of the Social Sciences*. Oxford: Blackwell.

Manners, I. (2003) 'Europaian studies', *Journal of Contemporary European Studies*, 11(1): 67–83.

Marks, G., Hooghe, L. and Blank, K. (1996a) 'European integration from the 1980s: state-centric v. multi-level governance', *Journal of Common Market Studies*, 34(3): 341–78.

Marks, G., Nielsen, F., Ray, L. and Salk, J. (1996b) 'Competencies, cracks and conflicts: regional mobilization in the European Union', in G. Marks, F.W. Scharpf, P.C. Schmitter and W. Steeck (eds), *Governance in the European Union*. London, Sage. pp. 40–63.

McLean, I. (2003) 'Two analytic narratives about the history of the EU', *European Union Politics*, 4(4): 499–506.

Mearsheimer, J.J. (2001) 'Methodological parochialism vs. methodological pluralism', Annual Conference of the American Political Science Association, San Francisco, CA, 31 August.

Milner, H.V. (1998) 'Rationalizing politics: the emerging synthesis of international, American and comparative politics', *International Organization*, 52(4): 759–86.

Milward, A.S. (1992) *The European Rescue of the Nation-State*. London: Routledge.

Milward, A.S. and Sørensen, V. (1993) 'Interdependence or integration? A national choice', in A.S. Milward, F.M.B. Lynch, F. Romero, R. Ranieri and V. Sørensen (eds), *The Frontier of National Sovereignty: History and Theory 1945–1992*. London: Routledge. pp. 1–32.

Moravcsik, A. (1997) 'Does the European Union represent an n of 1?', *ECSA Review*, 10(3). Available online at: http://www.eustudies.org/N1debate.htm, accessed 15 March 2006

Moravcsik, A. (1998) *The Choice for Europe: Social Purpose and State Power from Messina to Maastricht*. Ithaca, NY: Cornell University Press.

Moravcsik, A. (1999a) 'The Choice for Europe – Current commentary and future research; a response to James Caporaso, Fritz Scharpf and Helen Wallace', *Journal of European Public Policy*, 6(1): 168–79.

Moravcsik, A. (1999b) 'The future of European integration studies: social theory or social science?', *Millennium: Journal of International Studies*, 28(2): 371–91.

Moravcsik, A. (2001a) 'Bringing constructivist integration theory out of the clouds: has it landed yet?', *European Union Politics*, 2(2): 226–40.

Moravcsik, A. (2001b) 'Constructivism and European integration: a critique', in T. Christiansen, K.E. Jørgensen and A. Wiener (eds), *The Social Construction of Europe*. London: Sage. pp. 176–88.

Moravcsik, A. (2005) 'The European constitutional compromise and the neofunctionalist legacy', *Journal of European Public Policy*, 12(2): 349–86.

Murphy, C.N. and Nelson, D.R. (2001) 'International political economy: a tale of two heterodoxies', *British Journal of Politics and International Relations*, 3(3): 393–412.

Murray, A.J.H. (1997) *Reconstructing Realism: Between Power Politics and Cosmopolitan Ethics*. Edinburgh: Edinburgh University Press.

Pahre, R. (2005) 'Formal theory and case-study methods in EU studies', *European Union Politics*, 6(1): 113–43.

Paterson, W.E. and Rollo, J. (2004) 'Editorial', *Journal of Common Market Studies*, 42(1): 1–4.

Pollack, M.A. (2005a) 'Theorizing EU policy-making', in H. Wallace, W. Wallace and M.A. Pollack (eds), *Policy-Making in the European Union*, 5th edn. Oxford: Oxford University Press. pp. 13–48.

Pollack, M.A. (2005b) 'Theorizing the European Union: international organization, domestic polity or experiment in new governance?', *Annual Review of Political Science*, 8: 357–98.

Richardson, J. and Lindley, R. (1994) 'Editorial', *Journal of European Public Policy*, 1(1): 1–7.

Rosamond, B. (2000) *Theories of European Integration*. Basingstoke and New York: Macmillan and St. Martin's Press.

Rosamond, B. (2005) '*The Uniting of Europe* and the foundation of EU studies: revisiting the neofunctionalism of Ernst B. Haas', *Journal of European Public Policy*, 12(2): 237–54.

Rosenthal, G.G. (1999) 'The study of Europe in the United States: the Makins Report', *ECSA Review*, 12(1). Available online at: http://aei.pitt.edu/57/01/makinsforum.htm, accessed 7 September 2006.

Ruggie, J.G. (1993) 'Territoriality and beyond: problematizing modernity in international relations', *International Organization*, 47(1): 139–74.

Ruggie, J.J., Katzenstein, P.J., Keohane, R.O. and Schmitter, P.C. (2005) 'Transformations in world politics: the intellectual contributions of Ernst B. Haas', *Annual Review of Political Science*, 8: 271–96.

Rumford, C. and Murray, P. (2003) 'Globalization and the limitations of European integration studies: interdisciplinary considerations', *Journal of Contemporary European Studies*, 11(1): 85–93.

Sandholtz, W. and Stone Sweet, A. (eds) (1998) *European Integration and Supranational Governance*. Oxford: Oxford University Press.

Schimmelfennig, F. (2004) 'Liberal intergovernmentalism', in A. Wiener and T. Diez (eds), *European Integration Theory*. Oxford: Oxford University Press. pp. 75–94.

Schmidt, B.C. (1998) *The Political Discourse of Anarchy: a Disciplinary History of International Relations*. Albany, NY: SUNY Press.

Schmidt, B.C. (2002) 'On the history and historiography of international relations', in W. Carlsnaes, T. Risse and B.A. Simmons (eds), *Handbook of International Relation*. London: Sage. pp. 3–22.

Schmidt, S.K. (2000) 'Only an agenda setter? The European Commission's power over the Council of Ministers', *European Union Politics*, 1(1): 37–62.

Schmitter, P.C. (2004) 'Neo-neo-functionalism?', in A. Wiener and T. Diez (eds), *European Integration Theory*. Oxford: Oxford University Press. pp. 45–74.

Schneider, G. and Aspinwall, M. (2001) 'Moving beyond outworn debates: a new institutionalist research agenda', in M. Aspinwall and G. Schneider (eds), *The Rules of Integration: Institutionalist Approaches to the Study of Europe*. Manchester: Manchester University Press. pp. 177–87.

Schneider, G., Gabel, M. and Hix, S. (2000) '*European Union Politics* Editorial statement', *European Union Politics*, 1(1): 5–8.

Shaw, J. and More, G. (eds) (1995) *New Legal Dynamics of European Union*. Oxford: Clarendon Press.

Smith, S. (2000a) 'International theory and European integration', in M. Kelstrup and M.C. Williams (eds) *International Relations Theory and the Politics of European Integration: Power, Security and Community*. London: Routledge. pp. 33–56.

Smith, S. (2000b) 'The discipline of international relations: still an American social science?', *British Journal of Politics and International Relations*, 2(3): 374–402.

Smith, S. (2004) 'Singing our world into existence: international relations theory and September 11', *International Studies Quarterly*, 48(3): 499–515.

Tsoukalis, L. (1980) 'Editorial', *Journal of Common Market Studies*, 18(3): 215–6.

van Kersbergen, K. and van Waarden, F. (2004) '"Governance" as a bridge between disciplines: cross disciplinary inspiration regarding shifts in governance and problems of governability, accountability and legitimacy', *European Journal of Political Research*, 43(2): 143–71.

Verdun, A. (2005) 'An American/European divide in European integration studies: bridging the gap with international political economy (IPE)', in E. Jones and A. Verdun (eds), *The Political Economy of European Integration: Theory and Analysis*. London: Routledge. pp. 11–38.

Wagner, P., Wittrock, B. and Whitley, R. (eds) (1991) *Discourses on Society: The Shaping of the Social Scientific Disciplines*. Dordrecht: Kluwer.

Wallace, H. (2000) 'Studying contemporary Europe', *British Journal of Politics and International Relations*, 2(1): 95–113.

Wallace, H. (2002) 'Europeanisation and globalisation: complementary or contradictory trends?', in S. Breslin, C. Hughes, N. Phillips and B. Rosamond (eds), *New Regionalisms in the Global Political Economy: Theories and Cases*. London: Routledge. pp. 137–49.

Weiler, J.H.H. (1991) 'The transformation of Europe', *Yale Law Journal*, 100(8): 2405–83.

Wendt, A. (1999) *Social Theory of International Politics*. Cambridge University Press.

Wendt, A. (2001) 'Driving with the rearview mirror: on the rational science of institutional design', *International Organization*, 55(4): 1019–49.

Wessels, W. (2006) 'Cleavages, controversies and convergence in European Union studies', in M. Cini and A.K. Bourne (eds), *Palgrave Advances in European Union Studies*. Basingstoke: Palgrave Macmillan. pp. 233–46.

White, B. (2001) *Understanding European Foreign Policy*. Basingstoke: Palgrave.

White, J.P.J. (2003) 'Theory guiding practice: the neo-functionalists and the Hallstein EEC Commission', *Journal of European Integration History*, 9(1): 111–31.

Whitley, R. (1984) *The Intellectual and Social Organization of the Sciences*. Oxford: Clarendon Press.

Wiener, A. and Diez, T. (2004) 'Taking stock of integration theory', in A. Wiener and T. Diez (eds), *European Integration Theory*. Oxford: Oxford University Press. pp. 237–48.

Williams, M.C. (2005) *The Realist Tradition and the Limits of International Relations*. Cambridge: Cambridge University Press.

Wincott, D. (1995) 'Institutional interaction and European integration: towards an everyday critique of liberal intergovernmentalism', *Journal of Common Market Studies*, 33(4): 597–609.

Wæver, O. (1998) 'The sociology of a not so international discipline: American and European developments in international relations', *International Organization*, 52(4): 687–727.

Wæver, O. (2003) 'The structure of the IR discipline: a proto-comparative analysis', Annual Convention of the International Studies Association, Portland, OR, 25 February–1 March.

2

Rational Choice and EU Politics

MARK A. POLLACK

INTRODUCTION

Rational choice approaches to politics did not originate in the study of the European Union (EU), nor is 'rational choice' as such a theory of European integration or of EU politics.[1] Rational choice, like constructivism, should be understood as a broad approach to social theory, capable of generating an array of specific theories and testable hypotheses about a range of human behaviors. Over the past two decades, rational choice theories have made rapid inroads into the study of EU politics, most notably through the application of rational choice institutionalism to the study of EU decision-making. In this Chapter, I provide a brief introduction to rational choice theory, examine the application of rational choice analyses to EU politics, assess the empirical fruitfulness of such analyses and identify both internal and external challenges to the rational choice study of the EU.

The chapter is organized in five parts. In the first, I briefly summarize rational choice as a 'second-order' theory of human behavior and discuss the development of rational choice institutionalism (RCI), which has been the most

influential branch of rational choice in EU studies. This section also discusses some of the most common criticisms of rational choice as an approach to human behavior, with an emphasis on its purported methodological 'pathologies' and (lack of) empirical fruitfulness, and its alleged inability to theorize about endogenous preference formation or change. The second section briefly considers the range of first-order rational choice theories of European Union politics, starting with traditional integration theories and continuing through liberal intergovernmentalist, RCI and other mid-range theories of EU politics. In the third section, I address empirical applications of rational choice theories, noting the charges of methodological pathologies but also suggesting that rational choice approaches have produced progressive research programs and shed light on concrete empirical cases including the legislative, executive and judicial politics of the EU, as well as on other questions such as public opinion and Europeanization. Rational choice-inspired empirical work on the EU, I argue, has been predominantly progressive, not pathological. The fourth section examines some of the challenges to rational choice theories, including rationalism's purported 'ontological blindness' to a range of empirically important issues, including most notably the issues of endogenous preference formation and change. Like Checkel's review of constructivist theory (in this volume), I do not focus primarily on the rationalist-constructivist debate in EU studies, but I do suggest, against several recent analyses, that the rationalist-constructivist debate in EU studies has largely been a useful and pragmatic one, which has forced rationalists to confront difficult issues like endogenous preference formation and sources of change. A brief fifth section concludes.

RATIONAL CHOICE AS A SECOND-ORDER (META-) THEORY

Rational choice is, in Wendt's terms, a 'second-order' theory, concerned with ontological and epistemological questions such as 'the nature of human agency and its relationship to social structures, the role of ideas and material forces in social life, the proper form of social explanations and so on'.[2] By contrast with such broad, second-order social theories, 'first-order' theories are 'substantive', 'domain-specific' theories about particular social systems such as the family, Congress, the international system or the EU. Such first-order theories are derived from and should be consistent with the broader second-order theories to which they belong, but they go beyond second-order theories in identifying particular social systems as the object of study, in making specific assumptions about those systems and their constituent actors and in making specific causal or interpretive claims about them (Wendt 1999: 6; Snidal 2002: 74–5).

As a second-order theory, the rational choice approach relies on several fundamental assumptions about the nature of individual actors and of the social world that they constitute. At this broadest level, rational choice is 'a methodological approach that explains both individual and collective (social) outcomes in terms of *individual goal-seeking under constraints* ...' (Snidal 2002: 74, emphasis in original). This formulation, in turn, contains three essential

elements: (1) methodological individualism, (2) goal-seeking or utility-maximization and (3) the existence of various institutional or strategic constraints on individual choice.

The first of these elements, methodological individualism, means simply that rational choice analyses treat individuals as the basic units of social analysis. By contrast with 'holist' approaches that treat society as basic and derive individual characteristics from society, rational choice approaches seek to explain both individual and collective behavior as the aggregation of individual choices. Individuals, in this view, act according to preferences that are assumed to be fixed, transitive and exogenously given.

Second, individuals are assumed to act so as maximize their expected utility, subject to constraints. That is to say, individuals with fixed preferences over possible states of the world calculate the expected utility of alternative courses of action and choose the action that is likely to maximize their utility. This 'logic of consequentiality' provides a distinctive approach to human action and stands in contrast to both the 'logic of appropriateness', in which action is guided by the aim of behaving in conformity with accepted social norms, and the 'logic of arguing', where actors engage in truth-seeking deliberation, accepting 'the power of the better argument' rather than calculating the utility of alternative courses of action for themselves (Risse 2000).

Third and finally, individuals choose under *constraints*. That is to say, individuals do not directly choose their ideal states of the world, but weigh and choose among alternative courses of action within the constraints of their physical and social surroundings, and often on the basis of incomplete information. Rational choice institutionalist analyses, for example, emphasize the institutional constraints on individual behavior, exploring how formal and informal institutions shape and constrain the choices of individual actors, while game theorists emphasize the strategic context of individual choices in settings where each individual's payoff varies with the choices made by others.[3]

Rational choice, at this broad, second-order level of analysis, is not a theory of EU politics or even of politics more generally, but an umbrella for a family of first-order theories that marry these basic assumptions to an additional set of substantive assumptions about, *inter alia*, the nature of the actors, their preferences and the institutional or strategic settings in which they interact. Rational choice approaches can, for example, take individuals, organizations or states as their basic unit of analysis. They can adopt a 'thick' conception of rationality, in which actors are assumed to be narrowly self-interested, or a 'thin' conception, in which rational-actors may be self-interested or altruistic and may seek a variety of goals such as wealth, power or even love (Ferejohn 1991). Rational choice models can also differ in terms of their assumptions about individual preferences, the institutional and strategic situations in which individuals interact and the quality of the information available to actors seeking to maximize their individual utility. Many rational choice theories – including an increasing number in EU studies – are formulated as formal models, which express theoretical models in mathematic terms.[4] In many other cases, however, theories with rationalist assumptions are formulated and expressed verbally, with little or no use of formal modeling, i.e. 'soft' rational choice.

Given the very basic second-order assumptions laid out above and the considerable variation within rational choice in terms of substantive assumptions, we should understand rational choice, not as a single theory, but as a family of first-order theories connected by common assumptions and methodology. For this reason, as Wendt (1999) and Checkel (this volume) point out with regard to constructivism, *rational choice as a second-order theory cannot be either supported or falsified by empirical evidence.* It is, rather, the first-order or mid-range theories of politics derived from rational choice that do – or do not – provide testable hypotheses and insights into the politics of various political systems, including the European Union.

Rational Choice Institutionalism

Over the past two decades, perhaps the leading strand of rational choice literature – and certainly the most influential in EU studies – has been that of rational choice institutionalism, in which formal and (to a lesser extent) informal institutions have been reintroduced to the rational choice study of American, comparative and international politics. The contemporary RCI literature can be traced to the effort by American political scientists in the 1970s to re-introduce institutional factors, such as the workings of the committee system, into formal models of majority voting in the US Congress. Such scholars number examined in detail the 'agenda-setting' powers of the Congressional committees, specifying the conditions under which agenda-setting committees could influence the outcomes of certain Congressional votes. Congressional scholars also developed principal-agent models of legislative delegation of authority to the executive, to independent regulatory agencies and to courts, analysing the independence of these various 'agents' and the efforts of Congressional 'principals' to control them. More recently, Epstein and O'Halloran (1999) and Huber and Shipan (2003) have pioneered a 'transaction-cost' approach to the design of political institutions, hypothesizing that legislators deliberately and systematically design political institutions to minimize the transaction costs associated with making public policy. Throughout this work, rational choice theorists have studied institutions both as independent variables that channel individual choices into 'institutional equilibria' and as dependent variables or 'equilibrium institutions' chosen or designed by actors to secure mutual gains.

Although originally formulated in the context of American political institutions, these models are applicable across a range of other comparative and international political contexts. In recent years, for example, comparativists have applied RCI concepts to the comparative study of the design of political institutions (Huber and Shipan 2003); the significance of 'veto points' and 'veto players' in public policy-making (Tsebelis 2002); and the delegation of powers to independent agencies and courts (Huber and Shipan 2003). In international relations, the RCI approach has proven a natural fit with the pre-existing rationalist research program of neoliberal institutionalism and has informed a number of important works on topics including the rational design of international institutions (Koremenos et al. 2003), the delegation of powers to international organizations (Pollack 2003; Hawkins et al. 2006) and forum-shopping among various IOs (Jupille and Snidal 2005). Not surprisingly, RCI has also proven to be one of the fastest-growing theories of European integration and EU politics, as we shall see presently.

Critiques of Rational Choice Theory

Despite its rapid gains across a range of fields in political science, rational choice as an approach has been subject to extensive critique in recent years. Snidal (2002: 73), in his review of rational choice approaches to IR, usefully distinguishes between 'internal critiques', which accept the basic approach but debate 'how to do rational choice' in methodological terms, and 'external critiques', which identify alleged weaknesses in the approach as a whole. There are several 'internal' critiques of rational choice, according to Snidal, including an ongoing debate about the virtues and vices of formalization, but the most contentious debate of recent years has been the debate over empirical testing and falsification of rational choice theory launched by Green and Shapiro (1994) in their book, *Pathologies of Rational Choice Theory: A Critique of Applications in Political Science*. Unlike many critics of rational choice, these authors do not object to the core assumptions of the approach or to the use of formal models, and they applaud the scientific aspirations of most rational choice scholars. Instead, as their subtitle suggests, Green and Shapiro (1994: 33) focus on empirical applications of rational choice models, arguing that empirical work by rational choice theorists is subject to a 'syndrome of fundamental and recurrent [methodological] failings' which call into question the contribution of the rational choice enterprise to the study of politics. Specific weaknesses identified by the authors include the following:

- Rational choice theories are often *formulated in abstract and empirically intractable ways*, with heavy reliance on unobservable factors and with insufficient attention paid to the difficulties of operationalizing the hypothesized variables.
- Rational choice theorists often engage in *post hoc* or *'retroductive' theorizing*, seeking to develop rational choice models that might plausibly explain a set of known facts or an empirical regularity. At the extreme, Green and Shapiro argue, this can become an exercise in 'curve-fitting', in which assumptions are manipulated to fit the data, but no subsequent effort is made to test the resulting model with respect to data other than those used to generate the model.
- When they move from theory to the empirical world, rational choice theorists often *search for confirming evidence* of their theory, engaging in 'plausibility probes' or illustrations of the theory and selecting cases that are likely to confirm, rather than falsify, their hypotheses.
- When engaging in empirical tests (or illustrations) of their hypotheses, rational choice scholars frequently *ignore alterative accounts and competing explanations* for the observed outcomes and/or test their hypotheses against *trivial or implausible null hypotheses* (for example, the notion that political behavior is entirely random).
- Finally, in the rare instances in which 'no plausible variant of the theory appears to work', rational choice scholars engage in *'arbitrary domain restriction'*, conceding the inapplicability of rational choice in a given domain and, hence, arbitrarily ignoring the theory-infirming evidence from that domain (Green and Shapiro 1994: 33–46).

Green and Shapiro (1994: 7) survey rational choice applications to American politics, where they believe that much of the most sophisticated work has been done, and they find that, even here, most empirical work 'is marred by unscientifically chosen samples, poorly conducted tests, and tendentious interpretations of results'.

Green and Shapiro's critique has been subject to numerous responses from rational choice scholars, who suggest that the authors 'misunderstand the theory, overlook its achievements or adhere to naïve methodological standards' in their indictment of rational choice (Friedman 1996a: 5).[5] For our purposes in this chapter, however, Green and Shapiro's critique serves as a useful cautionary note: While there is little dispute in EU studies that rational choice has made increasing headway into the field, it remains to be seen whether rational choice models have made a genuine contribution to our empirical understanding of EU politics, or whether empirical applications of rational choice to the EU have been subject to the methodological failings identified by Green and Shapiro.

By contrast with these internal critiques, 'external critiques' have been directed at the rational choice by both constructivists (particularly in IR theory) and psychologists (most often associated with behavioral economics), who argue that rational choice emphasizes certain problems and sets aside other issues by assumption, resulting in 'ontological blind spots' and inaccurate renderings of the empirical world. Rational choice is 'found deficient in explaining who the key actors are, in explaining their interests, explaining the origin of institutions, or explaining how these change' (Snidal 2002: 74). In EU studies, this external critique is most common among the growing number of constructivist scholars who argue that EU institutions shape not only the behavior but also the preferences and identities of individuals and member states in Europe (Sandholtz 1996; Checkel 2005a, b; Lewis 2005). The argument is stated most forcefully by Christiansen et al. (1999: 529), who argue that European integration has had a 'transformative impact' on the interests and identities of individuals, but that this transformation 'will remain largely invisible in approaches that neglect processes of identity formation and/or assume interests to be given exogenously'. Similarly, because of its focus on institutional equilibria, other critics have suggested that rational choice is blind to endogenous change, such as appears to be commonplace within the EU.

Later in this Chapter, I examine how the rational choice study of EU politics has responded to these internal and external critiques. With regard to the internal critiques, I examine the empirical contribution of rational choice analyses to five discrete areas of study in EU politics, asking whether these studies have fallen prey to Green and Shapiro's methodological pathologies. With regard to external critiques, I inquire into the ability of rational choice theories to address the issues of endogenous preference formation and change. First, however, I consider the role of rational choice analysis in the development of theories of European integration and EU politics.

FIRST-ORDER THEORIES OF EUROPEAN INTEGRATION AND EU POLITICS

How has rational choice, as a second-order theory, influenced and shaped the study of the European Union, including first-order theories of European integration and EU politics? Ideally, at this stage one could review the history of European integration theory, identifying the various theories as rationalist or not rationalist, and weighing the fruitfulness of each of the two categories. Unfortunately, as Jupille (2005: 220) points out, such an endeavor is complicated by the fact that 'scholars are not always explicit about [their] metatheoretical commitments, which makes it hard to identify what is on offer, what is being rejected, and what is at stake'. In the neofunctionalist-intergovernmentalist debates of the 1960s and 1970s, the primary differences between the two bodies of theory were substantive, focusing primarily on the relative importance of various actors (national governments vs supranational and subnational actors) and on the presence or absence of a self-sustaining integration process. The neofunctionalist/intergovernmentalist debate was *not* primarily about second-order questions, and indeed the basic assumptions of each theory – the relationship between agents and structure, the logic of human behavior, etc. – were often left undefined. Haas's (1958, 2001) neofunctionalism, for example, assumed that both the supranational Commission and subnational interest groups were sophisticated actors capable of calculating their respective bureaucratic and economic advantage and acting accordingly, and in this sense Haas laid the groundwork for future rationalist theories of integration (Moravcsik 1998). By the same token, however, Haas's (2001) theory also focused on the possible transfer of 'loyalties' from the national to the European level, without specifying clearly the nature of such loyalties, and constructivists have subsequently come to identify their work with this strand of neofunctionalist theory (Risse 2005).

Intergovernmentalist theory, in turn, drew largely from the soft rational choice tradition of realist theory, identifying the EU's member governments implicitly or explicitly as rational actors who were both aware of and capable of forestalling the transfer of authority to supranational institutions in Brussels (Hoffmann 1966). By contrast with later rational choice work, however, early intergovernmentalist works seldom specified a clear set of preferences for member governments, beyond a generic concern for national sovereignty, and they typically neglected to model the strategic interaction between governments and the supranational agents they had created.

In the 1990s, intergovernmentalist theory gained a clearer set of microfoundations with Moravcsik's (1998) 'liberal intergovernmentalism'. In various writings, and particularly in his book, *The Choice for Europe*, Moravcsik refined intergovernmentalism into an explicitly rationalist theory in which actors were clearly specified, and predictions about outcomes made, at various levels of analysis. Specifically, Moravcsik (1998: 9) nests three complementary middle-range theories within his larger rationalist framework: (1) a liberal model of preference formation, (2) an intergovernmental model of international bargaining and (3) a model of institutional choice (drawn largely from the RCI literature reviewed above) stressing the importance of credible commitments.

As noted earlier, however, the rational choice study of the European Union is most closely associated with rational choice institutionalists who have sought to model both the workings and the choice of EU institutions. Beginning in the late 1980s, authors such as Scharpf, Tsebelis and Garrett sought to model in rational choice terms the selection and above all the workings of EU institutions, including the adoption, execution and adjudication of EU public policies.[6] Like the broader literature from which these studies drew inspiration, RCI scholars have theorized EU institutions both as dependent variables – as the object of choices by the EU's member governments – and as independent variables that have shaped subsequent policy-making and policy outcomes.

While much of this literature has been applied to the workings of EU institutions, the growing literatures on Europeanization and on EU enlargement have also drawn on rational choice institutionalism to generate hypotheses about the ways in which, and the conditions under which, EU norms and rules are transmitted from Brussels to the domestic politics and polities of the various member states (Schimmelfennig and Sedelmeier 2005a; Börzel and Risse, this volume).

Furthermore, as Ray, Raunio and Richardson make clear in their respective chapters on public opinion, political parties and organized interests (this volume), rational choice theories of politics have also informed the study of the attitudes and the behavior of subnational actors in the EU. The sources of these theoretical approaches have been varied, including Eastonian models in the public opinion literature, spatial models of party competition in the political parties literature and Olsonian collective action models in the study of EU organized interests, and in all three cases rational choice approaches continue to co-exist with alternative approaches. In each case, however, the respective EU literatures have become more theoretically oriented over time and rational choice theories have played a key role in the study of domestic and transnational behavior by individuals, parties and organized interests.

HAVE RATIONAL CHOICE THEORIES BEEN EMPIRICALLY FRUITFUL IN EU STUDIES?

The growing presence of rational choice theory in EU studies, however, raises an additional set of questions: Has rational choice been empirically fruitful, in the sense of generating testable first-order hypotheses about outcomes in EU politics? Have these hypotheses been subjected to careful and systematic testing, free from the 'pathologies' identified by Green and Shapiro? And, if so, have rationalist hypotheses found support in rigorous empirical testing? While a complete response to such questions is beyond the scope of this chapter, the chapters in this volume – each of which provides a thorough review of the scholarship undertaken in a particular area of EU studies – provide a useful starting point for at least a preliminary answer. Indeed, a careful reading of the chapters of this book will reveal that rational choice theory now has been applied to virtually every area of EU politics. Nevertheless, it is fair to say that rational choice theory employs a 'positive heuristic' that directs the analyst's attention to particular types of questions, and so the contribution of rational choice has not been uniform across questions or issue-areas (Lakatos 1970: 135).

Reflecting the widespread importation of RCI into EU studies, rational choice applications have made the greatest headway in the study of EU institutions, and in particular in the areas of legislative, executive and judicial politics. In each of these areas, scholars have been able to draw on a series of 'off-the-shelf' theories and models, and previous reviews have focused largely on these areas (see e.g. Jupille and Caporaso 1999; Dowding 2000; Moser et al. 2000; Aspinwall and Schneider 2001; Pollack 2004; Hix 2005; Scully 2005). As noted above, however, rational choice theories are no longer limited to the study of formal EU institutions, but have begun to be applied to other questions, such as the Europeanization of domestic politics and public opinion toward the EU, among others. In this section, I review the empirical applications and tests of rational choice theories in each of these five areas, drawing largely from the excellent reviews of these areas in the chapters of this book.[7] By and large, as we shall see, the balance sheet in these five areas is positive: while there is some evidence that the positive heuristic of rational choice theories has directed scholars' attention to certain questions to the exclusion of

others, and while some work in each of these fields has been characterized by one or another of Green and Shapiro's methodological pathologies, across the five areas rational choice theories have generated specific, testable hypotheses and the resulting empirical work has dramatically improved our understanding of EU politics and largely (although not invariably) supported the rationalist hypotheses in question.

Legislative Politics

Without doubt the best-developed strand of rational choice theory in EU studies has focused on EU legislative processes. Drawing heavily on theories and spatial models of legislative behavior and organization, students of EU legislative politics have adapted and tested models of legislative politics to understand the process of legislative decision-making in the EU. This literature, as McElroy points out in her chapter (this volume), has focused on three major questions: legislative politics within the European Parliament; the voting power of the various states in the Council of Ministers; and the respective powers of these two bodies in the EU legislative process.

The European Parliament (EP) has been the subject of extensive theoretical modeling and empirical study over the past two decades, with a growing number of scholars studying the legislative organization of the EP and the voting behavior of its members (MEPs), adapting models of legislative politics derived largely from the study of the US Congress. The early studies of the Parliament, in the 1980s and early 1990s, emphasized the striking fact that, in spite of the multinational nature of the Parliament, the best predictor of MEP voting behavior is not nationality but an MEP's 'party group', with the various party groups demonstrating extraordinarily high measures of cohesion in roll-call votes. These MEPs, moreover, were shown to contest elections and cast their votes in a two-dimensional 'issue space', including not only the familiar nationalism/supranationalism dimension but also and especially the more traditional, 'domestic' dimension of left–right contestation (Hix 2001). Still other studies have focused on the legislative organization of the EP, including not only the party groups but also the Parliament's powerful committees, whose members play an important agenda-setting role in preparing legislation for debate on the floor of Parliament (Kreppel 2001). Perhaps most fundamentally, these scholars have shown that the EP can increasingly be studied as a 'normal parliament' whose members vote predictably and cohesively within a political space dominated by the familiar contestation between parties of the left and right (Hix et al. 2002).

By contrast with this rich EP literature, McElroy notes, the rational choice literature on the Council of Ministers has until very recently focused primarily on the question of member-state voting power under different decision rules. In this context, a number of scholars have used increasingly elaborate formal models of Council voting to establish the relative voting weights – and hence the bargaining power – of various member states under various qualified majority voting (QMV) voting formulae. The use of such voting-power indexes has led to substantial debate among rational choice scholars, with several scholars criticizing the approach for its emphasis on formal voting weight at the expense of national preferences (Albert 2003). Whatever the merit of voting-power indexes, it is worth noting that the study of Council decision-making appears to be an area in which the use of off-the-shelf models has – at least initially – focused researchers' attention onto a relatively narrow set of questions, at the expense of other questions of equally great substantive interest. In recent years, however, a growing number of scholars have begun to examine voting and coalition patterns in the Council, noting the puzzling lack of minimum-winning coalitions, the extensive use of unanimous voting (even where QMV is an option) and the existence of a North–South cleavage within the Council.[8]

Third and finally, a large and ever-growing literature has attempted to model in rational choice terms and to study empirically the inter-institutional relations among the Commission (as agenda setter) and the Council and Parliament, under different legislative procedures. Over the course of the 1980s and the 1990s, the legislative powers of the EP have grown sequentially, from the relatively modest and non-binding 'consultation procedure' through the creation of the 'cooperation' and 'assent' procedures in the 1980s and the creation and reform of a 'co-decision procedure' in the 1990s. This expansion of EP legislative power and the complex nature of the new legislative procedures has fostered the development of a burgeoning literature and led to several vigorous debates among rational choice scholars about the nature and extent of the EP's and the Council's respective influence across the various procedures. The first of these debates concerned the power of the European Parliament under the cooperation procedure. In an influential article, Tsebelis (1994) argued that this provision gave the Parliament 'conditional agenda-setting' power, insofar as the Parliament would now enjoy the ability to make specific proposals that would be easier for the Council to adopt than to amend. Other scholars disputed Tsebelis's model, arguing that the EP's proposed amendments would have no special status without the approval of the Commission, which therefore remained the principal agenda setter. This theoretical debate, in turn, motivated a series of empirical studies which appeared to confirm the basic predictions of Tsebelis's model, namely that the Parliament enjoyed much greater success in influencing the content of legislation under cooperation than under the older consultation procedure (Kreppel 1999).

A second controversy emerged in the literature over the power of Parliament under the co-decision procedure introduced by the Maastricht Treaty (co-decision I) and reformed by the Treaty of Amsterdam (co-decision II). In another controversial article, Tsebelis (1997) argued that, contrary to common perceptions of the co-decision procedure as a step forward for the EP, Parliament had actually *lost* legislative power in the move from cooperation to co-decision I. By contrast, other rational choice scholars disputed Tsebelis's claims, noting that alternative specifications of the model predicted more modest agenda-setting power for the EP under cooperation and/or a stronger position for the EP in co-decision. Here again, quantitative and qualitative empirical analyses have provided at least tentative answers to the question of EP influence across the various legislative procedures, with the most extensive study suggesting that the EP has indeed enjoyed greater legislative influence under co-decision I than under cooperation, largely at the expense of the Commission (Tsebelis et al. 2001). In any event, the Treaty of Amsterdam subsequently simplified the co-decision procedure, creating a genuinely bicameral co-decision II procedure.

To some observers, these debates have verged on scholasticism, focusing more on model specification than on the empirical reality of legislative decision-making, and coming around to empirical testing relatively late in the day (Crombez et al. 2000; Garrett et al. 2001). Taken as a whole, however, the debate over the EP's legislative powers, like early work on the internal organization of the Parliament, has both clarified the basic theoretical assumptions that scholars make about the various actors and their preferences *and* motivated systematic empirical studies that have generated cumulative knowledge about the EU legislative process.

Executive Politics

The study of EU executive politics, Tallberg points out in his chapter, is not the exclusive preserve of rational choice scholars. Neofunctionalists and intergovernmentalists have been debating the causal role of the executive Commission for decades, and the Commission has been studied as well by sociological institutionalists, by students of political entrepreneurship and by normative democratic theorists. Nevertheless, as Tallberg also points out, RCI and principal-agent analysis have emerged over the past decade as the dominant approach to the study of the Commission and other executive actors such as the European Central Bank and the growing body of EU agencies.

These studies generally address two specific sets of questions. First, they ask why and under what conditions a group of (member-state) *principals* might delegate powers to (supranational) *agents*, such as the Commission, the European Central Bank or the Court of Justice. With regard to this first question, principal-agent accounts of delegation hypothesize that member-state principals, as rational actors, delegate powers to supranational organizations primarily to lower the transaction costs of policymaking, in particular by allowing member governments to commit themselves credibly to international agreements and to benefit from the policy-relevant expertise provided by supranational actors. Utilizing a variety of quantitative and qualitative methods, the empirical work of these scholars has collectively demonstrated that EU member governments do indeed delegate powers to the Commission and other agents largely to reduce the transaction costs of policymaking, in particular through the monitoring of member-state compliance, the filling-in of 'incomplete contracts' and the speedy and efficient adoption of implementing regulations (Moravcsik 1998; Franchino 2002, 2004, 2007; Pollack 2003). By contrast with these positive results, however, scholars have found little or no support for the hypothesis that member states delegate powers to the Commission to take advantage of its superior expertise (Moravcsik 1998; Pollack 2003).

In addition to the question of delegation, rational choice institutionalists have devoted greater attention to a second question posed by principal-agent models: What if an agent – such as the Commission, the Court of Justice, or the ECB – behaves in ways that diverge from the preferences of the principals? The answer to this question in principal-agent analysis lies primarily in the administrative procedures that the principals may establish to define *ex ante* the scope of agency activities, as well as the oversight procedures that allow for *ex post* oversight and sanctioning of errant agents. Applied to the EU, principal-agent analysis leads to the hypothesis that agency autonomy is likely to vary across issue-areas and over time, as a function of the preferences of the member governments, the distribution of information between principals and agents, and the decision rules governing the application of sanctions or the adoption of new legislation. By and large, empirical studies of executive politics in the EU have supported these hypotheses, pointing in particular to the significance of decision rules as a crucial determinant of executive autonomy (Pollack 1997, 2003; Tallberg 2000, 2003).

In sum, the rational choice, principal-agent approach has indeed, as Tallberg argues, come to dominate the study of the Commission and other executive actors in the past several decades. This principal-agent literature, like other rational choice approaches, can be criticized for its focus on a particular set of (albeit very important) questions about the relationship between principals and agents and for its neglect of other equally important questions such as the internal workings of executive organizations like the Commission. Furthermore, as Hix argues in his contribution to this volume, the traditional PA assumption that the Commission is an outlier with particularly intense preferences for greater integration may be misleading in the post-Maastricht era where the EU has already placed markers in nearly every area of public policy. Nevertheless, principal-agent models have provided a theoretical framework to ask a series of pointed questions about the causes and consequences of delegating executive power to EU actors, and they have directed scholars' attention to factors such as transaction costs, information asymmetries and the operation of formal rules and administrative law, that had been neglected or indeed ignored by earlier studies. Just as importantly, challenges such as Hix's can be accommodated within the rational choice tradition and can generate additional testable hypotheses that promise to advance further our systematic knowledge of executive politics in the EU.

Judicial Politics

In addition to the lively debate about the nature of EU executive politics, rational choice institutionalists have also engaged in an increasingly sophisticated research program into the nature of EU judicial politics and the role of the European Court of Justice,

examined by Conant in this volume. Writing in the early 1990s, for example, Garrett (1992) first drew on principal-agent analysis to argue that the Court, as an agent of the EU's member governments, was bound to follow the wishes of the most powerful member states. These member states, Garrett argued, had established the ECJ as a means to solve problems of incomplete contracting and monitoring compliance with EU obligations, and they rationally accepted ECJ jurisprudence, even when rulings went against them, because of their longer-term interest in the enforcement of EU law. In such a setting, Garrett and Weingast (1993: 189) argued, the ECJ might identify 'constructed focal points' among multiple equilibrium outcomes, but the Court was unlikely to rule against the preferences of powerful EU member states.

Responding to Garrett's work, other scholars argued forcefully that Garrett's model overestimated the control mechanisms available to powerful member states and the ease of sanctioning an activist Court, which has been far more autonomous than Garrett suggests, and that Garrett's empirical work misread the preferences of the member governments and the politics of internal market reform. Such accounts suggest that the Court has been able to pursue the process of legal integration far beyond the collective preferences of the member governments, in part because of the high costs to member states in overruling or failing to comply with ECJ decisions, and in part because the ECJ enjoys powerful allies in the form of national courts, which refer hundreds of cases per year to the ECJ via the 'preliminary reference' procedure (Mattli and Slaughter 1995, 1998; Stone Sweet and Brunell 1998; Stone Sweet and Caporaso 1998; Alter 2001). In this view, best summarized by Stone Sweet and Caporaso (1998: 129), 'the move to supremacy and direct effect must be understood as audacious acts of agency' by the Court. Responding to these critiques, rational choice analyses of the ECJ have become more nuanced over time, acknowledging the limits of member-state control over the Court and testing hypotheses about the conditions under which the ECJ enjoys the greatest autonomy from its national masters (Garrett 1995; Garrett et al. 1998; Kilroy 1999; Pollack 2003).

More recently, as Conant points out, the literature on the ECJ and legal integration has increasingly moved from the traditional question of the ECJ's relationship with national governments toward the study of the ECJ's other interlocutors, including most notably the national courts that bring the majority of cases before the ECJ and the individual litigants who use EU law to achieve their aims within national legal systems. Such studies have problematized and sought to explain the complex and ambivalent relationship between the ECJ and national courts, as well as the varying litigation strategies of 'one-shot' litigants and 'repeat players' before the courts (Mattli and Slaughter 1998; Alter 2001; Conant 2002). These and other studies, influenced largely (although not exclusively) by rational choice models, have demonstrated the complexities of ECJ legal integration, the inter-relationships among supranational, national and subnational political and legal actors, and the limits of EU law in national legal contexts.

Europeanization in Member States and Candidate Countries

In contrast to the previous sections, which focused on the behavior and policies of EU institutions, an increasing number of studies have focused in recent years on the effects of the EU on domestic politics within the EU's old and new member states – the 'Europeanization' literature reviewed in this volume by Börzel and Risse. Perhaps most interestingly for our purposes here, Börzel and Risse (2000, this volume) have suggested that Europeanization could be theorized in terms of two distinct mechanisms, the one derived from rational choice and emphasizing a logic of consequences, the other derived from sociological institutionalism and emphasizing a logic of appropriateness. In the former, rationalist version, 'the misfit between European and domestic processes, policies and institutions provides societal and/or political actors with new opportunities and constraints in the pursuance of their interests'. Whether these

actors could in turn secure domestic changes is hypothesized to depend on two key factors emphasized in off-the-shelf RC theories: the existence of multiple veto players and facilitating formal institutions providing resources and opportunities to various domestic actors. By contrast, the sociological perspective theorized that European norms and rules might exert an influence through persuasion and socialization, with domestic outcomes being mitigated by factors such as the existence of domestic 'norm entrepreneurs' to mobilize domestic support and a political culture conducive to consensus-building and cost-sharing (Börzel and Risse 2000: 2). Rationalism and constructivism meet here, not as colliding meta-theories, but as first-order theories that predict different mechanisms of Europeanization and different facilitating factors that would explain the variable impact of 'Europe' in different domestic settings.

The explicit derivation and testing of competing rationalist and constructivist hypotheses, moreover, has not been limited to the study of Europeanization in the 'old' member states, but has turned since the late 1990s in a concerted fashion to the impacts of the EU on the candidate and new member countries of southern and eastern Europe. Students of EU enlargement had for some time framed many of their research questions in terms of the rationalist-constructivist debate, including a number of studies that grappled with the EU's decision to enlarge and the substantive terms of enlargement negotiated with the candidate countries (Schimmelfennig and Sedelmeier 2002). Toward the end of the 1990s and into the current decade, many of these scholars turned to studying the effects of the EU on candidate and new member countries.

In the most extensive such study, Schimmelfennig and Sedelmeier (2005a) led a team of researchers who sought explicitly to test alternative rationalist and constructivist hypotheses about the effect of EU membership on the new member states in central and eastern Europe. Drawing on previous rationalist and constructivist work, Schimmelfennig and Sedelmeier (2005b) derived three distinct models of the mechanisms driving the Europeanization of the candidate/new member countries of central and eastern Europe. The first, 'external incentives' model was derived from rational choice models of bargaining, focusing on the asymmetrical bargaining power of the EU and its applicant states and in particular on EU 'conditionality', namely the EU's insistence that candidate countries apply the *acquis communautaire* as a prerequisite to membership. Against this rationalist model, the authors put up two competing constructivist or sociological institutionalist accounts – a 'social learning' model predicated on a 'logic of appropriateness' and focusing on the socialization of state and civil-society actors in the target countries, and a 'lesson-drawing' model in which dissatisfied governments in central and eastern Europe actively seek out and import EU practices, with the Union itself playing an essentially passive role.

Schimmelfennig and Sedelmeier's findings, based on a series of case studies cutting across multiple countries and multiple issue-areas, provide striking support for the external incentives model. While various studies in the larger project found some instances of socialization and/or lesson-drawing in the absence of conditionality, the authors conclude that, on balance, 'the external incentives provided by the EU can largely account for the impact of the EU on candidate countries'. Observed variations in rule adoption, moreover, are explained in large part by the independent variables hypothesized in the external incentives model, including most notably a credible membership perspective and clear political conditionality (Schimmelfennig and Sedelmeier 2005c: 210–11). Other recent studies employ varying theoretical frameworks and focus on different aspects of the Europeanization process, but here too the general finding is that explicit and credible political conditionality is the most important source of EU leverage and policy change in the new and candidate countries, with socialization and lesson-drawing having a much weaker and more variable impact (Jacoby 2004; Kelley 2004; Vachudova 2005; Schimmelfennig 2005; Zürn and Checkel 2005).

In sum, the growing literatures on Europeanization and enlargement are striking for two features, both of which augur well for the field. First, scholars have generally adopted a pragmatic, 'tool-kit' approach to rational choice and constructivist theories, deriving distinctive causal mechanisms and scope conditions for Europeanization from each theory and testing them with care and precision. Second, in these studies, external incentives in the form of political conditionality have emerged as the best predictor of policy change in old as well as new member states, and the scope conditions associated with rational choice theory have performed well in explaining variation across both issue-areas and countries.

Public Opinion and European Integration

The scholarly literature on EU public opinion, analysed in this volume by Ray, was relatively late to develop, due in large part to the emphasis by early integration theorists on elite attitudes, with mass opinion frequently depicted as a 'permissive consensus' within which elites could pursue integrative schemes (Haas 1958; Lindberg and Scheingold 1970). In recent decades, however, the EU public-opinion literature has blossomed, driven in part by events (direct elections of the European Parliament, dramatic referenda on European integration in EU member states) and in part by the availability of Eurobarometer polling data.

The EU public opinion literature, as Ray points out, has been largely problem-driven and theoretically eclectic, drawing on rational-choice models alongside socialization, political communications and other theoretical approaches to generate competing hypotheses about the determinants of public support for the EU. This eclectic approach can be traced back to Lindberg and Scheingold's (1970) pioneering work on EU support for European integration, in which an essentially rationalist or 'utilitarian' support (based on calculation of tangible economic benefits from integration) was contrasted with 'affective' support rooted in a more 'diffuse and emotional' response to the European project. This distinction has remained a fundamental feature of the subsequent literature, which continues to derive and competitively test hypotheses from diverse theoretical traditions about the determinants of public support for European integration, EU institutions and EU policies.

The rational-choice approach to EU public opinion, which Ray associates with the study of utilitarian support, has itself been theoretically and methodologically diverse, with various scholars identifying different independent variables as determinants of public support and operationalizing both dependent and independent variables in different ways using various survey questions from Eurobarometer and other data sources. Some utilitarian models, for example, have focused on EU fiscal transfers or on objective economic conditions at the national level as predictors of support, while others have identified the objective socioeconomic characteristics of individuals or else subjective individual evaluations of economic costs and benefits, as the best measures of utilitarian support. There is, in other words, no single 'rational choice theory' of EU public opinion, but a huge variety of first-order theories and hypotheses, each of which has been subjected to empirical testing, typically using quantitative analyses of Eurobarometer survey data. The complex and sometimes inconclusive empirical findings of this literature are summarized by Leonard, who notes that the most robust findings point to the importance of socioeconomic status ('human capital') and subjective economic perceptions as predictors of support for European integration. The impact of such utilitarian factors is not uncontested, with some studies arguing that identity is at least as strong a predictor of public opinion toward the EU as economic interest (Hooghe and Marks 2004), but the central place of rational-choice or utilitarian models in the literature is clear.

Perhaps the most striking feature of the public opinion literature for our purposes is its close approximation of Green and Shapiro's (1994) ideal type of social-scientific research. Unlike some other, more theoretically driven areas of EU research, work on EU public opinion has indeed been problem-driven and theoretically eclectic, with even strongly rationalist scholars like Gabel (1998) testing affective and other sources of support alongside utilitarian hypotheses. Furthermore, while one can question the operationalization of variables or the selection of data in any individual study, the public opinion literature as a whole has steered well clear of Green and Shapiro's methodological pathologies, relying as it has on multivariate statistical testing of competing hypotheses drawn from distinct theoretical approaches.

The Empirical Fruitfulness of Rational Choice Theory

In sum, rational choice theory appears – at least in the five areas examined here – to have been an empirically fruitful as well as a theoretically innovative approach to the study of EU politics. While some literatures have indeed focused for extended periods on model specification in the absence of hard empirical data, over time each of the above literatures has produced specific, testable hypotheses about the relative power of legislative, executive and judicial actors, about the determinants of public opinion toward the EU and about the effects of the EU on domestic politics in the member and candidate states. Just as importantly, moreover, most of the rational choice literature in EU studies appears to have avoided the pathologies identified by Green and Shapiro. While individual studies might derive formal models in the absence of empirical testing or conduct superficial empirical work designed to support or illustrate rather than test theories, many scholars in each of the literatures reviewed above have identified concrete, measurable dependent and independent variables; collected systematic quantitative and qualitative data to test their hypotheses; reported findings (including negative and puzzling findings) honestly; and revised and derived new theories in light of those findings.

By and large, moreover, the hypotheses generated by the various first-order (or middle-range) rationalist theories have found empirical support: MEPs do respond to institutional incentives in their voting behavior; the Commission does appear to enjoy variable influence according to the factors emphasized by principal-agent analysis; the Court of Justice does enjoy extraordinary (but not boundless) discretion vis-à-vis the member governments; individuals do appear to base their opinions of the EU in large part on a calculation of expected utility; and member and candidate countries do appear to respond most consistently to material incentives provided by the EU. While the debates in all these areas remain ongoing, the best rational choice work of the past decade has been empirically as well as theoretically rigorous and fruitful and has advanced our understanding of EU politics from the Brussels institutions to the member governments to individual opinions and behavior.

CHALLENGES FOR RATIONALIST ANALYSIS OF THE EU

Still, the reader may ask, what do rational choice approaches leave out or ignore in their study of EU politics? In addition to the 'internal' critique of poor empirical work, rational choice has also been subject to an 'external' critique, which emphasizes its limited domain of application and its 'ontological blindness' to important questions. Indeed, even within the five issues examined above, we noticed a tendency for rational choice approaches to focus, at least initially, on questions that are most amenable to study using off-the-shelf models while paying less attention to other equally important questions. Looking beyond our five selected issues, the external critique from constructivism raises three inter-related issues that I examine, very briefly, in this section. I consider first whether the purported 'great debate' between rationalism and constructivism has been a metatheoretical dialogue of the deaf or a useful controversy and I then go on to consider the ability of rational choice approaches to theorize about endogenous preference formation and endogenous sources of change, respectively.

Rationalism vs Constructivism: A Useful Controversy

Within both international relations and EU studies, the past decade has witnessed a marked change in the presentation of the field. By the late 1990s, and into the early 2000s, it was commonplace for scholars to depict both IR and EU studies as being characterized by a new 'great debate' between rational choice and constructivism, displacing earlier debates such as that between neofunctionalism and inter-governmentalism (Katzenstein et al. 1998; Christiansen et al. 1999; Moravcsik 1999; Checkel and Moravcsik 2001).

By the start of the current decade, however, a number of scholars noted the drawbacks of engaging in a grand meta-theoretical debate between rationalism and constructivism in both IR theory and EU studies. In an influential essay, Fearon and Wendt (2002) focused on the potential pitfalls of organizing the field of international relations around an ontological or empirical debate between rationalism and constructivism writ large. Such an approach, they argue, 'can encourage scholars to be method-driven rather than problem driven in their research', leading scholars to ignore important questions or answers that do not fit easily into the grand debate (Fearon and Wendt 2002: 52). In place of such a debate, the authors suggest that scholars approach rational choice and constructivist approaches pragmatically, as analytical 'tool-kits' that 'ask somewhat different questions and so bring different aspects of social life into focus' (Fearon and Wendt 2002: 53). The study of international politics may indeed be characterized by the existence of two second-order theories, but scholars' empirical work need not – and indeed should not – be organized purely in terms of a zero-sum battle between competing paradigms. Rather, the authors suggest, scholars can and should engage in problem-driven research, drawing on first-order theories from either or both approaches as appropriate.

Within EU studies, scholars have similarly warned against a metatheoretical dialogue of the deaf, seeking instead to encourage dialogue between the two approaches and focusing debate on first-order questions that can be resolved through careful empirical work. Moravcsik (1999), for example, rejects the call for 'more metatheory', calling instead for theorists to articulate 'distinct falsifiable hypotheses' and to test these hypotheses against competing theories from other approaches.

Along similar lines, three EU scholars (Jupille et al. 2003) have recently put forward a framework for promoting integration of – or at least a fruitful dialogue between – rationalist and constructivist approaches to international relations. Rationalism and constructivism, the authors argue, are not hopelessly incommensurate, but can engage each other through 'four distinct modes of theoretical conversation', namely:

(1) competitive testing, in which competing theories are pitted against each other in explaining a single event or class of events;
(2) a 'domain of application' approach, in which each theory is considered to explain some sub-set of empirical reality;
(3) a 'sequencing' approach, in which one theory might explain a particular step in a sequence of actions (e.g. a constructivist explanation of national preferences) while another theory might best explain subsequent developments (e.g. a rationalist explanation of subsequent bargaining); and
(4) 'incorporation' or 'subsumption', in which one theory claims to subsume the other.

Looking at the substantive empirical work in their special issue, Jupille et al. find that most contributions to the rationalist/constructivist debate utilize competitive testing, while only a small number have adopted the domain of application, sequencing or subsumption approaches. Nevertheless, they see substantial progress in the debate, in which both sides generally accept a common standard of empirical testing as the criterion for useful theorizing about EU politics.

Similarly, the review of empirical applications in EU studies conducted above suggests that the rationalist/constructivist debate has not been a dialogue of the deaf but a 'useful controversy', forcing scholars on both sides to articulate clear assumptions, test their hypotheses against competing explanations and specify alternative causal mechanisms for phenomena like Europeanization. In addition, the rationalist-constructivist debate has pressed rational-choice theorists to address two vital issues that have been at the margins of the approach: endogenous preference formation and change.

Endogenous Preference Formation

One of the central bones of contention between rationalists and constructivists – both generally and in EU studies – has been the issue of endogenous preference formation. To some extent, this debate has been muddied from the outset by a lack of clarity about the meanings of the terms 'exogenous' and 'endogenous'. For many theorists, exogeneity and endogeneity are characteristics of theories – what they seek to explain and what they leave unexplained. In this view, to say that actor preferences are 'exogenously given' means that the theorist makes no attempt to explain preferences, but simply adopts assumptions about them in order to theorize and make predictions about some other dependent variable or explanandum, such as actor behavior or policy outcomes. By contrast, other theories 'endogenize' actor preferences, in the precise sense of making those preferences the explanandum or dependent variable of the study. Rational choice theorists are typically seen to take the first approach, adopting simplifying assumptions about actor preferences (and hence making them exogenous to the theory, which makes no effort to explain them), whereas constructivists tend to place actors' identities and interests at the center of the analysis and attempt to explain them, frequently with regard to the social contexts that actors inhabit (Fearon and Wendt 2002: 60).

Muddying the waters, however, a slightly different interpretation of exogeneity and endogeneity has arisen in the debate between rational choice institutionalists and constructivists in IR and EU studies. In these institutionalist accounts, a number of constructivist authors have argued that the preferences of various national actors are endogenous *to the international institution* in question, e.g. that actor preferences are shaped (at least in part) by interaction and socialization at the international level (e.g. Sandholtz 1996; Checkel 2005a, b, Lewis 2005). In contrast, scholars who believe that national preferences are formulated domestically and are unaltered by interaction at the international level are often depicted as claiming that national preferences are exogenous *to international institutions*.

This distinction – between preferences being exogenous or endogenous to a *theory*, as opposed to being exogenous or endogenous to an *international institution* – matters in assessing the purported 'ontological blindness' of rationalism to this question. If we take the first approach, urged on us by Fearon and Wendt (2002: 60), the question is whether rational choice theories are clearly capable of 'endogenizing' – of seeking to explain – preferences, including the 'national preferences' of states in the international system. If it could be shown that rational choice is truly incapable of theorizing national preferences as an explanandum, then we might argue that the correct relationship between the two approaches may be 'domain of application' or 'sequencing' relationship, in which constructivists focus on explaining preferences and rationalists limit their efforts to modeling interactions among actors with exogenously given preferences.

Such a neat division of labor, however, does not stand up to careful scrutiny. Rational choice theorists have not abandoned the effort to explain actor preferences, particularly in international relations and in EU studies, where *national* preference formation has been a significant object of study for rationalists as well as constructivists. Within EU studies, for example, Moravcsik's (1998) liberal theory of national preference formation seeks to explain national preferences through the aggregation of individual and producer preferences by national governments and clearly endogenizes national preference formation in this sense. More broadly, rational choice theorists in IR have theorized explicitly and in a variety of ways about the endogenous formation of national preferences, including a range of models that focus on political and economic coalitions, principal-agent relations, audience costs and the effects of regime types and institutional rules on the aggregation of individual preferences at the national level (Snidal 2002: 84–5). By and large, such accounts retain simplifying assumptions about *individual* preferences, focusing instead on the creation of testable hypotheses about the impact of factors such as economic change and domestic institutions on the aggregation of individual preferences into

national preferences. Evolutionary game theorists go even further, seeking to explain individual preference formation through mechanisms of complex learning and selection (Gerber and Jackson 1993; Fearon and Wendt 2002: 65). Clearly, then, rational choice theory is *not* blind to the question of endogenous preference formation, nor have rationalists been unproductive in formulating and testing first-order theories about it.

Hence, when rationalists in EU studies and international relations are charged with blindness toward endogenous preference formation, it is typically in the second and more narrow sense, i.e. that rationalists are unable to theorize about the purported socializing impact of international/EU institutions on states (or on their representatives). Here, critics of rational choice are on firmer ground: Moravcsik's (1998) liberal intergovernmentalism, the most prominent rationalist theory to problematize and explain national preferences, does indeed rule out any socializing impact of international interaction on national preferences, in favor of a purely domestic process of preference formation. Even here, however, rational choice theory is not entirely irrelevant to the study of socialization in EU institutions, and indeed a recent special issue of *International Organization* usefully formulates and tests three distinct mechanisms of socialization drawn from rational choice theory ('strategic calculation'), sociological institutionalism ('role playing') and Habermasian communicative rationality ('normative suasion') (Checkel 2005a, b). The contributors to the volume take a problem-driven approach, drawing pragmatically from various theoretical approaches to identify different mechanisms of socialization as well as the scope conditions for their operations, and their approach to rationalist theory is open-minded rather than exclusionary. On the one hand, editor Jeffrey Checkel suggests that rational choice theories are limited to explaining certain elements of international institutions, including 'behavioral adaptation' (typically as a response to political conditionality and other incentives offered by international institutions) and simple learning (in response to new information provided by international institutions), while true socialization (understood as the internalization of norms and a shift from a logic of consequences to a logic of appropriateness) appears to lie outside the core assumptions of the rational choice approach. 'While ... the ontological differences separating rationalism and constructivism are often overstated', he argues, 'the former is nonetheless ill-equipped to theorize those instances in which the basic properties of agents are changing' (Checkel 2005b: 810).

On the other hand, despite these limitations, several of the volume's authors argue that rational choice theory is capable of theorizing important elements of the socialization process and that the empirical findings of the project are in each case subject to a 'double-interpretation', in which empirical outcomes can be construed as consistent with a rational choice as well as a constructivist explanation (Johnston 2005; Zürn and Checkel 2005). Several of the studies in the volume, for example, point to the central importance of material incentives, which emerge as a stronger predictor of sustained compliance than socialization without such incentives, and a general finding of the project is that the researchers did not 'see as much socialization as expected' – findings clearly consistent with even a thick rational choice perspective (Zürn and Checkel 2005: 1068; see also Kelley 2004; Schimmelfennig 2005; Schimmelfennig and Sedelmeier 2005c). Furthermore, they argue, even findings that appear at first glance to be clearly in support of the constructivist approach, such as the emergence of a culture of compromise with the EU's Committee of Permanent Representatives, can be plausibly interpreted in thin-rationalist terms as instances of political delegation, diffuse reciprocity or simple learning (Zürn and Checkel 2005: 1056–1065). For all of these reasons, Zürn and Checkel echo Fearon and Wendt (2002) in advocating a pragmatic approach to the rationalist/constructivist divide, in which overlaps are acknowledged and differences highlighted through a careful dialogue among first- and second-order theories of international politics.

In sum, rational choice theory is certainly capable of theorizing endogenous preference formation, particularly insofar as *national* preferences are derived from the aggregation of individual preferences through domestic political institutions; and even the study of international socialization can benefit from the articulation of a discrete set of rationalist hypotheses which may fall short of predicting changes in the core preferences of actors, but nevertheless provide compelling explanations for a wide range of related empirical phenomena.

Theorizing Change

A final weakness of rational choice analysis is its purported inability to theorize change – or more precisely to theorize 'endogenous' change. Here again, we encounter some diversity in the use of the terms exogenous and endogenous. If we take Fearon and Wendt's (2002) definition, invoked above, then a theory that endogenizes change is one that seeks to theorize about and explain the sources of change, whereas a theory that exogenizes change is one that takes the source of change – say, the rise of a new great power, or a change in relative prices on world markets – as an assumption and seeks to examine the effects of that source on an existing equilibrium. The key difference, again, is whether the source of change is taken as an unexplained independent variable (hence, exogenous) or is explained in some way by the theory (endogenous).

Within institutionalist theory, by contrast, the terms endogenous and exogenous have taken on a distinct, if overlapping, meaning. In this view, carefully articulated by Helfer (2006), exogeneity and endogeneity are defined in reference to the institution or organization being studied. In this view, widely shared by institutionalist IR scholars, 'change emanating from IO officials and staff is properly labeled as "endogenous" whereas that change resulting from shifts in state preferences or from alterations to the economic, political or social environment is appropriately described as "exogenous"' (Helfer 2006: 4).

Regardless of which of these definitions we accept, it has become commonplace to suggest that rational choice theories, with their emphasis on stable equilibria from which no actor has an incentive to depart, place a theoretical emphasis on stability rather than on change. Indeed, if the definition of an institutional equilibrium is that 'no one has an incentive to deviate from the behavior associated with the institution', then by definition 'any changes in self-enforcing institutions must have an extraneous origin' (Greif and Laitin 2004: 633). Thus, to the extent that rational choice models do address change, such change is typically attributed to exogenous shocks that (temporarily) upset an equilibrium and lead (eventually) to a new equilibrium (Helfer 2006: 4).

Looking specifically to EU studies, it appears that even the best rational choice work shares this tendency to either neglect the issue of change or to attribute change to exogenous shocks. Moravcsik's (1998) *The Choice for Europe*, for example, problematizes both national preferences and institutional change, but his analysis traces the primary sources of change to exogenous developments in the global economy. Similarly, Carrubba and Volden's (2001) formal model of change in Council voting rules, while also addressing directly the issue of change, attributes those changes to exogenous (unexplained) changes in the number of member states, changes in legislative procedures and changes in policy areas under consideration, each of which can affect the Council's ability to pass legislation and thus provide member states with a rational incentive to consider changes to the Council's voting rules and weights. These works, unlike much rational choice work on the EU, do theorize a process of change, but the sources of change remain exogenous – both to the institutions of the Union and more broadly to the theories being advanced. Given the rapid pace of institutional and policy change in the European Union over the past several decades, this relative inattention to endogenous sources of change – which has long been the bread-and-butter of neofunctionalist theory – seems a surprising lacuna.

As a variant on RCI, historical institutionalism seems a more promising approach to studying change within institutions like the EU. By contrast with rational choice's focus on stable equilibria, historical institutionalism has focused on the effects of institutions *over time*, and in particular at the ways in which a given set of institutions, once established, can shape or constrain the behavior of the actors who established them. Political institutions and public policies, in this view, are frequently characterized by 'increasing returns', insofar as those institutions and policies create incentives for actors to stick within and not abandon existing institutions, adapting them only incrementally to changing political environments. Insofar as political institutions and public policies are in fact characterized by increasing returns, Pierson (2000, 2004) argues, politics will be characterized by certain inter-related phenomena, including: inertia or lock-ins, whereby existing institutions may remain in equilibrium for extended periods despite considerable exogenous change; a critical role for timing and sequencing, in which relatively small and contingent events that occur at critical junctures early in a sequence shape and constrain events that occur later; and path-dependence, whereby early decisions provide rational incentives for actors to perpetuate institutional and policy choices inherited from the past, even when the resulting outcomes are manifestly inefficient. Such theories, while rejecting the equilibrium analysis of much rational-choice work, frequently adopt basic assumptions about actors and institutions that are fully consistent with those of rational choice (North 1990; Pierson 2000, 2004).

Historical institutionalism has been widely applied to the study of the European Union over the past two decades, with a particular emphasis on the path-dependent development of the EU and its policies. Scharpf's (1988) pioneering study of the 'joint-decision trap' in EU policy-making, for example, demonstrated how, under certain conditions of intergovernmentalism, unanimity voting and a status-quo default condition, inefficient EU policies such as the Common Agricultural Policy could persist and resist reform for extended periods. Similarly, Pierson's (1996) study of EU social policy argued that EU member states had effectively lost control of the policy, thanks to a combination of short time horizons, unintended consequences, change-resistant decision rules and policy adaptation by the beneficiaries of existing EU policies. Generalizing from these studies, we might hypothesize that, *ceteris paribus*, EU institutions and policies will be most resistant to change (a) where their alteration requires a unanimous agreement among member states or the consent of supranational actors like the Commission or the Parliament; and (b) where existing EU policies mobilize cross-national bases of support that raise the cost of reversing or revising them.

By and large, however, these 'first-generation' historical institutionalist works have been more effective in explaining *continuity* (often in the face of exogenous shocks) than in explaining endogenous *change*. For this reason, both rational choice and historical institutionalists have devoted increasing attention in recent years to the challenge of theorizing endogenous sources of change as well as stability. Within historical institutionalism, a growing 'second-generation' literature has focused on the central claim that existing institutions and policies may produce not only *positive* feedbacks that stabilize and reinforce existing equilibria, but also *negative* feedbacks that create pressures for institutional and policy change. Such feedbacks, it is argued, can produce changes that are gradual in timing but ultimately transformative in effect (Streeck and Thelen 2005; Hall and Thelen 2006; Immergut 2006). Welfare-state programs, for example, may be structured such that the value of benefits erodes over time, and this benefit erosion in turn may lead to a decline in public support for those programs – a clear negative feedback in an issue-area long characterized by the predominance of positive feedback (Immergut 2006).

Within rational choice, the most concerted effort to theorize endogenous sources of institutional change has come from Greif and Laitin (2004), who offer a model of endogenous change that draws upon game-theoretic equilibrium models but introduces a dynamic theory of institutional change. In a standard game-theoretic model, the authors suggest, institutions and their associated behaviors are endogenized (explained), while the environmental context for any given institution (say a given level of technology or the global economy or the global balance of power) is theorized as an exogenous set of 'parameters' that help to define the equilibrium outcome within that institution. In this context, however, it is possible that the workings

of an institution can in turn affect the value of its parameters – or what Greif and Laitin call 'quasi-parameters' – which in turn may affect the internal equilibrium of the institution, either reinforcing it or undermining it. *Self-reinforcing* institutions, in this view, are those that change the quasi-parameters of the institution so as to make the institution and the individual behaviors of the actors within it more stable in the face of exogenous changes. *Self-undermining* institutions, in contrast, are those that change the quasi-parameters such that a previously stable equilibrium is undermined; these institutions, in Greif and Laitin's (2004: 34) terms, 'can cultivate the seeds of their own demise'. Further developing Greif and Laitin's ideas, Büthe (2006) has suggested that the actions of the EU's supranational agents can similarly be theorized as an endogenous source of change, either reinforcing or undermining the Union's institutional and policy equilibrium over the long term.

Despite their differences, both recent developments in historical institutionalism and Greif and Laitin's theory of endogenous change make two central points: First, institutions may produce *feedback effects* that, over time, can lead to change in the institution itself. Second, these feedback effects may be *positive*, thus promoting a reinforcement of institutionalized cooperation, or they can be *negative*, undermining institutions and policies and possibly leading to their demise. Existing studies of the EU – drawing from theoretical sources including neofunctionalism, historical institutionalism and constructivism – have generally emphasized positive feedback, in which an initial integrative act can lead to functional spillover (Haas 1958), gaps in member-state control (Pierson 1996; Pollack 2003), long-term socialization of elites (Haas 1958; Checkel 2005a) and the negotiation of informal agreements that are subsequently codified over time (Farrell and Héritier 2005). The notion that EU institutions might have negative or self-undermining feedback effects has been explored less systematically,[9] yet the Union's ongoing constitutional crisis and the long-term decline in public support for further integration suggest that negative feedback should be the focus of greater attention in future studies of institutional change.

At the same time, however, both rational choice and other scholars should beware of the temptation to 'endogenize' all sources of change within a single theory or to attribute all change within the European Union to positive or negative feedback effects from the EU itself. As Immergut (2006: 6) aptly observes, 'Although exogenous change sounds like a fancy word for an *ad hoc* explanation, there are many interesting and systematic exogenous sources of change'. Indeed, while scholars should be attentive to possible feedback effects from European integration, it is both possible and likely that 'exogenous' factors, including political and economic changes on the world stage or critical elections within one or more member countries, have served and may continue to serve as the most important sources of change in the EU, and that the feedback effects of European integration may be rare or weak compared with other domestic and/or global sources of change.

CONCLUSIONS

There is an old expression to the effect that when you have a hammer, every problem looks like a nail. Critics of rational choice in EU studies have often argued that formal modelers in particular have approached the EU almost exclusively through the lens of their off-the-shelf theories, asking only narrow questions about those aspects of the EU that resemble, say, domestic legislatures or principal-agent relationships. There is, I have argued in this chapter, some truth to this claim: rational choice theorists have followed a positive heuristic that has pointed them toward the study of strategic interaction within institutional constraints and away from other questions such as socialization, deliberation and identity change.

Nevertheless, the picture presented in this chapter is broadly speaking a positive one, with respect to both rational choice analysis and the field of EU studies as a whole. With regard to the former, we have seen how, over the past several decades, students of the EU have adapted rational choice theories of politics with increasing sophistication to the myriad of specific questions we can ask about European integration and EU politics. Moreover, I have argued, the empirical record of these theories has been, on balance, positive and progressive, not pathological. While we do find some evidence of elaborate models subjected to cursory testing (or no testing at all), the broader picture is one in which scholars draw on rational choice theories (and other theories) to generate testable hypotheses about concrete political outcomes across a range of subject areas. Even in areas that have been considered to be outside the domain of application of rational choice, such as endogenous preference formation and change, rational choice theories have (alongside constructivists) contributed to the development of a sophisticated research program on EU socialization, as well as pioneering (alongside historical institutionalists) a revitalized discussion on the endogenous sources of change in the EU. Much remains to be done in these areas and the work reviewed here is in many cases suggestive rather than conclusive, but the claim that rational choice is 'ontologically blind' to such questions has not been borne out.

With regard to the health of the field overall, it is striking that the rational choice/constructivist divide in EU studies, which many scholars feared would descend into a metatheoretical dialogue of the deaf, has instead proven healthy to the field and to rationalist and constructivist theorists on both sides of the divide. To a very large extent, students of EU politics have taken a pragmatic and problem-driven approach: identifying an important problem, searching the existing literature (both rationalist and constructivist) for relevant insights and hypotheses and seeking to test those hypotheses through careful empirical analysis. This is the approach taken in much of the literature on public opinion, Europeanization, Eastern enlargement and socialization, and the same approach should be applicable to the full range of research questions in EU studies.

The case for rational choice, finally, can be made more forcefully. Thoughtful rational choice theorists over the past decade have argued that rational choice models should be most powerful within a certain domain, in which the stakes of individual decisions are considerable (making the calculation of expected utility worthwhile), the informational context is relatively rich (making calculation of expected utility possible) and the rules of the game are clearly and formally spelled out (Ferejohn and Satz 1996; Fiorina 1996). The European Union, whether we call it an international regime or a polity-in-the-making, has all of these characteristics, suggesting that EU politics is a promising forum for the elaboration and testing of rational choice theories even beyond the core areas explored in this chapter (Jupille 2004; Hix 2005). Put differently, across the full range of its activities, EU politics does indeed look like a nail – and we as a discipline would do well to get some hammers.

NOTES

1. The author is grateful to Ben Rosamond and Knud Erik Jørgensen for comments on an earlier draft of this chapter.

2. Rational choice, as Elster (1986) notes, is both a normative and a positive theory. In normative terms, rational choice theory does not dictate the ends or aims to which individuals should strive, but it does 'tell us what we ought to do in order to achieve our aims as well as possible'. In contrast, rational choice as a positive theory adopts a particular set of assumptions about actors and about their social context and seeks to generate testable hypotheses about human behavior. Despite the significance of the normative aspect, I focus here on rational choice exclusively as a positive theory, inquiring whether rational choice theories have advanced our understanding of EU politics.

3. This is, of course, a severely compressed discussion of a theoretical approach whose basic tenets remain to some extent contested. For good discussions see e.g. Elster (1986), Ferejohn (1991) and Snidal (2002).

4. The use of such models has been controversial, with critics accusing modelers of simply restating in simplified form basic insights already familiar to substantive experts in the field. However, as Snidal (2002: 77–8) has argued, formal models of collective action and international cooperation have produced non-intuitive or counter-intuitive findings that went largely against dominant views and generated specific predictions about both the obstacles and the solutions to collective action problems. For good discussions on the role of formal models in EU studies, see e.g. Hug (2003) and Pahre (2005).

5. For a useful collection of responses to Green and Shapiro's critique, see e.g. the essays collected in Friedman (1996b).

6. Foundational works in the RCI canon include Scharpf (1988), Garrett (1992), Tsebelis (1994) and Garrett and Tsebelis (1996). For useful reviews of institutionalism in EU

studies, see e.g. Jupille and Caporaso (1999), Dowding (2000), Aspinwall and Schneider (2001) and Pollack (2004).

7. I am grateful to Andrew Moravcsik for suggesting the empirical fruitfulness of rational choice theory as a central focus of this chapter.

8. For an up-to-date study of the state of the art in the study of the Council, see Hayes-Renshaw and Wallace (2006); recent rationalist work on the Council that looks beyond the voting-power approach includes Mattila and Lane (2001), Mattila (2004) and the chapters in Thomson et al. (2006).

9. Lindberg and Scheingold's (1970) notion of 'spillback' is a notable, but underdeveloped and little-noted, exception.

REFERENCES

Albert, M. (2003) 'The voting power approach: measurement without theory', *European Union Politics*, 4(3): 351–66.

Alter, K.J. (2001) *Establishing the Supremacy of European Law: The Making of an International Rule of Law in Europe*. New York: Oxford University Press.

Aspinwall, M. and Schneider, G. (eds) (2001) *The Rules of Integration: Institutionalist Approaches to the Study of Europe*. New York: Manchester University Press.

Börzel, T.A. and Risse, T. (2000) 'When Europeanization hits home: Europeanization and domestic change', RSC Working Paper No. 2000/56, Robert Schuman Centre for Advanced Studies, European University Institute, Florence. Available online at: http://www.iue.it/RSCAS/WP-Texts/00_56.pdf, accessed 16 July 2006.

Büthe, T. (2006) 'Institutional persistence and change in international delegation', paper prepared for the Workshop on Delegating Sovereignty, Duke Law School, 3–4 March 2006.

Carrubba, C.J. and Volden, C. (2001) 'Explaining institutional change in the European Union: what determines the voting rule in the Council of Ministers?', *European Union Politics*, 2(1): 5–30.

Checkel, J.T. (ed.) (2005a) 'International institutions and socialization in Europe', special issue of *International Organization*, 59(4).

Checkel, J.T. (2005b) 'International institutions and socialization in Europe: introduction and framework', *International Organization*, 59(4): 801–26.

Checkel, J.T. and Moravcsik, A. (2001) 'A constructivist research programme in EU studies?', *European Union Politics*, 2(2): 219–49.

Christiansen, T., Jørgensen, K.E. and Wiener, A. (1999) 'The social construction of Europe', *Journal of European Public Policy*, 6(4): 528–44.

Conant, L. (2002) *Justice Contained: Law and Politics in the European Union*. Ithaca, NY: Cornell University Press.

Crombez, C., Steunenberg, B. and Corbett, R. (2000) 'Understanding the EU legislative process: political scientists' and practitioners' perspectives', *European Union Politics*, 1(3): 363–81.

Dowding, K. (2000) 'Institutionalist research on the European Union: a critical review', *European Union Politics*, 1(1): 125–44.

Elster, J. (1986) 'Introduction', in J. Elster (ed.), *Rational Choice*. New York: New York University Press. pp. 1–33.

Epstein, D. and O'Halloran, S. (1999) *Delegating Powers: A Transaction Cost Politics Approach to Policy Making under Separate Powers*. New York: Cambridge University Press.

Farrell, H. and Héritier, A. (2005) 'A rationalist-institutionalist explanation of endogenous regional integration', *Journal of European Public Policy*, 12(2): 273–90.

Fearon, J. and Wendt, A. (2002) 'Rationalism vs. constructivism: a skeptical view', in W. Carlnaes, B. Simmons and T. Risse (eds), *Handbook of International Relations*. New York: Sage. pp. 52–72.

Ferejohn, J. (1991) 'Rationality and interpretation: parliamentary elections in early Stuart England', in K.R. Monroe (ed.), *The Economic Approach to Politics: A Critical Assessment of the Theory of Rational Action*. New York: Harper Collins. pp. 279–305.

Ferejohn, J. and Satz, D. (1996) 'Unification, universalism, and rational choice theory', in J. Friedman (ed.), *The Rational Choice Controversy*. New Haven: Yale University Press.pp. 71–84.

Fiorina, M.P. (1996) 'Rational choice, empirical contributions and the scientific enterprise', in J. Friedman (ed.), *The Rational Choice Controversy*. New Haven: Yale University Press.pp. 85–94.

Franchino, F. (2002) 'Efficiency or credibility? Testing the two logics of delegation to the European Commission', *Journal of European Public Policy*, 9(5): 677–94.

Franchino, F. (2004) 'Delegating powers in the European Community', *British Journal of Political Science*, 34(2): 449–76.

Franchino, F. (2007) *The Powers of the Union: Delegation in the EU*. New York: Cambridge University Press, forthcoming.

Friedman, J. (1996a) 'Introduction: economic approaches to politics', in Friedman (ed.), *The Rational Choice Controversy*. New Haven: Yale University Press. pp. 1–23.

Friedman, J. (ed.) (1996b) *The Rational Choice Controversy: Economic Models of Politics Reconsidered*. New Haven: Yale University Press.

Gabel, M.J. (1998) *Interests and Integration: Market Liberalization, Public Opinion, and European Integration*. Ann Arbor: University of Michigan Press.

Garrett, G. (1992) 'International cooperation and institutional choice: the European Community's internal market', *International Organization*, 46(2): 533–60.

Garrett, G. (1995) 'The politics of legal integration in the European Union', *International Organization*, 49(1): 171–81.

Garrett, G. and Tsebelis, G. (1996) 'An institutional critique of intergovernmentalism', *International Organization*, 50(2): 269–99.

Garrett, G. and Weingast, B. (1993) 'Ideas, interests, and institutions: constructing the European Community's internal market', in J. Goldstein and R. Keohane (eds), *Ideas and Foreign Policy*. Ithaca: Cornell University Press. pp. 173–206.

Garrett, G., Kelemen, R.D. and Schulz, H. (1998) 'The European court of justice, national governments, and legal integration in the European Union', *International Organization*, 52(1): 149–176.

Garrett, G., Tsebelis, G. and Corbett, R. (2001) 'The EU legislative process: academics vs. practitioners - round 2', *European Union Politics*, 2(3): 353–66.

Gerber, E.R. and Jackson, J.E. (1993) 'Endogenous preferences and the study of institutions', *American Political Science Review*, 87(3): 639–56.

Green, D.P. and Shapiro, I. (1994) *Pathologies of Rational Choice Theory: A Critique of Applications in Political Science*. New Haven: Yale University Press.

Greif, A. and Laitin, D.D. (2004) 'A theory of endogenous institutional change', *American Political Science Review*, 98(4): 633–52.

Haas, E.B. (1958) *The Uniting of Europe: Political, Social and Economical Forces 1950–1957*. London: Stevens & Sons Limited.

Haas, E.B. (2001) 'Does constructivism subsume neo-functionalism?', in T. Christiansen, K.E. Jorgensen and A. Wiener (eds), *The Social Construction of Europe*. London: Sage Publications. pp. 22–31.

Hall, P.A. and Thelen, K. (2006) 'Varieties of capitalism and institutional change', *APSA European Politics & Society: Newsletter of the European Politics and Society Section of the American Political Science Association*, 5(1): 1, 3–4. Available online at: http://www.apsanet.org/~ep/news letter.html, accessed 21 August 2006.

Hawkins, D., Lake, D.A., Nielsen, D. and Tierney, M.J. (eds) (2006) *Delegation and Agency in International Organizations*. New York: Cambridge University Press.

Hayes-Renshaw, F. and Wallace, H. (2006) *The Council of Ministers*, 2nd edn. London: Palgrave.

Helfer, L.R. (2006) 'Theories of change in international organizations', Paper presented at the Conference on 'Delegating Sovereignty: Constitutional and Political Perspectives', Duke University, 3–4 March 2006. Available online at: http://www.law.duke.edu/publiclaw/workshop/papers.html, accessed 21 August 2006.

Hix, S. (2001) 'Legislative behaviour and party competition in EP: an application of nominate to the EU', *Journal of Common Market Studies*, 39(4): 663–88.

Hix, S. (2005) *The Political System of the European Union*, 2nd edn. New York: Palgrave.

Hix, S., Noury, A. and Roland, G. (2002) 'A "normal" parliament? Party cohesion and competition in the European Parliament, 1979–2001', EPRG Working Paper, No 9. Available online at: http://www.lse.ac.uk/Depts/eprg/working-papers.htm, accessed 21 August 2006.

Hoffmann, S. (1966) 'Obstinate or obsolete? The fate of the nation-state and the case of western Europe', *Dædalus*, 95(3): 862–915.

Hooghe, L. and Marks, G. (2004) 'Does identity or economic rationality drive public opinion on European integration?', *PS: Political Science and Politics*, 37(3): 415–20.

Huber, J.D. and Shipan, C.R. (2003) *Deliberate Discretion: The Institutional Foundations of Bureaucratic Autonomy*. New York: Cambridge University Press.

Hug, S. (2003) 'The state that wasn't there: the future of EU institutions and formal models', *European Union Politics*, 4(1): 121–34.

Immergut, E. (2006) 'From constraints to change', *APSA European Politics & Society: Newsletter of the European Politics and Society Section of the American Political Science Association*, 5(2): 4–6.

Jacoby, W. (2004) *The Enlargement of the European Union: Ordering from the Menu in Central Europe*. New York: Cambridge University Press.

Johnston, A.I. (2005) 'Conclusions and extensions: toward mid-range theorizing and beyond Europe', *International Organization*, 59(4): 1013–44.

Jupille, J. (2004) *Procedural Politics: Issues, Influence, and Institutional Choice in the European Union*. New York: Cambridge University Press.

Jupille, J. (2005) 'Knowing Europe: metatheory and methodology in European Union studies', in M. Cini and A.K. Bourne (eds), *Palgrave Advances in European Union Studies*. New York: Palgrave. pp. 209–32.

Jupille, J. and Caporaso, J.A. (1999) 'Institutionalism and the European Union: beyond international relations and comparative politics', *Annual Review of Political Science*, 2: 429–44.

Jupille, J. and Snidal, D.A. (2005) 'The choice of international institutions: cooperation, alternatives and strategies', unpublished paper.

Jupille, J., Caporaso, J.A. and Checkel, J.T. (2003) 'Integrating institutions: rationalism, constructivism, and the study of the European Union', *Comparative Political Studies*, 36(1–2): 7–40.

Katzenstein, P.J., Keohane, R.O. and Krasner, S.D. (1998) 'International Organization and the study of world politics', *International Organization*, 52(4): 645–85.

Kelley, J. (2004) 'International actors on the domestic scene: membership conditionality and socialization by international institutions', *International Organization*, 58(2): 425–58.

Kilroy, B. (1999) 'Integration through law: ECJ and governments in the EU', PhD dissertation, UCLA.

Koremenos, B., Lipson, C. and Snidal, D. (eds) (2003) *The Rational Design of International Institutions*. New York: Cambridge University Press.

Kreppel, A. (1999) 'The European Parliament's influence over EU policy outcomes', *Journal of Common Market Studies*, 37(3): 521–38.

Kreppel, A. (2001) *The European Parliament and Supranational Party System: A Study in Institutional Development*. New York: Cambridge University Press.

Lakatos, I. (1970) 'Falsification and the methodology of scientific research programs', in I. Lakatos and A. Musgrave (eds), *Criticism and the Growth of Knowledge*. New York: Cambridge University Press. pp. 91–196.

Lewis, J. (2005) 'The Janus face of Brussels: socialization and everyday decision making in the European Union', *International Organization*, 59(4): 937–71.

Lindberg, L.N. and Scheingold, S.A. (1970) *Europe's Would-Be Polity: Patterns of Change in the European Community*. Englewood Cliffs, NJ: Prentice Hall.

Mattila, M. (2004) 'Contested decisions – empirical analysis of voting in the EU council of ministers', *European Journal of Political Research*, 43(1): 29–50.

Mattila, M. and Lane, J.-E. (2001) 'Why unanimity in the Council?', *European Union Politics*, 2(1): 31–52.

Mattli, W. and Slaughter, A.-M. (1995) 'Law and politics in the European Union: a reply to Garrett', *International Organization*, 49(1): 183–90.

Mattli, W. and Slaughter, A.-M. (1998) 'Revisiting the European Court of Justice', *International Organization*, 52(1): 177–209.

Moravcsik, A. (1998) *The Choice for Europe: Social Purpose and State Power from Messina to Maastricht*. Ithaca, NY: Cornell University Press.

Moravcsik, A. (1999) 'Is something rotten in the state of Denmark? Constructivism and European integration', *Journal of European Public Policy*, 6(4): 669–81.

Moser, P., Schneider, G. and Kirchgässner, G. (eds) (2000) *Decision Rules in the European Union: A Rational Choice Perspective*. New York: St. Martin's Press.

North, D. (1990) *Institutions, Institutional Change and Economic Performance*. New York: Cambridge University Press.

Pahre, R. (2005) 'Formal theory and case-study methods in EU studies', *European Union Politics*, 6(1): 113–45.

Pierson, P. (1996) 'The path to European integration: a historical institutionalist analysis', *Comparative Political Studies*, 29(2): 123–63.

Pierson, P. (2000) 'Increasing returns, path dependence, and the study of politics', *American Political Science Review*, 94(2): 251–67.

Pierson, P. (2004) *Politics in Time: History, Institutions and Social Analysis*. Princeton: Princeton University Press.

Pollack, M.A. (1997) 'Delegation, agency, and agenda-setting in the European Community', *International Organization*, 51(1): 99–134.

Pollack, M.A. (2003) *The Engines of European Integration: Delegation, Agency, and Agenda Setting in the EU*. Oxford: Oxford University Press.

Pollack, M.A. (2004) 'The new institutionalisms and European integration', in A. Wiener and T. Diez (eds), *European Integration Theory*. New York: Oxford University Press. pp. 137–56.

Risse, T. (2000) '"Let's argue!" Communicative action and world politics', *International Organization*, 54(1): 1–39.

Risse, T. (2005) 'Neo-functionalism, European identity, and the puzzles of European integration', *Journal of European Public Policy*, 12(2): 291–309.

Sandholtz, W. (1996) 'Membership matters: limits of the functional approach to European institutions', *Journal of Common Market Studies*, 34(3): 403–29.

Scharpf, F.W. (1988) 'The joint-decision trap: lessons from German federalism and European integration', *Public Administration*, 66(3), 239–78.

Schimmelfennig, F. (2005) 'Strategic calculation and international socialization: membership incentives, party constellations, and sustained compliance in central and eastern Europe', *International Organization*, 59(4): 827–60.

Schimmelfennig, F. and Sedelmeier, U. (2002) 'Theorising EU enlargement: research focus, hypotheses, and the state of research', *Journal of European Public Policy*, 9(4): 500–28.

Schimmelfennig, F. and Sedelmeier, U. (eds) (2005a) *The Europeanization of Central and Eastern Europe*. Ithaca: Cornell University Press.

Schimmelfennig, F. and Sedelmeier, U. (2005b) 'Introduction: conceptualizing then Europeanization of central and eastern Europe', in F. Schimmelfennig and U. Sedelmeier (eds), *The Europeanization of Central and Eastern Europe*. Ithaca: Cornell University Press. pp. 1–28.

Schimmelfennig, F., and Sedelmeier, U. (2005c) 'Conclusions: the impact of the EU on the accession countries', in F. Schimmelfennig and U. Sedelmeier (eds), *The Europeanization of Central and Eastern Europe*. Ithaca: Cornell University Press. pp. 210–28.

Scully, R.M. (2005) 'Rational institutionalism and liberal intergovernmentalism', in M. Cini and A.K. Bourne (eds), *Palgrave Advances in European Union Studies*. New York: Routledge. pp. 19–34.

Snidal, D. (2002) 'Rational choice and international relations', in W. Carlnaes, B. Simmons and T. Risse (eds), *Handbook of International Relations*. New York: Sage. pp. 73–94.

Stone Sweet, A. and Brunell, T.L. (1998) 'Constructing a supranational constitution: dispute resolution and governance in the European Community', *American Political Science Review*, 92(1): 63–81.

Stone Sweet, A. and Caporaso, J.A. (1998) 'From free trade to dupranational polity: the European Court and integration', in W. Sandholtz and A. Stone Sweet (eds), *European Integration and Supranational Governance*. New York: Oxford University Press. pp. 92–133.

Streeck, W. and Thelen, K. (2005) 'Introduction: institutional change in advanced political economies', in W. Streeck and K. Thelen (eds), *Beyond Continuity: Institutional Change in Advanced Political Economies*. New York: Oxford University Press. pp. 1–39.

Tallberg, J. (2000) 'The anatomy of autonomy: an institutional account of variation in supranational influence', *Journal of Common Market Studies*, 38(5): 843–64.

Tallberg, J. (2003) *European Governance and Supranational Institutions: Making States Comply*. London: Routledge.

Thomson, R., Stokman, F.N., König, T. and Achen, C. (eds) (2006) *The European Union Decides: The Empirical Relevance of Policy-Making Models*.

New York: Cambridge University Press, forthcoming.

Tsebelis, G. (1994) 'The power of the European Parliament as a conditional agenda setter', *American Political Science Review*, 88(1): 129–42.

Tsebelis, G. (1997) 'Maastricht and the democratic deficit', *Aussenwirtschaft*, 52(1): 29–56.

Tsebelis, G. (2002) *Veto Players: How Political Institutions Work.* Princeton: Princeton University Press.

Tsebelis, G., Jensen, C.B., Kalandrakis, A. and Kreppel, A. (2001) 'Legislative procedures in the European Union', *British Journal of Political Science*, 31(4): 573–99.

Vachudova, M.A. (2005) *Europe Undivided: Democracy, Leverage, and Integration after Communism.* New York: Oxford University Press.

Wendt, A. (1999) *Social Theory of International Politics.* New York: Cambridge University Press.

Zürn, M. and Checkel, J.T. (2005) 'Getting socialized to build bridges: constructivism and rationalism, Europe and the nation-state', *International Organization*, 59(4): 1045–79.

3

Constructivism and EU Politics

JEFFREY T. CHECKEL

INTRODUCTION

The complexities and challenges for a chapter such as this are captured in the very phrase 'social construction of Europe'. Should the emphasis be on Europe – thus suggesting the *sui generis* nature of the post-war European project and the special, regional-specific (constructivist) conceptual tools needed to study it? Or, should it be on the words social construction, implying a particular analytic orientation that can be applied across regions – including but not limited to Europe and the EU?

This essay comes down heavily in favour of the latter, as this would seem a natural choice. After all, within political science, constructivism's origins and two-decade long gestation were within the subfield of international relations, not in EU studies (Adler 2002; see also Haas 2001). The latter in fact only discovered it quite recently (Christiansen et al. 2001).

I thus view constructivism as a particular analytic orientation that, in this case, is applied to Europe. This leads me to evaluate the literature under review in a certain way. I am less interested in ascertaining whether we have or are developing a specific constructivist theory of

integration – something to compete with intergovernmentalism or neofunctionalism. Indeed, I would argue this is precisely not the development to be encouraged (see also Risse 2004a: 174). Rather, I ask how constructivist insights as applied to Europe are shedding light on issues – the nature of political order, the (re) construction of identity, the formation of political community – of more general interest.

My bottom line is that constructivists studying Europe and their counterparts elsewhere (mainly located in North America) have much to gain from a more sustained encounter and dialogue. Conventional constructivists need to get serious about meta-theory and power, while interpretative and critical/radical ones would do well to take more care in operationalizing arguments at the level of methods. As such weaknesses are largely off-setting – where one side is weak the other is strong – they will be more easily addressed to the extent that constructivists overcome their internal divisions. Furthermore, all constructivists will benefit from a more systematic integration of domestic politics into their arguments.

The remainder of this essay is organized as follows. I begin with a discussion of three types of constructivist scholarship – their generic features and how they are being applied to the EU and the study of Europe – highlighting key differences among them. The core of the essay is four sections each using a different prism – epistemology, methods, power, domestic politics – to evaluate constructivist scholarship on Europe. I conclude with a plea for bridge building among different constructivist scholars studying the EU as well as the broader international arena.

SOCIAL CONSTRUCTIVISMS: CONVENTIONAL, INTERPRETATIVE AND CRITICAL/RADICAL

Constructivist approaches to the study of Europe are trendy. Deliberation, discourses, norms, persuasion, identity, socialization, arguing – such concepts are now frequently invoked in debates over the past and future of the European project. To make better sense of such terms – and the very different ways in which they are employed – I distinguish among conventional, interpretative and critical/radical variants of constructivism (Checkel 2004: 230–1; see also Adler 1997; Ruggie 1998; Christiansen et al. 2001: 1–21).

Conventional constructivism, which is the school dominant in the US, examines the role of norms and, in fewer cases, identity in shaping international political outcomes. These scholars are positivist in epistemological orientation and strong advocates of bridge building among diverse theoretical perspectives; the qualitative, process-tracing case study is their typical methodological starting point. Institutional and organizational theory (March and Olsen, forthcoming; see also Finnemore 1996b; Trondal 2001), as well as sociology (Finnemore and Sikkink 1998; Barnett and Finnemore 1999, 2004; Wendt 1999) are sources of theoretical inspiration.

Within EU studies, conventional constructivism has been applied in a variety of ways. Caporaso et al. (2003a, b), for example, have explored the functioning of EU institutions with the explicit goal of building bridges between rationalist and sociological work (see also Beach 2005). Lewis (1998, 2005) has

examined the causal effect of norms by focusing on mechanisms of persuasion and role playing, and done so in a hard case for constructivism – the EU's highly intergovernmental Committee of Permanent Representatives, or COREPER.

Interpretative constructivism, which enjoys greater popularity in Europe, explores the role of language in mediating and constructing social reality. Given its commitment to various forms of post-positivist epistemologies, this role is not explanatory in the sense that A causes B. Rather, constructivist scholarship of this sort asks 'how possible' questions. For example, instead of examining what factors caused what aspects of a state's identity to change – as would the conventional mainstream (Checkel 2001) – interpretative constructivists would explore the background conditions and linguistic constructions (discourses) that made any such change possible in the first place. In an interpretative study of German identity, Banchoff (1999) argues precisely that his analytic task is not to 'establish the effects of identity on state action'. Rather, it is to 'demonstrate the content of state identity in a particular case – a necessary first step in the constructivist analysis of action' (Banchoff 1999: 271).

Put differently, interpretative constructivists are committed to a deeply inductive research strategy that targets the reconstruction of state/agent identity, with the methods encompassing a variety of linguistic techniques. Consider Hopf's recent study of Soviet and Russian identity. He begins not with some hypotheses or theory about what might cause that identity to change, as would scholars with a strong commitment to positivist methods (Laitin 1998). Rather, Hopf seeks to uncover Soviet-Russian identity as it emerges from a variety of texts, ranging from novels to minutes of Politburo meetings; his methods are textual and narrative. Furthermore, and to the extent possible, he engages in no prior theorization, instead letting the texts speak for themselves, as it were (Hopf 2002).

Critical/radical constructivists maintain the linguistic focus, but add an explicitly normative dimension by probing a researcher's own implication in the reproduction of the identities and world he/she is studying. Discourse-theoretical methods are again emphasized, but with a greater emphasis on the power and domination inherent in language. For both interpretative and critical/radical constructivists, key sources of theoretical inspiration lay in linguistic approaches – Wittgenstein, say – and continental social theory – Habermas, Bourdieu and Derrida, among others (Hopf 1998; Price and Reus-Smit 1998; Neumann 2002).

To continue with the example of Germany, a critical/radical constructivist might argue as follows,

> German military involvement abroad, within an approach that starts from norms [as would most conventional constructivists – JTC], becomes the result of a reasoning process within a given and unquestioned norm structure. And the use of the military becomes the only feasible alternative in a world limited by material conditions, such as the possibility of death. In other words, by attempting to start from 'reality' the status quo is privileged as independent, and binding conditions that limit our possibilities are asserted (Zehfuss 2002: 254–5).

The scholarly enterprise is not neutral. Our choices, be they analytic (starting with given norms) or methodological (adopting the foundationalist assumption that there exists a reality external to our theorizing) are not innocent. They have consequences for which we, as scholars, should bear responsibility. This politicized view of the academy – which is heavily indebted to the insights of Derrida – is far, far removed from the problem-driven, 'let's-just-get-on-with-the-research' perspective of the conventional constructivist.

Post-positivist constructivists – be they interpretative or critical/radical – explore the EU and European institutions in a manner quite different from their conventional counterparts. Instead of starting with certain givens – say, a set of social norms – and exploring their causal impact on outcomes, they might explore the discursive practices that make possible certain EU norms in the first place (Schwellnus 2005a). For these scholars, language becomes much more fluid. Thus, in studying the politics of integration through a linguistic prism, the focus would be less on language as acts of persuasion (as conventional

constructivists would argue – Gheciu 2005b) and more on underlying speech acts, structures of argumentation, or discursive power structures (Diez 1999; Waever 2004).

Another strand of post-positivist constructivist theorizing on Europe bases itself on the critical social theory of Jürgen Habermas.[1] If the buzzwords for conventional constructivists are norms and identity, and those for interpretative and critical/radical scholars are power and discourse, then for Habermasians studying Europe, they are deliberation and legitimacy (Eriksen and Fossum 2000; Neyer 2003; CIDEL 2005). While conventional constructivists would be interested in exploring the degree to which supranational institutions like the Commission affect the values and identities of social agents (Hooghe 2005), Habermasians would instead ask what kind of identity the EU should possess if it is to be a democratic and legitimate entity (Fossum 2003; Eriksen and Fossum 2004).

This review in hand, we can now explore in more detail constructivist contributions to EU studies and the challenges they face.

THE TROUBLE WITH POSITIVISM

The conventional constructivists who study Europe or the EU are empirically oriented scholars who just want to get on with it – that is, conduct research on the fascinating world of European politics. The paradigm wars and meta-theoretical bloodletting are for others. 'To get on with it', they often rely on a method known as process tracing.

> The process-tracing method attempts to identify the intervening causal process – the causal chain and causal mechanism – between an independent variable (or variables) and the outcome of the dependent variable. ... Process tracing forces the investigator to take equifinality into account, that is, to consider the alternative paths through which the outcome could have occurred, and it offers the possibility of mapping out one or more potential causal paths that are consistent with the outcome and the process-tracing evidence in a single case (Bennett and George 2005: 206–7).

The use of this method has allowed mainstream constructivists to advance nuanced, carefully documented claims on, say, the socializing power of European institutions (Lewis 2005). Indeed, one leading text sees process tracing as a central element in the constructivist methodological tool kit (Bennett and George 2005: 206).[2]

This is all fine and good, but empirical insight on Europe is being purchased at the expense of a very basic lack of meta-theoretical clarity. By meta-theory, I refer here not so much to ontology, which means to advance claims about existence, as to epistemology or how we come to know. On the level of ontology, virtually all constructivists are on the same page, recognizing the deeply social nature of the world around us. However, as the last section indicated, there is no common epistemological ground for constructivists.

In fact, process tracing would appear to be fundamentally at odds with the interpretative epistemologies at the core of constructivist social theory (Guzzini 2000: 155–62; see also Checkel 2005c). It only works if you hold things constant in a series of steps: A causes B; B then causes C; C then causes D; and so on. Such an approach simply cannot capture the recursivity and fluidity of post-positivist epistemologies. Not surprisingly, the very few interpretative constructivists who do employ process tracing are careful to separate it from the discursive and narrative techniques at the heart of their approach (Hopf 2002).

Why is this a problem for conventional constructivists? After all, they made a conscious choice to ground their scholarship in positivism – one that has had significant empirical pay-offs. Yet, there are both principled and practical reasons for being worried about such a move. On the former, questions of philosophy and conceptual coherence do matter, even in subfields such as EU studies or American IR, where neglect of such topics is widespread (Wight 2002: 26–37). Mixing apples and oranges can be a recipe for intellectual disarray. Put bluntly, without more attention to basic philosophical issues, conventional constructivists are setting themselves up for a reprise of Legro and Moravcsik's (1999) superb and on-the-mark critique of the conceptual confusion that characterizes contemporary realist scholarship. Their title – 'Is

Anybody Still a Realist?' – could simply be replaced by 'Is Anybody Still a Constructivist?'

In practical terms, this lack of attention to questions of epistemology is seriously limiting the bridge building efforts of conventional constructivists, a much cherished goal to which I return below.

If these principled and practical issues are such problems, why have they received very little attention to date? Two factors are at work, one generic to American IR scholarship, and one specific to conventional constructivism. For the former, meta-theory has not been a topic of primary concern for many years. Moreover, the normalization of epistemological discourse – 'we're all positivists, so why talk about epistemology' – in mainstream US international relations journals such as *International Organization* and *International Studies Quarterly* furthers this sense that all is in order.

An example is helpful. For over a decade, one of the most influential – if not the most influential – treatises on methods and design for American IR has been King et al.'s (1994) *Designing Social Inquiry*. This book was and is used by many conventional constructivists – and has helped these scholars significantly at the levels of research design and methods. While King et al. was the subject of many reviews, their focus was telling. They examined and questioned not the manuscript's underlying positivist philosophical basis, but its practical suggestions. The critique was 'in house' (positivist), as it were (Johnson 2006: 227, 236–40).

Only now are we seeing the first, detailed assessments that question the positivist epistemological basis of King et al., exploring how this seriously limits the utility of their advice for qualitative researchers, including conventional constructivists (Johnson 2006; Lebow 2006; Lebow and Lichbach 2006). Consider the centrally important question of causation. King et al. endorse a view of it that renders irrelevant the causal mechanisms that are crucial for so many conventional constructivists (Johnson 2006: 236–7). If this is indeed the case, why have the latter been content to accept such a state of affairs?

At this point, my story intersects with the second, conventional-constructivist-specific, reason for why epistemology has been neglected. Virtually all conventional constructivists have taken their theoretical and meta-theoretical inspiration from the work of Alexander Wendt. A consistent theme in Wendt's writing has been that the real meta-theoretical issues to address are more ontological than epistemological, and that once we agree on ontology – as most constructivists do – the rest (epistemology) will fall into place (Wendt 1999). While this view has more recently come under attack (Chernoff 2002, 2005: ch. 2), it was appealing to many as it allowed constructivists to get on with their work without getting caught up in the complicated and at times highly personalized world of epistemological debate.

Yet, such debate and epistemological reflection can no longer be avoided. My section heading was no mistake – there *is* a 'trouble with positivism'. As many interpretative and critical/radical constructivists have noted (Zehfuss 2002: chs. 1, 6; and, especially, Guzzini 2000), conventional constructivists do need more carefully to explicate their epistemological assumptions. This is true in general and all the more so for those who endorse methods like process tracing. And such a rethink will likely require a turn to postpositivist philosophies of science.

To develop this line of criticism, I consider the debate about bridge building between rational choice and constructivism, and how it has been applied to EU studies. This has been an exciting and, increasingly, controversial topic among constructivists in recent years. Researchers have followed up general calls for bridge building (Adler 1997) with increasingly sophisticated conceptual schemas for fitting constructivism better with its rivals. These include ideas on how one can integrate the ideational and the material, game theory and social constructivism, strategic-choice and cognitive perspectives, and other-regarding and self-interested behaviour (Katzenstein et al. 1998; Lebow 2001; Lepgold and Lamborn 2001; Fearon and Wendt 2002; Hemmer and Katzenstein 2002). At the level of research

designs and strategies, scholars have been equally creative, advocating notions of sequencing, domains of application and scope conditions as ways to integrate constructivism with its theoretical rivals (March and Olsen, forthcoming).

Most importantly, though, a growing number of empirical projects are testing these integrative schemes and designs on a variety of different topics in Europe or EU studies. These include institutional theory and the European Union (Caporaso et al. 2003a); compliance and European regional organizations (Kelley 2004); compliance and the European Union (Boerzel 2002; Tallberg 2002; Beach 2005); international institutions and socialization in Europe (Checkel 2005b); and the transposition of EU directives (Dimitrova and Rhinard 2005; Mastenbroek 2005). Collectively, these bridge-building efforts demonstrate that scholars have gotten down to the hard work of better specifying their alternative constructivist and rationalist theories, thus providing more complete yet still methodologically sound explanations for understanding developments in the EU or Europe more generally.

The point of increasing controversy is that the bridges being built have just one lane, going from conventional constructivism to rational choice (Zehfuss 2002: chs.1–2). Given that in principle they could have two lanes (with the second going from conventional constructivism to interpretative and critical/radical work) we need to understand better why this is not happening. If conventional constructivists are metatheoretically inconsistent, then these bridge builders face a more practical problem of constructing multi-lane bridges. In both cases, however, the culprit is positivism (see also Friedrichs 2003: 2–7).

Epistemology is thus not so easy to get around, and this is all the more true at the day-to-day, empirical levels. To see why, return to the Caporaso et al., EU/institutional-theory process-tracing, bridge-building project. Caporaso and collaborators had hoped to include one or more interpretative constructivists doing work on European integration. As they thought about it more, however, worries arose. How would they integrate these individuals into the collaboration? Would their emphasis on why questions unfairly limit and constrain the interpretative focus on how? How would (could?) interpretative constructivists implement a process-tracing technique within their own discursive studies?

In the end, they chose not to include such scholars, not out of sinister motives to delegitimize research agendas, but out of a practical concern to finish within a reasonable time frame. In the project's introduction, they discuss this dilemma.

> This choice bears an inevitable cost in the practical exclusion of a body of scholarship of a different epistemological bent. We thus knowingly proceed partially and incrementally, aware of the terrain left uncovered. If Aspinwall and Schneider are right in suggesting that transcending epistemological differences represents a bridge too far, then our choice is one that prevents the best (epistemological agreement) from being the enemy of the good (intraepistemological, intertheoretical progress) (Caporaso et al. 2003b: 24–5).

This is not an ideal state of affairs. Basically, it implies that we build bridges where we can control for epistemology, which, in turn, means they have only one lane – be it in the study of EU institutions or elsewhere. As Sil (2000: 354) has argued more generally, continuing epistemological disagreements 'militate against the emergence of a genuinely collaborative, truly integrated field of comparative analysis' (see also Forum Debate 2003).

This is where interpretative and critical/radical constructivists studying Europe can offer their conventional colleagues a helping hand. The former, who tend to highlight much more questions of meta-theory,[3] could well argue that the conclusions in that last paragraph are too bleak. Indeed, if one takes epistemology – in its various post-positivist guises – more seriously, there may be hope for the process tracers and bridge builders.

One possible post-positivist starting point would be scientific realism. The latter is a philosophical position, one that should be sharply distinguished from the various forms of theoretical realism in IR. Developed by philosophers such as Hilary Putnam and Roy Bashkar, it is the 'view that the objects of scientific theories are objects that exist independently of investigators' minds and that the

theoretical terms of their theories indeed refer to real objects in the world' (Chernoff 2005: 41). For many scientific realists, these 'real objects' are precisely the causal mechanisms highlighted in conventional constructivist, process-tracing case studies of European institutions (Risse-Kappen 1995; Schimmelfennig 2003, for example). Scientific realism is also epistemologically opportunist in that 'no one method, or epistemology could be expected to fit all cases' (Wight 2002: 36; more generally, see Lane 1996).

With such qualities, it would seem ideally placed both to give process tracing conceptual grounding and – equally important – create an epistemological platform broad enough to unite nearly all constructivists in a renewed effort at (multi-lane) bridge building. Indeed, pragmatic realism – as Adler (2002: 98) calls it – may 'provide a way to consolidate the common ground within IR constructivism'.

Given such conceptual foundations, process tracers and bridge builders can then begin to ask hard questions about their community standards – standards anchored in a philosophically coherent base. What counts as good process tracing? How do we know process tracing when we see it? How can discourse/textual and process-tracing approaches be combined in any bridge building effort (see also Hopf 2002)? Does bridge building require a special methodology of its own?

Answers to such questions need not only come from scientific realism. Analytic eclecticism (Katzenstein and Sil 2005), various forms of pragmatism (Cochran 2002; Johnson 2006) or conventionalism (Chernoff 2002, 2005) can achieve the same end. That end is to give IR – in my case, constructivists studying Europe – a middle-ground philosophy and epistemology that can fill the vast methodological space between American-style positivism and European post-structuralism (see also Lebow and Lichbach 2006: ch.1).

METHODS AND THE LINGUISTIC TURN

In recent years, there have been a growing number of calls by both conventional and interpretative constructivists for greater attention to methods (Milliken 1999; Adler 2002: 109–11; Neumann 2003). This trend needs to continue, with future methodological discussions transcending the positivist-interpretive epistemological divide (see also Lin 1998; Caprioli 2004).

The importance of such boundary crossing can be seen in the following example, taken from my own, conventional constructivist work on new citizenship and membership norms in Europe. I have been concerned with tracking the initial development of these norms within committees of several European regional organizations. My hunch was that arguing dynamics played some role in these settings, thus shifting the preferences of national agents. In theorizing such processes, I turned to a laboratory-experimental literature on persuasion taken from social psychology, from which I developed hypotheses on the roles of agent properties (for example, their degree of authoritativeness) and of privacy in promoting persuasion (Checkel 2001; see also Johnston 2001, 2007). To test these arguments, I relied on a traditional positivist methodological tool kit – process tracing, triangulation across sources and interviews (Checkel 2003).

When I presented my findings at several meetings, however, interpretative constructivists pointed to a theoretical-methodological gap in the analysis. Particular agents are not only persuasive because they are authoritative or because they argue in private. Their arguments are also persuasive because they are enabled and legitimated by the broader social discourse in which they are embedded. Did a particular agent's arguments in a particular committee resonate with this broader social discourse?

Constructivist colleagues were thus suggesting that I had lost sight of the (social) structural context. In positivist-empiricist terms, I had a potential problem of omitted variable bias, while, for interpretivists, the issue was one of missing the broader forces that enable and make possible human agency. Whatever you call it, the point and lesson are the same. To provide a more complete account of persuasion's role, it will be necessary to supplement my positivist methodologies with others grounded in interpretative techniques (see also Jacobsen 2003: 58). This theme of epistemological cross-fertilization can be developed in more detail by exploring how various constructivists studying the EU and Europe have operationalized the linguistic turn.

Taking Language Seriously

Knowledgeable readers may be puzzled by this subtitle. Do not constructivists already take language very seriously? After all, it is a central analytic category in their narratives and causal stories. Interpretative and critical/radical constructivists focus on discourse, speech acts and textual analysis. The conventional sort, by theorizing roles for arguing, persuasion and rhetorical action, see language as a causal mechanism leading to changes in core agent properties. Thus, the question is not 'whether language is important; the question is rather *which* approach to language' – and, I would add, how to use it as a practical research tool (Fierke 2002: 351 [emphasis in original]).

For interpretative and critical/radical scholars studying the EU and Europe, a central challenge is to continue the methodological discussion begun by individuals like Milliken and Neumann. Among the issues that should be addressed are the proper balance between textual approaches and those emphasizing practice (Hopf 2002: 269–70; Neumann 2002), and the degree to which these scholars need explicitly to describe and justify the sources and techniques they use to reconstruct discourses (Milliken 1999). On the latter, I am not suggesting a positivist primer that puts discourse into variable language or seeks to establish a single way of conducting such analyses. Rather, the time is ripe for further debate about best practices for those working with discourse and texts.

The importance of such a move is highlighted by two examples, one specifically on the EU and one on Europe more generally. On the former, Schwellnus has recently developed an innovative argumentative approach for exploring the role of norms in the process of EU enlargement. Convincingly showing the limitations of conventional constructivist approaches to EU enlargement that view arguments as causes for action (Schimmelfennig 2003), Schwellnus adopts an interpretative stand-point that instead explores the role of arguments in providing reasons and justifications for action. This is then applied to the case of Polish accession to the EU and the issue of minority rights. Schwellnus (2005a, b: 62–70) thus begins to operationalize and apply empirically arguments about arguing.

A key phrase in that last sentence is 'begins to operationalize'. Indeed, the reader is often left wondering how the rich textual analysis was actually conducted. How do we know that certain arguments about minority rights became dominant? What was the pool of source material? What were the counting rules? How were choices made by the author? We are never told, which is a pity for it undercuts the plausibility of the story Schwellnus so nicely otherwise tells. Put differently, the reader needs to know the (interpretive) community standards to which the author adheres when applying his argument empirically. Given that his is decidedly not an 'anything goes' post-modern project, these issues must be addressed.

A second example concerns the exercise (or lack thereof) of German military power in a radically changed post-Cold War Europe. In a richly empirical study, Maja Zehfuss offers a critical/radical constructivist account of contemporary Germany's role in international military operations. Her goal is not to explain why German policy took certain directions – intervening or not in a disintegrating Yugoslavia in the 1990s, say. Consistent with an epistemological underpinning that draws upon the work of scholars like Derrida, Zehfuss instead shrinks the gap between analyst and object, exploring the political responsibility of scholars in studying and interpreting German policy in particular ways. In this manner, she captures the ethical and critical dimensions that are so often missing in conventional and interpretative constructivist studies on the EU or Germany more specifically (Banchoff 1999; Rittberger 2001: ch. 5).

Zehfuss's method for connecting theory and empirics is discourse analysis. Yet, quite surprisingly – and especially for a volume with such a strong empirical focus – the reader is given no indication for how this analysis will be conducted. Surely, Zehfuss has some rules or hunches for identifying when normative commitments are 'shared amongst a number of people', for recognizing 'prominent narratives', or for how she identifies and reconstructs instances of 'shared meaning' (Zehfuss 2002: 120–2, 127–8). Her silence raises questions about the validity and reliability of the reconstructions, which, as Hopf (2002) so nicely shows, are key issues for critical/radical constructivists as well.

In sum, interpretative and critical/radical constructivists studying the EU and Europe could profit from more sustained attention to methods (see also Waever 2004: 213–14). Here, their conventional constructivist counterparts might offer a useful role model regarding methodological self-awareness.[4] The point would not be to mimic the particular methods employed by the latter. Process tracing is not what Zehfuss's study requires! Rather, the goal would be to state, operationalize and adhere to the appropriate community methodological standards given the questions asked (see also Hopf 2006; Lebow 2006: 10). This is precisely the achievement of the best conventional constructivist work on the EU or Europe more generally (Farrell and Flynn 1999; Parsons 2003; Smith 2004b; Lewis 2005; Sedelmeier 2005).

Taking Arguing Seriously

For a second group of conventional and interpretive constructivists, the challenge is of a different sort. In this case, it is time for a discussion and debate between proponents of arguing-deliberation and persuasion perspectives. Both groups are united in a concern for exploring how social communication and language can affect the outcomes and dynamics of European and international politics. Both also operate with a much thicker conception of language than rational choice scholars – one where language constitutes the identities and interests of actors, and not merely constrains them.

Despite such common ground, the two groups disagree on the best micro-mechanism for studying language. Students of arguing draw upon Habermas' theory of communicative action (Lynch 1999, 2002; Risse 2000; Sjursen 2002; Forum 2005), while proponents of persuasion make use of insights drawn from social psychology and communications theory (Johnston 2001; Checkel 2003).

This debate should have a theoretical, methodological and empirical component. Theoretically, a key question is whether Habermas' social theory can be specified and operationalized in such a way as to allow for the development of a robust empirical research programme. Risse (2000) has suggested this is possible. However, scholars like Johnston have questioned the very basis of Habermas' theory, arguing that the real heavy lifting in his approach is done by persuasion (Johnston 2001). It is thus not the force of the better argument that changes minds, as students of Habermas would claim. Rather, arguments carry the day when advanced by individuals with particular characteristics who operate in particular kinds of institutional settings that are conducive to persuasion.

Methodologically, a central challenge for proponents of both arguing and persuasion is recognizing it when they see it. While scholars like Johnston (2007) have proposed specific methodological strategies, we still have only preliminary empirical tests of them, especially as applied to Europe and the EU (Sjursen 2002; Checkel 2003; Pollack 2003). Moreover, there is continuing and worrying confusion on the question of agency. In particular, do robust explanatory claims about arguing and persuasion need to control for actor motives? Habermasians answer in the negative (Schwellnus 2005a), while students of persuasion suggest that 'getting between the earlobes' is both necessary and possible (Johnston 2001; Gheciu 2005b).

Empirically, a key question is how publicity affects dynamics of arguing and persuasion. Students of arguing see publicity's role as critically important. Making arguments publicly – to an audience – means one must provide reasons and give justifications. This very act renders unimportant the search for motivations as publicity induces an agent to behave in a way that is perceived as impartial and credible, even if – deep down – he/she is being strategic and hypocritical (Eriksen and Fossum 2000: 48–9; Kleine and Risse 2005: 11–12). Moreover, the gap between what is publicly stated and privately believed will likely shrink over time as preferences are adapted to behaviour (Elster 1998: 111; see also Zürn and Checkel 2005: 1053–4). Theorists of persuasion argue the exact opposite. That is, publicity creates a situation where agents are more likely to play to the audience and 'grand stand' than to rethink their basic preferences. In contrast, privacy creates a setting where actors can truthfully speak their minds and argue in a principled way (Checkel 2001; Johnston 2001; see also Kleine and Risse 2005: 12).

Ironically and very much in keeping with a central theme of this essay, both sides in this debate would benefit by rethinking, or perhaps better said, broadening their respective epistemological starting point. For Habermasians, a turn to positivism would have two benefits. For one, it might better alert them to the highly instrumental view of theoretical concepts they are developing (Wight 2002: 29, 41), and how this will lead them down the same problematic theory-building route as the rational choice theorists they so often criticize. The latter build their theories – in a very instrumental fashion – on 'as if' assumptions. Agents act as if they are egoistical and self-interested.

If agent motivations are likewise bracketed as we develop theories on the role of arguments, we end up with the same type of 'as if' reasoning, only now assuming that agents are other-regarding and moved by the force of the better argument. In both cases, the result is weak substantive theory that tells us little about how preferences are actually constituted (see also Wendt 1999: 119–22).

For students of European institutions, this matters – tremendously. From numerous sources – memoir literature, observations of the recent constitutional convention, interviews – we know that arguments and elements of deliberation are present and seem to play an important role in the integration process. Missing is the substantive theory that might better tell when and under what conditions they matter. Here, a little positivism could help. Indeed, substantive theories about arguing and deliberation do exist, but are being developed by IR scholars who have integrated Habermasian insights with elements of positivism (Lynch 1999, 2002; Mueller and Risse 2001; Crawford 2002; Deitelhoff and Mueller 2005; Kleine and Risse 2005).

There is a second – an equally important – reason why a bit of positivism might be healthy for Habermasian students of the EU. Many of these scholars, like Habermas himself, are normative theorists. Yet, the best normative theory updates its arguments in light of new empirical findings – findings typically anchored in a positivist epistemological frame. On the hotly debated question of publicity, for example, several recent projects, which examine both European and international institutions, report that publicity has precisely the negative affects predicted by persuasion theorists (Deitelhoff and Mueller 2005: 174; Naurin, forthcoming; see also Stasavage 2004: 696, *passim*). This result must have some bearing on the normative argumentation. As Lebow (2006: 17–18) so nicely puts it, 'normative theorizing must deal with facts just as empirical research must address norms. They do not inhabit separate worlds'.

Proponents of persuasion in this debate face the opposite problem – a surfeit of substantive, problem-solving theory. These scholars have advanced hypotheses for when persuasion should have causal force and begun developing methodological tools for measuring such dynamics in the European context (Gheciu 2005a; Lewis 2005). Absent, however, is critical-ethical reflection concerning the implications of their findings.[5]

Consider recent conventional constructivist work on persuasion that assesses the socializing power of European institutions – that is, the degree to which bodies like the European Commission induce a (partial) shift in the allegiances and identities of national agents. Are such value shifts normatively desirable? What are the implications for democratic and legitimate governance within and beyond the European nation state? These questions are centrally important, but remain unanswered (Checkel 2005b; see also Zürn and Checkel 2005: 1072–4). To address them, recourse to critical epistemologies and perspectives will be necessary; positivism and problem-solving theory will not be enough.

CONCEPTUAL LACUNA – WHERE'S POWER?

Those familiar with the EU literature – and especially that on its foreign and security policy – might question whether there is any such conceptual gap. We have numerous studies of normative or civilian power Europe, and of the EU's will and ability to exercise soft power (Manners 2002; Hyde-Price 2004; Smith 2004a; Sjursen 2006b). Missing in this discussion and in much of the constructivist literature on Europe and the EU more generally, however, is an understanding of power that is both more hard-edged and multi-faceted. By hard-edged, I simply mean the compulsive face of power (the ability of A to get B to do what B otherwise would not do).

By multi-faceted, I refer to conceptions of power that go beyond this standard coercive-compulsive notion to capture its institutional and productive dimensions as well. Specifically, institutional power is actors' control of others in indirect ways, where formal and informal institutions mediate between A and B; working through the rules of these institutions, A constrains the actions of B. Productive power is generated through discourse and the systems of knowledge through which meaning is produced and transformed (Barnett and Duvall 2005: 51, 55, *passim*; see also Bially Mattern 2004, 2005: ch. 4).

It is the students of deliberation and conventional constructivists studying the EU who have been especially remiss in neglecting power's role. With Habermasian studies of deliberation and arguing in EU institutions, one gets the sense that compulsory power is present but nonetheless ignored (Joerges and Neyer 1997a, b; Neyer 2003; Magnette 2004). As Hyde-Price (2006: 218, citing E. H. Carr) argues more specifically on deliberative studies of EU foreign and security policy, there often seems to be an 'almost total neglect of power'. It makes matters no better to invoke power, but to do so in ways that run counter to common-sense understandings. One analyst, for example, defines the EU's 'communicative power' as the ability of its policies and principle to endure critical public scrutiny (Sjursen 2006a: 174).

Thus, while Habermas may enjoin us to background power (Risse 2000), reality is more complex. One need not be a hard-nosed inter-governmentalist or bargaining theorist to recognize the plain truth that arguments are often used to shame, twist arms and compel, as a growing conventional constructivist literature in IR and EU studies confirms (Keck and Sikkink 1998; Risse et al. 1999; Schimmelfennig 2003).

For sure, compulsory-coercive power is mentioned in many of these Habermasian studies. However, they are typically not designed to test competitively the 'power of the better argument' against the power-based alternative explanation, where arguments are used to compel. Given that empirical research in this tradition appears to draw upon a standard positivist toolkit (Haacke 2005: 185–6; Romsloe 2004; Sjursen 2004: 117), such competitive testing is a requirement, not an option (see also Pollack 2003).

Conventional constructivist studies of persuasion and socialization in the EU provide a second example of power's under-specified role, in this case, missing its institutional and productive dimensions. The earlier critique (above) of my own work on persuasion was precisely about a neglect of productive power. Yes, acts of persuasion occurred in the institutional settings studied (Checkel 2001, 2003), but productive power – the background, discursive construction of meaning (see also Doty 1993: 299) – likely played a role as well. It did this by enabling and legitimating the arguments of individual persuaders.

In addition, institutional power would seem to play a central, albeit unspecified, role in conventional constructivist studies of socialization within European institutions (Checkel 2005b). All too often, this work reifies institutions, imbuing them with fixed values and meaning, but not asking from where these came or why certain ones are simply absent (see also Johnston 2005). Why does the EU, say, promote one conception of minority rights vis-à-vis candidate countries, but refuse to apply this same standard to its own member states (Schwellnus 2005a, b)? Perhaps this discrepancy (and hypocrisy) is explained by the exercise of institutional power, in this case, the ability to keep certain issues off the EU agenda.

The bottom line is that both Habermasians and conventional constructivists studying the EU need to bring power back in, and should do so in two ways. Epistemologically, they will need to draw upon insights from interpretive and critical/radical forms of constructivism, where power plays a much more central role (Waever 2004). In disciplinary terms, they should look to IR theory, where there is renewed interest in the conceptualization and study of power (Guzzini 1993; Barnett and Duvall 2005; Bially Mattern 2005; Hurrell 2005).

DOMESTIC POLITICS AND THE EUROPEAN PROJECT

There is an understandable temptation when studying the EU and other European institutions not to worry too much about – or, more formally, to bracket off – domestic politics. After all, much is happening in Europe – supranational polity building, the creation of the Euro, socialization beyond the nation state, the constitutionalization of the EU, the creation of an European identity – that is strongly suggestive of a Westphalian system being transformed and of a nation state in retreat. While recognizing the undeniable importance of such trends and facts, it would be a signal mistake for scholars to neglect the domestic and national. Unfortunately, all too many researchers – be they classic integration theorists or constructivists – commit precisely this error (see also Zürn and Checkel 2005: 1068–72).

Start with those integration warhorses – neofunctionalism and intergovernmentalism. Both focused overwhelmingly on the European level, seeking to explain supranational loyalty transfers or interstate bargaining, respectively. More recent approaches such as supranationalism, policy networks and institutional analysis have continued the European-level focus, albeit with a broader range of dependent variables – from the emergence of European governance structures to the multi-layered nature of European policymaking (Diez and Wiener 2004).

In all this work, systematic attention to, let alone explicit theorization of, domestic politics is notable mainly by its absence. For sure, the domestic is present in integration theory. As Haas argued many years ago, 'nationally constituted groups' – largely in the form of political elites – play a central role in integration (Risse 2005: 293, quoting from Haas 1958).

More recently, the starting point for Moravcsik's liberal intergovernmentalism is a clear specification of domestic interests. Yet, these are simply read off a country's structural position in the global political economy (Moravcsik 1998). Such arguments by Haas and Moravcsik, while intriguing, are not the same as a theory of domestic politics. A similar theoretical gap is also found in Europeanization studies (Caporaso et al. 2001: ch. 1) and work on multi-level governance (Hooghe and Marks 2001).[6]

Do constructivists studying the EU or Europe avoid this trap, instead robustly theorizing the domestic political? It would appear not. Consider recent work on two quintessentially constructivist topics – socialization and identity. A central finding of this research is that domestic politics play a key, if under-theorized, role in any socialization dynamic or process of identity change in the EU or in Europe more generally. Depending upon the author and his/her disciplinary and epistemological orientation, European identity or socialization experiences appear to be shaped

decisively by a wide array of domestic factors – deeply entrenched social discourses, previous bureaucratic experience, or the structure of national institutions (Risse and Maier 2003).

Several examples highlight the extent of this theoretical under-specification. In her study of NATO and socialization, Gheciu (2005a, b) argues that noviceness plays an important role in determining the likelihood of successful socialization. Using a more explicit domestic politics language, one might simply argue that noviceness is all about measuring the degree of national bureaucratic or cultural embeddedness of particular individuals.

Schimmelfennig (2005) theorizes that socialization outcomes promoted by the EU and other European institutions are heavily influenced by the structure of domestic party constellations. Quantitative studies of identity change and socialization within the Commission (Hooghe 2005) or within Council working groups (Beyers 2005) exercise great care in controlling for the independent effect of domestic factors, be these prior national bureaucratic experiences, exposure to federal national structures, or the like.

While all this attention to the domestic political should be welcomed, more needs to be done (see also Gourevitch 2002). At this point, the tendency is too often for ad-hocism to prevail, where domestic factors are added, but unguided by some broader and overarching theoretical argument. Such arguments – be they about elites, institutions or pluralism – are readily found in work on comparative politics, a point made forcefully over a decade ago by Milner (1992). More recently, Cortell and Davis (2000: 83–4) have argued that '[f]urther research into the relationship between the effects of socializing forces on the international system and states' domestic politics is required because it remains poorly understood'. If students of international relations are going to push comparativists to give up an exclusive focus on 'methodological nationalism' in which national political systems are compared as if they were independent of each other (Zürn 2002: 248), then it is only fair to ask that students of integration – constructivists or otherwise – reciprocate by systematically building arguments about domestic politics into their approaches.

In making these connections to the domestic, EU constructivists should dynamically integrate factors across different levels of analysis – national and European, in this case. Dynamic means that one goes back and forth across levels, emphasizing the simultaneity of international and domestic developments. This stands in contrast to an additive or residual variance approach – for many years the norm among integration and IR theorists – where the researcher explores one level at a time, explaining as much as possible there, before considering factors at other levels (Moravcsik 1993; Mueller and Risse-Kappen 1993).

To see the difference, consider again Hooghe's (2005) study of socialization and identity change within the European Commission. Her main finding is that much of the European-level socialization we see in the Commission is in fact a product of prior, national socialization. The approach here is basically additive, which suits her design well. Yet, an intriguing possibility is that those national-level experiences are themselves enmeshed with and shaped by European factors. A dynamic integration of the two levels could better capture such interplay (see also Risse 2005: 305).

For sure, there are complicated methodical issues involved in any such integration. With conventional constructivists, their positivist understanding of explanation presents a problem and challenge. After all, to argue and show that A is a cause of B requires that something be held constant, which is seemingly at odds with the dynamic approach sketched above. Yet, work on feedback loops (Johnston 2005) and bracketing techniques (Finnemore 1996a) suggests this particular problem is surmountable (see also Martin and Simmons 1998: 749; Katzenstein 2003: 737–9).

Interpretive and critical/radical constructivists, in contrast, would seem ideally placed to exploit the benefits of such a dynamic integration of the domestic and European. The recursivity at the heart of their epistemological world view allows precisely for an exploration of the simultaneity of international and domestic developments (Diez 1999; see also Price 1997). While no interpretivist himself, Risse has recently made a remarkably similar claim in regards to constructivist research on European identity. In what he calls a marble cake model, the various components of an individual's identity cannot be separated on different levels; rather, different components – German and European, say – 'influence … mesh and blend into each other' (Risse 2005: 296; see also Risse 2004b: 251–2).

Such a dynamic approach would benefit constructivist research on the EU/Europe in two ways. First, an emphasis on simultaneity and cross-cutting influences would keep the focus on process, where it should rightly be, given existing biases toward structural accounts in the literature. This is as true of conventional constructivist studies of European socialization (Checkel 2005a) as it is of interpretive analyses offering highly structural readings of European identity focused either on discourses (Rosamond 2001) or public spheres (Fossum and Trenz 2005).

Second, a dynamic, cross-cutting approach might better alert constructivist students of EU socialization to an understudied element in their analyses – feedback effects. What happens to the socializing agents or structures themselves – the EU Commission and Council, or the Committee of Permanent Representatives, say – when they attempt (and perhaps fail) to socialize a target group? There is a tendency for the causal arrows to point mainly in one direction: from socializer to socializee. To take one example, if would be a fascinating follow-on study to Gheciu's exploration of NATO's socializing role in Romania and the Czech republic to consider the effect on NATO if her 'baby generals' talked back, thus reversing the causal arrows (see also Johnston 2005, on emergent property effects).

My arguments on the importance of domestic politics in EU constructivist research find support in three closely related literatures. Among IR constructivists, there is now a growing recognition that, as Hopf so nicely puts it, 'constructivism [starts] at home', which in more operational terms means that 'domestic society … must be brought back into any constructivist account of world politics' (Hopf 2002: 1, 278).[7]

Within the field of European studies, two similar – and very recent – trends are at work. Scholars of integration are coming to recognize that the EU – and theory about it – is to some extent becoming a victim of its own success. The deepening of integration over the past decade and the current process of constitutionalization have spawned increasing domestic political resistance to and mobilization against the European project. In turn, this has led prominent theorists of integration to add a strong domestic politics-politicization element to their arguments. In the context of integration theory, Leon Lindberg's permissive consensus appears to have been transformed into its opposite – a constraining dissensus (Hooghe and Marks 2004: 5; see also Diez and Wiener 2004: 238–46).

In addition, new work on Europeanization emphasizes domestic cultural context, theorizing and documenting how religious communities that are at once both deeply national and transnational are likely to slow the degree of Europeanization in an enlarged European Union (Byrnes and Katzenstein 2006).

CONCLUSIONS – CAN'T WE GET ALONG BETTER THAN THIS?

To talk of a constructivist scholarly community studying Europe is to invoke an oxymoron. The devil is in that word community, for it implies shared standards and identity. As suggested throughout this essay, such common community standards – especially at the level of epistemology and methods – do not exist.[8] This state of affairs suggests two ways forward. The first is the path of least resistance, which means to let present trends continue. Conventional constructivists studying Europe could continue their courtship of the rationalist (US) mainstream, while Habermasian deliberation theorists could create their own life world disconnected from empirical reality – to take just two examples. However, down this path lie group think, closed citation cartels and, most important, intellectual closure.

The second way forward is more ambitious and intellectually challenging. It is a way defined by bridge building – not between rational choice and constructivism, but *within* the community of constructivist scholars studying Europe. As an American-trained academic who has lived and worked in Europe since 1996, I am often struck by the parochialism of much of the constructivist scholarship on both sides of the Atlantic.

Clearly, there are understandable (and hard to change) sociology-of-knowledge reasons why national or regional academic communities develop in certain ways (Waever 1998). Yet, the way forward – defined as better knowledge of the (European) world around us – is by connecting these diverse communities. Constructivists studying the EU have an extraordinary, real time, laboratory for addressing issues – political order within and beyond the nation state, the construction of community, the formation of actor identity and interests – of central concern to the broader disciplines. By anchoring their research programmes in these larger disciplinary frames and by speaking more to each other, they could learn an awful lot.

My call here is for conceptual and metatheoretical *pluralism* in the constructivist study of Europe – not unity. The latter would be a recipe for a make-everyone-happy analytic and conceptual mush. Rather, the point is to encourage dialogue, conversation and mutual learning – about epistemologies, methods, power and domestic politics. Done properly, such a bridging exercise could turn the tables a decade hence, with EU constructivists teaching their disciplinary colleagues a few new tricks. Indeed, the ultimate sign of success would be if that adjective EU in front of constructivists were to vanish.

ACKNOWLEDGEMENTS

I thank Knud Erik Jørgensen and Mark Pollack for detailed and helpful comments on earlier drafts. Parts of this chapter were previously published in *Review of International Studies*, 30 (2004).

NOTES

1. Not all the scholars named here would accept the designation constructivist, preferring instead to self-identify as students of deliberative democracy. I include them because, like constructivists, their underlying ontology is deeply social and they view language – arguing and deliberation, in their case – as constitutive of actor identity.

2. For sure, conventional constructivists employ methods other than process tracing – quantitative-statistical techniques or survey research, say (Finnemore 1996b). However, irrespective of methodological choice, the epistemological tension outlined below remains.

3. Consider the *European Journal of International Relations*. Recent volumes of this important outlet for interpretive and critical/radical constructivists contain a good number of essays specifically devoted to philosophy of science and epistemology.

4. For example, conventional constructivists are playing an active role in the new – and highly successful – qualitative methods organized section within the American Political Science Association. (Symposium 2004).

5. This same imbalance – where positive, substantive theory far outstrips critical reflection – is found in conventional constructivist work on EU enlargement (Schimmelfennig and Sedelmeier 2002, 2005; Schimmelfennig 2003; Kelley 2004).

6. To be fair to students of Europeanization, their focus is the effects of Europe on the nation state and its domestic politics. The latter is thus their dependent variable, which one typically does not attempt to theorize.

7. Here, IR rationalists are ahead of their constructivist counterparts, as they have been working to theorize the domestic political for nearly a decade (Keohane and Milner 1996, Milner 1997, Martin 2000, for example).

8. This is where Moravcsik's (2001) hard-hitting but largely fair critique of constructivist research on the EU goes astray. He assumes a universality of (positivist) community standards where in fact none exists.

REFERENCES

Adler, E. (1997) 'Seizing the middle ground: constructivism in world politics', *European Journal of International Relations*, 3(3): 319–63.

Adler, E. (2002) 'Constructivism and international relations', in W. Carlsnaes, T. Risse and B. Simmons (eds), *Handbook of International Relations*. London: Sage Publications. pp. 95–118.

Banchoff, T. (1999) 'German identity and European integration', *European Journal of International Relations*, 5(3): 259–90.

Barnett, M. and Duvall, R. (2005) 'Power in international politics', *International Organization*, 59(1): 39–76.

Barnett, M. and Finnemore, M. (1999) 'The politics, power and pathologies of international organizations', *International Organization*, 53(4): 699–732.

Barnett, M. and Finnemore, M. (2004) *Rules for the World: International Organizations in Global Politics*. Ithaca, NY: Cornell University Press.

Beach, D. (2005) 'Why governments comply: an integrative compliance model that bridges the gap between instrumental and normative models of compliance', *Journal of European Public Policy*, 12(1): 113–42.

Bennett, A. and George, A. (2005) *Case Studies and Theory Development in the Social Sciences*. Cambridge, MA: MIT Press.

Beyers, J. (2005) 'Multiple embeddedness and socialization in Europe: the case of council officials', *International Organization*, 59(4): 899–936.

Bially Mattern, J. (2004) 'Power in realist-constructivist research', *International Studies Review*, 6(2): 343–6.

Bially Mattern, J. (2005) *Ordering International Politics: Identity, Crisis and Representational Force*. New York: Routledge.

Boerzel, T. (2002) 'When states do not obey the law: non-compliance in the European Union', Paper presented at the ARENA Research Seminar, 6 June. Oslo: ARENA Centre for European Studies, University of Oslo.

Byrnes, T. and Katzenstein, P. (eds) (2006) *Religion in an Expanding Europe*. Cambridge: Cambridge University Press.

Caporaso, J., Checkel, J.T. and Jupille, J. (eds) (2003a) 'Integrating institutions: rationalism, constructivism and the study of the European Union', Special Issue of *Comparative Political Studies*, 36(1–2): 5–231.

Caporaso, J., Checkel, J.T. and Jupille, J. (eds) (2003b) 'Integrating institutions: rationalism, constructivism and the study of the European Union – introduction', *Comparative Political Studies*, 36(1–2): 7–41.

Caporaso, J., Cowles, M.G. and Risse, T. (eds) (2001) *Transforming Europe: Europeanization and Domestic Change*. Ithaca, NY: Cornell University Press.

Caprioli, M. (2004) 'Feminist IR theory and quantitative methodology: a critical analysis', *International Studies Review*, 6(2): 253–69.

Checkel, J.T. (2001) 'Why comply? Social learning and European identity change', *International Organization*, 55(3): 553–88.

Checkel, J.T. (2003) "Going native' in Europe? Theorizing social interaction in European institutions', *Comparative Political Studies*, 36(1–2): 209–31.

Checkel, J.T. (2004) 'Social constructivisms in global and European politics: a review essay', *Review of International Studies*, 30(2): 229–44.

Checkel, J.T. (2005a) 'International institutions and socialization in Europe: introduction and framework', *International Organization*, 59(4): 801–26.

Checkel, J.T. (ed.) (2005b) 'International institutions and socialization in Europe', Special Issue of *International Organization*, 59(4): 801–1079.

Checkel, J.T. (2005c) 'It's the process stupid! Process tracing in the study of European and international politics', in A. Klotz (ed.), *Qualitative Methods in International Relations*. Syracuse, NY: Maxwell School, Syracuse University.

Chernoff, F. (2002) 'Scientific realism as a metatheory of international politics', *International Studies Quarterly*, 46(2): 189–207.

Chernoff, F. (2005) *The Power of International Theory: Reforging the Link to Foreign Policy-Making through Scientific Enquiry*. New York: Routledge.

Christiansen, T., Jørgensen, K.E. and Wiener, A. (eds) (2001) *The Social Construction of Europe*. London: Sage Publications.

CIDEL (2005) *Towards a Citizens' Europe? Report from the European-Wide Research Project Citizenship and Democratic Legitimacy in the European Union (CIDEL)*. Oslo: Arena Centre for European Studies, University of Oslo.

Cochran, M. (2002) 'Deweyan pragmatism and post-positivist social science in IR', *Millennium*, 31(3): 525–48.

Cortell, A. and Davis, J. (2000) 'Understanding the domestic impact of international norms: a research agenda', *International Studies Review*, 2(1): 65–90.

Crawford, N. (2002) *Argument and Change in World Politics: Ethics, Decolonization and Humanitarian Intervention*. Cambridge: Cambridge University Press.

Deitelhoff, N. and Mueller, H. (2005) 'Theoretical paradise – empirically lost? Arguing with Habermas', *Review of International Studies*, 31(1): 167–79.

Diez, T. (1999) 'Speaking 'Europe': the politics of integration discourse', *Journal of European Public Policy*, 6(4): 598–613.

Diez, T. and Wiener, A. (eds) (2004) *European Integration Theory*. Oxford: Oxford University Press.

Dimitrova, A. and Rhinard, M. (2005) 'The power of norms in the transposition of EU directives', *European Integration Online Papers*, 9(16). Available online at: http://eiop.or.at/eiop, accessed 2 December 2005.

Doty, R.L. (1993) 'Foreign policy as social construction. A post-positivist analysis of US counterinsurgency policy in the Philippines', *International Studies Quarterly*, 37(3): 297–320.

Elster, J. (ed.) (1998) *Deliberative Democracy*. Cambridge: Cambridge University Press.

Eriksen, E.O. and Fossum, J.E. (eds) (2000) *Democracy in the European Union: Integration through Deliberation?* London: Routledge.

Eriksen, E.O. and Fossum, J.E. (2004) 'Europe in search of legitimacy: strategies of legitimation assessed', *International Political Science Review*, 25(4): 435–59.

Farrell, H. and Flynn, G. (1999) 'Piecing together the democratic peace: the CSCE and the 'construction' of security in post-cold war Europe', *International Organization*, 53(3): 505–36.

Fearon, J. and Wendt, A. (2002) 'Rationalism v. constructivism: a skeptical view', in W. Carlsnaes, T. Risse and B. Simmons (eds), *Handbook of International Relations*. London: Sage Publications. pp. 52–72.

Fierke, K. (2002) 'Links across the abyss: language and logic in international relations', *International Studies Quarterly*, 46(3): 331–54.

Finnemore, M. (1996a) *National Interests in International Society*. Ithaca, NY: Cornell University Press.

Finnemore, M. (1996b) 'Norms, culture and world politics: insights from sociology's institutionalism', *International Organization*, 50(2): 325–48.

Finnemore, M. and Sikkink, K. (1998) 'International norm dynamics and political change', *International Organization*, 52(3): 887–917.

Forum (2005) 'A useful dialogue? Habermas and international relations', *Review of International Studies*, 31(1): 127–209.

Forum Debate (2003) 'Are dialogue and synthesis possible in international relations?' *International Studies Review*, 5(1): 123–53.

Fossum, J.E. (2003) 'The European Union: in search of an identity', *European Journal of Political Theory*, 2(3): 319–40.

Fossum, J.E. and Trenz, H.-J. (2005) 'The EU's fledgling society: from deafening silence to critical voice in European constitution making', Paper presented at the ARENA Research Seminar, 4 October. Oslo: ARENA Centre for European Studies, University of Oslo.

Friedrichs, J. (2003) 'Middle ground or half-way house? Social constructivism and the theory of

European integration', Unpublished Mimeo. Bremen: School of Humanities and Social Sciences, International University Bremen, 4 March.

Gheciu, A. (2005a) 'Security institutions as agents of socialization? NATO and post-cold war central and eastern Europe', *International Organization*, 59(4): 973–1012.

Gheciu, A. (2005b) *NATO in the 'New Europe': The Politics of International Socialization After the Cold War*. Stanford: Stanford University Press.

Gourevitch, P. (2002) 'Domestic politics and international relations', in W. Carlsnaes, T. Risse and B. Simmons (eds), *Handbook of International Relations*. London: Sage Publications. pp. 309–28.

Guzzini, S. (1993) 'Structural power: the limits of neorealist analysis', *International Organization*, 47(3): 443–78.

Guzzini, S. (2000) 'A reconstruction of constructivism in international relations', *European Journal of International Relations*, 6(2): 147–82.

Haacke, J. (2005) 'The Frankfurt school and international relations: on the centrality of recognition', *Review of International Studies*, 31(1): 181–94.

Haas, E.B. (1958) *The Uniting of Europe: Political, Social and Economic Forces, 1950–57*. Stanford, CA: Stanford University Press.

Haas, E.B. (2001) 'Does constructivism subsume neo-functionalism?', in T. Christiansen, K.E. Joergensen and A. Wiener (eds), *The Social Construction of Europe*. London: Sage Publications. pp. 22–31.

Hemmer, C. and Katzenstein, P. (2002) 'Why is there no NATO in Asia? Collective identity, regionalism and the origins of multilateralism', *International Organization*, 56(2): 575–608.

Hooghe, L. (2005) 'Several roads lead to international norms, but few via international socialization: a case study of the European Commission', *International Organization*, 59(4): 861–98.

Hooghe, L. and Marks, G. (2001) *Multi-Level Governance and European Integration*. Boulder, CO: Rowman & Littlefield.

Hooghe, L. and Marks, G. (2004) 'The neofunctionalists were (almost) right: politicization and European integration', Paper presented at the ARENA Research Seminar, 5 October. Oslo: ARENA Centre for European Studies, University of Oslo.

Hopf, T. (1998) 'The promise of constructivism in international relations theory', *International Security*, 23(1): 171–200.

Hopf, T. (2002) *Social Construction of International Politics: Identities and Foreign Policies, Moscow,*

1955 and 1999. Ithaca, NY: Cornell University Press.

Hopf, T. (2006) 'The limits of interpreting evidence', in R.N. Lebow and M. Lichbach (eds), *Theory and Evidence*, ch.3. New York: Palgrave-Macmillan.

Hurrell, A. (2005) 'Power, institutions and the production of inequality', in M. Barnett and R. Duvall (eds), *Power and Global Governance*. Cambridge: Cambridge University Press. pp. 33–58.

Hyde-Price, A. (2004) 'The EU, power and coercion: from "civilian" to "civilising" power', Paper presented at a CIDEL-ARENA workshop on From Civilian to Military Power: The European Union at a Crossroads, October. Oslo: Arena Centre for European Studies, University of Oslo.

Hyde-Price, A. (2006) '"Normative" power Europe: a realist critique', *Journal of European Public Policy*, 13(2): 217–34.

Jacobsen, J.K. (2003) 'Duelling constructivisms: a post-mortem on the ideas debate in IR/IPE', *Review of International Studies*, 29(1): 39–60.

Joerges, C. and Neyer, J. (1997a) 'From intergovernmental bargaining to deliberative political processes: the constitutionalisation of comitology', *European Law Journal*, 3(3): 273–99.

Joerges, C. and Neyer, J. (1997b) 'Transforming strategic interaction into deliberative problem-solving: European comitology in the foodstuffs sector', *Journal of European Public Policy*, 4(4): 609–25.

Johnson, J. (2006) 'Consequences of positivism: a pragmatist assessment', *Comparative Political Studies*, 39(2): 224–52.

Johnston, A.I. (2001) 'Treating international institutions as social environments', *International Studies Quarterly*, 45(4): 487–516.

Johnston, A.I. (2005) 'Conclusions and extensions: toward mid-range theorizing and beyond Europe', *International Organization*, 59(4): 1013–1044.

Johnston, A.I. (2007) *Social States: China in International Institutions*. Princeton: Princeton University Press.

Katzenstein, P. (2003) 'Same war–different views: Germany, Japan and counterterrorism', *International Organization*, 57(4): 731–0.

Katzenstein, P. and Sil, R. (2005) 'What is analytic eclecticism and why do we need it? A pragmatist perspective on problems and mechanisms in the study of world politics', Paper presented at the Annual Convention of the American Political Science Association, September. Washington, DC.

Katzenstein, P., Keohane, R. and Krasner, S. (eds) (1998) '*International Organization* at fifty:

exploration and contestation in the study of world politics', Special Issue of *International Organization*, 52(4): 645–1061.

Keck, M. and Sikkink, K. (1998) *Activists Beyond Borders: Advocacy Networks in International Politics*. Ithaca, NY: Cornell University Press.

Kelley, J. (2004) *Ethnic Politics in Europe: The Power of Norms and Incentives*. Princeton: Princeton University Press.

Keohane, R. and Milner, H. (eds) (1996) *Internationalization and Domestic Politics*. Cambridge: Cambridge University Press.

King, G., Keohane, R. and Verba, S. (1994) *Designing Social Inquiry: Scientific Inference in Qualitative Research*. Princeton: Princeton University Press.

Kleine, M. and Risse, T. (2005) 'Arguing and persuasion in the European Convention', Draft Report. Berlin: Otto Suhr Institute for Political Science, Free University Berlin.

Laitin, D. (1998) *Identity in Formation: The Russian-Speaking Populations in the Near Abroad*. Ithaca, NY: Cornell University Press.

Lane, R. (1996) 'Positivism, scientific realism and political science: recent developments in the philosophy of science', *Journal of Theoretical Politics*, 8(3): 361–82.

Lebow, R.N. (2001) 'Thucydides the constructivist', *American Political Science Review*, 95(3): 547–60.

Lebow, R.N. (2006) 'What can we know? How do we know?', in R.N. Lebow and M. Lichbach (eds), *Theory and Evidence*, ch. 1. New York: Palgrave-Macmillan.

Lebow, R.N. and Lichbach, M. (eds) (2006) *Theory and Evidence*. New York: Palgrave-Macmillan.

Legro, J. and Moravcsik, A. (1999) 'Is anybody still a realist?' *International Security*, 24(2): 5–55.

Lepgold, J. and Lamborn, A. (2001) 'Locating bridges: connecting research agendas on cognition and strategic choice', *International Studies Review*, 3(3): 3–30.

Lewis, J. (1998) 'Is the 'hard bargaining' image of the Council misleading? The Committee of Permanent Representatives and the local elections directive', *Journal of Common Market Studies*, 36(4): 479–504.

Lewis, J. (2005) 'The Janus face of Brussels: socialization and everyday decision making in the European union', *International Organization*, 59(4): 937–72.

Lin, A.C. (1998) 'Bridging positivist and interpretivist approaches to qualitative methods', *Policy Studies Journal*, 26(1): 162–80.

Lynch, M. (1999) *State Interests and Public Spheres: The International Politics of Jordan's Identity*. New York: Columbia University Press.

Lynch, M. (2002) 'Why engage? China and the logic of communicative engagement', *European Journal of International Relations*, 8(2): 187–230.

Magnette, P. (2004) 'Coping with constitutional incompatibilities: bargains and rhetoric in the convention on the future of Europe', Paper presented at the ARENA Research Seminar, 2 March. Oslo: Arena Centre for European Studies, University of Oslo.

Manners, I. (2002) 'Normative power Europe: a contradiction in terms?', *Journal of Common Market Studies*, 40(2): 235–58.

March, J. and Olsen, J.P. (forthcoming) 'The logic of appropriateness', in R. Goodin, M.L. Moran and M. Rein (eds), *Handbook of Public Policy*. Oxford: Oxford University Press.

Martin, L. (2000) *Democratic Commitments: Legislatures and International Cooperation*. Princeton, NJ: Princeton University Press.

Martin, L. and Simmons, B. (1998) 'Theories and empirical studies of international institutions', *International Organization*, 52(3): 729–58.

Mastenbroek, E. (2005) 'What role for politics? Applying neo-institutionalism to EU transposition', Paper presented at the Joint Sessions of the European Consortium for Political Research, April. Granada, Spain.

Milliken, J. (1999) 'The study of discourse in international relations: a critique of research and methods', *European Journal of International Relations*, 5(2): 225–54.

Milner, H. (1992) 'International theories of cooperation among nations: strengths and weaknesses (a review essay)', *World Politics*, 44(3): 466–96.

Milner, H. (1997) *Interests, Institutions and Information: Domestic Politics and International Relations*. Princeton, NJ: Princeton University Press.

Moravcsik, A. (1993) 'Integrating international and domestic theories of international bargaining', in P.B. Evans, H. Jacobson and R. Putnam (eds), *Double-edged Diplomacy. International Bargaining and Domestic Politics*. Berkeley, CA: University of California Press. pp. 3–42.

Moravcsik, A. (1998) *The Choice for Europe: Social Purpose and State Power from Messina to Maastricht*. Ithaca, NY: Cornell University Press.

Moravcsik, A. (2001) 'Constructivism and European integration: a critique', in T. Christiansen, K.E. Joergensen and A. Wiener (eds), *The Social Construction of Europe*. London: Sage Publications. pp. 176–88.

Mueller, H. and Risse, T. (2001) *Arguing and Persuasion in Multilateral Negotiations*. A grant proposal to the Volkswagen foundation, 6 August. Berlin: Otto Suhr Institute for Political Science, Free University Berlin.

Mueller, H. and Risse-Kappen, T. (1993) 'From the outside in and from the inside out: international relations, domestic politics and foreign policy', in D. Skidmore and V. Hudson (eds), *The Limits of State Autonomy: Societal Groups and Foreign Policy Formulation.* Boulder, CO: Westview Press. pp. 25–48.

Naurin, D. (forthcoming) 'Backstage behavior? Lobbyists in public and private settings in Sweden and the European Union', *Comparative Politics.*

Neumann, I. (2002) 'Returning practice to the linguistic turn: the case of diplomacy', *Millennium,* 31(3): 627–51.

Neumann, I. (2003) 'From meta to method: the materiality of discourse', Unpublished Manuscript. Oslo: Norwegian Institute of International Affairs.

Neyer, J. (2003) 'Discourse and order in the EU: a deliberative approach to multi-level governance', *Journal of Common Market Studies,* 41(4): 687–706.

Parsons, C. (2003) *A Certain Idea of Europe.* Ithaca, NY: Cornell University Press.

Pollack, M. (2003) 'Deliberative democracy or member-state control mechanism? Two images of comitology', *Comparative Political Studies,* 36(1–2): 125–55.

Price, R. (1997) *The Chemical Weapons Taboo.* Ithaca, NY: Cornell University Press.

Price, R. and Reus-Smit, C. (1998) 'Dangerous liaisons? Critical international theory and constructivism', *European Journal of International Relations,* 4(3): 259–94.

Risse, T. (2000) "Let's argue!": communicative action in world politics', *International Organization,* 54(1): 1–40.

Risse, T. (2004a) 'Social constructivism and European integration', in T. Diez and A. Wiener (eds), *European Integration Theory.* Oxford: Oxford University Press. pp. 159–76.

Risse, T. (2004b) 'European institutions and identity change: what have we learned?', in R. Herrmann, T. Risse and M. Brewer (eds), *Transnational Identities: Becoming European in the EU.* Boulder, CO: Rowman & Littlefield Publishers. pp. 247–72.

Risse, T. (2005) 'Neo-functionalism, European identity, and the puzzles of European integration', *Journal of European Public Policy,* 12(2): 291–309.

Risse, T. and Maier, M. (eds) (2003) 'Europeanization, collective identities and public discourses', Draft Final Report Submitted to the European Commission. Florence, Italy: European University Institute and Robert Schuman Centre for Advanced Studies.

Risse, T., Ropp, S. and Sikkink, K. (eds) (1999) *The Power of Human Rights: International Norms and Domestic Change.* Cambridge: Cambridge University Press.

Risse-Kappen, T. (1995) *Cooperation among Democracies: The European Influence on US Foreign Policy.* Princeton, NJ: Princeton University Press.

Rittberger, V. (ed.) (2001) *German Foreign Policy since Unification: Theories and Case Studies.* Manchester: Manchester University Press.

Romsloe, B. (2004) *EU's External Policy: Are the Lilliputians Impotent or Potent? The Case of Crisis Management in the Amsterdam Treaty.* ARENA Working Paper 04/22. Oslo: Arena Centre for European Studies, University of Oslo.

Rosamond, B. (2001) 'Discourses of globalization and European identities', in T. Christiansen, K.E. Jørgensen and A. Wiener (eds), *The Social Construction of Europe.* London: Sage Publications. pp. 158–75.

Ruggie, J.G. (1998) 'What makes the world hang together? Neo-utilitarianism and the social constructivist challenge', *International Organization,* 52(4): 855–885.

Schimmelfennig, F. (2003) *The EU, NATO and the Integration of Europe: Rules and Rhetoric.* Cambridge: Cambridge University Press.

Schimmelfennig, F. (2005) 'Strategic calculation and international socialization: membership incentives, party constellations, and sustained compliance in central and eastern Europe', *International Organization,* 59(4): 827–60.

Schimmelfennig, F. and Sedelmeier, U. (eds) (2002) 'European Union enlargement – theoretical and comparative approaches', Special Issue of *Journal of European Public Policy,* 9(4): 499–665.

Schimmelfennig, F. and Sedelmeier, U. (2005) *The Europeanization of Central and Eastern Europe.* Ithaca, NY: Cornell University Press.

Schwellnus, G. (2005a) 'Dynamics of norm-construction and resonance in the context of EU enlargement: minority rights in Poland', PhD Thesis. Belfast: Faculty of Legal, Social and Educational Sciences, Queen's University Belfast.

Schwellnus, G. (2005b) 'The adoption of nondiscrimination and minority protection rules in Romania, Hungary and Poland', in F. Schimmelfennig and U. Sedelmeier (eds), *The Europeanization of Central and Eastern Europe.* Ithaca, NY: Cornell University Press. pp. 51–70.

Sedelmeier, U. (2005) *Constructing the Path to Eastern Enlargement: The Uneven Policy Impact of EU Identity.* Manchester: Manchester University Press.

Sil, R. (2000) 'The foundations of eclecticism: the epistemological status of agency, culture and structure in social theory', *Journal of Theoretical Politics*, 12(3): 353–87.

Sjursen, H. (2002) 'Why expand? The question of legitimacy and justification in the EU's enlargement policy', *Journal of Common Market Studies*, 40(3): 491–513.

Sjursen, H. (2004) 'Changes to European security in a communicative perspective', *Cooperation and Conflict*, 39(2): 107–28.

Sjursen, H. (2006a) 'What kind of power?' *Journal of European Public Policy*, 13(2): 169–81.

Sjursen, H. (2006b) 'The EU as a 'normative power': how can this be?' *Journal of European Public Policy*, 13(2): 235–51.

Smith, K.E. (2004a) 'Still 'civilian power EU'?', Paper presented at a CIDEL-ARENA workshop on From Civilian to Military Power: The European Union at a Crossroads, October. Oslo: Arena Centre for European Studies, University of Oslo.

Smith, M. (2004b) 'Institutionalization, policy adaptation and European foreign policy cooperation', *European Journal of International Relations*, 10(1): 95–136.

Stasavage, D. (2004) 'Open-door or closed-door? Transparency in domestic and international bargaining', *International Organization*, 58(4): 667–703.

Symposium: Discourse and Content Analysis (2004) *Qualitative Methods: Newsletter of the American Political Science Association Organized Section on Qualitative Methods*, 2(1): 15–39.

Tallberg, J. (2002) 'Paths to compliance: enforcement, management and the European Union', *International Organization*, 56(3): 609–44.

Trondal, J. (2001) 'Is there any social constructivist – institutionalist divide? Unpacking social mechanisms affecting representational roles among EU decision-makers', *Journal of European Public Policy*, 8(1): 1–23.

Waever, O. (1998) 'The sociology of a not so international discipline: American and European developments in international relations', *International Organization*, 52(4): 687–728.

Waever, O. (2004) 'Discursive approaches', in T. Diez and A. Wiener (eds), *European Integration Theory*. Oxford: Oxford University Press. pp. 197–216.

Wendt, A. (1999) *Social Theory of International Politics*. Cambridge: Cambridge University Press.

Wight, C. (2002) 'Philosophy of social science and international relations', in W. Carlsnaes, T. Risse and B. Simmons (eds), *Handbook of International Relations*. London: Sage Publications. pp. 23–51.

Zehfuss, M. (2002) *Constructivism in International Relations: The Politics of Reality*. Cambridge: Cambridge University Press.

Zürn, M. (2002) 'From interdependence to globalization', in W. Carlsnaes, B. Simmons and T. Risse (eds), *Handbook of International Relations*. London: Sage Publications. pp. 235–54.

Zürn, M. and Checkel, J.T. (2005) 'Getting socialized to build bridges: constructivism and rationalism, Europe and the nation-state', *International Organization*, 59(4): 1045–79.

4

Another Europe is Possible: Critical Perspectives on European Union Politics

IAN MANNERS

INTRODUCTION

Over the past two decades critical perspectives on the study of the European Union have blossomed in ways unimaginable from within the intellectual straitjacket of traditional political science during the Cold War era. The multitude of vistas provided by scholars working on European Union politics across the social sciences means that I can only provide a limited view of this vast wealth of critical perspectives. What becomes clear in writing this chapter is that EU politics, as found at EU Studies Associations across Europe and beyond, represents only a small portion of a now much broader and diverse field of social science.

Despite over five decades of European integration to analyse and a huge array of attempts to explain these processes, the EU is now more diverse and less well understood than ever. This is not to say that those who study EU politics are searching for one explanation or model, simply that traditional approaches based on assumptions and techniques developed to analyse political systems during the

Cold War look increasingly out of touch with contemporary EU politics. As EU referenda constantly remind us, many EU citizens (and non-citizens) are critical of the EU as a neo-liberal political project, similar to the way in which traditional political science fails to challenge or change existing structures of power and injustice.

As the two previous chapters have demonstrated, traditional approaches are forced to make many *ceteris paribus* assumptions in their analysis of the EU as an arena for political and social choice. In contrast, critical perspectives question the starting assumptions of political science by constantly raising these three questions – what is being studied? (ontological questions); what can we know? (epistemological questions); and how are we going to know? (methodological questions) (Hay 2002: 61–3). For critical scholarship, the answers to these questions are always political rather than neutral, as Jupille (2006) illustrates when he uncritically seeks to naturalize rational choice theory as a metatheory.

Critical scholars understand that if politics is power, then political science involves the study of the processes and consequences of the way power is acquired, distributed, and exercised (Hay 2002: 73). For critical theorists the centrality of power in pre-determining the questions asked and the theories used is summed up thus: 'theory is always *for* someone and *for* some purpose' since 'theory constitutes as well as explains the questions it asks (and those it does not ask)' (Cox 1981: 128; Hoskyns 2004: 224). In contrast to the discussions of the two previous chapters which attempt to apply theories to political questions without questioning the broader power consequences, critical theories are distinctively *political* theories in that they understand the political nature of political enquiry.

Critical scholars therefore seek to escape the intellectual straitjacket of traditional political science by questioning assumptions about political systems and institutions, economistic rationalities and methodologies, all of which have evolved out of the interest of earlier political scientists in the US political system and its foreign policy (see Manners 2003a; Smith 2004; Kinnvall 2005). But more than anything else, critical scholars share a commitment to uncovering preconceptions about historical reality and the contextual nature of knowledge, and they seek to change politics. In this respect all four critical perspectives on EU politics can be characterized by a dedication to emancipation – the freeing of humans and knowledge from the negative consequences of modernity.

The rest of the chapter sets out to examine the contribution of critical perspectives to the study of European Union politics. As stated at the outset, it will not be possible to include all critical perspectives and contributions, but I will hope to provide insights from four perspectives. The term 'perspective' is chosen with care – many of the scholars encountered here are not easily located in one theoretical 'school' or 'tradition', in addition to which the boundaries between perspectives are highly permeable and contested. Unfortunately, I was not able to include as many perspectives as I might have wished, and regret the absence of the Marxist perspectives of world systems, regulation and state theories, as well as post-colonial scholarship and work on race and

racism (for examples see Cole and Dale 1999; Tausch and Herrmann 2001; Chafer and Cooper 2003; Jessop 2004; Bailey 2006). In addition, I will undoubtedly exhibit an English-language bias in this chapter, which is also to be regretted.

The first perspective, historical materialisms, consists of critical approaches which draw explicitly on the intellectual heritage of Karl Marx and Antonio Gramsci (see Rupert and Smith 2002, for a good overview). The second perspective, Frankfurt Critical Theories, involves critical approaches which can be identified with the intellectual heritage of the Institute of Social Research in Frankfurt, including the work of Max Horkheimer, Theodor Adorno, and Jürgen Habermas (see Jay 1996, for a good overview). The third perspective, postmodern sciences, includes critical approaches which can be located within the critiques of modernity initiated by Friedrich Nietzsche, Michel Foucault, and Jacques Derrida, amongst others (see Weber 2005, for a good overview). Finally, feminist perspectives comprise of critical approaches which seek to question gender and power, and to promote social change (see Steans 2006, for a good overview). The ordering of the perspectives reflects a journey from more positivist to more post-positivist political science, with feminist perspectives including liberal, radical, and post-structuralist approaches, rather than any judgement on the relative merits of the differing perspectives.

HISTORICAL MATERIALISMS

Historical materialist perspectives on EU politics have grown out of the work of Marx, although prior to the end of the Cold War they were broadly ignored by traditional integration theory (Rosamond 2000: 81; Smith 2002: 264; Hoskyns 2004: 226). Remarkably, this relative lack of engagement has occurred despite the socialist origins of federalists such as Altiero Spinelli and Mario Albertini. During the Cold War a few scholars interrogated the processes of European integration from a

Marxist perspective, including Mandel (1970), Galtung (1973), and Holland (1980). What these scholars shared was a critique of the ahistorical and decontextual nature of contemporary integration studies and a commitment to paying greater attention to the larger scale dynamics of capitalism which drove capital concentration (larger companies) and their relationship to the dominance of the elite political class.

The end of the Cold War brought renewed energy to historical materialist approaches as scholars turned their attention away from Marxist theorizing of the capitalist state, and towards two differing perspectives on transnational human social and economic relations termed Open Marxism and Neo-Gramscianism. Although both perspectives share a historical materialist understanding of the capitalist context of social, economic and political relations, they differ in the relative primacy they give to early Marx's emphasis on human social relations compared to Gramsci's emphasis on critical economy (see Bieler and Morton 2003; see also 'Americanism and Fordism' in Gramsci 1971: 277–318).

Open Marxism

Open Marxist scholars, led by the work of Werner Bonefeld, Peter Burnham, Guglielmo Carchedi, Bernard Moss, and Hazel Smith, have sought to examine EU politics in terms of class, imperialism, labour commodification, and institutionalist bias. Open Marxism places an emphasis on Marx's open-ended class struggle within nation states. Bonefeld and Burnham have argued that the politics of monetary union can be explained by the attempts of the capitalist classes within member states to reinvigorate 'capital accumulation' (investment in capital goods and associated reproduction of capitalist social relations) while de-politicizing fiscal restraint and other 'competitive pressures' on the national working classes (Burnham 1999; Bonefeld 2001). Moss places much emphasis on the EU as a neo-liberal construction which serves, and is shaped by, the rivalries of the capitalist classes

of its member states (Moss and Michie 1999; Moss 2004). Carchedi's (2001) work focuses on the interplay between class relations and the EU's imperialist relations with the rest of the world. Carchedi (2001: 30–4) moves beyond a statist Marxist position when he argues that the Commission serves a 'transnational capitalist class' through a network of lobbying groups.

Both Hazel Smith and Gustav Peebles interrogate the way in which the EU treaties commodify labour through the harmonization of labour-power rules (Peebles 1997; Smith 2002). Smith (1998, 2002: 265–6) has also gone further than most Marxists in identifying the 'institutionalist bias' manifest in work on EU politics. This institutionalist bias involves two institutionalist fallacies of overemphasizing the study of institutional decision making and allowing the EU institutions to determine the constitution of the field of study, a criticism sometimes shared with non-Marxists.

The Open Marxist approach has revived political questions of 'who is the EU for?' – in particular by analysing the way in which European integration serves the political elite of one or several member states. Such scholarship argues that the single market and the single currency have changed the political relations between national ruling elites and national working classes. The growth of anti-capitalist groups and actions since the 1990s, together with the revival of parties of the left in Europe, illustrates the extent to which Open Marxist arguments over the role of the EU in reinforcing national class distinctions resonates with the wider European public (although see Mau 2005; Rhodes 2005; Sykes 2005, for non-Marxist political economy).

Neo-Gramscian Perspectives

Neo-Gramscian scholars such as Stephen Gill, Hans-Jürgen Bieling, Andreas Bieler, Adam David Morton, Bastiaan van Apeldoorn, Alan Cafruny, and Magnus Ryner adopt a transnational historical materialist perspective in analysing EU politics with particular reference to the 'sphere of production' in its widest sense.

In contrast to Open Marxism, Neo-Gramscian perspectives emphasize the role of 'social forces, engendered by the production process, as the most important collective actors' (Bieler and Morton 2001: 17), in particular transnational forces at the European and global level. Gill (1998, 2003) has argued that economic and monetary union has, since the early 1990s, constitutionalized neo-liberal discipline within the EU and contributed to the formation of a neo-Gramscian 'transnational historical bloc' which socially and politically embeds neo-liberalism. Bieling extends Gill's argument by looking at the impact of EU neo-liberalism on industrial relations, in particular at the way in which trade union organizations have been incorporated into 'competitive corporatism' (Bieling and Steinhilber 2000). Outside of the 'Amsterdam School' of international political economy, Bieler and Morton (2001) have led the way in arguing for neo-Gramscian perspectives on European Union politics. Bieler and Morton (2004) go further than simply advocating neo-Gramscian perspectives by raising the possibilities of counter-hegemonic EU strategies by labour and social movements, particularly within the context of the European Social Forum.

van Apeldoorn (2002), following van der Pijl and the Amsterdam School, argues that the EU and its processes of integration are embedded in neo-liberal discipline shaped by the hegemony of a transatlantic, transnational class as manifest in the role of the European Roundtable of Industrialists (for good overviews of the work of Robert Cox, Stephen Gill, and the Amsterdam School see Gill 1993; Overbeek 2004). From this perspective, van Apeldoorn et al. (2003: 32) engage in a neo-Gramscian critique of mainstream theories of European integration with an emphasis on the ways in which neofunctionalist, intergovernmentalist, multi-levelled, and liberal constructivist approaches lack 'a more comprehensive, critical, transnational, historical, and materialist theory of European integration'. Cafruny and Ryner (2003: vii–viii) capture much of the emancipatory ethic of the slogan that 'Another Europe is Possible' when they raise the question of whether the European attempts to create a fortress of resistance to US-led, transnational neo-liberal hegemony now lie in ruins. What they argue, like most neo-Gramscian scholars, is that the EU itself needs to become more social-democratic, turning to successful social democratic models such as Sweden 'for inspiration in the search for emancipatory alternatives to neo-liberalism' and 'establish regulatory policies across a wide array of international regimes' (Cafruny 2003: 300; Ryner 2004: 115).

By developing historical materialist ideas about the post-Cold War EU, Neo-Gramscian scholars are raising critical questions about the role of hegemonic practices in EU politics. Such scholarship both challenges traditional integration theories for their decontextualized neo-liberalism, and argues that neo-liberal capitalism has become transnationalized, particularly within the EU and across the Atlantic. The growth of the World Social Forum and European Social Forum since 2001 illustrates the way in which widely-held beliefs about the transnationalization of neo-liberal politics are reconfiguring both political participation and academic study in the EU. In particular, the widely shared ESF banner of 'Another Europe is Possible' became the rallying cry of the anti-Constitution forces in the referenda rejections during 2005, a cry no political scientist can ignore.

CRITICAL THEORIES

Critical Theories originating in the Frankfurt Institute of Social Research have attempted to develop, and then move beyond Marx in order to advance a critical theory of society that responds to the alienation of advanced capitalist society and questions 'traditional' theories (McCarthy 1981; Bernstein 1985; see also Diez and Steans 2005, for a more recent review). Like historical materialist perspectives, Frankfurt Critical Theories have remained largely disconnected from European integration theory (Hoskyns 2004: 226–7). This disconnection is increasingly addressed by the impact of probably the most widely known and read scholar on the EU: Jürgen Habermas.

The Frankfurt School has given rise to at least two perspectives based on the work of Max Horkheimer and Theodor Adorno here termed 'critical social theory', and the later work of Habermas here termed 'deliberative theory'.

Unlike historical materialist perspectives, Critical Theories did not have to contend with the intellectual and ideological consequences of the end of communism in the same way – indeed outside of EU studies, Frankfurt Critical Theory became widely accepted during the 1980s and 1990s, with Habermas (1986, 1989, 1992) as one of the prime sources of contemporary social theory. It was only during the 1990s that the social, cultural and political consequences of European union, globalization, and Europeanization began to be addressed and understood from a Critical Theory perspective (see Habermas 1992; Delanty 1995; Linklater 1998). My differentiation between the perspectives of Habermasian 'deliberative theory' and earlier Frankfurt 'critical social theory' needs explanation in the context of EU political science. Both perspectives share a concern for understanding and challenging the social production of knowledge; historicizing and contextualizing subjectivity; and a commitment to progress and emancipation as the goals of research (see Warleigh 2003: 52). However, by following Habermas's advocacy of 'communicative action' in the public sphere, it is clear that deliberative theorists are more interested in the liberal promotion of deliberative democracy than the critical questioning of the sociocultural production of human knowledge characteristic of critical social theory. In contrast, critical social theory is a more diverse collection of scholars who share Horkheimer and Adorno's agenda of progressive and radical critique of modern society (see Calhoun 1995).

Deliberative Theory

Following Habermas, scholars such as Deirdre Curtin, Andrew Linklater, Christian Jörges, Jürgen Neyer, Kirstin Jacobsson, Erik Oddvar Eriksen, John Erik Fossum, Helene Sjursen, and Alex Warleigh have sought to use his ideas

to understand the development of deliberative processes and democracy within a post-national EU polity. Deliberative theorists are interested in understanding, and advocating, the European Union as a post-national and cosmopolitan democracy where citizenship and democracy can and should be developed beyond the Westphalian state on the basis of 'constitutional patriotism'. Habermas has developed his themes of communicative action and constitutional patriotism to argue that, in the face of globalization and terrorism, the EU is 'the only normatively satisfactory alternative as a socially and economically effective European Union, constituted along federalist lines – an alternative that points to a future cosmopolitan order sensitive to both difference and social equality' (Habermas 2001: xix). For Habermas the EU would 'aim toward a common practice of opinion- and will-formation, nourished by the roots of a European civil society, and expanded into a European-wide political arena' and 'inspire the Kantian hope for a global domestic polity' (Habermas 2001: 100; Habermas and Derrida 2003: 297).

Linklater (1998) and Curtin (1997) were amongst the earliest scholars to develop Habermasian thinking in order to explore the EU in terms of cosmopolitan citizenship and deliberative democracy. Linklater (1996: 85) argues that critical theory and discourse ethics are 'explicitly concerned with an emancipatory project with universalist aspirations which transcend national frontiers' which he finds immanent in the cosmopolitan democracy, citizenship and civilising process of the EU. Curtin (2003: 58) draws on Habermas's link between 'communicative action, deliberation and civil society', arguing that EU post-national democracy should be built on deliberation in the public sphere. Similarly, Christian Jörges, Jürgen Neyer, and Kirstin Jacobsson have also used deliberative theory to analyse comitology, legitimacy and order in the EU and to argue that deliberative processes have a different basis of legitimacy to those of representative politics (Jacobsson 1997; Jörges and Neyer 1997; Neyer 2003).

Since 2000 the ARENA group of Erik Oddvar Eriksen, John Erik Fossum, and Helene Sjursen have played a leading role in bringing together

Habermasian deliberative theorists to interrogate and advocate deliberative democracy in the EU, including questions of 'democratic deficit', a European public sphere, foreign policy, and reflexivity in the European polity (Eriksen and Fossum 2000; Sjursen 2002, 2006; Eriksen 2005). Scholars following Habermas's lead are keen to explore the relationships between communicative action, public sphere, citizenship, deliberation, and cosmopolitan democracy (for example Warleigh 2003).

Over the past 15 years, Habermas and the Deliberative Theorists have moved the theoretical debates in EU politics beyond arguments over how best to analyse EU politics towards how best to achieve cosmopolitan and deliberative democracy in a post-national EU polity. In this respect, Deliberative Theorists are working with crucial political questions in a post-Cold War Europe very much concerned with questions of democratic deficit, legitimacy and citizenship within both EU member states and the EU institutions themselves. In the aftermath of the EU democratic deficit debates of the 1990s, and the EU counterterrorist debates of the 2000s, liberal concerns regarding such questions are clearly paramount to EU political science.

Critical Social Theory

Critical social theory (CST) perspectives on EU politics are led by the work of a diverse range of scholars including Gerard Delanty, Chris Rumford, Craig Calhoun, Seyla Benhabib, Pierre Bourdieu, and Niilo Kauppi (see discussion in Manners and Whitman 2003: 394–397). In a wide variety of ways these scholars have sought to draw on Adorno and Horkheimer's critical theory, together with Berger and Luckmann's social constructionism, in the study of Europe whilst taking 'the risk of trying for liberation, for equality, justice, and all the other problematic terms that join with freedom to make up the most popular normative and political path for critical theory' (Calhoun 1995: xvi).

Gerard Delanty and Chris Rumford have taken the lead in bringing social theory and

political sociology to the study of Europe and EU politics (Delanty 1995; Rumford 2002; Delanty and Rumford 2005). Delanty begins his work with reference to a central question for EU politics posed in Adorno and Horkheimer's (1979) *Dialectic of Enlightenment*: 'An indictment of an entire civilization, this celebrated work of the "Frankfurt School" of critical theory poses the question of the very possibility of a European identity in the wake of the Holocaust' (Delanty 1995: x). Delanty and Rumford (2005: 185, 188) argue that

> the transformations of the current period, conveniently summarized under the heading of globalization, have made much conventional social scientific theorizing about Europe redundant. ... There is now a cosmopolitan aspect to society in Europe which was not previously evident. ... A cosmopolitan perspective holds many attractions, not least of them being that a major problem in the way Europe is studied, perhaps *the* problem, is that the political and social science associated with the nation-state still pervades EU studies.

Alongside Delanty and Rumford, Calhoun (2001, 2003) has advanced a critical perspective on EU politics with particular emphases on the politics of identity, democratic integration, and the public sphere in Europe. Calhoun (2001: 38) argues that in EU politics it is important 'to build institutions that encourage and protect multiple, discontinuous, sometimes conflicting public spaces and modes of public engagement rather than attempt to nurture or impose some unified European culture'. He also suggests that 'the EU has an international (that is, global or supra-European) identity', but one that is 'always subject to construction and reconstruction' as part of the politics of EU identity (Calhoun 2003: 269–70).

Benhabib (2002, 2004) examines the politics of migration and citizenship in the EU from a CST perspective, arguing for 'moral universalism' and 'cosmopolitan federalism'. Benhabib examines the way the 'disaggregation of citizenship' in the EU has produced mixed results, arguing that, while a promising development for post-national EU citizens, for large groups of 'third country' nationals such disaggregation is dangerous (Benhabib 2002: 38). Instead, she advocates moral universalism based on Habermasian discourse ethics, which involves the recognition of the rights of all to speech and participation in moral conversation (Benhabib 2004: 13). For Benhabib cosmopolitan federalism involves multiple iterations of cosmopolitan norms between the layers of international law and democratic legislatures, of which the EU is at the forefront (Benhabib 2004: 176–7).

From a more radical perspective, Bourdieu (1998, 2001) has played a role as an observer and actor in EU politics by arguing for a 'reasoned utopia' and instigating Raisons d'Agir in 1995, both of which contributed to the creation of ATTAC and the European Social Forum. Bourdieu was a Critical Theorist *par excellence* in that he saw no separation between social science scholarship and commitment to a European social movement – 'I can assert that intellectuals are indispensable to social struggles, especially nowadays given the quite novel forms that domination assumes' (Bourdieu 1998, 2001: 20). Bourdieu formulated the question which he believed 'ought to be at the centre of any reasoned utopia concerning Europe: how do we create a *really European Europe*, one that is free from all the dependence on any of the *imperialisms?*' (Bourdieu 1998: 129–30).

Following in Bourdieu's footsteps, but developing his structural theory of politics into a theory of European integration, is Kauppi's (2005) 'structural constructivist' work on EU politics. Kauppi's work primarily focuses on the European Parliament as a revolutionary site which contributes to changing the structural features of member state (specifically French and Finnish) political fields by introducing new institutions and practices. Kauppi (2005: 22) argues that in order to understand the dislocating effects of European integration on political fields we should develop Bourdieu's structural constructivist theory of politics because it 'offers powerful instruments for a critical analysis of political power' and 'remedies some of the weaknesses of most versions of social constructivism, such as their diffuse conception of power and ideational notion of culture'. For Kauppi (2005: 22), a structural constructivist theory of European integration moves beyond existing

theories in order to 'examine the European Union as a multi-levelled and polycentric evolving field'.

Critical Social Theorists have begun to raise some difficult questions in the study of EU politics, in particular regarding the politics of identity, culture, imperialisms, and ethnicity. Such politics are by no means new to the integration process, but what is new is the way in which CST problematizes these questions in the context of the EU, rather than its constituent member states. Alongside the work of Habermas, the CST scholars considered here are read far more widely than most work cultivated within EU political science, which does raise the question of why there has not been more engagement between critical theory and EU politics? Alongside the contributions of Open Marxism and Neo-Gramscianism, the wider public reception of CST scholars (for example, Bourdieu through the French left, Raisons d'Agir, ATTAC, and the ESF) also illustrates the extent to which, prior to about 2001, the content of EU political science was fairly out of touch with contentious EU politics.

POSTMODERN SCIENCES

Lyotard's (1984) 'postmodern science' involves perspectives aimed at 'producing not the known, but the unknown' in order to 'wage a war on [the] totality' of metanarratives (in Manners 2003b: 254–5). In parallel with historical materialisms and Critical Theories, postmodern sciences have largely been avoided by traditional integration theory which has been mainly interested in 'producing the known' in the form of meta-narratives (all encompassing stories) about EU politics. Since the early 1990s postmodern scientific perspectives have increasingly contributed to the study of EU politics through the engagement of scholars such as Jacques Derrida and Julia Kristeva, as well as the more recent contributions of EU scholars using methods such as genealogy, governmentality, and deconstruction from Friedrich Nietzsche, Michel Foucault, and Derrida.

Postmodern scientific perspectives have probably benefited more than historical materialist and Critical Theoretical perspectives from the loosening of political science's intellectual straitjacket in the post-Cold War era. In discussing postmodern scientific perspectives care must be taken not to simply equate postmodern with poststructural – 'In keeping with current conventions, I treat postmodernity as a broad term encompassing a complex historical condition, and poststructuralism as a reference to a more specific response to philosophical dilemmas that have become especially pressing under postmodern conditions' (Rob Walker in Manners 2003b: 254 n. 62). Hence, most of the scholarship I shall consider here should be considered poststructural rather than postmodern, although there are exceptions. Unlike the previous perspectives, I shall differentiate between three different perspectives on the basis of work which argues the postmodern condition of the EU, work that follows Nietzsche and Foucault's ideas on genealogy and governmentality, and that which follows Derrida's ideas on deconstruction.

Postmodern Condition

Although numerous scholars have emphasized the postmodern characteristics of the EU (for example, Ruggie's (1993) 'postmodern international political form'), scholars such as Ian Ward and Peter van Ham have led the way in analysing the postmodern condition of the EU. Drawing on Lyotard and Derrida, Ward (1995: 15) argues that 'the European Union can best be understood as a postmodern text, and perhaps a postmodern polity' because 'from a political perspective, the European Union apparently continues to defy objective determination'. Ward's (2003) approach is informed by, and develops, the Critical Legal Studies movement by going beyond sovereignty. Ward argues that in order to more fully understand Europe and develop a public philosophy we need to think beyond sovereignty, democracy and constitutionalism towards 'a sense of justice which lies "beyond" rather than "before" the law' (Derrida 1992b in Ward 2001: 40).

van Ham's (2001) study of *European Integration and the Postmodern Condition* has given us probably the most comprehensive attempt to interrogate questions of governance, democracy, and identity from a postmodern perspective. van Ham's work is multifaceted, in line with Lyotard's definition of the postmodern as 'incredulity toward meta-narratives' (Lyotard in van Ham 2001: 9), but does try to 'come to an understanding of the vastness of political life on a European scale, reading the process of European integration a postmodern attempt at framing disorder' (van Ham 2001: 22). One interesting point he makes is that EU politics is one increasingly shaped by identity/affinity politics where cultural production and the 'brand state' are determining features.

Undoubtedly, one of the myths of EU political science has been the mantra of postmodern science having neither ambition nor power to analyse EU politics. In analysing the EU's postmodern condition, the scholarship discussed here seeks to understand how the unbundling of sovereignty, territory, and governance has significant consequences for EU politics. In particular, the assumptions of modern-state form clearly need to be problematized in a world increasingly characterized by global economic competition, overlapping international jurisdiction, and radical cultural changes which seem to turn fundamentalist beliefs into just causes. But the assumptions of this postmodern condition are not simply relativizing – the scholarship considered here goes beyond analysis and towards advocacy, in particular through rethinking justice and democracy.

Genealogy and Governmentality

Drawing on the works of Nietzsche and Foucault, scholars such as Stefan Elbe, William Walters, Jens Henrik Haahr, and Henrik Larsen have used approaches based on genealogy, governmentality, and discourse to understand the EU as a site of power relations. From this perspective, the EU is the location where knowledge and power meet, with consequences for the understanding of the past, present, and future through disciplining, governing, and discursive practices.

For Elbe (2003: 114), Nietzsche provides a perspective from which to look beyond the evil of European nationalisms, to become 'good Europeans' who 'would find their meaning in the diverse and enigmatic aspects of existence'. Such diversity is itself practiced through the notion of perspective, as Nietzsche (1998: 98) argued that 'perspectival seeing is the *only* kind of seeing there is, perspectival "knowing" the *only* kind of "knowing"'. It is this diversity of Nietzschean perspectival knowing that Ruggie (1993: 172) argued is constitutive of the EC and its analysis: 'it may constitute the first "multi-perspectival polity" to emerge since the advent of the modern era [where] the concept of multiperspectival institutional forms offers a lens through which to view other possible instances of international transformation today' (see Rumford and Murray 2003; Bohman 2004, on multi-perspectival approaches). Elbe has sought to develop a Nietzschean perspective on EU politics through engaging in genealogical reflections on European nihilism, nationalism, and the idea of Europe. Drawing on Nietzsche, Elbe (2001: 260) reminds us that 'genealogy is a specific type of historical inquiry' which is 'primarily concerned with providing a *history of the present*' and which insists 'on the necessity of allowing for a plurality of appropriations'. Undoubtedly, Elbe's most important reading of Nietzsche is in his argument that

> a vision of Europe that is deeply meaningful and not excessively technocratic … would be an idea that could contribute to a peaceful European community not because Europeans would share an identical and homogenous conception of what it means to be European, but because they would share a deep and valued experience of autonomy (Elbe 2003: 119).

In their discussions of *Governing Europe*, Walters and Haahr's (2005: 16–17) genealogical perspective is located in Michel Foucault's reading of genealogy as the excavation of singular events in order to understand the construction of the present (see also Elbe 2001: 260 n. 3). Walters and Haahr's (2005: 5) approach is based on Foucauldian 'governmentality [which] combines discourse analysis with a focus on the history of governing. As such it allows us to situate the study of European integration in relation to the much broader history of rationalities, arts and techniques of government'. By adopting a perspective of governmentality, they interrogate EU politics through the power/knowledge themes of political analysis, including the forms, relationality, and technologies of power, before using these themes in the genealogy of the genesis of the EC, the common market, justice and home affairs, and the open method of coordination (Walters and Haahr 2005). In denaturalizing EU politics, Walters and Haahr (2005) argue that 'European integration can be reframed in terms of the governmentalization of Europe', and suggest that histories of EU freedom and security are two of the narratives to be found in their work.

Also located in the work of Foucault, although with an emphasis on discourse analysis rather than genealogy or governmentality, are Henrik Larsen's studies of member state and EU foreign policies. Larsen's (1997: 2) work is primarily aimed at developing 'a theoretical framework for dealing with beliefs in FPA [Foreign Policy Analysis] which takes into account the languages in which beliefs are expressed and their social nature'. Moving beyond the analysis of member state foreign policy, Larsen argues that 'along the lines of Foucault a discourse is understood as a limited range of possible statements promoting a limited range of meanings. Discourses constrain what it is possible to say' within Danish and EU foreign policy (Larsen 2002: 287; 2005).

Methods of genealogy and governmentality provide a means of analysing and understanding the power of the EU to shape the idea of Europe, European identity, the market, internal affairs, and foreign affairs. From this perspective, European integration theories are unconvincing in explaining how EU politics develops in the way it does, but by engaging in a historical revealing of the present it becomes possible to understand how EU politics assumed the governmental mentalities of technocratic coordination. Similarly, by analysing the discursive constructions of regulation and policy, we can begin to make sense of legal, economic, cultural, regional, and neighbourhood policies as power politics. However, power politics here is not the ability to shape the agenda, or negotiation, but the preferences themselves.

Deconstruction

Post-structuralist scholarship informed and inspired by the work of Foucault and Derrida is to be found in the work of a number of EU politics scholars exploring the construction and structure of truth, threat, self, and other. What this scholarship shares is a commitment to deconstructing narratives within Europe and the EU in order to understand and reveal alternative truths and possibilities. Undoubtedly Derrida's own work is significant in this respect, with his scholarship on Europe and the EU emphasizing the extent to which, more than anything else, European integration is and should be a journey towards the other (Derrida 1992b; Borradori 2003). Such a journey, argues Derrida (1992b: 29, 48), 'is necessary to make ourselves the guardians of an idea of Europe, of a difference of Europe, *but* of a Europe that consists precisely in not closing itself off in its own identity and advancing itself in an exemplary way toward what it is not … to advance itself as a heading for the universal essence of humanity'. Crucially, for Derrida, this other heading is towards a 'new figure of Europe' recalling the memory of a European promise to its 'advanced non-theological political culture' in order to contribute to cosmopolitan democracy, international law, and emancipation for all (Derrida 1992b: 48, 76–8; Borradori 2003: 113, 116, 140, 170).

Kristeva's (1982, 1991) psychoanalytic post-structuralism argues that the other is always part of the self – an abject-foreigner which is part of our conscious and unconscious selves. Kristeva's work uses psychoanalysis to understand 'the creation of self as an internal psychological process' in which 'the other exists in our minds through imagination even when he or she is not physically present' (Kinnvall 2004: 753). Kristeva's (1982: 4–5, 155–6) work helps to understand the way in which Europeans deal with the horrors of fascism and Nazi crimes, such as Auschwitz, by abjecting (rejecting the abjectness) of their past selves and projecting them onto others. Kristeva (1991: 191–2) advocates recognizing that 'the foreigner is within us' and 'by recognizing *our* uncanny strangeness we shall neither suffer from it nor enjoy it from the outside'. Kristeva (1991: 192–5; 2000) sees European integration as part of a cosmopolitan ethic that recognizes the strangers to ourselves, the othering practices of nationalism, and a different type of freedom.

Beyond Derrida and Kristeva, and within the study of EU politics, Diez's (2001) post-structuralist work has probably made the greatest impact towards an understanding of 'the politics of integration discourse'. Diez's (1997, 1999) studies of 'speaking Europe' have sought to understand the role of language in constructing EU politics, as well as the implications of using Foucault and Derrida to deconstruct and open up space for alternative EU constructions or horizons. Diez's (2002, 2005) work goes beyond the deconstruction of integration discourses to understand the construction of EU self and others in world politics through his examination of discourse of EU 'normative power' and relations with Turkey and Cyprus.

Focusing on post-structuralist understandings of EU securitizations in the areas of migration and policing, Jef Huysmans and Didier Bigo both engage in critical approaches to the study of liberty and security. Huysmans's (2000) work emphasizes the way in which the incorporation of migration issues into the EU has been 'securitized' in the sense that immigration and asylum, the Schengen and Dublin arrangements, and the third pillar of the TEU have been politicized as 'threats' to European and national securities. Challenging 'spill-over' accounts for European integration, Huysmans (2005) argues that a Foucauldian emphasis on the technologies of government and control provide a means of better understanding the securitization of the area of freedom, justice, and security. Similarly, Bigo's (1996) work emphasizes the way in which ad hoc intergovernmental arrangements for policing Europe such as Trevi and Schengen are linked together in the third pillar of the TEU and Europol, with the effect of aggregating and securitizing previously discrete policing issues. Bigo draws on Bourdieu's theory of field to argue that the EU's security field increasingly securitizes and wraps together internal and external issues like a Möbius ribbon, where the borders between issues such as migration, asylum, crime, unemployment, religious zealotry, terrorism, and failed states become difficult to detect (Bigo and Guild 2005).

In using deconstruction to analyse and understand EU politics, post-structural scholars are seeking to denaturalise stories about European integration which are spoken as common sense. Hence, stories about where the EU is heading, what it is, what it does, and how it becomes more secure, are all interrogated in the search for emancipation. But deconstruction is but the first step, as the release from naturalized truths also brings responsibilities regarding where and what the EU should be heading/doing/securing. Thus, post-structural scholars advocate the alternative possibilities of EU politics in terms of non-theological political culture, reconciliation with otherness, reflexive *foreigning* policy, and the desecuritizing of migration and criminal matters in EU politics.

FEMINIST PERSPECTIVES

Feminist perspectives on EU politics address the most omnipresent aspect of all politics – the construction of difference, in particular, gender differences. Feminist perspectives are the strongest in terms of participants and contribution, but the most discriminated against in terms of exclusion from traditional EU political science. This may strike many as nonsensical, given the high profile of women in the discipline of EU politics. Clearly we must not confuse women with feminists. Rather, feminist scholarship highlights the pervasiveness of power relations embedded in social institutions such as EU political science and the EU institutions themselves – despite the

many successful examples we can think of, gender equality is nowhere near being achieved. The perspectives considered here broadly share the position that: 'Feminism is characterized by a focus on gender as a central organizing principle of social life; an emphasis on the concept of power and the ways that it affects social relations; and an unwavering commitment to progressive social change' (Millns and Whitty 1999: 35, in Shaw 2000: 412).

Like all the perspectives considered here, feminist scholarship on the EU was to be found during the Cold War era, as part of second wave feminism during the 1970s and 1980s (see Hoskyns 1985; Vallance and Davies 1986; Buckley and Anderson 1988; Prechal and Burrows 1990; Pillinger 1992). Similarly, the post-Cold War period has seen an eruption of feminist work which seeks to contribute to and reconfigure EU politics and EU political science, including more liberal feminism emphasizing rights and equality, as well as more radical feminism focusing on gender constructions and patriarchy (see Elman 1996; Hoskyns 1996a; Monk and Garcia-Ramon 1996; Rees 1998). This differentiation between the politics of equality and the politics of difference partially reflects the 'Wollstonecraft dilemma' within feminist perspectives – should feminists seek equal rights, or recognition and support for difference? (Rees 1998: 29; Lombardo 2003). However, the range of feminist scholarship goes far beyond this differentiation to also include, for example, constructionist, critical, and poststructural feminisms (see Shaw 2000: 412; Kronsell 2005: 1036 n. 3). Unfortunately, it is simply not possible for me to attempt to cover most of this feminist scholarship, so instead I will try to illustrate what feminist perspectives bring to EU political science by looking at some examples of work on EU policies, and work on EU politics. Whereas the former has tended to focus on equal rights, the latter tends to focus on the institutionalization of masculinity and the implications this has for power relations within the EU. Broadly speaking, EU feminist scholarship has followed three different routes to gender equality, emphasizing equal treatment, positive action/discrimination, and gender mainstreaming (Rees 1998; Booth and Bennett 2002). My overview of feminist scholarship and theorizing should be seen as complementary to Elisabeth Prugl's chapter on gender policy-making in this volume. As is clear, it is important not to compound women, gender, and feminism (see discussion in Carver et al. 1998; Weber 2005: 81–101).

Feminist EU Policies

Feminist scholarship on EU policies began with an emphasis on article 119 of the Treaty of Rome which asserted 'that men and women should receive equal pay for equal work' (Elman 1996: 1; Rees 1998: 1). Article 119 on equal treatment became the first focal point of feminist EU scholarship following activism in Belgium on behalf of Gabrielle Defrenne which established the direct effect of the equal pay principle in 1976 (Hoskyns 1996b: 15–17). Further scholarship focused on equal treatment law and policies during Hoskyns's 'hard times' of the 1980s, concerning pay, employment, social security, self-employment, pregnancy, and parenthood (Fredman 1992; Gregory 1992; Hoskyns 1992).

The end of the Cold War division of Europe saw new feminist scholarship on EU enlargement, including perspectives from central Europe (Havelkova 2000; Watson 2000; Bretherton 2001; Matynia 2003; Pető and Manners 2006). What this work shared are fairly unremitting critiques of the way in which EU enlargement policies has failed to mainstream gender equality and of the way in which central European feminists were often sidelined in the process. In particular, bitter criticisms have been raised over the way in which the EUs liberalizing approach often colluded with central European reactionary politics to roll-back the achievements of socialist equality and reproductive rights for women (Alsop and Hockey 2001; Matynia 2003).

More recent work on EU policies has begun to address the external actions of the Union, in particular with an emphasis on development policy

and ACP relations (Turner 1999; Painter and Ulmer 2002; Lister 2003). Scholarship here focuses on the inclusion of gender in development relations since 2001, highlighting the problems of existing institutional structures attempting to adapt to new practices without sufficient funding, staff, or training in order to do so. Painter and Ulmer (2002) argue that the policy of attempting to mainstream gender into development cooperation has sought to promote gender 'everywhere', but in practice the absence of resources, trained staff, legal provisions, and the abandonment of positive discrimination has led to gender being 'nowhere'.

Feminist scholarship on EU policies has led the way in bringing critical voices to the study of the EU, with particular emphases on gender, social, and rights policies, as well as more limited interest in enlargement and development policies. What is interesting about these feminist perspectives is the way in which the more critical work originated from within legal studies, then spread to social policy and political science. What is also clear is that most of the writers are participants, reaffirming the critical, emancipatory aims of feminist scholarship. However, with the end of the Cold War, and the 1980s pre-occupation with the market, feminist scholarship turned towards questions of politics in the EU.

Feminist EU Politics

Despite the creation of the EC Women's Bureau/Equal Opportunities Unit in Commission DG Employment and Social Affairs (1976/1994), the Advisory Committee on Equal Opportunities (1982), and the first two Action Programmes on the Promotion of Equal Opportunities (1982–85 and 1986–90), by the 1990s it became clear that they were 'failing to bring change to women's lives' (Booth and Bennett 2002: 437). During the 1980s the Actions Programmes and the creation of an equality networks by the Commission moved the agenda from equal treatment to positive action, with an emphasis on addressing the question of disadvantage in gender equality.

A number of feminist scholars have charted how women's policy networks, in particular the European Women's Lobby (EWL) created in 1990, together with the Women's Committee of the European Parliament have been influential in promoting positive action, as well as moving the gender equality debate into the development of gender mainstreaming during the 1990s (Bretherton and Sperling 1996; Cockburn 1997; Mazey 1998). What this scholarship argues is that the networking together of the EWL, the EP Women's Committee, the Equal Opportunities Unit, and the Advisory Committee together with the European Trades Union Congress and a much wider network of interested organizations and activist scholars has contributed towards the third debate of EU feminism – gender mainstreaming.

Rather than 'tinkering' with equal treatment legislation, or 'tailoring' positive action measures, gender mainstreaming is advocated by feminist scholars as a means of 'transforming' the pre-existing malestream organizations, structures, and norms in order to 'feminize the mainstream' (Rees 1998: 42–6). As Rees summarizes, 'the essence of the mainstreaming approach is to seek to identify these hidden, unrecognized and unremarked ways in which systems and structures are biased in favour of men, and to redress the balance' (Rees 1998: 189). The first step towards challenging the 'malestream' in EU politics began with the coincidence of the fourth and fifth Action Programmes on the Promotion of Equal Opportunities (1996–2000 and 2001–05), and feminist scholarship on integrating gender – a coincidence of 'intellectual and 'real world' mainstreaming' (Mazey 2000).

This coincidence of feminist mainstreaming has contributed to a series of significant interventions in EU politics, including the work of Beveridge et al. (2000), Mazey (2001), Shaw (2000; 2002), Liebert with Sifft (2003), and contributions to Rossilli's (2000) edited volume. One interesting aspect of the mainstreaming approach has been the calling into question of the EU's gender representation of the EU and its constitution through a process of gender auditing. Scholars such as Diaz and Millns

(2007) and Hoskyns (2003) critically analysed the convention and Constitution for Europe from a feminist perspective, arguing that both were unrepresentative of women and women's views, as well as suggesting this would result in ratification problems. However, there is also a critique to be raised against gender mainstreaming which has often remained focused on implementation issues rather than power challenges and shifts.

The last bastion for feminist analysis is undoubtedly European integration theory, although even this fortress has been recently breached (Hoskyns 2004; Kronsell 2005). Hoskyns (2004: 224) argues that gender-sensitive integration theory would have to start with social relations, be honest about subjectivity, and 'it would need to be one that sought to theorize change, transformation, and power, and had a broad definition of the political'. Discouragingly, Hoskyns concludes that 'both the core of EU policy-making and many of the key concepts in theorizing European integration remain virtually untouched' which is where Annica Kronsell's feminist analysis takes off (Hoskyns 2004: 233; Kronsell 2005: 1023). Kronsell systematically critiques existing malestream theories of 'national interest'; transnational, multilevel, and network governance; and institutional norms in order to envision integration from a feminist viewpoint. In conclusion, Kronsell (2005: 1035–6) argues that existing integration theories leave the 'male-as-norm unquestioned and invisible' and 'work from a simplistic view of power'.

Feminist perspectives on EU politics are now raising the most important and interesting questions about the EU as a democratic, participatory, and just polity. Feminist scholarship has gone beyond an emphasis on rights and policies, towards the gendered nature of the polity itself. Such studies revolve around questions of gender mainstreaming, representative politics, gender auditing, and integration theory. Feminist perspectives have undoubtedly been encouraged and facilitated by the growth of European networks such as EWL and ATHENA, as well as the launching of wall-breaking new journals such as the *European Journal of Women's Studies*, the *Journal of*

European Public Policy, and *Feminist Legal Studies*.

CONCLUSION: CRITICAL, NOT MONSTROUS

> Many circumstances can conspire to extinguish scientific discoveries, especially those that cause discomfort about our culture's sacred norms. As a species we cling to the familiar, comforting conformities of the mainstream. However, 'convention' penetrates more deeply than we tend to admit. Even if we lack a proper name for and knowledge of the history of a specific philosophy or thought style, all of us are embedded in our own safe 'reality'. Our outlooks shape what we see and how we know (Margulis 1998: 3, in Manners 2003a: 67).

As I suggest from the outset, the wide variety of critical perspectives on EU politics considered here do not present a parsimonious (i.e. thrifty) means to post-Cold War EU political science. The multitude of perspectives which I briefly, and undoubtedly unfairly, represented here do not provide cheap, quick, or even particularly new ways of understanding EU politics in the 21st century. But what they do share is a means of challenging the comfortable conventions of Cold War political science which has sought to extinguish the critical understanding of the EU in its current context. As Lynn Margulis has suggested in the 'natural' sciences, the familiar conformity of mainstream science can conspire to extinguish new discoveries – it is often found to be producing not the unknown, but reproducing the known.

Critical perspectives also share a concern for the role of power in their analyses – the power to pre-determine the questions asked, the power to pre-determine the theories used, and the power to shape what is and is not allowed in EU politics. A fuller understanding of this power in EU political science becomes clearer when asking what EU political science is not considered 'normal science'? Which papers are not included in an EU political science conference? Which articles are inadmissible in which EU political science journals? Which EU political scientists will not get which jobs? Critical perspectives have no shared accounts for this power – for some it is class and capital, for others it is hegemony and culture, whilst others still look to identity and difference. But what critical perspectives do share in this respect is a concern to emancipate humans from the conditions created by traditional explanations for the modern European Union.

Bringing these three shared concerns together – critical of conventions; critical of power; and concerned with emancipation – I would reiterate that the critical perspectives discussed here present distinctively *political* theories. Just as history is written by the winners, and knowledge reflects power, so conventional EU political science reproduces these power structures. Critical perspectives are thus political in that they understand they are not just analysing, but fighting power conformities, in order to more fully understand EU politics.

Clearly these perspectives are not new in political science, but they are relatively new to EU political science, reflecting the loosening of the intellectual straitjacket. Thus, these critical perspectives provide a means to re-connect EU political science to the rest of the social sciences in a political way. They also offer the opportunity to escape the normative wasteland and monstrous claims of 'normal science' of economistic pathologies – that path leads only to tighter straightjackets (see Strange 1991; Green and Shapiro 1996). Examples of these types of claims include the stories told by Dowding (2000: 139), Schneider et al. (2002: 5), and Pollack (2005: 35) that rational choice theory, comparative politics, and positivism are the new 'normal science' of EU politics. Such claims are hilariously summed up in Hix's (2005: 13) assertion that 'the basic theoretical assumptions of modern political science can be expressed in the following 'fundamental equation of politics': preferences + institutions = outcomes' (see also Manners 2003a: 71–3). It is worth noting that most of the contributions to this volume would not fit this definition of 'normal science'.

Finally, I am not arguing that critical perspectives bring more parsimonious, less falsifiable, or more generalizable explanations. I am not claiming a new turn in theory, or the achievement of a Kuhnian paradigm of 'normal science' (Kuhn 1962). The critical perspectives I have discussed here are simply multi-perspectival – they see EU politics from a variety of perspectives; they know EU politics from a multitude of vistas. These critical perspectives are political theories that acknowledge the presence of other political theories, and should not be considered 'one-eyed monsters – one-eyed because they [are] oblivious of politics; monsters because they [are] so arrogant towards all outsiders' (Strange 1991: 33 in van Ham 2001: 11). And most important of all, they make another Europe possible.

ACKNOWLEDGEMENTS

I am particularly grateful to Catarina Kinnvall, Annica Kronsell, Björn Fägersten, Andreas Bieler, Adam David Morton, and the editors, as well as Torbjörn Bergman, Vivienne Boon, Sverker Gustavsson, Anders Hellström, and Magnus Jerneck for their helpful comments.

REFERENCES

Adorno, T. and Horkheimer, M. (1979) *Dialectic of Enlightenment*. London: Verso.

Alsop, R. and Hockey, J. (2001) 'Women's reproductive lives as a symbolic resource in central and eastern Europe', *European Journal of Women's Studies*, 8(4): 454–71.

Bailey, D. (2006) 'Governance or the crisis of governmentality? Applying critical state theory at the European level', *Journal of European Public Policy*, 13(1): 16–33.

Benhabib, S. (2002) 'In search of Europe's borders: the politics of migration in the European Union', *Dissent*, 49(4): 33–9.

Benhabib, S. (2004) *The Rights of Others: Aliens, Residents and Citizens*. Cambridge: Cambridge University Press.

Bernstein, R. (1985) *Habermas and Modernity*. Cambridge: Polity.

Beveridge, F., Nott, S. and Kylie, S. (2000) *Making Women Count: Integrating Gender into Law and Policy-making*. Aldershot: Ashgate.

Bieler, A. and Morton, A.D. (eds) (2001) *Social Forces in the Making of the New Europe: The Restructuring of European Social Relations in the Global Political Economy*. Basingstoke: Palgrave.

Bieler, A. and Morton, A.D. (2003) 'Globalisation, the state and class struggle: a 'critical economy' engagement with open Marxism', *British Journal of Politics and International Relations*, 5(4): 467–99.

Bieler, A. and Morton, A.D. (2004) '"Another Europe is possible"? Labour and social movements at the European Social Forum', *Globalizations*, 1(2): 305–27.

Bieling, H.-J. and Steinhilber, J. (eds) (2000) *Europäische Konfiguration: Dimensionen einer kritischen Integrationstheorie*. Münster: Westfälisches Dampfboot.

Bigo, D. (1996) *Polices en réseaux: L'expérience européenne*. Paris: Presses de la Fondation nationale des sciences politiques.

Bigo, D. and Guild, E. (2005) *Controlling Frontiers: Free Movement into and Within Europe*. Aldershot: Ashgate.

Bohman, J. (2004) 'Constitution making and democratic innovation: the European Union and transnational governance', *European Journal of Political Theory*, 3(3): 315–37.

Bonefeld, W. (2001) *Politics of Europe: Monetary Union and Class*. Basingstoke: Palgrave.

Booth, C. and Bennett, C. (2002) 'Gender mainstreaming in the European Union: towards a new conception and practice of equal opportunities', *European Journal of Women's Studies*, 9(4): 430–46.

Borradori, G. (2003) *Philosophy in a Time of Terror: Dialogues with Jürgen Habermas and Jacques Derrida*. Chicago, IL: University of Chicago Press.

Bourdieu, P. (1998) 'A reasoned utopia and economic fatalism', *New Left Review*, 227: 125–30.

Bourdieu, P. (2001) *Firing Back: Against the Tyranny of the Market 2*. London: The New Press.

Bretherton, C. (2001) 'Gender mainstreaming and EU enlargement: swimming against the tide?' *Journal of European Public Policy*, 8(1): 60–82.

Bretherton, C. and Sperling, L. (1996) 'Women's networks and the European Union: towards an inclusive approach?' *Journal of Common Market Studies*, 34(4): 487–508.

Buckley, M. and Anderson, M. (eds) (1988) *Women, Equality and Europe*. London: Macmillan.

Burnham, P. (1999) 'The politics of economic management in the 1990s', *New Political Economy*, 4(1): 37–54.

Cafruny, A. (2003) 'Europe, the United States, and neoliberal (dis)order: is there a coming crisis of the Euro?', in A. Cafruny and M. Ryner (eds), *A Ruined Fortress? Neoliberal Hegemony and Transformation in Europe*. Lanham, MD: Rowman and Littlefield. pp. 285–305.

Cafruny, A. and Ryner, M. (eds) (2003) *A Ruined Fortress? Neoliberal Hegemony and Transformation in Europe.* Lanham, MD: Rowman and Littlefield.

Calhoun, C. (1995) *Critical Social Theory.* Oxford: Blackwell.

Calhoun, C. (2001) 'The virtues of inconsistency: identity and plurality in the conceptualization of Europe', in L.-E. Cederman (ed.), *Constructing Europe's Identity: The External Dimension.* Boulder, CO: Lynne Rienner. pp. 35–56.

Calhoun, C. (2003) 'The democratic integration of Europe: interests, identity, and the public sphere', in M. Berezin and M. Schain (eds), *Europe without Borders: Remapping Territory, Citizenship, and Identity in a Transnational Age.* Baltimore: Johns Hopkins University Press. pp. 243–74.

Carchedi, G. (2001) *For Another Europe: A Class Analysis of European Economic Integration.* London: Verso.

Carver, T., Cochran, M. and Squires, J. (1998) 'Gendering Jones: feminisms, IRs, masculinities', *Review of International Studies*, 24(2): 283–97.

Chafer, T. and Cooper, N. (eds) (2003) 'Special issue on post-colonialism', *Journal of Contemporary European Studies*, 11(2): 159–229.

Cockburn, C. (1997) 'Gender in an international space: trade union women as European social actor', *Women's Studies International Forum*, 20(4): 459–70.

Cole, M. and Dale, G. (eds) (1999) *The European Union and Migrant Labour.* Oxford: Berg Publishers.

Cox, R. (1981) 'Social forces, states and world order: beyond international relations theory', *Millennium: Journal of International Studies*, 10(2): 126–55.

Curtin, D. (1997) *Postnational Democracy: The European Union in Search of a Political Philosophy.* The Hague: Kluwer Law International.

Curtin, D. (2003) 'Private interest representation or civil society deliberation? A contemporary dilemma for European Union governance', *Social and Legal Studies*, 12(1): 55–75.

Delanty, G. (1995) *Inventing Europe: Idea, Identity, Reality.* Basingstoke: Macmillan.

Delanty, G. and Rumford, C. (2005) *Rethinking Europe: Social Theory and the Implications of Europeanization.* London: Routledge.

Derrida, J. (1992a) 'Before the law', in D. Attridge (ed.), *Acts of Literature.* London: Routledge. pp. 181–220.

Derrida, J. (1992b) *The Other Heading: Reflections on Today's Europe.* Indianapolis: Indiana University Press.

Diaz, M.M. and Millns, S. (2007, forthcoming) 'Gender auditing the Constitution for Europe', in M.M. Diaz and S. Millns (eds), *Gender Equality and the Future of the European Union.* Basingstoke: Palgrave.

Diez, T. (1997) 'International ethics and European integration: federal state or network horizon?', *Alternatives*, 22: 287–312.

Diez, T. (1999) *Die EU lesen: Diskursive Knotenpunkte in der britischen Europadebatte.* Opladen: Leske und Budrich.

Diez, T. (2001) 'Speaking 'Europe': the politics of integration discourse', in T. Christiansen, K.E. Jørgensen and A. Wiener (eds), *The Social Construction of Europe.* London: Sage. pp. 85–100.

Diez, T. (ed.) (2007) *The European Union and the Cyprus Conflict: Modern Conflict, Postmodern Union.* Manchester: Manchester University Press.

Diez, T. (2005) 'Constructing the self and changing others: reconsidering "normative power Europe"', *Millennium: Journal of International Studies*, 33(3): 613–36.

Diez, T. and Steans, J. (eds) (2005) 'Forum on Habermas and international relations', *Review of International Studies*, 31(1): 127–209.

Dowding, K. (2000) 'Institutionalist research on the European Union', *European Union Politics*, 1(1): 125–44.

Elbe, S. (2001) '"We good Europeans …': genealogical reflections on the *idea* of Europe', *Millennium: Journal of International Studies*, 30(2): 259–83.

Elbe, S. (2003) *Europe: A Nietzschean Perspective.* London: Routledge.

Elman, R.A. (ed.) (1996) *Sexual Politics and the European Union: The New Feminist Challenge.* Oxford: Berghahn.

Eriksen, E.O. (ed.) (2005) *Making the European Polity: Reflexive integration in the European Union.* London: Routledge.

Eriksen, E.O. and Fossum, J.E. (eds) (2000) *Democracy in the European Union: Integration Through Deliberation?* London: Routledge.

Fredman, S. (1992) 'European Community discrimination law: a critique', *Industrial Law Journal*, 21: 119–35.

Galtung, J. (1973) *The European Community: A Superpower in the Making.* London: Harper Collins.

Gill, S. (ed.) (1993) *Gramsci, Historical Materialism and International Relations.* Cambridge: Cambridge University Press.

Gill, S. (1998) 'European governance and new constitutionalism: economic and monetary union and alternatives to disciplinary neoliberalism in Europe', *New Political Economy*, 3(1): 5–26.

Gill, S. (2003) 'A neo-gramscian approach to European integration', in A. Cafruny and M. Ryner (eds), *A Ruined Fortress? Neoliberal Hegemony and Transformation in Europe.* Oxford: Rowman and Littlefield. pp. 47–70.

Gramsci, A. (1971) *Selections from the Prison Notebooks.* London: Lawrence and Wishart.

Green, D. and Shapiro, I. (1996) *Pathologies of Rational Choice Theory: A Critique of Applications in Political Science.* New Haven, CT: Yale University Press.

Gregory, J. (1992) 'Equal pay/comparable worth: national statues and case law in Britain and the USA', in P. Kahn and E. Meehan (eds), *Equal Pay/Comparable Worth in the UK and USA.* London: Macmillan.

Habermas, J. (1986) *The Theory of Communicative Action: Reason and the Rationalization of Society, Vol. 1.* Cambridge: Polity.

Habermas, J. (1989) *The Theory of Communicative Action: Critique of Functionalist Reason, Vol. 2.* Cambridge: Polity.

Habermas, J. (1992) *The Structural Transformation of the Public Sphere: Inquiry into a Category of Bourgeois Society.* Cambridge: Polity.

Habermas, J. (2001) *The Postnational Constellation: Political Essays.* Cambridge: Polity.

Habermas, J. and Derrida, J. (2003) 'February 15, or what binds Europe together: a plea for a common foreign policy, beginning in the core of Europe', *Constellations*, 10(3): 291–7.

Havelkova, H. (2000) 'Abstract citizenship? Women and power in the Czech Republic', in B. Hobson (ed.), *Gender and Citizenship in Transition.* Basingstoke: Palgrave. pp. 118–38.

Hay, C. (2002) *Political Analysis: A Critical Introduction.* Basingstoke: Palgrave.

Hix, S. (2005) *Political System of the European Union*, 2nd ed. Basingstoke: Palgrave.

Holland, S. (1980) *UnCommon Market: Capital, Class and Power in the European Community.* London: Macmillan.

Hoskyns, C. (1985) 'Women's equality and the European Community', *Feminist Review*, 20: 71–88.

Hoskyns, C. (1992) 'The European Community's policy on women in the context of 1992', *Women's Studies International Forum*, 15(1): 21–8.

Hoskyns, C. (1996a) *Integrating Gender: Women, Law, and Politics in the European Union.* London: Verso.

Hoskyns, C. (1996b) 'The European Union and the women within: an overview of women's rights policy', in R.A. Elman (ed.), *Sexual Politics and the European Union.* Oxford: Berghahn. pp. 13–22.

Hoskyns, C. (2003) *Gender Equality and the Convention: A Comment.* London: The Federal Trust.

Hoskyns, C. (2004) 'Gender perspectives', in A. Wiener and T. Diez (eds), *European Integration Theory.* Oxford: Oxford University Press. pp. 217–36.

Huysmans, J. (2000) 'The European Union and the securitization of migration', *Journal of Common Market Studies*, 38(5): 751–77.

Huysmans, J. (2005) *The Politics of Insecurity: Security, Migration and Asylum in the EU.* London: Routledge.

Jacobsson, K. (1997) 'Discursive will formation and the question of legitimacy in European politics', *Scandinavian Political Studies*, 20(1): 69–90.

Jay, M. (1996) *The Dialectical Imagination: History of the Frankfurt School and the Institute of Social Research, 1923–50.* Berkeley, CA: University of California Press.

Jessop, B. (2004) 'The European Union and recent transformations in statehood', in S.P. Riekmann, M. Mokre and M. Latzer (eds), *The State of Europe: Transformations of Statehood from a European Perspective.* Frankfurt: Campus.

Jupille, J. (2006) 'Knowing Europe: metatheory and methodology in European Union studies', in M. Cini and A. Bourne (eds), *European Union Studies.* Basingstoke: Palgrave. pp. 209–32.

Jörges, C. and Neyer, J. (1997) 'Transforming strategic interaction into deliberative problem-solving', *Journal of European Public Policy*, 4(4): 609–25.

Kauppi, N. (2005) *Democracy, Social Resources and Political Power in the European Union.* Manchester: Manchester University Press.

Kinnvall, C. (2004) 'Globalization and religious nationalism: self, identity, and the search for ontological self', *Political Psychology*, 25(5): 741–67.

Kinnvall, C. (2005) '"Not here, not now": the absence of a European Perestroika movement', in K.R. Monroe (ed.), *Perestroika!: The Raucous Rebellion in Political Science.* New Haven, CT: Yale University Press. pp. 21–44.

Kristeva, J. (1982) *Powers of Horror: An Essay in Abjection.* New York: Columbia University Press.

Kristeva, J. (1991) *Strangers to Ourselves.* New York: Columbia University Press.

Kristeva, J. (2000) 'Europe divided: politics, ethics, religion', in *Crisis of the European Subject.* New York: Other Press. pp. 111–62.

Kronsell, A. (2005) 'Gender, power and European integration theory', *Journal of European Public Policy*, 12(6): 1022–40.

Kuhn, T. (1962) *The Structure of Scientific Revolutions.* Chicago: University of Chicago Press.

Larsen, H. (1997) *Foreign Policy and Discourse Analysis: France, Britain and Europe.* London: Routledge.

Larsen, H. (2002) 'The EU: a global military actor?' *Cooperation and Conflict,* 37(3): 283–302.

Larsen, H. (2005) *Analysing the Foreign Policy of Small States in the European Union: The Case of Denmark.* Basingstoke: Palgrave.

Liebert, U. and Sifft, S. (eds) (2003) *Gendering Europeanisation.* Brussels: Peter Lang Publishers.

Linklater, A. (1996) 'Citizenship and sovereignty in the post-Westphalian state', *European Journal of International Relations,* 2(1): 77–103.

Linklater, A. (1998) *The Transformation of Political Community.* Cambridge: Polity.

Lister, M. (2003) 'Gender, development and EU foreign policy', in H. Mollett (ed.), *Europe in the World.* London: British Overseas NGOs for Development. pp. 95–9.

Lombardo, E. (2003) 'EU gender policy: trapped in the 'Wollstonecraft dilemma'?' *European Journal of Women's Studies,* 10(2): 159–80.

Lyotard, J.-F. (1984) *The Postmodern Condition: A Report on Knowledge.* Minnesota: University of Minnesota Press.

McCarthy, T. (1981) *The Critical Theory of Jürgen Habermas.* Cambridge, MA: MIT Press.

Mandel, E. (1970) *Europe vs. America? Contradictions of Imperialism.* London: New Left Books.

Manners, I. (2003a) 'Europaian studies', *Journal of Contemporary European Studies,* 11(1): 67–83.

Manners, I. (2003b) 'The missing tradition of the ES: including Nietzschean relativism and world imagination in extranational studies', *Millennium: Journal of International Studies,* 32(2): 241–64.

Manners, I. and Whitman, R. (2003) 'The 'difference engine': constructing and representing the international identity of the European Union', *Journal of European Public Policy,* 10(3): 380–404.

Margulis, L. (1998) *The Symbiotic Planet: A New Look at Life on Earth.* London: Orion.

Matynia, E. (2003) 'Provincializing global feminism: the Polish case', *Social Research,* 70(2): 499–530.

Mau, S. (2005) 'Democratic demand for a social Europe? Preferences of the European citizenry', *International Journal of Social Welfare,* 14(2): 76–85.

Mazey, S. (1998) 'The European Union and women's rights: from the Europeanization of national agendas to the nationalization of a European agenda?' *Journal of European Public Policy,* 5(1): 131–52.

Mazey, S. (2000) 'Introduction: integrating gender – intellectual and 'real world' mainstreaming', *Journal of European Public Policy,* 7(3): 333–45.

Mazey, S. (2001) *Gender Mainstreaming in the EU: Principles and Practice.* London: Kogan Page.

Millns, S. and Whitty, N. (eds) (1999) *Feminist Perspectives on Public Law.* London: Cavendish.

Monk, J. and Garcia-Ramon, M.D. (eds) (1996) *Women of the European Union: The Politics of Work and Daily Life.* London: Routledge.

Moss, B. (ed.) (2004) *Monetary Union in Crisis: The European Union as Neo-Liberal Construction.* Basingstoke: Palgrave.

Moss, B. and Michie, J. (eds) (1999) *Single European Currency in National Perspective: A Community in Crisis?* Basingstoke: Palgrave.

Neyer, J. (2003) 'Discourse and order in the EU', *Journal of Common Market Studies,* 41(4): 687–706.

Nietzsche, F. (1998) *On the Genealogy of Morals: A Polemic.* Oxford: Oxford Paperbacks.

Overbeek, H. (2004) 'Transnational class formation and concepts of control: towards a genealogy of the Amsterdam project in international political economy', *Journal of International Relations and Development,* 7(2): 113–41.

Painter, G. and Ulmer, K. (2002) *Everywhere and Nowhere: Assessing Gender Mainstreaming the European Community Development Cooperation.* London/Brussels: One World Action and APRODEV.

Peebles, G. (1997) '"A very eden of the innate rights of man"? A Marxist look at the European Union treaties and case law', *Law and Social Inquiry,* 22(3): 581–618.

Petó, A. and Manners, I. (2006) 'The European Union and the value of gender equality', in S. Lucarelli and I. Manners (eds), *Values and Principles in European Union Foreign Policy.* London: Routledge. pp. 97–113.

Pillinger, J. (1992) *Feminising the Market: Women's Pay and Employment in the European Community.* Basingstoke: Macmillan.

Pollack, M. (2005) 'Theorising EU policy-making', in H. Wallace, W. Wallace and M. Pollack (eds), *Policy-Making in the European Union,* 5th ed. Oxford: Oxford University Press. pp. 13–48.

Prechal, S. and Burrows, N. (1990) *European Community Law Relating to Gender Discrimination.* Aldershot: Dartmouth.

Rees, T. (1998) *Mainstreaming Equality in the European Union.* London: Routledge.

Rhodes, M. (2005) '"Varieties of capitalism" and the political economy of European welfare states', *New Political Economy,* 10(3): 363–70.

Rosamond, B. (2000) *Theories of European Integration.* Basingstoke: Macmillan.

Rossilli, M. (ed.) (2000) *Gender Policies in the European Union.* Brussels: Peter Lang.

Ruggie, J.G. (1993) 'Territoriality and beyond: problematizing modernity in international relations', *International Organisation*, 47(1): 139–74.

Rumford, C. (2002) *The European Union: A Political Sociology.* Oxford: Blackwell.

Rumford, C. and Murray, P. (2003) 'Do we need a core curriculum in European Union studies?' *European Political Science*, 3(1): 85–92.

Rupert, M. and Smith, H. (eds) (2002) *Historical Materialism and Globalisation: Essays on Continuity and Change.* London: Routledge.

Ryner, M. (2004) 'Neo-liberalization of social democracy: the Swedish case', *Comparative European Politics*, 2: 97–119.

Schneider, G., Gabel, M. and Hix, S. (2002) 'Editorial note', *European Union Politics*, 3(1): 5–6.

Shaw, J. (2000) 'Importing gender: the challenge of feminism and the analysis of the EU legal order', *Journal of European Public Policy*, 7(3): 406–31.

Shaw, J. (2002) 'The European Union and gender mainstreaming: constitutionally embedded or comprehensively marginalised?' *Feminist Legal Studies*, 10(3): 213–26.

Sjursen, H. (2002) 'Why expand?: The question of legitimacy and justification in the EU's enlargement policy', *Journal of Common Market Studies*, 40(3): 491–513.

Sjursen, H. (2006) 'The European Union as a 'normative power': how can this be?' *Journal of European Public Policy*, 13(2): 235–51.

Smith, H. (1998) 'Actually existing foreign policy – or not? The European Union and Latin America', in J. Peterson and H. Sjursen (eds), *A Common Foreign Policy for Europe?* London: Routledge. pp. 152–68.

Smith, H. (2002) 'The politics of regulated liberalism: a historical materialist approach to European integration', in M. Rupert and H. Smith (eds), *Historical Materialism and Globalisation: Essays on Continuity and Change.* London: Routledge. pp. 257–83.

Smith, S. (2004) 'Singing our world into existence: international relations theory and September 11', *International Studies Quarterly*, 48: 499–515.

Steans, J. (2006) *Gender and International Relations: Issues, Debates and Future Directions*, 2nd ed. Cambridge: Polity Press.

Strange, S. (1991) 'An eclectic approach', in C. Murphy and R. Tooze (eds), *The New International Political Economy.* Boulder: Lynne Rienner. pp. 33–49.

Sykes, R. (2005) 'Crisis? What crisis? EU enlargement and the political economy of European Union social policy', *Social Policy and Society*, 4(2): 207–15.

Tausch, A. and Herrmann, P. (2001) *Globalization and European Integration.* Hauppauge, NY: Nova Science Publishers.

Turner, E. (1999) 'The EU's development policy and gender', in M. Lister (ed.), *New Perspectives on European Union Development Cooperation.* Oxford: Westview. pp. 29–58.

Vallance, E. and Davies, E. (1986) *Women of Europe: Women MEPs and Equality Policy.* Cambridge: Cambridge University Press.

van Apeldoorn, B. (2002) *Transnational Capital and the Struggle over European Integration.* London: Routledge.

van Apeldoorn, B., Overbeek, H. and Ryner, M. (2003) 'Theories of European integration: a critique', in A. Cafruny and M. Ryner (eds), *A Ruined Fortress? Neoliberal Hegemony and Transformation in Europe.* Lanham, MD: Rowman and Littlefield. pp. 17–45.

van Ham, P. (2001) *European Integration and the Postmodern Condition: Governance, Democracy, Identity.* London: Routledge.

Walters, W. and Haahr, J.H. (2005) *Governing Europe: European Integration and Political Reason.* London: Routledge.

Ward, I. (1995) 'Identity and difference: the European Union and postmodernism', in J. Shaw and G. More (eds), *New Legal Dynamics of European Union.* Oxford: Clarendon Press. pp. 15–28.

Ward, I. (2001) 'Beyond constitutionalism: the search for a European political imagination', *European Law Journal*, 7(1): 24–40.

Ward, I. (2003) *A Critical Introduction to European Law.* London: Lexis Nexis.

Warleigh, A. (2003) *Democracy in the European Union: Theory, Practice and Reform.* London: Sage.

Watson, P. (2000) 'Politics, policy and identity: EU eastern enlargement and east–west differences', *Journal of European Public Policy*, 7(3): 369–84.

Weber, C. (2005) *International Relations Theory: a Critical Introduction*, 2nd ed. London: Routledge.

5

Disciplinary Perspectives on EU Politics: History, Law, Economics and Sociology

Introduction

The subject of this volume is the *politics* of the European Union, and the primary disciplinary perspective of the book is that of political science. The discipline of political science, as we have seen in the last three chapters, incorporates a broad range of approaches to social-scientific inquiry, and should not be seen itself as a single, monolithic 'approach' to the study of the EU. Nevertheless, we would argue that related disciplines have made significant contributions to our understanding of the process of European integration, the workings of the EU as a political system, and the public policy outputs of that system. Even in a volume devoted primarily to EU politics, therefore, room should be made for a careful analysis of the contributions of neighbouring academic disciplines to our common object of study. Accordingly, this chapter features four relatively short essays by leading scholars from the disciplines of history, law, economics, and sociology, each examining the particular perspective(s) and the specific

contributions of their respective disciplines to the study of EU politics.

In the first essay, Alan S. Milward deftly examines both the tensions and the complementarities between history and political science as approaches to the study of the European Union. Whereas political science frequently studies current events and seeks to theorize and to generalize about patterns in social life, Milward suggests, historians most often focus on the more distant past (often defined by the opening of access to historical archives), privileging detail and accuracy in the analysis of specific events over generalization. Despite these inherent tensions, Milward argues, historians and political scientists studying the EU have increasingly asked similar questions, particularly about the process of political integration begun in the 1950s and still underway, and the prospect exists for mutual learning, as political scientists draw on historical accounts and historical records, and historians employ methods common to the social sciences. Historical accounts of the European project emerged, in the first instance, largely as a corrective to some of the more far-reaching claims of neofunctionalism, chronicling the significance of the EUs member governments, and of traditional high-politics concerns, in the creation and pursuit of the European project. Perhaps most importantly, Milward concludes, the sources and the methods of historical inquiry – as employed both by historians and by political scientists – remain central to our understanding of the integration process and the nature of the EU's 'supranational' system of governance.

In the second essay, Ramses Wessel examines the distinctive contribution of legal scholarship to the study of the EU. The significance of the EU legal order – the 'constitutionalization' of the Treaties by the European Court of Justice, the establishment of key legal principles like direct effect and supremacy, and the impressive level of compliance with EU legislation by the member states – has long been recognized by legal scholars, who have been present in EU studies, alongside political scientists, for many decades. In this context, Wessel focuses on the distinctive contribution of legal scholarship, which, he argues, focuses on the analysis and interpretation of the EU legal order as manifested in primary (or treaty), secondary (legislative) and case law. Akin to political scientists, many legal scholars have focused on the institutional structure of the EU, paying particular attention to the legal competences of the EU and its various institutional actors, the institutional balance among them, and the hard (binding) or soft nature of their legal acts. Other legal scholars, by contrast, have focused largely on the various substantive areas of EU law, with impressive concentrations of expertise emerging in areas such as free movement, competition, environment, and external relations law. While much of this scholarship has been in the legal positivist tradition of doctrinal interpretation, Wessels also detects a growing diversity and interdisciplinarity among EU legal scholars, who increasingly place law in its social context, examine broader constitutional questions, and

incorporate approaches from critical legal studies and post-modernism, asking new questions and building links to scholars from other disciplines.

The discipline of economics, according to Patrick Crowley and David Mayes in the third essay, has been largely model-based and 'scientific', which has discouraged the study of individual areas (such as Europe) and particular policy problems in the EU. As the authors also point out, however, economists have made selective forays into EU studies, providing distinctive analyses of fundamental policy problems such as the creation and operation of the European internal market, the design of Economic and Monetary Union, and the Stability and Growth Pact. Such analyses, while limited largely to 'headline' issues, have provided important scholarly and policy-relevant insights into questions like the size and content of an Optimal Currency Area in Europe, the design of the European Central Bank, the necessity and efficacy of the Stability and Growth Pact. Such studies, together with a smaller number of genuinely interdisciplinary studies in political economy, have offered a distinctive perspective on some of the core policy questions facing the EU at the start of the 21st century.

Turning to the discipline of sociology, in the final essay, Adrian Favell notes that, while sociological claims were central to the analyses of early integration theorists like Ernst Haas and Karl Deutsch, contemporary sociologists have been slow to take up the challenge of studying the possible emergence of an EU or pan-European society. Nevertheless, in a far-reaching survey of the field, Favell finds multiple sociological contributions to EU studies, including not only the relatively well-known application of sociological institutionalism to EU institutions, but also the application of organizational sociology, the analysis of a European public sphere and European identity, and rich empirical studies by sociologists of an emerging European 'political field'. Such pioneering approaches, Favell argues, point to the promise of sociology for illuminating the 'bottom-up', societal aspects of an integration process that has been studied, by political scientists and others, primarily from the top-down.

History, Political Science and European Integration

ALAN S. MILWARD

The relationship between history and political science is constrained by different methods and purposes of research. Political science seeks to reach generalized theoretical statements of explanation of particular trends, events or patterns of political behaviour which will serve as theoretical hypotheses for further research into related topics. History, in contrast, seeks the particular, which limits the scope of generalized theory. History privileges detail and suspects generalization of privileging inaccuracy. Political science suspects history of emphasizing the singular and the exceptional which merely obfuscate theory and generalization. Political science focuses much of its enquiry on recent or contemporary issues. History, in contrast, is constrained by the propensity of governments and other institutions and organizations to keep their written records secret for some time. In western European countries this is typically for 30 years after the event, thus severely limiting historical research into issues where political science is less impeded in its search for conclusions.

Nevertheless, both disciplines explore similar issues and frequently seek to homogenize their respective conclusions. Political science takes much material from written history. Historians often use social science methodologies. Both disciplines lie open to the criticism that the hypotheses from which their research springs are often philosophically marred and that their methods do not satisfactorily test their hypotheses. In Britain in the 1970s ministers and officials were persuaded that the very term 'social science' infringed an imaginary Academic Trade Descriptions Act. Later, in the 1980s, postmodernists and deconstructionists tended to reject the idea that historical research could produce conclusions which had more than a merely personal meaning. It took some time before the cage of this literary theory was broken open and the history of politics escaped into favour as a subject with something worthwhile to say.

Given their vulnerability, it seems wiser for the two disciplines to spend more time thinking usefully about each others' methods. That this is possible and advantageous is revealed by the persistent efforts of both to explain a contemporary development of major significance, the causes of the proliferation of supranational institutions in Europe. In its range and explanatory power the dialogue on this theme between them has been truly fertile. It has established wider perimeters within which a better understanding of the real nature and trajectory of 'integrated' Europe can be reached.

The initial tendency of historians, when faced with the growing phenomenon of political integration in Europe, was to explain it by a post-war resurgence of the role of idealism in foreign policy. It was interpreted as an effort to master the recent catastrophic past by achieving a political union of European states. Popular accounts of the European Communities incorporated this historical interpretation and there are still capable scholars who hold to the view that 'the idea of Europe' continued to drive integration forward. Parsons (2003), for example, who writes both as historian and political scientist, in a study which does credit to his ability as a historical researcher, adheres to that view because of the persistence of the idea in mobilizing policy at crucial moments. The written historical records of governments show only the persistence of some independent minds in trying to create something akin to a federal union. In the records of foreign policy formulation their influence appears minimal.

Political scientists, however, preferred in the two decades after 1945 what they construed as a more realistic view of such major political change. They connected it to the inter-war concept of functionalism, the argument that the state is ultimately shaped by the functions which it exists to fulfil. In so far as western European states had similar functional objectives, integration was driven forward by co-operation in their pursuit. Ernst Haas and Leon Lindberg, in their pioneering works, concentrated on the formation and function of the European Coal and Steel Community (ECSC) and argued that the fulfilment of that organization's function of regulating the coal and steel markets of western Europe pointed to a widespread acceptance that supranational regulation was the way forward to a much desired peace in Europe as well as to serving the politico-economic needs of the member-states of the Community (Haas 1958). For Haas and Lindberg, the ECSC was the archetype of similar institutions which would be created by the same need for medium-level international regulation. Functionalism was essentially an intellectual response to the evident dysfunctionality of European states in the years 1918–39. It made good sense after 1945 to turn to an interpretation of international politics which delineated a more peaceful and cooperative European order with a common institutional structure which would resolve its international technical problems by one common response.

The theory and practice of functionalism suggested that solutions would be more easily reached because the problems were essentially technical, of a relatively low level of political importance. They would be left outside the media spotlights of the nations, in a different place and by functionaries who were relatively little known. Haas, who adumbrated all these new possibilities so systematically as to make them into a theory, compared the incipient development of the regulatory supranation to that of an ideal federal system, the implication being that such was its destiny. Lindberg (1963), whose work supported Haas's efforts, was more cautious about Haas's views of the European future, although supportive of his heuristic comparison. Both attributed the political dynamics of the new Europe to 'spillover'. Any agreed technical solution would require, they argued, further technical solutions to make it function fully. Thus, the Europe of

such political solutions would increase as a rational and progressive one. The prime example of this progression seemed in the works of Haas and Lindberg to be the achievement of the common market of the first six member-states of the European Economic Community (EEC) and its commitment in the Treaty of Rome (1957) to a common tariff on its frontiers.

It was at this point that historical research began to offer an altogether different interpretation of the purpose of the European Communities and the common market by showing the primacy of high-level politics, the diplomacy of war and peace, in their formation. The EEC's purpose was, so historians began to argue, the long subjection of the German Federal Republic to the victorious Allied founders of the new Western Europe, and the purpose of that subjection was to hold divided Germany in place until a peace treaty which could be signed by all four occupying powers became possible. As far as the supranational aspects of the new Europe were concerned, the high-level decision-making would be by its constituent nation-states, with Germany not excluded but, nevertheless, an occupied state and a member only on approval (Gillingham 1992; Milward 1992; Spierenburg and Poidevin 1994).

It followed from this that the management of the common market would be ultimately determined by the same high-level political objectives that had governed its creation. The removal of internal barriers to trade within the common market was a process carefully regulated by the member-states (Milward and Brennan 1996; Brusse 1997). The settlements within the EEC were regulated by the European Payments Union with the same political objectives in mind (Kaplan and Schleiminger 1989; Eichengreen 1995). Tariff setting was in practice, Moravcsik (1998) was to show, a form of intergovernmental liberalism resting nevertheless on 'social purpose and state-power'. The state was far from merging into a new form of governance and international relations.

The achievement, albeit gradual, of a common tariff on the borders of the EEC, brought into being in 1958 by the Treaty of Rome, led to a rapid increase in trade values and volume between the member-states. Customs union theory, first developed by Viner (1950), had made just such a prediction. Indeed it is on the dynamic effects of customs union theory that Baldwin (1995) rests his argument that the Common Market of the EC/EU has been the prime cause of its own expansion. Idiosyncratic shocks to trade have consistently, he argues, generated demands for wider membership in the EEC/EC/EU.

Customs union theory always held open the possibility of an economic theory of integration being sufficiently powerful to replace much of the detail of political science and history in causal explanation. Were matters so simple, Norway, however, would by now be a long-established member of the European Union. Domestic political policy choices can evidently outweigh the allegedly inexorable force of increasing trade benefits. Viner readily admitted that customs unions could be protectionist as well as liberalizing. Gains from trade have been proportionately greater for trade within the boundaries of the EC than between non-member states and the EC. The proportion of Spain's total exports directed to the 12-country EC over its first 6 years of membership doubled. Over the 6 years before entry it stagnated. The share of Greek exports directed to the nine-country EEC stagnated over its first 7 years of membership. Over Portugal's first 2 years of membership the share of its total exports directed to EC markets increased promisingly; over the next 4 years it stagnated in spite of the growth of its exports to Spain. Simple interpretations of customs union theory are obviously not reliable for forecasting.

To suppose that EU tariff policies have been more or less a linear progression towards liberalization from 1958 to the present is also an untenable simplification. The radical change in policy, a determined attack on tariffs on manufactures linked to a programme to establish free movement for services and, not so successfully, for public procurement became effective only from 1 July 1987 with Ireland's ratification of the Single European Act. Not surprisingly, there is, because of national governments' protection of their own policymaking papers, as yet no detailed, research-based

history of the changes wrought by that Act. That void will not be filled until the true extent of state bargaining over these issues has been shown. 'Free Trade' is but a slogan. To measure its extent would be, no doubt, to reveal that state power and social purpose have not been renounced in the supranation, but remain as influences on governance.

Functionalism has survived, although it received serious blows from Haas's gradual rejection in his later works of some of its principles and importance. He came to question the linking of research into institutions of the EC/EU with the concept of institutional and human path-dependency. It imposed too sharp limits on the freedom of human will. In its place, he suggested, because behaviour is shaped by institutions, the sociological theory of how 'actors' construct their interests as a result of the historical context shaping their perception should be deployed (Haas 1968). Few historians would contest such a method; it would open a bridge between history and political science and would leave some room for what could be salvaged from the seeming wreckage of functionalism.

With Haas's reconsideration of functionalist theory it might well seem as though there had been up to that point no fruitful interaction between history and political science, unless destruction is counted as being fruitful. It might seem as though functionalism had been retained only because of its links to the emotional appeal of federalism. That was indeed one reason why political science did cling to it and to its teleological connotations, although what historians brought to light, when they were not themselves federalists, was the impossibility of the existing working methods of the EC transforming themselves into one federal government. However, Haas's interest in the sociological bases of political power meant also an interest in the legal rules within which decisions must be made. The 'actor' acted only within a coalition where he was placed and it was only within that coalition where political power resided.

In part, the concept of political power existing in such coalitions was evidently determined by the overall structure of government. European supranational governance in the last decade of the twentieth century was construed by Majone (1996a, 2001) as a late phase in the regulatory state foreshadowed by social purposes of 40 years earlier. With tasks delegated to 'agencies', under what rules did agencies act? In this light, the EC/EU could be understood as an aspect of the 'regulatory state' within a European pattern which chose the EC/EU as an 'agency' (Majone 1996b). This set of assumptions can ask important questions of the European Commission. Within the EC/EU, were the actors in the Commission a force for an advance towards federalism? Were they responsible for the Community's expansions?

Functionalism does not seem to have been a strong enough force to have underlain the five frontier expansions of the EC/EU after 1972. Historical research has not adequately explained them either. Customs union theory only explains how it could have happened, but not why it did. Did the spread of governance through delegation encourage 'actors', in this case the bureaucrats of the European Commission, to promote expansion? Did the regulatory state carry within it the seeds of its expansion geographically and of its 'governmental' powers?

Stone Sweet and Sandholtz (1997: 299) are insistent that intergovernmental bargaining is embedded in processes 'sustained by the expansion of transnational society, the pro-integrative activities of supranational organizations, and the growing density of supranational rules', a situation they believe that inevitably reduces the control of member-states over outcomes (see Rosamond 2000: 127). The impulse towards expansion in that case comes from outside the supranational organizations. Their statement seems to depend, like much functionalist argument, more on belief than evidence. Could Majone's account of the EC/EU as a regulatory state confirm or supersede their belief? The issues raised by this resurgence or persistence of functionalism inside specific aspects of supranational governmental agencies are susceptible, following Majone's lead, to discovery or rebuttal by historical research. This has already generated one illuminating study

which admirably blends the research techniques of history and political science, Pollack's (2003) detailed attempt to test the hypotheses of Majone and the beliefs of Stone Sweet and Sandholtz.

The agents Pollack selects in his search for 'the engines of integration' are the Commission of the European Communities, the European Court of Justice, and the European Parliament. The latter two are agencies set to watch over the Council of Ministers and the Commission. For that purpose the European Court of Justice has members nominated by member-states, but the member-states have little effective redress against decisions which are unfavourable to them. The European Parliament, Pollack finds, is more dependent on the Commission as the executive power than, to take a comparable example, is the Congress of the USA on the Presidency. The European Parliament, seemingly weak compared to Congress, has, nevertheless, rid itself of one executive and made that executive's successor feel Parliament's weight. Member-states are therefore unhappy at having to depend to some extent on the support of the European Parliament as an agency and happier to delegate to the Commission. In short, the rules are such that agency theory is difficult to deploy. The word 'agency' probably itself needs a better definition or a new word to replace it.

In spite of these conceptual problems Pollack is quite clear that the European Commission and the European Court of Justice each have not only an agenda of their own but also a certain freedom to pursue it. With more delegation, he implies, the Commission would have to further expand its own agenda. The European Court of Justice has expanded its agenda without much difficulty. In spite of these convolutions, Pollack's approach generates results which can be accepted as historical evidence. Within the same convoluted rules the Commission did in the first 20 years of the Lomé Conventions – not one of the EC/EU's more successful initiatives – strive to retain that programme in the face of mounting disillusion from member-states (Milward 2005).

Agency theory remains, nevertheless, rather ill-defined by historical standards, because the question why government has hived off so much of its former daily administrative activity to 'agencies' is neither fully investigated nor answered. Pollack follows economic theory in assuming that delegation to agencies reduces overall transaction costs. No-one, historian or political scientist, has, so far as I am aware, convincingly shown this to be the case. Institutional history never seems to leave room for enquiry outside the walls of the institution and its present attempts to deploy sociological theory seem to encourage this weakness. One plausible reason for the spread of delegation as a system of governance may be to shuffle off government's responsibility. There seems to be more scope for disciplinary interaction than is offered by the rather narrow questions posed about the internal institutional history of the EC/EU. Its 'external effects' on the member-states, if studied in the same way, might provoke a more useful interaction.

To a certain extent the return to functionalism has promoted a return to the study of the member-states' interactions with each other, rather than with the EC/EU's own machinery. Much in this respect is due to Katzenstein (1985), whose work has been more historically-based than most political science. His study of the behaviour of smaller European states in world markets for industrial goods deals knowledgeably with industrial policy, demonstrating, among other things, that there still was industrial policy in the early 1980s (Katzenstein 1985). Subsequently, he has made an interesting case for Germany's structural congruence with small states with which it has had to deal so closely in history since, at the latest, the mid-19th century, Austria, Belgium, Luxembourg,

and Switzerland in particular. These relationships have produced not only similar practices but also similar institutions in their dealings with the EC/EU, of which Switzerland is not a member-stae (Katzenstein 1997). It is becoming fashionable to call such a process 'Europeanization' and to see 'Europeanization' as a substitute for, or an alternative to, revived functionalism. How far this approach will be able to live with and deploy historical research remains to be seen (Featherstone and Radaelli 2003). Ironically, the argument that the European Union mainly owes its existence to individuals of persistent and fervent vision, who have been set on making it the central organ of a European federation, remains as one established explanation of the supranation's incomplete existence, although neither political science nor history give that argument much credence. One reason may be that the political science of European integration, while it has changed so frequently, has never entirely abandoned the teleology of a European federation. Another may be that speculation about the future is more interesting theoretically than evidence from the past. An excess of writing usually forbodes the end of a love affair. In the love story of contemporary Europe the lovers have as yet scarcely come to grips with each other. History, when it prophesies, refers to the past. Political science is more inclined to prophesy by extrapolating present trends. In spite of their complicated past relationships, both disciplines have brought together a discerning set of approaches to explaining the present and the future of supranational governance in Europe, more shaded and realistic than economic theory has offered.

A Legal Approach to EU Studies

RAMSES A. WESSEL

WHAT IS A LEGAL APPROACH TO EU STUDIES?

To lawyers European law is the mother of all academic disciplines that are relevant for studying Europe. After all, the European treaties are the *alpha* and the *omega*: they started the whole process of European integration and they ultimately define its limits in terms of competences. This view is not always shared by other disciplines. In fact, while politics, economics and even sociology are considered to represent important dimensions of the European integration process, some see law as merely a tool to make the other dimensions work. In these views one hears the echo of a particular perspective on law in relation to the relations between states: why indeed should one bother to study international law in the area of foreign affairs? After all, as repeated by Henkin (1979: 2)

> as for the diplomat and the maker of foreign policy, they do not appear to consider international law important. International law is convenient for formalizing routine diplomatic practices so as to give free rein to the art of diplomacy; it is often an acceptable minor obstacle in the pursuit of policy; it is not a significant restraint on a nation's freedom to pursue important national interests as it sees them.

In fact, as Boyle (1985) and other authors hold, the involvement of lawyers in international politics can even be regarded as counterproductive because of the '*mélange* of inherently debilitating characteristics fundamental to legal education and training, to the processes of legal reasoning, to the practice of law, and to the legal profession' (Boyle 1980: 194).

These views may be the result of a *prima facie* absence of law in the relations between states. Unlike domestic society, the world, in the eyes of many observers, seems to lack structured rules, institutions and procedures to regulate the relations between states. From this vantage point, international relations – when based on legal norms at all – are based on the 'law of the jungle'. Legal analysis, in this view, is not to be isolated from the political set-up that dominates it, since this would lead to artificial theorizations not having much in common with reality (Scott 1994).

The aim of the present section is to contribute to an understanding of legal approaches to the European integration process and, thus, to the contribution of legal science to EU studies. It is asserted that – on an analytical level – one should be able to isolate putative legal arguments from political ones in order to get to grips with the whole range of norms, habits, deals, and commitments that exist between the EU Member States as well as between them and the European Union. In short, what lawyers do is determine whether the facts they are confronted with are also 'legal facts' in the sense that they form part of a *legal order* (*ordre juridique* or *Rechtsordnung*) and, if so, how one should interpret the phenomena encountered in the light of the special rules and mechanisms set by that order. It is these special rules, mechanisms, and consequences that – whenever they exist – have always justified (and even rendered essential) the separate analysis of the legal framework governing the European integration process.

At the same time, it is clear that the links between the legal approach and the political, social or economic approaches to European integration are essential. After all, the whole idea of French Foreign Minister Schuman in 1950 was political and the means – as well as most of the substantive norms in the EC Treaty – are mainly economic and social (Diebold 1959; Koopmans 1991). Nevertheless, interdisciplinary research has proven to be difficult and European law has its own practitioners, journals, conferences, and discourse.

How to Recognize Law in EU Studies?

Indeed, what European lawyers study are legal norms and competences. But, how do they distinguish their 'legal' order from the 'political', 'economic', or 'moral' order that exists simultaneously? A legal order is mostly conceived of as an abstraction, a way of looking at a number of inter-related norms in a coherent fashion. Moreover, there are no generally accepted criteria defining a legal order, or even defining 'law'. What we are dealing with is different ways to interpret and classify norms. In the words of Bengoetxea (1993: 37): 'the law is composed of *Rechtssätze* or norms in the form of legal precepts, i.e. legal or normative statements – what legal dogmatics or legal science does, with the help of a certain legal theory, is to order, clarify, and structure those sentences into norm-propositions forming a coherent whole or legal order'.

While the past 15 years in particular has revealed an interest of some legal researchers to look beyond the traditional doctrinal approaches of European law (see *infra* section 3), European legal scholarship seems to be influenced mostly by *legal positivism*. The basic idea behind legal positivism is that there is no imperative relationship between 'what is' and 'what ought to be'. In accepting this assumption, legal positivists focused in particular on the internal structure of the legal system. While in Austin's (1998; Raz 1970) view, for instance, a law was perceived as a general command of a sovereign addressed to his subjects – which excluded the more complex relations between different laws – other and subsequent approaches, in particular those presented by Kelsen (1949) and Hart (1961), stressed the systemic links between different norms. Unlike approaches in which a direct link between legal norms and moral considerations is thought to be essential (Fuller 1973; Dworkin 1977; Finnis 1980), *legal positivism* has always offered lawyers a more practical criterion for the determination of the *existence* of a *legal* norm: systemic validity (MacCormick 1998: 341). 'By "validity" we mean the specific existence of

norms. To say that a norm is valid, is to say that we assume its existence or – what amounts to the same thing – we assume that it has "binding force" for those whose behaviour it regulates' (Kelsen 1949: 30; 1991: 171, 213). Hence, according to Kelsen, a norm is valid if it is based on another valid norm, resulting in a 'chain of validity' – ultimately leading to a 'basic norm'. Since this *basic* norm cannot be based on another norm, its existence is presupposed. 'All norms whose validity may be traced back to one and the same basic norm form a system of norms, or an *order*' (Kelsen 1961: 111).

With Austin and Benthem, Kelsen saw all norms as *prescriptive* and thus as *imperative* (Raz 1970: 156). Hart contested this view in stating that there are also prescriptive norms which are not necessarily imperative norms, but which, nevertheless, guide human behaviour. These norms may be called *power-conferring norms* and have proved to fulfil a key function in European law. In Hart's (1961: 81) terms,

> Under rules of the one type, which may well be considered the basic or primary type, human beings are required to do so or abstain from certain actions, whether they wish to or not. Rules of the other type are in a sense parasitic upon or secondary to the first; for they provide that human beings may by doing or saying certain things introduce new rules of the primary type, extinguish or modify old ones, or in various ways determine their incidence or control their operations. Rules of the first type impose duties; rules of the second type confer powers [...].

Nevertheless, Hart is in agreement with Kelsen that the legal order is a complex system of interconnected norms. In his view, however, the determination of a valid norm requires a second rule, identifying the first one as valid. Hart (1961: 95) called this identification rule the *rule of recognition*: 'a rule for conclusive identification of the primary rules of obligation'. Like Kelsen's *basic norm*, the existence of the *ultimate* rule of recognition is not dependent on other laws in the legal system: 'whereas a subordinate rule of a system may be valid and in that sense "exist" even if it is generally disregarded, the rule of recognition exists only as a complex, but normally concordant, practice of the courts, officials, and private persons in identifying the law by reference to certain criteria. Its existence is a matter of fact' (Hart 1961: 110).

This explains the focus of European lawyers on norms and competences that can somehow be traced back to the treaties and it, subsequently, explains the pivotal position of the treaties in the legal approach to EU studies. As we will see, the legal dimension is not merely about case law of the European Court of Justice. Indeed, regardless of the value of the approach of, for instance, Kelsen in offering tools for the identification of (valid) legal EU norms, its main weakness is obvious. The existence of a legal system ultimately depends on its acceptance in practice (Ruiter 1993: 19). In Kelsen's (1967: 11) view 'a general legal norm is regarded as valid only if the human behaviour that is regulated by it actually conforms with it, at least to some degree. A norm that is not obeyed by anybody anywhere, in other words a norm that is not effective at least to some degree, is not regarded as a valid legal norm. A minimum of effectiveness is a condition of validity' (see also Kelsen 1991). Hence, the answer to the question why a particular EU norm is valid in the legal system is: 'because the system is valid'. Why then is the system valid? 'Because it is accepted in practice'. Kelsen (but Hart also) has thus based his concept of a legal system on assumptions or presuppositions which derive their validity from the fact that they are accepted in practice. Ruiter (1993: 52–4) seems to be following the same line when he insists on the need for the surrounding community to acknowledge a legal performance. He uses the concept of legal norms as *presentations* purporting to be made true by general acceptance. Validity in that sense would seem to depend on a general acceptance in the form of a social practice based on a common belief in the actual existence of the legal norm. This, in fact, seems to be an accurate description of how European lawyers select their objects of study.

Despite the fact that many European lawyers have indeed become 'Court watchers', the earlier observations reveal that the scope of European law extends far beyond the interpretations provided by the European Court of Justice. While most common law systems indeed base their concept of legal order on the notion that 'it is by examining the courts' opinions that one finds the laws on which they act' (Raz, quoted by Bengoetxea 1993: 39), this cannot mean that the addressees of the norms are only the courts, for if the rules (norms) did not exist for the public at large how were they to regulate their activities in legally relevant affairs. Norms exist before they are applied by the courts. The validity of the source does not depend on its being recognized by the courts: *the norm is recognized and applied precisely because it is valid*. What the courts determine is the meaning or content of the norm. However, most European norms and rules will never be part of a case before the Court. Their analysis depends on academics that are trained to present an interpretation that is meaningful in relation to all other norms that together make up the EU legal order.

What is European Law?

While there has been much debate among legal theorists whether the international system could also be regarded as a legal order (Hart 1961; Mosler 1976; Combacau 1986) – thus implicitly questioning the role of law beyond the state – with regard to the European system this question was answered by the European Court of Justice already in the early years of the integration process. In the leading case Costa-ENEL, that 'by contrast with ordinary international treaties, the EEC Treaty has created its own legal system' (Case 6/64 1964). This case – together with the increasing complexity of the discipline – has also caused European law to develop into a field separate from both national and international law (Pescatore 1974; Koopmans 1986, 1991; Schwarze 2001). In that sense, one may argue that the birth of 'European law' was inherent to the far-reaching agreements laid down in the Community treaties in the 1950s. Indeed, '[t]he construction of a genuine legal order is, naturally, also the construction of a genuine academic discipline' (Schepel and Wesseling 1997: 183).

The previous section revealed the mainstream answer to the question whether or not a norm forms part of any particular international legal order. Obviously the norm must allow for it to be traced back to an (explicit or implicit) treaty provision. If the general findings are subsequently translated to the EU legal order, any identification of legal norms – and thus the focus of European law – should be based on the following trio (Ruiter 1993: 93):

1. treaty norms are legal norms;
2. norms authorized by legal norms are legal norms; and
3. only norms specified in 1 and 2 are legal norms.

This allows us to define European law – or more precisely: the Law of the European Union – as the institutional and substantive norms laid down in the EU and EC treaties (*primary law*), in the decisions based on either those treaties (*secondary law*) or on other decisions (*tertiary law*), including the *case law* of the European Court of Justice. Irrespective of the complexity of most European issues, the legal approach thus has a very specific focus: treaties, decisions, and case law. As in any other domain, the main function of the legal approach is analysis and interpretation. European lawyers are interested in the question how a particular field is regulated and how the different norms and rules are to be interpreted. While 'law' is sometimes considered to be a 'normative' science, it is above all the analysis and interpretation of norms that is at stake rather than their creation on the basis of for instance moral values or political, economic, or social needs. Mainstream legal science is based on the 'positive' starting points described above and the job of legal scientists is to study the legal order and to interpret and place into context the new developments in that order. In that sense the legal approach is 'value free'; it deals with democracy, legitimacy, human rights, or the internal market, but it did not invent these concepts. The 'normative' dimension is defined by political science, economics or sociology; law basically studies the results of the debates on these concepts as they are laid down in legal rules. This is not to say that European law does not take into account any principles or

even values. These principles or values, however, may become part of the legal system – either because they are included in the treaty (see for instance the references to human rights in the treaties and many EU decisions), or because we allow a Court of Justice to acknowledge or introduce them as legal principles.

Obviously, however, European law was created by politicians and lawyers coming from different legal traditions. The influence of these legal traditions – and in particular those of the original six Member States – are still visible in the European legal order (Koopmans 1991). Thus, initially there was a dominant influence of French administrative law, which is still visible in the provisions on actions for annulment of Community decisions or in the form of the judgement and the role of the individual advisory opinion by one member of the Court. In the early years the European Court even followed the case law of the French *Conseil d'Etat* quite closely. The flexibility known to for instance Dutch and German lawyers was also visible, while the German influence has particularly been essential in the development of some of the current legal principles of Community law, such as the principles of proportionality (*Verhältnismässigkeit*) or loyalty (*Bundestreue*). These days, one may add the principle of subsidiarity to that list. As the UK only acceded to the Community in 1973, it took a while for the *common law* tradition to be able to play a role in the further development of the European legal order. Due to its main characteristics – 'courts climb from the facts to the rules to be applied, rather than deducing rules from principles or from more general rules' (Koopmans 1991: 503) – the common law influence could in particular be discovered in procedural matters, such as more attention for oral hearings and dialogue between 'bar and bench'.

Despite its disciplinary boundaries and the influence of different legal traditions, European law has developed into an academic field with specialists on detailed areas, which have almost become sub-disciplines, such as European environmental law, competition law, trade law, justice and home affairs law, foreign and security policy, or the free movement of goods (Craig and DeBurca 1999).

While the basic characteristics are known to every European lawyer, it has become impossible to stay a generalist and cover the full scope of 'European law'. Both the extensive case law and the often technical aspects of EU regulation have caused for specialists to emerge in almost all fields. It is interesting to witness a development that is similar to the specialization in law that took place ages ago at the national level.

KEY THEMES IN EUROPEAN LEGAL STUDIES

What do European Lawyers Spend Their Time On?

The number of available text books on EU law is amazingly high. In the UK in particular, almost all university lecturers seem to have published their own text book. In the international debate, the colleagues from the UK obviously dominate. This is partly due to the fact that they are able to write in their own language, but also to the fact that European law has been firmly established in all Law Schools and plays a prominent role in both the academic debate and in politics (Hunt and Shaw 2000). While the quality of the work in for instance Germany or Italy is by no means lower than that of the British, these countries are only slowly entering the international debate and have long stuck to publications in their own language.

It is striking that the many text books do not differ too much and that there seems to be a consensus on the relevant themes. The leading ones (Arnull et al. 2000; Craig and De Búrca 2003) have changed their titles from 'European Community Law' to 'European Union Law', while others have maintained 'EC Law' as a label (Steiner and Woods 2003). While a use of the term 'EU' fits the popular terminology better, most text books do not devote much space to the Union as such, but have continued to almost entirely restrict themselves to the Community pillar. Indeed, for 'hard core' Community lawyers, the non-Community pillars of the EU (Common Foreign and Security Policy and Police (CFSP) and Cooperation in Justice and Home Affairs (JHA)) are not regarded as forming part of European law. The fact that they fall outside the Community, are more intergovernmental in nature, and come close to other forms of cooperation under international law, made it difficult to fit them into the traditional doctrinal themes studied by Community lawyers. By now, the unity of the European legal order and the inter-relationship between the three pillars seems to be more accepted (Wessel 2003). Important reasons are the apparent connection between the political and economic external relations of the Union, the difficulty to make a clear distinction between the JHA issues in the third pillar and the so-called area of freedom and justice covered by the EC treaty, as well as the signing of the Treaty on establishment of a Constitution for Europe (2004), in which the pillar structure as well as the distinction between the European Community and the European Union is abandoned.

General courses on European Union law are similar all over the world. Most of the courses follow the doctrinal themes covered by the text books (see below). The increasing complexity of EU law, however, made it necessary to offer special specialization courses. Thus in most Law Schools courses are offered in for instance European Environmental Law, European Competition Law, or External Relations Law. In addition a difference is sometimes made between European Institutional Law (on the institutional structure, the types of decisions, the decision-making procedures, and legal protection) and European Substantive Law (on competition and the free movement of goods, persons, services, and capital). While it is difficult to separate institutional questions from substantive ones, the bottom line is that some European lawyers are mainly interested in how the rules are made, while others focus on the content of the rules. Again, others choose to specialize in a thematic field and know everything there is to know about the Economic and Monetary Union (EMU), Telecommunications Law, Intellectual Property, or European Defence Policy.

Institutional Themes

A major theme in European law is the role of the institutions in the decision-making process. After a historical introduction (in which the basic treaties are introduced), most text books start with a chapter on the institutional structure. It is in the analyses of the role of the institutions that connections with other disciplines are easily made. The way in which the Council operates or the powers of the European Parliament are recurring themes in EU law and allow a joining of the more general debate on democracy and legitimacy. Contrary to other disciplines, however, law is less interested in how decisions are made in practice, but rather poses the question of whether the relevant actors were competent, taking into account the legal treaty basis of the decision. If there would be one term to distinguish the legal approach from any other approach, it would be 'competence'. Many legal questions are somehow related to this notion: did the institutions have a competence to adopt the decision, was the right legal basis used, can an 'implied' competence be construed, does an external competence (vis-à-vis non-Member States) exist, and is the Community exclusively competent or do Member States still have something to say?

Closely related is the legal nature of the instruments. While other disciplines may show a tendency to take the overall possibilities of the Union to influence the behaviour of states into account, lawyers show a clear preference for the formal instruments: the Directive, the Regulation, and the Decision. The instruments of the second and third pillars play a less prominent role and soft law (ranging from Commission policies to the open method of coordination) is an area that is only studied by a select group of scholars (Senden 2004). Most legal questions concern the legal effects of the instruments in the legal order of the Member States. In that respect the Directive is, without doubt, the most important one (Prechal 2005) and questions include the possibilities to invoke a Directive after the implementation period has passed or the possibilities for damage claims.

While some answers to legal questions can be found on the basis of legal reasoning, it is much easier once the European Court of Justice has settled an issue. The case law of the Court therefore forms an inextricable part of the habitat of the European lawyer. (Un)fortunately, however, the case law of the Court is often multi-interpretable, allowing many European lawyers to give their own interpretations and to start a debate on the possible consequences of the Court's verdict. The importance of these analyses can, however, not be overestimated. As European law has become almost incomprehensible to laymen, lawyers are indispensable in analysing and interpreting the many complex rules and regulations. An important dimension of European law is related to legal protection. Citizens and companies are not only confronted with the rules made in Brussels, but equally have a right to invoke them to their own benefit. The key concepts of 'direct effect' (the question of whether a Community norm may be invoked before a national judge) and 'supremacy' (the priory that should be given to a Community norm once it conflicts with a national norm) are therefore central in many analyses on legal protection (De Witte 1999).

With the ongoing institutionalization of world trade law and the coming of age of the EU's foreign, security, and defence policy, the external relations law of the Union has developed into a specialization focusing on the relations between the European Community (and the Union) with third states and other international organizations, such as the United Nations or the World Trade Organization (Eeckhout 2005). The central question in this domain concerns the delimitation of competences, both vertically (between the EU/EC and its Member States) and horizontally (between the Community and the other two Union-pillars) (Wessel 2000b).

Substantive Themes

Two themes dominate the debate on substantive issues: the internal market and competition. As the internal market (or, in treaty terms, the common market) is traditionally seen as forming the heart of the European Community, it may very well be the area that has received the most attention in European law. The rules on the internal market boil down to the establishment of a European area without internal economic borders and with a common policy along the external border. The lion's share of the debate is devoted to the free movement of goods and in particular the forbidden quantitative restrictions on intra-Community trade (Weiler 1999b). The notion that 'all trading rules enacted by Member States, which are capable of hindering, directly or indirectly, actually or potentially, intra-Community trade are to be considered as measures having an effect equivalent to quantitative restriction' (Case 8/74, *Dassonville*) resulted in a complex legal puzzle, in which national rules on product characteristics (such as the German purity rules for beer) could be regarded as hampering trade between the Member States. This has turned the free movements of goods area into an area for which technical legal expertise has become essential.

The same – although maybe to a lesser extent – holds true for the free movement of persons. While this area originally was close to the free movement of goods, as persons were only relevant when they turned out to be 'workers', it has developed into a special branch (O'Leary 1999). This is mainly due to the fact that the European Union has become more active in the regulation of the rights of other persons (such as students or third country nationals) and the substantive development of the notion of 'European citizenship' by the European Court of Justice (Staples 1999; Schönberger 2005).

A final – and still booming – substantive theme concerns competition law. From an institutional perspective this area is also interesting as the rules on competition allow the European Community to directly impose obligations on companies and are increasingly set up in a 'multilevel' fashion, with tasks for both Community and national authorities. In fact, the competition regime aims to bind individual companies to the internal market rules for Member States. The rule – and the subsequent academic debate – on competition are possibly even more technical than those on

the free movement of goods. Their means are the control of anti-competitive behaviour by cartels and the prevention of abuse by undertakings of a dominant position. Closely related are the rules on financial state aid. While many of the competition rules are food for practicing lawyers, the academic debate has a tough job in keeping up with the interpretations of the Court and an analysis of new sets of rules (Bellamy and Child 2001).

DIFFERENT APPROACHES IN EUROPEAN LEGAL STUDIES

Taking Other Academic Disciplines Seriously

As argued above, European legal scholarship has long succeeded to remain primarily doctrine-led, with a dominance of positivist theories (Hunt and Shaw 2000). In the orthodox legal approach to European studies, integration was conceived of as a 'legal process driven by legal interpretation rather than political decision' (Schepel and Wesseling 1997: 166). Judging by the publications on EU law – and in particular the available textbooks – this is still the way most European lawyers approach their object of study. Nevertheless, the past 15 years or so revealed a broadening of the academic discipline in the sense that the legal analysis was more frequently placed in the context of other academic disciplines, in particular political science, public administration, and sociology. This had, no doubt, something to do with the more general trend to stress the importance of interdisciplinary research projects, but it also had a distinctive dynamic.

After the somewhat 'slower' decades in the European integration process (the 1970s and 1980s), the end of the 1980s and the beginning of the 1990s showed an unprecedented speed following first the Single European Act (entry into force in 1987) with a clear focus on the completion of the internal market and, second, the signing of the Treaty on European Union (entry into force 1993), which was generally perceived as an important 'constitutional' step in the integration process. These developments seemed to herald a phase in which some members of the European legal community developed a vulnerability to (or on a more positive note, an openness towards) the analyses made by political scientists, political philosophers, and sociologists with regard to issues such as the legitimacy of the EU, a possible democratic deficit, the absence of transparency, the European polity, or constitutional questions relating to for instance citizenship or flexibility. By now it has become quite easy to find publications on EU law which are less doctrinal, place the law in context, or use the methods of critical legal studies or post-modernism (Hunt and Shaw 2000). While one may argue that what these approaches primarily do is borrow insights from other disciplines to put the more orthodox views into perspective, their emergence can be seen as a sign that the European legal discipline has finally matured and increasingly shows similarities to both national and international law, which have always drawn upon a variety of methods. Nevertheless, it seems fair to stress that these alternative approaches remain exceptional. They have, however, been indispensable in building bridges towards other academic disciplines and in including lawyers in the overall discourse on European integration – something that occurred relatively late (Snyder 1990; Schepel 1998; an early example is Cappelletti et al. 1986).

A particular debate that was joined only recently by some European lawyers concerns 'governance'. Considering the popularity of the term in studies on public administration, political science, and sociology, there seemed no way to escape coining the concept in legal studies as well. The very fact that the notion is used in some legal circles underlines the fact that legal scholarship is indeed more open to the influence of other disciplines these days. The most relevant dimension of governance is the 'multilevel' variant. While lawyers tend to stress the separate existence of legal orders (as the legal order defines the competences of those who govern – see supra section 1), there is some awareness that the concept of multilevel governance comes close to the way the relationship between the Community legal order and the national legal orders is traditionally perceived: separate, but inseparable (Craig 1999; Bernard 2002; Pernice 2002; Hirsch Ballin and Senden 2005; Wessel 2006). At the same time, the notion of 'governance' is occasionally used in the meaning of 'good governance'. In particular after the publication of the Commission's White Paper on European Governance (2001), some studies started to look for a translation of good governance into legal principles (Curtin and Wessel 2005). Finally, the concept returns (although not always explicitly) in studies which focus on the executive function of the EU institutions, both with regard to the actors (regulatory agencies, comitology) and the instruments they use (soft law) (Joerges and Vos 1999; Vos 2000; Senden 2004).

Constitutional Approaches

Together with the increase of measures necessary to attain the objective of a Europe without internal borders by 1992 (initiated by the 1986 Single European Act), the signing of the 1992 Treaty on European Union may very well have boosted the broadening of the legal approach to European integration. As Weiler (1999a: 238) reminded us: 'It started with a bang: the signing of the Treaty on European Union at Maastricht in February 1992. It ended in a whimper: its entry into force in November 1993: a low, anti-climatic moment in the history of contemporary European integration, not its crowning achievement; a would-be triumph turned sour'. After so many years of an overall acceptance of the European project, something had changed. 'Maastricht, justly hailed as a remarkable diplomatic achievement, was met in many European streets with a sentiment ranging from hostility to indifference. [...] The Member States of the European Community are being swept by an electorate which is increasingly frustrated, alienated, and angry with politics as usual. And "Europe", once *avant garde*, has, it seems, become just that: politics as usual'.

While in their writing on the new Union treaty many European lawyers still concentrated on the more doctrinal issues – with a strong emphasis on the institutional structure of the new EU and the implications of its legal status (Curtin 1993; Wessel 2000a; Curtin and Dekker 2002), the general atmosphere in which the Union was perceived as a further step towards a European Federation (although the 'F-word' itself was carefully omitted in the treaty text), without a simultaneous transfer or creation of the traditional values, checks and balances, had an influence on European legal scholarship as well (Bankowski and Scott 2000; Schwarze 2001). The 'constitutional' approach, which in earlier days had largely been limited to studies which were still 'close to the Court', took account of the debate among political scientists and political philosophers on legitimacy, democracy, citizenship, and human rights (MacCormick 1993; Grimm 1995; Shaw 1996; Scott 1998; Craig 1999). Many of the publications attempt to take political ideas aboard by making translations into legal concepts. Thus, democracy and legitimacy, for instance, found concrete applications in how to make the Union more transparent or how to reorganize the system of representative democracy (Curtin 1996, 1997; Verhoeven 2002). Other 'constitutional' issues are the challenges and threats of the new possibilities for flexible cooperation and multi-speed Europe (Schrauwen 2002), the emergence of the European citizen (Shaw 1998; Schönberger 2005) and the need for the EU to formally be bound by the same human rights standards as its Member States (Alston 1999).

Thus, the debate which arose in the margin of the negotiations on the 2004 Treaty establishing a Constitution for Europe was far from new. By that time European legal scholarship was quite used to placing its arguments in the broader interdisciplinary constitutional debate, although a focus on the legally relevant questions was clearly maintained (Hartley 2002; De Witte 2003; Dehousse and Coussens 2003; Pernice and Poiares 2004; Eijsbouts and Reestman 2005). Indeed, the debate as it could be followed at conferences on European law and in European legal journals was – and still is – mainly on purely legal issues: the changes in the provisions in relation to the current treaty texts, the contradictions in the treaty texts, and the consequences for legal practice.

But, above all, it is about what lawyers do best: trying to make sense of legal texts by using their own means of interpretation and by explaining (and arguing about) how provisions are to be read and applied.

While the 'constitutional' approach is clearly visible in the academic debate, it had a marginal influence on the way we teach European law. While some text books devote some space to constitutional values or principles (Shaw 2000) and others even attempt to make use of political theory, philosophy and international relations and use the term constitutional law in their title (Douglas-Scott 2002; Lenaerts and Van Nuffel 2005), most of the textbooks on EU law deal with the issues in the traditional ('orthodox') doctrinal fashion.

Critical Approaches and the Law-in-Context

Even more marginal in European legal scholarship are some of the alternative approaches that play a role in almost all other legal disciplines. While the critical legal studies, for instance, have played a role in international law for some time, it never really developed as a separate approach in European law. Like most 'critical studies', the critical legal studies are mostly critical towards the discipline itself and the way in which it approaches and analyses the issues. It often attempts to deconstruct the arguments made by mainstream studies in order to see whether or not the relevant questions are posed (Kennedy 1994). At other occasions, they analyse a debate or a process and critically examine the arguments (Kennedy and Webb 1993). While critical studies and post-modernism are these days credited as important approaches to the study of European law, their influence on how European law is studied has remained marginal. The same holds true for the way we teach European law. Among the hundreds of textbooks on EU law, I know of only one which explicitly takes a critical approach, the reason being – according to its preface – that 'European law, like indeed any other area of law, warrants the most rigorous critical examination' (Ward 2003). The author phrases the special character of the critical approach as follows: '[…] such a critique remains both "internal", in its desire to uncover inconsistencies and injustices, and "external", in its deployment of broader critical and sceptical commentaries from beyond the narrow confines of legal scholarship. The role of the sceptic remains one that could be constructive, and such a role must be interdisciplinary and contextual'.

While critical legal studies are sometimes placed under the heading of 'law-in-context', the latter term is usually reserved for the approach that explicitly links law to society (Shaw 1997). Law-and-society scholarship enjoys great popularity among other academic disciplines as it accepts the existence of blurred boundaries between law and morality, law and tradition, law and economics, law and politics, and law and culture (Twining 1997; Selznick 2003). The characteristics of the approach are nicely repeated by Selznick (2003: 177):

> We see how legal rules and concepts, such as those affecting property, contract, and conceptions of justice, are animated and transformed by intellectual history; how much the authority and self-confidence of legal rules fit into broader contexts of custom and morality. In short, we see law as in and of society, adapting to its contours, far less self-regulating and self-sufficient, than often portrayed by its leaders and apologists. [...] Indeed, for a well-ordered legal system, nothing is more important than social support.

So far, the law-in context approach has not established itself as a separate school in EU law. One reason may be that the approach focuses on law as such and the discourse is not related to a particular area of the law. The 'contextual' approach in European law is therefore above all visible in the interdisciplinary approaches to legal studies, which seek to develop an understanding of the role of law within the wider context of European integration (Snyder 1990; Shaw and More 1995; Armstrong and Shaw 1998; Weiler 1999a).

CONCLUSION

Not related to the social sciences, European law has traditionally found difficulty in connecting to other disciplinary approaches to European integration. European law – like any other branch of law – has its own world, its own methods and, above all, its own research priorities. From the outset European law has been characterized by a doctrinal approach, in which reflection was related to the solution of legal questions, rather than to putting the legal approach itself into perspective. This explains the marginal role of alternative approaches, such as critical legal studies or the law-in-context approach.

The legal approach of EU studies is characterized by a strong focus on legal texts: treaties, decisions and case law. European legal scholarship is busy solving the legal puzzles that emerge from the texts. Indeed, it is about norms – but orthodox European law is not a normative science. While some regard law as a means to make Europe 'better', in the sense of more democratic, more legitimate or with a stronger focus on human rights or social standards, mainstream European law is interested in studying the 'positive' law as it is to be found in the legal texts.

Nevertheless, the past 15 years has shown an increasing interest in interdisciplinary research. While there have always been lawyers borrowing insights developed in other academic disciplines, their number seems to have increased as the European integration process started to pose new questions that could not be answered on the basis of a mere legal analysis.

As European law has developed into a discipline with many specializations it is difficult to name landmark studies. A study on one aspect of the free movement of goods may have had an influence on the group of specialists in that research area, but none on other European lawyers. Nevertheless, it seems fair to say that if a poll would be organized on the most influential publications in European law, those of Joseph Weiler would be in the higher ranks. A reason may very well be the combination of a strong doctrinal and the reflective approach that seems to be lacking in so may other studies. At the same time, *EU Law* by Craig and De Búrca (2003) is generally considered to be the leading text book. These publications continue to be quoted and have certainly left their mark on the collective conscience of European legal scholarship.

Contributions From Economics

PATRICK M. CROWLEY AND DAVID G. MAYES

Unlike political scientists, economists do not officially recognize regional specialties as a sub-discipline. The label 'European' in economics is as likely to be applied to one's origin as to the subject of research, which means that those with an interest in European issues are as likely to be specialists in econometrics as economic historians, and forays into European issues for economists looking for a 'real world' application of some otherwise unlikely configuration of circumstances or actors are not unusual.

Economics, as many commentators (both inside and outside the discipline) have noted, has become increasingly model-based and 'scientific', which presents problems for explorations of institutional features of the European Union, as this type of work does not naturally lend itself to quantification and characterization in terms of a set of equations. Indeed, Colander (2001) laments the loss of a more 'artistic' side of economics that revolves more around 'policy-based' economics rather than the pseudo-scientific positive economics that Milton Friedman argues for. An expansion of this more 'policy-based' approach would perhaps provide more useful contributions to European Studies (such as those done by the UK HM Treasury (2003) on UK membership of EMU).

In terms of the relationship between the economic work that has been done on European politics, much of it now increasingly follows the headline events in Europe. In fact, until or unless features of the integration process come into the limelight, most economists routinely ignore them. Examples of such developments would be the Maastricht criteria and the Stability and Growth Pact (SGP): it was only when these two accords became controversial that economists started to analyse them in greater detail. It is in this sense that political events appear to precede economic analysis, suggesting that much of the integration framework in Europe has not been formulated

directly by academic economists, but rather as a compromise between the various stances of member states when these agreements are negotiated. Indeed, when analysing the attribution of policy prerogatives between EU-level institutions and national ones, Alesina et al. (2005) find that the assignment of policies at different levels of government in the EU is inconsistent with economic theory.

Economic studies on European issues are now common, largely due to the success of the Centre for Economic Policy and Research (CEPR), which arranges conferences around economic themes that are germane to Europe (www.cepr.org). Even so, although the economic and political sciences are closely linked in terms of much of their subject matter, interdisciplinary work between the two is still rare, partly because the positivist notion of economics encourages economists to ignore (or at best downplay) political issues (see Crowley 2001, for a counter-example to this).

In this short review, we first address the theory of economic integration, and then move on to look at monetary union. EU fiscal policy is the subject of the fourth section, followed by a catch-all section which looks at other areas of integration. We finish with a brief section looking at the contributions from political economy on the EU. We do not try to be comprehensive in the areas of our focus, but instead attempt to give only an overview of the contributions of economic analysis in each area. We have to omit the large volume of valuable micro-economic work that has gone into the framing of the detail of EU law.

THE THEORY OF ECONOMIC INTEGRATION

As far as economists are concerned, there are essentially two forms of economic integration: multilateral and bilateral. The former takes place under what was the GATT (General

Agreement on Tariffs and Trade) (now part of the WTO trade rounds) and the latter takes place between countries under article 24 of the GATT. Article 24 of the GATT permits countries to accelerate the freeing-up of trade between members as long as restrictions on trade in goods and services with other countries are not increased – this is essentially the framework for regional integration. Balassa (1961) first formulated a vision for economic integration which comprised the following steps: customs union or free trade in goods and services, common market, economic union, monetary union, and political union. Crowley (2006) has updated Balassa's framework and analyses it from both a political and economic perspective. Although this process has been heavily criticized by economists such as Bhagwati and Krueger (1995) as being suboptimal, the fact that the multilateral process is slow and unpredictable gives countries an incentive to extract welfare gains more rapidly through regional integration, which has in turn led to a proliferation of regional integration agreements. We next provide a brief review of each step in the economic integration template.

Canadian economist Viner (1950), in a classic analysis of customs unions, showed that they both create new trade between the participants, and also divert trade away from other countries that are not part of the customs union. So, from a welfare standpoint, the world is better off only if this trade creation exceeds the trade diversion. Balassa (1967) was the first to try and estimate this for the European Union (or EEC as it then was) and found that there was net trade creation (see Mayes 1978, for a critical survey of the range of estimates and methods used).

After the customs union was implemented as part of the Treaty of Rome, the single market or what became known as the '1992 project' was really the next stage in the economic integration process. Baldwin (1989) and Flam (1992) both estimated the gains in terms of the freeing-up of restrictions between member states *ex-ante*, and found that they were unambiguously positive (Baldwin estimated an extra 0.9% in growth over what it otherwise would have been).

Economists such as Winter (1991) have pointed out that, although the EU is a net trade creator, the welfare costs of the Common Agricultural Policy (CAP) substantially offset the gains from trade in other areas, and may completely outweigh the benefits from the customs union. More recently Allan et al. (1998) used general equilibrium modelling techniques to estimate, *ex-post*, the welfare effects from the single market, and have concluded that the benefits could be significant (ranging up to 15% of GDP for a country like Portugal). Allington et al. (2004) have found that the single market combined with the single currency have together acted to narrow price differentials among participants in EMU significantly.

MONETARY UNION

The intellectual path towards monetary union and the economic and political experiences are heavily intertwined. Monetary union was not the ambition of European economic integration in the 1950s but instead the free movement of capital. In history, as currencies developed out of barter they needed to be something that was scarce, reasonably transportable and capable of straightforward authentication. Precious metals had the advantage over gems that they could be stamped with a design. Despite centuries of governments trying to expand their purchasing power by debasing currencies, the 19th-century norm became currencies that were based first on silver and later on gold. To quite some extent the fact that the effigies on the coins differed was unimportant. They were exchangeable simply because they could be weighed. Similarly by the time of the first world war a small number of currencies, led by the pound sterling, had come to dominate the world system as a unit of account for international transactions. Although single currencies tended to be more the result of conquest and commercial convenience, currency unions across national borders developed because there was a convenience gain and little downside difference. At the same time the international system was characterized by free trade.

The economic theory of the time therefore tended to follow the practice. Price levels and economic activity evolved according to the ability to pay internationally based on the stock of gold or silver. It was really only with the collapse of the system during the first world war and then the economic difficulties encountered with returning to the gold standard after the war that ideas began to change (Keynes 1923). The principal insight was that the costs of trying to drive prices down in order to achieve a given parity were unacceptable. However, by the same token the costs of hyperinflation were also unacceptable and quite enough to topple governments. The attempt to return to the pre-war order finally collapsed with the Great Crash. Experience with floating exchange rates was then rather uncomfortable and protection in trade and controls on capital movements were needed to try to protect the value of the currency.

The system designed toward the end of the second world war and enshrined in the Bretton Woods agreement therefore tried to return to the world fixity of exchange rates – within narrow bands – with respect this time to the US dollar which in turn was exchangeable at a fixed price for gold. However, in the event of severe pressure countries could, in what was intended to be exceptional circumstances, change their exchange rates (devalue because the costs of deflation are asymmetrically high). Indeed the UK exercised this option in 1949. This framework had not been overturned by the time of the negotiations for the EEC and EFTA and economic theory matched it. Although the ultimate aim was the complete removal of both trade protection and capital controls multilaterally as well as more rapidly within the trading areas, the prevailing levels were so high that major reductions could be made with little expected impact. Hence, possible adjustment costs were not the focus in the literature of the day. Triffin (1960) was probably the most effective in raising the issues about the imbalances between countries and the issues of the fixed rate system. Although Meade (1957) had advocated that a greater degree of flexibility in the exchange rate was necessary, within bounds, as other means of adjustment to economic shocks, such as labour mobility, were not very effective and slow moving. There were of course strong advocates of a more flexible approach (Friedman 1953).

With the work of Mundell (1961) and McKinnon (1963) the question was inverted. Instead of asking how much exchange rate flexibility was necessary to cope with shocks, they explored what the characteristics were of an area that could operate with a single currency (an Optimal Currency Area, or OCA). This involved setting out the features of an economy that would make adjustment costs sufficiently small for them to be acceptable. These include substantial mutual trade, being subject to similar shocks and cycles, mobility of capital and labour, a diversified economy, and a similar approach to policy. Since then the theory has been spelt out more clearly (Kenen 1969), allowing for example for more flexibility in wages and prices.

With the collapse of the Bretton Woods system at the end of the 1960s the EU simply tried to recreate the international system at the European level following the Werner Report of 1970 (for a good discussion, see Hallerberg, this volume). The rapid collapse of that system and the literature explaining the difficulties very much occurred in parallel (Fleming 1971; Corden 1972). However, when the European Monetary System (EMS) and its associated Exchange Rate Mechanism (ERM) came into being in 1979, it was a repeat of the same formula, with the exception of the creation of the Ecu as the numeraire at the heart of the system. Although in most respects a symbolic calculation device and not particularly distinguishable from its predecessor, the ERM raised the possibility of single currency.

Ironically, as the EMS developed, so understanding in the literature came of the impossibility of what it was trying to achieve – the trinity of free capital mobility, an independent monetary policy and a fixed exchange rate (Walter 1976; Fratianni and Peeters 1978, and the contributions therein; Padoa-Schioppa 1987). As the 1980s progressed so the member states nevertheless managed to converge their monetary policies to that of Germany, the crucial step being the policy turnaround in France in 1986 and the adoption of the *franc fort* (Ardy et al. 2005). It was only with the Single European Act of 1987 that monetary union became a clear goal as such.

The path to monetary union, however, continued to be driven by practical considerations rather than economic benefits. Estimates of the gains from a single currency were second-order, comprising some reduction in transaction costs, improved functioning of markets and reduction in uncertainty (this is most clearly set out in the Commission's assessment at the time of the Maastricht decision to go ahead; *One Market One Money* 1992). The Delors Committee of central bank governors, with just two academic advisers, therefore mapped out a framework of how to operate such a currency with a balance between national interests and central control in a system of central national central banks and a European Central Bank (Delors 1989). The sequence of how it would be achieved through stages with abolition of barriers and convergence on common inflation, and interest rates, with little exchange rate fluctuation came in for considerable academic criticism – the greatest criticism being reserved for the requirements for fiscal discipline (a debt ratio below 60% and a deficit of less than 3%). The Delors report itself, however, brought together a compendium of academic contributions, focusing mainly on the practicalities.

While the remaining difficulties were addressed in the run up to the Maastricht Treaty (Ernst and Young/NIESR 1991; Mayes and Begg 1991, for example) there was fairly widespread scepticism even among proponents (Britton and Mayes 1992) that many member states would manage to alter their structures fast enough to converge in the timetable laid down. The debate about how convergence should be driven (HM Treasury 1989) has continued, very much in line with the political stance in the member states, with the academic debate in the UK and Sweden, for example, favouring convergence first and membership second and many other countries including the new member states seeing an emphasis on membership itself being the necessary disciplining force (Mayes and Suvanto 2002).

What has become very clear is that OCA theory has to be treated in terms of what countries look like after the event rather than their prior position when they are subject to a whole range of barriers and restrictions (Schelkle 2001). Indeed, the work of Rose (2000) and Rose and Engel (2002) comparing a wide range of countries has shown that previous currency unions have been subject to striking endogenous convergence (as exemplified within Canada compared to across the border with the US, despite shorter distances; McCallum 1995; Helliwell 1998).

More recently much of the emphasis in the economic literature has been on assessing the performance of the ECB compared to other central banks, as in the CEPR Monitoring the European Central Bank series, and on the Stability and Growth Pact and the relationship with fiscal policy discussed in the next section. It is really inflation targeting and behaviour outside the Euro area that has driven the discussion of monetary policy in the literature (Rogoff 1985; Taylor 1993; Walsh 1995). De Grauwe (1997) offers a good analysis of the whole topic.

THE STABILITY AND GROWTH PACT

There are no specific plans for fiscal union in the EU (although Costa and De Grauwe (1999) detail the possible ramifications of tax convergence), and in practice the harmonization of indirect taxes is increasingly unlikely, as Eastern European countries are opposed to such moves. Nevertheless, the issue of economic union, and how this influences fiscal policy if harmonization is not agreed upon, given the mobility of factors of production within the EU, is an important issue (see Sinn 2003).

Putting aside economic integration, there are restrictions on fiscal policy in place in the EU as specified by the Stability and Growth Pact (SGP). Politically, this agreement was probably enacted to allay fears in Germany over potential laxity in Europe-wide fiscal policy when high-debt countries were clearly going to be permitted to join EMU under

Maastricht, thereby eliminating the 'end games' problem inherent in the Treaty (see Fratianni et al. 1992). These restrictions officially limit the latitude of governments to run budget deficits beyond the 3% level for prolonged periods of time.

These limits on budget deficits are controversial for many economists, simply because there appears to be little rationale for choosing specifically a 3% level, and also because most economists agree that for fiscal stability and sustainability, the emphasis should be placed on the public debt (the sum of all past deficits), rather than the current deficit. The criticisms that economists had levelled at the Maastricht Treaty convergence criteria (see Buiter et al. 1993, for example) were also valid criticisms for the SGP (Buiter 2005), but political expediency demanded that the spirit of the Maastricht convergence criteria be maintained after the inception of EMU. The prevailing view among economists was that, although the SGP was perhaps inappropriate for the question at hand, the effects on member states would not be burdensome (Eichengreen and Wyplosz 1998), and that it was superior to a situation where there were no limits imposed on fiscal policy.

The institutional context of the SGP is not typical of most EU policies that involve punitive sanctions. When the SGP was agreed upon in Dublin in 1996, the decision was taken not to include its specificities into the Treaty of Amsterdam (essentially an extension to Maastricht), but rather to adopt the SGP formally as two European Council regulations, a Directive and an opinion. The SGP was 'interpreted' as constituting the 'excessive deficit procedure' which was in the original Maastricht Treaty: but as the details of the SGP were not placed in the actual Treaty they could be changed by a qualified majority vote on the European Council or over-ridden by the Council if they so wished.

As is well known to scholars of European integration, the SGP was indeed over-ridden when the SGP came under scrutiny in 2003, as several member states repeatedly ran budget deficits in excess of the 3% of GDP limit. After warnings by the Commission, in early 2004 the official sanctions procedure was due to start

against France and Germany. This led to a mini-crisis of sorts in 2004 when a vote was taken on the European Council to essentially hold the SGP in abeyance. The ensuing debate on what was to be done with the SGP prompted an outpouring of research from both political scientists and economists, with important contributions from Begg and Schelkle (2004), Buiter and Grafe (2003), Buti et al. (2003), Eichengreen (2003), Hughes-Hallett et al. (2003), and Wyplosz (2005). It is clear from these contributions that there was little agreement among economists on whether the SGP should be reformed, and if so how it should be reformed.

The reforms to the SGP that were agreed upon in March of 2005 (European Commission 2005) have now been implemented, and they largely amount to cosmetic changes to the SGP, with the process before penalties are imposed now extended, and a less demanding definition of a 'severe downturn' (which suspends the implementation of the procedure) now in place. Consideration of debt levels is now to be included in any assessment, and the definition of other 'exceptional circumstances' has been widened to include 'financial contributions to fostering international solidarity and to achieving European policy goals, notably the unification of Europe'.

Clearly the SGP is still not the most appropriate arrangement for fiscal policy coordination in the EU, and there is therefore a distinct likelihood that the current arrangements will be further modified or scrapped at some point in the future (Pisani-Ferry 2002). Crowley and Rowley (2006) explore the events that might trigger further modifications to the pact.

INTEGRATION OF MARKETS

The heart of economic integration has been the process of steady removal of barriers in the markets for goods, services, labour, and capital and the creation of the framework for a 'single market'. Progress up until the 1980s had been very slow, to the point that a paradigm shift was required if momentum was going to be maintained after tariffs had been removed and the first expansion fully absorbed. The shift, when it came, was however rather more industry-inspired than driven by academic advance, although the industrial economics literature provided a helpful background (see e.g. Baumol et al. 1982) which has influenced the nature of competition policy in many countries. The pressure in the GATT to identify both what trade in services constituted and the nature of barriers also provided a helpful background (Mayes and Bramson 1987; Feketekuty 1988).

The intellectual jump was from trying to agree what constituted a common acceptable standard for products or qualifications, sector by sector across the markets, to identifying the nature of barriers to open competition. These were then listed (Commission 1985) following a paper by the European Roundtable and the routes to addressing them suggested by a specific deadline – 1992. These only required a regulatory framework that had to go through the usual legislative process for basic measures for consumer and worker protection. Much of the rest was then left for industry to decide where standard setting was necessary and for competition among rules to determine which systems appeared to work best (Macmillen et al. 1987; Pelkmans and Winters 1988). This was cast very much as a bonfire of regulatory barriers to freer trade and competition and was successful as such in capturing the imagination of euro-sceptics like the British so that the Single European Act was passed, which proved a landmark for closer integration over the ensuing 20 years (Young, this volume).

However, this message did not capture the popular imagination either generally or among legislators and much of industry outside the major cross-border firms, and required a deliberate attempt to put the economic justification together (Emerson et al. 1992), although this is much better known by its popular version, the Cecchini (1988) Report.

The single market initiative also proved to be much less effective in lowering barriers than anticipated and took much longer than expected (Sutherland 1992; Mayes and Hart 1994). The Commission also shied away from making quantitative assessments of benefits after it was shown that its methodology was producing negative results (Mayes and Burridge 1993). Indeed, it is worth focusing on the example of financial services which has required a second wave of intellectual development, this time drawing on network economics (Shy 2001; Rochet and Tirole 2002; Mayes and Wood 2006). The original (passport) principle applied was that an institution licensed in one member state could operate across borders in others without the need for relicensing. It was thought that this would enable each financial firm to operate across the EU under its home country rules and that the process of competition would lead to a convergence on the most efficient rule system (Woolcock 1994).

This original paradigm for reducing regulation has proved to be erroneous, particularly in the financial sector, and regulation has increased at EU and national level. Furthermore, the most effective barriers to cross-border activity, including mergers and acquisitions, were not removed, so the passport principle did not offer enough help for firms to operate in the other member states. This therefore generated a repeat of the original process of identifying barriers (Giovannini 2001, 2003) but an innovative way of addressing them through a hierarchy of committees harmonizing regulation whose conclusions were fast-tracked through the European Parliament for a finite period – the Lamfalussy process. The academic community has responded by emphasizing the importance of game theory, principal–agent relationships, and the role of incentives (Kaufman 1994; Herring 1997).

Competition among rules and regulatory arbitrage have not been particularly effective and convergence of rule systems has come rather more through agreements among authorities than through market forces. Trying to find a basis for establishing a single payment and securities settlement system in Europe has been hampered by the fact the models applied by the main players are incompatible. The group led by Deutsche Börse has constructed a 'vertical silo' approach linking the system all the way from securities trading down through payment, settlement and the securities depository (Schmiedel and Schönberger 2005). The alternative idea of there being open competition and access at each stage – trading, payment, settlement, and depository – is a contradictory idea that would remove the efficiencies the company gains from the vertical silo. Nevertheless, inhibiting choice means that the only way to get a single market is to have a single monopoly supplier, something that is vigorously resisted by those existing providers who fear they would not be that supplier.

The passport principle has generated complications because of the conflict between the roles of the home country in supervising such cross-border activity and the role of host countries in maintaining financial stability (Mayes and Vesala 2000; Schoenmaker 2003). This has therefore led to calls for an abandonment of the idea of competition and cooperation among authorities and the delegation of authority to the ECB and other EU-level organizations, since it is impossible to reconcile the conflicting incentives and interests (Schoenmaker and Goodhart 2006). Thus 20 years after the original 5-year programme, horizons for completion of the internal market at a level comparable, say, to the US, still look more than 5 years ahead. How banks actually go about cross-border activity has proved different from what had been expected (Dermine 2005). The expectation was that the regulatory structure would encourage Europeanization (Di Giorgio and Di Noia 2003) but in practice it has struggled, in many respects, because the major cross-border banks have become so large relative to GDP that they are a threat either to their host or home countries (Eisenbeis and Kaufman 2005). Solving this problem, particularly without the existence of substantial fiscal transfers and self-insurance across borders, would require further major steps of institution building (Nieto and Wall 2005; Mayes 2006). As with monetary union, 'completing the internal market' is proving difficult to achieve without a more federal fiscal and institutional structure. Institutional economics, public choice theory, and a wide range of other ideas from network economics, industrial organization, and principal–agent relationships have shown that the extent of market 'failures' is far more complex and persistent than envisaged at the time of the Single European Act (Dewatripont and Tirole 1994).

POLITICAL ECONOMY OF EUROPEAN INTEGRATION

There is very little work that has been done on European integration that combines elements from both political science and economics (what we label as 'political economy'). From an economics standpoint, perhaps Alberto Alesina, in a series of recent papers on Europe using research on the size of nation states and their economic influence has perhaps made the most impact. In Alesina and Wacziarg (1999) the process of European political integration is modelled and is found to illustrate a general principle that economic integration requires setting up European institutions endowed with the authority to enact Europe-wide policies. However, when countries can take advantage of scale effects thanks to economic integration, the need for political integration in Europe is reduced. To reconcile these views, a model for the optimal allocation of prerogatives across levels of government is proposed which is characterized by cross-border spillovers, so that some centralization of policies may be needed to internalize the externality. So the trade-off amounts to weighing up the gains from centralization against the costs from imposing the same policies upon heterogeneous groups. The authors analyse the institutional incentives at play for the allocation of political prerogatives in Europe and conclude that the EU has gone too far on most issues. This paper, together with Alesina et al. (2005) informs another paper by Alesina and Perotti (2004) which looks at the current state of the EU and the need for a European Constitution, both through the prism of economics. Their conclusions are that there are overlapping institutional jurisdictions between EU institutions and member states, and second that there is a heavy reliance on government intervention and policy coordination, which is perhaps misplaced.

Other important contributions in this area include joint work done by Mark Hallerberg and a variety of scholars including Jurgen Von Hagen, and focus on fiscal policy in member states of the EU, and how this is shaped by the political nature of the decision-making process in these member states coupled with the SGP. Hallerberg (2004) contains an extensive analysis of member state budgetary processes and Hallerberg et al. (2004) analyse the budgetary processes given the SGP. Hallerberg and Strauch (2002) also confirm that there is evidence of electoral cycles in fiscal policy in many EU member states.

CONCLUSIONS

There are two main routes by which economics is likely to continue to contribute to maximizing the benefits that can be obtained from European integration. The first comes from the continuing development of the theories relating to the economics of institutions, network economics, public choice, learning, principal-agent relationships and incentives, game theory, and so on, all of which deal with relationships between people and groups and the impact of the barriers that divide them, whether stemming from information, experience, custom, market structure, or the regulatory framework. Perhaps the most important insight economics offers is that people are forward-looking but their rates of time preference differ. Hence, striking bargains is a complex and continuing process.

The second route sounds more mundane but is the bread and butter of economic analysis, namely, the continuing empirical investigation of problems, applying the developing sophistication of theory, modelling and statistical and econometric methods. Whether it is Eurosystem monetary policy or CESR (Committee of European Securities Regulators) handling the minutiae of financial market integration, economic analysis is helping us understand decision-making and the outcome of policy. Much of this has occurred through the deliberate involvement of outside economists by the Commission in spelling out the framework for advance, exemplified most obviously in the five volumes of papers behind Emerson et al. (1989), but also in a whole host of small initiatives like the Maas Group (1995) on the introduction of the single currency, which preceded the Green Paper on the practical arrangements.

There is therefore no need to chase the elusive idea of an overarching theory or advocate ever wider interaction among the different disciplines in their approach to European integration, although the latter is obviously desirable in its own right if only to learn from others. The economics of the European Union continues to advance as an empirical and practical matter. Sometimes the theorist leads the practitioner but often the well known epithet applies: 'An economist is someone who sees something happening in practice and then tries to work out if it could (or should) happen in theory'.

The Sociology of EU Politics

ADRIAN FAVELL

A problematic absence characterizes sociology's relationship with EU studies. Although potentially one of the disciplines that might bring a much needed 'bottom up' view of the origins and sources of European integration – along with social history, anthropology, social psychology, human geography – its contributions have been scattered and marginal. Dominant understandings of European integration remain wedded to the resolutely 'top down' view of IR theory, law, diplomatic history, and public policy analysis. Sociological claims and argumentation were very much at the heart of the classic studies of Haas (1958) on elite socialization to the European project, or Deutsch et al. (1957) on increased interaction between nationals of the continent, as the two surest routes to regional integration. Yet today sociologists barely feature among the participants at mainstream EU conferences.

The short answer for why this is, is that sociologists are still wedded to 'society' as their principle unit of analysis. By this, they typically mean societies as historically formed, culturally distinct nation-states, and the EU is certainly *not* a nation-state-society in this sense. For all the theoretical talk among social theorists about transnational or global processes, very few of them have applied these ideas to European integration. Most empirical sociologists, on the other hand, study processes (of stratification, race relations, assimilation, education, etc.) *within* one society. For many American sociologists, the sociology of America is *still* the sociology of the modern world. Comparativists, meanwhile, typically use data that is identified and counted on a society-by-society basis, so that the variation they study is always cross-national (Breen and Rottman 1998). European scholars might be better attuned, but look for quantitative empirical data and you find even the EU's own statistical system – Eurostat, Eurobarometer, etc. – reproduce the mindset of 'methodological nationalism' (Wimmer and

Glick Schiller 2002). It is, in fact, very difficult to systematically study pan- or trans-national social structures and phenomena, because of the way nation-states have carved up the world and its populations, statistically speaking.

The possible emergence of contrasting models of economy and society in Asia, Europe, and North America, should suggest the development of a different, comparative macro-sociology on regional integration. Yet much of the pioneering work of this kind has in fact come from political economists or human geographers working in a 'regional studies' mode (i.e. Dunford 1998; Mattli 1999; Bagnasco and Le Galès 2000; Rodríguez-Pose 2002). A few exceptional works have sought to develop a pan-European sociological agenda, notably Kaelble (1990), Mendras (1997), Therborn (1995), and Crouch (1999). These look at the underlying economic and social structure of Europe on a regional scale, both historically and spatially (see also Klausen and Tilly 1997; Berezin and Schain 2003; Bettin Lattes and Recchi 2005). Also of note is work inspired by Rokkan's approach to Europe (Bartolini 2005). Empiricists will find better, non-state-centric data sources for this, and better ways of measuring pan-national structures: whether of European public opinion, classes and occupations, elite social power, values, or (most straightforwardly) behavioural convergence across the continent (say, as tourists or consumers). This would be the agenda for a future sociology of Europe. Here, I will focus on the somewhat narrower question of what a sociology of EU *politics* might look like.

'SOCIOLOGICAL' IR: EUROPEANIZATION AND THE CONSTRUCTION OF 'EUROPEAN IDENTITY'

One group of scholars describing themselves as 'sociological' have made a big splash in the heartland of EU studies: the social constructivists in IR theory. Inspired by Katzenstein's (1996) 'rummaging in the graveyard of sociological studies', Wendt's (1999) monumental 'social theory of international relations', and a wave of work emphasizing the impact of transnational human rights on global political change (Klotz 1995; Risse 1995; Keck and Sikkink 1997), a mainly younger generation of qualitatively inclined researchers have turned to norms, values, culture, and identity to explain policy-making and institutional change (see Christiansen et al. 2001; Checkel, this volume). A challenge has been laid down to the reductive, rationalist mainstream of political science. The EU is a fertile ground for these questions, given the massive efforts of the European institutions to influence European public opinion, and induce participation or cross-national behaviour, thereby encouraging the formation of 'European identity' as an antidote to national belonging and growing Euroscepticism. Numerous prominent IR theorists have thus sought to address the Europeanization question as a 'thick' cultural institutionalist one of constructing 'identity'. Archetypal studies in this vein have, for example, related variations in the stance of national elites on policies such as EMU or citizenship, to the residual impact beyond interests of national 'political cultures' (Risse 2001), the variable 'resonance' of international norms or ideas (Checkel 2001), or the impact of ideas and norms on EU enlargement (Schimmelfennig 2003). A connected 'sociological' tendency has been the re-emergence of theorizing that emphasizes the emergent functional properties of the European political system: pointing to the impact of institutional 'isomorphism', whereby 'routinized behaviours' and 'governing concepts' set by the EU institutions shape national and regional practices in a multi-levelled system of governance (Kohler-Koch and Eising 1999; Jachtenfuchs 2001).

It is odd to hear terminology and argumentation that is so reminiscent of the 'bad old days' of Parsonian political science – the paradigm laid down by the functionalist sociology of Talcott Parsons – when national politics was studied as if it expressed the logic of holistic, self-regulating 'systems', action was guided by mysterious, faceless 'norms', and variation understood in terms of reified 'political cultures'. This was before economics, not sociology, became the master paradigm for modern political science, a moment captured in Brian Barry's famous and spectacularly bloody destruction of Parsons, and Parsonian political scientists such as Easton, or Almond and Verba (Barry 1971). It was Barry's book – which has long represented the last word for political scientists on the merits of sociology – that dug the graveyard of which Katzenstein speaks. Ironic, then, that the constructivists have returned so ingenuously to a Parsonian idiom, whether theorizing about processes of 'social learning', the 'reflexive' nature of 'norms', or the 'constitutive' role of 'social meanings' in the development of 'collective consciousness' – to take some archetypal formulations. Giddens' structurationist theory is often the preferred citation for notions in this lineage (Wendt 1999), as are structuralist and post-structuralist notions of discourse and culture (Diez 1999). Such grand theories, redolent of the 1970s and 1980s, are every bit as peripheral to mainstream empirical sociology today as structural functionalism, and look very clumsy in comparison to the disaggregative approaches to 'culture', 'social structure', and 'institutions' – the analysis of social mechanisms, networks, or social cognition – that are its leading theoretical edge. The constructivist emphasis on specifying the cultural or institutional impact of political identities has, however, at least put the long neglected, classically Parsonian, question of political socialization firmly back on the table.

In the light of this, the value of the constructivist turn should be judged empirically, not in terms of its contribution to social theory. Problematically, where these theories are operationalized, they have tended to be so in terms of 'discourse' and exclusively textual sources, rather than in terms of systematic attitudinal or behavioural data. In Risse's work on EMU, for example, the sources go no further than the *ad hoc* interpretative analysis of elite discourse, and heuristic 'cultural' descriptions of national politics (Risse et al. 1999). It is interesting that in more recent work, he has now joined forces with social psychologists

(Herrmann et al. 2004). This collection represents an important selection of work on the question of 'European identity', that links experimental studies with quantitative surveys of public opinion (Bruter 2004; Citrin and Sides 2004). It also showcases another form of 'sociologizing' political science: EU analysts who have interviewed elite European officials, to determine the social and political profile of these archetypal 'highly Europeanized' European citizens (Hooghe 2002; Laffan 2004; see also Checkel 2005). These studies have revealed an interesting interplay between the strongly socializing impact of work in the Commission or Permanent Representation, for example, and the nationally defined duties of organizational and political roles that bureaucrats otherwise have to fulfil. One emerging message from these identity studies, at least, is that strong national and European 'identities' need not be mutually incompatible or zero sum in nature (Risse 2004: 249).

Such work on European identity remains fixated on national variation, and on a normative notion of European identity (participatory citizenship) very remote from the everyday lives of European citizens. One quite unique study by a sociologist that goes further is Diez Medrano's (2003) historical, discursive, and ethnographic investigation on the variation of national opinions between and within Spain, Germany, and the UK. He puts into action a frames-based approach influenced by social movements research, that emphasizes the constitutive role of national repertoires and media representations, and which in effect backs up some of the constructivist claims. The strength here lies in its methodological closeness to the ground – the terrain of ordinary Europeans' lives seen through in-depth interviews – rather than imperiously observed elite discourses. A number of French political sociologists too have developed interesting work of this kind on European identity (Duchesne and Frognier 2002), and European citizenship (Strudel 2002). The borders of sociology here blend with numerous other kinds of work on 'identities' in cultural studies and anthropology (Borneman and Fowler 1997). Notable among these are ethnographic, phenomenological studies of European identity as it is constructed through interaction at borders (Anderson and O'Dowd 1999; Meinhof 2004), or in institutional contexts (the work of Abélès (1996) or Shore (2000) on the Commission.

THE ECONOMIC SOCIOLOGY OF INTERNATIONAL INSTITUTIONS

Much of the interest in European identity is driven by a quite frankly normative view of European integration that feels compelled to answer concerns about democratic legitimacy. These political and philosophical debates are strikingly disconnected from the underlying market-driven process of European integration, whereas by far and away the bulk of legislative and legal activities of the European institutions is concerned with the political construction of the single market. A very different doorway into EU studies for sociologists, then, would be to apply the theories and tools of economic sociology – in dialogue with political economy – and look at the EU as a distinctive type of economic system, a distinctive form of capitalism among others, with its own market institutions. Extraordinarily, this has been a challenge only really picked by one economic sociologist, Neil Fligstein, who, in a series of single (Fligstein 2003) and jointly authored pieces (Fligstein and Mara-Drita 1996; Fligstein and McNichol 1998; Fligstein and Stone Sweet 2002), has mapped out a comprehensive economic insitutionalist reading of European integration.

Fligstein's touchstone is the historical creation of the market in the US: the epoch when the progressive movement established the model of the federal free trade area and rules of corporate governance that laid the foundations for America's extraordinary economic success in the 20th century. This model indeed remains an inspiration for the EU's own regional trade integration – particularly the core idea of breaking down barriers to the four freedoms of movement (of goods, capital, services, and persons) – but the EU today in fact dwarfs the American model as a natural experiment in the political construction of a single market.

The EU presents the most highly evolved example of an international governance structure in the global economy today, with an extraordinarily high degree of regional economic interdependence, and intra-member state trade (Fligstein and Mérand 2002). Fligstein portrays the European Union in terms of classic Weberian economic sociology, looking at how markets emerge, stabilize, and are transformed as a sociological process. Against neo-liberal accounts of the market, he emphasizes the deliberate political construction and structuring of this 'free' market: in terms of property rights, governance structures, rules of exchange, and conceptions of corporate control (Fligstein 2001). The EU in fact goes far beyond the removal of trade barriers and tariffs, and the promotion of competition across national borders over products and services. It is developing rules of exchange about common standards, insurance, liability, and ownership across borders; health and safety standards; standards of employment practices and workers' rights; and environmental norms. His view echoes Majone's analysis of the EU as 'regulatory state', shifting politics away from institutions and party politics into new technical arenas (Majone 1996a). One scholar in the sociology of science, Barry (2001), has given this standardization process a strikingly original reading, influenced by French philosophers Foucault, Callon, and Latour, detailing the way the EU has created new forms of political power and conflict through its creation of a knowledge-driven space of mobility and trade.

Barry sees the EU's obsession with technological 'harmonization' as a hallmark of neo-liberalism. Fligstein indeed substantiates the corporate influence on the EU, charting how the Commission has been able to successfully mobilize state and business actors in specific sectors (especially export-oriented industries, such as food, transportation, pharmaceuticals, chemicals) where standardized competition and more open markets were desirable (Fligstein and Mara Drita 1996). Much of the building of a European market has been about the opening of Europe for global firms, enabling the implantation of American and Japanese firms. Yet this self-evident facet of globalization is complicated by the fact that many of the EU's stated positions on corporate takeovers, social rights, the environment, privacy, and so on, differ sharply from the norms promoted by successive US administrations (see also Zeitlin and Herrigel 2000). The EU thus may well prove a crucial case in refuting the inevitability of neo-liberal theories of economic development that predict only an all-American future under globalization.

PUBLIC SPHERE ANALYSIS

Another greatly overlooked area in the study of the EU, particularly amenable to sociological analysis, is the media: public debate and communication in 'civil society', as the place in which opinions (and perhaps identities) are formed (see de Swann 1993; Schlesinger 1999). Certainly, the still heavily nationalized media in Europe is a crucial barrier to the emergence of any European voice – let alone a 'European identity' – and it remains an absent channel of democratic legitimation. Habermas's (1969) historical analysis of the public sphere is the master paradigm here, along with his later reflections on Europe as a postnational or cosmopolitan project (Habermas 2001; see for example, Delanty 1998; Delanty and Rumford 2005; Eriksen 2005). Habermas's account of modern liberal democracy sees the progressive enlarging of the circle of democratic inclusion, as driven by the necessity of inner elites couching arguments and justifications in the ever more universal terms of a 'public' audience. Trenz and Eder (2004) put this dynamic to work on the problem of the democratic deficit, arguing that the very deficiencies of 'closed' elite policy making in the EU are provoking the emergence of a contestatory public sphere across Europe. Although often hostile and sceptical to the European project, these reactions will in fact induce the further successful democratization of the EU's institutional forms.

Trenz and Eder's 'democratic functionalism' notably challenges the self-contained 'bureaucratic' arguments about the potential rational legitimacy of elite institutions, popular in discussions on comitology and regulatory efficiency (Cram 1997; Neyer 2000). The notion of institutional reflexivity may indeed point to some of the virtuous dynamics induced by the incomplete and inadequately democratic nature of the EU, but the 'democratic spillover' they speak of must surely underestimate the destructive potential of growing anti-EU sentiment, nowadays unlikely to be satisfied with co-option in the integration project. Effective links are drawn, however, with parallel social movements research, such as Tarrow's (1995) studies of the Europeanization of conflict (see also Marks and McAdam 1996; Rootes 1999; Imig and Tarrow 2001; Balme and Chabanet 2002). Such work has focused on the variable effectiveness with which unions, NGOs, environmental campaigners, and others have been able to articulate their interests (or not) at the European level, via opportunity structures that open up when elites within the Commission need expert external third party validation.

Another notable empirical operationalization of public sphere theories is the huge EUROPUB project (Koopmans and Statham 2002). Setting up a cross-national quantitative analysis of public 'claims making' related to various areas of European policy, via a longitudinal analysis of carefully selected newspaper articles reflecting European campaigns and debates, the project very effectively pinpoints which policies are more Europeanized in the public sphere, and the degree to which the framing of debates varies across key member states. Their findings document the disadvantaged access many weaker actors have to inner EU circles (Koopmans and Erbe 2004) – at least in so far as national media coverage reflects accurately actual EU politics, which is debatable. They also show how and when national medias might be prepared to frame debates in more international or universal terms, changes which in turn induce actors to pitch their claims in these terms (Statham and Gray 2005), and the degree to which 'new media', such as the internet, might be facilitating new forms of Europeanized communication.

Discourse analysts foreground communication as a form of political action in its own right, relying on a methodology that rates newspaper articles quantitatively as a mirror of political mobilization or claims making. Epistemological doubts here have to be traded off against the need for an effective operational empirical strategy. Similar doubts might be pointed to in other similar work, such as Soysal's pathbreaking and already much discussed study on the historical Europeanization of school textbooks (Schissler and Soysal 2004). But it is encouraging that evidence for a European social learning process – a notion at the core of the constructivist argument – is now being looked for in 'everyday' texts and discourses, rather than just selectively focusing on top-down EU directives or information drives. Other fertile areas for thinking about the sociological impact of harmonization include the impact of the Bologna process on standardization of European education, and the Erasmus/Socrates schemes on the social trajectories and identities of European students (King and Ruiz-Gelices 2003). Recchi and the PIONEUR project (Recchi et al. 2003) survey the mobile intra-EU migrant population as prototypical 'pioneers' of sociological integration; linked to this, Favell (2006) homes in on the experiences of free moving urban professionals in the EU. Nearly all such work when conducted has stressed the continued impact of national cognitive schemes within a tentative Europeanization of practices. For all the talk of Europeanizing norms, ideas and values, in the end it still seems that Europeanized behaviour amongst ordinary people is best predicted by material and spatial aspects of integration project – such as residence close to the border (Gabel 1998), engagement in cross-border commerce and transactions (Therborn 1995: 194–206), or involvement in 'parapublic' European cross-national associations and activities, such as town twinning and sports clubs (Krotz 2002).

ANALYSIS OF THE EUROPEAN POLITICAL 'FIELD'

A final much overlooked contribution to the 'sociological' analysis of EU politics hails from

France. French political science, as practiced for example in the corridors of the various Instituts d'Études Politiques in France, exists in an almost parallel universe to hegemonic anglo-American forms. One of its distinct strengths lies in the way it practices a routinely 'sociological' approach to understanding politics. Political sociology, in fact, is a subfield that has almost dropped entirely out of mainstream Anglo-American political science, largely because contemporary mainstream political science after Downs is an edifice erected on the theoretical fiction that voting preferences are always *revealed*, not socially *formed*. *En revanche*, French political science centres on the empirical analysis of the socio-economic and spatial determinants of voting choices of the electorate, often using a sophisticated combination of quantitative and qualitative methods.

France, then, has been a creative place for rethinking EU politics, particularly under the influence of a Bourdieusian style analysis of the European 'political field' (*champ politique*) (Bourdieu 1981). This combines a materialist concern with the underlying reasons why actors do things, with a socio-spatial notion of political conflict and competition. Political actions are thus 'moves' within a protean 'field', in which actors seek to monopolize resources, reproduce insider advantages, control gate keeper access to the Commission or Parliament, or discursively dominate weaker players through the strategic deployment of ideas and values. Brussels is a particularly fertile terrain for this kind of study, in which the success of certain NGOs or lobbying organizations can be directly linked to the specific organizational contours of insider politics in the city: a *modus operandi* dictated by the specific socially determined 'culture' of Europeanized actors in the city, developing a 'habitus' of successful political behaviours, quite in distinction from their national counterparts (see Favell 1998, on the immigration politics field). The great advantage of this approach lies in the way it eliminates the normative, overtly pro-European inflections of the democracy and citizenship literature, and offers an unsentimental analysis of the careers and organizational strategies of key European players, stressing the interplay of structure and agency in a much more empirically specifiable form than structurationist theory.

A volume in French by Guiraudon (2000) has done much to bring together disparate but high quality work of French political scientists, and put them in dialogue with the most congenial authors writing in English, such as Fligstein, Tarrow and Favell. Georgakakis (2000) on Commission scandals, Dorandeu and a research team in Strasbourg on the careers of European lawyers (Dorandeu and Georgakakis 2001), Joana and Smith's (2002) work on the Commission, Baisnée and Marchetti (2000) on European journalists, all offer good examples. Other related studies include Bigo's (1996, 1998) work on cross-national policing and security, Mérand's (2003) work on military officers and EU defence cooperation, Schnabel (1998) on the Collège de l'Europe at Bruges, and Schepel and Wessering's (1997) caustic socio-analysis of ECJ judges, all works that offer insider anatomies of specific professional groups and practices at the core of the European project. Two other works in English, by Kauppi (2005) and Rumford (2002), also bring an unfashionable political sociology to the study of the EU, stressing the operation of power and ideology in the workings of European institutions. All these authors reject the naïve analysis (and self-representation) of the worlds of media, law, or NGOs, as a 'mirror' of society, the embodiment of 'universal' norms, or the selfless advocates of 'civil society', respectively. Rather, each is read as political sites of contestation, in which actors are strategically constructing bounded fields of social power in their own right, at the same time as building successful, remunerative careers in these emergent professions. On a critical note, one can point to the usual weaknesses associated with Bourdieu and company. It offers a path towards an 'airless', rather cynical analysis, that stresses conflict and domination, and which takes an aggressively disaffected view of actors who themselves might see their own actions in terms of the purest benevolent or professional motives.

It is exactly in this respect, however, that the EU has been such a novel political environment. It has empowered lobbyists and campaigners of all kinds, and inspired new organizational forms in its own image. Corporations, regions, even classic agents of the state, such as senior police officials, have been induced by the EU to pursue goals and new professional networks in ways quite distinctive from the settled patterns and hierarchies of power concentrated around national government. It is the unformed, protean nature of Brussels that enables this, the way the intense heat and light of European politics enables new and ambitious actors to emerge on a brand new political stage. Much of this takes place well beyond the eye of national medias, and is a politics not detected by the Habermasian programme. This is all true of EU politics inside its institutional settings, but even then politicians often crave the narcissistic theatre and drama of national politics, because that is what national media portray as important.

Indeed, this media-led distortion of where power lies and what democracy is has itself become a significant sociological influence on the obsession with democratizing the EU. The European media (as well as populist intellectuals, such as Siedentop 2001) increasingly equate democracy with plebiscitory referenda, or presidential style elections, castigating the EU's political 'deficit' in these terms. This should come as no surprise, from a Bourdieusian point of view (Bourdieu 1996). For a knowledge-based politics that takes place between experts behind closed doors, or a justice-based politics that relies on courts to enforce individual rights against states or nationalist public opinion, is also one in which the social power of journalists is substantially reduced.

CONCLUSION

Outside of the IR constructivist debate, awareness of these sociological contributions is low, indeed marginal to the main thrust of EU studies. The issue is less that EU studies needs to become sociological, more that practicing sociologists need to get involved and be present in EU studies debates. They will bring new methods and empirical research

questions, and not only the abstract social theory for which the discipline is unjustly renowned. Sociologists in fact have European Journals and associations of their own (*European Societies, Innovation*, European Consortium for Sociological Research), but they do not attend mainstream EU studies events. With the current interest in varieties of institutionalism, networks analysis, and complexity theory, social structural and/or social psychological approaches are clearly ascendant trends, and the critique of individualism and rationalism in mainstream economics and political science is only likely to rediscover sociological argumentation as it moves away from these dogmas. The time is thus ripe for a sociological analysis of EU politics. The scattered examples presented here from economic sociology, 'public sphere' and 'political field' style work look particularly fertile, empirically speaking. It is to be hoped, at least, that that such 'sociological' analysis will not only be pursued by IR theorists reinventing the Parsonian wheel.

REFERENCES

Abélès, M. (1996) 'La communauté européenne: une perspective anthropologique', *Social Anthropology*, 4(1): 33–45.

Alesina, A. and Perotti, R. (2004) 'The European Union: a politically incorrect view', *Journal of Economic Perspectives*, 18(4): 27–48.

Alesina, A. and Wacziarg, R. (1999) 'Is Europe going too far?' *Journal of Monetary Economics*, 51(1): 1–42.

Alesina, A., Angeloni, I. and Schuknecht, L. (2005) 'What does the European Union do?' *Public Choice*, 123(3–4): 275–319.

Allan, C., Gasoriek, M. and Smith, A. (1998) 'The competition effects of the single market in Europe', *Economic Policy*, 27: 439–86.

Allington, M., Kattuman, P. and Waldmann, F. (2004) 'One market, one money, one price: price dispersion in the EU', University of Cambridge Judge Institute of Management Working Paper, Cambridge, UK.

Alston, P. (ed.) (1999) *The EU and Human Rights*. Oxford: Oxford University Press.

Anderson, J. and O'Dowd, L. (1999) 'Borders, border regions and territoriality: contradictory meanings, changing significance', *Regional Studies*, 33(7): 593–604.

Ardy, B., Begg, I., Hodson, D., Maher, I. and Mayes, D. (2005) *Adjusting to EMU*. Basingstoke: Palgrave-MacMillan.

Armstrong, K. and Shaw, J. (eds) (1998) *Integrating Law*. Special Issue of the *Journal of Common Market Studies*, 36(2).

Arnull, A., Dashwood, A., Ross, M. and Wyatt, D. (2000) *Wyatt and Dashwood's European Union Law*, 4th ed. London: Sweet & Maxwell.

Austin, J. (1998) *The Province of Jurisprudence Determined*, ed. by D. Campbell and Ph. Thomas. Aldershot, etc.: Ashgate.

Bagnasco, A. and Le Galès, P. (eds) (2000) *Cities in Contemporary Europe*. Cambridge: Cambridge University Press.

Baisnée, O. and Marchetti, D. (2000) 'Euronews, un laboratoire de la production de l'information "européenne"', in V. Guiraudon (ed.), *Sociologie de l'Europe: élites, mobilisations et configurations institutionnelles*, special edition of *Cultures et conflits*, no. 38–39. Paris: L'Harmattan. pp. 121–52.

Balassa, B. (1961) *The Theory of Economic Integration*. Homewood, IL: Richard D Irwin.

Balassa, B. (1967) 'Trade creation and trade diversion in the European common market', *Economic Journal*, 77: 1–21.

Baldwin, R. (1989) 'The growth effects of 1992', *Economic Policy*, 9: 247–82.

Baldwin, R.E. (1995) 'A domino theory of regionalism', in R.E. Baldwin, P. Haaparranta and J. Kiander (eds), *Expanding Membership of the European Union*. Cambridge: Cambridge University Press. pp. 25–33.

Balme, R. and Chabanet, D. (eds) (2002) *L'action collective en Europe*. Paris: Presses de Science Po.

Bankowski, Z. and Scott A. (eds) (2000) *The European Union and its Order: The Legal Theory of European Integration*. Oxford: Blackwell.

Barry, A. (2001) *Political Machines: Regulating a Technological Society*. London: Athlone Press.

Barry, B. (1971) *Sociologists, Economists and Democracy*. Chicago: Chicago University Press.

Bartolini, S. (2005) *Restructuring Europe: Centre Formation, System Building, and Political Structuring Between the Nation State and the European Union*. Oxford: Oxford University Press.

Baumol, W., Panzar, J. and Willig, R. (1982) *Contestable Markets and the Theory of Economic Structure*. New York: Harcourt Brace.

Begg, I. and Schelkle, W. (2004) 'The Pact is dead: long live the Pact', *National Institute Economic Review* No. 189, London, UK.

Bellamy, C. and Child, G. (2001) *European Community Law of Competition*. 5th ed. London: Sweet and Maxwell.

Bengoetxea, J. (1993) *The Legal Reasoning of the European Court of Justice: Towards a European Jurisprudence*. Oxford: Clarendon Press.

Berezin, M. and Schain, M. (eds) (2003) *Europe Without Borders: Remapping Territory, Citizenship, and Identity in Transnational Age*. Baltimore, MD: Johns Hopkins University Press.

Bernard, N. (2002) *Multilevel Governance in the European Union*. The Hague: Kluwer Law International.

Bettin Lattes, G. and Recchi, E. (eds) (2005) *Comparing European Societies: Towards a Sociology of the EU*. Bologna: Monduzzi.

Bhagwati, J. and Krueger, A. (1995) *The Dangerous Drift to Preferential Trade Agreements*. Washington, DC: American Enterprise Institute Press.

Bigo, D. (1996) *Polices en reseaux: l'experience européenne*. Paris: Presses de sciences po.

Bigo, D. (1998) 'Europe passoire et Europe forteresse: la sécuritisation/humanitarisation de l'immigration', in A. Réa (ed.), *Immigration et racisme en Europe*. Brussels: Editions Complexe. pp. 203–241.

Borneman, J. and Fowler, N. (1997) 'Europeanization', *Annual Review of Anthropology*, 26: 487–514.

Bourdieu, P. (1981) 'La répresentation politique: élements pour une théorie du champ politique', *Actes de Recherches en Sciences Sociales*, 36/37: 3–24.

Bourdieu, P. (1996) *Sur la télévision*. Paris: Liber.

Boyle, F.A. (1980) 'The irrelevance of international law: the schism between international law and international politics', *California Western International Law Journal*, 10: 193–219.

Boyle, F.A. (1985) *World Politics and International Law*. Durham, NC: Duke University Press.

Brada, J. and Mendez, J. (1988) 'An estimate of the dynamic effects of economic integration', *The Review of Economics and Statistics*, 70(1): 163–8.

Breen, R. and Rottman, D. (1998) 'Is the national state the appropriate geographical unit for class analysis?' *Sociology*, 32(1): 1–21.

Britton, A. and Mayes, D. (1992) *Achieving Monetary Union*. London: Sage.

Brusse, W.A. (1997) *Tariffs, Trade and European Integration 1947–1957. From Study Group to Common Market*. New York: St. Martin's Press.

Bruter, J. (2004) *Citizens of Europe? The Emergence of a Mass European Identity*. London: Palgrave.

Buiter, W. (2005) 'The "sense and nonsense of Maastricht" revisited: what have we learnt about stabilization in EMU?', Paper based on a public lecture given in the Seminal Contributions to the Political Economy of European Integration Seminar Series, LSE, London, UK.

Buiter, W. and Grafe, C (2003) 'Patching up the pact: some suggestions for enhancing fiscal sustainability and macroeconomic stability in an enlarged European Union', *Economics of Transition*, 12(1): 67–102.

Buiter, W., Corsetti, G. and Roubini, N. (1993) 'Excessive deficits: sense and nonsense in the Treaty of Maastricht', *Economic Policy*, 16: 8–60.

Buti, M., Eijffinger, S. and Franco, D. (2003) 'Revisiting the stability and growth pact: grand design or internal adjustment?' *European Economy* (Economic Paper No. 180).

Cappelletti, M., Seccombe, M. and Weiler J. (eds) (1986) *Integration through Law. Vol. 1: Methods, Tools and Institutions; Book 1: A Political, Legal and Economic Overview*. New York and Berlin: Walter de Gruyter.

Cecchini, P. (1988) *The European Challenge: The Benefits of a Single Market*. Aldershot: Gower.

Checkel, J. (2001) 'The Europeanisation of citizenship?' in M. Green Cowles, J. Caporaso and T. Risse (eds), *Transforming Europe: Europeanization and Domestic Change*. Ithica, NY: Cornell University Press. pp. 180–97.

Checkel, J. (2005) 'International institutions and socialization in Europe', special edition of *International Organization*, 59(4): 801–1079.

Christiansen, T., Jørgensen, K.-E. and Wiener, A. (eds) (2001) *The Social Construction of Europe*. London: Sage.

Citrin, J. and Sides, J. (2004) 'More than nationals: how identity choice matters in the new Europe', in R.K. Herrmann, R. Risse and M.B. Brewer (eds), *Transnational Identities: Becoming European in the EU*. Lanham, MD: Rowman and Littlefield. pp. 161–85.

Colander, D. (2001) *The Lost Art of Economics: Essays on Economics and the Economics Profession*. Cheltenham, UK and Northampton, MA: Edward Elgar.

Combacau, J. (1986) 'Le droit international; bric-à-brac ou système?' *Archives de philosophy du droit*, 31: 85–105.

Commission (1985) *Completing the Internal Market*, White Paper from the Commission to the European Council, COM(85)310 Brussels, 14 June.

Corden, M. (1972) 'Monetary integration', Princeton Studies in International Finance, No. 93, International Finance Section Princeton University, April.

Costa, C. and De Grauwe, P. (1999) 'EMU and the need for further economic integration', in W. Meeusen (ed.), *Economic Policy in the European Union*. Cheltenham: Edward Elgar. pp. 27–48.

Craig, P. (1999) 'The nature of the community: integration, democracy and legitimacy', in P. Craig and G. de Búrca (eds), *The Evolution of EU Law*. Oxford, Oxford University Press. pp. 1–50.

Craig, P. and De Búrca, G. (1999) *The Evolution of EU Law*. Oxford: Oxford University Press.

Craig, P. and De Búrca, G. (2003) *EU Law: Text, Cases and Materials*. Oxford: Oxford University Press.

Cram, L. (1997) *Policy Making in the European Union: Conceptual Lenses and The Process of Integration*. London: Routledge.

Crouch, C. (1999) *Social Change in Western Europe*. Oxford: Oxford University Press.

Crowley, P. (2001) 'The institutional implications of EMU', *Journal of Common Market Studies*, 39(3): 385–404.

Crowley, P. (2006) 'Is there a logical integration sequence after EMU?' *Journal of Economic Integration*, 21(1): 1–20.

Crowley, P. and Rowley, R. (2006) 'The future political and economics consequences of the revisions to the SGP', in P. Crowley (ed.), *EU Economic Policy at the Dawn of the Century*. New York: Nova Science. pp. 39–56.

Curtin, D.M. (1993) 'The constitutional structure of the Union: a Europe of bits and pieces', *Common Market Law Review*, 30: 17.

Curtin, D.M. (1996) 'Betwixt and between: democracy and transparency in the governance of the European Union', in J. Winter, D.M. Curtin, A.E. Kellermann, B. de Witte and L. Neville Brown (eds), *Reforming the Treaty on European Union – The Legal Debate*. The Hague: Kluwer Law International. pp. 95–121.

Curtin, D.M. (1997) *Postnational Democracy: the European Union in Search of a Political Philosophy*. The Hague: Kluwer Law International.

Curtin, D.M. and Dekker, I.F. (2002) 'The constitutional structure of the European Union: some reflections on vertical unity-in-diversity', in P. Beaumont, C. Lyons and N. Walker (eds), *Convergence and Divergence in European Public Law* Oxford: Oxford University Press. pp. 59–78.

Curtin, D.M. and Wessel, R.A. (eds) (2005) *Good Governance and the European Union: Some Reflections on Concepts, Institutions and Substance*. Antwerp: Intersentia.

De Grauwe, P (1997) *The Economics of Monetary Integration*. Oxford: Oxford University Press.

de Swann, A. (1993) 'The evolving European language system: a theory of communication potential and language competition', *International Political Science Review*, 14(3): 241–55.

De Witte, B. (1999) 'Direct effect, supremacy and the nature of the legal order', in P. Craig and G. De Búrca (eds), *The Evolution of EU Law*. Oxford, Oxford University Press. pp. 177–213.

De Witte, B. (ed.) (2003) *Reflections on the Constitutional Treaty for Europe*. Florence: European University Institute.

Dehousse, F. and Coussens, W. (2003) 'The convention's draft constitutional treaty: old wine in a new bottle?' *Studia Diplomatica*, 51(1–2): 5–76.

Delanty, G. (1998) 'Social theory and European transformations: is there a European society?' *Sociological Research Online*, 3(1): 1–24.

Delanty, G. and Rumford, C. (2005) *Rethinking Europe: Social Theory and the Implications of Europeanization*. London: Routledge.

Delors, J. (1989) *Report of the Committee for the Study of Monetary Union in the European Community*. Luxembourg: OOPEC.

Dermine, J. (2005) 'European banking integration: don't put the cart before the horse', mimeo, INSEAD, September.

Deutsch, K.W., Burrell, S.A., Kann, R.A., Lee Jr, M., Lichterman, M., Lindgren, R.E., Loewenheim, F.L. and van Wagenen, R.W. (1957) *Political Community and the North Atlantic Area: International Organization in the Light of Historical Experience*. Princeton, NJ: Princeton University Press.

Dewatripont, M. and Tirole, J. (1994) *The Prudential Regulation of Banks*. Cambridge, MA: MIT Press.

Di Giorgio, G. and Di Noia, C. (2003) 'Financial market regulation and supervision: how many peaks for the Euro area?' *Brooklyn Journal of International Law*, 28(2): 463–93.

Diebold, W. (1959) *The Schuman Plan: A Study in Economic Co-operation, 1950–1959*. New York: Praeger.

Diez, T. (1999) 'Speaking "Europe": the politics of integration discourse', *Journal of European Public Policy*, 6(4): 598–613.

Diez Medrano, J. (2003) *Framing Europe: Attitudes to European Integration in Germany, Spain and the United Kingdom*. Princeton, NJ: Princeton University Press.

Dorandeu, R. and Georgakakis, D. (2001) *L'Europe sur le métier: Acteurs et professionalisation de la construction européenne*. Strasbourg: Presses Universitaires de Strasbourg.

Douglas-Scott, S. (2002) *Constitutional Law of the European Union*. Harlow: Longman.

Duchesne, S. and Frognier, A.-P. (2002) 'Sur les dynamiques sociologiques et politiques de l'identification à l'Europe', *Revue française de science politique*, 52(4): 355–73.

Dunford, M. (1998) 'Economies in space and time: economic geographies of development and underdevelopment and historical geographies of modernization', in B. Graham (ed.), *Modern Europe: Place, Culture, Identity*. London, Arnold. pp. 53–88.

Eeckhout, P. (2005) *External Relations of the European Union: Legal and Constitutional Foundations*. Oxford: Oxford University Press.

Eichengreen, B. (ed) (1995) *Europe's Post-War Recovery*. Cambridge: Cambridge University Press.

Eichengreen, B. (2003) 'Institutions for fiscal stability', University of California–Berkeley, CA, USA. Working Paper PEIF-14.

Eichengreen, B. and Wyplosz, C. (1998) 'The Stability Pact: more than a minor nuisance?' *Economic Policy*, 26: 65–114.

Eijsbouts, W.T. and Reestman, J.H. (eds) (2005) 'The new European constitution: themes and questions', special issue of *European Constitutional Law Review*, 1.

Eisenbeis, R. and Kaufman, G. (2005) 'Bank crisis resolution and foreign-owned banks', *Federal Reserve Bank of Atlanta Economic Review*, 4: 1–18.

Emerson, M., Aujean, M., Catinat, N., Goybet, P. and Jacquemin, A. (1989) *The Economics of 1992*. Oxford: Oxford University Press.

Emerson, M., Gros, D., Italianer, A., Pisani-Ferry, J. and Reichenbach, H. (1992) *One Market One Money*. Oxford: Oxford University Press.

Eriksen, E.O. (2005) 'An emerging European public sphere', *European Journal of Social Theory*, 8(3): 341–63.

Ernst and Young/NIESR (1991) *A Strategy for the ECU*. London: Kogan Page.

European Commission (2001) *White Paper on European Governance*. COM(2001) 428 def., 25 July 2001.

European Commission (2005) *Public Finances in EMU 2005; European Economy* n° 3/2005, November.

Favell, A. (1998) 'The Europeanisation of immigration politics', *European Integration online Papers*, 2(10): 1–24. Also published in V. Guiraudon (ed.) (2000) *Sociologie de l'Europe: élites, mobilisations et configurations institutionelles*, special edition of *Cultures et conflits*, no. 38–39. Paris: L'Harmattan. Available online at: http://eiop.or.at/eiop/pdf/1998-010.pdf, accessed 10 September 2006.

Favell, A. (2006) *Eurostars and Eurocities: Free Moving Urban Professionals in an Integrating Europe.* Oxford: Blackwell.

Featherstone, K. and Radaelli, C.M. (eds) (2003) *The Politics of Europeanization.* New York: Oxford University Press.

Feketekuty, G. (1988) *International Trade in Services: An Overview and Blueprint for Negotiations.* Cambridge: Ballinger.

Finnis, J. (1980) *Natural Law and Natural Rights.* Oxford: Clarendon Press.

Flam, H. (1992) 'Product markets and 1992: full integration, large gains?' *Journal of Economic Perspectives,* 6(4): 7–30.

Fleming, J.M. (1971) 'On exchange rate unification', *Economic Journal,* 81: 467–88.

Fligstein, N. (2001) *The Architecture of Markets: An Economic Sociology of Twenty First Century Capitalist Societies* (Princeton, NJ: Princeton University Press).

Fligstein, N. (2003) 'The political and economic sociology of international economic arrangements', in N. Smelser and R. Swedberg (eds), *Handbook of Economic Sociology.* Princeton, NJ: Princeton University Press.

Fligstein, N. and Mara-Drita, I. (1996) 'How to make a market: reflections on the attempt to create a single market in the European Union', *American Journal of Sociology,* 102(1): 1–33.

Fligstein, N. and McNichol, J. (1998) 'The institutional terrain of the EU', in A. Stone Sweet and W. Sandholtz (eds), *European Integration and Supranational Governance.* Oxford: Oxford University Press. pp. 59–91.

Fligstein, N. and Mérand, F. (2002) 'Globalization or Europeanization? Evidence on the European economy since 1980', *Acta Sociologica,* 45(1): 7–22.

Fligstein, N. and Stone Sweet, A. (2002) 'Constructing polities and markets: an institutionalist account of European integration', *American Journal of Sociology,* 107: 1206–43.

Fratianni, M. and Peeters, T. (1978) *One Money for Europe.* London: MacMillan.

Fratianni, M., Von Hagen, J. and Waller, C. (1992) 'The Maastricht way to EMU', Essays in International Finance 187, Princeton University, New Jersey, USA.

Friedman, M. (1953) 'The case for flexible exchange rates', in M. Friedman (ed.), *Essays in Positive Economics.* Chicago: University of Chicago Press. pp. 157–203.

Fuller, L.L. (1973, 1969) *The Morality of Law.* New Haven, CT: Yale University Press.

Gabel, M. (1998) *Interests and Integration: Market Liberalization, Public Opinion, and European Union.* Ann Arbor: University of Michigan Press.

Georgakakis, D. (2000) 'La démission de la Commission Européenne: scandale et tournant institutionnel (oct 1998–mar 1999)' in V. Guiraudon (ed.), *Sociologie de l'Europe: élites, mobilisations et configurations institutionelles,* Special edition of *Cultures et conflits,* no. 38–39. Paris: L' Harmattan. pp. 39–59.

Gillingham, J. (1992) *Coal, Steel and the Rebirth of Europe. The Germans and French from Ruhr Conflict to Economic Community, 1945–1955.* Cambridge: Cambridge University Press.

Giovannini, A. (2001) *Cross-Border Clearing and Settlement Arrangements in the European Union.* Brussels: European Commission.

Giovannini, A. (2003) *Second Report on EU Clearing and Settlement Arrangements.* Brussels: European Commission.

Grimm, D. (1995) 'Does Europe need a constitution?' *European Law Journal,* 1: 282.

Guiraudon, V. (ed.) (2000) *Sociologie de l'Europe: élites, mobilisations et configurations institutionelles,* special edition of *Cultures et conflits,* no. 38–39. Paris: L'Harmattan.

Haas, E.B. (1958) *The Uniting of Europe: Political, Social, and Economic Forces, 1950–1957.* Stanford: Stanford University Press.

Haas, E.B. (1968) *The Uniting of Europe: Political, Social and Economic Forces 1950–1957,* 2nd ed. Stanford: Stanford University Press.

Habermas, J. (1969) *Strukturwandel der Öffentlichkeit: Untersuchungen zu einer Kategorie der bürgerlichen Gesellschaft.* Frankfurt-am-Main: Suhrkamp.

Habermas, J. (2001) *The Postnational Constellation: Political Essays.* Boston, MA: MIT Press.

Hallerberg, M. (2004) *Domestic Budgets in a United Europe: Fiscal Governance from the end of Bretton Woods to EMU.* Ithaca, NY: Cornell University Press.

Hallerberg, M. and Strauch, R. (2002) 'On the cyclicality of fiscal policy in Europe', *Empirica,* 29: 183–287.

Hallerberg, M., Strauch, R. and Von Hagen, J. (2004) 'The design of fiscal rules and forms of governance in European Union countries', ECB Working Paper 419, December, Frankfurt.

Hart, H.L.A. (1961, 1994) *The Concept of Law.* Oxford: Clarendon Press.

Hartley, T.C. (2002) 'The constitutional foundations of the European Union', *The Law Quarterly Review,* 117(10): 225–46.

Helliwell, J. (1998) *How Much Do National Borders Matter?* Washington, DC: Brookings.

Henkin, L. (1979, 1968) *How Nations Behave: Law and Foreign Policy*. New York: Columbia University Press.

Herring, R. (1997) 'Prospects for international cooperation in the regulation and supervision of financial services', in *Developments in Supervision and Regulation*. ICMB Occasional Studies no. 8, Geneva.

Herrmann, R.K., Risse, R. and Brewer, M.B. (eds) (2004) *Transnational Identities: Becoming European in the EU*. Lanham, MD: Rowman and Littlefield.

Hirsch Ballin, E.M.H. and Senden, L.A.J. (eds) (2005) *Co-actorship in the Development of European Law-making: The Quality of European Legislation and its Implementation and Application in the National Legal Order*. The Hague: T.M.C. Asser Press.

HM Treasury (1989) *An Evolutionary Approach to Economic and Monetary Union*. London: HMSO.

HM Treasury (2003) *Submissions on EMU from Leading Economists*. London: HM Treasury.

Hooghe, L. (2002) *The European Commission and the Integration of Europe*. Cambridge: Cambridge University Press.

Hughes Hallett, A., Lewis, J. and Von Hagen, J. (2003) 'Fiscal policy in Europe, 1991–2003: an evidence-based analysis', London: CEPR.

Hunt, J. and Shaw, J. (2000) 'European legal studies: then and now', in D. Hayton (ed.), *Law(s) Futures*. Oxford: Hart Publishing. pp. 117–33.

Imig, D. and Tarrow, S. (eds) (2001) *Contentious Europeans: Protest and Politics in an Emerging Polity*. Lanham, MD: Rowman and Littlefield.

Jachtenfuchs, M. (2001) 'Theorizing European integration and governance: the governance approach to European integration', *Journal of Common Market Studies*, 39(2): 245–64.

Joana, J. and Smith, A. (2002) *Les commissaires européennes: technocrates, diplomates ou politiques?* Paris: Presses de sciences po.

Joerges, C. and Vos, E. (eds) (1999) *EU Committees: Social Regulation, Law and Politics*. Oxford: Hart.

Kaelble, H. (1990) *A Social History of Western Europe 1880–1980*. Dublin, Gill and Macmillan.

Kaplan, J.J. and Schleiminger, G. (1989) *The European Payments Union. Financial Diplomacy in the 1950s*. Oxford: Clarendon Press.

Katzenstein, P. (ed.) (1996) *The Culture of National Security: Norms and Identity in World Politics*. New York: Columbia University Press.

Katzenstein, P.J. (1985) *Small States in World Markets: Industrial Policy in Europe*. Ithaca, NY: Cornell University Press.

Katzenstein, P.J. (1997) *Tamed Power. Germany in Europe*. Ithaca, NY: Cornell University Press.

Kaufman G (1994) *Reforming Financial Institutions in the United States*. Boston: Kluwer Academic.

Kauppi, N. (2005) *Democracy, Social Resources and Political Power in the European Union*. Manchester: Manchester University Press.

Keck, M. and Sikkink, K. (1997) *Activists Beyond Borders: Transnational Advocacy Networks in International Politics*. Ithaca, NY: Cornell University Press.

Kelsen, H. (1949, 1961) *General Theory of Law and State*. Cambridge, MA: Harvard University Press.

Kelsen, H. (1967) *The Pure Theory of Law and State*. Cambridge, MA: Harvard University Press.

Kelsen, H. (1991) *General Theory of Norms*. Oxford: Oxford University Press.

Kenen, P.B. (1969) 'A theory of optimum currency areas: an eclectic view', in R.A. Mundell and A.K. Swoboda (eds), *Monetary Problems of the International Economy*. Chicago: University of Chicago Press. pp. 41–60.

Kennedy, D.W. (1994) 'A new world order: yesterday, today, and tomorrow', *Transnational law and Contemporary Problems*, 4: 329–75.

Kennedy, D. and Webb, D.E. (1993) 'The limits of integration: eastern Europe and the European Communities', *Common Market Law Review*, 30: 1095–117.

Keynes, J.M. (1923) *A Tract on Monetary Reform*. London: MacMillan.

King, R. and Ruiz Gelices, E. (2003) 'International student migration and the European "year abroad": effects on European identity and subsequent migration behaviour', *International Journal of Population Geography*, 9: 229–52.

Klausen, J. and Tilly, L. (eds) (1997) *European Integration in Social and Historical Perspective*. Lanham, MD: Rowman and Littlefield.

Klotz, A. (1995) *Norms in International Relations: The Struggle Against Apartheid*. Ithaca, NY: Cornell University Press.

Kohler-Koch, B. and Eising, R. (eds) (1999) *The Transformation of Governance in the European Union*. London: Routledge.

Koopmans, R. and Erbe, J. (2004) 'Towards a European public sphere? Vertical and horizontal dimensions of a Europeanised political communication', *Innovation*, 17(2): 97–118.

Koopmans, R. and Statham, P. (2002) 'The transformation of political mobilisation and communication in European public spheres: a research outline (EUROPUB)', European Research proposal. Available online at: http://europub.wz-berlin.de, accessed 10 September 2006.

Koopmans, T. (1986) 'The role of law in the next stage of European integration', *International and Comparative Law Quarterly*, 35: 925–31.

Koopmans, T. (1991) 'The birth of European law at the crossroads of legal traditions', *American Journal of Comparative Law*, 39: 493.

Krotz, U. (2002) 'Ties that bind? The parapublic underpinnings of Franco-German relations as construction of international value'. Harvard University CES Working Paper 02/4. Available online at: http://www.ces.fas.harvard.edu/publications/Krotz4.pdf, accessed 10 September 2006.

Laffan, B. (2004) 'The European Union and its institutions as "identity builders"', in R.K. Hermann, R. Risse and M.B. Brewer (eds), *Transnational Identities: Becoming European in the EU*. Lanham, MD: Rowman and Littlefield. pp. 75–96.

Lenaerts, K. and. van Nuffel, P. (2005) *Constitutional Law of the European Union*. London: Sweet and Maxwell.

Lindberg, L.N. (1963) *The Political Dynamics of European Economic Integration*. Stanford, CA: Stanford University Press.

Maas, C. (1995) *Progress Report on the Preparation of the Changeover to the Single European Currency*. Brussels, 10 May.

MacCormick, N. (1993) 'Beyond the sovereign state', *Modern Law Review*, 56(1): 1–18.

MacCormick, N. (1998) 'Norms, institutions, and institutional facts', *Law and Philosophy*, 3: 301–45.

Macmillen, M., Mayes, D.G. and van Veen, P. (1987) *European Integration and Industry*. Tilburg: Tilburg University Press.

Majone, G. (1996a) *Regulating Europe*. New York: Routledge.

Majone, G. (1996b) *The European Community as a Regulatory State*, Collected Courses of the Academy of European Law. Vol. V, Book 1, pp. 321–419. The Hague: Martinus Nijhof.

Majone, G. (2001) 'Two logics of delegation: agency and fiduciary relations in EU governance', *European Union Politics*, 2(1): 103–22.

Marks, G. and McAdam, D. (1996) 'Social movements and the changing structure of political opportunity in the European Union', *West European Politics*, 19(2): 249–78.

Mattli, W. (1999) *The Logic of Regional Integration: Europe and Beyond*. Cambridge: Cambridge University Press.

Mayes, D. (1978) 'The effects of economic integration on trade', *Journal of Common Market Studies*, 17(1): 1–25.

Mayes, D. (2006) 'Cross-border financial supervision in Europe: goals and transition paths', *Sveriges Riksbank Economic Review*, 206(2): 58–89.

Mayes, D. and Begg, I. (1991) *Achieving Economic and Social Cohesion as a Precondition for Monetary Union*. European Parliament.

Mayes, D. and Bramson, M. (1987) 'Barriers to trade in services', OECD Occasional Paper, Paris.

Mayes, D. and Burridge, M. (1993) 'The impact of the internal market programme on European economic structure and performance', Working Paper E2, Strasbourg: European Parliament.

Mayes, D. and Hart P. (1994) *The Single Market Programme as a Stimulus to Change: Comparisons Between Britain and Germany*. Cambridge: Cambridge University Press.

Mayes, D. and Suvanto, S. (2002) 'Beyond the fringe: Finland and the choice of currency regime', *Journal of Public Policy*, 22(2): 161–82.

Mayes, D. and Vesala, J. (2000) 'On the problems of home country control', *Contemporary Politics and Economics of Europe*, 10(1): 1–26.

Mayes, D. and Wood, G. (2006) *The Structure of Financial Regulation*. London: Routledge.

Mayes, D.G., Macmillen, M. and van Veen, P. (1987) *Integration and European Industry*. Tilburg: Tilburg University Press.

McCallum, J. (1995) 'National borders matter: Canada–US regional trade patterns', *American Economic Review*, 85(3): 615–23.

McKinnon, R.I. (1963) 'Optimum currency areas', *American Economic Review*, 53: 717–25.

Meade, J.E. (1957) 'The balance of payment problems of a European free trade area', *Economic Journal*, 67: 379–96.

Meinhof, U. (2004) 'Europe viewed from below: agents, victims and the threat of the other', in R.K. Hermann, R. Risse and M.B. Brewer (eds), *Transnational Identities: Becoming European in the EU*. Lanham, MD: Rowman and Littlefield. pp. 214–46.

Mendras, H. (1997) *L'Europe des Européens*. Paris: Gallimard.

Mérand, F. (2003) 'Dying for the Union? Military officers and the creation of a European defence force', *European Societies*, 5(3): 253–82.

Milward, A.S. (1992) *The European Rescue of the Nation-State*. London: Routledge.

Milward, A.S. (2005) *Union and Economics in the History of the European Union*. The Graz Schumpeter Lectures. London: Routledge. pp. 80–115.

Milward, A.S. and Brennan, G. (1996) *Britain's Place in the World. A Historical Enquiry into Import*

Controls 1945–60. London and New York: Routledge.

Moravcsik, A. (1998) *The Choice for Europe. Social Purpose and State Power from Messina to Maastricht*. Ithaca, NY: Cornell University Press.

Mosler, H. (1976) 'The international society as a legal community', *Receuil des Courts* 1974, 140: 1–47.

Mundell, R.A. (1961) 'A theory of optimum currency areas', *American Economic Review*, 51: 509–17.

Neyer, J. (2000) 'Justifying comitology: the promise of comitology', in K. Neunreither and A. Wiener (eds), *European Integration after Amsterdam: Institutional Dynamics and Prospects for Democracy*. Oxford: Oxford University Press. pp. 112–28.

Nieto, M. and Wall, L. (2005) 'Institutional preconditions for a successful implementation of supervisors' prompt corrective action: is there a case for a banking standard in the EU?', mimeo, Bank of Spain

O'Leary, S. (1999) 'The free movement of persons and services', in P. Craig and G. De Búrca (eds), *The Evolution of EU Law*. Oxford: Oxford University Press.

Padoa-Schioppa, T. (1987) *Efficiency, Stability, Equity*. Oxford: Oxford University Press.

Parsons, C. (2003) *A Certain Idea of Europe*. Ithaca, NY: Cornell University Press.

Pelkmans, J. and Winters, L.A. (1988) *Europe's Domestic Market*. London: Pinter for RIIA.

Pernice, I. (2002) 'Multilevel constitutionalism and the European Union', *European Law Review*, 27: 511–29.

Pernice, I. and Poiares, M. (eds) (2004) *A Constitution for the European Union: first comments on the draft of the European Convention*. Baden-Baden: Nomos.

Pescatore, P. (1974) *The Law of Integration: Emergence of A New Phenomenon in International Relations, based on the Experience of the European Communities*. Leiden: Sijthoff.

Pisani-Ferry, J. (2002) 'Fiscal discipline and policy coordination in the Eurozone: assessment and proposals', Ministerie van Financien, Budgetary Policy in E(M)U: Design and Challenges, The Hague.

Pollack, M.A. (2003) *The Engines of European Integration. Delegation, Agency and Agenda Setting in the EU*. Oxford and New York: Oxford University Press.

Prechal, A. (2005) *Directives in EC Law*, 2nd rev. ed. Oxford: Oxford University Press.

Raz, J. (1970) *The Concept of a Legal System: An Introduction to the Theory of a Legal System*. Oxford: Clarendon Press.

Recchi, E., Tambini, D., Baldoni, E., Williams, D., Surak, K. and Favell, A. (2003) 'Intra-EU migration: a socio-demographic overview'. Working Paper WP3. PI NEUR project, 'Pioneers of European Integration from Below: Mobility and the Emergence of European Identity among National and Foreign Citizens in the EU', 1–47. Available online at: http://www.obets.ua.es/pioneur/, accessed 10 September 2006.

Risse, T. (ed.) (1995) *Bringing Transnational Relations Back In: Non-State Actors, Domestic Structures and International Institutions*. Cambridge: Cambridge University Press.

Risse, T. (2001) 'A European identity? Europeanization and the evolution of nation-state identities', in M. Green Cowles, J. Caporaso and T. Risse (eds), *Transforming Europe: Europeanization and Domestic Change*. Ithica, NY: Cornell University Press. pp. 198–216.

Risse, T. (2004) 'European institutions and identity change: what have we learned?', in R.K. Hermann, R. Risse and M.B. Brewer (eds), *Transnational Identities: Becoming European in the EU*. Lanham, MD: Rowman and Littlefield. pp. 247–72.

Risse, T., Engelmann-Martin, D., Knope, H.-J. and Roscher, K. (1999) 'To Euro or not to Euro? EMU and identity politics in the European Union', *European Journal of International Relations*, 5(2): 147–87.

Rochet, J.-C. and Tirole, J. (2002) 'Cooperation among competitors: some economics of payment card associations', *Rand Journal of Economics*, 33(4): 549–70.

Rodríguez-Pose, A. (2002) *The European Union: Economy, Society, and Polity*. Oxford: Oxford University Press.

Rogoff, K. (1985) 'The optimal degree of commitment to an intermediate monetary target', *Quarterly Journal of Economics*, 100(4): 1169–89.

Rootes, C. (1999) 'The transformation of environmental activism: activists, organisations and policy makers', *Innovation*, 12(2): 153–73.

Rosamond, B. (2000) *Theories of European Integration*. Basingstoke and New York: Palgrave.

Rose, A (2000) 'One market, one money: the effect of common currencies on trade', *Economic Policy*, 30: 7–46.

Rose, A. and Engel, C. (2002) 'Currency unions and international integration', *Journal of Money Credit and Banking*, 34(4): 1067–89.

Ruiter, D.W.P. (1993) *Institutional Legal Facts: Legal Powers and their Effects*. Dordrecht: Kluwer Academic Publishers.

Rumford, C. (2002) *The European Union: A Political Sociology*. Oxford: Blackwell.

Schelkle, W. (2001) 'The optimum currency area approach to European monetary integration: framework of debate or dead end?', European Institute Paper no 3, South Bank University.

Schepel, H. (1998) 'The mobilisation of European Community law', in J. Brand and D. Strempel (eds), *Soziologie des Rechts – Festschrift für Erhard Blankenburg*. Baden-Baden: Nomos. pp. 433–55.

Schepel, H. and Wesseling, R. (1997) 'The legal Community: judges, lawyers, officials and clerks in the writing of Europe', *European Law Journal*, 3(2): 165–88.

Schimmelfennig, F. (2003) *The EU, NATO and the Integration of Europe: Rules and Rhetoric*. Cambridge: Cambridge University Press.

Schissler, H. and Soysal, Y. (eds) (2004) *The Nation, Europe and the World: Textbooks and Curricula in Transition*. New York: Berghahn.

Schlesinger, P. (1999) 'Changing spaces of political communication: the case of the European Union', *Political Communication*, 16(3): 263–79.

Schmiedel, H. and Schönberger, A. (2005) 'Integration of securities market infrastructure in the EU', ECB Occasional Paper 33, July.

Schnabel, V. (1998) 'Elite européennes en formation: les étudiants du collège de Bruges et leurs études', *Politix*, 43: 33–52.

Schoenmaker, D. (2003) 'Financial supervision: from national to European?' *Financial and Monetary Studies*, 22(1).

Schoenmaker, D. and Goodhart, C. (2006) 'Problems in burden sharing in the EU', Sveriges Riksbank, 14 February.

Schönberger, Chr. (2005) *Unionsbürger: Europas föderales Bürgerrecht in vergleichender Sicht*. Berlin: Mohr Siebeck.

Schrauwen, A. (2002) *Flexibility in Constitutions. Forms of Closer Cooperation in Federal and Non-Federal Settings*. Groningen: Europa Law Publishing.

Schwarze, J. (ed.) (2001) *The Birth of a European Constitutional Order*. Baden-Baden: Nomos.

Scott, J. (1998) 'Law, legitimacy and EC governance: prospects for "partnership"', *Journal of Common Market Studies*, 36: 175.

Scott, S.V. (1994) 'International law as ideology: theorizing the relationship between international law and international politics', *European Journal of International Law*, 5: 313–25.

Selznick, P. (2003) '"Law in context" revisited', *Journal of Law and Society*, 30: 177–86.

Senden, L. (2004) *Soft Law in European Community Law*. Oxford: Hart Publishing.

Shaw, J. (1996) 'European Union legal studies in crisis? Towards a new dynamic', *Oxford Journal of Legal Studies*, 16: 231.

Shaw, J. (1997) 'Social-legal studies and the European Union', in P. Thomas (ed.), *Socio-Legal Studies*. Aldershot: Dartmouth.

Shaw, J. (1998) 'The interpretation of European Union citizenship', *Modern Law Review*, 61: 293.

Shaw, J. (2000) *The Law of the European Union*, 3rd ed. London: Palgrave.

Shaw, J. and More, G. (eds) (1995) *New Legal Dynamics of European Union*. Oxford: Oxford University Press.

Shore, C. (2000) *Building Europe: The Cultural Politics of European Integration*. London: Routledge.

Shy, O. (2001) *The Economics of Network Industries*. Cambridge: Cambridge University Press.

Siedentop, L. (2001) *Democracy in Europe*. Oxford: Oxford University Press.

Sinn, H.-W. (2003) *The New Systems Competition*, Yrjö-Jahnsson Lectures. Oxford: Basil Blackwell.

Snyder, F. (1990) *New Directions in European Community Law*. London: Weidenfeld and Nicolson.

Spierenburg, D. and Poidevin, R. (1994) *The History of the High Authority of the European Coal and Steel Community. Supranationality in Operation*. London: Weidenfeld and Nicolson.

Staples, H. (1999) *Legal Status of Third Country Nationals Resident in the EU*. The Hague: Kluwer Law International.

Statham, P. and Gray, E. (2005) 'The public sphere and debates about Europe in Britain: internalised and conflict driven?' *Innovation*, 18(1): 61–81.

Steiner, J. and Woods, L. (2003) *EC Law*. Oxford: Oxford University Press.

Stone Sweet, A. and Sandholtz, W. (1997) 'European integration and supranational governance', *Journal of European Public Policy*, 4(3): 197–317.

Strudel, S. (2002) 'Les citoyens européens aux urnes: les usages ambigus de l'article 8B de la traité de Maastrict', *Revue internationale de politique compare*, 9(1): 47–63.

Sutherland, P. (1992) 'The internal market after 1992. Meeting the challenge', Brussels: Report to the Commission by the High Level Group on the Operation of the Internal Market.

Tarrow, S. (1995) 'The Europeanisation of conflict: reflections from a social movements perspective', *West European Politics*, 18(2): 223–51.

Taylor, J.B. (1993) 'Discretion versus policy rules in practice', *Carnegie-Rochester Conference Series on Public Policy*, 39: 195–214.

Therborn, G. (1995) *European Modernity and Beyond: The Trajectory of European Societies, 1945–2000*. Thousand Oaks, CA: Sage.

Trenz, H.-J. and Eder, K. (2004) 'The democratising dynamics of a European public sphere: towards a theory of democratic functionalism', *European Journal of Social Theory*, 7(1): 5–25.

Triffin, R. (1960) *Gold and the Dollar Crisis*. New Haven, CT: Yale University Press.

Twining, W. (1997) *Law in Context: Enlarging a Discipline*. Oxford: Clarendon Press.

Verhoeven, A. (2002) *The European Union in Search of a Democratic and Constitutional Theory*. The Hague: Kluwer Law International.

Viner, J. (1950) *The Customs Union Issue*. New York: Carnegie Endowment for International Peace.

Vos, E. (2000) *European Administrative Reform and Agencies*. Florence: European University Institute.

Walsh, C. (1995) 'Optimal contracts for central bankers', *American Economic Review*, 85: 150–67.

Walter, N. (1976) 'Capital controls and the autonomy of national demand management: the German case', in A.K. Swoboda (ed.), *Capital Movements and Their Control*. Leiden: Sijthoff. pp. 163–70.

Ward, I. (2003) *A Critical Introduction to European Law*. London: Lexis Nexis Butterworths.

Weiler, J.H.H. (1999a) *The Constitution of Europe. 'Do the New Clothes have an Emperor?' and other Essays on European Integration*. Cambridge: Cambridge University Press.

Weiler, J.J.H. (1999b) 'The constitution of the common market place: text and context in the evolution of the free movement of goods', in P. Craig and G. De Búrca (eds), *The Evolution of EU Law*. Oxford: Oxford University Press. Ch. 10, pp. 349–76.

Wendt, A. (1999) *The Social Theory of International Politics*. Cambridge: Cambridge University Press.

Werner, P (1970) *Report to the Council and the Commission on the Realization by Stages of Economic and Monetary Union in the Community*. Supplement to the *Bulletin of the European Communities*, November.

Wessel, R.A. (2000a) 'Revisiting the international legal status of the EU', *European Foreign Affairs Review*, 5: 507–37.

Wessel, R.A. (2000b) 'The inside looking out: consistency and delimitation in EU external relations', *Common Market Law Review*, 37: 1135–71.

Wessel, R.A. (2003) 'The constitutional relationship between the European Union and the European Community: consequences for the relationship with the member states', in J.J.H. Weiler and A. von Bogdandy (eds), *Jean Monnet Working Papers*. Available olnie at: www.jeanmonnetprogram.org/papers/03/030901-09.html, accessed 8 September 2006.

Wessel, R.A. (2006) 'The multilevel constitution of European foreign relations', in N. Tsagourias (ed.), European and International Aspects of Constitutionalism. Cambridge: Cambridge University Press (forthcoming).

Wimmer, A. and Glick Schiller, N. (2002) 'Methodological nationalism and beyond: nation-state building, migration and the social sciences', *Global Networks*, 2(4): 301–34.

Winter, A. (1991) 'International trade and "1992": an overview', *European Economic Review*, 35: 367–77.

Woolcock, S. (1994) *The European Single Market: Centralisation or Competition Among National Rules*. London: RIIA.

Wyplosz, C. (2005) 'Fiscal policy: institutions versus rules', *National Institute Economic Review*, 191: 70–84.

Zeitlin, J. and Herrigel, G. (eds) (2000) *Americanization and its Limits: Reworking US Technology and Management in Post-War Europe and Japan*. Oxford: Oxford University Press.

PART II

The European Union as Polity

6

The European Union as a Polity (I)

SIMON HIX

INTRODUCTION

Since the work of Max Weber and others at the start of the twentieth century, it was almost universally accepted that politics and government could only take place within a 'state': a hierarchical political organization, with the sovereign power to make and enforce decisions on a (preferably) homogenous society. A century later, these ideas now seem rather quaint! The Weberian state largely existed in a particular geographic region of the world (the far western periphery of the Eurasian continent) and in a rather short period of human history (from the seventeenth to the mid-twentieth centuries). And, with the global devolution of power to regions, localities and non-state organizations, and the delegation of authority to supranational bodies such as the European Union and the World Trade Organization, political power is now dispersed or 'shared'. This does not mean that the 'state' does not exist. But, it does mean that politics and government now exist in many contexts either outside or beyond the classic state (cf. Badie and Birnbaum 1983).

This is precisely the situation with the EU where, in the second half of the twentieth century, the western European nation-states voluntarily delegated significant executive, legislative and judicial powers to a new set of institutions at the European level, and so established a new polity. The EU is the first genuine 'supranational polity', and so is *sui generis*, by definition. But, at one level, all polities are unique. The US has a unique form of federalism, Britain has a unique form of parliamentary government, and so on. At another level, all polities face a common set of issues, such as how far power is centralized, how decisions should be made at the centre, or who wins and who loses in the policy process. Put this way, if the EU is not a unique case (an 'N of 1'), it can be treated as just another (although admittedly strange) modern polity.

The recognition of the EU as 'just another polity' enabled a new generation of scholars to approach the EU from the fields of comparative politics and comparative public policy (e.g. Scharpf 1988; Attinà 1990; Streeck and Schmitter 1991; Sbragia 1992; Alter and Meunier-Aitsahalia 1994; Tsebelis 1994; Bowler and Farrell 1995; Crombez 1996; Majone 1996;

McKay 1996; Pierson 1996; van der Eijk and Franklin 1996; Hooghe and Marks 1998). This new generation brought a new set of research questions (cf. Hix 1994, 1998). Until the early 1990s, the main focus had been to explain bargaining between the member states, power relations between the member states and the supranational institutions, and the general long-run process of economic and political integration in Europe, mainly from the field of international relations. A whole new set of research questions have now been added to this list, such as how does executive power work, which actors are most influential in the EU legislative process, how independent from political control is the European Court of Justice, why do some citizens support the EU while others oppose it, why does the EU produce some policy outcomes but not others? These questions, and many others, are bread-and-butter issues in comparative government and comparative public policy, and these fields have an established analytical tool-kit to help answer them. Hence, treating the EU as a polity has enabled researchers to answer new questions, apply new empirical techniques, discover new facts, draw new analytical inferences, and bring together scholarship in international relations and comparative politics in the study of the EU.

As a result, the last decade has seen a rapidly growing set of literature that approaches the European Union as a polity. It is impossible and would be inappropriate to review all this research here.[1] This research has provided insights and cumulative knowledge about *inter alia* the design of the EU institutions, politics within and between the EU institutions, the aims and impact of the policy outputs of the EU, and the mechanisms of democratic control of the EU. In this essay I aim to build on this literature and its findings to provide a general overview of how the EU works as a 'polity'. Section 2 consequently looks at the allocation of policy powers between the member states and the EU level. Section 3 looks at the design and operation of agenda-setting and veto powers among the EU institutions: the Council, Commission, Parliament, and Court of Justice. In other words, these two sections look at the

two classic dimensions of the institutional design of democratic polities (e.g. Lijphart 1999). Sections 3 and 4 then look at how this particular institutional design shapes politics and democratic accountability in the EU.

The key points of this analysis are as follows. The basic institutional ('constitutional') architecture of the EU is extremely stable, and a myriad of checks-and-balances ensure that there are few losers from EU policies. Nevertheless, the design of EU constrains domestic policy choices, and it is difficult to change EU policies once they have been adopted. Direct democratic control on the EU is also extremely weak. As a result, in the coming years, the EU faces a challenge: how to undertake significant policy reforms in a system that does not provide a direct democratic mandate for such reforms.

ALLOCATION OF COMPETENCES BETWEEN THE STATES AND THE EU: AN UPSIDE-DOWN POLITY

In the EU, as in all multi-level polities, some policy competences are allocated to the central level of government while others are allocated to the lower (member state) level. From a *normative* perspective, policies should be allocated to different levels to produce the best overall policy outcome. For example, if there is an internal market then the abolition of internal trade barriers must be tackled at the centre. Policies where state decisions could have a negative impact on a neighbouring state (an 'externality'), such as environmental standards or product standards, are also best dealt with at the centre. Similarly, policies where preferences are homogeneous across citizens in different localities, such as basic social and civil rights, could be dealt with centrally (Alesina et al. 2001). And, the centre should be responsible for setting interest rates as well as income distribution from rich to poor states, on the grounds that central monetary policies inevitably constrain the tax and welfare policies of the states (Brown and Oates 1987; Oates 1999) – although the centre should provide hard budgetary constraints on state expenditures (to prevent high deficits) and regulatory and expenditure policies should be de-centralized, to foster policy competition and innovation (Weingast 1995; Quin and Weingast 1997).

From a *positive* perspective, in contrast, the allocation of competences is the result of a specific constitutional and political bargain, and how actors with different policy goals have behaved within this bargain (Riker 1975; McKay 1996, 2001). For example, social democrats usually prefer regulatory and fiscal policies to be centralized (to allow for income redistribution and central value allocation), whereas economic liberals prefer strong checks-and-balances on the exercise of these policies by the central government. In addition, some constitutional designs are more rigid than others. For example, the states can be protected against 'policy drift' to the centre via a clear catalogue of competences and independent judicial review of competence disputes. Nevertheless, under all constitutional designs, the division of competences is never completely fixed, and the long-term trend in most multi-level polities has been policy centralization.

For example, consider the evolution of competences in the EU and the US. Both polities started with a low level of policy centralization. However, policy centralization occurred remarkably quickly in the EU compared to the US, and in some areas faster than others (Pollack 1995, 2000). By the end of the 1990s, most regulatory and monetary policies were decided predominantly at the EU level. In contrast, most expenditure, citizen, and foreign policies were controlled by the states. In the US, in contrast, foreign policies were centralized before economic policies. In the area of regulatory policies, the harmonization of rules governing the production, distribution and exchange of goods, services and capital is now more extensive in the EU than in the US (Donohue and Pollack 2001). For example, in the field of social regulation, where there are few federal rules in the US, the EU has common standards covering working hours, rights

of part-time and temporary workers, workers consultation, and so on. Also, after the high point of regulatory policy-making by Washington in 1980, the 1990s saw the deregulation of US-federal regimes and increasing regulatory competition between the states (Ferejohn and Weingast 1992). Finally, in the area of taxation, whereas the EU has harmonized sales tax, there are no EU rules governing the application of income tax. In the US, in contrast, there are few federal restrictions on the application of consumption taxes by the states, but income taxes are levied by both the state and federal authorities.

These variations stem from very different social, political and historical experiences. But, given these differences in the US and EU, there has been a remarkably similar experience in the area of socio-economic policies. A normative perspective would predict that market integration must be tackled at the centre. From a positive perspective, however, in both the EU and the US, basic constitutional provisions guaranteeing the removal of barriers to the free movement of goods and services have been used by the central institutions to establish new common standards in other areas, such as social rights, and the gradual integration of other economic powers, such as a single currency, and constraints on fiscal policies. Meanwhile, the direct redistributive capacity of the US federal government remained limited until the 1930s, while the direct redistributive capacity of the EU is tiny compared to the expenditure power of the EU member states (the EU budget is only approximately 1% of EU GDP).

As a result, both the EU and the US developed as 'regulatory states' rather than 'redistributive' or 'welfare' states (cf. Skowronek 1982; Majone 1993, 1996). In the US, the regulatory capacity of the central government gradually developed between the late nineteenth century and the end of the 1970s. In the EU it took a much shorter time: between the late 1960s and the mid-1990s. But, once the single market was completed and the EU was given the necessary policy competences to regulate this market, a new European 'constitutional settlement' had effectively been established: where the European level of government is responsible for the creation and regulation of the market (and the related external trade policies); the domestic level of government is responsible for taxation and redistribution (within constraints agreed at the European level); and the domestic governments are collectively responsible for policies on internal security (justice and crime) and external security (defence and foreign). This settlement was essentially set up by the Single European Act, and then amended by the Maastricht Treaty. The subsequent reforms (in the Amsterdam and Nice Treaties and even in the draft Constitutional Treaty which was signed in June 2004) have not altered the settlement substantially. For example, the draft Constitution proposed to establish a catalogue of competences which would lock-in the existing quasi-constitutional settlement: with a separation between exclusive competences of the EU (for the establishment the market); shared competences between the EU and the member states (mainly for the regulation of the market); 'coordination competences' (covering macro-economic policies, interior affairs, and foreign policies), and exclusive competences of the member states (in most areas of taxation and expenditure).

Nevertheless, as Moravcsik (2001: 163–4) points out:

> The EU plays almost no role – at most a weak sort of international cooperation – in most of the issue-areas about which European voters care most, such as taxation, welfare state provision, defence, high foreign policy, policing, education, cultural policy, human rights, and small business policy ... The EU was designed as, and remains primarily, a limited national institution to coordinate national regulation of trade in goods and services, and the resulting flows of economic factors. ... The EU constitutional order is not only barely a federal state; it is barely recognizable as a state at all.

The concentration of policy-making capacity at the lower level of government rather than at the higher level of government means that democratic politics in the EU is 'upside down' compared to most other multi-level polities: where citizens, parties, politicians, and the media are primarily interested on the electoral battles for national political office and only secondarily concerned with the battles for European political office. For example, voters care much more about whether their taxes will increase or whether healthcare spending will be increased than whether the EU single market is more neoliberal or highly regulated. Likewise, politicians and political parties would rather win national government office and national parliamentary elections than be nominated to the EU Commission or increase their representation in the European Parliament. This consequently explains why European Parliament elections in almost every EU member state are always 'second order national elections': mid-term polls on the popularity of the governing party or parties in the member state rather than about the performance and policies of the parties in the European Parliament (Reif and Schmitt 1980; van der Eijk and Franklin 1996). This also explains why the outcome of most referendums on EU questions (whether to join the EU, to join the single currency, or to ratify an EU treaty) are influenced as much, if not more, by domestic political considerations than the preferences of citizens on the specific EU question on the ballot (Franklin et al. 1995; Hug 2002).

Nonetheless, the policy competences at the EU level have significant indirect distributional consequences at the domestic level. As a result of the EU single market and EU competition policies, the EU has forced member states to reduce their intervention in the economy. For example, as a result of the EU, air transport, telecommunications, energy supply and financial services have been significantly liberalized, often against the preferences of influential domestic vested interests. Moreover, in the area of social regulation, the EU has tended to establish voluntary common standards, rather than harmonized standards at a relatively high level (which the EU has done in the area of environmental regulation), which has allowed those states with low levels of social protection to continue these policies (esp. Streeck 1995, 1996). And, in the area of monetary policy, the Stability and Growth Pact, the excessive deficits procedure, and the system of multilateral surveillance present significant constrains on EMU member states' fiscal policy choices. There is little evidence that these policies have lead to 'social dumping': where member states with higher levels of social protection and taxation have been forced to cut these provisions under the threat of capital flight to states with lower production costs. Nevertheless, the particular mix of market (de)regulation and monetary policies at the European level presents significant constraints on welfare compromises and choices at the domestic level, and in particular forces member states to hold-down tax rates on capital and non-wage labour costs (Scharpf 1997, 1999).

This presents particular problems for democratic politics in the EU. On the one hand, voters, parties, and the media have few incentives to mobilize around the policy issues at stake at the European level, as the EU-level policies are not particularly salient. On the other hand, the low salience EU-level policies have significant constraints on the choices citizens and politicians can make in highly salient economic and social policies. This partly explains the concerns about the 'democratic deficit' in the EU. However, the problems resulting from the particular allocation of competences in the EU polity are confounded by the design and operation of the decision-making institutions at the European level.

SEPARATION OF POWERS AT THE CENTRE: A HYPER-CONSENSUS POLITY

A key factor determining how policies are made by polities is how far agenda-setting and veto power is centralized or dispersed (cf. Lijphart 1999). At one extreme, a polity can have a single agenda-setter and veto-player, as in the classic 'majoritarian' model of single-party government, executive dominance of the legislature, a weak second chamber, and a weak judiciary. At the other extreme, a 'consensus' polity tends to have multiple veto-players, either through proportional representation and coalition governments (particularly where a grand-coalition is prevalent), or a separation

of powers between the executive (president) and the legislature (congress), or 'strong bicameralism', or a system of independent judicial review, or a combination of these factors (e.g. Tsebelis 1995, 2002). However one might measure it, policy-making in the EU is at the extreme end of the majoritarian-consensus spectrum, and is perhaps more consensus-oriented in its design than any polity in the history of democratic government!

In the first place, agenda-setting power – in terms of who initiates policies – is split between two institutions. The European Council, which brings together the heads of state and government of the EU member states, decides on Treaty reforms (which determine the allocation of policies to the EU level) and sets the medium-term policy agenda (by inviting the Commission to initiate legislation in a particular policy area). The European Commission, meanwhile, has a formal monopoly on the initiative of most EU legislation.

In much of the literature on European integration and EU politics, the Commission is regarded as having significantly different preferences from the EU member states. In the early neo-functionalist theories, the Commission was thought to be ideologically committed to European integration (cf. Lindberg and Scheingold 1970). In more recent literature, the Commission was assumed to be more favourable towards EU regulation than almost all EU member states, either to promote its own institutional interests or because it is allied to a particular set of social or economic interests who expect to benefit from new EU rules (e.g. Sandholtz and Zysman 1989; Majone 1996; Cram 1997; Pollack 1997a, 2003). If the Commission has outlying preferences, it is likely to be able to use its agenda-setting powers to secure significant changes to the policy status quo. This at least partially explains the rapid development of EU integration in the late 1980s, following the delegation of significant agenda-setting power to the Commission in the Single European Act.

Nevertheless, recent research suggests that the Commission is not in fact a preference-outlier. Below the level of the politically appointed Commissioners, Hooghe (1999, 2001) has found that the main predictors of the policy preferences of the senior officials in the Commission's bureaucracy are their national origins and national party affiliations. At the political level, the member state governments choose 'their' Commissioners. Most of these politicians are strongly tied to the political parties who chose them and seek to return to domestic politics after their careers in the Commission. Hence, the Commissioners are likely to reflect the preferences of the parties and governments who nominated them. And, since the college of Commissioners decides by a majority vote, the Commission should initiate policies that are preferred by the median member of the Commission, and the median member of the Commission is likely to have relatively centrist policy preferences on both of the main dimensions of EU politics – EU integration, and the left-right (esp. Crombez 1997; Hug 2003).

The Commission President might be an influential agenda-setter inside the Commission, and so be able to influence the policies initiated by the Commission. However, until the Nice Treaty entered into force in 2003, the Commission President was chosen by unanimity amongst the member states. With a unanimity rule, the member state closest to the policy status quo (usually the least integrationist member state) was able to choose the Commission President. In the selection of most recent Commission Presidents, Britain was the least integrationist member state. As a result, Margaret Thatcher was able to veto Claude Cheysson in favour of Jacques Delors (who she felt was more free-market and less federalist!), John Major vetoed Jean-Luc Dehaene in favour of Jacques Santer, and Tony Blair proposed Romano Prodi.

In other words, the Commission is likely to initiate policies that are relatively centrist. And, if the Commission, as the agenda-setter, is centrally-located rather than located at one of the extremes, then the influence of the Commission on policy outcomes is less then one might expect. If the Commission is a preference-outlier, with strongly 'integrationist' or strong 'market regulation' preferences, it would propose legislation that would promote faster European integration or a high level of European regulation. In contrast, if the Commission is already located within, or close to, the set of policies that have already been adopted and cannot be changed (the win-set), the Commission will only want to initiate legislation in those areas where the existing policy status quo is rather extreme.

Furthermore, the powers of the EU agenda-setters are heavily constrained by the rules of the EU legislative process as they are currently designed. Under the institutional design of the Treaty of Rome and the Single European Act, the Commission was extremely powerful (e.g. Tsebelis and Kreppel 1998). This was because legislation was mainly adopted by the EU Council, with only limited input by the European Parliament. The introduction of the so-called 'cooperation procedure' in the Single European Act gave the European Parliament two readings of legislation, but the Commission maintained the right to decide whether to accept or reject the Parliament's proposed amendments and the Council remained the final legislative chamber, deciding whether to accept or reject the final proposal of the Commission (cf. Moser 1996; Tsebelis 1994). Where unanimity was required in the Council, the Commission had to satisfy the member state government that was closest to the status quo, and so could not change many existing policies. However, where only a qualified-majority was required in the Council (as in the adopted of most of the legislation for the creation of the single market), the size of the set of policies that a majority in the Council preferred to the status quo was considerably bigger, which gave the Commission the power to move policy outcomes closer to its policy preferences – regardless of whether its preferences were extremely integrationist or centrist (cf. Garrett 1992; Steunenberg 1994; Crombez 1996).

This was changed by the Maastricht, Amsterdam, and Nice Treaties, which significantly reduced the agenda-setting power of the Commission, and increased the number of veto-players in the EU's legislative system. The Maastricht Treaty, in 1993, introduced the co-decision procedure. This procedure introduced the rule that if the European Parliament and Council disagree after two readings of legislation, a 'conciliation committee' is convened, of equal representatives of the Parliament and Council. Then, after the conciliation committee, the European Parliament can reject the legislation outright. In other words, for the first time, the Maastricht Treaty established the European Parliament as a veto-player.

The Amsterdam Treaty, in 1999, then reformed and extended the co-decision procedure: increasing the power of the European Parliament within the procedure and extending the procedure to most areas previously covered by the cooperation procedure. And, the Nice Treaty, in 2003, further extended the co-decision procedure and raised the threshold for passing legislation by a qualified-majority in the Council.

These reforms established that in most policy areas the EU has a tri-cameral legislative system: where legislation is initiated by the Commission, and can then be amended beyond the Commission's intentions by a majority in the European Parliament and a qualified-majority in the Council. Adding the European Parliament as an independent agenda-setter and a veto-player, and raising the qualified-majority threshold in the Council have made it more difficult for EU legislation to be adopted (by reducing the set of policies that are acceptable to all three actors), and so have reduced the agenda-setting powers of the Commission (Crombez 2001; Tsebelis and Yataganas 2002). This intuition is also supported by empirical research, which has shown that while the move from unanimity to qualified-majority voting in the Council generally reduced the length of time it took to adopt legislation, involving the European Parliament increased the time needed (Schulz and König 2000; cf. Golub 1999) – empirical research has not yet analysed the impact of the increase in the qualified-majority threshold in the Council by the Nice Treaty.

In addition to the checks-and-balances between the Council and the Commission in the initiation of legislation, and the multiple veto-players in the legislative process, the EU has a highly developed system of judicial review. The European Court of Justice (ECJ) was originally established in the Treaty of Rome to oversee the behaviour of the Commission and the implementation of EU legislation by the member states. Also, there is no clear hierarchy of competences or norms in the EU Treaties, or a clear right of the ECJ to exercise what constitutional lawyers call 'competence-competence' (the ability to decide when there is a dispute over who has competence in a given policy area). However, the initial powers of the ECJ and the lack of clear constraints on the EU judiciary, have allowed the ECJ to develop as a powerful political actor (e.g. Mancini 1989; Weiler 1991). Although the ECJ has rarely struck-down EU legislation once it has passed, it certainly has the right to do so if the legislation is beyond the scope of the EU Treaties or is in breach of some fundamental norms, as set out, for example, in the (non-binding) Charter of Fundamental Rights of the European Union.

In other words, it is remarkable that the EU is able to do anything! The governments must first agree unanimously to add a policy competence to the EU. Having made this decision, the governments then decide (by unanimity) either to pass legislation in this policy area by unanimity (after a proposal from the Commission) or to allow legislation to be adopted by the co-decision procedure (where laws must be supported by majorities in all three of the EU's legislative institutions – the Commission, the Council and the European Parliament). Then, finally, the ECJ can reject the legislation if it breaches the competences of the EU.

The positive side of this elaborate system of checks-and-balances is that nothing can be done by the EU without overwhelming 'consensus' amongst all the main member states, political parties, and interest groups. In stark contrast to a classic majoritarian system of government, no single party-political or member state majority can 'govern' at the EU level against the interests of a particular minority. Diffuse interests, such as women's groups, labour unions or environmental groups, who are normally less able to mobilize to influence government than concentrated (mainly producer) interests, are well-represented in the EU policy-making process, in the Commission, the Council, the European Parliament, and the ECJ (e.g. Pollack 1997b; Greenwood 2003). As a result, the fear that the EU would impose a business interest-biased form of pluralism on the social democratic models of corporatism at the national level is extremely overblown (esp. Streeck and Schmitter 1991). Business interests are simply incapable of dominating in a system with so many access points and institutional veto-players.

Nevertheless, there are several negative consequences of such a hyper-consensual form of government. First, when legislation is hard to pass, courts, bureaucracies and independent agencies have a high degree of discretion in the implementation of legislation (e.g. Weingast 1996; Tsebelis 2002). In a majoritarian system, if a court makes a ruling, or a bureaucracy or agency implements a law in a way that the government or legislative majority does not like, the government or legislative majority can simply pass a new piece of legislation. In the EU, in contrast, if the ECJ makes a ruling that a proportion of governments or an interest group do not like, or if the Commission over-implements a legislative act, it is highly unlikely that new EU legislation will be passed to overturn the action of the ECJ or the Commission (Tsebelis and Garrett 2001). Hence, when applying or implementing EU law, national and European judges and bureaucrats have very little fear of political reprisal.

Second, although no particular group can govern against the interests of a minority, the flip-side is that, in a hyper-consensus system, it is easy for minority interests to block reforms that command overwhelming support. For example, in the US, which has a form of non-majoritarianism that is not as extreme as in the EU, healthcare reform or gun-control legislation has been repeatedly blocked by concentrated interests. The problem in the EU context is that once legislation is adopted for the first time (from an extreme status quo position), the checks-and-balances allow any concentrated

interest to block reform. Scharpf (1988) first observed this with the Common Agricultural Policy, which faced what he called a 'joint-decision trap'. But, the problem is now universal in the EU, for example in the reform of single market regulations, the reform of labour market rules, or the reform of the EU budget. Once policy has been adopted it is 'locked-in', unless the preferences of all the actors change so dramatically that the new status quo is well outside the set of feasible policies that can be adopted.

Third, with a weakened Commission as a result of the high thresholds for passing legislation, and a fragmented structure of governance in the European Council (where the Presidency rotates every 6 months), the EU suffers from a severe lack of political leadership. Jacques Delors was the exception. He was not only a clever politician, but he was helped by the particular institutional environment in which he found himself. At that time, it was relatively easy for the Commission to force legislation through the Council (under the consultation or cooperation procedures). Also, the task of the Delors Commission was to pass a lot of new legislation to create the single market, which meant that almost anything the Commission proposed was preferred by almost all member states to the existing status quo (of no single market).

Since the perceived failure of the Santer Commission, the governments have tried to increase the authority of the Commission President, by allowing the Commission President to veto the governments' nominees as Commissioners and then to allocate portfolios among the nominated Commissioners. This has strengthened the power of the Commission President inside the Commission. However, these changes have not addressed the problem that the Commission has been significantly weakened as a result of the reforms of the legislative procedures, which have reduced the Commission's agenda-setting powers. These reforms also have not addressed the problem that the main issue now is to reform legislation and programmes that have already been adopted, which is extremely difficult in the new hyper-consensus model of EU government.

Having said that, one unintended consequence of the Nice Treaty is that, as a result of the change in the way the Commission is now 'elected', the EU has the potential to become slightly more majoritarian. The Nice Treaty provided for the Commission President and the Commission to be nominated by a quali-fied-majority rather than unanimity in the European Council, and then (as before) passed by a simple majority in the European Parliament. At the time of the Nice Inter-governmental Conference, this reform seemed a rather small minor change, mainly to address the concern that enlargement to 25 member states would make it very difficult to agree on a Commission President. However, this change has the potential to be quite profound: by establishing that the same political majority (in the Council and European Parliament) can elect the agenda-setter and then adopt legisla-tion proposed by the agenda-setter. So, if the same political majority was able to control all three of the EU's legislative institutions (the Commission, the Council, and the Parliament), the EU might be able to overcome the constraints of the hyper-consensual deci-sion rules. This, however, is likely to be a rare condition, given the tendency for European Parliament elections to produce majorities opposed to those in the Council.

POLITICS IN THE EU IN TWO RECENT PERIODS

To illustrate how the EU polity works in prac-tice we can look at two recent periods: (1) the creation and regulation of the single market in the mid-1980s to the mid-1990s; and (2) the reform of the European social model as part of the so-called 'Lisbon Agenda' in the late 1990s and at the start of the new millennium. There were three significant differences in the way the EU worked between these two periods. First, the institutional design of the EU changed. In the late 1980s and early 1990s, with the cooperation procedure and the exten-sion of qualified-majority voting in the Council, the Commission had significant

agenda-setting power. By the late 1990s, however, with the new co-decision procedure the EU institutions were more hyper-consensual.

Second, the location of existing policies (the status quo) was different. In the late 1980s and early 1990s, when the aim was to adopt many new laws to create and regulate a single market, virtually all actors preferred any EU legislation to the status quo (of no single market rules). By the late 1990s, in contrast, the main policy aim was to reform national and EU regula-tions, where some governments and parties preferred to move existing EU legislation left-wards (for example, to adopt new EU social regulations or tax harmonization), while others preferred to move existing EU legisla-tion rightwards (for example, to pass rules liberalizing labour markets).

Third, the location of some of the key actors changed. In the late 1980s and early 1990s, of the three largest member states, French socialist President François Mitterrand advocated a 'social dimension' to the single market pro-gramme, and was largely supported in this agenda by Helmut Kohl's Christian democratic-liberal coalition in Germany. At the other extreme, Margaret Thatcher's conservative gov-ernments supported the single market but adamantly opposed EU social regulations – 'we did not roll back the state in London to have it re-imposed through the backdoor from Brussels', as she put it in her famous Bruges speech. Thatcher was marginalized, though, as the median member of the Delors Commission was considerably to the left of her, and the majority in the European Parliament was on the centre-left, dominated by a coalition of socialists (Party of European Socialists), lib-erals (European Liberal, Democrat and Reform Party), greens (Green group), and radical left MEPs (European United Left) (particularly in the 1989–94 period).

In the late 1990s the situation was quite dif-ferent. This time, Gerhard Schröder's social democrat-green government was furthest to the left of the three largest member states – and, as a result, was outvoted most in the Council in this period (Mattila and Lane 2001). French President Jacques Chirac was a conservative, but on the issue of reform of the welfare state and

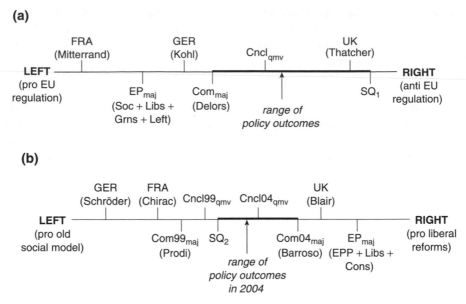

Figure 6.1   *Politics in the EU. (a) Creation and Regulation of the Single Market (mid-1980s to mid-1990s). (b) Reform of the European Social Model (late 1990s to early 2000s). Note: SQ_1, SQ_2 = policy status quos in period 1 and period 2, respectively; $Cncl_{qmv}$, $Cncl99_{qmv}$, $Cncl04_{qmv}$ = pivotal member of the Council under qualified-majority voting; EP_{maj} = pivotal member of the European Parliament under simple-majority voting; and Com_{maj}, $Com99_{maj}$, $Com04_{maj}$ = pivotal member of the European Commission under simple-majority voting.*

labour markets was closer to more traditional socialists than social democrat modernizers like Wim Kok or Tony Blair. The Blair government, meanwhile, was on the centre-right at the EU level: supporting liberal reforms (such as the Takeover Directive) and opposing new EU social regulations (such as the Working Time Directive). Nevertheless, the majority in the Council changed between 1999–2004, as many of the centre-left governments that dominated the Council in the late 1990s were replaced by centre-right governments.

The changing make-up of the Council was then reflected in the changing make-up of the Commission, since the governments choose the Commissioners. Whereas the 1999–2004 Commission led by Romano Prodi had a centre-left majority, the 2004–09 Commission led by José Manuel Barroso had a centre-right majority. Nonetheless, after the 1999 and 2004 European elections, the European Parliament was dominated by a centre-right coalition of Christian democrat/conservatives (European People's Party-European Democrats), liberals

(Alliance of Liberals and Democrats for Europe), and national-conservatives (Union for a European of Nations).

Figure 6.1 illustrates the basic structure of politics in these two periods. The first thing to note is that the main dimension of politics in the EU is similar to the classic 'left-right' dimension of EU politics, although with a slightly different meaning to the dimension in the two periods (cf. Hix 1999; Marks and Steenbergen 2002). This way of conceptualizing EU politics is quite different to the traditional view in European integration studies, where most theorists assumed that the main dimension of conflict was the speed and nature of European integration, with some member states and the EU institutions supporting faster integration and other member states supporting slower integration (e.g. Hoffmann 1966; Moravcsik 1998). In the creation of the single market, the left–right and the pro/anti-integration dimensions were related, with the left generally supporting more EU (social) regulation and the right generally supporting less (and voluntaristic) regulation (esp.

Hooghe and Marks 1998). In the late 1990s, however, the relationship between the dimensions is less clear. For example, while the right generally opposed more EU social regulation and tax harmonization they were also in favour of the EU forcing the member states to liberalize their service sector, labour markets and takeover rules, and the left had the reverse set of preferences. Empirical research also supports this conception of EU politics, in that the main dimension of voting behaviour in the European Parliament and the EU Council is the left–right and not the pro/anti-integration dimension (Mattila 2004; Hix et al. 2005, 2006).

A second issue of note in the figure is the relative location of the pivotal actors in the Council and the European Parliament in the two periods. Because European Parliament elections tend to be mid-term national contests, fought on the battle for national government office rather than on issues on the EU agenda, these elections tend to be won by opposition parties (Marsh 1998). As a result, while governing parties are represented in the Council, opposition parties tend to dominate the European Parliament. For example, in the late 1980s, the majority of governments in the Council were on the centre-right and the left won the 1989 European elections. Similarly, in the late 1990s, the Council was dominated by centre-left governments and the European People's Party emerged as the largest group in the 1999 European elections. As a result, like many polities with executive and legislative elections at different times (cf. Alesina and Rosenthal 1994), 'divided government' is the norm in the EU. This consequently compounds the consensual design of the EU, by ensuring that the preferences of two of the main veto-players are usually far apart.

It is easy to see from the structure of institutional rules, the locations of the status quos, and the locations of the actors that it was much easier for the EU to adopt legislation in the 1980s and early 1990s than in the late 1990s and early 2000s. In the earlier period, with a considerable distance between the pivotal member of the Council ($Cncl_{qmv}$ in Figure 6.1a) and the status quo (SQ_1), the Commission could propose any policy in the range

Com_{maj}–SQ_1 and it would be accepted by the Council and a majority in the European Parliament (although this was not necessary until the Maastricht Treaty in 1993).

The situation was rather different in the late 1990s. Following the 1999 European elections, the EU was 'gridlocked'. The Prodi Commission and the Council majority were to the left of most policy status quos whereas the European Parliament majority was now to the right of most status quos. This period consequently saw several high-profile battles between the three EU institutions, for example on the End-of-Life Vehicle Directive, where the centre-right majority in the European Parliament watered-down a highly regulatory Commission proposal which had been supported by a socialist-green coalition in the Council.

Following the 2004 European elections and the investiture of the Barroso Commission, the EU moved out of gridlock. Barroso was the first Commission President to be elected under the Nice Treaty rules, by a qualified-majority instead of unanimity. Had unanimity been used, Chirac and Schröder would probably have been able to secure the election of their preferred candidate, the Belgian Prime Minister Guy Verhofstadt. However, France and Germany were forced to accept Barroso when it was clear that he had the support of a qualified-majority. In early 2005, for the first time, the EU had a centre-right majority in the Council, the European Parliament and the Commission. With a Council majority ($Cncl04_{qmv}$ in Figure 6.1b) and a European Parliament majority (EP_{maj}) now to the right of the status quo (SQ_2), the Barroso Commission could propose liberal reforms (in the range SQ_2–$Com04_{maj}$) that would pass through the Council and the European Parliament.

However, Barroso's initial legislative agenda, which included a quite liberal Services Directive, had to be delayed because of opposition in France to 'Anglo-Saxon' EU reforms. France could have been outvoted (as it had been in the election of Barroso). But, France was due to hold a referendum on the EU Constitution, and the main opposition to the Constitution was from the left. Hence, the potential for genuine majoritarian politics in the EU was thwarted by collective agreement not to undertake reforms that would make any member state worse during the ratification of the Constitution, and so provoke opposition in that country.

These case studies consequently illustrate the difficulty of making policy in the EU's hyper-consensus polity. With a weakened Commission, a powerful European Parliament, a high voting threshold in the Council, and a majority in the European Parliament that is likely to be the opposite colour to the majority in the Council, the EU is only likely to be able to adopt policies in those areas where existing policies are strongly undesirable for all concerned (for example, a fragmented financial services market). Where the policy status quo is more centrist, as in the bulk of existing single market legislation, the EU is likely to be gridlocked.

The Nice Treaty, which allowed for the Commission President to be elected by a qualified-majority in the European Council, injected an element of majoritarianism into the system. However, the first time the EU experienced 'unified government' – with a centre-right majority in the Commission, the Council, and the European Parliament in 2004–05 – policy-making was stalled. This was partly a collective choice by the EU institutions while the member states and the Commission focused on ratifying the EU Constitution. But, this also reflected the difficulties of a particular party-political majority 'governing' in such a consensus-oriented polity. The problem is that those on the minority side (such as the French government in 2004–05) questioned the legitimacy of the liberalizing agenda pursued by the new centre-right majorities in the Commission, Council, and European Parliament. Even when unified-government does exist in the EU, there simply is no democratic 'mandate' to move policy in a particular direction.

DEMOCRACY IN THE EU: NO MANDATE FOR ACTION

The final problem for the EU polity is perhaps the most intractable: the so-called 'democratic deficit'. A huge amount has been written about this issue since the question arose in the late 1980s (for an excellent review and critique see Moravcsik 2002). Also, there is no single definition of the EU democratic-deficit (cf. Weiler et al. 1995; Siedentop 2000). Nevertheless, most contemporary commentators make one or more of the following claims.

First, European integration has increased the power of the executive at the expense of national parliamentary control. EU decisions are made primarily by executive actors: the Commission and national ministers in the Council. This has meant a decrease in the power of national parliaments, as governments can ignore their parliaments when making decisions in Brussels or can be out-voted in the Council (where qualified-majority voting is used) (e.g. Andersen and Burns 1996).

Second, the reduction of the power of national parliaments has not been compensated by increased power of the European Parliament. Despite the Treaty reforms, which have strengthened the power of the European Parliament, the Council still dominates the Parliament in the legislative process and in the adoption of the budget. Also, EU citizens are not as well connected to their MEPs as to their national parliamentarians (e.g. Williams 1991; Lodge 1994).

Citizens are not able to vote on EU policies, except in periodic referendums on EU membership or treaty reforms. National elections are fought on domestic rather than European issues, and parties collude to keep the issue of Europe off the domestic political agenda (Hix 1999; Marks et al. 2002). European Parliament elections are also not about Europe, as parties and the media treat them as mid-term national contests, as discussed.

The EU is 'too distant' and too complex. The Commission is neither a government nor a bureaucracy, and is appointed through an obscure procedure rather than elected by the people or a parliament (cf. Magnette 2001). The Council is the only legislature in the democratic world that makes decisions in secret. The European Parliament is impenetrable because of the multilingual nature of debates. And, the policy process is technocratic rather than political (Wallace and Smith 1995).

As a result of all these factors, the EU adopts policies that are not supported by a majority of citizens in many (or even most) member states, such as a neo-liberal regulatory framework for the single market, a neo-monetarist framework for EMU, and massive subsidies to farmers through the Common Agricultural Policy (e.g. Scharpf 1997, 1999).

However, these arguments are not universally accepted. In particular, Giandomenico Majone and Andrew Moravcsik have vehemently criticized these claims. As discussed, Majone sees the EU is essentially a 'regulatory state', which does not engage in redistributive or value-allocative policies (Majone 1998, 2000, 2002a, b). Following from this, because regulatory policies should be pareto-improving (benefiting everyone) rather than redistributive, EU policy-making should be isolated from the standard processes of majoritarian democratic politics – in the same way that courts and central banks should be independent of legislatures and executives. From Majone's perspective, the problem for the EU is less a democratic deficit, than a 'credibility crisis' or 'legitimacy deficit'. The solution, he believes, is procedural rather than more fundamental. What the EU needs is more transparent decision-making, ex-post review by courts and ombudsmen, greater professionalism and technical expertise, rules that protect the rights of minority interests, and better scrutiny by private actors, the media, and parliamentarians at both the EU and national levels. A more 'democratic' EU, dominated by the European Parliament or with a directly elected Commission President, would politicize regulatory policy-making. And, politicization would result in redistributive rather than pareto-efficient outcomes, and so undermine rather than increase the legitimacy of the EU (cf. Dehousse 1995).

Moravcsik (2002) goes even further, presenting an extensive critique of all the main democratic-deficit claims. Against the argument that power has been centralized in the executive, Moravcsik points out that national governments are the most directly accountable politicians in Europe. Against the critique that the executives are beyond the control of representative institutions, he argues that the most significant institutional development in the EU in the past two decades has been the increased powers of the European Parliament in the legislative process and in the selection of the Commission. He also argues that EU policy-making is more transparent than most domestic policy-making processes, that the EU technocrats are forced to listen to multiple societal interests, that there is extensive judicial review of EU actions by both the ECJ and national courts, and that the European Parliament and national parliaments have increasing scrutiny powers, which they are not afraid to use. Finally, against the so-called 'social democratic critique' that EU policies are systematically biased against the median voter, Moravcsik argues that the EU's system of checks-and-balances ensures that an overwhelming consensus is required for any policies to be agreed. As a result, free market liberals are just as unhappy with the centrist EU policy regime as social democrats.

But, there are at least three reasons why democracy, in terms of competitive elections to choose policies and leaders, is better than the sort of 'enlightened technocracy' advocated by Majone and Moravcsik. First, in either majoritarian or more consensual models of democracy, competitive elections guarantee that policies and elected officials respond to the preferences of citizens (Powell 2000). Electoral contests provide incentives for elites to develop rival policy ideas and propose rival candidates for political office. They also allow citizens to punish politicians who fail to implement their electoral promises or who are dishonest or corrupt (Fearon 1999). Where the EU is concerned, policies might be in the interests of citizens when they were first agreed, but without electoral competition there are few incentives for the Commission or the governments to change these policies in response to changes in citizens' preferences.

Second, political competition is an essential vehicle for fostering political debate, which in turn promotes the formation of public opinion on different policy options. Without the policy debate that is an inherent by-product of electoral competition, voters would not be able to form their preferences on complex policy issues. An example of this in the EU is the debate about structural reform of the European economy. The EU has the legal instruments and powers to force member states to liberalize their labour markets. But, without a public debate, the public cannot form opinions about the options for the EU, and the EU institutions do not have the incentives or the legitimate mandate to undertake such reforms.

Third, elections have a powerful formative effect, promoting a gradual evolution of political identities. For example, in the history of American and European democracies, the replacement of local identities by national identities occurred through the process and operation of mass elections and party competition (Key 1961; Rokkan 1999). In the EU, rather than assuming that a European 'demos' is a prerequisite for genuine EU democracy, a European democratic identity could only form through the practice of democratic competition; where citizens accept being on the losing side in one particular contest in the expectation that they will be on the winning side in the not too distant future (Habermas 1995).

The EU may be able to produce policy outputs that are close to some notional European-wide median voter. However, this is insufficient to guarantee public support for the EU polity. In times of economic growth, non-democratic regimes are as stable as democratic regimes. However, when the regime fails to continue to provide such benefits, for example in an economic downturn, non-democratic regimes tend to be far less stable than democratic regimes (Acemoglu and Robinson 2001; Przeworski 2004). This is because in non-democratic regimes the citizens blame the regime as a whole for the failed policies, whereas in democratic regimes citizens blame the current government of the day, which they can replace, rather than the regime as a whole.

However, because the powers of the governments to run the EU would be significantly reduced by either a more powerful European Parliament or an elected Commission President, it is unlikely that the governments will transform the EU into a genuine competitive-democracy any time soon. The proposed EU Constitution, which the 25 governments agreed to unanimously, would not have made any significant changes in this respect. Nevertheless, we may reach a point when European citizens turn against the EU polity for its repeated policy failures, the lock-in of unpopular policies, and the constant institutional gridlock. Only then might governments consider more dramatic reform.

CONCLUSION

One perspective, as cogently argued by Moravcsik (2003), is that 'if the EU ain't broke why fix it?' The European Union is a remarkable achievement. It is a historically unique experiment in the creation of a supranational polity, with some of the powers of a traditional 'state', at least in the fields of economic, social and environmental regulation. The EU has guaranteed prosperity, economic growth, political stability, and security in western Europe for the past 50 years and, as a result, has been a magnet to states in southern, eastern, and south-eastern Europe to undertake democratic political reforms and free market economic reforms in order to join it. The EU has also played its part in the global political economy, promoting global trade integration, economic and political development, and integration in other regions of the world.

Nevertheless, judged by the standards of modern democratic polities, the EU has some serious problems. The policy mix of the EU – with the regulation of the single market and monetary policies at the European level and taxation and spending at the national level – severely constrains the policy choices of national governments. The EU decision-making system, with its hyper-consensus structure of checks-and-balances, is incapable of enacting policy reforms which might force national governments to take on vested interests that are preventing them from liberalizing their labour markets (particularly in France, Germany and Italy). And, without a more democratic and competitive contest over the policy-agenda of the EU, there is no mandate for political leadership at the European level.

It may be unfair to judge the EU by these standards, as it has been designed precisely to constrain 'politics', with no clearly identifiable winners and losers. However, these are the standards by which many of Europe's citizens judge it. As a result, support for European integration has steadily declined since its peak in the early 1990s. In the wake of the Dutch and French rejections of the EU Constitution, it seems that the majority of EU citizens are relatively sceptical towards most things 'European'. The challenge for the EU is how to deliver the things Europe's citizens want – a functioning single market, economic growth, and structural reforms – without also reforming the institutional design to establish a more directly democratic system of accountability.

NOTE

1. For a book-length survey of recent research on the EU as a 'political system' see Hix (2005).

REFERENCES

Acemoglu, D. and Robinson, J.A. (2001) 'A theory of political transitions', *American Economic Review*, 91(4): 938–63.

Alesina, A. and Rosenthal, H. (1994) *Partisan Politics, Divided Government, and the Economy*. Cambridge: Cambridge University Press.

Alesina, A., Angeloni, I. and Schuknecht, L. (2001) 'What does the European Union do?', NBER Working Paper No. 8647, Cambridge, MA: National Bureau of Economic Research.

Alter, K.J. and Meunier-Aitsahalia, S. (1994) 'Judicial politics in the European Community: European integration and the pathbreaking Cassis de Dijon decision', *Comparative Political Studies*, 26(4): 535–61.

Andersen, S.S. and Burns, T. (1996) 'The European Union and the erosion of parliamentary democracy: a study of post-parliamentary governance', in S.S. Andersen and K.A. Eliassen (eds), *The European Union: How Democratic Is It?* London: Sage. pp. 227–51.

Attinà, F. (1990) 'The voting behaviour of the European Parliament members and the problem of Europarties', *European Journal of Political Research*, 18(3): 557–79.

Badie, B. and Birnbaum, P. (1983 [1979]) *The Sociology of the State*, translated by A. Goldhammer. Chicago, IL: University of Chicago Press.

Bowler, S. and Farrell, D. (1995) 'The organization of the European Parliament: committees, specialization and co-ordination', *British Journal of Political Science*, 25(2): 219–43.

Brown, C.C. and Oates, W.E. (1987) 'Assistance to the poor in a federal system', *Journal of Public Economics*, 32(3): 307–30.

Cram, L. (1997) *Policy-Making in the EU: Conceptual Lenses and the Integration Process*. London: Routledge.

Crombez, C. (1996) 'Legislative procedures in the European Community', *British Journal of Political Science*, 26(2): 199–218.

Crombez, C. (1997) 'Policy making and Commission appointment in the European Union', *Aussenwirtschaft*, 52(1/2): 63–82.

Crombez, C. (2001) 'Institutional reform and co-decision in the European Union', *Constitutional Political Economy*, 11(1): 41–57.

Dehousse, R. (1995) 'Constitutional reform in the European Community: are there alternatives to the majoritarian avenue?', in J. Hayward (ed.), *The Crisis of Representation in Europe*. London: Frank Cass. pp. 118–36.

Donohue, J.D. and Pollack, M.A. (2001) 'Centralization and its discontents: the rhythms of federalism in the United States and the European Union', in K. Nicolaïdis and R. Howse (eds), *The Federal Vision: Legitimacy and Levels of Governance in the United States and the European Union*. Oxford: Oxford University Press. pp. 73–117.

Fearon, J. (1999) 'Electoral accountability and the control of politicians: selecting good types versus sanctioning poor performance', in A. Przeworksi, S.C. Stokes and B. Manin (eds), *Democracy, Accountability and Representation*. Cambridge: Cambridge University Press. pp. 55–97.

Ferejohn, J.A. and Weingast, B.R. (1992) 'A positive theory of statutory interpretation', *International Review of Law and Economics*, 12(2): 263–79.

Franklin, M., van der Eijk, C. and Marsh, M. (1995) 'Referendum outcomes and trust in government: public support for Europe in the wake of Maastricht', in J. Hayward (ed.), *The Crisis of Representation in Europe*. London: Frank Cass. pp. 101–17.

Garrett, G. (1992) 'International cooperation and institutional choice: the European Community's internal market', *International Organization*, 46(2): 533–60.

Golub, J. (1999) 'In the shadow of the vote? Decision making in the European Community', *International Organization*, 53(4): 733–64.

Greenwood, J. (2003) *Interest representation in the European Union*. London: Palgrave.

Habermas, J. (1995) 'Comment on the paper by Dieter Grimm: "Does Europe need a constitution"', *European Law Journal*, 1(3): 303–7.

Hix, S. (1994) 'The study of the European Community: the challenge to comparative politics', *West European Politics*, 17(1): 1–30.

Hix, S. (1998) 'The study of the European Union II: the "new governance" agenda and its rival', *Journal of European Public Policy*, 5(1): 38–65.

Hix, S. (1999) 'Dimensions and alignments in European Union politics: cognitive constraints and partisan responses', *European Journal of Political Research*, 35(1): 69–106.

Hix, S. (2005) *The Political System of the European Union*, 2nd ed. London: Palgrave.

Hix, S., Noury, A. and Roland, G. (2005) 'Power to the parties: cohesion and competition in the European Parliament, 1979–2001', *British Journal of Political Science*, 35(2): 209–34.

Hix, S., Noury, A. and Roland, G. (2006) 'Dimensions of politics in the European Parliament', *American Journal of Political Science*, 50(2): 494–511.

Hoffmann, S. (1966) 'Obstinate or obsolete? The fate of the nation state and the case of western Europe', *Daedalus*, 95(4): 862–915.

Hooghe, L. (1999) 'Supranational activists or intergovernmental agents? Explaining the political orientations of senior Commission officials to European integration', *Comparative Political Studies*, 32(4): 435–63.

Hooghe, L. (2001) *The European Commission and the Integration of Europe: Images of Governance*. Cambridge: Cambridge University Press.

Hooghe, L. and Marks, G. (1998) 'The making of a polity: the struggle over European integration', in H. Kitschelt, P. Lange, G. Marks and J. Stephens (eds), *The Politics and Political Economy of Advanced Industrial Societies*. Cambridge: Cambridge University Press. pp. 70–100.

Hug, S. (2002) *Voices of Europe: Citizens, Referendums, and European Integration*. Lanham, MD: Rowman Littlefield.

Hug, S. (2003) 'Endogenous preferences and delegation in the European Union', *Comparative Political Studies*, 36(1–2): 41–74.

Key, V.O. (1961) *Public Opinion and American Democracy*. New York: Knopf.

Lijphart, A. (1999) *Patterns of Democracy: Government Forms and Performance in Thirty-Six Countries*. New Haven, CT: Yale University Press.

Lindberg, L. and Scheingold, S. (1970) *Europe's Would-Be Polity: Patterns of Change in the European Community*. Harvard, MA: Harvard University Press.

Lodge, J. (1994) 'The European Parliament and the authority-democracy crisis', *Annals of the American Academy of Political and Social Science*, 531: 69–83.

Magnette, P. (2001) 'Appointing and censuring the Commission: the adaptation of parliamentary institutions to the Community context', *European Law Journal*, 7(3): 289–307.

Majone, G. (1993) 'The European community between social policy and social regulation', *Journal of Common Market Studies*, 31(2): 153–70.

Majone, G. (1996) *Regulating Europe*. London: Routledge.

Majone, G. (1998) 'Europe's "democratic deficit": the question of standards', *European Law Journal*, 4(1): 5–28.

Majone, G. (2000) 'The credibility crisis of community regulation', *Journal of Common Market Studies*, 38(2): 273–302.

Majone, G. (2002a) 'The European Commission: the limits of centralization and the perils of parliamentarization', *Governance*, 15(3): 375–92.

Majone, G. (2002b) 'Delegation of regulatory powers in a mixed polity', *European Law Journal*, 8(3): 319–39.

Mancini, F. (1989) 'The making of a constitution for Europe', *Common Market Law Review*, 26(4): 595–614.

Marks, G. and Steenbergen, M. (2002) 'Introduction: understanding political contestation in the European Union', *Comparative Political Studies*, 35(8): 879–92.

Marks, G., Wilson, C. and Ray, L. (2002) 'National political parties and European integration', *American Journal of Political Science*, 46(3): 585–94.

Marsh, M. (1998) 'Testing the second-order election model after four European elections', *British Journal of Political Science*, 28(4): 591–607.

Mattila, M. (2004) 'Contested decisions: empirical analysis of voting in the European Union Council of Ministers', *European Journal of Political Research*, 43(1): 29–50.

Mattila, M. and Lane, J.-E. (2001) 'Why uanimity in the Council? A roll call analysis of Council voting', *European Union Politics*, 2(1): 31–52.

McKay, D.H. (1996) *Rush to Union: Understanding the European Federal Bargain.* Oxford: Clarendon.

McKay, D.H. (2001) *Designing Europe: Comparative Lessons from the Federal Experience.* Oxford: Oxford University Press.

Moravcsik, A. (1998) *The Choice for Europe: Social Purpose and State Power from Messina to Maastricht.* Ithaca, NY: Cornell University Press.

Moravcsik, A. (2001) 'Federalism in the European Union: rhetoric and reality', in K. Nicolaïdis and R. Howse (eds), *The Federal Vision: Legitimacy and Levels of Governance in the United States and the European Union.* Oxford: Oxford University Press. pp. 161–90.

Moravcsik, A. (2002) 'In defense of the "democratic deficit": reassessing the legitimacy of the European Union', *Journal of Common Market Studies*, 40(4): 603–34.

Moravcsik, A. (2003) 'The EU ain't broke', *Prospect*, March: 38–45.

Moser, P. (1996) 'The European Parliament as a conditional agenda-setter: what are the conditions? A critique of Tsebelis (1994)', *American Political Science Review*, 90(4): 834–8.

Oates, W.E. (1999) 'An essay on fiscal federalism', *Journal of Economic Literature*, 37(4): 1120–49.

Pierson, P. (1996) 'The path to European integration: a historical institutionalist analysis', *Comparative Political Studies*, 29(2): 123–63.

Pollack, M.A. (1995) 'Creeping competence: the expanding agenda of the European Community', *Journal of Public Policy*, 14(1): 97–143.

Pollack, M.A. (1997a) 'Delegation, agency and agenda setting in the European Community', *International Organization*, 51(1): 99–134.

Pollack, M.A. (1997b) 'Representing diffuse interests in EC policy-making', *Journal of European Public Policy*, 4(4): 572–90.

Pollack, M.A. (2000) 'The end of creeping competences? EU policy-making since Maastricht', *Journal of Common Market Studies*, 38(3): 519–38.

Pollack, M.A. (2003) *The Engines of Integration: Delegation, Agency, and Agency Setting in the European Union.* Oxford: Oxford University Press.

Powell, G.B. (2000) *Elections as Instruments of Democracy: Majoritarian or Proportional Visions.* New Haven, CT: Yale University Press.

Przeworski, A. (2004) 'Economic development and transitions to democracy', mimeo, New York: New York University.

Quin, Y. and Weingast, B.R. (1997) 'Federalism as a commitment to preserving market incentives', *Journal of Economic Perspectives*, 11(4): 83–92.

Reif, K. and Schmitt, H. (1980) 'Nine second-order national elections: a conceptual framework for the analysis of European election results', *European Journal of Political Research*, 8(1): 3–45.

Riker, W.H. (1975) 'Federalism', in F.I. Greenstein and N.W. Polsby (eds), *Handbook of Political Science*, Vol. 5. Reading, MA: Addison-Wesley.

Rokkan, S. (1999) *State Formation, Nation-Building, and Mass Politics in Europe: The Theory of Stein Rokkan*, selected and rearranged by P. Flora, S. Kuhnle and D. Urwin. Oxford: Oxford University Press.

Sandholtz, W. and Zysman, J. (1989) '1992: recasting the European bargain', *World Politics*, 42(1): 95–128.

Sbragia, A.M. (ed.) (1992) *Euro-Politics: Institutions and Policymaking in the 'New' European Community.* Washington, DC: The Brookings Institution.

Scharpf, F.W. (1988) 'The joint-decision trap: lessons from German federalism and European integration', *Public Administration*, 66(3): 277–304.

Scharpf, F.W. (1997) 'Economic integration, democracy and the welfare state', *Journal of European Public Policy*, 4(1): 18–36.

Scharpf, F.W. (1999) *Governing in Europe: Effective and Democratic?* Oxford: Oxford University Press.

Schulz, H. and König, T. (2000) 'Institutional reform and decision-making efficiency in the European Union', *American Political Science Review*, 44(4): 653–66.

Siedentop, L. (2000) *Democracy in Europe.* London: Allen Lane.

Skowronek, S. (1982) *Building a New American State: The Expansion of National Administrative Capacities.* Cambridge: Cambridge University Press.

Steunenberg, B. (1994) 'Decision-making under different institutional arrangements: legislation by the European Community', *Journal of Institutional and Theoretical Economics*, 150(4): 642–69.

Streeck, W. (1995) 'From market making to state building? Reflections on the political economy of European social policy', in S. Leibfried and P. Pierson (eds), *European Social Policy: Between Fragmentation and Integration.* Washington, DC: The Brookings Institution. pp. 389–431.

Streeck, W. (1996) 'Neo-voluntarism: a European social policy regime?', in G. Marks, F.W. Scharpf, P.C. Schmitter and W. Streeck (eds), *Governance in the European Union.* London: Sage. pp. 64–94.

Streeck, W. and Schmitter, P.C. (1991) 'From national corporatism to transnational pluralism: organized interests in the single European market', *Politics and Society*, 19(2): 133–64.

Tsebelis, G. (1994) 'The power of the European Parliament as a conditional agenda-setter', *American Political Science Review*, 88(1): 128–42.

Tsebelis, G. (1995) 'Decision making in political systems: veto players in presidentialism, parliamentarism, multicameralism and multipartyism', *British Journal of Political Science*, 25(3): 289–325.

Tsebelis, G. (2002) *Veto Players: How Political Institutions Work.* Princeton, NJ/New York: Princeton University Press/Russell Sage Foundation.

Tsebelis, G. and Garrett, G. (2001) 'The institutional foundations of intergovernmentalism and supranationalism in the European Union', *International Organization*, 55 (2): 357–90.

Tsebelis, G. and Kreppel, A. (1998) 'The history of conditional agenda-setting in European institutions', *European Journal of Political Research*, 33(1): 41–71.

Tsebelis, G. and Yataganas, X. (2002) 'Veto players and decision-making in the EU after Nice: policy stability and bureaucratic/judicial discretion', *Journal of Common Market Studies*, 40(2): 283–307.

van der Eijk, C. and Franklin, M. (eds) (1996) *Choosing Europe? The European Electorate and National Politics in the Face of Union.* Ann Arbor, MI: University of Michigan Press.

Wallace, W. and Smith, J. (1995) 'Democracy or technocracy? European integration and the problem of popular consent', *West European Politics*, 18(3): 137–57.

Weiler, J.H.H. (1991) 'The transformation of Europe', *Yale Law Journal*, 100(2): 2403–83.

Weiler, J.H.H., Haltern, U.R. and Mayer, F. (1995) 'European democracy and its critique', *West European Politics*, 18(3): 4–39.

Weingast, B.R. (1995) 'The economic role of political institutions: market-preserving federalism and economic development', *Journal of Law and Economic Organization*, 11(1): 1–31.

Weingast, B.R. (1996) 'Political institutions: rational choice perspectives', in R.E. Goodin and H.-D. Klingeman (eds), *A New Handbook of Political Science*. Oxford: Oxford University Press. pp. 167–91.

Williams, S. (1991) 'Sovereignty and accountability', in R.O. Keohane and S.Hoffmann (eds), *The New European Community: Decisionmaking and Institutional Change*. Boulder, CO: Westview. pp. 155–76.

7

The European Union as a Polity (II)

MARKUS JACHTENFUCHS

INTRODUCTION

One of the eternal themes of the study of the European Union consists in the issue of whether the EU is an N of 1. This debate is not about whether the EU has particular characteristics which make it unique in some holistic way. In that sense, nobody would deny that there is only one EU as there is only one United Nations, one US and one United Airlines. Events, decisions, policies, or institutions are always unique in this sense, but few scholars would deny that they can nevertheless be analysed scientifically. Despite much controversy in the philosophy of science, most social scientists attempt to explain something by relating it to more general laws. Thus, the real debate is not about whether the EU is unique and needs a special theory in order to explain it or whether important aspects of the EU can be explained by general theories. Instead, the debate is about *which* general theories are more powerful for explaining the most relevant aspects of the European Union: theories of international relations or theories of domestic politics.

For those who argued in favor of international relations, this analytical perspective followed from the fact that the EU was not a state but a creation of independent states. For those who argued in favor of domestic politics, the EU was so untypical an international organization that theories of international relations seemed inapplicable. This split goes back to the early days of integration theory. Both Haas (2004) and his counterpart Hoffmann (1966) have tried to explain the European Union from the vantage point of international relations theory whereas Lindberg and Scheingold (1970) have instead written about 'Europe's Would-Be Polity' from a domestic politics perspective. Nowadays, Moravcsik (1998) takes sides with Haas and Hoffmann while further refining their approaches, whereas Hix (2005) has joined Lindberg and Scheingold in analysing the political system of the EU.

Both perspectives have made important contributions to the better understanding of the EU. Yet each of them has blind spots that the other approach does not necessarily cover. The international relations perspective essentially regards the EU as a highly institutionalized negotiating system among states which still possess the monopoly of the legitimate use of force, control vast financial resources and enjoy a high degree of political legitimacy. The comparative politics perspective insists that politics and policy-making in the EU bears few if any traces of anarchy and the security dilemma which are so crucial to international relations but closely resembles normal politics in Western democracies (c.f. the debate between Hix (1994, 1996) on the one hand and Hurrell and Menon (1996) on the other). The debate between these two competing perspectives sometimes obscures the fact that the dividing line between the two subdisciplines of political science is eroding. Ideally, a more general approach to political science should be able to offer an integrated view (Scharpf 1997a; Milner 1998).

Such a widely accepted integrated theory of political science is not yet available. We should therefore keep in mind that the respective conceptual lenses of international relations or comparative politics might overlook important parts of the European Union which are nevertheless relevant and can be explained scientifically. Regarding the European Union as a *system of multi-level governance* has in recent years become a prominent way of achieving that goal. Although it has developed out of the comparative politics view, it offers the potential to cover blind spots of both international relations and comparative politics approaches while remaining open to their central insights and to testing and empirical scrutiny by considering the Euro-Polity as part of a larger set of governance systems.

THE EU AS A SYSTEM OF MULTI-LEVEL GOVERNANCE – THE INTELLECTUAL ORIGINS

The Aftermath of Grand Integration Theory

New perspectives on an issue often develop out of an inability of prevailing perspectives to deal with the issues researchers are interested in. They do not refute prevailing theories by testing and falsifying them but simply ignore them and start something new, often without offering alternative grand theories in the first place. This was the situation of European integration studies in the 1970s. The passionate debate in the 1960s about whether European integration could be better explained by autonomous state actors (intergovernmentalism) or social processes (neofunctionalism) was withering away (Puchala 1972; Haas 1975). Why the Euro-Polity had emerged and what significance it had for international relations became less interesting to the majority of scholars. Instead, the actual functioning of this polity – its policies – seemed to be a more promising field of research (c.f. Jachtenfuchs 2001, for an overview).

The dependent variable of a large part of European integration studies shifted from the polity to its policies, symbolized by the publication of the first edition of 'Policy-making in the European Community' (Wallace et al. 1977). Most policy studies initially focused on the Community level only. A notable exception is Puchala (1984: 7), who argued that EC policy-making could only be adequately understood if 'the shifting of policy debates back and forth between international and domestic arenas' was taken into account (c.f. Bulmer 1983).

German–American Approaches to Comparative Federalism

The symbolic reference point for the start of the multi-level perspective in EU studies is Scharpf's (1988) 'Joint-Decision Trap'. Scharpf (1988: 239) started from the observation that the process of European integration seemed to be caught in a stable status quo characterized by 'frustration without disintegration and resilience without progress'. With respect to the development of the Euro-Polity, this approach defied both neofunctionalism and intergovernmentalism. The EU, it was argued, produced suboptimal policy-outputs without failing altogether (as intergovernmentalism would expect) but at the same time without being able to reform itself (as neofunctionalism would anticipate). This situation, Scharpf argued, was the systematic result of a particular institutional configuration linking the European and the member state level. Similar observations could be made with reference to German policy-making. In essence, the representation of the *institutional* self-interests of constituent governments in central decision-making processes lead to the joint-decision trap: Constituent governments resist efficiency-oriented policy reforms when their institutional self-interests might be threatened.

What is important for EU studies is the novel perspective it introduced. Scharpf compared the EU with Germany – unusual for both IR scholars and comparativists – but adopted a purely analytical perspective without arguing that the EU was a state or that it could or should become one. The analytical categories used – decision styles, decision rules, institutional configurations, etc. – are to a large degree of a very general nature and not specific to international relations, comparative politics, or EU studies. The underlying idea is a political system consisting of two interrelated layers – this is the analytical definition of federalism without the normative teleology of Euro-federalism. Due to the structural similarities between German and European federalism, it is not surprising that conceptualizing the European Union as a multi-level system has become particularly popular in Germany (Benz 2000; Scharpf 2001; Jachtenfuchs and Kohler-Koch 2003; Kohler-Koch 2003). In addition, German authors are used to living in a 'semi-sovereign state' (Katzenstein 1987) and thus find it easy to accept the idea of their country being part of a larger multi-level system of governance.

This is different for US authors. Living in a superpower gives a lot of plausibility to the idea that states control international organizations and that the EU is controlled by the Big Three (France, Germany, and the UK) – a perspective which is arguably not shared by many Germans. As a result, the American debate about the European Union has to a considerable degree been dominated by approaches inspired by international relations (c.f. Pollack 2001). But the US is not only a superpower, it is also a federal system, although the levels of government are more clearly separated than they are in Germany or in the EU. Early American attempts to approach the EU as a multi-level or federal polity came primarily from legal scholars, probably because already in the 1980s, lawyers had written about the quasi-federal structure of the European legal order (Stein 1981; Weiler 1981, 1982). This made it easier for lawyers than for political scientists to move away from the international relations/international law perspective. The transatlantic 'Integration Through Law' project produced a number of monographs comparing the legal order of the US and the EU (Cappelletti et al. 1985; Rehbinder and Stewart 1985) as federal systems. A major theme in these studies was the structural tension between two levels of government in federal systems and the resulting need for conflict resolution and adjudication by judges and the legal order.

American political scientists joined in later. Here, the symbolic reference is Sbragia's (1992a) edited volume on 'Euro-Politics' to which a number of comparativists contributed. Drawing on the literature on comparative federalism and also on Scharpf's argument about the 'joint-decision trap', Sbragia (1992b, 1993) made a general plea for looking at the EU in terms of interlocked levels of government. Marks (1992, 1993) argued that major financial redistributions in the EU, the so-called 'structural policy', could not adequately be explained by approaches derived from international relations relying on interstate bargains but only if the EU was conceptualized as a system of multiple actors and decision-making arenas. Together with Hooghe, he further developed and extended this approach (Hooghe 1996; Marks et al. 1996; Marks and Hooghe 2000; Hooghe and Marks 2001, 2003).

These works, which were discussed here only in an exemplary fashion, made an important contribution to the better understanding of European integration. They paved the way to a better understanding of the European Union without resorting to an international relations perspective but without falling back to *sui generis* terminology. They have also led to the widely accepted view that institutional developments, political processes and substantive policies in the European Union can be better understood by regarding the EU as a system of two interlocking levels of government with a strong role for its member states. Finally, they have contributed to an increasing awareness among comparativists that cross-national studies of politics or policy-making in EU member states cannot ignore any more the impact of the EU on national patterns of politics and policy, as is the case in domestic multi-level systems. But, in order to see what difference a multi-level perspective on the EU makes, it is necessary to summarize the main findings about the nature of the multi-level EU polity.

WHAT DOES THE EU LOOK LIKE?

Considering the EU as a political system allows one to apply the comparative method (Peters 1998) and thus to gain substantive and sound new analytical insights without entering the highly controversial normative debate about whether the EU could or should become a state. Although the notion of a 'political system' only makes real sense if it is not used synonymously with the notion of a 'state', this concurrent usage is often the rule. Historically, it is the result of the debate between international and comparative approaches to the EU. In order to strengthen their case against international approaches, comparativists easily overstate the similarities between the EU and ideal-typical Western democratic states. Unintentionally, this could lead to the same teleology that was criticized with reference to neofunctionalism: At least in normal times when no intergovernmental conferences take place, the EU very much looks like a state, and like a rather unitary one: It adopts public policies, different institutions execute these policies, legislate, and adjudicate, interest groups and political parties compete for influence and power, and so on. All these processes do indeed take place, and it makes perfect sense to

analyse them from a point of view of comparative politics.

Still, these similarities should not make us forget that the EU is not a state and that it is rather different even from strongly federal states like the US or Germany. These are the differences highlighted by a multi-level governance perspective. What makes up the distinctiveness of the EU as a polity is not a single feature taken alone but their combination.

No Monopoly of Force, No Monopoly of Taxation

Max Weber's argument that the state is distinct from all other forms of political organization by its possession of the monopoly of the legitimate use of force is still convincing (Poggi 1990: Ch. 2). Historically, gaining effective control over the means of force (and over financial resources) was the decisive advantage that territorial entities had over their competitors (Tilly 1975; Reinhard 1999). In many respects, the EU as a polity is not very different any more from the polities of its member states. This is particularly striking if we look at the development of the Euro-polity in scope and depth from the beginning in the 1950s until the present (c.f. Hix 2005: 20–1). But, despite impressive developments in the field of justice and home affairs as well as in foreign and security policy, particularly since the early 1990s, the 'government' of the European Union does not control an army and it does not control a police force. On the contrary, military and police remain under the exclusive authority of the member states.

The EU would probably have an integrated army under the control of some kind of European government had the European Defense Community been adopted in the 1950s. But it failed in 1954, and the impressive development of military cooperation in the EU after decades of stagnation is not aiming at its resurrection. Instead, it is about intensive inter-state cooperation in clearly limited areas of security policy (Wagner 2003). The member states retain the last word about the use of the means of force.

This is also the case with regard to the police. The creation of Europol (Occhipinti 2003) has strongly contributed to the institutionalization of cooperation among police authorities and member states. The harmonization of criminal law, exchanges of information, executive cooperation, for instance in 'joint investigation teams', and most notably the European Arrest Warrant certainly go much beyond the traditional notion that, in military and police matters, state sovereignty is still intact. In fact, the monopoly of force of the member states becomes increasingly embedded into a larger institutional setting within the political system of the EU (Jachtenfuchs 2005). But there is no sign of an emerging competition for the monopoly of force between the central EU institutions and the member states. This is the decisive difference between the political system of the European Union and federal states. The latter usually have centralized military forces. The federal level also has either its own police forces or at least a firm constitutional grip on the police forces of lower levels of government (Bayley 1985).

However, political systems cannot rely on coercion alone in order to maintain themselves and to pursue public policies. Even in international relations, the 'managerial school' of compliance argues that the threat of force is not sufficient to achieve compliance with jointly agreed rules (Raustiala and Slaughter 2002). Hierarchy combined with force may become increasingly dysfunctional as a mode of governance in modern, highly differentiated societies. But having no monopoly of force at all is different from having it without using it most of the time. In the Euro-Polity, the threat and the actual use of force is not available for the center even in extreme circumstances. Governance and politics take place in a system which is in the last resort exclusively based on voluntary agreement.

Besides the monopoly of force, the second resource that the modern state has successfully claimed during its development is control over taxation. In the major industrialized countries, the tax take as a share of GDP rose to about 40%. As a result, states have enormous financial resources at their disposal. Like the monopoly of force, the monopoly of taxation is under pressure from globalization and Europeanization (Genschel 2005). But it still exists. The financial resources available to the EU are by far smaller than the financial resources available to the member states and to a large degree consist of member state contributions. As a result, the EU level has only rather limited financial resources at its disposal. Although politics does not simply and exclusively consist of spending money, having it makes a big difference, as large infrastructure projects or a redistributive welfare state with massive effects on political affiliation (Flora and Heidenheimer 1981) are feasible options only for the member states.

A Hierarchical Legal System

While the EU has no monopoly of force and no monopoly of taxation, it has a hierarchical legal system and a supranational constitutional order, most concisely expressed by the doctrines of 'direct effect' and of 'supremacy' (Weiler 1999; Alter 2001). According to the first, EU Treaties and secondary legislation do under certain conditions create direct individual rights and obligations without having to be transposed into national law. According to the second, European Union law is superior to national law, including national constitutional law. Both doctrines have met with considerable resistance but are now by and large accepted both by the political and the legal actors of EU member states.

As a result, the structure of the EU's legal system can to some degree compensate for the lack of a monopoly of force. In the first place, intentional non-implementation is not a promising option for member states resisting a certain policy. Due to the direct-effects doctrine, EU rules can create individual legal rights even if they are not implemented. These rights can be claimed from domestic courts. If states resist a legal act of the EU, it does not oppose a 'foreign' legal order by domestic courts and thus risks jeopardizing its own judicial system. Decision-making and implementation thus take place under the shadow of legal hierarchy. This considerably raises the costs for non-implementation. Although European law is still not like domestic law, mainly because its degree of political internalization is lower, it clearly has a higher legal quality than international law (Zürn and Wolf 1999). As a result, compliance is not systematically lower in the European Union than in territorial states (Zürn and Joerges 2005).

Weak Political Parties

In established democracies, political parties, interest groups and the media are the most common intermediary institutions between citizens and government. Of these, political parties are arguably the most important ones as they establish a rather direct link between individual political preferences and political action.

The development of the Euro-Polity has clearly stimulated the organization and coherence of political parties at the EU-level. Whereas the first wave of literature which appeared on the occasion of the first direct elections to the European Parliament in 1979 has shown limited programmatic and organizational coherence despite great expectations in this direction (Reif et al. 1980), organizational structures, programmatic coherence, and voting coherence of European level political parties have greatly increased since then (Gabel and Hix 2002; Hix et al. 2005). Although party politics at the European level thus increasingly looks like party politics at the national level, party politics is less relevant on the European level than it is on the member state level. This is so for several reasons.

In the first place, European elections in many member states are still second-order national elections (Reif and Schmitt 1980). Overall turnout in elections to the European Parliament has been steadily declining since 1979, and electoral campaigns are not about alternative choices for European public policies but mainly about national political issues. Apart from major European constitutional choices which often have a high mobilization potential, even major issues of European Union politics do not figure prominently in domestic debates and party politics. And, despite the increasing degree of programmatic integration on the left–right scale, the national cleavage is still very strong with respect to grand constitutional questions (Jachtenfuchs 2002). This is typical for territorially segmented systems such as the European Union.

The European Parliament as the arena where party politics takes place in the European Union is only one player in the EU legislative process. Although there are signs of a slow move away from the early technocratic image towards a more political view, the European Commission is not responsive to popular elections and thus does not show a strong ideological profile. This applies even more to the Council, which constantly changes its political composition as a result of different national election dates. The Council is not a corporate actor but a collective actor with constantly shifting composition. Thus, the Euro-Polity follows neither the model of a party government nor the model of a presidential system. Instead, it is a negotiating system with a limited role for political parties and a very strong role for national governments and their institutional and socioeconomic interests.

Negotiation is a mode of collective decision-making fundamentally different from voting which is prevalent in parliamentary politics (Scharpf 1997a: 151–70; Elster 1998). Whereas, in voting, the winning majority 'takes all' and thus has to make fewer compromises even if it is a coalition, negotiation ideal-typically requires the consent of all players and thus a larger readiness for compromise than voting. Although the Council increasingly decides by qualified majority, votes are still the exception rather than the rule and are used as a means to decide only after the failure of negotiations when compromises have already been made. As a result, the Euro-Polity still has a strong tendency to moderate socioeconomic cleavages and thus to reduce the role of political parties.

Weak Coupling of Levels of Government

The implicit understanding of much of the scientific and the political literature on the EU as a multilevel system assumes neatly separated levels of government, usually two – the EU-level and the member state level. There are several sources of this idea, ranging from fiscal federalism to the Catholic doctrine of subsidiarity. The basic thrust of the argument is that governmental activity can and should be organized at different territorial levels, depending on the issue at stake, in order to maximize policy-making efficiency and citizen involvement: Whereas garbage collection should be organized at the local level, defense should be located at the highest level of the political system. The merits and problems of this idea as a normative theory are not at issue here. As an analytical model, however, the concept of the EU consisting of independent levels of government is misleading as it supposes that each level of government has the resources and powers to carry out its tasks without having to rely on other levels.

The reality of the EU corresponds more to the German system of two interlocked levels of government than to an idealized US model of two clearly separated levels. The most illustrative case for this argument is the Council. In terms of decision-making, the Council was the overwhelmingly important body and remains crucial even after the constant rise of the European Parliament. Although the Council is an institution at the EU level, it represents national governments responsive to national electorates on national issues. It is not an equivalent to the US Senate which does not consist of state governors but of Senators specifically elected for it. Instead, the Council is closer to the German *Bundestag*, which consists of representatives of the *Länder* governments elected in *Länder* elections. In the terminology of Sbragia (1993), the representation of territorial interests in the European Union is much stronger than in federal states.

The EU does not only lack a monopoly of force that could be used to implement laws against open resistance, it also lacks the personnel and the powers to implement its laws in normal times. Instead, it has to rely on the member states to implement its laws and policies and to collect its resources (even the so-called 'own resources').

But the EU is also different from German federalism with respect to the relationship between the two main levels of government. Whereas, in Germany, both levels are tightly coupled, they are only loosely coupled in the EU (on the concept of 'coupling', c.f. Orton and Weick 1990). Strict coupling in the context of German federalism means that representatives of *Länder* governments in the *Bundesrat* have precise mandates for their negotiation strategy from which they usually will not deviate. The reason for this behavior is that both levels of government in German federalism are linked through political parties which exist as integrated organizations at both levels. The logic of party interests thus often supersedes the logic of territorial interests. As a result, the *Bundesrat* becomes involved into the power game at the federal level, a situation which is most visible when the respective majorities in the *Bundestag* and in the *Bundesrat* differ.

This is different in the EU context. Although several attempts have been made to coordinate the positions of the large party groups before major European Council meetings, Euro-parties usually have no influence on the positions of negotiators in the sectoral Council meetings which are responsible for the day-to-day governance of the EU. As a result, negotiating positions of governmental representatives in the EU Council are not linked to an overall political struggle at the EU level. Instead, negotiators in the Council have much more leeway than negotiators in the *Bundesrat*. In the European Union, the EU and the member state level are only loosely coupled (Benz 2000, 2003).

CONSEQUENCES FOR POLICY-MAKING AND POLITICS

These particular features of the EU multilevel system – the lack of a monopoly of force and of taxation, the hierarchical legal system, the weakness of political parties and the loose coupling of levels of government – have specific consequences for policy-making and political processes in the European Union.

A Specific Mode of Governance: Negotiation and Deliberation

Elster (1998: 5) has argued that there are only three pure forms of collective decision-making: voting, bargaining or negotiation, and deliberation (c.f. Scharpf 1997a). In political reality, there are often mixed or combined forms such as deliberations followed by a vote, mixtures of negotiation and deliberation, or negotiations in the shadow of a vote. The typical decision-making mode for democracies is voting (Dahl 1989: 135–62). Voting is a very efficient means of decision-making as it produces clear decisions quickly (if we neglect the problems of cyclical majorities). For this reason, the increased resort to majority voting is usually presented as a means to increase the decision-making efficiency of the EU and to prevent it from collapse in the face of an ever-expanding membership. However, voting does not change the preferences of the participants, it does not require compromises between the different positions, and it creates winners and losers. Hence, the acceptance of the majority decision by the minority is a structural problem. The factors usually identified for favoring acceptance are the realistic prospect of also being part of the majority in a not too distant future and a collective identity which makes losing easier as it takes place in a community.

The European Union is very heterogeneous in terms of both socio-economic development and of cultural identity. Decisions need to be accepted by all participants and can only be enforced through legal procedures (in the areas where the European Court of Justice has jurisdiction) but not through the use of force. This is why its decision-making procedures are characterized by the search of consensus, with the exception of voting in the European Parliament. The Commissioners, although formally entitled to adopt decisions by simple majority, usually try to reach agreement by consensus (Hix 2005: 41). The Council also tries to avoid voting (Mattila and Lane 2001) although qualified majority voting is possible in an increasing number of areas. Whereas, in the democratic state, voting is the major decision-making rule, in the European Union it is negotiation and deliberation.

Negotiation also does not change participants' preferences. Contrary to voting, however, it requires compromises and avoids losers as all participants have to sacrifice something in order to reach an agreement. It is therefore likely to be more frequent in decentralized systems with weak hierarchical elements such as the European Union than in more hierarchical systems. Indeed, negotiation prevails in the EU with the Council being the incarnation of a negotiation system. The Council decision-making process on all levels – from the ministerial level to COREPER and the Council working groups – is a highly institutionalized negotiation process. The same applies to the Comitology system (Joerges and Vos 1999) and to a large degree to relations between the Commission, the Council, and the European Parliament. The various 'dialogues' with societal actors are also partly negotiations. Beate Kohler-Koch has argued that the EU system is characterized by consociation instead of majoritarianism (c.f. Lijphart 1999) as a constitutional principle and by the prevalence of individual interests over the common good (Kohler-Koch 1999). As a result, outcomes are negotiated in consensus-oriented arenas with various participants (c.f. the contributions in Kohler-Koch and Eising 1999).

Deliberation, Elster's third mode of collective decision-making, involves changing preferences. Deliberation is the process of arriving at cognitive and normative agreements among participants by mutual conviction alone. It creates no losers and does not even require actors to 'give in' to a negotiation outcome which does not correspond to their preferences. Instead, deliberation leads to a change of actors' preferences so that in the end they all agree on a common course of action because they are convinced that this is the best and right collective decision even if they would have liked another outcome initially. Collective agreements reached through deliberation are thus self-enforcing and not vulnerable to unilateral action (which is a weakness of negotiated agreements). They are ideal for heterogeneous polities such as the EU but they also carry a heavy price in the form of high time requirements or the risk of non-decisions.

Deliberation is a difficult concept, mostly because the transition from social macro-theories to empirical research is very difficult and has not yet led to much agreement about how to operationalize deliberation. There is also no clear demarcation from related concepts such as a 'problem-solving' negotiation style or 'arguing'. In addition, distinguishing between deliberation and negotiation not only requires fine-grained and detailed empirical analysis (e.g. Holzinger 2001), but also access to the verbatim proceedings of the respective bodies (Elster 1992). Although micro-analytical analyses of the meetings of EU bodies are rare, there is clear evidence that negotiations among member states are not characterized by pure negotiation but also have a major deliberation component (Lewis 1998). This seems to be particularly strong in Comitology, where 'deliberative supranationalism' partly replaces inter-governmental bargaining (Joerges and Neyer 1997a, b; Gehring 1999).

A System-Specific Policy Mix?

The EU is a multilevel political system consisting of two interlinked levels of governance with relatively weak political parties and a weak collective identity. Like any institutional setting, this particular type of polity may have specific consequences for policy-making and governance.

Several attempts have been made to classify the multitude of substantive policy fields in a few groups in order to be able to systematically relate them to political processes and political institutions. The distinction between redistributive and regulatory policies based on Lowi's (1964, 1972) proposals is of particular relevance for the EU. Distributive policies, Lowi's third category, will be neglected here as hardly any policies nowadays simply distribute an inexhaustible resource across constituencies and thus create only winners without taking it from anybody. This classification is not comprehensive as it does not cover foreign and security policies as well as what in Euro-speak

is called 'justice and home affairs'. But it captures a key feature of the political system of the European Union, namely its systematic difficulties to carry out redistributive policies and the ensuing focus on regulatory policy-making.

Redistributive policies are characterized by the explicit transfer of resources from one party to another by public agents. By definition, they fail to meet the Pareto criterion and make some actors worse off than before the policy was initiated. They create winners and losers in a zero-sum logic of political interaction and lead to more conflictual political processes. Examples from the EU include agricultural policies or regional policy. The prime example from the member states is the welfare state. Regulatory policies set standards for certain behavior by market participants. They do not make direct use of financial resources and are intended to be Pareto-improving. Examples include environmental standards, technical regulations, or standards for health and safety in the workplace.

Regulatory policies also have financial consequences. But the key difference between regulatory and redistributive policies is that, in the latter case, the financial effects are intentional and clearly visible. In the field of regulatory policies, differential financial effects also exist but are in many cases unintended consequences of policies aiming at other goals. Often, the redistributive effects of regulatory policies are not clearly visible and are not borne by the addressees of the regulation but can be shifted onto others. In addition, regulatory policies often require a high degree of professional knowledge (e.g. when new pharmaceuticals or chemicals have to be assessed) which make their financial consequences even less visible.

Majone (1994, 1996) has forcefully argued that the European Union is very strong in regulatory policy-making but weak in redistributive policy-making. His analysis has now become a folk-theorem of European Union studies. Although the EU has a number of major redistributive policies (agriculture, regional policy, research, and development) which clearly surpass what can be found in other international institutions, these policies by far do not match the amount of redistribution linked to the welfare state. Whereas EU spending is leveled at about 1% of the EU's GDP, governmental spending in its member states on average amounts to almost half of the national GDP (Hix 2005: 272). At the same time, EU regulatory policies have steadily grown in scope and depth. In Majone's (1993) words, the EU is strong in social regulation but weak in social policy. This is not only an issue for policy-making. As the EU has structural difficulties to develop into a redistributive welfare state or to surpass a relatively modest level of public spending, it forgoes a major source of political support which is extensively used by the member states and constitutes a major step in their development (Zürn and Leibfried 2005). Majone and others have argued that this focus on regulatory policy-making is caused by structural properties of the Euro-polity. In other words, even if the governments of all member states wanted to create an EU-wide welfare state, they would face major difficulties. Why?

The main reason lies in the lack of democratic legitimacy of the European Union. Redistributive policies take resources from some actors and give them to others. Thus, they make actors worse off than before. Regulatory policies are much more unlikely to do so as their prime target is overall efficiency improvement and financial effects are only secondary and often less visible. However, policies need to be regarded as legitimate in order to be accepted by citizens and social groups. This is even more true in a system which cannot draw on the monopoly of force as a means of last resort.

Although the functioning of executive and legislative bodies at the EU level closely resembles their equivalents on the member state level, democratic political processes in the EU are weaker than in the democratic state. Large-scale and generalized redistributive policies would require solidarity between citizens of different nations. Neither intergovernmental decision-making of democratically elected governments in the Council nor parliamentary politics in the EP are sufficient to legitimate

far-reaching redistribution on the EU level. The EU does not possess the collective identity of a *demos* in whose name these decisions could be taken nor political parties strong enough to mediate between EU-level decisions and citizens' preferences (Weiler et al. 1995; Kielmansegg 2003; c.f. Majone 2005). As a result, its potential for redistribution is far smaller than the respective potential in the member states (Scharpf 1999). In sum, the growth of the policy-making powers of the EU has by and large followed the EU's capacity to legitimate the respective decisions. Conversely, the growth of regulatory policy-making in the Euro-Polity can be explained precisely by the relative autonomy of the Commission in particular and the relative weakness of political parties.

The Problem-Solving Capacity of the Euro-Polity

The above paragraph has only dealt with an inbuilt bias of the Euro-Polity to deal with regulatory policies rather than with redistributive policies. The respective literature did not make strong claims about the quality of these policies. With the ever increasing growth of EU policy-making, however, several authors have claimed that the EU systematically produces suboptimal policy outcomes, in other words that all other things being equal the quality of public policies is worse in the EU than in the member states.

The most substantive statement of this thesis is the 'joint-decision trap' (Scharpf 1988). The joint-decision trap is a decision-making pathology. As long as member state governments are represented in EU-level decision-making and (quasi-)unanimity is the decision rule, policies will be suboptimal and, worse, the system will remain incapable of self-reform. In recent years, it has been argued that the joint-decision trap is not without escape (Peters 1997; Blom-Hansen 1999) and that the introduction of qualified majority rule has removed one of the criteria for its application.

Still, the literature was full of suspicion that the EU was not a political system like any other but instead was highly selective in dealing with certain issues and specific (and possibly sub-optimal) in its outcomes. Scholars were concerned with the potential misrepresentation of diffuse interests (Pollack 1997), empty spots in the EU's agenda (Streeck 1995), or the prevalence of 'negative' over 'positive' integration (Scharpf 1996). However, after a decade of detailed empirical work on the problem-solving capacity of the EU, initial hypotheses about lowest-common-denominator outcomes between member states in most cases cannot be upheld. On the contrary, some EU policies unexpectedly even had adopted high standards (Eichener 1997).

As is usually the case in scientific debates, bold initial statements become more refined in the course of the debate as concepts become more sophisticated or problematized and more empirical results are available. In this debate, the problematization mainly concerned the concept of 'problem-solving' and the general issue of how to assess the substantive outcomes of a policy. The dilemma for political scientists in this respect is that on the one hand they cannot simply ignore the outcomes of public policies altogether but that on the other hand as political scientists they lack the professional competence for assessing most of these outcomes (c.f. Young 1999: 11–23). Although it is certainly true that the professional competence of political scientists relates to interaction results only (Scharpf 1997a: 11), political scientists have frequently made judgments about the successes of public policies, often without properly defining the criteria for success or failure (Mayntz 1987: 188). Even extreme cases are controversial: Is the Common Agricultural Policy a disaster or does it have the latent function of a social policy for a declining sector in profound structural change which avoids both major social hardships and food shortages (Rieger 2000)?

Still, even with these qualifications, the debate about the problem-solving capacity of the European Union (Scharpf 1997b) has by and large led to the result that the problem-solving capacity of the EU has effectively managed to escape deadlock (Héritier 1999). As a matter of fact, analyses show that conditions

for unsuccessful policy-making such as uncooperative actor constellations, insufficient capacities for implementation, or lacking public support are not limited to the European Union but are also present in the member states. Hence, the argument that the EU systematically and across the board leads to inferior outcomes is not supported. There is even substantial evidence that in a number of policy fields, the EU performed much better than expected (Grande and Jachtenfuchs 2000), even in the field of social policy where expectations were low (Falkner 2003).

Although there is no general theory linking the EU's problem-solving capacity to its institutional structure, it may be that the surprisingly high problem-solving capacity of the EU has to do with some of its system properties. One possible candidate is the relatively weak role of political parties and political competition in EU policy-making. Contrary to the situation in German federalism, this avoids specific issues to be superseded by party competition and the logic of adversarial politics. In addition, the EU has shown a high degree of institutional differentiation and of splitting up and combining issues and assigning them to appropriate institutional arenas (Gehring 1999, 2002). In this perspective, the relatively fluid and complex world of EU committees in the broadest sense is not an indicator of chaos or member state dominance but functional for problem-solving.

Against this generally positive view of EU policy-making which may be due to a certain bias towards positive cases is Scharpf's (2003) position that the high consensus requirements of negotiated solutions and the impossibility of majoritarian solutions in the EU prevent the adoption of policies in a number of areas such as foreign and security policies or the means to cope with the erosion of national welfare states due to the integrated European market. As a result, Scharpf claims, the EU is incapable of acting in a number of areas where the member states have lost their autonomous capacity to act due to European integration. While in the field of market regulation the balance is rather positive, the EU is still rather ineffective in areas requiring strong legitimation – a resource that the Euro-Polity only possesses to a limited extent.

CONCLUSION

The European Union is a highly institutional-ized system of governance. As such, it can be compared with other systems of governance. However, in order to come to meaningful rela-tionships between causes and effects, the nature of this system of governance as a potential causes of political processes and public policies has to be spelled out in detail as not much follows from broad classifications such as 'inter-national organization' or 'political system'. Analysing the EU as a multi-level system of gov-ernance tries to bridge the gap between the international relations and the comparative politics view of the European Union with a broader and more general concept. Still, the label itself does not lead very far if it is not accompanied by a more detailed description of the characteristic features of such a multi-level system. From these features – the lack of a monopoly of force and taxation, a hierarchical legal system, a weak role of political parties, and a loose coupling of the two main system levels – a number of rather specific conclusions can be drawn with regard to a specific mode of gover-nance, typical patterns of policy-making or the overall problem-solving capacity of the EU. Such an approach in the last resort is not spe-cific to EU studies any more but operates at the level of theories of the middle range or of ana-lytical toolkits inviting comparisons with other systems of governance having similar proper-ties. This comparison is essential. The European Union constitutes a laboratory for studying many of the features of modern governance and politics. In order to realize this potential and avoid the potential parochialism of studying e.g. American, German, or Swedish politics, stu-dents of European Union politics should not only refer to general political science theories and concepts but also seek comparisons with international as well as domestic institutions, processes and substantive policies outside the European Union.

ACKNOWLEDGMENT

I would like to thank Mark Pollack for helpful and constructive comments.

REFERENCES

Alter, K. (2001) *Establishing the Supremacy of European Law. The Making of an International Rule of Law in Europe.* Oxford: Oxford University Press.

Bayley, D.H. (1985) *Patterns of Policing. A Comparative International Analysis.* New Brunswick: Rutgers University Press.

Benz, A. (2000) 'Politische Steuerung in lose gekop-pelten Mehrebenensystemen', in R. Werle and U. Schimank (eds), *Gesellschaftliche Komplexität und kollektive Handlungsfähigkeit.* Frankfurt and New York: Campus. pp. 99–126.

Benz, A. (2003) 'Mehrebenenverflechtung in der Europäischen Union', in M. Jachtenfuchs and B. Kohler-Koch (eds), *Europäische Integration*, 2nd ed. Opladen: Leske und Budrich. pp. 317–51.

Blom-Hansen, J. (1999) 'Avoiding the "joint-decision trap". Lessons from intergovernmental relations in Scandinavia', *European Journal of Political Research*, 35(1): 35–67.

Bulmer, S. (1983) 'Domestic politics and European Community policy-making', *Journal of Common Market Studies*, 21(4): 349–63.

Cappelletti, M., Seccombe, M. and Weiler, J.H.H. (eds) (1985) *Integration Through Law. Europa and the American Federal Experience*, 3 Vols. Berlin and New York: de Gruyter.

Dahl, R.A. (1989) *Democracy and its Critics.* New Haven: Yale University Press.

Eichener, V. (1997) 'Effective European problem-solving. Lessons from the regulation of occupa-tional safety and of environmental protection', *Journal of European Public Policy*, 4(4): 591–608.

Elster, J. (1992) 'Arguing and bargaining in the federal convention and the assemblée constituante', in R. Malnes and A. Underdal (eds), *Rationality and Institutions. Essays in Honour of Knut Midgaard on the Occasion of his 60th Birthday, February 11, 1991.* Oslo: Universitetsforlaget. pp. 13–50.

Elster, J. (1998) 'Introduction', in J. Elster (ed), *Deliberative Democracy.* Cambridge: Cambridge University Press. pp. 1–18.

Falkner, G. (2003) 'Zwischen Gestaltungslücke und integrativen Kooperationseffekten. Wohlfahrtsstaat und Integration aus Sicht des historischen

Institutionalismus', in M. Jachtenfuchs and B. Kohler-Koch (eds), *Europäische Integration*, 2nd ed. Opladen: Leske und Budrich. pp. 479–511.

Flora, P. and Heidenheimer, A.J. (eds) (1981) *The Development of Welfare States in Europe and America*. New Brunswick: Transaction Publishers.

Gabel, M. and Hix, S. (2002) 'Defining the EU political space. An empirical study of the European elections manifestos, 1979–1999', *Comparative Political Studies*, 35(8): 934–64.

Gehring, T. (1999) 'Bargaining, arguing and functional differentiation of decision-making. The role of committees in European environmental process regulation', in C. Joerges and E. Vos (eds), *EU Committees. Social Regulation, Law and Politics*. Oxford and Portland: Hart. pp. 195–217.

Gehring, T. (2002) *Die Europäische Union als komplexe internationale Organisation*. Baden-Baden: Nomos.

Genschel, P. (2005) 'Globalization and the transformation of the tax state', *European Review*, 13(Special Issue 1): pp. 53–71.

Grande, E. and Jachtenfuchs, M. (eds) (2000) *Wie problemlösungsfähig ist die EU? Regieren im europäischen Mehrebenensystem*. Baden-Baden: Nomos.

Haas, E.B. (1975) *The Obsolescence of Regional Integration Theory*. Berkeley: Institute of International Studies, University of California, Research Series No. 25.

Haas, E.B. (2004) *The Uniting of Europe. Political, Economic, and Social Forces 1950–1957*, 3rd ed. Notre Dame: University of Notre Dame Press.

Héritier, A. (1999) *Policy-making and Diversity in Europe. Escaping Deadlock*. Cambridge: Cambridge University Press.

Hix, S. (1994) 'The study of the European Community. The challenge to comparative politics', *West European Politics*, 17(1): 1–30.

Hix, S. (1996) 'Comparative politics, international relations and the EU! A rejoinder to Hurrell and Menon', *West European Politics*, 19(4): 802–4.

Hix, S. (2005) *The Political System of the European Union*, 2nd ed. Houndsmills: Palgrave Macmillan.

Hix, S., Noury, A. and Roland, G. (2005) 'Power to the parties. Cohesion and competition in the European Parliament, 1979–2001', *British Journal of Political Science*, 35(2): 209–34.

Hoffmann, S. (1966) 'Obstinate or obsolete? The fate of the nation-state and the case of western Europe', *Daedalus*, 95: 862–915.

Holzinger, K. (2001) 'Verhandeln statt Argumentieren oder Verhandeln durch Argumentieren? Eine empirische Analyse auf der Basis der Sprechakttheorie', *Politische Vierteljahresschrift*, 42(3): 414–46.

Hooghe, L. (ed.) (1996) *European Integration and EU Cohesion Policy. Building Multilevel Governance*. Oxford: Oxford University Press.

Hooghe, L. and Marks, G. (2001) *Multi-Level Governance and European Integration*. Oxford: Rowman and Littlefield.

Hooghe, L. and Marks, G. (2003) 'Unravelling the central state, but how? Types of multi-level governance', *American Political Science Review*, 97(2): 233–43.

Hurrell, A. and Menon, A. (1996) 'Politics like any other? Comparative politics, international relations and the study of the EU', *West European Politics*, 19(2): 386–402.

Jachtenfuchs, M. (2001) 'The governance approach to European integration', *Journal of Common Market Studies*, 39(2): 245–64.

Jachtenfuchs, M. (2002) *Die Konstruktion Europas. Verfassungsideen und institutionelle Entwicklung*. Baden-Baden: Nomos.

Jachtenfuchs, M. (2005) 'The monopoly of legitimate force, denationalization, or business as usual?' *European Review*, 13(Special Issue 1): 37–52.

Jachtenfuchs, M. and Kohler-Koch, B. (eds) (2003) *Europäische Integration*, 2nd ed. Opladen: Leske und Budrich.

Joerges, C. and Neyer, J. (1997a) 'From intergovernmental bargaining to deliberative political processes. The constitutionalisation of comitology', *European Law Journal*, 3(3): 273–99.

Joerges, C. and Neyer, J. (1997b) 'Transforming strategic interaction into deliberative problem-solving, European comitology in the foodstuffs sector', *Journal of European Public Policy*, 4(4): 609–25.

Joerges, C. and Vos, E. (eds) (1999) *EU Committees. Social Regulation, Law and Politics*. Oxford; Portland: Hart.

Katzenstein, P.J. (1987) *Policy and Politics in West Germany. The Growth of a Semi-Sovereign State*. Philadelphia: Temple University Press.

Kielmansegg, G.P. (2003) 'Integration und Demokratie', in M. Jachtenfuchs and B. Kohler-Koch (eds), *Europäische Integration*, 2nd ed. Opladen: Leske und Budrich. pp. 49–83.

Kohler-Koch, B. (1999) 'The evolution and transformation of European governance', in B. Kohler-Koch and R. Eising (eds), *The Transformation of Governance in the European Union*. London: Routledge. pp. 14–35.

Kohler-Koch, B. (ed.) (2003) *Linking EU and National Governance*. Oxford: Oxford University Press.

Kohler-Koch, B. and Eising, R. (eds) (1999) *The Transformation of Governance in the European Union.* London: Routledge.

Lewis, J. (1998) *The Institutional Problem-Solving Capacities of the Council: The Committee of Permanent Representatives and the Methods of Community.* Köln: MPIFG Discussion Paper 98/1.

Lijphart, A. (1999) *Patterns of Democracy. Government Forms and Performance in Thirty-six Countries.* New Haven: Yale University Press.

Lindberg, L.N. and Scheingold, S.A. (1970) *Europe's Would-Be Polity. Patterns of Change in the European Community.* Englewood Cliffs: Prentice Hall.

Lowi, T. (1964) 'American business, public policy, case studies, and political theory', *World Politics*, 16(4): 677–715.

Lowi, T.J. (1972) 'Four systems of policy, politics, and choice', *Public Administration Review*, 32(4): 298–310.

Majone, G. (1993) 'The European Community between social policy and social regulation', *Journal of Common Market Studies*, 32(2): 153–70.

Majone, G. (1994) 'The rise of the regulatory state in Europe', *West European Politics*, 17(3): 77–101.

Majone, G. (ed) (1996) *Regulating Europe.* London: Routledge.

Majone, G. (2005) *Dilemmas of European Integration. The Ambiguities and Pitfalls of Integration by Stealth.* Oxford: Oxford University Press.

Marks, G. (1992) 'Structural policy in the European Community', in A.M. Sbragia (ed.), *Euro-Politics. Institutions and Policymaking in the 'New' European Community.* Washington: The Brookings Institution. pp. 391–411.

Marks, G. (1993) 'Structural policy and multilevel governance in the EC', in A.W. Cafruny and G.G. Rosenthal (eds), *The State of the European Community*, Vol. 2. The Maastricht Debates and Beyond. Boulder: Lynne Rienner. pp. 391–411.

Marks, G. and Hooghe, L. (2000) 'Optimality and authority. A critique of neoclassical theory', *Journal of Common Market Studies*, 38(5): 795–816.

Marks, G., Hooghe, L. and Blank, K. (1996) 'European integration from the 1980s. state-centric v. multi-level governance', *Journal of Common Market Studies*, 34(3): 341–78.

Mattila, M. and Lane, J.-E. (2001) 'Why unanimity in the Council? A roll call analysis of Council voting', *European Union Politics*, 2(1): 31–52.

Mayntz, R. (1987) 'Politische Steuerung und gesellschaftliche Steuerungsprobleme', in R. Mayntz (ed.), *Soziale Dynamik und politische Steuerung.*

Theoretische und methodologische Überlegungen. Frankfurt a.M.: Campus. pp. 186–208.

Milner, H.V. (1998) 'Rationalizing politics. The emerging synthesis of international, American, and comparative politics', *International Organization*, 52(4): 759–86.

Moravcsik, A. (1998) *The Choice for Europe. Social Purpose and State Power from Messina to Maastricht.* Ithaca: Cornell University Press.

Occhipinti, J.D. (2003) *The Politics of EU Police Cooperation. Toward a European FBI?* Boulder: Lynne Rienner.

Orton, J.D. and Weick, K.E. (1990) 'Loosely coupled systems. A reconceptualization', *Academy of Management Review*, 15(2): 203–23.

Peters, B.G. (1997) 'Escaping the joint-decision trap. Repetition and sectoral politics', *West European Politics*, 20(2): 22–36.

Peters, B.G. (1998) *Comparative Politics. Theory and Methods.* New York: New York University Press.

Poggi, G. (1990) *The State. Its Nature, Development and Prospects.* Stanford: Stanford University Press.

Pollack, M.A. (1997) 'Representing diffuse interests in EC policy-making', *Journal of European Public Policy*, 4(4): 572–90.

Pollack, M.A. (2001) 'International relations theory and European integration', *Journal of Common Market Studies*, 29(2): 221–44.

Puchala, D. (1972) 'Of blind men, elephants and international integration', *Journal of Common Market Studies*, 10(3): 267–84.

Puchala, D.J. (1984) *Fiscal Harmonization in the European Communities National Politics and International Cooperation.* London and Dover: Pinter.

Raustiala, K. and Slaughter, A.M. (2002) 'International law, international relations and compliance', in W. Carlsnaes, T. Risse and B.A. Simmons (eds), *Handbook of International Relations.* London: Sage. pp. 538–58.

Rehbinder, E. and Stewart, R. (1985) *Environmental Protection Policy.* Berlin/New York: de Gruyter.

Reif, K. and Schmitt, H. (1980) 'Nine second-order national elections. A conceptual framework for the analysis of European election results', *European Journal of Political Research*, 8(1): 3–45.

Reif, K., Cayrol, R. and Niedermayer, O. (1980) 'National political parties, middle level elites and European integration', *European Journal of Political Research*, 8: 91–112.

Reinhard, W. (1999) *Geschichte der Staatsgewalt. Eine vergleichende Verfassungsgeschichte Europas von den Anfängen bis zur Gegenwart.* München: Beck.

Rieger, E. (2000) 'The common agricultural policy. Politics against markets', in H. Wallace and W. Wallace (eds), *Policy-Making in the European Union.* Oxford: Oxford University Press. pp. 179–210.

Sbragia, A.M. (ed.) (1992a) *Euro-Politics. Institutions and Policymaking in the 'New' European Community.* Washington: The Brookings Institution.

Sbragia, A.M. (1992b) 'Thinking about the European future. The uses of comparison', in A.M. Sbragia (ed.), *Euro-Politics. Institutions and Policymaking in the 'New' European Community.* Washington: The Brookings Institution. pp. 257–91.

Sbragia, A.M. (1993) 'The European Community. A balancing act', *Publius,* 23(3): 23–38.

Scharpf, F.W. (1988) 'The joint-decision trap. Lessons from German federalism and European integration', *Public Administration,* 66(3): 239–78.

Scharpf, F.W. (1996) 'Negative and positive integration in the political economy of European welfare states', in G. Marks, F.W. Scharpf, P.C. Schmitter and W. Streeck (eds), *Governance in the European Union.* London: Sage. pp. 15–39.

Scharpf, F.W. (1997a) *Games Real Actors Play. Actor-Centered Institutionalism in Policy Research.* Boulder: Westview.

Scharpf, F.W. (1997b) 'Introduction. The problem solving capacity of multi-level governance', *Journal of European Public Policy,* 4(4): 520–38.

Scharpf, F.W. (1999) *Governing in Europe. Effective and Democratic?* Oxford: Oxford University Press.

Scharpf, F.W. (2001) 'Notes towards a theory of multilevel governing in Europe', *Scandinavian Political Studies,* 24(1): 1–26.

Scharpf, F.W. (2003) *Problem-solving Effectiveness and Democratic Accountability in the EU.* Köln: MPIfG Working Paper 03/1, February 2003.

Stein, E. (1981) 'Lawyers, judges, and the making of a transnational constitution', *American Journal of International Law,* 75(1): 1–27.

Streeck, W. (1995) 'Politikverflechtung und Entscheidungslücke. Zum Verhältnis von zwischenstaatlichen Beziehungen und sozialen Interessen im europäischen Binnenmarkt', in K. Bentele, B. Reissert and R. Scheettkat (eds), *Die Reformfähigkeit von Industriegesellschaften. Fritz W. Scharpf – Festschrift zu seinem 60. Geburtstag.* Frankfurt a.M.: Campus. pp. 101–28.

Tilly, C. (ed.) (1975) *The Formation of National States in Western Europe.* Princeton: Princeton University Press.

Wagner, W. (2003) 'Why the EU's common foreign and security policy will remain intergovernmental. A rationalist institutional choice analysis of European crisis management policy', *Journal of European Public Policy,* 10(4): 576–95.

Wallace, H., Wallace, W. and Webb, C. (eds) (1977) *Policy-Making in the European Communities.* London: Wiley.

Weiler, J.H.H. (1981) 'The Community system. The dual character of supranationalism', *Yearbook of European Law,* 1: 267–306.

Weiler, J.H.H. (1982) 'Community, member states and European integration. Is the law relevant?' *Journal of Common Market Studies,* 21(1/2): 39–56.

Weiler, J.H.H. (1999) *The Constitution of Europe. 'Do the New Clothes Have an Emperor?' and Other Essays on European Integration.* Cambridge: Cambridge University Press.

Weiler, J.H.H., Haltern, U.R. and Mayer, F.C. (1995) 'European democracy and its critique', *West European Politics,* 18(3): 4–39.

Young, O.R. (1999) *Governance in World Affairs.* Ithaca and London: Cornell University Press.

Zürn, M. and Joerges, C. (2005) *Law and Governance in Postnational Europe. Compliance Beyond the Nation-State.* Cambridge: Cambridge University Press.

Zürn, M. and Leibfried, S. (2005) 'Reconfiguring the national constellation', *European Review,* 13(Special Issue 1): 1–36.

Zürn, M. and Wolf, D. (1999) 'European law and international regimes. The features of law beyond the nation state', *European Law Journal,* 5(3): 272–92.

8

Legislative Politics

GAIL MCELROY

INTRODUCTION

Characterizing the ways in which legislation is made in the European Union is a complicated business. Different decision rules apply in different policy domains and the full array of legislative procedures can be bewildering for the uninitiated. The balance of power between the principal institutions varies under each legislative procedure, necessitating different strategies and imposing different bargaining requirements on the main actors. An exhaustive account of legislative politics in the European Union (EU) is beyond the scope of a single chapter; the details of the various legislative processes are admirably documented in several texts (for comprehensive accounts see Nugent 2003; Hix 2005; Wallace et al. 2005). Rather, this chapter aims to examine some of the more recent controversies that have arisen in the legislative politics literature and to identify areas which are under-researched and neglected by current research agendas.

Inevitably, the complexity of the processes by which legislation comes into force and the manner in which the institutions interact with each other has led to the development of several different literatures. It would be impossible to summarize all that has been done but I hope to identify the major recent research developments in three principal areas: (1) the growing literature on intra-parliamentary politics in the European Parliament (EP), (2) the power indices literature assessing member-state influence in the Council of Ministers, and (3) the literature on inter-institutional bargaining. More specifically, this chapter focuses on the key debates over the nature of policy competition in the European Parliament, whether or not the power indices approach provides useful insights into the legislative politics of the Council, and whether the inter-institutional arrangement is truly bicameral, and why these three literatures fail to speak to each other. In addition, I will consider what the study of legislation in the EU has to offer political science as a discipline more generally.

The sub-field of legislative politics has traditionally been dominated by studies of the US Congress and in particular by analyses of the activities of the House of Representatives (Gamm and Huber 2002). This congressional research has generated a remarkable body of scholarship, which is proving very influential in the nascent study of legislative politics in the EU. While the EU is certainly not the first setting to be examined in the context of legislative theories developed in Congress (Müller 2000; Carey 2002; Chaisty 2005; Kim and Loewenberg 2005), it may be more influential in feeding back into Congressional studies, given the apparent similarities between the two systems. It is remarkable that our understanding of legislative politics is largely dictated by the experience of one particular legislative body and in our desire for comparison there is a danger that we will stretch the parallels too far. There are key differences between the two political systems that must be given due consideration in any comparison. In particular, the weak (if not absent) electoral connection in the political system of the EU contrasts radically with the US. In addition, the asymmetry in powers between the Council and Parliament contrasts markedly with the more balanced relationship between the Senate and House of Representatives. Finally, there is no strict executive-legislative division of powers in the EU, which is the hallmark of the US presidential system. Any study of legislative politics in the EU is inevitably complicated by the dual role of the Council as both a legislative and executive body. There is a danger that legislative scholars will blindly adopt legislative theories developed in the context of the US in their desire to underscore the normalcy of politics in the EU. The true promise and potential of EU scholarship is that it provides a testing ground for extant theories of legislative behavior, reinforcing what we already know, offering the possibility of falsification and most importantly the opportunity to broaden the trends in legislative studies in general.

Our understanding of legislative politics in the EU is in its infancy, the system is complicated and the environment is in a constant state of flux. But taken more broadly the understanding of legislative politics in political science is less developed than one might think, given the study of legislatures is as old as the discipline itself, dating perhaps to the work of Bagehot (1867). As already outlined legislative theory is largely dictated by the American experience and even here much revolves around analyses of roll call behavior and the evolution and the functioning of the committee system. The focus on legislative behavior in pure parliamentary systems, which has been less instructive for the EU scholars, concerns itself primarily with cabinet behavior and coalition formation and dissolution and is not generally concerned with the behavior of individual legislators. What remains in the legislative literature beyond this is largely descriptive and oriented towards single legislatures, and is not consciously concerned with comparison or theorizing, with some notable exceptions (Döring 1995; Döring and Hallerberg 2004). In contrast, recent work on legislative politics in the EU has been explicitly comparative and for this reason it is of interest to scholars of legislative politics in general, not just European Union specialists.

This chapter proceeds as follows: The next section looks at recent developments in legislative politics within the European Parliament, examining in the process the burgeoning literature on roll call analyses, recent work on committee behavior and identifying areas that are under-researched. The explosion of work on the Parliament has been perhaps the most notable feature of EU legislative studies in recent years and as a result the bulk of this chapter is dedicated to this. Following this we turn to examine the voluminous power index literature and consider the value of these studies for legislative understanding in the Council and the EU in general. Finally, we conclude with an examination of the work on interinstitutional relations, with a particular focus on the spatial modeling literature. We end with a brief discussion of the failure of these literatures to speak to each other and consider the promising future of EU legislative politics.

LEGISLATIVE POLITICS IN THE EP

The recent increase in the application of legislative theories rooted in Congress to the EU has been most marked in studies of the European Parliament. These studies of the EP have been marked by a concerted and conscious effort to examine the legislative process in a comparative context, which is a welcome development for legislative politics in general. The work of the various scholars connected with the European Parliamentary Research Group is at the forefront of this movement with the explicit aim to 'connect research on the European Parliament to the general study of legislative behavior and institutions in political science'.[1]

Those interested in comparative legislative politics focus their attention on the EP, as opposed to the Council, as a body which has more obvious and immediate similarities with other assemblies: it is directly elected, it has an increasingly elaborate internal organization, it holds plenary sessions, has a party structure, and perhaps most importantly is reasonably transparent. Another key advantage in studying the EP is that it has even more key internal features in common with Congress, from whence most of our theories of legislative politics hail, than the German Bundestag, the British House of Commons, or the Swedish Riksdag. These similarities between the internal organization of the European Parliament and Congress make comparison easier than between a typical European parliament and Congress. Neither body has a government resting on a vote of no confidence; political parties are less cohesive in both chambers than is typically the case in the national assemblies of Europe; and in both chambers the work of members is concentrated in committee. However, the danger of the dominance of one institution in the field of legislative studies is that there are biases created in the types of questions posed and answered and that assumptions of comparability may be stretched too far. The differences in both institutions are important, as they structure individual action and limit the range of possible outcomes.

One of the more interesting features of the EP for instance is the weakened electoral connection. The electoral connection is the first and most fundamental of the legislative politics in Congress (Fiorina 1974; Mayhew 1974). This is not something to be dismissed in passing or explained away, it makes for very interesting comparison. To the extent that electoral incentives shape much of the behavior of political actors in Congress, it leaves open the question of what motivates MEPs in the European Parliament. The connection between MEPs and their voters is extraordinarily weak. It is well documented that elections to the European Parliament are not run on the basis of European issues but are best interpreted as classic 'second-order elections' (Reif and Schmitt 1980; Franklin et al. 1996; Marsh 1998; Schmitt 2005). Knowledge of the activity of political groups and their members is negligible among the citizenry of Europe, although Bowler and Farrell (1993) find that members elected in the single member districts in the UK and under preferential STV in Ireland are more responsive to their constituents than those elected in larger constituencies under list PR, suggesting that the electoral connection is not entirely irrelevant. Nonetheless, election-centered legislative behavior is clearly not an optimal assumption for legislative scholars in the EP. It is not even clear what constitutes an MEP's electoral constituency. Thomassen and Schmitt (1997), in their study of representation in the EU, treat the national party as the MEP's natural constituency. But Scully (2000) underscores the independence of MEPs from their national party when he demonstrates that the complexity of the EP ensures that it is both very difficult and inefficient for national parties to bind their members tightly to predetermined policy positions. Raunio (2000) found that the links between members and their national parties have increased over time but his findings show that MEPs are still largely independent of their parties: MEPs are not instructed how to vote but they nevertheless have gained more political weight in their domestic parties (see also Chapter 12 by Raunio, this volume).

Another interesting ramification for legislative behavior arising from the weakened electoral connection concerns the establishment of party discipline. MEPs are in the unusual legislative situation that the body that ensures their nomination (the national party) is distinct from the body that can guarantee their career advancement in the Parliament itself (the political group). The literature on party discipline tends to focus on electoral incentives as a means of inducing party loyalty, but the European Parliament provides a particularly interesting case study as these inducements are weak, if not missing altogether. If a party can control the nomination process, it can monitor the cohesion of the party through the selection and de-selection of 'problem' candidates (Gallagher and Marsh 1988). Control over access to the ballot is one of the primary methods of ensuring party discipline in parliamentary democracies. The more centralized the process the higher we should expect cohesion to be, all other factors being equal (Bowler et al. 1996). The political groups in the EP currently have no control over the nomination of candidates. National parties in each of the 25 member states control access to the ballot. The political groups in the European Parliament are clearly greatly disadvantaged vis-à-vis their national counterparts in the mechanisms they have at their disposal to enforce unity. The prospects for cohesion appear quite bleak. For these reasons scholars of comparative political parties invariably conclude that the political groups in the European Parliament are weak and ineffectual when compared with their national counterparts in the parliaments of Western Europe (Fitzmaurice 1988; Dehousse 1989; Lodge 1989; Wessels 1991).

Yet recent analysis suggests that cohesion levels are rising in the EP (Hix et al. 2005). What mechanism is driving this process and does this offer us insights into party discipline in other arenas? Political parties in established democracies typically exhibit such high levels of unity that the question of how and why such discipline arises has, until recently, received surprisingly little attention (Bowler et al. 1999). But in emerging legislatures the process of transforming rudimentary party organizations into disciplined parties is not inevitable. A crucial subject for any scholar of party politics is how such discipline is established. What mechanisms are used to achieve this end? How party discipline arises and how it is sustained are questions that should concern all scholars of legislative politics. Our knowledge of these topics, however, is surprisingly limited, especially outside the Anglo-American world (Bowler et al. 1999).

The political groups have played a crucial role in the organization of the Parliament from the beginning in terms of committee assignments, organizing the legislative agenda, and allocating speaking time and resources (Oudenhove 1965; Fitzmaurice 1975; Pridham and Pridham 1979; Niedermayer 1983; Bardi 1994; Corbett et al. 2003). There is growing evidence to suggest that this internal control of the organization by the political groups has been effectively used to promote cohesion and discipline in the political groups (McElroy 2003). In particular the control of the assignment process to the highly evolved committee system is one example of political group power. Scarrow (1997) finds that the number of careerist MEPs, who view the Parliament as their principal political arena, is increasing with time and MEPs who wish to make a career in the EP, via party promotion, may need to toe the party line. The European Parliament is a particularly apt arena in which to demonstrate the importance of internal advancement in a political actor's motivations, as it is one of the few contexts in which the electoral connection is not obviously paramount (McElroy 2003). It is almost certainly the case that intra-parliamentary incentives operate in all legislative bodes to encourage cohesion but often these are dwarfed by electoral considerations. The study of the European Parliament allows legislative scholars to more neatly isolate the internal and electoral factors in an actor's motivation structure, with implications for the general study of legislative behavior.

Roll Call Voting, Voting Behavior and the Rise of Cohesion in the EP

The study of legislative behavior in Congress has relied heavily on the analyses of roll call votes (RCVs). A recent growth area in legislative behavior in the EP has been afforded by the application of the technical tools developed for Congress to analyse RCVs. The EP, unlike many of its national counterparts in the member states, makes regular use of this particular voting procedure and it provides a good testing ground for these tools. The roll call analyses in the EP have been used to a variety of ends, to establish the nature of the policy space in the EP (Hix et al. 2005), to examine levels of cohesion (Raunio 1997; Kreppel 2002a), to establish ideal points of legislators (Voeten 2005; McElroy 2006), and to examine inter-group coalitions (Hix and Lord 1997; Kreppel 2000; Hix et al. 2003). These studies of MEP voting behavior have broadly concluded that voting cohesion is on the rise (Attina 1990; Raunio 1997), that the two largest parties both collude and compete depending on the need for unity in the EP (Kreppel 2000), and that political group affiliation is a better predictor of voting behavior than nationality (Hix 2002; Noury 2002), though there is some evidence to suggest that the party groups cannot prevent whole national delegations defecting (Brzinski 1995; Faas 2003). The most comprehensive analysis of RCV to date (Hix et al. 2005) concludes that cohesion in the Parliament has risen concomitantly with increasing powers of the Parliament. In addition, recent studies also demonstrate that the principal axis of competition in the European Parliament is left–right (rather than a national territorial dimension or pro-anti EU dimension) and that legislative politics is more competitive than consensual (Hix et al. 2007). These findings are echoed by scholars such as Tsebelis and Garrett (2000), Kreppel and Tsebelis (1999), and Kreppel (2000), who have described the EP policy space as uni-dimensional with the traditional left–right or 'regulation' dimension dominating. These findings about the dimensionality of EP policy space have been largely confirmed in a recent expert survey (McElroy and Benoit 2006) which finds that left and right issues cluster into two orthogonal component sets, the dominant one related to the classic national left and right issues from national party politics, and the second related clearly to EU issues.

The findings that the EU policy space largely mirrors that of national-level competitions are viewed as cause for optimism by those who look to the EP for alleviation of the democratic deficit in the European Union (Hix 1999; Noury and Roland 2002). If political parties are the motors of political competition in industrialized democracies and competitive party democracy is essential for the future of Europe (Thomassen et al. 2002), the RCV analyses present a rosy picture of 'politics as normal' already having emerged in the EP. The roll call evidence suggests, contrary to public perception, that trans-national political groups have already emerged as key actors in the European political space. There is clearly scope for further development of roll call analyses through the use of more sophisticated techniques such as the use of Monte Carlo Markov Chain (MCMC) models and in particular the more considered use of roll calls on particular substantive issues. One further interesting development in the 2004 European elections was the emergence for the first time of interest-group scores, equivalent to the powerful ADA scores in the US, by the environmental association Friends of the Earth. Perhaps this development points to a growing awareness of the importance of the activities of MEPs.

However, there are grounds to exercise caution in the interpretation of these roll call results. There are well-documented problems inherent in use of roll calls in terms of their strategic nature (Koford 1989) but particular problems arise with their use in the EP. Roll calls are used only about a third of the time (Corbett et al. 2003), in comparison to Congress where they are the norm. Roll call analyses may be a reasonable tool for studying legislative politics in the latter assembly but in the case of the EP where they are used only for a minority of votes we should be very concerned about the process by which they are generated. Carrubba et al. (2006) suggest that extreme caution is required in the interpretation and generalization of roll call analyses in the EP. Their work finds evidence for pooling concerns, the asymmetric use of roll calls under different legislative procedures, selection concerns, and the calling of RCVs disproportionately by particular parties. In general they find that RCVs are being called in less important legislative issue-areas and that

RCVs are not a representative sample of total votes in EP. Hug (2006) expresses similar concerns about the use of RCVs for the analysis of MEP legislative behavior. Overall these results suggest that roll call analyses may be a poor measure of levels of cohesion in EP and that the positive view of politics operating as normal in the EP may be a somewhat premature conclusion. This is not to argue that the use of roll calls should be abandoned but rather their use necessitates an explicit model of the process by which roll calls are generated. Ringe (2005) also cautions against the interpretation of voting as revealing policy preferences in the EP, suggesting that translation of ideology into policy decisions is not direct but structured by context, actors, and process. The use of roll call votes to isolate ideal points may be most problematic; roll calls are strategic and may reveal nothing more than how an MEP voted on a particular bill. However, it must be allowed that true preferences are unobservable in general and the use of alternative measures such as elite surveys to measure MEPs preferences have also been plagued by methodological problems such as very poor response rates (on surveys of MEPs see Scully and Farrell 2003; Scully 2005).

EP Organization

Parliaments are large and unwieldy bodies and increasingly the only way such large chambers can function is to divide into specialized committees (Laundy 1989). One area in which there are very strong comparative possibilities between the EP and Congress lies in the area of legislative organization. The comparative study of legislative committees has been surprisingly weak until recently, despite the fact that all legislatures work to some degree or other through these institutions. As with all legislatures, much of the real deliberation in the EP takes place outside of the plenary sessions in Strasbourg.

Committees have played a central role in the European Parliament from the outset. The Common Assembly of the European Coal and Steel Community recognized that committees would help alleviate the problems inherent in coordinating work in an Assembly which was scheduled to meet in plenary only a handful of times each year. To this end, it created seven committees to conduct Assembly business in January of 1953, and this committee model has continued through to today. Most of the activity of MEPs is now concentrated in the 20 parliamentary committees that meet in Brussels, not in the debating chamber. As is the case with the US Congress, the European Parliament in committee is the European Parliament at work. The assignment of MEPs to committees in the EP is heavily constrained by the Rules of Procedure. Committee prestige is largely dictated by the degree of legislative powers the EP has in the committee's policy jurisdiction and chairs of committees with these powers are highly sought after. Assignments and official positions on 'neutral' committees are far less desirable; these tend to be weak, non-legislative committees and are referred to as neutral because membership does not come at the cost of a position on another committee. This hierarchy of prestige grants the party leaders some power vis-a-vis their members as they lack many of the traditional incentives for fostering party discipline. Not only has the committee system expanded to provide 'jobs for the boys', control over the committee assignment process and committee chairs has been strongly tightened over the years. The committee system provides the political groups with an important source of patronage in addition to acting as a source of policy expertise.

Theories of legislative organization developed in the context of Congress suggest that committee systems are formed to either solve co-ordination problems among representatives by facilitating logrolling among members or alternatively to facilitate legislative efficiency. The former *distributional* approach predicts that members deliberately join committees in order to exercise disproportionate influence over the policy areas under the committee's jurisdiction (Shepsle and Weingast 1987). Committee members share a desire for high levels of benefit from the policies that lie within the jurisdiction of their committee (*high-demand preference outliers*). The alternative *informational*

(Krehbiel 1990) approach argues that committees are created to provide a greater number of legislative arenas for policy development and output in legislatures which are overburdened. This efficiency is enhanced by members' specialization in particular policy sub-fields. Informational theorists (Gilligan and Krehbiel 1990; Krehbiel 1991) dispute the degree of autonomy that the distributional approach ascribes to committees, arguing that most legislation must pass a majority vote on the floor of the house in order to be enacted. Given what we know about the origins of committees in the EP, the informational approach seems initially more plausible. Legislation in the European Union tends to be a complex, bargained outcome between multiple institutions. The Parliament has traditionally enjoyed fewer legislative powers than the Council of Ministers (see below), and any informational advantages developed through committee expertise would clearly improve the bargaining power of the EP. Such specialization may have been particularly important in the early days of the Parliament when it acted as a mere consultative assembly. Informational advantages brought about by specialization were perhaps the only means by which it could challenge the legislative authority of the Council. Finally, the lack of 'pork' to distribute, coupled with the lack of strong constituency ties in European elections (discussed above), removes many of the incentives that traditionally are seen to produce distributive gains.

Analyses of the role and importance of the parliamentary committees is very much in its infancy but evidence so far suggests that the assignment process is tightly controlled to ensure representative committees (McElroy 2006). Whitaker (2005) demonstrates that national parties tend to higher levels of representativeness on powerful committees and that national parties are more observant of their MEPs' behavior on these committees. Kaeding (2004), however, shows that the distribution of reports does not mirror the composition of the full plenary. Both of these analyses use small samples at particular time points and there is significant room for further research on the report allocation and the assignment processes

in general. McElroy (2002) demonstrates that the committee assignment process is used by parties to control members. There has been little if any systematic analysis of the committee meetings themselves, committee minutes, committee reports or committee voting.

One of the more interesting features of European Parliament committee system is the use of the committee 'rapporteur'. The position of rapporteur stems from the Continental European experience and there is no direct equivalent in the Anglo-Saxon democracies. When a committee receives a piece of draft legislation, it first appoints a rapporteur. It is the job of the rapporteur to prepare initial discussion on the draft legislation within the committee, to present a draft text to the committee, and ultimately to present the final report to plenary. At the committee stage of the legislative game, a rapporteur is a committee member appointed to draft a report which serves as the basis for legislative bargaining in the plenary. In principle, for any given piece of legislation, the rapporteur's work can have a direct and non-trivial impact on the character and fate of that legislation. Are rapporteurs an 'informational' device that reflects the desire of the legislature to acquire valuable information about a piece of legislation at a small cost? Are they a 'distributional' device which facilitates gains from trade between legislators? Or are rapporteurs 'partisan' in the sense that they further their party's agenda? Several recent studies of the rapporteur system in the EP examine the allocation of reports at the aggregate level. Benedetto (2005) and Mamadouh and Raunio (2001, 2003) examine the level of proportionality in the allocation of reports on dimensions such as nationality, party group, and national party affiliation and find that the process does not adhere to a strict proportionality norm. Hoyland (2006) shows that the aggregate number of reports allocated to a national party is higher for a national governing party (one represented in the Council of Ministers) than for a domestic opposition party. Another strand of studies explores the allocation of reports with individual-level analyses. In his study, Hausemer (2005) finds that the allocation of reports is a function of their salience for each party group. Within each group, committee chairs and preference outliers usually obtain the less salient reports, while the more salient ones are allocated to loyal MEPs. Moreover, the largest party group generally gets the most salient reports, while MEPs from smaller national parties (within a party group) also get more salient reports. Interestingly, Benedetto (2005) did not find a significant relationship between MEPs' pro- or anti-European views and their likelihood of obtaining salient reports. In a series of papers, Kaeding (2004, 2005) also examines the allocation of reports to individual MEPs. He finds evidence supporting both the informational and distributive perspective on legislatures with respect to report allocation. Looking at the consequences of rapporteurship allocations, Hoyland (2005) shows that the party affiliation of the rapporteur affects the likelihood that the report will be adopted on first reading by the Council of Ministers. Specifically, rapporteurs who belong to a governing party are at an advantage under the Codecision II procedure. But clearly there is much work to be done in this field.

Interesting work remains to be done in legislative organization in the EP. Topics such as jurisdictional battles between the committees, the role of the powerful rapporteur and the powerful and informal position of the party coordinator remain under-researched. In addition, one way in which the EP differs radically from the 'textbook Congress' (Mezey 1993) is the apparent absence of a seniority system operating at the committee level (Bowler and Farrell 1995), but it will be interesting to examine changes in this practice across time as the EP has become significantly more powerful in the past 10 years.

The Potential of EP Studies

Despite the recent growth in intra-parliamentary work in the past decade, the analysis of the EP as an institution is still in its infancy and there are many important areas of legislative research that are as yet relatively untouched. One such area that has received surprisingly little attention to date is the evolution of the rules of procedure of the EP and the development of internal organization in general. Apart from some work by Williams (1995) and Kreppel (2002a), there are few critical analyses of the internal evolution of the Parliament. Historical accounts of the formal impact of the various treaties on the EP abound but more analytical accounts are notably absent. In the period 1979–2002 there were considerably more than 1,000 rule changes proposed by the Rules Committee (PE 229.204 1999; PE 304.283 2001). Some of these changes were certainly inspired by significant revisions of the EU Treaties, but many more were seemingly technical (Judge and Earnshaw 2003: 197). The sheer volume of procedural proposals is noteworthy; a great deal of parliamentary time has been dedicated to the structuring of the institution. The formal rules of the legislative game have been highly contested over the course of the past 30 years. Standard accounts of the Parliament's history and development have almost exclusively adopted a functional (or macro-historical) approach (Lodge 1983; Corbett et al. 2003; Judge and Earnshaw 2003). The macro approach to questions of procedural choice specifies treaty revisions, increases in membership, and the escalation in workload as the root cause of organizational evolution. These posit that the institution developed as an adaptation to new circumstances, increased workloads, and new legislative powers. Traditional accounts of these major rule changes focus on the Parliament's attempts to increase its influence vis-à-vis the other European institutions such as the Council – the so-called *institutional imperative*. For example, Lodge (1983: 33) argues that these internal procedural changes rested 'on the premise that the EP has a moral and political obligation to EC voters to represent their interests by affecting the content of EC legislation'. Romer (1993: 2–3) identified a 'philosophy' behind the rules which has sought to strengthen the EP's position in the legislative process 'from the beginning to the final decision' as well as ensuring that internal organization is more efficient and more widely maximizes its inter-institutional impact.

It is clear that macro shocks in the form of treaty revisions necessitated internal adjustments. Undoubtedly, pressure from outside and the burden of work are important factors in explaining much of the institutional change in the EP, but it does not provide a complete account. The evolution of rules and norms were not merely a reflection of this necessity but also reflected issues internal to the Parliament itself. The history of the European Parliament is marked by lengthy battles over what appear to be organizational minutiae. The amount of effort and parliamentary time devoted to changing rules does not accord with a non-partisan account of procedural choice. In addition, the timing of many changes does not accord with changes in the external environment. The first direct elections to the Parliament took place in June 1979 and with them the membership of the Parliament doubled in size from 198 members to 410. The Rules of Procedure, which contained a mere 54 rules immediately prior to the elections, had more than doubled to 116 by May 1981. The Parliament did not gain any new powers at this time; the reorganization at this stage is primarily an internally driven process. The debates of Parliament reveal that frequently the two largest parties – the European People's Party (EPP) and the Party of the European Socialists (PES) – have acted in concert to shape the rules to their collective benefit. Rule evolution was to a significant degree the product of purposive, partisan action on the part of key players. Rules and matters of procedural choice are 'intelligent means to preconceived ends … they are chosen by individuals to accomplish particular purposes' (Gamm and Shepsle 1989: 40). Procedural matters may not be very important in legislatures that possess a large and cohesive majority (Binder 1997), but where such conditions are absent, as in the EP, legislative rules become important tools for actors who wish to build and sustain stable and cohesive parties. The debates of the European Parliament have, in general, not been subject to significant analyses and much interesting work remains to be done here.

The role of norms and informal institutions is also underdeveloped, though anecdotal evidence suggests these are no less important in the EP than in Congress. Johansson and Raunio (2005) identify the crucial part played by coalitions of leading personalities in the development and institutionalization of the Europarties. Johansson (2002) finds that informal networks and party elites in the EPP were crucial in the 'grand bargain' over the Single European Act. Johansson (1997) and Bowler and Farrell (1999) find that while the party groups lack a set of 'commonly accepted norms' to guide MEPs' behavior, coalition formation within and between groups is the product of extended negotiations and a culture of compromise. There is much scope for further analyses of these crucial but poorly understood aspects of legislative politics in the EP.

INTRA-COUNCIL POLITICS

Unfortunately the comparative study of the Council, in contrast to the European Parliament, has proven more problematic for legislative scholars, given its dissimilarity to traditional upper houses. Conventionally the Council is seen as the defender of national interests (Thomson et al. 2004) though there is evidence that internal operations do reveal some supranational elements (Beyers and Dierickx 1998; Lewis 1998). Nevertheless, the fact that parties are not the dominant actors in the Council makes analysis very difficult for legislative scholars, and typically analysis is done with the country as the primary unit. Work on internal workings of the Council is also hampered by the lack of transparency of its workings. Voting records are not as easily accessible as in the EP and the incidence of voting is also much less frequent.

Political decision-making within the Council has been subjected most notably to voting power studies. These studies have generated a methodologically sophisticated debate on the national distribution of power in the Council of Ministers. Power indices have been applied in a variety of settings but undoubtedly the EU studies have given rise to the largest body of literature on the topic (for an overview see Felsenthal and Machover 2001). Much of this debate has hinged on the existence of different, rival power indices, notably the Shapley and Shubik (1954) and the Banzhaf (1965) indices, and their respective merits and demerits (see Brams and Affuso 1985; Lane and Maeland 1995; Bindseil and Hantke 1997; Berg 1999; Brauninger and Konig 2001; Laruelle and Valenciano 2001; Nurmi et al. 2001; Pajala and Widgren 2004).

The first studies on voting power in the Council of Ministers appeared in the aftermath of the first round of enlargement (Johnston 1977) but there was a veritable boom in the power indices literature in the 1980s and 1990s, with frequent EU enlargements and treaty revisions allowing for new voting distributions to be evaluated. In particular, the computation of the power indices of different coalitions and alignments of states under different assumptions has generated an extensive exchange (c.f. Hosli 1995, 1996; Johnston 1995; Turnovec 1996; Berg and Lane 1997; Moberg 2002). This debate over power indices has found evidence for the proposition that under qualified majority voting the smaller states are over-represented (Felsenthal and Machover 1997) but the larger member states are still more likely to belong to a winning coalition (Hosli 1995; Widgren 1995), that under the recent voting power changes instituted by the Nice Treaty the medium sized members states fare poorly, and that the passage of legislation has been slowed down (Aleskerov et al. 2002; Moberg 2002).

However, the lack of transparency in decision-making and negotiations in the Council has left the predictions from the vast power indices literature to go largely untested until recently (Pajala and Widgren 2004). Recent work on budget transfers by Baldwin et al. (2000, 2001) suggests that power indices have good explanatory power. Their findings suggest that an index such as the Shapley-Shubik explains EU budget allocations more satisfactorily than do measures of income or proportion of agriculture in a country's GDP. Another pioneering empirical test of the power indices model is offered by Kauppi and Widgren (2004), who evaluate whether the

power measures explain members' shares of EU budget allocation. They conclude that 'at least 60% of the budget expenditures can be attributed to selfish power politics and the remaining 40% to the declared benevolent EU budget policies' (Kauppi and Widgren 2004: 221). Nonetheless, empirical tests of the predictions of these voting power models are still surprisingly few in number, given the immense amount of scholarly effort and energy devoted to the topic.

In recent years, there has been considerable disagreement about the usefulness of the whole power indices enterprise and substantial difference over how much insight it truly provides into intra-Council legislative decision-making. Criticism of the power indices debate have come most notably from Tsebelis and Garrett (1996), Garrett and Tsebelis (1996, 1999a, b, 2001), and Steunenberg et al. (1999), while a less provocative and more placatory assessment has been offered by Napel and Widgrén (2001, 2002, 2004). Garrett and Tsebelis (1999a, b) argue that the power index approach crucially fails to take account of preferences and proposal rules and additionally makes the unjustified assumption that all coalitions are equally probable. They further argue that applying measures of *a priori* voting power to the EU decision-making process in the Council of Ministers is wholly inappropriate as it fails to take account of the complex institutional framework and various important procedural elements. They suggest that this approach tells us little about a national actors' ability to further their preferences.

Another staunch critic of power indices is Albert (2003: 351), who argues that they should 'not even be considered as part of political science', claiming that they are unfalsifiable and a branch of probability theory at best. Responses to these criticisms include recent work by Rusinowska and de Swart (2002, 2003), who have developed a relatively unknown measure, the Hoede-Bakker index (Hoede and Bakker 1982), that is similar to the Banzhaf and Shapley-Shubik indices but which purportedly takes account of actors' preferences. Felsenthal and Machover (2001) suggest that it is important to investigate the distribution of power within the Council and there is nothing in power index analysis that prevents the use of composite decision rules. But the debate is far from resolved.

An alternative approach to intra-Council decision-making has been to examine roll calls in the Council itself. Mattila and Lane's (2001) analysis of these votes reveals a North–South division, though they find that unanimity in voting is the norm and suggest that log rolling is a possible explanation for this. Further analysis by Mattila (2004) suggests that there are two dimensions prevalent in Council roll calls, rather similar to those outlined in EP studies above: the traditional left–right dimension and the independence vs integration dimension. Pro-integration governments are least likely to raise their voice against the Council majority and left-wing governments are also more likely to fall in line.

What remains problematic for the power indices literature (and for roll call analyses) is the fact that many decisions in the Council are made without recourse to an actual vote. It has been established that a culture of compromise and consensus prevails in the Council (Westlake 1995; Hayes-Renshaw and Wallace 1997; Lewis 1998, 2000; Moberg 2002), though it is not clear whether or not the existence of the potential for a vote influences the consensual bargaining process. Perhaps the power indices debate has run its course, and it is time to extend our knowledge of intra-Council decision-making through the use of alternative approaches (for an alternative approach see Thomson et al. 2006).

LEGISLATIVE BARGAINING AMONG THE COUNCIL, COMMISSION, AND THE EP

To fully understand how legislation is made in the EU necessitates an examination of the strategic interaction among the three main institutional actors – the Council, Commission, and Parliament. Studying each institution in isolation provides valuable insights, but the danger is that one ignores the influence of the full structure of decision-making on internal choices.

Of course studying the legislative process as a whole can be overwhelming in its complexity: this is the case in any bicameral system, but particularly so in the EU.

The precise role and influence of the main institutions under various legislative procedures has been the subject of a great deal of theoretical debate in the past 10 years. The use of simplified formal, in particular spatial models, of the legislative process has been instructive in mapping this complex world of inter-institutional relations. Bargaining models have been the choice of several scholars (Bueno de Mesquita 1994; Stokman and Van Oosten 1994), non-cooperative voting games have been favored by others (Steunenberg 1994; Tsebelis 1994; Crombez 1996), while a co-operative voting model was adopted by Hosli et al. (2002). One of the recurrent questions that characterize this literature is the debate over the power of the EP under the various legislative procedures. While the cooperation procedure has now largely been replaced by the co-decision procedure, the power of the EP under cooperation generated a considerable volume of literature, centering on the importance of parliamentary agenda-setting powers vis-á-vis veto powers. Tsebelis (1994) influentially argued that the EP was 'a conditional agenda setter' due to the parliament's ability to present a 'take it or leave it' stance. However, Moser (1996), Steunenberg (1994), and Crombez (1996) contested Tsebelis' claim, positing that cooperation gave the EP little muscle in the absence of support from the Commission.

The first version of the co-decision procedure established by Maastricht was the subject of analysis by Steunenberg (1994, 1997), Tsebelis (1995), Schneider (1995), Crombez (1997), and Scully (1997a, b, c), while the Treaty of Amsterdam version ('co-decision II') has been subjected to analyses by Steunenberg (1997), Rittberger (2000), Tsebelis and Garrett (2000), Crombez (2001), and Laruelle (2002). Tsebelis (1997), Garrett (1995), and Tsebelis and Garrett (2000) argued, contrary to conventional wisdom, that the EP effectively lost power with the transition from cooperation to co-decision. They claim that the Parliament's power to set the agenda has been removed and replaced by the veto. Crombez (2000b) disagrees, claiming that the changes in the decision-making process are moving the EU towards a 'genuinely bicameral system'. Corbett (2000) concurs and his analysis suggests that the Parliament's influence on legislation is far greater under co-decision than cooperation. Scully's (1997a) analysis similarly finds in favor of co-decision. These differences in predictions largely reflect different modeling assumptions. For instance, Crombez (2000a) assumes that Parliament takes the lead in the co-decision procedure and specifically in the conciliation committee, whereas Steunenberg and Dimitrova (1999) have the Council Presidency as the first mover, drafting bills. In their overview of the various procedural models, Selck and Steunenberg (2004) find that the model in which the EP is first mover in the models performs best despite the formal order of the legislative process laid down in the treaties. They find overall in favor of the theoretical claims that Parliament is a genuine co-legislator with the Council.

A slew of empirical studies were generated by the formal debate to test the power of the EP to influence policy-making in the EU. These can be divided into two broad camps, case studies that demonstrate how the EP manages to win through despite opposition from the Council (Earnshaw and Judge 1993; Golub 1996; Jacobs 1997; Rittberger 2000) and quantitative studies (Golub 1999; Tsebelis and Kalandrakis 1999; Schulz and Konig 2000; Tsebelis et al. 2001; Kreppel 2002b). König and Poter (2001) offer one of the few direct tests of hypotheses derived from formal models but their results are inconclusive. More generally, Schulz and König (2000) find that the increased involvement of the EP in the decision-making process has slowed it down but this may be balanced by extension of QMV in the Council (Golub 1999; Jordan et al. 1999).

While spatial models are necessarily stylized versions of the decision-making process, one of the major problems with the spatial approach is that we know too little about

preferences of actors. Incompatible predictions about legislative outcomes arise in part from the different assumptions about preference structure of the Council, Commission, and European Parliament (Dowding 2000; König and Pöter 2001; Selck 2004). The key concepts used in spatial models such as the location of the status quo and the various actors' preferences are empirically difficult to measure, which undermines their falsifiability (Steunenberg 2000; Bueno de Mesquita 2004). One can never be certain if and when a spatial model fails an empirical test whether to conclude that the theory is falsified or rather to reject the secondary assumption that the measures of policy preferences are satisfactory.

Future work should explicitly consider what we already know about preference formation inside these three bodies (Hörl et al. 2005). For instance, the procedural literature treats the Commission as unitary (Crombez 1996; Tsebelis and Garrett 2000), but the limited case study evidence we have undermines this (Cram 1994, 1997). Thomson et al. (2004) further argue that preference configurations adopted in models should also take account of substance of decisions being made. Interestingly, the underlying assumptions about the main dimensions of the policy competition in many of the spatial models (attitudes to integration) does not cohere necessarily with the evidence of the principal dimension of competition from studies of intra-Council and Parliament decision-making. On the basis of their research, Kreppel (2000) and Kreppel and Tsebelis (1999) suggest that the conflicts between the Council and EP are based on an ideological disagreement over the issue of regulation, with the Council advocating less and the EP more, rather than over integration.

One interesting feature of inter-institutional relations that has so far received little attention is the conciliation committee which meets when the EP and Council fail to agree a legislative text under the co-decision procedure. In an analysis of particular directives, Garman and Hilditch (1998) demonstrate the importance of exploratory meetings in the conciliation process. Rasmussen (2005) tests the assumptions of the principal-agent model on delegation in the conciliation process and finds 'irresponsible behavior by the EU conciliation committee is rare, contrary to the usual prediction of the principal-agent framework', but more work analysing results is to be done. Rasmussen and Shackleton (2005) similarly find that delegation has not proved to be a hazardous strategy for the EP contrasting the experience here with that of Congress and the Bundestag where previous work suggests that members of conference committees' exercise disproportionate influence on the policy process. The question of which legislative body dominates in the committee is largely unexplored to date, though Napel and Widgren (2006) find evidence to suggest that the Council prevails. Nevertheless, the institution of the conciliation committee remains largely unstudied, no doubt in large part due to its comparative youth, but it offers a fruitful avenue for further analysis in the future, both qualitatively and quantitatively. Observational studies of the EU legislative process are relatively rare but the conciliation committee suggests itself as a prime candidate for such an approach.

CONCLUSION

Our understanding of legislative politics in the EU is still relatively underdeveloped; the system is complicated and the environment is in a constant state of flux. We know increasingly more about the internal workings of the European Parliament but the internal workings of the Council and Commission are still surprisingly mysterious. In examining the literature on legislative politics in the Council one is struck by the dominance of power index studies, perhaps at the expense of other interesting research questions. Meanwhile, research on intra-institutional decision-making inside the Commission is most marked by its absence. Clearly legislative scholars are very excited by the possibilities of studying the European Parliament and the broader insights it provides into legislative behavior more generally. Its internal organization offers great scope to scholars interested in the origins and evolution of institutions, given the rapid change it has undergone from a mere consultative body to a fully legislative assembly. It is also an excellent environment in which to examine post-election career advancement. Understandably, legislative scholars have latched onto the similarities between the EP and Congress in order to test theories of legislative behavior developed in the latter assembly and this has been undoubtedly a boon to legislative scholars on both sides of the Atlantic. But we should not, in our enthusiasm for comparison, ignore the notable differences between both institutions. One of the primary criticisms that can be leveled at the field of legislative studies, writ large, is that it has been dominated by the study of the US Congress. More generally, an emerging body of scholars is arguing forcefully that the relationship between the European Parliament and Council is that of a classic two-chamber political system (akin in particular to the Congressional model) within which the Council of Ministers remains the dominant actor (Nentwich and Falkner 1997; Tsebelis and Money 1997; Hix 1999, 2005; Neunreither 1999; Muntean 2000). The most influential proponent of this viewpoint forcefully states that the EU has a 'classic two chamber legislature in which the Council represents the states and the European Parliament represents the citizens' (Hix 2005: 72). However, perhaps it is a little to early to reach such a sanguine conclusion, since the lack of a constitutionally defined separation of powers, the dual role of the Council as both executive and legislature, and the absence of a tidy division of responsibilities between the main institutions (Lenaerts 1991; Kohler-Koch and Eising 1999) mean that the legislative politics in the EU is exceptionally complex. In our desire for comparison we ignore at our peril some crucial and interesting differences that are critical in structuring actors' preferences and the range of possible outcomes over which they bargain.

NOTE

1. http://www.lse.ac.uk/collections/EPRG/, accessed 18 March 2006.

REFERENCES

Albert, M. (2003) 'The voting power approach: measurement without theory', *European Union Politics*, 4(3): 351–66.

Aleskerov, F., Avci, G., Iakouba, V. and Turem, Z.U. (2002) 'European Union enlargement: power distribution implications of the new institutional arrangements', *European Journal of Political Research*, 41(3): 379–94.

Attina, F. (1990) 'The voting behaviour of the European Parliament members and the problems of the Europarties', *European Journal of Political Research*, 18(4): 557–79.

Bagehot, W. (1867) *The English constitution*. London: H. S. King and Co.

Baldwin, R., Berglof, E., Giavazzi, F. and Widgren, M. (2000) 'The EU reforms for tomorrow's Europe', CEPR Discussion Paper 2623.

Baldwin, R., Berglof, E., Giavazzi, F. and Widgren, M. (2001) 'Nice try: should the treaty of Nice be ratified?' *Monitoring European Integration* 11. London: Centre for Economic Policy Research.

Banzhaf, J.F. (1965) 'Weighted voting doesn't work: a mathematical analysis', *Rutgers Law Review*, 19: 317–43.

Bardi, L. (1994) 'Transnational party federations, European parliamentary party groups, and the guilding of Europarties', in R. Katz and P. Mair (eds), *How Parties Organize: Change and Adaptation in Party Organizations in Western Democracies*. Sage: London. Pp. 357–72.

Benedetto, G. (2005) 'Rapporteurs as legislative entrepreneurs: the dynamics of the co-decision procedure in Europe's Parliament', *Journal of European Public Policy*, 12(1): 67–88.

Berg, S. (1999) 'On voting power indices and a class of probability distributions: with applications to EU data', *Group Decision and Negotiation*, 8(1): 17–31.

Berg, S. and Lane, J.E. (1997) 'Measurements of Voting Power, Individual and Systemic Properties', NEMEU Working Paper No. 97-1, University of Twente, Enschede.

Beyers, J. and Dierickx, G. (1998) 'The working groups of the Council of the European Union: supranational or intergovernmental negotiations?' *Journal of Common Market Studies*, 36(3): 289–317.

Binder, S. (1997) *Minority Rights, Majority Rule: Partisanship and the Development of Congress*. Cambridge: Cambridge University Press.

Bindseil, U. and Hantke, C. (1997) 'The power distribution in decision-making among EU member states', *European Journal of Political Economy*, 13: 171–85.

Bowler, S. and Farrell, D.M. (1993) 'Legislator shirking and voter monitoring – impacts of European-Parliament electoral systems upon legislator voter relationships', *Journal of Common Market Studies*, 31(1): 45–69.

Bowler, S. and Farrell, D.M. (1995) 'The organizing of the European Parliament – committees, specialization and coordination', *British Journal of Political Science*, 25: 219–43.

Bowler, S. and Farrell, D.M. (1999) 'Parties and party discipline within the European Parliament: a norms based approach', in S. Bowler, D.M. Farrell and R.S. Katz (eds), *Party Discipline and Parliamentary Government*. Columbus: Ohio State University Press. pp. 208–22.

Bowler, S., Farrell, D.M. and Katz, R.S. (1999) 'Party cohesion, party discipline and parliaments', in S. Bowler, D.M. Farrell and R.S. Katz (eds), *Party Discipline and Parliamentary Government*. Columbus: Ohio State University Press. pp. 3–22.

Bowler, S., Farrell, D.M. and McAllister, I. (1996) 'Constituency campaigning in parliamentary systems with preferential voting: is there a paradox?' *Electoral Studies*, 15(4): 461–76.

Brams, S. and Affuso, P. (1985) 'New paradoxes of voting power in the EC Council of Ministers', *Electoral Studies*, 4(1): 135–9.

Brauninger, T. and Konig, T. (2001) *Indices of Power*. Version 2.0. Konstanz: University of Konstanz.

Brzinski, J.B. (1995) 'Political group cohesion in the European Parliament 1989–1994', in C. Rhodes and S. Mazay (eds), *The State of the European Union*, Vol 3. London: Longman. pp. 135–58.

Bueno de Mesquita, B. (1994) 'Political forecasting and expected utility model', in B. Bueno de Mesquita and F. Stokman (eds), *European Community Decision-Making*. New Haven, CT: Yale University Press. pp. 71–104.

Bueno de Mesquita B. (2004) 'Decision-making models, rigor and new puzzles', *European Union Politics*, 5(1): 125–38.

Carey, J. (2002) 'Parties and coalitions in Chile in the 1990s', in S. Morgenstern and B. Nacif (eds), *Legislative politics in Latin America*. Cambridge: Cambridge University Press. pp. 222–53.

Carrubba, C., Gabel, M. Murrah, L., Clough, R., Montgomery, E. and Schambach, R. (2006) 'Off the record: unrecorded legislative votes, selection bias and roll call vote analysis', *British Journal of Political Science*, 36(4): 691–704.

Chaisty, P. (2005) 'Party cohesion and policy-making in Russia', *Party Politics*, 11(3): 299–318.

Corbett, R. (2000) 'Academic modelling of the co-decision procedure: a practitioner's puzzled reaction', *European Union Politics*, 1(3): 73–91.

Corbett, R., Jacobs. F. and Shackleton, M. (2003) *The European Parliament*, 5th ed. London: John Harper Publishing.

Cram, L. (1994) 'The European Commission as a multi-organization: social policy and IT policy in the EU', *Journal of European Public Policy*, 1(2): 195–217.

Cram, L. (1997) *Policy Making in the EU*. London: Routledge.

Crombez, C. (1996) 'Legislative procedures in the European Community', *British Journal of Political Science*, 26: 199–228.

Crombez, C. (1997) 'The co-decision procedure in the European Union', *Legislative Studies Quarterly*, 22(1): 97–119.

Crombez, C. (2000a) 'Institutional reform and co-decision in the European Union', *Constitutional Political Economy*, 11: 41–57.

Crombez, C. (2000b) 'Understanding the EU legislative process – co-decision towards a bicameral union', *European Union Politics*, 1(3): 363–8.

Crombez, C. (2001) 'The Treaty of Amsterdam and the co-decision procedure', in G. Schneider and M. Aspinwall (eds), *The Rules of Integration: Institutional Approaches to the Study of Europe*. Manchester: Manchester University Press. pp. 101–22.

Dehousse, R. (1989) '1992 and beyond: the institutional dimension of the internal market programme', *Legal Issues of European Integration*, 1: 109–36.

Döring, H. (ed.) (1995) *Parliaments and Majority Rule in Western Europe*. New York: St. Martin's.

Döring, H. and Hallerberg, M. (2004) *Patterns of parliamentary behaviour: passage of legislation across Western Europe*. Aldershot: Ashgate.

Dowding, K. (2000) 'Institutional research on the European Union: a critical review', *European Union Politics*, 1(1): 125–44.

Earnshaw, D. and Judge, D. (1993) 'The European Parliament and the sweeteners directive: from footnote to inter-institutional conflict', *Journal of Common Market Studies*, 31: 103–16.

Faas, T. (2003) 'To defect or not to defect? National, institutional and party group pressures on MEPs and their consequences for party group cohesion in the European Parliament', *European Journal of Political Research*, 42(6): 841–66.

Felsenthal, D.S. and Machover, M. (1997) 'The weighted voting rule in the EU's Council of Ministers, 1958–95: intentions and outcomes', *Electoral Studies*, 16(1): 33–47.

Felsenthal, D.S. and Machover, M. (2001) 'Myths and meanings of voting power – comments on a symposium', *Journal of Theoretical Politics*, 13(1): 81–97.

Fiorina, M. (1974) *Representatives, roll calls, and constituencies*. Lexington, MA: Lexington Books.

Fitzmaurice, J. (1975) *The Party Groups in the European Parliament*. Lexington, MA: Lexington Books.

Fitzmaurice, J. (1988) 'An analysis of the European Community's co-operation procedure', *Journal of Common Market Studies*, 26(4): 389–400.

Franklin, M.N., van de Eijk, C. and Oppenhuis, E. (1996) 'The institutional context: turn-out', in C. van de Eijk and M.N. Franklin (eds), *Choosing Europe: the European electorate and national politics in the face of union*. Ann Arbor: University of Michigan Press. pp. 306–31.

Gallagher, M. and Marsh, M. (1988) *Candidate selection in comparative perspective: the secret garden of politics*. London: Sage.

Gamm, G. and Huber, J. (2002) 'Legislatures as political institutions: beyond the contemporary congress', in I. Katznelson, H.V. Milner and A.W. Finifter (eds), *Political science: the state of the discipline* (Centennial ed.). London: W.W. Norton. pp. 313–41.

Gamm, G. and Shepsle, K. (1989) 'Emergence of legislative institutions – standing committees in the House and Senate, 1810–1825', *Legislative Studies Quarterly*, 14(1): 39–66.

Garman, J. and Hilditch, L. (1998) 'Behind the scenes: an examination of the importance of the informal processes at work in conciliation', *Journal of European Public Policy*, 5(2): 271–84.

Garrett, G. (1995) 'From the Luxembourg compromise to co-decision – decision-making in the European-Union', *Electoral Studies*, 14(3): 289–308.

Garrett, G. and Tsebelis, G. (1996) 'An institutional critique of intergovernmentalism', *International Organization*, 50(2): 269–99.

Garrett, G. and Tsebelis, G. (1999a) 'Why resist the temptation to apply power indices to the European Union?' *Journal of Theoretical Politics*, 11(3): 291–308.

Garrett, G. and Tsebelis, G. (1999b) 'More reasons to resist the temptation of power indices in the European Union', *Journal of Theoretical Politics*, 11(3): 331–8.

Garrett, G. and Tsebelis, G. (2001) 'Even more reasons to resist the temptation of power indices in the EU', *Journal of Theoretical Politics*, 13(1): 99–105.

Gilligan, T.W. and Krehbiel, K. (1990) 'Organization of informative committees by a rational legislature', *American Journal of Political Science*, 34(2): 531–64.

Golub, J. (1996) 'State power and institutional influence in European integration: lessons from the packaging waste directive', *Journal of Common Market Studies*, 34(3): 313–39.

Golub, J. (1999) 'In the shadow of the vote? Decision making in the European Community', *International Organization*, 53(4): 733–64.

Hausemer, P. (2005) 'Representation and committee reports in the European parliament', School of Public Policy Working paper Series # 15, University College London. Available online at: http://www.ucl.ac.uk/spp/download/publications/spp-wp-15.pdf, accessed 7 September 2006.

Hayes-Renshaw, F. and Wallace, H. (1997) *The Council of Ministers*. London: Macmillan.

Hix, S. (1999) 'Dimensions and alignments in European Union politics: cognitive constraints and partisan responses', *European Journal of Political Research*, 35(1): 69–106.

Hix, S. (2002) 'Parliamentary behavior with two principals: preferences, parties, and voting in the European Parliament', *American Journal of Political Science*, 46(3): 688–98.

Hix, S. (2005) *The political system of the European Union*, 2nd ed. Basingstoke: Palgrave Macmillan.

Hix, S. and Lord, C. (1997) *Political parties in the European Union*. New York: St. Martin's press.

Hix, S., Kreppel, A. and Noury, A. (2003) 'The party system in the European Parliament: collusive or competitive?' *Journal of Common Market Studies*, 41(2): 309–31.

Hix, S., Noury, A. and Roland, G. (2005) 'Power to the parties: cohesion and competition in the European Parliament, 1979–2001', *British Journal of Political Science*, 35: 209–34.

Hix, S., Noury, A. and Roland, G. (2007) *Democratic Politics in the European Parliament*. Cambridge: Cambridge University Press.

Hoede, C. and Bakker, R.R. (1982) 'A theory of decisional power', *Journal of Mathematical Sociology*, 8(2): 309–22.

Hörl, B., Warntjen, A. and Wonka, A. (2005) 'Built on quicksand? A decade of procedural spatial models on EU legislative decision-making', *Journal of European Public Policy*, 12(3): 592–606.

Hosli, M.O. (1995) 'The balance between small and large – effects of a double-majority system on voting power in the European Union', *International Studies Quarterly*, 39(3): 351–70.

Hosli, M.O. (1996) 'Coalitions and power: effects of qualified majority voting in the Council of the European Union', *Journal of Common Market Studies*, 34(2): 255–73.

Hösli, M., van Deemen, A.M.A. and Widgrén, M. (2002) *Institutional Challenges in the European Union*. London: Routledge.

Hoyland, B. (2005) 'Government opposition in bicameral negotiations: decision making in European Union's co-decision procedure', EPRG Paper, No. 12. Available online at: http://www.lse.ac.uk/collections/EPRG/working-papers.htm, accessed 7 September 2006.

Hoyland, B. (2006) 'Allocation of co-decision reports in the 5th European Parliament', *European Union Politics*, 7(1): 30–50.

Hug, S. (2006) 'Selection effects in roll call votes', CIG Working Paper No. 19. Available online at: http://igov.berkeley.edu/workingpapers/papers0506.html#jun, accessed 8 April 2006.

Jacobs, F. (1997) 'Legislative co-decisions: a real step forward?' Paper presented at the Fifth Biennial Conference of the European Community Studies Association, Seattle.

Johansson, K.M. (1997) 'Veränderte Bedeutung der Politischen Fraktionen', in E. Kuper and U. Jun (eds), *Nationales und Integrative Politik in Transnationalen Parlamentarischen Versammlungen*. Opladen: Leske and Budrich. pp. 265–314.

Johansson, K.M. (2002) 'Party elites in multilevel Europe – the Christian Democrats and the Single European Act', *Party Politics*, 8(4): 423–39.

Johansson, K.M. and Raunio, T. (2005) 'Regulating Europarties – cross-party coalitions capitalizing on incomplete contracts', *Party Politics*, 11(5): 515–34.

Johnston, R.J. (1977) 'National sovereignty and national power in European institutions', *Environment and Planning*, 9: 569–77.

Johnston, R.J. (1995) 'The conflict over qualified majority voting in the European Union Council of Ministers – an analysis of the UK negotiating stance using power indexes', *British Journal of Political Science*, 25: 245–54.

Jordan, A., Brouwer, R. and Noble, E. (1999) 'Innovative and responsive? A longitudinal analysis of the speed of EU environmental policy making, 1967–97', *Journal of European Public Policy*, 6(3): 376–98.

Judge, D. and Earnshaw, D. (2003) *The European Parliament*. Basingstoke: Palgrave Macmillan.

Kaeding, M. (2004) 'Rapporteurship allocation in the European Parliament – information or distribution?' *European Union Politics*, 5(3): 353–71.

Kaeding, M. (2005) 'The world of committee reports: rapporteurship assignment in the European Parliament', *Journal of Legislative Studies*, 11(1): 82–104.

Kauppi, H. and Widgren, M. (2004) 'What determines EU decision making? Needs, power or both?' *Economic Policy*, 19(39): 221–66.

Kim, D.H. and Loewenberg, G. (2005) 'The role of parliamentary committees in coalition governments – keeping tabs on coalition partners in the German Bundestag', *Comparative Political Studies*, 38(9): 1104–29.

Koford, K. (1989) 'Different preferences, different politics – a demand-and-structure explanation', *Western Political Quarterly*, 42(1): 9–31.

Kohler-Koch, B. and Eising, R. (1999) *The transformation of governance in the European Union.* London: Routledge.

König, T. and Pöter, M. (2001) 'Examining the EU legislative process: the relative importance of agenda and veto power', *European Union Politics*, 2(3): 329–51.

Krehbiel, K. (1990) 'Are congressional committees composed of preference outliers', *American Political Science Review*, 84(1): 149–63.

Krehbiel, K. (1991) *Information and legislative organization*. Ann Arbor, MI: University of Michigan Press.

Kreppel, A. (2000) 'Rules, ideology and coalition formation in the European Parliament: past, present and future', *European Union Politics*, 1(3): 340–62.

Kreppel, A. (2002a) *The European Parliament and Supranational Party System: a study in institutional development.* Cambridge; New York: Cambridge University Press.

Kreppel, A. (2002b) 'Moving beyond procedure – an empirical analysis of European Parliament legislative influence', *Comparative Political Studies*, 35(7): 784–813.

Kreppel, A. and Tsebelis, G. (1999) 'Coalition formation in the European Parliament, *Comparative Political Studies*, 32(8): 933–66.

Lane, J.E. and Maeland, R. (1995) 'Voting power under the EU constitution', *Journal of Theoretical Politics*, 7(2): 223–30.

Laruelle, A. (2002) 'The EU decision-making procedures: some insight from non cooperative game theory', in M.O. Hosli, A.M.A. van Deemen and M. Wiberg (eds), *Institutional Challenges in the European Union*. London: Routledge. pp. 89–112.

Laruelle, A. and Valenciano, F. (2001) 'Shapley-Shubik and Banzhaf indices revisited', *Mathematics of Operations Research*, 26(1): 89–104.

Laundy, P. (1989) *Parliaments in the modern world.* Aldershot: Dartmouth.

Lenaerts, K. (1991) 'Some reflections on the separation of powers in the European Community', *Common Market Law Review*, 28(1): 11–35.

Lewis, J. (1998) 'Is the 'hard bargaining' image of the council misleading? The Committee of Permanent Representatives and the local elections directive', *Journal of Common Market Studies*, 36(4): 479–504.

Lewis, J. (2000) 'The methods of community in EU decision-making and administrative rivalry in the Council's infrastructure', *Journal of European Public Policy*, 7(2): 261–89.

Lodge, J. (1983) *Institutions and Policies of the European Community*. London: Frances Pinter.

Lodge, J. (1989) 'The European Parliament from assembly to co-legislator, changing the institutional dynamics', in J. Lodge (ed.), *The European Community and the Challenge of the Future.* London: Pinter. pp. 58–79.

Mamadouh, V. and Raunio, T. (2001) 'Allocating reports in the European Parliament: how parties influence committee work', EPRG Paper, No 7. Available online at: http://www.lse.ac.uk/collections/EPRG/working-papers.htm.

Mamadouh, V. and Raunio, T. (2003) 'The committee system: powers, appointments and report allocation', *Journal of Common Market Studies*, 41(2): 333–51.

Marsh, M. (1998) 'Testing the second-order election model after four European elections', *British Journal of Political Science*, 28: 591–607.

Mattila, M. (2004) 'Contested decisions: empirical analysis of voting in the European Union Council of Ministers', *European Journal of Political Research*, 43(1): 29–50.

Mattila, M. and Lane, J.E. (2001) 'Why unanimity in the Council? A roll call analysis of council voting', *European Union Politics*, 2(1): 31–52.

Mayhew, D.R. (1974) *Congress: the electoral connection*. New Haven, CT: Yale University Press.

McElroy, G. (2002) 'Committees and party cohesion in the European Parliament', EPRG Paper, No 8. Available online at: http://www.lse.ac.uk/collections/EPRG/working-papers.htm, accessed 6 September 2006

McElroy, G. (2003) 'In pursuit of party discipline: committee and cohesion in the European Parliament', PhD Dissertation, University of Rochester.

McElroy, G. (2006) 'Committee representation in the European Parliament', *European Union Politics*, 7(1): 5–29.

McElroy, G. and Benoit, K. (2006) 'Party groups and policy positions in the European Parliament', *Party Politics*, 12(6): 691–714.

Mezey, M.L. (1993) 'Legislatures: individual purpose and institutional performance', in A. Finiter (ed.), *The State of the Discipline II*. Washington, DC: APSA. pp. 335–64.

Moberg, A. (2002) 'The Nice Treaty and voting rules in the council', *Journal of Common Market Studies*, 40(2): 259–82.

Moser, P. (1996) 'The European Parliament as a conditional agenda setter: what are the conditions? A critique of Tsebelis (1994)', *American Political Science Review*, 90(4): 834–8.

Müller, W.C. (2000) 'Political parties in Parliamentary democracies: making delegation and accountability work', *European Journal of Political Research*, 37(3): 309–33.

Muntean, A.M. (2000) 'The European Parliament's political legitimacy and the Commissions misleading management: towards a parliamentarian European Union?' *European Integration online Papers (EIoP)*, http://eiop.or.at/eiop/texte/2000-005.htm, accessed 6 September 2006.

Napel, S. and Widgren, M. (2001) 'Inferior players in simple games', *International Journal of Game Theory*, 30(2): 209–20.

Napel, S. and Widgren, M. (2002) 'The power of a spatially inferior player', *Homo Oeconomicus*, 19: 327–43.

Napel, S. and Widgren, M. (2004) 'Power measurement as sensitivity analysis – a unified approach', *Journal of Theoretical Politics*, 16(4): 517–38.

Napel, S. and Widgren, M. (2006) 'The inter-institutional distribution of power in EU co-decision making', CESinfo Working Paper,#1347. Available online at: http://opus.zbw-kiel.de/volltexte/2005/2609/pdf/cesifo1_wp1347.pdf, accessed 18 March 2006.

Nentwich, M. and Falkner, G. (1997) 'The Treaty of Amsterdam: towards a new institutional balance', *European Integration online Papers* (EIoP), 1(15). Available online at: http://eiop.or.at/eiop/texte/1997-015a.htm.

Neunreither, K. (1999) 'The European Parliament', in L. Cram, D. Dinan and N. Nugent (eds), *Developments in the European Union*. London: Macmillan. pp. 62–83

Niedermayer, O. (1983) *Europäische Parteien? Zur grenzüberschreitenden Interaktion politischer Parteien im Rahmen der Europäischen Gemeinschaft*. Frankfurt: Campus Verlag.

Noury, A. (2002) 'Ideology, nationality and Euro-parliamentarians', *European Union Politics*, 3(1): 33–58.

Noury, A. and Roland, G. (2002) 'More power to the European Parliament', *Economic Policy*, 17(35): 279–319.

Nugent, N. (2003) *The government and politics of the European Union*, 5th ed. Basingstoke: Macmillan.

Nurmi, H., Meskanen, T. and Pajala, A. (2001) 'Calculus of consent in the EU Council of Ministers', in M. Holler and G. Owen (eds), *Power Indices and Coalition Formation*. Boston, Dordrecht, London: Kluwer. pp. 291–313.

Oudenhove, G.V. (1965) *The political parties in the European Parliament: the first ten years, September 1952–September 1962*. Leiden: A. W. Sijthoff.

Pajala, A. and Widgren, M. (2004) 'A priori versus empirical voting power in the EU Council of Ministers', *European Union Politics*, 5(1): 73–97.

Pridham, G. and Pridham, P. (1979) *Towards transnational parties in the European Community*. London: Policy Studies Institute.

Rasmussen, A. (2005) 'EU conciliation delegates: responsible or runaway agents?' *West European Politics*, 28(5): 1015–34.

Rasmussen A. and Shackleton, M. (2005) 'The scope for action of European Parliament negotiators in the legislative process: lessons of the past and for the future', Paper prepared for the Ninth Biennial International Conference of the European Union Studies Association, Austin, Texas, March.

Raunio, T. (1997) *The European Perspective: Transnational Party Groups in the 1989–1994 European Parliament*. London: Ashgate.

Raunio, T. (2000) 'Losing independence or finally gaining recognition? Contacts between MEPs and national parties', *Party Politics*, 6(2): 211–23.

Reif, K. and Schmitt, H. (1980) 'Nine second order national elections: a conceptual framework for the analysis of European election results', *European Journal of Political Science*, 8(1): 3–45.

Ringe, N. (2005) 'Policy preference formation in legislative politics. Structures, actors and focal points', *American Journal of Political Science*, 49(4): 731–45.

Rittberger, B. (2000) 'Impatient legislators and new issue-dimensions: a critique of the Garrett-Tsebelis 'standard version' of legislative politics', *Journal of European Public Policy*, 7(4): 554–75.

Romer, H. (1993) *Guidelines for the Application of the Rule Changes*. Secretariat, Group of the European People's Party. Brussels: EPP.

Rusinowska, A. and de Swart, H. (2002) 'On some properties of the Hoede-Bakker index', Mimeo, Tilburg University.

Rusinowska, A. and de Swart, H. (2003) 'Generalizing and modifying the Hoede-Bakker index', Mimeo, Tilburg University.

Scarrow, S.E. (1997) 'Political career paths and the European Parliament', *Legislative Studies Quarterly*, 22(2): 253–63.

Schmitt, H. (2005) 'The European Parliament elections of June 2004: still second-order?' *West European Politics*, 28(3): 650–79.

Schneider, G. (1995) 'The limits of self reform: institution building in the European Union', *European Journal of International Relations*, 1: 59–86.

Schulz, H. and Konig, T. (2000) 'Institutional reform and decision-making efficiency in the European Union', *American Journal of Political Science*, 44(4): 653–66.

Scully, R.M. (1997a) 'The EP and the co-decision procedure: a reassessment', *Journal of Legislative Studies*, 3(3): 58–73.

Scully, R.M. (1997b) 'The EP and co-decision: a rejoinder to Tsebelis and Garrett', *Journal of Legislative Studies*, 3(3): 93–101.

Scully, R.M. (1997c) 'Positively my last words on co-decision', *Journal of Legislative Studies*, 3(4): 144–6.

Scully, R. (2000) 'Democracy in the European Union: integration through deliberation?' *Journal of Common Market Studies*, 38(3): 542.

Scully, R. (2005) *Becoming Europeans? Attitudes, Behaviour, and Socialization in the European Parliament*. Oxford: Oxford University Press.

Scully, R and Farrell, D. (2003) 'MEPs as representatives: individual and institutional roles', *Journal of Common Market Studies*, 41(2): 269–88.

Selck, T.J. (2004) 'On the dimensionality of European Union legislative decision-making', *Journal of Theoretical Politics*, 16(2): 203–22.

Selck, T.J. and Steunenberg, B. (2004) 'Between power and luck – the European Parliament in the EU legislative process', *European Union Politics*, 5(1): 25–46.

Shapley, L. and Shubik, M. (1954) 'A method of evaluating the distribution of power in a committee system', *American Political Science Review*, 48: 787–92.

Shepsle, K.A. and Weingast, B.R. (1987) 'The institutional foundations of committee power', *American Political Science Review*, 81(1): 85–104.

Steunenberg, B. (1994) 'Decision-making under different institutional arrangements – legislation by the European-Community', *Journal of Institutional and Theoretical Economics-Zeitschrift Fur Die Gesamte Staatswissenschaft*, 150(4): 642–69.

Steunenberg, B. (1997) 'Codecision and its reform: a comparative analysis of decision-making rules in the European Union', in B. Steunenberg and F. van Vught (eds), *Political Institutions and Public Policy*. Amsterdam: Kluwer. pp. 205–29.

Steunenberg, B. (2000) 'Seeing what you want to see: the limits of current modeling on the European Union', *European Union Politics*, 1(3): 368–73.

Steunenberg, B. and Dimitrova, A. (1999) 'Interests, legitimacy and constitutional choice: the extension of the codecision procedure in Amsterdam', NEMEU Working Paper 99-2. Enschede: University of Twente.

Steunenberg, B., Schmidtchen, D. and Koboldt, C. (1999) 'Strategic power in the European Union – evaluating the distribution of power in policy games', *Journal of Theoretical Politics*, 11(3): 339–66.

Stokman, F. and van Oosten, R. (1994) 'The exchange of voting positions: an object-oriented model of policy networks', in B. Bueno de Mesquita and F. Stokman (eds), *European Community Decision-Making: Models, Applications and Comparisons*. New Haven, CT: Yale University Press. pp. 105–27.

Thomassen, J. and Schmitt, H. (1997) 'Policy representation', *European Journal of Political Research*, 32(2):165–84.

Thomassen, J., Noury, A. and Voeten E. (2004) 'Political competition in the European Parliament: evidence from roll call and survey analyses', in G. Marks and M. Steenbergen (eds), *European Integration and Political Conflict*. Cambridge: Cambridge University Press. pp. 141–64.

Thomson, R., Boerefijn, J. and Stokman, F. (2004) 'Actor alignments in European Union decision making', *European Journal of Political Research*, 43(2): 237–61.

Thomson, R., Stokman, F., Achen, C.H. and König, T. (2006) *The European Union Decides*. Cambridge: Cambridge University Press.

Tsebelis, G. (1994) 'The power of the European Parliament as a conditional agenda setter', *American Political Science Review*, 88(1): 128–42.

Tsebelis, G. (1995) 'Conditional agenda-setting and decision-making inside the European Parliament', *Journal of Legislative Studies*, 1(1): 65–93.

Tsebelis, G. (1997) 'Maastricht and the democratic deficit', *Aussenwirtschaft*, 52: 29–56.

Tsebelis, G. and Garrett, G. (1996) 'Agenda setting power, power indices, and decision making in the European Union', *International Review of Law and Economics*, 16(3): 345–61.

Tsebelis, G. and Garrett, G. (2000) 'Legislative politics in the European Union', *European Union Politics*, 1(1): 9–36.

Tsebelis, G. and Kalandrakis, A. (1999) 'The European Parliament and environmental legislation: the case of chemicals', *European Journal of Political Research*, 36(1): 119–54.

Tsebelis, G. and Money, J. (1997) *Bicameralism*. Cambridge: Cambridge University Press.

Tsebelis, G., Jensen, C.B., Kalandrakis, A. and Kreppel, A. (2001) 'Legislative procedures in the European Union: an empirical analysis', *British Journal of Political Science*, 31(4): 573–99.

Turnovec, F. (1996) 'Weights and votes in European Union: extension and institutional reform', *Prague Economic Papers*, 2: 161–74.

Voeten, E. (2005) 'Legislator preferences, ideal points and spatial models in the European Parliament', Centre for Institutions and Governance Working Paper Series. University of Berkeley. Available online at: http://igov.berkeley.edu/workingpapers/series1/No6_Voeten.pdf, accessed 20 March 2006.

Wallace, H., Wallace, W. and Pollack, M.A. (2005) *Policy-making in the European Union*, 5th ed. Oxford: Oxford University Press.

Wessels, W. (1991) 'The EC Council: the Community's decision-making centre', in R. Keohane and S. Hoffmann (eds), *The New European Community*. Boulder, CO: Westview. pp. 133–54.

Westlake, M. (1995) *The Council of the European Union*. London: Cartermill.

Whitaker, R. (2005) 'National parties in the European Parliament – an influence in the committee system?' *European Union Politics*, 6(1): 5–28.

Widgren, M. (1995) 'Probabilistic voting power in the EU Council – the cases of trade-policy and social regulation', *Scandinavian Journal of Economics*, 97(2): 345–56.

Williams, M. (1995) 'The European Parliament: political groups, minority rights and the 'rationalisations of parliamentary organisation. A research note', in H. Döring (ed.), *Parliaments and Majority Rule in Western Europe*. New York: St. Martin's. pp. 391–404.

9

Executive Politics

JONAS TALLBERG

INTRODUCTION

Had this handbook been published a decade ago, it is highly unlikely that it would have featured a chapter on executive politics. The issues addressed by students of executive politics today were still largely framed in terms of regional integration, and the theoretical approaches that nowadays dominate research on executive politics were still waiting to be imported from the general study of political science. This comparison of early and recent scholarship well summarizes the general argument of this chapter: the growing tendency of EU scholars over the last decade to conceptualize the EU as a polity or political system has produced a relatively distinct field of executive politics, concerned with issues of delegation, agency, and accountability, dominated by rational choice approaches to executive politics, and possible to describe as one of the liveliest areas of research on EU politics.

The term executive politics is derived from the classic constitutional framework, where the legislature decides, the executive enacts, and the judiciary adjudicates. While these powers in some political systems are concentrated in the hands of distinct political actors, the EU boasts a more complex division of power, not least as regards the organization of the executive. In the EU, executive power is vested both in the member states, responsible for implementing EU legislation through their own bureaucracies, and in a set of supranational organs, which have been delegated important competences in the formulation and enactment of EU policy. This organization has sometimes been described as a dual executive. While this description is empirically accurate, the scholarly literature on executive politics has tended to fall into two separate categories, depending on whether it addresses member states or supranational organs as executives. This chapter focuses exclusively on the delegation of power to the three main forms of supranational executives – the European Commission, the European Central Bank (ECB), and the European agencies – whereas Chapter 25 of this volume partly is devoted to the literature on member state implementation.

This chapter proceeds in the following steps. In the next section, I provide a brief intellectual history of the study of executive politics in the EU. Simplifying slightly, I divide this intellectual history into three consecutive phases, where the first consists of regional integration theorists debating the role of the Commission, the second of detailed empirical studies of the Commission as policy entrepreneur, and the third of the last decade's research on delegation, agency, and accountability in an EU polity of multiple, supranational executives. I conclude from this survey that it is since the mid-1990s that the study of EU politics can boast research on executive politics comparable to that produced in the context of domestic political systems. Concentrating on this body of literature, the subsequent two sections outline the dominant theoretical approaches in the modern study of executive politics, and describe the main areas of empirical research. The theoretical survey explains how rational choice institutionalism, mainly in the shape of principal-agent (P-A) analysis, has developed into the dominant approach in research on executive politics, but also describes how sociological institutionalism and normative democracy theory challenge the assumptions and conclusions of the rational choice approach. The empirical overview identifies the main areas of research and debate with reference to the Commission, the ECB, and the European agencies.

EXECUTIVE POLITICS: A BRIEF INTELLECTUAL HISTORY

Whereas executive politics only recently has become an established term in the study of EU politics, the theoretical issues addressed under this rubric have a longer intellectual history. Both in their early and more recent variants, the grand theories of European integration spoke to the role and influence the EU's supranational institutions.

The Legacy of Integration Theory

In the 1950s, 1960s, and early 1970s, the first generation of neofunctionalists and intergovernmentalists debated whether the powers conferred on the Commission enabled this supranational executive to influence European integration. Neofunctionalist scholars generally

submitted that the Commission was instrumental to the progression of integration, by encouraging societal demands for European policies, formulating policy proposals, and cultivating a process of spill-over (e.g. Haas 1958; Lindberg and Scheingold 1970). The Commission's political skills *par excellence* included goal articulation, transnational coalition-building, technical expertise, task expansion, and brokerage. Early intergovernmentalist scholarship turned sharply against this picture of the supranational institutions as engines and facilitators of European integration. In his seminal critique of neofunctionalism, Hoffmann (1966) submitted that the authority of the Commission was limited in scope, conditional on member-state approval, reversible if proven unacceptable in its results, and unlikely to be extended to domains of key importance to national interests.

When the debate between neofunctionalism and intergovernmentalism resurfaced in the late 1980s and early 1990s, following the internal market initiative and the relaunch of European integration, the dispute over the role of the supranational institutions partly took a new direction. Drawing on theoretical developments in the study of international cooperation, intergovernmentalist scholars conceptualized the EU as an international regime, whose institutions fulfilled important functional tasks for national governments but lacked the power to pursue their own political agendas (Hoffmann 1982; Moravcsik 1991, 1993). The bone of contention subsequently shifted to the question of independent causal influence. Did the supranational institutions only perform the functions they had been delegated, or had they in fact developed roles for themselves that went beyond those that governments intended? Examining the Commission's functions, Moravcsik (1993) did not find any scope for independent initiative. In the same vein, Garrett (1992) contended that the Commission tended to show restraint in pursuing its own interests, preferring instead to adapt its proposals to the preferences of the most powerful governments. By contrast, Sandholtz and Zysman (1989), in a revamped neofunctionalist argument, argued that the Commission had successfully exercised political leadership in the run-up to the Single European Act (SEA), mobilizing transnational business and persuading national governments in favor of the project. Similarly, Stone Sweet and Sandholtz (1997) presented the supranational institutions as vital actors in the construction of what they referred to as supranational governance.

The Commission as Policy Entrepreneur

Yet the most important development during the early 1990s for the study of executive politics was not the re-emergence of the grand theory debate, but the move away from the conception of European integration as the exclusive analytical domain of international relations theorists. Approaching EU politics from the sub-disciplines of public policy and comparative politics, scholars increasingly conceived of the EU as a polity, political system or system of governance, whose internal policy-making processes and policy development was of prime analytical importance. Together with the fast-moving political developments in the late 1980s and early 1990s, epitomized by the SEA and the Maastricht Treaty, this turn in the study of EU politics bred two strands of literature that spoke to issues of executive politics.

The first body of literature focused on the Commission as policy entrepreneur. The strong tendency in this literature to take an optimistic, and to some extent uncritical, view of the Commission's contribution to policy development sometimes led these contributions to be interpreted as closet neofunctionalism. Yet the ambition of this research in the public policy tradition was different from that of regional integration theory, as it mainly attempted to map the evolution of individual policy areas. Based on case studies, scholars testified to the Commission's role as entrepreneur in a large number of policy sectors, such as the internal market (Sandholtz and Zysman 1989), telecommunications policy (Sandholtz 1992), social policy (Cram 1993, 1997), equal

opportunities policy (Mazey 1995), regional policy (Hooghe and Keating 1994; Smyrl 1998), research policy (Peterson 1995), technology policy (Cram 1997), competition policy (McGowan 1997), and energy policy (Matlary 1997). Other scholars chose to highlight the Commission as policy manager, generally claiming that its capacity in this respect was considerably weaker than its capacity for policy entrepreneurship (Metcalfe 1992; Laffan 1997).

The second strand of literature focused on the executive itself, attempting to unveil the inner workings of the Commission. An important impetus for the development of this line of research was the high profile of the Commission under the presidency of Jacques Delors from 1985–94. Much of this work was descriptive in orientation, depicting how the Commission was structured and how it operated in principle and practice. These rich descriptions answered to a demand among scholars and policy-makers for analysis of the Commission, which hitherto had been the object of little detailed research (for an early exception, see Coombes 1970). Within this literature, which burgeoned in the mid-1990s and has continued to expand in the last decade, we find broad volumes on the Commission as an institution (Cini 1996; Edwards and Spence 1997; Nugent 1997, 2001; Dimitrakopoulos 2004), monographs on the Delors Commission (Grant 1994; Ross 1995; Drake 2000), as well as oft-cited contributions on the Commission generally (Ludlow 1991), the Commission president (Drake 1995), the Commission cabinets (Ross 1994; Donnelly and Ritchie 1997), the Commission college (MacMullen 1997; Smith 2003), and the Commission bureaucracy (Stevens and Stevens 2001), especially its administrative culture (Abèles et al. 1993; Cini 1997; McDonald 1997) and political views (Hooghe 2001).

Delegation, Agency, and Accountability

Even if the reorientation of EU studies toward middle-range theorizing had begun already in the first half of the 1990s, it was first in the second half of this decade that theories and methods of comparative politics became fully integrated into the study of EU executive politics. Simplifying only slightly, it is first from the late 1990s and onwards that we can truly speak of a study of executive politics in the EU, comparable to that of research on executive politics in domestic political systems.

This development took place against the backdrop of a political evolution in Europe that made the study of executive politics increasingly central to the general understanding of EU politics. Whereas the Commission previously had been the only supranational body vested with executive power, the member states on 1 January 1999 conferred exclusive authority over monetary policy to the ECB, and from the mid-1990s onwards set up a growing number of European regulatory agencies. Simultaneously, the political debate about democracy and legitimacy in the EU grew more intense in the late 1990s, raising questions about the accountability and control of the EU's supranational executives.

Rational choice institutionalism quickly became established as the dominant theoretical approach in this third wave of research on executive politics, concerned with issues of delegation, agency, and accountability. Drawing on the work of rational choice theorists in the study of American politics, EU scholars conceived of the relationship between the member states and the supranational institutions as a principal-agent relation, which raised theoretical questions about the sources of delegation and the degree of agent autonomy. The work of Majone (1996) and Pollack (1997, 2003) was especially important in this regard, demonstrating how the import of theoretical tools from the study of legislative-executive relations in the US could help shed new light on longstanding issues of debate, such as the influence of the EU's supranational institutions. Principal-agent theory was seen as offering a neutral theoretical language that did not *a priori* discriminate against the propositions of either neofunctionalism or intergovernmentalism, but permitted EU scholars to generate conditional generalizations about supranational influence, based on empirical patterns of variation across institutions, issue areas, and time.

Over time, students of EU executive politics have supplemented the initial focus on agency and autonomy with attention to issues of delegation and discretion, mirroring developments in the study of American executive politics (Pollack 2002). Furthermore, EU scholars have broadened the empirical scope to address the new supranational executives on the scene – the ECB and the European agencies – posing similar questions about the sources of delegation and the degree of autonomy. Finally, rational choice institutionalism, while still heavily influential, has been challenged in competing accounts informed by sociological institutionalism and normative democracy theory. The study of executive politics today constitutes one of the true growth areas in EU studies. As I will show in the subsequent sections, scholars over the last decade have produced an impressive body of research on issues of delegation, agency, and accountability in executive politics.

THEORETICAL APPROACHES TO EXECUTIVE POLITICS

Rational choice institutionalism, in the shape of P-A analysis, constitutes the dominant approach in the study of EU executive politics. Yet it does not stand unchallenged. Sociological institutionalism competes with P-A analysis on positive grounds, offering alternative hypotheses on the sources of delegation and the influence of executive actors. Democratic theory challenges P-A analysis on normative grounds, problematizing whether delegation to non-majoritarian institutions is democratically desirable and legitimate.

Rational Choice Institutionalism

The strong position of rational choice institutionalism in the study of EU executive politics owes much to the import of theories and methods from the literature on legislative-executive relations in American politics, which in turn was the first area of political research to recognize the wider applicability of the analytical tools of the new institutional economics. Since the early 1980s, P-A analysis has been the favored theoretical approach of American politics scholars for understanding the delegation of powers by the US Congress to the regulatory agencies of the executive branch, and the autonomy of the latter vis-à-vis their legislative principals. The study of EU politics in general, and executive politics in particular, constitute the contractual paradigm's most recent frontier in political science (for overviews, see Doleys 2000; Tallberg 2002; Kassim and Menon 2003).

The analytical core of P-A theory is the principal-agent relation, which arises whenever one party (principal) delegates certain functions to another party (agent), in the expectation that the agent will act in ways desired by the principal. P-A theory posits that this relationship is inherently problematic, since what is optimal for the principal is not necessarily optimal for the agent, who may have private interests at heart. Furthermore, principals rarely enjoy full insight into the actions of their agents, which provides the agents with an opportunity to pursue their own interests at the expense of the principals' – to 'shirk' in the P-A vocabulary. However, principals are not helpless in the face of agent shirking. Through the establishment of control mechanisms, involving forms of monitoring and sanctioning, principals may induce agents to comply with their wishes.

In the standard application of the P-A model to EU politics, scholars have conceptualized the member states as principals who have delegated certain powers to the supranational institutions and subsequently been confronted with a control problem.[1] The framing of the relationship between states and supranational institutions in these terms has focused the attention of EU scholars on the two issues of central analytical importance in P-A analysis, namely why principals delegate power to agents, and the extent to which agents can take advantage of their discretion to pursue private preferences.

The general answer offered by rational choice institutionalism to the first question is functionalist in orientation. Delegation is explained in terms of the anticipated effects for the delegating party, and is likely to take place when the expected benefits outweigh the expected costs. More specifically, the P-A literature emphasizes a set of transaction-cost reducing motivations for delegation, notably: (a) facilitating credible policy commitments, as delegation to agents insulated from the day-to-day pressure of electoral politics allows politicians to bind themselves to a given policy; (b) reducing information asymmetries, as the creation of institutions and agencies in technical areas of governance gives politicians access to policy-relevant expertise; and (c) improving decision-making efficiency, as agents manage detailed rule-making, thus saving politicians' time and effort for more general policy decisions (see, e.g. McCubbins and Page 1987; Epstein and O'Halloran 1999). In the study of executive politics in the EU, scholars have sought to test whether these reasons for delegation accurately capture the functions conferred on the supranational institutions. Furthermore, rational choice institutionalists have engaged in a debate about the relative explanatory power of alternative logics of delegation, contrasting credibility-based and efficiency-based reasons for delegation.

As an offshoot to this research on the sources of delegation, scholars in recent years have paid increasing attention to the degree of discretion allocated to agents within their delegated powers (Epstein and O'Halloran 1999; Huber and Shipan 2002). Discretion is commonly understood as the net of the powers delegated to agents, and the various forms of control mechanisms established by principals (delegated powers – control mechanisms = discretion). All principal-agent relationships are likely to involve some level of agent discretion, since control mechanisms are costly to institute and operate. The question that primarily has motivated P-A theorists is how to explain variation in the degree of discretion, which thus is conceptualized as a question of institutional design. Referring back to the reasons for delegation, this research hypothesizes that the degree of discretion is positively related to the demand for credible commitments and the demand for policy-relevant expertise. Inspired by the work of American politics scholars, students of executive politics have begun to explore the pattern and sources of discretion in the EU delegation.

Shifting to the agency stage, P-A analysis suggests that agent autonomy constitutes an effect of the extent and efficacy of control mechanisms. The general literature offers a set of well-established categorizations of forms of oversight (McCubbins and Schwartz 1984; McCubbins et al. 1987). First, it is common to distinguish between *ex ante* administrative procedures and *ex post* oversight procedures as two complementary forms of control mechanisms. Administrative procedures define the scope of the agent's activity, the legal instruments at its disposal, and the kind of procedures it has to follow. Oversight procedures, for their part, consist of institutional mechanisms for monitoring agent behavior and sanctioning potential shirking. A second influential distinction is that between 'police-patrol' oversight and 'fire-alarm' oversight, where the first consists of centralized, active, and direct monitoring on the part of the principal, and the second of decentralized, reactive, and indirect monitoring through parties affected by the agent's actions. With regard to sanctions, P-A theorists have identified an array of potential instruments, including cutting an agent's budget, reversing appointments, overriding decisions through new legislation, and revising an agent's institutional mandate. Drawing on these general categorizations and inventories, students of EU politics have sought to identify the kinds of mechanisms set up by member state principals for controlling their supranational agents, and, on this basis, generated specific hypotheses about the scope for agency and autonomy.

Sociological Institutionalism

In recent years, scholars inspired by sociological institutionalism, broadly interpreted, have challenged the assumptions and propositions of rational-choice theorists on delegation and agency in executive politics. Even if these challenges yet do not amount to a coherent alternative approach to delegation, they generate competing expectations on key issues of executive politics. Three areas of challenge, criticism, and competition may be isolated (see, also, Thatcher and Stone Sweet 2002; Pollack 2003: ch. 1).

First, sociological institutionalists have challenged, theoretically and empirically, the core assumptions about principals and agents as rational, unitary actors with fixed and exogenous preferences. At a general theoretical level, sociological institutionalists subscribe to the notion of actor behavior being governed by a sociological 'logic of appropriateness', rather than a rationalist 'logic of consequences' (March and Olsen 1989). In the political world of appropriateness, actors are not driven by strategic calculations on how to maximize expected utility, but by a wish to do the right thing in a given institutional context, where identities, expectations, norms, and roles define what constitutes appropriate behavior. The preferences guiding the behavior of executive actors, by consequence, are best viewed as endogenous and malleable, subject to definition and redefinition in an evolving institutional context, and open to processes of persuasion and socialization. At a more specific level, sociological institutionalists highlight the empirical inaccuracy and analytical pit-falls of the unitary actor assumption, by pointing to important social processes *within* agencies and institutions. Internal organizational cultures, conceptualized as shared belief systems, values, ideologies, and identities, are seen as influencing the perception of appropriate administrative behavior and the interpretation of institutional interest. In the study of EU executive politics, the best expression of this perspective on actor behavior is the research on the inner workings of the Commission, which problematizes the process of preference aggregation, introduces culture and ideology as fundamental variables, and thus questions the unitary actor approach, even if reference rarely is made to sociological institutionalism directly.

Second, sociological institutionalists have questioned the rationalist claim that delegation takes place in response to specific functional needs, and is driven by the desire to reduce transaction costs. Instead, sociological institutionalists perceive of institutional design as a process where low priority is given to concerns of efficiency, relative to concerns of legitimacy (DiMaggio and Powell 1983; Powell and DiMaggio 1991; Scott et al. 1994). Principals delegate power to agents because this form of institutional design is widely accepted as legitimate and appropriate – not necessarily because it is the most efficient. In the sociological account, the growing tendency of democratically elected politicians to delegate authority to independent institutions at the national and international level is thus best explained as an example of institutional isomorphism, or the spread of organizational models across domains through processes of emulation and diffusion. In the study of EU politics, this perspective on the sources of delegation is still relatively underdeveloped, with research on the origin and design of the ECB as the best example.

Third, sociological institutionalists take a very different position on the process through which actors influence political outcomes. In contrast to P-A theorists, who emphasize delegated powers, control mechanisms, and resultant zones of discretion as determinants of the scope for autonomous influence, sociological institutionalists underline alternative mechanisms and processes, such as informal agenda-setting, persuasion through good arguments, and moral authority (Kingdon 1984; Risse 2000; Barnett and Finnemore 2004). If actors' perceptions of interests, alternatives, problems, and solutions are malleable, then informal authority and the power of the better argument become important sources of influence. More generally, decision-making, in the sociological account, is better viewed as deliberation and problem-solving than as strategic interaction between utility-maximizing actors. Drawing on these theoretical notions, some students of EU politics have questioned the accuracy of the rationalist conception of the relationship between the member states and the Commission as one of control and autonomy, and presented an alternative perspective that highlights processes of persuasion, deliberation, and joint problem-solving.

Normative Democratic Theory

Normative democratic theory offers a third approach to issues of executive politics, and a second theoretical challenge to rational choice institutionalism. Yet, unlike sociological institutionalism, which shared the positive approach of P-A analysis to questions of delegation, democratic theory addresses the normative aspects of executive politics. Normative democratic theory is not a unified approach, but consists of several different strands of theory, often described as alternative models of democracy, which offer competing prescriptions for how the ideal democracy should be designed. One common distinction in the literature, with clear parallels in the debate about democracy at the EU level, is the trichotomy of competitive democracy, participatory democracy, and deliberative democracy (see, e.g. Elster 1986; Karlsson 2001).

At a general level, democratic theory challenges positive approaches to executive politics by highlighting the normative implications of delegation from democratically elected governments to non-majoritarian institutions, neither directly accountable to the voters nor to their elected representatives. These are issues that rational choice institutionalists either have neglected or regarded as unproblematic. Normative concerns have received limited attention in the scholarly debate about legislative-executive relations in the US. Similarly, P-A theorists in EU studies have remained wedded to positive questions, even if there is an unstated assumption in the broader literature on European integration that the delegation of power to supranational institutions has been instrumental to the process of European unification, and thus good for Europe.

More specifically, it is the ideals of the model of competitive or majoritarian democracy that present the most interesting challenge to the positive perspective of P-A theory. Highly simplified, this model of democracy stresses the opportunities for citizens to choose between competing political elites with alternative agendas (Schumpeter 1943; Dahl 1967). It is this model of democracy that in different versions informs the design of representative government in national political systems. In a strict interpretation of this theory, delegation to non-majoritarian institutions risks undermining desirable principles of democratic governance. First, the act of delegation in itself means that part of the authority to govern is shifted from the realm of democratic contestation to the realm of technocratic governance, especially if this power is difficult to effectively retrieve. Second, the mechanisms for holding non-majoritarian institutions democratically accountable are by definition absent or underdeveloped. And third, the political room for maneuver enjoyed by non-majoritarian institutions may give rise to autonomous actions contrary to the interests of the democratic representatives who empowered them.

While not unique to the EU, these problems of democratic legitimacy have received particular attention in Europe, where the delegation of power to supranational institutions and agencies often is considered one component of the EU's 'democratic deficit' (e.g. Lord 1998; Höreth 1999; Schmitter 2000; Arnull and Wincott 2003). Problems typically mentioned include technocratic decision-making, lack of transparency, insufficient public participation, exploitation of supranational discretion, and inadequate mechanisms of control and accountability. This is a critique that has been directed at all three main forms of supranational executive power in the EU. Furthermore, this critique most often comes attached with specific prescriptions for how to address this part of the democratic deficit, with proponents of competitive or majoritarian democracy generally endorsing a parliamentarization of the EU, through an enhanced role of the European Parliament (EP) in the formulation of legislation, the appointment of the Commission, and the control of all supranational executives.

Whereas the large majority of rational choice institutionalists have remained silent in this normative debate, some have taken a stance in defense of non-majoritarian institutions (Majone 1996, 1998, 1999; Moravcsik 2002). These theorists have emphasized the virtues of delegation as government *for* the

people, rather than its limits in terms of government *by* the people. First, they stress that delegation to non-majoritarian institutions is normatively justifiable since it tends to produce better outcomes for citizens, by raising the efficiency of decision-making, securing political rights against majority rule, and offsetting imperfections in majoritarian institutions. Second, these theorists point out that delegation to supranational institutions mainly takes place in those areas that are excluded from democratic control in most national political systems as well, and thus serves to replace the increasingly ineffective efforts of national bureaucrats. Third and finally, they emphasize that non-majoritarian institutions in fact are subject to forms of control, even if these do not involve direct democratic accountability. Foremost among these are procedural requirements, which offer a source of legitimacy.

THE EMPIRICAL STUDY OF EXECUTIVE POLITICS

The empirical research on executive politics in the EU is primarily concerned with the Commission, but the literature on the ECB and the European agencies is growing. The overview in this section restricts itself to the theoretically informed empirical research on delegation, agency, and accountability that has been produced during the last decade.

The European Commission as EU Executive

The literature on the Commission as executive may conveniently be divided into three thematic areas of research: (a) delegation and discretion; (b) agency and influence, and (c) delegation and democracy.

Delegation and Discretion

Member governments' delegation of executive power to the Commission is one of the growth areas in the study of executive politics. EU scholars have sought to identify the reasons for delegation, the specific functions delegated, and the degree of discretion enjoyed by the Commission within these powers. P-A analysis has constituted the main approach in this research, which has featured few theoretical alternatives. Rather, the most vibrant scholarly exchange has taken place between rational choice institutionalists debating what functional motives best explain the powers delegated to the Commission. This research may be divided into two strands, depending on whether it is delegation of treaty-based powers or delegation through secondary legislation that is addressed.

The literature in the first category testifies to a close fit between the functionalist predictions of rational choice institutionalism and the actual powers delegated to the Commission in the treaties. The observation of a close match was first forwarded by Pollack (1997), and this conclusion subsequently has been strengthened by research on the negotiations of the founding treaties (Rittberger 2001), as well as in-depth studies of the Commission's treaty-based powers of agenda setting, enforcement, and implementation.

First, scholars have argued convincingly in favor of a rationalist interpretation of the Commission's unusual agenda setting role, stressing either the logic of credible commitments or the need to reduce information asymmetries (Moravcsik 1998; Majone 2001; Pollack 2003). According to the first interpretation, often considered most consistent with the data, the member states pre-committed themselves to a particular agenda of supranational integration, when delegating a monopoly on formal agenda setting to the Commission. According to the second interpretation, the conferral of an agenda-setting role on the Commission helps to reduce technical information deficits, by allowing the member states to profit from the policy expertise of the Commission in the formulation of EU legislation.

Second, research on the Commission's function as 'guardian of the treaties' strongly suggests that delegation in this area can be adequately explained by the logic of credible commitments (Tallberg 2003). The discretion accorded to the Commission is exceedingly extensive, since EU governments effectively have abstained from establishing means of controlling this institution in the enforcement of state compliance. Furthermore, historical data testify that EU governments indeed have been motivated by the desire to safeguard their commitments, when delegating enforcement powers to the Commission.

Third, research into the delegation of issue-specific implementation powers through the treaties suggests that the logic of credible commitments is at play here as well (Pollack 2003). In the particular areas where member governments have chosen to delegate far-reaching implementation powers to the Commission, and allowed the supranational executive extensive discretion, such as competition policy and external trade policy, the Commission's tasks typically are designed to safeguard state commitments.

In the second strand of research on delegation, scholars examine the conferral of implementation powers to the Commission through secondary legislation. The questions that drive this work are why the Council delegates implementation authority to the Commission in some issue areas, but not others, and why this authority tends to be accompanied with varying levels of discretion for the Commission? Drawing on the work of P-A theorists in the US context, EU scholars have developed and tested hypotheses about executive delegation in the Europe (Franchino 2002, 2004, forthcoming). The findings indicate that variation in the amount of delegation and discretion depend on several factors: the level of conflict within the Council, the decision rule operating in the Council, the degree of conflict between the Council and the Commission, and the complexity of the policy area. Formulated in terms of rationales of delegation, this research suggests that the delegation of implementation authority to the Commission through secondary legislation is motivated both by a demand for efficient policy-making and by a demand for credible-commitment devices.

Agency and Influence

EU governments' means of controlling the Commission, and this institution's ability to exploit its discretion for the advancement of a supranational political agenda, were the areas of executive politics that first received the close attention of EU scholars. The literature is dominated by P-A analysis, but also features work informed by sociological institutionalism.

The research on control mechanisms has been characterized by the dual ambition to map empirically the oversight mechanisms established by EU governments, and to demonstrate how this system of control may be understood in the analytical categories of rational choice institutionalism. Pollack (1997, 2003) has presented the most comprehensive inventory of control mechanisms, whereas other researchers have offered in-depth treatments of the design, evolution, or use of specific control mechanisms (e.g. Gabel and Hix 2002; Costa et al. 2003; Tallberg 2003). Expressed in P-A terms, EU governments have established a system of police-patrol oversight through the comitology committees that supervise Commission implementation, as well as a system of fire-alarm oversight in the shape of institutional checks, administrative law, and judicial review. The sanctions available to the member states, too, are familiar from legislative-executive relations in American politics, and include powers of appointment and censure, the possibility of cutting the Commission's budget, the right to overrule Commission decisions through new legislation, the option of non-compliance, and the ultimate possibility of revising the Commission's institutional mandate at the next review of the EU treaties.

The design of the system of comitology committees is a topic that has generated an impressive amount of research. Part of the explanation for the interest in this relatively arcane part of EU politics is the presence of an alternative, sociological account to the claims advanced by rational choice institutionalists. In two frequently cited articles, Joerges and Neyer (1997a, b) argue that the comitology committees, rather than constituting control

mechanisms for member governments, provide fora for national and supranational experts to meet, deliberate, and engage in joint problem solving. Joerges and Neyer submit that deliberative problem-solving is the empirically most accurate description of the actual workings of comitology, even if these committees originally may have been set up to secure governments a voice in the adoption of EU regulation. Rational choice institutionalists have responded to this challenge by investigating empirically the Council's choice of comitology procedure, generally concluding that member governments carefully calculate the likely consequences of alternative comitology procedures, and thus tend to perceive this system as a control mechanism (Dogan 1997, 2000; Franchino 2000a, b; Pollack 2003).

The research on supranational agency and influence has been driven by the question of when, where, and how the EU's supranational institutions are capable of implementing their favored political agendas. This literature stretches across all three main functions of the Commission, and across a range of issue areas. The predominant methodological approach has been comparative case studies, generally involving process-tracing and often including counterfactual analysis. An overall conclusion in this research is that independent influences are more likely to appear where the Commission enjoys greater degrees of discretion within its delegated powers. Furthermore, this literature strongly suggests that the Commission is relatively more constrained than the European Court of Justice (ECJ), but that the close cooperation of this institution often features as a key component in those cases where the Commission succeeds in pursuing a supranational agenda unsupported by member governments (Schmidt 2000; Tallberg 2000; Pollack 2003). These are findings that contrast with the earlier literature on policy entrepreneurship, which was considerably more optimistic about the Commission's influence in EU politics.

Empirical studies of the Commission's capacity to exploit its formal agenda-setting power for private purposes indicate that the requirement of member state approval in the Council (as well as the approval of the Parliament in many cases) constitutes a serious constraint that highly limits the scope for independent supranational influence (Pollack 2003: chs. 5–6). Rationally anticipating the risk of having its legislative proposals dismissed by the Council, the Commission tends to present proposals with a high likelihood of adoption. Research on the enforcement function of the Commission shows how the guardian of the treaties, in tandem with the ECJ, has been able to exploit its discretion for purposes of strengthening the EU's enforcement regime (Tallberg 2000, 2003). Finally, research on the Commission's power of implementation points to relatively greater scope for supranational influence, but also to variation across issue areas. In the field of external trade, the Commission's mandate is matched with state control through the Council's 133 Committee, reducing the scope for autonomous action (Meunier and Nicolaïdis 1999; Nicolaïdis 1999; Meunier 2000; Pollack 2003: ch. 5). In the area of competition policy, the literature indicates relatively greater scope for agency and influence, often secured with the benign help of the ECJ (Schmidt 1998, 2000; Pollack 2003: ch. 5).

Delegation and Democracy

A third broad strand of research on the Commission as executive actor addresses the normative dimension of this institutional arrangement. This literature is intimately bound up with the political debate about the democratic credentials of the EU, which has grown particularly intense over the last decade. The scholarly debate on this subject offers two main positions.

The first perspective, shared by proponents of competitive or majoritarian democracy on the European level, emphasizes the negative implications of delegation to the Commission, the low legitimacy of this supranational executive, and the virtues of a parliamentarization of the Commission and the EU (e.g. Dehousse 1995; Mancini 1998; McKay 1999). This argument tends to be developed through a comparison with national political systems,

which yields the conclusion that delegation to the Commission has created an executive that possesses exceptional control over the political agenda, and is relieved of standard forms of democratic accountability. The placing of a monopoly on formal agenda setting in the hands of a bureaucracy means that citizens are deprived of the possibility to influence the political agenda of the EU executive through the normal route of electoral contestation, involving competing elites and alternative political agendas. By the same token, the procedures for appointing and dismissing the Commission effectively entails that this executive cannot be voted out of office, should citizens be disappointed with its performance.

This analysis translates into a distinct normative position on the democratization of the EU, which is seen as best achieved through a parliamentarization of the Union. In the political debate, this standpoint is generally associated with a federalist vision of the EU. The most important components of this reform alternative are the development of the Parliament into a full-blown co-legislator next to the Council in a bicameral legislative structure, and the transformation of the Commission into a true European government, appointed by and accountable to the Parliament.

The second distinct position in the normative debate about the Commission's executive power defends the status quo and cautions against an increasing politicization and parliamentarization of the Commission. The most consistent advocate of this perspective is Majone (1998, 2000, 2002), who warns that the progressive parliamentarization of the Commission risks compromising its credibility as an independent regulator, without necessarily enhancing its democratic legitimacy (see also Moravcsik 2002). If EU governments delegate powers to the Commission mainly in order to secure credible policy commitments, then the subjection of the Commission to stronger parliamentary control would risk undoing the virtues of this arrangement. No longer insulated from political pressure and majoritarian swings, the Commission would be unable to function as an impartial long-term guarantor of collective decisions, with negative effects for the credibility and consistency of EU policy.

Rather than strengthening the Commission's democratic accountability through the development of a European parliamentary system, representatives of this normative position propose that greater recognition be given to the legitimacy that flows from appropriate procedural requirements (Majone 1998, 1999). Procedural legitimacy, in this context, requires that powers be delegated to the Commission through democratic procedures, that the leadership of the Commission is selected by elected politicians, that the Commission's decision-making must follow well-defined procedures, and that its decisions must be justified and open to review.

The European Central Bank as EU Executive

The establishment of the ECB as the joint central bank of the member states in the euro zone constitutes an exceptional example of monetary delegation. As such, it obviously raises intriguing questions for EU scholars. To date, empirical research on this topic mainly has been preoccupied with the 'why' question. How can we explain that states protective of national sovereignty agreed to delegate exclusive authority of monetary policy to a supranational central bank, simultaneously abstaining from the most conventional means of control? By contrast, the other prominent question in research on delegation – the scope for autonomous influence – so far has not featured as a topic, even if the ECB's conduct of monetary policy has been the subject of studies by economists.[2]

Existing research on EU governments' motives for delegating executive power in monetary affairs to the ECB features two alternative answers. Rational choice institutionalists typically present the establishment and design of the ECB as motivated by the functional logic of credible commitments, and support this argument with data on the negotiation of the

Maastricht Treaty (Moravcsik 1998; Majone 2000). By placing the power over monetary policy in the hands of an independent central bank, and charging this bank with the objective of securing price stability, EU governments committed themselves to a non-inflationary monetary policy.

The alternative interpretation, informed by sociological institutionalism, has been most pointedly expressed by McNamara (2002), who questions the functional rationale of delegation. Instead, the ECB is viewed as the latest expression of the diffusion across industrialized countries of the independent central bank as an organizational model (see, also, Verdun 1999; Marcussen 2000). In McNamara's (2002: 48) account, governments choose to delegate not because of narrow functional benefits but rather because delegation has important legitimizing or symbolic properties which render it attractive in times of uncertainty or economic distress. The spread of central bank independence should be seen as a fundamentally social and political phenomenon, rooted in the logic of organizational mimicry and global norms of neoliberal governance.

This argument provides the best example in the literature on executive politics of how the general propositions of sociological institutionalism can be used to formulate a theoretically coherent alternative to P-A analysis with respect to specific empirical areas of delegation.

Another strain in the literature asks normative, rather than positive, questions about the delegation of monetary policy to the ECB. Indeed, this is the area of research on the ECB as executive actor that boasts the liveliest scholarly debate. The point of contention in this normative exchange is the appropriateness of central bank independence in view of democratic theory (for analyses of this debate, see de Haan and Eijffinger 2000; Elgie 2002; Jabko 2003).

Critics of the existing arrangement typically highlight the lack of transparency in ECB decision-making, and the lack of accountability vis-à-vis both member governments and the European Parliament (e.g. Verdun 1998;

Berman and McNamara 1999; Buiter 1999). EU governments in the negotiation of the statutes allegedly went further than necessary in the crafting of the Bank's independence. Even compared to other independent central banks, the ECB lacks in democratic accountability. The records of its proceedings are secret, and its statutes can only be revised through the unanimous agreement of all EU governments on a new EU treaty, subsequently ratified in all member states.

Defenders of the ECB's independence typically stress the rationale of this arrangement in terms of maintaining the credibility of the bank and its capacity to function as the impartial guarantor of the public's long-term interest, as well as the mechanisms of transparency and accountability that do exist (e.g. Majone 1998; Issing 1999). The legitimacy of the ECB, in this view, is not primarily derived from the democratic properties of its decision-making procedures, but from its capacity to fulfill the monetary policy objectives set by member governments when founding the Bank. Furthermore, defenders emphasize how the ECB in practice has strengthened its accountability and transparency beyond what the treaty requires, by appearing before the Parliament, and by publishing information on monetary policy.

The European Agencies as EU Executives

The establishment of European agencies is often described as one of the most important developments in EU regulatory policy since 1990. Whereas the first of these agencies were set up already in the mid-1970s, it was during the 1990s and early 2000s that the European agencies truly emerged as new actors on the EU executive scene. Between 1990–2004, the EU established 14 regulatory agencies, bringing the total number of agencies within the EU's first pillar of cooperation up to 16. In addition, since the late 1990s, the EU has created two agencies in the second pillar of foreign and security policy, as well as two agencies in the third pillar of police and judicial cooperation. The large-scale establishment of European agencies raises

a set of important questions for students of executive politics. The areas that so far have been subject to the most detailed work are the sources of the new wave of agency creation, as well as the design of these agencies. By contrast, the operation of the agencies, including questions of autonomy and influence, has received more limited attention.

Research on the political causes behind the establishment of the new agencies emphasizes the role of the Commission in promoting this development, and member states' acceptance of this initiative after having secured intergovernmental control of the new mini-executives (Everson 1995; Dehousse 1997; Kreher 1997; Shapiro 1997; Kelemen 2002). In this account, the EU's internal market initiative created a demand for regulatory activity that the Commission, with its limited staff, was hard-pressed to supply on its own. The creation of independent agencies constituted a solution that met the Commission's dual objectives of expanding the EU's governing capacity and off-loading some of the Commission's highly technical and resource-intensive regulatory activities.

Studies of agency design demonstrate that the powers delegated, as well as the control mechanisms established, vary extensively among the different European agencies (Majone 1997; Everson et al. 2001). The agencies within the first pillar of EU cooperation fall into multiple categories, depending on the nature of their responsibilities: providing services to industries, gathering and disseminating information, promoting cooperation between industries and trade unions, or performing specific executive tasks for the EU. Likewise, control mechanisms differ across the agencies, with variation in funding arrangements, administrative procedures, and oversight mechanisms. Some see the absence of a one-size-fits-all institutional structure as preliminary evidence that these agencies have been designed with specific functional benefits in mind (Pollack 2003: 396). However, we will have to await the results of future research for a definitive assessment.

The European agencies, too, have been the topic of a normative debate, in this case about the democratic appropriateness of delegating executive power to independent agencies staffed with experts and unaccountable to the electorate. Critics of the delegation of regulatory tasks to European agencies typically express concern about the speed and extent of this development, as well as the little thought that allegedly has been given to the democratic control of these agencies. As one leading theorist of democracy at the European level puts it, 'these emerging patterns of guardianship could represent a rather considerable future hazard for Euro-democratization' (Schmitter 2000: 88).

Rational choice institutionalists tend to perceive of the democratic credentials of these agencies as less important, given the functional benefits they promise. Furthermore, they emphasize that independent regulatory agencies in the US successfully derive legitimacy from the democratic statutes through which they are created, the procedures they must follow in their activities, and the mechanisms of ex post control available to the legislature (Everson 1995; Majone 1998). To the extent that such well-designed instruments of procedural accountability could be fashioned with respect to the European agencies, delegation of executive power to these mini-executives should be considered equally legitimate.

CONCLUSION

This chapter began with the observation that the study of executive politics in the EU over the last decade has matured into a relatively coherent research field, characterized by close theoretical links to the general study of executive politics, and worthy of a chapter of its own in an ambitious volume on EU politics. Venturing beyond the safe ground of the past and the present, I conclude this chapter by expressing three optimistic expectations about the direction of research in this area over the coming decade.

First, there is scope for more detailed empirical work on the motives, modes, and consequences of delegation to supranational executives in the EU. Even if the research in some areas is beginning to reach cumulative strength, the field still features untested propositions and assertions that have gained the status of empirical truths. The last decade of research illustrates the merits of an eclectic methodological approach, involving comparative case studies as well as aggregated quantitative research. Thematically, the variation in the organization of executive power across institutions, issue areas, and time in the EU offers a rich and promising empirical testing ground. Furthermore, as history teaches us, developments in the actual politics of the EU have tended to expand the research agenda.

Second, the field is likely to develop, and indeed would benefit from, a higher level of theoretical contestation. Whereas the attention accorded to the normative aspects of delegation in recent years have produced a healthy debate between rational choice institutionalists and democratic theorists, there is still considerable scope for a more well-developed dialogue with sociological institutionalism. The sociological approach to delegation remains unnecessarily underdeveloped theoretically and under-tested empirically. In view of the spread of delegation as a mode of governance in the EU, there is great potential for more systematic, empirical testing of the sociological propositions about institutional isomorphism.

Third, there is a potential for the study of executive politics in the EU to become a hotbed for theory development and refinement. In this area, as in many others, the field of EU studies has tended to be on the receiving end, importing theoretical tools from comparative politics and international relations. Yet, just like research on American politics, the study of executive politics in the EU may generate theoretical insights of general applicability. In this context, the special features of EU executive politics – multiple principals, multiple agents, and supranational policy-making – are likely to be particularly exploitable. Indeed, research generated in the EU context already has helped to inspire greater attention to issues of delegation and agency in the study of international organizations.

ACKNOWLEDGEMENTS

For helpful comments I would like to thank Hans Agné, Fabio Franchino, Hussein Kassim, Mark Pollack, and the participants of the research seminar on European politics at the Department of Political Science, Stockholm University.

NOTES

1. Note, however, that there are alternative conceptualizations. In the study of EU implementation, scholars either have reversed the standard role configuration (Commission as principal and national bureaucracies as agents) or extended the basic model (member governments as principals that engage the supranational institutions as supervisors, which oversee the implementation by national bureaucracies as agents) (Peters 1997; Tallberg 2003). Furthermore, in the study of parliamentary democracy in Europe, scholars describe a chain of delegation from voters to national parliamentarians, to national governments, and to the EU institutions (Strøm et al. 2003).

2. This absence of research on agency is best explained by the perception of ECB shirking as a non-issue, given the bank's own preference in favor of price stability – the target chosen by its principals for the conduct of monetary policy.

REFERENCES

Abèles, M., Bellier, I. and McDonald, M. (1993) 'Approche Anthropoligique de la Commission Européenne', unpublished report for the European Commission.

Arnull, A. and Wincott, D. (eds) (2003) *Accountability and Legitimacy in the European Union.* Oxford: Oxford University Press.

Barnett, M. and Finnemore, M. (2004) *Rules for the World: International Organizations in Global Politics.* Ithaca, NY: Cornell University Press.

Berman, S. and McNamara, K.R. (1999) 'Bank on democracy: why central banks need public oversight', *Foreign Affairs*, 78: 2–8.

Buiter, W.H. (1999) 'Alice in Euroland', *Journal of Common Market Studies*, 37(2): 181–209.

Cini, M. (1996) *The European Commission: Leadership, Organisation, and Culture in the EU Administration.* Manchester: Manchester University Press.

Cini, M. (1997) 'Administrative culture in the European Commission: the cases of competition and environment', in N. Nugent (ed.), *At the Heart of the Union: Studies of the European Commission.* Basingstoke: Macmillan. pp. 71–88.

Coombes, D. (1970) *Politics and Bureaucracy in the EC: A Portrait of the Commission of the EEC.* London: Allen & Unwin.

Costa, O., Jabko, N., Lequesne, C. and Magnette, P. (eds) (2003) 'Special Issue: The diffusion of democracy – emerging forms and norms of democratic control in the European Union', *Journal of European Public Policy*, 10(5).

Cram, L. (1993) 'Calling the tune without paying the piper? Social policy regulation: the role of the Commission in European Union social policy', *Policy and Politics*, 21: 135–46.

Cram, L. (1997) *Policy-Making in the EU: Conceptual Lenses and the Integration Process.* London: Routledge.

Dahl, R.A. (1967) *A Preface to Democratic Theory.* Chicago: University of Chicago Press.

de Haan, J. and Eijffinger, S.C.W. (2000) 'The democratic accountability of the European Central Bank', *Journal of Common Market Studies*, 38(3): 393–407.

Dehousse, R. (1995) 'Constitutional reform in the European Community: are there alternatives to the majoritarian avenue?' *West European Politics*, 18(3): 118–36.

Dehousse, R. (1997) 'Regulation by networks in the European Community: the role of European agencies', *Journal of European Public Policy*, 4: 246–61.

DiMaggio, P.J. and Powell, W.W. (1983) 'The iron cage revisited: institutional isomorphism and collective rationality in organizational fields', *American Sociological Review*, 48: 147–60.

Dimitrakopoulos, D.G. (ed.) (2004) *The Changing European Commission.* Manchester: Manchester University Press.

Dogan, R. (1997) 'Comitology: little procedures with big implications', *West European Politics*, 20: 31–60.

Dogan, R. (2000) 'A cross-sectoral view of comitology: incidence, issues, and implications', in T. Christiansen and E. Kirchner (eds), *Europe in Change: Committee Governance in the European Union.* Manchester: Manchester University Press. pp. 45–61.

Doleys, T.J. (2000) 'Member states and the European Commission: theoretical insights from the new economics of organization', *Journal of European Public Policy*, 7(4): 532–53.

Donnelly, M. and Ritchie, E. (1997) 'The College of Commissioners and the cabinets', in G. Edwards and D. Spence (eds), *The European Commission*, 2nd ed. London: Catermill.

Drake, H. (1995) 'Political leadership and European integration: the case of Jacques Delors', *West European Politics*, 18(1): 140–60.

Drake, H. (2000) *Jacques Delors: Perspectives on a European Leader*. London: Routledge.

Edwards, G. and Spence, D. (eds) (1997) *The European Commission*, 2nd ed. London: Catermill.

Elgie, R. (2002) 'The politics of the European Central Bank: principal-agent theory and the democratic deficit', *Journal of European Public Policy*, 9(2): 186–200.

Elster, J. (1986) 'The market and the forum: three varieties of democratic theory', in J. Elster and A. Hylland (eds), *Foundations of Social Choice Theory*. Cambridge: Cambridge University Press. pp. 103–32.

Epstein, D. and O'Halloran, S. (1999) *Delegating Powers: A Transaction Cost Politics Approach to Policy Making under Separate Powers*. Cambridge: Cambridge University Press.

Everson, M. (1995) 'European agencies: hierarchy beaters?' *European Law Journal*, 1(2): 180–204.

Everson, M., Majone, G., Metcalfe, L. and Schout, A. (2001) 'The role of specialized agencies in decentralising EU governance', report for the European Commission. Available online at: europa.eu.int/comm/governance/areas/group6/contribution_en.pdf, accessed 8 September 2006.

Franchino, F. (2000a) 'Control of the Commission's executive functions: uncertainty, conflict and decision rules', *European Union Politics*, 1(1): 63–92.

Franchino, F. (2000b) 'The Commission's executive discretion, information, and comitology', *Journal of Theoretical Politics*, 12(2): 155–81.

Franchino, F. (2002) 'Efficiency or credibility? Testing the two logics of delegation to the European Commission', *Journal of European Public Policy*, 9(5): 677–94.

Franchino, F. (2004) 'Delegating powers in the European Community', *British Journal of Political Science*, 34: 269–93.

Franchino, F. (forthcoming) *The Powers of the Union: Delegation in the EU*. Cambridge: Cambridge University Press.

Gabel, M. and Hix, S. (2002) 'The European Parliament and executive politics in the EU: voting behaviour and the commission president investiture procedure', in M. Hosli, A. Van Deemen and M. Widgrén (eds), *Institutional Challenges in the European Union*. London: Routledge.

Garrett, G. (1992) 'International cooperation and institutional choice: the European Community's internal market', *International Organization*, 46(2): 533–60.

Grant, C. (1994) *Delors: Inside the House that Jacques Built*. London: Nicholas Brealey.

Haas, E.B. (1958) *The Uniting of Europe: Political, Social and Economical Forces 1950–1957*. London: Stevens & Sons Limited.

Hoffmann, S. (1966) 'Obstinate or obsolete? The fate of the nation-state and the case of western Europe', *Dædalus*, 95(3): 862–915.

Hoffmann, S. (1982) 'Reflections on the nation-state in western Europe today', *Journal of Common Market Studies*, 21: 21–37.

Hooghe, L. (2001) *The European Commission and the Integration of Europe: Images of Governance*. Cambridge: Cambridge University Press.

Hooghe, L. and Keating, M. (1994) 'The politics of European Union regional policy', *Journal of European Public Policy*, 1(3): 367–93.

Höreth, M. (1999) 'No way out for the beast? The unresolved legitimacy problem of European governance', *Journal of European Public Policy*, 6(2): 183–205.

Huber, J.D. and Shipan, C.R. (2002) *Deliberate Discretion? The Institutional Foundations of Bureaucratic Autonomy*. Cambridge: Cambridge University Press.

Issing, O. (1999) 'The Eurosystem: transparent and accountable or "Willem in Euroland"', *Journal of Common Market Studies*, 37(3): 503–19.

Jabko, N. (2003) 'Democracy in the age of the Euro', *Journal of European Public Policy*, 10(5): 710–39.

Joerges, C. and Neyer, J. (1997a) 'From intergovernmental bargaining to deliberative political process: the constitutionalization of comitology', *European Law Journal*, 3: 273–99.

Joerges, C. and Neyer, J. (1997b) 'Transforming strategic interaction into deliberative problem-solving: European comitology in the foodstuffs sector', *Journal of European Public Policy*, 4: 609–25.

Karlsson, C. (2001) 'Democracy, legitimacy and the European Union'. PhD dissertation, Uppsala University.

Kassim, H. and Menon, A. (2003) 'The principal-agent approach and the study of the European Union: promise unfulfilled?' *Journal of European Public Policy*, 10(1): 121–39.

Kelemen, R.D. (2002) 'The politics of "Eurocratic" structure and the new European agencies', *West European Politics*, 25(4): 93–118.

Kingdon, J.W. (1984) *Agendas, Alternatives, and Public Policies*. Boston, MA: Little, Brown.

Kreher, A. (1997) 'Agencies in the European community: a step towards administrative integration in Europe', *Journal of European Public Policy*, 4: 225–45.

Laffan, B. (1997) 'From policy entrepreneur to policy manager: the challenge facing the European Commission', *Journal of European Public Policy*, 4: 422–38.

Lindberg, L.N. and Scheingold, S.A. (1970) *Europe's Would-Be Polity. Patterns of Change in the European Community*. Englewood Cliffs, NJ: Prentice-Hall.

Lord, C. (1998) *Democracy in the European Union*. Sheffield: Sheffield University Press.

Ludlow, P. (1991) 'The European Commission', in R.O. Keohane and S. Hoffmann (eds), *The New European Community: Decisionmaking and Institutional Change*. Boulder, CO: Westview Press. pp. 85–132.

Macmullen, A. (1997) 'European Commissioners 1952–1995: national routes to a European elite', in N. Nugent (ed.), *At the Heart of the Union: Studies of the European Commission*. Basingstoke: Macmillan. pp. 27–48.

Majone, G. (1996) *Regulating Europe*. London: Routledge.

Majone, G. (1997) 'The new European agencies: regulation by information', *Journal of European Public Policy*, 4(2): 262–75.

Majone, G. (1998) 'Europe's "democratic deficit": the question of standards', *European Law Journal*, 4(1): 5–28.

Majone, G. (1999) 'The regulatory state and its legitimacy problems', *West European Politics*, 22(1): 1–24.

Majone, G. (2000) 'The credibility crisis of Community regulation', *Journal of Common Market Studies*, 38(2): 273–302.

Majone, G. (2001) 'Two logics of delegation: agency and fudiciary relations in EU governance', *European Union Politics*, 2(1): 103–21.

Majone, G. (2002) 'The European Commission: the limits of centralization and the perils of parliamentarization', *Governance*, 15(3): 375–92.

Mancini, G.F. (1998) 'Europe: the case for statehood', *European Law Journal*, 4(1): 29–42.

March, J.G. and Olsen, J.P. (1989) *Rediscovering Institutions: The Organizational Basis of Politics*. New York: The Free Press.

Marcussen, M. (2000) *Ideas and Elites: The Social Construction of Economic and Monetary Union*. Aalborg: Aalborg University Press.

Matlary, J.H. (1997) *Energy Policy in the European Union*. Basingstoke: Macmillan.

Mazey, S. (1995) 'The development of EU equality policies: bureaucratic expansion on behalf of women?' *Public Administration*, 73(4): 591–609.

McCubbins, M.D. and Page, T. (1987) 'A theory of congressional delegation', in M.D. McCubbins and T. Sullivan (eds), *Congress: Structure and Policy*. New York: Cambridge University Press.

McCubbins, M.D. and Schwartz, T. (1984) 'Congressional oversight overlooked: police patrols versus fire alarms', *American Journal of Political Science*, 28(1): 165–79.

McCubbins, M.D., Noll, R.G. and Weingast, B.R. (1987) 'Administrative procedures as instruments of political control', *Journal of Law, Economics, and Organization*, 3(2): 243–77.

McDonald, M. (1997) 'Identities in the European commission', in N. Nugent (ed.), *At the Heart of the Union: Studies of the European Commission*. Basingstoke: Macmillan. pp. 49–70.

McGowan, L. (1997) 'Safeguarding the economic constitution: the Commission and competition policy', in N. Nugent (ed.), *At the Heart of the Union: Studies of the European Commission*. Basingstoke: Macmillan. pp. 145–66.

McKay, D. (1999) *Federalism and the European Union*. Oxford: Oxford University Press.

McNamara, K.R. (2002) 'Rational fictions: central bank independence and the social logic of delegation', *West European Politics*, 25(1): 47–76.

Metcalfe, L. (1992) 'After 1992: can the Commission manage Europe?' *Australian Journal of Public Administration*, 51: 117–30.

Meunier, S. (2000) 'What single voice? European institutions and EU–U.S. trade negotiations', *International Organization*, 54(1): 103–35.

Meunier, S. and Nicolaïdis, K. (1999) 'Who speaks for Europe? The delegation of trade authority in the EU', *Journal of Common Market Studies*, 37(3): 477–501.

Moravcsik, A. (1991) 'Negotiating the Single European Act', *International Organization*, 45(1): 651–88.

Moravcsik, A. (1993) 'Preferences and power in the European Community: a liberal intergovernmentalist approach', *Journal of Common Market Studies*, 31(4): 473–524.

Moravcsik, A. (1998) *The Choice for Europe: Social Purpose and State Power from Messina to Maastricht*. Ithaca, NY: Cornell University Press.

Moravcsik, A. (2002) 'Reassessing legitimacy in the European Union', *Journal of Common Market Studies*, 40(4): 603–24.

Nicolaïdis, K. (1999) 'Minimizing agency costs in two-level games: lessons from the trade authority controversies in the United States and the European Union', in R.M. Mnookin and L.E. Susskind (eds), *Negotiating on Behalf of Others*. Thousand Oaks, CA: Sage. pp. 87–126.

Nugent, N. (ed.) (1997) *At the Heart of the Union: Studies of the European Commission*. Basingstoke: Macmillan.

Nugent, N. (2001) *The European Commission.* Basingstoke: Palgrave.

Peters, B.G. (1997) 'The Commission and implementation in the European Union: is there an implementation deficit and why?', in N. Nugent (ed.), *At the Heart of the Union: Studies of the European Commission.* Basingstoke: Macmillan. pp. 187–202.

Peterson, J. (1995) 'EU research policy: the politics of expertise', in C. Rhodes and S. Mazey (eds), *The State of the European Union, Volume 3, Building a European Polity?* Boulder, CO: Lynne Rienner.

Pollack, M.A. (1997) 'Delegation, agency, and agenda-setting in the European community', *International Organization,* 51(1): 99–134.

Pollack, M. (2002) 'Learning from the Americanists (again): theory and method in the study of delegation', *West European Politics,* 25(1): 200–19.

Pollack, M.A. (2003) *The Engines of European Integration: Delegation, Agency, and Agenda Setting in the EU.* Oxford: Oxford University Press.

Powell, W.W. and DiMaggio, P.J. (eds) (1991) *The New Institutionalism in Organizational Analysis.* Chicago, IL: The University of Chicago Press.

Risse, T. (2000) '"Let's argue!": communicative action in world politics', *International Organization,* 54(1): 1–39.

Rittberger, B. (2001) 'Which institutions for Europe? Explaining the institutional design of Europe's first community', *Journal of European Public Policy,* 8: 673–708.

Ross, G. (1994) 'Inside the Delors cabinet', *Journal of Common Market Studies,* 32(4): 499–523.

Ross, G. (1995) *Jacques Delors and European Integration.* Cambridge: Polity Press.

Sandholtz, W. (1992) 'ESPRIT and the politics of international collective action', *Journal of Common Market Studies,* 30(1): 1–21.

Sandholtz, W. and Zysman, J. (1989) '1992: recasting the European bargain', *World Politics,* 42(1): 95–128.

Schmidt, S.K. (1998) 'Commission activism: subsuming telecommunications and electricity under European competition law', *Journal of European Public Policy,* 5(1): 169–84.

Schmidt, S. (2000) 'Only an agenda setter? The European Commission's power over the council of ministers', *European Union Politics,* 1(1): 37–61.

Schmitter, P. (2000) *How to Democratize the European Union...and Why Bother?* Lanham: Rowman & Littlefield Publishers.

Schumpeter, J.A. (1943) *Capitalism, Socialism, and Democracy.* London: Allen & Unwin.

Scott, W.R., Meyer, J.W., and associates (1994) *Institutional Environments and Organizations: Structural Complexity and Individualism.* London: Sage.

Shapiro, M. (1997) 'The problem of independent agencies in the United States and the European Union', *Journal of European Public Policy,* 4: 276–91.

Smith, A. (2003) 'Why European Commissioners matter', *Journal of Common Market Studies,* 41(1): 137–55.

Smyrl, M.E. (1998) 'When (and how) do the commission's preferences matter?' *Journal of Common Market Studies,* 36(1): 79–100.

Stevens, A. and Stevens, H. (2001) *Brussels Bureaucrats? The Administration of the European Union.* Basingstoke: Palgrave.

Stone Sweet, A. and Sandholtz, W. (1997) 'European integration and supranational governance', *Journal of European Public Policy,* 4(3): 297–317.

Strøm, K., Müller, W.C. and Bergman, T. (eds) (2003) *Delegation and Accountability in Parliamentary Democracies.* Oxford: Oxford University Press.

Tallberg, J. (2000) 'The anatomy of autonomy: an institutional account of variation in supranational influence', *Journal of Common Market Studies,* 38(5): 843–64.

Tallberg, J. (2002) 'Delegation to supranational institutions: why, how, and with what consequences?' *West European Politics,* 25(1): 23–46.

Tallberg, J. (2003) *European Governance and Supranational Institutions: Making States Comply.* London: Routledge.

Thatcher, M. and Stone Sweet, A. (2002) 'Theory and practice of delegation to non-majoritarian institutions', *West European Politics,* 25(1): 1–22.

Verdun, A. (1998) 'The institutional design of EMU: a democratic deficit?' *Journal of Public Policy,* 18: 107–32.

Verdun, A. (1999) 'The role of the Delors committee in the creation of EMU: an epistemic community?' *Journal of European Public Policy,* 6(2): 308–28.

10

Judicial Politics

LISA CONANT

Scholarly interest in European Union (EU) judicial politics emerged with the European Coal and Steel Community (ECSC) and expanded dramatically with the Single European Act (SEA). As a supranational court, the Court of Justice of the European Communities (ECJ) attracted the attention of legal and political observers who were curious to assess the prospects for transcending sovereignty. Early accounts of the role of law were not optimistic (Scheingold 1965, 1971), however, and when the momentum of integration slowed in the 1970s, political scientists abandoned the study of the ECJ altogether. Meanwhile, legal scholarship uncovered a transformation of European law: the Treaty of Rome functioned as a constitution since it conferred rights and obligations on individuals and states alike and reigned supreme over national law (Stein 1981; Weiler 1982; 1991; Everling 1984; Hartley 1986). Only later did political scientists discover this development as progress toward the internal market and single currency rekindled interest in the integration project. Parallel to the broader EU literature, a debate between rational choice institutionalists and neofunctionalists ensued as scholars

adapted theories of international organization and regional integration to frame the first explanations of EU judicial authority (Garrett 1992; Burley and Mattli 1993). This international relations debate, with its focus on the relative power of the member states and supranational legal institutions, animates much of the EU judicial politics literature. The renewal of interest in legal integration coincided with a newfound interest in the political role of courts around the world, and political scientists began to study EU judicial politics in light of domestic public-law literatures (Conant 2002; Kelemen 2003). An increasing number of scholars have adopted a comparative approach, developing arguments that are as relevant to national courts as they are to the supranational ECJ. I will argue that the EU legal system shares a closer institutional affinity with domestic, rather than international, legal systems. As a result, future scholarship could more fruitfully explore the dynamics of EU judicial politics by taking theoretical inspiration from the nuanced studies of judicial politics in domestic settings.

The chapter proceeds in three sections. The first provides an overview of the initial accounts of EU judicial politics, which generated a debate addressing the puzzles of international relations theory. The second summarizes the empirical findings of subsequent scholarship that tests competing expectations and extends the analysis into the domain of comparative politics. Finally, the third section and conclusion discuss an emerging literature that situates EU judicial politics within a domesticated political context, which generates questions that reach beyond the classic concerns of integration theory.

DOES EU JUDICIAL POLITICS TRANSCEND SOVEREIGNTY? DECLARING AND THEORIZING THE TAMING OF THE SHREW

The ambitions of the Treaty of Paris, which first established the ECJ to adjudicate ECSC disputes, inspired scrutiny by political scientists. Observing an institutional structure that was prone to gridlock, Stuart Scheingold expected that aggrieved parties would regularly engage the Court to overcome paralysis in the legislative institutions (1965). Later accounts emphasize this dynamic as one that generates opportunities for the ECJ to impose its choices (Tsebelis and Garrett 2001), but Scheingold argued that the inability of the legislative institutions to respond to demands for change could saddle the ECJ with a disproportionate burden and lead to a situation in which the law on the books and the law in practice become increasingly disparate (1965). In a subsequent study, Scheingold (1971: 47) found little evidence that the ECJ could impose legal solutions on difficult problems and identified a considerable 'gap between the assertive rhetoric of the Court of Justice and the modest role judges have played in the policy process'. As the demands of unanimous voting in the Council of Ministers slowed progress in the 1970s, scholarly interest waned and political scientists abandoned the ECJ as a subject of inquiry.

Meanwhile, legal scholars identified how ECJ decisions limited sovereignty and forged a new supranational legal order. Most importantly, the doctrine of direct effect transformed European treaties and legislation from traditional international laws that governed inter-state relations into a set of higher-order legal norms that bind private and public actors alike, and the doctrine of supremacy subordinated national law to European law. Observing that states originally rejected these principles, legal scholars attribute the ultimate acceptance of a directly effective and supreme European legal order to factors such as the functional necessity that all states obey the same rules, unanimous consent of member states to European provisions, respect for judicial independence, confidence in the neutrality and legitimacy of legal processes, and deference to the national courts that enforce many ECJ judgments (Stein 1981; Weiler 1982, 1991; Everling 1984; Hartley 1986).[1]

The striking claims of this legal literature, along with the SEA's rejuvenation of integration, renewed interest in EU judicial politics among political scientists. In a review essay of public law scholarship, Martin Shapiro lamented that two decades of neglect had caused American political science to miss 'arguably the most significant judicial instrument of political development in the twentieth century' (Shapiro 1993: 368). Volcansek (1992) observed that the ECJ played a crucial role in supranational policymaking in a special issue on judicial politics in *West European Politics*. In a subsequent special issue on European constitutional politics in *Comparative Political Studies*, Shapiro and Stone Sweet (1994: 408) argued that the ECJ 'has been a major player in the state-building enterprise. There are few instances as observable and as important as the ECJ case of a court building itself as a political institution, and building the whole set of institutions of which it is a part'.

The specter of a supranational court eliciting the obedience of states was puzzling from the perspective of traditional international relations theories. Geoffrey Garrett advanced one of the first explanations of EU judicial politics in his account of the internal market program of 1992. Addressing debates in international organization and political economy, Garrett developed a rational choice institutionalist explanation of the

ECJ's role. In this account, the ECJ's mandate derives from its collective utility in enforcing pre-established bargains related to trade liberalization and efficiently filling gaps in the 'incomplete contract' of European law. Garrett initially claimed that the ECJ encourages compliance by aligning its decisions with the preferences of the most powerful member states (Garrett 1992, 1995). Garrett and his collaborators later refined their position on judicial strategy, arguing that a tension between legal consistency and politically acceptable rulings generates strategic interactions that preserve the appearance of judicial autonomy while simultaneously respecting member state interests. Finally, the ECJ tolerates periodic non-compliance to ward off formal efforts to reverse its case law or limit its jurisdiction (Garrett et al. 1998). Consistent with realist approaches to international relations, member states submit to nothing that poses a serious threat to their interests.

Garrett ultimately abandoned this adversarial dichotomy between supranational and national institutions and developed a model to explain interactions of the EU institutions within the evolving rules established by the treaties. In this account, the ECJ enjoyed a great deal of autonomy to push integration forward in the era prior to the SEA because member states needed to agree unanimously to all reforms. Although qualified majority voting simplified efforts to overturn unwelcome ECJ decisions legislatively, the shift toward a genuinely bicameral legislative regime with the increase in the power of the European Parliament should mean a return to substantial gridlock and therefore greater autonomy for the ECJ (Tsebelis and Garrett 2001). Relying entirely on a logic of institutional rules that could be applied within domestic political contexts, the most recent rational choice institutionalism has left the international relations framework behind and situated the EU in the realm of comparative politics.

Widespread acceptance that the ECJ acts as an authoritative institution emerged in the context of a scholarly dialogue among these rational choice institutionalists and other scholars. Garrett's early dismissals of the

ECJ's autonomy inspired a challenge by neofunctionalists who contended that legal integration eroded the dominance of states. Adapted from Ernst Haas' pioneering work, the neofunctionalist legal dynamic involves a technocratic network of experts (lawyers, national judges, law professors, ECJ judges) that conspires with societal actors (private litigants) who have an incentive to promote regional cooperation. Blending legal and political logic, Anne-Marie Slaughter and Walter Mattli argue that the ECJ appeals to shared professional norms and self-interests to co-opt national judiciaries and constrain national governments. In this account, convincing legal argumentation legitimates ECJ rulings in the eyes of legal professionals, and the ability of national judges to refer questions of EU law to the ECJ for preliminary rulings – combined with the direct effect and supremacy of EU law – creates or expands national judges' opportunities to exercise judicial review. Meanwhile, law professors generate a market for their European expertise in universities by stressing the importance of ECJ case law, and lawyers benefit from an additional avenue to protect their clients' interests. Finally, national governments accept ECJ decisions because legal justifications 'mask' the implications of rulings and 'shield' the ECJ and its accomplices from attack (Burley and Mattli 1993; Mattli and Slaughter 1995). While this neofunctionalist account challenged rational choice institutionalists to take legal consistency seriously, the debate also led neofunctionalists to recognize the intrusion of politics in the law. Although Mattli and Slaughter reject the notion that judges can legitimately deploy overtly political arguments, they nonetheless accept that courts cannot stray too far from majority political preferences if they wish to avoid legislative efforts to restrict their jurisdiction. By arguing that judges avoid such political attacks (Mattli and Slaughter 1998), the neofunctionalists converged toward the rational choice institutionalists and also situated the logic of EU judicial politics within a broader comparative framework that is relevant beyond the unique supranational context.

The audacious claims of supranational judicial power, alongside the theoretical debate between rational choice institutionalists and neofunctionalists, sparked new research agendas. This early literature remained largely theoretical and descriptive, with next to no systematic empirical testing of competing accounts. Subsequent waves of scholarship test competing claims against empirical evidence and specify theoretical expectations related to more complex institutional relations.

OPENING UP THE BLACK BOX: INTERACTIONS BETWEEN LAW, POLITICS, AND SOCIETY

Much of the literature explaining EU judicial politics remains framed to speak to the international relations debate about the relative power of EU and national institutions. The first empirical tests of competing hypotheses from this debate emerged just as the theoretical accounts began to converge. A literature specifying the nature of interactions between law, politics, and society in the EU has focused on: (1) quantitative and qualitative analysis of ECJ case law; (2) the participation of national courts in the EU legal system; and (3) the institutional dynamics that generate variable degrees of autonomy.

Analysis of ECJ Case Law: Neofunctionalism vs. Rational Choice Institutionalism

Alec Stone Sweet and Thomas Brunell developed the neofunctionalist account by specifying the origins of variations in societal demand for legal integration and testing the relationship between intra-EU trade, national court references to the ECJ, and density of EU legislation. In this account, societal interactions generate conflicts over the underlying rules governing exchange relations. EU judges and legislators resolve these disputes by creating new legal norms to govern transactions. By decreasing contracting costs, the new rules encourage more exchange, which ultimately leads to more conflicts that reactivate the initial cycle. The rising tide of cross-border transactions in the EU, combined with the operation of EU institutions, fuel the expansion of EU law and promote the autonomy of the ECJ. To test the hypothesis that societal demands drive legal integration, Stone Sweet and Brunell created a data set of all national court references from 1961 to the mid-1990s, which they coded by country and court of origin, date of referral, and subject matter (available at http://www.iue.it/RSCAS/Research/Tools/ReferencesECLaw/Index.shtml). Relating this data to trade flows, Stone Sweet and Brunell find strongly positive linear relationships between: (1) the level of trade between member states and the total number of references their courts send to the ECJ; and (2) intra-EU trade flows, the production of EU secondary legislation, and rising national court references (Stone Sweet and Brunell 1998a). Since they did not eliminate references that have nothing to do with trade, however, the model includes spurious correlation. Another study that correlated sources of societal demand for EU law, including the volume of trade and the size of EU migrant worker populations, to references related to those subjects found weaker and less conclusive relationships (Golub 1996a).

Scholars have begun to examine ECJ case law systematically in order to test the competing claims in the literature concerning the extent to which: (1) societal actors can successfully deploy the EU legal system against national governments; and (2) the ECJ rules to placate member states or to promote European integration and its own autonomy. Stone Sweet and Brunell tracked the outcomes of ECJ preliminary rulings in 91 cases on social policy from their data set of references in order to determine the propensity of the ECJ to rule for or against member states as it evaluated alleged violations of EU law. They found that litigants disproportionately attacked national rules that represented the lowest common denominator positions in Council legislation, and that the ECJ ruled against member states in 53 per cent of its decisions and aligned its judgment with the position advocated by the European Commission in 88 per cent of cases (Stone Sweet and Brunell 1998a: 76). Interpreting this to confirm ECJ autonomy and allegiance with societal interests and other EU institutions, Stone Sweet and Brunell support the neofunctionalist position. Stone Sweet's recent book elaborates this model in greater depth and adds a parallel case study of the environment to analyses of trade and social provisions (2004).

In another study drawn from the same data set, Rachel Cichowski examined 36 environmental disputes that originated in national-court references to the ECJ from 1976 to 1996 and found that litigants disproportionately attacked the member states who either opposed EU environmental cooperation (e.g. France), took the most cavalier attitude toward implementation (Italy), or upheld strict standards that generate obstacles to trade (Netherlands). Parallel to the study of social policy, the ECJ did not hesitate to confront member states, declaring national violations of EU law in 47 per cent of all environmental litigation and siding with the position of the European Commission 97 per cent of the time. The ECJ was less likely to reject the manner in which national governments transposed EU environmental directives, however, finding national practices to be incompatible with EU law in only 18 per cent of these cases. Finally, when faced with a conflict between environmental protection and free trade, the ECJ favored free trade norms in 66 per cent of cases (Cichowski 1998: 396–7). Cichowski's study supports a neofunctionalist reading of interactions between societal interests, EU institutions, and member states, therefore, but its nuances also suggest a Court that defers to national efforts to comply with EU rules and favors the business interests within society over those of environmentalists and citizens.

Bernadette Kilroy completed the largest study of ECJ case law to date on the relationship between ECJ decisions and member state preferences. Her original data set includes 293 randomly selected ECJ judgments on the free movement of goods and social provisions from 1958 to 1994. This data set is the first to include not only the preliminary rulings that derive from national-court references, but also direct actions, which are cases litigated at the ECJ and/or Court of First Instance that are initiated by an EU institution, member state, or private party who is directly targeted by an action of an EU institution. After coding documented observations and ECJ decisions, Kilroy used an ordered probit analysis to estimate the likely effect of the independent variable, such as an observation that supports a national measure, on the dependent variable: the ECJ decision to declare a violation of EU law or not. Parallel to the findings of those advocating the neofunctionalist approach, Kilroy found that the ECJ declared a national violation of EU law in 55 per cent of cases, upheld national law in 36 per cent of cases, and took an intermediate position in the remainder of judgments. Furthermore, Kilroy did not find any evidence to support Garrett's hypothesis that the ECJ is most likely to rule in favor of the preferences of larger member states. Kilroy's findings do suggest, however, that the expression of support for a national rule by any member state other than Italy (whose compliance record is notoriously bad) increases the likelihood that the ECJ will not declare a violation of EU law (Kilroy 1999: 400). The hypothesis that the ECJ would defer to member states if a qualified majority of them expressed support for a national position was not testable since too few cases included observations from a qualified majority. Kilroy argues that her findings support the hypothesis that the ECJ rules to avoid noncompliance with its rulings, however, because the expression of a position by a simple majority, a blocking minority, or even a smaller coalition of member states has a statistically significant effect on the probability of a particular type of ECJ ruling. She found that the probability of the ECJ upholding a national rule was only 23 per cent when no member state makes an observation, but increased to: (1) 73 to 96 per cent when a simple majority of member states articulates support for a national rule; and (2) 56 per cent in the case of support from a blocking minority (Kilroy 1999: 405–6). This evidence supports the hypothesis on which rational choice institutionalists and neofunctionalists largely converged: the ECJ is unlikely to rule against majority preferences.

Further tests of the contending theories yield conflicting results. R. Daniel Kelemen examined all ECJ cases adjudicating disputes about competing trade and environment norms up through 1997 and found evidence to support the 'convergence' hypothesis that courts are strategic actors seeking to maintain their legitimacy by avoiding rulings that will be rejected. Advancing a view of EU judicial politics that is relevant to a broader comparative context, Kelemen situates his study in the context of the positive political theory of courts pioneered by scholars of US courts and compares the EU case to GATT/WTO dispute resolution panels. The small number of cases in this area allowed qualitative analysis of the political and economic interests at stake in each dispute. Kelemen found that ECJ decisions accommodate political demands when political pressures to uphold national measures are high and legal pressures to invalidate are low. In cases where political and legal pressures were low or mixed, however, ECJ decisions were mixed as well, but Kelemen concludes, in contrast to Cichowski (1998), that the ECJ has not routinely ruled against national environmental standards in disputes alleging trade barriers (Kelemen 2001).

In contrast to the conclusions of Kilroy and Kelemen, recent analyses of ECJ case law find support for neofunctionalism. To examine the impact of ECJ decisions on the intergovernmental Council of Ministers, Margaret McCown analysed 25 cases brought by the European Parliament in its efforts to gain standing to challenge other EU institutions and increase its legislative powers. McCown advances the hypothesis that judicial precedents influence how litigants subsequently premise, structure, and sequence their arguments in legal proceedings, with the result that gradual changes in litigants' positions lead to the incremental acceptance of once unwelcome ECJ rules. McCown argues that the effectiveness of making arguments that are embedded in past ECJ case law leads litigants to accept prior principles while they simultaneously try to qualify and distinguish the facts of new cases in order to achieve new outcomes. Tracking the response of the Council of Ministers to Parliamentary legal challenges, McCown concludes that intergovernmental actors do not attack ECJ decisions directly, but defensively argue in favor of narrow readings of past precedents. Over time, this results in a process of dispute resolution that is increasingly based on the acceptance of previous case law (McCown 2003). While framing her inquiry and results in terms of the adversarial dichotomy between intergovernmental and supranational institutions, McCown draws comparisons between the impact of precedents and the operation of informal institutions that are relevant to broader debates in comparative politics.

In one of the most recent studies of ECJ case law, Cichowski examined all 88 ECJ preliminary rulings related to social provisions from 1971 to 1993 and found that 56 per cent of judgments declared a national provision to be in violation of EU law. Once again, the ECJ did not shy from confronting more powerful member states, declaring violations against the four largest member states in 57 per cent of cases. Similar to other studies, the European Commission's observations were the most likely (91 per cent) to predict the ECJ's decision. Finally, Cichowski uses the number of member states submitting observations as an indicator of the political and financial significance of a dispute, where a larger number of observations indicates a case with more substantial policy implications. Although she does not provide information about how many observations it takes to get assigned to a low or high magnitude ranking, Cichowski claims that the ECJ declared national practices to be in violation of EU law in 100 per cent of cases with the highest magnitude ranking, in contrast to declaring violations in only 52 per cent of cases with the lowest magnitude ranking (Cichowski 2004: 495–500). Cichowski interprets her findings to support neofunctionalist claims that legal integration operates to diminish member state control over the evolution of EU law and empower individuals in their pursuit of self-interest.

Discrepancies in the findings of these studies, however, limit the number of definitive conclusions this literature produces. Although all of the analyses of case law involve similar schemes to code cases and examine some combination of the same policy areas (free movement of goods, social provisions, environment), methodological differences and case selection nonetheless generate contradictory findings. First, Kilroy's regression analysis (probit) of direct actions and preliminary rulings yields a fundamentally different result than Cichowski's descriptive statistics on preliminary rulings in that Kilroy finds that the expression of support for a national rule by any member state except Italy decreases the chance that the ECJ declares a violation of EU law (Kilroy 1999: 400) while Cichowski draws attention to the fact that the ECJ declared violations in all cases in which many member states made observations (2004: 499–500). By counting observations, but not coding who sided with whom, however, Cichowski is unable to track the influence that member state observations might have had on the ECJ. For instance, member states may intervene in a case in order to express their disapproval of another member state's national law and their agreement with the European Commission. If the ECJ then declared a violation, it would be siding with one or more member states against another. Moreover, proponents of neofunctionalism limit their case-law analyses to preliminary rulings, presumably on the grounds that these cases arise from society in national courts. The fact that direct actions constitute just under half of all ECJ cases, however, makes neofunctionalist claims about ECJ autonomy suspect since nearly half of the possible cases are missing from the analysis. Second, Kelemen's qualitative analysis of the politics behind direct actions and preliminary rulings concerning environmental disputes leads him to conclude that the ECJ responds affirmatively to political pressure and does not systematically favor free trade over environmental protection (2001), while Cichowski's more quantitative coding of member state observations and ECJ preliminary rulings in environmental disputes leads her to conclude that the ECJ acts autonomously of member states and privileges free trade norms (1998).

Consensus emerged on two findings nonetheless: the ECJ does not appear to favor larger over smaller member states and is most likely to agree with the legal analysis of the European Commission. The first finding suggests that the ECJ operates as any legitimate court should, with a healthy degree of fairness. The second finding is parallel to the similarly high success rate of the US Solicitor General in federal litigation, which is broadly indicative of the advantages gained by repeat players (Galanter 1974) who possess specialized information and control over prosecution in the case of infringement proceedings (included in Kilroy's and Kelemen's studies). The remaining disagreement about the responsiveness of the ECJ to member state interests might be fruitfully read outside the international relations frame, as an indication that the ECJ is a typical judicial institution that periodically must consider political factors in its legal deliberations.

The Participation of National Courts in the EU Legal System: Contested and Variable?

A second focus of empirical inquiry in EU judicial politics includes the role that national courts play. Many accounts address the puzzle of an apparently effective supranational legal system, but their explanations tend to be grounded in political dynamics that travel well to domestic settings. Karen Alter advanced neofunctionalist analysis by specifying national judicial interests to cooperate with the ECJ, but her explanation of judicial competition also contributes more broadly to comparative understandings of judicial politics. Observing that national supreme courts sit at the apex of national legal hierarchies and therefore face demotion in the event of the supremacy and direct effect of EU law, interpreted conclusively by the ECJ, Alter problematized the earlier neofunctionalist assumption that the EU legal system empowers all national judges. National supreme courts could traditionally reverse unwelcome decisions by lower-court judges, but a reference by a lower court to the ECJ for a preliminary ruling circumvents national review processes. The EU legal system offered the opportunity to exercise judicial review to all national judges, but Alter demonstrates that lower-court judges faced the strongest incentive to send references to the ECJ because they experienced empowerment relative to their past position and superior national judges by doing so. Using qualitative case studies of French and German courts, Alter demonstrates that the stream of references from lower courts led higher courts to begin to send their own references in an effort to influence the ECJ because nothing could stop the tide of lower-court references and supreme courts shied from the controversy that overt defiance threatened (Alter 1996, 2001). Alter and Weiler (1994) attribute much of the success of the ECJ in gaining compliance with its rulings to the fact that national courts enforce over half of all ECJ rulings through this decentralized reference procedure. Broader aggregate studies of reference activity confirm the greater propensity of lower and intermediate national courts to send references to the ECJ (Stone Sweet and Brunell 1998b; Conant 2002: 85).

Existing research on British judges' responses to the opportunity for empowerment through the EU legal system produces mixed results. Although references for preliminary rulings from courts in the United Kingdom (UK) approximated those of France during the first decade and a half of each state's membership, UK references subsequently grew more slowly and remain disproportionately low in comparison to the UK's population size and intra-EU trade activity (Weiler and Dehousse 1992; Golub 1996a; Stone Sweet and Brunell 1998a; Conant 2001: 106; Jupille and Caporaso 2005). In a recent study tracking UK judgments in the Lexis database, Joseph Jupille and James Caporaso note an increase in the presence of words and principles associated with EU law including 'Europe(an)', 'judicial review', and 'proportionality'. The authors attribute the steady increase in the presence of these terms overtime, and steep rate of growth after 1998 and especially 2000, to a process of Europeanization that is reconfiguring domestic sovereignty in favor of the British judiciary (Jupille and Caporaso 2005). These findings remain tentative, however, because the mere

presence of a word in a judgment does not mean that it was a legal basis on which a decision turned, 'Europe(an)' catches references to the European Convention on (and Court of) Human Rights, and 'judicial review' catches references to the traditional British practice of judicial review of administrative action for conformity with Parliamentary statute. The authors try to focus on European judicial review processes by tracking the presence of both terms in the same judgments, but even here, the uptick in references could be an artifact of the 1998 passage of the Human Rights Act and its 2000 incorporation of European Convention norms into national law.[2] Future research could examine the rate at which UK courts invoke precise EU legal bases over time. Damian Chalmers' study of all reported UK national court judgments on EU law from 1973 to 1998, which may just miss the surge that Jupille and Caporaso observe, suggests that British judges have not embraced opportunities for judicial empowerment. After analysing the content of all judgments, Chalmers demonstrates that UK courts typically apply EU provisions without directly addressing the status of incompatible national provisions, and judges entertained the question of whether national legislation might need to be suspended in only *two* cases (Chalmers 2000).

Despite trends of increasing interaction between national courts and the EU legal system, a growing body of research demonstrates that national judges contest many EU legal developments. Doctrinal analyses have demonstrated that many national courts did not readily accept the ECJ's rulings on direct effect and supremacy (Slaughter et al. 1998), and some constitutional courts that accepted the basic operation of the EU legal system nonetheless justified EU legal supremacy according to their own terms in order to leave the door open to reassert domestic constitutional norms (Boom 1995; Alter 1996: 479; Conant 2002: 93; Ruggiero 2002). In a study of British courts resolving environmental disputes, Jonathan Golub demonstrates that British judges interpreted EU law independently, refraining from sending references to the ECJ when they wanted to shield domestic practices from unwelcome ECJ rulings (Golub 1996b). Such strategic action by national courts is confirmed in a broader study as well. Stacy Nyikos examined national-court references, ECJ responses to those references, and national-court implementation of preliminary rulings to explore how *all* judges try to increase their autonomy. Building on Alter's contribution, Nyikos finds that national courts include opinions with their questions in an effort to influence the ECJ, the ECJ redefines issues in cases by adding or suppressing questions, and national courts typically comply with ECJ decisions but also evade unwelcome decisions by re-referring issues or reinterpreting the facts of cases (Nyikos 2000). While her research challenges the notion of a clear European judicial hierarchy, it also normalizes EU judicial politics by comparing strategies of issue definition to practices of the US Supreme Court.

More generally, existing research on national judicial practices indicates independent and variable approaches to EU legal interpretation. Data compiled on national court rulings related to EU law from the *Synopsis of the Work of the Court of Justice*, the *Annual Report of the Court of Justice*, and the European Commission's *Annual Report to the European Parliament on Monitoring the Application of Community Law* show that the overwhelming majority of all national court decisions on EU law are independent decisions that do not involve references to the ECJ (Conant 2002: 81–2). Subsequent analysis of French, German, and UK case law, drawn from the legal data bases Jurifrance (now Legifrance), Juris, and Lexis, show that national courts in all three states are more likely to interpret EU treaty provisions independently than to cite ECJ case law. All court systems except the French 'judiciary' courts were also more likely to cite EU regulations and directives than to cite ECJ case law (Conant 2002: 82–3). Analysis of the European Commission's survey of national court decisions indicates that national courts vary in the extent to which they look to ECJ preliminary rulings as sources of precedent to guide their decisions (Conant 2002: 66–8), and comparison of national court and ECJ rulings

related to nationality discrimination in public-sector employment and social benefits demonstrate that national courts do not necessarily refer cases that involve uncertainty about the meaning of EU law or follow ECJ principles in areas where ECJ case law exists (Conant 2002: 173–4, 209–10). Chalmers' comprehensive study of EU legal claims in UK courts shows that efforts to invoke EU law are more successful when EU law extends state powers to control behavior or reinforce private legal relationships and less successful when EU law prevents the state's promotion of collective ties, application of criminal sanctions, or protection of private property rights. These tendencies have meant that it has been easier to enforce EU sex equality provisions, which consolidate employment contracts, and more difficult to enforce free movement of persons rights, which threaten collective ties, or EU environmental and competition laws, which often disrupt private contracts (2000).

National courts' participation in the EU legal system has created a decentralized system to enforce EU law, but scholars have only begun to scratch the surface of this Europeanized judicial politics. Given that references for preliminary rulings represent the tip of an iceberg of national court interpretation of EU law, much more research on independent national judicial review of EU law is in order. Researching national case law systematically and comparatively poses many challenges because data bases on national case law possess variable analytical search capabilities (e.g. Lexis and Juris enable legal basis searching while Legifrance does not), include different fractions of the reported judgments in a country (e.g. Legifrance is more comprehensive than Lexis and Juris), operate in the languages native to the countries whose case law they index, and are not available for all member states, which leaves archival research based on much more labor-intensive searching the only option. Despite these challenges, EU judicial politics scholars should try to look beyond an exclusive focus on ECJ case law and national court references in order to explore how the majority of EU law is actually adjudicated, avoiding the blind spots associated with a disproportionate focus on a central high court and its 'constitutional' judgments, a problem Shapiro laments in the US public law literature (Gillman 2004).

Institutional Design and the Relationship between Principals and Agents

A third stream of scholarship responding to the legal integration debate specifies factors related to institutional design that privilege various organizational actors. While Garrett's rational choice institutionalism portrayed the ECJ as an agent of member state principals, with a relative emphasis on the ways in which principals constrain their agent, a number of scholars have deployed principal-agent analysis to highlight agency slippage that facilitates judicial autonomy. Alter (1998) demonstrates that member state principals intended the system of national-court references for ECJ preliminary rulings to be a mechanism to challenge EU law, not national law, but they were unable to reverse the ECJ's conversion of this system into a means of enforcing EU law because the unanimity rules that govern treaty revision and many forms of secondary legislation preserve ECJ choices that benefit at least a single member state. By enticing national courts to send references to the ECJ and apply EU law on their own, the ECJ became a principal that established its own agents of enforcement in the member states.

In a further theoretical refinement, Jonas Tallberg brings in the 'supervisor' role from institutional economics to argue that the member states *collectively* act as a principal who adopts beneficial common policies, the European Commission and ECJ jointly act as supervisors who monitor compliance, and the member states *individually* act as agents who must implement common policies. Because two principal-agent relationships become subject to shirking – between principal and supervisor and between supervisor and agent – the range of strategies to maintain autonomy increases for both the ECJ and member states. Tallberg's analysis of state efforts to prevent and reverse the ECJ's declaration of the principle

of state liability confirms the difficulty of using treaty revision to reverse unwelcome ECJ rulings, but his research on national responses to the doctrine of state liability show that inaction has kept this remedy largely ineffective (Tallberg 2000). Parallel to Kilroy's analysis, therefore, gaps in member state implementation can act as a check on the ECJ.

Mark Pollack explicitly extends principal-agent analysis of EU judicial politics beyond the international relations debate to a broader context by comparing the constraints and opportunities of the ECJ to those faced by its national counterparts. While he finds that EU treaties delegated the classic functions emphasized by principal-agent theory – monitoring, enforcement, and incomplete contracting – to the ECJ, Pollack's comparison of the ECJ to national constitutional courts reveals that the supranational court enjoys relatively more discretion. Furthermore, member states have strategically reacted to the ECJ in this account, not by reversing past encroachments on their prerogatives, but by defining ongoing delegations of power in more limited and precise ways (Pollack 2003). In another study with broader implications for comparative politics, Dorothee Heisenberg and Amy Richmond analyse the institutional design of the ECJ and European Central Bank, arguing that the more open-ended mandate of the ECJ, while politically easier to achieve, provided the Court with an opportunity to expand its competence incrementally. This facilitated judicial empowerment but has also left the ECJ more vulnerable to political accusations that it illegitimately exceeds its mandate (Heisenberg and Richmond 2002).

DOMESTICATING THE EU AND ITS SCHOLARSHIP

This scholarship on institutional design, combined with empirical research on national court activity, cast doubt on the utility of efforts to determine whether it is the ECJ or member states that reign supreme in EU judicial politics. An increasing number of studies discussed in the preceding section, despite a focus on the novelty of a supranational legal order, nonetheless draw comparisons to other political contexts in ways that bring EU studies out of a narrow focus on a unique regional experiment. In this section, I review the growing literature that abandons the national vs. supranational dichotomy and links EU judicial politics to the broader realm of comparative politics through explicit comparisons with domestic political contexts.

Specifically, scholars have begun to ask new questions that are marginal to integration theory and derive instead from the more general judicial politics literature as they explore the factors that: (1) condition access to justice and the propensity to litigate; (2) influence the broader impact of legal developments on political outcomes; (3) characterize the organizational operation of the ECJ; and (4) affect the democratic legitimacy of the EU.

Access to Justice and Propensity to Litigate

Individual access to EU legal norms through national courts, although indirect, facilitates relatively expedient justice in the EU in comparison to other venues such as the European Court of Human Rights (ECHR), where individuals must exhaust domestic remedies before appealing 'directly' to the ECHR (Conant 2006). Studies of the sectoral concentration of references for preliminary rulings (Harlow and Rawlings 1992; Chalmers 2000; Conant 2001) and citations to ECJ case law (Conant 2002), however, demonstrate that commercial enterprises, societal interest organizations, and public enforcement agencies are the most likely to gain access to courts to enforce EU legal norms because these actors are most likely to possess the knowledge and financing necessary to engage in successful litigation. Close examination of the disproportionate concentration of UK references on EU gender equality provisions reveals the concerted efforts of a public enforcement agency, the Equal Opportunities Commission, and organized labor to sponsor litigation (Harlow

and Rawlings 1992; Alter and Vargas 2000; Conant 2001). Moreover, disproportionately high rates of UK social security references are backed by Social Security Tribunals designed to minimize the costs of bringing disputes and Citizens' Advice Bureaux that provide a unique form of legal aid (Conant 2001). Individual access to organizational support, therefore, is often crucial to achieve practical access to justice in the EU. Furthermore, relatively conservative rules on standing in EU disputes reduce opportunities for litigation that are often available in domestic settings (Alter 2000; Conant 2002).

Apart from questions of resources and standing, attitudes and practices related to litigation condition the extent to which actors seek EU legal redress: states with higher levels of domestic litigation, such as Germany, also have higher rates of EU litigation (Conant 2001), and nearly 90 per cent of interest groups operating in the EU prefer to avoid litigation as a political strategy (Kelemen 2003).

Impact of Legal Developments on Policy Reform

Research based on case studies of legal and political developments in a number of different policy areas demonstrates that innovative ECJ case law does not exert any automatic impact on outcomes outside the court room. In their research on the famous Cassis de Dijon case, Karen Alter and Sophie Meunier find that ECJ interpretation developing the novel mutual recognition approach to regulatory harmonization did not create direct policy effects. The judicial mechanism to implement mutual recognition influenced only 115 products prior to the SEA. Yet Alter and Meunier argue that the ECJ case triggered the European Commission to advocate the replacement of harmonization with mutual recognition, which then triggered the mobilization of groups who supported and opposed this change. The political struggle ultimately culminated in the SEA compromise to apply mutual recognition on top of a base of minimally harmonized standards (Alter and Meunier 1994).

In case studies examining the ECJ's application of competition rules to traditionally monopolized sectors including telecommunications, electricity, and air transport, and efforts to prohibit nationality discrimination in access to public-sector employment and social benefits, my research also demonstrates that innovative ECJ interpretation remains relevant to litigants alone until a broader mobilization of support for judicial principles develops. Building on US public law and organizations scholarship, I specify the patterns of legal and political mobilization that are most likely to contribute to broad policy changes and deduce the likelihood for various forms of mobilization according to the magnitude and distribution of consequences associated with ECJ interpretation: Intense interest in high-magnitude costs and benefits that are concentrated is likely to inspire collective political and legal mobilization by organized actors that may largely ratify (telecommunications) or delay and dilute (electricity and air transport) judicial choices, while intense interest in high-magnitude costs and benefits that are diffused is likely to inspire individual legal mobilization that is unlikely to affect outcomes beyond the courtroom (most of the social benefits litigation) unless institutional support emerges to sustain legal pressures to reform broader policy (public-sector employment). In these accounts, actors most advantaged in political arenas retain important advantages over actors who are disadvantaged in political arenas because the ability to organize collective action, track official developments, and raise funds are valuable in political and legal arenas (Conant 2002, 2003, 2004). Tanja Börzel's case study examining the enforcement of EU environmental law in Germany and Spain reveals the same empowerment of the already powerful within EU legal arenas (Börzel 2006).

R. Daniel Kelemen draws on studies of regulatory federalism in the US to argue that the development of EU rights and fragmented European regulatory process encourage adversarial legalism in the EU, which is characterized by detailed and prescriptive rules, transparency and disclosure requirements, formal and adversarial dispute resolution, costly legal contestation, frequent judicial intervention in administration, and frequent litigation by public authorities and private parties (Kelemen 2003). In case studies on equal treatment, free movement, securities regulation, and environmental protection, Kelemen demonstrates that adversarial legalism is beginning to manifest itself in a variety of policy areas in the EU (Kelemen 2006).

Organizational Operation

Scholars have started to investigate the organizational operation of EU judicial politics in comparative terms. Sally Kenney, for example, examines the ECJ as an organization, drawing on organizational and feminist theory pioneered in domestic political settings. In a study based on interviews and observation of oral hearings at the ECJ, Kenney explores the role of référendaires (law clerks) and contrasts their activities to law clerks in the US Supreme Court. While some of the differences between clerks in the two settings derive from the international status of the ECJ, such as the importance of providing linguistic and EU legal expertise, most of the distinctions emerge from contrasts in the ways in which the two courts handle their case loads. Kenney finds that ECJ law clerks contribute to the efficient operation of the organization, promoting consistency and consensus, rather than acting as gatekeepers who screen cases for a court with docket control, as is true of US Supreme Court law clerks. This, along with the practice of collegiate ECJ judgments, mitigates concerns about excessive influence that characterize scholarship on US Supreme Court law clerks (2000). In another organizational analysis, Kenney asks why it took so long for member states to appoint women to the ECJ. Applying the feminist concept of gender mainstreaming, Kenney traces the history of appointment practices and identifies the 1995 United Nation's women's conference in Beijing, the 1995 membership of Nordic states championing gender equality, and the European Parliament's support for gender equality as catalysts that contributed to shifts in the perceived legitimacy of an all-male bench (2002). These studies open up the black box of the ECJ, disaggregating the Court into its constituent actors.

A recent volume edited by Michael Zürn and Christian Joerges compares compliance in the EU with Germany and the WTO in the policy areas of state aid, food regulation, and fiscal redistributive policy. Contributors argue that effective monitoring and enforcement mechanisms and a high degree of legalization lead to higher compliance rates, regardless of the level of governance. Indeed, EU organizational mechanisms outperformed those of the domestic and global cases examined in this project (2005).

The Rule of Law and Democratic Legitimacy

A literature that evaluates the democratic legitimacy of EU judicial politics is developing links to broader comparative assessments of democracy. Using Eurobarometer surveys of public opinion, Gregory Caldeira and James Gibson test hypotheses about diffuse and specific sources of support for courts from the US politics literature to evaluate the institutional legitimacy of the ECJ. As a relatively obscure institution, they argue that the ECJ is unlikely to build support by satisfying 'constituent demands', but the Court may find its decisions affecting its perceived legitimacy as it comes under future scrutiny. Without much information on the ECJ, ordinary citizens form their views based on the ECJ's connection to the EU and its broader political and legal values. Gibson and Caldeira find that the European Parliament has little legitimacy to transfer to the ECJ, and that national high courts, while enjoying greater legitimacy, are not necessarily able to transfer it to the EU level. Finally, because the ECJ does not yet enjoy widespread support, it has few resources to elicit compliance in controversial cases (Caldeira and Gibson 1995, 1997; Gibson and Caldeira 1995, 1998). Anke Grosskopf develops this analysis further, comparing public support for established courts including the US Supreme Court and West German Federal Constitutional Court with newly emerging courts including the Federal Constitutional Court in East Germany and the ECJ in East and West Germany. In contrast to Gibson and Caldeira, Grosskopf demonstrates that constitutional courts inhabit an 'interconnected support universe' that facilitates the transfer of legitimacy from national courts to the supranational level. She concludes by arguing that the ECJ faces more legitimacy challenges as a result of being a fairly new court, rather than being a supranational court (Grosskopf 2001).

Other studies of democratic legitimacy focus on the extent to which the ECJ upholds the rule of law by ensuring the legality of EU institutions, provides a new space for citizen participation in the political process, and acts as a counter-majoritarian institution. Clifford Carrubba designs a formal model that, assuming there is some legitimacy cost for a non-compliant government, assesses the likelihood that the ECJ can guarantee that no EU body acts above the law. He draws on the findings of Gibson and Caldeira – that mass publics remain largely unaware of the ECJ and do not yet manifest much support – to conclude that the ECJ is not yet in a good position to hold member states legally accountable (Carrubba 2003). By contrast, empirical research indicates that legal compliance in the EU is comparatively high, but this does not yet translate into broader democratic legitimacy (Zürn and Joerges 2005).

A recent special issue of *Comparative Political Studies* explores how EU litigation constitutes a form of individual participation in EU governance. Through access to the ECJ, individuals gain a new opportunity to advocate their interests in an international arena formerly dominated by states (Cichowski and Stone Sweet 2003; Alter 2006; Börzel 2006; Cichowski 2006; Conant 2006; Kelemen 2006). While such access represents an advance, it remains far from representative. Substantial asymmetries in the capacity of citizens to invoke EU law continue to limit the ECJ's impact on democratization in the EU (Conant 2002, 2004, 2006; Costa, 2003; Kelemen 2003, 2006; Börzel 2006).

Finally, the bold claims of neofunctionalists, asserting the autonomy of the ECJ and its insulation from national governments – who are democratically elected whatever other faults they might possess – suggest that the EU has been captured by an imperious judiciary freed from majority will. Given the limited impact of innovative ECJ rulings, however, and the need for a broader mobilization of support before ECJ principles operate as policy principles (Alter and Meunier 1994; Conant 2002), EU judicial politics may not be quite as counter-majoritarian as neofunctionalists imply.

CONCLUSION

All courts that resolve constitutional and administrative litigation find themselves in a position to rule against governments who control the mechanisms of coercion that enable enforcement (Fisher 1961; Conant 2002). But coercion and force are only relevant to a small fraction of legal relationships, typically reflecting a crisis rather than the norm (Bickel 1962). The high volume of the ECJ's case load in comparison to all other international courts, with the exception of the European Court of Human Rights that also enjoys a large docket (Alter 2006), along with habitual compliance (Conant 2002; Zürn and Joerges 2005), suggest that the ECJ is a legitimate court that can be compared more fruitfully to domestic courts than international institutions. As a result, nuanced studies of domestic judicial politics should inspire more of the future scholarship on EU judicial politics.

Observers of domestic political contexts emphasize how individuals and organizational actors continually contest the balance of power within existing institutional arrangements and the actual political outcomes that these institutions produce (e.g. Bickel 1962; Fisher 1988). I see no reason why EU politics is distinctive in this regard. The development of the EU as a functioning political system layered above existing national states is phenomenally distinctive, but there is little reason to believe that its internal institutional dynamics defy those of all other democratic polities. Explanations of the emergence of a viable political system need not declare the permanent supremacy of any single layer in a complex institutional structure. Instead, these explanations may explore how legal and political outcomes evolve over time in ways that reflect the interactions of various institutional venues and different constellations of interest and power. Rather than asking which level of government imposes the last word, it may be more interesting to explore how the 'last word' is actually a moving target evolving from the disputes of actors who face distinctive opportunities and constraints in promoting their goals through authoritative institutions. Research on the largely uncharted territory of national judicial review of EU law could uncover important insights here and contribute to a more complete understanding of EU judicial politics. Case studies on EU gender equality (Kenney 1995; Cichowski 2001), abortion politics (Millns and Thompson 1994), minority and immigrant rights (Guiraudon 1998, 2000; Marko 2003), and the research surveyed in the preceding section have begun to situate courts in a broader political context, with judges as one actor among others contributing to outcomes. Showing how judicial influence can vary depending on differences in the configuration of interests and institutions, I follow Shapiro in arguing that this type of research is most likely to advance our understanding of EU judicial politics (Gillman 2004).

NOTES

1. The remainder of this review focuses on the political science literature. For an interdisciplinary discussion of the divide between legal and political scholarship, see Alter et al. (2002).

2. This occurrence would be consistent with the authors' broader argument about the reconfiguration of UK sovereignty by an external legal force.

REFERENCES

Alter, K. (1996) 'The European Court's political power', *West European Politics*, 19: 458–87.

Alter, K. (1998) 'Who are the "masters of the treaty"?' *International Organization*, 52: 121–47.

Alter, K. (2000) 'The European union's legal system and domestic policy', *International Organization*, 54: 489–518.

Alter, K. (2001) *Establishing the Supremacy of European Law*. New York: Oxford University Press.

Alter, K. (2006) 'Private litigants and the new international courts', *Comparative Political Studies*, 39: pp. 22–49.

Alter, K. and Meunier-Aitsahalia, S. (1994) 'Judicial politics in the European Community', *Comparative Political Studies*, 26: 535–61.

Alter, K. and Vargas, J. (2000) 'Explaining variation in the use of European litigation strategies', *Comparative Political Studies*, 33: 452–82.

Alter, K., Dehousse, R., and Vanberg, G. (2002) 'Law, political science and EU legal studies', *European Union Politics*, 3: 113–36.

Bickel, A. ([1962] 1986) *The Least Dangerous Branch*. Reprint. New Haven, CT: Yale University Press.

Boom, S. (1995) 'The European Union after the Maastricht decision', *American Journal of Comparative Law*, 43: 177–226.

Börzel, T. (2006) 'Participation through law enforcement', *Comparative Political Studies*, 39: 128–52.

Burley, A. and Mattli, W. (1993) 'Europe before the court', *International Organization*, 47: 41–76.

Caldeira, G., and Gibson, J. (1995) 'The legitimacy of the Court of Justice in the European Union', *American Political Science Review*, 89: 356–76.

Caldeira, G. and Gibson, J. (1997) 'Democracy and legitimacy in the European Union', *International Social Science Journal*, 49: 209–24.

Carrubba, C. (2003) 'The European Court of Justice, democracy, and enlargement', *European Union Politics*, 4: 75–100.

Chalmers, D. (2000) 'The much ado about judicial politics in the United Kingdom', Harvard Jean Monnet Working Paper 1/100.

Cichowski, R. (1998) 'Integrating the environment', *Journal of European Public Policy*, 5: 387–405.

Cichowski, R. (2001) 'Judicial rulemaking and the institutionalization of European Union Sex Equality Policy', in A. Stone Sweet, W. Sandholtz and N. Fligstein (eds), *The Institutionalization of Europe*. New York, NY: Oxford University Press. pp. 113–36.

Cichowski, R. (2004) 'Women's rights, the European Court, and supranational constitutionalism', *Law and Society Review*, 38: 489–512.

Cichowski, R. (2006) 'Introduction: courts, democracy, and governance', *Comparative Political Studies*, 39: 3–21.

Cichowski, R. and Stone Sweet, A. (2003) 'Participation, representative democracy, and the courts', in B. Cain, R. Dalton and S. Scarrow (eds), *Democracy Transformed?* Oxford, UK: Oxford University Press. pp. 192–220.

Conant. L. (2001) 'Europeanization and the courts', in M. Green Cowles, J. Caporaso and T. Risse (eds), *Transforming Europe*. Ithaca, NY: Cornell University Press. pp. 97–115.

Conant, L. (2002) *Justice Contained*. Ithaca, NY: Cornell University Press.

Conant. L. (2003) 'Europe's no fly zone?', in T. Börzel and R. Cichowski (eds), *The State of the European Union*. New York, NY: Oxford University Press. 6: 235–54.

Conant, L. (2004) 'Contested boundaries', in J. Migdal (ed.), *Boundaries and Belonging*. New York, NY: Cambridge University Press. pp. 284–317.

Conant, L. (2006) 'Individuals, courts, and the development of European social rights', *Comparative Political Studies*, 39: 76–100.

Costa, O. (2003) 'The European Court of Justice and democratic control in the European Union', *Journal of European Public Policy*, 10: 740–61.

Everling, U. (1984) 'The member states of the European Community before their Court of Justice', *European Law Review*, 9: 215–41.

Fisher, L. (1988) *Constitutional Dialogues*. Princeton, NJ: Princeton University Press.

Fisher, R. (1961) 'Bringing law to bear on governments', *Harvard Law Review*, 74: 1130–40.

Galanter, M. (1974) 'Why the 'haves' come out ahead', *Law and Society Review*, 9: 95–160.

Garrett, G. (1992) 'International cooperation and institutional choice', *International Organization*, 46: 533–60.

Garrett, G. (1995) 'The politics of legal integration in the European Union', *International Organization*, 49: 171–81.

Garrett, G., Kelemen, R. and Schulz, H. (1998) 'The European Court of Justice, national governments, and legal integration in the European Union', *International Organization*, 52: 149–76.

Gibson, J. and Caldeira, G. (1995) 'The legitimacy of transnational legal institutions', *American Journal of Political Science*, 39: 459–89.

Gibson, J. and Caldeira, G. (1998) 'Changes in the legitimacy of the European Court of Justice', *British Journal of Political Science*, 28: 63–91.

Gillman, H. (2004) 'Martin Shapiro and the movement from "old" to "new" institutionalist studies in public law scholarship', *Annual Review of Political Science*, 7: 363–82.

Golub, J. (1996a) *Modeling Judicial Dialogue in the European Community*. Working Paper, RSC 96/58. Florence, IT: European University Institute.

Golub, J. (1996b) 'The politics of judicial discretion', *West European Politics*, 19: 360–85.

Grosskopf, A. (2001) 'A supernational case', *Dissertation Abstracts International, A: The Humanities and Social Sciences*, 61(9): 3750–A. (Available from UMI, Ann Arbor, MI. Order No. DA9985047.)

Guiraudon, V. (1998) 'Third country nationals and European law', *Journal of Ethnic and Migration Studies*, 24: 657–74.

Guiraudon, V. (2000) 'European courts and foreigners' rights', *International Migration Review*, 34: 1088–125.

Harlow, C. and Rawlings, R. (1992) *Pressure through Law*. New York, NY: Routledge.

Hartley, T. (1986) 'Federalism, courts and legal systems', *American Journal of Comparative Law*, 34: 229–47.

Heisenberg, D. and Richmond, A. (2002) 'Supranational institution-building in the European Union', *Journal of European Public Policy*, 9: 201–18.

Jupille, J. and Caporaso, J. (2005) *The Second Image Reversed*. Unpublished manuscript.

Kelemen, R. (2001) 'The limits of judicial power', *Comparative Political Studies*, 34: 622–50.

Kelemen, R. (2003) 'The EU rights revolution', in T. Börzel and R. Cichowski (eds), *The State of the European Union*. New York, NY: Oxford University Press. 6: 221–34.

Kelemen, R. (2006) 'Suing for Europe', *Comparative Political Studies*, 39: 101–27.

Kenney, S. (1995) 'Pregnancy discrimination', *Wisconsin Women's Law Journal*, 10: 351–402.

Kenney, S. (2000) 'Beyond principals and agents', *Comparative Political Studies*, 33: 593–625.

Kenney, S. (2002) 'Breaking the silence', *Feminist Legal Studies*, 10: 257–70.

Kilroy. B. (1999) 'Integration through the law', PhD Dissertation. University of California, Los Angeles. (Available from UMI, Ann Arbor, MI. Order No. AAT 9940492.)

Marko, J. (2003) 'Minority protection through jurisprudence in comparative perspective', *Journal of European Integration*, 25: 175–88.

Mattli, W. and Slaughter, A. (1995) 'Law and politics in the European Union', *International Organization*, 49: 183–90.

Mattli, W. and Slaughter, A. (1998) 'Revisiting the European Court of Justice', *International Organization*, 52: 177–209.

McCown, M. (2003) 'The European Parliament before the bench', *Journal of European Public Policy*, 10: 974–95.

Millns, S. and Thompson, B. (1994) 'Constructing British abortion law', *Parliamentary Affairs*, 47: 190–202.

Nyikos, S. (2000) 'The European Court of Justice and national courts', *Dissertation Abstracts International, A: The Humanities and Social Sciences*, 61(6): 2459–A. (Available from UMI, Ann Arbor, MI. Order No. DA9975557.)

Pollack, M. (2003) *The Engines of European Integration*. New York: Oxford University Press.

Ruggiero, C. (2002) 'The European Court of Justice and the German Constitutional Court', *Studies in Law, Politics, and Society*, 24: 51–80.

Scheingold, S. (1965) *The Rule of Law in European Integration*. New Haven, CT: Yale University Press.

Scheingold, S. (1971) *The Law in Political Integration*. Occasional Papers in International Affairs, No. 27. Cambridge, MA: Center for International Affairs, Harvard University.

Shapiro, M. (1993) 'Public law and judicial politics', in A. Finifter (ed.), *Political Science: The State of the Discipline*. Washington DC: American Political Science Association. pp. 365–81.

Shapiro, M. and Stone Sweet, A. (1994) 'Special issue: the new constitutional politics of Europe', *Comparative Political Studies*, 26: 397–561.

Slaughter, A., Stone Sweet, A. and Weiler, J. (eds) (1998) *The European Court and the National Courts – Doctrine and Jurisprudence*. Oxford, UK: Hart.

Stein, E. (1981) 'Lawyers, judges, and the making of a transnational constitution', *American Journal of International Law*, 75: 1–27.

Stone Sweet, A. (2004) *The Judicial Construction of Europe*. New York, NY: Oxford University Press.

Stone Sweet, A. and Brunell, T. (1998a) 'Constructing a supranational constitution', *American Political Science Review*, 92: 63–81.

Stone Sweet, A. and Brunell, T. (1998b) 'The European Court and the national courts', *Journal of European Public Policy*, 5: 66–97.

Tallberg, J. (2000) 'Supranational influence in EU enforcement', *Journal of European Public Policy*, 7: 104–21.

Tsebelis, G. and Garrett, G. (2001) 'The institutional foundations of intergovernmentalism and supranationalism in the European Union', *International Organization*, 55: 357–90.

Volcansek, M. (1992) 'The European Court of Justice', *West European Politics*, 15: 109–21.

Weiler, J. (1994) 'A quiet revolution', *Comparative Political Studies*, 26: 510–34.

Weiler, J. (1982) 'Community member states and European integration', *Journal of Common Market Studies*, 20: 39–56.

Weiler, J. (1991) 'The transformation of Europe', *Yale Law Journal*, 100: 2403–83.

Weiler, J. and Dehousse, R. (1992) 'Primus inter pares. The European Court and the National Courts'. Unpublished manuscript. Florence, IT: European University Institute.

Zürn, M. and Joerges, C. (eds) (2005) *Law and Governance in Postnational Europe*. Cambridge, UK: Cambridge University Press.

11

Organized Interests in the European Union[1]

JEREMY RICHARDSON

INTRODUCTION: SHOOTING WHERE THE DUCKS ARE

It is by now conventional wisdom to claim that the EU is *sui generis*. However, we need to recognize that the EU is now a relatively mature policy-making system. It is also a very *productive* policy-making system. In a sense, there is a policy-making engine at work within the EU that continues to churn out a mass of EU-level public policy that the 25 member states then have to implement. Thus the EU is a 'policy-making state' (Richardson 2005). Indeed, much of the criticism of the EU over the past decade (and part of the basis of the growing Euro-scepticism) has been centred upon the alleged 'excessive' policy-making role of the EU in general and of the Commission in particular. As Radaelli (1999) suggests, things began to change in the 1990s. Not just the quantity of EU legislation has been subject to challenge, but also its quality and the processes by which it is made. As he notes, the Amsterdam Treaty contains an entire title on the quality of EU legislation. Thus, 'good legislation requires

consultation, regulatory impact assessment, and systematic evaluation of the results achieved by European public policies. But it also requires transparency' (Radaelli 1999: 5). These 'process issues' were equally prominent in the Constitutional Convention and are in part addressed in the (as yet unratified) Constitutional Treaty (see Laffan and Mazey 2005; for a discussion of the implication of the rejection of the Constitutional Treaty see Majone 2006). The EU level is now the level at which a significant proportion of what used to be regarded as purely domestic policy-making takes place. Hix suggests that the EU sets over 80 per cent of the rules governing the exchange of goods, services and capital in the member states' markets (Hix 2005: 4), although Moravcsik is more doubtful, citing one study which estimated that the actual percentage of EU-based legislation is probably between 10 and 20 per cent of national rule-making (Moravcsik 2005: 17). Moravcsik also argues that many policy areas are still untouched by *direct* EU policy-making, such as social welfare, health care, pensions, education, defence, active cultural policy, and most law and order (Moravcsik 2005: 17, emphasis added). However, other authors see a stronger European influence (albeit often indirect) in at least some of these policy areas. For example, Greer's study of neo-functionalism in EU health policy concludes that:

> Once the European Court of Justice had decided that health systems are economic activities like any others, and therefore subject to internal market legislation, the conditions under which health systems gain and use resources changed dramatically, regardless of formal state protection or the existence of ECJ principles that limit the ability of EU law to wholly upset health systems (Greer 2006: 149).

This transference of power to a new venue (Baumgartner and Jones 1993) is the starting point for all studies of EU interest groups, even for those authors, such as Grant, who lean towards the view that the national route is still the main channel of EU lobbing for interest groups (Grant 2000: 106–15). It is the change in the locus of power that has provoked some profound changes in the behaviour of private actors in the policy process.

Thus, from the perspective of interest groups, the changing policy-making balance between nation states and the EU has obvious implications. Interest groups are a superb *weather vane* of power and tend to concentrate resources where decisions that might affect them directly are made, i.e. they tend to act rationally when allocating lobbying resources. As one lobbyist put it, interest groups tend to shoot where the ducks are! The practical reality for a huge number of interest groups within the EU is that if they are to influence public policy in their sector (or merely to get a decent warning of policy changes to which they will need to adjust) they need to act cross-nationally and get themselves to Brussels. They know that the policy environment under which they operate is increasingly determined outside the existing nation state boundaries. Interest groups tend to adopt a very practical approach to lobbying. They are aware of the big debates about such issues as federalism, enlargement, and the future direction of the Union and participate in those debates, but they have a very keen sense of day-to-day politics too. They know that while the big debates take place

the policy system still functions. Thus, the *logic of influence* simply drives them to the regional (and increasingly global) level if they are to stand a chance of influencing, let alone controlling, their organizational environment. Academic studies of interest groups in the EU have, first, tried to describe 'what is going on' (adopting a fairly light theoretical touch) and, secondly, (in later phases) develop some more robust and better-specified theoretical tools to explain it.

However, a central argument in this chapter is that more recent studies are merely echoing, in a more formal way, the implicit theoretical assumptions of earlier studies.

In the next section we analyse the general trajectory of the EU intermediation system and some of the theoretical approaches that have been mobilized to explain the growth of EU lobbying. There follows an analysis of the now sophisticated system of incentive structures at the EU level, which continue to 'drive' forward the lobbying system. We conclude with some reflections on what appears to be a rather clear pattern of continuity in studies of EU lobbying.

ANALYSING THE TRAJECTORY OF THE EU INTEREST INTERMEDIATION SYSTEM

The phenomenon of European lobbying is not at all new. Some fairly stable 'policy networks' involving ECSC officials and corporatist interests were apparent as early as the mid 1950s (Mazey 1992). However, the significant expansion of the Community's legislative competence following the adoption of the 1986 Single European Act (SEA), and subsequent Treaty reforms has prompted a sharp increase in the volume and intensity of interest group activity at the European level. Not surprisingly, academic research has tended to 'track' this real-world phenomenon. Most of the research can be more or less characterized as fitting within a rational-actor approach, assuming, as we suggest above, that groups act rationally to maximize their influence by directing their lobbying resources in an intelligent and informed way. Whilst other theoretical tools might have been used, such as focusing on affective as well as utilitarian reasons for supporting European integration (see Lindberg and Scheingold 1970) or, more recently, constructivist approaches in which identity rather than pure interest plays a major role (see Christiansen et al. 1999), this has not been the case. Alongside a rational-actor approach, neo-functionalism has also been a key theoretical building block of EU interest group studies. The observation by Ernst Haas in 1958 that, 'political integration is the process whereby political actors in several distinct national settings are persuaded to shift their loyalties, expectations and political activities toward a new centre, whose institutions possess or demand jurisdiction over the pre-existing national states' (Haas 1958: 16) is in many ways the intellectual thread running through the many studies of interest groups in the EU that have followed since then.

Thus, one of the earliest systematic studies of the emergence of a European interest group system was Kirchner's analysis of interest group formation at the EU level (Kirchner 1980a). This study cites Meynaud and Sidjanski's earlier study of European pressure groups, which found that many of these groupings established themselves at the Community level in response to the formation of a new centre of decision-making and as a result of advantages expected from Community action (Kirchner 1980a: 96–7). Sidjanski's study suggests that some of the groups were formed as the EEC's own institutions were created, others when it became clear that the EEC's regulatory powers could significantly affect different interests in society (Sidjanski 1970: 402). Clearly reflecting the neo-functionalist approach, Kirchner notes in the case of trade unions, there were also perceived *positive* benefits from European-level organisation. He suggests that one of the aims of the trade unions in mobilizing at the Euro-level 'is to promote, at the European level, the interests which become increasingly difficult to achieve at the national level' (Kirchner 1980b: 132). Kirchner's data imply that the development of the EU and the development of the EU interest group system went hand in hand.

Kirchner also notes that another phenomenon familiar from studies of national interest

groups systems was evident in the early years of the Union – namely that groups beget more groups. Once one set of interests is mobilized and organized to influence decision-makers, those interests in society who have not yet organized will see the need to do so; if they do not, they are leaving policy space exclusively occupied by rival interests. Interest group mobilisation is at least a means of 'risk avoidance' in the manner first suggested by David Truman in 1951. In an attempt to defend pluralism in the USA, he argued that over time interest group power would tend to reach some kind of equilibrium. This was partly because society was full of what he termed 'potential groups' which, when threatened by the successes of those interests already organized, would themselves become organized to defend their own objectives (Truman 1951: 31). Kirchner suggests that the mobilisation of trade unions at the European level is a classic example of this phenomenon (Kirchner 1977: 28). Thus, alongside neo-functionalism, pluralism has also been an important theoretical strand. Indeed, academic studies on EU interest intermediation fall firmly within the American tradition of interest group studies with a clear pluralist stance. For example Mazey and Richardson adopted an essentially pluralistic stance in their original edited volume on EC (as it then was) lobbying (Mazey and Richardson 1993) and more recently have argued that '... lobbying in the EU is likely to remain pluralistic, unpredictable and to favour those actors who can mobilize ideas and knowledge in order to "massage" the framing of public policies, who can manage a series of multi-level and shifting coalitions, and who can re-formulate their preferences rapidly...' (Mazey and Richardson 2005: 264–5). Within this broad theoretical approach, however, there has been widespread recognition that there can be imbalance in power, if not access. Thus, from early work by authors such as Sijanski (1970) and Kirchner (1980a, 1980b) through to more recent authors such as Coen (1997) there has been a recognition that business interests have probably exercised more actual power (in terms of policy outputs) than have what Pollack terms 'diffuse interests' (Pollack

1997: 572–3). In so far as the group system has emerged into a distinctive European policy style (Mazey and Richardson 1995) it has rarely if ever been seen as corporatist, however, but modelled more on pluralistic/consensual European models. In what is now the classic discussion of the possibilities of Euro-level corporatism, Wolfgang Streeck and Philippe Schmitter argued, rather convincingly, that there were limits to the degree of institutionalization of corporatist style concertation. They took this view because of the (claimed) absence of anything resembling a balance of class or sectoral interests at the European level. This is important because neo-corporatism assumes an underlying social structure that could be plausibly conceived of as polarized into two large classes: 'capital' and 'labour'. They argued that attempts to create Euro-corporatism failed, and a centralized pattern of interest politics did not emerge at the European level, despite their (probably wrong) belief that it was common at the national level (Streeck and Schmitter 1991: 133–64). Similarly, Michael Georges has argued that '… the Union still lacks the policy authority necessary to maintain traditional macro-corporatism, namely, the ability to use fiscal, social, or labour market policy to gain concessions from trade unions and business to assist in the negotiation of mutually acceptable compromises' (Georges 1996: 192–3). The corporatist debate is not quite dead, however, as studies move into a more detailed sectoral phase. Thus, Falkner's detailed study of EU social policy is entitled, *EU Social Policy in the 1990s: Towards a Corporatist Policy Community* (Falkner 1998) and reminds us that one of the key features of the EU policy process is sectorisation of policy-making, opening up the possibility of major cross-sectoral variations in policy styles. A more nuanced view of the EU policy process might yield a more varied range of modes of governance, including coercion, voluntarism, targeting and framework legislation (Treib et al. forthcoming).

Setting aside theoretical issues for the moment, the *empirical* story since 1980 has been one of rapid acceleration of Euro-interest group formation. By 1985, Alan Butt Philip

was reporting that 'almost five hundred Europe-wide pressure groups now devote their resources to influencing decisions taken by the EC' (Philip 1985: 1), but in 1986 Grote found rather more Euro-groups than Butt Philip had done the previous year – 654 in fact (Greenwood et al. 1992: 1). By February 2000, the Commission Secretary-General's list of non-profit making interest groups included some 800 groups. More recently, Mahoney's analysis of the so-called CONECCS dataset constructed by the Commission (see below page 237), identified some 700 groups in the civil society category alone (Mahoney 2004: 445). The growth in other types of Euro-level representation seems to have been almost exponential. Back in 1992, the Commission estimated that there were no less than 3,000 'special interest groups of varying types in Brussels, with up to 10,000 employees working in the lobbying sector' (Commission 1992: 4). In addition, the Commission estimated that at that time, over 200 firms had direct representation in Brussels, and approximately 100 lobbying consultancy firms were represented in Brussels. In 2003 Lahusen reported that the rate of formation of lobbying consultancy firms appeared to have slowed after the burst following the passage of the Single European Act of 1986, but that the sector was nevertheless continuing to expand by about 8-10 new organisations every year (Lahusen 2003: 197). Others have noted that regional interests have also become increasingly mobilized at the EU level. For example in 1996, Marks et al. note that '… the 1990s have seen the growth of a new and unheralded form of regional mobilization in the European Union…', with some 54 regional and local governments representing approximately three-sevenths of the population of the EU (Marks et al. 1996: 40). However, as Keating and Hooghe point out, both access and influence (by regional and local authorities) is unevenly distributed (Keating and Hooghe 2005: 283). Yet another range of interests exhibiting Europeanization of their strategies are the rather diffuse social movements in Europe. Over time they have been adept at exploiting opportunity structures as Kitschelt demonstrated in his study on anti-nuclear movements at the national level (Kitschelt 1986). But there is now evidence that, as with other interests, social movements have seen the potential benefits of Euro-level actions (see Tarrow 1998: 177; 2001). However, as Tarrow notes, it is safer to talk of tendencies and possibilities, rather than certainties and probabilities as 'weaker social actors continue to face imposing transaction costs when they attempt to organize across borders' (Tarrow 2001: 237). Ruzza is a little more optimistic about the capacity of what he terms 'movement coalitions' to influence the EU policy process (see Ruzza 2004: 26–55). Thus, we can see a long term trend, starting with pure economic interests (firms) and ending with fluid and broad based 'credit card' participation via various social movements.

It is difficult to gauge how reliable the data on numbers and types of all types of groups really is, or, indeed, how meaningful the numbers are given that we do not know how *active* in the lobbying process all of these groups and individuals are. However, it is also possible to argue that the true size of the Brussels-level lobbying industry could actually be *higher* than the Commission's estimate if the census were to include all those individuals who visit Brussels in order to lobby, but who are not based in Brussels. The number of people in this category almost certainly runs into many thousands.

As suggested above, descriptions of the growth of the EU lobbying system have often reflected neo-functionalist and pluralist approaches. Yet there is also another, and more important strand, running through nearly all of these studies. The studies are underpinned by the assumption, noted above, that interest groups have acted *rationally* in allocating scarce lobbying resources. From Sidjansky onwards, it is possible to fit most studies of the EU lobbying system within a (loose) rational-actor model. Moreover, the same rational-actor assumption is made for other actors, especially the EU's main institutions, the Commission, the Council, the European Parliament (EP), and the European Court of Justice (ECJ). Out of a rational calculation of self-interest, each of these institutions has, in

varying degrees, created incentives for interest groups to mobilize beyond their national borders. In other words there has often been a shared *interest* in the creation of an institutionalized EU-level group system. The incentives seem to point in the same direction. Sooner or later, those groups with sufficient resources to: (a) understand the EU policy process; and (b) then target lobbying resources accordingly, come to read, correctly, the power signals emitting from the new political system. In a sense, therefore, academic studies have often been describing (implicitly) groups as *learning* organizations, although it might be argued that studies which show groups still wedded to the national route are actually analysing learning *dysfunctions* within groups. (Interestingly the *process* by which groups do or do not learn seems to have been a relatively neglected in academic studies.)

EU INCENTIVE STRUCTURES

Public policy is not made in a vacuum. The process is always institutionalized in some way, whether through informal rules or via conventional public institutions such as cabinets, parliaments, courts or civil service bureaucracies. Thus, yet another strand in EU interest group studies has been resort to institutional approaches. Analysts of EU lobbying have always recognized that institutions (including informal rules) do indeed matter. Institutional arrangements are not neutral and certainly play a key role in structuring group behaviour. In particular at least some of the EU institutions have been active in developing incentive structures, which help condition group behaviour. We start our discussion of incentives with the European Commission, for two main reasons. First, it has a legal responsibility, under the Treaties, for making formal policy proposals to the other EU institutions such as the Council and European Parliament. Secondly, and more importantly, we know that bureaucracies occupy a special position in all public (and indeed private) policy-making systems. Whilst the specific origin of public policies is often unclear, and bureaucracies such as the European Commission are usually keen to deny that they are the main source of policy initiatives (reflecting their lack of legitimacy), we know that bureaucracies are almost invariably key players in the policy game. As Mazey argues, the Commission has always been active in helping to *create* an EU-level interest group systems. She suggests that this *constituency mobilisation* strategy is consistent both with theories of bureaucratic expansion and neo-functionalist models of European integration (Mazey 1995: 606, see also Mazey 1998).

More importantly, bureaucracies and interest groups have a mutual self interest in developing close relations, *even under circumstances of policy disagreement*. Mutual gains are to be had in the essentially long-running game in which EU institutions and organized interest groups are engaged. The mutuality of the relationship is aptly summarized in a quotation from the Commission's 2002 document, *General principles and minimum standards for consultation of interested parties by the Commission*. Thus:

> By fulfilling its duty to consult, the Commission ensures that its proposals are technically viable, practically workable and based on a bottom-up approach. In other words, good consultation serves a dual purpose by helping improve the quality of the policy outcomes and at the same time enhancing the involvement of interested parties and the public at large.

The Commission has a strong belief that consultation of interests represents a 'win-win' situation for all parties, i.e. that co-operation brings greater mutual gains. In fact, relations between the Commission, on the one hand, and an increasingly Europeanized interest group system on the other, appear to have developed along quite predictable lines. Indeed, despite the aforementioned reference to the EU as a *sui generis* political system, there is nothing new or unique about the EU's now well-developed interest intermediation system or about the way it has come about. This is in part underpinned by a legal obligation to consult. For example, Protocol No 7 on the application of the principles of subsidiarity and proportionality, annexed to the Amsterdam Treaty, states that the Commission should consult widely before proposing legislation, and, wherever appropriate, publish consultation documents. More recently, the new Constitutional Treaty also stresses the importance of open, transparent and regular dialogue between European institutions and representative associations and civil society. (Whatever the fate of the Constitution, it is almost unthinkable that this aspect of it will not survive, if only because the ideology which it reflects is already deeply embedded.)

Although the Commission is uniquely small in relation to its tasks and exhibits some fairly marked cultural diversity, it also has very familiar bureaucratic features, such as strong sectorization, serious problems of co-ordination, and, of special relevance here, a strong *penchant* for developing close relations with organized interests. The latter reflects the Commission's organizational ideology, which has arguably been more important than legal obligations in fostering the development of an EU-level interest group system. For their part, interest groups have been keen to exploit the Commission as a new *venue* or opportunity structure to gain influence over public policy-making. In practice, most interests are now organized at the European level and it is fair to argue that the EU interest group system is now very *dense* (albeit exhibiting varying degrees of density, in turn reflecting cross-sectoral differences (see Broscheid and Coen 2005).

That groups tend to focus on the bureaucratic arm of government is, of course, one of the central theoretical assumptions of interest group studies. Thus, interest group scholars (at least in Western Europe where legislatures have tended to be weak) have generally exhibited a bias towards studying the bureaucracy/interest group interface. This has been as true for EU interest group studies as it is for most national studies. Thus far more has been written about the relations between the Commission and interest groups than about the relationship between groups and the other EU institutions. This might be a reflection of the traditions in the discipline, mentioned above, or, more likely, that the evidence is that groups too see the Commission as generally the most important venue at which to shop. However, to assert at this time that groups still focus on the European Commission may seem odd in the light of the currently widespread belief that the Commission's powers have declined over the past decade or so. Decline has been attributed to a succession of Treaty reforms which have strengthened the European Parliament (Auel and Rittberger 2005), greater emphasis on intergovernmental solutions, and a shift in the European policy style towards what has been termed the Open Method of Co-ordination (OMC), which seems much less *dirigiste* (though actually present plenty of opportunities for group influence). Nevertheless, as indicated above, the founding Treaties of the EC state that the European Commission is the initiator of Community policies and, formally speaking, it has the sole right to propose Community legislation. The Commission is also the executive arm of Community governance ultimately responsible for ensuring the effective implementation of the policies decided upon by the Council of Ministers. The Commission therefore still plays a pivotal role in translating initiatives (from whatever source) into clear proposals. 'Commission watching' is an essential part of monitoring that crucial stage of the EU policy process, namely agenda-setting, as well as the detailed processing of issues through to Directives, regulations and soft law. The Commission is nothing if not politically skilled and, as an adaptive organization, it finds ways of 'legislating' in hard times.

Whether it is drafting hard or soft law, a key issue for Commission officials is how to 'manage' the process of consultation to which they are so deeply committed. They are in some respects victims of their own success: their steadfast commitment to consultation and openness has effectively created the oversupply of lobbying (Mazey and Richardson 2005: 253). Yet, the commission has recently introduced a number of measures designed to increase openness and transparency. These included earlier publication of the Commission's legislative programme, a commitment to ensure that target groups are aware of any new policy initiatives, and greater use of Green (consultative) Papers. Prior to 1990, the Commission

appears to have published only four Green Papers; in the following eight years approximately 50 were published. The Commission's Report, 'Better Lawmaking in 2003' records that in that year it published five Green Papers and 142 Communications, as well as 73 Reports.

More recently, use of the internet has become an increasingly important characteristic of the Commission's group management strategy. In April 2001, the Commission adopted a Communication on Interactive Policy Making. The so-called IPM initiative involves the development of two internet-based mechanisms to assist the consultation processes: a feedback facility, to allow existing networks to report to the Commission on a continuous basis; and an on-line consultation tool, designed to receive and store rapidly reactions to new initiatives. In 2003, for example, the Commission conducted 60 internet consultations through 'Your Voice in Europe', the Commission's single access point for consultations. As part of its policy on openness, contributions to open public consultations are published on the internet at the Your Voice in Europe portal. The Commission reported that it had received over 100 answers to its long questionnaire and nearly 700 answers to the online questionnaire.

The Commission has also created a web-based database of formal and structured consultative bodies in the field of civil society, the so-called CONECCS (Consultation, the European Commission and Civil Society). The database provides information on those Commission committees and other Commission frameworks through which civil society organisations are consulted in a formal or structured way and which are relatively permanent and meet at least once a year. For each group, the database lists its objectives, period of mandate, frequency of meetings, secretariat and chair of the body, as well as information on members and links to member organisations. This is a relatively recent development and cynics might wonder how important these bodies really are in terms of influencing policy outcomes, especially as CONECCS does not include what the Commission calls 'open consultation procedures'. These often less visible consultation exercises include bilateral contacts and/or *ad hoc* consultations between the Commission and groups.

In an attempt to allay public fears about the EU's democratic deficit, the Commission has, since the early 1990s, redoubled its efforts to achieve a more balanced institutionalisation of interest group intermediation, mainly through the construction of a series of inclusive social networks such as the Social Policy Forum. In 1997, the Commission adopted a Communication, *Promoting the Role of Voluntary Organizations and Foundations in Europe*, which stressed the need for NGOs to be consulted more widely and more systematically. As the Commission noted in 2002, this initiative underlined its intention to 'reduce the risk of the policy-makers just listening to one side of the argument or of particular groups getting privileged access'.

The Commission's need to demonstrate openness and transparency, driving it in a pluralistic direction, is paralleled by its need to mobilize a consensus in favour of technically sound and politically feasible policies. As Cram noted in her seminal study of the Commission, it can best be described as a 'purposeful opportunist' (Cram 1994). This notion of a purposeful organization is also reflected in more recent work by Broschild and Coen. They describe the Commission acting as both policy entrepreneur and *political* entrepreneur in response to the further explosion of lobbying after the Maastricht Treaty. In short, 'the Commission uses institutional engineering, in the service of political entrepreneurship' (Broschild and Coen 2003: 180–81).

As suggested earlier, academic studies of the EU interest intermediation system have exhibited a very strong bias towards the study of Commission/group relations (my guess is that over 90 per cent of academic studies fall into this category). Yet, as also suggested earlier, the balance of power among EU institutions has shifted. In so far as academic studies of lobbying have analysed the effects of these shifts in balance of power, they imply that groups will not pay less attention to the Commission but

that they will simply mobilize more lobbying resources so that they can cover more venues effectively. This seems plausible if one assumes rational action on the part of groups. Thus, once the high cost of setting up a Brussels office has been incurred, lobbying more institutions carries a low marginal cost. (Moreover, marginal costs of lobbying have almost certainly increased anyway for 'Commission-only lobbying' in that groups have learned over time not to rely solely on 'their' Directorate General (DG) but to also lobby other DGs that have a legitimate interest in the particular policy problem.)

In fact it is clear that groups are indeed rational enough to direct lobbying resources across the EU institutions even if resource allocation by certain groups such as big firms remains skewed toward the Commisson (see Coen 1997 for what is probably the earliest study to focus specifically on how groups allocate lobbying resources with the EU). Of, course, lobbying is a two-way relationship and we might expect that some institutions are more permeable than others. This is indeed the case. In terms of permeability, the Commission is followed (quite closely) by the European Parliament, it being no coincidence that both the Commission and the EP have considered regulating lobbying (though to no great effect) As Greenwood notes, attempts to formulate agreed formal written rules governing lobbying have not had a happy history. Thus it took the Parliament some seven years to agree, finally in 1996, a set of rules governing lobbying (Greenwood 1997: 96). Similarly, the Commission's approach to the possibility of formulating some kind of regulatory framework to govern lobbying has been very cautious and has resulted only in some fairly light 'rules' embodied in codes of practice (Preston 1998). In essence, neither institution wants to run the risk of being closed to influence, especially when the democratic deficit debate still rages. Next in the lobbying pecking order would come the ECJ and, some considerable way behind, the Council of Ministers, to which direct access is rather difficult (though not impossible, see below).

From a theoretical perspective, it might seem reasonable to argue that at least until its powers were increased very significantly, the European Parliament (EP) would be a relatively unattractive opportunity structure for interest groups. Why would groups have spent resources on lobbying a weak institution? In practice, the EP has, for a very long time (long before the more recent increases in its powers) attracted a great deal of lobbying activity – so much so, in fact, that the question of regulating lobbying has been a key issue within the EP for several years (as suggested above).

There are three obvious explanations for the apparent paradox of a relatively weak institution attracting an oversupply of lobbying. First, groups, as rational actors, recognize that the EU policy process demands a multi-track lobbying strategy – a 'belt and braces' approach to lobbying. Expressing a preference for one opportunity structure over another does not preclude some lobbying of less favoured structures. (The British case is instructive. Britain has one of the weakest legislatures in Western Europe yet all studies of national lobbying in Britain show that groups do not *ignore* parliament.) Just as EP elections are thought to be second-order elections, then so the EP has been, for many groups having good Commission contacts, a second-order lobbying target. Secondly, it seems likely that the EP attracts a disproportionate amount of lobbying from certain types of groups (environmentalists, women, consumers, animal rights) who, historically, may not have enjoyed such easy access to the Commission and/or their national governments. Thirdly, the EP's power in the EU policy process varies across policy sectors. Where there are effective EP committees, and legislative power is shared between the Council and the Parliament under co-decision making procedures, lobbying of the EP is likely to be more intense. The significant expansion of the EP's legislative role since 1986 has changed the calculation of the logic of influence by groups. As Kohler-Koch (1997) suggests, 'reflecting the new role of the EP as an important institution in the European decision-making process, the Parliamentarians are becoming a decisive target group for lobbyists ...' (Kohler-Koch 1997: 10).

Kohler-Koch's research suggests that interest groups and the Parliament can sometimes be effective 'advocacy coalitions' in the EU policy process, albeit sometimes coalitions of the weak. As she argues, changes in the Parliament's role, and in its relationship with groups, seem to be shifting the EP in the direction of a US Congress-type legislature. Similarly, Bouwen and McCown note that 'since the Treaty of Maastricht, the co-decision power has provided the European Parliament with real veto power in the legislative process' (Bouwen and McCown 2004: 4–5). The gradual increase in the EP's powers has, of course, further increased the complexity of the Brussels lobbying game. Few interests now dare risk leaving the parliamentary arena to their opponents and, hence, parliamentary hearings attract the full *melange* of stakeholders. Wessels, for example, has produced data showing that there are probably some 67,000 contacts between the EP and interest groups annually (Wessels 1999: 109). Following Kohler-Koch, he concludes that 'the more the EP becomes a veto-player, the more attention it receives' (Wessels 1999: 109). Similarly, Grant notes that business interests have realized that more attention needs to be paid to the EP, citing the example of the chemical industry's Euro-association, CEFIC, which appointed a full-time EP liaison officer in 1990 (Grant 2000: 118). Again we see studies of EU lobbying adopting a basic rational-actor approach, linked to institutional analyses, in trying to explain behavioral changes.

Reflecting a trend towards a more overt (and more robust in that testable hypotheses are formulated) specification of theoretical propositions, a more recent study by Bouwen finds the supply and demand model (in this case the supply and demand for 'access goods') useful for explaining interest group access to the EP. The access goods in question all relate to information, namely *expert knowledge, information about the European encompassing interest (i.e. the needs of the particular policy sector under discussion at any time) and information about the domestic encompassing interest*. His central thesis is that the crucial access good supplied to the EP by interest groups is not technical information (the access good that most researchers stress for Commission/group relations) but the European encompassing interest. This access good provides MEPs with the European perspective, which they need if an agreement is to be forged within the transnational groups in the EP (Bouwen, 2004a: 476–80). In addition, in order to increase their chances of re-election, MEPs also need the third access good, namely information on national needs and preferences. Thus, both European and national associations gain access to the EP by supplying goods which the EP demands, albeit sometimes rather different goods than those demanded by the Commission. Bouwen's study shows that the goods being traded are different but the trading process is, as with the Commission, based on mutual gains from co-operation, again echoing our suggestion of the underlining the dominance of the rational-actor approach to the analysis of the EU interest intermediation system. A continuing research theme is that actors face strong incentives to co-operate.

The crucial attention that interest groups pay to the EP is a direct reflection of its power as an institution. Similarly, the ECJ's attractiveness as a venue relates to its position in the EU's institutional hierarchy. Here, again, we see the EU interest intermediation system exhibiting some familiar features. In those political systems, such as the USA, which accord the judiciary a major role in the interpretation of legal and constitutional arrangements, recourse to the courts has long been a standard 'lobbying' strategy. In the EU, once the ECJ had acquired for itself a major role in the EU policy process it was inevitable that interest groups would devote more attention and resources to influencing ECJ rulings. As courts acquire power in the field of public policy so they present groups with a new option, namely a litigation strategy. The ECJ represents a perfect example of the 'venue shopping' theory of Baumgartner and Jones (1993). When groups fail to gain satisfaction at the national level, the Commission, EP or Council of Ministers, they have the option – albeit a costly one – of trying to bring a case before the Court, or of persuading the Commission to bring a case before the Court.

Using a standard supply and demand of goods as a theoretical model, Stone Sweet and Brunell have portrayed the Court as a 'supplying' institution – 'supplying integrative decisions in response to the demands of transnational actors such as businesses and individuals … who need European rules and those who are advantaged by European law and practices compared with national law and practices' (Stone Sweet and Brunell 1998: 72). Bouwen and McCown have analysed the conditions under which groups choose between litigation and lobbying strategies. The attraction of litigation (usually via the preliminary reference process under Article 234 of the Treaties) is that the activist case law of the ECJ provides 'interest groups with potentially powerful legal tools for promoting policy change' (Bowen and McCown 2004: 8). This strategy can bring about long-term policy change as 'interest groups that successfully litigate in order to shape EU policy, not only effect the removal on national rules, on the basis of EU law, but also typically shape the form of future legislation' (Bouwen and McCown 2004: 9; see also McCown 2005). Their research suggests that the most successful litigation strategy is not to bring a single case to the courts but to bring multiple cases, either in sequence or simultaneously in order to take advantage of the ECJ's tendency towards precedent based decision-making (see McCown 2005 and Bouwen and McCown 2004: 11). Although litigation strategies are used effectively by interest groups, Bouwen and McCown nevertheless conclude that the bias is still in favour of lobbying '… because of the differential resource threshold between the two influence strategies' (Bouwen and McCown 2004: 15). Yet again we see a rational-actor approach being used to explain group behaviour in that groups simply calculate costs against potential benefits. If costs are thought to be too high, they do not use the ECJ route or they see if costs can be shared amongst allies who are also potential beneficiaries.

An intergovernmental theorist would probably argue that the Council of Ministers should be the main European-level opportunity structure to be targeted by interest groups. Yet, it is the least *directly* accessible of all EU institutions. It is not just that institutions matter. Detailed institutional design is also crucial to groups. The Council is not *designed* to facilitate group access, unlike the Commission, which is in a serial process of designing group access. This makes lobbying more difficult (and presumably more costly). National groups make sure that they lobby 'their' national officials, who (the interest groups hope) will then ensure that their views are represented in the COREPER meetings – hence the description of members of COREPER as the 'lobbied lobbyists' (Spence 1993: 48). Euro-groups and those national associations and firms who really understand the importance of intergovernmentalism in EU policy-making typically lobby a range of national delegations in Brussels – particularly of those member states who are known to hold strong positions on any given policy issue. Acting rationally, they look for veto players in the particular policy game in which they are interested.

Bouwen's more recent comparative study of the business lobbying of EU institutions sheds more theoretical light on the dynamics of lobbying of the Council and is a rare example of research on lobbying and the Council. He finds that national associations and individual firms, rather than European associations, have the highest degree of access to the Council. Indeed, it appears that national associations have better access to the Council than either to the Parliament or the Commission (Bouwen 2004b: 358). He explains this bias by reference to his access goods theory (cited above). Basically, the Council needs information on the 'domestic encompassing interest', for instance the aggregate needs and interests of a sector in the domestic markets (Bouwen 2004b). Back to mutual gains again!

A second, common means of lobbying Council is for interest groups to lobby members of the many Council working groups. Rather like COREPER, this form of institutionalized 'issue processing' presents opportunities for detailed, technical arguments to be presented and for national representatives to be won over. The working groups are one of the boiler-houses of European integration. Composed of national officials 'congregating in their thousands every working day in Brussels, they (constitute) the backbone of the European system of integration ... they are performing the vital and frequently time-consuming technical groundwork for what will eventually become a piece of European legislation or policy' (Hayes-Renshaw and Wallace 1997: 98).

The third and most obvious means of influencing the Council is, of course, directly via national governments. Several authors see national governments as, in fact, the *main* opportunity structure for interest groups, not just as a means of influencing the Council but as the key opportunity structure through which groups can influence the EU policy process as a whole. For example, Grant has long been skeptical of the thesis that Brussels is the most effective lobbying arena (Grant 2000: 106–15). Similarly, Greenwood describes the 'national route' as the 'tried and tested ground for many organized interests' (Greenwood 1997: 32). Wessels also argues that 'a European route of interest intermediation is clearly not dominant' (Wessels 1999: 117). Bennett's survey data on the lobbying strategies of British business associations confirms this view of interest group behaviour. He found that the national route was the preferred Euro-lobbying strategy of the majority of associations (except federations). He, too, argues that this is perfectly rational: '[T]he preference for this route can be explained by its relative cheapness and its continuity of use of traditional channels of information and exchange that have developed from the period before European economic integration' (Bennett 1997: 85). His analysis indicates that groups are cost calculators, to some degree, and that there is also a degree of path dependency in the way that they behave. (I would add that his studies also show cognitive gaps, which might bear high but initially hidden costs to groups.)

More recently, writers such as Grossman (2004) and Schneider and Baltz have echoed 'the primacy of the national route' thesis. Indeed, Schneider and Baltz go so far as to suggest that the system is largely *étatist* and that groups are therefore generally weak in relation to national governments. Thus they conclude that 'although governments have to respect the interests of their stakeholders to some extent, they possess ample and largely uncontrolled discretion in EU affairs' (Schneider and Baltz 2004: 25). Clearly, the importance of national governments as an opportunity structure varies according to the policy issue, the type of interest group, the time, and the nature of the national government itself. The continued extension of qualified majority voting in the Council is, however, likely to erode still further the traditional ties between interest groups and national governments and to force interests to develop strategies independent of 'their' governments. Even when an interest group and its national government are on the same side in a policy development debate (often not a reasonable assumption), the group cannot rely on its national government being able to deliver the desired policy objective under QMV. A partner that was formerly a veto player in the policy game (under unanimity voting) is (under QMV) no longer a veto player. That surely changes the rational calculation of groups, especially if the potential policy pay-off is very high to the group on a given issue. Thus if an EU policy win would really deliver a big pay-off to a group (such as a multinational company) then a group is likely to risk a (probably temporary) disruption of good relations with a national government. Moreover, as cross-sectoral trade-offs between member states are not uncommon in last-minute EU bargaining, a national government may choose to 'dump' an interest group in favour of some other policy goal. Thus, both national governments and groups fully understand each other's predicaments. They are all engaged in a complex EU policy game with uncertain agendas and uncertain outcomes.

CONCLUSION: OLD WINE IN OLD BOTTLES?

The most striking aspect of a review of lobbying in the EU is the considerable degree of continuity in both the 'real world' of the EU interest intermediation system itself and the theoretical and conceptual tools used by academic researchers to describe it. If we take the 'real world' first, the trajectory of the lobbying system has been relatively unchanged since the days of the High Authority. Quite predictably, some interest groups (particularly business which had most to gain at that time) were very early to mobilize resources in order to gain influence at the new European policy-making venue. It is the growing importance of this venue that has been the driving force behind the creation of a mature interest intermediation system at the EU level. Intergovernmentalists and neo-functionalists can argue over how integration came about, and indeed, over how much integration has taken place, but it is beyond dispute that the EU has acquired for itself at least the policy-making attributes of a modern state across an increasingly wide range of policy sectors. The is now a huge *corpus* of EU law affecting a wide range of policy sectors and, as Hix notes, the EU policy process remains very productive in that 'on average more than 100 pieces of legislation pass through the EU institutions every year – more than most other democracies' (Hix 2005: 4). Even though it is conventional wisdom to argue that the EU lacks the coercive power of conventional states, I would argue that the EU does have a degree of 'coercive' power to enforce policy decisions due to the supremacy of EU law over national law. Also, the EU has a degree of steering capacity, via less coercive governance mechanisms, which means that 'power' can be exercised in the sense of getting other actors to change their behaviour. In practice, the erosion of national sovereignty (which clearly has taken place, over time) means the erosion of the power of the member states exclusively to decide much of their public policy via domestic policy-making processes and institutions. Whilst retaining the traditional coercive powers of the state, such as going to war, member states have in practice ceded many areas of hitherto domestic policy-making to the EU, albeit retaining a powerful role at the new transnational level at which policy is made. Whatever is the true figure for the amount of legislation that now emanates from the EU, it seems reasonable to assume that the *direction* of change is steady. For many policy areas, the locus of decision-making – and therefore power – has already shifted and it seems likely that other policy areas will gradually follow this pattern, albeit possibly along different paths. Also, as Stone Sweet argues, there appear to be no examples of rollback (Stone Sweet 2004: 236). Once a policy area has shifted to the regional (EU) level it is stuck there. That pressure groups should first see that the shift in the locus of power has taken place and, secondly, start to adjust their behaviour accordingly is totally unsurprising. In a sense, it is not a very interesting question to ask why do they lobby in Brussels as this is perfectly rational behaviour and replicates what we already know about group behaviour in national systems. The more interesting question (asked by researchers such as Bennett, Grant, and others cited above) perhaps, is why some groups do *not* lobby at the EU level. So, the real world phenomenon looks very familiar indeed.

Second, academic approaches to the study of the actual phenomenon have exhibited a similar degree of continuity in that the *basic* theoretical underpinnings appear not to have changed much over time. Sidjansky and others started the ball rolling with assumptions about rational behaviour of actors in response to shifts in the locus of power, namely that, sooner or later, groups would calculate that lobbying at the EU level was necessary and that not to lobby at that level was risky and potentially costly. Very many other studies have followed, building on this basic assumption and linking it to (particularly) the behaviour of the Commission as a self-interested actor behaving rationally, but also extending research into the other main EU institutions such as the EP, Council of Ministers, and ECJ. Basically, most academic studies have ended up using some kind of logic of influence/mutual gains model. So, has *anything* changed? Well, yes and no! The changes in approach that have taken place are not unique to interest group studies, however. They reflect broader changes in the political science discipline. Thus, if one looks at EU interest group studies over, say, the last ten years, one can detect a clear trend, namely

towards a much more explicit specifications of theoretical assumptions, a clearer specification of research questions, and more attempts to quantify evidence as a means of theory testing. All of this is very much to the good as it should be much easier for scholars to extract testable hypotheses from other scholars' work and then test them in other settings. If this sounds like two cheers for progress rather than three, it is! Why the missing third cheer? My worry is that we are not witnessing an accumulation of major blocks of new knowledge as such but merely a better methodology for telling us what we have known for rather a long time (such as lobbyists will try to influence the Commission if utility gains are expected; that lobbyists will consider the costs of lobbying; that lobbyists must present reliable information to the Commission. See Broscheid and Coen 2005). If we take the excellent work by Broscheid and Coen, and Bouwen as a fair benchmark of where EU lobbying studies are at just now, such researchers are certainly being more innovative in terms of methodology and are attempting to answer some more detailed research questions (such as 'why are some lobbying systems larger than others?' and 'what explains the presence, and number, of lobbying insiders in a subsystem?' (Broscheid and Coen 2005). Important questions are being asked but, perhaps inevitably with a sub-area that has been quite heavily researched for thirty years or more, the mapping as a result of the new research is likely to be more finely grained than earlier work, rather than radically different. It will be based on better data, better analysed. As with the EU interest intermediation system itself, however, research on that system is likely to bring incremental rather than radical change.

NOTE

1. This chapter draws substantially on the following works. Sonia Mazey and Jeremy Richardson, 'The Commission and the Lobby', in David Spence (ed.); Sonia Mazey and Jeremy Richardson, 'Interest groups and EU Policy-making' in Jeremy Richardson (ed.), *European Union. Power and Policy-making*, London: Routledge 2005.

REFERENCES

Auel, K. and Rittberger, B. (2005) 'Fluctuant nec mergunter. The European Parliament, national parliaments, and European integration', in J. Richardson (ed.), *European Union. Power and Policy-making*, 3rd ed. London: Routledge. pp. 122–45.

Baumgartner, F. R. and Jones, B. D. (1993) *Agendas and Instability in American Politics*. Chicago: University of Chicago Press.

Bennett, R. J. (1997) 'The impact of European integration on business associations: the UK case', *West European Politics*, 20(3): 6–90.

Bouwen, P. (2004a) 'The logic of access to the European Parliament', *Journal of Common Market Studies*, 42(3): 473–496.

Bouwen, P. (2004b) 'Exchange access good for access. A comparative study of business lobbying in the EU institutions', *European Journal of Political Research*, 43(3): 337–69.

Bouwen, P. and McCown, M. (2004) 'Lobbying versus litigation: political and legal strategies of interest representation in the European Union', Paper presented at the ECPR Standing Group on the European Union, Second Pan-European Conference on EU Politics, 24–26 June 2004, Bologna.

Broscheid, A. and Coen, D. (2003) 'Insider and outsider lobbying of the European Commission: an informational model of forum politics', *European Union Politics*, 4(2): 165–90.

Broscheid, A. and Coen, D. (2005) 'Lobbying systems in the European Union: a quantitative study', unpublished paper, November 2005.

Butt A. P. (1985) *Pressure Groups in the European Community*. London: University Association for Contemporary European Studies (UACES).

Christiansen, T., Jørgensen, K. E. and Weiner, A. (1999), 'The social construction of Europe', *The Journal of European Public Policy*, 6(4): 528–44.

Coen, D. (1997) 'The evolution of the large firm as a political actor in the European Union', *Journal of European Public Policy*, 4(1): 91–108.

Commission of the European Communities (1992) *An Open and Structured Dialogue*, SEC (1992) 2272 final. Brussels: European Commission.

Cram, L. (1994) 'The European Commission as a multi-organisation: social policy and IT policy in the EU', *Journal of European Public Policy*, 1(1): 195–218.

Falkner, G. (1998) *EU Social Policy in the 1990s: Towards a Corporatist Policy Community*. London: Routledge.

Georges, M. (1996) *Euro-Corporatism? Interest Intermediation in the European Community*. Lanham: University Press of America.

Grant, W. (2000) *Pressure Groups in British Politics*. Basingstoke, Macmillan.

Greer, S. (2006) 'Uninvited Europeanisation: neo-functionalism and EU health policy', *Journal of European Public Policy*, 13(1): 134–52.

Greenwood, J. (1997) *Representing Interests in the European Union*. Basingstoke: Macmillan.

Greenwood, J., Grote, J. and Ronit, K. (1992) 'Introduction: organized interests and the transnational dimension', in J. Greenwood, J. Grote, J. and K. Ronit (eds), *Organized Interests in the European Community*. London: Sage. pp. 1–41.

Grossman, E. (2004) 'Bringing politics back in: rethinking the role of economic interest groups in European integration', *Journal of European Public Policy*, 11(4): 637–56.

Haas, E. B. (1958) *The Uniting of Europe: Political, Economic and Social Forces, 1950–1957*. Stanford, CA: Stanford University Press.

Hayes-Renshaw, F. and Wallace, H. (1997) *The Council of Ministers*. London: Macmillan.

Hix, S. (2005) *The Political System of the European Union*, second edition. Basingstoke: Palgrave.

Keating, M. and Hooghe, L. (2005) 'By-passing the nation state? Regions and the EU policy process', in J. Richardson (ed.), *European Union. Power and Policy-making*, third edition. London: Routledge. pp. 269–86.

Kirchner, E. (1977) *Trade Unions as Pressure Groups in the European Community*. Farnborough: Saxon House.

Kirchner, E. (1980a) 'International trade union collaboration and the prospect for European industrial relations', *West European Politics*, 3(1): 124–37.

Kirchner, E. (1980b) 'Interest group behaviour at the Community level', in L. Hurwitz (ed.), *Contemporary Perspectives on European Integration*. London: Aldwich.

Kitschelt, P. H. (1986) 'Political opportunity structures and political protest: anti-nuclear movements in four democracies', *British Journal of Political Science*, 16(1): 57–85.

Kohler-Koch, B. (1997) 'Organised interests in the EU and the European Parliament', paper presented to the International Political Science Association XVIII Congress, Seoul, 17–21 August 1997.

Laffan, B. and Mazey, S. (2005) 'European integration – reaching an equilibrium?', in

J. Richardson (ed.), *European Union. Power and policy-making*, third edition. London: Routledge. pp. 31–54.

Lahusen, C. (2003) 'Moving into European orbit: commercial consultants in the European Union', *European Union Politics*, 4(2): 191–218.

Lindberg, L. N. and Scheingold, S. (1970) *Europe's Would-be Polity: Patterns of Change in the European Community*. Cambridge, MA: Harvard University Press.

McCown, M. (2005) 'Judicial law-making and European integration: the European Court of Justice' in J. Richardson (ed.), *European Union. Power and Policy-making*, third edition. London: Routledge. pp. 171–85.

Mahoney, C. (2004) 'The power of institutions: state and interest group activity in the European Union', *European Union Politics*, 5(4): 441–466.

Majone, G. (2006) 'The common sense of European integration', *Journal of European Public Policy*, 13(5): 607–26.

Marks, G., Neilson, F., Ray, L. and Salk, J. (1996) 'Competences, cracks and conflicts: regional mobilization in the European Union, in G. Marks, F. Scharpf, P. V. Scmitter, and W. Streeck (eds), *Governance in the European Union*. London: Sage. pp. 40–63.

Mazey, S. (1992) 'Conception and eolution of the high authority's administrative services (1952–1960)', in E.V. Heyen (ed.), *Yearbook of European Administrative History*. Baden-Baden: Nomos Verlagesellschaft. pp. 31–48.

Mazey, S. (1995) 'The development of EU equality policies: bureaucratic expansion on behalf of woman?', *Public Administration*, 73(4): 591–609.

Mazey, S. (1998) 'The European Union and women's rights: from the Europeanisation of national agendas to the nationalisation of a European agenda?', *Journal of European Public Policy*, 5(1): 131–52.

Mazey, S. and Richardson, J. (eds) (1993) *Lobbying in the European Community*. Oxford: Oxford University Press.

Mazey, S. and Richardson, J. (1995) 'Promiscuous policymaking: the European policy style?', in C. Rhodes and S. Mazey (eds), *The State of the European Union. Vol. 3: Building a European Polity?* Boulder: Lynne Rienner. pp. 337–59.

Mazey, S. and Richardson, J. (2005) 'Interest groups and EU policy-making: organizational logic and venue shopping', in J. Richardson (ed.), *European Union. Power and Policy-Making*, third edition. London: Routledge. pp. 247–68.

Moravcsik, A. (2005) 'The European constitutional compromise and the legacy of neo-functionalism', *Journal of European Public Policy*, 12(2): 349–86.

Pollack, M. A. (1997) 'Representing diffuse interests in EC policy-making', *Journal of European Public Policy*, 4(4): 572–90.

Preston, M. E. (1998) 'The European Commission and special interest groups', in P.-H. Claeys, C. Gobin, I. Smets and P. Winand (eds), *Lobbyisme, Pluralisme et Intégration Européenne*. Brussels: Presses Interuniversitaires Européennes. pp. 222–32.

Radaelli, C. (1999) *Technocracy in the European Union*. London: Longman.

Richardson, J. (ed.) (1982) *Policy Styles in Western Europe*. London: George Allen and Unwin.

Richardson, J. (2000) 'Government, Interest Groups and Policy Change', *Political Studies*, 48(5): 1006–25.

Richardson, J. (2005) 'Policy-making in the EU: interests, ideas and garbage cans of primeval soup', in J. Richardson (ed.), *European Union. Power and Policy-making*, third edition. London: Routledge. pp. 3–30.

Ruzza, C. (2004) *Europe and Civil Society. Movement Coalitions and European Governance*. Manchester: Manchester University Press.

Schneider, G. and Baltz, K. (2004) 'Paying the piper, calling the tune: interest intermediation in the pre-negotiations of EU legislation', paper presented at the Pan-European Conference of International Relations, the Hague, 9–11 September 2004.

Sidjanski, D. (1970) 'Pressure groups and the European economic community', in C. Cosgrove and K. Twitchett (eds), *The New International Actors: The United Nations and the European Economic Community*. London: Macmillan. pp. 222–36.

Spence, D. (1993) 'The role of the National Civil Service in European lobbying: the British Case', in S. Mazey, and J. Richardson (eds), *Lobbying in the European Community*. Oxford: Oxford University Press. pp. 47–73.

Stone Sweet, A. (2004) *The Judicial Construction of Europe*. Oxford: Oxford University Press.

Streeck, W. and Schmitter, P. C. (1991) 'From national corporatism to transnational pluralism: organised interests in the single European market', *Politics and Society*, 19(2): 133–64.

Tarrow, S. (1998) *Power in Movement*, second edition. Cambridge: Cambridge University Press.

Tarrow, S. (2001) 'Contentious politics in a composite polity', in D. Imig and S. Tarrow (eds),

Contentious Europeans. Lanham: Rowman and Littlefield. pp. 233–51.

Truman, D. (1951) *The Governmental Process: Political Interests and Public Opinion*. New York: Knopf.

Treib, O., Bähr, H. and Falkner, G. (forthcoming) 'Modes of Governance: A note towards a conceptual clarification', *Journal of European Public Policy*, 14(1).

Wessels, B. (1999) 'European Parliament and interest groups', in R. Katz and B. Wessels (eds), *The European Parliament, the National Parliaments, and European Integration*. Oxford: Oxford University Press. pp. 105–28.

12

Political Parties in the European Union

TAPIO RAUNIO[1]

European democracy is effectively party democracy. However, according to recent literature on political parties, they are gradually undergoing transformation: '[I]t would be an overstatement to write the parties' political obituary, but a pattern of partisan decline – or at least a transformation in the role played by parties – is increasingly apparent in almost all advanced industrial democracies' (Dalton and Wattenberg 2000: 3). The party transformation thesis is based primarily on the eroding linkage between parties and citizens. But while parties may not be as firmly rooted in civil society as before, no similar decline has occurred in the legislature and government. Indeed, the member states of the European Union (EU) continue to be governed by cohesive, disciplined parties.[2]

At the same time, the rapid constitutional transformation of the EU since the mid-1980s, in part brought about by the purposeful action of national parties themselves, has increased the relevance of parties in the EU political system. The strengthened role of the European Parliament (EP), both in terms of shaping EU legislation and of holding the Commission accountable, means that the party groups of

Europarties are in a much stronger position than before to influence the EU's policy process. As the Parliament must approve both the Commission President and the whole Commission before they take office, the old image of the Commission as a neutral supranational technocracy is gradually eroding, with both the media and researchers paying more attention to the partisan composition of the Commission. Nor should it be forgotten that the Council and the European Council, normally portrayed as intergovernmental institutions safeguarding national interests, are made up of politicians representing national government parties. In short, the further the EU moves away from 'diplomatic' intergovernmental negotiations to supranational democracy, the more its policies are shaped by political parties as opposed to just national governments.

The party politicization of EU has not gone unnoticed among political scientists. Quite the contrary, an increasing range of scholars has begun to analyse the role of parties in the EU system. This chapter examines the state of research on parties in the European Union. Adopting a bottom-up approach, the next section will first analyse research on political cleavages and on how the EU impacts on national party competition. This is essential in order to understand party behaviour at the European level. The third section explores the state of research on Europarties, with the fourth section then focusing on our knowledge of party behaviour in the EP. The concluding section outlines an agenda for future research. The main argument of the chapter is that the role of parties in the EU is still a rather new field of inquiry, with relatively little debate between competing schools of thought. However, recent research does clearly show that parties perform an increasingly important role in shaping the EU's agenda and legislation, particularly in the EP where party competition is increasingly structured along the left-right dimension.

EUROPEAN INTEGRATION AND POLITICAL CLEAVAGES

European integration presents a major challenge for national parties. Since the majority of main political parties in EU member states were established before the start of integration, the European issue has introduced a new dimension to their politics, both in terms of their ideologies and organization. Ideologically, parties both shape European integration by pursuing policy objectives at national and EU levels, and adapt to integration by operating in an environment increasingly influenced by the limits set by the constitution and legislation of the Union.

Lipset and Rokkan (1967) argued in their seminal work that the development of European party systems was shaped by critical junctures in history. These junctures resulted in social cleavages (class, religion, centre-periphery etc.), which in turn led to the formation of political parties representing distinct social and economic interests. Lipset and Rokkan, writing in the 1960s, argued that these party systems had become 'frozen'. European democracies, however, have changed rather fundamentally since the Second World

War. Economic development has gradually transformed European countries from industrial, or even predominantly agrarian societies to modern, post-industrial economies that are increasingly subject to global and particularly European regulation. New issues, such as environmental policy, human rights, and globalization have changed the agenda of politics.

While it probably would be an exaggeration to claim that the process of European integration forms such a critical juncture, the EU dimension, often defined as the anti/pro-integration continuum, does nonetheless arguably constitute the main new dimension in European politics, especially when examining developments since the late 1980s. Indeed, several scholars have (at least implicitly) argued that the European party-political space is nowadays based on two main dimensions – the old left-right cleavage and the new EU cleavage (e.g. Hix 1999; Hooghe and Marks 1999; Marks and Wilson 2000; Marks and Steenbergen 2002, 2004).

Research on policy representation has found European political parties to be fairly representative of their voters on the left-right dimension. Both comparative analyses and country studies testify that, by and large, European citizens are well represented on that key dimension of party competition.[3] However, the reality is altogether different when we examine attitudes towards European integration. This research has produced three main findings. First, European integration is clearly a destabilizing factor for national parties. Second, within parties the elites are far more supportive of integration than their electorates. And third, party policies on European integration are quite strongly related to parties' positions on the left-right dimension. These findings are connected to each other, as the divisive nature of the EU dimension provides incentives for parties to downplay European issues and to structure competition along the more familiar left-right dimension.

Regardless of the data used – surveys of citizens and members of parliament (MPs) (e.g. Thomassen and Schmitt 1999b), expert surveys (Ray 1999), or more descriptive approaches (e.g. Gaffney 1996) – research has clearly shown that national parties are ideologically less cohesive on integration than on traditional left/right issues. Perhaps more interestingly, within parties the elected representatives are considerably more supportive of integration than their voters, with the European dimension revealing a wide gap between citizens and MPs. The first comparative study on issue agreement on integration matters did, however, find considerable congruence of opinion. Comparing voters' perceptions of where parties stand and voters' own preferences from a survey carried out right after the 1989 EP elections, van der Eijk and Franklin (1991: 124) showed that most parties were representative of their voters in integration matters, with 'only a few parties' taking positions that were clearly out of line with the position of their voters.

Subsequent analyses have come to a somewhat different conclusion. Comparing the preferences of citizens and candidates in the 1994 EP elections in concrete policy issues about EU (abolishment of borders, unemployment, single currency), Thomassen and Schmitt (1997: 181) concluded that the elite and the electorate were 'living in different European worlds'. And, when comparing the views of MPs and MEPs (members of the European Parliament) and the citizens on those same issues, the same authors stated a couple of years later that 'across the board, voters' attitudes appeared to be less pro-European than those of the political elites, whether they were members of the European Parliament or of the national parliaments' (Thomassen and Schmitt 1999a: 206). In another article, based on elite and citizen survey data from 1979 and 1994, Schmitt and Thomassen (2000) showed that while the policy preferences of the voters and the parties did diverge, the issue agreement between voters and party elites about the general development of integration ('Are you for or against efforts being made to unify Europe?') was as high as on the left-right dimension. Thus they argued that while policy representation was failing in specific EU policy issues, it did seem to work fairly well as far as the overall development of integration is concerned. Finally, using

data from the 1999 European Election Study (EES), in which the voters were asked to place both themselves and the parties on the anti/pro-integration dimension, van der Eijk and Franklin (2004) showed that the diversity of opinion among the electorate was not reflected at the level of the parties. There was thus, according to those authors, 'potential for contestation' on EU issues, with the EU issue being a 'sleeping giant' in European politics. The study also showed the parties to be far more supportive of integration than the voters.

Turning to studies that seek to explain party positions on European integration, the main debate has centered on the relation between the EU dimension and the left-right cleavage. The standard finding has been that of an inverted U-curve, with opposition to European integration found at the extreme ends of the left-right dimension while more centrist parties are supportive of further integration. This means that party family is a powerful predictor of party positions on EU – with social democrats, liberals, and Christian democrats (and increasingly also greens) in favour of integration, and extreme right and left parties opposed to it (e.g. Hix and Lord 1997: 21–53; Taggart 1998; Marks and Wilson 2000; Marks et al. 2002; Taggart and Szczerbiak 2007a, b).

However, more recent research has partially challenged this argument, particularly as a result of the enlargement of the Union that took place in 2004. Using expert survey data from 1999, Hooghe et al. (2002) show that there is indeed a strong relationship between these two dimensions. However, they also show that another cleavage, the GAL (Green/alternative/libertarian)-TAN (traditional/authoritarian/nationalist) dimension is actually a stronger predictor of parties' EU positions. In a subsequent paper, based on similar expert survey data from 2002, Marks et al. (2006) confirm that parties' positions concerning European integration can indeed be inferred from their locations on the left-right and GAL/TAN dimensions, with opposition to further integration mainly found among extreme left and TAN parties. But, Marks et al. (2006) show that there are important differences between the 'old' member states and those that joined the Union in 2004. In the 'West', the leftist parties tend to be GAL parties while rightist parties are more TAN in their orientation. In the 'East', on the other hand, opposition to the EU is primarily concentrated among a group of left/TAN parties.[4]

While the research mentioned in this section clearly shows that European questions have in several EU countries led to severe conflicts among and within parties, European integration has nonetheless not altered the basic structure of national party systems by resulting in the formation of new parties. According to Mair (2000: 30), out of over 120 parties established in EU member states (excluding Greece, Portugal and Spain) to contest national parliamentary elections after the first direct EP elections held in each country, only three were formed 'with the explicit and primary intention of mobilising support for or against the EU'.[5] Mair also found that these parties were marginal players in their respective political systems, winning an average of only 1.5 per cent of the votes in national elections. Party members, at least on the elite level, have therefore decided not to defect to other parties despite the often considerable differences of opinion over Europe.

This is not surprising. Indeed, there are very strong reasons to expect that we would not witness the entry of new parties as a result of European integration – or any other issue for that matter. The main explanatory factor for the observed stability is that the established national parties have an interest in sustaining the status quo and the prevailing structures of party competition. It would be dangerous and potentially costly for parties to change existing structures of electoral contestation. After all, despite the gradual partisan dealignment, parties still have their 'natural' pools of voters and they have reputations for particular programmes and policy objectives. Giving the EU dimension a stronger role in the competition for votes would potentially lead to instability that might weaken the role of the main national parties (Marks and Steenbergen 2002: 881–2). As Hooghe et al. (2002: 970) argue:

Parties that are successful in the existing structure of contestation have little incentive to rock the boat, while unsuccessful parties, that is, parties with weak electoral support or those that are locked out of government, have an interest in restructuring competition. The same strategic logic that leads mainstream parties to assimilate the issues raised by European integration into the Left/Right dimension of party competition leads peripheral parties to exploit European integration in an effort to shake up the party system.

This section has explored the state of the research on how European integration has affected party systems at the national level and what factors explain parties' EU positions. The next two sections will investigate developments at the European level, starting with research on Europarties.

EUROPARTIES

The Maastricht Treaty assigned political parties a specific role to play in the political system of the European Union. According to the Treaty's Article 138a, 'Political parties at the European level are important as a factor for integration within the Union. They contribute to forming a European awareness and to expressing the political will of the citizens of the Union'. This 'Party Article' has also been included as Article I–46(4) in the Treaty establishing a Constitution for Europe: 'Political parties at European level contribute to forming European political awareness and to expressing the will of citizens of the Union.'

The constitutional recognition in the form of the Party Article in the Maastricht Treaty is directly linked to the subsequent development of Europarties. With the exception of the European People's Party (EPP) that had already been founded in 1976, the (con)federations of national parties were quickly turned into Europarties. The Confederation of Socialist Parties of the European Community (CSP), founded in 1974, was transformed into the Party of European Socialists (PES) in November 1992. The Federation of European Liberal, Democrat and Reform Parties, founded in 1976, became the European Liberal, Democrat and Reform Party (ELDR) in December 1993. The green parties established the European Federation of Green Parties (EFGP) in June 1993, changing their name to the European Green Party (EGP) in 2004. A newcomer is the Democratic Party of the Peoples of Europe – European Free Alliance (DPPE-EFA), a federation of regionalist parties established in 1998. Furthermore, plans both among radical left and right parties and among the various Eurosceptical parties to form their own Europarties are likely to get further impetus from the introduction in 2004 of public funding of Europarties from the EU's budget.[6] However, at least the various Eurosceptical parties or movements may find it difficult to agree on a common programme, as the objectives of these parties range from opposing further integration (for example, the June List in Sweden) to demanding their country's withdrawal from the Union (for example, the Independence Party in the UK).

Curiously enough, the early stages of transnational party cooperation are better covered by existing research than the period after the Maastricht Treaty. This applies in particular to theorizing about the development and constraints faced by European-level parties. The approaching first direct EP elections of 1979 had given a stimulus to co-operation among European national parties, and this received also the attention of a number of scholars. The two main works from that period are Pridham and Pridham (1981) and Niedermayer (1983), both of which also contain lengthy sections on party co-operation inside the European Parliament. Both volumes explored the establishment and work of the Europarties or transnational party federations, focusing in particular on the obstacles that stood in the way of truly supranational party politics. The diversity of national political cultures, the ideological discrepancies between parties belonging to the same federation, the lack of progress in European integration, the primacy of national over European politics, and the weak powers accorded to the EP were shown to influence the degree or quality of co-operation achieved among the parties both outside and within the Parliament.

During the 1980s scholarly interest in transnational parties declined, but the relaunch of the integration process in the early 1990s renewed interest in Europarties. This research has mainly focused on individual Europarties. Johansson (1997) analysed the rapprochement between conservative and Christian democratic parties in the EPP (see also Hanley 2002), while the more descriptive work by Jansen (1998) traces the evolution of EPP and its predecessors after the Second World War. Bomberg (1998) and Dietz (1997, 2000) examined European-level cooperation between green parties, both outside and inside the EP. Ladrech (2000) and Lightfoot (2005) in turn analysed the PES, arguing that traditional concepts of political parties are only partly applicable in the context of Europarties. According to Ladrech, Europarties are better understood as networks of like-minded national parties that facilitate information-sharing and, within certain constraints, also the advancement of policy objectives (see also Bardi 2002). The study by Lightfoot focused on the role of PES in two key policy areas (environment and employment) and in relation to Treaty amendments, and illustrates effectively how ideological differences among the member parties limit the ability of the PES to construct policy and thereby influence politics at the European level. The liberal party family has received least attention among scholars, with the only more extensive treatment being that of Sandström (2003), available unfortunately only in Swedish. Finally, Lynch (1998) and de Winter and Gomez-Reino Cachafeiro (2002) study the evolution of transnational party cooperation among the regionalist parties belonging to the DPPE-EFA.

This research on Europarties has largely focused on how an exogenous factor (deepening integration) has produced endogenous reforms within the Europarties – including the move to (qualified) majority voting as the main decision rule in the parties' executive bodies. The main findings of these individual case studies are also found in the comparative volumes edited by Bell and Lord (1998), Delwit et al. (2001),[7] and Johansson and

Zervakis (2002). Unfortunately this research suffers from two shortcomings. First, we still lack theoretical tools for understanding the nature of the Europarties. While most of the case studies do at least implicitly acknowledge the constraints and possibilities facing Europarties, none of them goes as far as to constructing a model or a theoretical framework that would enable us to sufficiently understand how and under what conditions Europarties are able impact on EU or national politics. The chapters on Europarties in Hix and Lord (1997), where the focus is primarily on the meetings of national party leaders in conjunction with the European Council meetings, and particularly Lightfoot (2005) and Ladrech (2000) are partial exceptions to the rule, as are the case studies by Johansson (1999, 2002a, 2002b) on the inclusion of the employment title in the Amsterdam Treaty and on the role of EPP in the negotiations resulting in the Single European Act and in the Maastricht Treaty. Moreover, Johansson and Raunio (2005) study the process resulting in the incorporation of the Party Article in the Maastricht Treaty, the subsequent clause in the Treaty of Nice, and the regulation on the introduction of public funding of political parties at the European level adopted in 2003. Applying insights from rational choice and historical institutionalism, they show how Europarties, both separately and together as coalitions, consistently and with determination exploited the 'incomplete contract', the Party Article in the Maastricht Treaty (see also Day and Shaw 2003). However, even these authors rely on selective case evidence as opposed to a more theory-driven model that would single out the conditions when Europarties can wield influence and when they cannot.

Secondly, there is a need for a comparative study that would explain variation among the five Europarties. So far such systematic comparison has only been applied to examining the ideologies of the Europarties. Adapting the content analysis method developed by the Manifesto Research Group (Budge et al. 2001), Hix (1999) and Gabel and Hix (2002) show in their analysis of Europarties' programmes that the Europarties have become ideologically increasingly similar, especially after social democrats (PES) and green parties (EGP) changed their attitudes to European integration. While support for deeper integration was stronger among the centre-right parties (EPP and ELDR) until the 1990s, since the Maastricht Treaty the centre-left (PES and also partially the Greens) have become the leading advocates of further centralization. However, these authors and Pennings (2002) also show that there are nonetheless quite considerable differences between the Europarties on the left-right dimension, thus offering real choices to the electorate. This comparative focus could logically be extended to the inner workings of the Europarties. The organizational aspects – e.g. staff, funding, formal decision rules – of Europarties have been analysed by several authors (Bardi 1992, 1994; see also Dietz 2000 and Johansson and Zervakis 2002), but we know relatively little in comparative terms about how Europarties operate and coordinate policy among the national member parties and whether this policy coordination results in changes in the ideologies of national member parties.

Having examined the state of research on Europarties outside the EP, the next section explores our knowledge of the (Europarties') party groups in the Parliament. The section is divided into two parts. The first part looks at research on MEP behaviour, with the latter then examining research on links between national parties and their MEPs.

PARTY POLITICS IN THE EUROPEAN PARLIAMENT

Compared with parties in EU member state legislatures, the party groups of the European Parliament operate in a very different institutional environment. There is no EU government accountable to the Parliament. There are no coherent and hierarchically organized European-level parties. Instead, MEPs are elected from lists drawn by national parties and on the basis of national electoral campaigns. The social and cultural heterogeneity of the EU is reflected in the internal diversity of the groups, with a total of 170 national parties from 25 member states winning seats in the Parliament in the 2004 elections. The party groups are thus structurally firmly embedded in the political systems of the EU member states. However, despite the existence of such factors, EP party groups have gradually over the decades consolidated their position in the Parliament, primarily through introducing procedural reforms that enable them to make effective use of EP's legislative powers. At the same time the shape of the party system has become more stable, at least as far as the main groups are concerned. One can thus speak of the 'institutionalization' of the EP party system (see also Chapter 8 in this volume).

Throughout its history the EP party system has been based on the left-right dimension. Initially the party system consisted of only three groups: socialists/social democrats (PES), Christian democrats/conservatives (EPP), and liberals (ELDR), the three main party families in EU member states. Since the first direct elections also the Greens and the group of the radical left parties, now titled the Confederal Group of the European United Left/Nordic Green Left (EUL-NGL), have become 'institutionalized' in the chamber. Moreover, Eurosceptical parties, parties whose main reason of existence is opposition to further integration, have formed a group under various labels since the 1994 elections.

Turning first to the period when the Parliament was not directly elected (until 1979), van Oudenhove (1965) examines the first decade of party politics in the Parliament. Fitzmaurice (1975) provides a clear and informative account of party groups, including chapters on individual groups, an analysis of their cohesion and the influence of external factors on their behaviour. After the introduction of direct elections, scholarly interest in the EP groups declined temporarily. However, since the early 1990s the EP groups have been subjected to rigorous scrutiny, making the European Parliament arguably one of the most-researched legislatures in the world. The volume by Hix and Lord (1997) contains informative chapters on EP groups, particularly

concerning group structure and coalition dynamics. But, the authoritative text on the development of EP groups is Kreppel (2002; see also Kreppel 2003). Kreppel analyses how the increase in the legislative powers of the EP has impacted on its party groups, and shows that it has resulted in the centralization of power in the hands of the two large party groups – PES and EPP – and in a dogmatic, conflictual style of politics being replaced by pragmatic co-operation between them in order to influence the EU legislative process. Based on a variety of data – the rules of the Parliament and its two largest groups, roll-call votes, interviews with MEPs and parliamentary staff, and distribution of committee chairs and rapporteurships – Kreppel shows how the two main party groups altered their voting behaviour in response to the EP becoming a real legislative body, and simultaneously introduced changes to the Parliament's rules that further marginalized the smaller party groups.

Moving to more detailed research on EP groups, much of this work has been based on roll-call data. Here the 'pioneering' contribution by Attinà (1990) deserves particular attention. Attinà measured group cohesion and voting likeness in the first and second terms of the directly elected Parliament, showing that the groups were able to achieve quite respectable levels of cohesion and that the left-right dimension was the main cleavage structuring voting in the Parliament (see also Quanjel and Wolters 1993; Bay Brzinski 1995). Raunio (1997) extended this approach to the 1989–94 Parliament, but as was the case with Attinà, his sample was fairly limited. Subsequent research by Hix and his colleagues has been far more ambitious, methodologically more sophisticated (primarily using the NOMINATE method developed by Poole and Rosenthal 1997) and based on larger numbers of recorded votes.[8] This research has produced two main findings. First, it has confirmed that the EP groups do continue to achieve rather high levels of cohesion. Reflecting its disagreements over European integration, the PES was prone to internal splits until the early 1990s, but has since become much more cohesive as the majority of European social democratic parties have adopted broadly similar views on both socio-economic matters and on the future of integration. The EPP, in turn, has become less cohesive since the mid-1990s as the group membership has been widened to include several conservative parties. Groups dominated by a single party have often reached very high levels of cohesion, while technical groups and the radical left groups have seldom made attempts to build common positions.

Second, the main cleavage structuring competition in the Parliament is the familiar left-right dimension, the main dimension of contestation in European democracies (e.g. Huber and Inglehart 1995). Noury (2002) and Thomassen et al. (2004) identify four dimensions of contestation in the chamber, but conclude that the dominant one is the left-right cleavage. Using the entirety of roll-call votes from 1979 to 2001, Hix et al. (2003, 2005) show that competition between party groups has been along a single left-right ideological dimension (see also Kreppel and Tsebelis 1999). Moreover, the EP has become more competitive as the institution has gained more legislative powers. While the primary decision rule in the Parliament is simple majority (50 per cent + 1 of those voting), for certain issues (mainly budget amendments and second reading legislative amendments adopted under the co-decision procedure) the Parliament needs to muster absolute majorities (50 per cent + 1 of *all* its members). The absolute majority requirement facilitates co-operation between the two main groups, EPP and PES, as the surest way of getting the required number of MEPs behind the Parliament's decision is when the two large groups agree on the issue. Co-operation between EPP and PES could also be regarded as a sign of 'maturity', as the Parliament needed to moderate its resolutions in order to get its amendments accepted by the Council and the Commission (Kreppel 2002). After all, the overwhelming majority of national ministers represented in the Council and members of the Commission are either social democrats or Christian democrats/ conservatives. However, after the 1999 EP elections this co-operation has played a lesser role than before, with EPP and PES opposing each other more often regardless of the voting rule (Hix et al. 2003, 2005; Kreppel and Hix 2003).

However, there is an important methodological caveat here. As recorded votes represent only a sample of the totality of votes in the Parliament, the representativeness of that sample is a crucial matter – particularly when studying conflict dimensions in the EP. Analysing both recorded and unrecorded votes in the EP, Carrubba et al. (2003) show that roll-call votes are biased both in terms of their importance (with important legislative votes under-represented) and their content (favouring thus particular policy areas at the expense of others). Carrubba et al. then argue that as roll-call data clearly under-represents legislative votes and certain policy areas, it does not enable us to draw any definitive conclusions about the levels of group cohesion or about the dimensionality of competition in the chamber. Roll-call votes are thus an essential source of information about MEP behaviour, but future research should explicitly acknowledge that results of such voting analysis can not – at least not without adequate complementary evidence – be generalized to apply to all issues processed by the Parliament.

Parliamentary committees have remained somewhat of a 'black box', but even here recent research has greatly improved our understanding of how EP committees function and how party groups influence committee proceedings. Research on EP committees has largely been driven by the debate between informational and distributional models of legislative politics derived from literature on the US Congress, with the studies on EP committees finding support for both perspectives. Bowler and Farrell (1995: 227) showed that 'the share of committee places is proportional by both nationality and ideological bloc. Within these limits, set by allocations along ideological or national lines, there is scope for the kinds of specialized membership and recruitment made in the US Congress'. The allocation of reports (that form the basis of EP resolutions) is roughly proportional to group strength in the Parliament (Mamadouh and Raunio 2003; but see Kaeding 2005), but also partly driven by distributive and informational concerns (Kaeding 2004, 2005; Benedetto 2005;

Hausemer 2005a, 2005b). The procedures for allocating committee chairs, seats and reports, all roughly based on proportionality, can be interpreted as mechanisms for the party groups to control the committees in a situation where the former are relatively weak, at least when compared to European national parliaments (Whitaker 2001; Mamadouh and Raunio 2003; Bowler and Farrell 1995). But, research also shows that national parties are key players in allocating committee seats and reports, and there are signs that they to an increasing extent use committee assignments to achieve their policy goals (Whitaker 2001, 2005; Mamadouh and Raunio 2003; Hausemer 2005a, 2005b).

Indeed, national party delegations are the cornerstones upon which the EP groups are based. Some groups are indeed no more than loose coalitions of national parties, while even in the oldest and most organized groups – EPP and PES – one can occasionally see divisions along national lines. Most national delegations have their own staff, elect their chairpersons, and convene prior to group meetings. MEPs can hence be regarded as agents serving multiple principals – voters, national parties, and their EP party groups. Arguably national parties constitute the most powerful principals as they control candidate selection, especially in countries that use closed lists. As Hearl and Sargent (1979: 11, 16, emphasis in original) argued on the eve of the first Euroelections:

> There is no MEP who does not owe his/her seat in both his/her national parliament and the European Parliament to a *national* political party. These national parties would therefore appear to constitute ideal foci for information links between MEPs and MPs of the same political party. Parties can also be expected to try to set up links in order to ensure that they are not affected adversely at home as a result of the actions or pronouncements of their European members ... the effect of direct elections, by making MEPs formally accountable directly to national electorates and no longer to national parliaments, will be to force the parties outside parliament to interpose themselves between the directly elected members and those who elect them in the same way as they now do in national politics.

However, examining research on links between national parties and their MEPs, the overall picture that emerges from the literature is primarily that of MEPs experiencing very little

actual control by national parties. Once elected to the Parliament, they lead a pretty independent existence and also have fairly low status in their national parties. Before the introduction of direct elections (1979) the linkage was solved by the dual mandate as members served simultaneously in the national legislature and the European Parliament. However, this did not mean that the flow of information between the two levels was satisfactory. The study by Hearl and Sargent (1979) showed that MEPs felt that domestic MPs were not really attentive to their European work, and as a result their freedom of action was much greater in the EP than in their national parliaments. This probably reflected the limited powers of the EC at that stage.

The move to direct elections did not seem to change the situation, at least not before the mid-1990s and the Maastricht Treaty. The volume edited by Morgan and Tame (1996) showed that MEPs in many countries were often largely ignored by their national counterparts during the 1980s, particularly in the run-up to the two Intergovernmental Conferences (IGC) held in 1990-91. Hix and Lord (1997: 60) meanwhile argued that 'most MEPs take part in domestic party congresses and vote in party leadership elections. Relative to national parliamentarians, however, the status of MEPs in the national party apparatus is weak'. Analysing the impact of Conservative and Labour MEPs on British EC policy, Thomas (1992) concluded that their influence was negligible. In her comparative study on green parties, Bomberg (1998) argued in turn that green MEPs did not receive adequate support from their national parties.

More recent research indicates that the linkage is gradually becoming stronger. The survey of national parties represented in the Parliament carried out in 1998 by Raunio (2000, 2002a) indicated that parties were gradually paying more attention to their MEPs. While the survey results were primarily restricted to a single point in time, the findings nevertheless suggested that information and control links between MEPs and their parties had increased as the EU and its Parliament had won more powers. Control of MEPs' behaviour was largely in the form of policy coordination and exchange of information. Less than one out of 10 parties gave MEPs voting instructions on a regular basis, just under one-third did so on issues of fundamental importance, and nearly half of the parties reported that they never 'mandate' their representatives.

Other studies have reached a broadly similar conclusion. Blomgren (2003) analysed the links between MEPs and parties in three smaller EU countries, Ireland, the Netherlands, and Sweden (three parties from each country). Blomgren (2003: 292) concluded that 'party organizations have not, generally speaking, created efficient means of coordinating between the MEPs and other groups within the parties. Most parties have quite meagre means of coordinating between the levels, or, for that matter, controlling the MEPs'. According to Blomgren most of the contacts between national and European levels rested upon personal relationships, with the contacts mainly initiated by MEPs. The low level of contacts or coordination was mainly explained by lack of interest from national parties, with Blomgren even detecting signs of growing hostility between MEPs and their parliamentary colleagues back home. Ovey (2002) examined how the British Labour Party and the German Social Democratic Party managed their links with MEPs from 1994 to 1999. According to Ovey the two parties established closer links with their MEPs, but both had difficulties in finding efficient ways of incorporating MEPs into party structures. While the parties became more interested in how their MEPs behaved and voted, particularly the Labour Party, the MEPs nevertheless enjoyed 'a free reign to a great degree' (Ovey 2002: 211). Messmer (2003) also studied the operation of the 'link system' established by the British Labour Party, which brings a section of Labour MEPs into close cooperation with the government and party leadership. Both Messmer and Ovey show that this link system enables the Labour Party leadership to place severe constraints on MEPs, including issuing voting instructions, especially in matters that are of high salience for the Blair government.

The only study so far that has attempted to 'model' linkages between national parties and their MEPs is the analysis of the frequency of voting instructions by Scully (2001). Using a principal-agent framework, Scully showed that 'mandating' was more common in parties that were located further from the centre of the left-right dimension, had larger delegations in the Parliament, were from unitary as opposed to federal countries, and in which MEPs had frequent contacts with party leadership. Holding government office may be an increasingly important variable here (see Ovey 2002; Blomgren 2003: 186–9; Messmer 2003). When a party is in government, it has a higher incentive than the opposition to learn about the mood in the Parliament as the outcome of legislative initiatives depends to an increasing extent also on the EP, notably so under the co-decision procedure. Hence the domestic party leadership may want to ensure that the voting behaviour of its MEPs is in line with the stand of the government. For example, the link system established by the British Labour Party was partly motivated by the need to ensure that the Labour MEPs do not vote against the position of the Labour government. However, Scully (2001) found that membership in the government did not have any impact on explaining the tendency to issue voting instructions.

In addition to studies focusing directly on links between MEPs and national parties, research on voting behaviour in the Parliament provides further evidence of the influence of national parties. It must be stressed that national parties, and not EP groups or Europarties, control, candidate selection: 'this selection procedure hence gives national parties the ultimate sanction over their MEPs; and ensures that where national party and EP party group allegiances conflict in the EP, the national party allegiance invariably wins out' (Hix and Lord 1997: 60; see also Hix and Lord 1996). Voting behaviour analysis indicates that when MEPs receive conflicting voting instructions from national parties and their EP groups, they are indeed more likely to side with their national party, particularly in parties where the leadership has better opportunities to punish and reward (through controlling candidate selection) its MEPs:

> Despite the fact that that the parliamentary principals in the EP control important benefits – such as committee assignments and speaking time – it is the principals that control candidate selection (the national parties) who ultimately determine how MEPs behave. When the national parties in the same parliamentary group decide to vote together, the EP parties look highly cohesive. But when these parties take opposing policy positions, the cohesion of the EP parties break down (Hix 2002: 696).

The decision to follow the national party rather than the EP group applies particularly to MEPs that are elected under institutions that facilitate strong party control over their representatives: closed lists, small district magnitude, and/or centralized candidate selection (Hix 2004). In a similar fashion, Faas (2003) shows that national party characteristics have a strong impact on MEP voting behaviour, with MEPs from parties that are more Eurosceptical, that have a centralized method of candidate selection, that invest more resources in the monitoring of their MEPs and/or that are in the government of their country being more likely to defect from party group lines. However, it is important to remember that none of the studies on voting behaviour claim that national parties back home would be explicitly instructing their MEPs how to behave. Nonetheless, they do show the importance of national parties for understanding how the EP and its party groups operate.

The existing research has thus produced two somewhat contradictory findings. On the one hand, national parties in general pay more attention to their MEPs, with particularly the case studies on British parties confirming this trend. On the other hand, MEPs often perceive themselves to be rather peripheral actors in their parties, complaining that their work is not taken seriously enough. However, one thing is clear: while MEPs are often ignored by their national parties, they are nevertheless firmly anchored in domestic politics, not least through their constituency-related activities. Most MEPs hold simultaneously various offices in their parties (either at the local, district, or national level) and maintain active links with their party organisations and voters. Moreover, it is interesting to note that overall the preferences of national MPs and MEPs over integration are quite similar, and that contrary to much accepted wisdom, MEPs do not 'go native' in Brussels, becoming considerably more pro-European than their party comrades back home (Scully 2005).

CONCLUSION

European integration has transformed party politics in Europe. The increase in the powers of the EU has strengthened the political weight and activity of the Europarties and their parliamentary groups in the European Parliament. At the same time it must be emphasized that membership in national parliament and particularly in government remain the most important channel for influencing decision-making in both domestic and European issues. Hence winning public office at the national level is still for most politicians the ultimate prize in European politics. The present situation is likely to persist for as long as there is no executive office at stake at the European level. Without any EU president or parliamentary government armed with considerable policy-making powers, the identity and dominant position of national parties is not threatened by the Europarties.

However, this does not mean that the EU would not impact on national parties. The review of literature in this chapter has shown that most of the research has focused on describing or explaining the EU policies of national parties. There is thus still a broad agenda for future research. First, we need information on how (or, indeed, if) EU impacts on the balance of power within the parties. Examining the organizational set-up of domestic parties, we can see that national parties have undergone only limited changes as a result of European integration. Most parties have established working groups on EU issues and appointed secretaries and spokespersons responsible for European affairs, and they do nominate candidates in European elections and choose delegates to represent them in the executive organs of the Europarties. However, these changes are limited in scope and do not alter the basic organizational structure of parties. But, beyond the surface the EU could indeed have altered the balance of power, for example through empowering the party leaders vis-à-vis the other party organs (Ladrech 2002: 398; Raunio 2002b).

More importantly, future research needs to address the question of salience. The only study that has examined the salience of European integration for parties cross-nationally is Steenbergen and Scott (2004). Based on expert surveys, they find significant variation among individual member states and parties and show that the salience of the EU has increased slightly as the EU has gained new powers. More specifically, future research could examine whether the EU impacts on party choice in national elections (Gabel 2000). At least in Great Britain the European issue emerged during the 1990s as a significant cleavage driving citizens' voting behaviour. The Conservative Party failed in its attempt to increase its vote share by adopting a highly Eurocritical position in the 1990s, with voters' perceptions of the party's position on the EU influencing negatively its electoral support (Evans 1998). In his subsequent work, Evans (2002) has shown that as the ideological differences between the two main British parties on traditional left-right axis have diminished, the European issue has emerged as a significant factor influencing voting behaviour in elections to the House of Commons. Tillman (2004) also argues that around the time (1994–6) when Austria, Finland, and Sweden joined the Union, the membership question influenced voting behaviour in these three countries. However, as Tillman himself admits, this may have resulted from the fact that the European issue was particularly salient in those countries during that time period.

Research on the European Parliament and its party groups has witnessed major progress during recent years. As the powers of the EP have been increased, so has our understanding of how the EP works and under what conditions it can influence supranational legislation. In fact, we now know more about the EP than about most national parliaments of the EU member states. Nonetheless, there are several aspects of the EP's work that remain under-researched, most importantly decision-making in committees and in party groups. Future research on the European Parliament and on Europarties could also benefit from more comparisons with the United States. After all, the EU resembles in many ways the American political system, with multiple veto-players, power-sharing and policy co-ordination between state and federal levels, and strong interest groups – but also weak and internally divided parties. Possible options would thus be to analyse the interaction between interest groups and EP groups or committees, and in particular the partisan linkages between the EP, Council and the Commission.

NOTES

1. I am grateful to Karl Magnus Johansson, Mark Pollack, and Knud Erik Jørgensen for comments on an earlier version of this chapter.

2. For more detailed information on the transformation of national parties, see the volumes edited by Dalton and Wattenberg (2000), Luther and Müller-Rommel (2002) and Webb et al. (2002).

3. For an excellent review of the policy representation literature, see Powell (2004).

4. For more information on the literature concerning cleavages in the European Union, see Marks and Steenbergen (2002, 2004).

5. Mair thus excluded anti/pro-EU parties that compete exclusively in EP elections. The Danish EP election system features two Eurosceptical lists, the June Movement and the People's Movement Against the EU, that do not contest seats in national parliamentary elections. In 1994 they won 25.5 per cent, in 1999 23.4 per cent, and in 2004 14.3 per cent of the votes. In France the party system in the EP elections has also differed partially from that found in national parliamentary elections. European elections have resulted in splits within parties, particularly among the Gaullists, with representatives from the same parties running for the Parliament from more than one list. In addition, in the 2004 elections specific Eurosceptical lists performed well in several countries, notably in the UK and in Sweden.

6. This change was based on the revised Party Article (191) included in the Treaty of Nice, which stipulates that 'Council, acting in accordance with the procedure referred to in Article 251 [co-decision procedure], shall lay down the regulations governing political parties at European level and in particular the rules regarding their funding'.

7. An English translation of the volume, originally published in French, is available at http://www.ulb.ac.be/soco/cevipol/Books%20Presentatin/The%20Europarties.htm.

8. See Hix et al. (2005) for a full list of references of this literature.

REFERENCES

Attinà, F. (1990) 'The voting behaviour of the European Parliament members and the problem of the Europarties', *European Journal of Political Research*, 18(4): 557–79.

Bardi, L. (1992) 'Transnational party federations in the European Community', in R. S. Katz and P. Mair (eds), *Party Organizations in Western Democracies, 1960–90*. London: Sage. pp. 931–73.

Bardi, L. (1994) 'Transnational party federations, European parliamentary party groups, and the building of Europarties', in R. S. Katz and P. Mair (eds), *How Parties Organize: Change and Adaptation in Western Democracies*. London: Sage. pp. 357–72.

Bardi, L. (2002) 'Parties and party systems in the European Union', in K. R. Luther and F. Müller-Rommel (eds), *Political Parties in the New Europe: Political and Analytical Challenges*. Oxford: Oxford University Press. pp. 293–321.

Bay Brzinski, J. (1995) 'Political group cohesion in the European Parliament, 1989–1994', in C. Rhodes and S. Mazey (eds), *The State of the European Union, Vol. 3*. London: Longman. pp. 135–58.

Bell, D.S. and Lord, C. (eds) (1998) *Transnational Parties in the European Union*. Aldershot: Ashgate.

Benedetto, G. (2005) 'Rapporteurs as legislative entrepreneurs: the dynamics of the codecision procedure in Europe's Parliament', *Journal of European Public Policy*, 12(1): 67–88.

Blomgren, M. (2003) *Cross-Pressure and Political Representation in Europe: A Comparative Study of MEPs and the Intra-Party Arena*. Umeå: Department of Political Science, Umeå University.

Bomberg, E. (1998) *Green Parties and Politics in the European Union*. London: Routledge.

Bowler, S. and Farrell, D.M. (1995) 'The organizing of the European Parliament: committees, specialisation and co-ordination', *British Journal of Political Science*, 25(2): 219–43.

Budge, I., Klingemann, H.-D., Volkens, A., Bara, J. and Tanenbaum, E. (eds) (2001) *Mapping Policy Preferences. Estimates for Parties, Electors, and Governments 1945–1998*. Oxford: Oxford University Press.

Carrubba, C.J., Gabel, M., Murrah, L., Clough, R., Montgomery, E. and Schambach, R. (2003) 'Off the record: unrecorded legislative votes, selection bias, and roll-call vote analysis', working paper, Emory University.

Dalton, R.J. and Wattenberg, M.P. (eds) (2000) *Parties without Partisans: Political Change in Advanced Industrial Democracies*. Oxford: Oxford University Press.

Dalton, R.J. and Wattenberg, M.P. (2000) 'Unthinkable democracy: political change in advanced industrial democracies', in R.J. Dalton and M.P. Wattenberg (eds), *Parties without Partisans: Political Change in Advanced Industrial Democracies*. Oxford: Oxford University Press. pp. 3–16.

Day, S. and Shaw, J. (2003) 'The evolution of Europe's transnational political parties in the era of European citizenship', in T. A. Börzel and R. A. Cichowski (eds), *The State of the European Union: Volume 6*. Oxford: Oxford University Press. pp. 149–69.

De Winter, L. and Gomez-Reino Cachafeiro, M. (2002) 'European integration and ethnoregionalist parties', *Party Politics*, 8(4): 483–503.

Delwit, P., Külachi, E. and Van De Walle, C. (eds) (2001) *Les federations européennes de parties: Organisation et influence*. Brussels: Editions de l'Universite de Bruxelles.

Dietz, T. (1997) *Die grenzüberschreitende Interaktion grüner Parteien in Europa*. Opladen: Westdeutscher Verlag.

Dietz, T. (2000) 'Similar but different? The European Greens compared to other transnational party federations in Europe', *Party Politics*, 6(2): 199–210.

Evans, G. (1998) 'Euroscepticism and conservative electoral support: how an asset became a liability', *British Journal of Political Science*, 28(4): 573–90.

Evans, G. (2002) 'European integration, party politics and voting in the 2001 election', *British Elections and Parties Review*, 12: 95–110.

Faas, T. (2003) 'To defect or not to defect? National, institutional and party group pressures on MEPs and their consequences for party group cohesion in the EP', *European Journal of Political Research*, 42(5): 841–66.

Fitzmaurice, J. (1975) *The Party Groups in the European Parliament*. Farnborough: Saxon House.

Gabel, M.J. (2000) 'European integration, voters and national politics', *West European Politics*, 23(4): 52–72.

Gabel, M.J. and Hix, S. (2002) 'Defining the EU political space: an empirical study of the

European elections manifestos, 1979–1999', *Comparative Political Studies*, 35(8): 934–64.

Gaffney, J. (ed.) (1996) *Political Parties and the European Union*. London: Routledge.

Hanley, D. (2002) 'Christian democracy and the paradoxes of Europeanization: flexibility, competition and collusion', *Party Politics*, 8(4): 463–81.

Hausemer, P. (2005a) 'Representation and committee assignments in the European Parliament. Paper presented at the Annual Meeting of the Midwest Political Science Association, Chicago, 7–10 April.

Hausemer, P. (2005b) 'Representation and committee reports in the EP', paper presented at the UACES/University of Leicester Workshop New Member States and the European Parliament: Research agendas in the enlarged EU, Leicester, 6–7 May.

Hearl, D. and Sargent, J. (1979) 'Linkage mechanisms between the European Parliament and the national parliaments', in V. Herman and R. Van Schendelen (eds), *The European Parliament and the National Parliaments*. Farnborough: Saxon House. pp. 3–31.

Hix, S. (1999) 'Dimensions and alignments in European Union politics: cognitive constraints and partisan responses', *European Journal of Political Research*, 35(1): 69–106.

Hix, S. (2002) 'Parliamentary behavior with two principals: preferences, parties, and voting in the European Parliament', *American Journal of Political Science*, 46(3): 688–98.

Hix, S. (2004) 'Electoral institutions and legislative behavior: explaining voting-defection in the European Parliament', *World Politics*, 56(1): 194–223.

Hix, S. and Lord, C. (1996) 'The making of a president: the European Parliament and the confirmation of Jacques Santer as President of the Commission', *Government and Opposition*, 31(1): 62–76.

Hix, S. and Lord, C. (1997) *Political Parties in the European Union*. Basingstoke: Macmillan.

Hix, S., Kreppel, A. and Noury, A. (2003) 'The party system in the European Parliament: collusive or competitive?' *Journal of Common Market Studies*, 41(2): 309–31.

Hix, S., Noury, A. and Roland, G. (2005) 'Power to the parties: cohesion and competition in the European Parliament, 1979–2001', *British Journal of Political Science*, 35(2): 209–34.

Hooghe, L. and Marks, G. (1999) 'The making of a polity: the struggle over European integration', in H. Kitschelt et al. (eds) *Continuity and Change in Contemporary Capitalism*. Cambridge: Cambridge University Press. pp. 70–97.

Hooghe, L., Marks, G. and Wilson, C.J. (2002) 'Does left/right structure party positions on European integration?' *Comparative Political Studies*, 35(8): 965–89.

Huber, J.D. and Inglehart, R. (1995) 'Expert interpretations of party space and party locations in 42 societies', *Party Politics*, 1(1): 73–111.

Jansen, T. (1998) *The European People's Party: Origins and Development*. Basingstoke: Macmillan.

Johansson, K.M. (1997) *Transnational Party Alliances: Analysing the Hard-Won Alliance Between Conservatives and Christian Democrats in the European Parliament*. Lund: Lund University Press.

Johansson, K.M. (1999) 'Tracing the employment title in the Amsterdam Treaty: uncovering transnational coalitions', *Journal of European Public Policy*, 6(1): 85–101.

Johansson, K.M. (2002a) 'Another road to Maastricht: the Christian Democrat Coalition and the quest for European Union', *Journal of Common Market Studies*, 40(5): 871–93.

Johansson, K.M. (2002b) 'Party elites in multilevel Europe: the Christian Democrats and the Single European Act', *Party Politics*, 8(4): 423–39.

Johansson, K.M. and Raunio, T. (2005) 'Regulating Europarties: cross-party coalitions capitalizing on incomplete contracts', *Party Politics*, 11(5): 515–34.

Johansson, K.M. and Zervakis, P. (eds) (2002) *European Political Parties between Cooperation and Integration*. Baden-Baden: Nomos.

Kaeding, M. (2004) 'Rapporteurship allocation in the European Parliament: information or distribution? *European Union Politics*, 5(3): 353–71.

Kaeding, M. (2005) 'The world of committee reports: rapporteurship assignment in the European Parliament', *Journal of Legislative Studies*, 11(1): 82–104.

Kreppel, A. (2002) *The European Parliament and the Supranational Party System: A Study of Institutional Development*. Cambridge: Cambridge University Press.

Kreppel, A. (2003) 'Necessary but not sufficient: understanding the impact of treaty reform on the internal development of the European Parliament', *Journal of European Public Policy*, 10(6): 884–911.

Kreppel, A. and Hix, S. (2003) 'From "grand coalition" to left-right confrontation: explaining the shifting structure of party competition in the European Parliament', *Comparative Political Studies*, 36(1–2): 75–96.

Kreppel, A. and Tsebelis, G. (1999) 'Coalition formation in the European Parliament', *Comparative Political Studies*, 32(8): 933–66.

Ladrech, R. (2000) *Social Democracy and the Challenge of European Union*. Boulder: Lynne Rienner.

Ladrech, R. (2002) 'Europeanisation and political parties: towards a framework for analysis', *Party Politics*, 8(4): 389–403.

Lightfoot, S. (2005) *Europeanizing Social Democracy? The Rise of the Party of European Socialists*. Abingdon: Routledge.

Lipset, S.M. and Rokkan, S. (1967) 'Cleavage structures, party systems, and voter alignments: an introduction', in S. M. Lipset and S. Rokkan (eds), *Party System and Voter Alignments: Cross-National Perspectives*. New York and London: The Free Press. pp. 1–64.

Luther, K.R. and Müller-Rommel, F. (eds) (2002) *Political Parties in the New Europe: Political and Analytical Challenges*. Oxford: Oxford University Press.

Lynch, P. (1998) 'Cooperation between regionalist parties at the level of the European Union: the European Free Alliance', in L. De Winter and H. Türsan (eds), *Regionalist Parties in Western Europe*. Routledge: London. pp. 190–203.

Mair, P. (2000) 'The limited impact of Europe on national party systems', *West European Politics*, 23(4): 27–51.

Mamadouh, V. and Raunio, T. (2003) 'The committee system: powers, appointments and report allocation', *Journal of Common Market Studies*, 41(2): 333–51.

Marks, G. and Steenbergen, M. (2002a) 'Understanding political contestation in the European Union', *Comparative Political Studies*, 35(8): 879–92.

Marks, G. and Steenbergen, M.R. (eds) (2002b) 'Dimensions of contestation in the European Union', special issue of *Comparative Political Studies*, 35(8).

Marks, G. and Steenbergen, M.R. (eds) (2004) *European Integration and Political Conflict*. Cambridge: Cambridge University Press.

Marks, G. and Wilson, C.J. (2000) 'The past in the present: a cleavage theory of party response to European integration', *British Journal of Political Science*, 30(3): 433–59.

Marks, G., Hooghe, L., Nelson, M. and Edwards, E. (2006) 'Party competition and European integration in East and West: different structure, same causality', *Comparative Political Studies*, 39(2): 155–75.

Marks, G., Wilson, C.J. and Ray, L. (2002) 'National political parties and European integration', *American Journal of Political Science*, 46(3): 585–94.

Messmer, W.B. (2003) 'Taming Labour's MEPs', *Party Politics*, 9(2): 201–18.

Morgan, R. and Tame, C. (eds) (1996) *Parliaments and Parties: The European Parliament and the Political Life in Europe*. London: Macmillan.

Niedermayer, O. (1983) *Europäische Parteien? Zur grenzüberschreitenden Interaktion politischer Parteien im Rahmen der Europäischen Gemeinschaft*. Frankfurt: Campus Verlag.

Noury, A. (2002) 'Ideology, nationality, and Euro-Parliamentarians', *European Union Politics*, 3(1): 33–58.

Ovey, J.-D. (2002) *Between Nation and Europe: Labour, the SPD and the European Parliament 1994-1999*. Opladen: Leske and Budrich.

Pennings, P. (2002) 'The dimensionality of the EU policy space: the European elections of 1999', *European Union Politics*, 3(1): 59–80.

Poole, K.T. and Rosenthal, H. (1997) *Congress: A Political-Economic History of Roll Call Voting*. New York: Oxford University Press.

Powell, G.B. Jr (2004) 'Political representation in comparative politics', *Annual Review of Political Science*, 7: 273–96.

Pridham, G. and Pridham, P. (1981) *Transnational Party Co-operation and European Integration: The Process Towards Direct Elections*. London: George Allen and Unwin.

Quanjel, M. and Wolters, M. (1993) 'Growing cohesion in the European Parliament', paper presented at the ECPR Joint Sessions, Leiden, April 1993.

Raunio, T. (1997) *The European Perspective: Transnational Party Groups in the 1989–94 European Parliament*. Aldershot: Ashgate.

Raunio, T. (2000) 'Losing independence or finally gaining recognition? Contacts between MEPs and national parties', *Party Politics*, 6(2): 211–23.

Raunio, T. (2002a) 'Beneficial cooperation or mutual ignorance? Contacts between MEPs and national parties', in B. Steunenberg and J. Thomassen (eds), *The European Parliament: Moving toward Democracy in the EU*. Lanham, MD: Rowman and Littlefield. pp. 87–111.

Raunio, T. (2002b) 'Why European integration increases leadership autonomy within political parties', *Party Politics*, 8(4): 405–22.

Ray, L. (1999) 'Measuring party orientations towards European integration: Results from an expert survey', *European Journal of Political Research*, 36(2): 283–306.

Sandström, C. (2003) *Liberalt partisamarbete i Europa: ELDR en ny typ av parti?* Umeå: Umeå University, Department of Political Science.

Schmitt, H. and Thomassen, J. (2000) 'Dynamic representation: the case of European integration', *European Union Politics*, 1(3): 318–39.

Scully, R. (2001) 'National parties and European Parliamentarians: developing and testing an institutionalist theory', *EPRG Working Paper* No. 6. Available online at: http://www.lse.ac.uk/depts/eprg, accessed 17 November 2005.

Scully, R. (2005) *Becoming Europeans? Attitudes, Behaviour and Socialization in the European Parliament.* Oxford: Oxford University Press.

Steenbergen, M. and Scott, D.J. (2004) 'Contesting Europe? The salience of European integration as a party issue', in G. Marks and M.R. Steenbergen (eds), *European Integration and Political Conflict.* Cambridge: Cambridge University Press. pp. 165–92.

Taggart, P. (1998) 'A touchstone of dissent: Euroscepticism in contemporary Western European party systems', *European Journal of Political Research*, 33(3): 363–88.

Taggart, P. and Szczerbiak, A. (eds) (2007a) *Opposing Europe? The Comparative Party Politics of Euroscepticism: Volume 1: Case Studies and Country Surveys.* Oxford: Oxford University Press.

Taggart, P. and Szczerbiak, A. (eds) (2007b) *Opposing Europe? The Comparative Party Politics of Euroscepticism: Volume 2: Comparative and Theoretical Perspectives.* Oxford: Oxford University Press.

Thomas, S.T. (1992) 'Assessing MEP influence on British EC policy', *Government and Opposition*, 27(1): 3–18.

Thomassen, J., Noury, A. and Voeten, E. (2004) 'Political competition in the European Parliament: evidence from roll call and survey analyses', in G. Marks and M. R. Steenbergen (eds), *European Integration and Political Conflict.* Cambridge: Cambridge University Press. pp. 141–64.

Thomassen, J. and Schmitt, H. (1997) 'Policy representation', *European Journal of Political Research*, 32(2): 165–84.

Thomassen, J. and Schmitt, H. (1999a) 'Issue congruence', in H. Schmitt and J. Thomassen (eds), *Political Representation and Legitimacy in the European Union.* Oxford: Oxford University Press. pp. 186–208.

Thomassen, J. and Schmitt, H. (1999b) 'Partisan structures in the European Parliament', in R. S. Katz and B. Wessels (eds), *The European Parliament, the National Parliaments, and European Integration.* Oxford: Oxford University Press. pp. 129–48.

Tillman, E.R. (2004) 'The European Union at the ballot box? European integration and voting behavior in the new member states', *Comparative Political Studies*, 37(5): 590–610.

Van der Eijk, C. and Franklin, M.N. (1991) 'European Community politics and electoral representation: evidence from the 1989 European Elections Study', *European Journal of Political Research*, 19(1): 105–27.

Van der Eijk, C. and Franklin, M.N. (2004) 'Potential for contestation on European matters at national elections in Europe', in G. Marks and M.R. Steenbergen (eds), *European Integration and Political Conflict.* Cambridge: Cambridge University Press. pp. 32–50.

Van Oudenhove, G. (1965) *The Political Parties in the European Parliament: The First Ten Years (September 1952 – September 1962).* Leyden: A.W. Sijthoff.

Webb, P. and Farrell, D. and Holliday, I. (eds) (2002) *Political Parties in Advanced Industrial Democracies.* Oxford: Oxford University Press.

Whitaker, R. (2001) 'Party control in a committee-based legislature? The case of the European parliament', *Journal of Legislative Studies*, 7(4): 63–88.

Whitaker, R. (2005) 'National parties in the European Parliament: an influence in the committee system?' *European Union Politics*, 6(1): 5–28.

13

Public Opinion, Socialization and Political Communication

LEONARD RAY

INTRODUCTION

This review will focus on the literature dealing with the role of the mass public in the process of European integration and the political life of the European Union. A recent work places the number of articles written on public opinion about European integration at over one hundred (Hooghe and Marks 2005). Theirs is a conservative estimate. I aim to orient the reader in this literature by identifying the major landmarks, indicating the sources of important currents, and alerting the reader to regions yet unexplored.[1]

The evolution of research on the mass public and European integration has been driven by a number of important factors, of which the most important are political/institutional developments, theoretical trends in EU studies, and the corpus of publicly available survey data. A quick timeline of the evolution of the field over the last 60 years would begin with the faith of European federalists in a popularly supported political union, enthusiasm which waned after the 1948 Hague Congress. The 1950s and 60s

saw the emergence of functional, transactionalist, and international relations theories of integration whose fortunes tracked the development and stagnation of the ECSC and EEC. In these approaches, mass attitudes were absent or played a subordinate role. Opinion data for this period was available only from ad hoc surveys or from the opinion polls conducted by the United States Information Agency. The 1970s saw tentative steps towards the study of the European Community as a polity, and early studies of mass attitudes which established the theoretical framework for much of the subsequent work. The Eurobarometer series of opinion surveys established in 1974 provided the raw material for serious comparative and time-series work in this area, and the institution of direct elections to the European Parliament, along with a series of referenda accompanying the first enlargement, provided ample justification that public opinion was a topic worth serious attention. These trends continued at a measured pace during the 1980s as the public opinion literature was relatively indifferent to the second and third expansion of the EU and to the Single European Act. The 1990s witnessed a veritable explosion of research on public attitudes in response to the high drama of the French and Danish referendums on the Treaty on European Union. Since 1992, dramatic events such as the fourth and fifth enlargement, the introduction of the single currency, and the rejection of the Constitutional Treaty in the French and Dutch referenda of 2005 have kept this field very active.

Research is this area is marked by substantial diversity. There is considerable variety in the object of study – ranging from opinions about specific policies and support for EU institutions, to opinions about integration in general, to transnational feelings of solidarity and identity. Work in this field is also theoretically eclectic, drawing upon such varied literatures as retrospective voting, value change, electoral studies, social psychology, and media studies. There is not, however, a great deal of methodological variety. Like the apocryphal drunk looking for lost keys under a streetlight, researchers have been drawn to the wealth of publicly available data sets, and particularly to the time series of Eurobarometer studies run on behalf of the European Commission. As a result, the majority of works are secondary analyses of mass survey data.

This chapter will begin with a historical sketch of the role of public opinion in the integration literature of the 50s and 60s before turning to some important works of the 1970s that introduced the terminology of 'permissive consensus' and 'affective vs. utilitarian support' which were quite popular with subsequent authors. More recent developments will be treated thematically, following the evolution of utilitarian, socialization, political communication, and identity approaches to mass attitudes. The chapter then reviews the literature on EU referenda and EP elections, areas where mass attitudes arguably have their most direct impact on European Union politics. I conclude with some thoughts on productive directions the field may take in the future. Particularly fruitful avenues for further research include the nature of a European identity, support for specific EU-level policy initiatives, and levels and sources of information about the EU.

FROM INTEGRATION THEORIES TO THE EC AS A POLITICAL SYSTEM

Many studies of public opinion about Europe open with a ritual invocation of the importance of the subject. This reflex is in part a response to the widespread impression that most of the early theories of integration assigned a quite minor role to mass attitudes.[2] In defense of their topic, scholars have invoked the democratic deficit, the increased salience of European issues following the Treaty on European Union, the frequency of referenda, the direct elections to the EP, and the need for legitimacy. I will revisit the relevance of public opinion after reviewing of the literature on the determinants of mass attitudes.

If one considers the federalist movement of the late 1940s as the earliest branch of integration theory, we must qualify the stereotype of early integration theory as indifferent to popular opinion. Federalism began with a bottom up conception of mass opinion as a driving force behind integration (Spinelli 1967). Federalists interpreted mass support for the vague goal of a 'United States of Europe' as evidence in favor of their tactic of European unification in one stroke through a constituent assembly. The lesson drawn by many from the modest outcome of the Congress of Europe of 1948 was that mass attitudes were too incoherent and vague to provide a basis for the creation of a federal Europe (e.g. Walton 1952; 1959). Indeed, while early federalists valued public opinion, they saw it as malleable enough to influence through elite-led organizations such as the European Movement.[3]

The functionalist approach to regional integration, most clearly identified with Ernst Haas, emphasized pragmatic cooperation in specific policy areas, in part as a reaction to the disappointing outcomes of federalist attempts to unify Europe at one stroke. The minimal role of the mass public in this theoretical approach was stated most dramatically by Ernst Haas who infamously wrote:

It is as impracticable as it is unnecessary to have recourse to general public opinion and attitude surveys ... It suffices to single out and define the political elites in the participating countries, to study their reactions to integration and to assess changes in attitude on their part (Haas 1958: 17).

For Haas this pessimism regarding the role of public opinion seemed justified given the mass public's shockingly low levels of information about the European Coal and Steel Community.

Another school of integration research, the transactionalist or communications school, viewed public attitudes as important and worth serious measurement. This approach, most closely identified with Karl Deutsch, considered communication and transaction flows as important markers for the creation of international community. In an early elaboration of his ideas Deutsch included 'feelings of confidence and trust' and 'attitudes of identification' as important sources of the mutual predictability required in an international community (1954: 54). But scholars in this tradition did not necessarily subscribe to a bottom-up model of integration any more than did the functionalists. As one author put it, 'bonds [of mutual understanding and confidence] first link national elites at a relatively early stage in the integration process; ultimately they also mark the merger of national mass populations into a single people' (Puchala 1968: 45–6). Major legacies of the transactionalist paradigm were the introduction of common identity ('we-feeling') as a theoretically important concept, and an exhaustive compilation of survey data.[4]

During the 1970s distinctive theories of regional integration went into decline, and the study of European integration became increasingly divided between the literature in international relations and an alternative 'governance' approach which treated the European Community as a polity (Jachtenfuchs 2001, this volume). Within an international relations framework, European integration was considered 'foreign policy' and the role ascribed to public opinion was correspondingly minor.[5] Despite eventual challenges to the 'Almond-Lippman consensus'[6] on the minimal impact of public opinion on foreign policy, even liberal intergovernmentalist approaches to the EU accorded the mass public little importance. As Moravscik explained in relation to the SEA:

Since Europe is a low priority issue for the voters of the three largest member states, it is implausible to posit a mechanism by which politicians launch policy initiatives to seek direct electoral advantage, except perhaps immediately before European elections. European integration thus remains an elite affair (Moravcsik 1991).

Even the constructivist literature, with its emphasis on 'identities', has focused on the identities of elites or of nations, and neglected studies of mass opinion and individual attitudes (Merlingen 2001). It is not the International Relations (IR) literature but the emerging governance approach where we find the works which lay the theoretical foundations for much of the literature on public opinion about the European Integration.

In the mid 1960s it was suggested that international systems such as those investigated by Deutsch and Haas were amenable to investigation with the tools of systems analysis (Alger 1963; Easton 1965: 173). Lindberg and Scheingold's (1970a) *Europe's Would-Be Polity* was a loose application of the Eastonian framework to the European Community. Two important theoretical concepts emerged from this work. The first was the notion that while public opinion did not drive the process of integration, it could act as a constraint should integration move in an unpopular direction. Borrowing vocabulary liberally from V.O Key (see Sinnott 1995 on this point), Lindberg and Scheingold concluded that a 'permissive consensus' in favor of integration had emerged among citizens of the six EEC member states allowing elites to make further moves towards integration. Many scholars have been concerned with the health of this 'permissive consensus', and have documented a marked weakening of support ever since the ratification debates surrounding the TEU.

Lindberg and Scheingold (1970a, b) also applied Easton's concept of regime support to the European Community. Expanding on Easton's original formulation, they distinguish between objects of support, and types of support. Their objects of support include the regime and the system (which Easton termed regime and political community), and identification with a social community (a concept borrowed from Deutsch rather than Easton).[7]

For each of these objects, they posit two types of support: utilitarian support 'based on some perceived and relatively concrete interest' and affective support which was 'a diffuse and perhaps emotional response' (1970a: 40). This distinction between affective and utilitarian support has become a mainstay of the literature[8] (Shepherd 1975; Inglehart and Rabier 1978; Inglehart et al. 1987; Mayhew 1980; Gabel 1998a).

TYPES OF ATTITUDE AND VARIETIES OF THEORETICAL APPROACH

The literature has examined a variety of attitudes related to European integration which go beyond the three objects of support identified by Lindberg and Scheingold (1970a) to include support for specific European-level policies.[9] Public opinion can range from attitudes about specific public policies (such as the single currency), to institutions (trust in the European Court of Justice), to the regime (Is membership in the European Union a good thing?), to the social community (Does the respondent identify as a European?). A variety of theoretical approaches have been employed to predict or explain opinions about these potential objects listed above. For ease of presentation, I will categorize these approaches to explaining public opinions under the following labels: utilitarian, representation, socialization, political communication, and identity approaches. In the remainder of this section I follow the evolution of research applying each of these approaches.

Utilitarian Benefits: Economics, Expectations and Support for the EU

The utilitarian approach applies the basic intuition of cost-benefit analysis to the evaluation of European integration. This approach has generally been applied to the impact of economic benefits on support for membership in the European Union, or for general efforts to unify Western Europe.[10] Several strategies have been employed in an attempt to distinguish those who benefit from European integration from those who see little reward from this

process. Following the logic of retrospective voting, it has been argued that utilitarian support for Europe will increase with positive objective economic outcomes. Alternately, individual-level subjective evaluations of economic conditions or of the benefits of the EU have been used. Other authors have examined prospective economic outcomes based on assumptions about the impact of integration on different social groups.

One obvious potential source of utilitarian benefits from integration is EU-level redistribution. The large British contribution to the EC budget was seen as an important explanation for low levels of support in the UK prior to the 'rebate'.[11] At the aggregate level, evidence of a measurable effect of the direct fiscal costs or benefits of European integration on support for the EU is inconclusive. Some quantitative analyses (Eichenberg and Dalton 1993; Bosch and Newton 1995) have found that net transfers to and from the EU budget cannot account for cross-national differences in support. Conversely, Anderson and Reichert (1996) find a significant effect of net transfers, and Gabel (1998a) finds a positive effect of CAP spending, while Bourantonis, Kalyvitis, and Tsoutsoplides find a positive effect for disbursements under the European Social Fund (1998).[12]

Research on objective economic conditions as predictors of support for the EU also yields mixed results. Here the most common economic indicators are the trinity of GDP growth, inflation, and unemployment, often supplemented with a measure of the extent of intra-EU trade.[13] Using data at the national level, Inglehart and Rabier (1978) found a positive correlation between industrial production and aggregate support for integration and a negative correlation between inflation and support for integration. The authors also test the effects of unemployment rates on support and find a negligible relationship. Eichenberg and Dalton (1993) likewise find significant effects for inflation, and for intra-EU trade, though not for unemployment. Anderson and Kaltenthaler (1996) actually find a strong effect of all three indicators (unemployment, GDP growth and inflation), while Anderson and Reichert report a positive effect of intra-EC trade (1996). Elsewhere, Anderson (1995) has noted substantial cross-national variation in the impact of GDP growth. Results using data at the regional level have been mixed. Duch and Taylor (1997) find that support for European integration is highest in regions with high levels of income, education, and employment, while Gabel and Whitten (1997) find that high regional unemployment actually increased support for the EU. They conclude that for unemployment, 'worsening economic conditions promote support for integration'. Enthusiasm for this research program has waned as recent analyses indicate that the effects of objective economic indicators erode substantially around the time of the Maastricht treaty ratification (Eichenberg 1998).

Some scholars, suspicious of the accuracy of perceptions of objective economic conditions, have used individual-level survey data on subjective evaluations of the economy. The earliest work in this tradition is Kriesberg (1959) who finds that Germans' opinions of the European Coal and Steel Community were related to their perceptions regarding the price of coal. Gabel and Whitten (1997) find that subjective evaluations of national and personal economic conditions have a stronger impact than objective conditions themselves. However, Anderson (1998) finds that perceived economic conditions are not related to support for the EU once support for the incumbent government is included in the model. He concludes that the influence of economic perceptions has an indirect effect via support for incumbent governments.

Another utilitarian approach has been to infer the likely consequences of integration from the social characteristics of individuals. Research has consistently found high socioeconomic status (generally measured as income, education, occupation, and/or employment) to be associated with support for the European Community (e.g. Puchala 1970a; Inglehart et al., 1987; Anderson and Reichert 1996).[14] Gabel and Whitten (1997) provide a utilitarian explanation for these socio-economic differences in support for the EU. In their view, individuals who possess higher 'human capital' (as indicated by educational attainment or occupation)

can expect to compete better in an expanded market than individuals with lower 'human capital'. Gabel (1998b) demonstrates the effectiveness of human capital predictors when compared to other theoretical explanations for EU support. Duch and Taylor (1997: 68) present a similar argument about the differential ability of the well off to take advantage of economic integration. As for the effects of income, Gabel and Palmer argue that 'EC citizens with higher income levels are also more likely to benefit from EC policies since they prefer low inflation, less public sector spending, and a larger and more open financial market' (Gabel and Palmer, 1995: 7). They also find that the elimination of internal borders leads to increased support from residents of border regions.

Two social groups have been difficult to incorporate into the utilitarian model of socio-economic interests without reference to national variation in policy outcomes. Women and farmers have relatively low levels of support for European integration, a finding which has puzzled some observers given the activity of the EU in the area of pay equity and CAP spending (Risse 2005). However, the opinions of farmers can be explained by cross-national variations in CAP spending (Gabel 1998a).[15] Nelsen and Guth (2000) offer an explanation for low levels of support among women based on female dependence on the welfare state. Their account fits well with a general model of expected utilitarian benefits from integration driven by expectations of policy convergence elaborated by Ray (2004). The volume and diversity of the utilitarian literature testifies to the importance of this type of approach in the broader discipline of political science. The most robust findings from this literature involve socio-economic differences and economic perceptions, while the effects of objective economic conditions vary according to model specification and data selection.[16]

Governance: Quality of National and Supranational Institutions

While the utilitarian approaches focus on tangible economic costs and benefits associated with European integration, another strand of theorizing emphasizes the political nature of the EU and its institutions. If the EU is a political system which carries out representative, judicial, and executive functions, then it may well be evaluated according to how well these functions are performed.

Two authors have recently applied this approach to model support for the EU as a whole. Sanchez-Cuenca (2000) argues that the political system of the EU is judged in relation to the perceived performance of national political systems. Establishing the general applicability of an old argument often made about Italy, he demonstrates that support for the EU is highest in nations whose domestic political system is perceived as corrupt. Rohrschneider (2002) further develops this argument by bringing perceptions about both levels of governance into the model. He argues that satisfaction with the domestic national system interacts with positive evaluations of supranational institutions. Rather than a direct influence on evaluations of the EU, satisfaction with domestic institutions raises the stakes for EU institutions, increasing the link between positive evaluations of EU level representation and support for the Union as a whole.

The literature on evaluations of specific EU-level institutions has been led by work on the European Court of Justice. Caldeira and Gibson (1995, 1997) ask whether the European Court of Justice has developed the required diffuse support to maintain its legitimacy in the face of unpopular decisions. Similar to the American case, they find effects of satisfaction with the performance of the Court, and of attachment to legal values. However, they find that in many countries, the Court is so unfamiliar that opinions are primarily derived from overall assessments of the EU. Later Gibson and Caldeira (1998) extend their analysis to include legitimacy of the EP as well as the ECJ. In addition to finding disturbingly low levels of legitimacy for the EP, they find no spill-over of legitimacy from national high courts to the ECJ, suggesting that – in the judicial realm – evaluations of national institutions have little impact on views of supranational ones.

Gelleny and Anderson (2000) address the popularity of the Presidency of the European Commission. Using data on evaluations of Jacques Delors from 1994, they find the European public very uninformed about one of the highest-profile Commission Presidents in recent memory. To the extent that individuals evaluate the Commission Presidency, they seem to do so on the basis of utilitarian considerations.

Work on the European Parliament has also emphasized a rather striking level of public ignorance about the only directly elected institution in the EU. Niedermayer and Sinnott find that on the eve of the fourth direct election to the EP, awareness about this institution was no different than during the run up to the first EP election (1995: 287). Gabel (2003) develops an explanation for support for the European Parliament and finds that support for EU membership, a European identity, and information about the EP all contribute to support for the institution. He finds minimal cross-national variation in support once these factors are controlled for. One possible explanation for the remaining cross-national differences is suggested by Johnston and Ray (2004). Examining the entire set of EU institutions, they find that trust in an EU institution does respond, in some cases, to objective measures of overrepresentation and underrepresentation. The analysis of preferences about specific EU institutions does assume a high level of knowledge about the internal structure and workings of EU institutions, knowledge that Gibson and Caldeira (1998) suggest may not be common. The approach, however, is important in an era when the basic institutional architecture of the Union is subject to codification in the proposed Constitutional Treaty.

Socialization: Familiarity and Childhood Socialization

In contrast to the cost-benefit rationality of utilitarian approaches, and strategic calculations of the governance approach, socialization models explain attitudes as a function of the social environment. A number of research programs can be grouped under the general heading of socialization models. Deutsch's transactionalist approach to integration theory would seem to fit under this rubric, as it assumes that increased interaction and communication gradually produces a social community characterized by mutual trust and shared identity. Other socialization approaches include opinion diffusion models which predict the spread of attitudes across a population and Inglehart's childhood socialization paradigm. Socialization approaches have been applied to explain both support for the existing European institutions and the emergence of European solidarity or identity. This approach is rarely used as a direct explanation for attitudes about specific policies.

Early integration theory expected an increase in mutual trust and identity to result from increased interaction. Trust has followed the expected pattern better than identity. During the first decade of the EEC, mutual regard and trust did increase, particularly between the French and Germans (Lindberg and Schiengold 1970a: 46–54; Puchala 1970b; Shepherd 1975: 67–83). After a dip in the mid 1970s, levels of trust resumed an upward trend (Handley 1981: 354–6; Niedermayer 1995). While European identity increased slowly in the 1970s (Handley 1981: 358) recent work has not found an association between length of EU membership and identification with Europe (Duchesne and Frognier 1995; Green 2000; Schild 2001).

Much of the literature from the 1960s and 1970s assumed that public support for integration would grow alongside familiarity with the institutions of the EEC. One piece of evidence cited in support of this 'attitudinal spillover' was the general upward trend in support for European integration (Puchala 1970a; Anderson 1995; Anderson and Kaltenthaler 1996).[17] Other authors have cited the difference in support between the six founding members and the three new members of the first enlargement as evidence that familiarity increases support for the EC (Mayhew 1980). The cross-national argument was weakened considerably with the expansion of the EEC to include Spain and Portugal, where support

levels were significantly higher than in the older members of Denmark and the UK.

Inglehart proposed a model which relies on childhood socialization rather than gradual acculturation. His earliest work on support for integration was a study of European youth (1967) who he found to be more pro-European and less nationalistic than their parents. By 1971 he had linked childhood socialization with Maslow's hierarchy of values to yield a theory of 'post-acquisitive' values, later re-baptized 'post-Materialist'. For Inglehart, post-materialist values influence support for European integration by lowering nationalism, and increasing 'cosmopolitanism'. Subsequent work found that while postmaterialism does seem to be associated with a 'European' identity, the relationship with support for European integration vanishes under controls for cognitive mobilization (Janssen 1991).[18] This divergence between effects on identity and support seems to have intensified, with Anderson and Reichert (1996) finding a negative effect of postmaterialism on support for integration, while Green (2000) finds postmaterialist values positively related to European identity.[19] Given this inconsistency in the impact of postmaterialism, the approach has fallen out of favor.

Political Communications: Elite Cues and Media Effects

Another approach argues that opinions reflect cues from political elites and the mass media. Martin Slater (1982) concludes that the euroskepticism of Norway, Denmark and the UK resulted from the orchestrated efforts of 'counter elites' who mobilized opposition to the EU. Analyses of UK party politics by Flickinger and Center (1993) and Rasmussen (1997) suggest that shifts in party positions did lead electorate opinion, and that the swing to a pro-EU position by the UK Labour party was particularly influential.

Early research also demonstrated significant differences in support for integration across supporters of different parties (Puchala 1970a) and these differences were linked to voters' perceptions of the position taken by their preferred party (Wildgen and Feld 1976). The notion that parties were sending cues to their electorates was, however, difficult to test further without cross-sectional data on party positions on European issues. Using estimates of party positions drawn from an expert survey, Ray (2003a) demonstrates that the impact of party cues varies significantly across types of parties and voters.

Research on EU-related referendums supports this view. Among others, analyses of the UK referendum of 1975 (Kitzinger 1975; Shepherd 1975), the 1986 Danish referendum on the SEA (Worre 1988), the 1992 Danish SEA referendum (Worre 1995), the 1994 membership referendum in Norway (Ray 1999), and the 2000 Danish referendum on Euro adoption (de Vreese and Semetko 2004a: 27) find that voters respond to the cues of their preferred political party. Establishing the direction of the causal relationship between voter opinion and party positions is difficult without panel data because of the possibility that parties react to changes in voter opinion, and the likelihood of issue voting. Using panel data from the Norwegian Storting election of 1993 and the EU membership referendum of 1994, Ray (1999) found that many individual survey respondents did shift their opinions in order to bring them into line with party cues. Likewise, in an analysis of panel data from the 2001 British national election Carey and Burton (2004) find significant effects of party cues on opinion change.

An alternative interpretation of the effects of partisanship identified incumbent parties as important sources of pro-EU cues.[20] Work by Inglehart and Rabier, (1978) as well as Franklin et al. (1994), and Anderson (1998) compared government and opposition parties and found opposition partisans to be relatively anti-European. However, Duch and Taylor (1997) find no such effect of incumbent support, and Ray (2003b) demonstrates that this effect seems to be restricted to the political context of EU-related referendums.

Another obvious source of cues is the mass media, though very little work was done in this field until quite recently. One of the earliest attempts to predict opinions about the EU with media cues was conducted by Dalton and Duval (1986). Using content analysis of European coverage from the Guardian newspaper during the 1970's, they find that positive or negative media coverage will move opinion in the corresponding direction, and that the effect of coverage persists for a few months. More recently, a comparative analysis of media coverage in the 1990s using a monthly content analysis produced for the European Commission also found that media tone can shape public attitudes (Norris 2000). A similar relationship is apparent for German media coverage and public approval of the Euro (Brettschneider et al. 2003). Carey and Burton (2004) examine the 2001 British national election, and find readers of pro-European newspapers differ from consumers of the Euroskeptic press.

An ambitious research program based at the Amsterdam School of Communications Research has embarked on a large-scale study of Europeanization and the news media, examining both structural changes in media systems in response to integration, and the influence of the media on public opinion. Central to their work on media effects is the concept of 'framing', in which selective emphasis of different elements can dramatically change the news coverage of any single event. In a comparison of British and German coverage of the introduction of the Euro, Semetko, de Vreese, and Peter (2000) document wide national differences in televised coverage of the launch of the single currency. British coverage was more negative in tone, and stressed the potential economic difficulties this move may cause for ordinary Britons while German coverage was more celebratory. de Vreese (2003) reports an intriguing experimental result where the framing of European issues was manipulated. He finds that framing the Euro as an economic or as a political issue has no effect on opinions, but framing the issue of enlargement in strategic terms does stimulate negative evaluations of enlargement. These effects, however, do not produce durable differences in support for enlargement. The 2000 referendum in

Denmark on adoption of the Euro provided an ideal environment for the study of media effects and issue framing. de Vreese and Semetko find that Danish media were influential in shaping the issues during this referendum (2004a), and that exposure to public broadcasting (which portrayed the Yes side negatively) was a significant predictor of vote choice in the referendum (2004b).

The Amsterdam group is also working on a cross-national analysis of media coverage in all 15 EU members during the 1999 EP elections (Semetko et al. 2000 cited in de Vreese 2000). Some results for Denmark, the Netherlands, and the UK suggest that the EP elections received little coverage compared to dramatic events elsewhere such as the conflict in Kosovo. What coverage there was echoed Tory campaign themes in the UK while stressing fraud in Denmark (de Vreese, 2003). The low salience of the EP has predictable consequences for turnout in EP elections, and raises questions about democratic accountability.

Identities: Nationalism – Obstinate or Obsolete? Europeanism Emergent?

Another important approach has examined the impact of identity. A common assumption is that there is some inherent incompatibility between European and national identities. The idea that constructing a European identity means the erosion of national identities (see Smith 1992; Shore 1993) justifies the use of nationalism as a predictor of opposition to European integration. Conversely, Guetzkow argues that supranational loyalty complements, rather than supplants, national loyalties (cited in Lodge 1978). This argument, buttressed by reference to the 'imagined' nature of political communities (Anderson 1983), implies that nationalism may not have negative consequences for support for Europe, but that 'Europeanism'—a European identity—will have positive consequences (assuming such a thing exists[21]).

The case for a negative effect of nationalism is made by Heath et al. (1999) who find that in the 1992 UK national election, British national

sentiment has a stronger effect on attitudes about Europe than on any of the other issue areas they examine. McLaren (2002) uses a Eurobarometer question on the 'cultural threat' posed by ethnic minorities to predict support for the EU, and finds that fear for one's national culture is an overlooked factor determining public attitudes towards Europe.

But other research suggests that national identity is not incompatible with support for the EU. Medrano and Gutierrez (2001) find positive relationships between regional and national identity and identification with Europe. Hansen and Petersen (1978) found that attachment to national symbols was not linked to opposition to Danish EEC membership in 1972. Two results highlight the importance of question wording in this area. McLaren (2004) replicates her earlier findings and finds markedly smaller effects of nationalism when using a Eurobarometer question about fears that the EU is a 'threat to national identity'. Schild (2001) examines data from France and Germany and finds no association between national pride and European identity during the 1980s when identity was measured as frequency of thinking of oneself as 'European'. But during the 1990's when identity was measured as a forced choice including exclusive and mixed identities, a strong negative correlation between national pride and European identity appears. Mixed results for national sentiment aside, possessing a European identity matters. European identity has been found to predict support for the EU (Hooghe and Marks 2005) and the EP (Gabel 2003).

The use of survey research to study European identity has been criticized both as a general technique (Smith 1992) and because the wording of the Eurobarometer questions is particularly problematic. Bruter departs from the mass survey paradigm in his work on European identity. He used focus groups of Europeans in three nations to explore the content of European identity (2004). This work suggests the existence of two components of European identity – a civic dimension and a cultural dimension. He then applies a very original experimental approach (Bruter 2003) to the question of European identity formation, and analyses the effect of positive or negative news on these types of identities, as well as the effect of exposure to European symbols such as the EU flag. He finds that exposure to EU symbols has a greater impact on cultural identity while exposure to positive news has a greater influence on civic identity. When combined with the media studies work demonstrating that much EU coverage has been negative (see above), this research suggests an explanation for the observed shifts in the Eurobarometer series.

DOES PUBLIC OPINION MATTER? DOMESTIC POLITICS, EP ELECTIONS, AND REFERENDA

Even before the 1970s, some argued that public opinion can influence EEC politics because the member states were democracies. Since 1972, EU-related referenda have provided an avenue for some European publics to influence, or at least stall, European integration. The direct elections of the EP since 1979 also hold out the promise of democratic accountability and responsiveness. The literature on each of these mechanisms of popular influence, however, suggest important caveats.

Domestic Democratic Politics

A domestic politics argument for mass influence assumes that elites will respond to public opinion. While the overall similarity between party and electorate positions on European issues has been established (Eijk and Franklin 1991), it is the direction of influence which is controversial. As early as 1966, Leon Lindberg's analysis of the European policy of Charles DeGaulle suggested that public opinion constrains political elites, particularly in the run-up to national elections. Clifford Carubba (2001) analysed the relationship between party positions and the opinions of target voters, and concludes that parties are positioning themselves in response to electorate opinion.

By contrast, other authors emphasize the freedom of action of elites. Martin Slater (1982) reviews community history in the 1960s and 70s, and concludes that the public has been largely irrelevant to developments, which were instead shaped by elites and reflected elite interests. He concluded that so long as national elites maintain a unified pro-integration consensus mass opinion will reflect that consensus, and will not influence the course of integration. Feld and Wildgen argued that elites did not perceive an electoral benefit from following mass opinion in formulating their own positions on European integration (1975). European issues have generally failed to spur durable realignments in domestic party systems (Mair 2000). Despite opposition to the Euro among the German public (Brettschneider et al. 2003) no German political party was successful in exploiting this issue electorally (Lees 2002).

Straddling the causal argument, Bernhard Wessels (1995a) and Ray (1998) find mixed results on the link between parties and voters. For Ray the direction of influence varies according to the characteristics of parties, and for Wessels, it varies according to the stage of the election cycle.

Direct Elections and the European Parliament

Skeptics have long warned that direct election of the European Parliament would be a disappointment. Arguing by analogy from Länder elections in Germany, and parliamentary by elections in France and the UK, Michael Steed (1971) argued that elections for a relatively powerless European Parliament could only serve as 'second-order' referenda on the performance of national governments. After the first EP elections in 1979, this conclusion was confirmed by Reif and Schmitt (1980; see also Reif 1997). Subsequent work on European elections has documented ever-decreasing levels of voter interest and turnout, and a persistent party and media focus on national issues during EP campaigns (Eijk and Franklin 1996; Semetko et al. 2000). This may explain the stunningly low salience of the EP documented by Gibson and Caldeira (1998).

Referendums

A voluminous literature has already emerged about EU-related referendums. With the French and Dutch rejections of the EU Constitutional Treaty in 2005, this literature is likely to grow even larger. Dozens of referenda on EU-related topics have been held since the first series of popular consultations about EEC expansion in 1972. While the referendum appears to offer voters an opportunity to influence the course of European integration, in reality, the referendum is a rare and blunt instrument, in which European issues can frequently be subordinated to myriad tactical concerns.

The issues debated during a referendum campaign may depart from the ostensible topic of the referendum (de Vreese and Semetko 2004a). Given the meager information most voters have about the European Union, it is difficult for them to evaluate the substantive content of the issue they are asked to decide. Many voters may respond by using the referendum to punish unpopular incumbent governments. With some nuances, this pattern has appeared repeatedly in EU-related referenda (Franklin et al. 1994; Franklin 2002).[22] Game-theoretic work on information assymmetry supports this thesis. Schneider and Weitsman (1996) demonstrate that opposition parties may chose to endorse or reject a treaty for strategic purposes. Hug and Sciarini (2000) and Hug (2002) analyse the entire series of EU-related referendums (up to 1994) and find a consistent association between incumbent support and voting in favor of a EU referendum, although the strength of the effect varies according to the institutional characteristics of the referendum.

TAKING STOCK

Over the course of a half-century of research on European integration, EU studies has come to embrace public opinion as an important topic for scholarly research. The relevance of public opinion is becoming an article of faith in the same way the 'permissive consensus' was two decades ago. The emergence of the Eurobarometer has facilitated rigorous cross-national and time-series analyses of public attitudes, and a growing number of scholars have been drawn to this field. Theories based on socialization and familiarity with the EU have not worn well, and utilitarian explanations have come to dominate the literature. Human capital and perceived benefits of membership have had particularly consistent effects. The transformation of an 'economic community' into a 'union' in 1992 marks the rise of political and identity variables which supplement, but do not supplant economic variables. I conclude with a few observations about what we have learned, what we still don't know, and what next directions for research would be the most promising.

Public Opinion about the EU is Not sui generis

Models of opinion change designed to capture aspects of a unique process of European integration (e.g. socialization, postmaterialism) have yielded disappointing results. While the EU itself may defy traditional theoretical approaches, opinions about the EU correspond in many ways to established theory. Theoretical insights drawn from the broader literature on public attitudes have proven very fruitful. A partial list includes economic voting models (e.g. Eichenberg and Dalton 1993), the literature on democratic transition (e.g. Rohrschneider 2002), support for the US judiciary (e.g. Caldiera and Gibson 1995), media studies (e.g. de Vreese 2003) and the policy response model of aggregate shifts in US policy mood (Franklin and Wlezien 1997).

The literature suggests that opinion about the EU, like public opinion more generally, is a very complex phenomenon. The determinants of public attitudes will differ across individuals of varying levels of interest and sophistication.

While utilitarian and governance models suggest that evaluations of the EU are relatively important for sophisticated individuals forming opinions in a low salience environment. When media sources and political actors begin to raise the volume on European issues, utilitarian evaluations can fade into the background as political communications become more effective. All potential influences weaken once attitudes become deeply entrenched – embedded in identities, and protected by well-developed rationalizations. We have learned to recognize the importance of contextual differences, political and media elites, and the stabilizing effect of identity formation.

Context Matters

We have come far from models of an undifferentiated process of identity formation and support as a result of socialization, familiarity, and communications flows. The nature of opinion and the processes which govern its evolution seem to vary considerably across space and time.[23] Context seems to matter over time. Our economic voting models evolve from a concern with inflation during the era of stagflation, to concern with unemployment during the sluggish price stability of the 1990s. The models lose traction with EMU suggesting that as the Union evolves, the determinants of support for the Union evolve as well (Gabel 1998c).

National context also matters. Nations vary in the degree to which Europe is a salient issue, the extent to which opinion is crystallized, and the extent of elite consensus. These differences introduce heterogeneity in the determinants of opinion. For example, elite division increases the effects of national identity (Hooghe and Marks 2005) and increases the impact of party cues (Ray 2003a). Variation in national political economy also alters the role of ideology, with leftists opposing the EU most strongly in social democracies (Ray 2004; Hooghe and Marks 2005).

There is variation also because of the immediate political context. Not only do salient political events such as referendums and elections seem to shift opinion (Handley 1981;

Eichenberg and Dalton 1993), they also seem to increase the influence of media and political cues on opinion formation (Ray 2003b).

Elites Matter

Another lesson from the research thus far is that elites matter. In an environment where few individuals have direct contact with the European Union, perceptions and evaluations are influenced by cues sent from the political and media systems. The effectiveness of these signals will vary. Political parties are most effective when they are united. Internal dissent vitiates the persuasiveness of a partisan message (Ray 2003a). While popular leaders can transfer their popularity to the European project, unpopular ones can transfer their unpopularity to the project as well (Franklin et al. 1994). The media can only affect opinion if they decide to cover the EU. There are strong disincentives to provide this coverage (de Vreese 2003).

NOW WHAT? IGNORANCE, IDENTITY, POLICY, AND THE IDENTITY-POLITY-POLICY TRIANGLE

Given what we know, what areas demand the most attention? I suggest that four areas in particular would be fertile ground for future work. These are ignorance, identity, policy, and the identity-polity-policy triangle.

Ignorance

Mass ignorance about the European Union is often masked in our results as individuals without opinions either vanish through listwise deletion of missing data, or make up answers suppressing the variance we can explain. But ignorance about the European Union has very real effects. According to Kritzinger (2003) ignorance makes EU perceptions derivative of national perceptions. Schneider and Weitsman put ignorance at the heart of their model of referendum strategy (1996).

We know relatively little about the causes of variation in knowledge about the EU. Suggestive research by Sinnott (1997) links knowledge to politicization – referenda and recent EU accession increase knowledge, while actual quality of information decreases with length of EU membership. de Vreese (2003) links information to the media system. Given the implications of information quality for our theories of preference formation, we should have more than a handful of studies to inform us about this area.

Identity

Most research on European identity has focused on the quantity or extent of European identification. But this leaves unclear the actual content of such an identity. Is European identity rooted in a common religious heritage (Nelsen et al. 2001)? Is it attachment to a particular model of society or a set of legal rights? Is it an emotional attachment to a set of symbols? Given the use of 'European identity' as a predictor in quantitative work, it would be good to have a clearer idea of the nature of this phenomenon. In this area, Green (2000) and Bruter (2004) are breaking new ground with qualitative studies of the meaning of European identity.

Policy

The EU is unlikely to vanish – whatever fate may await the Constitutional Treaty. It may be more productive to focus on conflicts over the desired policy outputs of the EU rather than on support for the continued existence of the organization. Early work in this field dwelt at some length on support for specific policies (e.g. Shepherd 1975: 134–53). Recently there has been a shift from a focus on overall support for the EU, to individual desires for specific types of policy outputs (Eichenberg and Dalton 1998; Gabel and Anderson 2002). Accompanying this shift is interest in the explanation of support for specific policies based on their expected costs or benefits (see

Ray 2004 for a model of policy expectations based on national differences). One reason for this interest may be the high salience since 1992 of EU monetary policy during the transition to the single currency.

The Identity-Polity-Policy Triangle

If we imagine evaluations of European identity (or social community), the EU polity, European institutions, and EU policies as located on a continuum from the most concrete (specific policy) to the most abstract (a European identity), we find great inconsistency regarding the causal links between evaluations at different levels. Some authors assume that causality flows upward, as the Eastonian model of specific support would suggest. For example, Gabel and Whitten (1997) argue that support for the EU is based on support for specific policies, and Kritzinger (2003) uses evaluations of EU institutions to predict general evaluations of European unification.

Conversely, general evaluations have been used to predict more specific ones. Hooghe and Marks (2005) use European identity to predict support for EU membership. Gabel (2003) predicts support for the EP using European identity while Caldeira and Gibson (1995) predict support for the ECJ with general support for the EU. Others model support for specific policies as a function of support for the EU, as the Eastonian concept of diffuse support would suggest. Teasing out the direction of causality in this type of situation is notoriously difficult, and existing methodologies involving instrumental variables and multiple stage estimation may prove insufficient. A breakthrough in this area may require new methodological strategies, with experimental methods (see Bruter 2003) as a strong alternative approach. If levels of European identity or of support for specific policies/institutions could be manipulated experimentally rather than simply observed, then new leverage can be brought to bear on an enduring ambiguity in theoretical accounts of support for the EU.

This chapter has attempted to summarize a half century of research on public opinion about European integration. The tempo of research in this area has increased dramatically over these decades. At the time of writing, the aftershocks of the French and Dutch rejection of the Constitutional Treaty were only beginning to be felt. One prediction can be made with confidence. This literature will grow even more rapidly over the next years. And perhaps we will even outgrow our ritual assertion that public opinion matters in EU studies.

NOTES

1. This review covers only the anglophone literature on the topic. Most of the comparative research on public opinion about the EU has appeared in English in international outlets. However, many EU related referendums were such dramatic events for domestic political actors that they have spawned a substantial literature in national outlets and tounges. Of particular importance are the Swiss, Norwegian, and Danish literatures on their particular national struggles with the question of EU membership.

2. Of course, modern scholarly denigration of the ability of the masses to influence political decision making is at least as old as Michels (1999). Page and Shapiro's 1983 article remains a classic work on the general problem of measuring the impact of public opinion on public policy. Conversely, if public opinion did not matter, the Commission and EP would not invest so much on the very expensive Eurobarometer survey series (Rabier 2003).

3. See Denis de Rougemont (1967) for a description of the hard work a small network of federalists put into persuading the public of the benefits, even the necessity of unification.

4. This focus on identity has led some to classify Deutsch as a precursor to constructivist approaches to IR (Adler 2002: 99) The data collected by Merritt and Puchala (1968) carried the field along until the advent of the Eurobarometers.

5. This argument is made by Kaase and Newton, among others (1995) p. 113. See Sinnott (1995) for an alternative view.

6. See Holsti (1992) on the Almond-Lippman consensus.

7. Easton took pains to distinguish his concept of political community from the definitions of community used by Deutsch and Haas (Easton 1965: 172). This is a distinction with a difference, as it relates to the important demarcation between state and nation.

8. Unfortunately, the questions used in our primary data source, the Eurobarometer, were really designed to produce a unidimensional guttman scale of support for Europe, and were not intended to tap into affective versus utilitarian support (Puchala 1973). However, Mayhew (1980: 198) and Gabel (1998a) present factor analytic results suggesting that the Eurobarometer indicators can be sorted into measures of affective and diffuse support.

9. For an exhaustive typology of potential kinds of attitude, and a discussion of typologies used in the literature see Niedermayer and Westle (1995: 50).

10. A recurring issue in this literature is the choice of an appropriate survey question to measure utilitarian support. See Eichenberg (1998) on this point.

11. For example, Inglehart, Rabier, and Reif (1987: 142), but Rasmussen (1997) questions whether the UK public ever rewarded Thatcher for securing the rebate in 1984.

12. Although their model is tested only for Greece. Hix (1999) points out that the European Union could use fiscal transfers to buy off opposition, a strategy which would actually direct more resources to the least supportive groups.

13. Ironically, trade data was first used by the tranactionalist school who interpreted trade flows as a measure of community rather than utilitarian benefit.

14. However, Bosch and Newton (1995) argue that cross-national variation in socio-economic effects undermines this approach.

15. The CAP has long suffered from negative perceptions – even in nations reputed to benefit from it (see Shepherd 1975: 111–3).

16. To date the most comprehensive statement of the utilitarian model remains Gabel's Interests and Integration (1998a)

17. The increase has, however, been uneven, with a period of stagnation in the mid 1970s (Inglehart and Rabier, 1978). The existence of a temporal trend may not, however, mean that familiarity with the European Union increases favorable opinions. An alternate interpretation would be the gradual diffusion through the public of the pro European ideas of 'cognitively mobilized' opinion leaders (Puchala 1968; Inglehart 1970; Wessels 1995b).

18. Ironically, cognitive mobilization had been a concept championed by Inglehart (1970).

19. Although Medrano and Gutierrez (2001) find no such effect in Spain.

20. This literature was inspired by work on referenda, during which incumbent parties were generally the ones campaigning for a pro-EU vote.

21. Deflem and Pampel (1996) point to persistent national differences in opinion about the EU as evidence that a European identity does not exist, while Duchesne and Frognier assert that it is only a 'vanguard' phenomenon (1995).

22. For a critique of this argument, see Siune, Svensson, and Tonsgaard (1994), Svensson (2002).

23. It is, of course, only the existence of the invaluable Eurobarometer survey series which allows us to make these comparisons.

REFERENCES

Adler, E. (2002) 'Constructivism and international relations', in W. Carlsnaes, T. Risse, and

B. Simmons (eds), *Handbook of International Relations*. Thousand Oaks, CA: Sage Publications. pp. 95–118.

Alger, C. (1963) 'Comparison of intranational and international politics', *The American Political Science Review*, 57(2): 406–19.

Anderson, B. (1983) *Imagined Communities: Reflections on the Origin and Spread of Nationalism*. London: Verso.

Anderson, C. (1995) 'Economic uncertainty and European solidarity revisited: trends in public support for European integration', in C. Rhodes and S. Mazey (eds), *The State of the European Union: Building a European Polity?* Boulder: Lynne Reinner. pp. 111–34.

Anderson, C. (1998) 'When in doubt, use proxies: attitudes toward domestic politics and support for European integration', *Comparative Political Studies*, 31(5): 569–601.

Anderson, C. and Kaltenthaler, K. (1996) 'The dynamics of public opinion toward European integration, 1973–93', *European Journal of International Relations*, 2(2): 175–99.

Anderson, C. and Reichert, S. (1996) 'Economic benefits and support for membership in the EU: A cross-national analysis', *Journal of Public Policy*, 15(3): 231–49.

Bosch, A. and Newton, K. (1995) 'Economic calculus or familiarity breeds content?', in O. Niedermayer and R. Sinnott (eds), *Public Opinion and Internationalized Governance*. Oxford: Oxford University Press. pp. 74–104.

Bourantonis, D., Kalyvitis, S. and Tsoutsoplides, C. (1998) 'The European Union and Greece: political acceptability and financial transfers', *Politics*, 18(2): 89–99.

Brettschneider, F., Maier, M. and Maier, J. (2003) 'From d-mark to Euro: the impact of mass media on public opinion in Germany', *German Politics*, 12(2): 45.

Bruter, M. (2003) 'Winning hearts and minds for Europe: news, symbols, and civic and cultural European identity', *Comparative Political Studies*, 36(10): 1148–79.

Bruter, M. (2004) 'On what citizens mean in feeling 'European': perceptions of news, symbols and borderless-ness', *Journal of Ethnic and Migration Studies*, 30(1): 21–40.

Caldeira, G.A. and Gibson, J.L. (1995) 'The legitimacy of the Court of Justice in the European Union', *American Political Science Review*, 89(2): 356–76.

Caldeira, G.A. and Gibson, J.L. (1997) 'Democracy and legitimacy in the European Union: the Court

of Justice and its constituents', *International Social Science Journal*, 49(2): 209–25.

Carubba, C.J. (2001) 'The electoral connection in European Union politics', *Journal of Politics*, 63(1): 141–58.

Carey, S. and Burton, J. (2004) 'Research note: the influence of the press in shaping public opinion towards the European Union in Britain', *Political Studies*, 52(3): 623–40.

Dalton, R.J. and Duval, R. (1986) 'The political environment and foreign policy opinions: British attitudes toward European integration, 1972–1979', *British Journal of Political Science*, 16(1): 113–34.

Dalton, R.J. and Eichenberg, R.C. (1998) 'Citizen support for policy integration', in W. Sandholtz and A. Stone Sweet (eds), *European Integration and Supranational Governance*. Oxford: Oxford University Press. pp. 250–83.

de Rougemont, D. (1967) 'The campaign of the European congresses', *Government and Opposition*, 2(July): 329–48.

de Vreese, C.H. (2003) *Framing Europe: Television News and European Integration*. Amsterdam: Aksant.

de Vreese, C.H. and Semetko, H. (2004a) *Political Campaigning in Referendums: Framing the Referendum Issue*. New York: Routledge.

de Vreese, C.H. and Semetko, H. (2004b) 'News matters: Influences on the vote in the Danish 2000 euro referendum campaign', *European Journal of Political Research*, 43(5): 699–722.

Deflem, M. and Pampel, F.C. (1996) 'The myth of postnational identity: popular support for European unification', *Social Forces*, 75(1): 119–43.

Deutsch, K. (1954) *Political Community at the International Level*. Garden City, New York: Doubleday and Company.

Duch, R. and Taylor, M. (1997) 'Economics and the vulnerability of pan-European institutions', *Political Behavior*, 19(1): 65–80.

Duchesne, S. and Frognier, A. (1995) 'Is there a European identity?', in O. Niedermayer and R. Sinnott (eds), *Public Opinion and Internationalized Governance*. Oxford: Oxford University Press. pp. 193–226.

Easton, D. (1965) *A Systems Analysis of Political Life*. New York: John Wiley and Sons Inc.

Eichenberg, R. (1998) 'Measurement matters: cumulation in the study of public opinion and European integration', paper presented at the annual meeting of the American Political Science Association in Boston, September 1998.

Eichenberg, R. and Dalton, R. (1993) 'Europeans and the European Community: the dynamics of

public support for European integration',
International Organization, 47(4): 507–34.

Eijk, C.V. and Franklin, M. (1991) 'European Community politics and electoral representation: evidence from the 1989 European elections study', *European Journal of Political Research*, 19: 105–27.

Eijk, C.V. and Franklin, M. (1996) *Choosing Europe?, The European Electorate and National Politics in the Face of Union*. Ann Arbor: University of Michigan Press.

Feld, W. and Wildgen, J.K. (1975) 'Electoral ambitions and European integration', *International Organization*, 29(2): 447–68.

Flickinger, R.S. and Center, M. (1993) 'British political parties and public attitudes toward the European Community: leading, following, or getting out of the way?', paper presented at the American Political Science Association annual meeting, 2–5 Sept Washington, DC.

Franklin, M. (2002) 'Learning from the Danish case: a comment on Palle Svensson's critique of the Franklin thesis', *European Journal of Political Research*, 41(6): 751–7.

Franklin, M. and Wlezien, C. (1997) 'The responsive public: issue salience, policy change, and preferences for European unification', *Journal of Theoretical Politics*, 9: 347–63.

Franklin, M., Marsh, M. and McLaren, L. (1994) 'Uncorking the bottle: popular opposition to European unification in the wake of Maastricht', *Journal of Common Market Studies*, 32: 455–72.

Gabel, M. (1998a) *Interests and Integration: Market Liberalization, Public Opinion, and European Union*. Ann Arbor: Michigan University Press.

Gabel, M. (1998b) 'Public support for European integration: an empirical test of five theories', *Journal of Politics*, 60(2): 333–54.

Gabel, M. (1998c) 'International economics and mass politics: market liberalization and public support for European integration', *American Journal of Political Science*, 42: 936–53.

Gabel, M. (2002) 'Public support for the European Parliament', *Journal of Common Market Studies*, 41(2): 289–308.

Gabel, M. and Anderson, C.J. (2002) 'The structure of citizen attitudes and the European political space', *Comparative Political Studies*, 35(8): 893–913.

Gabel, M. and Palmer, H. (1995) 'Understanding variation in support for European integration', *European Journal of Political Research*, (27): 3–19.

Gabel, M. and Whitten, G. (1997) 'Economic conditions, economic perceptions, and public support for European integration', *Political Behavior*, 19(1): 81–97.

Gelleny, R.D. and Anderson, C.J. (2000) 'The economy, accountability, and support for the President of the European Commission', *European Union Politics*, 1(2): 173–200.

Gibson, J.L. and Caldeira, G.A. (1998) 'Changes in the legitimacy of the European Court of Justice: a post-Maastricht analysis', *British Journal of Political Science*, 28(1): 63–-91.

Green, D.M. (2000) 'On being European: the character and consequences of being European', in M.G. Cowles and M. Smith (eds), *The State of the European Union: Risks, Reform, Resistance, and Renewal*. Oxford: Oxford University Press. pp. 292–322.

Haas, E. (1958) *The Uniting of Europe: Political, Social, and Economic Forces 1950-1957*. Stanford: Stanford University Press.

Handley, D.H. (1981) 'Public opinion and European integration: the crisis of the 1970s', *European Journal of Political Research*, 9: 355–64.

Hansen, P. and Petersen, N. (1978) 'Motivational bases of foreign policy attitudes and behavior: an empirical analysis', *International Studies Quarterly*, 22(1): 49–77.

Heath, A., Taylor, B., Brook, L. and Park, A. (1999) 'British national sentiment', *British Journal of Political Science*, (29)1: 155–75.

Hix, S. (1999) *The Political System of the European Union*. Basingstoke: Palgrave.

Holsti, H. (1992) 'Public opinion and foreign policy: challanges to the Almond Lippman Consensus', *International Studies Quarterly*, 32: 439–66.

Hooghe, L. and Marks, G. (2005) 'Calculation, community, and cues: public opinon on European integration', *European Union Politics*.

Hug, S. (2002) *Voices of Europe: Citizens, Referendums, and European Integration*. Lanham, MD: Rowman and Littlefield.

Hug, S. and Sciarini, P. (2000) 'Referendums on European integration: do institutions matter in the voter's decision?', *Comparative Political Studies*, 33(1): 3–36.

Inglehart, R. (1967) 'An end to European integration?', *The American Political Science Review*, 61(1): 91–105.

Inglehart, R. (1970) 'Cognitive mobilization and European identity', *Comparative Politics*, 3(1): 45–70.

Inglehart, R. and Rabier, J. (1978) 'Economic uncertainty and European solidarity: public opinion trends', *Annals of the American Academy of Political and Social Science*, 440(1): 66–97.

Inglehart, R., Rabier, J. and Reif, K. (1987) 'The evolution of public attitudes toward European integration: 1970–1986', *Revue d'integration europeenne /Journal of European Integration,* 10: 135–58.

Jachtenfuchs, M. (2001) 'The governance approach to European integration', *Journal of Common Market Studies,* 39(2): 245–64.

Janssen, J.I.H. (1991) 'Postmaterialism, cognitive mobilization and public support for European integration', *British Journal of Political Science,* 21(4): 443–68.

Johnston, G. and Ray, L. (2004) 'Institutional power and public opinion about EU institutions', paper presented at the annual meeting of the American Political Science Association, 27 August, Philadelphia Marriott Hotel, Philadelphia, PA.

Kaase, M. and Newton, K. (1995) *Beliefs in Government.* Oxford: Oxford University Press.

Kitzinger, U. (1975) *Diplomacy and Persuasion: How Britain Joined the Common Market.* London: Thames and Hudson.

Kriesberg, L. (1959) 'German public opinion and the European Coal and Steel Community', *The Public Opinion Quarterly,* 23(1): 28–42.

Kritzinger, S. (2003) 'The influence of the nation-state on individual support for the European Union', *European Union Politics,* 4(2): 219–41.

Lees, C. (2002) 'Dark matter': institutional constraints and the failure of party-based Euroscepticism in Germany', *Political Studies,* 50(2): 244–67.

Lindberg, L. (1966) 'Integration as a source of stress on the European Community system', *International Organization,* 20(2): 233–65.

Lindberg, L. and Scheingold, S. (1970a) *Europe's Would-Be Polity: Patterns of Change in the European Community.* New York: Prentice Hall Inc.

Lindberg, L. and Scheingold, S. (1970b) *Regional Integration: Theory and Research.* Cambridge, MA: Harvard University Press.

Lodge, J. (1978) 'Loyalty and the EEC: the limitations of the functionalist approach', *Political Studies,* (26)2: 232–48.

Mair, P. (2000) 'The limited impact of Europe on national party systems', *West European Politics,* 23(4): 27-51.

Mayhew, D.R. (1980) *Europeanism: A Study of Public Opinion and Attitudinal Integration in the European Community.* MA thesis Norman Paterson school of International Affairs, Carelton University, Ottowa Canada (July 1980).

McLaren, L.M. (2002) 'Public support for the European Union: cost/benefit analysis or perceived cultural threat?', *Journal of Politics,* 64(2): 551–66.

McLaren, L.M. (2004) 'Opposition to European integration and fear of loss of national identity: debunking a basic assumption regarding hostility to the integration project', *European Journal of Political Research,* (43)6: 895–912.

Medrano, J.D. and Gutiérrez, P. (2001) 'Nested identities: national and European identity in Spain', *Ethnic and Racial Studies,* 24(5): 753–78.

Merlingen, M. (2001) 'Identity, politics and Germany's post-TEU policy on EMU', *Journal of Common Market Studies,* 39(3): 463–83.

Merritt, R. and Puchala, D. (1968) *Western European Perspectives on International Affairs: Public Opinion Studies and Evaluations.* New York: Praeger.

Michels, R. (1999) *Political Parties: A Sociological Study of the Oligarchical Tendencies of Modern Democracy.* New Brunswick NJ: Transaction Publishers (Originally published 1962).

Moravcsik, A. (1991) 'Negotiating the Single European Act', *International Organization,* 45(1): 651–88.

Nelsen, B. and Guth, J. (2000) 'Exploring the gender gap: women, men, and public attitudes toward European integration', *European Union Politics,* 1(3): 267–91.

Nelsen, B., Guth, J. and Fraser, C. (2001) 'Does religion matter? Christianity and public support for the European Union', *European Union Politics,* 2(2): 191–217.

Niedermayer, O. (1995) 'Trust and sense of community', in O. Niedermayer and R. Sinnott (eds), *Public Opinion and Internationalized Governance.* Oxford: Oxford University Press. pp. 227–45.

Niedermayer, O. and Sinnott, R. (1995) 'Democratic legitimacy and the European Parliament', in O. Niedermayer, and R. Sinnott (eds), *Public Opinion and Internationalized Governance.* Oxford: Oxford University Press. pp. 277–309.

Niedermayer, O. and Westle, B. (1995) 'A typology of orientations', in O. Niedermayer, and R. Sinnott (eds), *Public Opinion and Internationalized Governance.* Oxford: Oxford University Press. pp. 33–41.

Norris, P. (2000) *A Virtuous Circle: Political Communications in Postindustrial Societies.* Cambridge: Cambridge University Press.

Page, B.I. and Shapiro, R.Y. (1983) 'Effects of public opinion on policy', *American Political Science Review,* 77(1): 175–90.

Puchala, D. (1968) 'The pattern of contemporary regional integration', *International Studies Quarterly,* 12(1): 38–64.

Puchala, D. (1970a) 'The common market and political federation in Western European public opinion', *International Studies Quarterly,* 14(1): 32–59

Puchala, D.J. (1970b) 'Integration and disintegration in Franco-German relations, 1954–1965', *International Organization*, 24(2): 183–208.

Puchala, D. (1973) 'Europeans and Europeanism in 1970', *International Organization*, 27(3): 387–92.

Rabier, J. (2003) 'Entretien avec M.Jacques-René Rabier, fondateur de l'Eurobaromètre Mardi, 21 october 2003'. Available at: http://europa.eu.int/comm/public_opinion/docs/entretien_rabier.pdf, accessed 23 May 2005.

Rasmussen, J. (1997) '"What kind of vision is that?" British public attitudes towards the European Community during the Thatcher era', *British Journal of Political Science*, 27(1): 111–118.

Ray, L. (1998) *Politicizing Europe: Political Parties and the Changing Nature of Public Opinion about the EU*. Doctoral Dissertation University of North Carolina at Chapel Hill.

Ray, L. (1999) 'Conversion, acquiescence, or delusion: the contingent nature of the party-voter link', *Political Behavior*, 21(4): 325–47.

Ray, L. (2003a) 'When parties matter: the conditional influence of party positions on voter opinions about European integration', *Journal of Politics*, 65(4): 978–94.

Ray, L. (2003b) 'Reconsidering the link between incumbent support and pro-EU opinion', *European Union Politics*, 4(3): 259–79.

Ray, L. (2004) 'Don't rock the boat: expectations, fears, and opposition to EU-level policy-making', in G. Marks and M. Steenbergen (eds), *European Integration and Political Conflict*. Cambridge: Cambridge University Press. pp. 51–61.

Reif, K. (1997) 'European elections as member state second-order elections revisited', *European Journal of Political Research*, 31(1): 115–24.

Reif, K. and Schmitt, H. (1980) 'Nine second order national elections: a conceptual framework for the analysis of European election results', *European Journal of Political Research*, 8(1): 3–44.

Risse, T. (2005) 'Neofunctionalism, European identity, and the puzzles of European integration', *Journal of European Public Policy*, 12(2): 291–309.

Rohrschneider, R. (2002) 'The democracy deficit and mass support for an EU-wide government', *American Journal of Political Science*, 46(2): 463–75.

Sanchez-Cuenca, I. (2000) 'The political basis of support for European integration', *European Union Politics*, 1(2): 147–171.

Schild, J.(2001) 'National v. European identities? French and Germans in the European multi-level system', *Journal of Common Market Studies*, 39(2): 331–50.

Schneider, G. and Weitsman, P. (1996) 'The punishment trap: integration referendums as popularity contests', *Comparative Political Studies*, 28(4): 582–607.

Semetko, H.A., de Vreese, C., and Peter, J. (2000) 'Europeanised politics – Europeanised media? European integration and political communication', *West European Politics*, 23(4): 121–41.

Shepherd, R. (1975) *Public Opinion and European Integration*. Westmead: Saxon House.

Shore, C. (1993) 'Inventing the "People's Europe": critical approaches to European Community "cultural policy"', *Man*, (28) 4: 779–800.

Sinnott, R. (1995) 'Bringing public opinion back in', in O. Niedermayer and R. Sinnott (eds), *Public Opinion and Internationalized Governance*. Oxford: Oxford University Press. pp. 11'32.

Sinnott, R. (1997) *European Public Opinion and the European Union: The Knowledge Gap*. Barcelona: Institut de Ciencies Politiques i Socials.

Siune, K., Svensson, P. and Tonsgaard, O. (1994) 'The European Union: the Danes said "no" in 1992 but "yes" in 1993: how and why?', *Electoral Studies*, 13(2): 107–16.

Slater, M. (1982) 'Political elites, popular indifference, and community building'. *Journal of Common Market Studies*, 21(1,2): 67–87.

Smith, A.D. (1992) 'National identity and the idea of European unity', *International Affairs*, 68(1): 55–76.

Spinelli, A. (1967) 'European Union and the resistance', *Government and Opposition*, 2: 321–9.

Steed, M. (1971) 'The European parliament: the significance of direct election', *Government and Opposition*, 6(October): 462–76.

Svensson, P. (2002) 'Five Danish referendums on the European community and European Union: a critical assessment of the Franklin thesis', *European Journal of Political Research*, 41(6): 733–50.

Walton, C. (1952) 'The fate of neo-federalism in Western Europe', *The Western Political Quarterly*, 5(3): 366–90.

Walton, C. (1959) 'The Hague "Congress of Europe": a case study of public opinion', *The Western Political Quarterly*, 12(3): 738–52.

Wessels, B. (1995a) 'Evaluations of the EC: elite or mass-driven?', in O. Niedermayer and R. Sinnott (eds), *Public Opinion and Internationalized Governance*. Oxford: Oxford University Press. pp. 137–162.

Wessels, B. (1995b) 'Development of support: diffusion or demographic replacement?', in O. Niedermayer and R. Sinnott (eds), *Public Opinion and Internationalized Governance*. Oxford: Oxford University Press. pp. 105–36.

Wilgden, J.K. and Feld, W.J. (1976) 'Evaluative and cognitive factors in the prediction of European unification', *Comparative Political Studies*, 9(3): 309–34.

Worre, T. (1988) 'Denmark at the crossroads: the Danish referendum of 28 February 1986 on the EC reform package', *Journal of Common Market Studies* 26(4): 361–88.

Worre, T. (1995) 'First no, then yes: the Danish referendums on the Maastricht Treaty 1992 and 1993', *Journal of Common Market Studies*, 33(2): 235–57.

14

Constitutional Politics

DARIO CASTIGLIONE AND JUSTUS SCHÖNLAU

INTRODUCTION

Constitutional Politics in the European Union may be thought of as a double oxymoron. The first paradox arises from the association of politics with constitutionalism, for constitutionalism is often understood as a (legal) limit to the means and ends of politics. The second apparent contradiction lies in linking the idea of the modern constitution – an institutional form developed in conjunction with the nation-state – with an organization, the EU, which is at best supra- or post-national. Obviously, in writing on constitutional politics as an aspect of European integration, we reject such stylized views. Nonetheless, both views stand to remind us that the very subject matter of this chapter is open to contestation. The first section of the chapter will therefore address the conceptual difficulties that are intrinsic to constitutional politics in the EU. The rest will attempt to sketch two broad narratives of 'constitutional politics', considered in several of their variants, as these have developed in political and academic discourse. The first narrative, which we call the 'constitutionalization narrative', and of

which we consider three different readings, focuses on the emergence of the European community/communities and their progressive transformation into the Union through a series of agreements and treatises. At the centre of this narrative there is the *emergence* of a constitutional order as the battleground for constitutional politics. The second narrative, which we call the 'supranational constitution narrative', and of which we consider two different readings, is more interested in the normative quality of the constitutionalization process, and therefore in the sense in which it is possible, if at all, to distinguish between *constitutional* and *normal* politics in the European context. At the centre of this second narrative there is the issue of constitutional *normativity*, and whether this results from the generative properties of a certain form of (constitutional) politics, or depends on the *nature* of the constitutional order itself. In either case, the question is whether the process of making the European constitution as a normative construct contributes to the legitimacy of the European Union.

Each of these two narratives cuts across a variety of disciplines – from constitutional law to political theory, from international relations to political science. Given the level of specialization of each of these literatures, we can only superficially touch on the more technical aspects of the various debates. In this chapter, we shall aim instead to offer an overview of the key analytical and theoretical issues that underlie the overlapping narratives that we have identified. We hope that our own meta-narrative will give a sense of what is at stake in discussions about European constitutional politics.

KEY CONCEPTS

We start by observing that, in examining the various literatures, one finds that 'constitutional politics' has no settled meaning. One of the available meanings takes constitutional politics to be an aspect of 'judicial power' (Stone Sweet 2000). This derives from the defining role that the written constitution and the process of judicial review of legislation have acquired in many modern democracies, following in particular the American model, but with reference also to a number of European *Rechtsstaat* traditions. The role that constitutional courts and the process of constitutional interpretation and adjudication play in limiting and re-directing legislation and policy making can be considered intrinsically *political*, and studied as a form of *politics*. This understanding of constitutional politics therefore focuses on the way in which political issues and policy making are influenced by the judicial process and by judicial actors, through means and modes of arguing that are typical of the judicial process and system, but that, in so far as they operate on substantive policies, can be considered political in the narrow sense, as determining the substance of the decisions and not just offering a 'frame' or the 'rules of the game' for arriving at the decisions themselves. A second meaning of constitutional politics takes a reverse view of the relationship between constitutional reality and politics by looking at ways in which political action contributes to the creation of a stable structure of rules, norms and expectations within which ordinary politics operates. The

focus here is on the capacity that political decisions and circumstances have to determine a higher order of rules and to produce a constitutional structure, even when this is not formalized as such. A third meaning, finally, identifies constitutional politics with the more specific processes of constitution making and constitutional transformation, and it looks at the particular qualities and normative purchase that political action has, or need to have, in order to produce a higher set of rules and laws. These three meanings of constitutional politics are not in complete opposition to each other. Indeed, they occasionally tend to coincide, so that, for instance, the exercise of judicial power can be seen as a form of constitution making; or constitution making can be considered as being successful only if and when political action generates the background conditions within which a more formalized document or set of norms acquire true constitutional status. As we shall see in the course of our discussion, all three meanings are at play in the way in which the EU has consolidated in some kind of polity.

The ambiguous meaning of 'constitutional politics' partly reflects ambiguities in the use of ideas of 'constitutionalism' and the 'constitution'. In one sense, constitutionalism is a modern political doctrine. It refers to a series of principled arguments for the limitation of political power in general and of government's sway over the life and rights of citizens in particular. Although one may conceive the means for the limitation of political power in many different ways, in the course of the last two centuries, these limitations and their underlying principles have been embodied in the institutions and practices of the modern constitutional state, with at their centre a written constitutional text (Castiglione 1995, 1996). By constitutionalism, in a second sense, one can thus refer to the complex of institutions that characterizes a constitutional regime; a form of state, and an organization of government, that is, that embodies the principles of constitutionalism. This double meaning is very similar to that which applies in the case of the term 'socialism', which is used to indicate either the ideology or the political regime – and occasionally both at the same time. There remains, however, some important difference between the analytical use of constitutionalism as a regime, and its normative meaning, so that discussions of European constitutionalism and its transformations (Weiler 1999), may be taken to refer to either the introduction of some kind of constitutional charter and constitutional law in the EU system of governance, or to a discussion of what kind of public philosophy should guide such a form of governance.

Although it would at first appear less evident, the ambivalence in the uses of constitutionalism also applies to the understanding of the constitution itself. In a more obvious sense a constitution is, as Paine said, 'a thing ... in fact': something that has 'a visible form', and can be quoted 'article by article' (1989: 81). But of course, Paine was here making a point against the Ancient and unwritten tradition of English constitutionalism. Even though, in its modern sense, the constitution is usually intended as a document setting out the higher law (or 'constitutive' rules) of a state; by the constitution a number of other 'things' are also intended, such as the act through which something is constituted, the basic norm according to which other laws and legislation can be judged, and the structure or inner characteristics defining a political order. Such a variety of meanings suggests that different roles are attributed to the constitution within organized legal and political systems, and that such roles can be looked at either analytically, as having a *function* within the system, or normatively, as determining how the system *ought to* work. Thus, to agree on what a constitution is or does may not be that easy, even when one takes it to be the linchpin on which the modern constitutional state rests. This distinction between the functional and normative role of the constitution is partly at the basis of the two narratives of constitutional politics we identify in this chapter, one more concerned with the way in which the EU has acquired a constitutional order, while the other more attentive to the legitimacy of such a constitutional order.

There is, of course, as mentioned at the beginning, the added complication that the EU, and the other institutional forms in which European integration has temporarily crystallized over the past 50 years, cannot readily be conceived as having state properties; or at least not in the same way in which one traditionally thinks of the state, as consisting (in broadly Weberian terms) in a unified territorial entity, where the central authority exercises a legal monopoly of force, and the citizenry accepts such an exercise as having some form of legitimacy (i.e. where power does not rest on force alone). In modern constitutional democracies, the constitution (in its various meanings) is said to be playing many important roles, such as: legitimating power, in so far as it seems to authorize it; or conferring unity to the legal and political system, by acting as the crucial link between these two systems of social organization (Luhmann 1996); or ensuring the loyalty of the citizens, by offering itself as a cultural and normative point of reference for the citizens' allegiance to the political system and their identification with the political community. In all these three roles, however, the capacity of the constitution to perform those functions is seen as dependent on the fact that there is some form of unified structure of power that the constitution helps putting together and organizing in some hierarchical form. This is precisely what is meant to be lacking at the European level, where certainly at the beginning of the integration process, and arguably still nowadays, authorization, legitimacy, integration, allegiance, and enforcement are fundamentally mediated by the member states, and therefore reflect the fragmented structure of power typical of the international system, and not (or not yet) the more unified and homogeneous one of the constitutional state. In order to talk meaningfully of constitutional politics in the EU (in either its functional or normative version), it is therefore necessary to make some sense of the divided image of the EU, as both an international organization and a polity in the making. *Hic Rhodus, hic salta!*[1]

THE EMERGENCE OF THE EUROPEAN CONSTITUTIONAL ORDER

One way, the most obvious one, of telling the story of constitutional politics in the EC/EU is to look at how the European constitutional order has come to life; or, as Alec Stone Sweet has put it, how has it happened that the EC/EU has metamorsophized 'from an international regime, founded on the precepts of international law, into a multi-tiered, quasi federal polity' (2000: 160). This is hardly an uncontested fact, but even those that hang on to the view that EU politics still operates as an international law regime (Grimm 1995), or that EU decision making is in essence intergovernmental (Moravcsik 1999), must offer some account of the consolidated nature of the community legal and institutional order, and of what Weiler has described as the virtual foreclosure to member states of the *exit* option from community obligations (1999: 31). Weiler himself has illustrated the emergence of European constitutionalism, meant as a constitutional regime, by looking at its 'geology', at how it was first conceptualized from a number of practical and theoretical perspectives (1999: 221–37). Following, in a slightly modified form, Weiler's own characterization of what he considers the three main approaches during the foundational phase, we here distinguish between a historical (an adaptation of what Weiler calls 'doctrine' approach), a legal, and a political reading of the emergence of the European constitutional order. These three readings offer a complex view of the 'constitutionalization narrative'. We shall look at them in the reverse order.

Neofunctionalism and Supranational Politics

The political science approach is probably the least self-consciously constitutional of these three readings, but it offered the first sustained attempt to identify a new kind of order, as this was emerging from the European integration process. This version of the constitutionalization narrative developed through a series of, often competing, 'grand theories' of European integration, starting with the intellectual breakthrough represented by neo-functionalism (Haas 1958). This is not the place where to re-assess that theory and its intellectual

history, but from a more specific constitutional perspective, its contribution can be summarized under several headings. For one, neofunctionalism entrenched the idea that there was a new, supranational dimension to politics. Interest formation and mediation were no longer taking shape exclusively within the two distinct, but mutually supportive sights of national statehood and the international arena. Moreover, the supranational dimension was not characterized by domination (as in the cases of imperial and colonial relationships), but it was emerging from the interactions of separate social and institutional actors, who operated (already at the national level) with a certain degree of autonomy, and who found it convenient to think of their interests and of the scope of their actions as something that reached beyond the nation state, connecting in this with other groups and institutions similarly operating with a regional framework in mind. Neo-functional theories and analyses propped up the idea of the new supranational dimension by suggesting that it had a dynamics of its own based on the concept of 'spillovers', and that its emergence was further reinforced by the very fact that it produced (and empowered) new institutional actors operating at the supranational level. Finally, both the mechanisms of functional development and adaptation, and the relative autonomy attributed to the supranational institutions overseeing integration, became part of a minoritarian, but self-conscious federal strategy for the promotion of the supranational level as an important, if not the dominant, political arena.

The partial demise of neo-functionalism, following a number of sustained attacks on some of its central tenets (Moravcsik 1999; Milward 2000) and the realization that its teleology of integration was not consistently and unequivocally sustained by either empirical analysis or general political developments, should not detract from the fact that neofunctionalism contributed to the conceptualization of the integration process, making this and the European institutions specific objects of analysis. Such analysis has since been carried forward through other methodological perspectives which, though rejecting some of the fundamental premises and guiding concepts of neo-functionalism, have nonetheless taken seriously the emergence of a supranational space and the autonomous role played by some of the European institutions. Neo-institutionalism, multi-level governance, and in a way constructivism, have offered a more nuanced way of conceiving the interactions between the national and the supranational levels, and how it is this mixture of levels, of institutional and normative constraints, and of competing constructions of political meaning that determines the constitutional underpinning of politics in the EU and the countries comprising it.

Judicial Constitutionalization

In spite of the increasing attention showed by political scientists to the structural elements in European integration and politics, a constitutional discourse was relatively slow to emerge in this literature. This may have something to do with the general inattention towards constitutional matters in much of political science and political theory for several decades after the middle of the twentieth century (Bellamy and Castiglione 1996). Not so amongst the lawyers. The second, and arguably the most influential reading of the constitutional narrative, is the one focused on the emergence of a new legal order at the European level, and how particularly the European Court of Justice was instrumental in fixing both its character and the way in which such a supranational legal order related to that of the member states. The story of the so-called 'judicial constitutionalization' has been told many times, and in a variety of forms, but its basic outline is undisputed (though its significance remains contested). At the centre of this version of the constitutionalization narrative there is the action of the European Court of Justice (ECJ) and how this, in the often quoted words of Eric Stein, 'fashioned a constitutional framework for a federal-type structure', while working in 'benign neglect' from its basis in 'the fairyland Duchy of Luxembourg' (1981: 1). The

constitutional order, in this case, is not (at least on the face of it) the product of a slow evolutionary process, as intended from a neo-functionalist perspective; nor is it the sedimentation of institutional logics and the way in which these both constrain and produce path-dependency. The constitutional order emerges instead as the by-product of a piecemeal, but purposive process of rationalization of the legal system through case law, in which the Court plays a pivotal role in its dealings with private litigants and national courts. The assumption here is that the de-facto legal system emerging from the integration process, the *acquis communautaire*, was given constitutional shape by the establishment of a series of ordering principles of European jurisprudence (for a general overview, see De Burca 1999). These principles are usually identified as the *supremacy*, and the *direct effect* doctrines (de Witte 1999); though one may also add *pre-emption* and the protection of human rights (Weiler 1999: 22–5; Mancini 2000: 7–14), and in a second period *indirect effect*, and *governmental liability* (Stone Sweet 2000: 163). Most of these doctrines are associated with particular legal cases and how the ECJ's rulings over them have become the corner stones of the new constitutional order. To deal only briefly with *supremacy* and *direct effect*: the doctrine of *supremacy*, first established in *Costa v ENEL* (ECJ 1964), maintains that community law has primacy over national law in view of the obligations that member states have incurred through agreements signed with other member states at the European level; and that national legislators cannot therefore legislate in a manner that is inconsistent with such agreements, while national judges have a 'duty to disapply' (de Witte 1999: 190) laws that may undermine such binding agreements. The doctrine of *direct effect*, first formulated in the *Van Gend en Loos* case (ECJ 1963) just before the *Costa* case, established instead the applicability at the national level of various legislative and regulative acts ('regulations', 'treaty provisions', and 'directives'). This would hold true even in those cases where national authorities either failed to make provisions for such application in a reasonable time, or the national law clashed with the spirit of the directives and regulations. Although the two rulings of the EJC (and others that have followed along the same path) remain controversial in their justification, their combined effect has been to suggest that there is a common legal order at the European level and that this has a kind of hierarchical structure that makes it similar to what applies at the national level.

There is an interesting ambivalence in this understanding of the judicial constitutionalization of the EU. On the one hand, it is clear that the constitutional order so conceived, as a coherent system organized around a number of key principles and doctrines, is the product of 'judicial creativeness'; on the other hand, the action of the ECJ is presented as nothing more than the rational interpretation and coherent systematization of principles already included in the acts and intentions of the national governments and the political actors who promoted and signed the EC/EU founding treaties, thus giving form and direction to the process of integration. The fact, of course, is that the difference between judicial 'creativeness' and judicial 'rationalization' depends on how one interprets what Stein called 'benign neglect', and on whether one assumes that such neglect has persisted over time, from the foundational phase of the 1960s and 1970s until nowadays (cf. also Weiler 1999: 191–2; de Witte 1999: 194–8). The relationship between the kind of constitutional jurisprudence defined by the ECJ, and the way in which this has been viewed by member states' governments and Parliaments, as well as by ordinary and constitutional courts at the national level, is an exceedingly complex story; but posing the problem in this terms makes it clear that the view of judicial constitutionalization as the single-handed product of the ECJ is an over-simplification in which both supporters and critics occasionally tend to fall. In any case, the view of the Court as the actor unpacking the logical implications of the intentions of the treaties' signatories, and of the 'fact' that the treaties themselves have created 'a Community of unlimited duration', with 'real powers stemming from a limitation of sovereignty or transfer of powers from the States to the Community' (ECJ 1964: 593), is something

that must necessarily rest on a particular reading of the history of treaty making in the EC/EU. This is indeed the third version of the constitutionalization narrative to which we referred at the beginning of this section, the one dealing with the chronicle of the formal and political acts through which member states have allegedly locked themselves in the course of the integration process.

From the Treaties to the Constitution

At the centre of this version there is the conceptual distinction between *treaty* and *constitution*, an issue to which we shall return, from a more theoretical perspective, in the next section. For the time being, we wish to look at the issue from a more historical perspective. This constitutional narrative is often conceived as a linear evolution from 'treaty' to 'constitution'; the effect of cumulative developments from the humble beginnings of functional co-operation in a few economic areas, most notably coal and steel, to the creation of an independent constitutional order beyond the nation state. In fact, a closer examination of the various phases seems to undermine such an image, showing surprising twists and turns along the line, and offering a much more complex picture of changes and continuities.

How the new European structure was to be set up ('constituted') and the particular instruments and processes used for this purpose, have been a matter of contention and experiment from the very beginning of the integration process. The rhetorical appeal to the idea of a 'constitution' was there at the outset. When the 'Schuman-Plan Conference' was created in 1950 to discuss how to implement the aims set out in the Schuman's Declaration of 9th May, one of the suggestions was to call the document '*Traité portant Constitution de la Communauté Européenne pour le charbon et l'acier*' (Schneider in Busek and Hummer 2004: 18). Later, even after the failure of the first European constitution (the European Political Community-Treaty) together with the European Defence Community (EDC), the 1957 Treaty of Rome made explicit reference to the aim of an 'ever closer union', showing that its underlying aspiration went beyond that of a common international treaty. Such a reading would suggest that the aspirations of the initial phase (from 1950 to the Treaty of Rome) were subsequently thwarted by the political reality of member states' increasing scepticism about the scale and ambition of change, which they clearly perceived as a threat to their own positions of power within such an emerging new regime. This was particularly evident in the French Parliament's rejection of the EDC Treaty, which at the time also seemed definitely to bury any idea of a political community. It may here be significant to note that the 'Schumann-Plan Conference' drafting the ECSC Treaty represented the first de-facto intergovernmental conference (chaired by Jean Monnet). Shortly afterwards, while planning the establishment of a political authority in charge of the European Defence Community, there were suggestions to entrust Parliamentarians with drafting a 'statute document' for a European Political Community – Europe's 'first constitution' (Griffith 2000). The Parliamentary Assembly of the Council of Europe urged to give such a mandate either to a committee of its own members (representing the six member states of the Coal and Steel Community), or to the Parliamentary Assembly of the ESCS itself; thus placing national Parliamentarians at the centre of the political/constitutional process (Schröder 1994). In the event, the foreign ministers of the 'six' decided to give the task to an 'ad hoc' committee, selected amongst the members of the ECSC parliamentary assembly, which was significantly named 'constitutional committee' (Dinan 1994: 27). The proposals advanced by this consultative group proved too ambitious, however, and their substance was considerably watered down during a series of intergovernmental meetings in 1953 and 1954. Eventually, these proposals came to nothing with the collapse of the proposed EDC.

The failure of the EDC project removed political integration from the official agenda for a number of years. The main focus now shifted towards narrower and more functional forms of integration, decided through technical treaties. And yet, the basic institutional structure of the coal and steel community, mixing intergovernmental and supranational institutions, remained in place, and became the blueprint for the formation of the European Economic Community. Although the Treaty of Rome was prepared by an intergovernmental committee chaired by the Belgian Foreign Minister Paul Henri Spaak, he was explicitly asked 'to call on the assistance of the High Authority of the ECSC, the general secretariat of OECE, of the Council of Europe and of the Conference of European Transport Ministers' (Fondation Spaak II 1984: 21). So the process of treaty-creation was not in the exclusive hands of the governments, but it already acquired a somewhat self-reflexive nature, in so far as it gave voice to the European institutions and to the kind of supranational interests that they had come to represent.

If judged from the perspective of treaty-creation, the period between 1957 and 1986 would seem uneventful. However, as we have seen in discussing the legal and political narratives, the lack of new treaties did not stop the development of European constitutional politics. From the more historical perspective we are now considering, a series of events contributed – if not directly, at least indirectly – to the development and consolidation of the supranational dimension. The question of qualified majority voting (with the 'empty-chair crisis', and the 'Luxembourg compromise'), the debates about the first round of enlargement in the 1970s, the implementation of the Treaty of Rome provision for the direct election of the European Parliament, and the reform of the community budget, as well as reports by Leo Tindemans (1976) and Pietro Adonnino (European Council 1985) on how to bring the integration project closer to the citizens, all testify to the fact that there was more to the EC than a series of intergovernmental treaties. The very logic of market integration seemed to require the (partial) abandonment of the unanimity principle, and the construction of a European-wide collective interest in a number of policy areas. As a consequence of such attempts at re-defining the boundaries within which to consider common interest and hence common policies, the question of the democratic nature of representation in the European institutions started to emerge as a widely discussed issue. Moreover, the introduction of direct elections to the European Parliament rather paradoxically made more, rather than less evident that there were unresolved questions of both political representation and political competence within the institutional structure of the community. It may therefore come as no surprise that the next major 'constitutional' initiative, namely the 1984 Spinelli draft constitution (European Parliament 1984), emerged from the European Parliament itself; even though the Parliament had no specific mandate for promoting such a document, while the document itself had no direct political and constitutional consequence.

And yet, the symbolic importance, or perhaps sheer timing, of the Spinelli's initiative should not be discarded altogether. With the introduction of the Single European Act came a significant acceleration to the series of intergovernmental conferences and treaty reforms, which in the past two decades have profoundly changed the relationship between the EU, the member states and the European citizens. The intergovernmental conferences have become, or at least have come to be perceived as the true markers of constitutional development in the EU. Even though the five IGC's since 1985 have differed considerably in terms of their 'constitutional' aspirations, their procedures, and their outcomes; their focus has invariably been on institutional reform. Moreover, in comparison to the past, the IGCs have become events where some form of genuine negotiation, and confrontation over different visions of the future of Europe, have taken place (Corbett 1987). By the time the upheavals of 1989 and the foundation of a new 'European Union' in 1991 had forced a more open 'constitutional' phase onto the European agenda, European integration had finally (and perhaps irrevocably) become an issue of genuine political contestation in almost all member states. In this context, the Maastricht ratification crisis marked the end of output legitimacy as the quasi-exclusive basis for an elite-driven integration process. However, as it had happened on previous occasions, the answer to the

sudden and unexpected popular interest in, but also reaction to, European supranational developments was a partial retreat from constitutional rhetoric and political ambition to narrower and piecemeal initiatives. The IGCs after Maastricht tended to present issues such as majority voting, enlargement, or the size of the commission in a de-politicized form, as 'leftovers' (i.e. unresolved technical questions). However, this gave a mixed message. Indeed, in order to deal with the 'leftovers', at Maastricht it was decided to fix yet another IGC within a set period of time, thus conferring to the IGCs a new role, as part of a continuous process of institutional adaptation and consolidation.

In spite of the more cautious attitudes triggered by the popular reactions to Maastricht, the age of constitutional politics seemed to have finally dawned on Europe. With the introduction of the Euro and a new unprecedented phase of enlargement, the debate about the 'future of Europe' became inevitable. This was reflected in the attempt to broaden participation during the negotiations for the Amsterdam Treaty, by involving the European and National Parliaments, and by engaging in an open discussion with 'civil society' organizations. Such an attempt could be considered as a way to find new kinds of ex-ante legitimacy in the operations of European institutions and for their reform. This move became more evident when, after the Cologne summit, in 1999, it was decided to stage another IGC and to set-up a completely new body (later called a 'Convention') to draft an EU Charter of Fundamental Rights. The new body comprised national and European Parliamentarians, national government and Commission representatives, and observers from other EU institutions and the European Court of Human Rights. Although it was not provided with a specific 'constitutional' mandate, it quickly became evident that a debate about fundamental rights in an assembly of this political standing would inevitably lead to a much wider discussion about the fundamentals of integration (Schönlau 2005). The results of this experiment were ambiguous. On the one hand, the text approved by the convention was not formally integrated in the treaty signed at the Nice IGC in 2000. This reinforced the impression that such ad hoc committees would remain subordinate to the IGC process and to intergovernmental negotiations. On the other hand, the 'Convention method', with its open and transparent proceedings, and its more upfront constitutional ambitions, seemed an important addition to the tool-set of European constitutional politics.

It was not long before this method was given a second chance. With enlargement increasing the pressure both to find a more adequate institutional structure in order to accommodate 25 member states without loosing in effectiveness, and to address growing concerns about the overall sense and purpose of integration, there seemed to be the need for a more decisive round of Treaty reform, after the perceived failures of Amsterdam and Nice. This was reflected in a speech given at the Humboldt University in May 2000, by the then German Foreign Minister. In it, Joschka Fischer forcefully proposed an overtly 'constitutional' path for the future of Europe. Comforted by the wave of interest and widespread approval that followed Fischer's speech, the Belgian presidency of the second half of 2001 proposed to launch a 'grand debate' on a new European institutional structure. This position was accepted in the Council, and a new Convention entrusted with the task of preparing such a debate, which, as the Council's resolution made clear, could perhaps have as an outcome a kind of constitutional document (European Council 2001).

In a sense, 50 years after the ECSC preparations, the European political debate had come full circle and acknowledged the need for an explicit 'constitution' within which to inscribe the integration process. In contrast to 50 years earlier, this time there was the recognition, at least in the public rhetoric, that such a development would need some form of direct democratic legitimacy. This could partly be achieved ex-ante, through the Convention process; and ex-post through popular or parliamentary ratification. With the Laeken declaration, the EU entered into the most explicitly constitutional phase of its development yet. It is at this juncture – meant here in a conceptual rather than merely historical terms – that a

second narrative of constitutional politics comes into its own. Such a narrative is no longer exclusively, or even primarily, concerned with the nature and effects of the constitutionalization process, but with its legitimacy and with the precise form that a European constitution should have. It is to this second narrative that we now turn.

THE SUPRANATIONAL CONSTITUTION AND ITS LEGITIMACY

As the 'historical' reading of the constitutionalization narrative suggests, the ideas of constitutionalism and of the constitution were present in the political debate from the very beginning of the integration process. Nevertheless, it took some time for the notion that the EC/EU had acquired some kind of, at least functional, constitution to be accepted. Weiler (1999: 3–9), for one, has remarked on this inversion of the traditional way of conceiving modern constitutionalism (but not, of course, of 'ancient' ideas of the constitution), by figuratively making use of the biblical passage in *Exodus* 24: 7, where the people of Israel are said to have declared their acceptance of the book of Covenant with the words: 'we will do, and hearken'. There would seem to be some incongruence in ante-posing the deeds ('we will do') to the act of listening and declaring one's willingness to obey ('and hearken'). In Weiler's metaphor, the 'doing' stands for the process of material constitutionalization, while the 'hearkening' represents the legitimate way in which a constitutional order is established: 'the deliberative process of listening, debating, and understanding' (1999: 5). This debate over the sources of legitimacy is at the core of what we here describe as the 'supranational constitution narrative'.

Such a narrative overlaps with the debate on the 'democratic deficit' (for a recent statement on this, cf. Føllesdal and Hix 2005) and with what has become the standard account of the way in which the democratic deficit in the EU has emerged as a consequence of the partial exhaustion, or inadequateness, of its output form of legitimacy (Beetham and Lord 1998; Scharpf 1999). Indeed, the idea of legitimacy has played an increasingly important role as a way of linking the theoretical-normative debates with the reality of ongoing integration (Bellamy and Castiglione 2003). At least since the early 1970s the question has been asked of how the current system or even further integration could be justified, in particular in the face of decreasing public support as measured by opinion polls. The realization grew that, apart from successful policy delivery (output legitimacy), also democratic input and probably some kind of social recognition (identification) were needed to maintain the legitimacy of the emerging European polity. Informal constitutionalization (through the ECJ or the gradual institutionalization of certain practices) was increasingly seen as playing an ambiguous role in the EU's 'quest for legitimacy' (de Burca 1996). On the one hand it was seen as necessary to develop and consolidate the system, thus ensuring its continuous functioning. On the other hand, it was criticized for excluding and further alienating the citizens from the process of integration, also provoking the occasional backlash from the member states as the guardians of the democratic interests of their citizens. As more questions were raised on how to ensure that a European-wide polity could be normatively legitimate, the very idea of democratic legitimacy in supranational conditions came under scrutiny. The same question obviously applied to democratic constitutionalism and the constitution (Zagrebelsky 2003; Dobson and Føllesdal 2004). Indeed, the debate over the nature of democratic legitimacy in the EU has inevitably got entangled with the question of whether Europe needed a written constitution (Habermas 2001).

Does Europe Need a Constitution?

In a strange way, the discussion about writing the European constitution took over from where the narrative of the neo-functionalists floundered, offering a moment of closure to the integration process as it had been described by the neo-functionalists. The constitution was an obvious, and theoretically unproblematic, aim for those who conceived the future of Europe in federal terms. Indeed, the constitution seemed to provide some 'meaning and purpose' (Nuotio 2004) to the integration process, determining once and for all what has been called its finalitè (Walker 2002). Since many identified the finalitè of the European integration process with the establishment of a new form of statehood at a supranational level, the constitution was conceived as the sanctioning that political integration was, on the whole, complete. By fixing the structure of internal power, assigning precise competences at national and supranational level, and between the various European institutions, the constitution would establish a new architecture of sovereignty within the EU and its member states. From such a perspective, the constitution would contribute to making the EU more legitimate, efficient and democratic. But if the constitution is meant to confer legitimacy to the EU as a state-like entity, where does the legitimacy of the constitution itself come from? The normative narrative of constitutional politics becomes therefore embroiled with the discussion of what is the nature and legitimacy of the 'constitution' in supranational conditions.[2]

This discussion has developed along two parallel lines of dispute, two faces, so to speak, of the same medal, involving, on the one hand, the identification of the 'constituent power' in the EU constitutional order; and, on the other, the characterization of the nature of the foundational document of such an order: whether this should be regarded as a 'treaty' between states, or as a 'constitution' of the European people. The German jurist Dieter Grimm has perhaps been the most authoritative and consistent voice arguing against the view that the European Union can, at this stage of its development, meaningfully give itself a constitution (Grimm 1995). Grimm remarks that the emergence of modern constitutions is intrinsically linked to the way in which positive law operates at two levels over the public domain. The first level establishes the legitimate source of state power and regulates the operations of government. The second level follows from the exercise of state power itself, but it acquires force in so far as state power has been bound by the rules set down at the first level. Grimm argues that this is not the way in which Community law has operated over the years, and that any attempt to constitutionalize it comes against the intractable question of who are the 'masters' of the Treaty, the ultimate repositories of sovereignty in the EU legal and political system – the true constituent power. According to Grimm, the 'constituent power' remains with the member states, who, as actors within an international system, are not subject to the constitutional discipline typical of first and second-order positive law, as it applies in constitutional states, where instead the constituent power dissolves itself into the 'constituted powers' as a result of the creation of a constitutional order. Grimm's argument here is that, due to the dominance of the separate state actors, the EU legal space lacks the distinctive structural properties of constitutional law. Attempts to introduce some form of constitutionalization remain partial and superficial until the EU can claim some form of self-sufficient statehood *independently from the member states*. According to this view, the European constitution cannot legitimate European statehood and democracy, since it presupposes some form of established statehood.

Even if we assume that Grimm is right in his analysis of the structural limits to be overcome in order for the EU to have a constitution, it could be argued that the post-Laeken process and the 'treaty establishing a Constitution for Europe' were meant to create the background political conditions for constitutional politics and constitutional law. This raises the other point of controversy, intriguingly captured by the decision made in the Convention to mix the languages of international and constitutional law by referring to the agreed document as both a 'treaty' and a 'constitution', or as they put it: a treaty establishing a constitution, where it remains unclear where the 'text' of the treaty ends and that of the constitution starts. This linguistic solution, however, only highlights the problem. As suggested by Bruno de Witte (2004), a close exegetical analysis of the language of the approved text, and of the

formal status of the document itself, seems to support the case that the way in which the document was both conceived and formulated is entirely within the tradition and language of international treaty making, showing the clear intention of the drafters to confirm, rather than weaken, the position of the member states as the 'high contracting parties', who have the power to bound themselves to the agreements set up in the treaty, within the limits set by their own *separate* constitutional orders. Such evidence, however, does not in itself seem conclusive, for there is nothing to prevent the possibility that a treaty may become the basis for a self-contained constitutional order, as it happened in the German case towards the end of the nineteenth century. In this respect, the intentions of the framers are of limited guidance. In fact, it is part of the 'constitutionalization' thesis to suggest that the passage from an international regime to a constitutional order has been on the whole unintended.

But there is another way of putting the sceptical argument against a federal Europe and against the idea that the EU is already in the position to give itself a constitution. This is generally known as the 'no-demos' thesis (Weiler 1999). Simply put, this argument suggests that without some kind of unified people there cannot be democracy – and therefore that any European state without a European people would necessarily be undemocratic. The issues commonly raised in relation to the 'no-demos' thesis are of three kinds. One concerns the deliberative presuppositions for democracy to operate. Such presuppositions comprise a diffuse and fairly integrated European public sphere, a working representative system at the European level, and even more obviously the ability to communicate and understand each other through a shared language. Although in some limited and/or rudimentary forms, these elements are already present in the EU, it is difficult to see how such conditions can operate beyond the narrow circle of European elites, something that would make it difficult for a European-wide political system to have a genuine popular character. The second issue raised by the 'no-demos' thesis concerns the way in which, in a democracy, people are prepared to accept collective decisions that have redistributive implications out of a sense of solidarity with the other members of the community. The nature and boundary of such solidarity are strongly contested, but historically in Europe democratic citizenship has developed in parallel to a solidaristic conception of the national community. A working democracy at the European level would therefore need some form of connective solidarity to ensure that people were willing to accept as legitimate the application of the majoritarian principle across a series of important policy decisions. The third issue, finally, is that of cultural diversity. Whereas the experience of democracy within the nation state has tended to coincide with a certain homogeneity of the people – or, more often, with a nation-building project, which relied on processes of democracy- and citizenship-formation in order to get firmly established – in the EU, cultural and national diversity is both pervasive and tends to be considered as a value worthy to be preserved rather than overcome.

In each of its forms, the 'no-demos' thesis once again proposes the question of sovereignty and the unresolved (perhaps unsolvable) question of the nature and role of the constituent power.[3] In the experience of national constitutionalism, the ultimate appeal to the demos, as both a unitary and self-constituting subject ('We, the people'), has played an important role as the alleged source of, and the legitimating influence over the exercise of power by the political and legal institutions – the 'constituted powers'. The question is whether this self-constituting model can be reproduced at a European level, in a situation in which the national demoi still cling both to the separateness of their interests and to demands for the recognition of their socio-cultural differences. It is here that the narrative of the 'supranational constitution' comes into its own. In other terms, if one does not start from the assumption that a quasi-federal structure is the natural *telos* of the integration process, how is it possible for constitutional politics to operate at a supranational level?[4] The answer to this question has taken two main forms, which represents the two divergent readings of the 'supranational constitution' narrative. One reading concentrates on the idea that the making of the constitution is the result of a *constitutional moment*; the other reading emphasizes the idea of the constitution as the result of a *process* of continuous negotiation and interpretation of constitutional law and of the underlying constitutional order – a process that requires time and that operates at different levels.

Constitutional Moments

The 'constitutional moment' version of the normative narrative has found inspiration in the work of the American constitutionalist Bruce Ackerman (1991), and has more recently been popularized in the idea that the European constitutional convention should be considered a New Philadelphia (Castiglione 2004; Walker 2004b). In both Ackerman's and the popular version, the writing of the constitution has an important 'generative' quality, which depends on the effect in time that the constitution has over the working of the political and legal systems. In other words, on how successful and long-lasting a constitution is. This implies a series of 'descriptive' statements, which can only be judged ex-post. But from a more normative perspective, the evaluation of a constitutional moment involves an assessment of the specific *generative* qualities of the constitutional moment, and of the way in which such generative qualities take *form*. Identifying the generative quality and the specific forms of constitutional moments is another way of posing the question of the sources of legitimacy. In other words, a constitutional moment is such, if it is capable of bringing into being the fundamental elements that give legitimacy to a polity and to its political regime. Here views may diverge on whether what matters is more an outcome-based assessment of legitimacy – a constitutional moment is therefore assessed on the kind of constitutional order it produces and on the substance of the constitutional document; or whether legitimacy is seen in more procedural terms – if, for instance, the constitutional moment succeeds in either mobilizing the citizenry or producing public deliberation and a higher form of consensus.

The Constitutional Convention has offered an interesting terrain for developing and debating the validity of the more procedural approach, and particularly the normative and socio-psychological basis for a deliberative approach to democracy and constitutionalism. A number of authors have engaged with the issue of the nature of discourse and agreement in politics, and what normative force principled deliberation and agreement (as opposed to contractual bargaining) may carry with them (see the contributions in Eriksen 2005; and Eriksen et al. 2004). By applying certain aspects of Habermas's communicative theory, they see the prolonged phase of institutional discussion and transformation in Europe since Maastricht as a way of constructing the unity of the European polity on the basis of a reflexive form of problem solving that makes appeal to shared norms and progressively entrenched commitments. From such a perspective, the introduction of the 'convention method' can be seen as a decisive improvement on the IGC, for it would seem to introduce a more dispassionate way of arguing about the organization of the European institutions, appealing to general reasons, instead of taking narrow national interests as the basis for log-rolling and the bargaining-type of intergovernmental politics dominating the signing of previous treaties in the history of European integration.

But this position presents some problems, for it offers an idealized view both of what happens in discussions on constitutional issues, and of the 'convention' experience itself, besides suggesting a somewhat artificial separation between constitutional questions and fundamental policy issues, thus assuming that the former are a better ground on which to build consensus at the European level. The normative quality of constitutional deliberation can be questioned from two distinct perspectives. The first does not necessarily imply a rejection of the analytic and normative contentions made by advocates of the superiority of constitutional deliberation. According to this view, although it is difficult to prove empirically that particular agreements are the result of rational deliberation, or that they reflect a rationally motivated consensus; it may still be true that the contextually induced restrains of constitutional deliberation create incentives through which agents are motivated to reach agreements based on more dispassionate principles and reasoning, and that such agreements have a strong 'integrative' function, establishing something stronger than a simple *modus vivendi*. From such a perspective, the work of the constitutional convention looks like a genuine attempt at substituting a more deliberative and supranational style of constitutional politics to the bargaining model based on strong national interests as instantiated in the practice of the IGCs. However, even though the process may look distinctive, it remains to be seen whether the outcome of the constitutional convention – i.e. the kind of constitutional document that it managed to produce – went beyond the kind of substantive compromises that have characterized much of treaty making in the EU (Magnette 2004). Indeed, the very fact that the constitutional draft prepared by the convention needed approval by the IGC may cast some doubt on the idea that the writing of the Constitutional Treaty represents a real break with past experience. Moreover, the stalling of the ratification process can be cited as further proof that the deliberative character of the process does not guarantee a consensual outcome.

Constitutional deliberation can also be questioned from a second, and normatively more radical, perspective. For, it can be argued that the negotiations in the constitutional Convention showed that a number of key constitutional questions can only be settled by 'normal' political means, and by trade-offs between policy-issues within a wider context; and that indeed such a bargaining style of politics is both unavoidable and justifiable, since political compromises are intrinsic to all forms of democratic politics. Compromises are not to be rejected because they may fall short of some idealized form of consensus, but need to be judged contextually and according to their capacity to favour social and political integration, besides producing distributive outcomes accepted by those involved. Compromise, and not consensus, is the form of agreement that better reflects political pluralism in modern times, and this is no different in either normal or constitutional politics (Bellamy and Schönlau 2004a, 2004b).

This second challenge undermines the *categorical* distinction between constitutional and normal politics, denying that they can be easily distinguished on the basis of their normative value. In the European case, some commentators go even further and question whether the recent phase of constitutional politics, which has focussed discussion on the EU institutional framework, and on what the EU is, or it should become, may be the best ground on which to build consensus at a European level. Andrew Moravcsik, for instance, maintains that talks on the constitution, far from consolidating the integration process, have opened up a Pandora box, risking destabilizing the 'constitutional settlement' reached throughout the 1990s (Moravcsik 2002, 2005a, b). This position, however, denies that there is a crisis of legitimacy in the EU, while assuming that its *de facto* supranational constitutional order needs no explicit normative basis, for it ultimately rests on the democratic legitimacy of the member states. Even allowing for Moravcsik's point on political prudence, it would seem difficult to maintain that the emergence of an explicit constitutional discourse in Europe is a largely manufactured event, particularly when one considers that it has developed within the context of an unprecedented process of enlargement, and that it follows from a phase of profound changes in the nature and extent of the economic integration process. If anything, the constitutional debate testifies of the need to find a new balance between the EU institutional structure and its policy-making ambitions. Arguably, Europe's constitutional moment should not be identified with the Laeken process of writing a documentary constitution, but with the new phase of political integration that started at Maastricht (Weiler 1999: 3–4). From such a perspective, the Convention and the Constitutional Treaty look more like the concluding acts of a protracted constitutional moment, whose fundamental features are not those enshrined in the articles of the constitutional text, but momentous political decisions such as the Enlargement, the introduction of a common currency, of an independent European Central Bank, and of the Stability Pact. It is partly ironic that such decisions are not regarded as 'constitutional', and that they have been taken with very little popular involvement, without a European-wide discussion (Weiler 2002). But as the ratification crisis of 2005 shows, in the eyes of the European public there is very little difference between what the EU *is* and what it *does*, so that at the moment of considering the ratification of the Constitutional Treaty many voters found it problematic to distinguish between what the Constitution *says* (i.e. what is in the actual text of the constitution) and what, in their view, it *stands for* (i.e. how they consider the European Union and its impact upon their everyday life). It is little surprising, therefore, that present and future enlargement, immigration, and social and economic policies – all issues that are not affected by the introduction of the Constitutional Treaty – have played such an important part in the way in which people voted in the French and Dutch referendums. It is a sign that constitutional politics cannot be limited to institutional matters, but it is inevitably entangled with some of the substantive issues associated with normal politics.

There is, however, another side to the idea that the normative character of constitutional politics needs a constitutional moment, something that breaks the routine of normal politics. This is connected with the importance of symbolism as part of constitutional politics. The point has been made forcefully by Jürgen Habermas, when he intimates that 'as a political collectivity, Europe cannot take hold in the consciousness of its citizens simply in the shape of a common currency. The intergovernmental arrangement at Maastricht lacks that power of symbolic crystallization which only a political act of foundation can give' (2001: 6). According to Habermas, the constitution can act as a catalytic point in the 'circular creation' of Europe as a political community, coming as the constitution does at the end of an already advanced process of social, economic and political integration, and, in turn, helping to

put in motion the construction of a European-wide civil society, a common public sphere, and a shared political culture (2001: 16–21). Underpinning this operation there is what Habermas calls 'constitutional patriotism', a form of allegiance to the political community, which rests on abstract and universal principles of a civic kind. A lively debate has developed around this idea and whether it may rightfully become part of a European identity (Friese and Wagner 2002; Lacroix 2002; Kumm 2005) but from Habermas's perspective, the main question is whether the focus on the constitution could help fostering such an allegiance. In other words, whether the writing of the constitution would be the key moment of a constitutional project aimed at enlarging our circle of solidarity at a European level and to create the conditions for a 'federation of nation-states' (Habermas 2001: 15).

In Habermas's and other supporters' view of the need for a constitution, as a strong normative and symbolic statement, the constitution is part of a constructivist gambit intended as the beginning of the process of construction of a political demos in Europe. But as Neil Walker has argued (2004a, 2004b, 2005) the way in which the Constitutional Treaty has taken shape did not reflect one single project or conception of the EU constitution and European constitutionalism. For Walker, a number of very different influences have shaped both the text and the form taken by the drafting process of the Constitutional Treaty, comprising positions expressing various shades of scepticism against constructive and documentary constitutionalism, and even extending to those who were in principle hostile to it. From such a perspective, the Constitutional Treaty reflects a compromise between different views, and is the basis for future political and intellectual battles. Thus the current debate on whether its text may be rescued after the defeats in the French and Dutch referendums is beside the point. The real issue is whether the halting of the constitutional moment simply signals a temporary retreat of constructivists and federalists constitutional projects, or it is the sign of a process of reversion of the broader constitutional agenda set at Maastricht.

Constitutional Processualism

The fuzzy definition of a European constitutional moment highlights the difficulties besetting any attempt to reproduce the traditional concepts of national constitutionalism at a European level. One of the key ideas of those who tend to emphasize the postnational character of the constitutional path in the EU is that constitution making in it cannot be characterized as an *event*, but as a *process* (Shaw 2003). This argument has many facets, involving different elements of constitutional politics. One is concerned with the relationship between formal and informal moments in the making of the constitutional order, emphasizing, for instance, how treaty reform in Europe cannot be seen as a simple succession of different treaties amending each others, and characterized by intergovernmental bargain (Greve and Jorgensen 2002; Farrell and Héritier 2003). A second element consists in a more systemic understanding of how both law and politics operate, but also of how they interact by producing a 'structural coupling' between them, so that constitutional politics is the result of various institutional dialogues and the way in which they come to interact (Greve and Jorgensen 2002). A third element concerns the way in which the development of European community law has changed the structural context in which different branches of law operate at the national level, forcefully impacting on the relationship between private and public law in the member states' legal systems, contributing to redrawing some of the boundaries between them, whilst in particular problematizing the relationship between private and public autonomy. This process is part and parcel of the open constitutionalization of the EU legal system (Joerges 1997; Joerges and Everson 2004).

The final and more evidently postnational element of this processual understanding of the constitutional politics in the EU is closely connected to the recognition of the fact that there are different demoi at the heart of the construction of the EU as a polity (Maduro 2003). Joseph Weiler (2001) has argued that Europe has already developed its constitutional *Sonderweg* by adopting a kind of toleration towards different national constitutional traditions, renouncing, that is, to look for a 'positive' common constitutional culture. Similar echoes can be found in other authors (Shaw 2003; Nuotio 2004) to apply to EU constitutionalism an open-textured and continuously negotiated (both internally and externally) method of constitution building. The principles that guide it, however, are still very much a matter of experiment and contention and may apply beyond the EU experience (Slaughter 2004). The basic intuition, however, is that the European constitutional order is a plural one, operating both at the supranational and at the national level, and encompassing both the national and the EU constitutions (Pernice and Kanits 2004). As Neil Mac Cormick says: 'a pluralistic analysis … shows the systems of law operative on the European level to be distinct and partially independent of each other, though also partially overlapping and interacting' (1999: 119). In itself, this is not a difficult state of affairs to perceive and analyse. The problem is how to conceive and operationalize conflict resolution in the context of such radical pluralism. This is indeed the challenge for constitutional politics in the EU.

NOTES

1. In the somewhat garbled and transformed sense of 'this is the crux of the matter' that Hegel and Marx conferred to Aesop's original: 'Hic Rhodus, hic saltus', meant instead as a challenge to the boasting of braggarts.

2. From a federalist perspective, the legitimacy of the constitution is not a real problem, or at least its legitimacy is no different from that attributed to the constitution of a state. There is here a difference between those who think that European statehood can be easily disjointed from nationhood, and that European democracy and constitutionalism therefore require a federal-like structure (Mancini 2000: XXVI), and those who take more seriously the conundrum of constitutionalizing a supranational entity.

3. The circularity that the issue of 'constituent power' poses to constitutionalism is similar to that raised by the possibility of establishing a democracy according to democratic means (Dahl 1989). In either case, something prior and discontinuous seems to be presupposed in order to establish a constitutional or a democratic regime.

4. This does not exclude that Europe's supranational constitution may not resemble traditional federal

constitutions. In fact, this is very likely. The issue here is not one of substance but of legitimacy. Discussions about the supranational constitution, even when they are in favour of a European constitution, start from the assumption that this cannot be justified on the basis of an already established statehood at the European level.

REFERENCES

Ackerman, B. (1991) *We the People. Foundations.* Cambridge, Mass.: Harvard University Press.

Beetham, D. and Lord, C. (1998) *Legitimacy and the European Union.* London: Longman.

Bellamy, R. and Castiglione, D. (1996) *The Constitution in Transformation.* Oxford: Blackwell.

Bellamy, R. and Castiglione, D. (2003) 'Legitimising the Euro-"polity" and its "regime": the normative turn in European studies', *European Journal of Political Theory*, 2(1): 1–34.

Bellamy, R. and Schönlau, J. (2004a) 'The normality of constitutional politics: an analysis of the drafting of the EU Charter of Fundamental Rights', *Constellations*, 11(3): 394–411.

Bellamy, R. and Schönlau, J. (2004b) 'The good, the bad and the ugly: the need for constitutional compromise and the drafting of the EU Constitution', in L. Dobson and A. Føllesdal (eds), *Political Theory and the European Constitution.* London, Routledge. pp. 56–74.

Castiglione, D. (1995) 'Contracts and constitutions', in R. Bellamy, V. Bufacchi, and D. Castiglione (eds), *Democracy and Constitutional Culture in the Unione of Europe.* London: Lothian Foundation Press. pp. 75–102.

Castiglione, D. (1996) 'The political theory of the constitution', in R. Bellamy and D. Castiglione (eds) *The Constitution in Transformation.* Oxford: Blackwell. pp. 417–35.

Castiglione, D. (2004) 'Reflections on Europe's constitutional future', *Constellations*, 11(3): 393–411.

Corbett, R. (1987) 'The 1985 intergovernmental conference and the Single European Act', in R. Pryce (ed.), *The Dynamics of European Union.* New York: Croom Helm. pp. 238–72.

Dahl, R.A. (1989) *Democracy and its Critics.* New Haven: Yale University Press.

de Búrca, G. (1996) 'The quest for legitimacy in the European Union', *The Modern Law Review*, 59: 349–76.

de Búrca, G. (1999) 'The institutional development of the EU: a constitutional analysis', in

P. Craig and G. de Búrca (eds), *The Evolution of EU Law*. Oxford: Oxford University Press. pp. 55–81.

de Witte, Bruno (1999) 'Direct effect, supremacy and the nature of the legal order', in P. Craig and G. de Búrca (eds), *The Evolution of EU Law*. Oxford: Oxford University Press. pp. 177–213.

de Witte, B. (2004) *The National Constitutional Dimension of European Treaty Revision – Evolution and Recent Debates*. The Second Walter van Gerven Lecture. Groningen: Europa Law Publishing.

Dinan, D. (1994) *Ever Closer Union?*, first edition. Houndmills, Basingstoke: Macmillan.

Dobson, L. and Føllesdal, A. (eds) (2004) *Political Theory and the European Constitution*. London and New York: Routledge.

ECJ (1963) Case 26/62 Van Gend and Loos vs. Nederlandse Administratie der Belastingen ECR 1.

ECJ (1964) Case 6/24 Costa vs. Enel ECR. 585.

Eriksen, E.O. (ed.) (2005) *Making the European Polity: Reflexive Integration in the EU*. London and New York: Routledge.

Eriksen, E.O., Fossum, J.E. and Menéndez, Augustín J. (eds) (2004) *Developing a Constitution for Europe*. London and New York: Routledge.

European Council (1985) 'Report from the ad hoc Committee on a People's Europe to the European Council (part one 29–30 March 1985 Brussels, part two 28–29 June Milan), *EC Bulletin* Supplement, 7/85.

European Council (2001) 'Declaration on the future of the EU', Annex to the Conclusions of the presidency, Laeken, 14–15 December.

European Parliament (1984) *Resolution of 14.2.1984 on the draft Treaty establishing the European Union* (OJ C 77, 19.3.1984, p. 5, rapporteur: Altiero Spinelli, 1–1200/1983).

Farrell, H. and Héritier, A. (2003) 'Formal and informal institutions under codecision: continuous constitution-building in Europe', *Governance*, 16(4): 577.

Fondation Spaak (1984) *Pour une Communauté Politique Européenne, Traveaux Préparatoires 1952–54, und 1955–57*. Bruylant: Bruxelles.

Friese, H. and Wagner, P. (2002) 'Survey article: the nascent political philosophy of the European polity', *The Journal of Political Philosophy*, 10(3): 342–64.

Føllesdal, A. and Hix, S. (2005) 'Why there is a democratic deficit in the EU: a response to Majone and Moravcsik'. *European Governance Papers* 1(2). Available at: http://www.connex-network.org/eurogov/pdf/egp-connex-C-05-02.pdf, accessed 10 March 2006.

Greve, M.F. and Jørgensen, K.E. (2002) 'Treaty reform as constitutional politics – a longitudinal view', *Journal of European Public Policy*, 9(1): 54–75.

Griffith, T. (2000) *Europe's First Constitution – The European Political Community 1952–54*. London: Federal Trust.

Grimm, D. (1995) 'Does Europe need a constitution?' *European Law Journal*, 1(3): 282–302.

Haas, E. (1958) *The Uniting of Europe*. Stanford: Stanford University Press.

Habermas, J. (2001) 'Why Europe needs a constitution', *New Left Review*, 11: 5–26.

Joerges, C. (1997) 'The impact of European integration on private law: reductionist perceptions, true conflicts and a new constitutional perspective', 3(4): 378–406.

Joerges, C. and Everson, M. (2004) 'Law, economics and politics in the constitutionalization of Europe', in E.O. Eriksen, J.E. Fossum and A.J. Menéndez (eds), *Developing a Constitution for Europe*. London and New York: Routledge. pp. 162–79.

Kumm, M. (2005) 'To be a European citizen: constitutional patriotism and the treaty establishing a constitution for Europe', in *The European Constitution: The Rubicon Crossed?*, ARENA Report No. 3/05. pp. 7–63.

Lacroix, J. (2002) 'For a European constitutional patriotism', *Political Studies*, 50(5): 944–58.

Luhmann, N. (1996) 'La costituzione come acquisizione evolutiva', in G. Zagrebelsky, P.P. Portinaro and J. Lüther (eds), *Il futuro della costituzione*. Turin: Einaudi. pp. 129–66.

Mac Cormick, N. (1999) *Questioning Sovereignty: Law, State, and Practical Reason*. Oxford: Oxford University Press.

Maduro, M.P. (2003) 'Europe and the constitution: what if this is as good as it gets?', in J.H.H. Weiler and M. Wind (eds), *European Constitutionalism Beyond the State*. Cambridge: Cambridge University Press. pp. 74–102.

Magnette, P. (2004) 'Deliberation or bargaining? Coping with constitutional conflicts in the Convention on the Future of Europe', in E.O. Eriksen, J.E. Fossum and A.J. Menéndez (eds), *Developing a Constitution for Europe*. London and New York: Routledge. pp. 207–25.

Mancini, G.F. (2000) *Democracy and Constitutionalism in the European Union*. Oxford: Hart Publishing.

Milward, A. (2000) *The European Rescue of the Nation State*, second edition. London: Routledge.

Moravcsik, A. (1999) *The Choice for Europe. Social Purpose and State Power from Messina to Maastricht*. London: UCL Press.

Moravcsik, A. (2002) 'In defence of the "democratic deficit": reassessing legitimacy in the European Union', *Journal of Common Market Studies*, 44(4): 603–24.

Moravcsik, A. (2005a) 'The constitution is dead, long live the constitution!', *Prospect*, 112.

Moravcsik, A. (2005b) 'The European constitutional compromise and the neofunctionalist legacy', *Journal of European Public Policy*, 12(2): 349–86.

Nuotio, K. (ed.) (2004) *Europe in Search of 'Meaning and Purpose'*. Helsinki: Forum Iuris, Faculty of Law University of Helsinki.

Paine, T. (1989) *Political Writings*. In B. Kuklic (ed.). Cambridge: Cambridge University Press.

Pernice, I. and Kanits, R. (2004) 'Fundamental rights and multilevel constitutionalism in Europe', *Walter Hallstein-Institut Paper* 7/04.

Scharpf, F.W. (1999) *Governing in Europe: Effective and Democratic?*. Oxford: Oxford University Press.

Schneider, H. (2004) 'Ursprünge und Vorläufer der gegenwärtigen "Verfassungsdiskussion" in der Europäischen Union', in E. Busek and W. Hummer (eds), *Der Europäische Konvent und sein Ergebnis – eine Europäische Verfassung*. Wien-Köln-Weimar: Böhlau Verlag.

Schönlau, J. (2005) *Drafting the EU Charter: Rights, Legitimacy and Process*. Basingstoke: Palgrave-Macmillan.

Schröder, H. (1994) *Jean Monnet und die amerkanische Unterstützung für die europäische Integration 1950–1957*. Frankfurt am Main: Verlag Peter Lang.

Shaw, J. (2003) 'Process, responsibility and inclusion in EU constitutionalism', *European Law Journal*, 9(1): 45–68.

Slaughter, A.-M. (2004) *A New World Order*. Princeton and Oxford: Princeton University Press.

Stein, E. (1981) 'Lawyers, judges and the making of a transnational constitution', *American Journal of International Law*, 75(1): 1–27.

Stone Sweet, A. (2000) *Governing with Judges. Constitutional Politics in Europe*. Oxford: Oxford University Press.

Tindemans, L. (1976) 'Report on European Union', *EC Bulletin*, Supplement 1/76.

Walker, N. (2002) 'The idea of a European Constitution and the finalité of integration', Faculdade de Direito da Universidade Nova de Lisboa, Francisco Lucas Pires Working Papers Series on European Constitutionalism, Working Paper 2002/01.

Walker, N. (2004a) 'The legacy of Europe's constitutional moment', *Constellations*, 11(3): 368–392.

Walker, N. (2004b) 'The EU as a constitutional project', *Federal Trust Online Constitutional Papers*, 19/04.

Walker, N. (2005) 'Europe's constitutional momentum and the search for polity legitimacy', *International Journal of Constitutional Law*, 4(2): 211–38.

Weiler, J.H.H. (1999) *The Constitution of Europe – Do the New Clothes have an Emperor? and other Essays on European Integration*. Cambridge University Press: Cambridge.

Weiler, J.H.H. (2001) 'Federalism with constitutionalism: Europe's *Sonderweg*', in K. Nicolaïdes and R. Howse (eds), *The Federal Vision. Legitimacy and Levels of Governance in the United States and the European Union*. Oxford: Oxford University Press. pp. 54–70.

Weiler, J.H.H. (2002) 'A constitution for Europe? Some hard choices', *Journal of Common Market Studies*, 40(4): 563–80.

Zagrebelsky, G. (ed.) (2003) *Diritti e Costituzione nell'Unione Europea*. Roma-Bari: Laterza.

15

Bringing Federalism Back In

R. DANIEL KELEMEN AND KALYPSO NICOLAIDIS

INTRODUCTION

In the past decade, comparative federalism has moved from the periphery of scholarship on the European Union to the mainstream. While pioneering scholars (see for instance Friedrich 1969; Forsyth 1981; Cappelletti et al. 1986; Scharpf 1988; Weiler 1991; Dehousse 1992; Sbragia 1992) have long applied insights from comparative federalism (or confederalism) to describe and explain the dynamics of European integration, the dominant theoretical perspectives on European integration rejected the relevance of federal comparisons. Intergovernmentalists had clear reasons to do so. From the intergovernmentalist perspective, European integration is driven by the same forces that explain the development of other international regimes (Moravcsik 1998), forces which differ in fundamental ways from the forces at work in domestic settings. From this perspective, any effort to gain comparative leverage on explaining European integration should be based on comparisons with other instances of regional integration (e.g. Mattli 1999), rather than with the experience of federal polities.

Scholars building on Haas' (2004) neofunctionalist tradition who do view the EU as a supranational polity in its own right have less compelling reasons to reject comparative federalism, but most have done so nonetheless. Some associate federalism with statehood and emphasize that because the EU lacks key elements of statehood, it cannot be studied as a federation. Such scholars have developed a new conceptual vocabulary associated with 'multi-level governance' (Marks et al. 1996; Hooghe and Marks 2001). Other 'institutionalist' scholars in the Haasian tradition seem to view an emphasis on the concept of federalism as a semantic distraction. For instance, Sandholtz and Stone Sweet's (1998: 9) study of the processes of 'institutionalisation' that drive European integration seeks to, 'avoid an argument about the precise nature of the EU polity and how it compares with other federal polities'. In short, the federalism lens on European integration has been considered either as privileging the descriptive over the explanatory (emphasizing the 'what' over the 'why') or as overly laden with normative connotations (suggesting what the EU should be rather than what it is).

Despite the best efforts of many EU scholars to steer research away from the dreaded F-word, it has continued to rear its head. The notion that federalism is relevant to understanding the EU has persisted for a number of reasons. First, as the EU has expanded its range of competences into realms typically associated with the nation state, comparisons with federal systems have become ever more plausible. Second, the language and analysis of subsidiarity and ideas related to identifying optimal divisions of authority between member states and the Union have clear parallels in federal systems. Third, political discourse has placed a spotlight on federalism. In particular, Joschka Fischer's controversial May 2000 speech on the EU's move toward federalism (Fischer 2000) stimulated widespread debate on the relevance of federal models for the EU, and the debate over the EU's draft Constitutional Treaty has again placed questions of European federalism centre stage.

Crucially, these trends have combined in partially freeing the federal paradigm from statehood (Elazar 1987; Nicolaidis 2001). Federalism has been defined in terms of leagues or collectivities of states each with a distinct identity (McKay 1999). The study of federalism addresses both the *why* (why federal unions emerge and survive) and the *what* (what forms and variants of political community they represent). Recently, more and more EU scholars have applied the lens of comparative federalism to the EU polity (see for instance Bednar et al. 1996; Koslowski 1999; Schmitter 2000; McKay 2001; Nicolaidis and Howse 2001; Zweifel 2002; Bogdanor 2003; Börzel and Hosli 2003; Kelemen 2003, 2004; Ansell and Di Palma 2004; Fabbrini 2005; Trechsel 2005a; Schain and Menon 2006; Halberstam and Maduro 2007). And conversely, scholars of comparative federalism have discovered the European Union and increasingly integrate the EU into their comparative studies of other federal systems (Friedman Goldstein 2001; Filippov et al. 2004; Rodden 2005; Bednar 2006). Indeed, interest in the EU has helped spark the renaissance in comparative federalism research in recent years, with some scholars arguing that, with more than half of the world's space and nearly half of its population governed by federal arrangements, an 'age of federalism' may be upon us (Hueglin and Fenna 2006).

The growing trend to apply tools and insights from the study of other federal systems to the EU is part of a broader trend to import tools and concepts from other branches of political science to EU studies. EU studies has never existed on an island completely unto itself; however, for years the field remained isolated on a *presqu'isle* with only a tenuous connection to 'mainland' political science. This isolation was encouraged by the fact that so much of EU studies focused on the macro-historical debate over the general explanation for European integration. Today, the literature on EU politics is focusing increasingly on mid-range theorizing, with authors focusing less on explaining why the EU came into existence and more on explaining how it operates in particular domains. However, the federal vision/lens can shed light on a wide range of areas, from questions of power allocation, to democratic legitimacy, to regulatory competition, to fiscal federalism, to party system development and identity formation. In these and other areas, comparative federalism can help EU scholars escape the barren empirical terrain inhabited by those who insist that the EU can only be viewed as a *sui generis* polity.

We divide the remainder of the chapter into four sections. The first section reviews earlier traditions in EU studies that invoked the concept of federalism. Section two explains the main reasons for the turn to federalism. The third section highlights emerging themes for federalism research and section four concludes.

THE EARLY PHASE: FEDERALISM IN ITS NORMATIVE GHETTO

Federalism as a Political Goal

The relevance of the federalism lens to European integration has been fiercely contested from the very inception of the EU, and remains so today. This is because, more than any other theoretical anchor to understanding the integration process, the notion of federal Europe is political and normative: a dream of what the European continent ought to be on the part of idealist thinkers and mainstream politicians alike in the interwar and immediate post-war era (Coudenhove-Kalergi 1938), when scarcely any book about Europe would fail to include the term *federal* in its title. An echo of these visions, the Hague conference of 1948 referred to the European federal project as a destiny, a *finalité politique*. But the choice made in the wake of the failure of the EDC and the run up of the Treaty of Rome, was that of another type of project, the step-by-step functionalism that has made the EU what it is today.

Nevertheless, the pre-war tradition of federalism never left the European scene and continued to inspire figures like Spinelli, Monnet and even Jacques Delors (Burgess 1993, 2000, 2003; Pinder 1998; Sidjanski 2000). Its appeal in the minds of continental politicians lay with the precise constitutional and democratic model it provided. Spinelli, in particular, was influenced by the British federalist literature stemming out of the Federal Union movement (Lord Lothian, Lionel Robbins and Sir William Beveridge among others), which he read on the island of Ventotene in 1939. As Burgess has noted, however, many (if not most) such statesmen in the post-war setting were reluctant to wear the federalist label, preferring instead '... to act as one rather than to use the word itself' (Burgess 2000: 74).

Consequently, the federalist strand in EU studies was weak for the first three decades of the project's life, with federal scholarship confined to a few key authors like Pinder and Burgess. Indeed, even as federal scholarship re-emerged in the 1980s it was tainted by its normative complexion and was viewed with a fair degree of scepticism in many quarters. This unfortunate impression was perhaps inevitable as the authors did indeed view federalism favourably, seeing it as a natural fit with the inherently global 'nature of problems' that confronted humankind; but this was reinforced by a formal definition of federalism integrating ideological positioning, philosophical statement and empirical fact (Burgess and Gagnon 1993). Federalism was defined as '... the recommendation and (sometimes) the active promotion of support for federation ... ideological in the sense that it can take the form of an overtly prescriptive guide to action' (Burgess 1993: 8). The federal scholars, on the other hand, felt outnumbered and outgunned by those arguing that the then EC was then, and (implicitly) would remain in the future, an inter-governmental enterprise, as opposed to one in which strong supra-national elements were developing and would develop further. There was much misunderstanding and mutual suspicion on both sides.

The Emergence of Federations

Unsurprisingly, a core theme of this early attempt to fit the EU in a comparative federalism framework was the question of why states or politicians decide to form political union in the first place and under what conditions federations are viable (Forsyth 1981; Burgess and Gagnon 1993). The subject attracted a great deal of attention in the 20 years following world war II in the context of state building in the defeated axis powers and the former colonies and the successful examples of federations in the New World (McKay 1999). Applying these insights to the emerging EU, two broad schools of thought emerged (McKay 1999).

The first explored what Karl Deutsch called 'the essential conditions' for a federation around the notion of *common interest* (Deutsch 1957; Wheare 1964). While the earliest benchmark had to do with a shared aversion to external threat, this was expanded to include the presence of an external military or diplomatic threat or opportunity for aggrandizement (Riker 1964, 1975). Lists of conditions were drawn and assessed such as Deutsch's mutual compatibility of main values, a distinctive way of life, a broadening political elite, increased economic growth, administrative capabilities and social communication. Or Watts (1966) and Wheare's (1956): (1) a sense of military insecurity; (2) a desire to be independent from foreign powers; (3) some previous political association; (4) geographical neighbourhood; (5) similarity of political institutions. But clearly in the EU as well as other unions, these were not universally necessary conditions and therefore held little explanatory power.

The second perspective treated federalism as an *ideology* and argued that these conditions are not sufficient either. In this view, objective conditions must be combined with the subjective beliefs of the actors involved, as it is the very commitment to the 'primary goal of federalism as an end in itself' on the part of some of them that will help transform the idea into reality (Franck 1968). In the same vein, Pinder (1995) emphasized the conscious action of federalists' support from specific interests, be they groups or particular member states. Burgess also offers a powerful revisionist critique of the established history of post-war integration, seeking to reassert the over-looked role that federalists played at many critical moments in the EU's development. He argued that '… inter-governmental approaches to explaining European integration, with their exclusive emphasis upon the role of states and governmental élites, effectively close off and shut out rival perspectives' (Burgess 2000: xiii). Most recently, Parsons (2003a) also argued for the rehabilitation of the federalist impulse in driving integration forward, attributing to the actions of purposeful supra-national agents at least equal importance to the self-interested actions of national governments. To some extent, neofunctionalism is infused with similar assumptions, emphasizing as it does the importance of support from specific interests generated by the internal logic of integration in various areas.

Both of these traditions, however, have failed to generate a cumulative research programme. Below we present four 'strategies of appropriation' that may facilitate 'bringing federalism back in' to EU studies in a manner that will stimulate well-focused, systematic and cumulative comparative research.

BRINGING FEDERALISM BACK IN: FOUR STRATEGIES OF APPROPRIATION

There are several proximate causes for the re-emergence of federalism as a conceptual lens for the EU in the 1990s. First and foremost, the combined momentum provided by the success of the 'Europe 1992' relaunch of the single market under Delors' leadership combined with the end of the Cold War seemed to project the union into a new era. There is little doubt that the Maastricht Treaty, as the initial institutional embodiment of this new state of affairs, represents the major turning point in this regard: substantively, as the newly relabelled 'Union' was then seen to fulfil minimal conditions for qualifying as an instance of federalism (Hesse and Wright 1996; McKay 1999); and politically, as for the first time, the federal nature of the enterprise became the explicit object of political bargaining. That the pace of integration continued to quicken in the 1990s with further widening of the scope of EU competences at Amsterdam and Nice in 1997 and 2000 appeared to provide mounting evidence that the EU was taking on a federal-type character – a diagnosis obviously contested and contestable (Moravcsik and Nicolaidis 1998; Moravcsik 2001).

As usual with the EU, developments in the real world were followed with a lag by developments in the field of EU studies. The few prior proponents of the EU-as-federal paradigm claimed to be vindicated, since in Burgess' words '… [today], the EU exhibits so many federal and confederal elements in its constitutional, legal, economic and political make-up that only the most ill-intentioned, not to say perverse, observers would attempt to deny it' (Burgess 2000: ix). Indeed, within a decade of Maastricht, courses and programmes on comparative federalism were created – as with the project COMFED bringing together six US and European universities. A number of collaborative projects brought scholars of the EU together with scholars of comparative federalism, and in particular US federalism (Nicolaidis and Howse 2001; Parsons 2003b; Fabbrini 2005; Trechsel 2005b; Halberstam and Maduro 2006; Menon and Shain 2006). And articles and monographs on comparative federalism including the EU alongside Switzerland, the US or Germany started to appear regularly (Friedman-Goldstein 2001; Kelemen 2001, 2004; McKay 2001; Zweifel 2002; Börzel and Hosli 2003; Sbragia 2004). Even established, yet contested federations like Canada or India began to look at the EU as a possible model for accommodating their-centrifugal pulls.

It would be a stretch to claim, however, that federalism has taken the field of EU studies by storm. While the standard international relations (IR)-based debate between functionalist, supranationalist and liberal intergovernmentalist approaches appears to have reached a substantial impasse, the EU remains an 'IR-object', with many treating the EU as the most advanced instance of regional integration or as a model for global governance (Nicolaidis and Howse 2002). Nevertheless, the small band of federal scholars in EU studies has recently been joined by a wider band of comparativists, who now include the EU within their universe of comparison (Hix 1994).

In short, scholars who argue for a federalism lens must address two conceptual challenges: how to accommodate the *distinctive* character of the EU while integrating it in the family of comparative federalism; and how to fend off the political and normative connotations of the term, implying a teleological rather than analytical focus. We identify four main strategies for addressing these challenges.

The first strategy we could term *constitutional* (Stein 1981; Cappelletti et al. 1986; Mancini 1989; Craig and de Burca 2002; Fabbrini and Sicurelli 2004; Stone Sweet 2004; Halberstam and Maduro 2006; Nicolaidis 2006). Mostly originating in constitutional law, and generally inspired by the European Court of Justice's role and jurisprudence, the strategy rests on the long-held diagnosis of constitutionalization of the treaties. Accordingly, the combination of direct effect and supremacy of EU law has created a direct link between citizens and the supra-national level of governance. In this view, the recent exercise of writing it all down *qua* Constitution merely makes explicit a long-term evolution. In reflecting the nature of the EU as it has evolved, the draft Constitution laid out the three basic principles of federalism as constitutional lawyers would have it (Nicolaidis 2007):

- Structurally, it describes a *multi-tier governance system* in which the member states are units that both constitute and belong to the federal whole, while remaining autonomous from it in a broad range of areas.

- Functionally, it establishes an explicit *division of power* between the constituent states and the federal whole, *la grande affaire* of federalism, and sets out the ways in which the boundary between them can be changed.

- Procedurally, it organizes an intense *mutual participation* between the respective legal orders involved – states shape the substance of federal supremacy while the federal level must acknowledge state autonomy.

There are limits, however, to this formal constitutional approach. First we can ask whether the failure to adopt an actual Constitution is not itself a testimony to the fact that the EU has not and should not reach this mature state (Moravcsik 2006). Even if the text was adopted it would fail to recognize explicitly the *federal* nature of the covenant, as the British government successfully argued for avoiding the use of this politically loaded expression, and would simply state the EU's *raison d'etre* – that we can achieve more by working together than working alone.

The second strategy we could term *disaggregative*. It accepts that the EU cannot be seen as an accomplished or mature federation, stressing instead that it exhibits *some* of the characteristics of a federal polity in certain policy areas, e.g. regulatory or fiscal federalism (see below). Here again, the decision on a common currency led at least those analysts already wedded to federalism to characterize Maastricht as 'the basis of a federal state' (McKay 1999). In this spirit, the majority in the Convention on the Future of Europe, including lawyers, defended the use of the word federal in its Article 1 as describing a decision-making process, but *not* the Union itself: the EU would be a Union of States administering common objectives 'in a federal way'. As such, the reference to federalism would cover only some of the Union's activities, like money, competition policy or external trade, and not others, like foreign policy or economic co-ordination. The latter would continue to be conducted under the so-called intergovernmental method, where the member states have the first and last word.

One teleological variant of this approach can be found in Pinder's distinction between *constitutional (or 'big bang')* and *incremental* federalism (Pinder 1995). Since the former, whereby a constituent assembly of people's representatives would have drawn up a federal constitution for ratification by European citizens, proved too ambitious for the post-war European, a form of *incremental federalism* was adopted. Here, the 'Monnet method' of integration via small steps is repackaged as *neofederalism*, the combination of a 'federal aim and steps towards it', which is '… in some respects a synthesis of the federalist and the neofunctionalist approaches' (Pinder 1995: 240–1).

The third strategy for bringing federalism back in can be termed *distributive*, in that it focuses on the distribution of power between the centre and the component units as well as among the component units themselves (Nicolaidis and Howse 2001; Kelemen 2003; Bednar 2004; Swenden 2004; Thorlakson 2006). Here the federal lens takes us back to an analysis of the system as a whole while trying to avoid the normative connotation of the constitutional approach. As usual, academic interest followed developments in the real world, with the increasing concern throughout the 1990s over the 'creeping competences' of the EU (Pollack 1994) and efforts to enforce the principle of subsidiarity proclaimed at Maastricht. Not surprisingly therefore, analysts in this vein have been especially preoccupied with the mechanisms designed to protect the rights and powers of the sub-federal units in the federal contract.

This focus on the distribution of authority rests on firm analytical grounds, often with a strong historical component. 'Who does what?', 'Who decides?', 'On what grounds?' and 'What explains the transfer of authority between levels of government?', are surely fundamental questions for all political systems of a federal nature. Under what kind of safeguards do states choose to part with some of their competences? Are different types of 'federal safeguards' (ascriptive, procedural, judicial, structural) functionally substitutable? Is the allocation of competences in a federal polity consistent with the principles adopted at its founding? One of the most important insights from studies of the distribution of authority in federal systems runs counter to the teleological centralizing tendency of the two strands of analysis we discuss above: the distribution of authority in federal systems moves in two-way 'cycles of federalism', with power sometimes shifting to the centre only to later pass back to the states (Donahue and Pollack 2001).

While much of the scholarship on distribution of authority focuses on explaining why authority *is* divided as it is, other work focuses on normative questions of how authority *should* be divided. Economists and institutionalists interested in federalism have produced an abundant literature, some of which we discuss below, on optimal design and 'optimal allocation' of competences, be they regulatory or fiscal. EU scholars have borrowed from this literature, focusing on how concerns regarding efficiency and legitimacy should be balanced and authority should be organized in a European Union (EU) composed of 25 member states, and which of the 'sharply different jurisdictional designs' (Hooghe and Marks 2003: 233) suggested by the literature are most relevant (Börzel and Hosli 2003).

A fourth and final strategy deployed to serve the cause of federalism, which we term *essentialist*, rests on a more philosophical premise, namely to ask what the idea or the concept of federalism actually refers to, what is in effect its 'essence'. Perhaps the starting assumption here is that the real debate should no longer be about whether the EU is federal, but *what kind of federalism* it represents, or indeed how the prevailing understanding of federalism should be reconfigured to accommodate the case of the EU and potential cases like it. The main challenge here is to do away with the mental association between federalism and statehood, which has come to spill over from the normative to the analytical domain. In effect, the door for using the federal lens can be opened most widely by the assumption that the EU is not, and will not likely become, a classic federation (Elazar 1987) or the reproduction of any national model at the supranational level (Nicolaidis and Weatherill 2003). In other words, it will instead inhabit the area of multi-state federalism, qualifying as a federal union, not a federal state (Nicolaidis 2004; Magnette 2005).

A variant on this strategy brings us back almost to the beginning, that is the classical distinction between federations and confederations, to the new confederalist school, which views federalism as encompassing the study of confederations and federations. In this regard, King's distinction between federalism and federation provided an early marker; for it is here that we see the embryo of the idea that integration may be '… leading to ultimately to some new form of federal organization' (King 1982; Burgess 1993: 4). This has provided the foundation for Pinder to take up Forsyth's concept of a federal union of States, and for Burgess to explore the avenue of re-conceptualizing confederation into a new or strong form (Burgess 2000). They may, ultimately, be talking about the same thing. Indeed, Forsyth defines federal union and confederation as synonyms and uses the terms interchangeably (Forsyth 1981). Defining the relationship between confederalism and federalism in the light of the actuality of the EU, and seeking to better understand how the concepts interrelate, is a central challenge for EU federal scholarship today (Law 2005).

TODAY: RESEARCH THEMES

In this section we review a number of topics addressed by scholars employing the lens of federalism to study the EU. We move from the areas in which this approach is most accepted, to the areas where it is most contested. We begin with a discussion of regulatory federalism and fiscal federalism in the EU, two well-established areas of research. We review recent contributions examining the EU's emerging party system from the perspective of comparative federalism. Finally, we discuss the relevance of federal models to questions of legitimacy, democracy and identity in the EU.

Regulatory Federalism

While the EU may remain a fiscal and foreign policy weakling, it is a regulatory powerhouse. Some EU scholars even characterize it as a 'regulatory state' (Majone 1996; McGowan and Wallace 1996). Applying the lens and the lessons of regulatory federalism to the analysis of EU regulation has emerged as an active area of research. Research on regulatory federalism in the EU has focused on a series of *normative* and *positive* questions. Scholars have borrowed from the literature on comparative federalism to ask what allocation of regulatory competences serves to maximize administrative efficiency and social welfare (Revesz 1997; Esty and Geradin 2001; Börzel and Hosli 2003). They have also asked what comparative federalism can tell us about the division of regulatory authority that is actually emerging in the EU, what legal and regulatory instruments structure the relationships between the federal centre and the states, and how these relationships affect the legitimacy of EU regulation (Bermann 1997; Halberstam 2001; Kelemen 2001, 2004; Majone 2001; Nicolaidis and Howse 2001; Börzel and Hosli 2003; Parsons 2003b).

The literature on regulatory federalism in the EU suggests that while the EU may be special, it is hardly unique: the EU faces many of the same regulatory challenges, and adopts variants of the same solutions, as other federal polities. The choices that EU regulators make – concerning when federal intervention is justified (the subsidiarity test), what form intervention should take (partial vs. total pre-emption of state authority), what regulatory instruments will be used (loose framework directives or detailed regulations) and, ultimately, the degree of discretion to allow member states in implementing – all echo choices made by regulators in other federal polities.

Viewing the EU in comparative perspective suggests that in the field of regulation, the EU is by no means the weak end of the federal continuum: in some policy areas, EU regulators enjoy a level of authority and exercise a degree of control over member states that clearly exceeds that of federal regulators in other well-established federations (Kelemen 2004).

Fiscal Federalism and Economic and Monetary Union

Arguably the best-developed literature on federalism is that on fiscal federalism, where analysts tend to focus on the efficient allocation of fiscal authority. In other words, how the authority to tax and spend *should* be allocated between levels of government in federal systems. Related to this normative concern are a series of positive questions and hypotheses concerning the likely impact of various alternative approaches to allocating authority.

The first widely shared argument of the fiscal federalism literature (building on Musgrave 1959 and Oates 1972) is that in order to maximize welfare, macro-economic stabilization functions and redistributive policies should be assigned to the federal level, while the provision of locally consumed public goods should be the responsibility of state and local governments. Only public goods with significant externalities and economies of scale should be centralized. Macro-economic stabilization should be centralized, because state governments lack the capacity to fulfil this function under conditions of deep integration. Redistributive policies should be centralized, because the mobility of households (both tax avoiders and benefit seekers) would limit the potential for redistribution by decentralized governments. By contrast, if local governments are responsible for providing locally consumed public goods, they can tailor such public goods more closely to local voters preferences. Moreover, as Tiebout (1956) argued, citizens can 'vote with their feet' and relocate to jurisdictions that provide the mix of local public goods and taxation most suited to their preferences. The literature on fiscal federalism also deals with questions of tax assignment, both in terms of which forms of taxation should be levied at which level of government and, crucially, in terms of the importance of imposing hard budget constraints on state governments. The essential conclusion here is that while there may be an important role for intergovernmental transfers in federal systems, decentralized governments must face a 'hard budget constraint'. If instead state governments can count on bail-outs from the federal government, they may easily succumb to the temptation to run excessive deficits, which in extreme cases may destabilize the entire economy.

While there is broad agreement on these basic principles, there is sharp disagreement concerning other implications of fiscal federalism, in particular concerning the costs and benefits of fiscal competition between jurisdictions. While some argue that fiscal competition can lead to destructive, 'race-to-the-bottom' tax competition that leads to sub-optimal levels of public good provision (Oates 2002), others insist on their positive role in restraining government spending (Hayek 1939; Brennan and Buchanan 1980; Weingast 1995).

These arguments will sound very familiar to anyone following contemporary debates in Europe concerning tax competition, 'social dumping', and the impact of EMU more broadly. From questions concerning whether EU control over monetary policy will eventually necessitate a greater centralization of fiscal power, to debates over whether the Stability and Growth Pact (SGP) should be scrapped, the literature on fiscal federalism has long informed thinking by scholars of European political economy.

Building on Musgrave and Oates, some scholars argue that fiscal federalism suggests that there is a strong case for transferring a number of redistributive and public goods-related policies – and the taxation capacity to fund those activities – to the European level (Inman and Rubinfeld 1992; Persson and Tabellinni 1996; Scharpf 1999; Tabellinni 2003). Official pronouncements – from the 1977 MacDougall Report on the feasibility of EMU to the 1989 Delors Report – have long relied on theories of optimal currency areas and fiscal federalism to, argue that EMU would need powerful fiscal capacity to deal with asymmetric shocks (Mundell 1961; Sachs and Sala-i-martin 1991).

Similarly, scholars have applied lessons from fiscal federalism to assess the credibility – and ultimately the desirability – of the SGP (Von Hagen and Eichengreen 1996; Rodden 2006) designed to enforce fiscal discipline among member states after the transition to EMU. While some observers have reacted to its recent violations by calling for the SGP to be strengthened, the lessons of fiscal federalism cast serious doubt on the need for the SGP in the first place. As Rodden (2006) explains, the literature on fiscal federalism suggests that in federations where the centre is vulnerable to pressure to bail out states that run excessive deficits, it is vital for the centre to impose limits on borrowing by states such as an even stronger SGP. However, the EU is not vulnerable to pressure for bail-outs. Its fiscal capacities remain so limited that neither voters nor creditors perceive implicit guarantees from the EU to bail out member states, and, will therefore discipline states themselves.

In sum, the literature on fiscal federalism is rich in theoretical models and empirical findings that can inform debates concerning EMU. This literature both provides indications of the challenges EMU is likely to face and offers insights that policy-makers can draw on in responding to those challenges.

Federalism and the EU Party System

Federalism also offers useful a lens on the political side. With the growing power of the European Parliament (EP), research on EP 'party groups' and more generally, the development of European parties and their relationship with national parties is also on the rise (see Chapter 12 in this volume). The rich literature on the role of party systems in federations, and the experience of other federal systems can provide useful comparative leverage for the study of the emerging European party system.

Some scholars have treated party systems as independent variables in explaining the dynamics of federalism. Riker (1964) emphasized how the decentralized structure of US political parties helped to defend state interests and maintain federalism in the face of centralizing pressures. Bermeo (2002) highlights the opposite dynamic, whereby the incorporation of regional interests into national political parties can help maintain federalism in systems threatened by centrifugal pressures.

Other scholars have treated party systems as dependent variables, shaped by broader developments in federal systems. In their historical study of Canada, Great Britain, India, and the United States, Kollman and Chhibber (2004) find that party systems develop by tracking the shifting allocation of power in the federation.

Applying their insights to the EU, one would predict that the increasing transfer of authority from the national to the EU level (Donahue and Pollack 2001) will be accompanied by a strengthening of the role of European-level parties. Indeed, though not framed in terms of comparative federalism, Kreppel's (2002) work suggests that the increasing legislative power led to increased centralization of party groups in the European Parliament.

Conversely, Hix et al.'s (2006) study of the development of parties in the European Parliament explicitly draws on the experience of federal systems. They use literature on the formation of national and regional parties in federal systems to develop hypotheses suggesting why, in a highly decentralized polity like the EU, regional conflicts would rarely be expected to emerge as major sources of cleavage in elections to the parliament at the federal level (2006: 79). Rather, this literature suggests that 'the left-right dimension should be the main dimension of conflict in the European Parliament and also the main axis of party and coalition formation' (2006: 87).

In a recent study, Thorlakson highlights the benefits of the comparative federalism approach to the study of the European Party system: 'First, it provides the analytic tools to assess linkages between national and European party systems. Second, it raises important questions such as how different models of federal aggregation and political competition at the federal level channel conflict and balance partisan and territorial competition through the linkage or separation of party organisations and party systems'. (Thorlakson 2005: 468–9) Her finding – that party systems at the state and federal level remain most 'incongruent' in federations where power is most decentralized – supports Kollman and Chibberr's conclusions. She emphasizes how such lack of congruence between the national and the emerging European party systems makes it difficult to build linkages between national parties and party groups in the EP. The literature on party systems in federations can both stimulate hypothesis formation and provide empirical material for comparative studies of the process of party formation at the European level.

Legitimacy, Democracy and Identity

A fourth strand of insights from federalism studies turns to the most fundamental macro-political question, namely the connection between legitimacy, democracy and identity in the formation and maintenance of the polity. While the legitimacy crisis of the EU, first made visible with Maastricht and reaching an apogee in the aftermath of the no votes on the European Constitution, spurred a great deal of scholarship on the so-called democratic deficit, scholars were slow to bring compara-tive federalism to bear on the issue.

To be sure, this is perhaps where federalism as a political project and federalism as an ana-lytical framework are most intertwined, since the diagnosis around the EU's lack of legiti-macy tends to revolve around whether it is – rightly or wrongly – taking on the features of a federal state. On the 'pro' side, a classic point of departure is to contrast the EU with the 1787 American settlement and the emergence of an indigenous ideology that may appropriately be termed federal democracy (Elazar 2001). Indeed, US federalism was not only seen by the founding fathers as a means of consolidating cooperation between the states, but also as means of deepening democracy within the states themselves through the appeal to the doctrine of 'dispersed sovereignty' or the idea that sovereignty belonged neither to the states nor to the federation, but to 'We, the People' (Magnette 2006). While the EU lacked such a democratic settlement at its origin – sover-eignty in this construct still rests with the member states – the adoption of a constitution would be a way to bring about a paradigm shift for Europe similar to that which was wrought two centuries ago in the former British colonies. On the 'anti-federal' side, the civic-republican school continues to stress that democracy in Europe was left to rest squarely with the state for good reasons (Lacroix 2002). In line with the *essentialist* strategy outlined above – redefining federalism as a non-statist construct – the question which animates fed-eral studies of the EU today is whether it is possible to adapt the federalist lens to an 'in-between' vision of democracy.

This line of thought can first be found in studies of federal citizenship in the EU which stress the asymmetry between its strong hori-zontal and weak vertical dimension (Magnette 1999). To be sure, a number of scholars of the EU have based their analysis on the three legal orders with which Kant defines a 'federation of free states', namely relations between citizens and state, relations between states and relations between nationals and a foreign state (Kant 1983; Magnette 1999; Cheneval 2005; Ferry 2000; Eleftheriadis 2001). But it is the third, cos-mopolitan order, characterized by systematic non-discrimination and mutual recognition, which has been perfected in the EU context, including an extraterritorial dimension at odds with territorially-based notions of democracy (Nicolaidis and Shaffer 2005). Indeed, the kind of institutional supranationalism that has characterized the EU differs from federalism most in the weakness of the direct link between citizens and the whole. While some authors focus on the institutional incarnation of such a direct link through the European Parliament, others ask what is the political foundation for federal citizenship beyond specific institutions, in terms of forms of participation and contes-tation linked to multi-level governance, as well as in terms of (objective) rights and (subjec-tive) feeling of belonging. While comparative federalism can shed light on all these dimen-sions of a nascent European citizenship, such citizenship remains in its infancy and is a far cry from that found in the other federal pro-jects (Beaud 2004; Christin et al. 2005).

The second strand of research concerns identity. Most analysts agree that in contrast to American federal unity, the EU is not founded on the fiction of a single people or even the idea that its creation would necessarily bring one about. There is sharp disagreement among EU scholars as to what degree of common European identity is necessary to stimulate and support further transfers of authority to the EU level, and how likely it is that such com-mon identity is to emerge (Cederman 2000). Scholars of identity politics in Europe recog-nize that 'Europeanness' may be mixed with national and subnational identities to form nuanced multiple identities (Choudhry 2001;

Risse 2001). Others argue that the irreducible diversity of not only cultural but also political identities in Europe is not antithetical to a federal vision, if such a vision is conceived as a federal union (rather than a federal state) and seeks to develop novel understanding of democracy, or demoi-cracy (Nicolaidis and Howse 2001; Nicolaidis 2004).

It is striking, however, that very little research has been conducted that seeks to draw lessons from the experience of identity formation in multi-national and multi-cultural federations (India, Nigeria, Belgium, Canada, Switzerland) for questions of 'European' identity formation in the EU. EU scholars may benefit greatly from asking what the experiences of other multi-national federal systems may have to teach us. Ultimately, federalism is about the primacy of the political and the idea that political legitimacy can only be found through a sustained equilibrium between unity and diversity, thus ensuring constitutional government in plural liberal democratic societies (Wheare 1963; Rosamond 2000). In this sense, it may offer more inspiration to EU studies as an ideal type than through any of its historical incarnations.

CONCLUSION: CRISIS? WHAT CRISIS? ON THE DURABILITY OF EU FEDERALISM

In the end the federalism lens may be most useful in helping us assess the trajectory of the EU in the *longue durée*. Politicians and pundits proclaim the EU to be in 'crisis' with astonishing regularity. Events great and small including 'No' votes in EU referenda, stalled budget talks, rising protectionism, attacks on the Euro from idiosyncratic Italian politicians, and even blockades on British Beef are treated by many as threats to the survival of the European Union. Likewise, many policy-makers and scholars suggest that the EU's current institutional arrangements will not function in an EU of 25 (or more) member states, and that without significant reforms, the EU's institutional machinery may grind to a halt. Is EU federalism indeed as fragile as the persistent reports of 'crisis' suggest? Are the EU's basic

institutions indeed in danger of collapsing under the weight of enlargement? More often than not, these questions are addressed on grounds of intuition and conjecture rather than theory and systematic comparative analysis. And yet, a potential guide to the fate of the EU lies at hand, in the study of stability and instability in other past and present federal systems.

At the most general level, the literature on federalism does suggest that those who fear for the EU's future may have a point. After all, most federations fail (Franck 1968; Lemco 1991). Federalism is inherently unstable because all federations face two fundamental dilemmas (Riker 1964; Bednar et al. 2001; De Figueiredo and Weingast 2005): they must prevent the two levels of government from undermining federalism, first by federal governments overreaching their competences, second by constituent states shirking on their commitments to the federation (Halberstam 2004). Unfortunately, institutions that help to resolve one of the dilemmas of federalism often exacerbate the other. While constitutions may provide for what appear to be rigid divisions of authority, in practice there is a continuous 'ebb and flow' of authority between states and the centre (Donahue and Pollack 2001; Filippov et al. 2004). To be durable, a federation must provide for a rigid enough division of authority to prevent one level of government from usurping the authority of the other, while remaining flexible enough to allow for shifts in the division of authority in response to economic, technological, socio-cultural and political developments (Nicolaidis 2001).

Recent work on the concept of self-enforcing federalism (Bednar et al. 2001; Filippov et al. 2004; De Figueiredo and Weingast 2005) suggests that one way to resolve this tension is for federal institutions to be self-enforcing in the short term and self-reinforcing in the long term. To be *self-enforcing*, they must create a structure of incentives in which no player wants to deviate from the rules and commitments of the federation, given their expectations about other players' behaviour. To be *self-reinforcing*, they must encourage behaviours that, over time, serve to expand the range of situations in which it is self-enforcing. So the single market is currently weakened, for instance, given growing expectations of protectionist defection, and the question is whether EU institutions still have the power to be self-reinforcing through rewards and punishments.

Whether and under what conditions one thinks the EU will fall apart depends on what one thinks holds it together. The literature on stability and change in federal systems suggests a number of common sources of institutional stability mentioned in this chapter, from the classic common external threats (Riker 1964), to a sense of federal comity or culture (Franck 1968; Elazar 1987), judicial enforcement of federalism disputes (Bzdera 1993; Bednar et al. 2001), structural safeguards (Bednar et al. 2001), or trans-state party systems (Riker 1964; Filippov et al. 2004). Which of these is most important in holding the EU together, and which is currently being strengthened or weakened, are key questions that can only benefit from a comparative perspective.

Assessments of the ultimate durability of the EU's institutional arrangements need not take place in a theoretical and empirical vacuum. Scholars who want to think systematically about the EU's short-term 'crises' and long-term prospects, can draw on recent theoretical work and the long historical record of successful and failed federal systems. Bringing federalism back in may not help make better predictions, but it is certainly a good way to stop obsessing about the EU's unique character and instead to begin shedding light on it in its proper global context, across time and space.

ACKNOWLEDGEMENT

We would like to thank John Law for his research assistance.

REFERENCES

Ansell, C. and Di Palma, G. (2004) *Restructuring Territoriality: Europe and the United States Compared.* New York: Cambridge University Press.

Beaud, O. (2004) 'Droits de l'homme et du citoyen et formes politiques. Le cas particulier de la Fédération', *Revue universelle des droits de l'homme,* 16(1–4): 16–26

Bednar, J. (2004) 'Authority migration in federations: a framework for analysis', *PS: Political Science and Politics,* July.

Bednar, J. (2006) *The Robust Federation.* MS: University of Michigan. Available at: http://www-personal.umich.edu/~jbednar/papers.htm, accessed 18 September 2006.

Bednar, J., Eskridge, W. and Ferejohn, J. (2001) 'A political theory of federalism', in J. Ferejohn, J.N. Rakove, and J. Riley (eds), *Constitutional Culture and Democratic Rule.* New York: Cambridge University Press. pp. 223–70.

Bednar, J., Ferejohn, J. and Garrett, G. (1996) 'The politics of European federalism', *International Review of Law and Economics,* 16: 279–94.

Bermann, G. (1997) *Regulatory Federalism: European Union and United States.* The Hague, Netherlands: Martinus Nijhoff Publishers.

Bermeo, N. (2002) 'A new look at federalism: the import of institutions', *Journal of Democracy,* 13(2): 96–110.

Bogdanor, V. (2003) 'Federalism and the nature of the European Union', paper prepared for the 'Governing together in the new Europe' conference, Robinson College, Cambridge, 12–13 April. Available at: http://www.riia.org/pdf/research/Europe/Bogdanor_Final.pdf, accessessed 4 April 2006.

Börzel, T. and Hosli, M. (2003) 'Brussels between Bern and Berlin: comparative federalism meets the European Union', *Governance,* 16(2):179–202.

Brennan, G. and Buchanan, J. (1980) *The Power to Tax.* Cambridge: Cambridge University Press.

Burgess, M. (1993) 'Federalism and federation: a reappraisal', in M. Burgess and A.-G. Gagnon (eds), *Comparative Federalism and Federation: Competing Traditions and Future Directions.* Toronto: University of Toronto Press. pp. 3–14.

Burgess, M. (2000) *Federalism and European Union: The Building of Europe, 1950– 2000.* Routledge.

Burgess, M. (2003) 'Federalism', in A. Wiener and D. Thomas (eds), *Theories of European Integration.* Oxford: Oxford University Press.

Burgess, M. and Gagnon, A. (eds) (1993) *Comparative Federalism and Federation.* Toronto: University of Toronto Press.

Bzdera, A. (1993) 'Comparative analysis of federal high courts: a political theory of judicial review', *Canadian Journal of Political Science,* 26(1): 3–29.

Cappelletti, M., Seccombe, M. and Weiler, J. (eds) (1986) *Integration Through Law: Europe and the American Federal Experience, Volume 1.* Berlin and New York: Walter de Gruyter.

Cederman, L.-E. (2000) 'Nationalism and bounded integration: what it would take to construct a European demos', EUI working article, RSC No. 2000/34. Fiesole, Italy: European University Institute.

Cheneval, F. (ed.) (2005) *Legitimationsgrundlagen der Europäischen Union.* Berlin, Lit Verlag.

Chhibber, P. and Kollman, K. (2004) *The Formation of National Party Systems: Federalism and Party Competition in Canada, Great Britain, India, and the United States.* Princeton: Princeton University Press.

Choudhry, S. (2001) 'Citizenship and federations: some preliminary reflections', in K. Nicolaidis and R. Howse (eds), *The Federal Vision: Legitimacy and levels of governance in the U.S. and EU.* Oxford, UK: Oxford University Press.

Christin, T., Hug, S. and Schulz, T. (2005) 'Federalism in the European Union: the view from below (if there is such a thing)', *Journal of European Public Policy,* 12(3): 488–508.

Coudenhove-Kalergi, R. (1938) *Europe Must Unite.* Glarus, Switzerland: Editions Ltd.

Craig, P. and de Burca, G. (2002) *EU Law: Text, Cases and Materials,* 3rd ed. Oxford: Oxford University Press.

De Figueiredo, R. and Weingast, B. (2005) 'Self-enforcing federalism', *Journal of Law, Economics and Organization,* 21(1): 103–35.

Dehousse, R. (1992) 'Integration v. regulation? On the dynamics of regulation in the European Community', *Journal of Common Market Studies,* 30: 383–402.

Deutsch, K.W. (1957) *Political Community and the North Atlantic Area.* Princeton, NJ: Princeton University Press.

Donahue, J. and Pollack, M. (2001) 'Centralization and its discontents: the rhythms of federalism in the United States and the European Union', in K. Nicolaidis and R. Howse (eds), *The Federal Vision: Legitimacy and Levels of Governance in the U.S. and EU.* Oxford, UK: Oxford University Press. pp. 73–117.

Elazar, D. (1987) *Exploring Federalism.* Tuscaloosa: University of Alabama Press.

Elazar, D. (2001) 'The United States and the European Union: models for their epochs', in K. Nicolaidis and R. Howse (eds), *The Federal Vision.* Oxford: Oxford University Press. pp. 31–53.

Eleftheriadis, P. (2001) 'The European Constitution and cosmopolitan ideals', *Columbia Journal of European Law,* 7: 21–39.

Esty, D. and Damien G. (eds) (2001) *Regulatory Competition and Economic Integration: Comparative Perspectives.* Oxford: Oxford University Press.

Fabbrini, S. (ed.) (2005) *Federalism and Democracy in the European Union and the United States. Exploring Post-National Governance.* London: Routledge.

Fabbrini, S. and Sicurelli, D. (2004) 'The federalization of the EU, the US and compound republic theory: the convention's debate', *Regional and Federal Studies,* 14(2): 232–54.

Filippov, M., Ordeshook, P.C. and Shvetsova, O. (2004) *Designing Federalism: A Theory of Self-Sustainable Federal Institutions.* New York: Cambridge University Press.

Fischer, J. (2000) 'From confederacy to federation: thoughts on the finality of European integration', speech at the Humboldt University, Berlin, 12 May. In C. Joerges, Y. Mény, and J.H.H. Weiler (eds), *What Kind of Constitution for What Kind of Polity? Responses to Joschka Fischer.* Florence: European University Institute.

Forsyth, M. (1981) *Unions of States.* Leicester: Leicester University Press.

Franck, T. (ed) (1968) *Why Federations Fail: An Enquiry into the requisites for Successful Federalism.* NY, USA: New York University Press.

Friedman-Goldstein, L. (2001) *Constituting Federal Sovereignty.* Baltimore: Johns Hopkins University Press.

Friedrich, C. (1969) *Trends of Federalism in Theory and Practice.* New York: Praeger.

Haas, E. (2004) *The Uniting of Europe: Political, Social, and Economic Forces, 1950–1957.* Notre Dame: University of Notre Dame Press.

Halberstam, D. (2001) 'Comparative federalism and the issue of commandeering', in K. Nicolaidis and R. Howse (eds), *The Federal Vision: Legitimacy and Levels of Governance in the U.S. and EU.* Oxford, UK: Oxford University Press. pp. 213–51.

Halberstam, D. (2004) *Beyond Competence: Comparative Federalism and the Duty of Cooperation.* The Federal Trust.

Halberstam, D. and Maduro, M. (eds) (2007) *The Constitutional Challenge in Europe and America: People, Power, and Politics.* Cambridge: Cambridge University Press.

Hayek, F. von (1939) 'The Economic conditions of interstate Federalism', *New Commonwealth Quarterly,* 5(2): 131–49. Reprinted in F. von Hayek [1957] *Individualism and Economic Order.* Chicago: University of Chicago Press.

Hesse, J.J. and Wright, V. (eds) (1996) *Federalizing Europe? The Costs, Benefits and Preconditions of Federal Political Systems*. Oxford: Oxford University Press.

Hix, S. (1994) 'The study of the European Community: the challenge to comparative politics', *West European Politics*, 17(1): 1–30.

Hix, S., Noury, A. and Roland, G. (2006) *Democratic Politics in the European Parliament*. Cambridge: Cambridge University Press.

Hooghe, L. and Marks, G. (2001) *European Integration and Multi-Level Governance*. Boulder: Rowman and Littlefield.

Hooghe, L. and Marks, G. (2003) 'Unraveling the central State, but how? Types of multi-level governance', *American Political Science Review*, 97(2): 233–43.

Hueglin, T. and Fenna, A. (2006) *Comparative Federalism: A systematic Inquiry*. Toronto: Broadview Press.

Inman, R. and Rubinfeld, D. (1992) 'Fiscal federalism in Europe: lessons from the United States experience', *European Economic Review*, 36: 654–60.

Kant, I. (1983) *Perpetual Peace, and other Essays on Politics, History and Morals*. Translated by Ted Humphrey. Indianapolis: Hackett Publishing Co.

Kelemen, R.D. (2001) 'The limits of judicial power: trade-environment disputes in the GATT/WTO and the EU', *Comparative Political Studies*, 34(6): 622–50.

Kelemen. R.D. (2003) 'The structure and dynamics of EU Federalism', *Comparative Political Studies*, 36(1–2): 184–208.

Kelemen. R.D. (2004) *The Rules of Federalism: Institutions and Regulatory Politics in the EU and Beyond*. Cambridge: Harvard University Press.

Kelemen. R.D. (2006) 'Federalism and democratization: the US and EU in comparative perspective', in A. Menon and M. Schain (eds), *The US and the EU in Comparative Perspective*. Oxford: Oxford University Press. Forthcoming.

King, P. (1982) *Federalism and Federation*. London: Croom Helm.

Koslowski, R. (1999) 'A constructivist approach to understanding the European Union as a federal polity', *Journal of European Public Policy*, 6(4): 561–78.

Law, J. (2005) 'The relationship between federalism and statehood', MSc Thesis, University of Oxford.

Lemco, J. (1991) *Political Stability in Federal Governments*. New York: Praeger.

Magnette, P. (1999) *La citoyenneté européenne*, Bruxelles: Editions de l'Université de Bruxelles.

Magnette, P. (2005) *What is the European Union? Nature and Prospect*. Basingstoke: Palgrave.

Magnette P. (2006) 'Comparing constitutional change in the US and the EU', in A. Menon and M. Schain (eds), *Federalism in Europe and the United States: A developmental perspective*. Oxford: Oxford University Press.

Majone, G. (1996) *Regulating Europe*. London: Routledge.

Majone, G. (2001) 'Regulatory legitimacy in the United States and the European Union', in K. Nicolaidis and R. Howse (eds), *The Federal Vision*. Oxford: Oxford University Press. pp. 252–76.

Mancini, G.F. (1989) 'The making of a constitution for Europe', *Common Market Law Review*, 26: 595–614.

Marks, G., Hooghe, L. and Blank, K. (1996) 'European integration since the 1980s. State-centric versus multi-level governance', *Journal of Common Market Studies*, 34: 343–78.

Mattli, W. (1999) *The Logic of Regional Integration: Europe and Beyond*. Cambridge: Cambridge University Press.

McGowan, F. and Wallace, H. (1996) 'Towards a European regulatory state', *Journal of European Public Policy*, 3(4): 560–76.

McKay, D. (1999) *Federalism and European Union: A Political Economy Perspective*. Oxford: Oxford University Press.

McKay, D. (2001) *Designing Europe: Comparative Lessons from the Federal Experience*. Oxford: Oxford University Press.

Menon, A. and Schain, M. (2006) *Federalism in Europe and the United States: A developmental perspective*. Oxford: Oxford University Press.

Moravcsik, A. (1998) *The Choice for Europe*. Ithaca, NY: Cornell University Press.

Moravcsik, A. (2001) 'Federalism in the European Union: rhetoric and reality', in K. Nicolaidis and R. Howse (eds), *The Federal Vision: Legitimacy and Levels of Governance in the United States and the European Union*. Oxford: Oxford University Press.

Moravcsik, A. (2006) 'What can we learn from the collapse of the European Constitutional project', *Politische Vierteljahresschrit*, 47(Jg Heft, S): 219–41.

Moravcsik, A. and Nicolaidis, K. (1998) 'Federal ideals vs constitutional realities in the Amsterdam Treaty', *Journal of Common Market Studies*, 36 (Annual Review): 13–38.

Mundell, R.(1961) 'A theory of optimum currency areas', *The American Economic Review*, 51(4): 657–65.

Nicolaidis, K. (2001) 'Conclusion: the federal vision beyond the federal state', in K. Nicolaidis and R. Howse (eds), *The Federal Vision:*

Legitimacy and Levels of Governance in the United States and the European Union. Oxford: Oxford University Press. pp. 439–82.

Nicolaidis, K. (2003) 'What is in a name? Europe's federal future and the convention on the future of Europe', Jurist EU, thinking outside the box editorial series, paper 5/2003. Available online at: http://www.fd.unl.pt/je/index.htm, accessed 18 September 2006.

Nicolaidis, K. (2004) 'We the peoples of Europe', *Foreign Affairs,* 83(6): 97–110.

Nicolaidis, K. (2006) 'Constitutionalizing the federal vision', in A. Menon and M. Schain (eds), *The US and the EU in Comparative Perspective.* Oxford: Oxford University Press. Forthcoming.

Nicolaidis, K. (2007) 'Paradise lost? The new European Constitution in the shadow of federalism', in D. Halberstam and M. Maduro (eds), *The Constitutional Challenge in Europe and America: People, Power, and Politics.* Cambridge: Cambridge University Press.

Nicolaidis, K. and Howse, R. (2001) *The Federal Vision: Legitimacy and Levels of Governance in the United States and the European Union.* Oxford: Oxford University Press.

Nicolaidis, K. and Howse, R. (2002) '"This is my utopia …": narrative as power', *Journal of Common Market Studies,* Special Anniversary issue, 40(4): 767–92.

Nicolaidis, K. and Shaffer, G. (2005) 'Transnational mutual recognition regimes: governance without global government', *Michigan Review of International Law,* 68: 267–322.

Nicolaidis, K. and Weatherill, S. (2003) *Whose Europe? National Models and the Constitution of the European Union.* European Studies at Oxford Series. Oxford: Oxford University Print.

Oates, W. (1972) *Fiscal Federalism.* New York: Harcourt Brace Jovanovich.

Oates, W. (2002) 'Fiscal and regulatory competition: theory and evidence', *Perspektiven der Wirtschaftspolitik,* 3: 377–90.

Parsons, C. (2003a) *A Certain Idea of Europe.* Ithaca, NY: Cornell University Press.

Parsons, C. (2003b) *Evolving Federalisms: The Intergovernmental Balance of Power in America and Europe.* Syracuse: Campbell Public Affairs Institute. Available online at: http://www.maxwell.syr.edu/campbell/Library%20Papers/EvovlingFederalisms.pdf, accessed 4 April 2006.

Persson, T. and Tabellini, G. (1996) 'Federal fiscal constitutions: risk sharing and redistribution', *Journal of Political Economy,* 104(5): 979–1009.

Pinder, J. (1995) *European Community: The Building of a Union.* Oxford: Oxford University Press.

Pinder, J. (1998) *Altiero Spinelli and the British Federalists.* London: Federal Trust.

Pollack, M.A. (1994) 'Creeping competence: the expanding agenda of the European Community', *Journal of Public Policy,* 14(2): 95–145.

Riker, W.H. (1964) *Federalism: Origin, operation, significance.* Boston: Little Brown.

Revesz, R. (1997) 'Federalism and environmental regulation: lessons for the European Union and the international community', *Virginia Law Review,* 83: 1331–46.

Riker, W. (1975) 'Federalism', in F.I. Greenstein and N. Polsby (eds), *The Handbook of Political Science,* Volume V: *Government Institutions and Processes.* Reading, MA: Addison Wesley.

Rodden, J. (2005) *Hamilton's Paradox: The Promise and Peril of Fiscal Federalism.* Cambridge: Cambridge University Press.

Rodden, J. (2006) 'Fiscal discipline in federations: Germany and the EMU', in P. Wierts, S. Deroose, E. Flores and A. Turrini (eds), *Fiscal Policy Surveillance in Europe.* New York: Palgrave MacMillan. Forthcoming.

Rosamond, B. (2000) *Theories of European integration.* New York: Palgrave.

Sachs, J. and Sala-i-martin, X.(1991) 'Fiscal federalism and optimum currency areas: evidence for Europe from the United States', NBER Working Paper, 3855, October.

Sandholtz, W. and Stone Sweet, A. (1998) 'Integration, supranational governance and the institutionalization of the European polity', in W. Sandholtz and A. Stone Sweet (eds), *European Integration and Supranational Governance.* Oxford: Oxford University Press. pp. 1–26.

Sbragia, A. (ed.) (1992) *Euro-politics: Institutions and Policymaking in the "New" European Community.* Washington, DC: Brookings.

Sbragia, A. (2004) 'Territory, representation, and policy outcome: the United States and the European Union compared', in C. Ansell and G. Di Palma (eds), *On Restructuring Territoriality: Europe and North America.* Cambridge: Cambridge University Press.

Scharpf, F. (1988) 'The joint decision trap: lessons from German Federalism and European integration', *Public Administration,* 66(3): 239–78.

Scharpf, F. (1999) *Governing in Europe: Effective and Democratic?* Oxford: Oxford University Press.

Schmitter, P. (2000) 'Federalism and the Euro-Polity', *Journal of Democracy,* 11(1): 40–7.

Sidjanski, D. (2000) *The Federal Future of Europe: From the European Community to the European Union.* University of Michigan Press.

Stone Sweet, A. (2004) *The Judicial Construction of Europe*. Oxford: Oxford University Press.

Swenden, W. (2004) 'Is the EU in need of a competence catalogue?', *Journal of Common Market Studies*, 42 (2): 371–92.

Tabellini, G. (2003) 'Principles of policymaking in the European Union: an Economic perspective', *CESifo Economic Studies*, 49(1): 75–102.

Thorlakson, L. (2005) 'Federalism and the European party system', *Journal of European Public Policy*, 12(3): 468–87.

Thorlakson, L. (2006) 'Building firewalls or floodgates? Constitutional design for the European Union', *Journal of Common Market Studies*, 44(1): 139–59.

Tiebout, C. (1956) 'A pure theory of local expenditures', *Journal of Political Economy*, 64(Oct): 416–24.

Trechsel, A. (ed.) (2005a) 'Special issue on EU federalism', *Journal of European Public Policy*, 12(3).

Trechsel, A. (2005b) 'How to federalize the European Union...and why bother', *Journal of European Public*, 12(3): 401–18.

Von Hagen, J. and Eichengreen, B. (1996) 'Federalism, fiscal restraints and European Monetary Union', *American Economic Review*, 2(86): 134–8.

Watts, R.L. (1966) *New Federations: Experiments in the Commonweath*. Oxford: Oxford University Press.

Weiler, J.H.H. (1991) 'The transformation of Europe', *The Yale Law Journal*, 100: 2403–83.

Wheare, K.C. (1956) *Federal Government*. Oxford: Oxford University Press.

Wheare, K.C. (1964) *Federal Government*, fourth edition. Oxford: Oxford University Press.

Weingast, B. (1995) 'The economic role of political institutions: market-preserving Federalism and economic development', *The Journal of Law, Economics and Organization*, 11(1): 1–33.

Zweifel, T. (2002) '...Who is without sin cast the first stone: the European Union's democratic deficit in comparison', *Journal of European Public Policy*, 9(5): 812–40.

16

Normative Political Theory and the European Union

ANDREAS FØLLESDAL

INTRODUCTION

In 2005 the French and Dutch referendum rejections of the European Union's Constitutional Treaty once again brought issues of the EU's legitimacy and identity to the forefront of political debate.[1] Does the EU suffer from legitimacy deficits? If so, what are their alleged symptoms, diagnoses and prescriptions? Is there, and should there be, a 'European identity'? Must Europeans share a core of values, traditions and rights – and should that requirement deny Turkey membership?

The expression of public concern in Europe for these issues of normative political theory underscores the value of such research both for doing and for understanding politics. This academic subdiscipline centrally seeks to evaluate the legitimacy of institutions and policies, and scrutinizes both the relevant standards, and the soundness of their normative grounds. The salience of such issues of normative political theory in the current political debate confirms a recognizable pattern: Perceived political crises increase the demand, supply and impact

of normative political theory. The insights of John Locke, Jean-Jacques Rousseau, Immanuel Kant, Mary Wollstonecraft, John Stuart Mill, Karl Marx, John Rawls, Jürgen Habermas and Susan Okin and others arose from, and informed, the political crises of the day.

Consider the alleged legitimacy deficit of the European Union (EU). Worries about a 'democratic deficit' did not emerge in response to the Constitutional Treaty. Indeed, the reverse may be argued: that concerns about such deficits actually added fuel to the calls for a constitution for the EU. Popular disquiet had already gained political salience in response to the contentious ratification process surrounding the Maastricht Treaty on European Union. Indeed such reactions were in line with the predictions of some scholars, who had warned of domestic backlashes in response to European integration (e.g. Keohane and Hoffmann 1991: 29).

What is at stake – for the EU and for academic subdisciplines? For some political theorists, legitimacy is centrally a matter of whether citizens have trust in the future compliance of other citizens and authorities, with institutions they believe to be normatively legitimate. Such trustworthiness in institutions and fellow citizens seems necessary for the long-term support for the multi-level political order, and for authorities' ability to govern. Disillusioned citizenry may fall prey to populist demagogues, with consequences all too familiar on this continent. Perhaps more likely, a general loss of political trust may also threaten a wide variety of institutions and practices – both at the domestic and European level. Normative political theory may contribute decisively in promoting such long-term stability:

> In so far as political philosophy does seek to persuade members of a system of the existence of a verifiable objective common good, it does serve, with respect to its possible political consequences, as a response that may aid in the growth of diffuse support (Easton 1965: 319 fn 3).

The normative legitimacy of the EU, and the public perception of such legitimacy, is also relevant for other research on European integration. For instance, some of these issues inform and are expressed by public opinion and political culture, both of which are crucial variables in several theories of European integration (Sinnott 1995: 24).

This review presents some of the central approaches and research issues of the political theory of the European Union. The 'normative turn in EU studies' (Bellamy and Castiglione 2003) is evident in several research topics addressed by normative political theorists. The first section gives a brief overview. Some of the highlights of the long, though meagre, pedigree of this field are sketched in the second section, and the more recent history is sketched in the third section. Popular and legal conflicts strengthened the claim of many politicians and scholars that the European Union suffered from a 'legitimacy deficit' in need of resolution. The fourth section dissolves this apparent consensus by exposing quite different accounts of symptoms, diagnoses and prescriptions with regard to this deficit. This section also illustrates how normative political theory engages with other subdisciplines of political science. The fifth section

seeks to provide a taxonomy of concepts of legitimacy, institutional mechanisms of legitimation, and objects of legitimacy. The sixth section combines several of these disjointed insights into a somewhat unified perspective. It incorporates empirical concepts of legitimacy as compliance in an account of citizens' political obligation to obey normatively legitimate political orders. Several concepts and mechanisms of legitimacy address the assurance problems that 'conditional compliers' face under complex structures of interdependence. These challenges are likely to increase with European integration, and merit careful study. The final section concludes with a sketch of some current normative research topics about the European Union. I shall suggest that several issues require scholars to rethink fundamental concepts and normative standards of the subdiscipline of normative political theory.

SOME TOPICS IN THE POLITICAL THEORY OF THE EU

At first glance it may seem that political theory and European integration are hardly on speaking terms. For instance, the Sage *Handbook of Political Theory* (Gaus and Kukathas 2004) makes no mention of the EU. Yet European integration raises profound issues of political theory, and has occasioned much political theory research.

One central topic is the implications of European integration for concepts such as the '*state*' and '*sovereignty*'. Europe is a prime site for changes to the institution of sovereign statehood. Final domestic legal authority and immunity from outside authorities have become less effective tools for effective control within the territory of each state, so governments have pooled some legal and political controls in order to achieve certain common objectives (Keohane 1995; Krasner 1999). How are we to assess such profound transformations of sovereignty, from a defining characteristic of a state to a bargaining chip? What are the normative implications if member states of the EU are no longer states in the received sense, or if the EU has itself taken on state-like features? Must, for instance, the EU be defended and assessed by similar standards of legitimacy as sovereign states? (MacCormick 1999).

Another topic of concern has been *the basic form* of the European political order. Should this 'polity' be regarded mainly as a confederal arrangement, or federal, or with a network structure? Or is the only empirically and normatively defensible solution to regard it as a political order *sui generis* – for now or for ever? The Constitutional Treaty would remove some obscurities by placing some legal competences more clearly with Member States or with the Union – a move toward a federal order by some accounts (Elazar 1987; Norman 1994; Kymlicka 1995; Choudhry 2001; Føllesdal 2001). What are we to make of allocating the competences according to a principle of Subsidiarity (Føllesdal 1998b)?

The assessment of the proper *values and objectives* that should or may be pursued by Europeans remains an important research task for normative political theory. The Constitutional Treaty identifies the central values of the Union, including:

> Respect for human dignity, freedom, democracy, equality, the rule of law and respect for human rights, including the rights of persons belonging to minorities. These values are common to the Member States in a society in which pluralism, non-discrimination, tolerance, justice, solidarity and equality between women and men prevail (Art I–2).

Article 3 of the Constitutional Treaty goes on to identify the objectives of the Union, including the promotion of peace, its values and 'the well-being of its peoples'. It shall also 'promote social justice and protection', 'economic, social and territorial cohesion, and solidarity among Member States' – whilst respecting Europe's 'rich cultural and linguistic diversity'. Much recent work by normative theorists addresses these various values and their relative weight. Is (further) integration necessary for peace? Should the EU be a counterforce to US military hegemony (Habermas and Derrida 2003)? What sort of freedom does and should the EU aim to promote (Dobson 2004)?

Another important normative issue is *distributive justice*. Given the objective of social justice and the frequent references to *the* 'European Social Model', how should European institutions distribute benefits and burdens among Europeans, and how should such decisions be made? To equalize living standards would entail politically unacceptable costs, since the newest member states GNP per capita (PPS) was only 35 to 76 per cent of the EU-15 average in 2002 (European commission 2005: 142). May more economic inequality be defended within a multi-level European political order than within a unified state, consistent with respecting the equal dignity of all European citizens?

Calls for a *European identity* may be more urgent insofar as a legitimate European order requires distribution and redistribution across Member State borders. Must Europeans share a nationality – and would this include a common culture (Føllesdal 2000)? Would a shared 'thin' political culture suffice for general support and compliance, even if it only includes the constitution, or its values (Habermas 1992)? Many hold that citizens of multinational federal orders need a shared 'overarching loyalty' for reasons of stability (Stepan 1999: 33). Can this common ground be maintained by carefully crafted institutions (Scharpf 1997a: 20), or must Europeans also share further, exclusive, values and objectives? The content of such a shared loyalty remains contested, as witnessed in the discussions concerning the *Borders of Europe* – especially with regard to Turkey's long-standing application: who are Europeans, and what normative commitments must unite them?

SOME HISTORY

Several recent contributions to the political theory of the European Union refer back to early philosophers who urged European integration. Their central concern was to find arrangements to end wars on that troubled continent.

Many 18th and 19th century theorists recommended confederal or federal arrangements. The 1713 Peace Plan of Abbé Charles de Saint-Pierre (1658–1743) would allow intervention to force states to join an established confederation and to quell rebellions. Jean-Jacques Rousseau (1712–1778) presented and critiqued Saint-Pierre's proposal. His alterntative included several conditions: all major power must be a member, the joint legislation must be binding, the joint forces must be stronger than any single state, and secession must be illegal. He agreed with Saint-Pierre that unanimity would have to be required for changes to the agreement. David Hume's (1711–1776) notion of 'Commonwealth' has recently been revived for the EU (MacCormick 1999: 143). In *Idea of a Perfect Commonwealth* (1752) Hume recommended a federal arrangement for deliberation of laws that would involve both sub-unit and central legislatures. Sub-units should enjoy several powers and partake in central decisions, but their laws and court judgments can always be overruled by the central bodies. Such a geographically large system would do better than small cities to prevent decisions based on 'intrigue, prejudice or passion' against the public interest.

Immanuel Kant (1724–1804) defended a confederation for peace among free states in *On Perpetual Peace* (1796). These thoughts have been revived and further developed by Jürgen Habermas (Habermas 1998) and others. Kant argued for a confederation rather than a treaty or an international state:

> merely to preserve and secure the freedom of each state in itself, along with that of the other confederated states, although this does not mean that they need to submit to public laws and to a coercive power which enforces them, as do men in a state of nature (Kant [1970] 1796: 104).

John Stuart Mill (1806–1873) may also have had Europe in mind when he recommended federations among 'portions of mankind' not disposed to live under a common government, to prevent wars among themselves and protect against aggression. He would also allow the center sufficient powers so as to ensure all benefits of union – including powers to prevent frontier duties to facilitate commerce (Mill [1861] 1958: ch. 17).

Several scholars of the mid 20th century were remarkably clear sighted with regard to European integration. Their explanations of integration may also help us understand the relative absence of normative theorists' interest until popular protests emerged in the 1990s. Ernst Haas, in 1958, defined political integration as a process that leads to 'political community' among political groups, who 'show more loyalty to their central political institutions than to any other political authority, in a specific period of time and in a definable geographic space'. (Haas 1958: 5). Scholars such as Stanley Hoffmann and Robert Keohane came to endorse Haas's claim that a central decision making process of the European Community is 'supranationality', a style of accommodation 'in which the participants refrain from unconditionally vetoing proposals and instead seek to attain agreement by means of compromises upgrading common interests' (Keohane and Hoffmann 1991: 15).

Haas also argued that the study of elites should take pride of place since the general population was either indifferent or ineffectual, and European integration only needed support from political elites. David Easton and others followed suit (Easton 1965). Leon Lindberg and Stuart A. Scheingold even claimed this as an example of what V. O. Key had coined a 'permissive consensus' in foreign policy, where the public defers to elites and experts' decisions (Key 1961: 32; Lindberg and Scheingold 1970). The reactions to the Maastricht Treaty on European Union challenged this assumption of popular albeit tacit consent, and may help explain why more normative political theorists turned to the issues of European integration.

THE MAASTRICHT TREATY ON EUROPEAN UNION: THE END OF POPULAR AND LEGAL CONSENSUS

The plight of the Constitutional Treaty is not the first time that popular dissatisfaction has replaced 'permissive consensus' about the speed or direction of European integration. Walter Hallstein, the first President of the Commission of the European Economic

Community, warned as early as 1969 that public support would be necessary in the long run – otherwise 'even those parts, which are already set up, could be jeopardized' (Papcke 1992 in Green 1999).

In 1991–1992, negative responses to the Treaty on European Union agreed in Maastricht questioned the presumption of broad tacit consent. Referendums on the Maastricht Treaty in Denmark and France caused wide ranging public debates and elite dissent concerning the proper ends and institutions of the European Communities. The treaty was rejected at a Danish referendum by a margin of 51–49 per cent in 1992, only to be accepted a year later when changed to allow Denmark the right to opt out of the single currency. In France the Treaty created serious cleavages within political parties. It barely passed in a referendum 51 to 49 per cent. The UK House of Commons passed the treaty only with great difficulty in 1993, and with important derogations regarding EMU that had been negotiated at Maastrict. This politicization of the integration process, together with falling popular support for European integration and lower participation rates at European Parliament elections, made governments attend much closer to public opinion (Everts and Sinnott 1995: 432).

In Germany and Denmark the Treaty ratification was also challenged on legal grounds. The treaties and legal structure of the European Community had undergone processes of 'constitutionalisation' with such milestones as the Doctrine of Direct Effect, the Doctrine of Supremacy of Community law, the Doctrine of Implied Powers and the Doctrine of Human Rights (Weiler 1991). These developments buttressed a self-understanding of the European Court of Justice as a constitutional court. The Maastricht Treaty expressed these legal and constitutional developments, and met legal resistance in domestic contexts.

The German Constitutional Court found the Treaty compatible with the German Constitution, but it insisted on its own right to protect fundamental rights, and its right to review whether European institutions acted within their limits. These requirements ran counter to the European Court's claim to have sole competence to ascertain the legality of European institutions. The German Constitutional Court also insisted that powers of the *Bundestag* could not be transferred without limits; nor should the Union decide whether such transfers were necessary to fulfil its aims, as Art. 235 would allow. Moreover, transfers of powers were not to reduce citizens' democratic influence over the state's authority. The continued influence of the Member States' peoples must be secured, either via national parliaments or by increasing European Parliament influence on European Community politics (German Constitutional Court 1993, Wallace 1993; MacCormick 1994; Abromeit 1998: 19–23; Weiler 1999).

The Danish Supreme Court found the Maastricht Treaty compatible with the Danish Constitution insofar as transfer of sovereign powers only occurred to a determinate and limited extent. The Supreme Court accepted further expansion of authority required for the objectives of the Union since that would require unanimous consent of the Council. Hence the Danish government would be able to exercise a preference to block that expansion. The Supreme Court also insisted that Danish courts retain the authority to determine the constitutionality – and hence applicability in Denmark – of EC laws, regardless of the findings by the European Court of Justice (Dansk 1998).

Many governments and EU officials have interpreted events to mean that the legitimacy of the EU was at stake. Politicians gradually came to fear that Europeans might refuse to accept future steps toward deeper European integration, and otherwise hamper governability. The recent Convention on the Future of Europe was in part a response to these fears, in order to pre-empt such scenarios and bolster future popular support.

As popular and legal challenges to the Treaty threatened future integration and enlargement, what started as a trickle of influential contributions to normative political theory (Scharpf 1988; Majone 1990; Mancini 1991; Smith 1991; Weiler 1991), gained in volume. Yet scholars disagree strongly about the symptoms, diagnoses and prognoses to address whatever legitimacy deficit there might be.

LEGITIMACY DEFICIT? SYMPTOMS, DIAGNOSES AND CURES

Alleged symptoms of a legitimacy deficit include on the one hand empirical findings regarding popular attitudes toward the EU to determine the extent of 'political community' in Haas's sense, and on the other hand normative assessments of its institutions. The symptoms range from Eurobarometer data on support for the existence of the European Union and of country membership therein; mistrust of other Europeans and EU institutions (Norris 1999a); 'variable implementation' or non-compliance with Union directives; disparities between elite and public support for membership; declining voter turnout for European Parliament elections (Sbragia 1999); to lack of parliamentary control of executive bodies at the EU level.

Some research on legitimacy in general tries to combine both empirical and normative approaches (Barker 2001: 8). This is also true of research specifically on the legitimacy of the EU. Christopher Lord and David Beetham argue that the same normative standards of legitimacy we know from liberal democratic states should also apply to the EU, its complexity and novel institutions notwithstanding (Lord and Beetham 2001). The EU has clearly fallen short of standards such as voter accountability and prominent human rights safeguards. Value dilemmas such as those between efficiency and accountability will not be removed but can at most be displaced.

These diagnoses of a legitimacy deficit have been contested. Some question the symptoms. Public opinion polls showed falling support for European integration in the 1990s, but European publics still seemed to be highly in favour of European integration. Low and falling turnout at European Parliament elections might not stem from wariness toward integration, but rather be due to lack of attention to European issues by political parties that instead tend to focus on domestic issues and national elections. The public is led to regard European issues and European elections as 'second-order' with less salience than national elections. National party elites even seem to collude to suppress debates about European level choices of policy and institutions, to avoid internal splits on the divisive issues of European integration (van der Eijk and Franklin 1996).

Some scholars argue that the EU does not suffer from a legitimacy deficit, democratic or otherwise (Majone 1998a; Moravcsik 2002, but see Føllesdal and Hix 2006). Even those who believe there is a legitimacy crisis diverge on their diagnoses. Some point to the lack of procedural 'input' legitimation due to citizens' lack of influence and control. Others may lament the lack of 'output' legitimation due to mismatches between citizens' preferences and politicians' delivery; or lack of political party articulation and contestation of central EU-level policies and matters of institutional design (van der Eijk and Franklin 1996; Schmitter 2000; Føllesdal and Hix 2006). Still others hold that one of the main problems is that European integration creates a legitimacy deficit within Member States who are no longer permitted or able to meet popular demands (Scharpf 1999). A further understanding of legitimacy concerns the self-legitimation by governments who make claims to authority addressed as much to themselves as to others, that they are justified in their rule. On this perspective, a legitimation deficit arises because the government of the EU – such as the Commission – legitimates itself inwardly in ways that cannot be sustained externally toward its subjects, given secrecy and lack of accountability (Barker 2001).

Some analysts are optimistic concerning the prognosis. Some warn against fixing something that 'ain't broke' (Weiler 2001), while others hold that only a European superstate can solve the democratic deficit (Sieberson 2004). Some trust alleged sightings of legitimizing deliberation in 'Comitology', the procedures for executing secondary legislation by committees of the European Commission where Member States are represented. Others worry about the legitimacy of these extremely complex procedures with skewed representation (Joerges 1999 vs. Wessels 1999). Some recommend that the EU focus on its role as a 'regulatory state', whose non-democratic independence pre-commits governments and hence bolsters the credibility of member states (Majone 1998a). Others fear that lack of common language, media or public discussions among the European citizenry without a shared identity or functioning political parties are crucial flaws, but disagree on the prospects of speedy improvements (Grimm 1995; Habermas [1995]1998; Abromeit 1998: 32).

No wonder that reflective scholars – not to mention politicians and civil servants – disagree about prescribed medications. Should there be more or fewer arenas of normatively salient and politically efficacious deliberation? Should there now be a written Constitution simplifying the structures of decision-making with a strengthened legal standing for the Charter on Fundamental Rights – or not (Skach 2005)? Do Member States need more discretion through the Open Method of Coordination, or a more efficient Commission securing the European interest over the conflicting national interests? Some suggest strengthening the European Parliament, others seek a stronger role for national parliaments (Neunreither 1994).

For a better grasp of the issues, options and areas of agreement and disagreement it may help to draw some distinctions. I shall suggest that different *concepts of legitimacy* support different, mutually incompatible prescriptions and proscriptions about institutional *objects* and how they can secure *legitimation*.

CONCEPTS, MEANS AND OBJECTS OF LEGITIMACY AND LEGITIMATION

The label 'legitimacy deficit' covers a broad range of issues, giving rise to different taxonomies (Easton 1965; Beetham 1991; Laffan 1996; Beetham and Lord 1998; Jachtenfuchs et al. 1998; Norris 1999a; Barker 2001; Lord and Magnette 2004). The literature seems to use four different fundamental *concepts* of what legitimacy is about, at least four institutional *means* of legitimation for expressing or achieving such legitimacy, regarding at least six different *objects* of legitimacy at varying levels of generality (Easton 1965; Norris 1999a).

We may say that laws or authorities are *legally legitimate* insofar as they are enacted and exercised in accordance with constitutional rules and appropriate procedures (Weiler 1991; Wallace 1993; Weiler 1995; Lenaerts and Desomer 2002). Laws or authorities are *socially legitimate* if the subjects actually abide by them and are so disposed. The EU's legitimacy is also sometimes treated as a matter of problem solving. Does the EU identify and implement solutions that actually secure certain goals otherwise unattainable? Finally, institutions are *normatively legitimate* insofar as they can be justified to the people living under them, and impose a moral duty on them to comply (Rawls 1993; Lehning 1997; Føllesdal 1998a; Michelman 2000). Normative theorists often take various forms of *normative legitimacy* to be fundamental, but overlook the other aspects at their peril. The four forms are interrelated, often compatible, and can be mutually re-enforcing. *Simple* rules and procedures may make it easier to determine the legality, compliance and justifiability of the EU (Magnette 2001). *Legal legitimacy*, for example in the form of constitutionalism and the rule of law, is often regarded as a necessary condition of the justifiability of a political order. On its own, *general compliance* is insufficient for normative legitimacy, since people may comply with unjust rule solely from fear of sanctions, lack of alternatives or unreflective habit. Yet compliance often requires that the population believe that the institutions are *normatively* legitimate (Easton 1965: 207–8; Beetham and Lord 1998: 10). Perceived normative legitimacy may also bolster the *problem-solving capacity* of governments – and of the EU (Dehousse 1999).

These four concepts of legitimacy may focus on different aspects of institutional arrangements that grant *legitimation* to authorities e.g. by means of express consent, affirmation or recognition by their subordinates or other legitimate authorities (Beetham 1991).

Legitimation through participation

Legitimation through participation might increase by including citizens, interest groups or experts in the decision process, for instance in referendums or committees (Easton 1965: 207–8; Andersen and Burns 1996: 245; Abromeit 1998; Beetham and Lord 1998: 10). Participation may certainly boost compliance, especially if the parties consulted can bind their members in forms of network governance (Kohler-Koch and Eising 1999).

Legitimation through democratic rule

One important form of participation is representative democracy, where citizens hold rulers accountable for their use of public power by selecting among competing candidate parties on the basis of informed discussion of their merits and objectives (Norris 1999a; Lenaerts and Desomer 2002). We should be careful to distinguish democracy from legitimacy (Mény 2002), but many critics argue that such measures are underdeveloped in the EU (Manin 1987: 352; Bellamy 1995: 167).

Legitimation through actual consent

Some writers also place great importance on institutional arrangements where the subordinates and other authorities expressly grant consent or affirm the authorities as legitimate, and where other legitimate authorities expressly recognize them (Habermas 1979: 200; Beetham 1991; Beetham and Lord 1998: 8)

Legitimation through output

The problem-solving or 'output' legitimation of the EU requires the ability to create de facto binding and sanctioned law, and the ability to make credible commitments e.g. through regulatory agencies, a common currency or an independent central bank (Beetham and Lord 1998; Majone 1998b; Scharpf 1999) or by creating arenas where diffuse constituents may pursue their interests.

The academic contributions about legitimacy, legitimation and the EU appear to address at least six different objects or institutional levels. Different concepts and institutional arrangements clearly apply better to some levels than others.

Discussions may concern:

- A particular political *decision* – a policy or piece of legislation. Questions of their legitimacy typically concern their legality or whether affected parties have otherwise *participated* or given *actual consent.*
- The *authorities* – the political actors: office-holders, a particular government or set of representatives – whose legitimacy is mainly an issue of legitimation, for example through *democratic* elections (Barker 2001: 32). Their problem-solving effectiveness may also be at stake.
- Particular *public institutions* such as the European Central Bank. Challenges to their legitimacy might be of all four kinds (Schmitt and Thomassen 1999: ch. 4).
- The *regime*, that is the political order as a whole, is challenged on all four counts, including lack of general compliance with the rules and authorities; its pedigree, its problem-solving capacity – as well as whether the regime can be justified to those subject to it.
- The regime *principles*, such as the objectives and ideals of the EU: general welfare, participation, and the rule of law; subsidiarity – and possibly social policies (Schmitt and Thomassen 1999: ch. 3). The central issues are matters of normative and problem-solving legitimacy as well as Legality – which was challenged by the German and Danish Constitutional Court decisions.
- The *political community* – the set of individuals who participate in and maintain common decision-making processes. Questions include whether there is a European 'demos', and whether it should include Turkish citizens. The legitimacy at stake here is typically normative.

There are important interconnections between the various concepts of legitimacy and legitimation regarding these six objects. Regarding *social legitimacy* in the form of political support, Easton notes the importance of *diffuse* institutional, regime and community support to ensure *specific* support – and presumably compliance with - particular decisions and authorities (Luhman 1969; Norris 1999b: 264). Diffuse support for the regime, in the form of an affective orientation to it *as* normatively legitimate, may arise either from below or from above; from acceptance of particular incumbents, or from the legitimating ideologies of the regime when it is seen to regularly yield output consistent with the regime objectives (Easton 1965: 290). Political theory about normative legitimacy may thus contribute to such diffuse support for the regime.

The different concepts of legitimacy and legitimation combined with an awareness of these different levels, can provide alternative, possibly complementary 'frames' for understanding the legitimacy challenges facing the EU. European integration and expansion may put both diffuse and specific support at risk. Support for the regime as a whole is not forthcoming 'from below' – witness the popular dissatisfaction with the Constitutional Treaty, especially in France and the Netherlands. Nor is there general agreement about the regime values and objectives of the EU – nor about whether the Union's 'outcome' achieves those objectives reasonably well.

Unfortunately, different 'frames' lead to different, mutually incompatible recommendations for institutional changes and the extent of integration (Kohler-Koch 2000). For instance, creative problem-solving efficiency, democracy and constitutionalism may conflict, even in principle (Lindberg and Scheingold 1970: 269; Elster and Slagstad 1988; Naurin 2004).

Some suggest sector-specific resolutions that vary between the Common Foreign and Security Policy (CFSP) and monetary policies (Lord and Magnette 2004: 190; Smismans 2004). Yet why should the sectors be legitimated in these different ways? Another approach seeks mutual adjustment of the four suggested concepts of legitimacy, and modify arrangements for legitimation according to the

popular or party support for various concepts (Jachtenfuchs et al. 1998). But why should such popularity be decisive, instead of considering the best reasons for some conceptions over others?

Normative theorists pursue several different strategies of reasoned reconciliation (Barker 2001). Some deny that problem-solving or compliance are plausible concepts of 'legitimation', and instead hold that normative legitimacy is fundamental. It is still appropriate to consider when, if at all, problem-solving and compliance are normatively relevant for legitimacy. Some argue that since the EU is 'sui generis' as a political order, democratic accountability is less appropriate than nonmajoritarian and 'post-parliamentary' standards and models of accountability (Majone 1994; Andersen and Burns 1996; Héritier 1999). In this vein some see EU phenomena such as comitology as embryonic arenas for 'deliberative politics' (Joerges 1999: 311).

The tradition of federalism suggests that the EU share many features with other federal arrangements – all of which are *sui generis*. So neither complexity nor uniqueness renders standard normative principles inappropriate (Beetham and Lord 1998). Still, the complexity and multi-level nature of the EU forces us to reconsider the reasons for requiring democratic accountability through elections. Perhaps we must look for functional equivalents.

A detailed account that brings together all relevant concepts, means and objects of legitimacy and legitimation in ways that resolve all tensions is beyond the scope of these reflections, – and beyond the scope of political theory. Still, we may benefit from an account that can guide discussions concerning trade-offs, scope and institutional design, by identifying some of the central arguments and appropriate considerations.

LEGITIMACY AND TRUSTWORTHINESS

In the following I sketch one such perspective on legitimacy. I suggest that we should distinguish between the normative legitimacy of a political order or regime, and the more demanding conditions for when citizens have a political obligation to abide by such rules and commands. The latter requires more than that the rules being normatively legitimate. Citizens have a political obligation only if such rules are also actually generally complied with.

On this account, a normative duty to obey political commands requires firstly, that the commands, rulers and regime are normatively legitimate, and secondly, that citizens also have reason to believe this, and have reason to trust in the future compliance of other citizens and authorities with such commands and regimes. I shall argue that all four concepts of legitimacy and the institutional arrangements of legitimation can enhance political trust and trustworthiness in a normatively legitimate EU, among 'contingent compliers'. Citizens have such political obligations primarily when the rules are legitimate, and they are generally complied with. That is, the rules must be part of an *institution* in the sense of a social practice according to publicly known formal and informal rules. That is: an institution exists when its rules specifying offices, rights, powers etc. are regularly acted on, and this is public knowledge (Rawls 1971: 55–56; North 1990). An institutionalist normative political theory takes as its central subject matter such institutions (Weale 1999: 20). For citizens to have a political obligation, then, they must have good reason to believe that the normatively legitimate rules are also generally complied with by others. This requires trust and trustworthiness.

Such trustworthiness in institutions and fellow citizens seems necessary for the long term support for the multi-level political order, and for authorities' ability to govern. Long-term support for the EU requires not only present compliance and support, but also long term trust in the general compliance of others – both citizens and officials - and a shared acceptance of the legality and normative legitimacy of the regime. Normative political theory may thus contribute decisively in promoting long term stability. Citizens' and authorities' publicly shared beliefs about *normative legitimacy* are central at several points to ensure trust.

But all four concepts of legitimacy, duly circumscribed, may serve to provide assurance among contingent compliers.

The need for trust and trustworthiness arises under circumstances of complex mutual dependence, where the regular co-operation by each depends on their conscious or habitual expectation of the regular co-operation of others. Trust and trustworthiness have become increasingly important among increasingly interdependent Europeans committed to mutual recognition of Member States' regulations, and subject to Qualified Majority Voting where majorities and minorities must be trusted to restrain themselves in the long term.

The truster must believe that it is in the interest of the trusted to act according to the shared expectations. Such interests may be of several kinds, bolstered by institutions. The trusted can act out of self-interest within institutions that sanction misbehaviour. The trusted can be known to act from a sense of appropriateness such that only certain actions seem open to their choice. Or the trusted person can be known to be other-regarding, with concern for the truster's well-being. One source of such trust has often been assumed to be a 'thick' sense of collective identity – which is absent among Europeans. This leads some to warn about the premature introduction of majority rule (Scharpf 1999: 9). Others observe that state building has sometimes preceded such 'national identities', and recall that political parties often have served such important integrating functions (Chambers 1963; Lipset and Rokkan 1967).

Another important motivation based on concern for others is found among 'contingent compliers'. They are prepared to comply with common, fair rules as long as they believe that others do so as well. They may for instance be motivated by what John Rawls called a *Duty of Justice*

> That they will comply with fair practices that exist and apply to them when they believe that the relevant others likewise do their part … (Rawls 1971: 336).

The theory of games explain how institutions may provide such assurance of general compliance by mixes of positive laws, transparency, shared practices, and socialization. These arrangements reduce the risks of, or suspicion of, others' defection, for instance by restricting the scope of valid majority rule by human rights. Institutions can also provide public mechanisms of socialising to certain preferences (Taylor 1987; Goodin 1992; Scharpf 1997b; Levi 1998; Rothstein 1998).

A conditional complier must believe that the policies and institutions in question are normatively legitimate, and that most others comply. The four different concepts of legitimacy discussed above play important roles. A plausible *public political theory* should defend the objectives and other normative standards of the political order, such as democracy, subsidiarity, solidarity, and human rights. The institutions should be *simple and transparent* enough for citizens to comprehend and assess them. The institutions should be *effective and efficient* in the sense of actually producing the normatively desired effects. The belief that most other actors will comply requires not only the widespread belief that a large proportion of individuals actually complies. A conditional complier must also have reason to regard the *future* compliance of sufficiently many others as highly probable. This is why politicians and academics may be right to worry about the long term consequences of an 'apparent' legitimacy deficit in the form of low levels of public support for institutions, policies and authorities. Various acts of legitimation by the government officials and by citizens may increase such support and trust. Institutions may contribute to such beliefs about future general compliance in several ways.

Educational systems and political parties can be known to socialize individuals to be conditional compliers with something like a duty of justice (Levi 1998; McKay 2001). Institutions can also boost expectations of other contingent compliers' future compliance, when the rules are seen to secure the intended, fair output, and cannot easily be abused (Rothstein 1998). Institutions that actually deliver according to their stated aims provide problem-solving legitimacy in the form of 'output legitimacy' (Scharpf 1999).

Institutions can also impose sanctions that modify citizens' incentives, to assure compliers that they will not be 'suckers':

> Government coercive capacity assures potentially supportive citizens that there will, in fact, be relative equality of sacrifice, [and] governmental institutions contribute to contingent consent (Levi 1998: 26; cf. Schmitter 2004).

Institutions may provide assurance even in the absence of formal sanctions when they monitor or report general compliance, or facilitate such reporting. These roles are enhanced by simplification and democratisation of EU institutions, and by enhanced transparency about their workings (Dehousse 1999; Héritier 1999).

To see some implications of this account, consider one of the alleged central tensions of the EU, between the objectives of effective and creative problem solving on the one hand, and transparency and democratic accountability on the other. We must pay close attention to the normative reasons for preferring democracy over other forms of governance in general – and then consider whether these reasons also hold for the EU.

One such argument may appeal to efficiency. But when comparing democratic arrangements to others on grounds of efficiency we cannot rely only on singular policy outcomes. We must know whether the alternative arrangements have mechanisms that will reliably continue to ensure acceptable outcomes in ways that provide crucial trustworthiness. One such mechanism essential to democracy is institutional design that allows an opposition (Dahl 1971). Party competition is crucial for opinion formation, informed policy choice and scrutiny of government (Schattschneider 1960: 68; Key 1961; Lipset and Rokkan 1967). Such arguments about the value of democratic arrangements entail further that democracy may be important both to provide 'input legitimacy' and to ensure 'output legitimacy.'

This focus on the need for institutions that create and maintain assurance among contingent compliers may shed light on how to alleviate the legitimacy deficits of the EU. There should be visible, effective channels for correcting or replacing authorities who pursue contested objectives and policies, also at the European level. Currently, the EU offers little room to present rival leadership and policy agendas, and national politics dominate EU elections. There are few national arenas for discussing issues of how the EU should develop and the policies it should pursue. Thus the electorate's views on European issues do not inform the agenda of European Parliament and EU policy making (van der Eijk and Franklin 1996). General objections that such changes threaten efficiency and problem solving legitimacy do not withstand scrutiny without further elaboration of the best alternatives. Democratic accountability or some other complex mechanisms seem necessary to maintain trust in the 'problem-solving' authorities, their objectives, means and good will.

CURRENT NORMATIVE RESEARCH ON THE EUROPEAN UNION

We finally review some of the topics of normative political theory that currently receive attention, and that are likely to remain high on the research agenda in the future processes of European integration. Some are listed in the first section (above), but here we may list the topics by their objects of legitimacy:

- The *authoritiess* – the political actors: should they be democratically accountable or not (Majone 1998a; Magnette 2000; Lord and Beetham 2001; Mény 2002; Moravcsik 2002; Schmitter 2000)?
- The legitimacy of particular *institutions* – for instance, should European courts be superior to national courts; what should be the proper powers and composition of Comitology (Lodge 1996; Dehousse 1999; Joerges 1999).
- The *regime*, that is the political order as a whole. The conceptual issues include notions of 'statehood' and 'sovereignty', and the basic form of this order. Questions about the legitimacy of this regime can be of the four different kinds. The concern may be about general compliance with the

rules and authorities; or an assessment of the consistency of procedural norms and authority structures that constitute the formal and informal rules of the game (Lenaerts and Desomer 2002; Bellamy and Castiglione 2003). Another central issue is of course the *problem-solving* ability of the system, where empirical evidence must tell whether the EU can actually obtain the objectives stated in the treaties, and whether it actually does so reasonably well (Majone 1994; Scharpf 1997a). Finally, we may be asking whether the regime *can be justified* to those subject to it (Lehning 1997; Weiler 1999).

- The regime *principles*. The research includes questions about the legitimacy of certain objectives, values and ideals of the EU, such as general welfare, participation, or the rule of law; and the scope of decisions and division of powers between the institutions (cf. Schmitt and Thomassen 1999; ch. 3). Should, for instance, the aims of the EU include (re)distributive social policies or military objectives? The central issues here seem to be matters of normative and problem-solving legitimacy. *Legality* is also at stake, at least in the sense that the member states' constitutions may restrict the powers of Union bodies. Thus the legality of the whole regime was challenged by the German and Danish Constitutional Court decisions, and their rulings constrain future development of the EU's objectives.
- The *political community*. Where should the borders of the European Union be drawn: who should participate in and maintain common decision-making processes for these ends? Issues about the appropriate role and content of a shared European identity may be relevant for this issue.

The following remarks expand on some of these issues, paying particular attention to attempts to enhance democracy and human rights in the EU.

The discussion about whether to democratize Union bodies has received much attention by political theorists. Many have applauded the slow increase of powers to the European

Parliament from Maastricht onwards in the Amsterdam Treaty, since this is said to reduce the democratic deficit. Authors particularly welcome changes that allow directly elected representatives to co-determine legislation and to hold the Commission accountable. (Lodge 1994, 1996; Wessels and Diedrichs 1999). However, even such measures are contested. Further clarification concerning normatively acceptable democratic institutions in the EU is required, if for no other reason that such vague and contested terms as 'democracy' may otherwise be misapplied and lend support to reforms on false grounds (Schmitter 2000).

Contributions in this field have addressed the grounds of democratic institutions, their irreplacability, and the appropriateness of majority rule. Some authors hold that individual autonomy should be secured, based on the assumption that self-determination is a fundamental human good. This entails that the EU must be a freedom-enabling order providing citizens opportunities for active participation to shape and sustain their institutions (MacCormick 1999: 164). Others may hold such self-determination to be a contested ideal of human flourishing, hence unsuited as a common normative basis. Several authors instead focus on individuals' interest in security against interference and against being subject to the arbitrary will of others (Pettit 1997; Abromeit 1998; Bellamy 1999). The Charter of Fundamental Rights may come to serve important functions in this regard. Some authors also argue that institutions should foster political involvement, both to keep the political order just, and to foster the appropriate human nature (Bellamy 1999). These may be important stabilizing mechanisms necessary to ensure the sustainability of such a just political order, and hence the subject of normative political theory.

One topic that requires further attention is the place of deliberation in the European political order. A controversial issue is whether and how public political deliberation affects citizens' fundamental preferences, as compared to other inputs on character formation, such as the civilising impact of hypocrisy (Elster 1998). One challenge is to disentangle and trace processes that occur while parties talk: when are they *arguing*, and when are they *bargaining*? – and how do we tell the difference? For instance, it is difficult to infer from observed changes over policy preferences whether what has occurred is modification of ultimate objectives – which is the main claim of some deliberative democrats – or part of bargaining in a broader sense. In either case it remains to be seen whether such shifts are to the normatively better, or simply to the group's own benefit. Another important concern is whether such preference transforming discussions should primarily happen within institutions with authority, or within 'civil society' in general (Nino 1996 vs. Dryzek 1990).

The reasons in favour of deliberation for interest formation rest on assumptions that are presently less plausible at the European level than at the national. The opacity of European institutions, the present lack of a well-developed European public space, and the relative absence of European political parties reduce the opportunities for character formation, and limit the informational bases and range of political choice. However, there is little reason to believe that these features are permanent, so such pessimism would seem premature.

But this does not yet provide an argument that decisions in general should be made in deliberating bodies, or that more deliberation among more individuals is always better – since a group may collude against others by what may appear to be deliberation. Nor does the need for preference modification require that we rank deliberation over preference aggregation, e.g. by votes. Preference formation and other tasks of deliberation do not replace or compete against voting. We can be concerned with deliberation and at the same time be aware of the need for 'post-deliberative democracy'. Indeed, this is not new: A broad range of democratic theorists have favoured open public debates for preference modification, learning and inclusion. Indeed, few theorists have been solely concerned with democracy as interest aggregation – though some recent deliberative theorists give that impression (Mill [1861]1958; Schumpeter [1943]1976; Schattschneider 1960; Key 1961: 449; Riker 2003: 172).

It remains to be determined when observed preference shifts in comitology are due to shifting expected payoffs, or shifts in ultimate objectives generally. We must also consider the risks involved, e.g. of collusion. Such risks – but perhaps also the benefits – may be greatly reduced by constraining comitology within other institutions such as the European Parliament. Others hold that institutionalized networks provide good opportunities for participation that enhances legitimacy (Héritier 1999). They may be among the many sites where private and public bodies can meet to deliberate about solutions to conflicts (Bellamy 1999). However, the institutionalist issues concerning trustworthiness reappear. How realistic is it that such networks will remain open, and not be skewed against emerging new points of view, preventing equal access to the agenda (Abromeit 1998)?

Some hold that associations in civil society play important roles in correcting skewed representation, providing information and socializing citizens. (Cohen and Rogers 1995). Some hold that democratic arrangements should be replaced (Dryzek 1990; Eriksen 2000: 44). Others more cautiously explore how these networks may supplement competitive elections and other traditional institutional staples of democracy (Cohen 2003), and how to maintain the undistorted arenas over time (Goodin 1992; Femia 1996). Majone also defends independent agencies only as subject to various checks (Majone 1998a). Thus, his suggestion is not to replace representative democracy, but rather to include bodies that are in turn under some form of democratic control.

Another important issue for the normative political theory of the EU is the legitimate role of such democratic principles as majority rule and the one-person-one-vote. It is not obvious that majoritarian decision-making is appropriate when segments of the population risk being in a permanent minority, especially if the majority cannot be trusted to always modify their views in light of the impact on minorities. And one-person-one-vote may not be appropriate under such circumstances. Skewed representation that favors minorities may be defensible. Hence, the appropriate modes of

securing responsive
within federal and oth
'plural' societies merit
1991; Lijphart 1999).

One means to pr
majority tyranny is h
But should public po
constrained by huma
national or Europea
scholars hold that co
rights are necessary f
order (MacCormick 1
such substantive cons
'unconstrained polit
norms and requirem
hold that democratic
promises should only
constraints that 'allo
their rights themselve
Such censure can be
disrespect of citizens'
erative capacities (Wa

Europeanization
new versions of this c
to make of internati
and adjudicate signato
dynamic interpretat
treaty texts go unche
ernance characteristi
further questions
human rights that
and risks of inte
regimes. To illustra
'human rights' stan
triggers for valual
actions by a wide
disobedience by cit
toring, non-militar
vention, and tra
Corporate Social Re

The roles of hu
even further issues.
not only constrain
own citizens and to
The legitimate po
vis-à-vis sub-units
merit scrutiny. So
should also regul
Member States, p
higher standards s

Parliament from Maastricht onwards in the Amsterdam Treaty, since this is said to reduce the democratic deficit. Authors particularly welcome changes that allow directly elected representatives to co-determine legislation and to hold the Commission accountable. (Lodge 1994, 1996; Wessels and Diedrichs 1999). However, even such measures are contested. Further clarification concerning normatively acceptable democratic institutions in the EU is required, if for no other reason that such vague and contested terms as 'democracy' may otherwise be misapplied and lend support to reforms on false grounds (Schmitter 2000).

Contributions in this field have addressed the grounds of democratic institutions, their irreplacability, and the appropriateness of majority rule. Some authors hold that individual autonomy should be secured, based on the assumption that self-determination is a fundamental human good. This entails that the EU must be a freedom-enabling order providing citizens opportunities for active participation to shape and sustain their institutions (MacCormick 1999: 164). Others may hold such self-determination to be a contested ideal of human flourishing, hence unsuited as a common normative basis. Several authors instead focus on individuals' interest in security against interference and against being subject to the arbitrary will of others (Pettit 1997; Abromeit 1998; Bellamy 1999). The Charter of Fundamental Rights may come to serve important functions in this regard. Some authors also argue that institutions should foster political involvement, both to keep the political order just, and to foster the appropriate human nature (Bellamy 1999). These may be important stabilizing mechanisms necessary to ensure the sustainability of such a just political order, and hence the subject of normative political theory.

One topic that requires further attention is the place of deliberation in the European political order. A controversial issue is whether and how public political deliberation affects citizens' fundamental preferences, as compared to other inputs on character formation, such as the civilising impact of hypocrisy (Elster 1998). One challenge is to disentangle and trace processes that occur while parties talk:

when are they *arguing*, and when are they *bargaining*? – and how do we tell the difference? For instance, it is difficult to infer from observed changes over policy preferences whether what has occurred is modification of ultimate objectives – which is the main claim of some deliberative democrats – or part of bargaining in a broader sense. In either case it remains to be seen whether such shifts are to the normatively better, or simply to the group's own benefit. Another important concern is whether such preference transforming discussions should primarily happen within institutions with authority, or within 'civil society' in general (Nino 1996 vs. Dryzek 1990).

The reasons in favour of deliberation for interest formation rest on assumptions that are presently less plausible at the European level than at the national. The opacity of European institutions, the present lack of a well-developed European public space, and the relative absence of European political parties reduce the opportunities for character formation, and limit the informational bases and range of political choice. However, there is little reason to believe that these features are permanent, so such pessimism would seem premature.

But this does not yet provide an argument that decisions in general should be made in deliberating bodies, or that more deliberation among more individuals is always better – since a group may collude against others by what may appear to be deliberation. Nor does the need for preference modification require that we rank deliberation over preference aggregation, e.g. by votes. Preference formation and other tasks of deliberation do not replace or compete against voting. We can be concerned with deliberation and at the same time be aware of the need for 'post-deliberative democracy'. Indeed, this is not new: A broad range of democratic theorists have favoured open public debates for preference modification, learning and inclusion. Indeed, few theorists have been solely concerned with democracy as interest aggregation – though some recent deliberative theorists give that impression (Mill [1861]1958; Schumpeter [1943]1976; Schattschneider 1960; Key 1961: 449; Riker 2003: 172).

It remains to be determined when observed preference shifts in comitology are due to shifting expected payoffs, or shifts in ultimate objectives generally. We must also consider the risks involved, e.g. of collusion. Such risks – but perhaps also the benefits – may be greatly reduced by constraining comitology within other institutions such as the European Parliament. Others hold that institutionalized networks provide good opportunities for participation that enhances legitimacy (Héritier 1999). They may be among the many sites where private and public bodies can meet to deliberate about solutions to conflicts (Bellamy 1999). However, the institutionalist issues concerning trustworthiness reappear. How realistic is it that such networks will remain open, and not be skewed against emerging new points of view, preventing equal access to the agenda (Abromeit 1998)?

Some hold that associations in civil society play important roles in correcting skewed representation, providing information and socializing citizens. (Cohen and Rogers 1995). Some hold that democratic arrangements should be replaced (Dryzek 1990; Eriksen 2000: 44). Others more cautiously explore how these networks may supplement competitive elections and other traditional institutional staples of democracy (Cohen 2003), and how to maintain the undistorted arenas over time (Goodin 1992; Femia 1996). Majone also defends independent agencies only as subject to various checks (Majone 1998a). Thus, his suggestion is not to replace representative democracy, but rather to include bodies that are in turn under some form of democratic control.

Another important issue for the normative political theory of the EU is the legitimate role of such democratic principles as majority rule and the one-person-one-vote. It is not obvious that majoritarian decision-making is appropriate when segments of the population risk being in a permanent minority, especially if the majority cannot be trusted to always modify their views in light of the impact on minorities. And one-person-one-vote may not be appropriate under such circumstances. Skewed representation that favors minorities may be defensible. Hence, the appropriate modes of

securing responsive and accountable rule within federal and other multi-level orders for 'plural' societies merit further scrutiny (Barry 1991; Lijphart 1999).

One means to protect minorities from majority tyranny is human rights protection. But should public power be constitutionally constrained by human rights, in the form of national or European judicial review? Some scholars hold that constitutionalized human rights are necessary for an acceptable political order (MacCormick 1999). Others are wary of such substantive constitutional constraints on 'unconstrained political debate' concerning norms and requirements (Dryzek 1990), and hold that democratic attempts at reaching compromises should only be secured by procedural constraints that 'allow individuals to fight for their rights themselves' (Bellamy 1995, 1999). Such censure can be said to express profound disrespect of citizens' sense of justice and deliberative capacities (Waldron 1998).

Europeanization and globalization create new versions of this classical issue. What are we to make of international bodies that monitor and adjudicate signatory states, by judges whose dynamic interpretations of near immutable treaty texts go unchecked? The multi-level governance characteristic of Europeanization puts further questions to a political theory of human rights that seeks to address the roles and risks of international human rights regimes. To illustrate, quite different sets of 'human rights' standards may be appropriate triggers for valuable but widely differing actions by a wide range of actors: justifiable disobedience by citizens, international monitoring, non-military pressure, military intervention, and transnational corporations' Corporate Social Responsibility.

The roles of human rights in the EU raise even further issues. In the EU, human rights do not only constrain governments vis-à-vis their own citizens and toward other sovereign states. The legitimate powers of central authorities vis-à-vis sub-units of a (quasi-)federation also merit scrutiny. Some human rights norms should also regulate the relations among Member States, possibly holding them to higher standards since they share values and objectives, while cautious about sanctions since the sub-units are internally democratic. In the EU, one related concern is the appropriate relationship between subsidiarity and human rights. Consider, for instance, that Art 7 of the TEU after Nice does not permit humanitarian intervention against human rights violations within a member state. Is this application of subsidiarity normatively defensible, or should EU bodies enjoy further powers of intervention?

CONCLUSION

The European Union challenges central tenets and raises central issues in normative political theory. Europeanization forces researchers to attend to fundamental concepts and values including the nature of the state and its justification, the reasons to value democracy and human rights, and how to maintain stable and just multi-level political orders. Such systematic reflections are sorely needed when politicians consider alternative strategies to enhance the transparency, responsiveness and fairness of EU institutions. They know that the Union must be justified toward all citizens and their representatives, at least at the time of Treaty ratification and in times of crises.

Political theory insists that the legitimacy and legitimation deficits are not only a matter of present public opinion registering low levels of political support for institutions, policies and authorities. Such a perception is indeed relevant for when citizens have a political obligation to obey normatively legitimate institutions, since they must have reason to trust the future compliance of other citizens and authorities. Trustworthiness in institutions and fellow citizens seems necessary for the long-term support for the multi-level political order, and for authorities' ability to govern. Normative political theory may thus help promote the long-term stability of a political order.

However, normative political theory offers only conditional support. If theorists find no common good for Europe and Europeans, or find that the EU – as a regime or some particular institution - fails to secure these objectives, these findings may erode what meagre support there is. Theorists might then even conclude that the regime lacks a moral right to obedience, and thus add their voices to calls for reform toward a political order that respects all as equals.

NOTE

1. I am grateful for constructive comments from J.P. Aus, R. Goodin, J.L. Marti, T.V. Olsen, H. Sjursen, U. Sverdrup, referees of the *Journal of Political Philosophy*, and the editors of this volume – especially K.E. Jørgensen. Some segments of the present overview originally appeared in *Journal of Political Philosophy* (Føllesdal 2006). I am grateful for permission.

REFERENCES

Abromeit, H. (1998) *Democracy in Europe: Legitimising Politics in a Non-State Polity*. New York: Berghahn Books.

Andersen, S.S. and Burns, T.R. (1996) 'The European Union and the erosion of parliamentary democracy: a study of post-parliamentary governance', in S.S. Andersen and K.A. Eliassen (eds), *The European Union: How Democratic Is It?* London: Sage. pp. 227–52.

Barker, R. (2001) *Legitimating Identities: The Self-Presentations of Ruler and Subjects*. Cambridge: Cambridge University Press.

Barry, B. (1991) 'Is democracy special?', in *Democracy and Power*. Oxford: Oxford University Press. pp. 24–60.

Beetham, D. (1991) *The Legitimation of Power*. London: Macmillan.

Beetham, D. and Lord, C. (1998) *Legitimacy and the European Union*. London: Longman.

Bellamy, R. (1995) 'The constitution of Europe: rights or democracy?', in R. Bellamy, V. Bufacchi and D. Castiglione (eds), *Democracy and Constitutional Culture in the Union of Europe*. pp. 153–75.

Bellamy, R. (1999) *Liberalism and Pluralism*. London: Routledge.

Bellamy, R. and Castiglione, D. (2003) 'Legitimizing the Euro-polity and its regime: the normative turn in EU studies', *European Journal of Political Theory*, 2(1): 7–34.

Chambers, W. (1963) *Parties in a New Nation*. New York: Oxford University Press.

Choudhry, S. (2001) 'Citizenship and federations: some preliminary reflections', in K. Nicolaïdis and R. Howse (eds), *The Federal Vision: Legitimacy and Levels of Governance in the US and the EU*. Oxford: Oxford University Press. pp. 377–402.

Cohen, J. (2003) 'Procedure and substance in deliberative democracy', in T. Christiano (ed.), *Philosophy and Democracy*. Oxford: Oxford University Press.

Cohen, J. and Rogers, J. (1995) *Associations and Democracy*. London: Verso.

Dahl, R.A. (1971) *Polyarchy: Participation and Opposition*. New Haven: Yale University Press.

Dansk, H. (1998) 'Dom i Sag I 361/1997 – "Grundlovssagen"', *Højesterets dombog*, 6 April.

Dehousse, R. (1999) 'Towards a regulation of transitional governance? Citizen's rights and the reform of comitology procedures', in C. Joerges and E. Vos (eds), *EU Committees: Social Regulation, Law and Politics*. Oxford: Hart. pp. 109–27.

Dobson, L. (2004) 'Conceptions of freedom and the European constitution', in L. Dobson and A. Føllesdal (eds), *Political Theory and the European Constitution*. London: Routledge. pp. 103–21.

Dryzek, J.S. (1990) *Discursive Democracy: Politics, Policy, and Political Science*. Cambridge: Cambridge University Press.

Easton, D. (1965) *A Systems Analysis of Political Life*. New York: Wiley.

Elazar, D.J. (1987) *Federalism As Grand Design: Political Philosophers and the Federal Principle*. Lanham, MD: University Press of America.

Elster, J. (1998) 'Deliberation and constitution making', in J. Elster (ed.), *Deliberative Democracy*. Cambridge: Cambridge University Press. pp. 97–122.

Elster, J. and Slagstad, R. (eds) (1988) *Constitutionalism and Democracy*. Cambridge: Cambridge University Press.

European Commission (2005) *Europe in Figures. Eurostat Yearbook 2005*. Luxembourg: Office for Official Publications of the European Communities.

Eriksen, E.O. (2000) 'Deliberative Supranationalism in the EU', in E.O. Eriksen and J.E. Fossum (eds), *Democracy in the European Union: Integration Through Deliberation?* London: Routledge. pp. 42–64.

Everts, P. and Sinnott, R. (1995) 'Conclusion: European publics and the legitimacy of internationalized governance', in O. Niedermayer and R. Sinnot (eds), *Public Opinion and Internationalized Governance*. Oxford: Oxford University Press. pp. 431–57.

Femia, J. (1996) 'Complexity and deliberative democracy', *Inquiry*, 39(3–4): 359–97.

Føllesdal, A. (1998a) 'Democracy, legitimacy and majority rule in the EU', in A. Weale and M. Nentwich (eds), *Political Theory and the European Union: Legitimacy, Constitutional Choice and Citizenship*. London: Routledge. pp. 34–48, 14.

Føllesdal, A. (1998b) 'Subsidiarity', *Journal of Political Philosophy*, 6(2): 231–59.

Føllesdal, A. (2000) 'The future soul of Europe: Nationalism or just patriotism? On David Miller's defence of nationality', *Journal of Peace Research*, 37(4): 503–18.

Føllesdal, A. (2001) 'Federal inequality among equals: a contractualist defense', *Metaphilosophy*. pp. 236–55.

Føllesdal, A. (in press) 'Legitimacy deficits of the European Union', *Journal of Political Philosophy*.

Føllesdal, A. and Hix, S. (2006) 'Why there is a democratic deficit in the EU: a response to Majone and Moravcsik', *Journal of Common Market Studies*, 44(3): 533–62.

Gaus, G.F. and Kukathas, C. (eds) (2004) *Handbook of Political Theory*. London: Sage.

German Constitutional Court (1993) 'Brunner v European Union Treaty', *BVerfGE*, 89: 155.

Goodin, R.E. (1992) *Motivating Political Morality*. Oxford: Blackwell.

Green, D. (1999) 'Who are the Europeans? – on European identity', *The State of the European Union (quotes from ECSA Paper)*.

Grimm, D. (1995) 'Does Europe need a constitution?', *European Law Journal*, 1(3): 282–302.

Haas, E.B. (1958) *The Uniting of Europe: Political, Economic and Social Forces 1950-1957*. London: Stevens and Sons.

Habermas, J. (1979) 'Legitimation problems in the modern state', in T. McCarthy (trans.) (ed.), *Communication and the Evolution of Society*. Boston: Beacon Press. Chapter 5.

Habermas, J. (1992) 'Citizenship and national identity: some reflections on the future of Europe', *Praxis International*, 12(1): 1–19.

Habermas, J. [1995] (1998) 'Does Europe need a constitution? Remarks on Dieter Grimm', *The Inclusion of the Other: Studies in Political Theory*. First printed as Remarks on Dieter Grimm's 'Does Europe need a Constitution?' *European Law Journal*, 1: 303–7. Cambridge, Mass.: MIT Press.

Habermas, J. (1998) *The Inclusion of the Other: Studies in Political Theory*, in P. de Greiff and C. Cronin (eds), Cambridge, MA: MIT Press.

Habermas, J. and Derrida, J. (2003) '"Unsere erneuerung" [Our renewal?]', *Frankfurter Allgemeine Zeitung*, 31 May.

Héritier, A. (1999) 'Elements of democratic legitimation in Europe: an alternative perspective', *Journal of European Public Policy*, 6(2): 269–82.

Hume, D. [1882] (1752) *Idea of a Perfect Commonwealth. Essays moral, political and literary.* London: Longmans Green.

Jachtenfuchs, M., Diez, T. and Jung, S. (1998) 'Which Europe? Conflicting models of a legitimate European political order', *European Journal of International Relations*, 4: 409–45.

Joerges, C. (1999) '"Good governance" through comitology?', in C. Joerges and E. Vos (eds), *EU Committees: Social Regulation, Law and Politics.* Oxford: Hart. pp. 311–38.

Kant, I. [1970] (1796) 'Perpetual peace: a philosophical sketch', in I. Kant's *Political Writings.* Caembridge: Cambridge University Press. pp. 93–130.

Keohane, R.O. (1995) 'Hobbes's dilemma and institutional change in world politics: sovereignty in international society', in H.-H. Holm and G. Sorensen (eds), *Whose World Order? Uneven Globalization and the End of the Cold War.* Boulder, CO: Westview Press. pp. 165–86.

Keohane, R.O. and Hoffmann, S. (1991) *The New European Community: Decisionmaking and Institutional Change.* Boulder: Westview Press.

Key Jr., O.V. (1961) *Public Opinion and American Democracy.* New York: Knopf.

Kohler-Koch, B. (2000) 'Framing: the bottleneck of constructing legitimate institutions', *Journal of European Public Policy*, 7(4): 513–31.

Kohler-Koch, B. and Eising, R. (eds) (1999) *The Transformation of Governance in the European Union.* London: Routledge.

Krasner, S.D. (1999) *Sovereignty: Organized Hypocrisy.* Princeton: Princeton University Press.

Kymlicka, W. (1995) *Multicultural Citizenship: A Liberal Theory of Minority Rights.* Oxford: Oxford University Press.

Laffan, B. (1996) 'The politics of identity and political order in Europe', *Journal of Common Market Studies*, 34(1): 81–102.

Lehning, P. (1997) 'Pluralism, contractarianism and Europe', in P. Lehning and A. Weale (eds), *Citizenship, Democracy and Justice in the New Europe.* London: Routledge. pp. 107–24.

Lenaerts, K. and Desomer, M. (2002) 'New models of constitution-making in Europe: the quest for legitimacy', *Common Market Law Review*, 39: 1217–53.

Levi, M. (1998) *Consent, Dissent and Patriotism.* New York: Cambridge University Press.

Lijphart, A. (1999) *Patterns of Democracy: Government Forms and Performance in Thirty-Six Countries.* Buy. New Haven: Yale University Press.

Lindberg, L.N. and Scheingold, S.A. (1970) *Europe's Would-Be Polity: Patterns of Change in the European Community.* Englewood Cliffs, NJ: Prentice-Hall.

Lipset, S.M. and Rokkan, S. (eds) (1967) *Party Systems and Voter Alignments.* New York: Free Press.

Lodge, J. (1994) 'Transparency and democratic legitimacy', *Journal of Common Market Studies*, 32(3): 343–68.

Lodge, J. (1996) 'The European Parliament', in S.S. Andersen and K.A. Eliassen (eds), *The European Union: How Democratic Is It?* London: Sage. pp. 187–214.

Lord, C. and Beetham, D. (2001) 'Legitimizing the EU: is there a "post-parliamentary basis" for its legitimation?', *Journal of Common Market Studies*, 39(3): 443–62.

Lord, C. and Magnette, P. (2004) 'E Pluribus Unum? Creative disagreement about legitimacy in the EU', *Journal of Common Market Studies*, 42(1): 183–202.

Luhman, N. (1969) *Legitimation Durch Verfahren.* Darmstadt: Luchterhand.

MacCormick, N. (1994) 'The Maastricht-Urteil: sovereignty now', *European Law Journal*, 1: 259–66.

MacCormick, N. (1999) *Questioning Sovereignty. Law. State, and Nation in the European Commonwealth .* Oxford: Oxford University Press.

Magnette, P. (2000) 'Towards "accountable independence"? Parliamentary controls of the European Central Bank and the rise of a new democratic model', *European Law Journal*, 6(4): 326–40.

Magnette, P. (2001) 'European governance and civic participation: can the European Union be politicised?', in C. Joerges, Y. Meny and J.H.H. Weiler (eds), *Symposium: Responses to the European Commission's White Paper on Governance.* Available online at: www.jeanmonnetprogram. org/papers/01/01061/html.

Majone, G. (1990) 'Preservation of cultural diversity in a federal system: the role of the regions', in M. Tushnet (ed.), *Comparative Constitutional Federalism. Europe and America.* New York: Greenwood Press. pp. 67–76.

Majone, G. (1994) 'The rise of the regulatory state in Europe', *West European Politics*, 17: 77–101.

Majone, G. (1998a) 'Europe's "democratic deficit": the question of standards', *European Law Journal*, 4(1): 5–28.

Majone, G. (1998b) 'State, market and regulatory competition: lessons for the integrating world economy', in A. Moravcsik (ed.), *Centralization or Fragmentation? Europe Facing the Challenges of Deepening, Diversity, and Democracy.* New York: Council on Foreign Relations. pp. 94–123.

Mancini, G.F. (1991) 'The making of the constitution of Europe', in R.O. Keohane and S. Hoffmann (eds), *The New European Community*. Boulder: Westview Press. pp. 177–94.

Manin, B. (1987) 'On legitimacy and political deliberation', *Political Theory*, 15: 338–68.

McKay, D. (2001) *Designing Europe – Comparative Lessons From the Federal Experience*. Oxford: Oxford University Press.

Michelman, F.I. (2000) 'W(h)ither the constitution?', *Cardozo Law Review*, 21: 1063–83.

Mill, J.S. [1958] (1861) *Considerations on Representative Government*. New York: Liberal Arts Press.

Moravcsik, A. (2002) 'In defence of the "democratic deficit": reassessing legitimacy in the European Union', *Journal of Common Market Studies*, 40(4): 603–24.

Mény, Y. (2002) 'De la démocratie en Europe: old concepts and new challenges', *Journal of Common Market Studies*, 41(1): 1–13.

Naurin, D. (2004) 'Transparency and legitimacy', in L. Dobson and A. Føllesdal (eds), *Political Theory and the European Constitution*. London: Routledge. pp. 139–50.

Neunreither, K. (1994) 'The democratic deficit of the European Union: towards closer cooperation between the European Parliament and the national Parliaments', *Government and Opposition*, 29: 299–314.

Nino, C.S. (1996) *The Constitution of Deliberative Democracy*. New Haven, Conn.: Yale University Press.

Norman, W.J. (1994) 'Towards a philosophy of federalism', in J. Baker (ed.), *Group Rights*. Toronto: University of Toronto Press. pp. 79–100.

Norris, P. (ed.) (1999a) *Critical Citizens: Global Support for Democratic Government*. Oxford: Oxford University Press.

Norris, P. (1999b) 'Institutional explanations for political support', in P. Norris (ed), *Critical Citizens: Global Support for Democratic Government*. Oxford: Oxford University Press. pp. 217–35.

North, D. (1990) *Institutions, Institutional Change and Economic Performance*. Cambridge: Cambridge University Press.

Papcke, S. (1992) 'Who needs European identity and what could it be?', in B. Nelson, D. Roberts and W. Veit (eds), *The Idea of Europe: Problems of National and Transnational Identity*. New York: Berg. pp. 61–72.

Pettit, P. (1997) *Republicanism: A Theory of Freedom and Government*. Oxford: Clarendon Press.

Rawls, J. (1971) *A Theory of Justice*. Cambridge, Mass.: Harvard University Press.

Rawls, J. (1993) *Political Liberalism*. New York: Columbia University Press.

Riker, W.H. (2003) 'Social choice theory and constitutional democracy', in T. Christiano (ed.), *Philosophy and Democracy*. Oxford: Oxford University Press. pp. 161–94.

Rousseau, J.-J. [1782] (1917) *A lasting peace through the federation of Europe (and the state of war)*, C.E. Vaughan (ed.), London: Constable.

Rothstein, B. (1998) *Just Institutions Matter: The Moral and Political Logic of the Universal Welfare State. Theories of Institutional Design*. Cambridge: Cambridge University Press.

Saint-Pierre, A.C. [1713] (1986) *Project pour render la paix perpjtuelle en Europe (Project to make peace perpetual in Europe)*. Paris: Fayard.

Sbragia, A.M. (1999) 'Politics in the European Union', in G.A. Almond, R.J. Dalton and Jr. G. Bingham Powell (eds), *European Politics Today*. New York: Longman. pp. 469–520.

Scharpf, F.W. (1988) 'The joint decision trap: lessons from German federalism and European integration', *Public Administration*, 66(3): 239–78.

Scharpf, F.W. (1997a) 'Economic integration, democracy and the welfare state', *Journal of European Public Policy*, 4(1): 18–36.

Scharpf, F.W. (1997b) *Games Real Actors Play: Actor-Centered Institutionalism in Policy Research*. Boulder, Co: Westview Preses.

Scharpf, F.W. (1999) *Governing in Europe: Effective and Democratic?* Oxford: Oxford University Press.

Schattschneider, E.E. (1960) *The Semi-Sovereign People: A Realist's View of Democracy in America*. New York: Holt, Rinehart and Winston.

Schmitt, H. and Thomassen, J. (eds) (1999) *Political Representation and Legitimacy in the European Union*. Oxford: Oxford University Press.

Schmitter, P.C. (2000) *How to Democratize the European Union – and Why Bother?* London: Rowman.

Schmitter, P.C. (2004) 'Is federalism for Europe a solution or a problem: Tocqueville inverted, perverted or subverted?', in L. Dobson and A. Føllesdal, (eds), *Political Theory and the European Constitution*. London: Routledge. pp. 10–22.

Schumpeter, J.A. [1976] (1943) *Capitalism, Socialism and Democracy*. London: Allen and Unwin.

Sieberson, S.C. (2004) 'The proposed European Union constitution – will it eliminate the EU's democratic deficit?', *Columbia Journal of European Law*, 10(2): 173–264.

Sinnott, R. (1995) 'Bringing public opinion back in', in O. Niedermayer and R. Sinnot (eds), *Public Opinion and Internationalized Governance*. Oxford: Oxford University Press. pp. 11–32.

Skach, C. (2005) 'We, the peoples? Constitutionalizing the European Union', *Journal of Common Market Studies,* 41(1): 149–70.

Smismans, S. (2004) *Law, Legitimacy and European Governance. Functional Participation in Social Regulation.* Oxford: Oxford University Press.

Smith, A.D. (1991) *National Identity.* London: Penguin.

Stepan, A. (1999) 'Federalism and democracy: beyond the US model', *Journal of Democracy,* 10: 19–34.

Taylor, M. (1987) *The Possibility of Cooperation.* Cambridge: Cambridge University Press.

van der Eijk, C. and Franklin, M. (eds) (1996) *Choosing Europe? The European Electorate and National Politics in the Face of Union.* Ann Arbor: University of Michigan Press.

Waldron, J. (1998) 'Judicial review and the conditions of democracy', *Journal of Political Philosophy,* 6: 335–55.

Wallace, H. (1993) 'Deepening and widening: problems of legitimacy for the EC', in S. Garcia (ed.), *European Identity and the Search for Legitimacy.* London: Pinter. pp. 95–105.

Weale, A. (1999) *Democracy.* New York: St. Martin's Press.

Weiler, J.H.H. (1991) 'The transformation of Europe', *Yale Law Review,* 100: 1–81.

Weiler, J.H.H. (1995) 'The state "Uber Alles" demos and telos in the German Maastricht Decision', Jean Monnet Working Paper no. 6/1995, Harvard University. Available online at: http://www.jeanmon netprogram.org/papers/95/9506ind.html, accessed 1 September 2006.

Weiler, J.H.H. (1999) *The Constitution of Europe.* Cambridge: Cambridge University Press.

Weiler, J.H.H. (2001) 'Federalism and constitutionalism: Europe's Sonderweg', *The Federal Vision: Legitimacy and Levels of Governance in the US and the EU.* Comments based on version published as Harvard Jean Monnet Working paper 10/00, in K. Nicolaidis and R. Howse (eds) Oxford: Oxford University Press. pp. 54–73.

Wessels, W. (1999) 'Comitology as a research subject: a new legitimacy mix?', in C. Joerges and E. Vos (eds), *EU Committees: Social Regulation, Law and Politics.* Oxford: Hart. pp. 259–69.

Wessels, W. and Diedrichs, U. (1999) 'The European Parliament and EU legitimacy', in T. Banchoff and M.P. Smith (eds), *Legitimacy and the European Union.* London: Routledge. pp. 134–52.

PART III

Politics and Policy-Making in the European Union

17

Overview: The European Union, Politics and Policy-Making

HELEN WALLACE AND WILLIAM WALLACE

THE HISTORICAL CONTEXT OF EU POLICY STUDIES

Politics within the European Union (EU), historically at least, has been mainly focused around the processes of building common policies and collective legislation. Analyses of these policy processes thus largely provide the basis for the varied interpretations in the academic literature of the overall character of EU politics, including its technocratic features and limited democratic mechanisms. As a partial and multi-layered polity without a clear centre of government the EU lacks many of the dimensions of contestation and democratic engagement that arise in a state where issues relating to the formation, roles, and responsibilities of government across society are continually present. In addition, the geopolitics of the foundational period, together with the pressures of post-war economic construction, served to suppress 'normal' politics on some policy issues. Only recently has the scope of EU politics broadened to incorporate 'constitutional' issues and more

explicit choices among societal preferences, such that, as Hix argues in Chapter 6, scholars can now increasingly identify the range of political features familiar from inside individual states.

The longer history of what we now know as the European Union (EU) is one of more segmented political contestation and engagement on specific policy issues – among states, within states, and across states. Somewhat frustratingly, we lack a comprehensive picture of how these segmented policy processes in the EU have developed over time. Instead we rely on partial accounts of individual policy areas, many based on thick description, interwoven with overarching assessments of the political essence of European integration, but many working from a narrow base of empirical observation. These include, on the one hand, analyses that seek to identify cumulative patterns of policy-making, and, on the other hand, interpretations of particular episodes or periods as crucially framing the development of the EU system. Striking examples of the latter include commentaries on the impacts of the 'empty chair crisis' of 1965–6 and of the alleged 'Eurosclerosis' of the 1970s on the politics of the then European Economic Community (EEC) (Hoffmann 1966; Haas 1975; Giersch 1985). But there remain many gaps in our knowledge of the 1960s, 1970s and early 1980s for which we have a much sparser analytical literature than the richer literature on subsequent periods.

Even the more recent scholarship of the last 15 years or so shows that the field has been subject to fashions both empirical and analytical, an obstacle to cross-temporal and cross-sectoral analysis. As regards policy areas, there have been successive waves of interest in, notably, the single market, then the environment and regional policy, latterly foreign policy, employment policy and migration issues, and so forth, as successive generations of scholars and students responded to topically interesting public policy dilemmas. Other policy domains remain much less well documented – agricultural policy is the most telling example. In addition, our knowledge of cross-country variations is patchy as regards either how EU policy issues were faced or how EU policies were implemented, hardly surprisingly given the linguistic and operational challenges of examining systematically all member states in an EU with expanding membership. A further challenge for scholars has been the differential availability of hard data, whether quantitative or qualitative. Differences in what material was most easily available produced a kind of methodological bias towards emphasizing the activities of the Commission and later the European Parliament and against investigating Council negotiations or the deliberations inside member governments – a crucial gap given the need to understand the nuances of bargaining among member governments. For the period up to the mid-1970s the ground is beginning to be covered by historians, now able to access original sources directly (see, for example, Knudsen 2001, 2006).[1] From the mid-1990s the situation has changed radically in that new rules and practices as regards 'transparency' are making more original documents available in real time. This opens up new opportunities for intellectual partnerships between historians and political scientists to reveal a more comprehensive picture (see, for example, Dinan 2006; Palayret et al. 2006).

Four other points need to be emphasized about the literature on EU policy-making. First, there is a recurrent fascination with micro-political processes within an institutional setting that many commentators regard as *sui generis* because of the experimental character of EU integration. Successive rounds of treaty reform have encouraged interest in fine-grained variations in institutional procedures. Second, political analyses of EU policy-making have paid a great deal of attention to the emergence of a whole new system of European law which bites into the legal and political systems of the member states (Mattli and Slaughter 1998; Stone Sweet and Caporaso 1998; Alter 2001).[2] This invites, however, an emphasis on the formal application of policies and a neglect of the substantive impacts of EU policies; implementation studies remain underdeveloped, despite some excellent exceptions (Siedentopf and Ziller 1988; Börzel 2003; Falkner et al. 2005). Third, economic analysis is not systematically incorporated into EU policy studies – with some notable exceptions as regards the impacts of the liberal and neoliberal turns in economic ideas which framed the development of the single market and the single currency (Pelkmans and Winters 1988; Tsoukalis 1997; McNamara 1998). More could be done to bring relevant insights from economic analysis into the assessment of EU policy-making, including its sometimes perverse economic outcomes. Fourth, despite the valuable and growing literature on Europeanization or EU-ization of national policy processes (Cowles et al. 2001; Graziano and Vink, forthcoming; and Chapter 25 in this volume) we still need to look harder at the bottom-up pictures of how national systems 'domesticate' EU policies, coopting and instrumentalizing them for domestic purposes (Wallace 1999).

ONE POLICY MODE OR SEVERAL?

Policy-making in the EU is not carried out through a single and predominant process but rather through several different and contrasting policy modes.[3] These different policy modes – we identify five – provide us with a helpful framework for commenting on the evolving literature on the subject. These modes are the product of: evolution and experimentation over time in the EU; changes in national policy-making processes; and developments in economic and social behaviour. Each policy mode reveals differences in the roles and behaviour of the various key actors, in their variety of approaches to policy dilemmas, and in the diversity of instruments used. In this chapter we deliberately do not locate these modes along a spectrum from supranational to intergovernmental, which is, in our view, an overly simplistic dichotomy.

In the context of the EU there are of course further complications: on the one hand, the debate continues about where to strike the balance between EU policy powers and those of the member states; and, on the other hand, EU policy-making takes place increasingly in the shadow of globalization. These two issues make it harder to separate out the EU processes clearly from the multi-layered processes within states and across the global system. Thus policy-makers in EU member states continually face choices about which policy forum to use for which policy purpose and they have to manage the connections – both political and practical – among these different fora. In so far as EU studies has become a specialist field, the scholarship probably understates and under-researches this 'forum-shopping' dimension (Jupille 2004, Jupille and Snidal 2005).

The five varied modes of EU policy-making which we identify are:

- a traditional Community method;
- the EU regulatory mode;
- the EU distributional mode;
- policy coordination; and
- intensive transgovernmentalism.

These modes can be found across the range of 'day-to-day' policy-making in the EU. They exclude the domain of constitutive politics or system-shaping as regards the overall political and institutional architecture of the EU,

aspects of which are covered in Part II of this volume. The five modes provide a useful way of setting out the different analytical frames that have developed to assess EU policy-making over the years, since few studies range across all five. Most studies in practice focus on the policy-making processes associated with one or other mode and, hence, their overall conclusions may not hold good across all modes of policy-making or across all substantive policy domains. Indeed it is part of our argument that the different policy modes which we observe empirically are influenced by the functional differences between policy domains, as indeed is typical of policy-making within states. It should, however, be noted that these policy modes coexist, vary over time and are not stable. Within all the modes we find examples of evolution and experimentation, as well as instances of both 'older' and 'newer' forms of governance.[4] The same policy domain may be addressed by more than one mode or may shift between modes. Moreover, there is no predominant developmental trend towards one mode rather than another.

A TRADITIONAL COMMUNITY METHOD

Much of the early literature on west European integration and the EU took as its starting point that a single predominant Community method of policy-making was emerging. This is a strong theme in the neofunctionalist writings, notably of Haas ([1958] 2004) and Lindberg (1963) and those who built on their analyses. Because of its early priority on the agenda of the original EEC, the common agricultural policy (CAP) set the template for this policy mode. This was defined by the late 1960s broadly as follows:

- a strong role delegated to the European Commission in policy design, policy-brokering, policy execution, and managing the interface with 'abroad';
- an empowering role for the Council of Ministers through strategic bargaining and package deals;

- a locking-in, or *engrenage*, of stakeholders, in this case the agricultural interests, through a form of cooption into a European process which offered them better rewards than national politics;
- an engagement of national agencies as the subordinated operating arms of the agreed common regime;
- a distancing from the influence of elected representatives at the national level, and only limited opportunities for the European Parliament (EP) to impinge;
- periodic, but defining, intrusion by the European Court of Justice (ECJ) or later the Court of First Instance (CFI) to reinforce the legal authority of the Community regime; and
- the resourcing of the policy on a collective basis, as an expression of sustained 'solidarity'.

This is the template which was widely argued to constitute a form of 'supranational' policymaking, in which powers – and to some extent loyalties – were transferred from the national to the EU level. It was structured by a kind of functionalist logic, in which those concerned with a particular policy sector could be encapsulated and build cross-national allegiances, but mediated by a form of politics in which political and economic elites colluded to further their various, and often different, interests. Other policy domains were soon identified as emerging examples of a similar mode of operation, notably competition policy and external trade policy, with some early commentary on the failure of other sectors to develop a similar dynamic, such as the case of stalled efforts to develop a common transport policy along similar lines (Lindberg 1963).

Interestingly this notion of a distinctive Community method came to set a frame of reference not only in the academic literature but also in the discourse of practitioners. Over the years many officials, especially in the Commission, and many advocates of closer political integration have used the phrase 'Community method' as shorthand for their aspirations to develop strong and clearly supranational forms of collective policymaking and as a kind of benchmark for

assessing achievement. Thus, for example, the Commission's White Paper on Governance of 2001 contains many allusions to the Community method as the preferred target in other policy domains from those which we have identified above. In the academic literature it is only rather recently that the merits and feasibility of extending the traditional Community method to other policy areas have begun to be systematically questioned, as in the recent overviews by Dehousse (2005) and Majone (2005).

There were, however, always critics of the underlying analysis. Thus the classical dichotomy of 'supranationalism' vs 'intergovernmentalism' drew much of its initial force from two arguments about the limitations of the original Community method. The first was that it might hold good for day-to-day and mundane decision-making, but that it would not stand up to the strain of dealing with 'high politics' on issues where there was fierce contestation among member governments, the core of Hoffmann's (1966) argument for recognizing the obstinacy of intergovernmentalism. The second argument was that the collusion on which such common policies were based also generated what Scharpf (1988) called a 'joint-decision trap', which set high obstacles to the revision of common policy once agreed, notably because in a regime of explicit or implicit unanimity rules there is an in-built bias against policy reform. This argument of course draws much empirical force from the repeated difficulties of reforming the CAP away from the foundational bargains of the 1960s in this field, a view that also finds further support from recent accounts of the lingering footprints of the Luxembourg Compromise in the fields of agricultural and trade policies, where forms of veto power persist (Meunier 2000; Hayes-Renshaw and Wallace 2006a). The criticisms gain even greater strength from the near consensus among economists that the CAP turned out to be an economically inefficient and market-distorting allocation of resources (for a recent commentary see Sapir et al. 2004). They also accord with the wider analysis by Milward (2000) of the limits to supranationalism.

How far the notion of a clearly supranational Community method, let alone its idealized version, accorded with reality, even in the case of agriculture, remains a matter for debate. There is actually a rather thin academic literature to which we can turn. There are few studies even from the early days of the EEC, apart from Lindberg's (1963) pioneering study and the studies by Averyt (1977) and Rosenthal (1975), although historians are beginning to fill out the picture for the early years (Knudsen 2001). Some political analyses (Rieger 2005; Roederer-Rynning 2006) suggest that the real story may be different, and one in which national politics determined rather more of the outcomes than the tale of supranational entrepreneurship implies. On the contrary these studies produce a picture in which in various ways national political and policy systems have 'domesticated' the CAP and contributed to the 'joint-decision-trap'. Furthermore it is striking that many of the institutional studies of EU policy-making that seek to characterize the evolving politics exclude data from the agricultural sector. Thus, for example, most studies of the European Parliament and of its increasing political impact leave aside the CAP case, since the EP still lacks legislative and budgetary powers in this domain. Nonetheless there is some evidence of changing policy dynamics even as regards the CAP. Recent scholarship (Roederer-Rynning 2003a) suggests that the redefinition of some agricultural issues as 'regulatory' – the safety of agricultural products or the environmental impacts of production – are beginning to alter the political and institutional factors at work. Interestingly, the common fisheries policy (CFP), which was intended to imitate the CAP regime and which included strong delegation of powers to manage quotas, does not fit the template very well either and moreover has had perverse economic and ecological outcomes (Lequesne 2004, 2005).

We should also note that competition policy, at least as recently 'modernized', no longer fits the template above of the traditional Community method, in that it now rests on a less overtly hierarchical system centred on the Commission than hitherto. Nonetheless some commentators argue that the Commission retains strong powers under the new networked arrangements with national competition authorities, but nowadays in a form of steered partnership that differs from the traditional Community method (Wilks 2005). It would perhaps be more sensible, given the modernization reforms, to consider competition policy as an example of the regulatory mode of EU policy-making rather than a version of the traditional Community method (see Chapter 19 in this volume). External trade policy perhaps remains a more faithful example of the traditional Community method, in which the Commission retains a strong role delegated to it by the principals in the member states (Meunier and Nicolaidis 1999; Woolcock 2005). Here too, however, there is a continued impact of the joint-decision-trap as regards the CAP, as well as evidence of fierce contestation on some issues among member governments that constrains the delegated power of the Commission (Meunier 2000, 2005). These observations indicate a gap in the scholarship on EU policy-making as regards what was once viewed as the traditional Community method. They also suggest that the stylized version of it needs to be modified.

It is also striking that there are few recent examples of new common policies being introduced according to versions of the traditional Community method, with a centralized and hierarchical institutional process, with clear delegation of powers and aimed at 'positive integration'. The single currency is perhaps the most apt example, although in this case the delegated institutional powers are centred on the European Central Bank (ECB) rather than on the Commission, and they apply only to the monetary strand of EMU and not to the economic strand (McNamara 2005). This form of delegation or partial delegation to function-specific operational agencies, rather than to the Commission, may be an emerging trend, which would benefit from cross-cutting analysis. Other interesting examples seem to be emerging in the fields of justice and home affairs (the instances of Europol and Eurojust) and of common foreign and security policy (the instance of the new European Armaments Agency).

Three concluding observations can be made on the nature of the politics relating to policies addressed by the traditional Community method. First, the politics concerned typically bifurcate: on the one hand, privileged techno-cratic management of day-to-day policy, both through EU institutions and in the member states, where the EU framework insulates the policy domain from 'normal' domestic politics; but, on the other hand, strategic bargaining among competing national interests on the core issues. Here, Peterson's (1995) account of different patterns of decision carries particular force, with its distinction between different types of decision: history-making, policy-setting, and day-to-day. Second, the democra-tic dimension is thin, given that the typical legal instruments of policy are directly applic-able regulations and decisions that do not need national transposition and that the powers of the EP are negligible (Meunier 2003; Roederer-Rynning 2003b). Third, the traditional Community method is being diluted over time by changes in the relevant policy regimes rather than reinforced.

THE EU REGULATORY MODE

During the 1980s, as the single European market developed, so an alternative policy mode emerged (Cowles 1994; Majone 1996; Young 2005; Chapter 19 in this volume). Its roots went back to the ambition of the Treaty of Rome to remove barriers between the national economies of the member states, building on the establishment of the customs union. Much of its driving force came from the international economy, which had made the search for competitiveness in both domestic and international markets critical to the ability of firms to adjust and to prosper. Within the US there were already traditions of both public regulation and private self-regulation that showed an alternative approach to market management. West Europeans began to exper-iment within countries and then collectively in

what was self-consciously called a 'new approach' to regulation. It turned out that the EU arena was especially amenable to the further development of a regulatory mode of policy-making, described by some commen-tators as a form of 'negative integration' (Scharpf 1994). On his reading the EU pro-vided more readily a mechanism for develop-ing collective market-making regulation that would constrain national welfare preferences than the opportunity to promote positive social welfare-oriented interventions. The strength of the European legal process, the machinery for promoting technical coopera-tion, and the initial distance from parliamen-tary interference were all factors that encouraged this further, and helped national policy-makers to escape some of the con-straints of politics that had built rigidities into national policy-making. The EU was, it seemed, particularly well-fitted for generating an over-arching regulatory framework that could combine international standards with country differences. Indeed, so successful was its implantation that this European approach has sometimes been promoted as a model for the development of broader global regulation.

This regulatory mode has been character-ized by:

- the Commission as the architect and defender of regulatory objectives and rules, increasingly by reference to economic crite-ria, and often working with the stakehold-ers and communities of experts;
- the Council as a forum (at both ministerial and official levels) for agreeing minimum standards and the direction of harmoniza-tion (mostly upwards towards higher stan-dards), to be complemented by mutual recognition of national preferences and controls, operated differentially in individ-ual countries;
- the European Court of Justice (ECJ) and the Court of First Instance (CFI) as the means of ensuring that the rules are applied reasonably evenly, backed by the national courts for local application, and enabling individual stakeholders to have

access to redress in case of non-application or discrimination;

- the EP as one of several means for prompting the consideration of non-economic factors (environmental, regional, social, and so forth), with increasing impact as its legislative powers have grown, but little leverage on the implementation of regulation; and
- extensive opportunities for stakeholders, especially economic actors, but sometimes other societal actors, to be consulted about, and to influence, the shape and content of European market rules.

This regulatory mode has been applied most obviously to the development of a single market without internal barriers, notably as regards free movement of goods and capital – there has been rather less impact on free movement of services or of intra-EU labour. To the extent that the EU has an industrial policy, it is mostly by using regulatory prompts and the competition regime to leverage industrial adjustment, with quite far-reaching effects in some sectors, such as the network utilities (Coen and Héritier 2005). In so far as the EU has a social policy, some (notably Leibfried 2005) argue that it is mainly constructed through legal regulation and market-making. Much of what the EU has done in the environmental domain (Jordan 2002; Lenschow 2005; Chapter 21 in this volume) has been by regulating industrial or agricultural processes. A cognate issue – biotechnology and food safety – has been similarly treated by the EU as a regulatory policy (Pollack and Shaffer 2005). Moreover, the EU's interactions with the rest of the world are an external reflection of its internal approach to regulation and industrial adjustment, and also of preferences emerging from domestic politics, as is evident in policies on enlargement, association with other neighbours, and external trade.

The expansion of this regulatory mode has been remarkable. Efforts to analyse it account for a good deal of the literature on EU policy-making since the 1980s, as regulation came to displace the traditional Community method as the predominant policy paradigm. Studies of EU regulation have the advantage of being able to draw together commentaries on policy-making and legislative or legal techniques with accounts of the economics of market forces. The subjects covered by EU regulation also lent themselves to a wide variety of micro case studies and to the exploration of contending approaches to the study of politics and policy-making, as Young sets out clearly in Chapter 19. Thus, on the one hand, there is now a richer literature on the politics surrounding EU policy-making. Some of this explores the exploitation of new institutional opportunities, notably for the EP to engage with policy through its increased legislative powers and for the European legal system to develop at both national and EU levels. In addition, the literature now covers in much more detail the evolving roles of various kinds of interest groups and stakeholders operating within and across states – and sometimes across the boundaries between the EU and the wider international economy. On the other hand, the literature has also been enriched by debates about the patterns and roles of the networks, coalitions, and alliances involved in EU regulatory policy-making, as well as by related techniques of deliberation, expert involvement, and so forth. In this respect EU policy-making has also been able to import insights from the wider literature on public policy analysis, thus moving the study of the EU into a broader comparative frame.

Nonetheless – as in the case of the commentary on the traditional Community method – there are criticisms of some of the underlying analytical assumptions. Thus, liberal intergovernmentalists, starting from Moravcsik (1998), have argued that decisions to develop the single market have depended and continue to depend on strategic bargains among member governments. Rational-choice institutionalists more broadly have insisted that member governments remain conscious principals despite the convenience of delegating some powers to the EU system. In such readings of the process supranational actors, however active and activist, remain constrained by how far and under what conditions policy powers are delegated to them (Pollack 2003). Furthermore, studies of compliance in the member states (e.g. Falkner et al. 2005) reveal uneven patterns of compliance and implementation among the member states and thus quite differentiated national outcomes from what are intended to be collective regulatory regimes. Moreover, Scharpf (1994) leads those critics who insist that regulatory policy-making as a form of negative integration incorporates a neo-liberal bias in its intrinsic methodology in so far as it is better suited for removing market barriers than for introducing positive policies to deal with market distortions or market failures.

Over now some 20 years of intensive experience in developing the single market we can observe changes in and limits to this regulatory mode. Thus, for example, it appears to have been particularly successful in dealing with product regulation (the characteristics of the goods concerned), and less robust in dealing with process standards (i.e. how the goods are produced), where differences either in levels of economic development or in societal preferences intervene (Young and Wallace 2000; Sedelmeier 2005). The mode has also had rather less purchase on the regulation of services, financial products, and utilities, where instead we see moves towards more decentralized, less hierarchical versions of regulation, reflecting differences in the character of markets. Here we see across the member states, and indeed in the global economy, the emergence of more-or-less independent regulatory agencies at arm's length from governments, as well as emerging forms of self-regulation. Within the EU there are experiments with: new quasi-independent regulatory agencies, such as the European Food Safety Authority; steered partnerships of national agencies working with the Commission, notably in the case of competition policy; transnational consortia of national regulatory bodies, for example in the energy sector: and looser networks of self-regulation, notably as regards the operation of financial markets or corporate governance.

It is thus becoming much harder to identify the contours of a single coherent EU regulatory model. The literature, amply set out in Chapter 19, thus needs to be read carefully both for its insights into specific regulatory regimes and for a better understanding of both the functional and the political limits to this EU policy mode. These latter provide part of the explanation for increasing recourse within the EU to softer modes of governance, whether because of political resistance to delegated hard regulation or because of its inappropriateness for certain policy purposes. In addition – notably within the context of a stagnant European economy – the increased politicization of debates on EU regulation must be highlighted, as evident in the sharp controversy about the EU Services Directive during and following the referendum campaign in France in 2005 over the Constitutional Treaty.

THE EU DISTRIBUTIONAL MODE

Distributional issues have been persistently highly politicized in the EU policy process, both causing dissensus among those involved and generating lively debates about how to analyse them. One set of issues concerns the allocation of budgetary resources to different groups, sectors, regions, countries, or relative spending priorities. The other set of issues concerns the economic impacts of EU policies, sometimes planned, sometimes unintended, sometimes progressive, and sometimes regressive.

In the early years of the EEC the language of 'financial solidarity' entered the political discourse, albeit subject to contested interpretations. This led to the commitment to fund the CAP collectively, making farmers and the food industry both the clients of European funding and the beneficiaries of high prices, gaining transfers of resources from both taxpayers and consumers. A lighter version of collective funding was introduced into the common fisheries policy (Lequesne 2005), and the European Social Fund, created by the Treaty of Rome (EEC), funded certain employment measures. Subsequent decisions to fund internal policies were limited to providing partial support alongside national expenditures, but significantly introducing elements of conditionality as regards their utilization. Over time the EU has also developed funding mechanisms to support various external policies as a form of 'collective goods'.

From the foundational period there were always fierce discussions over the distribution of burdens and benefits of participation in the EU, notably in the events that led to the 1965–6 'empty chair crisis' and in the period following British accession in 1973, in which attention came to focus on the budget as a measure of the impacts of EU membership. Laffan and Lindner (2005) and Lindner (2005) provide accounts of the difficult choices about how to establish financial arrangements, for both revenue and expenditure, that would be equitable between and acceptable to member states. This persists as a highly contentious issue in the EU, now greatly complicated by the arrival of ten new and less prosperous member states, with the December 2005 bargain on the Financial Perspective for 2007–13 as the next case study awaiting scholarly dissection.

This distributional mode is hard to identify simply since it operates at two levels, on the one hand periodic strategic bargains, and on the other hand the routines of regime, programme and project management, characterized by:

- the Commission as the proposer of appropriations, regime managers for agricultural products, and manager of programmes and projects in other sectors, in partnership with local and regional authorities or relevant sectoral stakeholders and agencies, and using financial incentives to gain leverage and to apply conditionality;
- member governments in the European Council making periodic strategic bargains with some redistributive elements, and following these up in regular Council sessions, under pressure from local and regional authorities or other stakeholders, by agreeing to specific spending instruments;
- an EP with teeth as regards both annual budgetary appropriations (although significantly not as regards agricultural guarantee expenditure) and specific instruments, such that MEPs often constitute an additional source of pressure from territorial

politics in the regions or from particular stakeholder groups;
- local and regional authorities benefiting from policy empowerment as a result of engaging in the European arena, with, from 1993 onwards, the Committee of the Regions to represent their concerns, and many of them with their own offices in Brussels;
- some scope for other stakeholders to be similarly coopted into the EU policy process; and
- periodic recasting on an inter-institutional basis of the EU budget to spend proportionately less on agriculture and to invest more in, first, cohesion, and, later, R&D, then external policies, but subject to strong revenue constraints.

The expansion of spending beyond the CAP on internal policy objectives came first with the 1973 enlargement and then again in the mid-1980s, prompted by the development of the single market and the need to consider its distributional impacts in terms of relative wealth and poverty, again in the context of enlargement. The term 'cohesion' was added to the policy-makers' vocabulary, signalling a commitment to mitigate economic and social divergence, and to assist disadvantaged regions and social groups. This appeared to mark a shift from haphazard distribution of resources to a planned redistribution through designed transfers of resources. The main spending mechanism was through the 'structural funds', discussed in Chapter 20 of this volume, with a focus on particular 'cohesion' countries and working not only with national authorities but also with agencies dealing with training and employment creation and with regional or local authorities. Since 2000 and the adoption of the Lisbon Strategy, a further macro policy objective has been used to make the case for increased EU expenditure on research and development in order to foster innovation. Here the reasoning is about developing collective goods rather than about explicit redistribution. In the external policy field over the past decade or so EU spending has increased both on measures to back up collective policy commitments and on programmes or projects subject to conditionality in the hope of altering behaviour by the receiving partners, in Europe and in the various associated third countries. There is a rich recent literature, both conceptual and empirical, exploring the ways in which conditionality operates, notably in relation to the new member states and the neighbours (Hughes et al. 2004; Schimmelfennig and Sedelmeier 2005; Sedelmeier 2005). This touches on interesting issues about the impact of the EU in shaping both systemic and policy developments within individual countries.

It was the opening for more direct contacts between the European and the infranational levels of government, and the politics that developed around them, that provoked the term 'multi-level governance' to characterize the EU process more generally (Marks 1993). It rested on two essential points: first, that national central governments could no longer monopolize the contacts between the member state and the EU levels of policy-making; and, second, that engagement at the European level created an opportunity to reinforce a phenomenon of regionalization. The implication was that the domestic polities of the member states were being partially reshaped as a consequence of EU policy-making, in which financial incentives could apply leverage on new political relationships. The multi-level governance approach inverted much of the discussion on how the EU worked; it emphasized politics on the ground, and shifted attention away from the Brussels-centred and entrepreneur-oriented images of, respectively, the Community method and the regulatory mode. Emphasis on the likely variation of policy outcomes implied by multi-level governance also proved a useful prompt to careful and comparative analysis of what then happened on the ground at the local/regional or stakeholder levels (Hooghe 1996; Smith 1998; Börzel 2003).

The multi-level governance approach is, however, not without its critics. Allen (2005) argues that the evidence does not add up to support the multilevel governance and regional empowerment analyses, in that infranational activity should not be confused with impact, and that central governments from the

member states have remained in the driving seat, including by 'domesticating' EU funding programmes within member states for intra-country purposes. Thus, the alternative story is one of strategic bargaining about EU revenue and spending, which has become more contested in the light of the enlarged membership since May 2004, and with a sharper focus on the net positions of member states rather than regional redistribution, with vying coalitions of net payers, historical beneficiaries, and vocal claimants from the new member states. Not surprisingly, the strategic bargaining dimension has attracted interest from political scientists and economists interested in bargaining models, on which there is now a considerable literature which seeks to assess relative voting power in this field (Thomson et al. 2006; see also the journal *European Union Politics* and Chapter 8 in this volume). One difficulty with this literature is that it does not incorporate entirely convincingly the relevance of different voting rules or empirical practice. Unanimity remains the formal rule on macro-budgetary decisions, and consensus-building persists as the predominant process in the Council and European Council in this field, with the shadow of the veto always present on core agricultural spending decisions (Heisenberg 2005; Hayes-Renshaw and Wallace 2006a, b). A further shadow is cast by the constraining impact on public budgets of the Maastricht criteria to govern EMU, which is shifting attention away from spending programmes towards other kinds of policy measures. These issues are well covered in the analytical literature, as explained in Chapter 20, and will no doubt continue to provide fertile ground for further research, including studies of how these issues play out in those new member states with high expectations of EU budgetary receipts.

However, other aspects of the distributional issues facing the EU remain to be explored in more detail. Here we can detect signs of new trends that will need to be evaluated analytically and which may correspond to neither the strategic bargaining version nor the multi-level governance patterns in the literature of the past decade or so. In particular there is increasing interest in developing a notion of collective goods, that is, investment in collective capabilities rather than in supporting nationally-segmented spending programmes; and there are pressures for greater spending on external responsibilities. As regards the former, the most obvious candidates in terms of political salience are: spending to promote innovation, research and development, linked to the Lisbon Strategy, as well as job creation measures; and measures to support justice and home affairs policies. The other new budgetary development is the sharp increase in EU spending as a result of its foreign policy activities, now running at 8–10% of the EU budget. Here we can see the arguments shifting away from how funds are distributed to individual member states towards the issue of the proportions in which individual member states contribute to collective programmes beyond the borders of the EU and which member states might be free-riders. The institutional and policy processes for developing and managing all of these areas of spending differ considerably from those that prevail for either agricultural or structural/cohesion policies. All-in-all, therefore, the distributional mode is being subjected to interesting changes, and ones that go to the heart of politics as well as policy-making across the EU and inside countries.

POLICY COORDINATION

A key contrast in the study of European collaboration has long been drawn between the EU policy modes outlined above, characterized by forms of intended hierarchy, and what in shorthand might be described as the 'OECD technique', described sometimes as 'heterarchy'. The Organization for Economic Cooperation and Development, the Paris-based club of western industrialized countries, has since the early 1960s provided a loose-knit forum within which its members could appraise and compare each other's ways of developing public policies. In its early years the Commission used this technique to pioneer light forms of cooperation and coordination in fields adjacent to core EU economic competences in order to make the case for

more direct policy powers. Policy coordination was, however, usually introduced as a mechanism of transition from nationally rooted policy-making to a collective EU regime. Thus, for example, in the 1970s the Commission promoted increasingly systematic consultations among member governments on environmental issues which led to many Council agreements to adopt legislation, ahead of the Commission's success in making a persuasive case for the Single European Act to assign explicit legislative powers to the EU in this field. Similar efforts have been made over the years in domains such as research and development or education policy. A long-standing feature of the EU has also been the attempt to promote the coordination of macro- and micro-economic policies. In the field of macro-economic policy in particular policy coordination from the 1970s onwards became a regular tool in its own right within the EU, as well as in some broader international settings, such as the Group of Seven (G7), OECD, and the International Monetary Fund (Bryant and Portes 1987; Putnam and Bayne 1987).

For the advocates of a strong EU, policy coordination might be a useful starting point, but it used to be seen as very much a second-best resting point, not least because it might imply a weakening of the distinctive features of the EU. However, since the late 1990s in particular the use of policy coordination techniques within the EU has expanded considerably as regards the topics covered and the argued merits of their utility. In particular the Open Method of Coordination (OMC) has emerged as an apparently novel tool for addressing a variety of socio-economic policy issues. This development has spawned a growing literature, as Chapter 24 explains. Indeed, some would argue normatively (Scott and Trubek 2002) that there is a case for understanding this development as the emergence of a new form of post-modern governance. We should also note that within individual European and other 'western' countries techniques of benchmarking and systematic cross-country comparison have become rather widely used, often unilaterally, i.e. without being locked into any form of transnational discipline.

The approach rests a great deal on the mobilization of expertise, the accumulation of technical arguments in favour of developing a shared approach, and the promotion of modernization and innovation, nested in practices of policy-learning and deliberative governance – persuasion and example rather than negotiation. The typical features are:

- the Commission as the developer of networks of experts or epistemic communities, and of stakeholders and/or civil society;
- the involvement of 'independent' experts as promoters of ideas and techniques;
- the use of benchmarking techniques imported from business practice as a device for systematic comparison and the raising of standards of performance;
- the convening of high-level groups in the Council, in brain-storming or deliberative rather than negotiating mode, often designed to develop forms of peer pressure; and
- dialogue (sometimes) with specialist committees in the EP, as the advocates of particular approaches (drawing on the greater willingness of MEPs, in comparison with their national counterparts, to probe some policy predicaments in depth).

Three factors then served to emphasize policy coordination as a technique and to promote its image as an experimental 'new' mode of governance. One was the move to a form of EMU with a single monetary policy but only a coordinated macro-economic policy. This prompted efforts to move on from the looser form of pre-EMU policy coordination to forms of more intense and more structured policy coordination through the Broad Economic Policy Guidelines and so forth (Sapir et al. 2004). A second impulse came from the Lisbon Strategy, adopted in March 2000, which specifically identified and elevated the OMC as a distinctive policy technique, using 'soft' policy prescriptions to shape behaviour, rather than 'hard' and often legally binding methods to induce compliance. OMC was to be used specifically in those fields of socio-economic (mainly micro-economic)

policy-making where the EU lacked – and was unlikely to gain – strong delegated policy powers. OMC, it was argued, could be a way of engaging member governments, relevant stakeholders, and civil society in iterative comparison, benchmarking, and continuous coordination as ends in themselves (Rodrigues et al. 2002; Rodrigues 2003; Kok 2004; Sapir et al. 2004). A third factor was the increasing recognition of cross-country variations in policy and economic performance, which made it harder to argue for uniform policy templates that would be applicable across the whole of the EU, especially an EU that would become even more diverse after the 2004 enlargement. These last two points are of particular relevance in the enlarged EU, where there is scope for further analytical work, for example, to compare policy coordination as a technique with the incentive- and conditionality-based techniques associated with spending programmes (see, for example, Schimmelfennig and Sedelmeier 2005).

The employment policy domain (Rhodes 2005) illustrates particularly well the debates and features that have propelled OMC as a technique. Here the main thrust of EU involvement is to compare national, local, and sectoral experiences of labour market adaptation. The object is not so much to establish a single common framework, but rather to share experience and to encourage the spread of best practice. In the now extensive literature and commentary on OMC we find hugely varying assessments of its effectiveness. These range between considerable scepticism as to the value of so 'soft' a form of joint policy-making, as argued in Chapter 24, and great enthusiasm for its success – and further potential – as a mechanism for extending EU influences into parts of the domestic policy processes of the member states where there remain deep obstacles to formal transfers of policy competences to the EU. Falkner et al. (2005) and Zeitlin et al. (2005) provide further insights into experience so far.

Judging between these competing assessments is especially hard against the backcloth of a sluggish European economy where causality and outputs are particularly hard to pin down. Many of the changes being sought are either to social behaviour or dependent on the recasting of domestic political bargains in the hope of improving economic performance. In this latter case the contested politics lie within countries rather than at the EU negotiating table. Enlargement of the EU also impinges, since the heterogeneity that it adds to the range of comparisons and indicators of socio-economic reforms makes the notion of common EU-wide policy templates particularly implausible – and perhaps inappropriate. A complication of these policy coordination techniques is that they diffuse and disperse political arguments and responsibilities among the relevant policy actors, making it harder to pin down where political 'ownership' rests or how to exercise political accountability. In so far as changing social behaviour is a key variable, it is also critically important for scholars to find ways of identifying any such change as a clear outcome of the use of policy coordination techniques – no small methodological challenge, and one which requires cross-temporal as well cross-country comparison. As regards OMC and the Lisbon Strategy these are still early days for achieving clarity, as is evident when one considers the timelines for judging the slow evolution of both the single market and the single currency projects, both under development since the 1960s.

INTENSIVE TRANSGOVERNMENTALISM

The literature on EU politics and policy-making is permeated by the alleged sharp dichotomy between supranationalism and intergovernmentalism, which we suggested earlier may be overly simplistic. It follows that we also argue that there is a compelling case for reassessing how intergovernmentalism is characterized, taking into account the evolution of several policy processes visible within the EU system. Throughout the history of the EU there have been examples of policy cooperation which have depended mainly on interaction between the relevant national policy-makers, and with relatively little of the classical treaty-based involvement of the EU institutions. This has been especially so in domains that touch sensitive issues of state sovereignty, and that lie beyond the core competences of the Union for market-making and market-regulating. Generally such cooperation has been described as 'intergovernmentalism' – by both practitioners and commentators. It has been widely regarded as a weaker and much less constraining form of policy development by both analysts and advocates of stronger EU policy regimes.

Nonetheless in the early 1970s policy cooperation did develop in two domains in particular – monetary and foreign policies – largely outside the orthodox EU institutional framework. In both domains heads of state or government were important actors. In some cases cooperation has been developed in groupings smaller than the whole EU membership. Franco–German bilateral cooperation was at some moments an important catalyst of policy advancement and latterly in the case of defence there was a Franco–British impulse (Morgan and Bray 1984; Simonian 1985; Howorth and Keeler 2003). From the mid-1980s until the mid-1990s, some EU governments chose to develop policy cooperation completely outside the EU framework so as to establish a common external border with liberalized internal borders through the Schengen Agreements, deliberately excluding some EU partners from the initial regime (Den Boer 1996). A recent example in a similar vein is the Prüm Convention, signed in May 2005 among only seven EU member states to develop cross-border cooperation to combat terrorism, crime, and illegal migration (Balzacq et al. 2006).

The term 'intergovernmental' does not, however, really capture the character of this policy mode in and around the EU, or at least not as used in the typical dichotomy in EU studies between 'supranational' and 'intergovernmental'. It resonates too much of cooperation among governments in many other international organizations, in which the intensity of cooperation is quite limited and the levels of mutual commitment and of collective discipline are low. In any case within international relations, Keohane and Nye (1974) coined the term 'transgovernmental' to identify patterns of relationships among countries that were not in the hands of foreign ministries and diplomatic services as the gatekeepers. As Webb (1983) argued, this term had considerable attraction for scholars of European integration, notably because of the extent to which the EU processes involved directly domestic policy actors and provided some opportunity structures for transnational coalition-building, sometimes by passing the traditional gatekeepers. We adopt the term 'intensive transgovernmentalism' here, however, for a more precise reason, namely to indicate that some of these transgovernmental relationships may also, on the one hand, fall outside the classical EU procedures and structures and, on the other hand, develop a momentum, an intensity of interactions, and a density of structured and productive collaboration. Some of our examples include traditional foreign or defence policy actors, while others include domestic policy actors. In these cases EU member governments have been prepared cumulatively to commit themselves to rather extensive engagements, some joint actions and some collective disciplines, but have judged the full EU institutional framework or the full EU membership to be inappropriate or unacceptable, or not yet ripe for adoption.

Intensive transgovernmentalism within the broad EU framework is characterized by:

- policy entrepreneurship from some national capitals and the active involvement of the European Council in setting the overall direction of policy;
- the predominance of the Council of Ministers (or an equivalent forum of national ministers) in consolidating cooperation;
- the limited or marginal role of the Commission;
- the exclusion of the EP and the ECJ from the circle of involvement;
- the involvement of a distinct circle of key national policy-makers;
- the adoption of special arrangements for managing cooperation, in particular the Council Secretariat;

- the opaqueness of the process, to national parliaments and citizens; but
- the capacity on occasion to deliver substantive joint policy.

Variants of intensive transgovernmentalism also occur outside the broad EU framework, sometimes on policy issues that are connected to EU policy arenas, and are characterized by:

- typically the use of conventions or separate treaties under international law as the primary legal instruments;
- sometimes a membership different from that of the EU (which can involve some non-EU member states, as was the case with Schengen);
- the central role being played by ministers and officials in rather closed circles of cooperation, and sometimes also other forms of inter-agency cooperation, with somewhat *ad hoc* secretariats, as for Schengen and Prüm;
- very limited access for national parliaments, though varied according to the constitutional rules of individual countries, and usually no transnational parliamentary forum, though the now residual WEU retains its parliamentary assembly;[5] and
- similarly limited opportunities for the involvement of societal groups or stakeholders, though again varied according to the constitutional rules of individual countries.

It might be tempting to dismiss these variants of intensive transgovernmentalism as simply weak forms of cooperation, and in the cases of explicitly 'extra-EU' cases this may often be the case. However, three factors challenge such a conclusion. First, this is the preferred policy mode in some other relatively strong European regimes. Nato is one obvious example; the European Space Agency is another, and very different, case. Both are instances where quite extensive and sustained policy collaboration has been achieved, albeit with evident limitations, and ones which offer European governments 'forum-shopping' opportunities. Second, within the EU this mode has in practice become a vehicle for developing extensive and cumulative cooperation, gradually with elements of a treaty foundation, but with a variety of experimental institutional arrangements. Indeed it is for this reason that the EU developed what became known as its three-pillar architecture, with the second and third pillars being, in our terms, 'transgovernmental'. Third, a policy domain may start in this mode of intensive transgovernmentalism and then move into a different mode.

The case of economic and monetary union (EMU) over the years is an interesting example of intensive transgovernmentalism as a transitional policy methodology. From the early 1960s the European Council, national finance ministers and officials, and central bankers between them produced such sustained intensity and dense structuring of cooperation that the idea of managing a single currency became feasible and eventually acceptable. Interestingly the development of EMU then bifurcated between, on the one hand, strong delegation to a collective regime for monetary policy with the ECB as the collective agent (Community method), and, on the other hand, processes of policy coordination (McNamara 2005). Thus, a period of intensive transgovernmentalism can lead to a shift from one policy mode to others. As in other policy fields, the shift to a more collective regime does not insulate a policy process from the contestation of high politics and processes of strategic bargaining. The arguments in autumn 2003 over whether or not the disciplines of the Stability and Growth Pact could be applied to erring member governments illustrate the forces of resistance to a collective regime, in this instance especially from larger member states (Annett et al. 2005; Ardy et al. 2005; Chapter 18 in this volume).

In the sphere of foreign policy first European Political Cooperation (EPC) from 1970, then from 1993 onwards the common foreign and security policy (CFSP) was built up (Wallace 2005b). Initially defence cooperation was left within two separate frameworks, Nato and Western European Union (WEU), with clear competition between these alternative frameworks, and with many parallel bilateral agreements between countries. However, since 1998 these frameworks have gradually been drawn together, with the Nato mode of policy cooperation setting many of the parameters for the way in which defence is being pulled into the EU setting. For many reasons the CFSP area continues to illustrate the continuing differences among EU member states of both policy preferences and policy capabilities, differences accentuated by the sharp arguments over the intervention in Iraq in 2003. These differences also pervaded the debates about EU treaty reform in 2002–04, where one of the key issues was about whether, and if so how, to enhance the EU's collective institutional capabilities to take forward CFSP and an associated collective defence capability. Interestingly, however, arguments about Iraq and about treaty reform notwithstanding, the process of intensive transgovernmentalism has proved more resilient and less voluntarist than appears at first sight. In practice there is these days more not less cooperation among EU governments on an array of foreign and defence policy issues, and at both the practical and the discursive level. The evolution of the EU joint military staff and the decision in early 2004 to set up a combined European Defence Agency are both interesting examples of cumulative transgovernmentalism, which coexist with continuing arguments about shifts from transgovernmentalism to 'communitarization'. In particular this is a policy field where systematic analysis is needed of the implementation of outcomes by way of joint actions achieved, or joint capacities created and sustained, or parallel deployment of national and collective funding mechanisms.

In the sphere of justice and home affairs (JHA) (Lavenex and Wallace 2005), two transgovernmental processes have emerged and to some degree converged. On the one hand, informal policy consultations, both bilateral and multilateral, have bred habits of increasingly intensive transgovernmental cooperation since the early 1970s. On the other hand, a wittingly separate treaty framework was constructed with loose *ad hoc* institutions under the Schengen Agreements, at first deliberately apart from the EU, then to be incorporated within the EU under the Treaty of Amsterdam. In addition events – both increased migration flows and increased challenges from terrorism and cross-border crime – have accentuated demand for more structured and more stringent policy cooperation. These developments have drawn together many of these different processes of cooperation as regards JHA. Increasingly business is transacted within the EU treaty framework, borrowing methodologies from other policy domains, including tools such as 'mutual recognition' to facilitate some joint regulation and methods such as benchmarking and peer review to promote improved management within member states. In addition, conditionality is being used especially to promote policy convergence and higher standards in the new member states so that they can also accede to Schengen. However, the Prüm Convention, according to some commentators (Balzacq et al. 2006), represents a process of reversion to less well-anchored methods of cooperation.

These three domains were among the most dynamic areas of EU policy development at the end of the 1990s and in the early 2000s. In each case the EU framework has become in a broad sense more accepted, but the detailed institutional arrangements are untypical. In the case of EMU, on the one hand, a ECB, a network of national banks, and a privileged Economic and Financial Committee of national finance officials have established a variant of the Community method, while, on the other hand, as regards macro-economic policy techniques of policy coordination predominate, with lingering elements of transgovernmentalism and European Council oversight. The heart of foreign and defence policy is the European Council, flanked by defence and foreign ministry ministers and officials, working with a secretariat so far located in the Council of Ministers (not the Commission), and a great deal of consultation among national capitals and parallel policy-making through national processes. In the case of JHA, we can now observe two tracks: on the one hand some issues have been drawn more tightly within the EU framework, with an increasing role for the

Commission and for EU legislative instruments; and, on the other hand, some policies are being developed primarily among the relevant national ministries and executive agencies. The expanded secretariat in the Council plays an important back up role, and some new agencies are being developed.

These three cases suggest that an important systemic change may be under way within the EU policy process. New areas of sensitive public policy are being assigned by EU member governments to forms of collective or pooled regimes, but using institutional formats over which they retain considerable control. These regimes have 'soft' institutions, though the arrangements for EMU have gone the furthest in hardening the institutional arrangements. Yet, these soft institutions sometimes seem capable of developing 'hard' policy, or at least to be aimed at creating the capacity to deliver 'hard' policy. However, these emerging variants of cooperation have not yet been extensively explored in terms of overarching theorizing. Typically there are different literatures in each of these three policy domains, each with different analytical lenses and empirical reference points. Majone (2005, especially Chapter 8) is virtually alone in suggesting that there is a new form of European governance emerging, one with distinctive features and with useful potential. On his reading this new form of governance is explicitly polycentric and involves different strategies of commitment from those associated with other EU policy modes. His analysis will surely provoke controversies, but ones which could be promising for the further development of critical analytical debate.

CONCLUSIONS

These five policy modes provide a typology – a set of ideal-types – for exploring the shifting patterns of EU policy-making. They also reflect changing fashions in political science, international relations, and public policy analysis. They further reflect changing fashions in the practice of public policy as well as the evolving policy challenges on the agendas of policy-makers, as they have developed in the EU over the past 50 years. Future scholarship would surely benefit from making more explicit these intellectual and contextual parameters that have shaped the way that policy-making in the EU has been studied. This is an encouraging conclusion rather than a discouraging one in so far as it suggests that there is a good deal of scope for new research, both theoretical and empirical, on not only new developments in EU policy-making but also the experiences of the past. As has been repeatedly emphasized in this chapter, our knowledge of the past is still full of holes and discontinuities in our understanding. In particular as historians begin to access sources on the post-foundational period of the EU and as more readily accessible primary sources become more widely available on the contemporary period, many opportunities are opened up for new research that could probe in finer detail and with sharper conceptual tools the varieties and intricacies of different policy modes.

NOTES

1. For an account of the historiography see Dinan (2006, Chapter 14).

2. For an overview of statistics on court cases, both ECJ and CFI, across years and across sectors see the compilation by Falke and Leibfried in Tables 3,4a, 3.4b and 3.5 in Wallace (2005a: 68–72).

3. This chapter draws on and elaborates Chapter 3 of Wallace et al. (2005), especially pp. 77–89, with the permission of Oxford University Press.

4. Analyses of the evolving patterns of governance in the EU lie at the heart of two major research programmes, both funded by the Sixth Framework Programme of the EU: CONNEX, details at http://www.connex-network.org/, and NEWGOV, details at http://www.eu-newgov.org/.

5. The WEU was incorporated into the second pillar of the EU system under the Treaty of Nice, but its Parliamentary Assembly continues to exist, with members drawn from 37 countries, i.e. some EU member states plus a range of 'affiliates', 'associates', 'permanent observers', 'affiliate permanent observers', 'affiliate associate partners', 'permanent guests' and 'special guests' (sic). It discusses various aspects of European security policy, as of course does the European Parliament and the Nato Parliamentary Assembly.

REFERENCES

Allen, D. (2005) 'Cohesion and the structural funds', in H. Wallace, W. Wallace and M.A. Pollack (eds), *Policy-Making in the European Union*. Oxford: Oxford University Press. pp. 213–42.

Alter, K. (2001) *Establishing the Supremacy of European Law: The Making of an International Rule of Law in Europe*. Oxford: Oxford University Press.

Annett, A., Decressin, J. and Deppler, M. (2005) 'Reforming the Stability and Growth Pact', Washington: IMF Policy Discussion Paper, PDP/05/2.

Ardy, B., Begg, I., Hodson, D., Maher, I. and Mayes, D.G. (2005) *Adjusting to EMU*. Basingstoke: Palgrave Macmillan.

Averyt, W.F. (1977) *Agropolitics in the European Community: Interest Groups and the Common Agricultural Policy*. New York: Praeger.

Balzacq, T., Bigo, D., Carrera, D. and Guild, E. (2006) *Security and the Two-Level Game: The Treaty of Prüm, the EU and the Management of Threats*. Brussels: Centre for European Policy Studies.

Börzel, T. (2003) *Environmental Leaders and Laggards in Europe. Why there is (not) a 'Southern Problem'*. Aldershot, VT: Ashgate.

Bryant, R.C. and Portes, R. (eds) (1987) *Global Macroeconomics: Policy Conflict and Cooperation*. Basingstoke: Macmillan.

Coen, D. and Héritier, H. (2005) *Refining Regulatory Regimes: Utilities in Europe*. Cheltenham; Edward Elgar.

Commission (2001) *European Governance: A White Paper*. COM (2001) 428 final.

Cowles, M.G. (1994) 'The politics of big business in the European Community: setting the agenda for a new Europe', PhD Dissertation, The American University, Washington, DC.

Cowles, M.G., Caporaso, J.A. and Risse, T. (2001) (eds) *Transforming Europe: Europeanization and Domestic Change*. Ithaca: Cornell University Press.

Dehousse, R. (2005) *La Fin de l'Europe*. Paris: Flammarion.

den Boer, M. (1996) 'Justice and Home Affairs: attachment without integration', in H. Wallace and W. Wallace (eds), *Policy-making in the European Union*. Oxford: Oxford University Press. pp. 389–410.

Dinan, D. (ed.) (2006) *Origin and Evolution of the European Union*. Oxford: Oxford University Press.

Falkner, G., Treib, O., Hartlapp, M. and Leiber, S. (2005) *Complying with Europe: EU Harmonisation and Soft Law in the Member States.* Cambridge: Cambridge University Press.

Giersch, H. (1985) 'Eurosclerosis', Kiel: Kiel Discussion Paper No. 112, October.

Graziano, P. and Vink, M. (eds) (forthcoming) *Europeanization: New Research Agendas.* Basingstoke: Palgrave Macmillan.

Haas, E.B. ([1958] 2004) *The Uniting of Europe. Political, Economic and Social Forces 1950–57.* Stanford, CA: Stanford University Press, reprinted by Notre Dame, IN: University of Notre Dame Press.

Haas, E.B. (1975) *The Obsolence of Regional Integration Theory.* Berkeley: Institute of International Studies.

Hayes-Renshaw, F. and Wallace, H. (2006a) 'Changing the course of European integration – or not?', in J.-M. Palayret, H. Wallace and P. Winand (eds), *Visions, Votes and Vetoes: The Empty Chair crisis and the Luxembourg Compromise 40 Years On.* Brussels: Peter Lang. pp. 301–20.

Hayes-Renshaw, F. and Wallace, H. (2006b) *The Council of Ministers*, 2nd ed. London: Palgrave Macmillan.

Heisenberg, D. (2005) 'The institution of 'consensus' in the European Union: formal versus informal decision-making in the Council', *European Journal of Political Research*, 44: 65–90.

Hoffman, S. (1966) 'Obstinate or obsolete? The case of the nation state and the case of western Europe', *Daedalus*, 95: 862–915.

Hooghe, L. (ed.) (1996) *Cohesion and European Integration: Building Multi-Level Governance in Europe.* Oxford: Oxford University Press.

Howorth, J. and Keeler, J. (eds) (2003) *Defending Europe: The EU, Nato, and the Quest for European Autonomy.* Basingstoke: Palgrave Macmillan.

Hughes, J., Sasse, G. and Gordon, G. (2004) *Europeanization and Regionalization in the EU's Enlargement to Central and Eastern Enlargement: The Myth of Conditionality.* Basingstoke: Palgrave Macmillan.

Jordan, A. (2002) *The Europeanization of British Environmental Policy. A Departmental Perspective.* Basingstoke: Palgrave Macmillan.

Jupille, J. (2004) *Procedural Politics: Issues, Influence and Institutional Choice in the European Union.* New York: Cambridge University Press.

Jupille, J. and Snidal, D. (2005) 'The choice of international institutions: cooperation, alternatives and strategies', unpublished manuscript, University of Colorado, 23 December.

Keohane, R. and Nye, J. (1974) 'Transgovernmental relations and international organizations', *World Politics*, 27(1): 39–62.

Knudsen, A.-C. (2001) 'Defining the policies of the Common Agricultural Policy: a historical study', PhD Dissertation, European University Institute, Florence.

Knudsen, A.-C. (2006) 'The politics of financing the Community and the fate of the first British membership application', *Journal of European Integration History*, 11(2): 11–30.

Kok, W. (2004) *The Kok Report on the mid-term evaluation of the Lisbon process.* Presented to the European Council, November, published December.

Laffan, B. and Lindner, J. (2005) 'The budget', in H. Wallace, W. Wallace and M.A. Pollack (eds), *Policy-Making in the European Union*, 5th ed. Oxford: Oxford University Press. pp. 191–212.

Lavenex, S. and Wallace, W (2005) 'Justice and Home Affairs', in H. Wallace, W. Wallace and M.A. Pollack (eds), *Policy-Making in the European Union*, 5th ed. Oxford: Oxford University Press. pp. 457–82.

Leibfried, S. (2005) 'Social policy', in H. Wallace, W. Wallace and M.A. Pollack (eds), *Policy-Making in the European Union*, 5th ed. Oxford: Oxford University Press. pp. 243–78.

Lenschow, A. (2005) 'Environmental policy', in H. Wallace, W. Wallace and M.A. Pollack (eds), *Policy-Making in the European Union*, 5th ed. Oxford: Oxford University Press. pp. 305–27.

Lequesne, C. (2004) *The Politics of Fisheries in the European Union.* Manchester: Manchester University Press.

Lequesne (2005) 'Fisheries policy', in H. Wallace, W. Wallace and M.A. Pollack (eds), *Policy-Making in the European Union*, 5th ed. Oxford: Oxford University Press. pp. 353–76.

Lindberg, L.N. (1963) *The Political Dynamics of European Economic Integration.* Stanford, CA: Stanford University Press.

Lindner, J. (2005) *Conflict and Change in EU Budgetary Politics.* London: Routledge.

Majone, G. (1996) *Regulating Europe.* London: Routledge.

Majone, G. (2005) *Dilemmas of European Integration: The Ambiguities and Pitfalls of Integration by Stealth.* Oxford: Oxford University Press.

Marks, G. (1993) 'Structural policy and multilevel governance in the EC', in A. Cafruny and G. Rosenthal (eds), *The State of the European Union, Vol 2.* Boulder, CO: Lynne Rienner. pp. 390–410.

Mattli, W. and Slaughter, A.-M. (1998) 'The ECJ, governments and legal integration in the EU', *International Organization*, 52(1): 177–210.

McNamara, K.R. (1998) *The Currency of Ideas: Monetary Politics in the European Union.* Ithaca: Cornell University Press.

McNamara, K.R. (2005) 'Economic and Monetary Union', in H. Wallace, W. Wallace and M.A. Pollack (eds), *Policy-Making in the European Union*, 5th ed. Oxford: Oxford University Press. pp. 141–60.

Meunier, S. (2000) 'What single voice? European institutions and EU–US trade negotiations', *International Organization*, 54(1): 103–35.

Meunier, S. (2003) 'Trade policy and political legitimacy in the European Union', *Comparative European Politics*, (1): 67–90.

Meunier, S. (2005) *Trading Voices: The European Union in International Commercial Negotiations*. Princeton: Princeton University Press.

Meunier, S. and Nicolaidis, K. (1999) 'Who speaks for Europe? The delegation of trade authority in the EU', *Journal of Common Market Studies*, 37(3): 477–501.

Milward, A. (with the assistance of Brennan, G. and Romero, F.) (2000) *The European rescue of the nation-state*, 2nd ed. London: Routledge.

Moravcsik, A. (1998) *The Choice for Europe: Social Purpose and State Power from Messina to Maastricht*. Ithaca: Cornell University Press.

Morgan, R. and Bray, C. (eds) (1984) *Partners and Rivals in Western Europe; Britain, France and Germany*. Aldershot: Gower.

Palayret, J.-M., Wallace, H. and Winand, P. (eds) (2006) *Visions, Votes and Vetoes: The Empty Chair crisis and the Luxembourg Compromise 40 Years On*. Brussels: Peter Lang.

Pelkmans, J. and Winters, L.A. (1988) *Europe's Domestic Market*. London: Royal Institute of International Affairs.

Peterson, J. (1995) 'Decision-making in the European Union: towards a framework for analysis', *Journal of European Public Policy*, 2(1): 69–93.

Pollack, M. (2003) *The Engines of Integration: Delegation, Agency and Agenda-Setting in the European Union*. Oxford: Oxford University Press.

Pollack, M.A. and Shaffer, G.C. (2005) 'Biotechnology policy', in H. Wallace, W. Wallace and M.A. Pollack (eds), *Policy-Making in the European Union*, 5th ed. Oxford: Oxford University Press. pp. 329–51.

Putnam, R. and Bayne, N. (1987) *Hanging Together: Cooperation and Conflict in the Seven-Power Summits*. London: Sage.

Rhodes, M. (2005) 'Employment policy', in H. Wallace, W. Wallace and M.A. Pollack (eds), *Policy-Making in the European Union*, 5th ed. Oxford: Oxford University Press. pp. 279–304.

Rieger, E. (2005) 'Agricultural policy', in H. Wallace, W. Wallace and M.A. Pollack (eds), *Policy-Making in the European Union*, 5th ed. Oxford: Oxford University Press. pp. 161–90.

Rodrigues, M.J. (2003) *European Policies for a Knowledge Economy*. Cheltenham: Edward Elgar.

Rodrigues, M.J., Lundvall, B., Esping-Anderssen, G., Soete, L., Castells, M., Telò, M., Tomlinson, M., Boyer, R. and Lindley, R.M. (2002) *The New Knowledge Economy in Europe: A Strategy for International Competitiveness and Social Cohesion*. Cheltenham: Edward Elgar.

Roederer-Rynning, C. (2003a) 'Impregnable citadel or leaning tower? Europe's Common Agricultural Policy at forty', *SAIS Review*, 23(1): 133–51.

Roederer-Rynning, C. (2003b) 'The European Parliament and agricultural change', *Journal of Common Market Studies*, 41(1): 113–36.

Roederer-Rynning, C. (2006) 'Agricultural policy', in P. Graziano and M. Vink (eds), *Europeanization: New Research Agendas*. Basingstoke: Palgrave Macmillan.

Rosenthal, G.G. (1975) *The Men Behind the Decisions*. Farnborough: D. C. Heath/Lexington Books.

Sapir, A., Aghion, P., Bertola, G., Hellwig, M., Pisany-Ferry, J., Rosati, D., Vinals, J. and Wallace, H. (2004) *An Agenda for a Growing Europe*. Oxford: Oxford University Press.

Scharpf, F.W. (1988) 'The joint-decision trap: lessons from German federalism and European integration', *Public Administration*, 66(3): 239–78.

Scharpf, F.W. (1994) 'Community and autonomy: multi-level policy-making in the European Union', *Journal of European Public Policy*, 1(2): 219–42.

Schimmelfennig, F. and Sedelmeier, U. (eds) (2005) *The Europeanizarion of Central and Eastern Europe*. Ithaca: Cornell University Press.

Scott, J. and Trubek, D. (2002) 'Mind the gap: law and new approaches to governance in the European Union', *European Law Journal*, 8(1): 1–18.

Sedelmeier, U. (2005) *Constructing the Path to Eastern Enlargement: The Uneven Policy Impact of EU Identity*. Manchester: Manchester University Press.

Siedentopf, H. and Ziller, J. (eds) (1988) *Making European Policies Work: The Implementation of Community Legisaltion in the Member States*. London: Sage.

Simonian, H. (1985) *The Privileged partnership: Franco-German Relations in the European Community, 1969–1984*. Oxford: Oxford University Press.

Smith, A. (1998) 'The sub-regional level: key battleground for structural funds', in P. Le Gales and

C. Lequesne (eds), *Regions in Europe*. London: Routledge. pp. 50–66.

Stone Sweet, A. and Caporaso, J. (1998) 'From free trade to supranational policy', in W. Sandholtz and A. Stone Sweet (eds), *European Integration and Supranational Governance*. Oxford: Oxford University Press. pp. 92–133.

Thomson, R., Stokman, F.N., Achen, C.H. and König, T. (2006) (eds) *The European Union Decides*. Cambridge: Cambridge University Press.

Tsoukalis, L. (1997) *The New European Economy Revisited*. Oxford: Oxford University Press.

Wallace, H. (1999) 'The domestication of Europe: contrasting experiences of EU membership and non-membership', *Sixth Daalder Lecture*. Leiden: Leiden University Department of Political Science.

Wallace, H. (2005a) 'An institutional anatomy and five policy modes', in H. Wallace, W. Wallace and M.A. Pollack (eds), *Policy-Making in the European Union*, 5th ed. Oxford: Oxford University Press. pp. 49–90.

Wallace, W. (2005b) 'Foreign and security policy', in H. Wallace, W. Wallace and M.A. Pollack (eds), *Policy-Making in the European Union*, 5th ed. Oxford: Oxford University Press. pp. 429–56.

Wallace, H., Wallace, W. and Pollack, M.A. (eds) (2005) *Policy-Making in the European Union*. Oxford: Oxford University Press.

Webb, C. (1983) 'Theoretical perspectives and problems', in H. Wallace, W. Wallace and C. Webb (eds), *Policy-Making in the European Community*, 2nd ed. Chichester: John Wiley. pp. 1–41.

Wilks (2005) 'Competition policy', in H. Wallace, W. Wallace and M.A. Pollack (eds), *Policy-Making in the European Union*, 5th ed. Oxford: Oxford University Press. pp. 113–39.

Woolcock, S. (2005) 'Trade policy', in H. Wallace, W. Wallace and M.A. Pollack (eds), *Policy-Making in the European Union*, 5th ed. Oxford: Oxford University Press. pp. 377–99.

Young, A. (2005) 'The single market', in H. Wallace, W. Wallace and M.A. Pollack (eds), *Policy-Making in the European Union*, 5th ed. Oxford: Oxford University Press. pp. 93–112.

Young, A. and Wallace, H. (2000) *Regulatory Politics in the Enlarging European Union: Weighing Civic and Producer Interests*. Manchester: Manchester University Press.

Zeitlin, J., Pochet, P. and Magnusson, L. (eds) (2005) *The Open Method of Coordination: The European Employment and Social Inclusion Strategies*. Brussels: Peter Lang.

18

Fiscal and Monetary Policy: Coordination and Integration in Macro-Economic Policy

MARK HALLERBERG

INTRODUCTION

Fiscal and monetary policies were not particularly relevant issues at the European level when the European Economic Community was formed. Discussions of some sort of 'monetary union' did arise in the 1960s, which culminated in the Werner Report in 1970. This document called for a move over three stages to the free movement of capital, the establishment of a community system of central banks, and an irrevocable fixing of exchange rates that would amount to a monetary union. On the fiscal side, the Report recommended that the Community set budget balance targets for the member states and make decisions on how countries would finance deficits or spend surpluses. The basic idea was that the Community would use fiscal policy to affect overall demand. The Report also suggested tax harmonization on levies that would affect the movement of capital, and it explicitly called for a harmonized value-added tax.

Economic and Monetary Union as designed under the Treaties of Maastricht and Amsterdam means that member states have implemented many of the monetary recommendations, but they have accomplished far less on the fiscal side. In this chapter, I consider the extent to which there exists a 'European' dimension to macro-economic policy. This dimension can take two forms. The first is coordination of policy. In this case, states are expected to act together to meet a given policy goal, such as stable exchange rates. A more advanced move along a European dimension is integration, where one or more supranational institutions make and execute policy. In 12 of the 25 member states today, for example, there is coordination of fiscal policy and integration of monetary and exchange rate policy. There is also coordination (albeit at a low level) of the three policy types among all European Union members.

In this chapter, I trace the development of macro-economic policy at the European level. Much of the literature understandably focuses on explaining both the content and the timing of Economic and Monetary Union. In the second section of the chapter, I examine competing explanations for the creation of EMU. There is a smaller, though still significant, literature on the fiscal side of macro-economic policy that I also discuss in the period through the creation of EMU. The third section discusses current policy and academic debates about the functioning of the European-level framework. There is general dissatisfaction with the functioning of the Stability and Growth Pact in particular, but there is no consensus about the general level of integration needed. More generally, the research on both the domestic and international implications of EMU (if any) is promising but still in its infancy. The normative literature on the overall desirability of EMU also is not clear about the overall consequences of EMU.

THE DEVELOPMENT OF EUROPEAN MACRO-ECONOMIC COORDINATION AND INTEGRATION, 1957–2002

There are several good treatments of the evolution of monetary cooperation in particular that serve as the basis for this section.[1] After reviewing what happened, I consider arguments about *why* the development took the form that it did in the following section. A first important point concerning macro-economic policy is that the relevant institutions at the European level have existed for decades. The Treaty of Rome already established the Monetary Committee, which was an advisory committee composed of representatives from the central banks and finance ministries of each state. It helped prepare the regular meetings of the ECOFIN Council, which is composed of the economic and finance ministers. At the central bank level, the Committee of Governors of Central Banks began meeting in 1964. The European Commission, for its part, had its country desk officers monitor macro-economic policy as early as 1960.

The first proposals for monetary cooperation at the European level came from the European Commission in 1962. As Kaelberer (2001) nicely details, the Second Action Programme (or Hallstein Initiative) suggested a common currency for European Economic Community members by 1970 at the latest. Economists at the time also discussed whether a monetary union was desirable. One impulse for these discussions was certainly the Common Agricultural Policy. So-called 'green currencies' were created to allow the CAP to function.

The Werner Report arose in a climate of international monetary tension. The Bretton Woods system, which had led to mostly fixed currencies within Europe and across the Atlantic to the US dollar and to gold, was in crisis, and it would soon collapse. The initial European response was the so-called 'snake', which was followed by the 'snake in the tunnel', with the 'snake' the European currencies in close alignment while the 'tunnel' was a band of rates against the US dollar. Each of these systems in the early 1970s tried to establish some level of currency stability among European Community members as well as, potentially, among select non-member trading partners as well.[2] By 1974, however, the French franc and Italian lira fell out of the system, and it became a *de facto* D-mark zone. At this time, there was no coordination, let alone integration, in any of the three policy areas outside the area that Germany dominated.

Matters changed, however, soon after a summit meeting in 1978 between French President Valery Giscard d'Estaing and German Chancellor Helmut Schmidt. The meeting laid the groundwork for the establishment of the European Monetary System (EMS) in 1979. This second attempt at exchange rate coordination was generally a success. Some countries, such as Belgium and Italy, did devalue within the system on occasion, but currencies generally remained within the prescribed bands. The system functioned so well that the countries agreed in 1988 to narrow those bands (De Grauwe 2003), while the major outsider to EMS, the UK, finally joined the system in 1990.

The fact that member states could coordinate their exchange rate policies so effectively through the 1980s was useful for actors pushing for more coordination and more integration in the three policy areas. The Treaty of Maastricht, signed in December 1991, represents a high water mark for at least the intention of having a true European macro-economic policy. The Treaty famously established the conditions for Economic and Monetary Union (EMU). A new common currency would eliminate country-level exchange rate policies. An institutionally independent central bank based in Frankfurt would set monetary policy. Unlike central banks such as the Federal Reserve Bank of the US, which is supposed to consider both price stability and economic growth when making its decisions, the new European Central Bank would have a mandate to consider price stability only.

The Maastricht Treaty also mandated policy coordination in the run-up to what was formally known as Stage III of EMU. All states would need to be members of the EMS for 2 years prior to joining the common currency, which would limit their ability to use exchange-rate policy before they delegated it almost completely to the European Central Bank. On the monetary side, long-term interest rates as well as inflation rates would need to converge. Fiscal policy requirements focused on both the deficit and debt levels, with general government deficits expected to be no larger than 3% of GDP and general government debts no larger than 60% of GDP. Finally, on the institutional side, governments would need to make their central banks independent.[3]

There were also lesser-known parts of the Treaty that mandated regular coordination of all facets of macro-economic policy. As Article 99(1) of the Treaty stated, 'Member states shall regard their economic policies as a matter of common concern and coordinate them in the Council'. The Broad Economic Policy Guidelines, which would be written every year, would assist in this coordination. The Commission would draft them and ECOFIN would then pass them by qualified majority. After the year had passed, the Commission would then make recommendations to ECOFIN about whether member states had abided by the guidelines. In practice, the guidelines became both country-specific and detailed, with provisions dealing with topics like pension and labor market reforms.

Prospects of further integration, however, seemed to take a turn for the worse. Less than a year after the signing of Maastricht, the EMS faced its first significant crisis. On what became known as Black Wednesday and in the face of intensifying market pressure, the UK pulled the pound out of the EMS, with the Italian lira and Spanish peseta quickly following suit. Pressure then built on the French franc, and in summer 1993 its band within the EMS was widened. This development left only currencies in Denmark, the Benelux, and Germany as 'hard' currencies in the system. Moreover, the fiscal balances of most countries deteriorated to the extent that a monetary union based on the fiscal criteria would have included only Denmark and Luxembourg based upon 1994 figures.

In this climate, there were concerns about whether the Maastricht Treaty provided sufficient guidelines and rules to maintain fiscal discipline once the common currency was created. Responding to domestic pressure both from the public and from the Bundesbank, the German Finance Minister, Theo Waigel, proposed a 'Stability Pact' in fall 1995. While it was renamed as 'the Stability and Growth Pact' and some parts of the proposal were weakened, the core parts of the proposal became EU law after the states agreed to it at the Dublin Summit in December 1996 (Heipertz and Verdun 2004).[4]

The Pact's design includes preventive and corrective mechanisms. The emphasis for the preventive arm rests on the monitoring of Member State behavior. States were expected to submit economic plans in the form of 'convergence programs' already in 1994, but the content of those plans as well as their timing was not clear. Based on both the Stability and Growth Pact and on provisions member states agreed to at subsequent European Council meetings, the rules for either convergence programs (which non-euro members file) or stability programs (which euro members file) became clear. States would have to update their programs yearly in the late fall. The Commission, for its part, would critically review the programs and make recommendations to ECOFIN on whether the programs met European goals and whether the goals themselves were realistic. It is noteworthy that all member states, not just euro members, must file such programs and receive critical comments on them.

The corrective arm of the Pact was, and remains, more controversial. If ECOFIN supports a Commission recommendation that a country is found to have an excessive deficit and, importantly, that it is not making progress to eliminate the excessive deficit, that country can be required to make a non-interest bearing deposit with the Commission of up to 0.5% of its GDP. The general 'floor' the Pact sets is a deficit of 3% of GDP. If the country does not make correction, the deposit becomes a fine. 'Exceptional' circumstances, such as a decline in economic growth of 2% or, upon ECOFIN's approval, a decline of between 0.75–2%, would exempt a state. In terms of the broader themes of this chapter, this mechanism amounts to a form of enforced cooperation. While Eurostat does decide which accounting maneuvers (or, more pejoratively, 'tricks') can reduce a deficit and which cannot (Savage 2005), it is broadly left to the member states to decide the course of its fiscal policy once it knows what measures do not run afoul of the Treaties. Moreover, as the last section will indicate, even the deficit 'floor' has not been respected by some countries in practice in recent years.

With the institutional framework in place, the question then became what countries would join Stage III of EMU. When Maastricht was signed, many observers expected a small eurozone composed only of France, Germany, and the Benelux countries. The initial set of countries was therefore a surprise – based on macro-economic data from 1997, 11 of 15 member countries qualified in May 1998 for the introduction of the euro on January 1, 1999. They included countries with historic chronic fiscal problems, such as Belgium and Italy. A twelfth country, and the final member on the Mediterranean, Greece, qualified just 2 years later.

While the final section of the paper will discuss recent developments, it is noteworthy that the introduction of currency notes and coins after January 1, 2002, progressed so smoothly. There were fears both among academics and in the popular press of chaos. Customers would have difficulty telling the coins and bills apart, while counterfeiters would be able to take advantage of the confusion to flood the market with fake euros. In practice, the advertising campaigns that national governments, the European Central Bank, the European Commission, and private actors (especially banks) conducted were generally effective. While there remain some minor idiosyncrasies, such as Finland's decision not to circulate any coins smaller than five eurocents, the transition from national currencies to the euro was anticlimactic.

EXPLANATIONS FOR THE LEVEL OF COOPERATION AND INTEGRATION

There are a plethora of rival explanations for the course and development of cooperation and integration in the European Union. This section reviews those arguments. A general problem with any assessment of the rival arguments is that we have relatively few events we can use to rule one theory superior to another. With such a 'small problem', the argument in any one piece can only be suggestive.

Moving from the general to the specific, the first set of theories considers geo-political variables. Henning (1998) focuses on the role of the US in encouraging greater levels of cooperation in Europe. At times when the US worked to stabilize the international monetary system, pressure on European countries to cooperate in monetary affairs was low. In the early 1960s, for example, the Kennedy Administration worked actively to maintain gold parity of the dollar. When the US took actions that destabilized the world monetary order, pressure increased on continental politicians to strengthen intra-European cooperation to insulate economies from American, and American-centered, decisions. Henning's article traces four cases of American stabilization and seven cases of American disruptions to explain both the evolution of European cooperation as well as the decision at Maastricht to introduce a common currency.

Kaelberer (2001) makes a similarly geopolitical argument, but his discussion is centered on European power relations. Countries with 'strong' currencies have leverage over those with 'weak' currencies because weak-currency countries must worry about reserve requirements that their strong counterparts do not face. The country with the strongest currency, Germany, has the most privileged position given low inflation and the strength of the d-mark, and it largely gets what it wants in terms of the level of monetary integration.

Moravcsik's (1998) sweeping discussion of European integration adds a more complete domestic argument. He does assume that member states make most of the important decisions through the negotiations of each Treaty, so to explain outcomes one needs to know what the member states wanted. In his view, why their negotiation strategies took the form that they did depends upon the relevant domestic interest groups. To take but one example, during the negotiations prior to Maastricht, Germany had the least room to maneuver. While its employer groups and unions generally supported monetary unification, the Bundesbank together with a majority of the public opposed it. The fact that Germany was more constrained domestically than other countries that would participate, and that it could live with the status quo if there were no changes, meant that it would get its way on most issues. Moravcsik and Kaelberer are therefore in agreement that Germany was the big winner from EMU.[5]

Other authors pay particular attention to the role that interest groups play in the policy debate leading up on Economic and Monetary Union. Frieden (2002) is the exemplar of this approach. He concentrates on the trade and investment benefits of a common currency, not on the monetary implications, and he traces how these benefits affected the strategies of interest groups. The principal benefit of EMU was that it eased the costs of cross-border trade and investments. Internationally engaged producers (and in particular specialized manufacturers) and investors would lobby for stable exchange rates and would favor monetary union. The principal cost was that policymakers could no longer use exchange rates to relieve competitiveness pressures. Both import-competing and export-oriented firms would support continued flexibility in the exchange rate. A difficulty with this type of research is how to measure the size and strength of interest groups. Using the proxy variables of manufactured exports to the d-mark zone and the trade balances as proxies for the two groups, he finds that increases in manufactured exports leads to greater currency stability while deterioration in trade balances leads to more flexibility.

Like Frieden, Gabel (2001) considers whether support for monetary integration depends upon the material interests of the people in question, but he focuses on the individual, rather than the interest group, level. Based on survey evidence, he finds that material interests matter – people who fit a profile of benefiting from European integration, such as those in the tradables sector, higher income people, and people in border areas, were all more likely to support EMU. Looking at preferences towards inflation more generally and not just in a European context, Scheve (2004) finds that the relative tolerance of inflation varies across populations. His analysis of individual-level survey data suggests that people place greater priority on fighting inflation where there has been more price volatility. Consistent with Frieden's results on preferences towards a stable currency, stronger financial sectors lead to greater inflation aversion.

Any discussion of the material benefits of integration would be deficient without discussing work in economics. The optimal currency area (OCA) literature considers which countries would be better off in aggregate if they adopted a joint currency. If economies are generally in sync, one monetary policy will be effective to address macro-economic concerns. As economic cycles diverge, it is harder to adopt a 'one size fits all' approach. What happens if there is an asymmetric shock that hits one country but not others? Two factors can make a common currency still manageable. If there are inter-regional (or inter-country) transfers, fiscal policy can smooth out the shock. Similarly, if there is real labor mobility, people can simply move from the area that experiences the shock to the area that is growing. A common critique one sees concerning Europe is that there are almost no inter-country transfers while labor mobility is, despite the 'freedom of labor' guaranteed in the Treaty of Rome, quite low. Mundell's (1961) classic article on optimal currency areas focused mostly on a union between the Canadian and US dollars, but he suggested at the time that a monetary union in Europe would not be optimal because of the limited labor mobility on the continent. Later scholars have evaluated which countries should join the euro. In particular, De Grauwe (2003) is somewhat more optimistic. While a eurozone of 25 countries clearly would not constitute an optimal currency area, De Grauwe assumes that a eurozone close to the number of members that did join comes closer to fitting an optimal currency area. Moreover, he suggests that the size of the currency area may be at least in part endogenous – countries that join the eurozone are likely to have their business cycles harmonize, which in turn increases the benefits from joining the common currency (see also Frankel and Rose 1998).[6]

The previous arguments generally focus on states as the relevant actors (even if interest groups ultimately determine the position a given state takes) and assume that material benefits are central. Several authors, in contrast, emphasize the additional role played by supranational actors. Another set of authors, which sometimes overlaps with the first group, considers material interests as not primary, positing an independent causal role for ideas. Verdun (1999), for example, writes about the role of the Delors Committee in setting the agenda on EMU. In a combination of supranational and ideational argument, she envisions the Committee as a classic epistemic community, where the members shared a common world view. Sandholtz (1993), for his part, considers five sets of explanations. While he finds some empirical support for more

traditional arguments like domestic politics and concerns about price stability, he also takes seriously the role of 'spillovers' from the 1992 program. A fully functioning internal market, so neo-functionalists would expect, would require a monetary union. Moreover, foreign policy beliefs, namely a desire to bind Germany firmly to the west shortly after German reunification (especially on the part of German policymakers), led to support for greater integration in some form.

The work that is most associated with a study of beliefs and EMU is that of McNamara (1998). She argues that a consensus about the most desirable type of monetary policy was necessary before there could be a common currency. In particular, the relevant policymakers converged to neo-liberal ideas that inflation was an unqualified 'bad'. This shift in thinking was necessary before countries would participate in a German-led EMS. The success of EMS reinforced this set of beliefs and made EMU possible. Dyson and Featherstone (1999), however, describe more ideological discord. They see a continued conflict after the beginning of Stage III of EMU between neo-liberals, who worry that EMU is not strong enough to guarantee stability and fiscal rigor, and neo-Keynesians, who fret that EMU is too deflationary and leads to lower growth.

The preceding arguments focus almost exclusively on monetary and/or exchange rate policy and say little about the development of fiscal policy through the beginning of EMU.[7] Indeed, there is little written on fiscal policy issues in the scholarly literature. There are some useful narratives for individual countries.[8] In addition, a few authors examine explicitly the question whether efforts to reach Maastricht criteria explain the general improvement of state finances at the end of the 1990s. Dafflon and Rossi (1999) argue that accounting tricks largely explained the seemingly healthy budgets one observed so there is nothing left to explain. Hallerberg (2004), in contrast, sees the improvement as real. He concludes that entry into the EMU may have been a useful carrot in a few countries, but overall the relative health of domestic fiscal institutions was more crucial than any

European-level incentives. Most writing on fiscal policy at the European level discusses the design and early operation of the Stability and Growth Pact. Eichengreen and Wyplosz (1998) assume that states will test the limits of the Pact but not overstep them significantly. Willett (1999), among others, worries that the fines included in the Pact framework are not enforceable. He suggests a more flexible, and more enforceable, agreement. As we shall see in the next section, Willett's desire for a more flexible Pact has certainly been met through a 2005 reform, but the jury remains out on whether it will now be more enforceable.

CURRENT AND FUTURE CHALLENGES

By many measures, Economic and Monetary Union has been a success. The currency circulates widely. After an initial weakness against the dollar and yen, the euro has strengthened to the point where many domestic producers fear that it is too strong. The European Central Bank is alive and well, and no one seriously doubts its independence. One of the biggest changes was one that was unanticipated. Capital markets became much more integrated than before (Eichengreen 2000). More controversially, Rose (2000) suggests that monetary integration has big trade benefits as well, and, in his co-authored review of the literature, he indicates that others have found trade effects in Europe after EMU in particular even though EMU remains young (Rose and Stanley 2005). The main complaint among populations is a common perception that there was a one-time increase in prices during the transition from domestic paper currencies to the euro. While restaurants used the printing of new menus to adjust prices, official statistics from the ECB suggest that the change in prices in aggregate was small. From a policy standpoint, despite this success EMU faces three challenges now and in the near future: reform of the Stability and Growth Pact, domestic economic reforms, and the recent enlargement of the Union from 15 to 25 countries.

While the policy and academic literatures undoubtedly overlap, the academic literature faces at least four challenges as well. The first is to explain the functioning, and the relative power, of the European Union-level institutions in macro-economic policy-making. The second is to consider the domestic effects of Economic and Monetary Union. The third is to evaluate the international implications of EMU. The final one is a normative consideration of the desirability of EMU as it now functions. In the following section, I consider both the policy and academic challenges in turn.

Given the paucity of literature on fiscal policy prior to EMU, there is an irony that the main concern in policy circles since 1999 has been in this field. There is general dissatisfaction with the Stability and Growth Pact both among policy-makers and academics. Most notably in policy terms, it has failed to keep budget deficits below 3% in some countries. The big countries have been especially remiss – France and Germany have had deficits above this figure from 2002–05, while Italian finances were clearly in trouble at the beginning of 2006. Smaller countries as well, such as Portugal and especially Greece (with a deficit of 6.6% in 2004), have had continued fiscal difficulties. There have also been questions whether the Pact has been enforced according to the letter of the law. The European Commission took the Council of Ministers to the European Court of Justice in January 2004 after the Council agreed with the Commission's assessment of the fiscal situation in France and Germany, but it suspended the sanctions mechanism of the Pact. In its July 2004 decision, the Court agreed with the Commission that the Council should not have suspended the punishment mechanism, but it also noted that the Council does have discretion more generally (European Commission 2004; *Financial Times*, January 13, 2004).

In practice, the discussion of reforms of the Stability and Growth Pact became more closely linked with overall domestic reforms, which combines really two challenges into one. There is a general (and correct) sense that a series of reforms, which often (but not always) can be fit under the 'Lisbon Agenda', are needed to make Europe more competitive in an increasingly globalized economy. As a preparatory step, in June 2004 the European Council stressed in a Declaration that the overall goal rested on the two pillars of sound budgetary positions and increasing the growth potential of each country.

A true 'reform' of the Pact, however, did not come until March 2005. In both the policy and the academic literature, there have been a series of proposals about what went wrong and what can be fixed (e.g. Buti et al. 2003; Hodson and Maher 2004; Schuknecht 2004; Schelkle 2005), but the reform of the Pact that the Member States ultimately agreed to does not follow any one set of recommendations. In terms of the preventive arm, the focus is on the medium-term budgetary objective (MTO). This objective is to provide a safety margin above the 3% deficit floor, assure sustainability of debt burdens and, after taking both of these objectives into account, allow public investment. The states can also consider the impact of any structural reforms on budgetary performance when assessing the fiscal performance of a given country, with health, pension, and labor market reforms mentioned explicitly.[9] A careful reader will note that these objectives are rather vague. Indeed, while the small states and the Commission had advocated one rule to fit all countries,[10] the large states wanted individual targets, and they got their way in the design of the MTOs. The states propose their own MTOs according to these guidelines in their stability or convergence programs, which in turn are then subject to Commission and Council review. The Council may decide to ask a country to strengthen its MTO. Once the MTO is in place, states that are below it should make efforts to meet it, with those efforts greater in good economic times than in bad times. The expectation is that states in the eurozone or that participate in ERM-II should make adjustments equal to at least 0.5% of GDP in cyclically adjusted terms.[11]

As anticipated in the June 2004 European Council Declaration, the Stability and Growth Pact does now consider more explicitly the importance of domestic economic reforms, and other steps have been taken as well.[12] The Broad Economic Policy Guidelines have been combined with the Employment Guidelines into the Integrated Guidelines. The intent is to detail both macro- and micro-policies that together can encourage greater economic growth. Whether the combination of the two will increase the profile of the Integrated Guidelines remains to be seen.

The final policy challenge concerns the enlargement of the eurozone following the enlargement of the European Union in 2004. The big question concerns when one or more of the ten new members will join the eurozone. The earliest any one country could join is 2 years after its accession. Slovenia seems to be on track to adopting the euro in 2007 as of this writing, with Estonia and Lithuania wanting to join as well as soon as possible. Seven countries have also pegged their currencies through ERM-2 to the euro. Other countries, however, are less certain. Hungary in particular has failed to meet its deficit targets in its convergence programs, and the expectation is that it will not join before 2010. The European Central Bank also faces possible reform. The Governing Council now includes every central bank governor, but it is presumed that meetings could become unworkable once the eurozone expands beyond 15 members. The plan on the table is to establish a rotating system similar to the Federal Reserve Bank of the US, with larger members receiving more regular representation than smaller members.

The academic literature is still catching up to these developments. There are four challenges to these writers that complement the discussions on the policy side. The first is to explain from a positivist point of view the institutional structure under EMU. What is the balance of power among the different institutions and member states? How does EMU differ from other policy areas at the European level? These questions are especially relevant given that the institutional players for macroeconomic policy at the EU level differ from other policy areas. First and most obviously, the European Central Bank (ECB) was established to conduct monetary policy in the eurozone. There was a spate of literature comparing the new bank with other banks prior to EMU and/or offering policy advice (e.g. Estella and Mishkin 1997; Taylor 1999). De Grauwe

(2003: 1) contends that 'since the start of its operations in 1999, the ECB has been scrutinized intensely'. There have been many evaluations of the Bank's behavior (e.g. Issing et al. 2001; von Hagen and Brückner 2001; De Grauwe 2003) from a policy perspective with a focus on what exactly the Bank is doing and whether what it is doing is desirable, and there remains a continued focus on whether the Bank is appropriately transparent (Issing 1999; Eijffinger and Hoeberichts 2002; de Haan et al. 2004, 2005) given that it is does not release the minutes of its Board deliberations with a delay as does the Bank of England or the Federal Reserve Bank of the US. There is nevertheless a paucity of good material on how the Bank has made decisions in practice, and on the Bank more generally in relation to other European Union institutions.

There are two additional institutions that deserve more treatment in the literature. While the economic and finance ministers meet together on the ECOFIN Council, the Eurogroup for its part brings together those ministers just from eurozone countries to discuss matters of importance to the eurozone. Similarly, the Economic and Financial Committee largely supplants the ambassadors on the Committee of Permanent Representatives (COREPER) in preparing ECOFIN meetings. Does the informal tenor of the Eurogroup meetings provide 'peer pressure' that has any real effect on the behavior of individual ministers when they go back home? Does supplanting the representatives of foreign ministries with those from finance (or similar) ministries affect what ECOFIN Councils discuss and on which they reach agreements? As for the ECB, a real problem confronting scholars is secrecy, given that the meetings of each of these bodies are held in secret. Yet the academic literature on them is again sparse (Puetter 2004, is an exception).

The second challenge is to explain the impact of EMU on domestic politics. Can one describe a 'Europeanization' of macroeconomic policy like one can for other fields? This is the welcome task of Dyson's (2002) edited volume, which considers cognitive effects of EMU on the nature of domestic debates as well as who is affected at the national level. The

book's chapters cover the European and global contexts, domestic contexts in four big and two small member states, and, in a cross-sectional discussion, sectoral and state policies. It is a terrific collection of chapters, but there is plenty of room for the consideration of additional policy areas (relationship between different levels of government, pensions, etc.) as well as additional cases; Enderlein's (2006) discussion of the effects of EMU on fiscal and wage institutions is an excellent start.

An intriguing hypothesis at the domestic level is that EMU is affecting the very basis of democracy, namely elections. Clark and Hallerberg (2000) expect that budget balances will worsen prior to elections more under EMU as countries in the eurozone effectively face a fixed exchange rate and, and the Mundell-Fleming model would predict, can manipulate the economy through fiscal policy expansions. EMU may also affect the timing of those elections. Incumbents have an incentive to hold elections at roughly the same time to benefit from the temporary increase in growth as a big country like Germany experiences its 'political business cycle' prior to its own election, and those growth effects spill over to that country's European trading partners (Sadeh 2006).[13]

The third challenge is to consider the effects of EMU on the international scene. Does coordination of economic policy in Europe have tangible effects on the balance of international monetary power? Will the euro rival, or even supplant, the role of the dollar? Scholars before the introduction of the currency (Henning 1997; Mundell 1998) envisioned the possibility of a trilateral world that included the yen as well as the dollar and euro and considered what challenges that would bring. Part of a special issue of the *Journal of Policy Modeling* (2000, Volume 22, Number 3) debated the experiences of the euro on the world stage after its first year of existence and concluded that the euro's initial international impact was less than many observers had predicted. Cohen (2003), for his part, argues that there are structural reasons why the euro will never supplant the dollar, which include the inertia of monetary behavior, the level of transaction costs, an anti-growth bias under EMU, and EMU's ambiguous governance institutions. The euro remains a young currency, but more work should be done on what exactly its role is relative to others and how this role may evolve. The final challenge is a normative one, namely whether the current institutional structure is desirable. The design of the European Central Bank certainly heightened the concerns of some scholars about democratic accountability. Berman and McNamara (1999) worry that the Bank is unaccountable, and that its creation bucks the world-wide trend towards greater democracy. They also find the Bank's mandate too narrow. Like the Federal Reserve Bank of the US, they argue that the Bank should consider both economic output and price stability, not just price stability, when making its decisions. Verdun (1998) considers EMU an improvement over the previous period when Germany essentially set policy alone, but, absent any European institution besides the ECB, she worries about whom populations will hold responsible when the distribution of costs and benefits to monetary adjustments are uneven. Jones (2002: ch. 3), in contrast, argues that the issue of a 'democratic deficit' in this case is simply beside the point. Voters do not consider tradeoffs between inflation and unemployment, or for that matter tradeoffs across a range of macro-economic outcomes. What they do care about is low inflation, high employment, and the distribution of resources. If the new institutional framework makes it unclear which institution is doing what, in fact, voters may never coalesce around what set of policies a single institution like the ECB should promote in the first place. One nice facet of Jones' book is that it considers the legitimacy and accountability of EMU as a whole, issues that deserve much more attention.

CONCLUSION

This chapter reviewed the development of European-level macro-economic policy both in terms of coordination and in terms of

integration. EMU means that integration in exchange rate and monetary policy has proceeded the furthest in the 12 countries that now constitute the eurozone. Fiscal policy, in contrast, has amounted only to coordination, and even then there are questions whether the coordination has been effective. One goal of fiscal policy coordination is to avoid any future bailouts of particular countries in the eurozone. If the 'no bailout' pledge in the Maastricht Treaty would be credible, markets would realize that all debt in the eurozone is not equal, and it would price the various bonds based on country, rather than European-level, risk. Indeed, one of the reasons for including the fiscal criteria in the first place was a general consensus among members at the time that market discipline had failed due to the debt crisis in Latin America (Bini-Smaghi et al. 1994). To increase pressure on governments, ECB President Trichet said in November 2005 that the Bank would accept bonds from countries for refinancing operations that rating agencies devalued below an A-rating. Yet bond rating in the countries with the greater fiscal difficulties, such as Greece, Italy, and Portugal, have rarely exceeded 30 basis points of more secure German bonds. It may take a crisis for markets to provide the discipline that the Stability and Growth Pact so far has failed to provide.

On the academic side, a casual comparison of the different parts of this essay indicates that the literature is more 'thick' on the origins of than on its operation. They may be to be expected given the youth of EMU, but much more research is necessary to get a handle on what the European Union-level institutions really do, what the domestic consequences are, and whether the entire set-up remains viable or whether another set of reforms will be necessary.

NOTES

1. They include Ludlow (1982), Padua-Schioppa (1994), Helleiner (1994), Buiter et al. (1998), Dyson and Featherstone (1999), and De Grauwe (2003).
2. Andrews (1997) indicates that Switzerland participated in early talks concerning the formation of the snake.

3. Sweden's refusal to make its bank independent is the formal reason why the country has not joined EMU.

4. The legal basis for the Pact today includes five Council Regulations, one European Council Resolution, and the Protocol on the Excessive Deficit Procedure annexed to the Treaties; see the Commission's analysis at http://europa.eu.int/comm/economy_finance/about/activ ities/sgp/sgp_en.htm, accessed 27 January 2006.

5. There is at least one state-centered approach that contends that France, rather than Germany, was the winner (see Garrett 2001).

6. An opposite view comes from Feldstein (1997), who predicted that the differences in optimal monetary policy across countries would not converge and would be so great that armed conflict could result.

7. The one exception to this general rule is Hallerberg (2004). He considers explicitly whether the European level, and in particular Economic and Monetary Union, affected fiscal policy directly (through lower deficits) and indirectly (through fiscal institutional reforms).

8. See, e.g. Strauch and von Hagen (1999) on Germany, Chiorazzo and Spaventa (1999), Sbragia (2001), and Stolfi (2006) on Italy; and Donnelly (2004) on France, Germany, and Spain.

9. Economic and Finance Committee (2005).

10. European Commission (2005).

11. That is, the actual deficit could increase and a state could still meet this objective because economic growth was weak in a given year.

12. The British, who remain outside the eurozone, agree with the linking of the domestic reform and fiscal discipline. Tony Blair's speech to the European Parliament in July 2005 is revealing: 'Fourth, and here I tread carefully, get a macro-economic framework for Europe that is disciplined but also flexible. It is not for me to comment on the Eurozone. I just say this: if we agreed real progress on economic reform, if we demonstrated real seriousness on structural change, then people would perceive reform of macro policy as sensible and rational, not a product of fiscal laxity but of common sense. And we need such reform urgently if Europe is to grow'.

13. Kayser (2006) finds a convergence of electoral timing beginning already with the European Monetary System.

REFERENCES

Andrews, D. (1997) 'France, Switzerland, and the European currency snake: the ins and the outs, 1974–1975', Paper presented at the 5th Biennial International Conference of the European Community Studies Association, Seattle, Washington, May.

Berman, S. and McNamara, K. (1999) 'Bank on democracy: why central banks need public oversight', Foreign Affairs, 28: 2–8.

Bini-Smaghi, L., Padoa-Schioppa, T. and Papdia, F. (1994) The Transition to EMU in the Maastricht Treaty. Princeton Essays in International Finance, No. 194.

Buiter, W., Corsetti, G. and Pesenti, P. (1998) Financial Markets and European Monetary Cooperation. The Lessons of the 1992–93 ERM Crisis Cambridge: Cambridge University Press.

Buti, M., Eijffinger, S. and Franco, D. (2003) 'Revisiting the Stability and Growth Pact: grand design or internal adjustment?', CEPR Discussion Papers 3692.

Chiorazzo, V. and Spaventa, L. (1999) 'Prodigal son or a confidence trickster? How Italy got into EMU', in D. Cobhan and G. Zis (eds), From EMS to EMU. New York: St. Martin's. pp. 129–56.

Clark, W.R. and Hallerberg, M. (2000) 'Mobile capital, domestic institutions, and electorally induced monetary and fiscal policy', American Political Science Review, 94(2): 323–46.

Cohen, B.J. (2003) 'Global currency rival: can the euro ever challenge the dollar?' Journal of Common Market Studies, 41(4): 575–95.

Dafflon, B. and Rossi, S. (1999) 'Public accounting fudges towards EMU: a first empirical survey and some public choice considerations', Public Choice, 101: 59–84.

De Grauwe, P. (2003) The Economics of Monetary Integration, 5th ed. Oxford: Oxford University Press.

De Haan, J., Amtenbrink, F. and Waller, S. (2004) 'The transparency and credibility of the European Central Bank', Journal of Common Market Studies, 42(4): 774–94.

De Haan, J., Amtenbrink, F. and Waller, S. (2005) The European Central Bank: Credibility, Transparency, and Centralization. Cambridge, MA: MIT Press.

Donnelly, S. (2004) Reshaping Economic and Monetary Union: Membership Rules and Budget Policies in Germany, France, and Spain. Manchester and New York: Manchester University Press.

Dyson, K. (ed.) (2002) European States and the Euro: Europeanization, Variation, and Convergence. New York and Oxford: Oxford University Press.

Dyson, K. and Featherstone, K. (1999) The Road to Maastricht: Negotiating Economic and Monetary Union. New York and Oxford: Oxford University Press.

Economic and Finance Committee (2005) 'Specifications on the implementation of the Stability and Growth Pact and guidelines on the format and content of stability and convergence programmes', October.

Eichengreen, B. (2000) 'The euro: one year on', *The Journal of Policy Modeling*, 22(3): 355–68.

Eichengreen, B. and Wyplosz, C. (1998) 'The Stability Pact: more than a minor nuisance?' *Economic Policy*, 13(26): 65–114.

Eijffinger, S. and Hoeberichts, M. (2002) 'Central bank accountability and transparency: theory and some evidence', *International Finance*, 5(1): 73–96.

Enderlein, H. (2006) 'Adjusting to EMU: the impact of supranational monetary policy on domestic fiscal and wage-setting institutions', *European Union Politics*, 7(1): 113–40.

Estella, A. and Mishkin, F.S. (1997) 'The predictive power of the term structure of interest rates in Europe and the United States: implications for the European central bank', *European Economic Review*, 41(7): 1375–401.

European Commission (2004) *Public Finances in EMU*. Brussels: Directorate-General for Economic and Financial Affairs.

European Commission (2005) *Public Finances in EMU*. Brussels: Directorate-General for Economic and Financial Affairs.

Feldstein, M. (1997) 'EMU and international conflict', *Foreign Affairs*, 76(6): 60–73.

Frankel, J. and Rose, A. (1998) 'The endogeneity of the optimum currency criterion', *Economic Journal*, 108(July): 1009–25.

Frieden, J. (2002) 'Real sources of European currency policy: sectoral interests and European monetary integration', *International Organization*, 56(4): 831–60.

Gabel, M. (2001) 'Divided opinion and common currency: the political economy of public support for EMU', in B. Eichengreen and J. Frieden (eds), *The Political Economy of European Monetary Unification*. Boulder: Westview Press. pp. 49–76.

Garrett, G. (2001) 'The politics of Maastricht', in B. Eichengreen and J. Frieden (eds), *The Political Economy of European Monetary Unification*. Boulder: Westview Press. pp. 111–30.

Hallerberg, M. (2004) *Domestic Budgets in a United Europe: Fiscal Governance from the End of Bretton Woods to EMU*. Ithaca, NJ: Cornell University Press.

Heipertz, M. and Verdun, A. (2004) 'The dog that would never bite? What we can learn from the origins of the stability and growth pact', *Journal of European Public Policy*, 11(5): 765–80.

Helleiner, E. (1994) *States and the Reemergence of Global Finance*. Ithaca, NJ: Cornell University Press.

Henning, C.R. (1997) *Cooperating with Europe's Monetary Union*. Washington, DC: Institute for International Economics.

Henning, C.R. (1998) 'Systemic conflict and monetary integration in Europe', *International Organization*, 52(3): 537–74.

Hodson, D. and Maher, I. (2004) 'Soft law and sanctions: economic policy co-ordination and reform of the Stability and Growth Pact', *Journal of European Public Policy*, 11(5): 798–813.

Issing, O. (1999) 'The Eurosystem: transparent and accountable', *Journal of Common Market Studies*, 37: 503–20.

Issing, O., Gaspar, V., Tristani, O. and Angeloni, I. (2001) *Monetary Policy in the Euro Area: Strategy and Decision-Making at the European Central Bank*. Cambridge: Cambridge University Press.

Jones, E. (2002) *The Politics of Economic and Monetary Union: Integration and Idiosyncracy*. Lanham: Rowman & Littlefield.

Kaelberer, M. (2001) *Money and Power in Europe: The Political Economy of European Monetary Cooperation*. Albany: State University of New York Press.

Kayser, M.A. (2006) 'Trade and the timing of elections', *British Journal of Political Science*, 36(3): 437–57.

Ludlow, P. (1982) *The Making of the European Monetary System: A Case Study in the Politics of the European Community*. London and Boston: Butterworth Scientific.

McNamara, K. (1998) *The Currency of Ideas*. Ithaca, NJ: Cornell University Press.

Moravcsik, A. (1998) *The Choice for Europe*. Ithaca, NJ: Cornell University Press.

Mundell, R.A. (1961) 'A theory of optimum currency areas', *The American Economic Review*, 51(4): 657–65.

Mundell, R.A. (1998) 'What the euro means for the dollar and the international monetary system', *Atlantic Economic Journal*, 26(39): 227–37.

Padua-Schioppa, T. (1994) *The Road to Monetary Union in Europe*. Oxford: Oxford University Press.

Puetter, U. (2004) 'Governing informally: the role of the Eurogroup in EMU and the Stability and Growth Pact', *Journal of European Public Policy*, 11(5): 854–70.

Rose, A. (2000) 'One market, one money: estimating the effect of common currencies on trade', *Economic Policy*, 30: 7–46.

Rose, A.K. and Stanley, T.D. (2005) 'A meta-analysis of the effect of common currencies on international trade', *Journal of Economic Surveys*, 19(3): 347–65.

Sadeh, T. (2006) 'Adjusting to EMU: electoral, partisan and fiscal cycles', *European Union Politics*, 7(6): 347–72.

Sandholtz, W. (1993) 'Choosing union: monetary politics and Maastricht', *International Organization*, 47(1): 1–39.

Savage, J. (2005) *Making the EMU*. Oxford: Oxford University Press.

Sbragia, A. (2001) 'Italy pays for Europe: political leadership, political choice, and institutional adaptation', in M.G. Cowles, J. Caporaso and T. Risse (eds), *Transforming Europe: Europeanization and Domestic Change*. Ithaca: Cornell University Presss. pp. 79–96.

Schelkle, W. (2005) 'The political economy of fiscal policy coordination in EMU: from disciplinarian device to insurance arrangement', *Journal of Common Market Studies*, 43(2): 371–91.

Scheve, K. (2004) 'Public inflation aversion and the political economy of macreconomic policymaking', *International Organization*, 58: 1–34.

Schuknecht, L. (2004) 'EU fiscal rules: issues and lessons from political economy', European Central Bank Working Paper no. 421 (December).

Stolfi, F. (2006) 'The Europeanization of Italy's budget institutions, 1960–2001: a bottom-up approach', PhD Dissertation, University of Pittsburgh.

Strauch, R. and von Hagen, J. (1999) 'Tumbling giant: Germany's experience with the Maastricht criteria', in D. Cobhan and G. Zis (eds), *From EMS to EMU*. New York: St. Martin's. pp. 129–56.

Taylor, J.B. (1999) 'The robustness and efficiency of monetary policy rules as guidelines for interest rate setting by the European Central Bank', *Journal of Monetary Economics*, 43(3): 655–79.

Verdun, A. (1998) 'The institutional design of EMU: a democratic deficit?' *Journal of Public Policy*, 18: 107–32.

Verdun, A. (1999) 'The role of the Delors committee in the creation of EMU: an epistemic community?' *Journal of European Public Policy*, 6(2): 308–28.

Von Hagen, J. and Brückner, M. (2001) 'Monetary policy in unknown territory: the European Central Bank in the early years', Center for European Integration Studies (ZEI), Working Paper B-18.

Willett, T.D. (1999) 'A political economy analysis of the Maastricht and stability pact fiscal criteria', in M. Hutchinson, S. Jensen and A. Hughes Hallett (eds), *Fiscal Aspects of European Monetary Integration*. Cambridge: Cambridge University Press. pp. 37–66.

19

The Politics of Regulation and the Internal Market

ALASDAIR R. YOUNG

INTRODUCTION

The single market programme is probably the most far-reaching and ambitious regulatory project in the world. It has both profoundly affected the relationship between the state and market within European states and fundamentally shifted authority for much microeconomic management from the member states to the European Union. As a consequence, the single market, and with it the politics of regulation, have become central to what the European Union does and have shaped how we understand what kind of political entity it is.

As with traditional states, the study of regulation in the EU has focused on core questions of whose interests prevail in the policy process and what the effects of regulatory changes are. The common question of which political actors are most influential is given extra piquancy by the EU's character as neither a state nor an international organization (Sbragia 1992; Kohler-Koch 1999; Wallace 2005; and see Chapters 6 and 7). The EU's unusual character and the centrality of

regulation to the European project also provoke additional questions associated with the appropriate location of authority and the implications for the EU's legitimacy.

Although there were a few early pioneers (Dashwood 1977, 1983), interest in the politics of regulation in the EU really only took off in the wake of the launch of the internal (or single European) market programme in 1985. The study of the politics of European regulation, therefore, is a relatively recent endeavour (Majone 1994). Although the study of EU regulatory politics only really bloomed in the 1990s, it has developed into a vigorous and diverse field of study, with new issues receiving attention as their real-world salience increases. This attention, however, has been concentrated on a relatively limited range of, admittedly important, policy decisions. Further, most accounts focus on single case studies. Together these tendencies limit our capacity to understand the nuances of EU regulatory politics.

After clarifying what this chapter does and does not cover, I discuss how the single

European market programme fits into theories of European integration. I will then examine the characterization of the EU as a 'regulatory state' before discussing the political implications of different types of regulation and modes of economic integration. I will then examine the answers that have been advanced to the core traditional questions – Which political actors are most important? And whose interests prevail? – before considering whether the answers to these questions suggest that the EU represents a new form of governance. I will also consider the limited literature on the politics of the EU's competition policy, which is both more similar to regulatory policy within states than most EU regulatory activity and directed at creating a common market. To round out the picture, I will also examine the role of regulation in the EU's external relations (see also Chapter 27). In the light of the central discussion of EU regulatory politics, I will argue that much of the discussion of the EU's legitimacy crisis is misframed and, consequently, exaggerates the scale of the problem. I will conclude by elaborating on the limitations in the literature mentioned above and suggesting how they might be addressed.

THE BOUNDARIES OF REGULATION AND THE SINGLE MARKET

For the purposes of this chapter, regulation involves public actors adopting and policing rules aimed at disciplining the behaviour of economic actors. The chapter thus focuses on the legal instruments of regulation that have been at the heart of the single market programme, rather than the newer, 'softer' forms of regulation (Knill and Lenschow 2003).[1] Regulation is usually seen as aiming to improve the efficiency of the economy by correcting market failures, such as information asymmetries, negative externalities (such as pollution), and monopolies (Majone 1994). Consequently, regulation is an immensely broad field, many aspects of which are addressed in detail in other chapters of this volume. I will therefore limit my discussion

here to the regulatory activity most directly affected by the attempts to build a single European market. That is, it will focus on the politics of regulation as they apply directly to the removal of regulatory barriers to trade in goods and services. This means leaving aside some of the flanking policies, such as environmental protection as an end in itself (see Chapter 21), social policy (see, for example, Chapter 22), and labour market regulation (touched on in Chapter 24). Furthermore, the focus will be on the European level rather than on how regulation at the European level has affected state-market relations in the member states (see Chapter 25).

THE SINGLE MARKET AND INTEGRATION THEORY

Before turning to the politics of how the single market works, it is worth exploring the debate about its origins and how this contributed to broader debates about the process of European integration. The crux of this debate is about which actors were most influential in launching the single market programme: supranational actors or member governments. Framed this way the debate is between neo-functionalism and liberal intergovernmentalism. There is an associated debate about the importance of ideas, which is most developed in the emphasis on supranational actors, versus the bargaining power of states pursuing clear preferences, although some see ideas as important in shaping how the states sought to realize those preferences. Framed this way the debate is between constructivism and rationalism. These linked tensions about which actors matter and the importance of ideas and norms also motivate the debates about the dynamics of regulatory politics in the single market.

The neofunction-intergovernmentalist debate about the origins of the single market is rather miscast as the different camps seek to explain different aspects of the project (Armstrong and Bulmer 1998; Young 2005). Those analysts who concentrate on the single European market programme – the substance of the project – tend to stress the role of supranational actors and ideas. Those that concentrate on the Single European Act – the institutional reforms to facilitate the realization of the project – tend to stress the role of the member states. As a consequence, it is possible that both accounts are right, but explain different things (Armstrong and Bulmer 1998: 19; Young 2005). Nonetheless, the debate endures and is worth examining in some detail because of its continuing relevance for and resonance with debates about how the EU makes regulatory policy.

In particular, it is worth noting that even among those who emphasize the importance of supranational actors there are differences about which actors matter more, also a central concern of the debates over EU regulatory politics. Some, such as Cowles (1994) and van Apeldoorn (2001, 2002) emphasize the importance of transnational business interests, especially the European Roundtable of Industrialists (ERT), in shaping the EU agenda in favour of the completion of the single market. Sandholtz and Zysman (1989) and Jabko (2006) cast the Commission in the leading role.

Analysts who focus on the SEA, by contrast, emphasize bargaining among the member governments. Moravcsik (1991, 1998), in particular, argues that the SEA was the product of interstate bargaining, principally between the British, French, and German governments, although the preferences of these governments were influenced by business interests responding to increasing economic interdependence. Garrett (1992) argues that the member governments were willing to accept limits on their policy autonomy because they were engaged in an extended cooperative project and wanted to be able to ensure that their partners would comply with agreements. Cameron (1992) concludes that ultimately the member governments were the crucial actors, although he concedes that supranational actors, such as the Commission, ECJ, and big business, may have influenced their preferences.

Majone (1994, 1996) contends that the interaction of both supranational actors, particularly the Commission (supply side), and the member states (demand side) is necessary

to explain the transfer of regulatory authority to the EU that the single market programme implied. More specifically, he argues that because the EU's budget is so limited, the Commission must seek to develop through task expansion, hence its 'entrepreneurial' promotion of the single market. The Commission was supported by internationally-oriented European firms, which wanted to avoid dealing with multiple, competing national regulations. The member states were willing to delegate regulatory authority to the EU in order to minimize transaction costs – associated with identifying interlocutors, bargaining, and, particularly, policing, monitoring and enforcement – and flesh out the relational contract of the EC Treaty (agenda setting). These pressures persist and help to explain the continuing, albeit at a diminished rate, transfer of regulatory authority to the EU level even after the bulk of the formal single market programme has been adopted.

The preceding discussion has focused on the debate about why regulatory policy authority was shifted to the EU. That, however, is only part of the story. The other part concerns why that common policy took the form it did. This is where the role of ideas becomes prominent. Strikingly, however, the discussion of the role of ideas in the launch of the single market programme does not really engage with the broader constructivist-rationalist debate. This is because all of the accounts of ideas in the single market programme depict them more in terms of affecting understandings of ends–means relationships than changing underlying preferences. The key differences, therefore, revolve around the interaction between actors and ideas. Liberal intergovernmental authors tend to emphasize a convergence of policy preferences around neo-liberal economic ideas during the early 1980s (Sandholtz and Zysman 1989; Majone 1991; Moravcsik 1991; Cameron 1992). Others, however, stress the role of supranational institutions in promoting particular ideas. Garrett and Weingast (1993) contend that the idea of mutual recognition, developed by the European Court of Justice in its *cassis de Dijon* ruling, provided a focal point for agreement among member governments that favoured liberalization. Alter and Meunier-Aitsahalia (1994) and Pollack (2003a) recognize that the idea of mutual recognition was important, but stress the Commission's entrepreneurial exploitation of this idea as a formula for liberalization.

Both Jabko (2006) and van Apeldoorn (2001, 2002), however, stress that there was not one unambiguous understanding of the single market programme. There was a neo-liberal vision of boosting economic efficiency by liberalizing trade between and within the member states, but there was also a more competitiveness-oriented vision, in which the creation of the single market, not least through enabling European firms to take advantage of greater economies of scale, would enable European firms to compete more effectively with their international rivals, notably in Japan and the US. European market liberalization, therefore, served quite different purposes for different governments and different economic actors. While Jabko (2006) contends that the Commission strategically exploited the ambiguity about the meaning of the market in order to advance European integration, van Apeldoorn (2001, 2002) contends that there was a clash between competition and competitiveness factions within the ERT, which the competitiveness faction initially won, but was unable to realize because of opposition from neo-liberal member states.

THE EU AS A 'REGULATORY STATE'

The success of the single market programme has been such that many authors see it as a defining feature of the EU (Majone 1994; Begg 1996; Gottweis 1999; Egan 2001). In fact, regulation is so central to the EU's functioning that it can usefully be considered a 'regulatory state' (Majone 1994, 1996; McGowan and Wallace 1996; Egan 2001). According to McGowan and Wallace (1996: 563), a regulatory state attaches greater importance to the processes of regulation than to other forms of policy-making, it focuses on rule-making and it has 'an attachment to the rule of law and, normally, a

predilection for judicial or quasi-judicial solutions'.

This is theoretically significant because it situates the EU's regulatory politics within a comparative politics framework. Majone (1996: 55) explicitly states that conceptualizing the EU as a regulatory state is 'heuristically useful' as it opens the door to comparison with the other prominent example of a 'regulatory state', the US, and to the extensive literature on regulatory politics in the US.

Although it is extremely useful to situate EU regulatory politics in a comparative framework, care needs to be taken when applying the lessons from the study of politics in the US to the EU. Crucially, the EU, unlike the US, is rarely directly involved in regulating the activities of firms or individuals; there has only been a very limited transfer of regulatory powers to the EU (Eberlein and Grande 2005). Rather European rules often focus on regulating the (national) regulators (McGowan and Wallace 1996), although the EU also makes extensive use of detailed legislation in areas of social regulation (Kelemen 2004).

Further, care needs to be taken that, in focusing on decision-making at the EU level (where the 'regulatory state' analogy is strongest), we do not lose sight of the multilevel character of EU regulatory governance. The comparative federalism literature provides a corrective to this within the context of comparative politics (Nicolaïdis and Howse 2001; Kelemen 2004), as does the focus in international political economy on the interaction between domestic and international politics (Katzenstein et al. 1998; Friedman and Martin 2002).

In addition, it is dangerous in the EU context to equate regulatory policy-making with technocratic policy-making (Harcourt and Radaelli 1999). As the single market programme involves reconciling different national regulatory approaches, each of which embodies complex compromises and reflects national attitudes and preferences, there is contestation about the objectives of regulation, not just its means. These are intensely political issues. When combined with the fact that regulation (and de- and re-regulation) creates winners and losers, it is not surprising that the politics of regulation in the EU are often vigorous and that the legitimacy of EU regulation is questioned.

DIFFERENT TYPES OF REGULATORY POLITICS

One of the important lessons from the US study of regulation is that different types of regulation are characterized by different types of politics. One basic distinction is between economic regulations, which govern entry to and competition within particular sectors, and social regulations, which are aimed at addressing negative externalities (such as pollution) and information asymmetries (e.g. consumer protection). These different types of regulation distribute costs and benefits differently, and, therefore, are characterized by different types of politics (Wilson 1980). Where anticipated costs are concentrated and benefits are diffuse, as in social regulation and the liberalizing of economic regulations, 'entrepreneurial' politics are necessary to overcome the resistance of the better organized interests that will incur the costs of policy change. A political entrepreneur sees advantage in pursuing policy objectives that benefit large numbers of people who are not mobilized within the policy process (Derthick and Quirk 1986). With regard to economic regulation the benefits of being protected from competition are concentrated among the firms in the regulated sector. Where the costs are diffuse, as, for example, in airlines and telecommunications where the consumers are individuals, client politics, in which producers dominate, is likely, although Wilson (1980) notes that established civic interest groups can make such politics more transparent and therefore make producer dominance harder. In other cases, where the consumers are other firms, such as in road haulage and maritime transport, Lowi's (1964) characterization of regulatory politics as interest group politics prevails.

A second important difference between economic and social regulation is that at least since the 1970s they have been subject to very different ideational frameworks. The rise of neo-liberal economic ideas, and the critiques of regulatory economists, challenged the idea that markets should be protected from competition, thereby paving the way for deregulation in the US and the single market programme in the EU (Derthick and Quirk 1986; Majone 1991; Armstrong and Bulmer 1998). By contrast, the spread of post-material values in the US and western Europe contributed to greater support for social regulation (Vogel 1989; Weale 1992).

These different ideational frameworks have been buttressed by technological and scientific change. Technological developments have undermined the view that a number of industries, most notably in telecommunications, are natural monopolies and therefore cannot be subject to competition (Dyson and Humphreys 1990; Thatcher 1999). In contrast scientific advances have enhanced awareness of environmental problems and consumer safety issues and contributed to pressure to resolve them (Vogel 1989; Weale 1992). Thus economic and social regulation are characterized by different types of politics operating within different ideational frameworks.

THE POLITICS OF DIFFERENT TYPES AND MODES OF REGULATORY INTEGRATION

Although these broad trends and political dynamics broadly characterize regulatory politics in all countries, precisely how they translate underlying preferences into policies differs between countries. There are a number of reasons for this (Hancher and Moran 1989; Vogel 1995, 2003; Previdi 1997; Holmes and Young 2001): countries face different problems; they may have different historically and culturally influenced attitudes towards risk; and they have different constellations of interests and different political institutions for aggregating them.

With regard to social regulation, such differences, whether intentionally or not, can impede trade between states as all products must meet the standards of the state in which they are sold and all service providers must comply with the rules of the state in which they operate. Economic regulations, which are particularly common in services, also impede trade as they directly restrict access to (national) markets. Economic integration among states, therefore, requires overcoming these different national rules. The single market programme was intended to do precisely that.

There are, however, a number of different ways of addressing differences among national regulations. These different modes of economic integration engage different actors and take place within different institutional frameworks within the EU; they, therefore, have different political dynamics.

Negative and Positive Integration

Pinder (1968) posited that there are essentially two ways to remove regulatory barriers to trade: one is to simply remove them ('negative integration'); the other is to replace them with a common rule ('positive integration'). Negative integration can occur through a decision of the member governments, in which case it is not dissimilar to positive integration (see below). More commonly, however, it comes about through the European Court of Justice (ECJ) finding a national rule incompatible with the Treaty of the European Community, a process that began in the early 1970s. The most obvious manifestation of negative integration within the EU is the mutual recognition principle, which was articulated on the basis of the ECJ's 1979 *cassis de Dijon* judgement. The mutual recognition principle holds that, assuming the member governments' rules are equivalent in effect, products sold legally in one member state should be allowed to be sold in all member states.[2] Thus, with regard to negative integration, the ECJ is a key actor, as are those actors, usually firms, that challenge the national rules.

Most regulations, however, are aimed at delivering public policy objectives and, as discussed earlier, may not actually be equivalent in effect. Consequently, they cannot simply be eliminated or considered equivalent. As a result, in order to both liberalize trade and continue to realize desired public policy objectives, regulation must be shifted to the EU level – 'positive integration'. In this context, the member states' governments, the European Commission, and the European Parliament become the main players, with numerous interest groups seeking to influence them. Given its more overtly political nature, it is not surprising that the vast majority of the literature has examined the politics of positive integration.

What attention has been paid to the politics of negative integration has focused the implications of the ensuing regulatory competition for public policy objectives. This attention has been motivated by two related concerns. The first concern, now familiar in discussions of globalization, was whether increased economic exchange among the member states would put pressure on governments to relax their social regulations, which increase the costs of their domestic firms (Siebert and Koop 1993). Economic integration implies both increased competition from imports and greater opportunities for firms to relocate to less regulated, and therefore less costly, or lower taxed countries. Faced with the prospect of firms either going out of business or moving their activity (and jobs) to other member states, there was concern that governments would relax their social regulations. This could lead to a competitive 'race to the bottom' in which each member state sought to give its firms the greatest competitive edge. Thus, the concern was that national social regulations would be eroded.

The second, related, concern was that the high threshold for agreement and diversity of interests among the member states would make it difficult to adopt common social regulation to the EU level, which would eliminate the incentive for competitive deregulation among the member states. Thus, the EU's regulatory capacity would not be sufficient to compensate for the erosion of the member states' regulatory capacity resulting from negative integration (Scharpf 1988). The central thrust of these concerns was that the market would be strengthened at the expense of the state and that economic interests would prevail over other considerations.

Despite the plausibility of the underlying logics of these concerns, neither has, for the most part, been born out in the EU. A number of studies have found little evidence of regulatory competition among the member states (Woolcock 1994, 1997; Sun and Pelkmans 1995; Gatsios and Holmes 1997; Scharpf 1997, 1999). In large part this is because firms, for a variety of reasons, have not put the EU's member states under intense pressure to relax their regulatory regimes (Woolcock 1994). A central reason for this is that for most firms environmental regulations (Vogel 1997b) and health and safety regulations (Eichner 1997) do not significantly increase costs. Further, even when firms do press for changes, governments have strong incentives to resist them as the policies were adopted to address domestic political concerns in the first place (Sun and Pelkmans 1995; Scharpf 1997). Thus, negative integration does not appear to have extensively eroded the regulatory capacity of the member states.[3]

Moreover, a number of studies have established that the EU has demonstrated significant regulatory capacity in adopting quite stringent rules across a wide range of policy areas, including health and safety and environmental product regulations; environmental process regulations, and rules governing banking and insurance (Eichner 1993, 1997; Sbragia 1993; Vogel 1995; Peterson 1997; Pollack 1997; Scharpf 1997, 1999; Young 1997; Young and Wallace 2000). The political dynamics that explain this outcome are examined in detail in the section on the politics of positive integration below, but it is worth summarizing here the key explanatory factors: advocacy by particular member governments; sponsorship by supranational institutions, notably the Commission and European Parliament; and lobbying by constellations of civic and, crucially, producer interests. As will be explored below, these factors are more prevalent and influential in some circumstances than others. Consequently, there are some exceptions to this positive picture of EU regulatory capacity, most notably with respect to social policy,

industrial relations, and taxes on firms and capital (Scharpf 1997, 1999).

Types of Positive Integration

The overwhelming majority of the literature on the politics of EU regulation examines different types of positive integration. Most of that work concentrates on relatively few sectors within two types of positive integration: market making and approximation (see Table 19.1).

'Market-making' regulation (Scharpf 1999: 104) involves the adoption of EU-level rules to replace national economic regulations that restrict access to particular sectors, which are particularly common in services. It typically involves eliminating (gradually) national quantitative restrictions on market entry and replacing them with EU-level qualitative restrictions.

Regulatory approximation, arguably the high water mark of positive integration, involves replacing national product standards with detailed, common EU standards so that products can circulate freely within the single market. Approximation is reserved for those products that are too complex and/or politically sensitive to be left to the vagaries of negative integration.

Less attention has been paid to the 'new approach' to standardization and to 'home country control', its analogue in financial services regulation. Under the 'new approach' only minimum essential requirements are agreed politically at the EU level. Responsibility for developing detailed technical standards is delegated to the independent European standards bodies, but national and even firm standards that are certified to meet the essential minimum requirements are also acceptable, hence there is also an element of mutual recognition. Likewise, with regard to 'home country control', only minimum standards for the national regulation of financial services are agreed at the EU level. Financial service providers can operate throughout the single market regulated by the government of the country in which they have their headquarters (home). These approaches blur the distinction between

Table 19.1 *Partial survey of the literature on the politics of positive integration.*

	Type of regulation	
	Economic	Social
Market making	Air transport (Kassim 1996; Holmes and McGowan 1997; O'Reilly and Stone Sweet 1998; Aspinwall 1999) Road haulage (Young 1995; Héritier 1997; Aspinwall 1999; Schmidt 2002) Telecommunications (Dyson and Humphreys 1990; Schneider et al. 1994; Cram 1997; Sandholtz 1998; Schmidt 1998; Bartle 1999; Thatcher 1999, 2001; Levi-Faur 2004) Electricity (Schmidt 1998; Bartle 1999; Eising and Jabko 2001; Eising 2002; Padgett 2003; Levi-Faur 2004; Jabko 2006)	
Approximation		Automobile emissions (Boehmer-Christiansen 1990; Arp 1993; Tsebelis 1994; Sbragia 1996; Friedrich et al. 1998; Young and Wallace 2000) Food safety (Earnshaw and Judge 1993; Vogel 1995; Joerges and Neyer 1997; Krapohl 2003; Kelemen 2004; Ansell and Vogel 2006) Genetically modified crops (Gottweis 1999; Patterson 2000; Skogstad 2003; Pollack and Shaffer 2005) General product safety and consumer protection (Bomberg and Peterson 1993; Young 1997) Chemicals (Eckley and Selin 2004) Pharmaceuticals (Young and Wallace 2000; Kelemen 2004; Krapohl 2004; Permanand and Mossialos 2005) Tobacco (Arregui et al. 2004; Duina and Kurzer 2004)
'New approach'/ Home country control		Standards (Schreiber 1991; Egan 2001) Financial services, especially insurance (Moran 1994; Mitchell 1999; Schmidt 2002; Müller 2003)

Approach to positive integration

positive and negative integration because they involve a degree of positive integration in setting common minimum standards before mutual recognition applies.

The Spread of Regulatory Agencies

A relatively new feature of regulation in Europe, which is attracting a great deal of academic interest, is the proliferation of regulatory agencies (see, for example, Majone 2000; Kelemen 2002, 2004; Thatcher and Stone Sweet 2002; Coen and Thatcher 2005). Although this phenomenon is prevalent within individual EU member states and the emergence of supranational regulatory agencies is central to the characterization of the EU as a 'regulatory state', the delegation of regulatory powers to the EU level has actually been extremely limited. Even the most powerful European agencies, such as the European Medicines Evaluation Agency and the new European Food Safety Agency, do not have independent regulatory authority, but refer opinions to political committees for decisions (Krapohl 2004; Eberlein and Grande 2005). Perhaps not surprisingly, therefore, most of the literature on the European regulatory agencies has focused on why they were established rather than their impact on regulation.

THE POLITICS OF POSITIVE INTEGRATION

Despite the different types of positive integration and the variety of sectors that have been studied, there is a striking degree of accord about how regulatory politics within the single market work. Within that broad accord, however, there are important differences of emphasis. These differences are found in answers to the two distinct, but related, questions that have motivated most of the research: (1) which institutions are most important, particularly are supranational institutions more important than the member states? And (2) which societal actors' interests prevail? Taking the different answers to these two questions together leads to a third question – Does the EU represent a new form of governance? (Eising and Kohler-Koch 1999a).

Which Institutions are the Most Important?

To a significant extent the question about which institutions are most important is an echo of the neo-functionalist – liberal intergovernmentalist debate: do the EU's supranational institutions simply serve the interests of the EU member states or do they have an independent impact on outcomes? Within this broader discussion there is a subsidiary debate about the relative importance of the different EU institutions, particularly concerning the policy impact of the European Parliament.

Given the European Commission's exclusive formal right of initiating policies, it is not surprising that it is at the heart of EU regulatory politics. It is frequently characterized as a 'policy entrepreneur', which has its own interests and pursues them strategically (Majone 1996; Holmes and McGowan 1997; Pollack 1997; Schmidt 1998, 2000; Aspinwall 1999; Kohler-Koch 1999; Egan 2001). This emphasis on the Commission as a policy entrepreneur is striking, because the literature on US regulatory politics emphasizses the importance for deregulation (market making) and social regulation (approximation) of a policy entrepreneur championing the interests of diffuse actors against the resistance from vested interests (Wilson 1980; Derthick and Quirk 1986).

The existing literature provides a wide variety of explanations about why the Commission should be inclined to play such an entrepreneurial role. Majone (1996) emphasizes the Commission's non-majoritarian character, which insulates it from electoral politics so it can better consider the common good. This inclination is reinforced by the Commission's perception that pursuing popular policies is a prominent way to address concerns about its democratic legitimacy (Peters 1994; Young and Wallace 2000). Further, in order to advance the single market the Commission must challenge existing (national) arrangements, which tend to favour powerful interests (Majone 1996; Kohler-Koch 1999; Young and Wallace 2000). Further, by extending European regulatory activity the Commission increases the scope of its authority with respect to the member states (Majone 1994; Pollack 1997; Kohler-Koch 1999). Although these explanations of Commission entrepreneurship are different they are reinforcing rather than competing.

Although there is agreement that the Commission has interests distinct from those of the member states, the characterization of the Commission as a policy entrepreneur masks disagreement about how its interests interact with those of the member states. A number of authors stress the Commission's strategic use of its competition policy powers to undermine the viability of the status quo in air transport (Holmes and McGowan 1997; Aspinwall 1999), telecommunications (Cram 1997; Sandholtz 1998; Schmidt 1998), and a number of other sectors (Schmidt 2000), thereby paving the way for liberalization. The Commission has also been known to encourage actively coalitions of interests in order to build support its proposals, such as for liberalizing telecommunications (Sandholtz 1998). Other observers, however, tend to see the Commission playing an entrepreneurial role by selecting among a range of options for which a winning coalition is possible (Garrett and Tsebelis 1996; Majone 1996; Pollack 1997; Young and Wallace 2000).

There has been rather less attention paid to the impact of the European Parliament on regulatory policy-making, at least by those studying regulatory politics rather than the Parliament. Most of what literature there is focuses on the Parliament's impact on regulatory approximation, rather than market making, for example, on sweeteners (Earnshaw and Judge 1993), novel foods (Burns 2004), pharmaceutical advertising (Young and Wallace 2000), the EU's new food safety regime (Kelemen 2004) and, in particular, automobile emissions (Judge et al. 1994; Tsebelis 1994; Young and Wallace 2000). The Parliament has, however, been drawn into normative questions in conjunction with public service obligations associated with market making in public

utilities, such as electricity, gas, and postal services (Lord 2003).

The work focused on the Parliament's influence has stressed that the extent of the Parliament's impact on policy – through its agenda setting and veto powers – depends on its policy preferences in relation to those of the Commission and the member states, although crucially there is considerable disagreement about how much room for manoeuvre it has (Crombez et al. 2000; Garrett et al. 2001; Kasack 2004). This is significant because the Parliament is usually assumed to favour more European regulation and to defend diffuse interests (Pollack 1997; Young and Wallace 2000; Lord 2003), although these preferences may vary with the ideological composition of the Parliament (Lord 2003).

The Parliament has also used non-legislative powers to influence the single market. Its successful ECJ case against the Council for failing to adopt a common transport policy raised the spectre of court-imposed deregulation of road haulage. This raised the cost-of-no-agreement for those opposed to liberalization and, thereby, strengthened the hands of those that wanted more far-reaching liberalization (Young 1995; Héritier 1997; Aspinwall 1999; Schmidt 2002).

The example of road haulage highlights nicely the role of the ECJ in regulatory politics. As a court it does not play a direct role in the policy process. It can, however, have a profound impact on the contours of the policy adopted because it can eliminate the status quo as a viable alternative. In such circumstances, the issue is not whether there should be reform, but what form it should take.

In contrast to its role with respect to economic regulations, the ECJ has had an important impact on EU regulatory politics as a result of up-holding the legitimacy of national social regulations (Joerges and Neyer 1997). As a result, national rules that serve legitimate public policy objectives (as defined by Article 95 of the EC Treaty) and are not unnecessarily trade restrictive are permitted even if they interfere with the free movement of goods. Thus, the ECJ has required that member states justify their policies with respect to specific legitimate objectives (Joerges and Neyer 1997). In this situation, the status quo is a viable option and the member state with the more stringent standard is under no pressure to change it, while its trading partners' firms are excluded from its market or have to comply with different national standards. Thus, it is the ECJ's upholding of national regulatory autonomy that enables the dynamics of 'trading-up' to occur (Vogel 1995; Scharpf 1999; Young and Wallace 2000).

Although there is broad agreement that the member states are the most important players in EU regulatory politics, different authors emphasize different roles: 'leaders' or 'laggards'.[4] As 'leaders' the member states play a crucial role in putting issues on the EU's agenda by adopting national policies that disrupt the single market (Héritier 1996; Kelemen 2004; Scharpf 1999; Vogel 1995; Young and Wallace 2000).[5] As Gottweis (1999) stresses, however, the trade disrupting effect of national rules translates into pressure for a common policy only because of the accepted objective of creating a single market; impeding trade is not inherently a problem. The disruptive impact of national regulations on intra-EU trade has been an important factor in explaining much of the approximation of social regulations within the single market, including automobile emissions (Young and Wallace 2000); the ban on growth hormones in beef (Vogel 1995); the approval process for genetically modified crops (Young 2001); pharmaceutical regulation (Kelemen 2004); the EU's food safety regime (Kelemen 2004); and chemicals regulation (Eckley and Selin 2004), as well as occupational safety, which has been largely pursued through approximation of equipment standards (Scharpf 1997). In these accounts the focus is on how the EU's institutions facilitated the translation of the leader's policies to the EU level.

By contrast, with regard to market-making regulations the member states are usually depicted as 'laggards', resisting change (Young 1995; Héritier 1997; Holmes and McGowan 1997; Sandholtz 1998; Schmidt 1998, 2002; Aspinwall 1999; Eising and Jabko 2001; Eising 2002). To be sure there are member states that favour market-making regulations, usually

because they have already liberalized their national markets, but they are usually depicted as supporting the Commission against the 'laggards' rather than leading the charge (Young 1995; Holmes and McGowan 1997; Padgett 2003). In most of these accounts, therefore, the focus is on how the EU's supranational institutions and the broader institutional context of the EU enabled the opposition of the 'laggards' to be overcome.[6]

It should be noted, however, that this is not a universally shared view. Thatcher (2001) argues that the Commission and the member governments were largely in accord on the substance of telecommunications liberalization, but differed over 'constitutional' issues concerning the allocation of powers between the Commission and the Council. Bartle (1999) and Levi-Faur (2004) argue that broader processes of globalization and technological change were more significant than the EU context for explaining the liberalization of electricity and, particularly, telecommunications.

Which Societal Actors' Interests Prevail?

Although there is a significant degree of disagreement about which actors matter more in the policy process, there is considerable agreement that the process of building the single market has by-and-large benefited diffuse interests at the expense of vested (economic) interests (Bomberg and Peterson 1993; Majone 1996; Joerges and Neyer 1997; Pollack 1997; Young and Wallace 2000). There are several reinforcing explanations for this: one focuses on the preferences of the political actors discussed above (Bomberg and Peterson 1993; Pollack 1997); another emphasizes the relative openness of the EU's policy networks (Héritier 1996; Kohler-Koch 1999; Jachtenfuchs and Kohler-Koch 2004); and a third pays attention to the role of ideas, including public perceptions of policy failures (Weale 1992; Woolcock 2002; Vogel 2003). As these are reinforcing rather than competing explanations, some authors integrate all three (Majone 1996; Young and Wallace 2000).

As discussed above, the Commission and Parliament have incentives to promote policies that benefit diffuse interests. Although there is debate about precisely how much they matter in the policy process, they clearly have an impact. Further, the dynamics of market integration tend to enhance the influence of those member states that have policies more beneficial to diffuse interests – stringent social regulations and liberalized economic regulations. Thus, a range of political actors have incentives to promote diffuse interests and the power resources to do so.

In addition, the relative openness of policy networks at the EU level affords (organized) diffuse interests access to the policy process. Although the Parliament is very open to interest groups, the Commission, as the initiator of policy proposals, is the focus of most interest group activity and scholarly attention. There are several reasons why the policy networks surrounding the Commission are particularly open. Some of these are essentially accidental. For example, when the Commission enters new policy areas there are no firmly established networks of actors (Peters 1994). Further, because the Commission is not directly involved in policy implementation, EU policy networks are less stable than at the national level (Eising and Kohler-Koch 1999b), although they become more stable as EU activity in a policy area progresses (Mazey and Richardson 2001). In addition, because an EU policy will apply in all member states more actors with more diverse interests than within any one member state will be affected and are thus likely to mobilize to try to influence the policy (Young and Wallace 2000). As a side-effect of this, 'Baptist and bootlegger' coalitions between producer and civic interests may be particularly prevalent at the EU level as some firms seek to extend the regulations that they are used to the rest of the EU (Young and Wallace 2000).

EU policy networks are also open as a result of the Commission's strategic action. The Commission's policy-making staff is actually very small, so it depends on interest groups to provide it with information about problems and possible solutions (Young and Wallace 2000; Mazey and Richardson 2001). In addition, the Commission consults widely in order to enhance the credibility and legitimacy of its policy proposals in the eyes of the member states (Peters 1994; Kohler-Koch 1999; Mazey and Richardson 2001). More recently, the Commission has sought to enhance its legitimacy more broadly through encouraging interest group activity (Mazey and Richardson 2001; Greenwood and Young 2005).

As in the US context, prevailing political ideas have been important in shaping policy outcomes. With respect to market-making regulations neo-liberal economic ideas about boosting economic efficiency and, thereby, growth through freeing competition have had a role. This has been most evident in air transport (Holmes and McGowan 1997) and road haulage (Young 1995). The norm of the market was also significant in the liberalization of electricity (Eising and Jabko 2001; Jabko 2006).

Also as in the US, social regulations have been largely immune to the logic of neo-liberal ideas. With regard to social regulations different ideas have supported more comprehensive and more risk averse regulation. 'Ecological modernization', which, among other things, challenged the assumption that environmental protection was incompatible with economic growth and called for the objective of environmental protection to be integrated into other policies, has been influential in Europe (more so than in the US) and has facilitated the fit between creating a single market and stringent environmental (product) standards (Weale 1992; Weale and Williams 1992).

An outgrowth of ecological modernism, the 'precautionary principle', which justifies taking action to address uncertain but potentially significant risks before scientific proof has been established, is likely to tilt the policy-making presumption towards more stringent regulation (Majone 2002). Moreover, the 'precautionary principle' has subsequently been extended to human, animal, and plant health (Woolcock 2002). There are, however, some indications that the 'precautionary principle' has had an impact more at the level of discourse than in policy outputs, where the impact of 'leader' states has been more important (Eckley and Selin 2004). It is possible that the shift towards more stringent regulation in the EU is actually a political response to a crisis of legitimacy in European regulation in the wake of a number of high-profile regulatory failures (Vogel 2003; Ansell and Vogel 2006). Whether as a principled approach to regulation or as a political reaction to public distrust, social regulation within the EU takes place within an ideational context that favours more rather than less stringent regulation.

Although there is some disagreement about which are the most important factors explaining the tendency of EU policy to favour diffuse interests, there is a consensus that there is such a tendency. Further, it would seem that this tendency arises more by accident than by design.

EU Regulatory Politics as a New Form of Governance?

In light of the importance of the supranational institutions in EU regulatory politics and the relative openness of the EU's policy networks, some authors have argued that the EU represents a new form of governance – 'network governance' (Eising and Kohler-Koch 1999a: 6; Egan 2001). In effect there are two dimensions to this argument: one horizontal, the other vertical. The horizontal dimension concerns whether state-society relations at the EU level are substantially different from those found in conventional states. The vertical dimension concerns whether sustained participation in the crucible of EU policy-making transforms the way that actors, particularly the member governments, understand and pursue their preferences. This vertical dimension, therefore, intersects with the broader rationalist-constructivist debate.

As the preceding discussion of participation in the EU regulatory politics suggests, there is something different about interest representation at the EU level. First, interest groups are active and important in the policy process, which distinguishes the EU from statist systems. Second, the policy networks are often open and fluid, which distinguishes it from corporatist networks. Third, the Commission plays an activist role and is not simply refereeing among competing interests as implied in an ideal-type pluralist system (Majone 1996; Eising and Kohler-Koch 1999a; Egan 2001). Although Commission-society relations do appear to be distinct from these ideal types found in some EU member states, they are frequently compared to policy networks (Peterson 1995, 2004) or 'policy subsystems' (Sabatier 1998), which are found within traditional states, such as the UK and US.

The second dimension of the governance question is more controversial. The proponents of the network governance approach contend that at the EU level the actors are oriented towards the 'upgrading of common interests in the pursuit of individual interests' (Eising and Kohler-Koch 1999a: 6). This takes place through deliberation, argument, and persuasion – 'deliberative supranationalism' – which is made possible by the intensive, institutionalized interaction of individuals in the EU regulatory process (Joerges and Neyer 1997: 610).

Much of this characterization focuses on the issue networks around the Commission and, in particular, the comitology system, which brings together the Commission, member government, and other experts and stakeholders. There is a fair degree of agreement that at the policy formation stage, where the Commission is to the fore, expertise and persuasion are the currencies of influence (Héritier 1996; Joerges and Neyer 1997; Eising and Kohler-Koch 1999a; Young and Wallace 2000). Deliberation is arguably particularly likely in policy areas where there is a heavy emphasis on science and risk assessment (Pollack 2003b).

More controversial is the contention that the process of 'deliberative supranationalism' can lead to the member governments changing their positions. This is based on two widely accepted observations. First, the member governments almost always try to find consensus within the Council of Ministers (Young and Wallace 2000; Padgett 2003). Second, during the policy process member governments' positions sometimes change (Sabatier 1998; Eising and Jabko 2001; Eising 2002; Padgett 2003; Arregui et al. 2004; Duina and Kurzer 2004). Although there is a fair degree of agreement that these observations are accurate at least some of the time, there is disagreement about how prevalent they are and what motivates them. For instance, while some contend that the member governments seek consensus because of 'informal understandings of principles of conduct' (Eising and Jabko 2001: 747), others see such behaviour as consistent with the rationalist logic of diffuse reciprocity (Keohane 1986).

Significantly, even the advocates of the constructivist approach accept that there are times when the member governments will not compromise (Eising and Kohler-Koch 1999b; Joerges and Neyer 1997). In fact, Joerges and Neyer (1997) specify that 'deliberative supranationalism' is most likely to occur when the distributive consequences of a policy are unclear and so the member governments are unsure where their preferences lie. In practice, although 'market integration' is one of the areas in which network governance is claimed to be particularly prevalent (Eising and Kohler-Koch 1999a), explicit votes in the Council of Ministers are more common on single market issues than other policy areas (Hayes-Renshaw et al. 2005) and governments frequently do not change their positions at all (Arregui et al. 2004).

There is a range of non-constructivist explanations for why governments sometimes change their positions. Several authors (Sabatier 1998; Eising and Jabko 2001; Padgett 2003) stress policy learning, which is related to, but distinct from, deliberative supranationalism. Policy learning is related to deliberative supranationalism in that the EU framework provides an intensive forum for the exchange of ideas, but it is distinct in that policy learning, because it concerns understandings of ends-means relationships rather than preferences, is fully compatible with rationalist explanations. Alternatively, some (Arregui et al. 2004) emphasize the importance of bargaining dynamics, such as package deals or being faced with a situation where any deal is better than no agreement. It is in this respect that the Commission's use of its competition

policy rules to change the default condition can be significant.

Other explanations for changes in the member governments' positions come from explicitly treating them as the aggregates of domestic preferences. The process of negotiation within the EU, as in international negotiations more generally, tends to bring new actors into the policy process and may legitimize the positions of domestic critics of existing national policies, as a consequence of which the government's position may change (Eising and Jabko 2001; Eising 2002). In the case of tobacco advertising, it would seem that changes in the party composition of member governments led to shifts in positions (Duina and Kurzer 2004).

This discussion suggests that the case for deliberative supranationalism is stronger in the policy proposal stage than in the decision phase, as Krapohl (2003) found in his study of the EU's response to the BSE crisis. This is consistent with the view that a problem-solving approach characterizes only the process through which the Commission formulates its policy proposal, while decision-making in the Council is characterized by bargaining and compensation (Peterson 1995; Héritier 1996).

COMPETITION POLICY

Competition policy is not part of the single market programme and significantly predates it. It warrants discussion here for several reasons, however. First, the member states have delegated antitrust and merger control to the Commission, subject to procedural requirements, so the Commission's exercise of its competition policy authority is the closest the EU comes to an independent regulatory agency. As a result, it is central to the understanding of the EU as a 'regulatory state' (Wilks 2005b). Second, competition policy – at least its antitrust and merger control aspects – in the EU, like the single market programme, is aimed at market integration, but targets private barriers to trade (McGowan and Cini 1999; Wilks 2005b). In addition, as discussed above, the Commission has used its competition

policy powers to alter the political climate for market-making regulations.

The politics of EU competition policy has received relatively little, some would say surprisingly little, attention from political scientists (Allen 1983). Most of the politics literature focuses on reforms of the institutions of competition policy (Cini and McGowan 1998), particularly the 1989 Merger Control Regulation (McGowan and Cini 1999), the 1962 Regulation 17 (Allen 1983), and the 2003 Modernisation Regulation (Wilks 2005a). While Regulation 17 is depicted in terms of delegation from the member governments to the Commission (Wilks 2005a), in the Merger Control and Modernization Regulations the Commission is depicted as playing a leading role (McGowan and Cini 1999; Wilks 2005a, b).

The Commission's powers to approve mergers have received some attention from political scientists, not least because these decisions are often controversial, especially when they affect foreign firms. Significantly, delegating decision-making to the Commission has not resulted in pure technocratic policy-making (McGowan and Cini 1999). The 1989 Merger Control Regulation assigned decision-making power not to a technocratic body, but to the College of Commissioners and there is sufficient leeway in the decision-making criteria to permit non-competition policy objectives to sometimes prevail (Cini and McGowan 1998; McGowan and Cini 1999; McGowan 2000a; Wilks 2005b). Thus, competing policy objectives among directorates general, pressure from member governments, and lobbying by affected interests have influenced policy decisions (McGowan and Cini 1999).

Rather less attention has been paid to the Commission's anti-trust activities (McGowan 2000b), despite their relative importance in the Commission's workload (McGowan 2000a). The major exception has been with regard to the Commission's approval of 'block exemptions' from antitrust rules to permit cooperation among European firms. The most studied example of which concerned the block exemption for automobile distribution, which effectively permitted the continued segmentation of national markets after the creation of the single market,

which in turn enabled the member states to maintain national restrictions on Japanese automobile imports. Unusually for an antitrust decision, this case involved extensive lobbying by interest groups, notably consumers, and conflict between the different policy priorities of different parts of the Commission (Holmes and McGowan 1997; Young and Wallace 2000).

THE EXTERNAL DIMENSION OF EU REGULATION

The preceding discussion has focused upon political conflicts within the EU over regulatory policies. The politics of regulation also has an important external dimension. The single market has been extended beyond the borders of the EU in the European Economic Area and has provided the focal point for all of the enlargement negotiations since 1986 (Young and Wallace 2000; Sedelmeier 2005a, b). In addition, given the EU's generally liberal trade regime in manufactured goods, regulations are now the most important barriers to imports of goods and establish the conditions for foreign firms wishing to provide services within the EU. Consequently, single market measures have been the source of numerous trade disputes, particularly with the US (Woolcock 1991; Hocking and Smith 1997; Vogel 1997a; Petersmann and Pollack 2003; Young 2003, 2004; Princen 2004a, b). In addition, as alluded to above, EU competition policy decisions have had significant implications for foreign firms, including Boeing and Microsoft.

Further, the Commission has actively sought to export some of the EU's regulatory practices to the rest of the world. This has been most evident with respect to competition policy (Holmes et al. 1996; Cini and McGowan 1998; Damro 2001) and the 'precautionary principle' (Majone 2002; Woolcock 2002).

LEGITIMACY

Given the centrality of regulation to the EU's activity, it is not surprising that general concerns about the EU's lack of input legitimacy resonate in discussions of regulatory politics, even though the European Parliament's involvement in regulatory politics, where the co-decision procedure first and most extensively applies, is relatively significant (Eising and Kohler-Koch 1999b; Harcourt and Radaelli 1999; Skogstad 2003; Eberlein and Grande 2005). Two opposite approaches have been presented for addressing this problem. Majone (1996) has advocated creating truly independent regulatory agencies with proper mechanisms of accountability. Others have stressed deliberative supranationalism and network governance as ways of bolstering the EU's input legitimacy (Joerges and Neyer 1997; Eising and Kohler-Koch 1999b), and the Commission seems to have been moving in that direction (Greenwood and Young 2005).

A central problem with both these approaches, however, is that neither can cope with fundamental differences over desired outcomes. Technocratic decision-making works only when the decisions really are technical – how to realize desired objectives, not what the objectives should be (Harcourt and Radaelli 1999). Such agreement on objectives is often lacking within the EU. There are even competing visions of the appropriate objectives of competition policy – promoting competition or competitiveness (McGowan and Cini 1999). Skogstad (2003) explicitly speculates that network governance, and particularly deliberative supranationalism, may not work on ideologically charged issues, such as genetically modified crops. This is consistent with Ansell and Vogel's (2006) concept of 'contested governance', which applies to situations, such as EU food safety, in which contestation is not simply about what a particular rule should be, but also concerns who should make policy, on what basis and at which level of governance. Arguably, it is the attempt to reconcile fundamentally different preferences that is the heart of the EU's legitimacy crisis, rather than the lack of democratic input into common policies.

Further, the focus on the perceived procedural shortcomings of EU regulatory policy making is arguably misframed. To the extent that the EU is a regulatory state, comparing it to the democratic features of a traditional state is inappropriate. In fact, the European Parliament's participation in and scrutiny of EU regulation is actually significantly greater than that found in most EU member states, where regulatory decisions are taken largely by executives, albeit within established legal and administrative frameworks (Young and Wallace 2000). The apparently greater powers of national parliaments relate to their role in redistributive policies. Thus, the problems with the legitimacy of EU regulatory policy may have more to with what it tries to do than with how it does it.

FUTURE DIRECTIONS

There is a surprising degree of common ground among observers of EU regulatory politics. With a few exceptions (Gottweis 1999; van Apeldoorn 2002), studies of EU regulatory politics explicitly or implicitly adopt neo-institutionalist approaches. Where the differences arise is between the more rationalist and more sociological/constructivist variants. Even here, however, there is a degree of agreement, at least with regard to observed behaviour, if not with what motivates it.

The study of EU regulatory politics, however, suffers from its fragmentation and narrow focus. With a few exceptions (Majone 1996; Eising and Kohler-Koch 1999a, b; Scharpf 1999; Young and Wallace 2000), the study of EU regulatory politics focuses on detailed studies of individual pieces of legislation or sectors. Although these provide a wealth of information, this fragmentation of the field makes it very difficult to move beyond the rather crude questions about whether the member governments or supranational institutions matter more or whether actors engage in arguing or bargaining, to specifying the conditions under which these different factors prevail.

Further, as Table 19.1 illustrates, most of the analytical activity has been concentrated on relatively few sectors, where EU regulation has been most controversial. This creates two blind spots. The first concerns the vast majority of EU regulatory activity that has not been controversial. Why policies have not been controversial may be as revealing about the nature of regulatory politics in the EU as understanding why controversial decisions came out the way they did. The second blind spot concerns areas where integration has not occurred. As a consequence, more theoretically guided and explicitly comparative work across a much wider range of cases is necessary before we can really understand the politics of EU regulation.

NOTES

1. For discussions of different meanings of regulation in the European context see Begg (1996); Majone (1994); and McGowan and Wallace (1996).

2. A form of negotiated mutual recognition also applies with regard to professional services, as the member governments must agree that their professional qualifications are equivalent in effect (Lovecy 1999).

3. In an elaboration on this concern, Hay and Rosamond (2002) argue that whether the argument that intensified economic competition requires governments to change their policies is 'true' may matter less than whether it is deemed to be true or just useful to those employing it.

4. The use of 'leaders' and 'laggards' here is not precisely the same as Héritier's (1996), but it captures broadly the same idea.

5. Member states also play a 'leader' role with respect to process regulation, but the pressures for a common policy are different and emanate from the adopting state.

6. With regard to the role of supranational institutions performing a similar role in environmental process standards, see Chapter 21.

REFERENCES

Allen, D. (1983) 'Managing the common market: the Community's competition policy', in H. Wallace, W. Wallace and C. Webb (eds), *Policy-Making in the European Union*, 2nd ed. London: John Wiley & Sons. pp. 209–36.

Alter, K.J. and Meunier-Aitsahalia, S. (1994) 'Judicial politics in the European community: European integration and the pathbreaking *Cassis de Dijon* decision', *Comparative Political Studies*, 26(4): 535–61.

Ansell, C. and Vogel, D. (eds) (2006) *What's the Beef? The Contested Governance of European Food Safety*. Cambridge, MA: MIT Press.

Armstrong, K. and Bulmer, S. (1998) *The Governance of the Single European Market*. Manchester: Manchester University Press.

Arp, H. (1993) 'Technical regulation and politics: the interplay between economic interests and environmental policy goals in EC car legislation', in J.D. Leifferink, P.D. Lowe and A.P.J. Mol (eds), *European Integration and Enviromental Policy*. London: Belhaven Press. pp. 150–71.

Arregui, J., Stokman, F. and Thomson, R. (2004) 'Bargaining in the European Union and shifts in actors' policy positions', *European Union Politics*, 5(1): 47–72.

Aspinwall, M. (1999) 'Planes, trains and automobiles: transport governance in the European Union', in B. Kohler-Koch and R. Eising (eds), *The Transformation of Governance in the European Union*. London: Routledge. pp. 119–34.

Bartle, I. (1999) 'Transnational intersts in the European Union: globalization and changing organization in telecommunications and electricity', *Journal of Common Market Studies*, 37(3): 363–83.

Begg, I. (1996) 'Introduction: regulation in the European Union', *Journal of European Public Policy*, 3(4): 525–35.

Boehmer-Christiansen, S.A. (1990) 'Vehicle emission regulation in Europe – the demise of lean-burn engines, the polluter pays principle … and the small car?' *Energy and Environment*, 1(1): 1–25.

Bomberg. E. and Peterson, J. (1993) 'Prevention from above? The role of the European Community', in M. Mills (ed.), *Prevention, Health and British Politics*. Aldershot: Avebury. pp. 140–60.

Burns, C. (2004) 'Codecision and the European Commission: a study of declining influence?' *Journal of European Public Policy*, 11(1): 1–18.

Cameron, D. (1992) 'The 1992 initiative: causes and consequences', in A.M. Sbragia (ed.), *Euro-Politics: Institutions and Policymaking in the 'New' European Community*. Washington: Brookings Institution. pp. 23–74.

Cini, M. and McGowan, L. (1998) *Competition Policy in the European Union*. London: Routledge.

Coen, D. and Thatcher, M. (eds) (2005) 'The new governance of markets and non-majoritarian regulators', *Governance*, 18(3): 329–46.

Cowles, M.G. (1994) 'The politics of big business in the European Community: setting the agenda for a new Europe', PhD dissertation, The American University, Washington, DC.

Cram, L. (1997) *Policy-Making in the European Union: Conceptual Lenses and the Integration Process*. London: Routledge.

Crombez, C., Steunenberg, B. and Corbett, R. (2000) 'Forum section: Understanding the EU legislative process: political scientists' and practitioners' perspectives', *European Union Politics*, 1(3): 363–81.

Damro, C. (2001) 'Building an international identity: the EU and extraterritorial competition policy', *Journal of European Public Policy*, 8(2): 208–26.

Dashwood, A. (1977) 'Hastening slowly: the Communities' path towards harmonization', in H. Wallace, W. Wallace and C. Webb (eds), *Policy-Making in the European Commuities*. John Wiley & Sons. pp. 273–99.

Dashwood, A. (1983) 'Hastening slowly: the Communities' path towards harmonization', in H. Wallace, W. Wallace and C. Webb (eds), *Policy-Making in the European Commuities*, 2nd ed. John Wiley & Sons. pp. 177–208.

Derthick, M. and Quirk, P.J. (1986) *The Politics of Deregulation*. Washington, DC: Brookings Institution.

Duina, F. and Kurzer, P. (2004) 'Smoke in your eyes: the struggle over tobacco control in the European Union', *Journal of European Public Policy*, 11(1): 57–77.

Dyson, K. and Humphreys, P. (1990) 'Introduction: politics, markets and communication policies', in K. Dyson and P. Humphreys (eds), *The Political Economy of Communications: International and European Dimensions*. London: Routledge. pp. 1–32.

Earnshaw, D. and Judge, D. (1993) 'The European Parliament and the Sweeteners Directive: from footnote to inter-institutional conflict', *Journal of Common Market Studies*, 31(1): 103–16.

Eberlein, B. and Grande, E. (2005) 'Beyond delegation: transnational regulatory regimes and the EU regulatory state', *Journal of European Public Policy*, 12(1): 89–112.

Eckley, N. and Selin, H. (2004) 'All talk, little action: precaution and European chemicals regulation', *Journal of European Public Policy*, 11(1): 78–105.

Egan, M. (2001) *Constructing a European Market*. Oxford: Oxford University Press.

Eichner, V. (1993) 'Social dumping of innovative regulation? Processes and outcomes of European decision-making in the sector of health and safety at work harmonization', EUI Working Papers in Political and Social Sciences (SPS) No. 92/28. Florence: European University Institute.

Eichner, V. (1997) 'Effective European problem-solving: lessons from the regulation of occupational safety and environmental protection', *Journal of European Public Policy*, 4(4): 591–608.

Eising, R. (2002) 'Policy learning in embedded negotiations: explaining EU electricity liberalization', *International Organization*, 56(1): 85–120.

Eising, R. and Jabko, N. (2001) 'Moving targets: national interests and electricity liberalization in the European Union', *Comparative Political Studies*, 34(7): 742–67.

Eising, R. and Kohler-Koch, B. (1999a) 'Introduction: network governance in the European Union', in B. Kohler-Koch and R. Eising (eds), *The Transformation of Governance in the European Union*. London: Routledge. pp. 3–13.

Eising, R. and Kohler-Koch, B. (1999b) 'Governance in the European Union: a comparative assessment', in B. Kohler-Koch and R. Eising (eds), *The Transformation of Governance in the European Union*. London: Routledge. pp. 267–85.

Friedman, J. and Martin, L.L. (2002) 'International political economy: global and domestic interactions', in I. Katznelson and H.V. Milner (eds), *Political Science: State of the Discipline*, III. New York: W.W. Norton. pp. 118–46.

Friedrich, A., Tappe, M. and Wurzel, R. (1998) 'The auto-oil programme: missed opportunity or leap forward?', Centre for European Union Studies Research Paper 1/98. Hull: The University of Hull.

Garrett, G. (1992) 'International cooperation and institutional choice: the European Community's internal market', *International Organization*, 46(2): 533–60.

Garrett, G. and Tsebelis, G. (1996) 'An institutional critique of intergovernmentalism', *International Organization*, 50(2): 269–90.

Garrett, G. and Weingast, B.R. (1993) 'Ideas, interests and institutions: constructing the European Community's internal market', in J. Goldstein and R.O. Keohane (eds), *Ideas and Foreign Policy: Beliefs, Institutions and Political Change*. Ithaca, NY: Cornell University Press. pp. 173–206.

Garrett, G., Tsebelis, G. and Corbett, R. (2001) 'Forum section: Understanding the EU legislative process: academics vs. practitioners – round 2', *European Union Politics*, 2(3): 353–66.

Gatsios, K. and Holmes, P. (1997) 'Regulatory competition and international harmonization', ESRC Global Economic Institutions Working Paper 36. London: Centre for Economic Policy Research, August.

Gottweis, H. (1999) 'Regulating genetic engineering in the European Union', in B. Kohler-Koch and R. Eising (eds), *The Transformation of Governance in the European Union*. London: Routledge. pp. 61–82.

Greenwood, J. and Young, A.R. (2005) 'EU interest representation or US-style lobbying?' in C. Parsons and N. Jabko (eds), *The State of the European Union, Volume 7: With US or Against US? European Trends in American Perspective*. Oxford: Oxford University Press. pp. 275–95.

Hancher, L. and Moran, M. (1989) 'Introduction: regulation and deregulation', *European Journal of Political Research*, 17(2): 129–36.

Harcourt, A. and Radaelli, C.M. (1999) 'The limits to EU technocratic regulation?' *European Journal of Political Research*, 35: 107–22.

Hay, C. and Rosamond, B. (2002) 'Globalisation, European integration and the discursive construction of economic imperatives', *Journal of European Public Policy*, 9(2): 147–67.

Hayes-Renshaw, F., van Aken, W. and Wallace, H. (2005) 'When and why the Council of Ministers of the EU votes explicitly', EUI Working Paper RSCAS No. 2005/25. European University Institute.

Héritier, A. (1996) 'The accommodation of diversity in European policy-making and its outcomes: regulatory policy as a patchwork', *Journal of European Public Policy*, 3(2): 149–67.

Héritier, A. (1997) 'Market-making policy in Europe: it's impact on member state policies: the case of road haulage in Britain, the Netherlands, Germany and Italy', *Journal of European Public Policy*, 4(4): 539–55.

Hocking, B. and Smith, M. (1997) *Beyond Foreign Economic Policy: The United States, the Single European Market and the Changing World Economy*. London: Pinter.

Holmes, P. and McGowan, F. (1997) 'The changing dynamic of EU–industry relations: lessons from the liberalization of European car and airline markets', in H. Wallace and A.R. Young (eds), *Participation and Policy-Making in the European Union*. Oxford: Clarendon Press. pp. 159–84.

Holmes, P. and Young, A.R. (2001) 'European lessons for multilateral economic integration: a cautionary tale', in Z. Drabek (ed.), *Globalization Under Threat: The Stability of Trade Policy and International Agreements*. Cheltenham: Edward Elgar. pp. 203–28.

Holmes, P., Kempton, J. and McGowan, F. (1996) 'International competition policy and telecommunications: lessons from the EU and prospects for the WTO', *Telecommunications Policy*, 20(10): 755–67.

Jabko, N. (2006) *Playing the Market: A Political Strategy for Uniting Europe, 1985–2005*. Ithaca, NY: Cornell University Press.

Jachtenfuchs, M. and Kohler-Koch, B. (1994) 'Governance and institutional development', in T. Diez and A. Wiener (eds), *European Integration Theory*. Oxford: Oxford University Press. pp. 97–115.

Joerges, C. and Neyer, J. (1997) 'Transforming strategic interaction into deliberative political process: the constitutionalization of comitology in the foodstuffs sector', *Journal of European Public Policy*, 4(4): 609–25.

Judge, D., Earnshaw, D. and Cowan, N. (1994) 'Ripples or waves: the European Parliament in the European Community policy process', *Journal of European Public Policy*, 1(1): 27–52.

Kasack, C. (2004) 'The legislative impact of the European Parliament under the revised co-decision procedure: environmental, public health and consumer protection policies', *European Union Politics*, 5(2): 241–60.

Kassim, H. (1996) 'Air transport', in H. Kassim and A. Mennon (eds), *The European Union and National Industrial Policy*. London: Routledge. pp. 106–31.

Katzenstein, P.J., Keohane, R.O. and Krasner, S.D. (1998) 'International organization and the study of world politics', *International Organization*, 52(4): 645–85.

Kelemen, R.D. (2002) 'The politics of "Eurocratic" structures and the new European agencies', *West European Politics*, 25(4): 93–118.

Kelemen, R.D. (2004) *The Rules of Federalism: Institutions and Regulatory Politics in the EU and Beyond*. Cambridge, MA: Harvard University Press.

Keohane, R.O. (1986) 'Reciprocity in international relations', *International Organization*, 40(1): 1–27.

Knill, C. and Lenschow, A. (2003) 'Modes of regulation and governance of the European Union: towards a comprehensive evaluation', *European Integration Online Papers*, 7(1): 1–22.

Kohler-Koch, B. (1999) 'The evolution and transformation of European governance', in B. Kohler-Koch and R. Eising (eds), *The Transformation of Governance in the European Union*. London: Routledge. pp. 14–35.

Krapohl, S. (2003) 'Risk regulation in the EU between interests and expertise: the case of BSE', *Journal of European Public Policy*, 10(2): 198–207.

Krapohl, S. (2004) 'Credible commitments in non-independent regulatory agencies: a comparative analysis of the European agencies for pharmaceuticals and foodstuffs', *European Law Journal*, 10(5): 518–38.

Levi-Faur, D. (2004) 'On the "net impact" of Europeanization: the EU's telecoms and electricity industries in comparative perspective', *Comparative Political Studies*, 37(1): 3–29.

Lord, C. (2003) 'The European Parliament in the economic governance of the European Union', *Journal of Common Market Studies*, 41(2): 249–67.

Lovecy, J. (1999) 'Governance transformation in the professional services sector: the case of market integration "by the back door"?', in B. Kohler-Koch and R. Eising (eds), *The Transformation of Governance in the European Union*. London: Routledge. pp. 135–51.

Lowi, T. (1964) 'American business, public policy, case studies and political theory', *World Politics*, 16(4): 677–715.

Majone, G. (1991) 'Cross-national sources of regulatory policymaking in Europe and the United States', *Journal of Public Policy*, 2(1): 79–106.

Majone, G. (1994) 'The rise of the regulatory state in Europe', *West European Politics*, 17(3): 77–101.

Majone, G. (1996) *Regulating Europe*. London: Routledge.

Majone, G. (2000) 'The credibility crisis of Community regulation', *Journal of Common Market Studies*, 38(2): 273–302.

Majone, G. (2002) 'What price safety? The precautionary principle and its policy implications', *Journal of Common Market Studies*, 40(1): 89–109.

Mazey, S. and Richardson, J. (2001) 'Institutionalising promiscuity: commission-interest group relations in the European Union', in A. Stone Sweet, W. Sandholtz and N. Fligstein (eds), *The Institutionalisation of Europe*. Oxford: Oxford University Press. pp. 71–93.

McGowan, F. (2000a) 'Competition policy: the limits of the European regulatory state', in H. Wallace and W. Wallace (eds), *Policy-Making in the European Union*, 4th ed. Oxford: Oxford University Press. pp. 115–47.

McGowan, F. and Wallace, H. (1996) 'Towards a European regulatory state', *Journal of European Public Policy*, 3(4): 560–76.

McGowan, L. (2000b) 'At the commission's discretion: Cartelbusting and Fining infringements under the EU's restrictive practices policy', *Public Administration*, 78(3): 639–56.

McGowan, L. and Cini, M. (1999) 'Discretion and politicization in EU competition policy: the case of merger control', *Governance*, 12(2): 175–200.

Mitchell, J. (1999) 'European Union policies and practices', *Journal of Consumer Studies and Home Economics*, 23(2): 65–88.

Moran, M. (1994) 'The state and the financial services revolution: a comparative analysis,' *West European Politics*, 17(3): 158–77.

Moravcsik, A. (1991) 'Negotiating the Single European Act: national interests and conventional statecraft in the European community', *International Organization*, 45(1): 19–56.

Moravcsik, A. (1998) *The Choice for Europe: Social Purpose and State Power from Messina to Maastricht*. London: UCL Press.

Müller, H. (2003) 'Interests or ideas? The regulation of insurance services and the European single market: trade liberalisation, risk regulation and limits to market integration', DPhil thesis, Falmer, University of Sussex.

Nicolaïdis, K. and Howse, R. (eds) (2001) *The Federal Vision: Legitimacy and Levels of Governance in the United States ands the European Union*. Oxford: Oxford University Press.

O'Reilly, D. and Stone Sweet, A. (1998) 'The liberalization and European reregulation of air transport', in W. Sandholtz and A. Stone Sweet (eds), *European Integration and Supranational Governance*. Oxford: Oxford University Press. pp. 164–87.

Padgett, S. (2003) 'Between synthesis and emulation: EU policy transfer in the power sector', *Journal of European Public Policy*, 10(2): 227–45.

Patterson, L.A. (2000) 'Biotechnology policy: regulating risks and risking regulation', in H. Wallace and W. Wallace (eds), *Policy-Making in the European Union*, 4th ed. Oxford: Oxford University Press. pp. 317–43.

Permanand, G. and Mossialos, E. (2005) 'Constitutional asymmetry and pharmaceutical policy-making in the European Union', *Journal of European Public Policy*, 12(4): 687–709.

Peters, B.G. (1994) 'Agenda-setting in the European community', *Journal of European Public Policy*, 1(1): 9–26.

Petersmann, E.-U. and Pollack, M.A. (eds) (2003) *Transatlantic Economic Disputes: The EU, the US and the WTO*. Oxford: Oxford University Press. pp. 595–602.

Peterson, J. (1995) 'Decision-making in the European Union: towards a framework for analysis', *Journal of European Public Policy*, 2(1): 69–93.

Peterson, J. (1997) 'States, societies and the European Union', *West European Politics*, 20(4): 1–24.

Peterson, J. (2004) 'Policy networks', in A. Wiener and T. Diez (eds), *European Integration Theory*. Oxford: Oxford University Press. pp. 117–35.

Pinder, J. (1968) 'Positive integration and negative integration: some problems of economic union in the EEC', *The World Today*, 24(3): 88–110.

Pollack, M.A. (1997) 'Representing diffuse interests in EC policy making', *Journal of European Public Policy*, 4(4): 572–90.

Pollack, M.A. (2003a) *The Engines of European Integration: Delegation, Agency and Agenda*

Setting in the EU. Oxford: Oxford University Press.

Pollack, M.A. (2003b) 'Control mechanism or deliberative democracy? Two images of comitology', *Comparative Political Studies*, 36(1–2): 125–55.

Pollack, M.A. and Shaffer, G.C. (2005) 'Biotechnology policy: between national fears and global disciplines', in H. Wallace, W. Wallace and M.A. Pollack (eds), *Policy-Making in the European Union*, 5th ed. Oxford: Oxford University Press. pp. 329–51.

Previdi, E. (1997) 'Making and enforcing regulatory policy in the single market', in H. Wallace and A.R. Young (eds), *Participation and Policy-Making in the European Union.* Oxford: Clarendon Press. pp. 69–91.

Princen, S.B.M. (2004a) 'Trading up in the transatlantic relationship', *Journal of Public Policy*, 24(1): 127–44.

Princen, S.B.M. (2004b) 'Exporting regulatory standards: the cases of trapping and data protection', in M. Knodt and S.B.M. Princen (eds), *Understanding the EU's External Relations.* London: Routledge. pp. 142–57.

Sabatier, P.A. (1998) 'The advocacy coalition framework: revision and relevance for Europe', *Journal of European Public Policy*, 5(1): 98–130.

Sandholtz, W. (1998) 'The emergence of a supranational telecommunications regime', in W. Sandholtz and A. Stone Sweet (eds), *European Integration and Supranational Governance.* Oxford: Oxford University Press. pp. 134–63.

Sandholtz, W. and Zysman, J. (1989) '1992: recasting the European bargain', *World Politics*, 42(1): 95–128.

Sbragia, A.M. (1992) *Euro-Politics: Institutions and Policymaking in the 'New' European Community.* Washington: Brookings Institution.

Sbragia, A. (1993) 'EC environmental policy: atypical ambitions and typical problems?', in A.W. Cafruny and G.G. Rosenthal (eds), *The State of the European Community, vol. 2: The Maastricht Debates and Beyond.* Boulder, CO: Lynne Rienner. pp. 337–52.

Sbragia, A. (1996) 'Environmental policy: the "push–pull" of policy-making', in H. Wallace and W. Wallace (eds), *Policy-Making in the European Union*, 3rd ed. Oxford: Oxford University Press. pp. 235–55.

Scharpf, F.W. (1988) 'The joint-decision trap: lessons from German federalism and European integration', *Public Administration*, 66(3): 239–78.

Scharpf, F.W. (1997) 'Introduction: the problem-solving capacity of multi-level governance', *Journal of European Public Policy*, 4(4): 520–38.

Scharpf, F.W. (1999) *Governing in Europe: Effective and Democratic?* Oxford: Oxford University Press.

Schmidt, S.K. (1998) 'Commission activism: subsuming telecommunications and electricity under European competition law', *Journal of European Public Policy*, 5(1): 169–84.

Schmidt, S.K. (2000) 'Only an agenda setter? The European Commission's power over the council of ministers', *European Union Politics*, 1(1): 37–61.

Schmidt, S.K. (2002) 'The impact of mutual recognition – inbuilt limits and domestic responses to the single market', *Journal of European Public Policy*, 9(6): 935–53.

Schneider, V., Dang-Nguyen, G. and Werle, R. (1994) 'Corporate actor networks in European policy-making: harmonizing telecommunications policy', *Journal of Common Market Studies*, 32(4): 473–98.

Schreiber, K. (1991) 'The new approach to technical harmonization and standards', in L. Hurwitz and C. Lequesne (eds), *The State of the European Community: Politics, Institutions and Debates in the Transition Years.* Boulder, CO: Lynne Rienner. pp. 97–112.

Sedelmeier, U. (2005a) 'Eastern enlargement: towards a European EU?', in H. Wallace, W. Wallace and M.A. Pollack (eds), *Policy-Making in the European Union*, 5th ed. Oxford: Oxford University Press. pp. 401–28.

Sedelmeier, U. (2005b) *Constructing the Path to Eastern Enlargement: The Uneven Policy Impact of EU Identity.* Manchester: Manchester University Press.

Siebert, H. and Koop, M. (1993) 'Institutional competition versus centralization: quo vadis Europe?' *Oxford Review of Economic Policy*, 9(1): 67–94.

Skogstad, G. (2003) 'Legitimacy and/or policy effectiveness? Network governance and GMO regulation in the European Union', *Journal of European Public Policy*, 10(3): 321–38.

Sun, J.-M. and Pelkmans, J. (1995) 'Regulatory competition and the single market', *Journal of Common Market Studies*, 33(1): 67–89.

Thatcher, M. (1999) *The Politics of Telecommunications: National Institutions, Convergence and Change.* Oxford: Oxford University Press.

Thatcher, M. (2001) 'The Commission and national governments as partners: EC regulatory expansion in telecommunications 1979–2000', *Journal of European Public Policy*, 8(4): 558–84.

Thatcher, M. and Stone Sweet, A. (eds) (2002) 'The politics of delegation: non-majoritarian institutions in Europe', special issue of *West European Politics*, 25(1): 1–22.

Tsebelis, G. (1994) 'The power of the European Parliament as a conditional agenda setter', *American Political Science Review*, 88(1): 128–42.

van Apeldoorn, B. (2001) 'The struggle over European order: transnational class agency in he making of 'embedded neo-liberalism', in A. Bieler and A.D. Morton (eds), *Social Forces in the Making of New Europe: The Restructuring of European Social Relations in the Global Political Economy*. Basingstoke: Palgrave. pp. 70–89.

van Apeldoorn, B. (2002) *Transnational Capitalism and the Struggle over European Integration*. London: Routledge.

Vogel, D. (1989) *Fluctuating Fortunes: The Political Power of Business in America*. New York: Basic Books.

Vogel, D. (1995) *Trading Up: Consumer and Environmental Regulation in a Global Economy*. Cambridge, MA: Harvard University Press.

Vogel, D. (1997a) *Barriers or Benefits? Regulation in Transatlantic Trade*. Washington, DC: Brookings Institution Press.

Vogel, D. (1997b) 'Trading up and governing across: transnational governance and environmental protection', *Journal of European Public Policy*, 4(4): 556–71.

Vogel, D. (2003) 'The hare and the tortoise revisited: the new politics of consumer and environmental regulation in Europe', *British Journal of Political Science*, 33: 557–80.

Wallace, W. (2005) 'Post-sovereign governance', in H. Wallace, W. Wallace and M.A. Pollack (eds), *Policy-Making in the European Union*. Oxford: Oxford University Press. pp. 483–503.

Weale, A. (1992) *The New Politics of Pollution*. Manchester: Manchester University Press.

Weale, A. and Williams, A. (1992) 'Between economy and ecology? The single market and the integration of environmental policy', *Environmental Politics*, 1(4): 45–64.

Wilks, S. (2005a) 'Agency escape: decentralization or dominance of the European Commission in the modernization of competition policy?' *Governance*, 18(3): 431–52.

Wilks, S. (2005b) 'Competition policy: challenge and reform', in H. Wallace, W. Wallace and M.A. Pollack (eds), *Policy-Making in the European Union*, 5th ed. Oxford: Oxford University Press. pp. 113–39.

Wilson, J.Q. (1980) *The Politics of Regulation*. New York: Basic Books.

Woolcock, S. (1991) *Market Access Issues in EC-US Relations: Trading Partners or Trading Blows?* London: Pinter.

Woolcock, S. (1994) *The Single European Market: Centralization or Competition among Rules?* London: RIIA.

Woolcock, S. (1997) 'Competition among rules in the European Union', in D.G. Mayes (ed.), *The Evolution of the Single European Market*. Cheltenham, Edward Elgar. pp. 66–86.

Woolcock, S. (2002) 'The precautionary principle in the European Union and its international trade effects', Paper for the Centre for European Policy Studies, February.

Young, A.R. (1995) 'Ideas, interests and institutions: the politics of liberalisation in the EC's road haulage industry', in D. Mayes (ed.), *The Evolution of Rules for a Single European Market, Part I: Industry and Finance*. Luxembourg: Office for Official Publications of the European Communities.

Young, A.R. (1997) 'Consumers in the single market: consumption without representation?' in H. Wallace and A.R. Young (eds), *Participation and Policy-Making in the European Union*. Oxford: Clarendon Press. pp. 206–34.

Young, A.R. (2001) 'Trading up or trading blows? US politics and transatlantic trade in genetically modified food', RSC Working Paper 2001–30. San Domenico di Fiesole: European University Institute, Robert Schumann Centre.

Young, A.R. (2003) 'Political transfer and "trading up": transatlantic trade in genetically modified food and US politics', *World Politics*, 55(4): 457–84.

Young, A.R. (2004) 'The incidental fortress: the single European market and world trade', *Journal of Common Market Studies*, 42(2): 393–414.

Young, A.R. (2005) 'The single market: a new approach to policy', in H. Wallace, W. Wallace and M.A. Pollack (eds), *Policy-Making in the European Union*, 5th ed. Oxford: Oxford University Press. pp. 93–112.

Young, A.R. and Wallace, H. (2000) *Regulatory Politics in the Enlarging European Union: Weighing Civic and Producer Interests*. Manchester: Manchester University Press.

20

The Politics of Redistribution

IAN BACHE

INTRODUCTION

Scholarship on the EU has not engaged very much with the concept of redistribution in a broad sense, but has tended to focus on a single redistributive policy area, that of regional policy.[1] This focus, while reflecting a narrow conceptualization of redistribution, relating to financial transfers between member states, is understandable because it takes a direct and relatively tangible form (accounts for a third of the EU budget). However, this focus overshadows the importance of the direct redistributive effects of both financial non-financial EU policies in other policy areas and on the EU's indirect effects on the redistributive policies of its member (and accession) states. This chapter considers both the narrow conceptualization of financial redistribution, covering the main debates over regional policy, before considering wider understandings of redistribution and how this research agenda might move forward. The starting point is to distinguish between redistribution and other areas of EU activity.

According to the classic statement by Lowi (1964), redistribution is one of three major categories of public policies, alongside distribution and regulation. Both distributive and redistributive policies involve public expenditure, while regulatory (rule-making) policies do not; this distinction provides the basis for the narrower categorization provided by Majone (1996b: 267) of non-regulatory and regulatory policies. The distributive label refers to spending on a wide range of public programmes and services generally aimed at particular sectors or 'clients' and distributive policy processes are often categorized as 'pork barrel': indeed, Lowi (1964: 690) suggested that '"patronage" in the fullest meaning of the word can be taken as a synonym for "distributive"'. By contrast, redistributive policies are generally aimed at broader categories: 'they are, crudely speaking, haves and have-nots, bigness and smallness, bourgeoisie and proletariat' (Lowi 1964: 691). Redistributive policies involve a transfer of resources to less advantaged social groups from more advantaged groups, whereas distributive policies do not. More broadly, the redistribution function may be taken to include 'all transfers of resources from one social group to another, as well as the provision of "merit goods", that is, goods such as elementary education or public financed medical care, that the government compels individuals to consume' (Majone 1996b: 267).

As Lowi acknowledged, these typologies are not straightforward. Regulatory and distributive policies may be redistributive in the longer term and thus, the typologies are most helpful in categorizing the short term. This is useful to highlight here because a theme of the discussion below is that it is both the regulatory aspects of structural policy, as well as the financial aspects that have been of redistributive significance. Moreover, as social constructivists would be quick to point out, different actors might categorize policies differently. An illustration was provided in an early response to Lowi's work: 'liberals in Congress might view the Poverty Program as a distributive issue (which would be an accurate classification, given Lowi's categories): conservatives on the other hand, might perceive such a program as redistributive' (Froman 1968: 50).

Pollack (2000) identified a growth of EU policy competences across Lowi's categories before a backlash in the 1990s. At this point the 'creeping competence' of the EU became more uneven, with distributive and redistributive policies hampered by firm financial ceilings while regulatory policies were exempt from such constraints. The financial costs of regulation are borne by those regulated, rather than those making the policies. Moreover, with a wider range of interests participating in EU politics, demand for regulation increased and supply was assured by the Commission's desire to expand EU competences.

Institutional factors are also seen to constrain the development of redistributive policies. Streeck (1996: 89–90) argued that the EU's ability to act in this sphere is 'severely limited' by the 'fundamentally intergovernmental system of governance' that 'favors the deregulatory, neo-liberal agenda of business over the interests of labor, which generally seeks re-regulation and protection at the EC level' (cited in Pollack 1997: 575). On this issue though, the weight of evidence is unclear. Pollack (1997) countered Streeck's argument by highlighting the many access points provided by supranational institutions to a broad range of social interests and the resulting EU policies that counter or compensate for the neo-liberal agenda. The development of regional policy illustrates the kinds of opportunities presented through the interaction between supranational institutions and domestic and national transnational interest organizations (see below).

THE NORMATIVE DIMENSION

Of course, constraints on redistribution in the EU are not only financial and institutional. There is also a normative dimension and one that relates to views on the very nature of the EU. Wallace (1980: 24) identified an essential difference between

> … those who see this as clearly a Community responsibility and those who argue that, whatever may be the role of the EC, it is and must remain relatively insignificant beside the responsibility of national governments, unless the EC were to change fundamentally and become a developed federation.

Related to this difference of view, issues of redistribution have become increasingly bound up with debates about the legitimacy of the EU. For some scholars (see Scharpf 1999), the failure of the EU to deliver on the 'output' side of democracy in terms of effective redistribution and social protection alienates the social groups that benefit least from European integration. On the other side of this argument, scholars have stated that, in the absence of strong majoritarian principles in the EU's institutional system, the very different legal and political traditions of the member states make it difficult to see how an effective and equitable set of redistributive policies could be developed. As such, 'a more active role of the European Union in income redistribution would not reduce the Union's democratic deficit, as many people would seem to think, but would on the contrary aggravate it' (Majone 1996a: 298–9). Therefore, there is a paradox at the heart of the legitimacy-redistribution issue: on the one hand it is difficult to justify greater redistribution without more effective and legitimate decision-making procedures, while on the other hand the very legitimacy of the EU is seen to be undermined by its ineffectiveness as a redistributive polity.

On a quite different tack, Guérot (2004) has suggested that the EU needs to shift its spending away from redistributive policies towards geo-strategic strategies to enhance its position as a political power. This approach would render issues like the Turkish accession 'unambiguously' advantageous, rather than complicated by the potential costs of extending existing redistributive policies.

In short, this issue is not simply about how well the EU delivers an agreed policy goal: it is a contentious and politicized domain, which has at its centre some of the key debates about the nature, purpose, and adequacy of the EU. However, many of these debates refer obliquely at best to redistribution: indeed, explicit references to the politics of redistribution in academic literature on the EU are rare in comparison with those on the politics of regulation. As such, there is no rich seam to mine for the purposes of this chapter in terms of an established literature explicitly on this theme. This is probably a significant omission in academic debates on the EU – a point that will be returned to in the conclusion. Instead, the focus here is on the closest thing we have: established (and some less established) debates on the politics of financial redistribution and specifically on what are considered to be the most redistributive instruments of EU finance: the structural funds.

THE STRUCTURAL FUNDS

A starting point for understanding the politics of redistribution in relation to the structural funds is the broader budgetary picture. Irrespective of the formula for determining national contributions, there has long been a political sensitivity around how much is paid in and how much is received in return. For example, Wallace (1980: 26) argued that 'from the outset an important strand in French policy was that the financial gains of EC membership should at least balance the financial contributions – the so-called principle of *juste*

retour'. That the Common Agricultural Policy (CAP), of which France is the major beneficiary, has swallowed up such a large proportion of the overall budget historically is testimony to this policy.

Of course, the notion of securing a fair return on contributions is not exclusively French. Perhaps even more famously, successive British governments have been keen to demonstrate a fair return for their EU contributions. In the first instance, the creation of ERDF owed a large part to the British accession (below), while the difficult issue of the British rebate has bounced up and down the EU's agenda since the 1970s. Following the 2004 enlargement, pressure on the Blair government to reduce the British rebate in the context of the accession of a number of poorer member states was met with an explicit link between this and the reform of CAP funding. This was unacceptable to the French government and the issue remained unresolved.

Over time, however, the budget has become less CAP-dominated and a shift towards the more redistributive structural funds has taken place. The proportion of agricultural support in the budget has declined from its high point of 80% in the 1980s to 44% by 2003 (Laffan and Lindner 2006: 30). For its part, structural funding grew from an initial allocation of less than 5% in 1975 (Marks 1992: 194) to over one-third of the total budget by 2000.

The breakthrough period for structural policy was the mid-1980s, with the impetus provided by the Single European Act (SEA) and the Iberian enlargement. The Commission cultivated an explicit link between the completion of the single market and the need for greater redistribution, which persuaded the net contributor governments. This led to a major overhaul of structural policy in 1988 (below) and later to the creation of a Cohesion Fund at Maastricht in 1991 to assist the poorest four member states to meet the criteria for Economic and Monetary Union (EMU).

But while the late 1980s and early 1990s witnessed growth in the EU budget and more generous allocations to redistributive instruments, governments applied the brakes later in the decade. At the level of 1.27% of EU GDP agreed for the funding period 2000–06, the overall EU budget remains relatively small in comparison with the spending of national governments; and thus does the potential for greater financial redistribution.

The Dominant Debate: Intergovernmentalism vs Supranationalism

There is no doubt that, in line with much else in the EU, the dominant theoretical debate on regional policy has revolved around the power struggle between national governments (individually and collectively) and supranational institutions (notably the Commission). As the main financial instrument of regional policy was not created until 1975, regional policy was not an explicit feature of the writings of early neofunctionalists: although, as we shall see later, their contribution to the study of the sector was far from irrelevant. But born at a high tide of intergovernmentalism, regional policy emerged as a 'virtual paragon of intergovernmentalism' (McAleavey 1992: 3). This view was seriously challenged with the reform of the structural funds in 1988, which spawned the neofunctionalist-inspired concept of multi-level governance. From the early 1990s onwards, multi-level governance presented an important conceptual challenge to intergovernmentalism, not only in relation to regional policy but also in capturing the nature of the EU as a whole.

Intergovernmentalism and multi-level governance remained central to debate on regional policy and, along with the bulk of structural funding, its coverage spread to the states of central and eastern Europe in run up to the 2004 enlargement and immediately after. During the same period the debate had also begun to broaden out in concert with a wider chorus of voices on EU developments. The progression and expansion of debate on regional policy is best understood in historical context; not least because this debate has often focused on and been shaped by a series of periodic reforms and their subsequent implementation.

The Early Years: A Virtual Paragon of Intergovernmentalism

While the Treaty of Rome acknowledged the EC's marked regional imbalances, it was not until the 1970s that serious attempts were made to address them at the European level. Agreement to create the European Regional Development Fund (ERDF) at the Paris Summit of 1972 reflected the increased salience of the issue in the context of the impending enlargement to include Britain, Denmark, and Ireland. The position of the British government was particularly important in pushing for the fund, being 'urgently in need of actions which could be used to show a sceptical public and Parliament that concrete benefits were resulting from common market membership' (Wise and Croxford 1988: 173). Other influential factors were a push towards EMU provided by the Werner Report (European Commission 1970) and Commission plans to control member states' aid to industries (see Bache 1998: 36–7).

Ironically perhaps, a report by Regional Policy Commissioner George Thomson in 1973 (European Commission 1973) set out the instrumental arguments for regional policy that have remained central to intergovernmental explanations since. It emphasized that the commitment to EMU was jeopardized by regional disparities. In the context of a common market, manipulation of the exchange rate of the national currency was one of the few policy instruments still available to governments seeking to strengthen lagging regions: EMU implied the loss of that instrument. Moreover, ongoing regional disparities threatened the viability of the common market and thus the very basis of the Community itself. This issue-linkage is a key theme in the history of regional policy and central to understanding the 'side-payments' argument that intergovernmentalists have advanced (below).

From the step towards a regional fund taken at Paris in 1972, it was a difficult journey to the creation of the ERDF. Agreement was reached in 1974, again in Paris, only when the Irish and Italian governments threatened to boycott the summit unless they were promised progress on the creation of the fund. The size of the fund (1.3 billion European Units of Account, or EUA) disappointed the demandeur member states, but they saw its creation as a breakthrough. The fund would usually provide up to half the cost of regional development projects in eligible regions: this contribution had to be matched by domestic financing. This 'match-funding' principle was designed to enhance coordination and complementarity between EC and domestic regional policies. It would have significance in debates both connected to redistribution and Europeanization.

Institutionally, national governments retained an important role at the EU level through representation on a Fund Management Committee, which would ultimately approved the projects funded: projects that were themselves submitted by national governments. Governments also insisted that the fund should be allocated according to national quotas rather than objective Community criteria. Each government demanded a quota, even though this meant that relatively prosperous regions in wealthier member states would receive funding at the expense of poorer regions elsewhere. This intergovernmental carve-up meant that funding was dispersed over 40% of the total EC population rather than concentrated on areas of greatest need. In terms of supranational principles, the additionality requirement stating that 'the Fund's assistance should not lead Member States to reduce their own regional development efforts but should complement these efforts' (European Commission 1975) would long be at the centre of controversy and academic debate over regional policy.

An intergovernmentalist consensus soon emerged to explain the creation of EC regional policy. Preston (1984: 68) described how 'the major protagonists saw the Fund issue in terms of national interest', while George (1985: 146) recorded that even for one of its major advocates (Britain), 'all that was being sought was an institutionalised subsidy … An integrated Community policy for regional policy was not on the agenda'. Wallace (1977: 147) noted how '… the Commission concentrated on constructing a package of rewards that would satisfy the demandeurs and persuade other member governments that the [E]RDF would further their interests too'. Each government insisted on a stake, however small, and 'none was prepared to forgo the possible leverage that a stake in the Fund would give it, both in bargaining over the Regional Fund and over other policy sectors' (Preston 1984: 84).

Not only were intergovernmentalist arguments prominent in explaining the EC-level deal, they also captured the nature of the implementation process. The Commission was concerned with the implementation of the additionality principle in a number of member states, although the UK emerged as a particular problem (Preston 1983; McAleavey 1992). The UK government's reluctance to pass on EC funds to the assisted regions was part of a 'determined reluctance to allow the availability of Community funds to become a resource in domestic politics except so far as it could be controlled by central government' (Wallace 1977: 154). As such, the implementation of additionality became an important barometer in measuring the relative strengths of national governments and the Commission over EU regional policy and, as such, informed later conceptual debate.

After 1975, the perception of EC regional policy as a 'virtual paragon of intergovernmentalism' did not begin to change until after the first major reform of regional policy in 1988. Up to that point, there was some limited evidence for supranational arguments: experiments with non-quota programmes after 1979 and the introduction of the multi-annual programming approach to administering funds in 1984 were examples of this. Thus, national governments were seen to shape the broad contours of regional policy, while the Commission, at times assisted by the European Parliament, made piecemeal progress by seeking to 'educate and cajole governments at the margins rather than to promote immediate and radical changes in national regional policies' (Wallace 1983: 97). But while supranational institutions played a role, there were no significant cross-sectoral or multi-level policy networks to speak of that were important to later conceptual developments. Wallace (1983: 97) noted that, there has been almost no scope for the direct involvement of extra-governmental interests, for regional lobbies or other pressure groups, much though they have lobbied and pronounced on the various proposals tabled and important as their influence may have been at national level.

The reform of the structural funds in 1988 provided a major opportunity for the Commission to strengthen the redistributive impact of regional policy. Perceptions about regional policy began to change after this reform.

The 1988 Reform and the Challenge of Multi-Level Governance

The accession of Spain and Portugal in 1985 meant a considerable widening of regional disparities in the EU, leading to a doubling of the population of regions with a per capita GDP of less than 50% of the Community average (European Commission 1989: 9). This in itself required an increase in regional allocations. However, in response to the concerns of the poorer regions about the effects of the SEA, Article 130A set out the need to strengthen 'economic and social cohesion' within the EC, in particular through 'reducing disparities between the various regions and the backwardness of the least favoured regions' (European Commission 1989: 11). Laffan and Lindner (2006: 12) argue that, 'the new articles on "economic and social cohesion" (Article, 130 SEA), promoted by the Commission and the poorer member states, proved a powerful peg for the Commission to develop its strategy on redistribution'. For the Commission, cohesion had a dual meaning: 'It summarized a novel policy rationale to deal more effectively with the old problem of regional economic disparities, but it also held a political promise to involve subnational actors more openly in European decision- making … subnational mobilization was crucial to its success' (Hooghe 1996b: 89).

Allocations to the structural funds would double in real terms between 1987–93, reaching almost 25% of the EU budget. Their operation would be guided by four complementary principles, which were essentially those the Commission had advocated throughout the development of regional policy. *Additionality* required that funds be spent in addition to planned domestic spending; *concentration* focused funds on areas of greatest need; *programming* required regions to develop strategic multi-annual plans to ensure coherence between projects funded; and *partnership* required that funds be administered through regional partnerships within each state, consisting of representatives of national government, regional (or local) government, and the European Commission.

In terms of the budgetary envelope agreed in 1988, an intergovernmentalist interpretation found favour among most commentators. The more prosperous member states strongly supported the completion of the single market and wanted this market extending to include Spain and Portugal. In this context, the likely paymaster governments accepted the doubling of the structural funds as a 'side-payment to Ireland and the Southern nations' in exchange for their political support on other issues (Moravcsik 1991: 62). Advocates of multi-level governance generally accepted this interpretation (Hooghe 1996a), although Marks (1992: 198) conceptualized the side-payment argument in neofunctionalist language, describing it as an illustration of *forced spillover* 'in which the prospect of a breakthrough in one arena created intense pressure for innovation in others'.

Consensus between scholars over other aspects of the 1988 reform is harder to find. For example, Hooghe (1996b: 100) argued that the Commission emerged 'as the pivotal actor in designing the regulations' through its 'monopoly of initiative on the institutional design'. A good example was the inclusion of the partnership principle in the regulations, which was the major innovation of the 1988 reform. In contrast, Pollack (1995) took an 'essentially intergovernmentalist' view, arguing that agreement could be explained by changes in the preferences of the various member states – in particular net contributors such as Britain, France, and Germany. The preferences of the net contributors changed in three ways. First, with the Iberian enlargement, the proportion of structural funds received by the 'big three' member states decreased significantly. This meant that for these governments, 'the idea of greater Commission oversight seemed less like an intrusion into the internal affairs of one's own state, where EC spending was minimal, and more like a necessary oversight of the poor member states where the bulk of EC money was being spent' (Pollack 1995: 372). Second, the Iberian enlargement made France, like Britain and Germany, a net contributor to the EC budget, thus giving the 'big three' governments a common interest in the efficient use of the structural funds. Third, the spiralling costs of both the CAP and the structural funds made the level and efficiency of EC spending a 'political issue' of increasing concern to the governments of France, Germany, and Britain in the 1980s (Pollack 1995: 372).

While there were disagreements over the architects of the reform, the effects of two of the principles agreed in 1988 proved especially relevant in the conceptual challenge to intergovernmentalism. These were the principles of partnership and additionality. The partnership principle provided the first formal requirement that local and regional authorities be involved in EC policy-making, while the additionality principle, which pre-existed the 1988 reform, was significantly clarified and strengthened in pursuit of more effective implementation (and thus redistribution). The effects of these principles became central to the development of multi-level governance (Marks 1993).

On partnership, the effects appeared fairly clear: any government seeking structural funds had to establish partnerships in each of its assisted regions consisting of supranational (Commission), national, and subnational actors. This structure was undeniably 'multi-level'. The conceptual debate around the significance of this development related to the extent to which it affected policy outcomes: that is, whether this was multi-level *governance* in any meaningful sense or simply multi-level *participation* (Bache 1999: 42). The answer depended largely on the domestic context.

The first major empirical study of the implementation of the partnership principle was coordinated by Hooghe (1996a). The study found that the implementation of the

principle had different effects in different member states, with the pre-existing distribution of power between central and subnational governments a key explanatory factor (for case studies, see Anderson 1996; Balme and Jouve 1996; de Rynck 1996; Grote 1996; Ioakimidis 1996; Laffan 1996; Morata and Munoz 1996; Nanetti 1996; Smith 1997). Indeed, there was some evidence of variations in the implementation of the principle within member states (Bache et al. 1996; Martin and Pearce 1999). The extent of variation encouraged engagement with the related concept of policy networks, with its focus on implementation and patterns of resource dependencies between actors within networks (Heinelt and Smith 1996; Rhodes et al. 1996; Ansell et al. 1997; Börzel 1997; Bache 1998; Adshead 2002). Thus, the implementation of the partnership principle promoted multi-level governance in the sense that 'supranational, national, regional and local governments are enmeshed in territorially overarching policy networks' (Marks 1993: 402). However, the variation across and within states pointed to the need to analyse and explain the distribution of power within those networks and its effect on policy outcomes.

On additionality, the pivotal case study arose from a dispute between the Commission and the UK government, when it became apparent that the latter had not changed its non-compliance with additionality despite the provisions of the 1988 reform. The details of the dispute are complex and have been well documented (McAleavey 1992, 1995; Marks 1993; Bache 1998) but a key dimension was the alliance of the Commission and British local authorities against the UK government: an alliance that led to a government climbdown to resolve the dispute ahead of the 1992 general election. In developing multi-level governance, Marks (1993: 403) argued that,

> Several aspects of the conflict – the way in which local actors were mobilized, their alliance with the Commission, and the effectiveness of their efforts in shifting the government's position – confirm the claim that structural policy has provided subnational governments and the Commission with new political resources and opportunities in an emerging multilevel policy arena.

Yet while the interaction between the levels of government was again indisputable, the outcomes from this interaction were less clear. A study of the implementation of the agreement reached at the end of the dispute demonstrated that little changed in terms of additional spending on regional development in Britain. Instead it appeared that while national government had been forced into a climbdown at one stage of the policy process, it reasserted its powers to avoid compliance at a later stage. In other words, the 'gatekeeping' role of national government extended deeply into the implementation process (Bache 1999).

Whatever the differences over the effects of these principles, the emphasis placed on policy implementation by multi-level governance and the related concept of policy networks was an important contribution to the study of the EU. It challenged state-centric theorists to address the significance of the implementation process, which was neglected in intergovernmentalist accounts of the EU. This challenge reflected a broader shift in the study of the EU in which the application of approaches from domestic and comparative politics began to challenge the traditional study of the EU as a process of integration drawing on approaches from international relations (see Hix 1994). In terms of theoretical development, a key lesson from the implementation of the 1988 reform was that:

> Analysts who want to predict developments in EU cohesion policy from the great bargains risk overlooking the ambivalence in the regulations; the active role of the European Commission, national administrations, and subnational actors in exploiting these ambiguities; and the effects of policy learning (Hooghe 1996b: 119).

A Europe of the Regions

In the period after the 1988 reform, debates on multi-level governance became interweaved with a burgeoning debate on the emergence of a 'Europe of the Regions' (Anderson 1990; Mazey and Mitchell 1993; Sharpe 1993; Harvie 1994; Scott et al. 1994; Jones and Keating 1995; Hooghe and Marks 1996; Loughlin 1996; Jeffery 1997; Keating 1998; Keating and Hooghe 1998; Le Galès and Lequesne 1998; Tommel 1998) and related strands on regional empowerment (Martin and Pearce 1993; Smyrl 1997; Bache and Jones 2000; Bailey and De Propris 2002a: Bourne 2003) and on the nature and significance of subnational mobilization (John 1994, 2001; Hooghe 1995; McAleavey and Mitchell 1995; Benington and Harvey 1998; Bomberg and Peterson 1998; John and McAteer 1998; Allen 2000, 2006; Jeffery 2000).

In the Europe of the Regions literature, there was a divide between those who saw the promotion of regions and regionalism as a conscious and deliberate Commission strategy to undermine the power of national governments and thus promote integration, and those who saw it as a tool of an effective regional policy. The first view was typically held by national politicians, not least those who were reluctant Europeans and were thus naturally suspicious of the Commission's motives. It was not a view strongly articulated in academic circles, although there was acknowledgement that the Commission 'might be said to have an institutional interest in the development of a new level of legitimate government, as a means of by-passing the member states' (Richardson 1998: vii). And it was evident that, consciously political or not, the idea of a 'Europe of the Regions' was embraced as a slogan by regional political actors and even by the Commission for a short while under the presidency of Jacques Delors (John 2001: 73). In the second view, Tommel (1998: 53) was clear that the goal was an effective regional policy rather than a political agenda: 'the Commission was not primarily concerned with consciously involving the regions in its decision-making and policy implementation procedures, let alone with "visions", "grand designs" or politically motivated strategies on how to reorganize the EU system or on how to modernize state behaviour and performance'.

On the related sub-themes of subnational mobilization and regional empowerment, a consensus emerged that paralleled the findings on multi-level governance and structural policy: there was evidence of participation and mobilization by regional actors, but the significance of this was often uncertain. Richardson

(1998: viii) suggested that, 'The story is one of much symbolic politics and institutional innovation and not much real redistribution of power between levels of government, other than to the supranational level'. Similarly, Hooghe and Keating (1994: 368) reported that, 'We find that there has been a great deal of regional mobilization but that its effectiveness is questionable'.

The 1993 Reform:
Intergovernmentalism Reasserted

If the 1988 reform of the structural funds advanced supranationalism and, to varying degrees, multi-level governance, the 1993 reform was generally viewed as a swing back towards intergovernmentalism (Pollack 1995: 378–84; Allen 2000, 2006). While some cautioned against exaggerating the significance of the changes in 1993 (Sutcliffe 2000: 291) in that the major principles of 1988 remained, evidence suggested that the Council secured significant modifications to these principles to reassert national government control over contentious aspects of implementation (Pollack 1995: 376).

In between structural fund reforms, the Cohesion Fund was agreed at Maastricht in 1991. This Fund was aimed at member states with a GDP of less than less than 90% of the Community average, not at specific regions. It would support up to 85% of the costs of projects, a higher intervention rate than with any of the structural funds. As with the structural funds, the Cohesion Fund – and the interim instrument established before the Fund came into operation – was subject to indicative allocations. The dominant interpretations of the creation and operation of the fund were intergovernmental (Scott 1995: 38; Morata and Munoz 1996). In particular, they emphasized the push given by poorer member states led by Spain – which would otherwise be a net contributor by 1993 – that an additional compensatory financial instrument was necessary in the context of moves towards EMU. It is notable in relation to these interpretations that the structural fund principles of partnership and additionality were far less visible in guiding the Cohesion Fund.

1999: Towards Enlargement

In the context of budgetary restraint noted earlier, the 1999 reform of the structural funds was an exercise in preparing the ground for the accession of countries from central and Eastern Europe, with an average GDP of typically around one-third of the EU average. The challenge was two-fold: securing member state agreement to a reduction in their structural fund allocations to facilitate enlargement; and agreeing measures to develop the institutional capacity and capability in the accession state that would allow them to deal with large-scale structural funding effectively. Not without the usual horse-trading, agreement was reached on the principle of large-scale transfer of structural funding away from existing member states to the new ones post-enlargement. On the second challenge, a number of instruments were put in place over the post-2000 period, notably PHARE (Poland and Hungary: Aid for Economic Restructuring) and SAPARD (Special Accession Programme for Agricultural and Rural Development).

The academic focus on the effects of these new instruments in the accession states was again on the degree of multi-level governance promoted. The picture portrayed was one of Commission influence over the use of the funds, the nature of institutional change required, the size of the territorial units, and the institutional capabilities required; and of the national governments concerned being 'eager to comply with the new rules of the game' (Bailey and de Propris 2002b: 319–20). While this picture raised the prospects for multi-level governance, the empirical evidence suggested that national government 'gatekeepers' remained 'firmly in control' of domestic sub-national actors, who were able to influence but not *significantly* influence the policy process (Bailey and de Propris 2002b: 319–20). This situation echoed the experience of centralized states in the period immediately after the introduction of the partnership principle (above).

The assumed degree of asymmetry in the relationship between the Commission and accession states led to scholars relating the terms of compliance for membership with the notion of 'conditionality' generally applied to north–south development programmes. However, the research here again reflected the importance of national actors and circumstances and the relative weakness of EU actors to enforce change that had also been identified in studies of the EU 15 identified above, with Hughes et al. (2004: 54) suggesting that 'national governments have a great deal of power to decide the institutional framework and means of implementation'. Also in line with earlier studies and reflecting the diversity of findings in relation to multi-level governance, the research revealed 'asymmetrical' regionalization in the countries of central and Eastern Europe, 'a convergence with the diversity of regional government in the Member States' (Hughes et al. 2004: 547).

THE WIDER CHORUS

Much of the debate on structural policy continues to focus on the governance effects, but is now often connected explicitly to the concept of *Europeanization* (for example, Benz and Eberlein 1999; Börzel 1999; Bache 2000; Thielmann 2000; Burch and Gomez 2003, 2006; Gualini 2003; Bache and Marshall 2004; Chapter 25, this volume). The concept of Europeanization is generally used to draw attention to and explain both convergent and divergent processes of domestic change through engagement with the EU. In the literature connecting Europeanization to structural policy, the concept of multi-level governance remains prominent, although there is a focus on effects of engagement with the structural funds on particular institutions and actors that takes the debate beyond its usual focus on regions. Examples of this include work on the Europeanization of local governance (Marshall 2005, 2006) and of the third sector (Chapman 2006; also on the structural funds and its effects on both urban governance and the third sector, see Tofarides 2003).

Much of what has been done under the name of Europeanization and structural policy to date has shared the focus of the Hooghe (1996a) study without adding significantly to the tools or concepts through which the process of change is understood. There is potential for this to be done in future research, for example by drawing out of the Europeanization literature the contrasting hypotheses based on varieties of new institutionalism (on other policy areas, see Schimmelfennig and Sedelmeier 2005) and categorizing and explaining different domestic responses to Europeanization pressures, such as transformation, absorption, accommodation, inertia, and retrenchment (see Börzel 2005). In addition, there is very little work that considers the Europeanization of regional *policy* itself rather than the governance dimension, although Conzelmann (1998, 2003, 2006) is an exception here. This is despite the potential of the match-funding requirement of regional policy to reshape domestic regional programmes that are often the source of co-funding.

Again linked to debates on multi-level governance are contributions on structural policy that engage with issues of democracy and legitimacy (Scott 1998; Bache and Olsson 2001; Olsson 2003). Scott (1998) argued that partnership offers promise to those concerned with the politics of inclusion by extending participation in the political process of those hitherto excluded. However, extending participation is a necessary but not sufficient condition for a more responsive democracy and her empirical research pointed to participation being extended to a range of agencies in her case study region in Scotland, but primarily to those whose funding and often very existence depended on central government. Bache and Olsson (2001) highlighted the implementation stage of structural policy-making as one in which significant decisions are taken in the distribution of funds, but one that is often distant from political or public debate and scrutiny. Olsson (2003) has outlined the potential contributions of three models for enhancing democracy in this context, namely parliamentarization, deliberation, and constitutionalization. Peters and Pierre (2004: 85) have characterized the democratic dilemma in the context of multi-level governance as a 'Faustian Bargain', in which 'core values of democratic government are traded for accommodation, consensus and the purported efficiency in governance'.

There is scope here for a fruitful exchange between those scholars with an explicit regional policy/multi-level governance focus and those researching democratic challenges in the context of governance more generally (e.g. Fung and Wright 2001; Papadopoulos 2003; Walti et al. 2004).

A relatively neglected area of research is that linking debates on structural policy with conceptualizations of the model of capitalism that characterizes the EU (but see Hooghe 1998; Bache 2001). The questions addressed here relate to analytical and normative arguments that counter-pose 'anglo-saxon' against 'continental' models; a field of enquiry that appeared likely to remain vibrant in the wake of the French rejection of the Constitutional Treaty in 2005 and explanations relating to the perceived threat to the French social model by British influence over the Treaty.

RATIONALISM VS REFLECTIVISM

Debates on regional policy have generally mirrored wider trends in debate on the EU. If the first phase was categorized as debate dominated by IR theories, and particularly intergovernmentalism, the second phase was marked by the emergence of approaches from public policy and comparative politics. Logically, therefore, debates on regional policy should begin to reflect the rationalist–reflectivist dichotomy central to much current analysis of the EU.

To some extent the rationalist–reflectivist dichotomy has always been a theme of debate, in relation to both regional policy and the EU more generally, with rationalism evident in intergovernmentalism and liberal intergovernmentalism while neofunctionalism and multi-level governance have taken broader view of the motivations and interests of actors and are concerned with the sociological concepts of

culture and political community. In recent work on structural policy, there has been more explicit acknowledgement of the reflectivist emphasis on the importance of social learning. Bache and Olsson (2001: 234) suggested that 'policy formulation is increasingly characterized by consensus-seeking and communicative rationality rather than political-ideological divides', while Benz and Fürst (2002: 21) identified 'regional policy learning as a precondition of regional development'. One outcome of such learning has been evidence over time of less resistance to the partnership principle (Kelleher et al. 1999; Bache 2004). Research on this dimension is relatively new and piecemeal and more comprehensive comparative and historical research is required for a firmer assessment of the development of national and regional preferences in the sector.

Similarly, while there has been no explicit application of constructivism to the impact of the structural funds, there is certainly a role for such analysis in the rhetoric around the 'Europe of the Regions' when analysis and politics became closely aligned. Indeed, a deconstruction of texts may offer much in clarifying the often blurred distinctions between analytical and normative uses of key concepts in the debate such as intergovernmentalism and multi-level governance. To even the careful reader, it is not often clear whether theorists are seeking to explain the nature of the emerging EU or shape its contours. From a similar perspective, it might be interesting to analyse the effect of the narrative of the regulatory state on the prospects for redistribution in the EU. As constructivism tells us, powerful narratives constrain possibilities for change and, as yet, there has been no significant counter-narrative promoting the potential for the EU as a redistributive polity. Possible future directions of regional policy research are developed further in the concluding section.

CONCLUSION

While the structural funds have had redistributive effects (Doménech et al. 2000), significant

Table 20.1   *Dimensions of financial redistribution.*

	Internal	External
Direct		
financial policies	E.g. redistributive effects of EU regional policy	E.g. redistributive effects of aid policies aimed at developing countries/candidate states
non-financial policies	E.g. transport policy, state aids policy	
Indirect	E.g. effects of EMU on domestic redistributive policies of member states	E.g. effects of EMU on domestic redistributive policies of neighbouring non-member states

disparities within the EU remain. For example, Getimis (2004: 8) reported that the average income per capita of the 10% of the population living in the most developed areas of the EU is 2.6 times higher than the average income per capita of the 10% of the population living in lagging regions. However, it is clear from the discussion above that it is not only the financial redistribution that academics have viewed as important in relation to EU regional policy, it is also about the impact on the redistribution of power within member states: and, specifically, between actors organized at different territorial levels and within different sectors. In this sense, we should be clear that ostensibly 'financial' policies such as the structural funds can also have non-financial redistributive effects: the regulation relating to 'partnership' is a key example here. We return to this below. For now though, we note that this focus has been central to the dominant intergovernmental-supranational debate. While this debate remains important, it has been joined by a number of others and scope for greater theoretical diversity remains.

Yet, while this chapter has identified gaps in the literature on EU regional policy, the main omission to be reported here relates to academic research and scholarly debate that engages explicitly with the EU as a redistributive polity: the focus has been narrower, on financial transfers through the structural funds. Yet, just as ostensibly 'financial' policies can redistribute non-financial power resources so 'non-financial' policies can have redistributive effects both financially and in other terms. Robinson (2004) made the case for the redistributive effects of transport policy, while EU

policy over national state aids to industry is an important but relatively neglected area of 'financial' redistribution (see Wishlade 1998; Conzelmann 2006). Moreover, EU policies can have direct redistributive effects beyond EU borders. These include financial transfers to accession and candidate states, and also transfers to developing countries through the EU's aid budget, which is presumably *the* most redistributive financial instrument of the EU.

In addition to considering the *direct* effects on financial redistribution of some EU policies, it may also be useful to consider the *indirect* effects of others in this regard: again, both within and beyond the EU's borders. For example, policies such as EMU are widely seen to have indirect effects on the abilities of national governments to deliver (redistributive) social and welfare policies, and similar constraints may be placed on neighbouring states whose domestic policies are shaped by changes in the regional economy.

In short, a broader debate just on EU financial redistribution might become more rounded if both *direct* and *indirect* dimensions of redistribution and *internal* and *external* dimensions are accounted for. In the case of the 'direct' category, a further subdivision between financial and non-financial (regulatory and distributive) policy instruments may also be helpful (Table 20.1)

In seeking to take a broader view of *what* might be redistributed other than finance, it is helpful to draw on the policy networks literature (for example, Rhodes 1997) to make a more refined distinction between financial and non-financial redistributive effects. If finance is understood as one type of power resource, then understanding non-financial resources as, variously, constitutional-legal, organizational, political, or informational resources (or some combination of these) provides some perspective on the relative importance of financial redistribution against a broader set of relevant categories.

The debate could go further still, to incorporate the cultural aspects of redistribution. As Powell (1999) has argued, 'the politics of redistribution is being challenged by cultural politics based on class, gender, race, age, disability and sexual orientation, that reflects the fractured nature of social identity'. As such, a wider debate on the politics of redistribution might be placed alongside a related debate on the politics of recognition.

Wherever we place our conceptual boundaries, in both its narrow and broad conceptualizations, the future of the EU as a redistributive polity remains uncertain. While on the one hand, enlargement may place greater pressure for redistribution because of the relative economic disadvantage in the new member states (Pollack 2000: 537), enlargement may also promote a degree of diversity within the EU that hinders the potential for agreement on further redistributive measures. The problematic ratification process of the Constitutional Treaty in 2005 brought little clarity to the picture, except to underline that the direct and indirect redistributive effects of the EU were under greater scrutiny than ever and looked set to have a pivotal position in debate over the future of the Union.

NOTE

1. This chapter focuses primarily on 'regional policy' as shorthand for the principles guiding the use of the main financial instrument of redistribution, the ERDF. However, the terms 'structural policy/funds' and 'cohesion policy/fund' are used where they are more accurate.

REFERENCES

Adshead, M. (2002) *Developing European Regions? Comparative governance, policy networks and European integration*. Aldershot: Ashgate.

Allen, D. (2000) 'Cohesion and the structural funds: transfers and trade-offs', in H. Wallace and W. Wallace (eds), *Policy-Making in the European Union*, 4th ed. Oxford: Oxford University Press. pp. 243–66.

Allen, D. (2006) 'Cohesion and the structural funds: competing pressures for reform?', in H. Wallace, W. Wallace and M. Pollack (eds), *Policy-Making in the European Union*, 5th ed. Oxford: Oxford University Press. pp. 212–41.

Anderson, J. (1990) 'Skeptical reflections on a Europe of regions: Britain, Germany, and the ERDF', *Journal of Public Policy*, 10(4): 417–47.

Anderson J. (1996) 'Germany and the structural funds: unification leads to bifurcation', in L. Hooghe (ed.), *Cohesion Policy and European Integration: Building Multi-level Governance*. Oxford: Oxford University Press. pp. 163–94.

Ansell, C., Parsons, C. and Darden, D. (1997) 'Dual networks in European regional development policy', *Journal of Common Market Studies*, 35(3): 347–75.

Bache, I. (1998) *The Politics of European Union Regional Policy: Multi-level Governance or Flexible Gatekeeping?* Sheffield: Sheffield Academic Press/UACES.

Bache, I. (1999) 'The extended gatekeeper: central government and the implementation of EC regional policy in the UK', *Journal of European Public Policy*, 6(1): 28–49.

Bache, I. (2000) 'Europeanisation and partnership: exploring and explaining variations in policy transfer', *Queen's Papers on Europeanisation*, 8. Available online at: http://www.qub.ac.uk/schools/SchoolofPoliticsInternationalStudies/FileStore/EuropeanisationFiles/Filetoupload,5297,en.pdf, accessed 17 July 2005.

Bache, I. (2001) 'Different seeds in the same plot? Competing models of capitalism and the incomplete contracts of partnership design', *Public Administration*, 79(2): 337–59.

Bache, I. (2004) 'Multi-level governance and European union regional policy', in I. Bache and M. Flinders (eds), *Multi-Level Governance*. Oxford: Oxford University Press. pp. 165–78.

Bache, I. and Jones, R. (2000) 'Empowering the regions? The political impact of EC regional policy in Britain and Spain', *Regional and Federal Studies*, 10(2): 1–20.

Bache, I. and Marshall, A. (2004) 'Europeanisation and domestic change: a governance approach to institutional adaptation in Britain', *Queen's Papers on Europeanisation*, 5. Available online at: http://www.qub.ac.uk/schools/SchoolofPolitics

InternationalStudies/FileStore/Europeanisation Files/Filetoupload,5456,en.pdf, accessed 18 July 2006.

Bache, I. and Olsson, J. (2001) 'Legitimacy through partnership? EU policy diffusion in Britain and Sweden', *Scandinavian Political Studies*, 24(3): 215–37.

Bache, I., George, S. and Rhodes, R.A.W. (1996) 'Cohesion policy and subnational authorities in the UK', in L. Hooghe (ed.), *Cohesion Policy and European Integration: Building Multi-level Governance*. Oxford: Oxford University Press. pp. 294–319.

Bailey, D. and De Propris, L. (2002a) 'The 1988 reform of the European structural funds: entitlement or empowerment?' *Journal of European Public Policy*, 9(3): 408–28.

Bailey, D. and De Propris, L. (2002b) 'EU structural funds, regional capabilities and enlargement: towards multi-level governance?' *Journal of European Integration*, 24(4): 303–24.

Balme, R. and Jouve, B. (1996) 'Building the regional state: Europe and territorial organization in France', in L. Hooghe (ed.), *Cohesion Policy and European Integration: Building Multi-level Governance*. Oxford: Oxford University Press. pp. 219–55.

Benington, J. and Harvey, J. (1998) 'Transnational local authority networking within the European union: passing fashion or new paradigm?', in D. Marsh (ed.), *Comparing Policy Networks*. Buckingham: Open University Press. pp. 149–66.

Benz, A. and Eberlein, T. (1999) 'The Europeanization of regional policies: patterns of multi-level governance', *Journal of European Public Policy*, 6(2): 329–48.

Benz, A. and Fürst, D. (2002) 'Policy learning in regional networks', *European Urban and Regional Studies*, 9(1): 21–35.

Bomberg, E. and Peterson, J. (1998) 'European Union decision making: the role of sub-national authorities', *Political Studies*, 46(2): 219–35.

Börzel, T. (1997) 'What's so special about policy networks? An exploration of the concept and its usefulness in studying European governance', *European Integration online Papers*, 1(16). Available online at: http://eiop.or.at/eiop/texte/1997-016.htm, accessed 4 August 2006.

Börzel, T. (1999) 'Towards convergence in Europe? Institutional adaption to Europeanization in Germany and Spain', *Journal of Common Market Studies*, 37(4): 573–96.

Börzel, T. (2005) 'Europeanization: how the EU interacts with its member states', in S. Bulmer and C. Lesquesne (eds), *The Member States of the European Union*. Oxford: Oxford University Press. pp. 45–76.

Bourne, A. (2003) 'The impact of European integration on regional power', *Journal of Common Market Studies*, 41(4): 597–620.

Burch, M. and Gomez, R. (2003) 'Europeanization and the English regions', *Paper for UACES/ESRC seminar series*. Sheffield, 2 May. Available online at: http://www.shef.ac.uk/ebpp/burchgomez.pdf, accessed 16 July 2005.

Burch, M. and Gomez, R. (2006) 'The English regions', in I. Bache and A. Jordan (eds), *The Europeanization of British Politics*. Basingstoke: Palgrave Macmillan. pp. 82–97.

Chapman, R. (2006) 'The third sector', in I. Bache and A. Jordan (eds), *The Europeanization of British Politics*. Basingstoke: Palgrave Macmillan. pp. 168–86.

Conzelmann, T. (1998) '"Europeanization" of regional development policies? Linking the multi-level governance approach with theories of policy learning and policy change', *European Integration online Papers*, 2(4). Available online at: http://eiop.or.at/eiop/texte/1998-004.htm, accessed 4 August 2005.

Conzelmann, T. (2003) 'Contested spaces: Europeanised regional policy in Great Britain and Germany', Draft paper prepared for the EUSA 8th Biennial International Conference. Nashville, Tennessee, 29 March.

Conzelmann, T. (2006) 'Regional development', in I. Bache and A. Jordan (eds), *The Europeanization of British Politics*. Basingstoke: Palgrave Macmillan. pp. 248–64.

de Rynck, S. (1996) 'Europe and cohesion policy-making in the Flemish region', in L. Hooghe (ed.), *Cohesion Policy and European Integration: Building Multi-level Governance*. Oxford: Oxford University Press. pp. 129–62.

Doménech, R., Maudes, A. and Varela, J. (2000) 'Fiscal flows in Europe: the redistributive effects of the EU budget', *Review of World Economics*, 39(2): 609–34.

European Commission (1970) *Report to the Council and the Commission on the realisation by stages of Economic and Monetary Union in the Community – "Werner Report"*. Brussels: European Communities.

European Commission (1973) *Report on the Regional Problems in the Enlarged Community*. Brussels: European Communities.

European Commission (1975) 'Preamble to regulation (EEC) No. 724/75 of March 18, establishing a European Regional Development Fund', OJ L73, 21/3/75.

European Commission (1989) *Guide to the Reform of the Community's Structural Funds*. Brussels/ Luxembourg: European Communities.

Froman, L. (1968) 'The categorisation of policy contents', in A. Ranney (ed.), *Political Science and Public Policy*. Chicago: Markham. pp. 41–52.

Fung, A. and Wright, E. (2001) 'Deepening democracy: innovations in empowered participatory governance', *Politics and Society*, 29(1): 5–41.

George, S. (1985) *Politics and Policy in the European Community*. Oxford: Clarendon Press.

Getimis, P. (2004) 'European enlargement, territorial cohesion and ESPD', Paper presented at the International Conference: Present and future of the European Spatial Development Perspective, Turin, 5 March.

Grote, J. (1996) 'Cohesion in Italy: a view on non-economic disparities', in L. Hooghe (ed.), *Cohesion Policy and European Integration: Building Multi-level Governance*. Oxford: Oxford University Press. pp. 256–93.

Gualini, E. (2003) 'Challenges to multi-level governance: contradictions and conflicts in the Europeanization of Italian regional policy', *Journal of European Public Policy*, 10(4): 616–36.

Guérot, U. (2004) 'The European paradox, widening and deepening in the European Union', *US-Europe Analysis Series*. The Brookings Institution, 15 May.

Harvie, C. (1994) *The Rise of Regional Europe*. London: Routledge.

Heinelt, H. and Smith, R. (eds) (1996) *Policy Networks and European Structural Funds*. Aldershot: Avebury.

Hix, S. (1994) 'The study of the European Community: the challenge to comparative politics', *West European Politics*, 17(1): 1–30.

Hooghe, L. (1995) 'Subnational mobilisation in the European Union', *West European Politics*, 18(3): 175–98.

Hooghe, L. (ed.) (1996a) *Cohesion Policy and European Integration: Building Multi-Level Governance*. Oxford: Oxford University Press.

Hooghe, L. (1996b) 'Building a Europe with the regions: the changing role of the European Commission', in L. Hooghe (ed.), *Cohesion Policy and European Integration: Building-Multi-Level Governance*. Oxford: Oxford University Press. pp. 89–128.

Hooghe, L. (1998) 'EU cohesion policy and competing models of capitalism', *Journal of Common Market Studies*, 36(4): 457–77.

Hooghe, L. and Keating, M. (1994) 'The politics of European Union regional policy', *Journal of European Public Policy*, 1(3): 367–93.

Hooghe, L. and Marks, G. (1996) 'Europe with the regions? Regional representation in the European Union', *Publius*, 26(1): 73–91.

Hughes, J., Sasse, G. and Gordon, C. (2004) 'Conditionality and compliance in the EU's eastern enlargement: regional policy and the reform of sub-national government', *Journal of Common Market Studies*, 42(3): 523–51.

Ioakimidis, P. (1996) 'EU cohesion policy in Greece: the tension between bureaucratic centralism and regionalism', in L. Hooghe (ed.), *Cohesion Policy and European Integration: Building Multi-level Governance*. Oxford: Oxford University Press. pp. 342–63.

Jeffery, C. (ed.) (1997) *The Regional Dimension of the European Union: Towards a Third Level in Europe?* London: Frank Cass.

Jeffery, C. (2000) 'Sub-national mobilization and European integration: does it make any difference?' *Journal of Common Market Studies*, 38(1): 1–23.

John, P. (1994) 'UK Sub-national offices in Britain: regionalization or diversification?' *Regional Studies*, 28(1): 739–46.

John, P. (2001) *Local Governance in Western Europe*. London: Sage.

John, P. and McAteer, M. (1998) 'Sub-national institutions and the new European governance: local authority strategies for the IGC', *Regional and Federal Studies*, 8(3): 104–24.

Jones, B. and Keating, M. (eds) (1995) *The European Union and the Regions*. Oxford: Oxford University Press.

Keating, M. (1998) 'Is there a regional level of government in Europe?', in P. Le Gales and C. Lequesne (eds), *Regions in Europe*. London and New York: Routledge. pp. 11–29.

Keating, M. and Hooghe, L. (1998) 'By-passing the nation-state? Regions and the EU policy process', in J. Richardson (ed.), *European Union: Power and Policy Making*. London: Routledge. pp. 216–19.

Kelleher, J., Batterbury, S. and Stern, E. (1999) *The Thematic Evaluation of the Partnership Principle: Final Synthesis Report*. London: The Tavistock Institute Evaluation Development and Review Unit.

Laffan, B. (1996) 'Ireland: a region without regions: the odd man out?', in L. Hooghe (ed.), *Cohesion Policy and European Integration: Building Multi-level Governance*. Oxford: Oxford University Press. pp. 320–41.

Laffan, B. and Lindner, J. (2006) 'The budget: who gets what, when and how', in H. Wallace, W. Wallace and M. Pollack (eds), *Policy-Making in the European Union*, 5th ed. Oxford: Oxford University Press. pp. 191–212.

Le Galès, P. and Lequesne, C. (eds) (1998) *Regions in Europe*. London and New York: Routledge.

Loughlin, J. (1996) 'Europe of the regions and the federalisation of Europe', *Publius*, 26(4): 141–62.

Lowi, T. (1964) 'American business, public policy, case studies and political theory', *World Politics*, 16(4): 677–715.

Majone, G. (1996a) *Regulating Europe*. London and New York: Routledge.

Majone, G. (1996b) 'A European regulatory state?', in J. Richardson (ed.), *European Union: Power and Policy-Making*. London and New York: Routledge. pp. 263–77.

Marks, G. (1992) 'Structural policy in the European Community', in A. Sbragia (ed.), *Euro-Politics: Institutions and Policymaking in the "New" European Community*. Washington, DC: The Brookings Institution. pp. 191–224.

Marks, G. (1993) 'Structural policy and multilevel governance in the EC', in A. Cafruny and G. Rosenthal (eds), *The State of the European Community, Vol. 2: The Maastricht Debates and Beyond*. Harlow: Longman. pp. 391–410.

Marshall, A. (2005) 'Europeanization at the urban level: local actors, institutions and the dynamics of multi-level interaction', *Journal of European Public Policy*, 12(4): 668–86.

Marshall, A. (2006) 'Local governance', in I. Bache and A. Jordan (eds), *The Europeanization of British Politics*. Basingstoke: Palgrave Macmillan. pp. 98–118.

Martin, S. and Pearce, G. (1993) 'European regional development strategies: strengthening meso-government in the UK?' *Regional Studies*, 27(7): 682–96.

Martin, S. and Pearce, G. (1999) 'Differentiated multi-level governance? The response of British sub-national governments to European integration', *Regional and Federal Studies*, 9(2): 32–52.

Mazey, S. and Mitchell, J. (1993) 'Europe of the regions? Territorial interests and European integration: the Scottish experience', in S. Mazey and J. Richardson (eds), *Lobbying in the European Community*. Oxford: Oxford University Press. pp. 95–121.

McAleavey, P. (1992) 'The politics of European regional development policy: the European Commission's RECHAR initiative and the concept of additionality', *Strathclyde Papers on Government and Politics*, 88.

McAleavey, P. (1995) 'European regional development fund expenditure in the UK: from additionality to subtractionality', *European Urban and Regional Studies*, 2(3): 249–53.

McAleavey, P. and Mitchell, J. (1995) 'Industrial regions and lobbying in the structural funds reform process', *Journal of Common Market Studies*, 32(2): 237–48.

Morata, F. and Munoz, X. (1996) 'Vying for European funds: territorial restructuring in Spain', in L. Hooghe (ed.), *Cohesion Policy and European Integration: Building Multi-level Governance*. Oxford: Oxford University Press. pp. 195–218.

Moravcsik, A. (1991) 'Negotiating the Single European Act', in R. Keohane and S. Hoffmann (eds), *The New European Community: Decisionmaking and Institutional Change*. Boulder-San Francisco-Oxford: Westview Press. pp. 41–84.

Nanetti, R. (1996) 'EU cohesion policy and territorial restructuring in the member states', in L. Hooghe (ed.), *Cohesion Policy and European Integration: Building Multi-level Governance*. Oxford: Oxford University Press. pp. 59–88.

Olsson, J. (2003) 'Democracy paradoxes in multi-level governance', *Journal of European Public Policy*, 10(2): 283–300.

Papadopoulos, Y. (2003) 'Cooperative forms of governance: problems of democratic accountability in complex environments', *European Journal of Political Research*, 42(4): 473–501.

Peters, G. and Pierre, J. (2004) 'Multi-level governance and democracy: a Faustian bargain?', in I. Bache and M. Flinders (eds), *Multi-Level Governance*. Oxford: Oxford University Press. pp. 75–92.

Pollack, M. (1995) 'Regional actors in an intergovernmental play: the making and implementation of EC structural policy', in S. Mazey and C. Rhodes (eds), *The State of the European Union, Vol. 3*. Boston: Lynne Riener. pp. 361–90.

Pollack, M. (1997) 'Representing diffuse interests in EC policy-making', *Journal of European Public Policy*, 4(4): 572–90.

Pollack, M. (2000) 'The end of creeping competence? EU policy-making since Maastricht', *Journal of Common Market Studies*, 38(3): 519–38.

Powell, F. (1999) 'Adult education, cultural empowerment and social equality: the Cork northside education initiative', *Widening Participation and Lifelong Learning*, 1(1). Available online at: http://www.staffs.ac.uk/journal/Volume1(1)/art-ab-1.htm, accessed 20 July 2005.

Preston, C. (1983) 'Additional to what? Does the UK government cheat on the European regional development fund?' *Politics*, 3(2): 20–6.

Preston, C. (1984) 'The politics of implementation: the European Community regional development fund and European Community regional aid to the UK 1975–81', Unpublished PhD thesis, University of Essex.

Rhodes, R. (1997) *Understanding Governance: Policy Networks, Goverannce, Reflexivity and Accountability*. Buckingham and Philadelphia: Open University Press.

Rhodes, R., Bache, I. and George, S. (1996) 'Policy networks and policy-making in the European union: a critical appraisal', in L. Hooghe (ed.), *Cohesion Policy and European Integration: Building Multi-Level Governance*. Oxford: Oxford University Press. pp. 294–319.

Richardson, J. (1998) 'Series editor's preface', in P. Le Galès and C. Lequesne (eds), *Regions in Europe*. London and New York: Routledge. pp. vii–ix.

Robinson, N. (2004) 'The European Union: towards a redistributive state?' Paper presented at the UACES Annual Conference, University of Birmingham, 6–8 September.

Scharpf, F. (1999) *Crisis and Choice in European Social Democracy*. Ithaca: Cornell University Press.

Schimmelfennig, F. and Sedelmeier, U. (eds) (2005) *The Europeanization of Central and Eastern Europe*. Ithaca, NJ: Cornell University Press.

Scott, A., Peterson, J. and Millar, D. (1994) 'Subsidiarity: a Europe of the regions v. the British constitution', *Journal of Common Market Studies*, 32(1): 47–68.

Scott, J. (1995) *Development Dilemmas in the European Community: Rethinking Regional Development Policy*. Buckingham–Philadelphia: Open University Press.

Scott, J. (1998) 'Law, legitimacy and EC governance: prospects for partnership', *Journal of Common Market Studies*, 36(2): 175–94.

Sharpe, L. (1993) 'The European meso: an appraisal', in L. Sharpe (ed.), *The Rise of Meso Government in Europe*. London and Newbury Park, CA: Sage Publications. pp. 1–39.

Smith, A. (1997) 'Studying multi-level governance: examples from French translations of the structural funds', *Public Administration*, 75(4): 711–29.

Smyrl, M. (1997) 'Does European community regional policy empower the regions?' *Governance*, 10(3): 287–309.

Streeck, W. (1996) 'Neo-voluntarism: a new social policy paradigm?', in G. Marks, F. Scharpf, P. Schmitter and W. Streeck (eds), *Governance in the European Union*. London: Sage. pp. 64–94.

Sutcliffe, J. (2000) 'The 1999 reform of the structural funds: multi-level governance or renationalisation?' *Journal of European Public Policy*, 7(2): 290–309.

Thielemann, E. (2000) 'Europeanisation and institutional compatibility: implementing European regional policy in Germany', *Queen's Papers on Europeanization*, 4. Available online at: http://www.qub.ac.uk/schools/SchoolofPoliticsInternationalStudies/FileStore/EuropeanisationFiles/Filetoupload,5301,en.pdf, accessed 20 July 2005.

Tofarides, M. (2003) *Urban Policy in the European Union: A Multi-Level Gatekeeper System*. Aldershot: Ashgate.

Tommel, I. (1998) 'Transformation of governance: the European Commission's strategy for creating a "Europe of the regions"', *Regional and Federal Studies*, 8(2): 52–80.

Wallace, H. (1977) 'The establishment of the Regional Development Fund: common policy or pork barrel?', in H. Wallace, W. Wallace and C. Webb (eds), *Policy-Making in the European Communities*. London: John Wiley and Sons. pp. 137–63.

Wallace, H. (1980) *Budgetary Politics: The Finances of the European Communities*. London: George Allen and Unwin.

Wallace, H. (1983) 'Distributional politics: dividing up the Community cake', in H. Wallace, W. Wallace and C. Webb (eds), *Policy-Making in the European Communities*, 2nd ed. London: John Wiley and Sons. pp. 81–113.

Walti, S., Kubler, D. and Papadopoulos, Y. (2004) 'How democratic is "governance"? Lessons from Swiss drug policy', *Governance*, 17(1): 83–113.

Wise, M. and Croxford, G. (1988) 'The European regional development fund: community ideals and national realities', *Political Geography Quarterly*, 7(2): 161–82.

Wishlade, F. (1998) 'Competition policy or cohesion policy by the back door? The Commission guidelines on national regional aid', *European Competition Law Review*, 19(6): 343–57.

21

Environmental Policy in the European Union: Bridging Policy, Politics and Polity Dimensions

ANDREA LENSCHOW

INTRODUCTION

Environmental policy has received tremendous attention among European Union scholars. Considering the relatively late appearance of the policy in the list of competencies of the EU and its comparatively marginal status in the economy-dominated policy repertoire, this is notable. Numerous environmental crises and accidents exciting citizens and scholars alike since the 1970s and the emergence of an environmental social movement in several European countries may be part of the explanation. Yet, even after green politics in Europe quieted and environmental policy gained a 'normal' status in the *acquis communautaire*, this attention never subsided. I will argue in this chapter that the study of environmental policy lends itself to contribute to several larger debates on the dynamics in EU policy-making and the nature of the EU polity.

For policy analysts, three questions are of particular interest: (a) How did the policy emerge and develop as a policy area? (b) What kind of decisions are being made? (c) How does the policy perform? Political scientists with a stronger interest in the political system of the EU, in turn, will wonder about the *structures of governance that can be found in this policy area*, hence the relations between the different levels of the polity as well as patterns of public–private interactions.

With regard to EU environmental policy *per se*, we note (a) its rapid expansion and step-wise institutionalization, (b) the agreement of regulatory standards often exceeding the so-called lowest common denominator (LCD) among the decision-makers, and (c) nevertheless increasing concern about the effectiveness of the policy. In tackling these questions and searching for explanations, the literature on EU environmental policy may be divided into three analytical phases.[1] First, research on environmental policy began from an international relations perspective, as was true for most EU-related analyses. The 'grand debate' between intergovernmental and neo-functional approaches to explain integration processes framed initial investigations of the emergence and spread of the policy. However, the institutional and legal set-up of the EU, the single market as the main reference point for policy makers in all fields, and the open constellation of actors joining together in policy making were soon identified as clearly distinct from other international organizations or regimes and analysts began to look for the characteristics of the 'domestic politics' of the EU. In this second phase authors borrowed conceptual vocabulary from especially institutional, ideational and policy network approaches (for the general analytical turn see Peterson 2001: 300ff).

Methodologically, EU environmental policy research during these first two phases was dominated by individual or comparative case studies. Those interested in the big picture of EU politics and polity development – in particular scholars outside the 'public policy community' – may have been disenchanted by the bias to piece-meal and rather 'microscopic' investigations of single policy items or limited instances of environmental pollution. But arguably, in recent years we have entered a third phase in researching EU environmental policy, which shifts attention towards the 'bigger picture' of European governance. EU governance, understood as a particular rule-making structure, consists of multiple layers, is characterized by policy fragmentation, and sits on shaky legitimatory grounds. Triggered by the performance question, the analysis of EU environmental policy pinpointed the close connection between policy reforms and polity features and dynamics. The process of policy-making and the choices of policy instruments in the environmental field indicate novel features in the EU polity, namely the rise of less hierarchical relations in governing the Union and shifts in the balance between public and private actors. Notably, these governance implications are not limited to Brussels, but reach 'upward' to the international level as well as 'downward' to the national and regional levels. The influential book-length study of EU environmental policy-making and the emergence of diverse policy styles in the policy repertoire

by Héritier et al. (1994, 1996) first signified this change of perspective.[2]

The chapter is structured in three parts, following the three research streams outlined above. The first will review the literature on the emergence of EU environmental policy and highlight the turn from integration to 'domestic' theories. The second will turn to the question of environmental policy performance, identifying three different perspectives that have been adopted in the literature – investigating the level of regulation, implementation and effectiveness. Finally, this chapter establishes the link between environmental policy-making and the more general process of a European policy-making. It is my intention to show that scholarship on EU environmental policy has not only picked up general discussions on EU policy-making and integration, but it has also been a driver for entering new debates.

EMERGENCE AND EXPANSION OF THE POLICY: MOVING FROM NICHES TO CENTRE STAGE

Environmental policy initially was not among the range of competencies that the Treaty of Rome attributed to the European Communities. Nevertheless, European environmental policy was 'founded' arguably already in the 1960s when directives were adopted to deal with dangerous substances, noise, and exhaust emissions of motor vehicles. In fact, the literature identifies several periods in the process of environmental policy expansion and institutionalization. During the 'founding period' from 1957–1972 (Zito 1999: 24) a few 'incidental measures' were passed (Hildebrand 1993: 17). The second period began with the adoption of the first (non-binding) environmental action programme in 1972; between that date and 1987, 118 major new pieces of environmental legislation were adopted (Jordan et al. 1999: 382), amounting to the early institutionalization of the policy field. EU environmental policy spread to cover all environmental media (air, water, soil) and major problem areas (such as waste, dangerous substances/chemicals, nature protection). 1987 was a watershed year in the evolution of European environmental policy in the sense that the Single European Act formally included environmental policy in the range of Community competencies, ending ambiguities as to the judicial status of environmental measures. Subsequently, until the early 1990s, the number of newly adopted pieces of legislation sky-rocketed and the annual rate of major innovations rose to around 10 (Jordan et al. 1999: 383).[3] The notion of the EU as a regulatory state reflects this growth of regulatory policy competency (Majone 1996; Young, this volume). Also thereafter the total number of new adoptions continues to be high (Haigh 2004), but the 'high-water mark' (Zito 1999: 28) for the passage of truly new and major items has now passed. Arguably, since the formulation of the fifth environmental action programme of the EU in 1992, the focus began to shift to selected priority areas (such as climate change or biodiversity), to attempts at streamlining or improving existing policies (e.g. in the field of water protection) and to 'mainstreaming' environmental objectives in EU policy-making.

In tracing the analytical accounts for this process of expansion and institutionalization of European environmental policy, I shall argue in this part of the chapter, we see a shift from integration to 'domestic politics' theories; the latter, in turn, may be roughly divided into actor- and institutionally-oriented approaches.

Integration Theories

While early scholarship on EU environmental policy in the 1980s was mostly devoted to the description of the emerging policy field and its ambiguous legal basis (Rehbinder and Stewart 1985; Johnson and Corcelle 1989), the history of quantitative and qualitative expansion of EU environmental policy constituted the first big theoretical puzzle for scholars in this field. It was first approached from an integration theory perspective, following either (liberal) intergovernmentalist or neofunctionalist lines of argument. Jonathan Golub most strongly took the intergovernmentalist position. Analysing

the process of adopting the Packaging Waste Directive (Golub 1996a) he found that attempts of supranational and societal actors to influence the policy-making process did not translate into real power, capable of moving member states to change policy positions. Hence, intergovernmental bargaining in the Council resulted in a directive reflecting the lowest common denominator (see also Huelshoff and Pfeiffer 1991, for a similar assessment). In his work on the UK's role in EU environmental policy making, Golub (1996b) maintains that concerns for the protection of national interests and state sovereignty have determined British behaviour in EU policy negotiations,[4] and presumably the behaviour of other member states as well.

The intergovernmentalist paradigm did not gain any dominance in explaining environmental policy-making in the EU, however, not least because the rather remarkable expansion of the field did not usually come at the price of LCD decisions. State-centred analyses more generally did come for rescue to resolve this puzzle. Such studies pointed to the interesting pattern of 'green member states' (Liefferink and Andersen 1998), 'pioneers' (Andersen and Liefferink 1997), or 'leaders' (Héritier 1996; Sbragia 1996) successfully pushing for the adoption of strict regulation. The influential study by Héritier et al. (1996) on the adoption process of several environmental directives and regulations identified 'first moving' member states as being able to set the European policy agenda and to strongly influence regulatory style and standards in the legislation to be decided. Liefferink and Andersen (1998: 256f) later refined the first mover terminology by distinguishing (a) between *direct* pushing of environmental policy and *indirect* strategies, typically via the internal market policies, as well as (b) *purposeful* approaches which are clearly directed at the EU level and *incremental* action rooted in domestic politics.

Neofunctional theory had been the second large point of reference in the earlier accounts of the development of EU environmental policy. But rarely was neofunctionalism treated as a coherent explanatory framework. In light of the peak of environmental policy adoptions following the single market programme, some authors identified the functional link between market integration and the harmonization of national environmental (or other regulatory) policy as one important explanatory factor, in the sense that European regulation served to level the playing field for national producers (e.g. Weale 1999). Most scholars writing in the tradition of neofunctionalism took the functional pressure as a given, however, and concentrated on actor-centred 'push factors'. A case in point were the contributions of an activist European Court of Justice (ECJ), which had interpreted the Treaty framework in an expansionist fashion and allowed environmental policy to enter the Community *acquis* by way of reference to functional linkages with already established competencies of the Community (Koppen 1993). Similarly, the Environmental Directorate-General of the European Commission had been building a role for itself by searching for new policy niches, exploiting political windows of opportunity for policy expansion and forming 'green alliances' within the institutional framework of the EU (e.g. Weale and Williams 1993: 61; Sbragia 2000). Also the second 'entrepreneurial' organ, the European Parliament (EP), received much attention (Judge 1993; Judge et al. 1994; Bomberg and Burns 1999) as insisting both on progressive environmental regulation (and implementation) as well as on being given the institutional powers to intervene. These studies shared the theoretical interest in establishing some link between functional expansion and the more general European integration project.[5]

The well-known criticism of the neofunctionalist paradigm as exaggerating the linear progression for task expansion has been voiced with regard to environmental policy analyses as well. Furthermore, the interest in such progression began to fade after environmental policy had been firmly established as a policy field in the EU and the institutional co-evolution – in the form of extending the rule of qualified majority voting (QMV) to most aspects of environmental policy and expanding parliamentary powers first to

cooperation (Maastricht), then to co-decision powers (Amsterdam) – slowly came to a close. Analytical attention shifted from the macroscopic view of the development of the policy area as a whole to more detailed studies of the policy-making process within EU institutions and between the EU level, member states and societal actors.

Organized Interests, Policy Networks and Epistemic Communities

While green political parties are widely ignored in the investigation of EU environmental policy-making (see below), environmental interest groups are not (Hull 1993; Mazey and Richardson 1993; Hey and Brendle 1994; Webster 1998). In part, the literature on lobbying and the influence of interest groups is framed as a critique of state-centric accounts. Environmental groups were shown to shape the policy agenda in Brussels and influence the decision-making process using a mix of strategies, ranging from political pressure and campaigns to the provision of policy advice and information. Case studies, for instance on the formulation of car emission policy, the 'greening' of the structural funds or the Union's marine policy (cf. Arp 1993; Long 1995; Lenschow 1997; Heard and Richards 2005, respectively), highlight how environmental groups managed to mobilize member states sympathetic to their concerns, raise awareness of environmental problems inside the Commission, and even shift the balance of interests inside the EP. The emergence of 'Euro-groups' in Brussels, typically organizing as a network of nationally organized NGOs, and their close interaction with the supranational organs of the Community has been read as supporting neofunctionalist theory suggesting that interest groups would form in response to functional spillover and play a central role in European political integration.

Increasingly, attention shifted towards the structure of interest intermediation in the EU, however, and with it to the literature of comparative politics. The study of environmental policy raised the issue of the relative influence of diffuse interests vis-à-vis the presumably privileged and better organized business interests. Mollifying normative concerns about biased representation, we are pointed to the existence of multiple access points in the EU system (Pollack 1997), sympathetic EU institutional actors (Marks and McAdam 1996) and the ample opportunities to make use and even change often instable interest constellations inside Community organs or even within the business community. It is in this context that the analysis of interest intermediation in the EU is frequently mixed with reflections on the role of ideas and discourses: It was shown that common interests between previously adversarial business and environmental groups emerged due to novel discourses on 'ecological modernization' (Weale 1992; Hajer 1995), 'sustainable development' (Lenschow 1999) or policy-specific frame shifts leading to a reinterpretation of policy positions among core actors (cf. Jachtenfuchs 1996; Lenschow and Zito 1998). Such frame shifts relied on the power of ideas at least as much as on political 'networking' and pressure.

Organizationally, environmental groups have adapted to the framework of interest intermediation in the EU by forming a 'grand coalition' and coordinating their activities in order to handle the workload and appear as cohesive as possible (Hey and Brendle 1994; Webster 1998). Indeed, Mazey and Richardson (1993: 109–10) argue that 'groups lobbying in this [i.e. the environment] sector face the same range of opportunities as other groups in the EC', and that, apart from the need to deal with more dispersed and more informal policy-making processes in the EU, the same 'fundamental rules of the game' apply as in national political systems.

Taking a broader perspective on green politics, however, and inquiring into the capacities or intentions of European groups and political parties to mobilize a larger public for environmental objectives, the differences between the EU and national systems are striking. Looking at parliamentary structures first, it is notable that the activities of the European Parliament's

Environment Committee received more attention than the contributions of the Green Party group within the EP (but see Bomberg 1998a). The strong representation of the Green Party (or parties) in the EP and its influence in policy-making has been reflected surprisingly little – in part, of course, because this representation indeed may have little to do with a EU-wide green mobilization but rather with the nature of European elections as largely second-order national contests.

Furthermore, there is no evidence of a (green) social movement emerging transnationally (Imig and Tarrow 2000; Rucht 2001). Rather, the multi-level system seems characterized by a division of labour, with environmental groups in Brussels following the more technocratic traits of policy-making, whereas national groups are more strongly grounded in society. This structure, of course, mirrors the elitist and technocratic bias in the neofunctionalist vision of integration: *Not green voters or environmental movements push environmental policy forward in the EU, but networks of self-declared policy advocates.* These networks are formed either on the basis of exchange relations with actors interacting strategically, or they reflect ties that are based on 'shared core beliefs' (Sabatier 1998) and may even result in the formation of epistemic communities (Zito 2001).

Institutional Perspectives

In light of the dramatic expansion of the policy, the emphasis on functional pull and actors' push for environmental policy is not surprising. But, there have been both empirical and analytical reasons to investigate the impact of institutional structures as well.

Empirically, authors wondered about the real impact of institutional reforms on environmental policy-making. The environmental policy field has been an interesting test case, given the gradual institutional co-evolution already mentioned. Did it make a difference to establish a *de jure* status for a *de facto* policy? Did QMV ease negotiations in the Council, contributing to more and faster decision-making? What has been the impact of the expanded legislative competencies of the EP?

The impact of the institutional framework on actors' strategies has been quite evident. Hence, in the period between the introduction of the environment title into the Treaty in 1987 and the extension of QMV to environmental policy, 'Treaty games' became a feature of policy-making with the Commission avoiding the procedurally less favourable environmental articles (ex) 130 r-t and continuing the 'market route' to environmental policy (via ex Art. 100a) (Hildebrand 1993; more differentiated: Hovden 2002). This institutional 'mess' was resolved in subsequent Treaty reforms (Wilkinson 1992; Jordan 1998), assisted by Court rulings supporting pro-integrationist strategies of the Commission and the Parliament (Koppen 1993). Most authors reflecting on the increasing embeddedness of environmental policy imply institutional lock-in effects.

A more complex picture emerges with regard to the impact of institutional changes on the efficiency of decision-making and the empowerment of the EP (Andersen and Rasmussen 1998; Jordan et al. 1999; Kasack 2004). Reflecting on post-Maastricht expectation that decision-making in environmental policy would ease due to the spread of QMV and the introduction of co-decision-making, Jordan et al. detect no uniform pattern or trend in the efficiency of decision-making across policy sub-areas. Andersen and Rasmussen show that co-decision-making counteracts the efficiency gains of QMV. Kasack finds that the simplification of the co-decision procedure in the Amsterdam Treaty did not increase adoption rates either; nor did it further empower the EP. The impact of the Nice Treaty – placing the large member states in a more powerful position and lowering the threshold for reaching decisions – still needs to be researched, although arguably it will be the increased membership of the EU and not the reformed procedures that will produce the notable impact (Homeyer et al. 2000; Jordan and Fairbrass 2001).

Besides these links between the institutional and procedural Treaty reforms and changes in policy-making as well as output, the more stable system characteristics of the European Union have also been shown to impact on policy-making. This literature is more strongly embedded in a 'meta-debate' on the distinct nature of the political system of the EU and its effects on actors' identities, interests, and values, hence both political strategies and policy choices. Here, environmental policy studies serve as illustrations for broader arguments. Hence, we learn about the peculiar institution of the EU presidency with its implications for European policy agendas (Andersen and Rasmussen 1998) and as triggers of 'European thinking' in the governments having the chair (Wurzel 1996). Weale (1996: 594) more pessimistically reflects on the EU 'system of concurrent majorities' where agreement is needed by a high proportion of participants extending from Commission, Council, and Parliament to functional constituencies. Accordingly, Weale suggests that system characteristics lead important decisions to fail or to be reached at sub-optimal levels. This is especially evident with regard to coordination with other policy sectors such as transport, industry and agriculture. Studies by me and others (Lenschow 1997, 2002a) highlight similar structural constraints, although showing a slightly less gloomy picture. While both the institutional (that is, fragmented) and the normatively market-biased structure of the EU pose severe constraints on policy coordination, there are limits to a complete 'lock-in' on the sectoral level. Héritier (1997) attributes these limits most pointedly to 'strategies of subterfuge' in a fluid polity, giving rise to informal politics.

All-in-all, the puzzle of task expansion in the environmental policy field has been tackled using a range of theoretical approaches, both from the European integration school and the canon of comparative politics and policy-making more generally. Given the dynamic and sometimes unexpected evolution of the policy, these studies helped advance theoretical positions more generally. Nevertheless, I shall argue below that truly novel and innovative perspectives were developed with respect to other empirical questions and puzzles.

THE PERFORMANCE OF THE POLICY: HIGH STANDARDS, BUT POOR IMPLEMENTATION?

Public policy derives much of its legitimacy from solving problems, although the assessment of problem-solving capacity and effectiveness may be a complex matter. The effectiveness of EU environmental policy has been analysed from three perspectives: (1) investigating the level of environmental standards defined by EU decision-makers; (2) analysing policy compliance and implementation; and (3) questioning the merits of traditional regulatory instruments. This succession of perspectives implies an increasing reflection on the nature of the multi-level system of the EU. At the same time, it is evident that the analysis of environmental outcomes are largely neglected by political scientists and left to other disciplines.[6]

Regulatory Standards and Regulatory Competition

Task expansion in the field of European environmental policy can only be meaningful from a problem-solving perspective if the agreements that have been reached in Brussels change the status quo, are capable of protecting the environment, and reduce already existing pollution levels and harmful practices. The literature on forms and strictness of EU environmental regulation can be divided into two strands, elaborating on different competitive dynamics among member states.

One point of departure is the economic theory of regulatory competition (e.g. Oates and Schwab 1988; van Long and Siebert 1991), which is applied to regulatory policy generally and predicts a 'race to the bottom' in cases where national barriers to trade are removed. National producers encounter international competitors who may benefit from less rigid – hence less costly – regulatory conditions at home. In the name of international competitiveness high regulating states are expected to reduce the regulatory burden on national industry. EU environmental policy serves to lower such competitive pressure and corresponding transaction costs among member states (Holzinger and Knill 2004). Assuming that the competitive logic nevertheless still applies to the process of setting EU standards, the theory expects LCD decisions.

Neither internationally (Vogel 1995; Jänicke 1998; Drezner 2001) nor in the EU (Holzinger 1994; Eichener 1997; Scharpf 1997) does the literature find much empirical support for races to the bottom, however. Staying within the rationalist and state-centric paradigm, Scharpf (1997) advanced the theory of regulatory competition by systematically modelling negotiation situations with respect to the distinction between product standards on the one hand, and production or process standards on the other. The theory now predicts high(er) environmental product standards in the EU because previously low regulating states face the credible threat of trade barriers (based on Article 30 of the Treaty) if they insist on their low standards. The option of declining market entry does not exist in the EU with respect to non-product standards and, hence, the theory predicts either fairly low minimum standards or the failure to reach any agreement. The empirical test ends inconclusively, however: On the one hand, we see a clear dominance of product over production standards in EU environmental policy; also, EU product standards typically exceed the LCD level. Running counter the expectations, however, a fair number of non-product directives on matters such as environmental impact assessments, public access to information, ecological auditing, and the protection of flora, fauna and natural habitats have been passed in the EU at demanding levels for member states (Héritier et al. 1996; Knill and Lenschow 1998). Hence, there is still reason to puzzle.

Surveying the literature, we find general and EU-specific attempts to explain these patterns. Holzinger (2002) and Bernauer with Caduff (2004) alert us to the need to investigate the real cost of regulation and the social context in which it may be imposed. The assumption that the preferences of cost-bearing producers determine the negotiation position of governments certainly ignores that environmental regulation creates benefits as well as costs for a society. The business community may be too heterogeneous and interest group politics too influential to generalize state positions simply on the basis of the regulatory status quo and the competitive situation of the country. Also, the EU is not easily comparable to other international cooperative settings like the WTO. During the pre-decision-making phase the central role of bureaucratic working groups and of independent advisory committees frames decision-making along technocratic and scientific as opposed to competitive lines (Eichener 1997; for a different assessment see Andersen and Rasmussen 1998). Not least, the option of QMV and the legislative role of the EP tend to operate against LCD dynamics.

Novel in the analysis of EU policy-making has been the observation of environmental policy scholars that *member states may not only compete over standards but also over regulatory styles and approaches*. Hence, the traditional dominance of a legalistic policy style and technology-based policy solutions in the EU has been attributed to Germany winning the (implicit) competition over setting the environmental policy agenda in Brussels. The emergence of procedural standards in the EU repertoire, by contrast, has been credited to the UK's 'waking up' to EU policy-making (Knill 1995; Héritier et al. 1996; Jordan 2002). In short, besides acting in the interest of economic competitiveness, member states follow a second logic of regulatory competition, namely to keep legal and administrative adaptation costs related to implementing EU regulation at a minimum. They may, therefore, pursue a 'first mover' strategy and attempt to 'shuttle in' national policy-makers to influential positions inside the Commission, in order to push national models onto the EU agenda. Consequently, we find types of regulatory policy (such as production and process standards) and levels of standards in the EU repertoire that would not have been expected from the narrowly economic regulatory competition perspective.

Policy Compliance and Implementation

There may be yet another reason for high and wide-ranging regulatory standards in the EU.

Patterns of lax implementation could explain member states' acceptance of potentially costly regulation (Macrory 1992; Eichener 1997; Jordan 1999). Implementation deficits, in turn, are linked to weak enforcement mechanisms in the EU. Underscoring this point, some authors have compared the EU to international regimes in policy implementation (Skjærseth and Wettestad 2002). Although the EU clearly differs from regimes in adopting legally binding directives and regulations, it lacks the capacity to control practical implementation as well as effective sanctioning mechanisms. Hence, similar to regimes it relies on softer social practices. These, however, may be particularly effective given the close and iterative decision-making context in the EU (cf. Young and Levy 1999). Regime scholars therefore tend to view the EU as a model structure featuring institutional characteristics to which regimes might aspire or as a test case for regime-theoretic propositions.

Such social practices fail if either the problem structure or the interest constellation prohibits 'good policy' that may be implemented effectively. The environmental problem at hand may be too complex, involving too many uncertainties or invoking too contrasting opinions for decision-makers to produce consistent and potentially effective negotiation results. Regime theorists would acknowledge the Council of Ministers to be vulnerable to such constellations like any other intergovernmental setting. They would expect the social capacity to overcome disagreement to be larger in the Council than in international regimes, however. Critical 'insider' observers of EU policy-making, by contrast, have gone so far to argue that implementation failure tends to be encoded in the decision-making practices in the EU (Weale et al. 2000: 296ff). Commission activism, symbolic politics in the Council and missing enforcement capacities have resulted in a long-lasting neglect of this part of the policy cycle (Jordan 1999: 74; similarly Collins and Earnshaw 1993; Snyder 1993; Tallberg 1999). Arguably, this neglect is mirrored in the presentation of the data on (non-) compliance, which have been claimed to produce statistical artefacts (Börzel 2001). However, these records are likely to underestimate the real extent of implementation failures as the problems coming to the attention of the Commission or the Court are strongly biased towards non-reporting or the incorrect transposition of EU directives into national law. They take too lightly the problems of practical implementation on the ground.

Recent implementation research has begun to focus on the issue of deficient practical implementation and identified the preference for top-down steering as a possible cause. Arguably, the dominant hierarchical and non-discretionary policy style on the EU level is not only the result of 'first mover' successes of countries with legalistic regulatory preferences like Germany but is more systemic in nature. As long as the market rationale of levelling the (regulatory) playing field for producers acts as a main motive for EU environmental policy, there will be some tendency to harmonize national standards. Secondly, non-discretionary measures may substitute for high levels of trust, especially in times with rising and increasingly heterogeneous membership, and help the Commission to compensate for weak enforcement structures (cf. Kelemen 2000). Such a top-down regulatory style, however, necessarily causes problems of implementation in a heterogeneous setting like the EU. Obligations formulated on the EU level may not fit into national legal and administrative systems and overtax local capacities or willingness to adapt (Knill and Lenschow 1998, 2000; Börzel 2000). *We may, in short, face a real dilemma in EU environmental governance!*

This issue was further pursued in two directions. First, it was deemed worthwhile to investigate the proclaimed shift towards 'new', softer and more flexible policy instruments. Second, the notion of fit (or misfit) between EU and national structures became influential in 'Europeanization' research more generally.

Choice of Policy Instruments and Modes of Governance

The discussion of soft modes of governance is very much *en vogue* in EU politics and academic reflection generally. Often this discussion focuses on the introduction of the open method of coordination (OMC) in social policy (see Rhodes and Citi, this volume). However, soft modes have spread widely and environmental policy has been an early field for experimentation. Here, the term 'new instruments' signifies the move to a more cooperative, less hierarchical governance approach and may be divided in two classes: *Economic instruments* cover eco-taxes, emission fees, emission certificates, state subsidies, tradable permits, and the like. *Context-oriented regulation* subsumes procedural law (i.e. information and participation rights) as well as cooperative or non-binding agreements between private and state actors or among private actors. Both forms emphasize the responsiveness to local conditions. Flexibility (not uniformity), participation (not top-down command), and learning (not sanctioning) are some keywords characterizing this new philosophy. Implementation gaps and evidence of deficient effectiveness of EU policy had raised concerns about the dominant hierarchical and legalistic style. Post-Maastricht debates about subsidiarity (Collier et al. 1993; Golub 1996c) and the emergence of a global deregulatory trend contributed to the reform agenda. Yet, national policy innovations including environmental incentive systems (e.g. eco-taxes and charges), information tools (e.g. eco-labels, eco-management) and greater involvement of private actors (by way of participation, co- or self-regulation) provided the models for EU-level proposals (Golub 1998; Mol et al. 2000; De Clercq 2002; Jordan et al. 2003). In quantitative terms, few so-called new policy instruments have been adopted so far (Héritier 2002; Holzinger et al. 2003). Nevertheless, quantitative data do not capture the varied scope of old and new policy instruments, with old-style instruments typically being much more specific than new incentive or information tools which aim at broader behavioural change.

The more critical question concerns the effectiveness of these new instruments, which returns us to the implementation literature. This literature hinted that *the widely assumed superiority of 'bottom-up' or 'new' approaches rests on very demanding assumptions.* The fact that new instruments allow for more discretion and flexibility does not mean that they are easier to handle. The contrary may be the case – particularly in countries with hierarchical legal and administrative cultures (Knill and Lenschow 2000). Furthermore, especially information and voluntary instruments strongly rely on the responsiveness of societal actors and some level of environmental mobilization; they are incapable of building such societal structures from scratch (Börzel 2000). Moreover, national experience with softer modes of governance suggests the need for some 'shadow of hierarchy' in order to keep actors committed to the policy objectives (Mayntz and Scharpf 1995; De Clercq 2002). For the future of EU environmental governance this points to the need for complementary instruments, mixing top-down and bottom-up elements (Hey et al. 2005). It also calls on the Commission to supervize new instruments, hence to develop new managerial capacities in Brussels. *Will therefore centralization be the consequence of new, softer regulation? This rather paradoxical prospect – if true – may take us out of the dilemma identified above and poses an interesting avenue for future research.* It also leads us to wider considerations of the system – as opposed to merely tools – of (environmental) governance in the EU.

POLICY MAKING AS POLITY-IN-THE-MAKING

We have seen above that the initial concern with European policies grew from a much wider interest in European integration. The rise of policy competencies in Brussels and the strengthening of supranational elements were taken as evidence for a European polity in the making. Recent scholarship on European environmental policy-making returns to the polity issue from a 'policy-up' perspective: In a more open-ended way it asks how policy-making interacts with the development of the political system of the European Union. There are three dimensions to this development. First, policy-making not only reflects but also shapes

governance structures in the EU. Second, EU policy-making and policies impact on the member states, both as actors involved in policy formulation and implementation and as political systems. Third, the EU has appeared as a new actor in international environmental politics and is potentially changing international governance. This final part will consider these polity dynamics in turn.

The Brussels Perspective

If we speak of an EU polity, we have not yet specified what kind of a polity is emerging in Europe. The term governance structure, which is often used to characterize the EU system, conveys that we are not faced with a state, but with a less formal and less hierarchical political structure. Such structures require new forms of coordination to bridge potential gaps between vertical levels and across horizontal fields of governance as well as between public and private actors. Earlier I referred to the network concept as highlighting the range of actors and their interactions in EU policymaking. Increasingly – and especially in the continental European literature – networks are looked at as elements of a governance structure. The concept is used to capture the fluid *forms* of connecting a multitude of actors in the EU generally (Peterson 2004) and with respect to environmental polic-making in particular (Héritier et al. 1996; Bomberg 1998b). Nevertheless, the network terminology is too encompassing to account for the very different constellations that have emerged in the environmental policy field. It also sidelines the one hierarchical structure that does prevail in EU environmental policy, namely the law. Below I will characterize the constellation of networks as it emerges from the literature on environmental policy.

We first observe informal and open networks particularly in the early policy formulation phase, when a wide range of interested parties might form (temporary) alliances to shape the problem perception among policymakers in Brussels and propose suitable solutions. This network formation is facilitated by the open structure of especially the Commission, allowing easy access to policy advocates. The small size of the Commission and its dependence on external information, on the one hand, and the Commission's power of policy initiative on the other hand, create the resource interdependence that has been argued to be the logical core to policy network building.

Second, we see more narrow, technocratic and stable forms of elite networks and policy communities, which become involved in the actual policy setting and implementation. These tend to be orchestrated top-down, serving the interests of the member states and the Commission. We find policy-specific networks including Commission officials and national administrators to bridge the gap between European law making and its local application. They have the double function of advising policy-makers on what is feasible on the ground as well as raising the level of acceptance among the policy 'receivers'. For instance, the implementation network (IMPEL) of Commission officials and representatives of relevant national (or local) authorities has become an important forum for considering the technical, administrative, and cultural feasibility of EU environmental proposals early in the game as well as for improving the capacity and willingness of local implementers through the exchange of experiences (cf. Dehousse 1992: 391). Especially the comitology committees, which are composed of member state and Commission representatives and assist the Commission in the development of implementation regulation, must be understood as bridges between the levels of political authority (Töller 2002).

Third, increasingly we see private stakeholder involvement taking new forms. It was already hinted in the previous part that new modes of governance emerge as alternatives to legally binding environmental law, introducing elements of private and corporatist-style governance operating in a shadow of hierarchy. In the area of technical standards and norms the EU has firmly institutionalized a 'new approach' of regulated self-regulation (Voelzkow 1996; Egan 2001) by delegating responsibilities

to the European standards bodies, CEN and CENELEC. We also observe increasing experiments with self- and co-regulatory environmental agreements of corporate actors. While some of these voluntary agreements merely serve as a bridge 'to initiate European policy-making in areas previously entirely reserved to member states' (Héritier 2002: 195), the development of public–private partnerships and their implications for 'traditional' governance in the EU will be important to watch (cf. Scheer and Rubik 2006). These forms most closely correspond to the network governance as described by Kohler-Koch (1999: 25f), with the 'state' acting as mediator or activator and actors negotiating as equal partners. Notions of equal, non-hierarchical partnerships must not blind anyone to the fact that these are rather exclusive public (in the case of comitology) or public–private networks. While they may be capable of closing the gap to the administrative and private (typically industry) addressees of European environmental policy, such networks raise democratic concerns. In the environmental field the EP as well as the non-business European NGO community has started to mobilize against such governance structures privileging technocratic elites and corporate actors,[7] insisting on either parliamentary control or more inclusive network structures.

When environmental policy is analysed as an area involving horizontal interdependencies, network governance assumes yet other characteristics. In this perspective, environmental policy depends on sectoral decision makers – for instance in transport or energy policy – to integrate environmental objectives into their respective policies. Environmental policy can only be effective if it is successfully 'mainstreamed'. But, such environmental policy integration (EPI) faces the same cognitive and institutional constraints as other forms of mainstreaming (on gender see Prugl, this volume). Comparing the EPI process in the reforms of the regional development fund, the cohesion fund and the common agricultural policy (CAP), I have argued that deeply embedded policy-specific norms – for instance associating environmental problems with smokestack industries or (regional) development with large investment projects – have hindered sectoral policy-makers from perceiving environmental destruction as 'their' problem. Sectoral perceptions were reinforced by segmented legal and institutional structures (e.g. the cohesion fund being formally linked to the EMU convergence criteria) and closed policy communities (Lenschow 1997). In recent years there have been attempts of 'macro-planning' EPI within the European Council, which has called on many Directorates-General in the Commission and sectoral councils to develop sectoral integration strategies, targets and timetables and to identify best practice examples. These macro-strategies mirror soft governance like the Open Method of Coordination (OMC) within EU institutions (Lenschow 2002b). But these initiatives too naively rely on the sectors to self-organize cross-sectoral networks (Schout and Jordan 2005: 218) and develop the skill of horizontal coordination. Policy actors have little intrinsic motivation and perceive neither real pressure nor incentives to build bridges connecting formerly separate policy 'homes'. The analysis of EPI hints that in the absence of hierarchical pressure soft governance at the macro-level needs to be accompanied by management on the meso- and micro-levels in order to produce the intended learning and reform processes.

In sum, the network metaphor has facilitated understanding various dynamics between policy making and building a governance system. While networks are built in light of the opportunities and constraints created by the institutional framework as well as the interests of central actors in the EU governance structure, they also become characteristic elements of the polity in the making. While networks responding to the vertical interdependencies in the EU come with a strong elitist and technocratic accent, networks to overcome horizontal fragmentation are still in their infancy, inhibited by strong institutional and cognitive barriers.

The Member State Perspective

Recent years have seen intense discussions about Europeanization, broadly defined as the impact of EU policies and polity structures on domestic structures. Research on environmental policy has been a main contributor to this literature; arguably it has even been a 'front runner'. There have been two sides to environmental Europeanization research: On the one hand, authors investigate the processes of member states – mostly governments and executives – learning to play the European policy game. National adaptation processes are observed in order to better understand the policy patterns emerging in Brussels. The 1996 study by Héritier et al. falls in this category; it explains the patchwork of European environmental policy with member states adjusting strategies and membership identities to the challenges of policy-making and implementation. Historically the most interesting case has been the UK, which moved from a passive to a pro-active role, implying far-reaching learning processes inside the executive (Jordan 2002). Germany, by contrast, had understood the first mover advantage early, yet may have failed to consolidate this position by, for instance, developing a European personnel policy. Jehlička and Tickle (2004) raise the interesting question how the new Eastern European members of the EU will play the game and what consequences this might have for future EU environmental policy. On the basis of expert interviews they identify two slightly contradictory patterns, namely passivity and reactivity, on the one hand, and support for new policy instruments and more effective policy integration, on the other hand (see also Schreurs 2004). The first pattern is expected by many, given that environmental policy does not rank high on the priority list of national policy-makers in Eastern Europe. The consequence would be a slow-down and potential re-nationalization of EU environmental policy-making (cf. Homeyer et al. 2000). The second pattern can be understood as aspects of the process of emancipation from an authoritarian past and a spreading liberal ideology. Whether it will be sustained depends on the capacity of these states to implement these soft and discretionary instruments, which – as outlined above – assume a certain level of societal responsiveness and organizational flexibility.

Most recent literature takes Europeanization as the dependent variable; hence it adopts the 'second image reversed' perspective to understand transformations of national governance or policy. Generally, this literature is dominated by institutional perspectives emphasizing the constraints to national adaptations. It comes in several distinct variants: Keywords are (mis)fit, veto points and capacities. EU environmental policy typically takes the form of a directive that needs to be transposed by national legislatures and, regardless of the type of instrument, it usually requires public administrations to implement the law on the ground. Extent and timing of implementation, but also the exact shape that is given to the policy, therefore depend on the performance of legislative and administrative actors. The analysis of veto points gives us a good idea of the procedural hurdles a directive needs to take and the potential that it is blocked, delayed or implemented in a minimalist fashion (cf. Haverland 2000). The concepts of 'fit' and 'misfit' alert us to the fact that EU directives may not pose the same legislative and administrative adaptation challenge to all member states. The argument is that legislators and administrators tend to resist high adaptation requirements and hence extensive Europeanization, especially if the 'core' of pre-existing and potentially affected policies and administrative procedures is institutionally deeply embedded and stable (Knill and Lenschow 1998, 2000; Knill 2001).

The analysis of institutional (mis-)fit and of the impact of administrative capacities – which has become particularly topical since the last expansion of the EU (cf. Carmin and VanDeveer 2004; Homeyer 2004) – makes explicit the close relationship between Europeanization of policy and that of governance structures such as legal traditions, administrative structures, procedures and interest intermediation. This goes beyond the more narrow concern of implementation studies. Jordan and Liefferink (2004: 237) have edited the most comprehensive study to date, which compares patterns of Europeanization in environmental policy and political structures across member states. While all countries have witnessed a pattern of Europeanization – more deeply with regard to policy content than concerning structures and policy styles – the group of 'strongly Europeanized' states is small, consisting of the UK, Ireland, and Spain. It will be interesting to see whether Eastern European states follow the example of the two 'cohesion countries'.[8] Importantly, so far *Europeanization did not result in the convergence* of policy or governance structures across member states, confirming the institutionalist insistence on the impact of path-dependency.

The International Perspective

Finally, the multi-level governance structure should be extended to cover the EU's role in international environmental politics. As international conventions are usually formal agreements between sovereign states, and as the EU obviously is not a state, this process involved the establishment of new procedures and routines both internationally and within the EU, challenging traditional multilateral practices (Sbragia and Damro 1999). International environmental policy-making is as much about procedures as about content – this is also reflected in the literature. The question of whether to accept the Community as a party to an international convention is controversial for non-EU partners and within the EU itself. Over the years, 'mixed agreements' with the Community and the member states as signatories have emerged as the normal pattern in international environmental agreements. Despite some persisting ambiguities, EU member governments have become increasingly willing to coordinate their positions and act collectively, while international partners have come to expect 'the Union' in some formation at the negotiation table.

This evolution is mirrored in the analytical approaches taken to study the EU in international agreements. Initially, the main puzzle was to explain how the member states reached agreement on a common position to be presented to other negotiating partners. We are alerted to preference constellations and rules – like the reciprocity rule or burden sharing arrangements – to facilitate agreement (Skjærseth 1994). In addition, institutional constellations, like the Commission mediating or the Presidency seeking a profile, can play a role (cf. Jachtenfuchs 1990). While such constellations are not specific to international environmental policy-making, Damro and Méndez (2003) suggest that exactly the mixed or 'dual representation', which seemed a compromise solution at first, gave the Community an intergovernmental as well as 'federal' external personality. Member states submitted to it as national interests seemed protected and were given added weight in the Union. In a next – empirical and analytical – phase EU leadership became an issue. Sbragia and Damro (1999: 53) argue that during the process of institutionalizing its formal position the EU evolved from a 'Vienna laggard to a Kyoto leader' in global environmental negotiations. EU member states had developed a collective spirit in the sense that they had become used to accepting national restrictions and even to agree on differential treatments among themselves. In the case of the Kyoto Protocol the intra-EU burden-sharing agreement, which allocates different greenhouse gas reduction commitments to the member states, strengthened the EU's negotiation position as it was able to commit itself to the toughest (collective) target of an 8% reduction. Jupille (1999) is less convinced about the collective maturity of the EU and argues that such leadership is dependent on favourable decision rules internally. Only if the EU decides on its international negotiation position through QMV will we see a tendency for the EU to push for international outcomes and succeed due to its bargaining weight. In either case, however, it is notable that the EU was willing and capable of developing international leadership in the 'soft' area of environmental policy, forcing international regimes to accommodate procedurally and substantively.

In the longer run such a leadership role depends on credibility, namely the EU's capacity to comply with its international commitments, like the Kyoto targets or the sustainable development agenda, effectively (cf. Lightfoot and Burchell 2005). Here, the excursion to the international expansion of EU environmental policy ends on familiar terrain – a potential implementation deficit which could undermine the project.

CONCLUSION

This chapter set out to review the contributions of EU environmental policy research to the general understanding of EU policy-making and governance. The reader will have noted that environmental policy scholars have 'danced at many parties'. In the early years, they have analysed policy through the lenses of the two grand theories and entered into similar debates as most other EU scholars. Later, most analysts made the turn toward a domestic politics perspective with the debate centring on the merits of actor-oriented or institutional approaches. Neither of these debates produced a clear 'winner'. But, especially the latter discussion produced real 'value added', as the analysis of this rapidly expanding policy field revealed the multi-faceted and fluid actor and institutional constellations characterizing the EU system of governance.

Many analytically motivated studies of EU policy focus on the 'making' of policy while performance assessments tend to be left to normative commentaries. Arguably, environmental policy research has been a 'front-runner' in theory-based performance or output studies. Interestingly, the issue of environmental standards is tackled mostly from a state-centric, rationalist perspective, whereas policy compliance and implementation are approached from an institutionalist angle. Especially in the latter case this theory-bias has triggered a lively debate also outside the field of environmental policy,[9] inviting comparative policy research in this area.

Furthermore, the 'performance question' contributed to widening the research perspective beyond mere policy towards governance and beyond Brussels toward impacts on the member states and (to a lesser extent) the international level. Especially the analysis of different policy instruments and of shifting actor constellations in environmental problem solving revealed not only a close, but also a very dynamic relationship between policy and polity making. In focusing on this interaction, the study of European environmental policy has made a turn from the policy level to the systems level of analysing the EU. This 'big picture' looks highly differentiated and even somewhat 'messy', more so than either a regime or a federal state. Hopefully, this chapter has demonstrated that (environmental) policy research has made a notable contribution to *understanding* this complex process and structure of governance in the EU.

ACKNOWLEDGEMENT

I am thankful to Marc Pollack, Duncan Liefferink and Andrew Jordan for valuable comments on earlier drafts of this chapter.

NOTES

1. These are not subsequent phases in the very strict sense of the word as they overlap and some authors have certainly pursued several streams in parallel.

2. The German title of the book 'Die Veränderung von Staatlichkeit' is revealing in this sense.

3. If new and amended laws were counted this number would rise to around 40 per annum (Zito 1999: 19).

4. Neither argument is uncontested. Haverland (2000) shows that the adoption of the packaging waste directive involved member states changing their initial positions. Jordan (2002) offers a detailed analysis of the – however slow – adaptation process in the British environment ministry. However, both authors relate their argument to the more recent Europeanization debate rather than general integration theories.

5. To the extent that the institutional interest of the supranational organ is identified as the primary driver for policy expansion – regardless of any general integrationist objectives these actors might embrace – this literature may be also characterized as neo-institutionalist (of the rational choice variant).

6. See, for instance, Glachant (2001) for an economists' perspective.

7. Interesting case studies to this effect focus on the so-called Auto-Oil Programme of the Commission, which had been hailed as a model for private involvement in environment policy-making (Friedrich et al. 2000; Warleigh 2000).

8. The Europeanization discussion has, in fact, contributed to a more differentiated and more favourable image of the southern and cohesion countries, which used to be considered 'laggards' in this policy field (cf. Pridham 1994; Börzel 2000).

9. See, for instance, Falkner et al. (2005) on social policy.

REFERENCES

Andersen, M.S. and Liefferink, D.J. (1997) *Issue in Environmental Policy. European Environmental Policy – The Pioneers*. Manchester: Manchester University Press.

Andersen, M.S. and Rasmussen, L.N. (1998) 'The making of environmental policy in the European Council', *Journal of Common Market Studies*, 36(4): 585–97.

Arp, H. (1993) 'Technical regulation and politics: the interplay between economic interests and environmental policy goals in the EC car emission legislation', in J.D. Liefferink, P.D. Lowe and A.P.J. Mol (eds), *European Integration and Environmental Policy*. London and New York: Belhaven Press. pp. 150–71.

Bernauer, T. and Caduff, L. (2004) 'In whose interest? Pressure group politics, economic competition and environmental regulation', *Journal of Public Policy*, 24(1): 99–126.

Bomberg, E. (1998a) *Green Parties and Politics in the European Union*. London and New York: Routledge.

Bomberg, E. (1998b) 'Issue networks and the environment: explaining European Union environmental policy', in D. Marsh (ed.), *Comparing Policy Networks*. Buckingham: Open University Press. pp. 167–84.

Bomberg, E. and Burns, C. (1999) 'The Environment Committee of the European Parliament: new powers, old problems', *Environmental Politics*, 8(4): 173–9.

Börzel, T.A. (2000) 'Why there is no 'southern problem'. On environmental leaders and laggards in the European Union', *Journal of European Public Policy*, 7(1): 141–62.

Börzel, T.A. (2001) 'Non-compliance in the European Union. Pathology or statistical artefact', *Journal of European Public Policy*, 8(5): 303–24.

Carmin, J. and Vandeveer, S.D. (2004) 'Enlarging EU environments: central and eastern Europe from transition to accession', *Environmental Politics*, 13(1): 3–24.

Collier, U., Golub, J. and Kreher, A. (eds) (1993) *Subsidiarity and Shared Responsibility. New Challenges for EU Environmental Policy*. Baden-Baden: Nomos.

Collins, K. and Earnshaw, D. (1993) 'The implementation and enforcement of European Community environment legislation', in D. Judge (ed.), *A Green Dimension for the European Community. Political Issues and Processes*. London: Frank Cass. pp. 213–49.

Damro, C. and Méndez, P.L. (2003) 'Emissions trading at Kyoto: from EU resistance to union innovation', *Environmental Politics*, 12(2): 71–94.

De Clercq, M. (ed.) (2002) *Negotiating Environmental Agreements in Europe: Critical Factors for Success*. Cheltenham: Edgar Elgar.

Dehousse, R. (1992) 'Integration v. regulation? On the dynamics of regulation in the European Community', *Journal of Common Market Studies*, 15(4): 383–402.

Drezner, D.W. (2001) 'Globalization and policy convergence', *The International Studies Review*, 3(1): 53–78.

Egan, M. (2001) *Constructing a European Market*. Oxford: Oxford University Press.

Eichener, V. (1997) 'Effective European problem-solving: lessons from the regulation of occupational safety and environmental protection', *Journal of European Public Policy*, 4(4): 591–608.

Falkner, G., Treib, O., Hartlapp, M. and Leiber, S. (2005) *Complying with Europe: Theory and Practics of EU Harmonization and Soft Law in the Multi-Level System*. Cambridge: Cambridge University Press.

Friedrich, A., Tappe, M. and Wurzel, R.K.W. (2000) 'A new approach to EU environmental policy-making? The auto-oil I programme', *Journal of European Public Policy*, 7(4): 593–612.

Glachant, M. (ed.) (2001) *Implementing European Environmental Policy. The Impacts of Directives in the Member States*. Cheltenham, UK and Northampton, USA: Edward Elgar.

Golub, J. (1996a) 'State power and institutional influence in European integration: lessons from the packaging waste directive', *Journal of Common Market Studies*, 34(3): 313–37.

Golub, J. (1996b) 'British sovereignty and the development of EC environmental policy', *Environmental Politics*, 5(4): 700–28.

Golub, J. (1996c) 'Sovereignty and subsidiarity in EU environmental policy', *Political Studies*, 44(4): 686–703.

Golub, J. (ed.) (1998) *New Instruments for Environmental Policy in the EU*. London and New York: Routledge.

Haigh, N. (2004) *Manual of Environmental Policy: The EU and Britain*. Leeds: Maney Publishing.

Hajer, M.A. (1995) *The Politics of Environmental Discourse. Ecological Modernization and the Policy Process*. Oxford: Oxford University Press.

Haverland, M. (2000) 'National adaptation to European integration: the importance of institutional veto points', *Journal of Public Policy*, 20(1): 83–103.

Heard, J. and Richards, J. (2005) 'European environmental NGOs: issues, resources and strategies in marine campaigns', *Environmental Politics*, 14(1): 23–41.

Héritier, A. (1996) 'The accommodation of diversity in European policy-making and its outcomes: regulatory policy as a patchwork', *Journal of European Public Policy*, 3(2): 149–67.

Héritier, A. (1997) 'Policy-making by subterfuge: interest accommodation, innovation and substitute democratic legitimation in Europe – perspectives from distinctive policy areas', *Journal of European Public Policy*, 4(2): 171–89.

Héritier, A. (2002) 'New modes of governance in Europe: policy-making without legislating?', in A. Héritier (ed.), *Common Goods. Reinventing European and International Governance*. Lanham: Rowman & Littlefield Publishers. pp. 185–206.

Héritier, A., Knill, C. and Mingers, S. (1996) *Ringing the Changes in Europe. Regulatory Competition and the Transformation of the State*. Berlin: de Gruyter.

Héritier, A., Mingers, S., Knill, C. and Becka, M. (1994) *Die Veränderung von Staatlichkeit in Europa*. Opladen: Leske + Budrich.

Hey, C. and Brendle, U. (1994) *Towards a New Renaissance: A New Development Model. Part A: Reversing the Roll-Back of Environmental Policies in the European Union*. Freiburg, Brussels: Eures and EEB.

Hey, C., Volkery, A. and Zerle, P. (2005) 'Neue umweltpolitische Steuerungskonzepte in der Europäischen Union', *Zeitschrift für Umweltpolitik und Umweltrecht*, 28(1): 1–38.

Hildebrand, P.M. (1993) 'The European Community's environmental policy, 1957 to '1992': from incidental measures to an international regime?', in D. Judge (ed.), *A Green Dimension for the European Community. Political Issues and Processes*. London: Frank Cass. pp. 13–44.

Holzinger, K. (1994) *Politik des kleinsten gemeinsamen Nenners? Umweltpolitische Entscheidungsprozesse in der EG am Beispiel des Katalysatorautos*. Berlin: Edition Sigma.

Holzinger, K. (2002) 'The provision of transnational common goods: regulatory competition for environmental standards', in A. Héritier (ed.),

Common Goods: Reinventing European and International Governance. Lanham: Rowman and Littlefield. pp. 57–79.

Holzinger, K. and Knill, C. (2004) 'Regulatory competition and regulatory cooperation in environmental policy: individual and interaction effects', *Journal of Public Policy*, 25(1): 25–47.

Holzinger, K., Knill, C. and Schäfer, A. (2003) 'Steuerungswandel in der europäischen Umweltpolitik?', in K. Holzinger, C. Knill and D. Lehmkuhl (eds), *Politische Steuerung im Wandel: Der Einfluss von Ideen und Problemstrukturen.* Opladen: Leske + Budrich. pp. 103–29.

Homeyer, I.V. (2004) 'Differential effects of enlargement on EU environmental governance', *Environmental Politics*, 13(1): 52–76.

Homeyer, I.V., Carius, A. and Bär, S. (2000) 'Flexibility or renationalization: effects of enlargement on EC environmental policy', in M.G. Cowles and M. Smith (eds), *The State of the European Union: Risks, Reform, Resistance and Revival.* Oxford: Oxford University Press. pp. 347–68.

Hovden, E. (2002) 'The legal basis of European Union policy: the case of environmental policy. *Environmental and Planning C: Government and Policy*, 20(4): 535–52.

Huelshoff, M.G. and Pfeiffer, T. (1991) 'Environmental policy in the EC: neofunctionalist sovereignty transfer or neo-realist gatekeeping', *International Journal*, 47(1): 136–58.

Hull, R. (1993) 'Lobbying Brussels: a view from within', in S. Mazey and J. Richardson (eds), *Lobbying in the European Community.* Oxford: Oxford University Press. pp. 82–92.

Imig, D. and Tarrow, S. (2000) 'Political contention in a Europeanising polity', *West European Politics*, 23: 73–93.

Jachtenfuchs, M. (1990) 'The European Community and the protection of the ozone layer', *Journal of Common Market Studies*, 18(3): 261–71.

Jachtenfuchs, M. (1996) 'Regieren durch Überzeugen: Die Europäische Union und der Treibhauseffekt', in M. Jachtenfuchs and B. Kohler-Koch (eds), *Europäische Integration.* Opladen: Leske+ Budrich. pp. 429–54.

Jänicke, M. (1998) 'Umweltpolitik – global am Ende oder am Ende global. Thesen zu ökologischen Determinanten des Weltmarktes', in U. Beck (ed.), *Perspektiven der Weltgesellschaft.* Frankfurt am Main: Suhrkamp. pp. 332–44.

Jehlička, P. and Tickle, A. (2004) 'Environmental implications of eastern enlargement: the end of progressive EU environmental policy?', *Environmental Politics*, 13(1): 77–95.

Johnson, S.P. and Corcelle, G. (1989) *The Environmental Policy of the European Communities.* London: Graham & Trotman.

Jordan, A. (1998) 'Step change or stasis? EC environmental policy after the Amsterdam summit', *Environmental Politics*, 7(1, Special Issue): 227–36.

Jordan, A. (1999) 'The implementation of EU environmental policy: a problem without a political solution?', *Environment and Planning C: Government and Policy*, 17(1): 69–90.

Jordan, A. (2002) *The Europeanization of British Environmental Policy. A Departmental Perspective.* Basingstoke: Palgrave.

Jordan, A. and Fairbrass, J. (2001) 'European Union environmental policy after the Nice summit', *Environmental Politics*, 10(4): 109–14.

Jordan, A. and Liefferink, D.J. (eds) (2004) *Environmental Policy in Europe. The Europeanization of national environmental policy.* London and New York: Routledge.

Jordan, A., Brouwer, R. and Noble, E. (1999) 'Innovative and responsive? A longitudinal analysis of the speed of EU environmental policy making, 1967–97', *Journal of European Public Policy*, 6(3): 376–98.

Jordan, A., Wurzel, R.K.W. and Zito, A.R. (2003) '"New" instruments of environmental governance: patterns and pathways of change', *Environmental Politics*, 12(1): 1–24.

Judge, D. (1993) '"Predestined to save the earth": the environment committee of the European Parliament', in D. Judge (ed.), *A Green Dimension for the European Community. Political Issues and Processes.* London: Frank Cass. pp. 186–212.

Judge, D., Earnshaw, D. and Cowan, N. (1994) 'Ripples or waves: the European Parliament in the European Community policy process', *Journal of European Public Policy*, 1(1): 27–52.

Jupille, J. (1999) 'The European Union and international outcomes', *International Organization*, 53(2): 409–25.

Kasack, C. (2004) 'The legislative impact of the European Parliament under the revised co-decision procedure: environmental, public health and consumer protection policies', *European Union Politics*, 5(2): 241–60.

Kelemen, R.D. (2000) 'Regulatory federalism: EU environmental regulation in comparative perspective', *Journal of Public Policy*, 20(3): 133–67.

Knill, C. (1995) *Staatlichkeit im Wandel. Großbritannien im Spannungsfeld innenpolitischer Reformen und europäischer Integration.* Opladen: Deutscher Universitätsverlag.

Knill, C. (2001) *The Europeanisation of National Administrations. Patterns of Institutional Change and Persistence.* Cambridge: Cambridge University Press.

Knill, C. and Lenschow, A. (1998) 'Coping with Europe: the impact of British and German administration on the implementation of EU environmental policy', *Journal of European Public Policy*, 5(4): 595–614.

Knill, C. and Lenschow, A. (eds) (2000) *Implementing EU Environmental Policies: New Directions and Old Problems.* Manchester: Manchester University Press.

Kohler-Koch, B. (1999) 'The evolution and transformation of European governance', in B. Kohler-Koch and R. Eising (eds), *The Transformation of Governance in the European Union.* London and New York: Routledge. pp. 14–35.

Koppen, I.J. (1993) 'The role of the European Court of Justice', in J.D. Liefferink, P.D. Lowe and A.P.J. Mol (eds), *European Integration and Environmental Policy.* London and New York: Belhaven Press. pp. 126–49.

Lenschow, A. (1997) 'Variation in EC environmental policy integration: agency push within complex institutional structures', *Journal of European Public Policy*, 4(1): 109–27.

Lenschow, A. (1999) 'Transformation in European environmental governance', in B. Kohler-Koch and R. Eising (eds), *The Transformation of Governance in the European Union.* London/New York: Routledge. pp. 39–61.

Lenschow, A. (ed.) (2002a) *Environmental Policy Integration. Greening Sectoral Policies in Europe.* London: Earthscan.

Lenschow, A. (2002b) 'New regulatory approaches in 'greening' EU policies', *European Law Journal*, 8(1): 19–37.

Lenschow, A. and Zito, A. (1998) 'Blurring or shifting of policy frames? The institutionalization of the economic-environmental policy linkage in the European Community', *Governance*, 11(4): 415–41.

Liefferink, D. and Andersen, M.S. (1998) 'Strategies of the 'green' member states in EU environmental policy-making', *Journal of European Public Policy*, 5(2): 254–70.

Lightfoot, S. and Burchell, J. (2005) 'The European Union and the world summit on sustainable development: normative power Europe in action', *Journal of Common Market Studies*, 43(1): 75–95.

Long, T. (1995) 'Shaping public policy in the European Union: a case study of the structural funds', *Journal of European Public Policy*, 2(4): 672–9.

Macrory, R. (1992) 'The enforcement of Community environmental laws: some critical issues', *Common Market Law Review*, 29: 347–69.

Majone, G. (1996) *Regulating Europe: Problems and Prospects.* London: Routledge.

Marks, G. and McAdam, D. (1996) 'Social movements and the changing structure of political opportunity in the European Union', *West European Politics*, 20: 111–33.

Mayntz, R. and Scharpf, F. W. (1995) 'Steuerung und Selbstorganisation in staatsnahen Sektoren', in R. Mayntz and F. Scharpf (eds), *Gesellschaftliche Selbstregulierung und politische Steuerung.* Frankfurt a.M.: Campus Verlag. pp. 9–38.

Mazey, S. and Richardson, J. (1993) 'Environmental groups and the EC: challenges and opportunities', in D. Judge (ed.), *A Green Dimension for the European Community? Political Issues and Processes.* London: Frank Cass. pp. 109–28.

Mol, A., Liefferink, D. and Lauber, V. (eds) (2000) *The Voluntary Approach to Environmental Policy. Joint Environmental Approach to Environmental Policy-making in Europe.* Oxford: Oxford University Press.

Oates, W.E. and Schwab, R.M. (1988) 'Economic competition among jurisdictions. Efficiency enhancing or distortion inducing?' *Journal of Public Economics*, 35: 333–54.

Peterson, J. (2001) 'The choice for EU theorists: establishing a common framework for analysis', *European Journal of Political Research*, 39: 289–318.

Peterson, J. (2004) 'Policy networks', in A. Wiener and T. Diez (eds), *European Integration Theory.* Oxford: Oxford University Press. pp. 117–35.

Pollack, M.A. (1997) 'Representing diffuse interests in EC policy-making', *Journal of European Public Policy*, 4(4): 572–90.

Pridham, G. (1994) 'National environmental policy-making in the European framework: Spain, Greece and Italy in comparison', *Regional Politics and Policy*, 4(1): 80–101.

Rehbinder, E. and Stewart, R. (1985) *Environmental Protection Policy, Vol. 2, Integration Through Law: European and the American Federal Experience.* Berlin, New York: De Gruyer.

Rucht, D. (2001) 'Lobbying or protest? Strategies to influence EU environmental policies', in D. Imig and S. Tarrow (eds), *Contentious European. Protest and Politics in an Emerging Polity.* Lanham: Rowman & Littlefield. pp. 125–42.

Sabatier, P.A. (1998) 'The advocacy coalition framework: revisions and relevance for Europe', *Journal of European Public Policy*, 5(1): 98–130.

Sbragia, A. (1996) 'Environmental policy: the 'push-pull' of policy-making', in H. Wallace and W. Wallace (eds), *Policy-Making in the European Union.* Oxford: Oxford University Press. pp. 235–56.

Sbragia, A. (2000) 'Environmental policy. Economic constraints and external pressures', in H. Wallace and W. Wallace (eds), *Policy-making in the European Union.* Oxford: Oxford University Press. pp. 293–316.

Sbragia, A.M. and Damro, C. (1999) 'The changing role of the European Union in international environmental politics. Institution building and the politics of climate change', *Environment and Planning C: Government and Policy,* 17(1): 53–68.

Scharpf, F.W. (1997) 'Introduction', *Journal of European Public Policy,* 4(4): 520–38.

Scheer, D. and Rubik, F. (eds) (2006) *Governance of Integrated Product Policy - in Search of Sustainable Production and Consumption.* Sheffield: Greenleaf Publishing Ltd.

Schout, A. and Jordan, A. (2005) 'Coordinated European governance: self-organizing or centrally steered?' *Public Administration,* 83(1): 201–20.

Schreurs, M. (2004) 'Environmental protection in an expanding European Community: lessons from past accessions', *Environmental Politics,* 13(1): 27–51.

Skjærseth. J.B. (1994) 'Climate policy of the EC: too hot to handle?' *Journal of Common Market Studies,* 32(1): 25–42.

Skjærseth, J.B. and Wettestad, J. (2002) 'Understanding the effectiveness of EU environmental polity: how can regime analysis contribute?' *Environmental Politics,* 11(3): 99–120.

Snyder, F. (1993) 'The effectiveness of European Community law. Institutions, processes, tools and techniques', *Modern Law Review,* 56: 19–54.

Tallberg, J. (1999) *Making States Comply. The European Commission, the European Court of Justice and the enforcement of the internal market.* Lund: Studentliteratur.

Töller, A.E. (2002) *Komitologie: theoretische Bedeutung und praktische Funktionsweise von Durchführungsausschüssen der Europäischen Union am Beispiel der Umweltpolitik.* Opladen: Leske + Budrich.

van Long, N. and Siebert, H. (1991) 'Institutional competition versus ex-ante harmonisation. The case of environmental policy', *Journal of Institutional and Theoretical Economics,* 147: 296–311.

Voelzkow, H. (1996) *Private Regierungen in der Techniksteuerung. Eine sozialwissenschaftliche Analyse der technischen Normung.* Frankfurt and New York: Campus.

Vogel, D. (1995) *Trading Up.* Cambridge and London: Harvard University Press.

Warleigh, A. (2000) 'The hustle: citizenship practice, NGOs and 'policy coalitions', in the European Union – the cases of Auto Oil, drinking water and unit pricing', *Journal of European Public Policy,* 7(2): 229–43.

Weale, A. (1992) *The new politics of pollution.* Manchester and New York: Manchester University Press.

Weale, A. (1996) 'Environmental rules and rule-making in the European Union', *Journal of European Public Policy,* 3(4): 594–611.

Weale, A. (1999) 'European environmental policy by stealth: the dysfunctionality of functionalism?' *Environment and Planning C: Government and Policy,* 17(1): 37–51.

Weale, A. and Williams, A. (1993) 'Between economy and ecology? The single market and the integration of environmental policy', in D. Judge (ed.), *A Green Dimension for the European Community. Political Issues and Processes.* London: Frank Cass. pp. 45–64.

Weale, A., Pridham, G., Cini, M., Konstadakopulos, D., Porter, M. and Flynn, B. (2000) *Environmental Governance in Europe.* Oxford: Oxford University Press.

Webster, R. (1998) 'Environmental collective action. Stable patterns of cooperation and issue alliances at the European level', in J. Greenwood and M. Aspinwall (eds), *Collective Action in the European Union.* London, New York: Routledge. pp. 176–225.

Wilkinson, D. (1992) *Maastricht and the Environment. The implications for the EC's environmental policy of the Treaty on European Union signed at Maastricht on 7 February 1992.* London: IEEP.

Wurzel, R.K.W. (1996) 'The role of the EU presidency in the environmental field: does it make a difference which member state runs the presidency?' *Journal of European Public Policy,* 3(2): 272–91.

Young, O. and Levy, M. (1999) 'The effectiveness of international evvironmental regimes', in O. Young (ed.), *The Effectiveness of International Environmental Regimes: Causal Connections and Behavioral Mechanisms.* Cambridge, MA: MIT Press. pp. 1–32.

Zito, A. (1999) 'Task expansion: a theoretical overview', *Environment and Planning C, Government and Policy,* 17(1): 19–35.

Zito, A. (2001) 'Epistemic communities, collective entrepreneurship and European integration', *Journal of European Public Policy,* 8(4): 585–603.

22

Gender and European Union Politics

ELISABETH PRÜGL

INTRODUCTION

A post-Westphalian entity, the European Union (EU) has disturbed the principle of state sovereignty and with it the patriarchal gender orders of its member states.[1] The specific impacts on women and men of the contemporary reorganization of political authority in Europe are a matter of debate. On the one hand, among international institutions, the EU stands out in its foregrounding of the goal of gender equality, listing 'equality between women and men' among its 'values' and 'objectives' in the new Constitutional Treaty (Articles I-2 and I-3) and having committed to mainstreaming gender considerations into all aspects of its operations. On the other hand, caught between the agendas of market liberalization and the preservation of European welfare states, it is a site of political struggle about European gender orders. The EU contributes to new forms of modernization that have found their expression in rhetorical commitments to gender equality

while producing inequality and difference in new ways.

An extensive literature on gender and EU politics discusses these matters. It ranges from descriptions of the development and scope of the EU's gender policies to analyses of policy-making and implementation in a multi-level polity, interpretations of gender regimes in sectoral and regional contexts, and discussions of the exclusionary effects of these policies in the EU's emerging constructions of citizenship. The following review of literature proceeds in three steps. First, I provide a brief historical overview of the formation of the EU's gender equality policy, setting the stage for an exploration of the scholarly literature. Second, I survey studies that seek to explain the creation and implementation of the EU's gender equality policies. The point of departure of many of these studies is the political agency of states, feminists, and EU institutions. Third, I survey studies of the EU as a gender order and of the various ways in which gender inhabits the European integration project. The focus of these studies is not only the EU's gender equality policies but a broad range of its policies. They tend to probe the discourses that inform EU politics and the gender regimes woven into the EU as a regulatory project. They conceptualize politics as biases in rules and as the discursive production of gender difference. I conclude with an assessment of the significance of a feminist approach to studying the EU for European integration theory more broadly.

The chapter suggests that the scholarly literature on gender politics in the European Union increasingly has moved from policy analysis towards discourse analysis, from asking 'how and why does the EU adopt and implement gender equality policies?' to asking 'how and why is gender difference constructed and gender inequality reproduced through EU policies?' The adoption of gender mainstreaming as the EU's favored approach to advancing gender equality has given further impetus to this shift. I argue that feminist constructivism is particularly useful in probing the extent to which the EU reproduces and modifies the patriarchal welfare state.

FROM EQUAL OPPORTUNITY TO GENDER MAINSTREAMING

A legal equality regime forms the center of the EU's gender equality policy. Hoskyns' (1996) landmark study provided the first comprehensive account of the development of this regime. She recounts its roots in Article 119 (now Article 141) of the Rome Treaty, its development through feminist uses of the law, its elaboration through a series of directives addressing equal pay and equal treatment in the 1970s and 1980s and through diverse rulings by the European Court of Justice (ECJ), affirming the direct applicability of Article 119. Today this legal regime encompasses a variety of soft law instruments in addition to Treaty provisions, directives, and court rulings (for useful recent compilations see Hantrais 2000a; Ellina 2003; Kettelhut 2003; Berghahn 2004).

The EU's equality regime has been built in stages, shifting approaches and expanding in scope over time. Scholars have described a three-stage movement from a focus on equal rights and treatment, to positive action, to gender mainstreaming (Rees 1998; Mazey 2001; Booth and Bennett 2002). The equal rights approach employed legislation (directives) and litigation to ensure that women were treated in a manner equal to men. A series of 'action programs' starting in the 1980s added a positive action approach supporting women in areas where they were disadvantaged in order to level the playing field. In particular, this meant funding educational and job-training programs to desegregate the labor market (Hoskyns 2000). In the 1990s, gender mainstreaming became the preferred strategy for achieving gender equality in the EU. This has involved the consideration of gender differences in all areas of policy-making and programming, from the stage of planning to implementation. While feminists and gender experts in the EU insist that gender mainstreaming is only one leg of a 'three-legged equality stool' (Booth and Bennett 2002), the approach has shifted the attention of advocates from hard to soft law and from legal to administrative strategies, and sometimes given governments an excuse to eliminate equal opportunity programs. Where the legislative approach used the power of the law to force member state compliance, gender mainstreaming relies on bureaucratic mechanisms such as reporting requirements and requirements for gender-disaggregated data to stimulate policy developments in the member states.

A change in the scope of the EU's gender regime paralleled this change in approaches. In the 1970s, the EU narrowly defined its competencies regarding gender equality as pertaining to labor market issues only. Feminist scholars criticized this understanding because it tended to take the male worker as the norm. Thus, EU directives include no consideration of divisions of unpaid labor or of labor market segregation, issues important to women and key obstacles to gender equality (Egan 1998). Over the years, and resulting in part from the introduction of gender mainstreaming, the EU has expanded the scope of its activism. It increasingly has concerned itself with measures that allow workers to reconcile work and family, passed a pregnancy directive, a parental leave directive, and directives on part-time and temporary work (Hantrais 2000b; Hoskyns 2000; Walby 2004). In December 2004, the EU furthermore adopted a Directive on Equal Treatment in Goods and Services, the first directive not focused on the labor market. It also has moved towards addressing equality in the political and civil arena. For example, the 2001–05 Community Framework Strategy on Gender Equality includes among objectives to be accomplished not only equality in economic and social life, but also 'equal representation and participation in decision-making (parity democracy); ... equality in civil life (human rights, gender-related violence, trafficking), and changing gender roles and overcoming stereotypes (in education, culture, media)' (Mazey 2002: 2).

Despite this broadening of focus, feminists have bemoaned that the EU's efforts have not gone far enough. According to Guerrina (2002), the Pregnant Workers Directive does not go beyond a superficial 'procedural' form of equality. And while the Parental Leave Directive addresses gender relations in the family by extending to men the right to leave to fulfil family obligations, it fails to provide a minimum standard for pay during leave. Existing economic hierarchies and unequal pay make it likely that women continue to take leave rather than men. Other EU documents make steps towards more 'substantive' equality, but typically these fall into the category of soft law.

How did gender equality get onto the EU agenda? How is one to explain its development? How is it being implemented? How is one to explain its limited outcomes? The following section shows how studies have drawn on theories of policy networks, social movements, and institutionalism in order to suggest answers to these questions (Mazey 2000).

MAKING GENDER EQUALITY POLICY

In probing the development of the EU's gender equality policy, Pierson (1998) has advanced an institutionalist argument, describing it as an instance of path-dependent developments, in which short-term government interests in the 1950s led to long-term unintended

consequences, i.e. EU leadership in gender equality policy. Pierson emphasizes governments' loss of control as a result of institutional processes. Ellina (2003) similarly relies on historical institutionalism to describe the evolution of the EU's gender policy as generating unanticipated results, emphasizing in addition the autonomy of supranational institutions.

But the development of the EU's gender equality policy has not always been a matter of a linear policy progression. Egan (1998: 25) has pointed out that the legal, incrementalist, and functionalist-inspired image in narratives of policy development fails to account for the 'oscillating or stop-go pattern of European integration'. Historical institutionalism cannot by itself explain this pattern and scholars often have adduced other 'politics' as a supplemental explanation. Egan (1998: 25) points out that the Court reacted to political pressure in the aftermath of its activist rulings on gender policy and, while not reversing itself (which would contradict the argument of path-dependency), it did move towards 'a more restrained promotion of women's rights'. Liebert (1999) similarly identifies political pressure as one explanation for a 'take-off' of gender equality policy in the 1990s. Member states were concerned about a gender gap in referenda on the Maastricht treaty; in addition the new Nordic member states made gender equality a priority of their EU agenda.

The autonomy of EU institutions figures in institutionalist explanations and in explanations that emphasize situational politics. According to Liebert (1999), the Commission strategically employed the gender gap in EU support to advance gender equality policy in the 1990s. Ellina (2003) concurs, suggesting that the Commission has acted autonomously by taking advantage of certain rules (such as qualified majority voting) and by creating an interest group constituency, including the European Women's Lobby (EWL). The increased power of the European Parliament in the 1990s may also have contributed to an acceleration of gender equality concerns (Liebert 1999).

However, other institutional innovations may have the opposite outcome. Van der Vleuten (2004) anticipates a slow-down in the EU's performance in the domain of gender equality as a result of new procedures and practices introduced in the Maastricht Treaty. Increased parliamentary powers may help advance gender equality, but the 'social agreement', which gives management and labor a role in supranational rulemaking, has led to directives on parental leave and part-time work reflecting the lowest common denominator. In addition, gender mainstreaming is difficult to enforce and the mechanisms of 'naming and shaming' are not employed to advance it. Finally, enlargement is likely to weaken equality policies because they carry substantial political, economic, and ideological cost for some of the new member states (see also Regulska 2003). Hoskyns (2000) anticipates a slow-down from yet another source. She suggests that the goal of gender equality may suffer as the Commission, under the watchword of subsidiarity, has lost its pre-eminent role as agenda setter and member states have reassumed control over policy mechanisms.

Scholars have used institutionalist arguments not only to explain policy-making at the European level but also the implementation of gender equality policies at the national level. Thus, in their classic formulation, Ostner and Lewis (1995) characterized national-level institutions as needles' eyes through which European-level policy prescriptions need to pass. The degree to which national institutions uphold the norm of the male breadwinner and the norm of the family as caregiver influences how equality policies are implemented, sometimes leading to a distortion of their intent. Mazey (1998: 145) agrees with this portrayal when she argues that 'national policy styles beget a dense "hinterland" of detailed programmes, policies and institutions and it takes a very long time for EU institutions and policies to permeate and change this hinterland significantly'. Caporaso and Jupille (2001) apply a similar logic in their case study of the implementation of EU gender equality policy in Britain and France, explaining 'domestic structural change' as resulting from 'goodness of fit' between existing European and domestic provisions, paired with the strength of national 'mediating institutions' (e.g. equality agencies or labor tribunals) and the quality of state–society relations. National policies function as a filter for EU policies, while institutions (state agencies and feminist organizations) appear as actors embedded in corporatist or pluralist state–society relations.

While institutionalist arguments have thus provided powerful explanations of policy-formation and implementation, feminist scholars of EU politics have drawn heavily on theories of social movements and policy-networks in addition, bringing into view the role of the women's movement and of women's networks as political agents. Hoskyns (1996) has highlighted women's activism in reviving Article 119, the role of the EWL in broadening the gender policy agenda, and the role of grass-roots women's organizing in raising issues of racial diversity. Similarly, Mazey (1998) has described the interaction between 'advocacy coalitions' and European institutions in defining new agendas and in developing 'sex equality policy'. Drawing on social movement theory, she describes the EU as an 'opportunity structure', an alternative policy arena for women. Feminist critique helped develop a 'policy frame' that has broadened over the years. The activism of EU institutions (particularly the ECJ and the Commission) constituted the opportunity structure within which these policies flourished. Changes in the external policy environment, i.e. the rise of neo-liberalism, ultimately limited the effectiveness of social legislation leading to gender mainstreaming as 'an attractive form of "policy succession"' (Mazey 2002: 20).

Various studies have used the social movements approach to explain the development of specific EU policies. For example, Locher (2005) draws on Woodward's (2003a) notion of a 'velvet triangle' consisting of femocrats and feminist politicians, academics and experts, and movement actors to explain the emergence of the EU policy on trafficking in women. She conceptualizes the triangle of actors as a feminist network that was able to advance potent policy frames (evoking bodily violations and the slave trade) in a context of opportunity (the Detroux scandal in Belgium and the entry of Nordic states into the EU). Helferich and Kolb (2001) add an interesting analysis of the way in which movement politics works in treaty negotiations. They describe the negotiations of the Amsterdam Treaty and the political environment of the 1990s (northern enlargement and a sense of crisis resulting from the ratification debates around the Maastricht Treaty) as an opportunity to advance feminist policy. In this context, the EWL worked strategically to develop a 'transnational feminist interest', which consisted of non-controversial goals among its diverse national member organizations. This allowed it to coordinate lobbying action at multiple levels and accomplish the insertion of broad gender equality goals into the Amsterdam Treaty including a commitment to gender mainstreaming as a guiding principle, a provision for equal pay for work of equal value, and a broad anti-discrimination provision.

Movement and network approaches also figure in literatures on the implementation of EU gender equality policies. For example, Liebert (2003a) combines elements from institutionalist explanations with those drawn from theories of social movements and policy networks to develop three types of 'mechanisms' that can explain the Europeanization of gender equality norms. The first consists of 'environmental mechanisms' generated externally by the EU, such as legal mechanisms demanding compliance, institutional monitoring, information campaigns, spillover mechanisms, or public pressure. The second consists of 'cognitive mechanisms', such as elite learning, strategic framing, and frame reflections. The third includes 'interactive mechanisms', involving policy discourse, norm entrepreneurs, epistemic communities, and policy advocacy coalitions, multi-level action coordination, and collective action mobilization. Liebert associates environmental mechanisms with institutionalism, and highlights the significance of the cognitive and interactive mechanisms in addition.

A collection of case studies illustrates how these mechanisms operate in different national contexts (Liebert 2003b). In France, Reuter and Mazur (2003) confirm Caporaso and Jupille's finding that the EU mattered little in French equality policy, but put the emphasis on public debates and the framings of domestic debates rather than on institutions. In contrast, Kodré and Müller (2003) show that environmental mechanisms were important in Germany where the implementation of European gender equality policy in the 1970s and 1980s advanced mostly as a result of legal pressure from the EU (and indeed against a reluctant government; see Berghahn 1998). There was little public debate on these changes before the 1995 'Kalanke case' in which the ECJ ruled against positive action, declaring that the Land of Bremen violated the EU's definition of equality when it gave preference to women over equally qualified men in situations where women were under-represented. But the case mobilized public debate on the EU in Germany, contributing to its drop in popularity, and to elite learning on gender equality issues. Discursive mechanisms also are central to the adoption of gender mainstreaming in Germany. The 'Open Method of Coordination' provides a venue for implementing gender mainstreaming, relying on the development of 'common benchmarks, requiring gender impact assessments, peer review and monitoring by the Commission' (Liebert 2002: 254; also Mazey 2002). Liebert (2002: 252) observes a continuing process of elite learning, influenced by transnational exchanges and contributing to 'slow, but ongoing reconstructions of gender roles in Germany'.

In Britain, public debate and framing have long mattered in implementing the EU's gender equality policy, as has feminist activism. While the British government opposed EU social policy initiatives, British feminists participated in the formulation of gender equality norms at the EU level. Both feminists and Euroskeptics mobilized around the domestic implementation of these norms, 'translating' EU directives into British domestic contexts and giving them a uniquely British spin. Conservatives resisted the EU's reconciliation policies and framed them as market distortions and as a case of social engineering. The Labour government implemented the policies but, like the Conservatives, did not consider them simply a matter of furthering equality. Instead Labour discourse framed reconciliation policies as labor market instruments rendering women, in Ilona Ostner's words, 'equally employable'. The emphasis was on increasing employment, not on reducing inequality (Sifft 2003).

Similar processes of a discursive embedding of EU gender policies are evident in Southern European states. For the post-authoritarian Spanish government, implementing gender equality norms was a matter of building a democratic and economically developed country and as such encountered little resistance (Valiente 2003). In Italy, EU gender equality norms met a gender regime that defined women largely as mothers. But the result was not simply a matter of squeezing equality norms through a domestic needle's eye. Instead, Italy in the 1990s developed creative new measures moving from the protection of maternity to the protection of the family and of the rights of children (Calloni 2003). Similarly, and somewhat unexpectedly, EU measures are changing the meaning of gender equality in Sweden, traditionally considered a pioneer in these matters. The ECJ has ruled that the policy of compulsory maternity leave and the use of quotas in appointing university professors contradicted EU norms, causing considerable public debate and fueling the pronounced Euroskepticism in the country. The combined effects of environmental and cognitive mechanisms are changing Swedish understandings of gender equality from a strict notion of sameness to allowing for difference (Sunnus 2003).

Liebert's interactive mechanisms of Europeanization emphasize the role of actors in networks and are especially visible in the implementation of gender mainstreaming. For example, Mazey (2002: 229) argues that gender mainstreaming constitutes an example of 'policy transfer' in which the European Commission plays the role of a 'policy entrepreneur', 'best practices' of member states are diffused, and the ideas and values of certain 'advocacy coalitions' win out. Liebert (2002) similarly points to the importance of advocacy networks in the spread of gender mainstreaming, but also suggests that public support is a necessary prerequisite for the state-level adoption of the practice. She points out that states

have embraced gender mainstreaming not as a result of legal measures or material incentives but as a result of 'knowledge-based inducements'.

This focus on networks leads to a breakdown of the simple distinction between processes of policy formulation and policy implementation. Advocates in networks often operate in a two-way process, as Sifft (2003) observed in her study of Europeanization in Britain. Here feminist advocates were two-level players using the EU to advance domestic agendas in a way described by Keck and Sikkink (1998) as a 'boomerang pattern'. Although the British government was fiercely opposed to gender equality directives, British advocates participated in the preparation and negotiation of the directives at the European level and ultimately sought their implementation in Britain through lobbying, mobilization, and litigation. Zippel (2004) further develops the boomerang metaphor in her study of the incorporation of sexual harassment into the amended Equal Treatment Directive of 2002. She concludes that the interaction between advocacy networks and states in a multi-level polity follows not only a boomerang pattern but is characterized by a 'ping-pong effect', a policy-cycle consisting of several phases. When advocates encounter obstacles at the national level, they turn to the EU to initiate soft law that requires national action. After a phase of implementation at the national level (which may or may not result in national legislation) activists orient themselves again towards the EU, providing impetus for creating stronger EU language.

In sum, studies of the making and implementation of the EU's gender equality policy have combined institutionalist approaches with a consideration of advocacy networks and movement strategies. They focus on institutions as both structures and agents, the interaction of networks with institutions (including EU and national institutions), and on movement politics of framing, interest formation, and multi-level advocacy. Researchers increasingly combine their studies of the politics of creating and implementing law with an analysis of discursive politics, a tendency that may reflect the influence of constructivist approaches popular in the field of International Relations (Mazey 2000; Shaw 2000; Locher and Prügl 2001a; Kronsell 2005). The following section moves to the foreground discursive analyses of EU gender politics, probing gender in laws, rules, and rhetorics and exploring the way in which EU gender politics encode new forms of difference and bias.

GENDER REGIMES AND THE EU

Feminists have sought to gauge the impacts of the EU's gender equality policy by probing changes in European gender orders, regimes, and discourses. While they have long criticized the narrowness of the EU's gender equality regime and its limited application to the area of employment, the recent expansion of the regime has led to more optimistic assessments, but also to an acknowledgement that the regime is embedded in other structures, most importantly global capitalism. Thus, Walby (2004: 23) argues that the EU has developed, in a path-dependent fashion, a 'new kind of gender regime … with distinctive patterns of gender inequality'. This regime is informed by 'two complexes of political activity and institutions' (p. 12) relevant to the EU's capitalist project: social inclusion and feminism. They have yielded a regime whose core is the regulation of employment (von Wahl 2005, speaks of the European Union as an 'equal employment regime'), but has moved from a narrow emphasis on equal treatment to a broader regulation of worker-careers. The recent directives on working time and atypical forms of employment (temporary and part-time) address the differential insertion of women and men into employment in the course of their life cycles. Furthermore, equality policies have migrated to other areas, in part as a result of gender mainstreaming, and the EU has taken initiative to further gender equality in areas including taxation, provision of benefits and welfare, policies relating to fertility and sexuality, and in combating violence against women.

Do these policies represent a move towards more gender equality in line with a broader global movement of cultural rationalization and modernization (Berkovitch 1999; Inglehart and Norris 2003)? Or do they represent a cooptation of feminist agendas into patriarchal and capitalist structures? While many feminists look towards the EU to further gender equality, scholars have bemoaned what Lombardo (2003) has called the 'Wollstonecraft Dilemma', i.e. the failure of a liberal feminist approach (that characterizes policy-making in the EU) to undermine structures of power.

One of the broadest critiques of the EU's gender regime along these lines develops the political economy approach suggested by Walby. It approaches the EU as an agent of neoliberal restructuring, whose policies of market liberalization, deregulation, and dismantling of the welfare state have had detrimental outcomes for women. The disproportionate opposition of women, especially in the Nordic states, to joining the EU and to the introduction of the Euro, brought into view the gender subtext of the neoliberal project (Liebert 1999; Rossilli 2000; Young 2002). Scholars following this line of argument have launched conceptual and empirical critiques. On a conceptual level, Young (2002: 307) has joined feminist economists to point to the gender biases in neo-liberal economics. These biases include a deflationary bias that counteracts efforts of employment creation, a commodification bias that has moved many public services into the private sector, and a male-breadwinner bias built into social services and tax systems. Because the EU advances 'disciplinary neoliberalism', it replicates these gendered biases. Its gender and market-making policies together amount to a 'liberalization' of existing gender orders, including a movement from 'dependency' to individualization made possible by a flexibilization of labor. This individualization leaves unresolved the issue of care labor: 'Despite its private seclusion, the reproductive work of the Fordist period was at least socially recognized. Now, with the flexibilization and informalization of the labor markets, child rearing has, once again, become an economic and social externality' (Young 2000: 95).

Young (2000) identifies negative integration as one of the mechanisms producing this outcome. Other feminists equally have criticized the EU for weakening national welfare states while failing to develop a social dimension. Ostner (2000: 27) has pointed out that the EU's gender equality policies have flourished only 'as far as they have fitted regulatory policies of negative integration in contrast to redistributive ones of positive integration'. She cites ECJ rulings that invariably have led to a more unfavorable treatment of women in instances where they previously were treated preferentially (e.g. equalizing working hours, night work, and retirement age) and for allowing governments to use equalization arguments to justify cut-backs (e.g. eliminating 'husband-only' benefits). She identifies the problem in the Court's emphasis on individual choice and in its interpretation of non-discrimination as being treated like a man.

Since the late 1990s, feminist scholars have bemoaned the cooptation of the EU's gender equality policies into its employment-creation agenda. Threlfall (2003) argues that the 'European Employment Strategy' amounts to 'the adoption of a new social model', that depends for its success 'almost exclusively on the responses and behavior of women'. The strategy's goal is to increase the percentage of the working-age population in employment, relying on women to join the labor force regardless of the types of jobs. A growth of flexible and part-time employment is a built-in expectation. Indeed, data show that higher levels of women's employment have resulted largely from a flexibilization of rules and a simplification of hiring practices rather than traditional forms of job creation. The European Employment Strategy in particular lacks a serious engagement with issues of child care and family-friendly hours (Threlfall 2005).[2] To the extent that these matters are discussed, they are increasingly framed no longer as a matter of equality policy but as a matter of active labor market policy or an effort to 'render the family more "employment-friendly"' (Ostner 2000: 38). What gets lost is the feminist demand for a more equal sharing of family labor.

Stratigaki (2004) documents this loss in her analysis of EU texts dealing with work and family issues, tracing the shift from a language of 'sharing' family responsibilities to 'reconciling' work and family. The original goal, informed by feminist demands, was to accomplish a more equal division of domestic and caring work. In contrast, the language of reconciliation has reframed the issue so that it encourages interventions that make it possible for both women and men to combine work and family. This has served to legitimize the flexibilization of labor relations, creating a secondary feminized labor market and leaving unchanged the distribution of unpaid labor in the family. Similar framings apparently operate at the national level. A comparative project analysing the 'organization of intimacy' across Europe has shown that 'measures that have originated in gender equality policies, such as child care services, part time work and parental leave are mostly legitimized through linking them with other goals such as flexible labor, more employment, more children or better functioning families' (Verloo et al. 2004: 21).[3]

Gender mainstreaming may have aggravated such tendencies towards the cooptation of feminist goals in the EU. Those who promote gender mainstreaming understand that 'inequality is structural and is deeply embedded in society's cultural expectations of men and women' (Beveridge et al. 2000: 388). Therefore, combating gender inequality requires changing structures, or what Connell (1987) has called 'gender regimes', in diverse social institutions. Gender mainstreaming seeks to do so by harnessing the power of the state as a public administrator and as a policy-maker interested in furthering equality between citizens. It requires that government programming and policy-making in all issue areas counteract discriminatory gender regimes and pursue the goal of gender equality. But the strategy has become the focus of considerable conceptual debate in feminist circles (Beveridge and Nott 2002).

Initial studies of gender mainstreaming in the EU show that implementation is highly uneven. Pollack and Hafner-Burton (2000: 440) found some DGs more open to gender mainstreaming than others. The difference seemed to lie in the core commitments of the DGs. Those DGs which have 'historically been interventionist in character, and relatively open to consideration of social justice issues', such as the Structural Funds and DGs charged with employment and development policy, have been receptive to gender mainstreaming. By contrast, 'the most strongly neo-liberal' DGs, including those focused on competition policy, have resisted gender mainstreaming. So have DGs in important areas such as agriculture, environment and transport, and in foreign policy (Braithwaite 2000; Woodward 2003b: 75). Because External Relations was in charge of enlargement negotiations, there was little gender mainstreaming in these negotiations (Bretherton 2001).

'Frame resonance' carries most of the weight in Pollack and Hafner-Burton's explanation, in addition to the presence or absence of gender advocates. But the unevenness of implementation also may point towards different gender regimes operating in different contexts, regimes that form part of a larger set of discursive commitments in different issue areas. Thus, Prügl (2005) suggests that gender regimes differ in economic sectors and that there are unique gender biases in the EU's agricultural policy: it has a long-standing, explicit commitment to family farming, an institution that thrives on its unequal gender order; it seeks to advance agricultural modernization, which has made women farmers into flexible farm laborers; and it seeks to promote rural diversification by commodifying rural women's caring and household labor, reproducing existing gender divisions of labor while promising wealth through entrepreneurship. Unlike in other areas of employment, in agriculture the EU has (re)produced a highly unequal gender regime that stabilizes some of the core commitments of the policy itself.

Researching the conditions under which gender mainstreaming can be successful has become a priority for many feminist researchers. Woodward (2003b) suggests that the success of GM is related to (a) the degree of an organization's commitment, often represented by a 'gender hero', i.e. a top power holder who convinces other top managers; (b) the level of 'sophistication' within an organization, including the degree to which an agency has produced research on gender equality, gender-sensitive data, and makes available gender training; (c) the level of resistance to gender initiatives within an agency; and (d) the degree to which gender experts play a role. She measures success by whether the inclusion of gender into policy-making and administration has become a given and her gauge is discursive, i.e. whether 'languages … have changed' (Woodward 2003b: 83). The Mainstreaming Gender Equality (MACEEQ) project probes precisely such change in languages. The results are sobering. Analysing the diverse meanings that 'gender equality' has taken in policy texts at the EU and national levels, scholars participating in the project have found 'strong processes of degendering' and the 'retraditionalizing' of gender roles, adding fuel to the suggestion that gender mainstreaming may be undermining feminist goals (Verloo 2005).

In order to counteract the tendency of cooptation, feminist scholars have called on the women's movement to take ownership of gender mainstreaming and for feminist NGOs to hold government agencies accountable. There is little evidence of such accountability politics to date. Indeed, Lang (2005: 23) has shown that European feminist networks lack the capacity to monitor gender mainstreaming, rarely have tried to generate public debate around the issue, and have not benefited from increased funding, as one might expect from the rhetoric. Instead, they have developed an 'individualized lobbying culture' that links them to the EU, but not to other feminist networks, and they often find themselves sidelined and on the defensive, having to justify a focus on women's issues not framed in terms of gender mainstreaming. Pudrovska and Ferree (2004) confirm that, judging from the dearth of links from its website to the websites of other transnational feminist organizations, the EWL is a remarkably parochial network. Furthermore, the EWL avoids the term 'feminist' and radical anti-system discourse, positioning itself as an EU insider.

Perhaps gender mainstreaming can become transformative only if it also enhances the participation and inclusion of women into decision-making, as Beveridge et al. (2000) propose. Indeed, the purpose of the strategy is not only to change regimes but also the way organizations operate, bringing to bear the distinct abilities of women and men. This includes the institutionalization of 'gender impact assessments', gender-sensitive indicators, gender budgets, and monitoring in addition to encouraging the participation of women in decision-making (Schmidt 2001). In the context of such demands, the dearth of women in positions of authority in the EU has become the subject of renewed attention. Their absence is particularly glaring in inter-governmental arenas such as the treaty negotiations of the 1990s (Hoskyns 1999). In the Constitutional Convention only 18 out of 105 (17%) members were women (Mateo Diaz 2004: 214), a striking statement considering that one purpose of the convention was to help overcome the EU's democratic deficit. Mateo Diaz and Millns (2004) suggest a link between this under-representation and the meager feminist gains in the Constitutional Treaty.

Women also are under-represented in the EU's supranational institutions. In 1997/98, they made up 18.7% in the Council, 26.5% in the European Parliament and 25% in the Commission (Abels and Bongert 1998: 10). According to EU personnel statistics, women accounted for 19.5% of Commission staff at grade level A (administration and management) in 2000, and for 22% in the Council Secretariat in 2002. Shaw (2002: 223) has high-lighted the persistent under-representation of women on the European Court of Justice. She argues that the Court has not adapted to 'the changed environment of gender mainstreaming', and that this is reflected in judgments that have failed to consider the differential real-life effects on women and men. Kenney (2002) forcefully makes the case for having women represented on the Court. While the logic of judging and of judicial independence seems to contradict the logic of equal representation, it is necessary to think about judging as making

choices about public policy, a practice that can benefit from diverse experiences and perspectives.

Ironically, a consideration of gender regimes, typically a theoretical starting point of feminists with structuralist inclinations, has led us back to liberal notions of women's representation, but the demands for such representation must be understood as embedded in strategic languages and in political cultures. The 'politics of presence' frame emerged in the Council of Europe, which has long dealt with human rights and 'the legal rights of individuals in relation to the domestic political arrangements of its member states, and with sustaining and strengthening the democratic character of the latter' (Lovecy 2002: 274). The frame gradually diffused to the EU, fueling demands for a 'balanced participation of women and men in decision-making processes' (Lovecy 2002: 279). This goes beyond the rights-focused liberalism in the EU's legislative approach to gender equality in the 1970s and 1980s, raising issues such as quotas and the demand for parity democracy (Krook 2001). While the rights-based approach put women on the defensive – they had to prove discrimination – the demand for parity reframes the issue in a way that makes existing inequalities in participation indefensible (Vogel-Polsky 2000). Demands for women's representation originating in international institutions thus are part of a discursive field, a multi-level terrain of rule-making that has impacted gender regimes in diverse sites.

Feminist legal scholars in particular have tended to conceptualize EU gender politics as the construction of rules in a multi-level social field, characterized by discursive mechanisms. For example, Kenney (2004) describes EU discourses on women in decision-making and discourses on equal opportunity as resources that helped feminists undermine the secretive process of selecting judges in the UK. Drawing on organizational theory, Wobbe (2003) similarly has conceptualized the EU's sex equality norms as evolving in an 'organizational field' populated by international organizations, European and national courts. The ECJ's ruling against the German military's exclusion of women is the result of a competition between these organizations for institutional legitimacy and social acceptability, leading to homogenization. In conceptualizing rule-making as a social process, these feminist legal approaches connect the European gender equality project to feminist practice. They theorize the multi-level European polity as a global legal and social space that is the site of contestation over gender politics.

Feminist theorizations of the patriarchal state provide an interesting complement to these approaches and are particularly prevalent in the German feminist literature. Thus, Schunter-Kleemann (1998) characterizes the EU as a masculinist project and as a men's club (*Männerbund*) that operates on the basis of secrecy and enacts male rituals of power with little concern for the effects of its policies on women. Kreisky (2001) sees other characteristics of this men's club in the militarism of the neoliberal language it favors. Sauer (2001a, c) has provided a wide-ranging treatment of what feminist state theory could mean at a time of state restructuring. She suggests a distinction between state and statehood (*Staatlichkeit*) where the former denotes the state as an apparatus and actor and the latter a particular constellation of rule and discourses of power. She suggests that solidified masculinity (*versachlichte Männlichkeit*) is part of the political norms, practices, and institutions that make up *Staatlichkeit* and defines the 'structural selectivity' of state norms and institutions. Focusing on the bureaucracy, Sauer (2001b) suggests that the statehood of the EU lies in its 'commissariat administration', a 'brotherhood' of national and international officers of the state developing a depoliticized hegemonial administrative culture, operating as 'bureaucratic entrepreneurs' in a context of secrecy and within exclusionary networks. The objective of this form of administration is the formation of an *imperium oeconomicum* built on the basis of gendered regulations. Gender mainstreaming is a strategy of gendering discourse of the EU bureaucracy and of articulating solidified masculinity. It also is an expression of the proliferating bureaucratization of modern life.

An approach to the EU as a state-like constellation of rules and rule considerably broadens the object under investigation. It opens up new fields of inquiry into the operations of power and gender and allows for an application of feminist theories of patriarchy to the EU, including considerations of the intersection of capitalism and patriarchy (as offered by Young) and of the masculinism of state bureaucracy (as offered by Sauer, Kreisky, and Schunter-Kleemann). It points in addition to a consideration of the EU legal order from the perspective of feminist state theory, as suggested by Shaw (2000). Mayrhofer's (2005) exploration of the pervasiveness of heterosexism in EU legislation is an example of what this type of analysis can accomplish. It finally should encourage a look at the EU as an emerging security state, bringing to bear feminist understandings of the constitutive power of gender in security discourses (see Prugl 2003).

CONCLUSION

The feminist literature on the EU depicts institutional mechanisms, political agents, and discursive constructions operating to establish equality policy and generate gendered regimes. The literature is diverse, asking different questions, and employing different concepts and methods. How has this literature contributed to understanding the European project?

Kronsell (2005) has argued that European integration theories for the most part cannot address the way in which gender operates in processes of regional integration because they assume a male norm and because they employ a 'rudimentary' understanding of power. She suggests that constructivism and multi-level governance provide alternative frameworks that may be more hospitable to feminist interventions. Mazey (2000) and Shaw (2000) join her in a hopeful assessment of constructivism's promise. Indeed, the review of literature offered here shows that studies of gender politics and the EU extensively draw on the image of multi-level governance, including the concepts of network and social movement. And they argue in a constructivist fashion, putting forward notions of framing, meaning-construction, discourse, regimes, rule-making, institutionalization, and process-oriented 'mechanisms'. Furthermore, there is an emerging theoretical debate about the way in which constructivism and discourse analysis can be made useful for understanding gender politics in the European Union (Elgström 2000; Bacchi 2004). Curiously, little of this debate has recognized the relevance of feminist theory.

Feminist theories often entail a constructivist ontology; indeed, feminism is part of constructivism's pedigree (Locher and Prügl 2001b). Feminist state theories perhaps provide a particularly useful starting point to understanding how the European Union participates in constructing gender. They show how feminist aspirations refract in the internationalized state, and how state politics create new gender realities. They show how patriarchy is mutating together with the state. More than the national patriarchal welfare state, the EU state is multifaceted and decentered, including a considerable variety of gender regimes both in member states and issue areas and allowing for the extensive co-existence of dispersed pockets of state feminism with bastions of technocratic gender blindness. The EU state thus promotes feminist goals, diverts them, and works against them all at once. Feminist state theory provides useful analytical tools to analyse gender construction in the complex European quasi-state.

From a feminist perspective, European integration involves the Europeanization of a socio-political space, including not only the creation of new political institutions, but also the reconfiguration of public and private gender relations and the development of new gender identities. Feminist constructivist approaches, including feminist state theory, ask questions about processes of gendering and degendering in the European reorganization of state–society relations; they probe laws, norms, practices, and discourses that construct new gender relations. Grounded in a feminist perspective, these approaches provide the knowledge base for a feminist critique of the contradictory and multiple ways in which the EU advances and obstructs feminist goals.

NOTES

1. For a theoretical elaboration of the connection between state and patriarchy, sovereignty and masculinism, see Hoffman (2001).

2. For an analysis of trends in flexible employment showing a proliferation of atypical jobs disproportionately taken by women, see Bettio et al. (2000).

3. These mechanisms of cooptation may not be entirely new: Guerrina (2002: 52) has interpreted the 1992 Pregnant Workers Directive and the 1996 Parental Leave Directive as policies 'to ensure the stability of population numbers and the future viability of the welfare state'. Similarly, Duncan (2002) has argued that the 'demographic time bomb', i.e. an aging population and low fertility have powered the EU's policy on reconciling work and family.

REFERENCES

Abels, G. and Bongert, E. (1998) 'Quo vadis, Europa? Einleitung: Stand und Perspektiven feministischer Europaforschung', *Femina Politica*, 2: 9–19.

Bacchi, C. (2004) 'Policy and discourse: challenging the construction of affirmative action as preferential treatment', *Journal of European Public Policy*, 11(1): 128–46.

Berghahn, S. (1998) 'Zwischen marktvermittelter Geschlechtergleichheit im europäischen "Herrenclub" und den patriarchalischen Traditionalismen von Mitgliedstaaten: Gibt es einen "Mehrwert" der europäischen Gleichheitsentwicklung für Frauen?', *Femina Politica*, 2: 46–55.

Berghahn, S. (2004) 'The influence of European Union legislation on labour market equality for women', *Advances in Life Course Research*, 8: 211–30.

Berkovitch, N. (1999) *From Motherhood to Citizenship: Women's Rights and International Organizations*. Baltimore: The Johns Hopkins University Press.

Bettio, F., Rubery, J. and Smith, M. (2000) 'Gender, flexibility, and new employment relations in the European Union', in M.S. Rossilli (ed.), *Gender Policies in the European Union*. New York: Peter Lang. p. 123.

Beveridge, F. and Nott, S. (2002) 'Mainstreaming: a case for optimism and cynicism', *Feminist Legal Studies*, 10(3): 299–311.

Beveridge, F., Nott, S. and Stephen, K. (2000) 'Mainstreaming and the engendering of policy-making: a means to an end?' *Journal of European Public Policy*, 7(3, Special Issue): 385–405.

Booth, C. and Bennett, C. (2002) 'Gender mainstreaming in the European Union', *The European Journal of Women's Studies*, 9(4): 430–46.

Braithwaite, M. (2000) 'Mainstreaming gender in the European structural funds', paper prepared for the Mainstreaming Gender in European Public Policy Workshop, University of Wisconsin-Madison, 14–15 October.

Bretherton, C. (2001) 'Gender mainstreaming and EU enlargement: swimming against the tide?' *Journal of European Public Policy*, 8(1): 60–81.

Calloni, M. (2003) 'From maternalism to mainstreaming: femocrats and the reframing of gender equality policy in Italy', in U. Liebert (ed.), *Gendering Europeanisation*. Brussels: P.I.E.-Peter Lang. pp. 117–84.

Caporaso, J. and Jupille, J. (2001) 'The Europeanization of gender equality policy and domestic structural change', in M. Green Cowles, J. Caporaso and T. Risse (eds), *Transforming Europe: Europeanization and domestic change*. Ithaca: Cornell University Press. pp. 21–43.

Connell, R.W. (1987) *Gender and Power*. Stanford: Stanford University Press.

Duncan, S. (2002) 'Policy discourses on "reconciling work and life" in the EU', *Social Policy and Society*, 1(4): 305–14.

Egan, M. (1998) 'Gendered integration: social policies and the European market', *Women and Politics*, 19(4): 23–52.

Elgström, O. (2000) 'Norm negotiations: the construction of new norms regarding gender and development in EU foreign aid policy', *Journal of European Public Policy*, 7(3): 457–76.

Ellina, C.A. (2003) *Promoting women's rights: the politics of gender in the European Union*. New York: Routledge.

Guerrina, R. (2002) 'Mothering in Europe: feminist critique of European policies on motherhood and employment', *The European Journal of Women's Studies*, 9(1): 49–68.

Hantrais, L. (2000a) 'From equal pay to reconciliation of employment and family life', in L. Hantrais, (ed.), *Gendered policies in Europe: Reconciling employment and family life*. Houndsmill, Basingstoke: Macmillan Press. pp. 1–26.

Hantrais, L. (ed.) (2000b) *Gendered policies in Europe: Reconciling employment and family life*. Houndsmill, Basingstoke: Macmillan Press.

Helferich, B. and Kolb F. (2001) 'Multilevel action coordination in European contentious politics: the case of the European women's lobby', in D. Imig and S. Tarrow (eds), *Contentious Europeans: protest and politics in an emerging polity*. Lanham, MD: Rowman and Littlefield. pp. 143–61.

Hoffman, J. (2001) *Gender and sovereignty: feminism, the state and international relations*. Houndsmill, Basingstoke: Palgrave.

Hoskyns, C. (1996) *Integrating gender: women, law and politics in the European Union*. London: Verso.

Hoskyns, C. (1999) 'Gender and transnational democracy: the case of the European Union', in M.K. Meyer and E. Prugl (eds), *Gender politics in global governance*. Lanham, MD: Rowman and Littlefield. pp. 72–87.

Hoskyns, C. (2000) 'A study of four action programmes on equal opportunities', in M. Rossilli (ed.), *Gender policies in the European Union*. New York: Peter Lang. pp. 43–59.

Inglehart, R. and Norris, P. (2003) *Rising tide: gender equality and cultural change around the world*. Cambridge, New York: Cambridge University Press.

Keck, M.E. and Sikkink, K. (1998) *Activists beyond borders: advocacy networks in international politics*. Ithaca, NJ: Cornell University Press.

Kenney, S.J. (2002) 'Breaking the silence: gender mainstreaming and the composition of the European court of justice', *Feminist Legal Studies*, 10(3): 257–70.

Kenney, S.J. (2004) 'Equal employment opportunity and representation: extending the frame to courts', *Social Politics*, 11(Spring): 86–116.

Kettelhut, J. (2003) 'Appendix: EU gender equality law, gender disparities in domestic labour markets, and public EU support', in U. Liebert (ed.), *Gendering Europeanisation*. Brussels: P.I.E.-Peter Lang. pp. 285–300.

Kodré, P. and Müller H. (2003) 'Shifting policy frames: EU equal treament norms and domestic discourses in Germany', in U. Liebert (ed.), *Gendering Europeanisation*. Brussels: P.I.E.-Peter Lang. pp. 83–116.

Kreisky, E. (2001) 'Die maskuline Ethik des Neoliberalism – Die neoliberal Dynamik des Maskulinismus', *Femina Politica*, 2: 76–91.

Kronsell, A. (2005) 'Gender, power and European integration theory', *Journal of European Public Policy*, 12(6): 1022–40.

Krook, M.L. (2001) 'Promoting gender balanced decision-making in the European union: international and transnational strategies for parity democracy', Paper presented at the European Community Studies Association International Conference, 31 May–2 June, Madison.

Lang, S. (2005) 'Framing the beast? Transnational women's networks and gender mainstreaming in the European union', Paper presented at the Annual Meeting of the International Studies Association, 1–5 March, Honolulu.

Liebert, U. (1999) 'Gender politics in the European Union: the return of the public', *European Societies*, 1(2): 197–239.

Liebert, U. (2002) 'Europeanising gender mainstreaming: constraints and opportunities in the multilevel Euro-polity', *Feminist Legal Studies*, 10: 241–56.

Liebert, U. (2003a) 'Between diversity and equality: analysing Europeanisation', in U. Liebert (ed.), *Gendering europeanisation*. Brussels: P.I.E.-Peter Lang. pp. 11–46.

Liebert, U. (ed.) (2003b) *Gendering europeanisation*. Brussels: P.I.E.-Peter Lang.

Locher, B. (2005) *Trafficking in women in the European Union: norms, advocacy networks, and policy change*. Wiesbaden: VS Verlag für Sozialwissenschaften.

Locher, B. and Prügl, E. (2001a) 'Feminism and constructivism: worlds apart or sharing the middle ground?' *International Studies Quarterly*, 45(1): 111–29.

Locher, B. and Prügl, E. (2001b) 'Feminism: constructivism's other pedigree', in K.M. Fierke and K.E. Jørgensen (eds), *Constructing International Relations: the next generation*. Armonk, NY, London: M.E. Sharpe. pp. 76–92.

Lombardo, E. (2003) 'EU gender policy: trapped in the "Wollstonecraft dilemma"?' *The European Journal of Women's Studies*, 10(2): 159–80.

Lovecy, J. (2002) 'Gender mainstreaming and the framing of women's rights in Europe: the contribution of the council of Europe', *Feminist Legal Studies*, 10: 271–83.

Mateo Diaz, M. (2004) 'The participation and representation of women in the debate on the future of the European Union', *South European Society and Politics*, 9(1): 208–22.

Mateo Diaz, M. and Millns, S. (2004) 'Die Rolle der Frau und die konstitutionelle Zukunft der Europäischen Union', *Femina Politica*, 1: 75–90.

Mayrhofer, M. (2005) 'heterosExUelle Ausrichtungen: Die Suprantionalisierung sexueller Normen im Kontext der EU-Integration', *Femina Politica*, 1: 36–47.

Mazey, S. (1998) 'The European Union and women's rights: from the Europeanization of national agendas to the nationalization of European agendas?' *Journal of European Public Policy*, 5(1): 131–52.

Mazey, S. (2000) 'Introduction: integrating gender – intellectual and 'real world' mainstreaming', *Journal of European Public Policy*, 7(3; Special Issue):333–45.

Mazey, S. (2001) *Gender mainstreaming in the EU: principles and practice*. London: Kogan Page Limited.

Mazey, S. (2002) 'The development of EU gender policies: toward the recognition of difference', *EUSA Review*, 15(3): 1–2.

Ostner, I. (2000) 'From equal pay to equal employability: four decades of European gender policies', in M. Rossilli (ed.), *Gender policies in the European Union*. New York: Peter Lang. pp. 25–42.

Ostner, I. and Lewis, J. (1995) 'Gender and the evolution of European social policies', in S. Leibfried and P. Pierson (eds), *European social policy: between fragmentation and integration*. Washington, DC: Brookings Institution. pp. 159–93.

Pierson, P. (1998) 'The path to European integration: a historical-institutionalist analysis', in W. Sandholtz and A. Stone Sweet (eds), *European integration and supranational governance*. Oxford: Oxford University Press. pp. 27–58.

Pollack, M. and Hafner-Burton, E. (2000) 'Mainstreaming gender in the European Union', *Journal of European Public Policy*, 7(3): 432–56.

Prügl, E. (2003) 'Gender and war: causes, constructions, and critique', *Perspectives on Politics*, 1(2): 335–47.

Prügl, E. (2005) 'Mainstreaming gender in the EU's agricultural market and rural development policies', Paper presented at the Annual Meetings of the International Studies Association, 1–5 March, Honolulu.

Pudrovska, T. and Ferree M.M. (2004) 'Global activism in "virtual space": the European women's lobby in the network of transnational women's NGOs on the web', *Social Politics*, 11(1): 117–43.

Rees, T. (1998) *Mainstreaming equality in the European Union: education, training and labour market policies*. New York: Routledge.

Regulska, J. (2003) 'Constructing supranational political spaces: women's agency in an enlarged

Europe', Paper presented at the Annual Meeting of the American Association for the Advancement of Slavic Studies, 20–23 November, Toronto.

Reuter, S. and Mazur, A.G. (2003) 'Paradoxes of gender-biased universalism: the dynamics of French gender equality discourse', in U. Liebert (ed.), *Gendering Europeanisation.* Brussels: P.I.E.-Peter Lang. pp. 47–82.

Rossilli, M. (2000) 'Introduction: the European Union's gender policies', in M. Rossilli (ed.), *Gender policies in the European Union.* New York: Peter Lang. pp. 1–23.

Sauer, B. (2001a) 'Das "bewundernswert Männliche" des Staates: Überlegungen zum Geschlechterverhältnis in der Politik', *Femina Politica*, 2: 50–62.

Sauer, B. (2001b) 'Vom Nationalstaat zum Europäischen Reich? Staat und Geschlecht in der Europäischen Union', *Feministische Studien*, 1: 8–20.

Sauer, B. (2001c) *Die Asche des Souveräns: Staat und Demokratie in der Geschlechterdebatte.* Frankfurt/M., New York: Campus Verlag.

Schmidt, V. (2001) 'Gender Mainstreaming als Leitbild für Geschlechtergerechtigkeit in Organisationsstrukturen', *Zeitschrift für Frauenforschung und Geschlechterstudien*, 19(1&2): 45–62.

Schunter-Kleemann, S. (1998) 'Währungsunion und Globalisierung oder der endgültige Abschied der Europäer vom Keynesianismus', *Femina Politica*, 2: 61–9.

Shaw, J. (2000) 'Importing gender: the challenge of feminism and the analysis of the EU legal order', *Journal of European Public Policy*, 7(3, Special Issue): 406–31.

Shaw, J. (2002) 'The European Union and gender mainstreaming: constitutionally embedded or comprehensively marginalised?' *Feminist Legal Studies*, 10: 213–26.

Sifft, S. (2003) 'Pushing for Europeanisation: how British feminists link with the EU to promote parental rights', in U. Liebert (ed.), *Gendering europeanisation.* Brussels: P.I.E.-Peter Lang. pp. 149–86.

Stratigaki, M. (2004) 'The cooptation of gender concepts in EU policies: the case of "reconciliation of work and family"', *Social Politics*, 11(1): 30–56.

Sunnus, M. (2003) 'EU challenges to the pioneer in gender equality: the case of Sweden', in U. Liebert (ed.), *Gendering europeanisation.* Brussels: P.I.E.-Peter Lang. pp. 223–54.

Threlfall, M. (2003) 'Is there a feminist perspective on the European employment strategy and guidelines?', Paper presented at the European Union Studies Association Conference, 26–29 March, Nashville, TN.

Threlfall, M. (2005) 'The European Employment Strategy and women's work', Manuscript, Loughborough University.

Valiente, C. (2003) 'Pushing for equality reforms: the European Union and gender discourse in post-authoritarian Spain', in U. Liebert (ed.), *Gendering europeanisation.* Brussels: P.I.E.-Peter Lang. pp. 187–222.

Van der Vleuten, A. (2004) 'Snail or snake? Shifts in the domain of EU gender equality policies', Paper presented at the Second Pan-European Conference on EU Politics of the ECPR Standing Group on the European Union, 24–26 June, Bologna.

Verloo, M. (2005) 'Studying gender equality in Europe', *European Studies Newsletter*, 34(3–4): 8–9.

Verloo, M., van Beveren, J., van Lamoen, I., Tertinegg, K. and Aliparanti, L. (2004) 'Framing the organisation of intimacy as a policy problem across Europe', Paper presented at the 2nd Pan-European Conference on European Politics of the ECPR Standing Group on the European Union, 24–26 June, Bologna.

Vogel-Polsky, E. (2000) 'Parity democracy-law and Europe', in M. Rossilli (ed.), *Gender Policies in the European Union.* New York: Peter Lang. pp. 61–85.

von Wahl, A. (2005) 'Liberal, Conservative, Social Democratic, or ... European? The European Union as equal employment regime', *Social Politics: International Studies in Gender State, and Society*, 12(1, Spring): 67–95.

Walby, S. (2004) 'The European Union and gender equality: emergent varieties of gender regime', *Social Politics*, 11(1): 4–29.

Wobbe, T. (2003) 'From protecting to promoting: evolving EU sex equality norms in an organisational field', *European Law Journal*, 9(1): 88–108.

Woodward, A. (2003a) 'Building velvet triangles: gender and informal governance', in T. Christiansen and S. Piattoni (eds), *Informal governance in the European Union.* Cheltenham, UK & Northampton, MA: Edward Elgar. pp. 76–93.

Woodward, A. (2003b) 'European gender mainstreaming: promises and pitfalls of transformative policy', *Review of Policy Research*, 20(1): 65–88.

Young, B. (2000) 'Disciplinary neoliberalism in the European Union and gender politics', *Political Economy*, 5(1): 77–98.

Young, B. (2002) 'On collision course: the European Central Bank, monetary policy, and the Nordic welfare model', *International Feminist Journal of Politics*, 4(3): 295–314.

Zippel, K. (2004) 'Transnational advocacy networks and policy cycles in the European Union: the case of sexual harassment', *Social Politics*, 11(1): 57–85.

23

The Politics of European Union Domestic Order

ANDREW GEDDES

INTRODUCTION

For a policy field such as internal security where the 'touch of stateness' has been particularly profound, the development of an EU politics of domestic order is a remarkable development (Weiler 1999: 270). This chapter looks at explanations for why, when, and how these developments occurred and at some of the key ideas that have underpinned this relatively new area for EU studies. Since the 1980s there has been 'a disjointed incrementalism *par excellence*' (Lavenex and Wallace 2005: 465) culminating with attempts to realize the 'big idea' of the Amsterdam Treaty, which was the creation of an Area of Freedom, Security and Justice (AFSJ). The rationale for action in the areas of policing, judicial co-operation, migration, and asylum was spelled out by the heads of government at the Tampere summit meeting in October 1999 when they contended that 'Justice and Home Affairs is essential given the worldwide challenges facing the Union such as restoring the rule of law, controlling migratory movements and combating organized crime. Above and beyond the strategic importance of a particular country, a global approach is required' (European Council 1999, for an update see European Council 2004). This political impetus was reinforced following the September 2001, March 2003 and July 2005 terrorist attacks on New York, the Pentagon, Madrid and London. In the wake of such cataclysmic events, JHA has been described as 'one of the most dynamic and expansionist areas of EU development' (Monar 2002: 165; see also Monar 2001; Apap 2004a; Walker 2004).

The more obvious analytical puzzle is to figure out how to make sense of all this apparent dynamism and expansion. For a field consumed by the pursuit of order there has been some disorderliness about the academic field dedicated to its study. This may be because the analysis of AFSJ is a relative newcomer on the EU scene and draws from a wide range of disciplinary perspectives, the main ones being law, political science, international relations, geography and sociology. The subject matter is quite diverse too ranging from judicial co-operation to labour migration and asylum. A developing policy consensus has, however, been detected with 'an attempt to *construct* a new kind of policy whole out of diverse parts' (Walker 2004: 8, emphasis in original). The underlying concern during the construction of this policy area has been with security. Key drivers on the 'demand side' of the market for security were the Tampere declaration and terror attacks; but to focus on drivers such as 9/11 alone would be to neglect some of the more fundamental dynamics of the EU's politics of domestic order that have created since the 1970s a 'supply' of security. Efforts will be made in this chapter to avoid some of the perils of hyper-presentism and too strong a focus on the demand side of the market for security because, while there is much that is new in this policy area, there is also much that draws from longer-standing debates about the state, security and order. There are also some analogies to other aspects of EU action, particularly AFSJ's burgeoning 'external' dimension that blurs the distinction between internal and external security and raises some similar issues to those seen in debates about the EU's CFSP and the nature, form and effects of European power expressed through relations with non-member states (Lavenex and Uçarer 2002; Pastore 2002; Boswell 2003; Geddes 2005).

To address the analytical puzzle of imparting some orderliness to what has been a nascent and somewhat disorderly field, the chapter looks at the practices that have developed in the area of AFSJ and at the conceptual foundations of these practices. In organizational terms this means that the chapter begins by analysing the core *concepts* associated with the state, security, order and borders that have animated the EU's pursuit of internal security. This is followed by a section that explores the *motors* such as terrorist attacks that have been seen to drive co-operation and integration, as well as exploring some longer-standing themes in EU security co-operation. We then explore the *levels* of governance across which this co-operation and integration occurs with implications for our understanding of borders and the territorial basis of state action and political organization. This leads to an assessment of the *processes* of integration and co-operation with consideration of underlying intergovernmental and supranational dynamics, as well as the distribution of power and authority between the executive, legislative and judicial branches of government. The next section looks at efforts to judge the *effects* of co-operation and integration that looks at some key normative questions concerning accountability, as well as asking how distinctly 'European' is JHA co-operation. The chapter concludes with some consideration of possible future developments in this area. It is argued that the politics of domestic order will remain high on the agenda and that, by doing so, it will expose classic territorial, organizational and conceptual dilemmas that go to the very heart of the European project and to the identities of both its member states and those resident on their territories.

CONCEPTS

Notions of the state, security and order have been central to the analysis of the EU politics of domestic order. The key referent for debates about security has been the state. While not going into the much more fundamental historical debate about the state, security, public order and social control (on this see Melossi 1990), it seems reasonable to depart from the observation that the debate about the meaning of security has broadened considerably since the end of the Cold War to include notions of societal, environmental and political security. By considering this broadening and analysing when, why and how the meaning of security and the identification of security threats has widened we can better understand the underlying conceptualization of the state in a 'protective union' (Kostakopoulou 2000). Analogous with some other areas of EU activity (such as the debate about power in CFSP) the word security has attracted a wide range of adjectives: 'personal', 'micro', 'macro', 'privatized', 'hard' and 'soft' are some of those on offer. It has been argued that the notion of personal security has been used to legitimate expanded EU action in the area of AFSJ (Koslowski 1998). A certain amount of populism has been seen as supporting the development of 'separate but interlocking security zones' that seek to ensure that 'People from the outside must be kept outside or brought under appropriate control and enforcement action' (Monar 2000: 5). A distinction has also been made between micro and macro security where macro is state-controlled security and driven by national militaries while micro-level risks come from private individuals (Grabbe 2000: 520). A privatization of security understood as an increased role for private actors has also been identified (on the privatization of migration control policies see Lahav (1998) and Guiraudon and Lahav (2000)). The distinction between hard (military) and soft (such as organized crime and illegal immigration) security is seen to provoke an 'uncertainty [that] is almost certain to continue progressively revolutionizing the assumptions that drive security policy' (Lindley-French 2004: 1). What all these perspective seem to have in common is a take on the transformed dynamics of the governance of security in the light of changed geo-political and institutional settings.

The adjectives appended to it do tend to leave open the question of the meaning of the word security itself and associated debates about fears and threats. It could be argued that a sure sign that an academic community has entered into the secure possession of a new concept is that a vocabulary has developed in terms of which the new concept can be publicly articulated and discussed (*pace* Skinner 1978: xii–xiii). Issue framing is clearly important. How then to capture these changes within a state-centred debate about security? In the 1990s a turf war within the sub-discipline of security studies broke out into a wider discussion about the meaning of security and processes of securitization. 'Traditional' security studies centred on the threats posed by states to each other with the security and identity of states dominating the understanding of what security could be and, more profoundly, the nature and identity of political communities (Walker 1990: 6). The end of the Cold War

impelled a debate about the continued relevance of this state-centred understanding of security in the face of what were seen at the time as a number of threats from Eastern Europe, such as the spectres of uncontrolled immigration and the menace of the Russian mafia. Work addressed a shift from traditional military themes in security studies to include references to societal, political, economic and environmental security (Buzan 1991; Ullman 1983; Wæver et al. 1993; Wæver 1996; Buzan et al. 1998; Huysmans 1998). A particularly notable contribution from the 'Copenhagen School' identified 'societal security', by which was meant that the identity of a people is threatened rather than that of the state (Wæver et al. 1993). The Copenhagen School was particularly focused on public discourse about security as a particular way of framing an issue as an 'absolute priority' (Wæver 1996: 106). Alternative approaches have analysed the ways in which bureaucratic networks have been integral to the propagation and development of an 'insecurity agenda' within an 'unsettled environment … manufactured so as to legitimize the activities of security agencies and frame social changes as manifestations of insecurity and chaos' (Bigo 2001: 149; see also Bigo 1996).

The broadening of the concept of security also has analytical implications as an increase in the number of properties covered by a concept (intension) can lead to a reduction in the class of entities to which the concept applies (extension) (Sartori 1970). 'Security' in this sense seems analogous to 'Europeanization' because a very wide range of empirical instances seem to have something to do with it (Radaelli 2000: 4–5). A post-foundational route out of this impasse has been identified by Huysmans (1998: 242), who argues that security has developed from a concept into a 'thick signifier', by which is meant something that 'does not describe social relations but changes them into security relations. The question is no longer if the security story gives a true or false picture of social relations. The question becomes: how does a security story order social relations? What are the implications of politicizing an issue as a security problem?' The question would also seem to become whether or not a 'security story' provides a convincing interpretation. Analysis of the securitization of migration explores the ways in which words such as 'foreigner' and 'asylum-seeker' are spoken of and written about as threats to cultural, racial, labour market and welfare state identities (Huysmans 2000, 2006).

The expanded security agenda and the profusion of work on new security threats also raises a second conceptual issue, the question of the underlying conceptualization of the state to which security has been classically conjoined as famously evident, for example, in writings of Hobbes for whom security was the main purpose of and justification for the state understood 'as an artificial man made for the protection and salvation of the natural man' (Hobbes [1650] 1957: 64). Ostensibly EU cooperation and integration in the area of JHA would appear difficult as it encroaches upon areas that are quintessentially 'domestic' and where there are highly distinct organizational (such as in the field of policing) and legal cultures with the EU in such terms 'barely recognizable as a state at all' (Moravcsik 2001: 163–4). If we try to draw out what the broadening of the concept of security means for the conceptualization of the state then we move in the direction of sociological understandings where the focus is placed not on what the state does or does not do or what it should or should not be but on those 'groups, organizations and individuals, who claim a state concept in order to furnish themselves, as well as other social actors with reasons and grounds for their own actions'. In these terms, the state is not a super-individual, but the 'organized and constrained actions of individuals' (Melossi 1990: 6). A particular argument about security is that population control has acquired a European dimension through the intensification of co-operation between security specialists and other officials and a European-level representation of threats. This then extends to what Foucault identified as the sovereignty-discipline-government triangle 'which has as its primary target the population and as its essential mechanism the apparatuses of security' (Foucault 1991: 102). If we then

consider the implications of this for sovereignty then 'the relationship between state and non-state sites is better viewed as heterarchical rather than hierarchical' (Walker 2004). While the state remains the key referent for many of the issues that are central to the EU politics of domestic order, it is also a central contention of much of the work on this issue that networks of expertise now transcend the borders of the member states with the result that quintessentially domestic issues have become a common European concern with some form of emergent multi-level governance of internal security.

The third key conceptual reference is to the notion of order, with some discussion about the possible emergence of a European public order (Lavenex and Wallace 2005). The core underlying dilemma in terms of the politics of domestic order has been identified as arising from the tension as the EU shifts from being a functional problem-solving organization to one that deals with fundamental questions such as policing, law and migration (Laffan 2001). Challenges to established politi-cal and legal orders can arise from the asser-tion of regional identities, forms of transnational legal and police co-operation, or in response to external challenges such as immigration. Changes in the political economic and social order contribute to a politics of uncertainty and to the assertion of national identities (Laffan 2001: 92). An identity, borders and orders 'triad' has been identified as a way of nudging IR theory in a direction that can capture mobility, fluidity and change in international politics (Lapid 2001). The AFSJ is on the cusp of these changes. Legal and political orders change as a result of European integration and raise a more general debate about European identity. Moreover, the issues raised expose various types of border within the European union, such as the borders of territory as the classic sites at which decisions about exclusion and inclusion are made, but also at key organizational borders such as those of work and welfare, and at more nebulous but vitally important conceptual borders of identity, belonging and entitlement (Geddes 2005).

MOTORS

Understandings of the state and security either implicitly or explicitly provide a frame for analyses of EU responses to security crises such as those following the terror attacks of 2001, 2003 and 2005. Such attacks can provide institutional opportunities and impel co-operation and integration, but 'security policy is never *compelled* by external events' (Walker 2004: 11). The demand for security has been matched by a supply of security; indeed, the supply was present before the terror attacks because security ideas and practices of longer provenance informed the response to these terror attacks and to a range of other issues such as migration and asylum. Put another way, the argument about compulsion tends to focus on the demand side of the 'market' for security. There is a supply side too embedded within the practices of security agencies.

If we consider the demand side first then three distinct sets of post-Cold War events are often seen as impelling EU internal security co-operation. As we shall see later, there were earlier drivers of EU internal security co-operation that underpinned the creation of the Trevi network from 1975 onwards focused on terrorism. The first of these post-Cold War factors followed the end of the Cold War and German reunification as enormous generators of insecurity based on (exaggerated as it turned out) claims about vast migration potential and the spread of organized crime on a potentially massive scale. In an account of JHA development in the 1990s it was asserted that migration, crime and policing ascended the EU agenda as a response to single market integration and to the end of the Cold War which 'unleashed a flood of immigrants from the east and seemed to open the way to criminal organizations from the east to move to the EU' (Turnbull and Sandholtz 2001). As a matter of fact, the scale of migration nowhere near matched some of the predictions (for an explosion of some of these myths, see Codagnone 1999). Of course there was immigration as a result of the post-Cold War geopolitical shake-up, but the issue was not so much mass or uncontrolled immigration, but

the fear of immigration and its effects that helped induce a response by member states dominated by security concerns as was evident by the creation of the Maastricht Treaty's Justice and Home Affairs pillar, by the continued development of the Schengen system, and then by the Amsterdam Treaty's incorporation of Schengen.

The second set of events on the demand side of the market for security occurred during the years that preceded the May 2004 enlargement. The tension between EU internal and external security policies was analysed in the run up to the 2004 enlargement with discussion of the damaging effects of the 'sharp edges' of Europe on accession states (Grabbe 2000). Others feared that the effects of enlargement such as the unleashing of large-scale migration would drive a 'hard' border mentality that was more likely to be counter-productive (Zielonka 2001).

The third set of events were the 9/11, 3/11 and 7/7 attacks. The 2001 attacks on the USA were particularly important because 'For Europe, 9/11 came as an unprecedented challenge to the role it has had most difficulty developing since its origins in the 1950s: its role as a security actor in both external and internal matters' (den Boer and Monar 2002). At the special meeting of the European Council on 21 September 2001, the member states called it 'an assault on our open, democratic and multicultural societies' (European Council 2001). The rapid progress on the European Arrest Warrant and the common definition of terrorist crimes were seen as representing the desire to be seen by the US as a credible partner as '11 September has clearly led to a significant cross-pillarization of the transatlantic security partnership, both practically and politically' (den Boer and Monar 2002: 14).

There seems to be a strong demand-side impetus, but the market for security has a supply-side too that can be traced back through analysis of internal security co-operation and the understandings of security that developed at EU level since the 1970s. These provided a base for the articulation and discussion of the response to later cataclysmic events such as the terror attacks that occurred during the first decade of the 21st century. EU responses were not entirely reactive. Indeed, if we were to probe the historical sociology of EU internal security co-operation more closely then it would be necessary to go back to at least the mid-1970s and the role of the Trevi group as a forum for discussion between member states about (initially) terrorism (Bigo 1992; Peek 1994). While the end of the Cold War and 'war on terror' have given a powerful impetus to the development of EU internal security co-operation, it is necessary to link these motors of policy development to underlying conceptualizations of the state, security and order, as well as to conceptualizations of the levels or domains across which JHA co-operation and integration have developed, which we now move on to consider.

LEVELS

The development of a European dimension to the governance of internal security has shaped and been shaped by the shifting meaning of territoriality and borders in Europe. EU internal security co-operation and integration is located along the 'domestic/foreign Frontier' where

> the international system is less commanding, but still powerful. States are changing, but they are not disappearing. State sovereignty has been eroded, but it is still vigorously asserted. Governments are weaker, but they can still throw their weight around. At certain times the public are more demanding, but at other times they are more pliable. Borders still keep out intruders, but at other times they are more porous (Rosenau 1997: 4).

Integral to this 'domestic/foreign Frontier' is the notion of territoriality. Although the supposed 'end of territories' has been proclaimed (Badie 1995) this would be a 'truly cataclysmic and improbable change' (Anderson 2002) because there is still a highly developed sense of territoriality in Europe as defined as 'a pattern of behaviour whereby living space is fragmented into more or less well-defined territories whose limits are viewed as inviolable for their occupants' (Glassner 1993). The end of the Cold War led to the creation of 12,000

km of new borders and changed the nature of these frontiers too (Anderson and Bort 2001: 2–3). There has not been a shortage of adjectives when borders are the subject of analysis. They may be 'hard', 'soft', 'sharp', 'open' or 'closed'. This does leave open the question of the meaning of the term border. A distinction has been made between territorial borders as the classic sites at which the sovereign power of the state to exclude is exercised; organizational borders of work, welfare and citizenship that are also important sites of inclusion and exclusion often within states; and conceptual borders of belonging and entitlement that are fuzzy but no less important mediators of the relationship between newcomers and host societies (Geddes 2005).

In practical terms, the EU internal security field is a multi-level and crowded policy space. To take one example of this, there is work on European policing that distinguishes between micro, meso and macro levels (Benyon et al. 1993). The macro-level (Europol) is actually quite distant from 'real' police work. Anderson (2002: 4) notes that those at the micro-level of police work see the macro-level as a 'politically inspired organization, not one set up because of police needs'. The meso level (the Schengen Information System) functions primarily as an information exchange. The development of cross-border information exchange networks is interesting in light of other dynamics as police forces become oriented 'towards information gathering, anticipatory engagement, pro-active intervention, systematic surveillance, and rational calculation of results [which] demonstrates an ethos comparable to that found in the commercial security sector' (Johnston 2000: 76). The micro level is evident through forms of cross-border co-operation such as juxtaposed police stations in Britain and France on either side of the channel tunnel.

The EU does provide a new institutional setting for these debates about borders and security, but there are reasons to doubt that territorial and border strategies developed by EU member states are simply examples of Europeanization. The EU is, of course, a unique international organization with decision-making capabilities distinct from those of other international organizations, but in terms of the character of the policy response there may be similarities between EU border strategies and those pursued by similar states facing similar dilemmas. EU border strategies may be more general examples of what in the context of NAFTA and US-Mexico border relations has been called 'boundary build-up' (Purcell and Nevins 2005). Boundary build-up occurs as a result of 'complex interchanges between state actors and groups of citizens [that] produced a deep set of concerns about the ethno-cultural, socio-economic, and bio-physical security of the nation, all of which are inherently geographical given their inextricable relationship to a particular territory. Boundary build-up is thus a territorial strategy to achieve security and assuage those concerns'. A NAFTA-ization of the US–Mexico border has been seen to develop as the US promotes 'extra-territorial opportunities for national territory-based capital whilst attempting to provide security against the social costs unleashed by globalization – especially immigration' (Nevins 2002; see also Andreas and Snyder 2000). EU efforts to consolidate external frontiers and co-opt neighbouring states within these actions can be likened to processes of boundary build-up in the face of external threats such as irregular migration and organized crime that challenge territorial, organizational and conceptual borders.

PROCESSES

Much work on JHA analyses the nuts and bolts of integration and co-operation. A drawback is that this work swiftly dates as analyses of the current state of play are swiftly overtaken by events. There is another point that can also be made in relation to processes of co-operation and integration that can be formulated as follows: to what extent does EU action differ from that undertaken in similar non-European states? As we have just seen there are similarities between 'boundary build up' in North America and the EU. Furthermore, if we take

the example of asylum-seeking migration, Australia has sought extra-territorial solutions to reduce asylum-seeking migration while EU member states have also looked at this (Noll 2003). In the area of migration policy more generally, it has been argued that modes of immigration politics in liberal democratic states may actually follow similar dynamics that are to do with the form of politics in those states rather than the result of regional integration (Freeman 1995). Freeman draws on approaches to regulatory politics to argue that the concentrated beneficiaries of migration such as business and the pro-migrant lobby have a greater incentive to mobilize than the diffuse bearers of costs (the general public). The result is that migration policies in liberal states are inherently rather than intermittently or contingently expansive in terms of admission and inclusive in terms of rights extended to newcomers. This powerfully counter-intuitive insight postulates general processes linked to politics within rather than between states. Similarly, a body of scholarship has compared the impact of embedded liberalism on the rights-base of migration politics and argued that legal processes at either national or international level have helped open social and political spaces for migrants (Hollifield 1992; Soysal 1994).

If we look more specifically at the EU we see that explanations for the underlying dynamics of the development of AFSJ reflect more general debates about supranational and inter-governmental dynamics, with co-operation typically characterized as intergovernmental given the dominant Council role and because the AFSJ deals with the 'hard core' of national sovereignty (Fijnaut 2004). Neo-functional perspectives have linked police co-operation to single market spillover (Occhipinti 2003) while another approach with roots in neo-functionalism identifies three mechanisms of institutional change (Turnbull and Sandholtz 2001). The first, endogenous source of change saw JHA ascend the EU agenda as a result of single market integration. This was reinforced by a second exogenous source of change linked to the new security challenges in post-Cold War Europe. A third, more intergovernmental element is identified when it is argued that German chancellor Helmut Kohl acted as a policy entrepreneur seeking EU solutions to German domestic migration problems. An intriguing Foucauldian spillover argument has been made that accounts for the move from an economic space to an internal security space in terms of political speech acts, discourses and the development of technologies of population control that, in the context of single market integration, bind freedom and security (Huysmans 2006).

Neo-functional accounts represent a point of divergence with the predominant strand within the literature that emphasizes 'intensive transgovernmentalism' with a minimal Commission role and member states in the driving seat. Intensive transgovernmentalism is used to denote 'the greater intensity and denser structuring where EU member governments have been prepared cumulatively to commit themselves to rather extensive engagement and disciplines, but have judged the full EU institutional framework to be inappropriate or unacceptable, or not yet ripe for adoption' (Wallace 2005: 87). Analysis of the development of EU migration policy has an intergovernmental orientation, but also draws from work on 'new governance' to analyse the motives for and implications of the movement of migration controls 'up' to supranational actors, 'down' to sub-national authorities and 'out' to private actors such as airlines, ferry operators and truck drivers who, through carrier sanctions and other measures, are co-opted as agents of the immigration control authorities (Lahav 1998; Guiraudon and Lahav 2000). Emphasis has been placed on strategic learning by state actors that motivate 'venue shopping' to escape domestic legal and legislative constraints on their capacity to regulate migration. Delegation is understood as 'a strategic adaptation to institutional constraints where the role of central administrations was being questioned and there had been an enlargement of the policy space (upwards and downwards) that made it both desirable and feasible' (Guiraudon 2001: 47). From a similar perspective, regulation and principal-agent approaches have been used to explain the

development of EU migration policy that ask why national principals would delegate authority to supranational agents and uses the costs of 'international regulatory failure' as an explanation. The shift from the weak intergovernmentalism of Maastricht to the more formal 'communitarization' of Amsterdam can then be explained by the costs of international regulatory failure arising from inefficient decision-making procedures (Stetter 2000).

In terms of the organization of the JHA field, there has been a proliferation of semi-autonomous special agencies and bodies where much of the co-operation is based on soft law and information exchange (Lavenex and Wallace 2005: 470–1). There is overlap too between national and supranational legal orders with the Schengen system as an integration 'black market', or 'laboratory', providing ideas and practices that later made their way into the EU (Peers 2000; Monar 2002). There is less use of 'traditional' forms of integration and more use of information exchange and co-ordination between national administrations. The relative absence of case law shifts the focus to implementation by states of their obligations in international public law (Peers 2000: 2–3).

A supranational/intergovernmental dichotomy can, however, be a rather crude way of looking at JHA policy dynamics because the relative balance between the two differs at the stages of initiation, adoption, the location of competencies, the intensity of measures adopted, the mode of implementation and the form of oversight (Walker 2004). A process rather than a levelled approach has been advocated as a way of understanding the dynamics of internal security co-operation (den Boer 1998). Studying process means identifying the actors, their intentions and 'the ways in which their discourse is transformed under the influence of bargains and external stimuli'. There are some methodological challenges with this approach given endemic secrecy in this policy area, but there is a web of groups that can influence the political process at what has been called the 'policy shaping level' (Peterson 1995) populated by civil servants from the relevant ministries in the member states who 'are indeed, the busy bees in the Third Pillar factory' (den Boer 1998: 14). This leads to the development of 'horizontal working relationships' that developed since the days of Trevi in the 1970s and 'grew into an issue network with shared knowledge and a narrow bureaucratic specialization' and the gradual supplanting of police officers and security specialists by senior civil servants (den Boer 1998: 15).

The distinction between intergovernmental/supranational elements in JHA while necessary is not a sufficient basis for understanding JHA cooperation. It is also vital to account for the distribution of executive, legislative and judicial authority. There is an important strand within the work on EU migration that points to the ways in which member states in the 1980s and 1990s sought alternative EU institutional venues that would allow them to escape domestic judicial and legislative constraints on the executive's capacity to regulate migration (Freeman 1998). The development of intensive transgovernmentalism at EU level privileged the executive branch of government while the European Commission remained weak and the European Parliament and European Court of Justice almost entirely marginal (Geddes 2000). Proposals in the constitutional treaty to strengthen the role of national parliaments in the scrutiny of internal security co-operation could be construed as a shift in the direction of intergovernmentalism, but such a shift would strengthen legislative authority in an area where national executives have been and still are the key players.

EFFECTS

This section explores accounts of the links between the institutional and ideational structures of an EU internal security field and an associated politics of domestic order. Within this field there are debates about accountability, rights, implementation and the EU's 'externalization' of policing and migration control to include non-EU countries. The question of how to control the controllers opens a discussion of rights and accountability. Another set of issues centre on the form of European power that is being exported to neighbouring states.

The first, 'democratic deficit' strand is particularly critical of executive dominance, the under-developed role of legislative and judicial institutions and EU fortress-like tendencies (Spencer 1990, 1995; Bunyan 1991; Webber and Fekete 1994; Geddes 1995). In a peculiar way, however, the debate about 'fortress Europe' arises precisely because Europe is not a fortress. This is not to say that Europe's borders are open. That would be an absurd proposition. Rather, Europe's borders are open at the margins to various forms of population mobility. It is these margins that are the core of the EU's politics of domestic order. There has been an 'inconsistent and sometimes contradictory' impact of globalization on internal security that can reinforce national interior ministries in their co-ordination role but give them diminished independent capacity to manage their security (den Boer 2002: 158).

Much of the academic work that has developed in these areas of accountability and scrutiny has a strong legal influence where the work of lawyers through training and socialization leads to an emphasis on 'exposition, representation, organization and refinement of the internal structure of the legal orders which are their object of study (Walker 2004: 11). A key theme has been accountability when the 'social bond that underpinned the Westphalian state is dissolving in a globalizing world and justice will not be seen to be done if the sphere of justice remains bounded by the state' (Anderson and Bort 2001: 11). This has opened a lively debate between those who identify the increased relevance of international laws and the diminished relevance of national sovereignty (see Soysal 1994; Jacobson 1996; Sassen 1998) and those who contend that, rather than being externally constrained, states have self-limited their sovereignty as a result of embedded liberal constitutional norms (Guiraudon 2000).

Rights, their meaning and their location are central to any discussion of JHA because 'classic civil liberties questions, such as freedom of assembly, rights during criminal procedure, privacy rights and, particularly in the case of asylum-seekers, freedom from torture or inhuman or degrading treatment' (Peers 2000: 2) are all highly pertinent. One particularly pertinent example of this is migrants' rights within which an immigrant integration agenda has acquired an EU dimension that has been linked to EU internal security through the attribution of competence to the Commission Directorate General dealing with AFSJ. It has been argued that the discussion of supranational rights for migrants 'touch only the fringe, not the core of the European project' (Joppke 1998: 30). The debate has moved on through EU legislation covering anti-discrimination, family reunion and the rights of long-term residents. Of particular interest is the underlying conceptualization of foreigners (or third country nationals in EU parlance) that these developments entail. A distinction has been made between three element approaches to immigrant integration: equal treatment and non-discrimination; citizenship and nationality; and linkages between admission policies and integration policies (Groenendijk 2004). The first of these – equal treatment and non-discrimination – has been most evident in EU action grounded in provisions of the Treaty of Rome that prohibited discrimination against citizens of member states on the grounds of nationality and gender-based discrimination as well as the 1976 Equal Treatment directive (Bell 2002). This understanding of integration is very closely linked to the core economic purposes of the EU and allows us to see very clearly the link between integration policies as pursued at EU level and the sources of legal, political and social power created by the Treaty framework. The second element – citizenship and nationality – remains largely a matter for the member states. The third element – linkage between admission and perceived integration capacities of new migrants – is identified as an important recent element of national approaches in Austria, Germany and the Netherlands and may form the base future developments with EU-wide implications.

Much of the work on the developing EU politics of domestic order has thus far concentrated on the construction of a new policy field with attention paid to structures, actors and processes and less to the penetration of more micro-level security practices. As the issue area has become more consolidated at EU level there is a shift in attention to implementation issues (Apap 2004b). Much of this discussion was impelled by the 2004 enlargement. Underlying issues here centre on diverse political and legal framework, as well as underlying levels of trust between the actors and agencies involved in EU internal security cooperation (Grabbe 2000; Zielonka 2001; Walker 2002; Apap 2004a; Lavenex 2004).

While important, the development of an accountability regime in the area of policing may not be quite so straightforward. How can such a regime be constituted in a sensitive area such as internal security? den Boer (2002: 280–1) makes a distinction between internal and external accountability. Internal accountability is based around internal organizational structures of 'responsibility, control, supervision and loyalty and is typically associated with the hierarchical lines of the traditional machine bureaucracy'. External accountability could and often is seen to imply accountability to citizens, but has also acquired new meaning related to the rise of the New Public Management and associated targeting, standards setting and the pursuit of 'value for money' that now characterizes debate about the delivery of public services in some member states.

The effects on external governance of the development of an EU politics of domestic order also raises the question of whether the 'unbundling of territoriality' has induced a shift from the politics of exclusion to the politics of inclusion that seeks to internalize rather than externalize disturbance from surrounding states and neighbours (Smith 1996; Lavenex 2004). In turn this opens a debate about the nature and form of European power, particularly the notion of Europe as a 'soft' or 'civilian' power – and here we see clear overlap with CFSP (Duchêne 1972; Manners 2002). The relationship with Europe's 'neighbourhood' is crucial too. A differentiated understanding of the politics of inclusion has been suggested based on the selective extension of the EU's legal boundary without the opening of its institutional boundaries in the form of membership (Lavenex 2004: 694). The EU can thus be understood as a civilian power through the 'attempt to tackle interdependencies through the external projection of internal solutions' (Lavenex 2004: 695) which means we understand the EU less in terms of common institutions, but as a security community (Deutsch 1957). The expectation of peaceful change within a security community is strongest when the sense of we-feeling or community is strongest and, as an extension of this, it could be argued that the essence of the insecurity community is the perception of threat to community and we-feeling. Threats to we-feeling and community may stem from broader changes in welfare states and labour markets that engender feelings of insecurity and for which immigration and immigrants may not be the main driver but for which they can be a convenient target or scapegoat (Geddes 2005).

CONCLUSION

There is little doubt that the EU's politics of domestic order has been quite a growth industry. There has been an explosion of interest in this area, which is hardly likely to dissipate given that the cross-border issues of crime, legal co-operation and migration seem likely to remain high on the EU agenda for many years to come. The analytical focus may also shift as the emphasis switches from a current strong emphasis on the construction of an EU policy domain to analysis of the implementation of policy in a situation with diverse political and legal frameworks, differing implementation capacities and, which, in turn, has been related to the development of trust between the various security agencies. To be sure, the quest for effectiveness will give rise to a plethora of communications, decisions, recommendations, green papers and all the other forms of output in which the EU specializes. Core underlying questions, however, include the deeper importance of these developments and the ways in which EU action can inform understanding of internal security in other states and regions. In terms of the

importance of these developments and in relation to the 'faces of Europeanization' (Olsen 2002), we do see both the penetration of national systems of governance and the export of EU norms and practices to surrounding states and regions. We also see attempts to constitute a European space of internal security that is not separate from member states, but is indicative of transitions in the state, security and order. In terms of the broader importance of these developments it is useful to reflect on the extent to which these developments are indicative of Europeanization understood not just as a process concentrated on distinct EU modes of governance and their effects but in terms too of the content of policy. In relation to border and population control strategies we have seen some similarities in 'boundary build-up' and the 'externalization' of internal security between the EU and similar states facing comparable dilemmas such as the USA and Australia.

These considerations of the importance of an emergent EU politics of domestic order strike at our understandings of Europe's borders and border relationships. These borders are not simply those of territory, although the reconfiguration of territoriality from a space of places to a space of flows (Castells 1996) has been a core underlying change linked to single market integration that has tightly bound security and freedom. There are two other types of border relationships that are central to the EU's politics of domestic order. The first of these is the organizational borders of legal and policing systems that have to some extent been penetrated by EU co-operation. There are other types of organizational border that are also integral to a discussion of order and security. These are Europe's borders of work and welfare. The politics of insecurity cannot be understood as a simple response to perceived external threats, such as immigrants as competitors for jobs or welfare state resources. The politics of insecurity is also embedded in deeper changes in key organizational borders and through them is linked to more general labour market and welfare state pressures. Migration and other external pressures are not on such a scale that they drive these pressures, but can often be a lens through which the effects of change can be observed. The second other type of border relationships beyond territory is conceptual borders of identity, belonging and entitlement. These may well be fuzzy, but are vitally important components of debates about the EU's politics of domestic order. Taken together, changes in border relationships between and within EU member states will define the EU's politics of domestic order and play a key role in the future direction of the European project and shape of European identities.

REFERENCES

Anderson, M. (2002) 'Trust and police co-operation', in M. Anderson and J. Apap (eds), *Police and Justice Co-operation and the New European Borders*. The Hague: Kluwer. pp. 35–46.

Anderson, M. and Bort, E. (2001) *The Frontiers of Europe*. Basingstoke: Palgrave Macmillan.

Andreas, P. and Snyder, T. (eds) (2000) *The Wall Around the West: State Borders and Immigration Controls in Europe and North America*. New York: Rowman and Littlefield.

Apap, J. (2004a) *Justice and Home Affairs Issues in the EU: Liberty and Security Issues After Enlargement*. London: Edward Elgar.

Apap, J. (2004b) 'Problems and solutions for new member states in implementing the JHA acquis', Centre for European Policy Studies Working Document No. 212, Brussels: Centre for European Policy Studies.

Badie, B. (1995) *La Fin des Territoires: Essai sur le Désordre International et sur le Utilité Social de Respect*. Paris: Fayard.

Bell, M. (2002) *Anti-Discrimination Law and the European Union*. Oxford: Oxford University Press.

Benyon, J., Turnbull, I., Willis, A., Woodward, R. and Beck, A. (1993) *Police Co-operation in Europe: An Investigation*. Leicester: Centre for the Study of Public Order.

Bigo, D. (ed.) (1992) *L'Europe des Police et de la Securité Intérieure*. Brussels: Editions Complexe.

Bigo, D. (1996) *Polices en Réseaux: Experiénce Européene*. Paris: Presses de la Fondation de Sciences Politiques.

Bigo, D. (2001) 'Migration and security', in V. Guiraudon and C. Joppke (eds), *Controlling a New Migration World*. London: Routledge. pp. 121–49.

Boswell, C. (2003) *European Migration Policies in Flux: Changing Patterns of Inclusion and Exclusion*. Oxford: Blackwell.

Bunyan, T. (1991) 'Towards an authoritarian European state', *Race and Class*, 32(3): 179–88.

Buzan, B. (1991) *People, States and Fear: An Agenda for International Security Studies in the Post-Cold War Era*. Hemel Hempstead: Harvester Wheatsheaf.

Buzan, B., Wæver, O. and de Wilde, J. (1998) *Security: A New Framework for Analysis*. Boulder, CO: Lynne Reinner.

Castells, M. (1996) *The Rise of the Network Society*. Oxford: Blackwell.

Codagnone, C. (1999) 'The new migration in Russia in the 1990s', in K. Koser and H. Lutz (eds), *The New Migration in Europe: Social Constructions and Social Realities*. Basingstoke: Macmillan. pp. 39–59.

den Boer, M. (1998) *Taming the Third Pillar. Improving the Management of Justice and Home Affairs Co-operation in the European Union*. Maastricht: European Institute for Public Administration.

den Boer, M. (2002) 'Towards an accountability regime for an emerging European policing governance', *Policing and Society*, 2(4): 275–89.

den Boer, M. and Monar, J. (2002) 'Keynote article: 11 September and the challenge of global terrorism to the EU as a security actor', *Journal of Common Market Studies*, Annual Review of the EU.

Deutsch, K. (1957) *Political Community and the North Atlantic Area*. Princeton: Princeton University Press.

Duchêne, F. (1972) 'Europe's role in world peace', in R. Mayne (ed.), *Europe Tomorrow: Sixteen European's Look Ahead*. London: Fontana. pp. 32–47.

European Council (1999) *Conclusions*. Tampere, Finland, October.

European Council (2001) *Conclusions*. Laeken, Belgium, October.

European Council (2004) *The Hague Programme: Strengthening Freedom, Security and Justice in the European Union*. Brussels: EC.

Fijnaut, C. (2004) 'Police co-operation and the area of freedom, security and justice', in N. Walker (ed.), *Europe's Area of Freedom, Security and Justice*. Oxford: Oxford University Press. pp. 241–82.

Foucault, M. (1991) 'Governmentality', in G. Burchell, C. Gordon and P. Miller (eds), *The Foucault Effect*. Hemel Hempstead: Harvester Wheatsheaf. pp. 87–104.

Freeman, G. (1995) 'Modes of immigration politics in liberal democratic states', *International Migration Review*, 29(3): 17–30.

Freeman, G. (1998) 'The decline of sovereignty: politics and immigration restriction in liberal states', in

C. Joppke (ed.), *Challenge to the Nation State: Immigration in Western Europe and the United States.* Oxford: Oxford University Press. pp. 86–108.

Geddes, A. (1995) 'Immigrant and ethnic minorities and the EU's democratic deficit', *Journal of Common Market Studies*, 33(2): 197–217.

Geddes, A. (2000) *Immigration and European Integration: Towards Fortress Europe?* Manchester: Manchester University Press.

Geddes, A. (2005) 'Europe's border relationships and international migration relations', *Journal of Common Market Studies*, 43(4): 787–806.

Glassner, M. (1993) *Political Geography.* London: Wiley.

Grabbe, H. (2000) 'The sharp edges of Europe: extending Schengen eastwards', *International Affairs*, 76(3): 519–36.

Groenendijk, K. (2004) 'Legal concepts of integration in EU migration law', *European Journal of Migration and Law*, 6(2): 111–26.

Guiraudon, V. (2000) 'European integration and migration: vertical policy-making as venue shopping', *Journal of Common Market Studies*, 38(2): 251–71.

Guiraudon, V. (2001) 'De-nationalising control: analyzing state responses to constraints on migration control', in V. Guiraudon and C. Joppke (eds), *Controlling a New Migration World.* London: Routledge. pp. 31–64.

Guiraudon, V. and Lahav, G. (2000) 'A reappraisal of the state sovereignty debate: the case of migration control', *Comparative Political Studies*, 33(2): 163–95.

Hobbes, T. (1957) *Leviathan.* Oxford: Clarendon Press.

Hollifield, J. (1992) *Immigrants, States and Markets: The Political Economy of Post-War Europe.* Cambridge, MA: Harvard University Press.

Huysmans, J. (1998) 'Security! What do you mean? From concept to thick signifier', *European Journal of International Relations*, 4(2): 226–55.

Huysmans, J. (2000) 'The European union and the securitization of migration', *Journal of Common Market Studies*, 38(5): 751–77.

Huysmans, J. (2006) *The Politics of Insecurity. Fear, Migration and Asylum in the EU.* London: Routledge.

Jacobson, D. (1996) *Rights Across Borders: Immigration and the Decline of Citizenship.* Baltimore, MD: Johns Hopkins University Press.

Johnston, L. (2000) 'Transnational private policing: the impact of global commercial security', in J. Sheptycki (ed.), *Issues in Transnational Policing.* London: Routledge. pp. 21–42.

Joppke, C. (1998) 'Immigration challenges the nation state', in C. Joppke (ed.), *Challenge to the Nation State: Immigration in Western Europe and the United States.* Oxford: Oxford University Press. pp. 5–48.

Koslowski, R. (1998) 'European migration regimes: established and emergent', in C. Joppke (ed.), *Challenge to the Nation State: Immigration in Western Europe and the United States.* Oxford: Oxford University Press. pp. 153–90.

Kostakopoulou, T. (2000) 'The "protective union": change and continuity in migration law and policy in post-Amsterdam Europe', *Journal of Common Market Studies*, 38(3): 497–518.

Laffan, B. (2001) 'The European union polity: a union of regulative, normative and cognitive pillars', *Journal of European Public Policy*, 8(5): 709–27.

Lahav, G. (1998) 'Immigration and the state: the devolution and privatisation of immigration control in the European Union', *Journal of Ethnic and Migration Studies*, 24(4): 675–94

Lapid, Y. (2001) 'Introduction. Identities, borders, orders: nudging international relations theory in a new direction', in M. Albert, D. Jacobson and Y. Lapid (eds), *Identities, Borders and Orders: Rethinking International Relations Theory.* Minneapolis: University of Minnesota Press. pp. 1–20.

Lavenex, S. (2004) 'EU external governance in 'wider Europe'', *Journal of European Public Policy*, 11(4): 680–700.

Lavenex, S. and Uçarer, E. (2002) *Migration and the Externalities of European Integration.* Lanham, MD: Lexington.

Lavenex, S. and Wallace, W. (2005) 'Justice and Home Affairs: towards a European public order?', in H. Wallace, W. Wallace and M. Pollack (eds), *Policy-Making in the European Union.* Oxford: Oxford University Press. pp. 457–80.

Lindley-French, J. (2004) 'The revolution in security affairs: hard and soft security dynamics in the twenty-first century', *European Security*, 13(1 and 2): 1–15.

Manners, I. (2002) 'Normative power Europe: a contradiction in terms?' *Journal of Common Market Studies*, 40(2): 235–58.

Melossi, D. (1990) *The State of Social Control.* Cambridge: Polity Press.

Monar, J. (2000) 'Justice and Home Affairs in a wider Europe: the dynamics of exclusion and inclusion', *ESRC One Europe or Several Working Paper*, 07/00.

Monar, J. (2001) 'The dynamics of Justice and Home Affairs: laboratories, driving factors and costs', *Journal of Common Market Studies*, 39(4): 747–64.

Monar, J. (2002) 'Justice and Home Affairs', *Journal of Common Market Studies*, Annual Review of the EU: 119–23.

Moravcsik, A. (2001) 'Federalism in the European Union: rhetoric and reality', in K. Nicolaïdis and A. Howse (eds), *The Federal Vision*. Oxford: Oxford University Press. pp. 161–90.

Nevins, J. (2002) *Operation Gatekeeper: The Rise of the 'Illegal Alien' and the Making of the US-Mexico Boundary*. New York: Routledge.

Noll. G. (2003) 'Visions of the exceptional: legal and theoretical issues raised by transit processing centres and protection zones', *European Journal of Migration and Law*, 5(3): 303–41.

Occhipinti, J. (2003) *The Politics of European Union Police Co-operation: Towards a European FBI?* Boulder: Lynne Reinner.

Olsen. J. (2002) 'The many faces of Europeanization', *Journal of Common Market Studies*, 40(5): 921–52.

Pastore, F. (2002) 'The asymmetrical fortress: the problem of the relations between internal and external security policies in the European union', in M. Anderson and J. Apap (eds), *Police and Justice Co-operation and the new European Borders*. The Hague: Kluwer. pp. 59–80.

Peek, J. (1994) 'International police co-operation within justified political and juridical frameworks: five theses on Trevi', in R. Morgan and J. Monar (eds), *The Third Pillar of the European Union: Co-operation in the Fields of Justice and Home Affairs*. Brussels: European Interuniversity Press. pp. 201–8.

Peers, S. (2000) *EU Justice and Home Affairs Law*. Harlow: Longman.

Peterson, J. (1995) 'Decision-making in the European union: towards a framework for analysis', *Journal of European Public Policy*, 2(1): 69–93.

Purcell, M. and Nevins, J. (2005) 'Pushing the boundary: state restructuring, state theory and the case of US–Mexico border enforcement in the 1990s', *Political Geography*, 24(3): 211–35.

Radaelli, C. (2000) 'Whither Europeanization: concept stretching and substantive change', *European Integration On-Line Papers*, 4(8), Available online at: http://eiop.or.at/eiop/texte/2000-008a.htm, accessed 3 October 2006.

Rosenau, J. (1997) *Along the Domestic-Foreign Frontier: Exploring Governance in a Turbulent World*. Cambridge: Cambridge University Press.

Sartori, G. (1970) 'Concept misinformation in comparative politics', *American Political Science Review*, 64(4): 1033–53.

Sassen, S. (1998) 'The *de facto* transnationalising of immigration policy', in C. Joppke (ed.), *Challenge to the Nation State: Immigration in Western Europe and the United States*. Oxford: Oxford University Press. pp. 49–85.

Skinner, Q. (1978) *Foundations of Modern Political Thought: Volume I*. Cambridge: Cambridge University Press.

Smith, M, (1996) 'The European union in a changing Europe: establishing the boundaries of order', *Journal of Common Market Studies*, 34(1): 5–28.

Soysal, Y. (1994) *Limits to Citizenship: Migrants and Post-National Membership in Europe*. Chicago: University of Chicago Press.

Spencer, M. (1990) *1992 and all that: Civil Liberties in the Balance*. London: The Civil Liberties Trust.

Spencer, M. (1995) *States of Injustice*. London: Pluto Press.

Stetter, S. (2000) 'Regulating migration: authority delegation in Justice and Home Affairs', *Journal of European Public Policy*, 7(1): 80–103.

Turnbull, P. and Sandholtz, W. (2001) 'Policing and immigration: the creation of new policy spaces', in A. Stone Sweet, W. Sandholtz and N. Fligstein (eds), *The Institutionalization of Europe*. Oxford: Oxford University Press. pp. 193–220.

Ullman, R. (1983) 'Redefining security', *International Security*, 8(1): 129–53.

Wæver, O. (1996) 'European security identities', *Journal of Common Market Studies*, 34(1): 103–32.

Wæver, O., Buzan, B., Kelstrup, M. and Lemaitre, P. (eds) (1993) *Identity, Migration and the New Security Agenda in Europe*. London: Pinter.

Walker, N. (2002) 'The problem of trust in an enlarged area of freedom, security and justice', in M. Anderson and J. Apap (eds), *Police and Justice Co-operation and the New European Borders*. The Hague: Kluwer. pp. 19–34.

Walker, N. (ed.) (2004) *Europe's Area of Freedom, Security and Justice*. Oxford: Oxford University Press.

Walker, R.B.J. (1990) 'Security, sovereignty and the challenge of world politics', *Alternatives*, 15(1): 3–27.

Wallace, H. (2005) 'An institutional anatomy and five policy modes', in H. Wallace, W. Wallace and M. Pollack (eds), *Policy-Making in the European Union*. 5th edn. Oxford: Oxford University Press. pp. 65–85.

Webber, F. and Fekete, L. (1994) *Inside Racist Europe*. London: Institute of Race Relations.

Weiler, J. (1999) *The Constitution of Europe: "Do the New Clothes Have an Emperor?" And Other Essays on European Integration*. Cambridge: Cambridge University Press.

Zielonka, J. (2001) 'How new enlarged borders will reshape the European union', *Journal of Common Market Studies*, 39(3): 507–36.

24

New Modes of Governance in the European Union: A Critical Survey and Analysis

MANUELE CITI AND MARTIN RHODES

INTRODUCTION

The emergence in the European Union of new modes of governance (NMG) such as the Open Method of Coordination (OMC) has produced a flurry of analyses concerning its nature and significance.[1] This extensive literature falls into four broad categories. A theoretical approach seeks to explain why such methods emerged and locates them in existing theories of European integration, policy-making and institutional change (for instance, Magnus Johansson 1999; Ioannou and Niemann 2003; Wessels 2003; Schäfer 2004). Then there is a strongly normative approach that extols the non-hierarchical, deliberative virtues of new modes of governance and 'soft' law and prioritizes the potential of the OMC as a font of 'social learning' (for instance, Cohen and Sabel 2003; Mosher and Trubek 2003; Sabel and Zeitlin 2003; Eberlein and Kerwer 2004). A third, more empirical approach assesses new modes in operation across different policy areas and countries (Zeitlin et al. 2005; for an overview, see de la Porte and Pochet 2003).[2] Finally, a more critical approach assesses the claims made on the OMC's behalf as an effective instrument of policy learning and transfer within the EU's multi-level polity (e.g. de la Porte 2002; Scharpf 2002, 2003; Héritier 2003; Kröger 2004; Eckardt 2005; Heidenreich and Bischoff in press).

The theoretical approach – concerned with explaining the emergence of new modes of governance in the EU – is probably the least developed, at least in terms of the quantity of work devoted to it. Ioannou and Niemann's (2003) survey suggests that a neo-functionalist approach can explain the emergence of the OMC, for example, via the 'spillover' from the development of the single market and EMU, and the consequent loss of national policy-making instruments for promoting employment growth (see also Scharpf 2002). However, intergovernmentalist and rational-choice institutionalist analyses are better at explaining why governments chose this particular alternative to the conventional Community Method of legislation and why they delegated so little authority to the European supranational authorities responsible for it. Indeed, Schäfer (2004: 13) argues that governments supported the soft-law OMC for 'sovereignty-protecting' reasons – 'because of its low degree of legalization and limited potential for unintended consequences'. The normative approach has been strongly inspired by two closely-related concerns: the idea that the OMC can contribute to alleviating Europe's democratic deficit and that it can bring the purported virtues of deliberative policy-making to the EU, via, for example, the involvement of what Eriksen and Fossum (2001) call 'strong publics' in promoting debate and the search for consensus and 'truth' via 'reasonable' discussion. However, such arguments raise several counter-positions: that even if the EU suffers from a 'democratic deficit', involving interest groups in a form of 'weak Euro-corporatism' would not necessarily do anything to correct it (in fact, the experience of national 'corporatism might suggest the opposite); that the legitimacy conveyed by deliberation may well lack real *political* legitimacy, both because it is divorced from the approval of general publics (i.e. through elections) and from the genuine expertise of policy-makers (Ryfe 2005); and that while those promoting deliberation believe it raises consciousness and fosters the search for 'truth', it may also generate the costs of 'wasted time, procrastination and indecision, stalling in the face of needed change, and unfair control of agendas' (Shapiro 2002).

In reality, there is nothing intrinsically democratic in deliberation processes as such. Indeed, the third, more empirically-focused literature, provides a wealth of detail about the ways in which particular new methods of governance, especially the multiple varieties of OMC, are conducted in practice, and provides ample material for assessing those normative claims (we refer to much of the empirical literature below, but see especially Govecor 2004). That assessment is carried out in the fourth approach which, more analytical and critical in its approach, brings a useful antidote to the normative perspective by revealing how little new modes of governance, and the OMC in particular, conform to deliberative ideals (de la Porte and Nanz 2004; Kröger 2004). This literature notes the challenges they pose to more traditional (and often more democratic) forms of decision-making, including the Community Method. Smismans (2004) refers to the OMC as the 'Open method of centralization' because of its centralising, non-democratic nature; it illustrates the low degree of integration or influence of such methods within national policy-making communities (Govecor 2004; Zeitlin and Pochet with Magnusson 2005); it considers the trade-offs between experimentalism and efficacy that inevitably afflict them; and it advocates the need to link 'soft' and 'hard' forms of governance – the first 'in the shadow' of the second, or as 'hybrid' instruments and processes – if real outcomes, rather than mere 'cheap talk', are to result (Scharpf 2002; Héritier 2003; Kröger 2004; Rhodes 2005; Trubek and Trubek 2005; Trubek et al. 2005).

Apart from our concern to provide a critical survey and review of this literature – we touch on all four streams in the literature, and comment on their most important arguments and claims in the analysis that follows – our aim is also to focus on what we consider to be one of its greatest deficiencies: the absence, hitherto, of any coherent framework for systematically assessing policy *effectiveness*, i.e., the capacity of new modes of governance for achieving stated policy objectives. In doing so we also bring into our account a parallel literature – that on policy diffusion and learning, a literature that is frequently referred to by studies of the OMC and other new modes of governance (it is central to many of the more normative studies), but one that is rarely integrated systematically into their analysis. It is important that we do this, for four reasons.

The first is that a key (though often rhetorical) question in much of the literature is: 'does, or can, the OMC' work? With few exceptions, however, there is little attempt to answer this question systematically. The second and closely related reason is that much analysis frames the question 'does, or can it, work' in terms of 'improving governance', defined largely in terms of openness, inclusion and extent of participation (see de la Porte and Nanz 2004 for a critique). The subsequent step is often to *assume* on the basis of fragmented evidence rather than clearly *ascertain* the contribution that these instruments can make to enhancing 'policy learning' as a major mechanism for advancing collective decision-making and regulation. Third, while the overwhelming focus of the literature is thus on the potential of NMG for what Scharpf (1998: 2) calls 'input legitimacy', whereby 'collectively binding decisions should originate from the authentic expression of the preferences of the constituency in question', much less well understood or considered (though see Scharpf himself in Scharpf 2002, and Bursens and Helsen 2005) is their capacity for achieving 'output legitimacy', i.e. the effective application of collectively binding decisions that serve a constituency's common interest. We argue that any instrument of policy, no matter how elaborately developed, will be ignored and abandoned unless 'output legitimacy' is also achieved or achievable.

A fourth and final reason for focusing on policy effectiveness is that in the absence of a frank and analytically-focused discussion of policy capacity, the literature and debate on new modes of governance and the OMC has tended to polarize on normative grounds. It is frequently linked to other but closely-related political debates on the desirability of a strengthened European 'social dimension' (i.e. a greater elevation of social welfare policy to the EU level) and the need to correct the EU's purported 'democratic deficit', as revealed by the debate on 'constitutionalizing' the OMC in the European convention (Tsakatika 2004; Moravcsik 2005; Trubek and Trubek 2005). While one popular academic thesis maintains that both input *and* output legitimacy can be achieved via deliberation and mutual learning (e.g. Sabel and Zeitlin 2003; Eberlein and Kerwer, 2004; see Zeitlin 2005a for a discussion), the opposing view (e.g. Chalmers and Lodge 2003) holds that the OMC fails miserably on both counts. For ultra-sceptics Alesina and Perotti (2004: 8) the OMC is largely an innocuous exercise in 'Euro-verbosity', but one with damaging 'Kafkian' dimensions. They

opine that not only is it a waste of time and money, but that it 'has set back the level of the debate and understanding by the public by giving the impression that some EU institutions actually know how to solve the problem of European employment if only national governments cooperated'. More sober, schematic assessments are clearly needed.

We argue that any analysis of the potential of NMG for policy *effectiveness* must begin by examining the links between policy inputs and outputs in the EU's multi-level polity. Within that architecture, policy confluence or convergence is determined both by supranational factors (i.e. common institutions, concerns and objectives) and by national factors (domestic interests and preferences, the costs of domestic implementation and openness to policy transfer). For that reason, two different variables need to be taken into account – one from a 'top-down' perspective, the other from a 'bottom-up' perspective. In so doing we respond to calls in the general EU policy literature as well as by OMC specialists for a focus on the two-way, reciprocal relationship between Europe and its member states rather than the search for one-way impacts (e.g. Boerzel 2003; Trubek and Trubek 2005: 356–7; Zeitlin 2005b: 16; Heidenreich and Bischoff in press). We also respond to calls (e.g. by Trubek et al. 2005) for the need to bridge the divide between rationalism and constructivism in studies of national and international governance when considering the influence of 'soft' and 'hard' law and the need for a synthetic approach in understanding the 'hybridity' of the two (cf. Abbott and Snidal 2000; Finnemore and Toope 2001. See Trubek and Trubek 2005 for a useful discussion of these two conceptions of law).

Thus, following an increasingly common method for understanding EU policy transposition or transfer (e.g. Boerzel and Risse 2003; Paster 2005; Schimmelfennig and Sedelmeier 2005; Epstein 2006), we characterize the interaction between top-down and bottom-up policy pressures and influences in terms of a 'logic of consequences' and a 'logic of appropriateness'. If we are to take the aspirations of policy makers seriously, the 'top-down' explanatory variable is the capacity of different

European modes of governance to induce national policy change towards common objectives. This may involve material incentives and coercion via hard law (*the logic of consequences*) and/or the non-coercive transposition of norms, ideas and 'collective understandings' via communication, socialization and social learning (*the logic of appropriateness*) (March and Olsen 1998). We call this *policy convergence capacity*.

As we argue below, this capacity varies in line with various combinations of policy instrument and the particular blending (or 'hybridity') of 'soft' and 'hard' law in any given new mode of governance. From a 'bottom-up' perspective, policy transfer is driven by national actors, interests and preferences, revealing both the logics of consequences *and* appropriateness. In the first instance, the adoption of a policy will depend on the balance of power between pro- and anti-EU reform coalitions and the degree of expectation that it will help resolve domestic policy problems. Policy makers will also be influenced by 'altered material payoffs' (Simmons and Elkins 2004) induced by external pressures, be they competitive (a desire to achieve the results delivered by the policy reform elsewhere) or coercive (as in conditionality or obligations in the EU under binding legal instruments). In the second instance, an ideational process of consensus-creation may involve learning via channels of communication and socialization, or even shifts in what Nedergaard (2005), who takes a social constructivist approach to studying the OMC, calls 'language-constituted relations', whereby new concepts become 'hegemonic' in a particular epistemic community - the main achievement of the OMC to date according to some analysts (e.g. Jacobsson 2004). Under such circumstances, 'altered reputational payoffs' are created either by a desire to conform to an ideational consensus or by cultural emulation linked to shared beliefs (Simmons and Elkins, 2004). We understand behaviour under both logics to be rational, however, and characterize them together as the *rationality of policy transfer*.

In the following we carry out our critical survey and review of the literature within an analysis of new modes of governance, policy convergence capacity and the rationality of policy transfer. In part one, we explain why the OMC is considered to be a 'new mode of governance' and place it alongside and differentiate it from other, pre-Lisbon, NMGs. In part two, we begin our exploration of the effectiveness of new modes of governance and the various OMCs by merging the different top-down factors found in the literature on policy transfer into a single explanatory variable – policy convergence capacity. In part three, we account for the rationality of policy transfer from a bottom-up perspective, and assess the scope conditions under which new, non-hierarchical modes of policy diffusion under new modes of governance can be effective. Part four concludes.

THE LISBON STRATEGY AND NEW MODES OF GOVERNANCE

The Lisbon European Council of March 2000 is remembered for two key innovations – a set of highly ambitious economic development objectives and the launching of the OMC. The objectives sought to make the EU 'the most competitive and dynamic knowledge-based economy of the world, capable of a sustainable economic growth, better work places and greater social cohesion' by 2010. The second formally 'elects' the OMC as the new 'soft-non-legislative' tool for achieving convergence on the declared goals. As defined by the Lisbon Council Presidency Conclusions, the OMC has four key elements (European Council 2000: 12):

- fixing guidelines for the Union combined with specific timetables for achieving the goals (…) in the short, medium and long terms;
- establishing, where appropriate, quantitative and qualitative indicators and benchmarks against the best in the world and tailored to the needs of different member states and sectors as a means of comparing best practice;

- translating these European guidelines into national and regional policies by setting specific targets; and
- periodic monitoring, evaluation and peer review organized as mutual learning processes.

The Lisbon summit and subsequent European Councils called for the Commission, Council and members states to extend the OMC to other areas. As a result, there are now explicit OMCs in social inclusion (adopted by the Nice Council in 2000), pensions (Stockholm 2001), health care (Göteberg 2001), research and innovation (Spring European Council 2003) and numerous other 'OMC-like' processes in information society, enterprise and e-business and education (de la Porte and Pochet 2003). Related new modes of 'soft' governance have also emerged in climate change policy for example (Usui 2005). A critical distinction needs to be made between these post-Lisbon innovations and the pre-Lisbon Luxembourg, Cardiff and Cologne processes – which, respectively, cover employment policy (in the European Employment Strategy, or EES), structural reform policy and wage monitoring – and the Broad Economic Policy Guidelines (BEPGs) in macro-economic policy (Ioannou and Nieman 2003). While the EES and the BEPGs are treaty-based, the other OMCs, and especially the 'OMC-like' processes, have a more ambiguous legal and institutional status.

At first sight, the OMC is merely a collection and reorganization of instruments and processes stemming from the tradition of soft law. Practices such as the benchmarking of national policies, peer review and monitoring are very similar to processes that have long been in use by international organizations, such as the OECD (Armingeon and Beyeler 2004; Casey 2004). Nor is the EU's use of soft law new as such: it has long been employed, in the form of recommendations, codes of practice, 'solemn declarations' and action programmes to preview, accompany or set the agenda for hard law measures (Rhodes 2005). Nevertheless, the OMC does depart from those previous examples in its ambitions and procedures.

Regarding ambitions, the OMC is considered superior by its advocates to both uncoordinated national 'free riding' and the hard-law-based Community Method (Rodrigues 2002; Vandenbroucke 2002). Under the OMC, member states are free to choose their own policy instruments, and consensus among governments on otherwise divisive policies should – at least in principle – be easier to reach. Second, the OMC is thought to allow advances with 'positive integration' now that 'negative integration' – the removal of national barriers to the freedom of movement of goods, services, capital and people – has reached its limits. By the early 21st century, the integration project had moved closer to the core areas of welfare states (e.g. immigration, fiscal and pension policies). Traditionally regulated by national social contracts, the top-down regulation and uniform application of EU law in these areas would not only be illegitimate but 'unthinkable' (Scharpf 2002). Elsewhere, in innovation policy, for example, the complexity and uniqueness of national systems render centrally-determined policies dysfunctional (Kaiser and Prange 2004). Third, advocates argue that the OMC provides a pragmatic answer to concerns about the legitimacy of the EU. Although medium and long-term political objectives are deliberated at the supranational level, the full content of policies is supposed to be shaped, implemented and democratically endorsed in the member states. As for procedures, attaining those objectives requires extensive process innovation (Borrás and Jacobsson 2004). Thus, the OMC is supposedly characterized by the following: it is an intergovernmental rather than Commission-led approach; it is therefore subject to political monitoring at the highest EU level (European Council and Council of Ministers); it is based on an iterative process that implies a higher commitment and degree of peer pressure than ad-hoc, soft-law processes; and whereas the latter have been confined to discrete, unconnected policy areas, the OMC is meant to recognize their functional inter-dependence and the potential for spillovers between them.

But as encoded by the Lisbon strategy, the OMC is only a template. Empirical reality reveals great variation: there are in fact as many new modes of governance (of both the OMC and non-OMC variety) as there are policy areas, each with their different histories, formats, procedures and rationales (CEC 2001; Radaelli 2003; Borrás and Jacobsson 2004):

- *Budgetary policy* coordination is based on quantitative parameters fixed by the Stability and Growth Pact. A multi-lateral surveillance procedure produces recommendations and a sanctioning mechanism for non-compliance can levy fines when budgetary deficits are exceeded. The policy cycle is based on an annual reporting and review process.
- *Macroeconomic policy* coordination is based on the Broad Economic Policy Guidelines and specific indicators against which national policies are evaluated or 'benchmarked'. There are no sanctions for non-compliance, but individual recommendations and 'peer pressure' can be applied. The policy cycle is based on an annual reporting and review process.
- *Employment policy* coordination is based on the Luxembourg Process. National Action Plans (NAPs) are evaluated against employment guidelines (quantitative targets and indicators) formulated within the European Employment Strategy (EES). There are no sanctions for non-compliance, but reliance on recommendations and 'peer pressure'. The policy cycle is annual.
- *Social inclusion policy* coordination is based on qualitative common objectives and benchmarking on quantitative indicators. There are no sanctions, but peer pressure can be applied. The policy cycle is biannual.
- *Pension reform policy* coordination is based on qualitative common objectives and strategy reports. Benchmarking is very limited, although peer pressure can be applied. There are no sanctioning mechanisms. The policy cycle is triennial.
- *Research and innovation policy* coordination is based on the benchmarking of national performance against common indicators (e.g. an innovation scoreboard or trend chart). Peer pressure is applied via the negative publicity given to the weakest performers.
- *'OMC-like' processes in information society, enterprise and e-business and education* in which open-ended, experimental forms of 'coordination' have emerged, primarily involving *ad hoc* agenda setting and policy framing by the European authorities.

The balance between 'hard' and 'soft' governance shifts rapidly and fully in favour of the latter as one descends this list. While budgetary, macro-economic and employment policy coordination are all cases of pre-Lisbon policy innovation, have treaty bases and operate to different degrees in what Scharpf (1997) calls the 'shadow of hierarchy', social inclusion, pensions and research and innovation are all 'pure OMCs'. In the former group, the logics of consequences and appropriateness are combined; in the latter group the second logic operates alone.

ASSESSING POLICY CONVERGENCE CAPACITY

There have been many more analyses of OMC processes than in-depth attempts to assess their national-level impact (though see Govecor 2004 and Zeitlin et al. 2005). The problem with measuring or even estimating the impact or influence of the 'pure OMCs' within the member states, as opposed to the EU-level of policy communities and policy dialogue, is twofold (Borrás 2004; Borrás and Greve 2004; Eberlein and Kerwer 2004; Heidenreich and Bischoff in press). First, 'impact' is hard to define. Should we consider as 'impact' the fact that different member states ascribe to common cognitive frameworks and devise common indicators for benchmarking progress towards common objectives? Or should we consider it exclusively in terms of national-level policy outcomes? If the former, then what is the importance of such a change and will it lead to effective reform? If the latter, is impact the national achievement of objectives and indicators or actual policy convergence? Second, it is difficult, and perhaps impossible to ascribe effects to the OMC itself, rather than to parallel processes or unrelated developments. Is

1. Simple benchmarking and/or recommendations   Lowest

2. Voluntary policy objectives + benchmarking & peer pressure

3. Voluntary policy objectives + benchmarking & peer pressure   **Policy**
   + structured coordination process   **Convergence**
                                                                                        Capacity
4. Legally-binding policy objectives (sanctions for non-compliance)
   + benchmarking & peer pressure + structured coordination process

5. Legally binding regulations   Highest

Figure 24.1   *Policy convergence capacity.*

an increase in a country's employment rate, for example, due to the EES/OMC or changing macroeconomic conditions? These complications also reveal one of the OMC's core weaknesses: meeting the demands of 'output legitimacy' through evidence-based assessment.

There have been few attempts to subject the OMC and other new modes of governance to systematic, variable-based analysis. Nonetheless, existing work (e.g. Radaelli 2003; Borrás and Greve 2004; Borrás and Jacobsson 2004) does alert us to two critical factors for understanding potential impact: the presence of sanctions and the extent of institutionalization. The Europeanization literature (e.g. Featherstone and Radaelli 2003; Radaelli 2003; Bulmer and Padgett 2005) also provides tools for understanding domestic change. The work of Börzel and Risse (2003) is especially useful in noting the importance of 'facilitating factors' for policy transfer, such as supportive and cooperative institutions and policy entrepreneurs. Impediments (e.g. multiple veto points) will also be important, as will the definitions and defence of national interests. Member states jealously guard their sovereignty and may have rational reasons for resisting further Europeanization – even in its 'soft' OMC guise (Schäfer 2004). As a result, securing compliance with European policies is always problematic – even under the Community Method and hard law (e.g. Conant 2002).

In order to analyse different types of NMG, we establish a single common variable for locating different policy instruments and their various combinations.[3] In Figure 24.1 we define

this variable in terms of five discrete steps, and calibrate convergence capacity accordingly.

Simple Benchmarking and/or Recommendations

The first step of the variable, where convergence capacity is lowest, includes instruments in the purest 'soft-law' tradition, such as recommendations and benchmarking. The Commission uses recommendations to take official positions or recommend certain courses of action regarding a national policy or policy outcome. This indirect instrument of pressure has no strength to compel and is often ignored, though in some cases it may have the effect of 'moral suasion'. Developed initially in the 1970s by corporations for evaluating company quality, productivity and competitiveness, benchmarking has also been adopted more recently by the public sector. The OECD has used benchmarking in its periodical reports for many years to assess and compare the policy performance of western countries (Casey 2004). In the EU, its use has been most prominent in EMU's Maastricht membership criteria and the Stability and Growth Pact (SGP). From there it has been extended (though in the absence of SGP-type sanctions) to employment policy, social policy and research and innovation (Arrowsmith *et al.* 2004).

In theory, benchmarking may exert a certain influence by 'naming and shaming' weak performers, especially when comparative data are able to trigger responses from a country's media, political-economic elite and public opinion. But recent analysis of the OECD's use of benchmarks to diffuse 'best practices' in employment and social policy reveals little efficacy at work (Armingeon and Beyeler 2004). Its convergence capacity in the EU is also likely to be low, especially in the absence of effective peer review and peer pressure and attention from the media and mass publics. Groenendijk (2004) distinguishes between three different types of benchmarking that could be successfully employed in EU policy-making: benchmarking for horizontal policy learning, benchmarking for vertical policy transfer and benchmarking for monitoring and surveillance. But, he argues, while current OMC benchmarking methods akin to the first two types are poorly designed and therefore fail to function as intended, the third cannot succeed unless linked to clear, minimum standards that are subject to enforcement.

Benchmarks are at their strongest when used to monitor and publicize national indicators and when linked to the potential for 'harder' policy interventions (as with deficit levels in the case of the Stability and Growth Pact – see below). They have 'moderate strength' when they take the form of non-binding guidelines and indicative targets and are also accompanied by monitoring and reporting requirements and the threat of legislation, as in the European Climate Change Programme (Usui 2005). They are at their weakest, as in education policy, where there are no concrete targets for individual countries, but merely 'reference levels' of average European performance. The latter have little real meaning and certainly no impact, apart perhaps from some kind of (unmeasurable) shaping or standardization of policy language when linked to the development of a transnational policy community (Gornitzka 2005).

Voluntary Policy Objectives + Benchmarking & Peer Pressure

This more complex form of OMC involves different types of instrument. First, unlike simple benchmarking, there is a clearly defined, though voluntary, set of objectives that member states freely decide to pursue – a public expression of will that implies a degree of commitment to

meeting them. Second, unlike in education policy, for example, benchmarking here is explicitly aimed at measuring national performance and progress towards common goals. Third, national performance is assessed through political monitoring at the highest level. Finally, there is an iterative process of joint progress evaluation, which in principle triggers reactions from other national leaders (peer pressure). This type of OMC has been used in research and innovation policy and pension reform. In the former, there are clearly stated political objectives (those of the Lisbon Strategy), the benchmarking of national performance (European innovation scoreboards and trend charts), as well as an annual review of national performance and the identification of best practices (in the Competitiveness Council). The pensions OMC is weaker: eleven broad common objectives have been agreed to and progress presented in 'national strategy reports' is reviewed periodically in the Employment, Social Policy, Health and Consumer Affairs Council. But benchmarking is still limited in effect, and the peer review mechanisms weak. Eckardt (2005: 247) concludes that although the OMC on pension reforms provides an additional input into the policy-making process, 'it does not fundamentally alter the incentive structure of national political markets'. Policy convergence capacity is therefore still very low. Conditions that might ensure greater efficacy are: (i) pressure for compliance at the national level from politico-economic elites and public opinion; and/or (ii) pressure on national executives when national policies are questioned in the Council of Ministers.

Voluntary Policy Objectives + Benchmarking & Peer Pressure + Structured Coordination Process

In step three, benchmarking constantly feeds mechanisms of peer review and pressure within a system of structured coordination – a process for coordinating national policies in line with common guidelines underpinned by national convergence plans. In principle, this process increases member state commitment to common goals. This is the case for employment policy – the European Employment Strategy (EES) – coordinated under the Luxembourg process. The latter is implemented through an annual cycle, which begins with the European Council's adoption of employment guidelines and priorities for national policy initiatives. Each state is responsible for formulating its own National Action Plan (NAP), which specifies the employment objectives to be pursued. The Commission and the Council then assess the NAPs in a joint employment report, issuing legally non-binding recommendations on the performance of individual states (for a detailed account, see Rhodes 2005). A similar approach is used in EU environmental governance, though the threat of legislation regarding emissions levels, for example, adds a strong 'shadow of hierarchy' to the process (Usui 2005). This combination of instruments is also found in macroeconomic policy, which has had a specific process of coordination since 1992. The common Broad Economic Policy Guidelines (BEPG) are elaborated annually by the European Commission and adopted by the Council (ECOFIN), while compliance and policy convergence is monitored through an annual review of national implementation reports. In principle, convergence capacity is more powerful given the combination of instruments within a structured and iterative policy process. It is not just the higher degree of institutionalization that counts, but the greater level of commitment secured from national executives via implementation reports. However, the absence of sanctions in cases of non-compliance still allows for important instances of deviation.

Legally-Binding Policy Objectives + Benchmarking & Peer Pressure + Structured Coordination Process

This is the most powerful form of non-legislative governance, because it establishes a legally-binding policy objective, while still leaving governments to choose their own paths and policies for implementation and convergence. Non-compliance is punishable by sanctions. But there is only one example of this mode of governance in the EU – budgetary policy under the Stability and Growth Pact (SGP). The SGP of 1997 established a threshold for national deficits of 3 per cent of GDP so as to avoid 'regional spillover' – the negative externality produced when an increase in the deficit spending of a given member state leads to a rise in Eurozone interest rates (Hodson and Maher 2001). The principal concern of the SGP was to safeguard sound government finances so as to strengthen, in turn, the conditions for price stability and sustainable growth.

The pact is enforced through a multilateral surveillance mechanism, in which each member state submits an annual stability and convergence programme to the Council of Ministers (ECOFIN) (Hodson 2004; Hodson and Maher 2004). In cases of non-compliance, a sanctioning mechanism is set in motion. In a first phase the Council makes recommendations to the member state, which are not made public. Then, if the Council establishes that there has been no effective action, it may make open recommendations that are widely publicized. If the member state persists in ignoring the Councils' recommendations, the Council may invite the European Investment Bank to reconsider its lending policy towards the member state; require the offending state to make a non-interest bearing deposit with the Community until the excessive deficit is corrected; and impose fines of an appropriate size. In addition, the Excessive Deficit Procedure allows the Council to issue an 'early warning' before a breach of the deficit limit has occurred.

The key distinguishing feature here is the incentive structure for compelling member-state compliance. Under the SGP, both 'competition incentives' (exposure to market sanctions for individual countries and the EU as a whole) and 'cooperation incentives' (peer pressure on poor performers) combine with the ultimate power of the entire 'club' to apply sanctions (Morelli et al. 2002). But in reality, the functioning of the pact – which has seen Portugal, France, Germany and Italy all breach the 3 per cent limit since 2001 – reveals the limits even of sanctions (which ECOFIN has proven reluctant to levy), the failure of markets to react adversely (suggesting that the formal sanctions were never seen as credible) and the ultimate reliance of the SGP on soft law (Hodson 2004; Hodson and Maher 2004). The 'near death' of the pact in 2004 has led some economists to advocate returning fiscal discretion to national governments and the achievement of discipline by peer pressure and bad publicity alone (Alesina and Perotti 2004: 15).

Nevertheless, Fritz Scharpf (2001) has argued that similar procedures could be adopted in other areas where looser forms of coordination have failed. Thus, the legislation of the Council and the Parliament under the Community Method could be limited to setting core objectives to be implemented at the national level, coupled with a form of open coordination in which member states would declare their intentions in a national plan. Their performance would be monitored by the Commission and evaluated by peer review. The Council would have the power to intervene with tighter legislation in the case of general implementation problems and initiate infringement proceedings along the lines of the SGP's excessive budget procedure. For Scharpf (2001, 2003), this method of coordination employed 'in the shadow of legislation' would allow European law to avoid the excessive detail that vexes member states, as well as an indiscriminate delegation of legislative competences the Commission. However, the proposal hits up against the problem that the functional pressures for extending an SGP-like process to social policy, for example, do not exist (Moravcsik 2005: 366). To the extent that member-state commitments have been secured under the SGP, they are closely linked to the negative externalities that can be created by a loss of fiscal discipline among its signatories. Such competition or cooperation incentives are not at all present in the same way for social policy.

Legally Binding Regulations

This is the classical mode of regulation, or Community Method, long employed for the development and consolidation of the EU's internal market. This method goes beyond inducing the convergence of national policies on common objectives, because it produces rules whose *content* is equally legally binding across all member states. It is conducive to the greatest degree of impact, even if evasion and implementation deficits are frequent and full convergence or harmonization does not always occur (Conant 2002).

This 'old' mode of governance was useful and effective for 'market making' policies, but is inappropriate (not to mention inadvisable) for 'market *correcting*' policies (Scharpf 2001). Market integration, although never completely conflict-free, was a widely-shared goal achieved through uniform rules of integration, liberalization and harmonization. Many of these policies were initiated by the Commission and the European Court of Justice in their roles as 'guardians of the Treaty', and they could count on the support of national actors expecting to benefit from access to a larger, liberalized European market. By contrast, uniform market-correcting regulations would be opposed by both national governments and actors, for at least three reasons: uniform policy convergence would undermine the 'social contracts' enshrined in their different welfare regimes; it would have deleterious effects on economic growth (firms, workers and consumers in Portugal and Greece, let alone the Czech Republic or Lithuania, cannot afford the environmental, labour or social standards deemed essential by their Finnish or Danish counterparts); and the inherent differences and political salience of national health and pension systems render EU harmonization unrealistic (Schludi 2003). Thus, this method has been abandoned as a tool for dealing with new EU integration challenges in favour of the new modes of intervention discussed above.

THE RATIONALITY OF POLICY LEARNING AND TRANSFER

One of the assumptions underlying the Lisbon Presidency's conclusions was that the OMC would bring about greater convergence on EU goals by spreading 'best practices' among member states. It was assumed that an increased exchange of information concerning each country's national policies and processes, and the periodic assessment of these achievements, would foster a process of 'mutual learning', which, in turn, would produce an alignment of national policies.

As the literature on new modes of governance reveals, however, the concept of policy learning is very ill-defined. In the context of EU policy making it has multiple mechanisms and meanings, including 'experience comparison' and knowledge diffusion through repetitive policy cycles, peer review and pressure, the development of a common policy discourse and common indicators, or even 'cognitive convergence' as well as the strategic use of knowledge for imitating successful models and practice. The scholarly study of the OMC has widely incorporated the concept of learning, but without specifying its scope or questioning its utility – or even considering the conditions under which it might actually function. Eberlein and Kerwer (2004), for instance, merge policy learning with a theoretical framework of 'democratic experimentalism' and 'directly-deliberative polyarchy' drawn from Sabel and Cohen (1997) and Dorf and Sabel (1998). This theory is based on a simple model in which a central 'forum' coordinates local deliberating units and distributes information about the effectiveness of different local-level policy experiments. At the end of the process, information on multiple, parallel experiments is successfully converted into 'best practices'. In essence, this notion of deliberation underpins both the European Commission's understanding of the OMC and many academic treatments of the subject. But while it may have heuristic and normative value, it seems largely innocent of the insights available from empirical studies of learning and policy diffusion and has been described as quite utopian regarding the potential for citizen participation (Shapiro 2002; Ryfe 2005).

Given the nature of the policy areas in which the OMC has been launched, any analysis of policy-making potential must take account of the role of bargaining, the centrality of

conflicting interests and the rationality of choices in policy transfer (Kröger 2004). Policy-makers are not seeking the truth, but power. They may be open to discussing best practices and successful foreign policy models, but will not accept blind commitments to processes and policies in areas as politically salient and sensitive as welfare-state recalibration and tax policy. Convergence on 'talk' hardly ever means convergence in decisions. No process of policy transfer from abroad is painless, and no domestic policy change is ever simple to implement; it always carries the possibility of failure, and always implies political costs. And since the transposition of successful policies or best practice is voluntary in all OMC processes, we need to assess the conditions under which it is rational for a member state to transfer a policy in the absence of coercion.

Scholars of public policy analysis such as Dolowitz and Marsh (1996, 2000) provide evidence of such processes worldwide. They classify different types of policy transfer according to six factors: the reasons for engagement in policy transfer, the actors involved, the content transferred, the source from which the lessons are drawn, different degrees of transfer, and the factors that restrict or facilitate the process. As in our own exercise above, they conceptualize policy transfer in terms of a scale of compulsion, running from lesson-drawing to outright coercion. But while they identify many of the factors facilitating non-coercive policy transfer – such as 'dissatisfaction with the status quo' or situations of 'conditionality' – they do not consider systematically the conditions for rational policy transfer. A more recent literature (Simmons and Elkins 2004; Elkins and Simmons 2005; Meseguer 2005; Way 2005; Epstein 2006) has begun to provide the basis for such an assessment.

Taking our cue from those innovations, we outline below five scope conditions under which it is rational for national policy makers to transfer a policy in the absence of coercion and a sixth, extremely broad condition for the *non-rationality* of transfer (Table 24.1). Although the first three rationality conditions are more conducive to a logic of consequences, and the latter two to a logic of appropriateness,

Table 24.1   *The rationality and non-rationality of policy transfer.*

Conditions for the rationality of policy transfe	• Policy failure and high degree of uncertainty
	• External conditionality
	• Functional interdependence
	• Consensus and normative consistency
	• Domestic receptivity
Conditions for the non-rationality of policy transfer	• Costs of policy transfer are higher than the expected benefs

in effect – and in contrast to unproductive efforts to separate these modes of behaviour, deriving from March and Olsen (1998) – we argue that *both* are always present (see Epstein 2006 for an extended discussion). We also argue that the more these conditions are present, and the more they reinforce one another, the more likely it is that actors will engage in some form of learning or emulation. However, policy-learning analysis alerts us to several provisos. First, 'bounded learning' – in which the analytical skills of actors are limited and subject to cognitive biases – is the norm. 'Rational learning', by contrast, in which analytical capabilities are maximal and shared by all actors, leading to convergence in policy decision making, is extremely rare. Second, there are many reasons why 'bounded learning' may go wrong, including the fact that policy makers (like most individuals) are 'cognitive misers' and often have difficulty assessing the consequences of various policies (Ryfe 2005). And third, strong evidence suggests that simple policy emulation – a 'blind' act that lacks the degree of reflection required to map 'best practice' or to consider the consequences for policy outcomes – is much more common than either rational *or* bounded learning (Dolowitz and Marsh 2000; Elkins and Simmons 2005; Meseguer 2005).

The first scope condition is *policy failure, uncertainty and insecurity*, circumstances in which policy makers realize that a policy is failing but are uncertain how to proceed. Failure may be imputable to changing external factors – when a country's innovation policy fails, for example not because it is inappropriate or ineffective, but because that country is 'falling behind' in international competition. It then becomes rational for policy makers to look around for effective policies and programmes elsewhere, and engage in policy transfer via learning or emulation. Following Way (2005), we use 'insecurity' to convey the tendency for governments or leaders with tenuous grips on power to jump on policy bandwagons and believe the claims made on behalf of new policy models by external actors – for example, international organizations, amongst which we can include the EU. The 'mimetism' or 'isomorphism' involved is driven as much by the search for legitimacy as for successful models, suggesting that the logic underpinning this process is as much one of appropriateness as it is of consequences (DiMaggio and Powell 1991: 69).

An example of this kind of policy transfer at work in the EU is the adoption of Economic and Monetary Union. The inflationary crisis of the 1970s revealed that governments could not easily keep the demand for inflation under control. One solution was to inhibit the *supply* of inflation by removing monetary policy discretion from the political system, and at Maastricht monetary policy was transferred from governments to a non-majoritarian institution – the European Central Bank – charged with maintaining price stability. EMU gained legitimacy as a policy solution at a time of great uncertainty and policy failure because there was a successful model – German monetary policy as administered by the Bundesbank – to emulate (Radaelli 2000; McNamara 2002).

In those policy areas where pure OMCs are being used, there are varying degrees of uncertainty. In labour policy, years of high rates of unemployment across Europe have arguably made policy makers highly susceptible to policy transfer, as has the common challenge of demographic change to the long-term sustainability of Bismarckian pension systems and escalating costs in health care. But as the example of EMU reveals, uncertainty is not enough: a successful and easily apprehended 'model' or policy alternative must also be available. We return to this issue below.

The second scope condition is *external conditionality*. Formally, conditionality is a mutual arrangement under which a government promises to implement certain policies in return for specified amounts of assistance – usually financial or technical – from an international organization or agency (Checkel 2001). The International Monetary Fund and the World Bank have long employed such instruments and incentives for persuasion, relying on lending programmes for encouraging policy transfer. In the EU, conditionality has been employed in negotiations with the Accession Countries: those countries that accept a process of reform for the incorporation of the *acquis communautaire* are entitled to proceed to the next stage of membership. The available incentives for policy transfer are thus not only financial but also eminently political, and can create conditions under which it is rational to transfer a policy. The degree of rationality will depend on the extent to which the target country relies on the resources promised in return for compliance. There have been some loose attempts to link the employment OMC with a degree of financial conditionality through new conditions on member state use of European Social Fund resources. From 2007 their use should conform to national EES obligations. Numerous proposals (e.g. by the Sapir and Kok Reports) to strengthen OMC-type instruments have proposed an even greater use of conditionality (Kok 2003; Sapir et al. 2004). But as a growing literature reveals, material conditionality and payoffs for compliance rarely function well or succeed in the absence of *socialization* (Epstein 2005). We return to this point below under conditions four and five.

The third scope condition is *functional interdependence*. Here, two or more countries adopt policies with potentially harmful, cross-border effects. Examples often referred to in the EU are fiscal, tax or labour policy where 'beggar-thy-neigbour' practices to redirect foreign investment flows could result in 'races-to-the-bottom' (Radaelli 2000). When such policies are harmful – both to those countries which participate in the 'race-to-the-bottom' and those that do not (for all countries there is a risk that capital income taxes, for example, will slowly diminish) – it becomes rational for all to collaborate to prevent a downward policy spiral. Indeed, the fear of such practices has been one of the major rationales for strong support of both centralized EU policies and OMCs in social and employment policy. But in the EU to date, neither a compulsory range of tax rates nor a single European tax system has been adopted by EU member states; nor has there been much progress in moving beyond an EU social or employment policy based on intergovernmental bargaining and the standard Community Method (Rhodes 2005). This could be because upward policy transfer is hampered, either by the bounded rationality of policy makers or by the salience of the policy itself at the national level. But equally important is that, by contrast with internal market competition policy and the EMU/SGP deficit criterion, negative externalities and the potential for downward policy spirals in other policy areas is actually quite limited (cf. Scharpf 2002). A rule of thumb for assessing the success of novel mechanisms of coordination in the EU is the presence of such externalities. In the absence of a much higher levels of cross-border labour flows, or trends for countries to diminish welfare spending in the search for competitive advantage, or greater evidence than presently exists for widespread tax competition, there are equally few incentives to compel serious national actor engagement in even the softer forms of social and employment policy coordination advanced under the EES/OMC (Moravcsik 2005).

The fourth scope condition, *consensus and normative consistency*, refers to the nature of the message being communicated, but also to that of the social and cultural environment in which the message is received. Analyses in areas ranging from privatization and trade liberalization to central bank independence have shown that policy makers engaged in policy transfer use cognitive short cuts, favour clear foreign models of success, and limit the number of changes to national circumstances as they seek to implement (or rather emulate) those models – all evidence of the prevalence of bounded as opposed to rational learning (Meseguer 2005). The clarity of principles involved in say, central bank independence (price stability and political autonomy), makes the CBI model highly conducive to transfer. The contrast with many of the forms of policy transfer envisaged under the EU's multiple OMCs is clear. To take the example of employment, beyond a general agreement to focus on supply-side reforms there is little consensus on how to improve Europe unemployment problems: there are at least several competing 'models' of labour market organization in the EU, each presenting different 'lessons' of how to achieve varying trade-offs between labour market flexibility and employment security. Nor does much normative or discursive consistency flow from expert opinion or 'deliberation' in the European Employment Strategy (EES) policy process (Nedergaard 2005), with major differences apparent over the desirable degrees and forms of labour market regulation. Many of the 'messages' contained in general EES strategy reports or specific recommendations to national authorities reveal rather transparent and ineffectual attempts to paper over such inconsistencies. Thus, the European Commission's (2003) report on *The Future of the European Employment Strategy* recommends both greater flexibility in contractual arrangements and restrictions on the segmentation of the labour market into different categories of workers – two clearly contradictory goals (Raveaud 2005; Rhodes 2005). Such inconsistencies may be responsible in part for what has been identified as 'asymmetric' policy learning across different member states (Büchs 2004). More normative consistency is displayed, however, in the social inclusion OMC, since combating poverty is less susceptible to ideological disputes.

The fifth scope condition is *domestic receptivity*. A lack of consensus and normative consistency in the 'policy message' is inevitable in a policy area as politically salient and contested as employment or pensions in a Union of 25 member states. But so too is diversity in the national contexts where that message is received, adding cultural and institutional differences to the already considerable organizational impediments to policy transfer. Both benchmarking and mutual learning face formidable obstacles under such circumstances. While benchmarking complex social systems – for example, labour markets and pensions – leads to reductive and often inappropriate targets and guidelines (Schludi 2003; Room 2005), mutual learning hits up against a barrage of differences across countries in rules, procedures and norms, not to mention cultural and cognitive understandings (Büchs 2004; Greonendijk 2004). As revealed by Casey and Gold (2005), these impediments have severely limited the transfer of employment policy content, instruments and programmes in the peer review process of the EES.

On the other hand, the recent literature on policy transfer is replete with examples of the ways in which domestic receptivity can be enhanced by international institutions, via both socialization and material incentives. While Epstein (2006) shows how international organizations can exploit the reputational payoffs or 'social recognition' for Central and Eastern European elites in gaining support for their policy reforms, Dai (2005) demonstrates how the EU has enhanced compliance with the soft law of international agreements regarding climate change by boosting the electoral leverage and informational status of pro-compliance constituencies. Many of the EU's OMCs rely on the creation of pan-European epistemic communities to diffuse new policy norms – Heidenrieich and Bischoff (in press) discuss their development in social and employment policy. They also use elements of social recognition and information resource empowerment to strengthen the hand of government officials (and sometimes also national NGOs) in domestic policy-making arenas.

Some important successes have been noted – especially in the creation of common notions and principles of policy assessment, backed up by new, standardized data sets regarding, for example, adequate pensions and poverty levels. There are also examples, as in the case of the social inclusion OMC, of national actors (in this case poverty action groups) being energized in lobbying for domestic policy change. But creating a strong national constituency in favour of a particular reform is much harder than promoting an epistemic community of officials and experts, or creating isolated islands of domestic support inside ministries and bureaucracies – the main achievement to date in the case of social and employment policy (see Kröger 2004 and Friedrich 2006 on social inclusion; Heidenreich and Bischoff, in press, on employment). Much more common are either what Johnson (2006) calls 'wormhole effects', that link specific national policy elites into a transnational network but do not engage other domestic political and economic actors (and therefore fail to facilitate the domestic receptivity for reform), or, the disturbance of existing power relations among elites, with quite different consequences for receptivity and policy outcomes from one country to the next, as Büchs (2004) discovers in her study of the EES.

Finally, the conditions for rational policy transfer should be analytically balanced by a set of conditions under which it is *not rational* to transfer a policy. There are indeed many different instances in which this may be true, but it is possible to group them into a common generic condition: *when the costs of policy transfer are higher than expected benefits.* 'Costs' and 'benefits' should not to be understood simply in economic terms. There can be heavy political or social costs in the adoption of a new policy, and the importance of those factors should never be discounted; indeed, they are routinely referred to in the peer review process of the most developed OMC, the European Employment Strategy, to explain why 'best practices' are so hard to identify and transfer (Casey and Gold 2005).[4]

Given these costs, as well as the loss of output legitimacy incurred from unfulfilled policy expectations, many policy makers are now unconvinced of the merits of the OMC when dealing with politically salient issues, notably unemployment. André Sapir, a key Commission policy adviser, and co-author of the influential *Agenda for a Growing Europe* (Sapir et al. 2004) has concluded that the

attempt to coordinate labour markets and social policy through the EES is 'probably an obstacle rather than catalyst for reform because it tends to blur the responsibility between national and EU authorities (…) and is a sure recipe for voters' dissatisfaction with the European Union' (Sapir 2005: 12–13).

CONCLUSION

The new challenges facing the European Union, such as those envisaged by the Lisbon Strategy, have led policy makers to adopt experimental, new modes of governance – namely the Open Method of Coordination – as the standard mode of policy making in certain policy areas. This is because new modes of governance allow in principle for the coordination and steering of national policies towards common EU objectives, while also respecting the autonomy and the diversity of each member state. The key factor to study, from a public policy point of view, has thus become the behaviour of member states in the 'space' created by these new modes, for example, the extent to which member states effectively make their policies converge on common goals. However, policy convergence through non-legislative instruments is a highly complex behavioural phenomenon whose explanation cannot be traced to either national or supranational factors but rather to a combination of both.

We have reviewed the literature on this subject from within a framework designed to address and bring some order to this complexity. We did so by integrating two different approaches: a top-down approach, which seeks to explain how different modes of governance have different degrees of policy convergence capacity; and a bottom-up approach, which shows how different degrees of policy convergence are the result of incentive and preference structures that, from a national point of view, make the transfer of policies 'rational'. Our main point in carrying out this exercise was not just to mobilize and synthesize some of the key insights from the more empirically and analytically-oriented literatures. It was also to critically assess more normative approaches. The latter have made great claims on behalf of new modes of governance, such as the OMC, specifically for its deliberative, democratic potential but also for its capacity to effectively move the European policy agenda forward via novel processes (peer review, policy learning etc.) in the post-Lisbon era. We have taken those claims seriously, and they largely inspired our attempts to link material with non-material (ideational) influences in understanding the potential for non-coercive forms of policy intervention and transfer.

Our conclusion is that theoretical and empirical research into new modes of governance and the voluntary adoption of policies need to move beyond normative preoccupations and reconsider the importance of the fundamental factors that drive the behaviour of national policy-makers. These include national interest, the rationality and utility of policy transfer, the political salience of policy areas and domestic costs of policy change. This list does not claim to be exhaustive. But an approach that considers the scope conditions under which non-coercive policy transfer can occur via mechanisms of socialization and material influence can provide, in future research, a deeper understanding of such innovations, as well as their potential for influencing national policies.

Our analysis suggests, however, that simple solutions are not available for enhancing the utility of new modes of governance such as the OMC. Increasing levels of participation and therefore the formal quality of deliberation in such processes – or politicizing the OMC, as the more normative literature has strongly advocated (for instance, Tsakatika 2004; Zeitlin 2005b) – will not necessarily have any effect in themselves on policy delivery and outcomes or even add to the political saliency of the method. Nor will a formal institutionalization of such procedures, either by giving them a stronger Treaty-base or by sanctifying them in the (presently defunct) European Constitution. As our analysis suggests, success actually depends on a complex combination of material and non-material conditions which are unlikely to be present in all policy areas, in all

member states or at all times. The contingencies influencing policy outcomes are therefore many, indicating that despite their recent proliferation, the employment of 'new' modes of governance may quickly revert to older, tried and tested, approaches to policy making when policy effectiveness proves lacking and the political salience of the issue area is high.

NOTES

1. The authors would like to thank Caroline de la Porte and Ingo Linsenmann for their comments on earlier drafts of this chapter
2. See also the Cologne-based Govecor project (www.govecor.org) that explores the emergence of new modes of socio-economic governance in the EU. Access to a wide range of pertinent literature can also be found on the OMC Research Forum site of the EU Centre of Excellence at the University of Wisconsin-Madison http://eucenter.wisc.edu/OMC/open12.html.
3. See de la Porte and Pochet (2002) for an earlier approach along these lines.
4. For detailed information, see EES Mutual Learning Programme http://www.mutual-learning-employment.net/peerreviews/

REFERENCES

Abbott, K. and Snidal, D. (2000) 'Hard and soft law in international governance', *International Organization*, 54(3): 421–56.

Alesina, A. and Perotti, R. (2004) 'The European Union: a politically incorrect view', *National Bureau of Economic Research*, Cambridge, Mass., Working Paper 10342 http://papers.nber.org/papers/w10342.pdf

Armingeon. K. and Beyeler, M. (2004) *The OECD and European welfare states.* Cheltenham UK and Northampton, MA, USA: Edward Elgar.

Arrowsmith, J., Sisson, K. and Marginson, P. (2004) 'What can "benchmarking" offer the open method of coordination?', *Journal of European Public Policy*, 11(2): 311–28.

Borrás, S. and Jacobsson, K. (2004) 'The open method of coordination and new governance patterns in the EU', *Journal of European Public Policy*, 11(2): 185–208.

Borrás, S. and Greve, B. (2004) 'Concluding remarks: new method or just cheap talk?', *Journal of European Public Policy*, 11(2): 329–36.

Börzel, T.A. and Risse, T. (2003), 'Conceptualizing the domestic impact of Europe', in K. Featherstone and C.M. Radaelli (eds), *The Politics of Europeanization*. Oxford: Oxford University Press. pp. 57–80.

Büchs, M. (2004) 'Asymmetries of policy learning? The European employment strategy and its role in labour market policy reform in Germany and the UK', paper presented to the ESPAnet Conference, University of Oxford, 9–11 September.

Bulmer, S. and Padgett, S. (2005) 'Policy transfer in the European Union: an institutionalist perspective', *British Journal of Political Science*, 35(1): 103–26.

Bursens, P. and Helsen, S. (2005) 'The OMC: a legitimate mode of governance?', paper presented to the EUSA 9th Biennial Conference, Austin, Texas, 31 March – 2 April.

Casey, B.H. (2004) 'The OECD jobs strategy and the European employment strategy: two views of the labour market and the welfare state', *International Journal of Industrial Relations*, 10(3): 329–52.

Casey, B.H. and Gold, M. (2005) 'Peer review of labour market programmes in the European Union: what can countries really learn from one another', *Journal of European Public Policy*, 12(1): 23–43.

Chalmers, D. and Lodge, M. (2003) 'The open method of coordination and the European welfare state', *ESRC Centre for Analysis of Risk and Regulation Discussion Papers*, 11 June, London School of Economics and Political Science. Available at: http://www.lse.ac.uk/collections/CARR/pdf/Disspaper11.pdf

Checkel, J.T. (2001) 'Why comply? Social learning and European identity change', *International Organization*, 55(3): 553–88.

Cohen, J. and Sabel, C. (2003) 'Sovereignty and solidarity: the EU and the US', in J. Zeitlin and D.M. Trubek (eds), *Governing Work and Welfare in a New Economy: European and American Experiments*. Oxford: Oxford University Press. pp. 345–75.

Commission of the European Communities (CEC) (2001) *European Governance. A White Paper*, *COM (2001)*, 428 final.

Conant, L. (2002) *Justice Contained: Law and Politics in the European Union*. Ithaca and London: Cornell University Press.

Dai, X. (2005) 'Why comply? The domestic constituency mechanism', *International Organization*, 59(2): 363–98.

De la Porte, C. (2002) 'Is the open method of coordination appropriate for organizing activities at European level in sensitive policy areas?', *European Law Journal*, 8(1): 38–58.

De la Porte C. and Nanz, P. (2004) 'OMC – a deliberative-democratic mode of governance? The cases of employment and pensions', *Journal of European Public Policy*, 11(2): 267–88.

De la Porte, C. and Pochet, P. (2002) 'Supple coordination at EU level and the key actors' involvement, in C. De la Porte and P. Pochet (eds), *Building Social Europe Through the Open Method of Coordination*. Brussels: P.I.E.-Peter Lang. pp. 27–68.

De la Porte, C. and Pochet, P. (2003) 'The OMC intertwined with the debates on governance, democracy and social Europe, research prepared for the Belgian Minister for Social Affairs and Pensions. Available online at: http://www.ose.be/files/docPP/researchOMC.pdf.

DiMaggio, P. and Powell, W. (1991) 'The iron cage revisited: institutional isomorphism and collective rationality in organizational fields', in W. Powell and P. DiMaggio (eds), *The New Institutionalism in Organizational Analysis*. Chicago: Chicago University Press. pp. 63–82.

Dolowitz, D.P. and Marsh, D. (1996) 'Who learns what from whom? A review of the policy transfer literature', *Political Studies*, 44(2): 343–57.

Dolowitz, D.P. and Marsh, D. (2000) 'Learning from abroad: the role of policy transfer in contemporary policy-making', *Governance: An International Journal of Policy and Administration*, 13(1): 5–24.

Dorf. M.C. and Sabel, C.F. (1998) 'A constitution of democratic experimentalism', *Columbia Law Review*, 48(2): 267–473.

Eberlein, B. and Kerwer D. (2004) 'New governance in the European Union: a theoretical perspective', *Journal of Common Market Studies*, 42(1): 121–42.

Eckardt, M. (2005) 'The open method of coordination on pensions: an economic analysis of its effects on pension reforms', *Journal of European Social Policy*, 15(3): 247–67.

Elkins, Z. and Simmons, B. (2005) 'On waves, clusters, and diffusion: a conceptual framework', *Annals of the American Academy of Political and Social Science*, 598(March): 33–51.

Epstein, R. (2005) 'The paradoxes of enlargement', *European Political Science*, 4(4): 384–94.

Epstein, R. (2006) 'Cultivating consensus and creating conflict: international institutions and the (de)politicization of economic policy in post-communist Europe', *Comparative Political Studies*, 39(8): 1019–42.

Eriksen, E.O. and Fossum, J.E. (2001) 'Democracy through strong publics in the European Union', ARENA Working Papers, WP 01/16.

European Council (2000) *Presidency Conclusions.* Lisbon European Council, 23–24 March.

Featherstone, K. and Radaelli, C.M. (eds) (2003) *The Politics of Europeanization.* Oxford: Oxford University Press.

Finnemore, M. and Toope, S. (2001) 'Alternatives to "legalization": richer views of law and politics', *International Organization,* 55(3): 743–58.

Friedrich, D. (2006) 'Policy process, governance and democracy in the EU: the case of the open method of coordination on social inclusion', *Policy and Politics,* 34(2): 367–83.

Gornitzka, Å. (2005) 'Can policies be coordinated cross-nationally in areas of national sensitivity? The embryonic case of education policy, Europe and the open method of coordination', Paper presented at the NOPSA conference, Reykjavik 11–13 August.

Govecor (2004) 'Self-coordination at the national level: towards a collective gouvernement économique', Final national reports. Available online at: http://www.govercor.org.

Groenendijk, N.S. (2004) 'The use of benchmarking in EU economic and social policies', Paper presented at the Danish Association for European Studies, University of South Denmark, Odense, 24–25 September.

Heidenreich, M. and Bischoff, G. (in press) 'The open method of coordination: a way to the Europeanization of social and employment policies?', *Journal of Common Market Studies,* forthcoming .

Héritier, A. (2003) 'New modes of governance in Europe: increasing political capacity and policy effectiveness?', in T.A. Börzel and R.A. Cichowski (eds), *The State of the European Union: Law, Politics and Society.* Oxford, Oxford University Press. pp. 105–26.

Hodson, D. (2004) 'Macroeconomic coordination in the Euro-area: the scope and limits of the open method', *Journal of European Public Policy,* 11(2): 231–48.

Hodson, D. and Maher, I. (2001) 'The open method as a new mode of governance: the case of soft economic policy coordination', *Journal of Common Market Studies,* 39(4): 719–46

Hodson, D. and Maher, I. (2004) 'Soft law and sanctions: economic policy coordination and reform of the stability and growth pact', *Journal of European Public Policy,* 11(5): 798–813.

Ioannou, D. and Niemann, A. (2003) 'Taking stock of the open method of co-ordination: nature, modus operandi and theoretical perspectives', Dresdner Arbeitspapierer Internationale Beziehungen, Technische Universität Dresden, Nr. 8.

Jacobsson, K. (2004) 'Soft regulation and the subtle transformation of states: the case of EU employment policy', *Journal of European Social Policy,* 14(4): 355–70.

Johnson, J. (2006) 'Two-track diffusion of central bank embeddedness: the politics of Euro adoption in Hungary and the Czech Republic', *Review of International Political Economy,* 13(3): 361–86.

Kaiser, R. and Prange, H. (2004) 'Managing diversity in a system of multi-level governance: the open method of coordination in innovation policy', *Journal of European Public Policy,* 11(2): 249–66.

Kok, W. (2003) 'Jobs, jobs, jobs: report of the employment taskforce', Brussels, November. Available online at: http://europa.eu.int/comm/employment_social/employment_strategy/pdf/etf_en.pdf.

Kröger, S. (2004) '"Let's talk about it": theorizing the OMC (inclusion) in light of its real life application', Paper for the 2004 meeting of the Jean Monnet Chair of the Institut d'Études Politiques, Paris, 11 June.

Magnus Johansson, J. (1999) 'Tracing the employment title in the Amsterdam Treaty: uncovering transnational coalitions', *Journal of European Public Policy,* 6(1): 85–101.

March J.G., and Olsen, J.P. (1998) 'The institutional dynamics of international political orders', *International Organization,* 52(4): 943–69.

McNamara, K. (2002) 'Rational fictions: central bank independence and the social logic of delegation', *West European Politics,* 25(1): 47–76.

Meseguer, C. (2005) 'Policy learning, policy diffusion, and the making of a new order', *Annals of the American Academy of Political and Social Science,* 598: 67–82.

Moravcsik, A. (2005) 'The European constitutional compromise and the neo-functionalist legacy', *Journal of European Public Policy,* 12(2): 349–86.

Morelli, P., Padoan, P.C. and Rodano, L. (2002) 'The Lisbon strategy to the new economy: some economic and institutional aspects', Paper presented to the XIV Villa Mondragone International Economic Seminar, Rome, 27 June.

Mosher, J.S. and Trubek, D.M. (2003) 'Alternative approaches to governance in the EU: EU social policy and the European employment strategy', *Journal of Common Market Studies,* 41(1): 63–8.

Nedergaard, P. (2005) 'The open method of coordination and the analysis of mutual learning processes of the European employment strategy', Working Paper no. 1, International Centre for

Business and Politics, Copenhagen Business School.

Paster, T. (2005) 'The new modes of governance: combining rationalism and constructivism in explaining voluntarist policy coordination in the EU', Österreichische Zeitschrift für Politikwissenschaft, 34(2): 147–61.

Radaelli, C.M. (2000) 'Policy transfer in the European Union: institutional isomorphism as a source of legitimacy', Governance, An International Journal of Policy and Administration, 13(1): 25–43.

Radaelli, C.M. (2003) The Open Method of Coordination: A New Governance Architecture for the European Union? Stockholm: Swedish Institute for European Policy Studies.

Raveaud, G. (2005) 'The European employment strategy: from ends to means', in R. Salais and R. Villeneuve (eds), Europe and the Politics of Capabilities. Cambridge: Cambridge University Press. pp.123–39.

Rhodes, M. (2005) 'Employment policy: between efficacy and experimentation', in H. Wallace, W. Wallace and M. Pollack (eds), Policy-making in the European Union, fifth edition. Oxford: Oxford University Press. pp. 279–304.

Rodrigues, M.J. (2002) 'Introduction: for a European strategy at the turn of the century', in M.J. Rodrigues (ed.), The New Knowledge Economy in Europe: A Strategy for International Competitiveness and Social Cohesion. Cheltenham: Edward Elgar. pp. 1–27.

Room, G. (2005) 'Policy benchmarking in the European Union: indicators and ambiguities', Policy Studies, 26(2): 117–32.

Ryfe, D.M. (2005) 'Does deliberative democracy work?', Annual Review of Political Science, 8: 49–71.

Sabel, C. and Cohen, J. (1997) 'Directly-deliberative polyarchy', European Law Journal, 3(4): 313–40.

Sabel, C. and Zeitlin, J. (2003) 'Networked governance and pragmatic constitutionalism: the new transformation of Europe'. Available online at: http://www.law.nyu.edu/kingsburyb/spring03/globalization/charlesabelpaper_updated.pdf.

Sapir, A. (2005) 'Globalization and the reform of European social models', background document for presentation at the ECOFIN Informal Meeting, Manchester 9 September. Available online at: http://www.bruegel.org/Repositories/Documents/publications/working_papers/SapirPaper080905.pdf.

Sapir, A. et al. (2004) An Agenda for a Growing Europe. Oxford: Oxford University Press.

Schäfer, A. (2004) 'Beyond the community method: why the open method of coordination was introduced to EU policy-making', European integration online papers (EIoP), 8/13. Available online at: http://eiop.or.at/eiop/texte/2004-013a.htm.

Scharpf, F.W. (1997) Games Real Actors Play: Actor-centred Institutionalism in Policy Research. Boulder, CO: Westview Press.

Scharpf, F.W. (1998) 'Interdependence and democratic legitimation', Max-Planck Institute for the Study of Societies, Working Paper 98/2, Cologne.

Scharpf, F.W. (2002) 'The European social model: coping with the challenges of diversity', Journal of Common Market Studies, 40(4): 645–70.

Scharpf, F.W. (2003) 'Legitimate diversity: the new challenge of European integration', in T.A. Börzel and R.A. Cichowski (eds), The State of the European Union: Law, Politics and Society. Oxford: Oxford University Press. pp. 79–104.

Schimmelfennig, F. and Sedelmeier, U. (2005) 'Introduction: conceptualizing the Europeanization of Central and Eastern Europe', in F. Schimmelfennig and U. Sedelmeier (eds), The Europeanization of Central and Eastern Europe. Ithaca and London: Cornell University Press. pp. 1–28.

Schludi, M. (2003) 'Chances and limitations of "benchmarking" in the reform of welfare state structures – the case of pension policy', University of Amsterdam, Amsterdam Institute for Advanced Labour Studies. Available online at: http://www.uva-aias.net/files/working_papers/WP10.pdf.

Shapiro, I. (2002) 'Optimal deliberation?', The Journal of Political Philosophy, 10(2): 196–211.

Simmons, B.A. and Elkins, Z. (2004) 'The globalization of liberalization: policy diffusion in the international political economy', American Political Science Review, 98(1): 171–89.

Smismans, S. (2004) 'EU employment policy: decentralization or centralization through the open method of coordination', EUI Working Paper, Law, 2004/1. Florence: European University Institute.

Trubek, D.M. and Trubek, L.G. (2005) 'Hard and soft law in the constitution of social Europe: the role of the open method of co-ordination', European Law Journal, 11(3): 343–64.

Trubek, D.M., Cottrell, P. and Nance, M. (2005) '"Soft law", "hard law" and European integration: toward a theory of hybridity', University of Wisconsin Law School, Legal Studies Research Paper Series, no. 1002, November.

Tsakatika, M. (2004) 'The open method of co-ordination in the European Convention: an opportunity lost?', in L. Dobson and A. Føllesdal (eds), *Political Theory and the European Constitution*. London: Routledge. pp. 91–102.

Usui, Y. (2005) 'New modes of governance and the climate change strategy in the European Union: implications for democracy in regional integration', paper presented at the 1st CREP International Workshop, Tokyo 12–13 September.

Vandenbroucke, F. (2002) 'Forward: sustainable social justice and "open co-ordination" in Europe', in G. Esping-Andersen (ed.), *Why We Need a New Welfare State*. Oxford: Oxford University Press, pp. viii–xxiv.

Way, C. (2005) 'Political insecurity and the diffusion of financial market regulation', *Annals of the American Academy of Political and Social Science*, 598: 125–44.

Wessels, W. (2003) '(Open) methods of self coordination: new modes of governance as a typical step in the evolution of the EU system', *Beitrag für den Arbeitskreis Politische Steuerung der Deitschen Vereinigung für Politsche Wissenschaft*, Mainz, 25 September. Available online at: http://www.govecor.org.

Zeitlin, J. (2005a) 'The open method of coordination in action: theoretical promise, empirical realities, reform strategy', in J. Zeitlin and P. Pochet with L. Magnusson (eds), *The Open Method of Coordination in Action: the European Employment and Social Inclusion Strategies*. Brussels: P.I.E.-Peter Lang (pp. 447–503).

Zeitlin, J. (2005b) 'Social Europe and experimentalist governance: towards a new constitutional compromise?', *European Governance Papers (EUROGOV)* No. C-05-04. Available online at: http://www.connex-network.org/eurogov/pdf/egp-connex-C-05-04.pdf.

Zeitlin J. and Pochet, P. with Magnusson, L. (eds) (2005) *The Open Method of Coordination in action: the European employment and social inclusion strategies*. Brussels: P.I.E.-Peter Lang.

25

Europeanization: The Domestic Impact of European Union Politics

TANJA A. BÖRZEL AND THOMAS RISSE

INTRODUCTION

From Ernst Haas's legendary contribution *The Uniting of Europe* in 1958 (Haas 1958) to Andrew Moravcsik's *The Choice for Europe* in 1998 (Moravcsik 1998), the study of European integration has consisted of trying to understand and explain the 'Brussels processes' – the dynamics of European policy-making and European integration.[1] This is not surprising, since a new polity was in the making and required analysis. These were also the days of the theoretical battles among the various 'isms', from federalism and (neo-)functionalism to (liberal) intergovernmentalism and, most recently, social constructivism (on the latter see Christiansen et al. 2001). Yet, the 'dependent variable' of these efforts always remained the same: The focus was on explaining the processes and outcomes of European integration itself.

This changed in about the mid-1990s. More and more scholars became interested in understanding the domestic impact of Europe. How

does European integration affect the domestic policies, politics, and polities of the member states? Does the European Union (EU) impact upon policy changes, institutional transformation, or even to identity changes – and under what conditions? Finally, what is the overall outcome of these changes? Should we expect policy and/or institutional convergence among the EU member states as resulting from the domestic impact of Europe, or should we rather anticipate continuing divergence?

With these questions, research on Europeanization was born. Today, the study of Europeanization has become quite a cottage industry, as exemplified by various edited volumes (Goetz and Hix 2000; Cowles et al. 2001; Featherstone and Radaelli 2003a; Bulmer and Lequesne 2005). Moreover, there have been dozens of journal articles and monographs on the subject covering comparisons between countries and between policy-areas. Finally, the study of Europeanization has not stopped at the member states, but has turned to the accession countries in the meantime (e.g. Lippert et al. 2001; Schimmelfennig and Sedelmeier 2005b) and even to non-member states such as Norway and Switzerland (Kux and Sverdrup 2000; Gstöhl 2002; Egeberg 2005).

In sum, Europeanization has quickly become an exciting research area without which the study of European Union politics is incomplete. In the following, we review the emerging literature on Europeanization. We begin with a history of the concept and the way it has been used in the literature. We then review the empirical findings with regard to transformations in domestic policies, institutions, and identities, as well as concerning the Eastern enlargement countries. The third part of the chapter evaluates the various efforts at theorizing Europeanization, thereby concentrating on the concept of 'goodness of fit', on the mediating factors leading to or preventing Europeanization, and the overall outcome of Europeanization in terms of convergence or divergence. Our chapter concludes with some remarks on what the study of Europeanization contributes to research on EU politics in general. We argue that a theory of the EU as a multi-level polity requires both a 'bottom up' and a 'top down' perspective and that the former is insufficient without the latter, and vice versa.

FROM IMPLEMENTATION TO EUROPEANIZATION: THE HISTORY OF A CONCEPT

As argued in the introduction, research on Europeanization has become quite fashionable in EU studies in recent years (see also Featherstone 2003: 5), showing a significant increase during the late 1990s. But it is not without predecessors. Among them are studies on the implementation of EU policies that emerged in the second half of the 1990s (Héritier et al. 1994; Héritier et al. 1996; Duina 1997, 1999; but see already Wallace 1984; Siedentopf and Ziller 1988). In the meantime, implementation studies have given way to and have been refined to research on compliance with EU law (Börzel 2003; Falkner et al. 2005; Zürn and Joerges 2005).

In the early 1990s, students of European integration became increasingly interested in the impact of European processes and institutions on the member states. The first studies essentially turned around the explanatory logics of the two major paradigms of European integration, liberal intergovernmentalism and neofunctionalism. If intergovernmentalism was right in assuming that member-state governments controlled European integration while supranational institutions themselves exercised little independent effect, the power of the member states would not be challenged. Rather, European integration should enhance the control of national governments over domestic affairs since it removed issues from domestic controversy into the arena of executive control at the European level (Milward 1992; Moravcsik 1994). Proponents of neofunctionalism suggested exactly the opposite, namely that the European Union provided domestic actors, such as regions and interest groups, with independent channels of political access and influence at the European level (Marks 1993; Marks et al. 1996; Sandholtz 1996).

Interestingly enough, the Europeanization research that took off from the mid-1990s on, did not take any of the European integration 'isms' as its point of departure (see e.g. Ladrech 1994; Meny et al. 1996; Rometsch and Wessels 1996; Schmidt 1996). Coming out of comparative politics rather than international relations, most studies took the multi-level governance (MLG) framework on European integration as their point of departure (cf. Kohler-Koch and Eising 1999; Hooghe and Marks 2001).

Unfortunately, though, there has been little agreement in the literature on Europeanization about the usage of the term (for the following see for example Olsen 2002; Featherstone 2003; Radaelli 2003, 2004; Bulmer and Radaelli 2005).

Europeanization is understood in at least three different ways:

1. 'The emergence and development at the European level of distinct structures of governance [...]' (Risse et al. 2001: 3): Thus, Europeanization refers to EU-level processes

in a somewhat broader understanding of European integration.

2. 'The process of influence deriving from European decisions and impacting member states' policies and political and administrative structures' (Héritier et al. 2001; also Ladrech 1994: 17): Here, Europeanization is understood as a 'top-down' process by which European-level institutions and decisions shape and transform the domestic politics and institutions of member states.

3. 'Processes of (a) construction, (b) diffusion and (c) institutionalization of [...] rules, procedures, policy paradigms, [...] and shared beliefs and norms which are first defined and consolidated in the making of EU public policy and politics and then incorporated in the logic of domestic discourse, identities, political structures, and public policies' (Radaelli 2003: 30; similarly Olsen 2002). In a way, this understanding of Europeanization encompasses both the first and the second usage of the term and conceives of Europeanization as both a 'bottom up' and a 'top down' process.

In the broadest understanding then, Europeanization research would encompass both the traditional research agenda of European integration studies trying to explain 'Brussels processes' and the somewhat newer research agenda focusing on the domestic impact of Europe and the European Union (no matter whether we refer to member states or non-member states, see below). We do not find this latter understanding particularly useful. If Europeanization entails both the evolution of European integration and its domestic impact, it ceases to be a researchable subject matter, no matter how often we use terms such as 'co-evolution' or 'mutual adapation' (see Gualini 2003: 6; also Radaelli 2004: 3).

As a result, we suggest to understand Europeanization in the second sense of the term which also resonates with common sense: Accordingly, Europeanization would refer to the 'domestic impact of Europe' – the various ways in which institutions, processes and policies emanating from the European level influence policies, politics, and polities at the

domestic level (be it member or non-member states). It does not matter, in our view, whether Europeanization is triggered by domestic factors and actors (in fact, they often are when domestic actors use European-level developments to push for policy changes in their country; cf. Börzel 2005). In other words, one must not assume that European-level actors actively seek domestic transformation of the policies and institutions in member states or accession countries in order to be able to discern Europeanization. Moreover, the domestic impact of Europe does not necessarily mean that it always works directly. First, in many cases, countries adjust to Europe or the EU, and other member states or accession countries then emulate this particular type of adaptation. Second, Europeanization may work horizontally, without travelling directly via Brussels, if one country responds to policy developments in another country, as the Netherlands (e.g. Maarten Vink 2002) and France (e.g. Tomei 2001: 44–7) did when German immigration laws became more restrictive in 1992–93. Last not least, this research agenda does not exclude at all that there is a feedback loop running from change at the domestic level back unto the European level. All we recommend is to use the term Europeanization as focusing on the dimensions, mechanisms, and outcomes by which European processes and institutions affect domestic-level processes and institutions. In other words, Europeanization adopts a 'second image reversed' perspective, replayed at the European level (see Gourevitch 1978).

If we understand Europeanization in such a way, research in this context needs to tackle three interrelated questions:

1. Where does the EU affect the member states (dimensions of domestic change)? This question refers to the 'dependent variable' of change, i.e. policies, politics, and polities, but also to the particular issue-areas influenced by European-level processes and structures.

2. How do the EU and other European institutions[2] affect the member states

(mechanisms of domestic change)? This concerns the particular causal processes and mechanisms by which European level decisions and institutions influence domestic decisions and institutions. Here, concepts such as the 'goodness of fit', intervening factors, and the like, come into play.

3. What is the effect of the European Union and other European institutions on the member states (outcome of domestic change)? Controversies about convergence and continuing divergence form the core issues relating to this question.

These three questions are explored, in turn, in the third, fourth, and fifth sections of the chapter, below.

DIMENSIONS OF DOMESTIC CHANGE

Europeanization as Policy Change

The impact of Europe on the policies of the member states is probably the most intensively researched area in the Europeanization literature (cf. Featherstone 2003). It is also the most diverse. Strongly influenced by the literature on EU policy-making, many studies evaluate the implementation of or compliance with EU policies rather than domestic change as such (Haverland 1999; Börzel 2003; Giuliani 2003; Falkner et al. 2005). That said, the implementation of EU policies often requires significant adaptations in the member states, particularly if they do not fit domestic structures (see below). But the dimensions of policy change remain often ill specified and vary significantly from study to study. While some adopt a more narrow definition of policy, focusing on policy content, instruments, and regulatory style (type of intervention and character of interest intermediation; Börzel 2003; Haverland 2003), others include administrative structures (Héritier et al. 1996; Héritier et al. 2001; Knill 2001; Jordan and Liefferink 2004), policy paradigms (e.g. core beliefs on the role of the state), and policy discourses (Kohler-Koch

2002; Harcourt 2003; Falkner et al. 2005). This seems logical since policies are deeply embedded in institutions and political processes. As a result, the Europeanization of public policies may also affect the polity and politics of the member states (Cowles et al. 2001; Dyson 2002).

While there is a growing number of theoretically well informed studies, these works are necessarily limited by the number of cases and the dimension of change they can analyse at a time. Consequently, we still miss the big picture. The vast part of the Europeanization literature compares only two or three member states, which often include the 'usual suspects', France, Germany and the UK (for exceptions see Jordan and Liefferink 2004; Falkner et al. 2005). The same is true for the policy areas where environmental, social or regional policies have gained much more attention than other first-pillar issues, such as agriculture, public health or culture. Even less is known about the domestic impact of Europe on foreign and security policy (but see e.g. Manners and Whitman 2000; Smith 2000; Tonra 2001), and justice and home affairs (but see the literature on the Europeanization of immigration and asylum policy above and Favell 1998; Lavenex 2001).

Nevertheless, the policy literature presents some common insights. First, the impact of Europe on the policies of the member states is differential. Some member states have undergone deeper policy changes than others. While this may vary across issue areas, the Southern European latecomers (Spain, Greece, Portugal) have been generally more affected (Featherstone 2001; Liebert 2003: 277–80; Jordan and Liefferink 2004; Falkner et al. 2005). Second, the domestic impact of Europe is mostly felt with regard to policy standards and policy instruments, while the institutionally more entrenched administrative structures, policy styles and policy paradigms have been less affected. Thus, EU policies have resulted in tighter environmental and social standards in all member states. They have also led to the introduction of new policy instruments, which are incentive-based and encourage societal participation in policy-making (Knill and Lenschow

2000) or prescribe cross-policy integration (Liebert 2003). Yet, even in areas, where the EU has made ample use of its far-reaching policy-making competencies, the member states have not converged towards a common policy model (Héritier et al. 2001; Liebert 2003; Jordan and Liefferink 2004; Falkner et al. 2005; Kassim 2005). Third, Europe has hit virtually all policy areas. First-pillar issues have naturally been more affected since they are subject to supranational policy-making (see below), whereas the EU's reach into the foreign and security policy and the justice and home affairs of the member states is limited by the intergovernmental institutions of the second and third pillar. Within the first pillar, however, the domestic impact does not systematically vary between market making (negative integration) and market correcting (positive integration) policies. Market correcting policies, such as environment or social regulation, are certainly more likely to require direct policy changes by prescribing specific policy standards and policy instruments (Knill and Lehmkuhl 1999). However, the removal of national barriers to foreign competition has made a more profound impact on member state policies that goes right to the core. While EU policies hardly stipulate templates for deregulation and privatization, the liberalization of national markets has changed the dominant policy paradigm in member states like France, Germany, and Italy, where the state used to be responsible for the provision of public utilities (Héritier et al. 2001).

Europeanization as Institutional Change

While students of EU policy-making were mostly interested in domestic policy change, comparativists focused on Europe-induced changes in specific domestic institutions, both formal and informal. They have analysed whether and to what extent European processes, policies, and institutions affect domestic systems of interest intermediation (Schmidt 1996; Héritier et al. 2001), intergovernmental relations (Jones and Keating 1995; Bache 1998; Börzel 2002), national bureaucracies (Page and Wouters 1995; Kassim et al. 2000, 2001) and

administrative structures (Wright 1994; Rometsch and Wessels 1996; Knill 2001; Massey 2004), regulatory structures (Majone 1997; Coen and Thatcher 2000; Thatcher 2000; Jordana et al. 2005), the relationship between executive and legislature (Andersen and Burns 1996; Norton 1996; Raunio and Hix 2000; Maurer and Wessels 2001), judicial structures (Slaughter et al. 1998; Conant, 2002), and macro-economic institutions (Dyson 2002; Schmidt 2002b). A few studies have analysed how Europeanization has changed the domestic polity as a whole, examining changes in the overall 'constellation of institutions, procedures and rules associated with parliamentary democracy in each of the member states' (Anderson 2002: 794; Schmidt 2006).

Despite the impressive number of studies, no clear picture has emerged. While some find that domestic institutions have largely withstood Europeanization (Anderson 2002; Olsen 2002), others contend that the EU has 'federalized' and 'pluralized' the member states (Schmidt 1999a,b, 2006). The disagreement somehow reproduces the debate between liberal intergovernmentalists, supranationalists, and proponents of multi-level governance in the late 1980s on whether European integration strengthens, weakens or transforms the state. When focusing on meso-level institutions, the findings appear less contradictory. Thus, national administrations have responded to the 'demands of EU membership' (Kassim 2003) but institutional adaptation differs significantly and is mediated by pre-existing institutions (cf. Hanf and Soetendorp 1998; Harmsen 1999; Kassim et al. 2000). Moreover, there is at least one finding that seems to be uncontested – Europeanization has strengthened the central executive at the expense of parliaments despite their increased involvement in EU policy-making (Rometsch and Wessels 1996; Kassim et al. 2000; Maurer and Wessels 2001).

Europeanization as Change of Politics

The politics dimension has been least explored in the Europeanization literature (Featherstone

2003). There are many studies on how domestic actors seek to channel their interests into the European policy-making process (Mazey and Richardson 1993; Marks and McAdam 1996; Greenwood and Aspinwall 1998). Less has been done on the Europeanization of electoral and party politics (Featherstone 1988; Greven 1992; Gabel 2000; see also the chapters by Raunio and Ray in this volume). Since the EU offers fewer opportunities and more constraints to parties than to interest groups, its impact on party systems of the member states has been limited (Mair 2000; Ladrech 2005). But even interest groups, many of which have made Europe part of their lobbying strategies, remain firmly embedded in their national systems of interest intermediation (Greenwood and Aspinwall 1998; Eising 2003). We hardly know anything about how the emergence of a European structure of political and societal interest representation impacts on processes of political contestation and interest aggregation in the member states. While Mair, for example, argues that Europeanization contributes to de-politicization, indifference, and political disengagement (Mair 2000; see also Schmidt 2006), Harcourt and Radaelli contend that European policy-making causes an increasing politicization at the domestic level (Harcourt and Radaelli 1999; Imig and Tarrow 2000).

Europeanization as Public Discourse and Identity Change

Research on 'Europeanization as discourse' has become part and parcel of the social constructivist research program pertaining to EU politics (see e.g. Christiansen et al. 2001; Hay and Rosamond 2002; Risse 2003). Most of this work concerns the policy discourses, frames, and narratives that construct meanings, legitimize, and accompany public policies (e.g. Radaelli 1999; Schmidt 2002a; Mörth 2003; Schmidt and Radaelli 2004). Political actors often reframe policy problems in European terms thereby actively constructing adaptational pressures and demanding policy changes in response to European pressures. The same holds true for the 'Europe made me

do it' legitimation of costly domestic policy changes whereby blame is being shifted to Brussels and to European institutions irrespective of whether domestic actors actively sought specific EU rules and regulations.

However, this type of legitimation only works if and when 'Europe' and European integration invoke positive connotations and strong public support in national public discourses. But what about Europeanization as identity change – the impact of European integration on the transformation of national collective identities? As with Europeanization research in general, scholarship on European identity has taken off in recent years from a variety of disciplinary perspectives (e.g. Breakwell and Lyons 1996; Eder and Giesen 1999; Risse 2002; Diez Medrano 2003; Marks and Hooghe 2003; Bruter 2004a; Herrmann et al. 2004). First, this research has empirically demonstrated that most Europeans hold multiple identities. 'Nation first, but Europe, too' is the dominant outlook in most EU member states, and people do not perceive this as contradictory (see Marks and Hooghe 2003; Citrin and Sides 2004). The real cleavage in mass public opinion is between those who exclusively identify with their nation, on the one hand, and those perceiving themselves as attached to both their nation and Europe, on the other hand. Support for European integration increases markedly, the more people identify with Europe and the EU, if only as a secondary identity.

Second, people clearly distinguish between Europe as a broader cultural concept, on the one hand, and Europe defined in civic or political terms, on the other (see Bruter 2004a, 2004b). 'Europe' as a civic and political space is largely defined by the EU and its institutions. Third, however, the Europeanization of nation-state identities comes in national colours. Europe and the EU resonate differently with existing narratives of historical traditions, memories, experiences, and symbols. Opinion poll data show an enormous variation between countries concerning the degree to which people identify with Europe and the EU. Moreover, given the variation in the discursive construction of Europe, Europe and the EU mean different things in different national contexts.

While we know quite a bit about the 'dependent variable' in this case, namely the extent to which people identify with Europe and the EU, it is far less clear how the process of European integration has affected identification processes over time. Unfortunately, the current state of the art does not yet allow for firm answers.

A pre-condition for the emergence of Europeanized identities is the Europeanization of public spheres. Citizens have usually no access to EU politics other than through their national media. What do we know about the Europeanization of national public spheres (for the following see Hodess 1997; Eder and Kantner 2000; Semetko et al. 2000; Trenz 2002; Koopmans and Erbe 2003; Kantner 2004)? Two findings seem to stick out. First, media reporting about the EU still pales in comparison to information about national and local politics, even though media observation of European events seems to have increased in recent years. Second, however, to the extent that media do report about Europe and EU politics, they use similar interpretive frames across national public spheres. While there are few European-wide media and while Europeans do not speak a common language, interpretive structures and meaning constructions do not differ much in the various public spheres, thus allowing for transnational communication in principle. Moreover, fellow Europeans are increasingly regarded as legitimate speakers in national public spheres.

Europeanization and EU Enlargement

Students of Europeanization have been awarded a real-world experiment recently in the context of the EU's Eastern enlargement process as a result of which it is increasingly examined in this framework (see Grabbe 2003; Goetz 2005; Schimmelfennig and Sedelmeier 2005b). Eastern enlargement is particularly well suited to test hypotheses about Europeanization for various reasons. First, the Central East European Countries (CEEC) have

followed different historical trajectories than the advanced Western European democracies, in particular concerning their recent transition from communism. Second, the CEECs have had little 'uploading' capacity in terms of the ability to influence EU decisions prior to accession. They had to merely 'download' the acquis communitaire that thus, created enormous need for adaptation (e.g. Lippert et al. 2001: 984). Finally and resulting from this, we would expect stronger convergence with particular EU policy models because of the speed with which the CEECs had to adjust to Europe, their openness to EU influence in the light of the post-communist transition process (Héritier 2005), and because of the breadth and scope of the EU agenda (Grabbe 2001: 1014, Hughes et al. 2001; Brusis 2002; Grabbe 2003: 306–8).

Yet, Europeanization studies of Eastern enlargement countries show a mixed picture that does not completely confirm the expectations. Most scholars agree that 'enlargement is the main driving force and the main condition of effective EU rule export in this region' (Schimmelfennig and Sedelmeier 2005a: 221). EU conditionality and the membership perspective provided a huge incentive for CEECs to adjust to Europe and to 'download' EU policies in the various sectors. At the same time, EU rules and norms had to be adopted in a rather inflexible way with regard to the single market and the various sectoral policies. In this sense then, Europeanization strongly resembles a one-way street and top-down process (see, however, Tulmets 2005, for a more balanced picture).

At the same time, the Europeanization of CEECs confirms some of the findings of the literature on the 'old' member states, particularly with regard to the impact on East European polities and politics. First, Europeanization has strengthened core executives across the board and increased their autonomy from domestic political and societal pressures (Goetz 2005: 272). It has also led to the development of a non-politicized civil service and to some degree of decentralization and regionalization, at least in comparison with the Communist legacy.

Second, however, the effects on institutions and politics vary considerably. As Frank Schimmelfennig and others demonstrate in particular, EU political conditionality only worked in cases of unstable democracies by strengthening liberal politics, while being irrelevant in those countries with strong democratic constituencies or in autocratically ruled states (Schimmelfennig 2005; see also Kelley 2004, on minority policies). In general, most studies on Europeanization in the East confirm the differential impact of Europe and the EU. There has been little institutional convergence around a single European model of governance, while divergent endogenous interests prevailed over external pressures at institutional convergence (Lippert et al. 2001; Grabbe 2003; Goetz 2005).

Third, as Klaus Goetz points out, while the institutional and policy effects on the CEECs have been immediate and fast because of accession conditionality (also Schimmelfennig and Sedelmeier 2005a), the long-term outcome might be much more shallow and also reversible (Goetz 2005: 262). Why should Eastern European countries invest in 'deep Europeanization' and lock in specific institutional arrangements given their generally weak state capacity and the enormous uncertainty surrounding enlargement (Grabbe 2003: 318–23)? Last but not least, the strong and 'top-down' accession conditionality could well have the unanticipated effect of hindering social learning and policy emulation so as to result in 'shallow Europeanization'.

In sum then, the Europeanization of CEECs shows some peculiarities with regard to the strong pressures for adaptation emanating from the EU and reinforced by conditionality. But the general picture emerging from the studies confirms largely the existing literature on Europeanization, particularly the emphasis on the differential impact of Europe.

THEORIZING EUROPEANIZATION

How can we explain the differential impact of Europe? Scholars have devoted considerable attention to developing conceptual frameworks which would help to explain Europeanization processes. As we argue below, these frameworks can be roughly divided between rationalist and constructivist approaches which posit distinctive microfoundations and causal mechanisms of Europeanization. Before we turn to these arguments, we want to briefly review the 'goodness of fit' proposition that has sparked so much debate among scholars of Europeanization.

Much Ado About (Almost) Nothing: Goodness of Fit

Irrespective of the theoretical approach chosen, most empirical studies quoted above find that there must be some 'misfit', 'mismatch', or incompatibility between European and domestic policies, processes, and institutions (e.g. Héritier et al. 1996; Knill and Lenschow 1998; Börzel 1999; Duina 1999; Risse et al. 2001). The 'goodness of fit' or congruence between the European and the domestic level determines whether we should expect domestic change in response to European policies, processes, and institutions. Only if European policies, institutions, and/or processes differ significantly from those found at the domestic level, is there any need for member states (or accession candidates) to change. Two types of misfit have been identified in the literature.

First, European policies might cause a 'policy misfit' between European rules and regulations, on the one hand, and domestic policies, on the other (cf. Héritier et al. 1996; Schmidt 2001; Börzel 2003). Here, policy misfits equal compliance problems. European policies can challenge national policy goals, regulatory standards, the instruments used to achieve policy goals, and/or the underlying problem-solving approach. Member state resistance to adapt domestic policies usually results in violations of European legal requirements. Policy misfit can also affect underlying institutions and political processes.

Second, Europe can cause 'institutional misfit' challenging domestic rules and procedures and the collective understandings attached to them (see e.g. Knill and Lenschow 2001a).

European rules and procedures, which give national governments privileged decision powers vis-à-vis other domestic actors, might conflict with the territorial institutions of highly decentralized member states which grant their regions autonomous decision powers (Börzel 2002). Europe might even threaten deeply collective understandings of national identity as it touches upon constitutive norms such as state sovereignty (Checkel 2001a; Risse 2001). At the same time, the more institutional congruence between the EU and domestic ways 'of doing things', the fewer requirements for institutional change and adaptation exist.

The 'goodness of fit' proposition as a starting point for theorizing the domestic impact of Europe has led to heated debates in the scholarly community and has been challenged on various grounds. Since much of the criticism is raised against our own contributions to the debate (particularly Risse et al. 2001; Börzel and Risse 2003; Börzel 2005), let us comment on the controversy and refine our argument.

First, Knill and Lehmkuhl argue that the relevance of misfit is limited to the EU's market-correcting policies, such as environmental regulations, which positively prescribe or impose a concrete model for domestic compliance. Market-making policies – or negative integration – by contrast, would leave the member states too much flexibility and discretion in order to exert pressure for adaptation (Knill and Lehmkuhl 1999; also Radaelli 2003; Bulmer and Radaelli 2005: 347). Second, Héritier et al. criticize the static perspective, which ignores that the goalposts of goodness of fit may change over time depending on the stage of the national policy process. Even if European policies initially fit domestic regulations, they may empower domestic actors to introduce changes that go against European requirements resulting in 'ex-post' misfit (Héritier et al. 2001). A third criticism focuses on the fragility of domestic institutions. If they are in a performance crisis or in endogenous transition, domestic institutions may not be sufficiently robust in order to be challenged by European policies, processes, and institutions (Knill and Lenschow 2001a). This applies, in

particular, to the Southern European member states and the Central and Eastern European accession countries, where EU membership has been associated with institution-building rather than institutional change. Finally, Thatcher argues that, in the case of the telecommunications sector, there has been little adaptational pressure emanating from Europe to explain the degree to which telecommunications has been liberalized and de-regulated in the various member states (Thatcher 2004, see, however, Schneider 2001).

So, what is the theoretical status of the 'goodness of fit' proposition? First, it is based on a standard social science proposition that can be found in cognitive psychology as well as in organizational and institutional analysis (irrespective of whether we are using a rational choice or a constructivist approach): Human beings as well as social institutions prefer continuity over change. As a result, transformations are not to be expected, unless there is some necessity for it. Thus, we shall only expect domestic change in response to European developments – our 'dependent variable' here – if there is some degree of misfit between domestic policies, processes, and institutions, on the one hand, and developments at the European level, on the other. This is the ontological status of the 'goodness of fit' proposition. Otherwise, the proposition is theoretically neutral, that is, it can serve as a starting point for both rationalist and constructivist accounts of Europeanization.

Second, nobody argued that a lacking congruence between European and domestic policies, processes, and institutions suffices to account for domestic change. Hence, the emphasis is on 'mediating factors' to explain Europeanization (see below). Third, 'goodness of fit' should not be reified as a static concept. There are, of course, cases in which EU rules and regulation directly exert compliance pressure in an almost hierarchical sense by prescribing particular and specific policy and/or institutional responses by the member states. Mostly, however, European rules and processes do not require specific domestic responses as a result of which the degree of 'misfit' is subject to interpretation and to creative usage (see also Radaelli 2004: 4, on this point).

This leads to a fourth point, which is the most important conclusion we draw from the extensive debate about the 'goodness of fit'. We agree with Sophie Jacquot and Cornelia Woll (Jacquot and Woll 2003) that 'misfit' or incongruence between European and domestic decisions, processes, and institutions does not necessarily imply pressure for adaptation as such.[3] Whether 'misfit' leads to pressure for domestic adaptation or not depends on the active intervention of actors, be it European or domestic. In this understanding, 'pressure for adaptation' is itself part and parcel of the process by which domestic change in response to Europe is being induced. When the European Commission opens infringement proceedings against a member state, policy misfit turns into adaptational pressure 'from above'. Likewise, domestic actors can employ policy misfit to push for policy changes 'from below' (Börzel 2003). Such differential empowerment is by no means confined to market-making policies. Domestic reform coalitions have been able to exploit the EU-induced liberalization of national markets to push for adaptations that go far beyond EU requirements (Héritier et al. 2001). In any case, there has to be some misfit for domestic actors to be empowered in the first place. Social constructivists might add that, thus, the degree to which 'misfit' results in political pressures for adaptation is itself subject to meaning construction in discursive processes.

In sum, the 'goodness of fit' proposition amounts to nothing more than an enabling condition for the domestic impact of Europe, a starting point without much causal weight in and of itself. Domestic change in response to Europe and the EU then requires domestic or European actors to actively construct 'adaptational pressures' and to engage in politics. This is where the causal story starts in earnest about processes of Europeanization.

Europeanization as a Process of Redistributing Resources

Resource-dependency approaches are based on rationalist institutionalism, which assumes that actors are rational, goal-oriented, and purposeful following a 'logic of consequentialism' (cf. March and Olsen 1989, 1998; Hall and Taylor 1996). As any individual or corporate actor is dependent on others to achieve his or her goals, actors have to exchange their resources to produce desired outcomes. The resource exchange is based on the mutual assessment of resources, strategies, and interests.

From this perspective, Europe is largely conceived as an emerging political opportunity structure which offers some actors additional legal and political resources to exert influence, while severely constraining the ability of others to pursue their goals (Kohler-Koch and Eising 1999; Hix and Goetz 2000; Héritier et al. 2001). Such changes in the political opportunities and constraints for domestic actors result in a redistribution of resources among them, empowering some over others. Those empowered are likely to actively construct an existing 'misfit' between European and domestic decisions, processes, and institutions into pressure for domestic adaptation. The 'differential empowerment' may not only alter domestic institutions but also change domestic policies and political processes.

Yet, even if European level developments have modified the domestic opportunity structures, domestic change is not automatic, but still faces constraints as well as enabling conditions. The Europeanization literature has identified two institutional factors that influence the capacities of domestic actors to exploit new opportunities and avoid constraints with opposite effects: multiple veto players and facilitating formal institutions. First, even under conditions of severe 'misfit', the existence of multiple veto points can empower domestic actors with diverse interests to avoid constraints and, thus, effectively inhibit domestic adaptation (Tsebelis 1995; Haverland 2000; Giuliani 2003). The more power is dispersed across the political system and the more actors have a say in political decision-making, the more difficult it is to foster the domestic 'winning coalition' necessary to introduce changes in response to Europeanization pressures.

Second, facilitating formal institutions can provide actors with material and ideational resources necessary to exploit European opportunities and thus promote domestic adaptation (Risse et al. 2001). The European political opportunity structure may offer domestic actors additional resources. But they are not able to deploy them when they lack the necessary action capacity. For example, public agencies and related complementary institutions in the UK helped women's organizations with the means to use EU equal pay and equal treatment directives in furthering gender equality (Tesoka 1999; Caporaso and Jupille 2001).

Europeanization as a Process of Socialization

Socialization approaches draw on the sociological strand of neo-institutionalism, which contrasts the rationalist 'logic of consequentialism' with a 'logic of appropriateness' (March and Olsen 1998). Actors are guided by collectively shared understandings of what constitutes proper – socially accepted behaviour in a given rule structure. Such collective understandings and intersubjective meaning structures influence the way actors define their goals and what they perceive as rational action. From this perspective, Europeanization entails processes of social learning by which domestic actors and organizations incorporate new rules, norms, practices, and meanings. Domestic actors are socialized into European norms and rules of appropriateness through processes of persuasion and social learning and redefine their interests and identities accordingly (cf. Checkel 2001b). This perspective also generates expectations about the differential impact of Europeanization, but it conceives of 'misfit' primarily in terms of incompatibilities of norms and meaning structures between Europe and the domestic level. Accordingly, 'adaptational pressures' refer to social understandings including discursive processes.

Again, two mediating factors account for the degree to which misfit leads to processes of socialization by which actors internalize new norms and develop new identities: norm entrepreneurs and cultural understandings. First, norm entrepreneurs mobilize at the domestic level to persuade actors to redefine their interests and identities in the light of the new norms and rules by engaging them in processes of social learning. Two types of norm- and idea-promoting agents can be identified. Epistemic communities are networks of actors with an authoritative claim to knowledge and a normative agenda (Haas 1992). They legitimate new norms and ideas by providing scientific knowledge about cause-and-effect relationships. Advocacy or principled issue networks are bound together by shared beliefs and values rather than by consensual knowledge (Sabatier and Jenkins-Smith 1993; Keck and Sikkink 1998). They appeal to collectively shared norms and identities in order to persuade other actors to reconsider their goals and preferences.

Second, the Europeanization literature has identified a cooperative political culture as facilitating domestic change. Informal institutions and cultural understandings entail collective understandings of appropriate behaviour that influence the ways in which domestic actors respond to pressures for Europeanization. A consensus-oriented or cooperative decision-making culture helps to overcome multiple veto points by rendering their use for actors inappropriate. For example, the litigational culture of Germany encouraged its citizens to appeal to national courts for the deficient application of Community Law, while such a culture was absent in France where litigation is much lower (Conant 2001, 2002). Moreover, a consensus-oriented culture allows for a sharing of adaptational costs, which facilitates the accommodation of pressure for adaptation. Rather than shifting adaptational costs upon a social or political minority, the 'winners' of domestic change compensate the 'losers' (Héritier et al. 2001; Börzel 2002).

So far, the Europeanization literature is inconclusive concerning whether the resource dependency model or the socialization model carries more causal weight. A recent study on the Europeanization of Central Eastern Europe appears to strongly confirm the rationalist model (Schimmelfennig and Sedelmeier 2005a) arguing against institutional inertia as theorized by sociological institutionalism. Yet, this study also points to the significance of mediating factors, in particular the presence of EU centred expert networks ('epistemic communities') as knowledge brokers.

Thus, these mediating factors and mechanisms that the Europeanization literature has identified as promoting or hindering domestic change in response to Europe, should not be regarded as mutually exclusive, but as complementary. For example, norm entrepreneurs or knowledge brokers who actively construct adaptational pressures emanating from Europe in order to change actors' interests and to induce domestic change, can still be facing active veto players in a political system which can only be overcome because of an existing cooperative culture. The mediating factors and causal mechanisms identified above often occur simultaneously, but they may also pull in different directions. Or they characterize different phases in processes of change. Future Europeanization research has to figure out how the causal mechanisms relate to each other (Olsen 2002; Börzel and Risse 2003).

Some have argued that the causal mechanisms identified above vary according to policy type (see Knill and Lehmkuhl 1999; Radaelli 2003; Bulmer and Lequesne 2005). In cases of positive integration or market-correcting policies, the EU could actually force member states to adapt because of legally binding prescriptions for domestic change ('vertical Europeanization'). In contrast, negative integration or market-making policies (Bulmer and Lequesne 2005) would not prescribe any specific policy changes as a result of which Europeanization would work more horizontally and indirectly through altering political opportunity structures and regulatory competition pressures.

We see little empirical evidence for these propositions. Empirical findings show that causal mechanisms do not systematically vary between policy types (see e.g. Schimmelfennig and Sedelmeier 2005b). Europeanization of a policy area can combine 'vertical' and 'horizontal' mechanisms (see the regulation of media markets as an example of negative integration, Harcourt 2003; and environmental

policy as a case of positive integration, Bugdahn 2005). Nevertheless, theory-guided research on the causal mechanisms of Europeanization has only begun, and it is far too early to come to firm conclusions as to what explains the observable variation in mechanisms.

THE OUTCOME OF DOMESTIC CHANGE

Deep Impact? The Scope of Domestic Change

The literature has convincingly demonstrated that Europeanization does indeed occur. Europe and the EU lead to domestic changes, which can be neither explained away by globalization pressures or endogenous national developments. Yet, the scope of change is far from clear and we still lack good explanations for the degree of change that European-level processes and institutions induce in domestic politics, policies, and polities. The literature broadly distinguishes between different outcomes regarding the degree of change (Cowles and Risse 2001; Héritier et al. 2001; Radaelli 2003, 2004), ranging from inertia as the absence of change all the way to substantial transformation, i.e., the replacement of existing policies, processes, and institutions by new and substantially different ones.

The theoretical approaches identified above generate different propositions about the scope of domestic change. They both take misfit as the necessary condition of domestic change and converge around the expectation that the lower the misfit, the smaller the pressure for adaptation is likely to be. Actors seeking to invoke the EU-level to justify and legitimate domestic reforms, require some significant misfit, which they may translate in greater domestic change than the degree of misfit might lead us to expect (Haverland 2000). But the two approaches depart on the effect of high misfit. For resource dependency, the higher the misfit, the more likely domestic reform coalitions will be empowered. Whether high misfit results in transformation then depends on the number of veto points and the existence of supporting institutions. Socialization approaches, by contrast, expect high misfit challenging core features of domestic policies and institutions to result in inertia since domestic actors will refuse to replace norms, rules, and practices by new ones (Knill[*] 2001). Actors are more open to learning and persuasion if new norms, rules, and practices resonate with the ones they are familiar with (Checkel 1999). Transformation should only occur under exceptional circumstances, such as performance crises (Olsen 1996) or if powerful norm entrepreneurs exist that are supported by coercive pressures.

It is too early to reach firm conclusions on these propositions. Yet, it seems to be clear from the empirical evidence that the EU's impact on domestic policy change has been far greater than its influence on domestic politics and institutions, with the possible exception of the new Eastern member states (see Grabbe 2003; Goetz 2005). Given the more than 40 years of continuously expanding EU policy-making power, the degree of domestic change induced by Europe appears to be limited.

The most common domestic impact of Europe appears to be absorption – the incorporation of European requirements into existing policies and institutions, or accommodation, that is the adaptation of existing policies and institutions without changing core features.[4] In the absence of norm entrepreneurs or facilitating institutions, inertia appears to be the first domestic reaction in cases of severe policy misfit. However, when the EU Commission starts infringement procedures and, thus, increases the adaptational pressure, member states often seek to absorb or accommodate European policies by 'patching up' the policy instruments that are not compatible with their existing arrangements. This often impairs the effective implementation of EU policies but leaves the core of the policy regime intact (Knill and Lenschow 2001a).

In contrast, transformative outcomes are likely in those cases in which national governments succeed in 'uploading' their preferences to the European level in order to introduce domestic reforms that have failed due to veto players. Thus, Europeanization often leads to

the domestic empowerment of governments (Moravcsik 1994; Dyson and Featherstone 1999; Haverland 2000). Transformative change is also likely if there is a strong domestic pro-reform constituency that succeeds in 'pulling down' the European policies to the domestic level (Héritier et al. 2001; Börzel 2003).

Interestingly enough, and in contrast to some expectations in the literature, EU-induced market liberalization reforms seem to have led to deeper domestic change including institutional transformation than positive integration, even though the EU does not prescribe policy models in these cases, but simply requires member states to open up to competition by deregulating their markets and by privatizing former state monopolies. In these cases, adaptational pressures often emanate from globalization rather than from the EU, but adaptation to these pressures would have been slower and less comprehensive without the EU stepping in (see Thatcher 2000). Moreover, the EU often helps diffusing certain policy models, such as regulatory agencies (Harcourt 2003).

While Europeanization as policy change has been profound in many cases, the impact on domestic institutions is still significant, but, in general, did not result in radically transforming state institutions (Anderson 2002; Olsen 2002). Moreover, the institutional impact of Europe tends to be differential and asymmetrical, affecting some member states more than others. Moreover, national core institutions such as the respective welfare systems or the territorial structures appear to be rather resistant to transformative change (Kassim 2005). These overall results strongly confirm historical institutionalist arguments concerning institutional inertia and path-dependent processes according to which we should expect radical institutional transformation only in exceptional cases of severe crises and critical junctures (see March and Olsen 1989; Pierson 1996).

Convergence or Divergence?

Is Europeanization making the European states more similar? The literature has found little evidence for a general homogenization or convergence across the board of domestic institutions, policies, and processes toward common models and approaches (Cowles and Risse 2001; Héritier et al. 2001; Featherstone and Radaelli 2003a; Bulmer and Lequesne 2005). This is not too surprising. The EU hardly prescribes a model to which member states would have to adjust. Even though EU policies may provide a template, they resemble a 'regulatory patchwork' rather than a coherent model combining different problem-solving approaches and policy instruments, sometimes even within one policy (Héritier 1996). In the absence of a uniform EU policy model, we should neither expect national policies to converge nor to profoundly transform. Moreover, EU directives are only framework legislation that, by design, grant the member states leeway to fit EU policies into their national arrangements. Often, EU policies constrain rather than bind member states in their policy choices (Radaelli 1997; Featherstone 1998). Finally, the effect of European policies, institutions, and processes is filtered through existing domestic institutions, policies and interests. The number of veto points, supporting formal institutions, norm entrepreneurs, and cooperative informal institutions mediate between the 'goodness of fit', the pressures for adaptation, and the outcome of domestic changes.

We should expect at best some 'clustered convergence' among European states facing similar pressures for adaptation because similar actors are empowered and are likely to learn from each other in searching effective ways of responding to European pressures (Börzel 1999). Since most studies only compare a limited number of countries and policies, the jury is still out whether Europeanization gives rise at least to clustered convergence.

Despite its differential impact, however, Europe has not caused divergence among states, either, driving them further apart. There are no indications that member state variation in their domestic institutions and policies has increased. The dominant finding is persistence and diversity that needs to be explained. Consequently, measuring convergence and

divergence may be of limited use in analysing the domestic impact of Europe, particularly since answers vary according to the level at which one looks for convergence or divergence (Knill and Lenschow 2001b; Kassim 2003: 90–2; Radaelli 2003: 51–2).

Finally, the convergence we do observe does not necessarily originate at the European level (Schmidt 2001; Schneider 2001). The EU is not always the driving force, but complements and may enhance global, but also national trends that were already affecting the nation-states. Globalization in particular appears to be the major rival for Europeanization in driving domestic change. While some studies have attempted to separate effects of Europeanization and globalization (e.g. Schneider 2001; Verdier and Breen 2001), it is often difficult to isolate the 'net effect' of Europe and to disentangle it from other sources of domestic change not only at the global, but also at the national and local level.[5] Careful process-tracing and attention to time-sequences should allow for separating out globalization and Europeanization effects. Concerning the liberalization of telecommunication markets, for example, one can demonstrate that EU member states such as the UK liberalized their markets even before the EU Commission became active in this area, while the liberalization of the Italian telecommunication markets would not have been possible without active EU involvement (Schneider 2001).

In the latter case, Europeanization served as an accelerator of larger globalization forces. In other cases, however, Europeanization works as a shield against globalization. The most prominent (and also most problematic) example is probably the Common Agricultural Policy (CAP), without which farming would probably not exist in some EU member states given the international market pressures. The recent debate about a 'European social model' is largely framed in terms of Europeanization as enabling the European welfare state to survive against the forces of globalization. Yet, the current state of the art of Europeanization research does not allow for firm conclusions on how Europeanization and globalization relate to each other.

CONCLUSIONS: TRIALS AND TRIBULATIONS OF THE EUROPEANIZATION RESEARCH

In the last two decades, research on Europeanization and domestic change has accelerated and asserted itself as a new and exciting research agenda in European Studies. Theory-building is still in progress. It is informed by different strands of research, including international relations, policy analysis, comparative politics, organizational theory, and discourse analysis. While Europeanization is a pluralistic and 'conversant research agenda' (Featherstone and Radaelli 2003b), it has yielded significant insights in the domestic impact of Europe which serves as a reference point for most studies and can be summarized in a few points:

1. European integration has had substantial effects on the policies, politics, and polities of the member states and beyond, irrespective of a country's size or deeply entrenched history of institutions. Old and new member states have been Europeanized, as well as big and small ones. Yet, the EU penetration into the member states is neither universal nor uniform but is marked by diversity and asymmetry.
2. While a certain 'misfit' between EU rules, policies, and institutions, on the one hand, and domestic policies and institutions, on the other hand, is a pre-condition for domestic changes, it is by no means sufficient. Most recently, research on Europeanization has started identifying mediating factors in a more systematic way that explain the variation in domestic transformation across countries and across policy-areas.
3. The overall outcome of Europeanization is neither convergence across the board nor continuing divergence. Rather, 'clustered convergence' among countries and policy-areas facing similar adjustment problems and similar mediating factors appears to be the overall result.

In conclusion, we would like to highlight one area that is still under-explored. While most of the work discussed in this chapter concentrates on 'vertical Europeanization', i.e. the domestic impact of European policies, rules, and meaning constructions, we know far less about 'horizontal Europeanization' or 'transnational cultural diffusion' (see Featherstone 2003: 7; also Radaelli 2003: 41). In many cases, Europeanization works 'sideways' through processes of emulation, mimicking, and lesson-drawing. EU member states often copy from their counterparts structures and procedures that have proved to be successful (Harmsen 1999; Radaelli 2000; Kassim 2003). Regulatory competition can also lead to horizontal Europeanization in the sense that 'best practices' are adopted by European states without any input from the EU or from Brussels-based institutions. Last not least, sociological institutionalists point out that frequent contact and interaction which is so common in a multi-level polity such as the EU should lead to institutional isomorphism as well as to collectively shared norms and understandings (Rometsch and Wessels 1996; Olsen 1997: 161). Yet, we know rather little about the dynamics of this type of Europeanization, which might be even more profound than Europeanization as 'adjusting to Brussels'.

NOTES

1. We thank the editors of this volume for their very useful comments. We also thank Tina Freyburg for research assistance.

2. For reasons of scope, we focus on the domestic impact of the EU exclusively. This does not mean, however, that we reduce the concept of Europeanization to EUization.

3. Here, the formulations in Risse et al. (2001), Börzel and Risse (2003), and Börzel (2005) have indeed been misleading.

4. For a more detailed overview over the different outcomes regarding scope and degree of change see Börzel (2005: 58–60).

5. For a discussion see for example Ross, who postulates among others that the support for further integration by the EU member states in the mid-1980s – when globalization pressure intensified – was based on ideas being totally different from those attached to globalization (Ross 1998).

REFERENCES

Andersen, S.S. and Burns, T. (1996) 'The European Union and the erosion of parliamentary democracy: a study of post-parliamentary governance', in S.S. Andersen and K.A. Eliassen (eds), *The European Union: How Democratic Is It?* London: Sage. pp. 227–51.

Anderson, J.J. (2002) 'Europeanization and the transformation of the democratic polity', *Journal of Common Market Studies*, 40(5): 793–822.

Bache, I. (1998) *The Politics of EU Regional Policy: Multilevel Governance or Flexible Gatekeeping?* Sheffield: Sheffield Academic Press.

Börzel, T.A. (1999) 'Towards convergence in Europe? Institutional adaptation to Europeanization in Germany and Spain', *Journal of Common Market Studies*, 37(4): 573–96.

Börzel, T.A. (2002) *States and Regions in Europe. Institutional Adaptation in Germany and Spain.* Cambridge: Cambridge University Press.

Börzel, T.A. (2003) *Environmental Leaders and Laggards in Europe. Why There is (Not) a Southern Problem.* London: Ashgate.

Börzel, T.A. (2005) 'Europeanization: how the European Union interacts with its member states', in S. Bulmer and C. Lequesne (eds), *The Member States of the European Union.* Oxford: Oxford University Press. pp. 45–69

Börzel, T.A., and Risse, T. (2003) 'Conceptualizing the domestic impact of Europe', in K. Featherstone and C.M. Radaelli (eds), *The Politics of Europeanization.* Oxford: Oxford University Press. pp. 57–80.

Breakwell, G.M. and Lyons, E. (eds) (1996) *Changing European Identities. Social Psychological Analyses of Change.* Oxford: Butterworth-Heinemann.

Brusis, M. (2002) 'Between EU requirements, competitive politics, and national traditions: re-creating regions in the accession countries of Central and Eastern Europe', *Governance: An International Journal of Policy and Administration,* 15(4): 531–59.

Bruter, M. (2004a) *Citizens of Europe? The Emergence of Mass European Identity.* London: Palgrave – Macmillan.

Bruter, M. (2004b) 'Civic and cultural components of a European identity. A pilot model of measurement of citizens levels of European identity', in R.K. Herrmann, T. Risse and M. Brewer (eds), *Transnational Identities. Becoming European in the European Union.* Lanham MD: Rowman and Littlefield. pp. 186–213.

Bugdahn, S. (2005) 'Of Europeanization and domestication: the implementation of the environmental information directive in Ireland, Great Britain and Germany', *Journal of European Public Policy,* 12(1): 177–99.

Bulmer, S. and Lequesne, C. (eds) (2005) *The Member States of the European Union.* Oxford: Oxford University Press.

Bulmer, S., and Radaelli, C.M. (2005) 'The Europeanization of national policy', in S. Bulmer and C.M. Radaelli (eds), *The Member States of the European Union.* Oxford: Oxford University Press. pp. 338–59.

Caporaso, J.A. and Jupille, J. (2001) 'The Europeanization of gender equality policy and domestic structural change', in M.G. Cowles, J.A. Caporaso and T. Risse (eds), *Transforming Europe. Europeanization and Domestic Change.* Ithaca. NY: Cornell University Press. pp. 21–43.

Checkel, J.T. (1999) 'Norms, institutions, and national identity in contemporary Europe', *International Studies Quarterly,* 43(March): 83–114.

Checkel, J.T. (2001a) 'The Europeanization of citizenship?', in M.G. Cowles, J.A. Caporaso and T. Risse (eds), *Transforming Europe. Europeanization and Domestic Change.* Ithaca, NY: Cornell University Press. pp. 180–97.

Checkel, J.T. (2001b) 'Why comply? Social learning and European identity change', *International Organization,* 55(3): 553–88.

Christiansen, T., Jørgensen, K.E. and Wiener, A. (eds) (2001) *The Social Construction of Europe.* London et al.: Sage.

Citrin, J. and Sides, J. (2004) 'More than nationals: how identity choice matters in the new Europe', in R.K. Herrmann, T. Risse and M. Brewer (eds), *Transnational Identities. Becoming European in the EU.* Lanham MD: Rowman and Littlefield. pp. 161–85.

Coen, D. and Thatcher, M. (eds) (2000) *Utilities Reform in Europe.* New York: Nova Press.

Conant, L.J. (2001) 'Europeanization and the courts: variable patterns of adaptation among national judiciaries', in M.G. Cowles, J.A. Caporaso and T. Risse (eds), *Transforming Europe. Europeanization and Domestic Change.* Ithaca, NY: Cornell. pp. 97–115.

Conant, L.J. (2002) *Justice Contained. Law and Politics in the European Union.* Ithaca NY: Cornell University Press.

Cowles, M.G. and Risse, T. (2001) 'Transforming Europe: conclusions', in M. G. Cowles, J.A. Caporaso and T. Risse (eds), *Transforming Europe. Europeanization and Domestic Change.* Ithaca, NY: Cornell University Press. pp. 217–38.

Cowles, M.G., Caporaso, J., and Risse, T. (eds) (2001) *Transforming Europe: Europeanization and Domestic Change.* Ithaca NY: Cornell University Press.

Diez Medrano, J. (2003) *Framing Europe: Attitudes toward European Integration in Germany, Spain, and the United Kingdom.* Princeton NJ: Princeton University Press.

Duina, F.G. (1997) 'Explaining legal implementation in the European Union', *International Journal of the Sociology of Law*, 25(2): 155–79.

Duina, F.G. (1999) *Harmonizing Europe. Nation-States within the Common Market.* New York: State University of New York Press.

Dyson, K. (ed.) (2002) *European States and the Euro.* Oxford: Oxford University Press.

Dyson, K. and Featherstone, K. (1999) *The Road to Maastricht. Negotiating Economic and Monetary Union.* Oxford: Oxford University Press.

Eder, K. and Giesen, B. (eds) (1999) *European Citizenship and the National Legacies.* Oxford: Oxford University Press.

Eder, K. and Kantner, C. (2000) 'Transnationale Resonanzstrukturen in Europa. Eine Kritik der Rede vom Öffentlichkeitsdefizit', in M. Bach (ed.), *Die Europäisierung nationaler Gesellschaften. Sonderheft 40 der Kölner Zeitschrift für Soziologie und Sozialpsychologie.* Wiesbaden: Westdeutscher Verlag. pp. 306–31.

Egeberg, M. (2005) 'The EU and the Nordic countries: organizing domestic diversity?', in S. Bulmer and C. Lequesne (eds), *The Member States of the European Union.* Oxford: Oxford University Press. pp. 185–208.

Eising, R. (2003) 'Interest groups in the European Union', in M. Cini (ed.), *European Union Politics.* Oxford: Oxford University Press. pp. 192–207.

Falkner, G., Treib, O., Hartlapp, M. and Leiber, S. (2005) *Complying with Europe. EU Harmonization and Soft Law in the Member States.* Cambridge: Cambridge University Press.

Favell, A. (1998) 'The Europeanisation of immigration politics', *European Integration online Papers (EIoP)*, 2(10). Available online at: http://eiop.or.at/eiop/texte/1998-1010a.htm.

Featherstone, K. (1988) *Socialist Parties and European Integration.* Manchester: Manchester University Press.

Featherstone, K. (1998) 'Europeanization and the centre periphery: the case of Greece in the 1990s', *South European Society and Politics*, 3(1): 23–39.

Featherstone, K. (2003) 'Introduction: in the name of "Europe"', in K. Featherstone and C. Radaelli (eds), *The Politics of Europeanization.* Oxford: Oxford University Press. pp. 3–26.

Featherstone, K. and Kazamias, G (eds) (2001) *Europeanization and the Southern Periphery.* London: Frank Cass.

Featherstone, K. and Radaelli, C. (eds) (2003a) *The Politics of Europeanization.* Oxford: Oxford University Press.

Featherstone, K. and Radaelli, C.M. (2003b) 'A conversant research agenda', in K. Featherstone and C.M. Radaelli (eds), *The Politics of Europeanization.* Oxford: Oxford University Press. pp. 331–41.

Gabel, M.J. (2000) 'European integration, voters and national politics', *West European Politics, Special Issue*, 23(4): 52–72.

Giuliani, M. (2003) 'Europeanisation in comparative perspective: institutional fit and national adaptation', in K. Featherstone and C. Radaelli (eds), *The Politics of Europeanisation.* Oxford: Oxford University Press. pp. 134–55.

Goetz, K.H. (2005) 'The new member states and the EU: responding to Europe', in S. Bulmer and C. Lequesne (eds), *The Member States of the European Union.* Oxford: Oxford University Press. pp. 254–84.

Goetz, K.H. and Hix, S. (eds) (2000) 'Europeanised politics? European integration and national political systems', *West European Politics, Special Issue*, 23(4). Essex: Frank Cass.

Gourevitch, P. (1978) 'The second image reversed: the international sources of domestic politics', *International Organization*, 32(4): 881–912.

Grabbe, H. (2001) 'How does Europeanization affect CEE governance? Conditionality, diffusion and diversity', *Journal of European Public Policy*, 8(6): 1013–31.

Grabbe, H. (2003) 'Europeanization goes east: power and uncertainty in the EU accession process', in K. Featherstone and C. Radaelli (eds), *The Politics of Europeanization.* Oxford: Oxford University Press. pp. 303–27.

Greenwood, J. and Aspinwall, M. (eds) (1998) *Collective Action in the European Union: Interests and the New Politics of Associability.* London: Routledge.

Greven, M. (1992) 'Political parties between national identity and Eurofication', in B. Nelson, D. Roberts and W. Veit (eds), *The Idea of Europe*. Oxford: Berg. pp. 75–95.

Gstöhl, S. (2002) *Reluctant Europeans. Sweden, Norway, and Switzerland in the Process of Integration*. Boulder: Lynne Rienner.

Gualini, E. (2003) *Multi-level Governance and Institutional Change. The Europeanization of Regional Policy in Italy*. Aldershot: Ashgate.

Haas, E.B. (1958) *The Uniting of Europe: Political, Social, and Economic Forces 1950–57*. Stanford, CA: Stanford University Press.

Haas, P.M. (ed.) (1992) 'Knowledge, power and international policy coordination', *International Organization, Special Issue*, 46(1).

Hall, P.A. and Taylor, R.C.R. (1996) 'Political science and the three new institutionalisms', *Political Studies*, 44: 952–73.

Hanf, K. and Soetendorp, B. (1998) *Adapting to European Integration. Small States and the European Union*. Harlow: Addison Wesley Longman.

Harcourt, A.J. (2003) 'Europeanization as convergence: the regulation of media markets in the European Union', in K. Featherstone and C. Radaelli (eds), *The Politics of Europeanization*. Oxford: Oxford University Press. pp. 179–202.

Harcourt, A.J. and Radaelli, C.M. (1999) 'Limits to EU technocratic regulation?', *European Journal of Political Research*, 35(1): 107–22.

Harmsen, R. (1999) 'The Europeanization of national administrations: a comparative study of France and the Netherlands', *Governance*, 12: 81–113.

Haverland, M. (1999) *National Autonomy, European Integration and the Politics of Packaging Waste*. Amsterdam: Thela Thesis.

Haverland, M. (2000) 'National adaptation to European integration: the importance of institutional veto points', *Journal of Public Policy*, 20(1): 83–103.

Haverland, M. (2003) 'The impact of the European Union on environmental policies', in K. Featherstone and C. Radaelli (eds), *The Politics of Europeanization*. Oxford: Oxford University Press. pp. 203–21.

Hay, C. and Rosamond, B. (2002) 'Globalisation, European integration and the discursive construction of economic imperatives', *Journal of European Public Policy*, 9(2): 147–67.

Héritier, A. (1996) 'The accomodation of diversity in European policy-making and its outcomes: regulatory policy as a patchwork', *Journal of European Public Policy*, 3(2): 149–67.

Héritier, A. (2005) 'Europeanization in east and west: a comparative assessment', in F. Schimmelfennig and U. Sedelmeier (eds), *The Europeanization of Central and Eastern Europe*. Ithaca, NY: Cornel University Press. pp. 199–209.

Héritier, A., Knill, C. and Mingers, S. (1996) *Ringing the Changes in Europe. Regulatory Competition and the Transformation of the State. Britain, France, Germany*. Berlin-New York: Walter de Gruyter.

Héritier, A., Mingers, S., Knill, C. and Becka, M. (1994) *Die Veränderung von Staatlichkeit in Europa. Ein regulativer Wettbewerb: Deutschland, Großbritannien und Frankreich in der Europäischen Union*. Opladen: Leske + Budrich.

Héritier, A., Kerwer, D., Knill, C., Lehmkuhl, D. and Teutsch, M. (2001) *Differential Europe – New Opportunities and Restrictions for Policy Making in Member States*. Lanham, MD: Rowman and Littlefield.

Herrmann, R.K., Brewer, M. and Risse, T. (eds) (2004) *Transnational Identities. Becoming European in the EU*. Lanham MD: Rowman and Littlefield.

Hix, S., and Goetz, K.H. (2000) 'Introduction: European integration and national political systems', *West European Politics, Special Issue*, 23(4): 1–26.

Hodess, R.B. (1997) 'The role of news media in European integration: a framework of analysis for political science', *Res Publica*, 39(2): 215–227.

Hooghe, L., and Marks, G. (2001) *Multi-Level Governance and European Integration*. Lanham MD et al.: Rowman and Littlefield.

Hughes, J., Sasse, G. and Gordon, C. (2001) 'The regional deficit in eastward enlargement of the European Union: top down policies and bottom up reactions', *One Europe or Several Working Papers*, 29.

Imig, D. and Tarrow, S. (2000) 'Political contention in a Europeanising polity', *West European Politics, Special Issue*, 23(4): 73–93.

Jacquot, S. and Woll, C. (2003) 'Usage of European integration – Europeanisation from a sociological perspective', *European Integration online Papers*, 7(12). Available online at: http://eiop.or.at/eiop/texte/2003-2012a.htm.

Jones, B. and Keating, M. (eds) (1995) *The European Union and the Regions*. Oxford: Clarendon Press.

Jordan, A. and Liefferink, D. (eds) (2004) *Environmental Policy in Europe. The Europeanization of National Environmental Policy*. London: Routledge.

Jordana, J., Levi-Faur, D. and Puig, I. (2005) 'The limits of Europeanization: regulatory reforms in the Spanish and Portuguese telecommunications and electricity sectors', *European Integration Online Papers*, 9(10). Available online at: http://eiop.or.at/eiop/texte/2005-10a.htm.

Kantner, C. (2004) *Kein modernes Babel. Kommunikative Voraussetzungen europäischer Öffentlichkeit.* Wiesbaden: VS Verlag für Sozialwissenschaften.

Kassim, H. (2003) 'Meeting the demands of EU membership: the Europeanization of national administrative systems', in K. Featherstone and C.M. Radaelli (eds), *The Politics of Europeanization*. Oxford: Oxford University Press. pp. 83–111.

Kassim, H. (2005) 'The Europeanization of member state institutions', in S. Bulmer and C. Lequesne (eds), *The Member States of the European Union*. Oxford: Oxford University Press. pp. 285–316.

Kassim, H., Menon, A., Peters, B.G. and Wright, V. (2000) *The National Co-ordination of EU Policy. The Domestic Level*. Oxford: Oxford University Press.

Kassim, H., Menon, A., Peters, B.G. and Wright, V. (2001) *The National Co-ordination of EU Policy. The European Level*. Oxford: Oxford University Press.

Keck, M. and Sikkink, K. (1998) *Activists Beyond Borders. Transnational Advocacy Networks in International Politics*. Ithaca NY: Cornell University Press.

Kelley, J.G. (2004) *Ethnic Politics in Europe. The Power of Norms and Incentives*. Princeton NJ: Princeton University Press.

Knill, C. (2001) *The Transformation of National Administrations in Europe. Patterns of Change and Persistence*. Cambridge: Cambridge University Press.

Knill, C. and Lehmkuhl, D. (1999) 'How Europe matters. Different mechanisms of Europeanization', *European Integration Online Papers*, 3(7). Available online at: http://eiop.or.at/eiop/texte/1999-1007a.htm.

Knill, C. and Lenschow, A. (1998) 'Coping with Europe: the impact of British and German administrations on the implementation of EU environmental policy', *Journal of European Public Policy*, 5(4): 595–615.

Knill, C. and Lenschow, A. (eds) (2000) *Implementing EU Environmental Policy: New Directions and Old Problems*. Manchester: Manchester University Press.

Knill, C. and Lenschow, A. (2001a) 'Adjusting to EU environmental policy: change and persistence of domestic administrations', in M.G. Cowles, J.A. Caporaso and T. Risse (eds), *Transforming Europe. Europeanization and Domestic Change*. Ithaca, NY: Cornell University Press. pp. 116–136.

Knill, C., and Lenschow, A. (2001b) '"Seek and ye shall find". Linking different perspectives on institutional change', *Comparative Political Studies*, 34: 187–215.

Kohler-Koch, B. (2002) 'European networks and ideas: changing national policies?', *European Integration Online Papers*, 6(6). Available online at: http://www.eiop.or.at/eiop/texte/2002-2006a.htm.

Kohler-Koch, B. and Eising, R. (eds) (1999) *The Transformation of Governance in the European Union*. London: Routledge.

Koopmans, R. and Erbe, J. (2003) 'Towards a European public sphere? Vertical and horizontal dimensions of Europeanised political communication', paper presented at the conference on Europeanisation of Public Spheres, Political Mobilisation, Public Communication, and the European Union, June 20–22, Wissenschaftszentrum, Berlin.

Kux, S. and Sverdrup, U. (2000) 'Fuzzy borders and adaptive outsiders. Norway, Switzerland and the EU', *Journal of European Integration*, 22: 237–70.

Ladrech, R. (1994) 'Europeanization of domestic politics and institutions: the case of France', *Journal of Common Market Studies*, 32(1): 69–88.

Ladrech, R. (2005) 'The Europeanization of interest groups and political parties', in S. Bulmer and C. Lequesne (eds), *The Member States of the European Union*. Oxford: Oxford University Press. pp. 317–37.

Lavenex, S. (2001) 'The Europeanization of refugee policies', *Journal of Common Market Studies*, 39(5): 851–74.

Liebert, U. (ed.) (2003) *Gendering Europeanisation*. Brussels: Peter Lang.

Lippert, B., Umbach, G. and Wessels, W. (2001) 'Europeanization of CEE executives: EU membership negotiations as a shaping power', *Journal of European Public Policy*, 8(6): 902–1012.

Mair, P. (2000) 'The limited impact of Europe on national party systems', *West European Politics*, Special Issue, 23(4): 27–51.

Majone, G. (1997) 'From the positive to the regulatory state: causes and consequences of changes in the model of governance', *Journal of Public Policy*, 17(2): 139–67.

Manners, I. and Whitman, R.G. (eds) (2000) *The Foreign Policies of the European Union Member States*. Manchester: Manchester University Press.

March, J.G. and Olsen, J.P. (1989) *Rediscovering Institutions*. New York: The Free Press.

March, J.G. and Olsen, J.P. (1998) 'The institutional dynamics of international political orders', *International Organization*, 52(4): 943–69.

Marks, G. (1993) 'Structural policy and multilevel governance in the European community', in A. Cafruny and G. Rosenthal (eds), *The State of the European Community II: Maastricht Debates and Beyond.* Boulder: Lynne Riener. pp. 391–410.

Marks, G. and Hooghe, L. (2003) 'National identity and support for European integration', unpublished manuscript, Chapel Hill, Berlin.

Marks, G. and McAdam, D. (1996) 'Social movements and the changing structure of political opportunity in the European Union', in G. Marks, F.W. Scharpf, P.C. Schmitter and W. Streeck (eds), *Governance in the European Union.* London, Thousand Oaks, New Delhi: Sage. pp. 95–120.

Marks, G., Hooghe, L. and Blank, K. (1996) 'European integration from the 1980s: state-centric v. multi-level governance', *Journal of Common Market Studies*, 34(3): 341–78.

Massey, A. (2004) 'Modernisation as Europeanisation: the impact of the European Union on public administration', *Policy Studies*, 25(1): 19–33.

Maurer, A. and Wessels, W. (eds) (2001) *National Parlaments on their Ways to Europe: Losers or Latecomers?* Baden-Baden: Nomos.

Mazey, S. and Richardson, J. (eds) (1993) *Lobbying in the European Community.* Oxford and New York: Oxford University Press.

Meny, Y., Muller, P. and Quermonne, J.-L. (eds) (1996) *Adjusting to Europe: The Impact of the European Union on National Institutions and Policies.* London: Routledge.

Milward, A. S. (1992) *The European Rescue of the Nation-State.* Berkeley, CA: University of California Press.

Moravcsik, A. (1994) 'Why the European community strengthens the state: domestic politics and international cooperation, working paper No. 52. Cambridge, Mass.: Harvard University.

Moravcsik, A. (1998) *The Choice for Europe: Social Purpose and State Power From Rome to Maastricht.* Ithaca NY: Cornell University Press.

Mörth, U. (2003) 'Europeanization as interpretation, translation, and editing of public policies', in K. Featherstone and C. Radaelli (eds), *The Politics of Europeanization.* Oxford: Oxford University Press. pp. 159–78.

Norton, P. (ed.) (1996) *National Parliaments and the European Union.* London: Frank Cass.

Olsen, J.P. (1996) 'Europeanization and nation-state dynamics', in S. Gustavsson and L. Lewin (eds), *The Future of the Nation-State.* London: Routledge. pp. 245–85.

Olsen, J.P. (1997) 'European challenges to the nation state', in B. Steunenberg and F.V. Vught (eds), *Political Institutions and Public Policy.* The Hague et al.: Kluver Academic Publishers. pp. 157–88.

Olsen, J.P. (2002) 'The many faces of Europeanization', *Journal of Common Market Studies*, 40(5): 921–52.

Page, E.C. and Wouters, L. (1995) 'The Europeanization of national bureaucracies?', in J. Pierre (ed.), *Bureaucracy in the Modern State. An Introduction to Comparative Public Administration.* Aldershot: Edward Elgar. pp. 185–204.

Pierson, P. (1996) 'Path dependence and the study of politics', paper presented at the American Political Science Association, Annual Meetings, San Francisco, CA.

Radaelli, C. (1997) 'How does Europeanization produce policy change? Corporate tax policy in Italy and the UK', *Comparative Political Studies*, 30(5): 553–75.

Radaelli, C. (1999) 'Harmful tax competition in the European Union: policy narratives and advocacy coalitions', *Journal of Common Market Studies*, 37(4): 661–82.

Radaelli, C. (2000) 'Policy transfer in the European Union', *Governance: An International Journal of Policy and Administration*, 13(1): 25–44.

Radaelli, C. (2003) 'The Europeanization of public policy' in K. Featherstone and C. Radaelli (eds), *The Politics of Europeanization.* Oxford: Oxford University Press. pp. 27–56.

Radaelli, C. (2004) 'Europeanisation: solution or problem?', *European Integration Online Papers*, 8(16).

Raunio, T. and Hix, S. (2000) 'Backbenchers learn to fight back: European integration and parliamentary government', *West European Politics*, 23(4): 142–68.

Risse, T. (2001) 'A European identity? Europeanization and the Evolution of Nation-State Identities', in M.G. Cowles, J.A. Caporaso and T. Risse (eds), *Transforming Europe. Europeanization and Domestic Change.* Ithaca, NY: Cornell University Press. pp. 198–216.

Risse, T. (2002) 'Nationalism and collective identities. Europe versus the nation-state?', in P. Heywood, E. Jones and M. Rhodes (eds), *Developments in West European Politics.* Houndsmills, Basingstoke: Palgrave. pp. 77–93.

Risse, T. (2003) 'Social constructivism and European integration', in T. Diez and A. Wiener (eds), *European Integration Theory.* Oxford: Oxford University Press. pp. 159–76.

Risse, T., Caporaso, J., and Cowles, M.G. (2001) 'Europeanization and domestic change. Introduction', in M.G. Cowles, J. Caporaso and

T. Risse (eds), *Transforming Europe: Europeanization and Domestic Change*. Ithaca NY: Cornell University Press. pp. 1–20.

Rometsch, D. and Wessels, W. (eds) (1996) *The European Union and the Member States: Towards Institutional Fusion?* Manchester and New York: Manchester University Press.

Ross, G. (1998) 'European integration and globalization', in R. Axtmann (ed.), *Globalization and Europe. Theoretical and Empirical Investigations*. London: Pinter. pp. 164–83.

Sabatier, P.A. and Jenkins-Smith, H.C. (eds) (1993) *Policy Change and Learning: An Advocacy Coalition Approach*. Boulder and Oxford: Westview.

Sandholtz, W. (1996) 'Membership matters: limits of the functional approach to European institutions', *Journal of Common Market Studies*, 34(3): 403–29.

Schimmelfennig, F. (2005) 'Strategic calculation and international socialization: membership incentives, party constellations, and sustained compliance in central and eastern Europe', *International Organization*, 59(4): 827–60.

Schimmelfennig, F. and Sedelmeier, U. (2005a) 'Conclusions: the impact of the EU on the accession countries', in F. Schimmelfennig and U. Sedelmeier (eds), *The Europeanization of Central and Eastern Europe*. Ithaca NY: Cornell University Press. pp. 210–28.

Schimmelfennig, F. and Sedelmeier, U. (eds) (2005b) *The Europeanization of Central and Eastern Europe*. Ithaca NY: Cornell University Press.

Schmidt, V.A. (1996) *From State to Market? The Transformation of French Business and Government*. Cambridge: Cambridge University Press.

Schmidt, V.A. (1999a) '"European federalism" and its encroachments on national institutions', *Publius*, 29(1): 19–44.

Schmidt, V.A. (1999b) 'National pattern of governance under siege: the impact of European integration', in B. Kohler-Koch and R. Eising (eds), *The Transformation of Governance in the European Union*. London: Routledge. pp. 155–72.

Schmidt, V.A. (2001) 'Europeanization and the mechanisms of economic policy adjustments', *European Integration Online Papers*, 5(6).

Schmidt, V.A. (2002a) 'Does discourse matter in the politics of welfare adjustment?', *Comparative Political Studies*, 35(2): 168–193.

Schmidt, V.A. (2002b) *The Futures of European Capitalism*. Oxford: Oxford University Press.

Schmidt, V.A. (2006) *Democracy in Europe. The EU and National Polities*. Oxford: Oxford University Press.

Schmidt, V.A and Radaelli, C. M. (2004) 'Policy change and discourse in Europe: conceptual and methodological issues', *West European Politics*, 27(2): 183–210.

Schneider, V. (2001) 'Institutional reform in telecommunications: the European Union in trans-national policy diffusion', in M.G. Cowles, J.A. Caporaso and T. Risse (eds), Transforming Europe. *Europeanization and Domestic Change*. Ithaca, NY: Cornell University Press. pp. 60–78.

Semetko, H.A., Vreese, C.H.D. and Peter, J. (2000) 'Europeanised politics – Europeanised media? European integration and political communication', *West European Politics*, 23(4): 121–41.

Siedentopf, H. and Hauschild, C. (1988) 'The implementation of community legislation by the member states: a comparative analysis', in H. Siedentopf and J. Ziller (eds), *Making European Policies Work: The Implementation of Community Legislation in the Member States. Volume 1: Comparative Syntheses*. London: Sage. pp. 1–87.

Slaughter, A.-M., Stone Sweet, A. and Weiler, J.H.H. (eds) (1998) *The European Court and the National Courts. Doctrine and Jurisprudence: Legal Changes in its Social Context*. Oxford: Hart.

Smith, M.E. (2000) 'Conforming to Europe: the domestic impact of EU foreign policy', *Journal of European Public Policy*, 7(4): 613–31.

Tesoka, S. (1999) *Judicial Politics in the European Union: Its Impact on National Opportunity Structures for Gender Equality (MPIfG Discussion Paper No. 99/2)*. Köln: Max-Planck-Institut für Gesellschaftsforschung.

Thatcher, M. (2000) *The Politics of Telecommunication. National Institutions, Convergence, and Change*. Oxford: Oxford University Press.

Thatcher, M. (2004) 'Winners and losers in Europeanization: reforming the national regulation of telecommunications', *West European Politics*, 27(1): 29–52.

Tomei, V. (2001) *Europäisierung Nationaler Migrationspolitik: Eine Studie zur Veränderung von Regieren in Europa*. Stutgart: Lucius and Lucius.

Tonra, B. (2001) *The Europeanization of National Foreign Policy: Dutch, Danish and Irish Foreign Policy in the European Union*. Aldershot: Ashgate.

Trenz, H.-J. (2002) *Zur Konstitution politischer Öffentlichkeit in der Europäischen Union. Zivilgesellschaftliche Subpolitik oder schaupolitische Inszenierung?* Baden-Baden: Nomos.

Tsebelis, G. (1995) 'Decision making in political systems. Veto players in presidentialism, parliamentarism, multicameralism and multipartism', *British Journal of Political Science*, 25(3): 289–325.

Tulmets, E. (2005) 'La Conditionnalité dans la Politique d'Elargissement de l'Union Européenne à l'Est: Un Cadre d'Appretissages et de Socialisation Mutuelle?', unpublished PhD. IEP – FU Berlin, Paris – Berlin.

Verdier, D. and Breen, R. (2001) 'Europeanization and globalization. Politics against markets in the European Union', *Comparative Political Studies*, 34(1): 227–62.

Vink, M.P. (2002) 'Negative and positive integration in European immigration policies', *EIoP*, 6 (13). Available online at: http://eiop.or.at/eiop/texte/2002-013a.htm.

Wallace, H. (1984) 'Implementation across national boundaries', in D. Lewis and H. Wallace (eds), *Policies into Practice: National and International Case Studies in Implementation*. London: Heineman Educational Books. pp. 129–44.

Wright, V. (1994) 'Reshaping the state: the implications for public administration', in W.C. Müller and V. Wright (eds), *The State in Western Europe. Retreat or Redefinition*. London: Frank Cass. pp. 102–37.

Zürn, M. and Joerges, C. (eds) (2005) *Compliance in Modern Political Systems*. Cambridge: Cambridge University Press.

PART IV

The European Union and the International System

26

Overview: The European Union and the World

KNUD ERIK JØRGENSEN

INTRODUCTION

Writing at a time when the final phase of the process of widening the European Union (EU) seems to be within reach, the geographical contours of the future domain of 'foreign affairs' are clearer than ever.[1] Furthermore, after more than two decades of almost constant treaty reform, the EU also seems to have reached its *grosso modo* final institutional form and only very few issue areas – for instance territorial defence and church affairs – remain outside the EUs portfolio of policies. Finally, the European Commission has celebrated the 50th anniversary of its external service (European Commission 2004). Combined, such a unique historical juncture seems to be particularly apt for reflections on the study of the EU and the world.

A general or comprehensive review of research on the EU and the world requires a focus on significant trends, key distinctions, surprising lacunae, broad avenues of inquiry and indispensable contexts. Furthermore, an overview is by its very nature required to be comprehensive in terms of temporal, spatial and linguistic coverage. Finally, an overview

should outline analytical dilemmas and challenges as well as point to possible solutions. In the following, I examine seven key issues which different scholars over time have addressed differently. I begin by looking at the explanandum, i.e. the phenomenon we aim at understanding. This is followed by reflections on the dimension of time, specifically the spectre of 'presentism', as well as retrospective and prospective perspectives. In the third part, I address the notoriously difficult issue of analysing the European Union either as a collective (a Union) or as a group of individual member states. Subsequently, I raise the question how the evergreen threat of dogma and possibility of progress has been handled. In the fifth section, I explore the 'world' part of the chapter's title, emphasizing that the EUs environment has been constantly changing and under-researched. Sixth, I claim that research on the EU and the world has been as heavily compartmentalized as European foreign policy-making and has come to resemble an archipelago. Finally, the issue of the field's own external relations will be addressed, for instance potentials and constraints of cultivating relations with other fields of research, including options for export and import.

DEFINING THE EXPLANANDUM

The present chapter has deliberately been enti-tled 'the EU and the world'. The simple reason for choosing such a title is that it promises broader scope, more analytical options and fewer inbuilt limits or biases. The characteris-tics of the field can be defined by means of four distinct ways of defining the explanandum (on this issue, see also Chapter 27).

Actor

The first kind of explanandum is the very com-mon focus on the EU as *an international actor*, including issues of identity, interests and poli-cies. Often this kind of research takes an onto-logical point of departure and constitutive explanation is a typical fashion of inquiry. In other cases, the EU simply substitutes states as the unit of analysis and studies are conducted by means of standard operating procedures. Given that the EU in historical terms is a new-comer to world politics, the actor-centric per-spective is a predictable and valuable way of proceeding and scholars from Sjöstedt (1977) and Hill (1996) to Bretherton and Vogler (2006) have offered three modes of inquiry. Notably, Sjöstedt (1977: 6) regards the EC as a would-be actor and, in general, invites deduc-tive analysis by creating a model for the mea-surement of actorness, '[t]he aim of this project is, therefore, to try to construct a model for the evaluation of the extent to which the EC is to be regarded as a genuine actor in the international system, or rather what indicators may be discerned pointing to the EC develop-ing in that direction'. When analysing the actors in Europe's foreign policy, Hill focuses on member states though he also includes the European Commission. Bretherton and Vogler (2006: 1) point out that they, in the first edi-tion of their book, wanted to explore the extent to which the EU functions as an actor, '[o]ur conclusion was that the importance of the Union in international affairs was greater than we had anticipated, but that its capacity as an actor was limited, in some policy areas more than others, by its distinctive character'. They

arrive at this conclusion by means of an induc-tive approach that begins with international environmental politics and development policy and thus goes beyond a narrow focus on traditional foreign policy. In general, actor-centric studies have been very popular, and the numerous different ways of approaching the actor document that the EU has been concep-tualized as an actor in a concerted yet dispersed fashion (see also Rummel 1982; Ginsberg 1989, 2001).

Interventions on the theme of actorness have their limits. While actors and agency no doubt is part of the story, it is far from being the full story. In relation to the agent-structure problem, the perspective is squarely on the agent side of things and, thus, similar to Waltz's (1979) second image.[2] In contrast, the second image reversed argument claims that, though actors might want to project character-istics and aspirations from the inside to the outside, the outside is not a pure receiver of such projections. On the contrary, the outside might strike back, influencing domestic insti-tutions and processes of policy-making (Gourevitch 1978; Zimmerling 1991). Over time, various external federators have been nominated, ranging from Gamal Abdel Nasser to Saddam Hussein ('The CFSP was born in Kuwait'). Also, external processes have been pointed to, including Americanization (once upon a time), superpower politics and, presently, processes of globalization (Rosamond 2007).

Policies

The EU cultivates an increasingly rich palette of policies (trade, development, security, neighbourhood, enlargement, defence, envi-ronment, etc.) and each of these policies has been more or less thoroughly reviewed (Grilli 1993; Holland 2002; Meunier 2005; Schimmelfennig and Sedelmeier 2005). Research on single policy areas has by far been the most popular design, whereas comparative policy studies have been relatively rare. Some take their point of departure in the official vocabulary and examine the EU's CFSP or

ESDP etc., and then the analytical problems begin, particularly because these abbreviations, despite their labels, represent institutions that *make* but *are* not proper policies. Others examine genuine policies or a collection of international policies. Unfortunately, policy implementation has not attracted much attention, whereas horizontal and vertical consistency, as well as cross pillar politics has at least been put on the agenda (Stetter, forthcoming 2007). The policy *process* (i.e., aspects of information, access, administration and culture) and the changing *politics* of foreign policy has received less attention (but see Tonra 2001; Hill 2003).

Relations

The third explanandum is foreign relations, that is something somewhat different from policies. Thus, the EU has a policy on China, but China also has a policy on the EU. Over time, the two parties have reached various agreements, and there is an increasingly dense economic exchange between the two members of international society. Combined, these elements constitute EU–China relations.[3] When scanning the globe for such relations, it becomes clear that the EU has developed a dense web of relations with states, regions and international organizations (Marsh and Mackenstein 2005). The EU cultivates conventional bilateral relations with most states around the world (US, China, Japan, Russia, India, etc.). Furthermore, the EU cultivates relations with regional groupings such as ACP countries, Mercosur, ASEAN, the Gulf Cooperation Council and ASEM (Holland 2002; Bersick 2004). The cultivation of these kinds of relations is part of the EU's call to fame and uniqueness as an international actor. Finally, the EU has gradually developed relations with all major international organizations and has actually made support of multilateral institutions one of its key objectives in world politics (European Union 2003). Whereas policy-makers aim at making policies that strengthen, reform or create multilateral institutions, analysts aim at understanding the evolving relationship between the EU and multilateral institutions. For political scientists it is somewhat embarrassing, but legal studies seem to be ahead of political science in this field (Raux 1966; Brückner 1990; Wessel 1999; Griller 2003; Govaere et. al. 2004; Eeckhout 2005). Within political science, studies have generally been rare and predominantly focused on the EU–UN relationship (Gregory and Stack 1981; Stadler 1993; Johansson-Nogués 2004). The presence of a few studies obviously does not make a tradition, and for a long time research coverage has neither been consistent, coherent nor systematic. However, the encounter between European policy-makers and the Bush administration has triggered a growing awareness of and interest in the EU's identity, interests and policies. In turn, the 'effective multilateralism' initiative has triggered a significant increase in research on multilateral institutions (Eide 2004; Biscop 2005; Cameron 2005; Ortega 2005; Elgstrøm and Smith 2006; Laatikainen and Smith 2006; Jørgensen 2007).

In terms of biases, most studies employ an inside-out perspective on foreign relations. Few studies try to understand others' perceptions of European foreign policy. The outsiders' view of their relations with the EU – including processes of recognition, perceptions etc. – has systematically been downplayed, i.e. scholars have not engaged in such work. However, African scholars tend to focus on the impact of the EU on African economics and politics (Gueye 1997). In general, the coordinates from where observations are made seems to matter. Karagiannis (2004: 7) thus points out that, 'living in one of the ACP countries, Zimbabwe, during the writing of this text has necessarily influenced my view of the European discourse'.

Polity

The fourth approach examines polity features, including patterns of governance, institutional dynamics, legal issues, the diplomatic service and organizational relations between member states' administrations and EU institutions.

Three major avenues of inquiry characterize polity-related research. First, the conventional, old-time legal-institutional approach is far from unknown, focusing as it does on treaties and legal provisions in order to explain what the EU is or does in world politics. Because the waves of treaty reform have kept coming in for decades, there has been no shortage in new provisions to be described or interpreted. Second, the emergence and development of a comprehensive European foreign policy system have increasingly been acknowledged. In this system, national foreign ministries are among the key units, but have not yet been thoroughly analysed as parts of such a system (for exceptions, see Güssgen 2002; Hocking and Spence 2004; Morisse-Schillbach, forthcoming). By contrast, the institutionalization of the conduct of European foreign policy has generated a considerable literature (Smith 2002; Terpan 2003). Third, the field has acquired its own Europeanization literature, focusing on the top-down flow of influence from the Euro-polity to national institutions and policy-making processes. This focus of research was launched by Tonra (2001) and further developed by Ekengren (2002); on Europeanization, see also Chapter 22). The EU's diplomatic service has been analysed in a surprisingly limited number of studies (Bruter 1999; Duke 2003) and the same characterizes normative issues of foreign policy, such as ethics, accountability, democracy and legitimacy (Manners 2002; Karagiannis 2004; Wagner 2005; Lucarelli and Manners 2006; Wessel 2006).

In principle, these different kinds of explanandum are inter-related. Scholars exploring actorness often include policies. Similarly, relations and policies tend to be difficult to keep apart. However, there is often an emphasis at play – i.e. some aspects more in focus than others – and considering all four kinds of explanandum might help to identify the emphasis in specific studies. The four kinds of studies – being complementary parts of a whole – each provide important yet limited insights. An overview of the field of study is therefore bound to go beyond each of the four options. In turn, this explains why a focus on the EU and the world is suitable for an overview with synthesizing aspirations.

PRESENTISM, RETROSPECTIVE AND PROSPECTIVE PERSPECTIVES

Many studies have a 'presentism' bias, i.e. research is over-determined by 'here and now plus the immediate future' concerns. This ubiquitous 'presentism' implies that the dimension of time is sliced into fragments of insight that, in turn, function as obstacles for general and synthesized knowledge. While such studies might win a bit in policy-relevance, they risk losing a lot in terms of analytical depth and rigour. Because 'presentist' studies always surf the latest wave of policy-making or institutional reform, it becomes difficult to conceive of change or transformation in analytical terms, meaning that such notions merely play a role as assumption, conviction or declaration. Furthermore, the heavy 'presentism' implies that long-run perspectives are relatively rare. Thus, no one has done a comprehensive study of the European Commission's role, including its changing conceptions of the EU in the world. Similarly, not many bridges between political science and historical research have been designed or built. Due to problems with access to archives, historical research always tends to be 30 years behind the latest wave, with the consequence that the disconnect between 'presentist' and historical research is complete.

Leaving 'presentism' behind, I turn to retrospectives. We know that the process of European integration was launched at a specific historical juncture of time, characterized by the four macro processes that in the following will be outlined. Retreat is one such process. Europe experienced at the time a significant retreat from the pre-eminent power position the continent had enjoyed for centuries. De-colonization implied formal sovereignty for most Third World countries and a new role for the European metropoles. A book title such as *Losing an Empire, Finding a Role* (Sanders 1990) did not only characterize the situation of the

UK but also a number of continental European states, actually a majority among the six founding states. However, there was a second version of retreat at play. Tilly (1975: 636) concludes a long comparative study of the European state tradition in the following way,

> if there is something to the trends we have described, they threaten almost every single one of these defining features of the state: the monopoly of coercion, the centralization, the formal coordination, even the differentiation from other organizations begin to fall away in such compacts as the European Common Market.

If Tilly is right, experiments with collective foreign policy-making are likely to be influenced by such changes.

Second, the process was launched during the Cold War, i.e. during a time when Europe was divided into 'East' and 'West'. Even Western Europe was characterized by significant divisions, as demonstrated by groupings such as the EC, EFTA, neutral and non-aligned states, democracies and authoritarian regimes (Spain, Portugal, Greece). The EC constituted a minor part of Europe, situated to the immediate west of the central front. For the Six, The Nine and the Twelve, security was provided by NATO or, in more brutal, yet accurate, terms by the US. European security dilemmas had been overlaid and reduced to just one which, in return, risked becoming the endgame of all endgames.

Third, the expansion of international society was perhaps not finished, but it was well underway (Bull and Watson 1984). The launch of the EC potentially threatened relations between European metropoles and their colonies for which reason Article 131 in the Rome Treaty was included. Once the colonies were decolonized they enjoyed formal sovereignty, and a post-colonial relationship with Europe had to be defined. During the following decades, the EC made ACP countries a privileged grouping within the Third World (Ravenhill 1985; Grilli 1993). The expansion of international society also profoundly changed Europe's status from *being* international society to being only a (powerful) *part* of it.

Fourth, the centuries long civilizing process had in a fundamentally devastating fashion been reversed during the 1930s and 1940s (Elias 1939). Whereas foreign affairs epistemes around 1900 were characterized by expansion, chauvinism and arrogance, images of decline crept in during the 1950s. Feelings of shame mixed with a sense of responsibility and hope played a key role in images of the Third World. Concerning relations with the US, acknowledgements of manifest *dependencia* were mixed with vague aspirations for independence.

In short, the EC was from the very beginning 'in the world' and some dimensions of a common foreign policy – development, trade and enlargement – have been cultivated ever since the signing of the Rome Treaty. The first book-length manuscript on EC external relations followed soon after (Pescatore 1961). Over time, more and more issue areas have been added to the portfolio of European foreign policy, including areas governed by the EPC/CFSP/ESDP institutions and environment. Indeed, all policies of EU domestic integration have an external policy dimension.

The prospective perspective is notoriously difficult to handle. On the one hand, the EU is marred by agony, flagellants, doubt and mental *dependencia*. Institutional inertia – at both European and national levels – is pronounced. European foreign policy is often assumed to be part of a possible future but certainly not part of the present or past. On the other hand, Europe is among the most dynamic and powerful continents in the world. Within a few decades, the EU has launched a common legal framework (the *acquis communautaire*), a single European market and a single currency, achieved continent-wide enlargement and redefined foreign relations both internally and externally. Europe represents state of the art technology ranging from Galileo and the Airbus enterprise to nanotechnology and biotech industries. In terms of military spending, the EU-25 is a global 2nd outnumbering the spending of Russia, China and Japan combined. If we consider achievements and potentials in a global perspective, it is no wonder that Rifkin (2004) opted for the title *European Dream*. Needless to say that the two scenarios or epistemes trigger fundamentally different conceptions of the EU and the world and they suggest contending foreign policy strategies.

INDIVIDUAL AND COLLECTIVE INTENTIONALITY

According to Hill (1983: xi), European Political Cooperation (EPC) had by the early 1980s, 'been studied predominantly from the point of view of its overall progress, as a collective phenomenon'. By contrast, he emphasizes, 'no one had examined the question in detail starting from the separate national traditions' (Hill 1983: xi). In this fashion, Hill touches one of the classic analytical dilemmas we face when analysing groups. Should one choose an individual or a collective point of departure? In terms of foreign policy analysis, the individual approach is commendable for its aspiration, i.e. linking national foreign policy traditions and the launch and development of common institutions such as EPC/CFSP (Hill 1996; Manners and Whitman 2001). Indeed, the emergence of EPC/CFSP did clearly not imply the withering away of national foreign policies. This development enables a two-tier focus on both national and European foreign policy, including the interplay between the two tiers in terms of actorness and policy-making. Furthermore, Hill points to a somewhat free-floating *Towards a European Foreign Policy* type of literature that characterized the 1970s.[4] However, whether this literature was as predominant at the time as claimed is at best unclear. Actually, the mainstream seems to be elsewhere, as most foreign policy analysts did research on national foreign policy without paying any attention to the emerging European dimension.

Despite Hill's analytical break-away from the claimed mainstream, others continued their efforts at understanding the 'overall progress' of European foreign policy 'as a collective phenomenon'. Hänsch (1997: ix) has quite rightly pointed out that, 'The EU's international role and influence as an entity rather than a collection of nation-states still frequently goes unacknowledged'. Similarly, Piening (1997: 1) states that 'the purpose of this book is to show how and why the European Union (EU) has come to assume the status of an emerging global power'. Twenty

years before, Feld (1976: ix) explained that the purpose of his book, 'is to examine and to analyse the impact and effects that a new economic colossus, the EC has had and is likely to have on the world's economic and political relations. Clearly, the community, which has grown from a limited experiment in regional integration into a major world power, has affected every nation of the globe either economically or politically'. The collective approach is currently represented by a veritable avalanche of publications, all claiming that the EU has become a significant world power, if not a superpower.[5] This literature does not necessarily vindicate Galtung's (1973) dystopian vision of a superpower Europe. Rather, it links to a perspective that has been around for a long time.

Both perspectives – individual and collective – have their limits and inherent problems. The collective perspective has produced remarkably constant assessments over time, but given that both the EU and the world have changed, this kind of consistency should be a source of concern. Furthermore, when an entity is assumed rather than demonstrated, the perspective is potentially misleading. Finally, adding numbers does not necessarily beat the logic of diversity as the issue area of development aid so clearly demonstrates. The EU-25 *is* the biggest aid provider in the world, but it is also true that concerted action is not particularly widespread as member states often forget they are part of a union. The individual approach risks reifying national traditions, attitudes and interests, i.e. assuming they have a foundational or essentialist nature. This risk is particularly pronounced when assumptions remain unexamined by contending theoretical perspectives. Furthermore, we have the classic relationship between member states and EU institutions (or principals and agents) in focus, and research has been obsessed with this vertical member states–EU relationship. In a way this one-dimensional focus is our form of the heavy emphasis on domestic factors in research on American foreign policy. Yet, the increasing number of member states makes it more difficult to conduct comprehensive studies of national and European foreign policy. In 1983, Hill was concerned about the readability of ten (country) case studies. Would they be indigestible? One thing is certain, the EU-25+ obviously multiplies the problems. There are various ways of avoiding the dilemma that emerges from the accession of ever more member states and a limit to the number of chapters. In many ways, the multi-volume solution – two or three volumes on national perspectives – is slightly unattractive. Given this, some take refuge in theoretical assumptions about key member states and conduct studies of German, French and British engagements in European foreign policy (Aggestam 2004), or they take their point of departure in actual foreign policy conducted by the Big-Three, cf. policy-making on Iran since 2003. Others construct more or less 'natural' groupings, claiming that it makes sense to bundle Nordic, Iberian, 'Eastern' or Benelux member states. Counterclaims, for instance that there is nothing natural to an Iberian grouping (Barbé 1996), are typically dismissed, and editorial convenience thus wins over justified substantive arguments. However, it becomes increasingly clear that studies in a new key are not only pragmatically necessary but also analytically desirable. Several such new keys are available.

One new key is to make foreign policy strategies our unit of analysis, i.e. focus on strategic thinking across member states. However, even research in a new key is marred by classic dilemmas. Should we conceptualize strategic thinking *da novo* or apply well-tested concepts? Some argue that for the case of the EU, we lack an analytical vocabulary. Though we find the notions 'Atlanticists' and 'Europeanists' among the concepts developed for European foreign policy, they clearly lack analytical depth. Holbraad (2003) makes use of two dimensions – 'nationalism' and 'internationalism' – combined with the three classical European political ideologies, i.e. conservatism, liberalism and socialism. In this fashion he creates a six-cell matrix and provides analyses of, for instance, liberal internationalist thinking, a tradition of thought that is not at all irrelevant for European foreign policy. In order to launch research on foreign policy strategies across countries, we will need

to develop a conceptual framework and carefully explicate each term employed. By contrast, others argue that analysts of American foreign policy have focused on foreign policy strategies for years and developed a range of taxonomies, such as the dichotomy 'isolationism' and 'internationalism', the latter tradition including both 'unilateral' and 'multilateral' strategies. Furthermore, they argue that we can apply these concepts on the case of Europe. In such a perspective, the Prodi Commission has been informed, *grosso modo*, by the kind of liberal internationalism that also informed the Clinton Administration's foreign policy. Actually, this family resemblance might explain some of the caustic neo-conservative analysis of European foreign policy (Kagan 2003). There is, thus, clearly some mileage in this approach. However, mechanic application is best if avoided because it is bound to omit some distinctly European strategies, for instance the legacy of the European colonial tradition, including the present commitment to development aid policy.

Concerning the two general approaches, it seems that a carefully crafted balance between application and *da novo* conceptualization is among the most promising avenues of inquiry. Concerning the individual and collective approaches, we are in essence dealing with a classic social science dilemma, and entire research traditions have been built on one or the other solution.

BETWEEN DOGMA AND THE SHOCK OF THE NEW

When the 1969 Hague Summit launched the EPC, some contemplated whether we were witnessing a renaissance of the Concert of Europe (Berger 1971). When Germany recognized Croatia in 1991, some observers claimed that we witnessed the return of a traditional European great power to a traditional game. This kind of *déjà vu* has been fairly common in reflections on the EU and the world. We observe something seemingly new, yet choose to refer to familiar images of the past. In the literature on the role of operational codes in foreign policy-making, a key distinction has been made between 'closed' and 'open' information processing. Scholars are probably not any different from their objects of study, implying that scholarly perceptions vary between closed and open information processing. Relations between dogma and the shock of the new have several aspects, but the following four seem particularly relevant for our field of study.

First, it might appear as a paradox, but theoretical reflection unintentionally contributes to the tendency of looking at new actors and developments through traditional lenses. Hence, realists spot national 'preferences', yet are bound to translate these into sacrosanct national 'interests'. They observe a seemingly strong international institution at work, yet have to explain the institution (away) by re-introducing explanations based on balance of power logic. When observing European integration, liberal scholars are inclined to spot complex interdependence come true. According to the liberal tradition, the origin of the chain of command is domestic politics (Moravcsik 1998). The importance of geopolitical factors is acknowledged, but these factors come second. Similarly, economic historians are disposed to think that economic factors are second to none when explaining European integration (Milward 1992). Finally, English School theorists neglect the EU altogether, or they regard the EU as the strongest international society ever seen (Buzan 2001). In summary, theoretical reflection does not guarantee analytical progress, but it does make progress a possibility. In this context, Keohane and Hoffmann (1990: 284) point out that it is unfortunate to skip theory, as 'attempts to avoid theory not only miss interesting questions but rely implicitly on a framework for analysis that remains unexamined precisely because it is implicit'.

Second, the question of dogma and the shock of the new is obviously related to issues of continuity and change. Whereas the former – dogma/new – concerns our reflections, the latter – change/continuity – concerns political practice. Because the latter cannot be directly tapped, it has to go through our conceptual lenses which, in turn, are difficult to employ without triggering an unintended shadow on the observed (cf. the exchange between Diez 1999 and Moravcsik 1999; see also Kaiser 1966). Ruggie (1989: 32) has described the dilemma in the following concise terms,

> How we think about transformation fundamentally shapes what we look for; what we look for obviously has an effect on what we find; if we look for signs of transformation through the lenses of the conventional structural approach of our discipline we are unlikely to conclude that anything much is happening out there; but we cannot say whether or not that conclusion is correct because the epistemological biases of that approach are such that it is ill-equipped to detect signs of transformation.

He adds that 'if change comes it will be the product of micro practices. Hence if we want to understand change or help to shape it, it is to these micro practices that we should look' (Ruggie 1989: 32). In any case, dogma is cultivated when change or transformation actually takes place but we stick to old analytical concepts or images.

Third, there is the evergreen Scylla and Charybdis dilemma of being too close or too far away from the language of political practice. When we are too close, we risk merely reproducing politics and lacking critical analytical distance to our subject matter. Thus, French policy-makers are prone to express concerns one day about a possible German 'Alleingang' (going it alone) and the next day they engage in French unilateral action. To the degree analysts reproduce such inconsistent behaviour, in their studies they obviously lack analytical rigour. The extreme opposite position is employment of purely abstract concepts without any linkage to real-world phenomena. That is, theories can become so alienated from reality that they buy sophistication at the cost of relevance (Bull 1969; Schneider and Seybold 1997).

Fourth, with some justification readers might expect that in this part of the handbook we finally arrive at reviewing research on EU external affairs. And, obviously, we do. But in a different sense, nothing could be more wrong. The prime reason can be found in the truly remarkable confirmation of Schmitter's (1969) classic externalization hypothesis, 'integrating units will find themselves increasingly compelled, regardless of original intentions, to adopt common policies vis-à-vis non-participant third parties'. With practically no exception, all previous chapters review research on policies or aspects of politics with external dimensions. It is a fact that, for instance environmental politics, Single European Market politics, the Common Agricultural Policy and migration politics all have significant external dimensions. Furthermore, we can hypnotize that we, in Brussels, will find fewer officials working inside the intuitive core of external political and economic relations (DG Relex, DG Development and DG Trade) than in DGs outside the presumed core (for instance in DG Environment, DG Agriculture, DG Enlargement etc.).[6] Whereas the EU is not an island in the sea of (world) politics, most scholars within EU Studies proceed as if this is the case, thus continuing the tradition Haas began with his first landmark study of European integration.

However, the inside/outside neglect is mutual. Research on European foreign policy has, thus, so far, not been systematically combined with research on European party politics or public opinion. This is surprising and unfortunate because European foreign policy seems foremost to be the specific kind of foreign policy that has been cultivated by centrist parties of various sorts. In other words, the development of a common European foreign policy has been a project sponsored by *via media* political forces such as Christian Democrats, Social Democrats and Liberals. In contrast, left wing socialists, orthodox communists and extreme right wing parties do not have many shares in the project. The mutual neglect can probably be explained by the somewhat awkward position of foreign policy analysis: neither considered a public policy nor proper international relations (Carlsnaes 2002). In the case of European foreign policy, this awkward position is even squared because European foreign policy is not national foreign policy and most analysts of traditional foreign policy have a limited interest in European foreign policy.

THE EXTERNAL ENVIRONMENT – A MOVING TARGET

In general, the external environment has been strangely downplayed in research on the EU and the world. Systemic factors, whether conceived of as polarity structure or international society, play a minor role, and systemic change also does not figure prominently on the research agenda or among explanatory factors. Generally, scholars do not pay attention to how the EU has been shaped by the environment. Instead, they aim at explaining how the EU aspires to shape the environment. This bias, combined with the previously mentioned tendency to presentism, explains the fact that it has played no major role and that the environment has always been a moving target.

Maps of Europe and the world, anno the signing of the Treaty of Rome, show that several European empires were most present in the world. These empires had world-wide interests and a world-wide reach. True, it was also an era of decline. Thus, when France signed the Treaty of Rome, it was only 3 years after the bitter military defeat at Dien Bien Phu in Vietnam and 5 years before the defeat in Algeria. The Italian trusteeship of southern Somalia and Dutch and Belgian colonial possessions also came to an end.[7] Shortly before joining the EC, the UK withdrew from 'east of Suez'. During two decades, the process of decolonization fundamentally redefined Europe's relations with the Third World.[8]

In general, the term 'neighbourhood' has meant very different things at different times. In Europe, the near abroad of the EC's founding six members included Comecon states, beginning only some 100 km east of Hamburg. Furthermore, EFTA was in some corners intended to be a counter-project to the EC. The Iberian Peninsula was the home of Spanish and Portuguese fascist regimes. Yet, the process of enlargement has been a more or less constant source of change. It has triggered self-reform as well as redefined the frontier and, thus, the immediate exterior. Successive enlargements have moved the boundary of the EU and created new European horizons. Hence, the accession of Spain and Portugal gave a boost to EU–Latin American relations. The accession of Sweden and Finland triggered a Northern Dimension policy. The 2004 accession added new dimensions to the EU's *Ostpolitik* and to the Mediterranean policy. In summary, each wave of accession has prompted a new EU's boundary and, hence, changed the coordinates of what is considered to be foreign affairs.

Furthermore, it is not only in spatial terms that foreign affairs have been a moving target. During the last 50 years, the meaning of most policies has also been changing. In his aptly entitled volume, *The Changing Politics of Foreign Policy*, Hill (2003) suggests the kind of change I have in mind. This type of 'phasing' calls for diachronic comparison. During most of the Cold War, a common European security policy was a rather modest affair and defense policy was almost absent. During the same period, development policy was not coated by a politics of conditionality, in particular because the game included a competitor ('East') sponsor, the Soviet Union and allies. Carlsnaes et al.'s (2004) aspiration was precisely to examine 'the changing nature of foreign policy', suggesting that the end of the Cold War and redefined relations between member states governments and EU institutions were the two key variables responsible for the changed nature of foreign policy.

Finally, it is noteworthy that the EPC was launched during the period of détente and, significantly, as a consequence of it. Similarly, the CFSP can be seen as a response to the fundamental change from Cold War conditions (bipolarity) to post-Cold War realities, i.e. unipolarity or emerging multipolarity. If we allow ourselves to differentiate among policy fields, we see that, within the field of trade, there is a largely bipolar structure (EU-US) in place, plus a multilateral framework (WTO) which the EU has been influential in defining.

In summary, the ever changing coordinates of the EU in the world have required thorough (re-)inventions of European identity, interests and policies.

BRIDGING AN ARCHIPELAGO OF KNOWLEDGE

Research on EU foreign affairs has traditionally been among the most compartmentalized fields of study.[9] Each major issue area has been covered and each important relationship to states, world-regions or international organizations has been described. Each institution has been thoroughly accounted for and the single case study has been king. In temporal terms, the ubiquitous *presentism* ensures that time is sliced in fragments that, in turn, become obstacles for general or synthesized knowledge. Perhaps all this should not come as a surprise. After all, Lowi (1992) once claimed that 'we become what we study'. This insight also applies to our field of study and perhaps reflects the compartmentalized institutional architecture and the pronounced diversity in terms of policy-making procedures. It is an irony of ironies that the attributes scholars use in order to characterize European foreign policy – lack of consistency, coherence, impact, power, coordination and high degree of disagreement – also characterize research.

The well-developed compartmentalization creates problems. The positive point of departure is that scholars engaged in the field of study have a shared understanding of the fact that foreign affairs are more relevant and significant than scholars focusing on EU–domestic politics typically are willing to admit. Furthermore, it is necessary to stress that my criticism of compartmentalization is not aimed at individual studies. It concerns the field of study as such. Hence, there is a great demand of knowledge of all the specifics, ranging from the European security strategy, the founding of the EDF, Singapore (trade) issues, the EU's role in former Yugoslavia and to the EU's status within ASEM (Lucarelli 2000; Bersick 2004; Dimier 2004; Biscop 2005; Damro 2006a, c). However, for the field of study, problems are legion. First, when it comes to generalizing findings, the odds of a compartmentalized field of study are not the best. For instance, when trying to generalize findings and make claims about the EU as an international actor or EU foreign relations, we tend to replicate the procedures of the blind men describing the elephant in Puchala's (1972) famous fable. The relationship between Europe and the world is such an elephant, and we are still grappling with understanding the general nature of the elephant and its impact on the world (and vice versa). Whenever we try, the dynamics described by Puchala are immediately activated and reaching a consensus understanding becomes tiresome if not impossible. In other words, with no interface between the isolated areas and a time horizon of a maximum 5–10 years, the outcome is bound to be merely an archipelago of knowledge about the EU and the world. Therefore, we have a rich underwood of specific studies, yet lack a critical mass of impressive 'high tree' studies that summarize and synthesize research.

Given the negative consequences of compartmentalization, it is worthwhile if not crucially important to consider possible solutions. In the following, I outline five research designs that promise to reduce compartmentalization and enhance synthesis and generalization. First, instead of pursuing studies of individual policies, comparative studies, aiming at explaining variation of e.g. influence across policies, is a relatively straightforward design. Second, instead of doing research on bilateral relations only, research on triangular relationships promises more synthesized findings. The case of the EU contemplating to lift the arms embargo on China can serve as an illustrative example. If such research includes the US, India or Russia, it would potentially generate more solid findings and in addition potentially generate added value for the policy community. Third, each Commission can be characterized by its own distinct mixture of continuity and change in terms of conceptions of foreign affairs. However, there have hardly been any comparative studies across time of the 12 commissions that have served during the last 50 years (1957–2007). Fourth, instead of the ubiquitous single case study, multiple case studies potentially produce more condensed knowledge, particularly when case selection has been prudently done (Moravcsik 1998; Héritier 1999; Meunier 2005). Finally, research designs mixing issue areas promise an

upgraded knowledge of world politics. Sørensen (1996) provides an illustrative example by linking two literatures: one on security, the other on development issues. He argues that the issue areas are intimately linked whereas the two literatures traditionally exist in worlds apart. A second illustrative example is the triangle of trade, development and agriculture policies that has a joint presence in the real world yet is often kept strictly separated in research.

THE REGIONAL AND UNIVERSAL PROCESS OF THEORIZING THE EU'S FOREIGN AFFAIRS

In this section, the field's own foreign relations will be examined with a special view to the issue of possible import or export of knowledge. A range of fields of study and disciplines appear to be promising analytical encounters. Before examining these encounters, it is worthwhile to point out that they will be seen from a specific point of view. The fact is that research on the EU's global engagements has always been a largely European affair. Focal points include actor characteristics, policy-making processes, stated intentions and measurement of success in terms of achieved objectives. In contrast, African scholars tend to focus on the effects on Africa of European policies (Gueye 1997). In the US, European studies have generally been characterized by ebbs and tides, including changing fashions regarding the virtue of area studies. Hot or not fads, foreign affairs have always been among the top-three most popular topics (Keeler 2005). The fact that the area has been a largely European affair implies that it predominantly has been influenced by the trends and diversity characterizing European political science.[10]

Political Science

One promising encounter is political science itself. Indeed, one of the mantras of the present time is that European studies should give up its identity as an area studies and instead adapt to the standards and methods of political science in a general sense. The plea deserves further reflection because no field of study is likely to thrive if left isolated from progress in other areas. Unfortunately, the mantra is based on the slightly misleading if not strange idea that neofunctionalism's roots in pluralist theory do not count as political science; that the integration theories developed within International Relations should be dismissed as genuine political science; and the dubious promise that after a long era in darkness, enlightenment will come, if only. … In short, the plea is a typical example of legitimizing a pet theoretical orientation by presenting a historiography of the field based on less than rigorous scientific standards (for further reflections on this issues, see Chapter 1).

International Relations

In the following, I examine the encounters between major theoretical orientations and the study of the EU in the world. According to realism, European integration is epiphenomenal to the systemic distribution of (military) power and to the balance of power logic. Hence, US predominant power and presence in Europe is a key to understanding contemporary European affairs. Without the presence of the US, security dilemmas will soon be activated and great power politics re-introduced. In other words, as long as the US has a military presence in Europe, then European security dilemmas will remain dormant. When the US eventually leaves, the security dilemmas and traditional European great power politics will return (Mearsheimer 1990, 1995, 2003). Mearsheimer, who is a patient analyst, is ready to wait and see if not the future will confirm predictions. Furthermore, due to the 'false promise of institutions' argument, the EU itself is nothing but a reflection of the European balance of power (Mearsheimer 1995). It follows that it is not worthwhile to analyse the EU as an actor who pursues international policies and cultivates relations with most states around the world. If it appears that the EU actually is a

player in world politics, it is because European great powers are lurking behind seemingly common positions. European scholars (and many others) are unable to acknowledge these inherent limits of the EU because they are all idealists (Mearsheimer 2005). In sum, realists have a distinct interpretation of European affairs. It is to their advantage that they keep an eye on state power and security dynamics but, in general, they tend to be several steps behind actual developments and their theoretical lenses provide formidable obstacles to catch up.

Turning to the English School, European integration or governance has never played any significant role as explanandum (Jørgensen, forthcoming). In many ways, the English School has been made by men (and a few women) of the British Commonwealth, not of Europe. They focus on major international relations issues rather than on EU specifics. Thus, Bull did research on superpower politics and arms control, not on EPC 'procedure as substitute for policy' (Wallace and Allen 1977). Finally, the English School has earned its distinctiveness as a major theoretical tradition due to its conception of international society, an anarchical society but a society nonetheless. Post-war Europe has consequently been a predominantly blank spot on the map. Actually, most of the few references to European integration have a quasi-realist nature. The pronounced blindness towards economic factors of all sorts ensures that the CAP, the Single European Market, European trade policies or globalization are all no-go areas. Furthermore, if European states fully integrate, it is really no big deal. The new Euro-state will be a new player, sure, but it will not change the nature of international society. When considering potentially fruitful encounters between the English School and our field of study, it is worth noticing that the English School contributes valuable reflections on the kind of world in which the EU has been raised and is currently growing up (but see Diez and Whitman 2002). Furthermore, the expansion of international society is intimately linked to de-colonization and to the globalization of the European model of sovereign statehood (Bull and Watson 1984). There is an interest in quasi-states (Jackson 2000: 294–315) but not specifically in EC–ACP relations; there is an interest in the UN (Roberts and Kingsbury 1993) but not specifically in the EU's policies vis-à-vis the UN. Finally, the classic debate between the liberally minded Dûchene (1972) and Bull (1982) has by now been transcended by reflections on normative power Europe (Manners 2002).

European integration and the liberal tradition have always been closely connected. Integration theories, including neofunctionalism, emerged from within the liberal tradition, and European integration has functioned as an intellectual eye-opener (Katzenstein et al. 1998). The classical integration theories had their heyday during the early phases of European integration. Theorists looked at Europe as a subsystem and debated whether integration was possible or likely or not. Key figures were Karl Deutsch, Ernest Haas, Stanley Hoffmann and Amitai Etzioni, four Europeans who, as émigrés in a new US setting, reflected on the fate of their old continent (informed by a dash of hope). However, liberal approaches foremost focus on the integration process, claiming that integration and cooperation is possible. Integration is seen as a universal process and non-European cases were considered (East Africa, Latin America, etc.). Hence, studies of regionalism can be seen as a contemporary version of the liberal vocation (see Chapter 29 in this volume; see also the Japanese project CREP directed by Tamio Nakamura and Yoichiro Usui). However, liberal-minded scholars have never shown much interest in the EU's foreign relations. Nye has published widely on soft power, but has consistently focused on the US rather than the EU. Moravcsik's work is a tribute to the role of domestic politics. In short, in the liberal universe the EU counts as one of those international institutions that matter, but state power rules the game implying in turn that the EU is not conceived of as an international actor in its own right. Therefore, liberal analysts run into trouble as soon as the Europolity and European governance enter the scene, i.e. as soon as the European experiment goes beyond zones of integration, complex interdependence or security communities. Put differently, once the EU emerges as an independent global player, or when traditional European international politics metamorphoses into EU domestic politics, scholars working within the liberal tradition are bound to back off. Given that the, in principle, most suitable theoretical tradition is currently running out of steam and relevance, it is hardly surprising that journalists, ambassadors and empiricists constitute the grouping that recognizes the EU as a significant international player.

Turning to the encounter between the tradition of foreign policy analysis and European foreign policy analysis, it is clear that the focal point becomes narrower and mutual interest should therefore in principle increase (Carlsnaes and Smith 1994; White 2001; Carlsnaes et al. 2004). However, this has not been the case. In this context, it is worth recalling that despite being among the top-three most popular topics to research (Keeler 2005), the fate of the foreign policy analysis literature is to be at the margin of what is perceived to be proper International Relations. Hence, the European foreign policy literature is estranged in a double sense. No wonder that the field of study has had a limited impact on the general foreign policy analysis literature (compare Carlsnaes 2002 and Chapter 28 in this volume). When moving from general foreign policy analysis to one of the specific issue areas, development policy, it is clear that political-administrative division lines and practices are reflected in scholarship. Concerning practice, national development agencies guard their turf against an increased EU role, and the EU's own development activities are perceived in most critical if not downright hostile fashions, sometimes presented in the form of time-for-closure arguments. Concerning development studies, it has been like the relationship between the EU and NATO during the Cold War, co-habitation in Brussels, but no relationship. Development studies have a pronounced national capital orientation, and EU cooperation has only been shown limited interest. Hence, we have a relatively well-organized field of study (cf. the professional organization EADI) and a rather small grouping of scholars with an interest in the EU and the Third World (Grilli 1993; Holland 2002). The unique north–south relationship – characterizing EU–ACP relations for a while – has also attracted some interest. However, with the redefined EU–ACP relationship, this research interest in a unique era is likely to disappear with the disappearance of the special relationship.[11]

In summary, there has been a predominantly one-sided relationship between the rather small research community doing research on the EU and the world and the broader research communities doing International Relations or Foreign Policy Analysis. To the degree the former community has conducted theory-informed research, it has drawn on theories developed by IR theorists who, for their part, have largely ignored findings. Consequently, the analytical spill back function has been largely defunct. Given that precisely this function is of key importance to avoid theoretical degeneration, this is serious business. The current state of affairs should therefore be regretted. Not only because the EU-focused community has much to inform the wider world-focused community, but also because it is responsible for avoiding IR theory to slide into dogma and for leaving the community's own implicit assumptions left unexamined.

Political Theory

In research on the EU and the world there is no shortage of employing political theory concepts. Just think of terms such as norms, ethics, legitimacy, values, responsibility, democracy, duty, rules and justice. Such concepts abound. Keeping the field's predominant research interest in policy-studies in mind, Kennan's (1995) quip – 'we do not primarily need policies, much less a single policy, we need principles, sound principles' – becomes an important reminder about focal points, biases and blank spots in political practice and in scholarly reflection. In other words, what has become of our interest in doing research on the 'sound principles' guiding policy-making? What about public philosophies and stated reasons for political action?

Brown (2002: 11) has identified a most intriguing triangle consisting of international relations, political theory and international political theory. He argues that 'international political theory is different from, although related to political theory, but it is also different from, and related to, international relations theory – although in rather different ways'. It seems to me that research on the EU and the world can benefit considerably from drawing on international political theory and contribute specific European insights to international political theorizing. There are several points of departure for such an endeavour. Given that the area has been under-researched for years, one obvious point of departure could be a reconstruction of former reflections, i.e. a critical reading of former literatures, yet focusing on the political theory dimension of arguments and observations. A second avenue of inquiry focuses on the slowly growing literature that takes key notions of political theory into consideration. Manners' (2000) study of the role of symbolism in European politics highlighted the distinction between substantive and symbolic objectives and took, as one of the first, symbolic representation seriously rather than denouncing it as window-dressing. The study paved the way for Manners' subsequent examination of normative power Europe and the EU's international identity (Manners 2002; Manners and Whitman 2003). Karagiannis (2004) provides a critical, political theory-inspired exploration of the EU–ACP relationship, focusing, most of the time, on the concept of responsibility. She explores what the notion entails? How is the relationship between responsibility and autonomy? How is the discourse on European development policy based on these and similar notions? In short, how should the public philosophy, that informs development policy, be characterized? Finally, in the words of Lucarelli and Manners (2006: 201), they 'sought to understand how values and principles shape, and are shaped by, EU foreign policy relations with the rest of the world'. They draw three main lessons, namely that the relationship between a political community and the external world is crucially important and that we should examine mutual influence; furthermore, that the peculiar translation of values into guiding principles is more significant than just a listing of values; and, finally, that the specific context of such translations is determined by historical experiences and cultural identity.

CONCLUSIONS TO GO

Monnet (1976) famously claimed that European integration is a 'key step towards the organization of tomorrow's world'. The citation illustrates that in political thinking there has always been a close connection between regional and global processes. Concerning political practice, the regional and the universal processes have also always been intertwined. The EU has always been in the world, has always tried to shape the world and has always been shaped by international factors. This said, it is also true that since the end of the Cold War there has been a fundamental increase in international engagements and both actor capability and policy portfolio have been significantly expanded. The policy field has become increasingly dynamic and complex linkages between EU–domestic and international policies have created ever more well-established patterns of behaviour.

If we look at the questions scholars typically ask, some are derived from the political agenda whereas others are inductively generated from empirical work; still others are derived from theoretical reflection. Whereas discourse of practice includes questions such as, 'would the introduction of a European foreign minister make a difference, e.g. concerning consistency or coherence? How do we avoid punching below our economic weight? What is the role of multilateral genes?', discourse of theory includes notions like distribution of power, balance of power, state behaviour, interdependence, identity, policies, interests, preferences. Although we cannot avoid some overlap between the questions, there is a considerable lack of correspondence between the three sets of questions. It is as if they have not encountered each other. This absent encounter has significantly influenced the state of the art.

Probably because the field of study has experienced an increasingly high growth rate, the significant differences concerning research interests, concerns and findings go less noticed than one might expect, and they have not triggered heated debates with well-defined fault lines of arguments.

The field has always been heavily compartmentalized, thus inadvertently but perfectly reflecting the politico-administrative dividing lines of political practice. In this sense we have become what we study and it seems immensely difficult to break well-established patterns of habit. The result is that the explanandum has been defined in a considerably dispersed fashion. The evergreen dilemma of analysing the European Union as a Union or as a group of individual member states adds to the problem of creating concerted analytical reflection. The field has been heavily influenced by 'presentism' and comparisons (diachronic or synchronic) of, for instance, the handling of foreign affairs by presidencies and commissions have been rare. This state of the art implies a rather limited transfer of insights to related fields of study such as general political science, foreign policy analysis and International Relations. Concerning the latter, the field displays intriguing lacunae of research on external influence on EU institutions and policy-making processes. Concerning political science, there is a striking absence of interest in the triangle consisting of foreign policy, political parties and public opinion (polls, surveys, media). There are considerable potentials for cultivating relations with other fields of research, implying that also concerning this aspect, political practice and analytical reflection share common features.

NOTES

1. I am particularly grateful to Derek Beach, Gorm Rye Olsen, Richard Whitman and my co-editors for their helpful comments of previous versions of the chapter.

2. The inventors of neofunctionalism and intergovernmentalism, respectively, were both ardent sceptics of structural approaches. Both Ernest Haas and Stanley Hoffman subscribed to a position that is basically a Weberian theory of action.

3. Although the notion 'external relations' conventionally and technically refers to EC external relations, I will nonetheless use the notion in a broader sense when writing about the network of EU external relations.

4. The 1970s literature includes Weil (1970) and Alting von Geusau (1974).

5. Some journalists, ambassadors, politicians and academics share the view that the EU is an emerging superpower (Guttman 2001; Haseler 2004; Reid 2004; Rifkin 2004; Leonard 2005; Schnabel 2005).

6. Such findings would be similar to an analysis of the distribution of manpower resources in Danish ministries. To the considerable surprise of the Ministry of Foreign Affairs, more people are working with foreign affairs in sector ministries than in the MFA (Nye Grænser 1995).

7. Germany was spared of these colonial traumas but, then, had other traumas to handle.

8. Spain and Portugal joined the EC in the late 1980s, yet kept their colonial possessions until the mid-1970s.

9. Division of labour is an old yet nonetheless still very useful invention. Compartmentalization is something entirely different from division of labour, in particular because it implies that there is no mutual acknowledgment of the other parts and hence no mutual engagement.

10. On the British study of politics, see Hayward et al. (1999); On German political science, see Bleek (2001) and Hellmann et al. (2003); On International Relations in Europe, see Jørgensen and Knudsen (2006).

11. See http://www.eu-ldc.org for debates and research on EU–LDC relations.

REFERENCES

Aggestam, L. (2004) 'A European foreign policy? Role cenceptions and the politics of identity in Britain, France and Germany'. Phd thesis, Stockholm University.

Alting von Geusau, F. (ed.) (1974) *The external relations of the EC: perspectives, policies and responses.* Lexington: Lexington Books.

Barbé, E. (1996) 'Spain: the uses of foreign policy cooperation', in C. Hill (ed.), *The Actors in Europe's Foreign Policy.* London: Routledge. pp. 108–29.

Berger, R. (1971) 'Vor der Wiedergeburt Europas à la Wiener Congress? Die Europa-Vorschläge Staatspräsident Pompidous', *Europa-Archiv*, 19: 665–72.

Bersick, S. (2004) *Auf dem Weg in eine neue Weltordnung? Zur Politik der interregionalen Beziehungen am Beispiel des ASEM-Prozesses.* Baden-Baden: Nomos.

Biscop, S. (2005) *The European Security Strategy.* London: Ashgate.

Bleek, W. (2001) *Geschichte der Politikwissenschaft in Deutschland.* München: Verlag C. H. Beck.

Bretherton, C. and Vogler, J. (1999/2006) *The European Union as a Global Actor.* London: Routledge.

Brown, C. (2002) *Sovereignty, Rights and Justice. International Political Theory Today.* Oxford: Polity.

Brückner, P. (1990) 'The European community and the United Nations', *European Journal of International Law*, 1: 174–92.

Bruter, M. (1999) 'Diplomacy without a state: the external delegations of the European Commission', *Journal of European Public Policy*, 6(2): 183–205.

Bull, H. (1969) 'International theory: the case for a classical approach', in K. Knorr and J.N. Rosenau (eds), *Contending Approaches to International Politics.* Princeton: Princeton University Press. pp. 20–38.

Bull, H. (1982) 'Civilian power Europe: a contradiction in terms', *Journal of Common Market Studies*, 21(1–2): 149–64.

Bull, H. and Watson, A. (1984) *The Expansion of International Society.* Oxford: Oxford University Press.

Buzan, B. (2001) 'The English school: an unexploited resource in IR', *Review of International Studies*, 27: 471–88.

Cameron, F. (2005) 'The EU and international organisations: partners in crisis management', EPC Issue Paper No. 41.

Carlsnaes, W. (2002) 'Foreign policy', in W. Carlsnaes, T. Risse and B.A. Simmons (eds), *Handbook of International Relations.* London: Sage. pp. 331–49.

Carlsnaes, W. and Smith, S. (eds) (1994) *European Foreign Policy: The EC and Changing Perspectives in Europe.* London: Sage Publications.

Carlsnaes, W., Sjursen, H. and White, B. (eds) (2004) *Contemporary European Foreign Policy.* London: Sage Publications.

Damro, C. (2006a) 'Institutions, ideas and a leadership gap: the EU's role in multilateral competition policy', in O. Elgström and M. Smith (eds), *The European Union's Role in International Politics.* London: Routledge. pp. 208–26.

Damro, C. (2006b) 'The EU and international environmental politics: the challenges of shared competence', in K. V. Laatikainen and K. E. Smith (eds), *The European Union and the United Nations.* Basingstoke: Palgrave. pp. 175–92.

Diez, T. (1999) 'Riding the AM-track through Europe, or: The pitfalls of a rationalist journey through European integration', *Millennium: Journal of International Studies*, 28(2): 355–69.

Diez, T. and Whitman, R. (2002) 'Analysing European integration: reflecting on the English school – scenarios for an encounter', *Journal of Common Market Studies*, 40: 43–67.

Dimier, V. (2004) 'Préfets d'Europe: le rôle des délégations de la Commission dans les pays ACP (1964–2004)', *Revue française d'administration publique*, 111: 433–45.

Duchêne, F. (1972) 'Europe's role in world peace', in R. Mayne (ed.), *Europe Tomorrow: Sixteen Europeans Look Ahead*. London: Fontana. pp. 32–47.

Duke, S. (2003) 'The convention, the draft constitution and external relations: effects and implications for the EU and its international role', EIPA Working Paper.

Eeckhout, P. (2005) *External Relations of the European Union: Legal and Constitutional Foundations*. Oxford: Oxford University Press.

Eide, E.B. (ed.) (2004) *Global Europe, Report 1: 'Effective Multilateralism': Europe, Regional Security and a Revitalised UN*. London: The Foreign Policy Centre.

Ekengren, M. (2002) *The Time of European Governance*. Manchester: Manchester University Press.

Elgstrøm, O. and Smith, M. (eds) (2006) *The European Union's Roles in International Politics: Concepts and analysis*. London: Routledge.

Elias, N. (1939/1960) *The Civilizing Process*. Oxford: Blackwell.

European Commission (2004) *Taking Europe to the world – 50 years of the European Commission's External Service*. Luxembourg: Office for Official Publications of the European Communities.

European Union (2003) *A Secure Europe in a Better World. European Security Strategy*. Brussels, 12 December.

Feld, W. (1976) *The European Community in World Affairs. Economic Power and Political Influence*. Washington: Alfred Publishing Co.

Galtung, J. (1973) *The European Community: A Superpower in the Making?* London: Allen and Unwin.

Ginsberg, R. (1989) *Foreign policy actions of the European Community*. Boulder, CO: Lynne Rienner Publishers.

Ginsberg, R.H. (2001) *The European Union in World Politics: Baptism by Fire*. Lanham, MD: Rowman & Littlefield.

Gourevitch, P. (1978) 'The second image reversed: the international sources of domestic politics', *International Organization*, 32: 881–912.

Govaere, I., Capiau, J. and Vermeersch, A. (2004) In-between seats. the participation of the European Union in international organizations', *European Foreign Affairs Review*, 9: 155–87.

Gregory, F. and Stack, F. (1981) 'The European community and international institutions', in J. Lodge (ed.), *Institutions and Policies of the European Community*. London: Pinter. pp. 240–51.

Griller, S. (2003) 'External relations', in B. de Witte (ed), *Ten Reflections on the Constitutional Treaty for Europe*. EUI, E-book, April 2003, pp. 133–57. Available online at: http://www.iue.it/RSCAS/Research/Institutions/EuropeanTreaties.shtml, accessed 25 August 2006.

Grilli, E. (1993) *The European Community and the Developing Countries*. Cambridge: Cambridge University Press.

Gueye, B. (1997) 'Africa', in G. C. Azzi (ed.), *Survey of current Political Science Research on European Integration Worldwide: 1994–1997*. Brussels: European Commission. pp. 339–44.

Güssgen, F. (2002) 'Resources for Europe? The transformation of foreign service organization(s) in France and Germany in the light of a European diplomatic capability (1970–2001)', PhD thesis, Florence: European University Institute.

Guttman, R.J. (2001) *Europe in the New Century: Visions of An Emerging Superpower*. Boulder, CO: Rienner.

Hänsch, K. (1997) 'Foreword', in C. Piening, C. (ed.), *Global Europe: The European Union in World Affairs*. Boulder: Lynne Rienner. p. ix.

Haseler, S. (2004) *Super-State. The New Europe and Its Challenge to America*. London: I.B.Tauris.

Hayward, J., Barry, B. and Brown, A. (1999) *The British Study of Politics in the Twentieth Century*. Oxford: Oxford University Press.

Hellmann, G., Wolf, K.-D. and Zürn, M. (2003) *Die neuen Internationalen Beziehungen. Forschungsstand und Perspektiven in Deutschland*. Baden-Baden: Nomos Verlagsgesellschaft.

Héritier, A. (1999) *Policy-Making and Diversity in Europe. Escape from Deadlock*. Cambridge: Cambridge University Press.

Hill, C. (ed.) (1983) *National Foreign Policies and European Political Cooperation*. London: Allen and Unwin

Hill, C. (ed.) (1996) *The Actors in Europe's Foreign Policy*. London: Routledge.

Hill, C. (2003) *The Changing Politics of Foreign Policy*. Basingstoke: Palgrave Macmillan.

Hocking, B. and Spence, D. (eds) (2004) *Foreign Ministries: Change and Adaptation*. Basingstoke: Palgrave.

Holbraad, C. (2003) *Internationalism and Nationalism in European Political Thought*. Basingstoke: Palgrave.

Holland, M. (2002) *The European Union and the Third World*. Basingstoke: Palgrave/Macmillan.

Jackson, R. (2000) *The Global Covenant: Human Conduct in a World of States*. Oxford. Oxford University Press.

Johansson-Nogués, E. (2004) 'The fifteen and the accession states in the UN general assembly: what future for European foreign policy in the coming together of the 'old' and 'new' Europe', *European Foreign Affairs Review*, 9: 67–92.

Jørgensen, K.E. (ed.) (forthcoming 2007) *The European Union and International Organizations*.

Jørgensen, K.E. and Knudsen, T.B. (eds) (2006) *International Relations in Europe. Traditions, perspectives and destinations*. London: Routledge.

Kagan, R. (2003) *Paradise and Power. America and Europe in the New World Order*. London: Atlantic Books.

Kaiser, K. (1966) 'L'Europe des Savants. European integration and the social sciences', *Journal of Common Market Studies*, 41(1): 36–46.

Karagiannis, N. (2004) *Avoiding Responsibility. The Politics and Discourse of European Development Policy*. London: Pluto Press.

Katzenstein, P. J., Keohane, R. and Krasner, S. (1998) 'International organization and the study of world politics', *International Organisation*, 52: 645–85.

Keeler, J. (2005) 'Mapping EU studies: the evolution from boutique to boom field, 1960–2001', *Journal of Common Market Studies*, 43(3): 551–82.

Kennan, G.F. (1995) 'On American principles', *Foreign Affairs*, 74(2): 116–26.

Keohane, R. and Hoffmann, S. (1990) 'European Community politics and institutional change', in W. Wallace (ed.), *Dynamics of European Integration*. London: Pinter. pp. 276–330.

Laatikainen, K.V. and Smith, K.E. (eds) (2006) *Intersecting Multilateralisms: The European Union at the United Nations*. Basingstoke: Palgrave.

Leonard, M. (2005) *Why Europe will run the 21st Century*. London: HarperCollins.

Lowi, T. J. (1992) 'The state in political science: how we become what we study', *The American Political Science Review*, 86: 1–7.

Lucarelli, S. (2000) *Western Europe and the Breakup of Yugoslavia. A Political failure in search of a scholarly explanation*. The Hague: Kluwer Law International.

Lucarelli, S. and Manners, I. (eds) (2006) *Values and Principles in European Union Foreign Policy*. London: Routledge.

Manners, I. (2000) *Substance and Symbolism. An anatomy of cooperation in the New Europe*. Aldershot: Ashgate.

Manners, I. (2002) 'Normative power Europe: a contradiction in terms?', *Journal of Common Market Studies*, 40(2): 235–58.

Manners, I. and Whitman, R.G. (eds) (2001) *The Foreign Policy of the European Union Member States*. London: Pinter/Cassell.

Manners, I. and Whitman, R.G. (2003) 'The "difference engine": constructing and representing the international identity of the European Union', *Journal of European Public Policy*, 10: 380–404.

Marsh, S. and Mackenstein, H. (2005) *The International Relations of the European Union*. London: Pearson/Longman.

Mearsheimer, J. (1990) 'Back to the future. Instability in Europe sfter the cold war', *International Security*, 15: 5–56.

Mearsheimer, J. (1995) 'The false promise of international institutions', *International Security*, 19(3): 5–49.

Mearsheimer, J. (2003) *The Tragedy of Great Power Politics*. New York: W.W. Norton & Company.

Mearsheimer, J. (2005) 'E.H. Carr vs idealism: the battle rages on', *International Relations*, 19(2): 139–52.

Meunier, S. (2005) *Trading Voices: The European Union in International Commercial Negotiations*. Princeton, NJ: Princeton University Press.

Milward, A. (1992) *The European Rescue of the Nation State*. London: Routledge.

Monnet, J. (1976) *Memoirs*. New York: Doubleday.

Moravcsik, A. (1999) *The Choice for Europe: Social Purpose and State Power from Messina to Maastricht*. London: UCL Press.

Morisse-Schillbach, M. (forthcoming) *Diplomatie und Europäische Außenpolitik: Europäisierungseffekte im Kontext von Intergouvernementalismus am Beispiel von Frankreich und Großbritannien*. Baden-Baden: Nomos.

Nye Grænser (1995) *Nye Grænser. Den danske udenrigstjeneste 1970–95*. Copenhagen: Ministry of Foreign Affairs.

Ortega, M. (ed.) (2005) 'The European Union and the United Nations – partners in effective multilateralism', *Chaillot Paper*, 78.

Pescatore, P. (1961) 'Les Relations extérieures des Communautés Européennes', *Recueil des Cours de l'Academie de Droit Internationals*, 103: 5–244.

Piening, C. (1997) *Global Europe: The European Union in World Affairs*. Boulder: Lynne Rienner.

Puchala, D. (1972) 'Of blind men, elephants and European integration', *The Journal of Common Market Studies*, 10(2): 267–84.

Raux, J. (1966) *Les Relations extérieures des Communautés Economique Européennes*. Paris: Editions Cujas.

Ravenhill, J. (1985) *Collective Clientelism: The Lomé Convention and North-South Relations.* New York: Columbia University Press.

Reid, T.R. (2004) *The United States of Europe. The New Superpower and the End of American Supremacy.* London: Penguin Books.

Rifkin, R. (2004) *The European Dream. How Europe's Vision of the Future is Quietly Eclipsing the American Dream.* Oxford: Polity.

Roberts, A. and Kingsbury, B. (1993) *United Nations, Divided International Relations.* Oxford University Press.

Rosamond, B. (2007) *Globalization and the European Union.* Basingstoke: Palgrave.

Ruggie, J.G. (1989) 'International structure and international transformation: space, time and method', in E.-O. Czempiel and J.G. Rosenau (eds), *Global Changes and Theoretical Challenges.* Massachusetts: Lexington. pp. 21–35.

Rummel, R. (1982) Zusammengesetzte Aussenpolitik. Westeuropa als Internationaler Akteur. Strassburg: Engel Verlag.

Sanders, D. (1990) *Losing an Empire, Finding a Role. British Foreign Policy Since 1945.* Basingstoke: Palgrave.

Schimmelfennig, F. and Sedelmeier, U. (2005) *The Politics of European Union Enlargement: Theoretical Approaches.* London: Routledge.

Schmitter, P. (1969) 'Three neo-functional hypotheses about international integration', *International Organization*, 23: 161–6.

Schnabel, R.A. (2005) *The Next Superpower? The Rise of Europe and Its Challenge to the United States.* Lanham: Rowman and Littlefield.

Schneider, G. and Seybold, C. (1997) 'Twelve tongues, one voice: an evaluation of European political cooperation', *European Journal of Political Research*, 31(3): 367–97.

Sjöstedt, G. (1977) *The External Role of the European Community.* Farnborough: Saxon House.

Smith M.E. (2002) *Europe's Foreign and Security Policy. The Institutionalization of Cooperation.* Cambridge: Cambridge University Press.

Sørensen, G. (1996) 'Development as a Hobbesian dilemma', *Third World Quarterly*, 17(5): 903–16.

Stadler, K.-D. (1993) *Die Europäische Gemeinschaft in der Vereinten Nationen: Die Rolle der EG im Entscheidungsprocess der UN-Hauptorgan am Beispile der Generalversammlung.* Baden Baden: Nomos.

Stetter. S. (forthcoming 2007) *Cross-Pillar Politics of the European Union: The Dynamics of Integration in EU Foreign and Interior Policies.* London: Routledge.

Terpan, F. (2003) *La politique étrangère et de sécurité commune de l'Union européenne.* Bruxelles: Bruylant.

Tilly, C. (ed.) (1975) *The Formation of National States in Western Europe.* Princeton: Princeton University Press.

Tonra, B. (2001) *The Europeanisation of National Foreign Policy.* Aldershot: Ashgate.

Wagner, W. (2005) 'The democratic legitimacy of European security and defense policy, European Union institute for security studies', *Occasional Paper*, No. 57, Paris.

Wallace, W. and Allen, D. (1977) 'Political cooperation: procedure as substitute for policy', in H. Wallace, W. Wallace and C. Webb (eds), *Policy-Making in the European Community.* Chichester: John Wiley and Sons. pp. 227–48.

Waltz, K. (1979) *Theory of International Politics.* Reading: Addison-Wesley.

Weil, G.L. (1970) *A Foreign Policy for Europe?* Bruges: College of Europe.

Wessel, R. (1999) *The European Union's Foreign and Security Policy: A Legal Institutional Perspective.* Den Haag: Kluwer Law International.

Wessel, R. (forthcoming, 2007) 'Accountability in EU foreign, security and defence policy: Shared competences, mixed responsibilities', in A. Dashwood and M. Maresceau (eds), *Recent Trends in the External Relations of the Union.* Cambridge: Cambridge University Press.

White, B. (2001) *Understanding European Foreign Policy.* Basingstoke: Palgrave.

Zimmerling, R. (1991) *Externe Einflüsse auf die Integration von Staaten. Zur politikwissenschaftliche Theorie regionaler Zusammenschlüse.* Freiburg: Verlag Karl Alber.

27

The European Union and International Political Economy: Trade, Aid and Monetary Policy

MICHAEL SMITH

INTRODUCTION

At the core of the study of international political economy (IPE) are two sets of questions. The first set addresses the relationships between actors in the IPE: the nature of the actors themselves, how they are arrayed, and how the linkages between them are expressed – in particular, the linkages and tensions between state authorities and other actors in international markets. The second set of key questions, which intersects with the first, relates to the outcomes of activity in the IPE: it addresses issues of authority, equity and efficiency, and the ways in which practices within the IPE contribute to the achievement of these outcomes. Around these two sets of questions there has arisen a very extensive literature about the evolution and the workings of the IPE, and about the tensions between the notion of an IPE (tending to carry implications of state-centrism) and the putative global political economy (GPE) which is seen as the broad outcome of processes of globalization in production, exchange and regulation.

This is not the place for a detailed exegesis of the IPE literature, which can be found in many texts (for example Spero and Hart 1997; Gilpin 2000; Frieden and Lake 2000; Palan 2000; Woods 2000; Gilpin and Gilpin 2001; Dicken 2003; Goddard et al. 2003; Kahler and Lake 2003; O'Brien and Williams 2004; Stubbs and Underhill 2005). But the two sets of questions outlined above are crucial to an understanding of the EU's role in the IPE, and thus fundamental to the investigation in this chapter. The EU's place in the IPE is challenging not only in the empirical sense, but also in the conceptual sense, for the simple reason that (on the one hand) it is not a state and that (on the other hand) it performs a number of vital state functions in the IPE. This creates a set of major ambiguities about the EU's role(s) in the IPE (Laffan et al. 2000: Chapter 4). In turn, this links to broader considerations of the EU's role(s) in the international arena, in which the Union can be seen firstly as a (sub)system of international relations in itself, secondly as a part of the process of international relations, and finally as an emergent power in international relations (Hill and Smith 2005: introduction and conclusion).

From the outset, the process of European integration has been a challenge to established concepts of IPE. In particular, it has posed a standing and strengthening challenge to the notion of IPE as being about the state/market relationship (Kahler 1995; Kapteyn 1996; Tsoukalis 1997, 2003; Scott 1998; Laffan et al. 2000; Jones and Verdun 2004). The idea that sovereignty over fundamental economic processes can be transferred from the national to the cross-national or supranational level does not of course do away with the role of states and national governments; but the unintended outcomes of initial integration processes can have major effects on the capacity of national authorities to recapture their autonomy. Thus, the initial discussion of European (economic) integration in terms of federalism and functionalism (see Chapter 1) and its development into ideas of neo-functionalism, transactionalism and complex interdependence raised precisely the central issues of IPE: what was the effect of this on the relationship between states and markets, and to what extent had the European integration process transferred state functions to the supranational level? Further, the integration process raised and continues to raise vital questions about how to conceptualize and explore the relationship between this new creation and the broader processes and politics of the IPE (Smith 2004b). It also raises important issues in the comparative study of regional integration efforts and the ways in which they articulate with change in the international economy (Cable and Henderson 1994; Coleman and Underhill 1998; Switky and Kerremans 2000; Teló 2001; Breslin et al. 2002; Schirm 2002); whilst this comparative dimension is not dealt with in detail here, it is a significant and growing part of the analytical context.

It can readily be seen that as a result, the study of the EU in the IPE raises some key issues both about the nature of the Union – its resources, roles and impacts – and about the nature of the IPE itself, especially the fluid balance between the 'international' and the 'global' in the contemporary era. These questions are not simply empirical: they concern key themes in this volume as a whole, such as the balance between rationalism and normative elements in the evolution of the EU and its roles in the world. In this chapter, the central aim is to review the literature and the debates in three key areas of the EU's engagement in the IPE – trade, aid, and monetary relations – and by so doing to cast light on the EU's evolving roles in the IPE. A second aim is to draw attention to continuing and emerging research agendas relating to the EU's role in the IPE, and this will be the focus in the conclusion to the chapter. Throughout the chapter, reference will be made to the three images of the EU noted above, in relation specifically to the IPE: the EU as a (sub)system of IPE, the EU as part of the process of the IPE, and the EU as an emergent power in the IPE.

TRADE

The EU's role in international trade is one of the most long established and institutionally developed of the Union's external policies. The EU has well-founded internal policy mechanisms and resources, it has an established role in the processes of IPE and it can claim with some justification to be a major trade power in the IPE. The purpose here is to go beneath these broad judgements, to look at the ways in which each of these areas has been the subject of academic debate and conceptual development, and to indicate some of the links to broader issues of international trade such as the role of 'domestic' politics and institutions and the impact of trade policies on the global arena (Milner 2002).

First, let us examine the EU's system of trade policy formation and implementation. The 'constitutional' foundations of EU trade policies were some of the first to be established, but the issue of competence, both in the legal and in the more broadly political sense, has remained open for a very long time. Partly this is because of the changing nature of the IPE, and in particular the growth of new forms of international exchange, especially trade in services; partly it is also because of the ways in which Member States have been relatively reluctant to go beyond the limited grants of competence made as long ago as the 1960s. Thus a key theme in the analysis of EU trade policies during the past decade has been the struggle for trade policy competence, and the tension between those who espoused a view of 'exclusive competence' and those who supported the 'mixed competence' view (Hayes 1993; Eeckhout 1994, 2004; Heidensohn 1995; Macleod et al. 1996; Meunier and Nicolaidis 2000; Elsig 2002). Viewed in purely legal terms, this was the subject of bargaining throughout the 1990s, with the final (so far) resolution being reached at the Nice intergovernmental conference of 2000. This effectively established that for all matters within the jurisdiction of the World Trade Organization (WTO) (which had succeeded the General Agreement on Tariffs and Trade (GATT) in 1995), the Commission would act on behalf of the Community, subject to mandates granted by the Council of Ministers.

But the legal and institutional situation is only part of the story in EU trade policy formation. Alongside the more legal and institutional analysis has gone a strand of investigation based strongly on theories of delegation and of principal-agent relationships (Meunier and Nicolaidis 1999; Meunier 2000, 2005; Kerremans 2006). Such analyses point out that over a very long period, but particularly in the 1990s, there has been a tension between 'agency drift' represented by the Commission and its need (or desire) to maximize its autonomy, and the desire of the Council as a collective principal to exercise control over the Commission as its agent. In this area, the EU is often seen as unique, but there is a growing sense in which such problems reflect the increasingly fractious nature of 'trade politics' in many major economies (Hocking and McGuire 2004).

Important work has been done within this broad framework on the ways in which the Commission can manipulate formal institutional assets but also more specific assets in the form of information, expertise and coalition-building capacity to increase its effective policy space and escape the surveillance of the Council. Such treatments of principal-agent relationships are complemented by those that focus on the processes of negotiation that take place within and between the Commission and the Council: here, the emphasis is on the ways in which bargaining assets are deployed, and especially on the ways in which negotiating mandates are shaped and implemented (Elgström and Jönsson 2005; Smith 2005c; see also Kerremans 2006). Such treatments are informed by the theory of multi-level games, and the need to form linkages between negotiations at different 'tables'. Thus for example, the rigidity of Commission negotiating positions within the WTO can be explored by reference to the terms on which negotiating mandates are granted, the difficulty in renegotiating the internal bargains on which negotiating mandates are based, and the need for Commission negotiators to address different and conflicting audiences (Meunier 1998, 2000, 2005).

The internal process of policy-formation – and thus the foundation of the EU's trade policy system – is thus contested at the level of constitutional grants of authority and at the more specific level of negotiating principles and practices. Unsurprisingly, this contestation has important implications for the conduct of trade policy and the implementation of agreements. The EU has developed a full set of 'trade tools' (McGuire 1999) in support of its trade policy objectives, but the deployment of these tools is conditioned by the balance of forces within the institutions and by the changing nature of the IPE more broadly. Thus, it is important to ask whether the EU is on balance an example of trade liberalism or trade protectionism (Hanson 1998; McGuire 1999; Young 2004b): as well as a series of institutional questions, this opens up key questions about the relationship between 'north' and 'south' in the Union (the north generally held to be less protectionist, the south more), about the impact of the changing membership of the Union (and particularly the impact of ten new Member States from 2004 onwards), and about the changing balance between technocracy and politicization in the EU on trade matters (Smith and Woolcock 1999; Smith 2001, 2004). It is broadly the case that studies of EU trade policy have focused on the distribution of 'domestic' preferences between Member States, the institutions and other powerful groupings, and that these have been seen as a major source of evidence with which to underpin explanations of trade policy actions. Little attention has been paid to the more explicitly normative aspects of trade policies – unlike, for example, the situation in analysis of the CFSP and enlargement (for exceptions see Elsig 2002; Niemann 2004). Whether this is a function of the specific institutional arrangements or the prevailing ideas in the IPE as a whole, or whether it says something about the EU in particular, is an important area for further study. In similar fashion, there are few studies of EU implementation of trade agreements (especially those reached within the context of the GATT/WTO), and thus future research might profitably focus on the ways in which institutional arrangements and domestic pressures have affected implementation. Such a focus could be extended to explore the ways in which agreements reflect specific constellations of ideas or the interests of broad economic and other forces, another underresearched area (although there has been some attention to the influence of neo-liberal ideologies on trade policy formation).

In relation to the second area of interest here – the EU and processes of international trade – it can be said immediately that the EU does have a major influence on the patterns and processes of international commerce. To put it simply, the EU is a very large trading bloc, which thus fundamentally shapes and reshapes the patterns of international trade, both in terms of composition and in terms of flows. This has effects in the first place on the functioning of the major multilateral trade bodies, and particularly the WTO (Heidensohn 1995; Jackson 1995; Krueger 1998; Bromley 2001;

Hoekman and Kostecki 2001; Aggarwal and Fogarty 2004). Whilst the original customs union of the EEC was only possible because of the provisions of the GATT, the WTO was born into a world in which the EU was an established fact, accounting for something like twenty per cent of world trade (excluding trade between the EU's Member States), and with a highly developed institutional and legal structure (Dent 1997). Thus the question of compatibility between the EU's internal structures and the multilateral framework has been a consistent preoccupation of analysts in this area (Woolcock 1993, 2000, 2005; see also Meunier and Nicolaidis 2005). At the level of the EU itself, there is a fairly consistent readiness to state the Union's commitment to and pursuit of multilateral principles, but it is often less easy to see this in terms of actual EU policy practice, for example in the use of anti-dumping regulations. So the question emerges, how complementary are the European and the global processes? The problem is that in some respects the EU's positions in multilateral fora are the externalization of policy problems encountered within the Union itself, for example of the reform of the Common Agricultural Policy (CAP), and that they are thus resistant to all but the most compelling of international pressures. In other cases, the EU's internal debate about constitutional arrangements for trade policy formation can be seen as affecting the Union's effective participation in the multilateral process; as for example in the debate about policy competence during the 1990s (Meunier and Nicolaidis 2000, 2005; Young 2000, 2002) or the problems attending the adaptation of trade rules adopted through complex bargaining processes (Young 2004b). One issue that arises from these areas of tension is that of the effectiveness of EU trade policy in itself: how far can it be seen as advancing agreed aims and fulfilling agreed mandates? At a much broader level, there is a question of leadership and legitimacy, to which we will return shortly.

Another dimension of the processes of international trade is the bargaining and negotiation surrounding particular trade disputes or relations with particular trading partners.

There is a large literature on the ways in which the EU enters into and handles international trade disputes; as in other areas, a significant part of the literature is legal in focus, but there is also a strong vein of analysis in terms of bargaining and negotiation theory (Young 2004a, 2004b, 2006; Ahnlid 2005). It is logical that as a major concentration of world trade and exchange, and one of the most attractive markets in the IPE, the EU will become engaged in a wide range of trade disputes. It is also clear that as noted above, the EU is well-armed with the traditional (and some new) trade weapons with which to handle these disputes, and that the Union is publicly committed to defence of and use of the multilateral system. There is a tension, though, between the EU's use of essentially unilateral measures of 'trade defence' such as anti-dumping and anti-subsidy regulations, and their use of the WTO dispute settlement apparatus. To use terms deployed by one analyst of the area, it is unclear what kind of player the EU is and in which game it is participating at any given time (Young 2004a). So there is a significant body of work that has grown up around the EU's use of a range of instruments and institutional channels in pursuit of trade policy objectives (McGuire 1999; Smith 2001).

There is also a large literature dealing with the EU's key trading relationships, only a small proportion of which can be mentioned here. Easily the largest group of studies surrounds the EU's relationship with the USA, which is the key bilateral relationship between the EU and the IPE. The process of 'competitive cooperation' (Smith 1998) between the EU and the US is central not only to the two direct participants but also to the whole of the IPE. It demonstrates not only the range of trade disputes that is bound to emerge from conditions of complex interdependence and integration, but also the ways in which choices are made about channels and instruments for the pursuit of trade advantage in the IPE. Thus, EU-US disputes are often characterized by unilateral behaviour, but often the very same disputes see resort to bilateral mechanisms for 'early warning' or crisis management, and to the multilateral system of the WTO in pursuit of advantage either through negotiation or through legitimation of essentially unilateral policy initiatives (Pollack 2003a, 2003b). This is often hard-ball IPE, but equally often it is moderated by considerations of reciprocity, of broader multilateral coalition building, of public-private interactions and by essentially problem solving modes of negotiation (Eichengreen 1998; Guay 1999; Pollack and Shaffer 2001; Petersmann and Pollack 2003; Pollack 2003a, 2003b; Smith 2005b).

Whereas the EU-US relationship is multi-faceted and pursued at many different levels, other major bilateral relationships between the EU and major partners in the IPE are less comprehensive. Thus, the EU and Japan have significant mutual trade interests, a number of areas of friction, and relatively less ambitious mechanisms of mutual management (Gilson 2000). The EU's relations with China are much less long standing, but have undergone a rapid deepening and widening since the early 1990s (Preston and Gilson 2001). Relations with Russia have been conducted on a relatively cautious basis, reflecting the political as well as the economic unevenness of the relationship (Gowan 2000). Each of these relationships does demonstrate the coexistence, already noted, of the unilateral, bilateral and multilateral modes of relations, and of bargaining and problem-solving processes, but none of them reaches the scope or intensity of the EU-US relationship. Importantly, however, it has become increasingly apparent that many of the most significant commercial relationships are themselves interdependent, thus posing a new set of policy problems for the EU as well as a potentially fruitful area for new forms of analysis. To take only one example, European and US policies towards China – and Chinese policies towards both the EU and the US – are not independent, and this fact leads to potential complexities, trade-offs and unintended consequences of policy-making in all three parties.

It is clear from the argument so far that the EU is a major trade power in the IPE (Meunier and Nicolaidis 2005). Often it is argued or implied that this is the only area in which the EU has a truly leading position within the world arena, reflecting its institutional strength, its market resources, its accumulated legitimacy and its capacity to deploy specific tools of trade policy. As a result, a significant literature has accrued around the study of the EU's aims and impact within the global trading system, and in particular the extent to which the EU is 'different' from traditional state actors in its aims and strategies or in its choice of instruments (Tsoukalis 2003; Aggarwal and Fogarty 2004; van den Hoven 2004; Smith 2005a; Kerremans 2006). On the one side, it is possible to view the EU as a traditional 'power', employing incentives and punishments through trade to encourage its partners or targets to comply, and deploying its structural power to demand concessions from those who would wish to gain access to its market. This is certainly the way it has appeared to many countries outside the North Atlantic area, subject as they have been to the EU's 'pyramid of privilege' (Hine 1985) in trading agreements (and see the next section on aid/development). On the other side, it is possible to analyse the EU's trade policies as essentially those of a 'trading state' (Rosecrance 1986, 1993), aimed at the use of multilateral and civilian methods to create stability and good trading conditions.

The image of the 'trading state' is still based on a set of assumptions about EU needs and strategic priorities, but it runs alongside a third image: that of the EU as a major contributor to global governance, here specifically the global governance of trade and the deployment of EU power in this cause. The rhetoric of EU policies is very much that of multilateralism, and of support for the WTO and other global institutions. But we have already noted that there is at least a potential tension between the EU's internal needs and development and the aims of the WTO; and it can also be noted that the EU's assiduous promotion of inter-regional relations, especially with East and Southeast Asia and with Latin America, could run counter to at least some of the WTO's global stipulations (Aggarwal and Fogarty 2004; Young 2004a; Meunier and Nicolaidis 2005). Likewise, the EU's pursuit of a wide range of trade agreements incorporating political conditionality, as has been noted by a number of

analysts (Youngs 2001; K. Smith 2004a), could create important contradictions with the broader multilateral system. The issue of whether trade agreements can be used as a lever of good governance or the observance of international human rights is raised in a particularly direct form by consideration of the EU as a trade power, provoking analysis in terms of normative considerations as well as those of more material policy objectives.

One final point should be made. Although the review conducted here has used the term 'trade policy' in a broad sense, it is clear from recent analysis that on the one hand trade has changed radically from the days when trade in goods could be assumed to be the whole of the story, and that on the other hand trade is only part of a broader commercial policy domain, which includes large elements of regulatory policy and of policy areas long assumed to be 'domestic' in their focus (Smith and Woolcock 1999; Damro 2001, 2006; Young 2000, 2002; Smith 2001; Morgan and McGuire, 2004). The EU's attention (for example) to competition policy, environmental policy, employment policy and other 'behind the border' issues has greatly broadened its engagement with the IPE and this has been reflected in the recent direction of analysis.

AID AND DEVELOPMENT POLICY

The European integration process has had an aid and development policy dimension since its inception (see above). Given that the initial six Member States included at least four with substantial colonial legacies, the creation of a customs union implied that special provisions in trade and other areas might be necessary for the ex-colonies; the addition of Britain in the 1970s and then Spain and Portugal in the 1980s added considerable weight to the ex-imperial dimension of the EC (Grilli 1993; Mayall 2005). From an analytical perspective, it is clear that the presence of historical, institutional, cultural and other ties between the ex-metropolitan countries and their ex-possessions was bound to shape the relationships between the EC and developing countries. In its turn, this set of developing relationships connected with broader developments in the IPE, and with analytical problems related to models of development and dependency, the role of international institutions and the processes of negotiation that characterize relations between industrial economies and the 'global south' (Maxfield 2002). In the post-Cold War period, the understanding of 'development' has itself been broadened to apply to countries from the former Soviet sphere, many of which have themselves become either members of the EU or closely linked to it.

History and change are thus potent factors conditioning the evolution of European aid and development policies. The first area in which this can be observed is in the construction of the EU's system for formulating and implementing aid and development policies (Grilli 1993; Holland 2002; Mayall 2005). This was in effect an outcome of the integration process – a means of handling the problems confronting a number of key Member States, most notably France. But the commitment of individual Member States to their national aid and development policies meant that from an early stage a key feature of the system was its 'mixity'; in other words, there was here none of the apparently exclusive grant of competence that was apparent in trade policy. Analysis of the policy domain thus took as a central assumption the coexistence of national and 'European' policies. As the Community developed, analysis also had to take on board the fact that the intensity and breadth of commitment of Member States was in fairly direct proportion to their imperial heritage (Arts 2004). Thus the key force in the initial development of policy was France (Claeys 2004); there was a radical extension of development policies through the first Lomé Convention of 1975 as a result of British accession; and the extension of development policies to Latin America and a range of other territories was a function of Spanish and Portuguese accession in 1986. The elaborate institutional apparatus established as a result of the Lomé process clearly set a new standard in development assistance, and much of the analysis of these

arrangements was premised on the assumption that a new form of North-South partnership had come into being.

But what sort of system was this? From the outset, a number of commentators focused on the fact that despite the claims of partnership, there was a strong whiff of neo-colonialism about the Lomé arrangements (Galtung 1972; Ravenhill 1985, 1995), whilst later analysts have also focused on the appropriateness of the structures and aims to African countries especially (Collier and Gunning 1995; Collier et al., 1997; Babarinde 1998). The EC extended unilateral trade and other concessions to the African, Caribbean and Pacific (ACP) partners, and set elaborate tests which they must pass in order to benefit from the rewards of partnership. Certain potential partners were excluded because they were too large, too needy or otherwise threatening. Arrangements for the stabilization of export prices or commodity prices were certainly as much in the interest of the EC as of the ACP countries. As a result, the literature on the Lomé system ranged between the highly critical and the partly self-congratulatory. It also tended to treat the 'development' policy area as rather self-contained, and not to see it in the context of broader EU trade and external policies.

During the 1980s and 1990s, there has been a strong move away from this position, towards analysis of the development policy area as a part of the 'external relations system' of the EC and then the EU and towards an emphasis on its interaction with other parts of the system such as trade policy, foreign and security policy and human rights policies (Collinson 1999; Holland 2002; K. Smith 2004a; Vanhoonacker 2005). The development policy domain has been analysed as part of the broader process of institutionalization of EU policies, and the interaction of national and European policies has been explicitly addressed (Lister 1997, 1999; Holland 2002; Arts and Dickson 2004). In addition, there have been important efforts to link the development policy system with the broader evolution of the post-colonial experience of EU Member States (Mayall 2005), and thus to explain the shape and scope of the system by reference to broader processes of international change. As yet, there has been no sustained effort to subject development policy to analysis through the lens of social constructivism and to show the ways in which it has come to represent certain value positions on the part both of actors in the EU system and of those in the broader Lomé framework, although some of the critical work mentioned earlier addresses these issues, as does some of the work on broader issues of conditionality (Youngs 2001; K. Smith 2004a). From 2000, the Lomé structures were replaced by those of the Cotonou Convention, which in its turn reflected a new consensus within the EU institutions about the direction of aid policies, involving conceptions of sustainable development and capacity-building (Holland 2002; Arts and Dickson 2004).

Given that the evolution of the EU's development policy system has been highly dependent on historical, cultural and other factors, and that it has been subject to conflicting value interpretations, how does a focus on this system help us to understand how the EU has related to the broader processes of the IPE? As noted above, one interpretation of the establishment of the EU development policy framework during the 1960s and 1970s was that this provided a new model for the conduct of relations between rich and poor countries. Thus the Lomé Conventions were interpreted by many commentators as a response to calls for a 'new international economic order' in the mid-1970s, providing a new set of institutional standards and forms of partnership (Grilli 1993; Lister 1997, 1999; Arts and Dickson 2004). As time went by, though, there was a more critical approach to the structures by those who saw them as decreasingly relevant to the needs of the developing countries – especially those who favoured trade remedies rather than the Lomé model of aid, and who pointed to the inherent contradictions between EU policies such as the CAP and the proclaimed aims of the development policy framework (for a selection of views see Arts and Dickson 2004). The decreasing effectiveness of unilateral trade preferences – a key feature of the initial Lomé model – was also noted, and the inefficiency of the structures for allocation and distribution of aid itself was a point of criticism (see for example Davenport 1992; Dickson 2004). These were in many cases criticisms that were increasingly made of the entire structure of 'western' aid and development policies, and thus the shifts in the Cotonou Convention towards models of sustainable development and capacity building could be interpreted as another response to changing international conditions.

The broad framework of EU aid and development policies is thus closely linked to the developing and changing international debate about development issues. At the more focused level of individual initiatives and negotiations, a range of other approaches is relevant. One prominent set of approaches has focused on negotiation processes, and especially on the conduct of asymmetrical negotiation and bargaining processes (Holland 2000; Stevens 2000; Forwood 2001; Elgström 2005), emphasizing the disparities between the EU and its partners and relating these to negotiation outcomes both at the broad (Cotonou) level and the more specific (sugar, bananas, etc.) level. One issue that emerges from these studies is on the one hand the extent to which EU-ACP negotiations can in effect be conducted as closed negotiations within the 'EU system' and on the other hand the ways in which they are linked strategically to broader processes of negotiation in the WTO or other contexts; to quote one author, it could be that in such contexts the ACP countries are just one of the crowd (K. Smith 2004b). This has become particularly problematic as the leverage of developing countries in the WTO itself has become more apparent. In the same area of analysis, there has been attention to the ways in which unilateral EU initiatives such as the 'everything but arms' measures adopted in 2001/2 can be incorporated into more generalized models of development and trade negotiations (Holland 2002).

Given what has been said about the EU system of aid and development policies, and about the ways in which they link to broader processes of IPE, what can be said about the EU's role as a power in this broad domain?

Some of the answer to this is implicit in the earlier discussion of the history behind EU policies. There is leverage in analyses that take on the implicit neo-colonial aspects of EU policies, and relate these to broader issues of dependency and exploitation: in this view, the EU is an aid superpower which acts as superpowers do, by dividing and ruling and exploiting and by selling a certain idea of development (Galtung 1972; Ravenhill 1985, 1995). This is countered by the view that puts the EU into the liberal 'global governance' camp, and which interprets the EU's aims as benign – or at least mixed - if not especially efficient or always effective (Holland 2002; Arts and Dickson 2004).

One argument that bears especially strongly on this, and which would bear further investigation, is the one from multi-level governance and multi-level negotiation: the evidence is that in formulating and pursuing aid and development policy, the European institutions have to engage in a complex balancing of preferences and institutional pressures, both from 'above' (the global institutions), from 'alongside' (other national development policies including those of the EU Member States themselves) and from 'below' (the broader debate and mobilization of NGOs, social movements and the like in pursuit of sustainable development). In this context, what is the power that the EU can mobilize? In many ways it seems to be the power to negotiate, to form linkages and to use linked institutions to put forward a package of development measures that respond to a logic of appropriateness rather than a logic of consequences simply framed in terms of an intra-EU consensus shaped around the lowest common denominator of Member State positions.

Finally, the impact of EU power in aid and development policies has been increasingly linked with theories of 'normative power' and the associated roles of norms and values in international aid and development issues (Manners 2002, 2006). The broad 'normative power' argument relies upon the assumption that the EU in itself represents and propagates certain normative positions – in this case, in favour of specific models of development, especially those associated with sustainable development and good governance practices. This can then be used as an analytical lever with which to explore EU policies on the broad issue of conditionality, and on the promotion of particular core values such as the abolition of the death penalty. More precisely, the role of norms and their association with power has been explored by a number of authors in their analysis of international development negotiations (Elgström 2005). Here, norms can be seen as pervading the negotiations and providing a source of bargaining leverage for the EU and its agents; they can also be seen as part of the outcomes of the negotiation process, when attention is focused on the generation, the promotion or the preservation of specific normative positions.

MONETARY RELATIONS

The EU's international monetary relations have been analysed increasingly in the past decade with the approach and then the implementation of EMU; and in the process, analysts have built upon increasing appreciation of the political and institutional complexities of international finance more generally (Cohen 2002). This is not of course to imply that 'Europe's money' was not a focus of attention in the 1960's, 1970s and 1980s. The gradual but fundamental shifts in international monetary power during the 1970s and 1980s in particular created a literature exploring the relationship between the European Monetary System and the US Dollar, which was associated with the broader IPE studies of the western system conducted by a number of scholars (Diebold 1972; Calleo and Rowland 1973; Kruse 1980; Ludlow 1982; Tsoukalis 1986). In the late 1980s and early 1990s, these studies were joined by others dealing with the monetary implications of the SMP, exploring the implications of the slogan 'one market, one money' that was propounded by the Delors Committee in its preparation of the case for EMU (Mayes 1993). As with other areas of the EU's involvement in the IPE, it is possible to explore the later development of monetary policy analysis through the three areas that have been at the core of this chapter: the EU as a (sub)system of the IPE, the EU as part of the process of IPE, and the EU as a power in the IPE.

The establishment of EMU as a core goal of the Union in the Maastricht Treaty (1991) set the scene for prolonged attention to the negotiations that framed the EU's system of monetary integration. Here, one of the key analytical distinctions (as in other areas of EU politics) was between the intergovernmentalist approach to EMU and the approaches that centred around institutionalist ideas encompassing a broader range of non-state influences. A number of large and important studies of the negotiations thus emerged during the 1990s (Dyson and Featherstone 1999; Dyson 2000; McNamara 2001), which had as their primary aim the explanation of why and how the institutional framework evolved in the way that it did. These were accompanied by studies analysing the process from the perspective of national priorities and policies and interstate bargaining, which for a variety of good reasons did not focus to a large extent on the international implications of the process or its product (Hösli 1998, 2000; Jones 1998, 2000; Cameron 1998; Dyson 2002). Later, there emerged a number of treatments which emphasized the non-material aspects of the EMU negotiations, and in particular the ways in which the idea of EMU became established almost in defiance of the 'facts' about national economic priorities and divergences of economic performance, creating issues of legitimacy and institutional capacity (Verdun 1998, 2000; Verdun and Christiansen 2000).

The performance of the EMU system itself became an increasing focus of attention after the introduction of the Euro and the associated Stability and Growth Pact in the late 1990s and early 2000s. It was at this point that the functioning of 'Euroland' as an international political economy became an explicit focus of analysis, and in particular the relationship between 'economic government' in the eurozone and the macro-economic needs of the zone for stability and the fight against inflation (Crouch 2000; Dyson 2000; Tsoukalis 2000,

2003; La Malfa 2002; Underhill 2002; Verdun 2002). As noted in Chapter 18, the contending pressures for and against the politicization of monetary management within EMU raised key questions about the role of institutions such as the European Central Bank (ECB) and the Economic and Financial Committee of the EU (Ecofin); in particular, there arose issues about the 'capture' or subversion of the institutions by national political needs, and about the resources available to monetary authorities in the absence of a developed fiscal policy for the eurozone.

How did this concern with the initiation and working of the Euro system link with the second of our issues: the relationship between the European process and the broader processes of the IPE? Whilst as noted above the primary interest of analysts during the 1990s was with the establishment of the system itself, there was a growing number of studies assessing the implications of EMU for the working of international finance and the management of currencies within the global arena. As might have been anticipated, one of the issues raised at an early stage was the extent to which EMU would be or would remain inward-looking (as was the case with the early stages of the SMP). A primary focus on the internal aspects of the process might then produce unintended and adverse consequences for the working of the international monetary system as a whole (Fratiani 2000). More particularly, the emphasis of the Euro system on financial stability and the reduction of inflation could have significant effects on the growth of world demand, and thus on the alignment of international currencies. As it happens also, the relatively poor economic performance of major eurozone countries such as France and Germany – arguably exacerbated by eurozone restrictions – has had important impacts on the capacity of the eurozone as a whole to play a role in international monetary management.

Alongside the issues of internalization and externalization raised by the preceding discussion, the establishment of the euro has been evaluated in terms of its impact on institutional frameworks within the IPE. From an early stage, it was noted by analysts that the initiation of EMU could have repercussions for the established international financial institutions, especially the International Monetary Fund (IMF) (Henning 1997; Eichengreen and Ghironi 1998; Fratiani 2000). The establishment of a major zone of fixed exchange rates among industrial economies, with potential for considerable enlargement as the EU itself enlarged, clearly created a significant new structure at the core of the IPE. In consequence, issues about representation and voting rights in major international institutions have been raised, and questions about the composition of national currency reserves and the operation of international financial markets and investment flows have been sharpened (McNamara and Meunier 2002), for instance in respect of Dollar or euro holdings by governments in Asia or the Middle East. In analytical terms, the questions are those of institutional development and adjustment, and of the extent to which processes of global economic governance can be adapted to take account of a major new actor (Bromley 2001).

Such questions relate closely to the final issue to be considered here: the implications of EMU for the EU's role as a power in the IPE. As far back as the 1970s, the question of monetary union had been considered in the context of relations between the (then) EC and the United States (Diebold 1972; Warnecke 1972), and this has not surprisingly been one of the key focuses of analysis in the recent past. A number of US analysts pointed out at an early stage that the euro could lead to a strong and continuing challenge to the Dollar as a medium of international exchange and to the privileges that have accompanied the Dollar's role as 'top currency' (Bergsten 1997; Henning 1997; Eichengreen and Ghironi 1998). This, it was well recognized, was not simply a technical issue – it concerned the political use of the Dollar in the cause of US hegemony, and thus a potential political challenge from a uniting Europe to the USA. The analyses carried out especially by US scholars seemed to point in the direction of a possible 'tripolar' international monetary system, or even to a bipolar one with the Japanese Yen reduced to marginal status (Bergsten 1997, 1999; Henning 1997).

Such a system would be inherently more volatile than a multipolar one, with major implications for the style of international monetary management.

As it happened, the early years of the euro seemed to contradict the idea that the EU could become a monetary 'superpower' in the IPE. After its launch in January 2000, the currency declined rapidly against the Dollar and seemed to some to be ill-equipped to compete with the US currency. Analysis as a result tended now to focus on the weakness of the currency and on the deficiencies of its political management arrangements (see above); this tended to overlook the fact that, as with established national currencies, the euro was reflecting the economic fundamentals and especially the stagnating economies of France, Germany and Italy (Jones 2000). When the euro not only revived against the Dollar but became increasingly strong against it in 2003–2004, analysts noted that this in turn reflected a number of political and economic fundamentals, including the political risk factors sharpened by the war in Iraq and the economic risks created by large deficits in the US balance of payments and federal budget (Cohen 2003). In terms of Political Science approaches, much of this analysis remained essentially at the strategic level, with the euro seen as a proxy for a national currency – but a currency with significant institutional and political limitations, as already noted.

In addition to these approaches, it is important to note that in the case of European monetary policy (as with trade and aid/development policy) there is a body of literature addressing the place of the euro in globalization. In particular, there is a strong strand of critical literature in which the euro is evaluated as part of a broad neo-liberal project, either one that is a reflection of US predominance or one that is in a sense 'home-grown' (Gill 1998; Cafruny 2003; Cafruny and Ryner 2003). Both institutionally and in terms of political linkages with the interests of large corporations, the euro can be assessed as a contribution to the malign influences of globalization and as part of an attack on the 'European social model'. But it is equally important to note that there is a literature on the ways in which the development of a European 'economic government' might be seen as a defence against the perils of globalization, and the euro a source of a growing European identity (Risse 2003) – an argument implicitly espoused by a number of continental European governments and by a number of commentators across the EU.

AGENDAS

This chapter has reviewed the study of the EU's role in the IPE in the light of two frameworks: first, the coexisting roles of the EU as a (sub)system of the IPE, as part of the process of the IPE and as a 'power' in the IPE; and second, the ways in which these roles can be identified in the specific policy areas of trade, aid/development and money. It is clear that a great deal of literature and political science analysis can be accommodated within these frameworks, and that the literature casts valuable light on the methodological and substantive issues that are raised. The intention in this concluding section is to indicate a number of research issues that have either been uncovered but not fully explored or that remain effectively concealed from the view of political science analysis. These issues form the core of an agenda for exploration of the EU's role in the IPE during the coming period. They include:

- Continued exploration of the EU's role in global (and regional) governance, including the role of 'external governance' through the application of EU norms and standards in other non-member societies or regions.
- Further attention to the ways in which EU-regionalism forms either a model for or a contrast to regionalism elsewhere in the world arena, with specific attention to trade, aid/development and monetary policies.
- The ways in which the EU's 'foreign economic policy' forms the basis for strategic action and potentially hegemonic practices in the IPE on behalf of the EU (and thus

the extent to which trade, aid/development and monetary policy form weapons for these kinds of practices).
- The ways in which 'normative power' can be identified and analysed within the EU's activities in the IPE, and linked with this the extent to which the deployment of ideas within EU foreign economic policies is a potent source of impact for the Union on the IPE as a whole or specific regions.
- In similar fashion, the ways in which 'regulatory power' can be analysed as part of the EU's armoury within the IPE, both in a materialist sense (examining the EU's capacity to extend regulation into other regions and compete with the US, for example) and in a non-materialist sense (EU regulatory power as part of or an extension of normative power).

More broadly, what has emerged from this review is a threefold set of conclusions in substance and methodology. First, the EU as a (sub)system of IPE displays a number of unresolved tensions centred on scope, competence, institutional capacity and continuing national divergence. To date, these have been analysed predominantly in terms of internal bargains and their conclusion (or non-conclusion), but increasingly they are also evaluated in terms of the normative consensus to which they give expression, and of the ways in which EU positions are socially constructed as well as materially founded. Second, the EU as part of the process of the IPE expresses important tensions between regionalism and globalism, but also has substantial but as yet inconclusive effects on the institutions and practices of the IPE. There is scope for extension of analysis in this area, including (as noted above) empirical exploration of the relationship between the EU's material presence in major processes of IPE and the ways in which the EU has affected the core discourses and practices of the IPE. Third, the EU as a 'power' in the IPE also displays unresolved tensions between its status as a civilian or normative/civilizing power and its aspiration (or the aspiration of major EU members) to create material effects on the balance of forces in the IPE. In particular, there is an issue about the EU's legitimacy as part of the governing arrangements of the IPE, and about the associated problem of leadership. There are still issues to be explored about what are the key constituents of EU power, and about what EU power might be used for – a normative as well as an empirical issue, which lends itself to exploration with a range of rationalist or non-rationalist approaches.

REFERENCES

Aggarwal, V. and Fogarty, E. (eds) (2004) *European Union Trade Strategies: Between Regionalism and Globalism*. Basingstoke: Palgrave/Macmillan.

Ahnlid, A. (2005) 'Setting the global trade agenda: the European Union and the launch of the doha round', in O. Elgström and C. Jönsson (eds), *European Union Negotiations: Processes, Networks and Institutions*. London: Routledge. pp.130–47.

Arts, K. (2004) 'Changing interests in EU development cooperation: the impact of EU membership and advancing integration', in K. Arts and A. Dickson (eds), *EU Development Cooperation: From Development to Symbol*. Manchester: Manchester University Press. pp. 101–12.

Arts, K. and Dickson, A. (eds) (2004) *EU Development Cooperation: From Development to Symbol*. Manchester: Manchester University Press.

Babarinde, O. (1998) 'The EU's relations with the south: a commitment to development?' in C. Rhodes (ed.), *The European Union in the World Community*. Boulder, CO: Lynne Rienner.

Bergsten, C.F. (1997) 'The dollar and the euro', *Foreign Affairs*, 76(4): 83–95.

Bergsten, C.F. (1999) 'America and Europe: clash of the Titans?' *Foreign Affairs*, 78(2): 20–34.

Breslin, S., Hughes, C., Phillips, N. and Rosamond, B. (eds) (2002) *New Regionalisms in the Global Political Economy*. London: Routledge.

Bromley, S. (2001) 'The European Union and global economic governance' in G. Thompson (ed.), *Governing the European Economy*. London: Sage/Open University. pp. 269–302.

Cafruny, A. (2003) 'Europe, the United States, and neoliberal (dis)order: is there a coming crisis of the Euro?', in A. Cafruny and M. Ryner (eds), *A Ruined Fortress? Neoliberal Hegemony and Transformation in Europe*. Lanham, MD: Rowman and Littlefield. pp. 285–305.

Cafruny, A. and Ryner, M. (eds) (2003) *A Ruined Fortress? Neoliberal Hegemony and Transformation in Europe*. Lanham, MD: Rowman and Littlefield.

Cable, V. and Henderson, D. (1994) *Trade Blocs? The Future of Regional Integration*. London: Royal Institute of International Affairs.

Calleo, D. and Rowland, B. (1973) *America and the World Political Economy: Atlantic Dreams and National Realities*. Bloominton, IN and London: Indiana State University Press.

Cameron, D. (1998) 'Creating supranational authority in monetary and exchange-rate policy: the sources and effects of EMU', in W. Sandholtz and A. Stone Sweet (eds), *European Integration and Supranational Governance*. Oxford: Oxford University Press. pp. 188–216.

Claeys, A.-S. (2004) '"Sense and sensibility": the role of France and French interests in European development policy since 1957', in K. Arts and A. Dickson (eds), *EU Development Cooperation: From Model to Symbol*. Manchester: Manchester University Press. pp. 113–32.

Cohen, B. (2002) 'International finance', in W. Carlsnaes, T. Risse, and B. Simmons (eds), *Handbook of International Relations*. London: Sage. pp. 429–47.

Cohen, B. (2003) 'Can the Euro ever challenge the dollar?', *Journal of Common Market Studies*, 41(4): 575–96.

Coleman, W. and Underhill, G. (eds) (1998) *Regionalism and Global Economic Integration: Europe, Asia and the Americas*. London: Routledge.

Collier, P. and Gunning, J. (1995) 'Trade policy and regional integration: implications for relations between Europe and Africa', *The World Economy*, 18(3): 387–410.

Collier, P., Guillaumont, P., Guillamont, S. and Gunning, J. (1997) 'The future of Lomé: Europe's role in Africa's growth', *The World Economy*, 20(3): 285–306.

Collinson, S. (1999) '"Issue-systems", "multi-level games" and the analysis of the EU's external commercial and associated policies: a research agenda', *Journal of European Public Policy*, 6(2): 206–24.

Crouch, C. (ed) (2000) *After the Euro: Shaping Institutions for Governance in the Wake of European Monetary Union*. Oxford: Oxford University Press.

Damro, C. (2001) 'Building an international identity: the EU and extraterritorial competition policy, *Journal of European Public Policy*, 8(2): 208–26.

Damro, C. (2006) 'Institutions, ideas and a leadership gap: the EU's role in multilateral competition policy' in O. Elgström and M. Smith (eds), *The European Union's Roles in International Politics: Concepts and Analysis*. London: Routledge. pp. 208–24.

Davenport, M. (1992) 'Africa and the unimportance of being preferred', *Journal of Common Market Studies*, 30(2): 233–51.

Dent, C. (1997) *The European Economy: The Global Context*. London: Routledge.

Dicken, P. (2003) *Global Shift: Reshaping the Global Economic Map in the 21st Century*. London: Sage.

Dickson, A. (2004) 'The unimportance of trade preferences' in K. Arts and A. Dickson (eds) *EU Development Cooperation: From Model to Symbol*. Manchester: Manchester University Press. pp. 42–59.

Diebold, W. (1972) *The United States and the Industrial World*. New York: Praeger.

Dyson, K. (2000) *The Politics of the Euro-zone: Stability or Breakdown?* Oxford: Oxford University Press.

Dyson, K. (ed.) (2002) *European States and the Euro: Europeanization, Variation and Convergence*. Oxford: Oxford University Press.

Dyson, K, and Featherstone, K. (1999) *The Road to Maastricht: Negotiating Economic and Monetary Union*. Oxford: Oxford University Press.

Eeckhout, P. (1994) *The European Internal Market and International Trade: A Legal Analysis*. Oxford: Clarendon Press.

Eeckhout, P. (2004) *External Relations of the European Union: Legal and Constitutional Foundations*. Oxford: Oxford University Press.

Eichengreen, B. (ed.) (1998) *Transatlantic Economic Relations in the Post-Cold War Era*. New York: Council on Foreign Relations.

Eichengreen, B. and Ghironi, F (1998) 'European monetary unification and international monetary cooperation', in B. Eichengreen (ed.), *Transatlantic Economic Relations in the Post-Cold War Era*. New York: Council on Foreign Relations. pp. 69–98.

Elgström, O. (2005) 'The Cotonou agreement: asymmetric negotiations and the impact of norms', in O. Elgström and C. Jönsson (eds) *European Union Negotiations: Processes, Networks and Institutions*. London: Routledge. pp. 183–99.

Elgström, O. and Jönsson, C. (eds) (2005) *European Union Negotiations: Processes, Networks and Institutions*. London: Routledge.

Elsig, M. (2002) *The EU's Common Commercial Policy: Institutions, Interests and Ideas*. Aldershot: Ashgate.

Forwood, G. (2001) 'The road to Cotonou: negotiating a successor to Lomé', *Journal of Common Market Studies*, 39(3): 485–506.

Fratiani, M. (2000) 'The international monetary system after the Euro', in A. Prakash and J. Hart (eds), *Responding to Globalization*. London: Routledge. pp. 151–70.

Frieden, J. and Lake, D. (eds) (2000) *International Political Economy: Perspectives on Global Power and Wealth*, 4th edn. London: Routledge.

Galtung, J. (1972) *The European Community: A Superpower in the Making*. London: George Allen and Unwin.

Gill, S. (1998) 'European governance and new constitutionalism: EMU and alternatives to disciplinary neo-liberalism in Europe', *New Political Economy*, 3(1): 5–26.

Gilpin, R. (2000) *The Challenge of Global Capitalism: The World Economy in the 21st Century*. Princeton: Princeton University Press.

Gilpin, R. and Gilpin, J. (2001) *Global Political Economy: Understanding the International Economic Order*. Princeton: Princeton University Press.

Gilson, J. (2000) *Japan and the European Union: A Partnership for the Twenty-First Century?* Basingstoke: Macmillan.

Goddard, C. R., Cronin, P. and Dash, K. (eds) (2003) *International Political Economy: State-Market Relations in a Changing Global Order*, 2nd edn. Basingstoke: Palgrave/Macmillan.

Gowan, P. (2000) *How the EU Can Help Russia*. London: Centre for European Reform.

Grilli, E. (1993) *The European Community and the Developing Countries*. Cambridge: Cambridge University Press.

Guay, T. (1999) *The United States and the European Union: The Political Economy of a Relationship*. Sheffield: Sheffield Academic Press.

Hanson, B. (1998) 'What happened to fortress Europe? External trade policy liberalization in the European Union', *International Organization*, 52(1): 55–85.

Hayes, J. (1993) *Making Trade Policy in the European Community*. London: Macmillan for the Trade Policy Research Centre.

Heidensohn, K. (1995) *Europe and World Trade*. London: Pinter.

Henning, C.R. (1997) *Cooperating with Europe's Monetary Union*. Washington, DC: Institute for International Economics.

Hill, C. and Smith. M. (2005) *International Relations and the European Union*. Oxford: Oxford University Press.

Hine, R. (1985) *The Political Economy of European Trade*. Brighton: Harvester-Wheatsheaf.

Hocking, B. and McGuire, S. (eds) (2004) *Trade Politics*, second edition. London: Routledge.

Hoekman, B. and Kostecki, M. (2001) *The Political Economy of the World Trading System: The WTO and Beyond*, second edition. Oxford: Oxford University Press.

Holland, M. (2000) 'Resisting reform or risking revival? Renegotiating the Lomé convention', in M. Green Cowles and M. Smith (eds), *The State of the European Union Volume 5: Risks Reform, Resistance and Revival*. New York: Oxford University Press. pp. 390–410.

Holland, M. (2002) *The European Union and the Third World*. Basingstoke: Palgrave/Macmillan.

Hösli, M. (1998) 'The EMU and international monetary relations: what to expect for international actors?', in C. Rhodes (ed.), *The European Union in the Global Community*. Boulder, CO: Lynne Rienner. pp. 165–91.

Hösli, M. (2000) 'The creation of the European economic and monetary union (EMU): intergovernmental negotiations and two-level games', *Journal of European Public Policy*, 7(5): 744–66.

Jackson, J. (1995) 'The EC and world trade: the commercial policy dimension', in W. Adams (ed.), *Singular Europe: Economy and Polity of the European Community after 1992*. Ann Arbor: University of Michigan Press. pp. 321–45.

Jones, E. (1998) 'Economic and monetary union: playing with money', in A. Moravcsik (ed.), *Centralization or Fragmentation? Europe Facing the Challenges of Deepening, Diversity, and Democracy*. New York: Council on Foreign Relations. pp. 59–93.

Jones, E. (2000) 'European monetary union and the new political economy of adjustment' in M. Green Cowles and M. Smith (eds), *The State of the European Union Volume 5: Risks, Reform, Resistance and Revival*. Oxford: Oxford University Press. pp. 127–45.

Jones, E. and Verdun, A. (2004) *The Political Economy of European Integration*. London: Routledge.

Kahler, M. (1995) *International Institutions and the Political Economy of Integration*. Washington, DC: Brookings Institution.

Kahler, M. and Lake, A. (eds) (2003) *Governance in a Global Economy: Political Authority in Transition*. Princeton: Princeton University Press.

Kapteyn, P. (1996) *The Stateless Market: The European Dilemma of Integration and Civilization*. London: Routledge.

Kerremans, B. (2006) 'Pro-active policy entrepreneur or risk minimizer? A principal-agent interpretation of the EU's role in the WTO', in O. Elgström and M. Smith (eds), *The European Union's Roles in International Politics: Concepts and Analysis*. London: Routledge. pp. 172–88.

Krueger. A. (ed.) (1998) *The WTO as an International Organization*. Chicago: Chicago University Press.

Kruse, D. (1980) *Monetary Integration in Western Europe: EMU, EMS and Beyond*. London: Butterworth.

Laffan, B., O'Donnell, R. and Smith, M. (2000) *Europe's Experimental Union: Rethinking Integration*. London: Routledge.

La Malfa, G. (2002) 'The orphaned Euro', *Survival*, 44(1): 81–92.

Lister, M. (1997) *The European Union and the South: Relations with Developing Countries*. London: Routledge.

Lister, M. (ed.) (1999) *New Perspectives on European Union Development Cooperation*. Boulder, CO and Oxford: Westview Press.

Ludlow, P. (1982) *The Making of the European Monetary System: A Case Study of the Politics of the European Community*. London: Butterworth.

Macleod, I., Hendry, I. and Hyett, S. (1996) *The External Relations of the European Communities: A Manual of Law and Practice*. Oxford: Clarendon Press.

McGuire, S. (1999) 'Trade tools: holding the fort or declaring open house?', in T. Lawton (ed.), *European Industrial Policy and Competitiveness: Concepts and Instruments*. Basingstoke: Macmillan. pp. 77–92.

McNamara, K. (2001) 'Where do rules come from? The creation of the European Central Bank', in A. Stone Sweet, W. Sandholtz and N. Fligstein (eds), *The Institutionalization of Europe*. Oxford: Oxford University Press. pp. 155–70.

McNamara, K. and Meunier, S. (2002) 'Between national sovereignty and international power: what external voice for the Euro?', *International Affairs*, 77(1): 849–68.

Manners, I. (2002) 'Normative power Europe: a contradiction in terms?' *Journal of Common Market Studies*, 40(2): 235–58.

Manners, I. (2006) 'Normative power Europe reconsidered', *Journal of European Public Policy*, 13(2): 182–99.

Maxfield, S. (2002) 'International development' in W. Carlsnaes, T. Risse and B. Simmons (eds), *Handbook of International Relations*. London: Sage. pp. 462–79

Mayall, J. (2005) 'The shadow of empire: the EU and the former colonial world', in C. Hill and M. Smith (eds), *International Relations and the European Union*. Oxford: Oxford University Press. pp. 292–316.

Mayes, D. (ed.) (1993) *The External Implications of European Integration*. London: Harvester-Wheatsheaf.

Meunier, S. (1998) 'Divided but united: European trade policy, integration and EC-US agricultural negotiations in the Uruguay round', in C. Rhodes (ed.), *The European Union in the World Community*. Boulder, CO: Lynne Rienner. pp. 193–211.

Meunier, S. (2000) 'What single voice? European institutions and EU-U.S. trade negotiations', *International Organization*, 54(1): 103–35.

Meunier, S. (2005) *Trading Voices: The European Union in International Commercial Negotiations*. Princeton, NJ: Princeton University Press.

Meunier, S. and Nicolaidis, K. (1999) 'Who speaks for Europe? The delegation of trade authority in the EU', *Journal of Common Market Studies*, 37(3): 477–502.

Meunier, S. and Nicolaidis, K. (2000) 'EU trade policy: the "exclusive" *versus* "shared" competence debate', in M. Green Cowles and M. Smith (eds), *The State of the European Union Volume 5: Risks, Reforms, Resistance and Revival*. Oxford: Oxford University Press. pp. 325–46.

Meunier, S. and Nicolaidis, K. (2005) 'The European Union as a trade power', in C. Hill and M. Smith (eds) *International Relations and the European Union*. Oxford: Oxford University Press. pp. 247–69.

Milner, H. (2002) 'International trade', in W. Carlsnaes, T. Risse and B. Simmons (eds), *Handbook of International Relations*. London: Sage. pp. 448–61.

Morgan, E. and McGuire, S. (2004) 'Transatlantic divergence: GE-Honeywell and the EU's merger policy', *Journal of European Public Policy*, 11(1): 39–56.

Niemann, A. (2004) 'Between communicative action and strategic action: the Article 113 Committee and the negotiations on the WTO basic telecommunications services agreement', *Journal of European Public Policy*, 11(3): 379–407.

O'Brien, R. and Williams, M. (2004) *Global Political Economy: Evolution and Dynamics*. Basingstoke: Palgrave/Macmillan.

Palan, R. (ed.) (2000) *Global Political Economy: Contemporary Theories*. London: Routledge.

Petersmann, E.-U. and Pollack, M. (eds) (2003) *Transatlantic Economic Disputes: The EU, the US, and the WTO*. Oxford: Oxford University Press.

Pollack, M. (2003a) 'The political economy of transatlantic trade disputes', in E.-U. Petersmann and M. Pollack (eds), *Transatlantic Economic Disputes: The EU, the US, and the WTO*. Oxford: Oxford University Press. pp. 65–118.

Pollack, M. (2003b) 'Managing system friction: regulatory conflicts in transatlantic relations and the WTO', in E.-U. Petersmann and M. Pollack (eds) *Transatlantic Economic Disputes: The EU, the US, and the WTO*. Oxford: Oxford University Press. pp. 595–602.

Pollack, M. and Shaffer, G. (2001) *Transatlantic Governance in the Global Economy*. Lanham, MD: Rowman and Littlefield.

Preston, P. and Gilson, J. (eds) (2001) *The European Union and East Asia: Interregional Linkages in a Changing Global System*. Aldershot: Edward Elgar.

Ravenhill, J. (1985) *Collective Clientelism: The Lomé Convention and North–South Relations*. New York: Columbia University Press.

Ravenhill, J. (1995) 'Dependent by default: Africa's relations with the European Union' in W. Harbeson and D. Rothschild (eds), *Africa in World Politics: Post-Cold War Challenges*. Boulder, CO and Oxford: Westview Press.

Risse, T. (2003) 'The Euro between national and European identity', *Journal of European Public Policy*, 10(4): 487–505.

Rosecrance, R. (1986) *The Rise of the Trading State: Commerce and Conquest in the Modern World*. New York: Random House.

Rosecrance, R. (1993) 'Trading States in a new concert of Europe', in H. Haftendorn and C. Tuschhoff (eds) *America and Europe in an Era of Change*. Boulder, CO and Oxford: Westview Press. pp. 127–46.

Schirm, S. (2002) *Globalization and the New Regionalism: Global Markets, Domestic Politics and Regional Cooperation*. Cambridge: Polity.

Scott, A. (1998) *Regions and the World Economy: The Coming Shape of Global Production, Competition and Political Order*. Oxford: Oxford University Press.

Smith, K. (2004a) *The Making of EU Foreign Policy: The Case of Eastern Europe*, 2nd edn. Basingstoke: Palgrave/Macmillan.

Smith, K. (2004b) 'The ACP in the European Union's network of regional relationships: still unique or just one in the crowd?', in K. Arts and A. Dickson (eds), *EU Development Cooperation: From Model to Symbol*. Manchester: Manchester University Press. pp. 60–79.

Smith, M. (1998) 'Competitive cooperation and EU-US relations: can the EU be a strategic partner for the US in the global political economy?', *Journal of European Public Policy*, 5(4): 561–77.

Smith, M (2001) 'The EU's commercial policy: between coherence and fragmentation', *Journal of European Public Policy*, 8(5): 787–802.

Smith, M. (2004a) 'The European Union as a trade policy actor' in B. Hocking and S. McGuire (eds) *Trade Politics*, second edition. London: Routledge. pp. 289–303.

Smith, M. (2004b) 'Foreign economic policy', in W. Carlsnaes, H. Sjursen and B. White (eds), *Contemporary European Foreign Policy*. London: Sage. pp. 75–90.

Smith, M. (2005a) 'Negotiating globalization: the foreign economic policy of the European Union', in R. Stubbs, and G. Underhill (eds), *Political Economy and the Changing Global Order*, third edition. Toronto: Oxford University Press. pp. 387–97

Smith, M. (2005b) 'The European Union and the United States of America: the politics of "bi-multilateral" negotiations', in O. Elgström and C. Jönsson (eds), *European Union Negotiations: Processes, Networks and Institutions*. London: Routledge. pp. 164–82.

Smith, M. (2005c) 'The Commission and external relations', in D. Spence (ed.), *The European Commission*, 3rd edn. London: John Harper. pp. 305–32.

Smith, M. and Woolcock, S. (1999) 'European Union commercial policy: a leadership role in the new millennium?', *European Foreign Affairs Review*, 4(4): 439–62.

Spero, J. and Hart, J. (1997) *The Politics of International Economic Relations*, 5th edn. London: Routledge.

Stevens, C. (2000) 'Trade with developing countries: banana skins and turf wars', in H. Wallace and W. Wallace (eds), *Policy-Making in the European Union*. Oxford: Oxford University Press. pp. 401–26.

Stubbs, R. and Underhill, G. (eds) (2005) *Political Economy and the Changing Global Order*, 3rd edn. Toronto: Oxford University Press.

Switky, R. and Kerremans, B. (2000) *The Political Importance of Regional Trading Blocs*. Aldershot: Ashgate.

Teló, M. (2001) *European Union and New Regionalism: Europe and Globalization in Comparative Perspective*. Aldershot: Ashgate.

Tsoukalis, L. (1986) (ed.) *Europe, America and the World Economy*. Oxford: Blackwell.

Tsoukalis, L. (1997) *The New European Economy Revisited*. Oxford: Oxford University Press.

Tsoukalis, L. (2000) 'Economic and monetary union: political conviction and economic uncertainty', in H. Wallace and W. Wallace (eds), *Policy-Making in the European Union*, 4th edn. Oxford: Oxford University Press. pp. 149–78.

Tsoukalis, L. (2003) *What Kind of Europe?* Oxford: Oxford University Press.

Underhill, G. (2002) 'Global integration, EMU, and monetary governance in the European Union: the political economy of the "stability culture", in K. Dyson (ed.), *European States and the Euro: Europeanization, Variation and Convergence*. Oxford: Oxford University Press. pp. 31–52.

Van den Hoven, A. (2004) 'The European Union as an international economic actor', in N. Nugent (ed.), *European Union Enlargement*. Basingstoke: Palgrave/Macmillan. pp. 213–25.

Vanhoonacker, S. (2005) 'The institutional framework', in C. Hill and M. Smith (eds), *International Relations and the European Union*. Oxford: Oxford University Press. pp. 67–90.

Verdun, A. (1998) 'Understanding economic and monetary union in the EU', *Journal of European Public Policy*, 5(3): 527–33.

Verdun, A. (2000) 'Monetary integration in Europe: ideas and evolution', in M. Green Cowles and M. Smith (eds) *The State of the European Union Volume 5: Risks, Reform, Resistance and Revival*. Oxford: Oxford University Press. pp. 91–109.

Verdun, A. (ed.) (2002) *The Euro: European Integration Theory and Economic and Monetary Union*. Lanham, MD: Rowman and Littlefield.

Verdun, A. and Christiansen, T. (2000) 'Policies, institutions and the Euro: dilemmas of legitimacy', in C. Crouch (ed.), *After the Euro: Shaping Institutions for Governance in the Wake of European Monetary Union*. Oxford: Oxford University Press. pp. 162–78.

Warnecke, S. (ed.) (1972) *The European Community in the 1970s*. New York: Praeger.

Woods, N. (ed.) (2000) *The Political Economy of Globalization*. Basingstoke: Macmillan.

Woolcock, S. (1993) 'The European *acquis* and multilateral trade rules: are they compatible?', *Journal of Common Market Studies*, 31(4): 539–58.

Woolcock, S. (2000) 'European trade policy: global pressures and domestic constraints', in H. Wallace and W. Wallace (eds), *Policy-Making in the European Union*, 4th edn. Oxford: Oxford University Press. pp. 373–400.

Woolcock, S. (2005) 'Trade policy: from Uruguay to Doha and beyond', in H. Wallace, W. Wallace and M. Pollack (eds), *Policy-Making in the European Union*, fifth edition. Oxford: Oxford University Press. pp. 377–400.

Young, A. (2000) 'The adaptation of European foreign economic policy: from Rome to Seattle', *Journal of Common Market Studies*, 38(1): 93–116.

Young, A. (2002) *Extending European Cooperation: The European Union and the 'New' International Trade Agenda.* Manchester: Manchester University Press.

Young, A. (2004a) 'What game? By which rules? Adaptation and flexibility in the EC's foreign economic policy', in M. Knodt and S. Princen (eds), *Understanding the European Union's External Relations.* London: Routledge. pp. 54–71.

Young, A. (2004b) 'The incidental fortress: the single European market and world trade', *Journal of Common Market Studies*, 42(2): 393–414.

Young, A. (2006) 'Punching its weight? The EU's use of WTO dispute resolution', in O. Elgström and M. Smith (eds), *The European Union's Roles in International Politics: Concepts and Analysis.* London: Routledge. pp. 189–207.

Youngs, R. (2001) *The European Union and the Promotion of Democracy: Europe's Mediterranean and Asian Policies.* Oxford: Oxford University Press.

28

European Foreign Policy

WALTER CARLSNAES

INTRODUCTION

Although the notion of a 'European Foreign Policy' (EFP) is currently an undisputed part of the study of European Union (EU) politics, it is a relatively recent addition to the disciplinary vocabulary of this field of research. Indeed, as recently as in the 1998 publication of the exhaustive *Encyclopedia of the European Union*, it is not even included as a subject-matter deserving to be defined or discussed by itself (Dinan 1998). The assumption underlying this omission is perhaps that since the phenomenon was presumed not to exist at that time, it did not merit attention as a topic or concept. This may or may not have been a credible stance to take a decade or so ago, even though one could find scholarly contributions using this concept already in the early parts of the 1990s.[1]

In any case, since then the situation has changed rapidly as well as radically. In a review article summing up the state of the art in EFP studies at the turn of the millennium, Ben Tonra was moved to conclude on the upbeat note that it 'is a pleasure to report on the health and strength of publication in the field ... The developing scholarship in this area is throwing up new conceptual challenges and is offering a widening variety of conclusions to some well-established questions' (Tonra 2000: 168). More recently, an edited volume pays this topic the tribute of entitling it *Rethinking European Foreign Policy* (Tonra and Christiansen 2004a). As its two co-editors note, a major reason for this need to reconsider an area of analysis which until recently seemed hardly to have existed at all is that 'foreign policy has been one of the areas in which European integration has made the most dynamic advances' (Tonra and Christiansen 2004b: 1). As we shall see below, this is also a period during which an increasing number of monographs and edited volumes have been published on various aspects of European foreign policy, as well as a plethora of articles in scientific and policy journals. This increasing scholarly focus on EFP over the past decade is a reflection of the rapid expansion in the scope and institutional capacity of EU foreign-policy making during this period, which to a considerable extent has developed in response to the pressures put on Europe during the post Cold War period, including the dissolution of the former Yugoslavia, increased instability along some of its borders, the security implications of enlargement and, subsequent to 11 September 2001, the threats posed by the 'new' terrorism.

This is not to say, however, that this is a field with a clear identity of its own and hence generally accepted analytical boundaries vis-à-vis other subfields of current EU scholarship. What is seen to emerge is a new form of foreign policy system, based not on traditional state boundaries but on a progressively robust form of transnational governance. Since, in the view of a considerable number of scholars, the growth of this complex and multilayered European foreign policy system represents a genuine novelty, it also poses a challenge to conventional foreign policy analysis. More specifically, what is at issue is the question of how to penetrate analytically a European constellation of states characterized by three different types of 'foreign' interactions cutting across both member state and European Union boundaries (see Soetendorp 1999; White 2001: 40–1).

The first of these is traditional *national* foreign policy, emanating from the separate and distinguishable foreign policy activities of the member states, which have arguably not decreased during the past decade despite a substantial increase in the scope of the other two types of relations. The second form of activity is EU foreign policy, referring to EU co-ordination of its *political* relations with the outside world, commonly described in terms of a commitment – building on the prior development of the intergovernmental system of European Political Cooperation (EPC), existing outside the competence and institutional framework of the European Economic Community (EEC) – to establish a Common Foreign and Security Policy (CFSP) as specified in the Treaty on European Union (TEU), signed in Maastricht in 1992 and figuratively expressed as Pillar II in the EU firmament. More recently the European Security and Defence Policy (ESDP) was launched to augment the CSFP, mainly in response to European powerlessness in the face of the blood-drenched dissolution of the former Yugoslavia. Finally, we also have EC foreign policy, which incorporates the more long-standing external *economic* relations lying within the domain of the first pillar.

The development of these foreign policy systems side by side has had important consequences for both the EU, its member states as well as for its neighbours and allies. New foreign policy decision systems have been formed, and new political alliances created on a European level, both of which in turn have affected the European political agenda. Furthermore, the EU is not a closed system within which integration only affects the borders between its member states. On the contrary, the Union also affects the boundaries of its member states vis-à-vis the rest of the world.

Thus, while EFP as a research focus is currently enjoying considerable attention, there are good reasons why it at the same time is less than well-consolidated in terms of its basic analytical assumptions as a field of study. Two fundamental factors – both of which underlie the issues of novelty and complexity discussed above – help to explain this situation. The first is the crucial issue of what kind of actor or entity the EU itself is, and how it should or can be analysed from the point of view of political science broadly defined. In other words: is it *sui generis*, or can it be classified and hence examined in terms of the conventional categories of our discipline? Insofar as this uncertainty pertains to the EU as a whole, it equally affects the study of 'European' foreign policy. In short, to the extent that the nature of the EU remains conceptually contested, the nature of its foreign policy system – however conceived – will also remain an issue of conceptual contention. Secondly, and closely related to this problem, while it would perhaps be natural to assume that once we have defined this field as 'foreign policy', we can without any real difficulty avail ourselves of the established analytical instruments of foreign policy analysis (FPA). However, this too is problematic, and for a simple reason: FPA does not consist of one toolkit but of many, some of which are – to say the least – not well synchronized with one another (see Carlsnaes 2002). Hence, to the extent that the nature of FPA remains contested, using it for analysing European foreign policy will inevitably lead to controversy and a lack of disciplinary identity. Both of these problems and how they manifest themselves within the field of EFP will be discussed in more detail below.

This overview of the field will proceed in the following manner. In the next section a discussion of some of the major research contributions during the early years of EFP studies will be presented, after which the focus will be placed on the current situation of the field. In both instances the aim is to highlight *how* European foreign policy has been studied, rather than presenting substantive empirical results of such research. In short, the discussion here will concentrate on second-order issues of conceptualization and analytic approaches in current research on European foreign policy, not on the historical development of EFP or on the status of empirical analysis itself. However, whereas the early years will be traversed in the form of tracing some major research trends, the current state of the art will be discussed in terms of brief presentations and analyses of seven book-length studies published after the turn of the millennium. In my view, they constitute the major, substantive contributions to the field during this short period, in particular since they combine both theory and empirical analysis.[2] After this – in the main part of the chapter – the discussion will be broadened by looking at the current status of FPA, and to what extent EFP can perhaps benefit from debates within the former. The chapter will then conclude with some brief comments summarizing the preceding discussion and looking ahead to the future prospects of this burgeoning field of EU studies.

APPROACHES IN EUROPEAN FOREIGN POLICY ANALYSIS

Compared to foreign policy analysis (see Carlsnaes 2002), the history of European foreign policy as a field of research is both considerably briefer and hence less complicated to delineate. Indeed, as suggested in the beginning of this chapter, EFP was not even established as a subject matter in its own right until around a decade or so ago. This does not

mean, however, that such an overview would be redundant in the present context, or that it would not be informative in the light of current approaches within the field. Thus, before focusing on the current condition of the field, a few general remarks on its earlier history will be offered.

The Early Years

The *first* aspect that needs to be emphasized here is that much of the earlier literature on EPC and its evolution is of a descriptive or policy-oriented kind, and that this pertains pretty much to pre-EFP studies of the CFSP as well. Two prominent and early scholars within the field, writing almost two decades ago, thus pointed to the failure of an 'academic community unable either to relate EPC into any meaningful systems theory, integration theory or international relations theory let alone create a new EPC general theory' (Weiler and Wessels 1988: 229). Arguing that 'although there has been plenty of academic discussion and extremely fruitful analysis of many facets of EPC, the term theory as such has, one gets the impression, often been studiously avoided' (Weiler and Wessels 1988: 232), resulting in 'too many case studies, *ad hoc* "lessons" from limited experiences and organizational description, but too little theoretical mediation' (Weiler and Wessels 1988: 230). A contemporary scholar, commenting on the above indictment in one of the most recently published volumes on our topic, writes as follows:

> One decade on from this self-critique, the literature on CFSP reveals that the academic community has made but modest progress towards providing such a coherent account and explanation of the CFSP experience. Arguably, the last decade has witnessed more theorizing on CFSP than the preceding two decades. Yet in analyses of CFSP, theorizing remains subordinate to case studies and organizational description ... (Øhrgaard 2004: 42).

The result is that 'the study of European foreign policy co-operation remains at a pre-theoretical stage, where individual concepts and partial explanations continue to appear to hold out the best promise for explaining CFSP' (Øhrgaard 2004: 42).

A notable early study of this kind is Simon J. Nuttall's magisterial analysis of EPC, first published in 1992 (Nuttall 1992), more recently updated in his equally detailed volume entitled *European Foreign Policy* (Nuttall 2001). A much more succinct introduction is to be found in a study by Fraser Cameron (1999), while the best current chapter-length presentation is William Wallace's very systematic contribution to *Policy Making in the European Union* (2005), one of the standard textbooks in the field of EU studies.

The *second* aspect that needs to be emphasized here is that the theorizing that has existed in the past has to a considerable degree hinged on the issue whether to view the EPC/CFSP as *sui generis* or not, and hence whether conventional international relations approaches are appropriate to this domain or whether 'new' forms of theorizing are called for. Two main stands have been taken on this question. On the one hand, the claim is made that insofar as EPC/CFSP is essentially intergovernmental in nature, it is not a unique form of co-operation and can hence be analysed with the help of current International Relations (IR) approaches such as realism, regime theory or neoliberal institutionalism (see, e.g. Hill and Wallace 1996). Features used as evidence for this view include, as Jørgensen has noted, 'the distribution of institutional power, politically binding rules, decision-making procedures, limited enforcement arrangements, and the Treaty on European Union's (TEU) structure'. In short, insofar as member states seem to control events, 'at the formal level of reasoning it seems difficult to question CFSP's inherent intergovernmentalism' (Jørgensen 1997a: 167). Some of the more notable contributions in this vein are early studies by Panayiotis Ifestos (1987), Alfred Pijpers (1991) and, in a more general vein, Stanley Hoffmann (2000). Although his main focus is on processes of economic integration rather than foreign policy or security issues, Andrew Moravcsik's massive and influential intergovernmental analysis of the development of the EU between 1955 and 1991 also belongs to this genre (1998).

The opposite and increasingly dominant position rests on the claim that although in formal institutional terms EPC/CFSP is clearly intergovernmental in character, 'the practices of European foreign policy co-operation which have emerged over the years, and the impact which they have had, even at the institutional level, are not easily captured by this term as traditionally defined in opposition to supranationalism' (Øhrgaard 2004: 28). Or as Wolfgang Wessels noted already in the early 1980's, 'even if EPC shares ... conceptual elements with historically familiar forms of diplomatic co-operation, the intensity and quality of EPC activities ... go beyond these accepted concepts in the way that makes this characterization appear no longer applicable in any satisfactory way' (quoted in Øhrgaard 2004: 28). The concomitant theoretical stand is that insofar as this is the case, current approaches based on sovereign states as utility-maximizing actors will be inadequate in explaining what is taken to be an unusual, if not unique, phenomenon. As noted recently by Helene Sjursen, writing more specifically about the shortcomings of realism:

> It is in fact difficult for the realist perspective to explain why the CFSP occasionally succeeds, why member states sometimes comply with common positions even if there is no evident gain for them in doing so, or why most member states seem to acknowledge that there will be no return to the pre-Maastricht situation of European Political Co-operation (Sjursen 2003: 38).

More specifically, Christopher Hill and William Wallace have pointed to the so-called *engrenage* effect of the day-to-day interpenetration of member governments and their officials, resulting in 'a progressive shift away from accepted models of state-to-state international relations, without moving too far towards the alternative accepted model of a federal state'. Although the Maastricht Treaty (on the insistence of France and Great Britain) kept the three pillars as far away from one another as practicable, the following has resulted:

> Habits of co-operation, accepted advantages of shared information, responses to common threats, cost saving through increased collaboration, have all significantly altered patterns of national policy-making. This is an intensive system of external relations, in which the co-operating actors which constitute the system intertwine (Hill and Wallace 1996: 12).

More recently Neil Winn and Christopher Lord have discussed this type of social dynamics in terms of the notion of 'transgovernmentalism', formed as a result of direct contacts between the foreign ministries of member states:

> What is striking about these contacts is, first, their intensity – the volume of 'traffic' that they are made to carry through the exchange of information and discussion of common positions – and, second, the way in which they link the foreign services of member states together at every level of their operation: foreign ministers, political directors, desk officers, delegations to other international bodies and embassies to non-EU countries (Winn and Lord 2001: 48–9).

Similarly Michael E. Smith has spoken of 'progressive adaptation in the midst of continuity' as 'a defining feature of EPC/CFSP', and hence how EU foreign policy could develop its own internal momentum in a manner not captured by convention IR theories of international co-operation (2004: 4, 22). It should be added that this process did not start with CFSP; on the contrary, as Winn and Lord suggest, 'it is probably fair to say that the whole of Title V by which CFSP is defined in the Treaty needs to be understood against the backdrop of those transgovernmental practices that had already been developed under EPC' (Winn and Lord 2001: 49).

A *third* division in earlier studies pertains to the question whether the focus should be strictly on EPC/CFSP or whether a broader tack should be taken, including within the ambit of the field also the 'external' relations of the EU as well as even broader aspects of foreign policy co-ordination in Europe. On this dimension a clear tendency from the narrower view to the broader view is noticeable over time. In its infancy, attention within the field concentrated on the detailed analysis of the unique decision-making processes and policy outputs within, first of all, EPC and later, the CFSP. Pre-eminent examples of this focus on decision-making and policy are studies by Holland (1997), Nuttall (1992) and Regelsberger et al. (1997).

More recently scholarly focus has shifted to a more 'holistic' or broader conception of the international actions and capacity of the EU. Although, as Tonra notes, these scholars acknowledge that important differences exist between CFSP and what are traditionally described as the 'external relations' of the Union, they argue that such distinctions should nevertheless not inhibit an analysis of all facets of the Union's international capacity 'when these are collectively deployed in support of the political interests, will and values of the member states' (Tonra 2000: 164). The foremost representatives of this shift in focus – all discussed in Tonra's overview – include Bretherton and Vogler (1999), Jørgensen (1997a), Petersen and Sjursen (1998), Piening (1997) and Smith (1999). As we shall see below, this is a focus that will gather strength as we move into the new millennium.

A *fourth* and final dimension which needs to be highlighted in this context is the distinction between approaches viewing the EU as an actor in some sense or other, and more structurally oriented traditions within the field. The 'EU-as-actor' approach, Brian White has recently written, 'concentrates on the impact of Europe on world politics. Working backwards, as it were, from impact, scholars have tried to identify what sort of an "actor" Europe is that has enabled it to be such an influential global player' (White 2004: 16–17). In his view, this approach has made two major empirical and conceptual contributions to the analysis of EU's international role. First of all, it has generated empirical data on the capabilities – both actual and potential – of the EU as a global actor (see, e.g. Whitman 1998; Bretherton and Vogler 1999). Secondly, despite a less than illustrious record in converting such capabilities into actual power and influence, this approach has generated a number of debates on how best to characterize the EC/EU – whether in terms of 'civilian power' (Duchêne 1972; Bull 1983; Hill 1990; Smith 1998); a 'superpower in the making' (Galtung 1973; Buchan 1993); an international 'presence' (Allen and Smith 1990); 'actorness' (Sjöstedt 1977; Hill 1993; Bretherton and Vogler 1999); or as an 'international identity' (Rhodes 1998; Whitman 1998).

Rather than focusing on actor-generated behaviour, structure-based approaches to the international role of the EU attempt 'to provide an explanation of actor behaviour as a function of the international institutions or other structures within which actors are located' (White 2004: 18). The structural focus here is essentially on institutions, both external and internal to the EU, and the thrust of the argument is to show how these determine European international co-operation. Studies of the explanatory role of external institutions can broadly speaking be located within interdependence theory and neo-liberal institutionalism (see, e.g. Allen et al. 1982; Ifestos 1987; Nuttall 1992; Regelsberger et al. 1997), while institutions internal to the EU have been studied in terms of how foreign policy decision-making has been institutionalized since the early years of EPC. Smith has recently described this process as follows:

> The key point here is that such actions are driven not only by external forces impinging on the EU, but also by an internal decision-making dynamic increasingly bound by institutionalization. They are the result of EPC/CFSP becoming, over time, much greater than the sum of its parts. EU foreign policy developed its own internal momentum which is not captured by most theories of international co-operation (Smith 2004: 22).

Where We Are Today

The overview by Tonra referred to in the beginning of this chapter ends with the suggestion that an 'analytical map' of the field is emerging, offering 'students of EU foreign policy and CFSP a number of paths for future, profitable research' (Tonra 2000: 168). Since he has covered much of the field up to the turn of the millennium, I will here focus on some of the major book-length contributions since then, using as my starting point his characterization – and indeed appreciation – of the field as going into different directions, 'offering us a widening variety of conclusions to some well-established questions' (Tonra 2000: 168). Has this process continued, and if so, in what manner and to what effect?

The discussion below will proceed as follows. I will start by first considering conceptual issues, including some of the central definitional aspects that of necessity are crucial to the analytical identity of any particular field of study. Are scholars talking about similar phenomena when discussing European foreign policy and its attendant aspects, or are they speaking past each other simply because they are discussing essentially different things? In short: what is the explanandum? After this I will focus on the types of explanatory factors – or explanans – adduced, that is, issues pertaining to the kind of analytical or explanatory frameworks being employed and hence, by implication, what kind of social science is being pursued. [3]

'Does the European Union have a foreign policy?' is the rhetorical title of the introductory chapter in Hazel Smith's volume on *European Union Foreign Policy* (Smith 2002). The question is certainly crucial to our concerns here, and her answer is unequivocal: the European Union does indeed have a foreign policy, and it is 'much the same as that of the nation-state' (Smith 2002: 7). She then goes on to outline six arguments for disposing of current objections to the very idea of a European Union foreign policy. These objections are grouped into two main categories, pertaining to either structural and/or institutional deficiencies, on the one hand, or to the capacity of the EU to pursue a foreign policy of its own, on the other. All six putative shortcomings – that the EU is not a sovereign entity, that it is a subordinate actor to its member states, that it lacks a centralized decision-making as well as military capacity, that it is not very effective in international crisis-management, and the so-called 'capability-expectations gap' argument – are given short shrift, leading to her conclusion that 'the European Union does indeed have a foreign policy and that it can be analysed in pretty much the same way as we can analyse that of any nation-state' (Smith 2002: 1).

What does Smith have in mind when she claims that there are no conceptual problems with the notion of the European Union possessing a foreign policy much the same as that of the nation-state? Her argument is very clear on this score: 'foreign policy' means the 'capacity to make and implement policies abroad which promote the domestic values, interests and policies of the actor in question', and since the EU does in her view possess all of these attributes, it ipso facto has a foreign policy. It can be characterized thus due to 'its developed philosophy based on liberal capitalist democracy, and its panoply of domestic competencies and policies on issues ranging from the common market to co-operation in policing and judicial matters' (Smith 2002 7–8). This view is certainly as far as it is possible to get from conceptions of European foreign policy as *sui generis,* and hence as not amenable to conventional foreign policy analysis.

Having disposed of the conceptual issues pertaining to the explanandum, her analytic approach is explicitly to eschew a procedural or institutional tack – to equate EFP with what 'emanates from the procedures of the Common Foreign and Security Policy' (Smith 2002: 8) – in favour of what she calls the 'geo-issue-area approach', involving foci which 'engage with either the geographical reach of the Union abroad or which attempt to evaluate the various issues with which the Union has involved itself abroad. Both these approaches treat the European Union as a conglomerate actor' (Smith 2002: 9). Beyond this empirically focused framework of analysis no particular theory is advanced in this study; instead, Smith notes that there are not really any 'theoretical obstacles to adopting the approach that the European Union has a foreign policy that it exercises throughout the world in a number of different issue-areas' (Smith 2002: 269).

Karen Smith's conceptualization of European foreign policy comes very close to the one espoused above. In her most recent study, entitled *European Foreign Policy in a Changing World* (Smith 2003), she provides the following formulation:

> 'Foreign policy' is defined widely here, to mean the activity of developing and managing relationships between the state (or, in our case, the EU) and other international actors, which promotes the domestic values and interests of the state or actor in question (Smith 2003: 2).

It is also made clear that this view means that EU foreign policy is not to be confined only to second pillar activities, that is, CFSP, including the more recently established ESDP, but also encompasses its two constituent pillars. Also in agreement with Smith's view, she claims that the EU has at its disposal many of the traditional foreign policy instruments used by states, in addition to some unique tools of its own (Smith 2003: 67).

Karen Smith's modus operandi is to structure her study around five foreign policy objectives of the EU – the promotion of regional co-operation; the promotion of human rights; the promotion of democracy and good governance; the prevention of violent conflict; and the fight against international crime – and to analyse these in terms of why and how they have been pursued. The ambition has been not only to shed light on how the EU has attempted to realize these objectives but also thereby to determine its international identity qua foreign policy actor; and inasmuch as the approach is essentially empirical and evaluative, little effort is spent on linking these concerns to a larger theoretical framework or to ongoing theoretical debates.

If both Hazel Smith and Karen Smith can be said to find the question of how to define EFP unproblematic, providing us with a no nonsense answer based on traditional conceptions of what – at least in their view – foreign policy analysis is all about, this cannot be said about Brian White's discussion of this issue in *Understanding European Foreign Policy* (2001). Whereas his two colleagues do not find it necessary to spend much effort on distinguishing between 'EU' and 'European' foreign policy, or to delve into definitional issues more generally, White goes to considerable lengths to grapple not only with the role of foreign policy analysis in EFP, but also in trying to untangle the three strands that, in his view, are intertwined in the latter: Community, Union and national foreign policy (White 2001: 40-1). Without providing us with a formal definition à la the two Smiths above, he argues that defining EFP in terms of any one or two of these would be too restrictive, since 'European governance in the foreign policy field appears to take all three forms'. Hence, if it 'is to be useful for analytical purposes, the concept has to encompass the fragmented nature of agency at the European level and the variety of forms of action' implied in the above classification (White 2001: 39). However, he is open to a development in which the three become increasingly interwoven over time;

and 'the more extensive the interrelationships between them, the more justified we are in using the label European foreign policy' (White 2001: 39).

The framework of analysis which White provides for his subsequent empirical analysis of EFP is based on the notion of a foreign policy system in action composed of an interrelated set of elements consisting of processes, issues, instruments, context and outputs. He has described this systems analysis approach as follows:

> The nature of the policy process is affected by the identity of the actors involved, the issues being dealt with, the policy instruments available and, not least, the context within which policy is made. These interrelationships in turn generate the outputs from the system (White, 2001: 40).

These elements – in the form of focused questions – are subsequently utilized in each of the empirically oriented chapters in order to give these a comparable structure, at the same time as the ambition is to indicate how these elements form interrelated components of a foreign policy system shorn of the state-centric realism of traditional FPA.

Roy H. Ginsberg, in *The European Union in International Politics* (Ginsberg 2001), will have no truck with talk about the EU having a foreign policy pretty much like that of the nation-state. 'Comparing and assessing EFP as if the EU were a state', he warns us, 'is a slippery slope' (Ginsberg 2001: 12). The reason for this is that 'the EU is a partially constructed international political actor, neither a state nor a political union of states', and hence 'lacks the attributes of cohesion, purpose, and continuity normally (but not always) associated with national foreign policies' (Ginsberg 2001: 9). This does not mean, however, that the EU is not engaged in foreign policy activities of various kinds. It certainly is, and his study is an impassioned examination – indeed, commendation – of the EU's 'baptism by fire' during the 1990's as a foreign policy actor engaged in a host of 'individual country, region-, and issue-based foreign policy activities' around the world (Ginsberg 2001: 9). More specifically, and this is as close as

he gets to a definition of EFP, such 'activity refers to the universe of concrete civilian actions, policies, positions, relations, commitments, and choices of the EC (and EU) in international politics' (Ginsberg 2001: 3).

In his extensive elaboration of a conceptual model for analysing EFP – one of the most extensive and intricate in the literature discussed here, inspired by Eastonian systems analysis – these various types of activities are conceptualized in the form of 'outputs' from a 'European foreign policy system' which includes all three EU pillars as well as the foreign policies emanating from within member states. However, the purpose of his book is not so much to analyse or to explain these foreign policy outputs as such as their international impact in the form of outcomes, that is, their external political effects.

In their study – entitled *EU Foreign Policy Beyond the Nation-State* (Winn and Lord 2001) – of how the three pillar structure (called 'pillarization') influences decision-making within the EU, Neil Winn and Christopher Lord opt for a relatively wide conception of EU foreign policy. Two reasons are offered for this choice, the one substantive and the other analytical. With respect to the former they write as follows: 'a wide conception of the EU's foreign policy is implicit in our focus on pillarization to the extent that the latter is supposed to institutionalize links between the external economic policy and the diplomatic démarches of CFSP' (Winn and Lord 2001: 16). In short, their empirical focus is on both the first and the second pillar, and on the institutional relations between the two in the pursuit of foreign policy. Analytically, they define 'foreign policy' itself in a manner that would facilitate comparison with the external activities of other political systems belonging to 'the same class of object' – in this instance, the class of 'foreign policy'. Consequently, they give this concept the following 'minimum' definition: 'purposive and sustained efforts to influence the international environment undertaken by a body that acts on behalf of a public, as opposed to purely private, interest' (Winn and Lord 2001: 17).

The empirical focus of the Winn and Lord study is on 'joint actions' – 'the main policy instruments established under CFSP' (Winn and Lord 2001: 174) – in order to analyse the operation of pillarization between 1993–98. This they do in the form of three in-depth case studies of such joint actions (the EU administration of Mostar, the implementation of the Dayton accords, and EU policy towards the Caucasus), in which they systematically employ three competing theories: rational action, policy networks and 'garbage can' approaches. They conclude that although FPA has much to recommend it, 'the EU is a multi-arena actor operating on a number of levels and therefore requires a number of theoretical tools to understand its multilayered complexity'. Hence, using models from comparative politics and public administration 'allows the theorist to look at insights into preference formation, agenda-setting, national foreign policy inputs, policy learning, strategic action, and backward-mapping implementation in another, and perhaps richer, light' (Winn and Lord 2001: 176). These approaches have allowed them to treat the EU foreign affairs system as a complex web of nodal interconnections, highlighting the EU system of governance, characterized as 'multi-level, multi-nodal, non-hierarchical, knowledge-based, and in some ways polity-like' (Winn and Lord 2001: 177). A major conclusion is that an 'increasing enmeshment of international actors through pragmatic responses to common foreign policy problems is the *leitmotif* of contemporary European foreign policy actions' (Winn and Lord 2001: 179). Thus, although they posit a definition of EU foreign policy premised on the notion of purposive behaviour, in the actual conduct of their study a much more complicated system of interrelated structures and processes – both internal and external – emerge, not unlike the systems approach endorsed by Ginsberg. This also explains their stress on the utility of comparative politics and public administration models of decision-making in the analysis of EU foreign policy.

Elke Krahmann's study of *Multilevel Networks in European Foreign Policy* (Krahmann 2003) has the most encompassing definition of 'European foreign policy' of the seven volumes under discussion here. While acknowledging that typically this concept has been understood – quoting Christopher Hill – as 'the sum of what the EU and its member states do in international relations', she nevertheless rejects this stipulation in favour of employing one that 'pertains to the decisions and actions of core European states and their multilateral organizations which are primarily concerned with the welfare of the region' (Krahmann 2003: 3). The reason for this new conceptualization is that European foreign policy cannot, she claims, be reduced to the actions of the EU alone, nor to those of its member states, since not only are these 'influenced by the United States and vice versa, but also there are key European foreign policy decisions taken and implemented by a broad range of national and multinational institutions, including the United Nations and NATO' (Krahmann 2003: 3).

As a consequence of this complex set of relationships and foreign policy decision-making processes characterized by the increasing multiplicity, diversity and interdependence of foreign policy actors, she proposes the use of a multi-level network approach to incorporate the behaviour of national, transnational and international actors within the European context. In her view, this behaviour can best be explained in terms of the notion of rational, utility maximizing actors attempting to influence one another's preferences in the pursuit of European foreign policies. In the empirical part of her book she uses this approach in three closely argued and technically sophisticated case studies of European foreign policy decision-making: the first focusing on the EU, the second on the transatlantic community and the third on the United Kingdom.

The final volume to be considered in this overview, and the one published most recently, is Michael E. Smith's *Europe's Foreign and Security Policy: The Institutionalization of Cooperation* (Smith 2004). He defines 'EU foreign policy', 'European foreign policy' or 'foreign/security policy co-operation' (these terms are used interchangeably) as co-operative actions characterized as follows:

(1) undertaken on behalf of all EU states toward non-members, international bodies, or global events or issues; (2) oriented toward a specific goal; (3) made operational with physical activity, such as financing or diplomacy; and (4) undertaken in the context of EPC/CFSP discussions (although the EC can also be involved) (Smith 2004).

The emphasis here is on institutionalized co-operation on the part of EU member states, specifically in situations in which 'states did not perceive themselves as having identical interests in a given choice situation, yet…attempted to adjust their foreign policies to accommodate each other' (Smith 2004: 18). Such policy co-ordination necessarily involves active efforts on the part of member states to achieve a common end, and is hence a highly purposive and conjoined type of activity heavily dependent on institutionalized forms of co-operation. His book is essentially focused on tracing and explaining the institutionalization of such co-operation in Europe since the early days of EPC.

This he does by way of explaining how changes in institutional context – in terms of intergovernmental, transgovernmental and supranational procedures – affect the propensity for co-operation, and then linking processes of institutionalization to an expansion of foreign policy co-operation among EU member states. The claim made is that 'there is a reciprocal relationship between institution-building and co-operation', and that in the case of EU foreign policy this has meant a 'progressive expansion of both the institutional mechanisms and substantive outcomes of cooperation' (Smith 2004: 239–40). Starting with its modest beginnings in EPC, this process has led to the institutionalization of a European foreign policy capacity – currently embodied in the CFSP – defined in terms of both regular, substantive policy outcomes and a set of explicit aspirations or goals.

Having sketched very briefly how these eight scholars have defined their object of analysis – the explanandum – it is time to return to the question raised in the beginning: do they speak past one another, or are their respective conceptualizations of the object of analysis in EFP compatible with one another? In other words,

are EFP scholars still moving into different directions, essentially pursuing different objects of analysis?

The short answer is clearly yes: even a quick comparison between them points to obvious differences in both scope and kind – for example, between, on the one hand, Ginsberg's very broad conception of 'outputs' incorporating all three pillars as well as member states' foreign policies, or Krahmann's even more encompassing notion of multilevel networks operating within and outside Europe, and, on the other hand, Michael E. Smith's narrow focus on policy-making within the institutional ambit of EPC/CFSP. This follows in the footsteps of the previous scholarship discussed by Tonra in terms of his distinction between studies focusing on either CFSP or on more holistic EFP approaches (Tonra 2000: 164). We also find a clear differentiation – also discussed by Tonra – between, on the one hand, studies viewing EFP as essentially *sui generis* (Michael E. Smith, Krahmann and Ginsburg) and, on the other, those that to considerable extent view it as comparable to, or at least compatible with, conventional foreign policy analysis (Hazel Smith, Karen Smith, Winn and Lord, and perhaps White).

What is the longer answer? Are these just surface differences pertaining essentially to terminological and/or conceptual issues, or are they indicative of more fundamental questions regarding explanation and theoretical understanding, pertaining to the nature and choice of feasible explanans? Once again the answer is in the affirmative, and since we are here dealing with a more deep-rooted division, I will elaborate briefly on these differences and what they can be said to indicate about the landscape of European foreign policy analysis.

For this purposes I will distinguish, first of all, between policy as 'output' and policy as 'action'. The former is a behavioural concept with 'objectivist' connotations, whereas the latter denotes purposive, goal-oriented behaviour and hence is based on an essentially interpretative type of epistemology. Secondly, a distinction will be made between two basic ontological conceptions of the nature of social systems, revolving around the issue of where the primary causal foundations or dynamics of social systems are assumed to be situated. Without going into the deeper meta-theoretical and controversial ramifications of this fundamental distinction in social theory, I will here simply distinguish between 'structure' and 'agency'.[4]

These two dimensions can be combined to render a simple two-by-two matrix (Table 28.1) that can be used to classify the conceptualizations of EFP discussed above. As I will briefly try to argue below, the seven studies reviewed here can be placed into the four cells provided by these two dimensions as follows.

Clearly, Ginsberg's conceptualization of the 'European Foreign Policy System' and his stipulation of policy as an 'output' of this system places him squarely in the upper left box. The stress on institutional factors, on complex webs of nodal interconnections, and on the role of various networks of interested actors seeking to influence the policy process, all with a strong structural thrust, place Winn and Lord in this category as well. Given the strong emphasis by Michael E. Smith on the institutionalized nature and dynamics of EFP, his is also a structural approach, but one with a conception of policy which is purposive and goal-oriented in nature. The latter also applies to both Hazel Smith and Karen Smith, but in both cases we have a strong focus on agency rather than on structure, in the sense that the actions involved are pursued by self-conscious and goal-oriented actors – in this instance the EU in some form or other. White is more difficult to categorize in terms of these criteria, but given the non-structural type of FPA that he advocates, with a focus on the decision-making behaviour of non-state actors in an interrelated and dynamic system producing foreign policy outputs, he ends up in the bottom left box. Finally, in view of the strong rational choice orientation of Krahmann's study, she too ends up in this box (although her approach is clearly very different from White's).

What does this classification of contemporary EFP scholarship tell us? In my view, essentially two things: that the differences between the major recent contributions to the field are considerably more *foundational* in character

Table 28.1 *Conceptualization of EFP.*

	Output	Action
Structure	Ginsberg	M. Smith
	Winn & Lord	
Agency	White	H. Smith
	Krahmann	K. Smith

than is perhaps assumed by most scholars working within it. In short, the above analysis suggests not only that they are talking about different *things*, but also that they are talking about them in different *ways*. Secondly, that if the notion of cumulation is valued above diversity and a 'widening variety of conclusions' (to quote Tonra (2000: 168) again), then we need to discuss and penetrate these aspects more than has been done in the past. One way of doing this is to latch on to recent discussions within FPA.

WHAT CAN WE LEARN FROM FOREIGN POLICY ANALYSIS?

What characterizes the condition of FPA today, and are there any essential lessons that EFP can learn from recent debates within the former? The answer to the first query is arguably that a consensus exists today on the nature of the explanandum, although it has taken a circuitous route for scholars to reach this point of relative agreement. In my view, this consensus boils down to a specification of the unit of analysis that emphasizes the purposive nature of foreign policy actions, a focus on policy undertakings and the crucial role of state-like boundaries (Carlsnaes 2002: 335; but see also Hill 2003: 3). This type of agreement has certainly been beneficial to FPA, and there is a strong prima facie case that a similar agreement within EFP would have equally positive effects. The crucial notions here are *purposive action, policy undertakings* and *international boundaries,* and it should not be an insuperable task to translate these into appropriate EFP terms.

This is the good news. The bad news is that here scholarly agreement within FPA ends. Indeed, as I have argued elsewhere, current approaches to foreign policy analysis are at

Table 28.2   *Four perspectives in foreign policy analysis.*

	Objectivism	Interpretativism
Holism	Structural perspective	Social-institutional perspective
Individualism	Agency-based perspective	Interpretative actor perspective

least as diverse as the studies exemplified above, and this essentially for similar meta-theoretical reasons (Carlsnaes 2002). These can be structured in terms of the following matrix (Table 28.2), in which the horizontal dimension pertains to issues of epistemology in social theory (essentially along the lines of Max Weber's celebrated distinction between *Erklären* and *Verstehen*), while the vertical dimension expresses the classical ontological choice between holistic and individualistic approaches to social science explanations.

In an overview of current FPA we find, first of all, an array of *agency-based* approaches to the study of foreign policy actions, focusing either on the role of individuals and groups in the foreign policy process or on the cognitive and psychological characteristics of decision-makers. So-called bureaucratic politics and liberal approaches can also be said to belong to this category. A second major group of current analytical frameworks is premised on a *structural* rather than agency-based perspective in the analysis of state behaviour. Various forms – old and new – of realism are to be found here, as well as neoliberal institutionalism, which in many respects is simply a benign version of the former. A third category of approaches, which have become increasingly prominent during the past decade and half, are premised on a *social-institutional* perspective (based on social constructivist premises), and here we can distinguish between a sociologically oriented ('thin' constructivism) and a more discursive strand. Finally, there is also what can be called an *interpretative actor* perspective within FPA, a more traditional mode of analysis essentially based on the reconstruction of the reasoning of individual or group decision-makers.

In view of this rich flora of alternative approaches to FPA, there is arguably little help for EFP to be had here. Two options seem to confront us: either to accept this state of affairs, both in FPA and in EFP, and to go whichever route suits our predilections best; or to opt for some form of synthetic approach which would do the trick by providing an integrative framework for – at best – both subfields. The former is by far the easier choice, whereas the latter requires a bridge-building effort in a terrain that would seem to have no natural location points to support such an overarching construction. This does not mean that such attempts have not been made.

My own view is that a synthetic framework for analysing foreign policy is indeed feasible, but that it has to be on a level of abstraction that does not substantively prejudge explanation in favour of any particular type or combination of empirical factors. Since I have elaborated on it elsewhere, I will here simply give a skeletal outline of the explanatory logic of such a suggested synthetic framework of analysis (Carlsnaes 1992, 1994, 2002). The starting point is the claim that while the meta-theoretical matrix used above is specifically designed for the purpose of classifying approaches to foreign policy analysis in terms of their most fundamental ontological and epistemological presuppositions, it is less suitable for empirical analysis itself as distinguished from meta-theoretical dissection. At the same time foreign policy action in 'real life' is arguably always a combination of purposive behaviour, cognitive-psychological factors in play and the various structural phenomena characterizing societies and their environments; hence explanations of actual foreign policy actions must be able to give accounts that do not by definition exclude or privilege any of these types of explanans. Insofar as the matrix used above does have such exclusionary implications, it simply will not be able to deliver the goods in this respect. Thus, rather than thinking in terms of a logic of mutual exclusion, I suggest that we instead conceptualize such a synthetic analytic framework in terms of a tripartite approach to foreign policy actions (the explanandum) consisting respectively of an

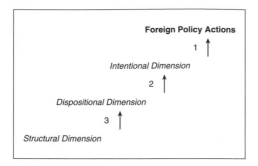

Figure 28.1 *Three levels for explaining foreign policy actions.*

intentional, a dispositional and a structural dimension of explanation (the explanans) (Figure 28.1).

Although conceptualized as analytically autonomous, these three dimensions should be viewed as closely linked in the sense that they can be conjoined in a logical, step-by-step manner to render increasingly exhaustive (or 'deeper') explanations of foreign policy actions.

This means, first of all, that a teleological explanation (arrow 1) in terms solely of the intentional dimension is fully feasible, based either on strict rationality assumptions or on more traditional modes of intentional analysis. It also means, however, that one can choose to 'deepen' the analysis by providing a causal determination (arrow 2) of policy – as opposed to an explanation wholly in terms of given goals and preferences – in which the factors characterizing the intentional dimension are themselves explained in terms of underlying psychological-cognitive factors which have, so to speak, disposed a given actor to have this and not that preference or intention. Finally, the third – and deepest – layer is based on the assumption that in so far as intentional behaviour is never pursued outside the crucible of structural determination, factors of the latter kind must always figure prominently and causally (arrow 3) in our accounts of the former. As conceived here, this link between structure and agency can be conceived as both of a constraining and of an enabling kind, causally affecting policy actions via its effects on the dispositional characteristics of the agents of policy.

Although this type of an integrative framework eschews the dichotomization of approaches discussed above, it does not as such imply the inapplicability of any of these. Indeed, approaches from all the four types of rock-bottom perspectives discussed above can be fully utilized: the 'structural' and 'social-institutional' when analysing causal links between the structural and dispositional dimensions; 'agency-based' perspectives when tracing causal patterns between the dispositional and the intentional dimension; and the 'interpretative actor' perspective when the purpose is to penetrate the teleological links between intentions and foreign policy actions.

Transferring this framework to the analysis of European foreign policy would in my view entail the following. Whenever trying to explain such policy, we should first of all specify it qua explanandum in the form of an explicit European undertaking in an issue-area or with regard to specific geographical area – in both instances beyond its borders. The EU and its member states have clearly engaged in many such undertakings over the years, and in this regard this behaviour is no different from that of a single state pursuing foreign policy actions.

Secondly, such actions can be analysed in terms of various levels of explanatory ambition, but whatever the ambition, the starting point must be a specification of the intention(s) behind the undertaking in question. This is not a causal issue, but one of teleology: what the action in question is intended to achieve. The reason why such a determination always needs to be made as a first step is that by definition one cannot describe purposive actions without invoking the reason(s) for them. This, too, is no different from the analysis of the foreign policies of states, since in neither case need such purposive behaviour be defined with reference to any particular type of institutional boundaries. Thirdly, issues of causality enter the picture the moment one wants to determine why certain purposes, goals, preferences or choices have been invoked, but not others. In seeking for these essentially dispositional factors there is, once again, in principle no difference between the analysis of foreign policies pursued by individual states and foreign policies pursued by states in consort in some form or other (as in EFP). Dispositions in this sense are not bound by any particular boundaries or institutional structures, since they pertain to the characteristics of single or joint decision-makers, be their roles national, international or transnational. Finally, structural factors as constraining and enabling characteristics determining to various degrees the dispositions of such decision-makers, and by extension their purposive behaviour in the form of policies, do not come pre-packaged in either nationally or internationally coloured boxes. Some such factors are essentially of a domestic nature, others not; but most often their causal effects are felt equally across the various boundaries defining international societies and their interactions. Here, as in the case of the two other dimensions discussed above, the issue of finding and characterizing the appropriate causal factor is empirical, not one of definition. It is in this sense that the levels of analysis issue – whether we are dealing with national, transnational or international actors or factors – does not predetermine the type of analysis that can be pursued.

CONCLUDING REMARKS

The argument above has been that the growth of EFP as a burgeoning field of analysis is characterized by a situation in which its major contemporary practitioners are pulling in different directions as a result of fundamentally different approaches to their subject matter. This applies both to their conceptualization of 'European foreign policy' qua explanandum and the types of explanatory analysis contained in these studies. Although this condition can be celebrated for producing a rich and variegated spectrum of studies, it can also be lamented for undermining the possibility of producing a cumulative body of knowledge. Insofar as EFP is a new field of study, but one with close and natural affinities with FPA as a major and long-standing body of research, the question was then raised whether inspiration for alleviating this problem could possibly be provided by current developments

within the latter. However, it was then argued that the very same problem was to be found also in contemporary studies of foreign policy in general, but that at least some attempts can be found within the field to bridge the existing divisions. One such suggestion was then discussed in some detail – my own stab at bridge-building – and this leaves us with the question whether and, in particular, how this suggestion could be applied to EFP. My concluding comments above are intended to suggest both an affirmative answer to the first question, as well as – in response to the second – a skeletal outline of how this can be achieved.

NOTES

1. See, e.g., Hill (1990) and the edited volume on *European Foreign Policy*, published in 1994 but building on a series of workshops initiated already at the beginning of that decade (Carlsnaes and Smith 1994). However, although this title may have been prescient of future developments in Europe, the fact is – as pointed out by several reviewers of the volume – that it is mainly concerned with the potential role of conventional foreign policy analysis in the study of the 'new' Europe rather than with EU foreign policy itself.

2. For recent collections of essays on this topic, see Carlsnaes et al. (2004), Tonra and Christiansen (2004), Knodt and Princen (2003) and Dannreuther (2004). Unfortunately Maria Strömvik's very recent and pertinent study of the collective foreign policy of the EU came too late into my hands to be included here (Strömvik 2005).

3. The rest of this chapter is to a considerable degree based on my review article in *European Union Politics* (Carlsnaes 2004).

4. For more extensive discussions of these concepts, see Carlsnaes (1992, 1994).

REFERENCES

Allen, D. and Smith, M. (1990) 'Western Europe's presence in the contemporary international arena', *Review of International Studies* 16: 19–38.

Allen, D., Rummel, R. and Wessels, W. (eds) (1982) *European Political Cooperation: Towards a Foreign Policy for Western Europe.* London: Butterworth Scientific.

Bretherton, C. and Vogler, J. (1999) *The European Union as a Global Actor.* London: Routledge.

Buchan, D. (1993) *Europe: The Strange Superpower.* Aldershot: Dartmouth.

Bull, H. (1983) 'Civilian power Europe: a contradiction in terms?', in L. Tsoukalis (ed.), *The European Community: Past, Present, Future.* Oxford: Blackwell. pp. 149–70.

Cameron, F. (1999) *The Foreign and Security Policy of the European Union: Past, Present and Future.* Sheffield: Sheffield Academic Press.

Carlsnaes, W. (1992) 'The agency-structure problem in foreign policy analysis', *International Studies Quarterly*, 36: 245–70.

Carlsnaes, W. (1994) 'In lieu of a conclusion: compatibility and the agency-structure issue in foreign policy analysis', in W. Carlsnaes and S. Smith (eds), *European Foreign Policy: The EC and Changing Perspectives in Europe.* London: Sage. pp. 274–87

Carlsnaes, W. (2002) 'Foreign policy', in W. Carlsnaes, T. Risse, and B.A. Simmons (eds), *Handbook of International Relations.* London: Sage. pp. 331–49.

Carlsnaes, W. (2004) 'Where is the analysis of European foreign policy going?', *European Union Politics*, 5: 495–508.

Carlsnaes, W. and Smith, S. (eds) (1994) *European Foreign Policy: The EC and Changing Perspectives in Europe.* London: Sage Publications.

Carlsnaes, W., Sjursen, H. and White, B. (eds) (2004) *Contemporary European Foreign Policy.* London: Sage Publications.

Dannreuther, R. (ed.) (2004) *European Union Foreign and Security Policy: Towards a Neighbourhood Strategy.* London: Routledge.

Dinan, D. (ed.) (1998) *Encyclopedia of the European Union.* Boulder: Lynne Rienner Publishers.

Duchêne, F. (1972) 'Europe's role in world peace', in R. Mayne (ed.) *Europe Tomorrow: Sixteen European Look Ahead.* London: Fontana. pp. 32–47.

Galtung, J. (1973) *The European Community: A Superpower in the Making?* London: Allen and Unwin.

Ginsberg, R.H. (2001) *The European Union in International Politics: Baptism by Fire.* Lanham: Rowman & Littlefield.

Hill, C. (1990) 'European foreign policy: power bloc, civilian model – or flop?', in R. Rummel (ed.) *The Evolution of an International Actor.* Boulder: Westview. pp. 31–55.

Hill, C. (1993) 'The capability-expectations gap', *Journal of Common Market Studies*, 31(3): 305–28.

Hill, C. (2003) *The Changing Politics of Foreign Policy.* Basingstoke: Palgrave Macmillan.

Hill, C. and Wallace, W. (1996) 'Introduction: actors and actions', in C. Hill (ed.), *The Actors in Europe's Foreign Policy.* London: Routledge. pp. 1–16

Hoffmann, S. (2000) 'Toward a common and security policy', *Journal of Common Market Studies*, 38: 189–98.

Holland, M. (ed.) (1997) *Common Foreign and Security Policy: The Record and Reforms.* London: Pinter.

Ifestos, P. (1987) *European Political Cooperation: Towards a Framework of Supranational Diplomacy?* Aldershot: Avebury.

Jørgensen, K.E. (ed.) (1997a) *European Approaches to Crisis Management.* London: Kluwer.

Jørgensen, K.E. (1997b) 'PoCo: the diplomatic republic of Europe', in K.E. Jörgensen (ed.), *Reflective Approaches to European Governance.* London: Macmillan Press. pp. 167–80

Knodt, M. and Princen, S. (eds) (2003) *Understanding the European Union's External Relations.* London: Routledge.

Krahmann, E. (2003) *Multilevel Networks in European Foreign Policy.* Aldershot: Ashgate.

Moravcsik, A. (1998) *The Choice for Europe: Social Purpose and State Power from Messina to Maastricht.* Ithaca: Cornell University Press.

Nuttall, S.J. (1992) *European Political Co-operation.* Oxford: Clarendon Press.

Nuttall, S.J. (2001) *European Foreign Policy.* Oxford: Oxford University Press.

Øhrgaard, J.C. (2004) 'International relations or European integration: is the CFSP sui generis?', in B. Tonra and T. Christiansen (eds), *Rethinking European Union Foreign Policy.* Manchester: Manchester University Press. pp. 26–44.

Peterson, J. and Sjursen, H. (eds) (1998) *A Common Foreign Policy for Europe? Competing Visions of the CFSP.* London: Routledge.

Piening, C. (1997) *Global Europe: The European Union in World Affairs.* Boulder: Lynne Rienner.

Pijpers, A. (1991) 'European Political Cooperation and the realist paradigm', in M. Holland (ed.), *The Future of European Political Cooperation: Essays on Theory and Practice.* London: Macmillan. pp. 8–26.

Regelsberger, E., de Schoutheete de Tervarent, P. and Wessels, W. (eds) (1997) *Foreign Policy of the European Union: From EPC to CFSP and Beyond.* Boulder: Lynne Rienner.

Rhodes, C. (1998) 'Introduction: the identity of the European Union in international affairs', in C. Rhodes (ed.), *The European Union in the World Community.* Boulder: Lynne Rienner. pp. 1–17.

Sjursen, H. (2003) 'Understanding the common foreign and security policy: analytical building blocks', in M. Knodt and S. Princen (eds), *Understanding the European Union's External Relations*. London: Routledge. pp. 35–53.

Sjöstedt, G. (1977) *The External Role of the European Community*. Farnborough: Saxon House.

Smith, H. (2002) *European Union Foreign Policy: What it is and What it Does*. London: Pluto Press.

Smith, K.E. (1998) 'The instruments of European foreign policy', in J. Zielonka (ed.), *Paradoxes of European Foreign Policy*. The Hague: Kluwer Law International.

Smith, K.E. (1999) *The Making of EU Foreign Policy*. Basingstoke: Macmillan.

Smith, K.E. (2003) *European Union Foreign Policy in a Changing World*. Cambridge: Polity Press.

Smith, M.E. (2004) *Europe's Foreign and Security Policy: The Institutionalisation of Cooperation*. Cambridge: Cambridge University Press.

Soetendorp, B. (1999) *Foreign Policy in the European Union*, London: Longman.

Strömvik, M. (2005) *To Act as a Union: Explaining the Development of the EU's collective Foreign Policy*. Lund: Lund Political Studies 142.

Tonra, B. (2000) 'Mapping EU foreign policy studies', *Journal of European Public Policy*, 7: 163–69.

Tonra, B. and Christiansen, T. (eds) (2004a) *Rethinking European Foreign Policy*. Manchester: Manchester University Press.

Tonra, B. and Christiansen, T. (2004b) 'The study of EU foreign policy: between international relations and European studies' in B. Tonra and T. Christiansen (eds), *Rethinking European Union Foreign Policy*. Manchester: Manchester University Press. pp. 1–9.

Wallace, W. (2005) 'Foreign and security policy: the painful path from shadow to substance', in H. Wallace, W. Wallace and M.A. Pollack (eds), *Policy-Making in the European Union*. Oxford: Oxford University Press. pp. 429–56.

Weiler, J. and Wessels, W. (1988) 'EPC and the challenge of theory', in A. Pijpers, E. Regelsberger, and W. Wessels (eds), *European Political Cooperation in the 1980's: A Common Foreign Policy for Western Europe?*. Dordrecht: Martinus Nijhoff.

White, B. (2001) *Understanding European Foreign Policy*. London: Palgrave.

White, B. (2004) 'Foreign policy analysis and the new Europe', in W. Carlsnaes, H. Sjursen, and B. White (eds), *Contemporary European Foreign Policy*. London: Sage Publications.

Whitman, R.G. (1998) *From Civilian Power to Superpower?* Basingstoke: Macmillan.

Winn, N. and Christopher, L. (2001) *EU Foreign Policy Beyond the Nation-State*. Basingstoke: Palgrave.

29

'The European and the Universal Process'? European Union Studies, New Regionalism and Global Governance

ALEX WARLEIGH-LACK

In one of his classic articles (Haas 1961), whose subtitle is of course echoed in the title of this chapter, Ernst Haas argued that the European experiment with international integration *should* be reproduced in other parts of the globe in the name of what we might now call 'good governance'. However, neofunctionalists such as Haas were ultimately less than sanguine about the feasibility of such mimicry (Nye 1971). They also considered that even if it were to occur, the spreading of the 'European model' would in all likelihood detract from 'universal' (or global) integration, because it would create various rival blocs instead of a single world system or one based explicitly on regional components – a relationship to which I return below (Haas 1961: 391–2). Focusing increasingly on the West European case as other regional integration processes failed, neofunctionalists eventually concluded that

what we now call the EU would be most unlikely to progress significantly beyond the stage it had attained by the late 1960s (Lindberg and Scheingold 1970), and as a theory of regional integration neofunctionalism fell from grace shortly thereafter (Haas 1975). The intergovernmentalist scholars who filled the theory vacuum for the remainder of EU studies' 'foundational period' (O'Neill 2000) argued that European integration was rife with endogenous limits, constituting a phenomenon which could demonstrate very little that would be of use in any discussion of global politics or international relations, except perhaps as a cautionary tale about the ultimate failure of any attempt to transcend national sovereignty as a means of political organization (Hoffmann 1982).

Why then does this chapter attempt to link the literature on European Union studies with that on regional integration elsewhere and also with a further set of literature on global governance? A clue is to be found in the previous paragraph: EU studies is no longer in its foundational period. Moreover, the erstwhile orthodox views set out above describing both the limits of European integration and the unlikelihood of regionalism succeeding in other parts of the globe have been ditched as a response to both the political, legal and economic development of the EU and the widespread phenomenon known as 'new regionalism'.[1] Moreover, in an era of globalization and the increasing number, importance and power of international organizations with a (near-) global scope, it has become commonplace to speak of a nascent 'global polity' (Ougaard and Higgott 2002). As Bob Dylan might have said, the times, they've been a-changing: the EU is more widely studied in its own right than ever before, has been examined as a source of ideas about how other regions might develop, and has even been taken as a model by scholars concerned with the reform of global institutions (Held 2004).[2]

Elsewhere (Warleigh 2004, 2006a) I have argued that scholars of both new regionalism (NR) and international relations (IR) have much to learn from a sustained engagement with EU studies, since its contemporary complexity and subtleties traduce the caricatured understanding of it they often have, and yield much of interest to the scholar of governance 'beyond the nation state' (to borrow yet another phrase from Ernst Haas [1964]). My focus in this piece, however, is rather the reverse – to ask whether the literatures on new regionalism and global governance have anything that might usefully be adopted by EU studies scholars. My argument is that such is indeed the case, and that by focusing on a broader range of actors and processes EU studies scholars will generate a fuller understanding of their dependent variable. This argument is made in more detail in section five of the chapter. Between here and there, the chapter proceeds as follows. In section two, I focus on defining EU studies rather more fully. In section three, I flesh out the relationship between EU studies and comparative regionalism studies.

And in section four, I situate EU studies in the context of the global governance literature.

UNDERSTANDING EUROPEAN UNION STUDIES: NORMAL SCIENCE OR AREA STUDIES?

How then do I understand the term 'EU studies'? Perhaps a useful first step would be to distinguish it from integration theory. The latter is, obviously, an attempt to generate a theory of a particular phenomenon (regional integration) and is properly a concern of neofunctionalism: strictly speaking, only neofunctionalists can speak of regional 'integration', since only they agreed that such was indeed their dependent variable. Intergovernmentalists have always been sceptical of the possibilities for 'integration' in the neofunctionalist sense of a non-coercive process whereby 'states cease to be wholly sovereign … (and) voluntarily mingle, merge, and mix with their neighbours so as to lose the factual attributes of sovereignty while acquiring new techniques for resolving conflict between themselves' (Haas 1970: 610; my parentheses). Such a process would involve the development of a new sense of political community and the supranationalization of decision-making, of which intergovernmentalists see little or no convincing evidence. Similarly, new regionalist scholars often have problems with neofunctionalism's insistence that regional integration must/should produce as its outcome a heavily institutionalized quasi-federal polity, as any other outcome in fact demonstrates an immature or gone-awry integration process (on the perceived imperfections of European integration, see Lindberg and Scheingold 1970; on neofunctionalism's hope for a state-like outcome for regional integration despite its proponents' wish to avoid teleology and emphasis on the 'sui generis' character of the EU, see Pentland 1973: 107). Hence, Söderbaum (2003: 8) argues that 'regional integration' is very much a 'first wave regionalism' concept. Thus, while many EU studies scholars use the term 'integration theory' as a label for their theoretical perspectives, it is necessary to remember that in many cases their endeavours are not really integration theory *proprement dit*.[3]

The notion of 'EU Studies' implies an approach more in keeping with the use of a range of perspectives than with a particular discipline, and with an understanding that although no piece of work is, or could be, entirely atheoretical, there is value in empirically-driven enquiry which might leave explicit theorizing to one side or see it as a subsequent, middle-range activity for which empirical work must first build the foundations (Bourne and Cini 2006).[4] Thus, many scholars in the field would perceive it as a form of area studies, even if they work themselves primarily within a single discipline. However, it should be noted that an influential group of scholars holds that EU Studies must conform to the rationalist social science ontology and epistemology which dominates the US mainstream, in order to produce research which is compatible with, and will be taken seriously by, scholars in that mainstream (for an interesting discussion, see Schneider and Aspinwall 2001). There is thus a 'normal science' versus 'area studies' divide in the field, but for the purposes of the present chapter I will ask the reader to understand EU studies as the pluri-disciplinary study of the European Union in terms of its history, identity, politics, law, economics, sociology and anthropology,[5] and also as the attempt to place the EU in both a broader (global/international) political-economic context, and in an ideational context which draws on thinking in the natural sciences where appropriate (Geyer 2003; Manners 2003). Such a perspective allows us to generate a holistic and penetrating understanding of our dependent variable. In that spirit, the next section situates EU studies in the context of the literature on comparative regionalism.

EU STUDIES AND THE NEW REGIONALISM

One of the most attractive features of early neofunctionalism was the ambitiousness of its effort to develop as a general theory of regional integration (see *inter alia* Haas 1961; Nye 1968; the essays in Lindberg and Scheingold 1971). 'Grand theories' such as this are no longer in fashion, but when scholars interested in the EU began to turn away from neofunctionalism in the 1970s they also became introspective: deliberate and sustained attention to regional blocs elsewhere fell off the agenda in favour of the bid to understand more about the quixotic Euro-polity. Thus, although neofunctionalism is still used in EU studies (Schmitter 2004), it is by no means the sole or even the dominant theoretical approach in the field. Moreover, when regional blocs began to form again, or take on new leases of life, in the mid-1980s, they were generally studied by academics who were particularly stringent in their claim that EU studies in general, and neofunctionalism in particular, were of very limited use in their work. In this section of the chapter I therefore attempt to provide a brief overview of the work on the 'new regionalism', setting out how the scholars involved have understood their field and the term 'region', before commenting on the development of work in this area to date.

Rethinking the Region and Regional Organization

Scholars of the 'new regionalism', then, have largely rejected neofunctionalism, even if the theory may yet yield insights that could be useful for them.[6] The general view in new regionalist studies – *pace* (Haas 2001) – is that the neofunctionalism is too rationalistic a perspective to yield helpful explanations of key independent variables such as the role of identity (Hettne 2003; Wunderlich 2004). Additionally, neofunctionalism is held to privilege an institutionalized version of regionalism, which many regions outside Europe have explicitly rejected as a normatively suitable model (Acharya 2002). Third, neofunctionalism espouses a teleology (i.e. integration projects *should* develop towards a regional polity/state), which screens out too many instances of contemporary regionalization to be generally applicable (Schulz et al. 2001). Fourth, neofunctionalism

Table 29.1   *Old and new regionalisms.*

'Old' regionalism	'New' regionalisms
Formed in bipolar Cold War context	Formed in multi-polar, globalized context
Dependent upon superpower patronage	Driven by the member states, not outsiders
Economically protectionist	Economically 'open'
Sector-specific	Multi-functional
No significant challenge to state sovereignty	Part of transformation of sovereignty

Source: Adapted from Hettne (2002), pp. 325–40. See www.tandf.co.uk/journals

sees an unnecessary rivalry between regional and global levels of organization, which makes it unable to explain how the two may in fact be mutually reinforcing (Fawcett 1995; Choi and Caporaso 2002). Finally, neofunctionalism relies too heavily on internal actors as a source of pressure for deepening regionalization, paying inadequate attention to the impact and roles of the global economy and third states (Calleya 1997; Söderbaum 2003).[7] Thus, for most NR scholars, neofunctionalism is ultimately reducible to an attempt to theorize a particular and temporally-specific instance of regionalization, namely that in (Western) Europe, whose central tenets reveal assumptions and epistemologies that are inappropriate for use in the early twenty-first century. As a result, they have tended to ignore EU studies in their work, considering it both too closely associated with neofunctionalism and too closely focused on one particular case of a more general phenomenon. There are a range of further sociology of knowledge issues that can further explain this oversight, and also the scarcity of global governance scholars' engagement with EU studies. The most important have been the dominance of US scholars and norms about 'good scholarship' in international relations studies and the fact that most new regionalist and global governance scholars have seen themselves as members of a broadly-defined IR community. The comparative politics turn in EU studies (which new regionalist scholars with a non-European focus often considered unsuitable for their work) is also important here (for a longer discussion, see Warleigh 2004; Higgott 2005; Warleigh 2006a).

Here is not the place to debate the strengths and weaknesses of neofunctionalism.[8] However, it must be noted that by seeking to move beyond neofunctionalism, and by eliding EU studies with that particular theoretical approach, new regionalist scholars have tended to set their field out as something qualitatively new with greater links to the literature in international relations in general, and international political economy in particular, than with EU studies.

The New Regionalism

Andrew Hurrell (1995) argued that the second wave of regionalism (i.e. that which occurred after 1985) produced entities with significant new characteristics, such as the membership of states from both the global 'North' and the global 'South' in the same regional organization, as in the case of NAFTA, the North American Free Trade Association, which brings together Canada, the USA and Mexico. Moreover, such organizations were far more diverse than neofunctionalism implied, with some of them eschewing formal institutionalization almost altogether, and with the development of a regional organization being deeply dependent upon a rise of regional consciousness/identity.

Set out in Table 29.1, the primary distinctions between the two eras of regionalism, it is argued, can largely be explained by the changed global context – the world economy and global politics were rather different from the 1950s by the time the 'second wave' of regionalism began in the mid-1980s (Fawcett 1995; Hettne and Söderbaum 2000). The Cold War was ending, and the USA shifted its preferences to favour certain forms of regional engagement; free trade rather than protectionism was the dominant economic ideology; and in the face of globalization many

Table 29.2   *The 'region-ness' spectrum.*

Variant	Characteristics
Regional Space	Geographic unit bound by trade and settlement links
Regional Complex	Embryonic economic interdependence
Regional Society	Based on shared rules, the input of non-state as well as state actors; may become formally institutionalized
Regional Community	Based on shared values and a transnational civil society, this form of region develops powers to act on its own initiative and is seen by outsiders as an actor in its own right
Region-State	Internally diverse, pluralist state in which national sovereignty is effectively replaced

Source: Adapted from Hettne and Söderbaum (2000), pp. 457–73. See www.tandf.co.uk/journals

states were prepared to sacrifice parts of their nominal sovereignty in order to gain, through collaboration with each other, a greater *de facto* influence over important policy issues. Consequently, the demands for regional organizations, and their evolutionary potential, had changed.

However, the diversity of such organizations made it difficult to reach a parsimonious definition of the term 'region'. Instead, scholars developed a spectrum of 'region-ness', which set out a range of possibilities for regional organizations while explicitly stating that no one point on the spectrum should be considered better than others, and that there should be no implication of teleology – regions will not necessarily evolve from one point in the spectrum to another in linear fashion, and may even shift back and forth (Hettne and Soderbaum 2000; Hettne, 2002). Table 29.2 illustrates this spectrum of 'region-ness'.

Furthermore, in terms of their relative importance in global politics, regions can be of three sorts: *core regions* (which are densely organized and exist to allow their member states to increase their role in the world political economy); *intermediate zone regions* (which imitate core regions and aspire to match them at the centre of the global political economy); and *peripheral zone regions*, where political turbulence and slow economic growth are the norm (Hettne 2001). There are thus several degrees of 'region-ness', and to understand the phenomenon of contemporary regionalism we must study them all.

The Evolution of New Regionalist Literature

New regionalist scholarship has principally developed through the use of international political economy literature and social constructivism, and within this body of work there is considerable diversity. First, there has been the self-conscious attempt to develop a new body of theory, the 'new regionalism approach' (NRA), drawing on international political economy and critical theory to examine state-society interaction in the context of the various regional organizations (Schulz et al. 2001: 12–13). Other scholars have taken a constructivist approach to the NRA (Hettne 2003; Wunderlich 2004), while others have studied new regionalism using social constructivism but not the NRA per se (Slocum and Van Langenhove 2004). Still other scholars have taken a more rationalist political economy perspective, again often outside the 'new regionalist approach' as such, even though their subject of study is the new regionalism (Taylor 1993; Mansfield and Milner 1999; Mattli 1999). Hence, there is the currently ubiquitous rationalist/constructivist debate in new regionalism studies, alongside (and perhaps as part of) the attempt to elaborate the NRA.

However, the evolution of new regionalist scholarship has not been free of problems. In fact, the 'new regionalist approach' has recently undergone significant revision, as many of the initially-apparent differences between 'old' and 'new' forms of regionalism have seemed less significant over time. This is not least because the EU itself is also an expression of 'new regionalism' – although it was founded in the 1950s, it was the EU's transformation by the Single European Act in 1985 that provoked the global return of regionalism (Fawcett 1995). Björn Hettne, the principal advocate of the NRA, has recently argued that the theoretically important differences between 'old' and 'new' forms of regionalism are few, and that the new regionalism approach has over-stated both the dependence of current regional organizations on globalization and such organizations' growth potential (Hettne 2003). Hence, the 'new regionalist approach' is being reconsidered, with many scholars arguing that comparative study of regional organizations is the best way to meet this objective (Hettne 2001; Laursen 2003a, 2003b; Söderbaum 2003). In this endeavour, the EU has been explicitly accepted as a comparator (Hettne 2002; Söderbaum and Shaw 2003), a fact which may herald a new era of collaboration between scholars of regionalism inside and outside Europe.

GLOBAL GOVERNANCE

Another set of scholars of international relations also has potential to inform the development of EU studies in useful ways. These are academics interested in the development of 'global governance', which they see as a clear departure from orthodox understandings of the international system, and one which represents many common characteristics with regional organizations of the various kinds discussed above. In this section of the chapter I seek to define the idea of global governance before tracing the development of the literature on the subject and presenting a brief analysis of its strengths and weaknesses.

Defining Global Governance

To understand the concept of global governance (explained in Table 29.3) it is necessary to delve back into recent political history. The end of the Cold War – metaphorically, '1989', when the Berlin Wall fell – is argued to mark a caesura in the development of international politics as a consequence of several simultaneously occurring factors. First, the end of the superpower rivalry between the USA and the Soviet Union, which reduced the insecurity of the international system; second, the spread of neoliberalism as an economic ideology to most parts of the globe, which reduced the variation between different governments' understandings of sound macroeconomic policy; third, a resulting sense of increased interdependence, in a context where individual states were seen to matter less than in the past, and transnational corporations to matter rather more; fourth, the rise of important issues which were held to require global action if they were to be addressed successfully, e.g. environmental problems such as climate change, or human rights protection; and fifth, the vast improvement in international communication possibilities through the ICT revolution (Desai 1995; Messner 2002; Woods 2002).

This process can be summed up as 'globalization', which Zürn argues is a qualitative shift away from interdependence, because states in the international system are no longer simply open or vulnerable to each other but are actually beginning to merge with each other: globalization points to the creation of an integrated world market and a global society in which power is increasingly exercised not just through the private sector but through cross-national links between 'regulatory agencies, courts, executives and increasingly also legislatures' (Zürn 2002: 241). Hence, globalization is producing a 'global polity' with four main characteristics (Higgott and Ougaard 2002: 2–4). First, there is increased interconnectedness between state actors, non-state actors of both public and private kinds, and sub-state actors. Second, network systems of decision-making, where sites of real power are hard to pinpoint, but through which authoritative decisions are made, are predominant. Third, there can be observed the development at popular and elite levels of a thin awareness of the planetary level as a necessary site for problem-solving. Fourth, there is a concomitant weakening of

Table 29.3 *Unpacking 'global governance'.*

'Global'	'Governance'	'Global governance'
The term 'global' means rather more than the term 'international'. The latter can mean relations between only two or three states, and certainly implies that states remain central units of analysis. The term 'global', by contrast, suggests that the unit of analysis should be world-wide, i.e. the institutions and processes which affect the whole planet.	The idea of 'governance' represents a perceived new way of making public policy. Governance scholars claim that public power is no longer monopolized by a strong central government in each nation state. Instead, partly for normative reasons such as the belief in decentralization or the liberation of market forces, and partly because the range and complexity of issues with which governments have to deal have greatly increased, new forms of decision-making have been created. These new forms and processes do not replace the state/the government, but they re-calibrate how the machinery of government is used. Governance involves alliance building and network-formation, i.e. the assembling of coalitions, both inside and outside formal political institutions. It emphasises collaboration (within networks) and rivalry (between networks). It makes policy-making less formal, but may increase the range of actors involved in the process.	'The evolving system of formal and informal political coordination across multiple levels from the local to the global - amongst public authorities (states and intergovernmental organizations) and private agencies (NGOs and corporate actors) seeking to realize common purposes or resolve collective problems through the making and implementing of global or transnational norms, rules, programmes, and policies'.

Source: Author (columns 1 and 2); McGrew (2005: 25) (column 3). 'Global governance' from Box 1.3: Key Concepts (p. 25) from 'The Globalization of World Politics: An introduction to world politics' by Baylis, J. and Smith, S. (2005). By permission of Oxford University Press.

the nation-state as a political actor. In turn, this network, contested, interconnected mode of decision-making is what constitutes *global governance* (Hardt and Negri 2000: 14).

For certain observers, global governance is extremely varied in its range and authority. Koenig-Archibugi (2002) argues cogently that in some policy areas there is no significant authority 'above' the nation state, and that in others there is a gap between what, in principle, a global governance system should logically provide and what it can actually deliver, given its truncated powers. Moreover, the various institutions and networks that carry out this global governance have overlapping competences, and in some policy areas different groups or networks compete for influence (Koenig-Archibugi 2002). Indeed, Rosenau (2002) goes so far as to speak of 'fragmegration' – the simultaneous globalization and localizing of politics, in which spheres of authority are changeable and changing. Hence, global governance is to be considered a contingent process, and one which is very much still in formation.

Global Governance: Characterizing the Literature

Just as the new regionalism distinguished itself from EU studies, global governance scholars consider their work to be different from the study field of international relations as it has traditionally been understood. These differences stem from the claim repeated above that '1989' changed the nature of the international system, and that as a result it became possible to embrace farther-reaching understandings of the scope of international politics (Nuscheler 2002). As a result, global governance work pays sustained attention to a broader range of actors than conventional international relations scholarship: the latter often still debates whether, for example, international institutions and organizations are influential, whereas global governance scholars take such influence as a given and have a much broader understanding of the range of actors which can be influential in international decision-making (O'Brien et al. 2000).

Two further points are worth making here. First, the literature on global governance is not afraid to be normative, i.e. to make recommendations for change in the ways global governance is structured on the basis of moral criteria (Luard 1990; Commission on Global Governance 1995). This is at odds with the rationalist mainstream in international relations scholarship. Second, scholars of global governance often take a stance based on critical theory; their goal is to examine the balance of power in global institutions and decision-making processes, pointing out where the structures and processes at global level serve to favour the interests of the powerful rather than the general good (Wilkinson and Hughes 2002).

The literature on global governance has had even less time to develop than that on new regionalism, because its empirical starting point is usually '1989'. Nonetheless, certain strengths and weaknesses can be noted, as can its relationship with EU studies. In the global governance literature's favour are its interdisciplinarity (political science is used in conjunction with economics, geography, philosophy and history – see for example the essays in Demko and Wood 1994; Desai and Redfern 1995), its explicit normative debate (mirroring in this respect the literature on globalization), its strong critical and reflexive strands, and its emphasis on contingency (e.g. O'Brien et al. 2000). On the negative side, the literature has yet to provide a single, agreed definition of 'global governance', and is in some cases overly-reliant upon normative exhortation to build its case (e.g. Luard 1990). Certain authors in the field appear to find important events in world politics, such as the unilateral assertion of power by the USA, just as difficult to explain as more orthodox international relations scholars found '1989' (see the wry reflections of Messner and Nuscheler 2002). Hence, global governance is still very much an evolving body of work. Indeed, some scholars have gone so far as to argue that the concept of 'governance' is simply unhelpful in IR, because in their view neither the international system nor the nation state model have been as radically altered as the idea of a global polity or

even global governance would suggest. For example, Welch and Kennedy-Pipe (2004) argue that the role of the US as global hegemon means there is no possibility of 'global governance' except that which is sanctioned by Washington and thus reducible to American power. Moreover, they argue that whatever may be happening domestically, the nation state retains its coherence when working in the international system.

Despite this sceptical strand of scholars, the contours of a relationship between Global Governance and EU studies are emerging. Zürn's work on globalization has many parallels with the contemporaneous analysis of the EU's impact on the governance of its member states (Kohler-Koch and Eising 1999). Moreover, global governance literature already acknowledges the potential of the EU as a source of ideas about how to rethink or restructure governance for a post-national world, although opinions differ about whether the EU is a positive model or not. For example, Linklater (2005) and Held (2004) respectively consider the EU as a model/civilizing project for international governance and as a source of ideas about how to rethink representative democracy for an international governance system. On the other hand, Mann (1998) cautions that the EU could also be an anti-model as it shows how hollowed-out societies can become in a context of multi-level, overlapping international network governance. In the final sections of the chapter I set out how I think EU studies scholars can profit from a more sustained engagement with this work, and with that of the new regionalism.

(WHAT) CAN EUROPEAN UNION STUDIES LEARN FROM NEW REGIONALISM AND GLOBAL GOVERNANCE?

Is it possible for EU studies scholars to engage meaningfully with those of new regionalism and global governance? There are genuine problems here of how to define a dependent variable. If it can be argued that EU studies and new regionalism scholars have essentially the same interests which are spiced up by local colour, the same does not hold quite so automatically for scholars of global governance: both sets of scholars are interested in post- or trans-national governance, but the global system is different from that of the EU in several key ways (for example, there is no hegemon in the EU, whereas the world system has the US in this role; the 'North–South' issues in global politics have only a tiny echo in the squabbles over the EU budget and redistributive policies). Moreover, the fact that most new regionalist and global governance scholars have generally used International Relations (IR) or International Political Economy (IPE) conceptual tools, whereas EU studies scholars increasingly use and adapt those of comparative politics if they are political scientists, and use the methods of other disciplines if such is their intellectual affiliation, will generate both epistemological and ontological problems that will be important to recognize even if they are not necessarily insuperable. On the other hand, it should be noted that global governance scholars explicitly and by definition seek to challenge both the state-centric focus of orthodox IR scholarship and its understanding of the limits of the international system. In this respect, there is room to learn from, and adapt, several aspects of EU studies scholarship, notably on issues such as the disaggregation of political authority, the nature and potential of international organizations, the transformative potential of international collaboration and organizations on national actors, institutions and legal systems, and democracy (Warleigh 2006a).

Nonetheless, if EU studies, new regionalism and global governance scholars are to fertilize each other's work they must concentrate primarily on what unites them and harness their differences as mutually instructive sources of learning through ongoing, critical research; and, as Van Kersbergen and Van Waarden (2004) demonstrate, there are limits to the capacity of governance studies to bridge inter- and intra-disciplinary barriers. If they are serious about learning from other groups of scholars studying post- or trans-national governance, EU studies scholars will therefore

have to engage with global governance issues more systematically.[9]

Sceptics might point out that EU studies scholars often fail to engage with their own area studies history, making their engagement with scholars outside their intellectual area at best unlikely. At the very least, the reluctance of many scholars to interrogate early EU studies literature means that it is often students in other areas who go furthest in meeting challenges that our own intellectual forebears set for us. For example, Ernst Haas (1970: 609) argued EU studies needed to adopt a greater focus on normative issues and foreign policy analysis, and yet the 'normative turn' in EU studies (Bellamy and Castiglione 2003) failed to materialize until 20 years later, when it was largely a result of the work of political theorists and legal scholars.[10] Similarly, it was new regionalism scholars who examined regionalism from the perspective of international political economy, although it must be admitted that many EU scholars devoted their attention to the EU's external relations (Keeler 2005). EU studies is only beginning to map itself as an area of study, and has yet to match the IR critique of its historiography (Ashworth 2002; Schmidt 2002); perhaps the 'normal science' versus interdisciplinarity debate will fulfil a similar function.

However, it should be recalled that a strength of EU studies is that it has never accepted the notion of a strict divide between 'the domestic' and 'the international'; the neofunctionalists (who were of course IR scholars interested primarily in the EU/regional integration) deliberately shaped the field of EU studies this way (Moravcsik 2005; Schmitter 2005). This fact can be utilized to justify a wider focus for EU studies than is the current norm, especially because the new regionalist and global governance literatures have assets that EU studies scholars would do well to simulate.

The new regionalist literature, in its divergent strands, has made many contributions to knowledge which are useful for EU studies specialists (Warleigh 2004: 308–9). It has given those interested in regional organization a far greater wealth of data and analytical tools than would have been gained simply through a narrow focus on EU studies, thereby helping the EU studies community out of their 'N=1' dilemma (the difficulty in making solid theory by depending on a single case study, i.e. the EU, which is the product of an assumption that the Union is unique and thus literally incomparable.) It has also reminded EU studies scholars that the global and international contexts are analytically important because they impact upon the EU's creation, essence and policy agenda. New regionalist studies provide EU scholars with a greater range of possibilities for testing emerging concepts; for example, one interesting way in which the concept of a 'normative power Europe' (Manners 2002) can be tested is by analysing the EU's relationships with other regional organizations, and whether they view the EU in this way. New regionalism studies will also allow EU scholars to test whether what may appear to be evidence of integration 'gone awry' (such as flexibility or the reliance upon informal politics) may in fact simply be standard features of contemporary regional organizations. By introducing concepts and approaches which have recently been outside the EU studies mainstream, such as global/international political economy, new regionalist scholars have enriched the conceptual toolboxes of their EU studies colleagues.[11]

A lesson that EU studies can learn from the global governance/globalization literature is how to engage with the public. How many EU studies scholars reach as many non-specialists as, for example, Naomi Klein or Joseph Stiglitz? Of course, to a certain extent, this is a function of the general public's view of the subject material; an unexpected finding in previous work I undertook was the consistent reporting by NGO officers that their members/supporters were far more interested in global politics than the EU, even when it was the latter which affected them most (Warleigh 2001). However, the reasons for this lack of resonance with the public are also partly explicable through an examination of EU studies' intellectual roots. As a result of the 'systematic social science' that Haas and his contemporaries introduced for us, EU studies is often afraid to be *engaged* in

the manner of, say, David Mitrany or, to give a contemporary equivalent, David Held. It is a weakness in our field that we have no equivalents of Held's 2004 book on global social democracy, which includes an actual plan of how to create such a system and a discussion of how it would work that is intelligible to the layperson and practitioner.

CONCLUSIONS AND PERSPECTIVES

How, then, should EU studies be re-thought? Throughout this chapter I have tried to show that EU studies scholars have much to learn from scholars in other cognate fields of enquiry. In order to derive maximum benefit from this, EU studies must rethink its dependent variable, and explicitly consider itself as a form of regionalism in the global political economy rather than the paradigm case of regionalism or a state-like polity. It must embrace far more than 'normal science', with its emphasis on positivism and hard rationalism, in order to develop multi-disciplinary (or even, as Rosamond (2005) argues, postdisciplinary) research programmes that can draw on as wide a range of perspectives as possible and speak to as many scholars as possible. It must strengthen its commitment to critical theories and methodologies, in order to develop deeper understandings but also to be able to engage both the public and policymakers by showing why our work *matters*.

Perhaps the best way to do this is via a common research programme between EU studies scholars and those of both the new regionalism and global governance. In order to make progress in their cooperation, however, scholars of the EU, other regionalization processes and global governance will need to address key questions about both what they study and how they study it. Building on an initial discussion by Richard Higgott (2005), I suggest that there are five key issues that could usefully be addressed as part of a common research agenda involving scholars from all three study areas.

The first two issues are methodological. First, how can we adapt state-based methodologies for use in the study of regional and global governance? EU studies shows that such methods can successfully be adapted for wider use, but iterated attention will have to be given to their adaptation for use in other global regions and at global level. The intellectual divide between the 'domestic' and the 'international' (or 'global') may well be increasingly untenable, but this does not automatically mean that state-based tools of analysis can simply be applied to global or regional governance without careful reworking (Warleigh 2006a). The second methodological issue is closely related to the first, and regards the question of how to undertake interdisciplinary study of supra- or transnational governance. Are all relevant disciplines sufficiently open to the very idea of such governance? Do scholars in these various disciplines understand either the world or how to study it in compatible ways? Thus, a useful research programme would involve inter-disciplinary cooperation between scholars of the EU, other global regions, and global governance on these fundamental issues of methodology, with the aim to develop a common framework for study and methodological compatibility. The beginnings of explicit cooperation between scholars of the EU and new regionalism offer an optimistic sign here (Warleigh 2006b).

The next three issues are perhaps more substantive, but not necessarily more important. They all relate to the need to understand the nature of contemporary regional and global governance, and the complex ways in which they relate to each other. Using critical theory, scholars should focus on the use of power in regional and global governance, and ask in whose interests the various organizations appear to work. By building up an empirically-informed analysis of this issue, it will then be possible to address the remaining two key issues. First, what are the links between global governance, regionalization, and the power of the USA – is 'global governance' in fact the expression of US imperial policy, or a response to it? Similarly, are regionalization processes a response to globalization and global governance from actors seeking to control their own destinies more directly, or part of the very process of globalization that disempowers them? Second, how can regional and global organizations and governance processes be made more legitimate? Collaborating in the use of normative theory, scholars can begin to address issues of participation, representation and accountability more successfully, thereby answering a key need to respond to both the EU's democracy deficit (which holds lessons for other global regions) and the protests of the anti-globalization community.

European Union Studies has come a long way from the days when those teaching it had to write their own textbooks because there weren't any,[12] and as scholars in that field we may be proud of what we can teach not just our students but scholars in cognate fields. But we must also remember what we can learn about the 'European process' from scholars of its 'universal' equivalents; governance 'beyond the nation state' is still sufficiently new to throw up challenges that we can only understand through collaboration.

NOTES

1. The links between the 'deepening' of European integration and the birth of 'new regionalism' are complex. It was arguably the *relance* of the EU which set the new regionalism in train elsewhere, a process which also means that the post-1987 EU is itself a form of 'new regionalism' (Fawcett 1995; Schulz et al. 2003). However, other scholars explain the rebirth of regionalism as a function of the end of the Cold War, the growth of interdependence, and the near-global triumph of neoliberal ideology (Ravenhill 2005: 127).

2. It should be noted that scholars of 'new regionalism' argue the EU must not be taken as *the* model of regionalism in the earlier Haasian manner (Acharya 2002; Hettne 2002).

3. 'European integration theory' (Diez and Wiener 2004: 7) might be understood as a half-way house term, focusing specifically on the EU/European context, but keeping the term 'integration' for the sake of its general recognition factor or as a result of its lingering in the collective conscious of both EU and IR scholars.

4. Bourne and Cini argue that the main disciplines in EU studies have so far been political science, law and economics, with growing contributions from history, anthropology, sociology and geography. It should be added that the 'normative turn' in EU studies has also seen significant contributions to the field from political theorists and philosophers (Warleigh 2003).

5. Other disciplines could of course be mentioned here, and are omitted only because the work on the EU of scholars in those fields has not yet been extensive – as pointed out by Bourne and Cini (2006).

6. For example, compare what follows immediately below with Ravenhill's (2005) account of the political and economic reasons for the advent of 'new regionalism', in which the similarities between neofunctionalism and Ravenhill's political economy approach are striking.

7. In the present revisionist stage in the development of the new regionalist approach, this feature of neofunctionalism may be less of a problem than previously anticipated because the relative importance of globalisation as a causal factor in new regionalism is being questioned.

8. For a range of perspectives on this, see Warleigh (1998); Rosamond (2000); Schmitter (2004).

9. See, for example, Rosamond 2005 for an argument that EU Studies work on globalisation is inconsistent and often narrow, indicating that EU scholars often, and ironically, have more difficulty extending their own 'fusion thesis' (Wessels 1997) to the global level than scholars of international political economy.

10. Of course, certain scholars produced work on normative issues in the interim, but not until the late 1990s did the issues of legitimacy and democracy become key issues in EU studies in general, and integration theory in particular (Bellamy and Warleigh 1998; Warleigh 2003).

11. This particular gap may be closing; see for example Cafruny and Rosenthal (2003).

12. This is a story recounted by Helen Wallace.

REFERENCES

Acharya, A. (2002) 'Regionalism and the emerging world order: sovereignty, autonomy, identity', in S. Breslin, C. Hughes, N. Phillips and B. Rosamond (eds), *New Regionalisms in the Global Political Economy*. London: Routledge. pp. 20–32.

Ashworth, L. (2002) 'Did the realist-idealist great debate really happen? A revisionist history of international relations', *International Relations*, 16(1): 33–51.

Bellamy, R. and Castiglione D. (2003) 'Legitimizing the "Euro-polity" and its "regime": the normative turn in EU studies', *European Journal of Political Theory*, 2(1): 7–34.

Bellamy, R. and Warleigh, A. (1998) 'From an ethics of integration to an ethics of participation', *Millennium*, 27(3): 447–70.

Bourne, A. and Cini, M. (2006) 'Introduction – defining boundaries and identifying trends in European Union studies', in A. Bourne and M. Cini (eds), *Advances in European Union Studies*, Basingstoke: Palgrave. pp. 1–18.

Cafruny, A. and Ryner, M. (eds) (2003) *A Ruined Fortress? Neoliberal Hegemony and Transformation in Europe*. Lanham, MA/Oxford: Rowman and Littlefield.

Calleya, S. (1997) *Navigating Regional Dynamics in the Post-Cold War World*. Aldershot: Dartmouth.

Choi, Y.J. and Caporaso, J. (2002) 'Comparative Regional Integration', in W. Carlsnaes, T. Risse and B. Simmons (eds), *Handbook of International Relations*. London: Sage. pp. 480–99.

Commission on Global Governance (1995) *Our Global Neighbourhood*. Oxford: Oxford University Press.

Demko, G. and Wood, W. (1994) *Reordering the World – Geopolitical Perspectives on the 21st Century*. Boulder: Westview Press.

Desai, M. (1995) 'Global governance', in M. Desai and P. Redfern (eds) *Global Governance: Ethics and Economics of the World Order*. London: Pinter. pp. 6–21.

Desai, M. and Redfern, P. (eds) (1995) *Global Governance: Ethics and Economics of the World Order*. London: Pinter.

Diez, T. and Wiener, A. (2004) 'Introduction: the mosaic of integration theory', in A. Wiener and T. Diez (eds), *European Integration Theory*. Oxford: Oxford University Press. pp. 1–21.

Fawcett, L. (1995) 'Regiobnalism in historical perspective', in L. Fawcett and A. Hurrell (eds), *Regionalism in World Politics: Regional Organization and International Order*. Oxford: Oxford University Press. pp. 9–36.

Geyer, R. (2003) 'European integration, the problem of complexity and the revision of theory', *Journal of Common Market Studies*, 41(1): 15–35.

Haas, E. (1961) 'International integration: the European and the universal process', *International Organization*, 15: 366–92.

Haas, E. (1964) *Beyond the Nation State*. Stanford: Stanford University Press.

Haas, E. (1970) 'The study of regional integration: reflections on the joy and anguish of pre-theorizing', *International Organization*, 24: 607–46.

Haas, E. (1975) *The Obsolescence of Regional Integration Theory*. Berkeley, CA: University of California Press.

Haas, E. (2001) 'Does constructivism subsume neofunctionalism?', in T. Christiansen, K.E. Jørgensen and A. Wiener (eds), *The Social Construction of Europe*. London: Sage. pp. 22–31.

Hardt, M. and Negri, A. (2000) *Empire*. Cambridge, MA: Harvard University Press.

Held, D. (2004) *Global Covenant: the Social Democratic Alternative to the Washington Consensus.* Cambridge: Polity.

Hettne, B. (2001) 'Regionalism, security and development: a comparative perspective', in B. Hettne, A. Inotai and O. Sunkel (eds), *Comparing Regionalisms: Implications for Global Development.* Basingstoke: Macmillan. pp. 1–53.

Hettne, B. (2002) 'The Europeanisation of Europe: endogenous and exogenous variables', *Journal of European Integration,* 24(4): 325–40.

Hettne, B. (2003) 'The new regionalism revisited', in F. Söderbaum and T. Shaw (eds), *Theories of New Regionalism: A Palgrave Reader.* Basingstoke: Palgrave. pp. 22–42.

Hettne, B. and Söderbaum, F. (2000) 'Theorising the rise of region-ness', *New Political Economy,* 5(3): 457–73.

Higgott, R. (2005) 'The theory and practice of global and regional governance: accommodating American exceptionalism and European pluralism'. GARNET Working Paper 01/05. Available at: http://www. garnet-eu.org, accessed 14 December 2005.

Higgott, R. and Ougaard, M. (2002) 'Introduction: beyond system and society – towards a global polity?', in R. Higgott and M. Ougaard (eds), *Towards a Global Polity.* London: Routledge. pp. 1–19.

Hoffmann, S. (1982) 'Reflections on the nation-state in Western Europe today', *Journal of Common Market Studies,* 21: 21–37.

Hurrell, A. (1995) 'Explaining the resurgence of regionalism in world politics', *Review of International Studies,* 21: 331–58.

Keeler, J. (2005) 'Mapping EU studies: the evolution from boutique to boom field, 1960–2001', *Journal of Common Market Studies,* 43(3): 551–82.

Koenig-Archibugi, M. (2002) 'Mapping global governance', in D. Held and A. McGrew (eds) *Governing Globalization: Power, Authority and Global Governance.* Cambridge: Polity. pp. 46–69.

Kohler-Koch, B. and Eising, R. (eds) (1999) *The Transformation of Governance in the European Union.* London: Routledge.

Laursen, F. (2003a) 'International regimes or would-be polities? Some concluding questions and remarks', in F. Laursen (ed.), *Comparative Regional Integration – Theoretical Perspectives.* Aldershot: Ashgate, pp. 283–93.

Laursen, F. (2003b) 'Theoretical perspectives on comparative regional integration', in F. Laursen (ed.), *Comparative Regional Integration – Theoretical Perspectives.* Aldershot: Ashgate, pp. 3–28.

Lindberg, L. and Scheingold, S. (1970) *Europe's Would-Be Polity.* Englewood Clifs, NJ: Prentice-Hall.

Lindberg, L. and Scheingold, S. (eds) (1971) *Regional Integration.* Cambridge, MA: Harvard University Press.

Linklater, A. (2005) 'Globalization and the transformation of political community', in J. Baylis and S. Smith (eds), *The Globalization of World Politics,* third edition. Oxford: Oxford University Press. pp. 709–25.

Luard, E. (1990) *The Globalization of Politics: The Changed Focus of Political Action in the Modern World.* Basingstoke: Macmillan.

Mann, M. (1998) 'Is there a society called Euro?', in R. Axtmann (ed.), *Globalization and Europe: Theoretical and Empirical Investigations.* London: Pinter. pp. 184–207.

Manners, I. (2002) 'Normative power Europe: a contradiction in terms?', *Journal of Common Market Studies,* 40(2): 235–58

Manners, I. (2003) 'Europaian studies?', *Journal of Contemporary European Studies,* 11(1): 67–83.

Mansfield, E. and Milner, H. (1999) 'The new wave of regionalism', *International Organization,* 53(3): 589–627.

Mattli, W. (1999) *The Logic of Regional Integration: Europe and Beyond.* Cambridge: Cambridge University Press.

McGrew, D. (2005) 'Globalization and global politics', in J. Baylis and S. Smith (eds), *The Globalization of World Politics: An Introduction to International Relations.* Oxford: Oxford University Press. pp. 19–40.

Messner, D. (2002) 'World society – structures and trends', in P. Kennedy, D. Messner and F. Nuscheler (eds), *Global Trends and Global Governance.* London: Pluto Press/Development and Peace Foundation. pp. 22–64.

Messner, D. and Nuscheler, F. (2002) 'World politics – structures and trends', in P. Kennedy, D. Messner and F. Nuscheler (eds), *Global Trends and Global Governance.* London: Pluto Press/Development and Peace Foundation. pp. 125–55.

Moravcsik, A. (2005) 'The European constitutional compromise and the neofunctionalist legacy', *Journal of European Public Policy,* 12(2): 349–86.

Nuscheler, F. (2002) 'Global governance, development and peace', in P. Kennedy, D. Messner and F. Nuscheler (eds), *Global Trends and Global Governance.* London: Pluto Press/Development and Peace Foundation. pp. 156–83.

Nye, J. (1968) 'Comparative regional integration: concept and measurement', *International Organization*, 22(4): 855–80.

Nye, J. (1971) 'Comparing common markets: a revised neofunctionalist model', in L. Lindberg and S. Scheingold (eds), *Regional Integration*. Cambridge, MA: Harvard University Press. pp. 192–231.

O'Brien, R., Goetz, A.M., Scholte J.A. (2000) *Contesting Global Governance: Multilateral Economic Institutions and Global Social Movements*. Cambridge: Cambridge University Press.

O'Neill, M. (2000) 'Theorising the European Union: towards a post-foundational discourse'. *Current Politics and Economics of Europe*. 9(2): 121–45.

Pentland, C. (1973) *International Theory and European Integration*. London: Faber and Faber.

Ravenhill, J. (2005) 'The study of global political economy', in J. Ravenhill (ed.), *Global Political Economy*. Oxford: Oxford University Press. pp. 3–27.

Rosamond, B. (2000) *Theories of European Integration*. Basingstoke: Macmillan.

Rosamond, B. (2005) 'Globalization, the ambivalence of European integration and the possibilities for a post-disciplinary EU studies', *Innovation*, 18(1): 23–43.

Rosenau, J. (2002) 'Governance in a new global order', in D. Held and A. McGrew (eds) *Governing Globalization: Power, Authority and Global Governance*. Cambridge: Polity. pp. 70–86.

Schmidt, B. (2002) 'On the history and historiography of international relations', in W. Carlsnaes, T. Risse and B. Simmons (eds) *Handbook of International Relations*. London: Sage. pp. 3–22.

Schmitter, P. (1971) 'A revised theory of regional integration', in L. Lindberg and S. Scheingold (eds), *Regional Integration*. Cambridge, MA: Harvard University Press.

Schmitter, P. (2004) 'Neo-neofunctionalism', in A. Wiener and T. Diez (eds), *European Integration Theory*. Oxford: Oxford University Press. pp. 45–74.

Schmitter, P. (2005) 'Ernst B. Haas and the legacy of neofunctionalism', *Journal of European Public Policy* 12(2): 255–72.

Schneider, G. and Aspinwall, M. (2001) 'Moving beyond outworn debates: a new institutional research agenda', in M. Aspinwall and G. Schneider (eds), *The Rules of Integration: Institutionalist Approaches to the Study of Europe*. Manchester: Manchester University Press. pp. 177–87.

Schulz, M., Söderbaum, F. and Ojendal, J. (2001) 'A framework for understanding regionalization', in M. Schulz, F. Söderbaum and J. Ojendal (eds), *Regionalizatioin in a Globalizing World*. London: Sage. pp. 1–21.

Slocum, N. and Van Langenhove, L. (2004) 'The meaning of regional integration: introducing positioning theory in regional integration studies', *Journal of European Integration*, 26(3): 227–52.

Söderbaum, F. (2003) 'Introduction: theories of new regionalism', in F. Söderbaum and T. Shaw (eds), *Theories of New Regionalism: A Palgrave Reader*. Basingstoke: Palgrave. pp. 1–21.

Taylor, P. (1993) *International Organization in the Modern World: The Regional and the Global Process*. London: Pinter.

Van Kersbergen, K. and Van warden, F. (2004) '"Governance" as a bridge between disciplines: cross-disciplinary inspiration regarding shifts in governance and problems of governability, accountability and legitimacy', *European Journal of Political Research*, 43(2): 143–71.

Warleigh, A. (1998) 'Better the devil you know? Synthetic and confederal understandings of European unification', *West European Politics*, 21(3): 1–18.

Warleigh, A. (2001) 'Europeanizing civil society: NGOs as agents of political socialisation', *Journal of Common Market Studies*, 39(4): 619–39.

Warleigh, A. (2003) *Democracy in the European Union: Theory, Practice and Reform*. London: Sage.

Warleigh, A. (2004) 'In defence of intra-disciplinarity: "European studies", the "new regionalism" and the issue of democratisation', *Cambridge Review of International Affairs*, 17(2): 301–18.

Warleigh, A. (2006a) 'Learning from Europe? EU studies and the re-thinking of "international relations"', *European Journal of International Relations*, 12(1): 31–51.

Warleigh, A. (2006b) 'Towards a conceptual framework for regionalisation: bridging "new regionalism" and "integration theory"', *Review of International Political Economy*, 13(5): 750–77.

Welch, S. and Kennedy-Pipe, C. (2004) 'Multi-level governance and international relations', in I. Bache and M. Flinders (eds), *Multi-level Governance*. Oxford: Oxford University Press. pp. 127–44.

Wessels, W. (1997) 'An ever closer fusion? A dynamic macropolitical view on integration processes', *Journal of Common Market Studies*, 35(2): 267–99.

Wilkinson, R. and Hughes, S. (eds) (2002) *Global Governance: Critical Perspectives*. London: Routledge.

Woods, N. (2002) 'Global governance and the role of institutions', in D. Held and A. McGrew (eds) *Governing Globalization: Power, Authority and Global Governance.* Cambridge: Polity. pp. 25–45.

Wunderlich, U. (2004) *Conceptualising the European Union: A New Regionalism Approach.* Paper to 34th UACES Annual Conference and 9th Research Conference, University of Birmingham, 6–8 September 2004.

Zürn, M. (2002) 'From interdependence to globalization', in W. Carlsnaes, T. Risse and B. Simmons (eds), *Handbook of International Relations.* London: Sage. pp. 235–54.

Subject Index

Name Index